D0212009

DAY BY DAY

The Twenties

Day by Day: The Twenties

Facts On File, Inc.
An Imprint of Infobase Publishing
132 West 31st Street
New York, NY 10001

Library of Congress Cataloging-in-Publication Data

Day by day : the twenties / Rodney P. Carlisle, general editor.
v. cm.
Includes bibliographical references and index.
Contents: v. 1. 1920-1924 -- v. 2. 1925-1929.
ISBN 978-0-8160-7183-8 (hbk. : alk. paper)
1. Nineteen twenties-Chronology. I. Carlisle, Rodney P. II. Title: Twenties.
D723.D43 2008
909.82'2--dc22
2007050850

Facts On File books are available at special discounts when purchased in bulk quantities for businesses, associations, institutions, or sales promotions. Please call our Special Sales Department in New York at (212) 967-8800 or (800) 322-8755.

You can find Facts On File on the World Wide Web at http://www.factsonfile.com

Photo Credits
Library of Congress: 1920 pages 2–3; 1921 pages 110–111; 1922 pages 238–239; 1923 pages 368–369; 1924 pages 480–481; 1925 pages 588–589; 1926 pages 702–703; 1927 pages 820–821; 1928 pages 928–929. Getty Images: 1929 pages 1034-1035

GOLSON BOOKS, LTD.

President and Editor	J. Geoffrey Golson
Creative Director	Mary Jo Scibetta
Managing Editor	Susan Moskowitz
Copyeditor	Jacqueline Frances Brownstein
Layout Editors	Kenneth Heller
	Susan Honeywell
	Stephanie Larson
Proofreaders	Julie Grady
	Joan K. Griffitts
Indexer	J S Editorial

Printed in the United States of America

VB GB 12 11 10 9 8 7 6 5 4 3 2 1

This book is printed on acid-free paper and contains 30 percent post-consumer recycled content.

DAY BY DAY

The Twenties

VOLUME 1

1920–1924

Rodney P. Carlisle, Ph.D.

General Editor

Facts On File
An imprint of Infobase Publishing

The Twenties Authors

John Barnhill

Thomas W. Collins

Justin Corfield

Pamela Gray

Ann Kordas

Caryn E. Neumann

Timothy Neeno

Luca Prono

Viva Nordberg Reynolds

Kathleen Ruppert

Robert Stacy

CONTENTS

VOLUME 1

VOLUME 2

INTRODUCTION

The decade of the 1920s seemed in many ways to represent the true beginning of the 20th century, in popular culture, in the arts, in politics, and in international affairs. As Americans dealt with the disillusionment that came out of World War I, they entered a new age. For some, it was the Jazz Age, the Roaring Twenties, marked by bathtub gin, speakeasies, jukebox music, with middle-class, well-brought up young women smoking cigarettes in public, wearing their skirts and their hair short. For others, shocked at such challenges to propriety, the times called for a return to strict standards, with revival of fundamental Christian values.

No matter how one felt about the excesses of the younger generation, for many it seemed to be a time of prosperity and opportunity, with startling changes that suggested that a new and modern world had arrived and the old had passed away. But for those on the lowest social edge, including recent immigrants, African Americans who had migrated to Northern cities and for millions of poorer white Americans throughout the nation, there was little evidence of economic good times. Working wages rarely approached a dollar an hour, while farm prices dropped and farmers faced foreclosures. Waves of unemployment hit some of the mills and factories of New England and the rest of the North, as changing fashions in clothing and shoes reduced the demand for textiles and heavy footwear.

The great Mississippi Flood of April 1927 revealed to a shocked nation the depth of poverty throughout parts of the South. As refugees fled and relief workers sought to rescue them, they discovered in isolated districts forms of peonage for African Americans that were little removed from slavery. For those who faced such conditions, the claims of prosperity seemed a distant myth.

While profits rose and there were signs of prosperity, the fact that real wages barely increased over the 1920s suggested that prosperity did not run very deep. The class disparity in the United States was severe, made worse by tough anti-labor practices. Textile mills in states with strong union traditions closed down, and new mills opened in Virginia and North Carolina. Labor spies turned in the names of malcontents seeking to organize, and potential union organizers were often promptly dismissed. Labor leaders were accused of flirting with Bolshevism, and whether or not they harbored Marxist ideas, the charge helped rally public opinion against unions.

Even with the gulf between rich and poor, the economy did show signs of prosperity, and investors and businessmen viewed the 1920s as a boom time. The gross national product grew from $74 billion in 1922 to over $104 billion by 1929. Per-capita income grew from $627 in 1922 to $857 by 1929, although that gain for working-class people was largely offset by inflation.

Through later decades of the 20th century, astute observers and historians looked back on the raucous decade of the 1920s and could see in it the beginnings of modernism in popular culture, in the arts, and in social movements. Clearly, with the end of World War I, the "Age of Innocence" was well over. Some of the trends that emerged in the 1920s had been brewing over the first two decades of the century, only to develop more fully in the Roaring Twenties. One of the sources for that burst of cultural activity was found in the disillusionment spawned by World War I.

In 1919, idealists hoped that the end of war would represent a victory for democracy and that the promise of the Versailles conference to produce a lasting international guardian of world peace in the form of the League of Nations would be fulfilled. Those hopes were dashed with the failure of the United States to ratify the Peace Treaty and with the refusal of the U.S. Senate to endorse Woodrow Wilson's plan to join the League of Nations.

In November 1919, for the first time in its history, the U.S. Senate voted to cut off debate by invoking cloture, and in a series of votes, defeated the Versailles Treaty and the Covenant of the League of Nations, with or without reservations. A bitter blow to Wilson, the votes represented not only a clash of ideas and ideals about international affairs, but a personal clash between Henry Cabot Lodge, the Republican elder statesman in the Senate, and Wilson. Lodge resented Wilson's assumption that he could negotiate treaties without prior advice from the Senate. Some senators believed that participation in the League of Nations would require American involvement in distant international conflicts, or that League resolutions would encroach on American sovereignty.

PRESIDENT WILSON PARALYZED

Wilson, partially paralyzed and incapacitated after a stroke during a speaking tour that he hoped would rally support for the League, was unable to marshal Senatorial support for the Treaty and the League Covenant. Exhausted and weakened, he had cut short his speaking tour in September 1919. Then, after his return to Washington, his wife found him, on October 2, paralyzed on the floor of a bathroom in their private quarters in the White House. Although he could receive visitors sitting down, Wilson was a broken and embittered man, leaving most of the affairs of government to others. During the next months, he demanded the resignation of some of his most trusted advisers, including his second Secretary of State, Robert Lansing, and his personal secretary Joseph Tumulty. The administration simply drifted along through the period October 2, 1919 through March 4, 1921.

The Republican nomination for President in the 1920 election went to the handsome, but easily-manipulated Warren G. Harding, Senator from Ohio. His running mate was Calvin Coolidge, the governor of Massachusetts who had won fame by breaking the Boston police strike of September 1919. Senator Lodge had called the strike the first step towards sovietizing the United States, and Massachusetts Governor Coolidge stated that there was no right to strike against the public safety by anybody, anywhere, any time.

The Democrats, suffering from Wilson's defeat in the Senate and disillusionment with his program, found the coalition of progressive forces that had supported him now in disarray. Part of that disarray was Wilson's own fault, since he had stood aside during the 19 months of American participation the war (April 6, 1917-November 11, 1918), allowing his attorney general, the military, and his office of public information to collaborate in suppressing dissent and anti-war activity. The victims of this attack on civil liberties were members of the left, especially the Socialists. However, those liberals who had been most active in supporting Wilson as the candidate who stood against war and for peace in 1916, found themselves on the receiving end of political repression during the frenzied period of the war.

With Wilson's support on the left dissolving, and with conservatives flocking to the Republican cause, Democratic candidate James Cox and his running mate Franklin Roosevelt had little chance. In an early campaign address, Warren Harding sounded a reassuring note. The country should return to "normalcy," a word he was said to have invented.

Despite the fact that his critics claimed that his speeches seemed a series of pompous phrases crawling over the landscape in search of an idea, with the concept of normalcy, Harding had captured the mood of the voters. Americans seemed tired of idealism, tired of international crises, tired of the high moral tone and intellectual demeanor of Wilson. Harding, by contrast, seemed an amiable and ordinary representative of middle America, ready to take the country back to a course of business as usual. Harding won the election in November 1920 by 16 million votes to James Cox's nine million. Eugene Debs, still in prison for exercising his right to free speech by opposing the draft, polled over 900,000 votes for President on the Socialist ticket. President Harding pardoned Debs as part of a general amnesty for imprisoned radicals on Christmas Day, 1921.

Even with Harding's pleasant style and his assurances of normalcy, the years that followed were marked in many ways more by departure from the past than by any return to a by-gone era. In fact, Republicans began to describe their economic plan and the apparent prosperity that evolved from it as the New Era. New Era prosperity was reflected in rising stock prices, greater volume of stock market trade, and a boom in real estate values in Florida and elsewhere. The prosperity gave rise to new fortunes and new ways of spending money.

The New Era was new in more profound ways. Prohibition, enacted during Wilson's tenure of office, engendered a strange legal climate in which otherwise law-abiding citizens found ways to break the law in order to get a cocktail, a bottle of beer, or a party lubricated with scotch, bourbon, or gin. Overnight, it seemed, ordinary behavior had become criminalized, wrenching social and cultural values in a new direction. The nation turned inward to consumerism and a cultural clash over manners and morals, and away from a focus on issues of world peace, democracy, and justice.

Although the disillusionment in foreign affairs ushered in a period of isolationism, many Americans still kept a nervous eye on developments abroad. Small wars racked Europe, between Greece and Turkey and between Russia and Poland, and military dictators emerged to stifle budding democracies. Vladimir Ilyich Lenin's Bolshevik brand of Communism came to dominate the newly formed Soviet Union. To many it seemed that the inspired idealism of Wilson had only contributed to worse calamities, rather than offering comprehensive remedies. War and autocracy were on the rise, not in decline.

In Italy, the population was embittered by the war. At Versailles, Wilson had denied Italian claims to the port of Fiume, and Italians believed they had been betrayed by the Americans and the other Allies. Aroused by this cause and by the emergence of an invigorated left, veterans and youth turned to the new Fascist party headed by Benito Mussolini who was elected to Parliament in 1921, and then named Prime Minister in 1922 after his followers dramatically marched on Rome. Mussolini offered an uncompromising brand of nationalism, and the new word, "totalitarianism" entered the vocabularies of the world, to represent the Fascist party claim that there should be a total commitment by all organizations to a single version of national identity. In 1926, Mussolini solidified his power by outlawing all political parties except his own.

Autocratic and dictatorial regimes replaced democracies across Europe through the decade. In 1920, a dictatorship by Regent Miklos Horthy took over in Hungary. In 1923, General Primo Rivera set up a military dictatorship in Spain, and the Greek monarchy was abolished. Hitler, having taken over the Nazi Party in Germany in 1921, failed in his attempt to lead a revolt in the beer hall putsch of 1923 and was arrested. While in prison, he wrote *Mein Kampf*, published in 1924 as a blueprint for his party's victory and for the return of Germany to great power status. In 1924 Lenin died, and after a power struggle, Joseph Stalin emerged as the dictator of the Soviet Union.

Autocracy seemed to spread to small as well as the large nations of Europe. In 1924, Ahmed Zogu led an invasion and seizure of power in Albania, proclaiming himself King Zog, with absolute powers, in 1928. The military took power in Portugal in 1926, and in 1928, Dr. Antonio Salazar began to emerge as the dictator there, taking power over all government budgets. The Portuguese system increasingly emulated Italy's. In 1929 in Yugoslavia, King Alexander declared himself royal dictator, abolishing the parliament.

MISGUIDED IDEALISM

In the face of such events, the deaths of some 106,000 American soldiers in battle and non-combat incidents, rather than a noble sacrifice to the causes of democracy and peace, seemed in retrospect to be the tragic cost of a misguided idealism. Neither democracy nor peace prevailed in Europe or around the world. The young survivors of the war, in the words of Gertrude Stein, were a Lost Generation, with up and coming writers like Ernest Hemingway as their spokesmen. Clusters of American intellectuals, finding Prohibition and the emergence of a triumphant boosterism to be symptoms of a bourgeois culture that suppressed individualism, sought out escape, either by emigrating to France or Spain or by seeking refuge in isolated art colonies within the United States that seemed more open to their Bohemian lifestyles

.

Turning their backs on the League of Nations and the travails of Europe, many middle-class Americans seemed to revel in the new-found freedoms that sprang from putting the innocent idealism and high moral tone of earlier decades behind them. Overnight it seemed, young people rejected the manners and mores of their parents, regarding their customs and restrictions as either "Puritan" or "Victorian," although neither actual Puritans nor real Victorians would recognize the stereotypes of themselves bandied about over cocktails and cigarettes in the emerging Bohemian salons of Greenwich Village in New York City, Taos in New Mexico, or Hollywood.

For many in the middle class, however, the 1920s were not so much an age of flaming youth, bootlegged or home-brewed liquor, and emulation of the jazz style of Harlem. For sectors of the middle class, the years from 1920 to 1930 were a decade of financial opportunity. Suddenly, it seemed, one could make money in the stock market or in Florida land speculation. Or, if not so well-off to be able to spare some savings for such speculations, the working middle class found evidence of new prosperity in the ability to purchase some wonderful new possessions on the installment, or pay-as-you-go plan.

With new Fords and Chevrolets still priced well under $1,000 and with a thriving used car market with top quality Cadillacs and Pierce Arrows in the range of $1,500, middle-income consumers could make payments and own an automobile. Young people found the cars a means of a welcome escape from the watchful eyes of elders, allowing visits to juke joints, roadhouses, or more romantic encounters in the back seat or in roadside motor cabins that began to spring up on country highways.

THE ELECTRIC LIFE

Other technical advances changed the home itself, with labor-saving appliances, such as washing machines, electric irons, and small kitchen appliances that sold well wherever homes were linked to the spreading electric power grid. In the mountains of Tennessee and in vast areas of the West and Midwest, where ranches and farms lay too far from the power lines to make it profitable for power companies to extend service, the pre-electric life still continued with kerosene lamps, woodstoves, and once-a-week hot baths.

But for the urban and suburban dweller, the 20th century was well underway.

Handy inventions entered the marketplace—electric hair dryers in 1920, Band-Aids in 1924, and Kool Aid, Aerosol spray, and the greatest thing since bread itself, sliced bread, in 1927. Construction and farm machinery made steady advances. The first bulldozer was manufactured in 1923.And in a hint of the bold new future, an obscure scientist, Dr. Robert Goddard, developed a liquid fueled rocket in 1927 that was the precursor of guided missiles and interplanetary launch vehicles.

Many of the technical innovations of the age fed into the cultural phenomena. The first licensed radio broadcast in the United States was in 1920, from station KDKA in Pittsburgh, but within five years, millions listened to music, evangelists, and baseball games, at first on headsets and then increasingly, sitting attentively near radio loudspeakers.

The movies flourished, generating a shared national culture that celebrated celebrities. Hollywood became adept at creating such figures, and other communities joined in the effort, with Atlantic City, New Jersey sponsoring a bathing-beauty contest in September 1921 that evolved into the Miss America Pageant, and New York City hosting radio shows that were re-broadcast across the nation over the new National and American broadcasting networks.

The movies of the era provided a cheap and thrilling form of entertainment. Sound to accompany films was not introduced until the release of *The Jazz Singer*, the first full-length film with a sound track, in 1927. However, silent films, usually accompanied by a hired piano player in the theater, had made household names of John and Lionel Barrymore, Lon Chaney, Clara Bow, Greta Garbo, Lillian Gish, Mary Pickford, Francis X. Bushman, Ronald Colman, Charlie Chaplin, W.C. Fields, and dozens of others. Some of the great classic films of the era survived to entertain audiences years after, including *The Cabinet of Dr. Caligari* (1920), *Greed* (1924), *The Gold Rush* (1925), *The General* (1926), *Metropolis* (1927), and *The Passion of Joan of Arc* (1928).

For some of the older generation, these pastimes seemed to be pandering to low-brow popular taste, but new fortunes were made as the creation and management of American culture was taken away from the staid publishing houses and concert halls of New England and New York, and turned over to mass marketing by the new media of radio, film, and phonograph records. The newspapers that adapted to the new mass taste survived and flourished, with the "yellow journalism" of press magnate William Randolph Hearst expanding as he took over more and more newspapers across the nation in the first of the national chains.

By 1930 Hearst owned over 20 daily papers and his empire gave every sign of continuing its growth. His columns were filled not only with crime, sex and divorce scandals, disasters, and celebrities, but also with a running commentary on politics and international affairs. His views and those of other press magnates at once reflected and shaped public opinion, compounded of a vaguely anti-Wall Street and anti-banker populism, support for private property and proper behavior, an undercurrent of anti-radicalism, and opposition to the League of Nations. The tone was one of almost prurient interest in the misbehavior of criminals, rogues, and loose women, allowing a kind of vicarious thrill while retaining one's self-respect as a paragon of morality.

Daily newspapers like Hearst's *San Francisco Examiner* and his *New York American* continued to dominate the media, with Hearst commanding some 10 percent of over 30 million readers of the daily press a day. Hearst's press and other newspapers fed into the fads of the era, sometimes capturing them, other times manufacturing them. An early fad was that of Emile Coue, a popular French psychologist who argued that simply repeating a phrase could change one's state of mind, a procedure technically known as autosuggestion. Coue's method was popularized by Dr. Milan Miladinovic in a book published in 1922. Fascination in Coue was matched by the pyramid schemes of Charles K. Ponzi, then by the game of Mah Jongg, then by the short-lived sensation surrounding Floyd Collins, trapped in a Kentucky cave. Other popular obsessions were more lasting. The crossword puzzle was first invented in 1913. It continued appearing in the *New York World*, with some limited success. Then in 1924, a new publishing house, Simon and Schuster, published a crossword puzzle book, and the craze swept the nation, in a fad that never died away.

Murders and court cases became national sensations. In 1922, near New Brunswick New Jersey, two dead bodies were discovered, those of Reverend Edward Hall, and Mrs. Eleanor Mills, known to be having an extra-marital affair with each other. The Hall-Mills murder case kept the nation riveted for months through 1922 and 1923, and remains unsolved to this day. Equally compelling was the 1924 case of the young brilliant men Nathan Leopold and Richard Loeb, who were found guilty of the murder of Bobby Franks in Chicago after a botched kidnapping and ransom attempt.

The case of John Scopes, found guilty of teaching evolution in Tennessee, riveted the nation in the hot summer of 1925. The Scopes trial reflected deeper divisions in the country, noted by reporters and by historians since: liberals and modernists supported Scopes, conservatives and fundamentalists supported the prosecution. William Jennings Bryan, three-time candidate for President, and Secretary of State for 27 months under Woodrow Wilson, jumped at the chance to assist the Scopes prosecution, having taken up the cause of Creationism. Clarence Darrow, long a defender of the underdog and liberal causes, assisted the defense. H.L. Mencken, sardonic writer and social commentator, described the carnival scene in the small town of Dayton, Tennessee, for the readers of his nationally syndicated column. Hot-dog vendors, bible salesmen, caged chimpanzees, and out-of-town crowds jammed the streets. Bryan, Mencken claimed, had set himself up as the Fundamentalist Pope. Sensational journalism colored the way Americans viewed the serious business of government. When Warren Harding died, August 2, 1923 of food poisoning on a trip from Alaska to San Francisco, newspapers planted suspicions that he had been murdered. Readers later hung on the story of Nan Britton, who published an account of her affair with the President and the subsequent birth of a daughter she claimed that he had fathered.

Other scandals had marked Harding's brief presidency, including the Teapot Dome affair, which continued in the headlines for years after Harding's death. That scandal involved United States Secretary of the Interior Albert B. Fall. He had accepted bribes and no-interest personal loans, and in exchange, he had arranged for the leasing of publicly-owned oil fields to specific oil companies without the required competitive bidding. While the leases were legal, taking bribes to arrange leases was a federal crime. Teapot Dome was the name of one of the oil fields in Wyoming, while Elk Hills, California was another that Fall leased to his benefactors.

MORE SCANDALS

Other scandals wracked the Harding administration. The head of the Office of Alien Property, Thomas Miller, was convicted of accepting bribes, while Charles Forbes, director of the Veterans' Bureau, took kickbacks and ran a bootlegging operation and illegal drug business on the side. At least two officials involved in the scandals committed suicide. Harding never profited from the behavior of his appointees, many of whom had been selected because they were old political cronies from Ohio. Yet he seemed unable to dismiss or control the behavior of his former poker-playing friends. Affability and amiability had served as assets during the Presidential campaign, but proved to be severe liabilities in the office of the Presidency.

By contrast, his successor, Calvin Coolidge maintained a taciturn, quiet and often solemn manner. Coolidge became notorious for his low-key style, sleeping a reputed 12-hours a day and choosing his words very carefully. He once remarked that he had never gotten in trouble for something he did not say. As President, Coolidge retained many of Harding's more qualified and prestigious appointments at the Cabinet level through the next two years, including Herbert Hoover as Secretary of Commerce, Andrew Mellon as Secretary of the Treasury, and Charles Evans Hughes as Secretary of State. Coolidge replaced Hughes with Frank Kellogg in 1925, but retained Mellon throughout his own second term of office, and Hoover until August 1928.

Coolidge handily won re-election in the 1924 election, as the Democrats were in disarray, divided between those who supported William Gibbs McAdoo and those backing Al Smith. McAdoo was the son-in-law of Woodrow Wilson and his Secretary of the Treasury, and hoped to capture the party nomination with support of former Wilsonians and the loyal Democratic state machines of the South. Al Smith, the reform governor of New York, had backing from the city political machines as well as from the liberal northern branch of the party. The two wings of the party were reflected in a vote at the convention to condemn the Ku Klux Klan, a measure that won with 545 votes to 542. Liberals and Northeastern Democrats backed Smith and the anti-Klan position, Conservatives and Southerners backed McAdoo and the Klan. The convention dragged on through a record 103 ballots without achieving the necessary two-thirds for either McAdoo or Smith, finally compromising on John Davis of West Virginia, former U.S. ambassador to Great Britain.

Progressives rallied around a third-party candidacy of Robert LaFollette in 1924. The election seemed a confirmation of confidence in the New Era, with Coolidge taking about 15 million votes and Davis about eight million. LaFollette polled over four million, the greatest third-party turnout since Theodore Roosevelt's Progressive run in 1912. LaFollette's campaign had been ill-planned and executed, and his defeat was widely regarded, rightly or wrongly, as the death-knell of third-party politics. Coolidge declined to be nominated in 1928, and Herbert Hoover, with background as a mining engineer and administrator of relief agencies in World War I, as well as an excellent record as Secretary of Commerce through 1920s, received the nomination of the Republicans in 1928. He resigned that post in order to accept the nomination and campaign for the presidency.

Al Smith won the Democratic nomination in 1928 and that campaign reflected the difficult issues that served as an undercurrent to the era. Although neither Hoover nor Smith were explicit in their opinions of Prohibition, it appeared that Smith would be willing to modify it in the direction of eliminating it, and Hoover would work to modify it to make it more effective and reasonable. The fact that Smith was a Catholic rarely entered the campaign explicitly, but his ties to city political machines, his opposition to the Klan, and his Catholic religion seemed responsible for destroying the Democrats' hold on the Solid South. Hoover had over 21 million popular votes to Smith's 15 million, and Hoover took 444 electoral votes while Smith won only 87. Smith lost his own state of New York to Hoover, and Hoover took Oklahoma, Tennessee, Texas, Virginia, North Carolina, Florida, and Kentucky.

Observers speculated whether it was Smith's religion, his opposition to the Klan and Prohibition, or the fact that for the first time, candidates' speeches were broadcast by radio that defeated him. Radio put Smith's New York accent in living rooms throughout the South and that may have been even more jarring than his liberal political views. It was also entirely possible that an outright majority of American voters preferred Hoover because they believed his own record of accomplishments and that of the Coolidge administration deserved endorsement.

By contrast to the war years under Woodrow Wilson and the years of the Great Depression under Franklin Roosevelt, the three Republican administrations of the 1920s appeared to represent an era of small government, lowered taxes, and pro-business anti-union policies. On closer examination however, such a characterization of the Harding, Coolidge, and Hoover years is quite inaccurate. When the details of legislation and administration for the decade are looked at objectively and in the day-to-day press, a different picture emerges.

Although tax rates declined, they did not return to the rates before the war. Federal spending and federal aid to the states continued to grow. The number of government-owned corporations with special functions ballooned. Agriculture suffered by contrast to industry, but government crop price-support programs began in the era in genuine efforts to ameliorate the plight of farmers.

LAW AND LABOR

Law enforcement by the federal government greatly expanded with Prohibition, and the prosecution of anti-trust cases continued. Neither type of law enforcement could be said to be symptomatic of a small-government bias. And although the administrations were clearly pro-business, their policies did provide some measures that addressed the concerns of labor, such as increased wages in the Post Office Department and the expansion of labor dispute mediation services and statistical services.

Examining the daily news of the era, the stereotype of the Harding, Coolidge, and Hoover years as a period of government retrenchment and simple conservativism gives way to a picture of continuing some of the Progressive goals and the continued emergence of agencies that became permanent parts of the American system of structured government-business relations.

A national income tax had been established in 1913, with the highest rate at seven percent, increased in 1916 to 77 percent as the nation prepared to enter the war. Under Harding and Coolidge the top rate was reduced in several steps to 25 percent by 1925. Even so, the 25 percent rate was far higher than the pre-war seven percent rate. Furthermore, the revenues were used to support a much higher level of federal spending on non-military agencies than prevailed in the Progressive Era before the war.

These areas included law enforcement (much of it devoted to enforcing Prohibition), commerce, agriculture, labor, immigration, public education and public improvements. By 1930, the budgets in all of these areas were two to three times what they had been in 1920. Furthermore, the federal government vastly increased its aid to state governments, from about $6 million in 1915 to about $109 million by 1930. Hoover remained in the presidency through March 5, 1933. Looking at the Hoover years, the federal aid to states climbed to over $230 million by 1932. Compared with later years these amounts were small, but compared with the miniscule amounts before the war, it is clear that the decade of the 1920s saw the precedent of federal support to the states well established.

New government agencies and government corporations, including those continued from the war years and those established during the 1920s showed that "big government" was here to stay. The Federal Land Bank, the Sugar Equalization Board, and the U.S. Housing Corporation, all created during the Wilson years were not dismantled in the 1920s. In 1923, the Agricultural Credits Act established 12 federally owned banks to provide loans for farmers. In 1924, the Inland Waterways Corporation was established, and in 1929 the Federal Farm Board was set up. Some of Hoover's measures to deal with business closures and unemployment survived into later years. The Reconstruction Finance Corporation, established in Hoover's administration in 1932 provided loans to both states and corporations as a means of providing relief to states and corporations, and was later retained by the Roosevelt administration as a major channel for federal aid to stimulate employment during the Depression. Federal construction projects, such as the Hoover Dam on the Colorado River, later renamed the Boulder Dam, began under the Republican administration in 1930.

As Secretary of Commerce under Coolidge, Herbert Hoover was responsible for the creation of two new agencies to regulate the booming new industries of aviation and radio. The Federal Aviation Administration (FAA) had its origin in 1926 as the Air Commerce Branch of the Department of Commerce, created under the Federal Air Commerce Act of that year. The Federal Communications Commission (FCC) had as its predecessor, the Federal Radio Commission established in 1927. Hoover, as a manager and activist administrator, took immediate charge of the Mississippi Flood situation, marshalling a fleet of hundreds of boats to rescue over 300,000 displaced African Americans and moving them to relief camps. His newsworthy competence in that crisis was still fresh in the minds of delegates to the Republican convention in 1928 when he received the presidential nomination.

Although farmers and ranchers did not fare very well through the 1920s, part of their problems derived from the growth of production overseas and the lowering of world agricultural prices. Even though the Harding, Coolidge, and Hoover administrations were reputed to be more oriented to industry than to the needs of farmers, several measures were passed and implemented through the decade to help keep up farm prices or to provide farm loans. Tariffs on imported farm products were included in the 1921 revenue act, and in 1922, the Capper-Volstead Act was passed, that exempted agricultural cooperatives from antitrust laws. The Department of Agriculture set up in 1926 the Division of Cooperative Marketing, a measure supported personally by Coolidge. The 1923 Agricultural Credits Act facilitated short-term loans from the Federal Farm Loan Board for farmers.

FEDERAL FARM BOARD

Direct price supports for farm commodities were more difficult to achieve. The Republican-controlled Congress passed the McNary-Haugen bill in Congress in 1927 and in 1928, but in both years this plan for agricultural price support was vetoed by Coolidge on what he regarded as constitutional grounds. However, in 1929, the Agricultural Marketing Act was passed and signed into law by Hoover after he had called Congress into special session to address the problem. That act created a Federal Farm Board empowered to purchase and store agricultural products with the purpose of directly supporting farm prices.

Enforcement of the law was another area in which the growth of the federal government reached into new areas. Prohibition was blamed in the popular press for the rise of organized crime, particularly in the person of crime boss Al Capone, who from his base in Cicero, Illinois, dominated bootlegging, prostitution, drug rackets and extortion in Chicago after spectacular gang fights there. Estimates of the number of gangsters killed in the gang wars in that city alone during the 1920s exceeded 500.

From the point of view of the federal government's role, Prohibition was responsible for a vast expansion of law-enforcement budgets and apparatus. The Bureau of Internal Revenue in the Treasury Department was supported by agents of the Customs Service, the Coast Guard, and the Department of Justice. In 1920, a Prohibition Unit was set up in the Bureau of Internal Revenue. In 1927, the Treasury Department had a separate Bureau of Prohibition. Since the budgets of all of these agencies and bureaus were usually included in the overall budget for the department or agency, it was difficult even at the time to identify exactly how much was being spent on law enforcement. Even so, the creation and expansion of these federal law enforcement agencies shows that the image of an inactive or passive federal government for the era was simply incorrect.

Although Theodore Roosevelt had earned a reputation as a "trust-buster," the growth of antitrust activity came well after his administration that ended in 1909. During T. R.'s administration from 1905 to 1909, the government brought some 39 cases against businesses engaged in price-fixing or other illegal monopolization activities. Over period 1910 through 1919, during the administration of William

Howard Taft and those of Woodrow Wilson, some 134 antitrust cases were initiated. In the so-called pro-business climate of the 1920s, there were an additional 125 antitrust cases initiated. The Progressive goal of preventing excessive monopolization by business did not die off under the three Republican presidents of the decade.

AFRICAN-AMERICAN MIGRATION

As African Americans migrated in great numbers from the South to northern cities during the war years, the effects of this mass movement were felt especially in Chicago, New York, St. Louis, and several other major cities of the northeast. Violent race riots, including a bitter eruption in East St. Louis in 1917 and another in Chicago in the summer of 1919 reflected the hostilities of whites to the newcomers' presence. As black neighborhoods in the cities continued to grow during the 1920s, these pockets of African-American culture began to develop a life of their own. Harlem in New York had a thriving black culture before World War I, and the emergence of jazz clubs in that section began to bring white customers in the 1920s.

In Newark, Harlem, Chicago, and smaller northern cities, store-front religions sprang up, developing into whole denominations, often viewed by outsiders as cults. Daddy Grace, an immigrant from the Cape Verde Islands, established the first United House of Prayer for All People in Wareham, Massachusetts in 1919, formally incorporated in Washington D.C. in 1926. Soon Houses of Prayer began to spread to other cities, offering a communal life style as well as salvation. A competing organization, founded by Father Divine, the Peace Mission Movement, called on its members to be celibate. Divine's Peace Missions, first appearing in Brooklyn in 1919, swelled in numbers, often attracting thousands to rallies. Estimates of the total in the movement varied from 50,000 to two million.

The secular leader, Marcus Garvey built a much wider organization through the 1920s, the United Negro Improvement Association (UNIA). Garvey had first arrived in the United States from Jamaica in 1915, seeking to work with and emulate Booker T. Washington. However, he founded his own organization that grew rapidly through the war years and especially after 1919. The UNIA attracted followers based on a promise of establishing black businesses and black organizations. The UNIA adopted the red, green, and black flag that became the symbol of African-American national identity.

Garvey's Black Star Line was set up to purchase ships to ply in trade to the Caribbean and to Africa, although it soon collapsed due to the mismanagement of the organization's affairs and some unwise ship purchases. Garvey was arrested and convicted of mail fraud in 1925, and incarcerated in the Atlanta Federal Penitentiary. In 1927, his sentence was commuted by President Coolidge, and Garvey was hastily deported to Jamaica. Nevertheless, the organization he founded continued to attract members for the next few years.

Lesser-known black leaders, including some who preached adherence to Islam or to Judaism flourished in the decade. It appeared to observers that many African Americans had migrated to the North in search of a promised land and in hopes of escaping the oppression of lynching and segregation in the South. Disappointed to find their physical well-being little improved, with unemployment, discrimination, poverty and bitter winter climates, and cut off from their traditional religious roots, they seemed ready to turn to the promises held out by such charismatic leaders as Grace, Divine, Garvey and others.

By the late 1920s, street agitators and religious leaders, as well as some in more traditional Christian churches, turned their attention to questions of unemployment and discrimination, forerunners of the civil rights activism of later decades. Other immigrants also faced discrimination and hostility, although as whites, their integration into main-stream America was somewhat easier to accomplish. Nevertheless, for first-generation migrants from southern

Europe and the Middle East during this period, hostility and prejudice were commonplace. Like African Americans, the new immigrants tended to seek out enclaves where others from their homelands had taken up residence. The Immigration Restriction Act of 1924 reflected an effort by Congress to establish immigration quotas that would favor those from the British Isles and northern Europe. Limiting immigration to two percent of the ethnic groups represented in the 1890 census, before the waves of southern Europeans and others had flooded into the United States in the first decade of the 20th century, the law also placed a total immigration cap of 154,000. The quotas allowed for Italians fell from 42,000 to just over 3,800. The law did not apply to countries in the Western Hemisphere, and it did not go into effect until 1929. Nevertheless, the meaning of the law was clear, both to immigrants and native-born citizens—the country had adopted a policy intended to reshape American ethnicity along the lines of 1890, not that of 1910 or 1920.

A case involving immigrants that caught the imagination of the American public and sympathizers around the world was that of Nicola Sacco and Bartomoleo Vanzetti. In April, 1920, a payroll truck was held up in South Braintree, Massachusetts, and the driver was killed. Italian immigrants, both radical abolitionists, Sacco and Vanzetti were arrested May 5, 1920 for the crime, attracting only local attention. However, when the well-known Socialist lawyer Fred Moore came to their defense based upon the suggestion that the courts and juries were biased against them as radicals and as Italians, their case soon began to attract international attention. Moore set out to publicize the case, by enlisting radical organizations and newspapers to come the defense of the two men. After a hard-fought, six-week trial that pitted Socialism and anarchism against patriotism, the two men were found guilty of robbery and murder on July 14, 1921.

Over the next six years, Moore and his successor as defense attorney, William Thompson, mounted a campaign of letter-writing and publicity. Despite protests from liberals and radicals from around the world, Sacco and Vanzetti were sentenced to death on April 9, 1927. The protests did result in the appointment of a commission in Massachusetts to review their case. However, the commission, after the exercise of some very dubious logic, found that there was no reason to recommend clemency to the governor, and the two were executed August 23, 1927.

Through the decade, intellectuals offered running commentary on the changing times, through novels, autobiographical sketches, essays and columns. One of the leading spokesmen of the revolt of the intellectuals against the oppressive imposition of middle-class living standards and standards of taste was H.L. Mencken. Building on his reputation from the *Baltimore Sun,* he went on to edit the *American Mercury,* which became an outlet for his comments on the silliness of the American mind.

Even though voters and much of the middle class appeared to believe that the nation enjoyed solid prosperity, there were indications of deep cracks in the façade. Aside from the disparity between the rich and poor, there were growing pockets of economic distress as in agriculture and factory and mining towns. Even more ominously, there were indications that all was not well on the scale of the world economy.

October 29, 1929, known as Black Tuesday, saw the beginning of a fall of stock prices that lasted for a full month. By the end of that period, bankruptcies spread from speculators to banks to corporations. The overall bear market continued through 1932. In fact, stock prices did not reach the levels they had held in 1929 until 1954. With credit drying up and investor confidence at low ebb, manufacturers cut back. The layoffs of workers spread, and unemployment rose, quickly driving down consumer spending. The last two months of the decade saw the beginnings of the Great Depression.

Rodney Carlisle, Ph.D.
General Editor

	World Affairs	Europe	Africa & The Middle East	The Americas	Asia & The Pacific
1920	The League of Nations begins operations.	The Ottoman Empire breaks apart. Under the Treaty of Sévres, large areas in Europe and the Middle East become independent states or mandates.... Holland refuses to give the Kaiser to the allies. He remains in exile until his death in 1941.... The monarchist Kapp Putsch fails in Germany.... Russia fights a war against Poland as well as a Red-White civil war.	Britain takes over the mandate for German East Africa. The mandate becomes Tanganyika.... Arabs rise against Britain in Iraq.	Venustiano Carranza resists turning the presidency over to Alvaro Obregon. When Obregon and others rise against him and declare the Republic of Sonora, he flees to Tlaxcalantongo, where he is assassinated.	Seeking home rule, Mohandas K. Gandhi begins his first non-cooperation campaign, including a boycott of British goods and the spinning of homespun.... An earthquake in China kills 200,000.
1921	At the Washington Disarmament Conference, the major powers agree to respect Chinese territorial integrity. They also commit to reduce warship tonnages.	King Karl violates treaty agreements and returns to Hungary. The legislature rejects the restoration of the Habsburg monarchy. A second attempt leads to mobilization of the Yugoslav army and Karl's exile.	England assumes the Belgian mandate in Tanganyika and splits Transjordan from Palestine, exempting the new emirate from the Balfour Declaration.... Spain engages in a protracted war with the Rif in Morocco.	Panama occupies territory claimed by Costa Rica.	Mohandas Gandhi begins a boycott of imported cloth as a pressure tactic for Indian independence.... China's Communist Party emerges.
1922	The Reparations Commission sets Germany's obligation at 132 billion gold marks. German inflation begins.... The major powers sign the Five-, Four-, and Nine-Power treaties.	Benito Mussolini's March on Rome succeeds. Italy becomes fascist.... Britain proclaims the Irish Free State, a self-governing component of the empire.... Ukraine becomes a Soviet Socialist Republic.	George Carnarvon and Howard Carter discover the unlooted tomb of King Tutankhamen in Egypt.... Britain terminates its protectorate of Egypt and Fuad I becomes Egyptian king.	Costa Rica invades Panama.	The Chinese Communist Party is officially formed.
1923	Ethiopia joins the League of Nations after Italy and France reassure Britain, concerned about slavery and arms trafficking in Ethiopia.	France and Belgium occupy the Ruhr to force Germany to pay reparations.... Adolf Hitler attempts the unsuccessful Munich Beer Hall Putsch.... The Soviet Union introduces forced labor camps, finds gold in Siberia, and begins economic recovery.	Britain assumes the Palestinian mandate.	Mexico agrees to recognize oil concessions in place prior to 1917. This easing of nationalization efforts improves relations with the U..S. and allows the U.S. to recognize the Obregon government.	A massive earthquake destroys a third of Tokyo.
1924	Charles Jewtraw wins the first event of the International Winter Sports Week (later renamed the first Winter Olympics) but the Nordic countries dominate.... Stars of the summer Olympics are Finland's Paavo Nurmi, who wins five distance-running gold medals and Johnny Weissmuller, who takes three swimming gold medals.	Adolf Hitler receives a five-year sentence, writes *Mein Kampf* in prison, and gets out after eight months.... Vladimir Lenin dies. Joseph Stalin takes power in the Soviet Union.	Abdul Aziz Ibn Saud leads the Wahhabi to power in Saudi Arabia.... Britain represses risings in Egypt and Iraq.... Spain struggles against the Rif.	U.S. Marines withdraw from the Dominican Republic, which enters the League.... U.S. Marines intervene in a Honduran civil war.	Japan gives up tariff and extraterritoriality in Siam.... Anti-Hindu riots occur in India.... The Hanapepe Massacre sees Hawaiian police kill striking Filipino sugar workers.... Australia enacts compulsory voting.
1925	The Locarno Conferences convene as nations seek mutual security.	Adolf Hitler forms a 27,000 member Nazi Party.... German scientists develop a method of creating synthetic gasoline.	France consolidates two mandates in forming Syria.... The African Sleeping Sickness Conference convenes outside Africa.	U.S. Marines leave Nicaragua after 13 years.... Colombia's effort to create a Caribbean airline stumbles due to U.S. indifference.	Sun Yat-sen dies.... Under the name Rama VII Prajadhipok becomes ruler of Siam. He will be the last Siamese emperor.
1926	Germany joins the League of Nations but leaves in 1933.	Fascist youth organizations form in Germany and Italy.... A British company manufactures the first compound fertilizers using nitrogen, potassium, and phosphorous.... In Switzerland, the Pro Juventute Foundation begins taking Roma children from their parents without consent. The program lasts until 1973.... Turkey bans the fez and polygamy.	Lebanon becomes a republic..... France and Spain defeat the Rif.... Ibn Saud secures his hold on Saudi Arabia.... Reza Khan becomes Shah of Iran.	The U.S. sends Marines to Nicaragua to stabilize the revolt-torn country. Marines remain until 1933.	Chiang Kai-shek becomes head of the Chinese Nationalists.
	A *Includes developments that affect more than one world region, international organizations and important meetings of world leaders.*	B *Includes all domestic and regional developments in Europe, including the Soviet Union.*	C *Includes all domestic and regional developments in Africa and the Middle East.*	D *Includes all domestic and regional developments in Latin America, the Caribbean, and Canada.*	E *Includes all domestic and regional developments in Asian and Pacific nations (and colonies).*

U.S. Politics & Social Issues	U.S. Foreign Policy & Affairs, Defense	U.S. Economy & Environment	Science, Technology & Nature	Culture, Leisure & Lifestyle	
The U.S. government engages in a "Red Hunt" and deports hundreds of radicals.…Police arrest Nicolo Sacco and Bartolomeo Vanzetti for murder and robbery.…Tennessee ratifies the Nineteenth Amendment. Women receive the right to vote.…Clarence Darrow, Helen Keller, Jane Addams, and others form the American Civil Liberties Union.	The Senate fails to find a compromise, killing ratification of the Treaty of Versailles.…The Harding administration implements the Emergency Quota Immigration Act restricting immigration to three percent of the 1910 population.	KDKA, Pittsburgh, transmits the first commercial radio broadcast.…Illinois Bell and Indiana Bell telephone companies form.	In Writtle, England, Guglielmo Marconi opens the world's first radio station, and Robert Goddard begins his work in rocketry.…William Draper Harkins theorizes that a subatomic particle, the neutron, exists.…Thomas Hunt Morgan postulates that chromosomes carry genetic information.	In sports, the Yankees buy Babe Ruth from Boston, Cleveland beats Brooklyn in the World Series, Ottawa wins the Stanley Cup over Seattle, and Paul Jones wins the Kentucky Derby. NCAA football champion is 9-0 California, and pro champions are the 9-0-3 Akron Pros.…Eugene O'Neill's *Beyond the Horizon*, his first full-length play, wins a Pulitzer Prize. The Harlem Renaissance begins. With Prohibition, the speakeasy replaces the saloon.…The Dada movement starts.	1920
New government agencies are the Veterans Bureau and the Bureau of the Budget.…The first burial at the Tomb of the Unknown Soldier in Arlington National Cemetery occurs.	By joint resolution, Congress declares that World War I is over.	Unemployment reaches 11.7 percent. The federal budget tops $5 billion. A first-class stamp costs two cents.…The discovery of oil near Signal Hill makes California a leading oil-producing state.…Western Union begins transmitting wirephotos.…The boll weevil destroys the profitability of cotton.	Vitamins D and E are discovered.…Albert Einstein wins a Nobel Prize for his discovery of the photoelectric effect.…Canadian John Larson invents the polygraph.	The Giants beat the Yankees in the World Series, Ottawa wins the Stanley Cup, and California shares the football title with 8-0 Cornell.…Miss America is Margaret Gorman of Washington, D.C.…Fatty Arbuckle's career ends after his arrest for manslaughter.…Rudolf Valentino becomes a star after debuting in *The Sheik*.	1921
The U.S. Post Office destroys 500 copies of newly published *Ulysses* by James Joyce.	The Washington Conference establishes ratios for the major powers' capital ships and restricts submarine and gas warfare.…The Fordney-McCumber Tariff goes into effect with the highest rates in U.S. history.	Unemployment is down to 6.7 percent. The federal budget is down to $3.29 billion. The United Mine Workers of America strike for six months. The public mood becomes increasingly anti-union.…The first radio commercial sells for $100 for 10 minutes.	Frederick Banting and Herbert Best isolate insulin, which regulates the body's use of sugar. Herbert McLean Evans discovers human growth hormone in the pituitary gland.…French children are first to receive the new tuberculosis vaccine.	The Lincoln Memorial opens in Washington, D.C.…The Giants beat the Yankees again, California shares its third football title, and Toronto St. Pats beats Vancouver in hockey.…Eugene O'Neill's *Anna Christie* and Booth Tarkington's *Alice Adams* win Pulitzer Prizes.…*Reader's Digest* begins publication.	1922
The revived Ku Klux Klan becomes a political force.…President Warren Harding dies. Vice President Calvin Coolidge becomes president.…The first legal birth control clinic in the U.S. opens in New York.	The first U.S. dirigible, *Shenandoah*, makes its maiden flight.	Unemployment is at 2.4 percent, and the federal budget is $3.14 billion.…The A.C. Nielson begins providing audience ratings for radio advertisers.…Kodak introduces home movie equipment.	Vladimir Zworykin patents the iconoscope, the first television transmission tube.…Tests at San Quentin reveal that scopolamine is a "truth serum," not just a childbirth anesthetic.…	The Yankees finally beat the Giants in the World Series.…Bessie Smith cuts her first single. The Cotton Club opens in Harlem. It features black performers and white audiences.…Rin Tin Tin becomes a star.…*Time* magazine debuts.	1923
Albert Fall, Harry Doheny, and Harry Sinclair are indicted for conspiracy and bribery in the Teapot Dome scandal.…Nathan Leopold and Richard Loeb confess to murdering their cousin. Bobby Franks.…Aimee Semple Macpherson opens her Angelus Temple.	The 1924 Immigration Act establishes quotas of 2 percent of the 1890 census, provides a 150,000 ceiling in 1927, and excludes Asians.….Anti-American demonstrations in Japan occur in the aftermath of U.S. unilateral abrogation of the 1907 Gentlemen's Agrement.	International Business Machine arises from a reorganization of Computer Tabulating Recording Company.…The federal budget is $2.9 billion. Unemployment is up to five percent.	Edwin Hubble demonstrates that spiral nebulae consist of stars.…George and Gladys Dick link streptococcus to scarlet fever.	Washington wins the World Series against the New York Giants.…Undefeated Notre Dame is undisputed national college football champion.…Macy's sponsors its first Thanksgiving Day parade.…George Gershwin's *Rhapsody in Blue* debuts. Walt Disney produces his first cartoon. Imports of mah jongg sets top $1.6 million as the craze peaks.	1924
Wyoming's Nellie Tayloe Ross becomes the first U.S. woman governor.…The Tennessee trial of John Scopes highlights the evolution debate and media frenzy.…Al Capone becomes head of Chicago's bootlegging operation.	The dirigible *Shenandoah* breaks up.…Billy Mitchell's court martial occurs.	The Chrysler Corporation forms.….The first motel, the Milestone Motel, opens in California.…Ford buys the Stout Metal Airplane Company and begins producing the Ford Trimotor in 1926.	Vladimir Zworykin patents the first television color tube.…Scottish John Logie Baird transmits human features over television.…The Tri-state tornado, the worst in U.S. history, sweeps through Missouri, Illinois and Indiana, killing 689.…Werner Heisenberg and Niels Bohr develop quantum mechanics.	*The Smith Family* becomes radio's first soap opera. Edna Ferber's *So Big* wins a literature Pulitzer while George Bernard Shaw wins the literature Nobel Prize.…Notable movies are Sergei Eisenstein's innovative *Potemkin* and the record $3.95 million *Ben Hur*.…The Charleston and cloche became fads. Jazz conquers Europe.	1925
Father Charles Coughlin begins a 20-year radio broadcasting career.	The Thompson Commission calls for more autonomy for the Philippines but reports that independence is not yet feasible.…The Army Air Corps is activated.	Unemployment is 1.8 percent and the federal budget remains below $3 billion.…RCA, GE, and Westinghouse form the National Broadcasting Company (NBC).	A.A. Michelson uses mirrors to measure the speed of light.…Richard Byrd and Floyd Bennett claim to have flown over the North Pole.…Robert Goddard launches his first liquid-fuelled rockets. Anti-freeze allows use of automobiles year round.…Electrical recording is a major improvement over tinny-sounding acoustic recording.	The Book-of-the-Month Club begins selling books by mail to subscribers.…Martha Graham debuts her dance ensemble, 18 barefoot and provocatively-clad women.	1926

F	G	H	I	J
Includes campaigns, elections, federal-state relations, civil rights and liberties, crime, the judiciary, education, healthcare, poverty, urban affairs, and population.	*Includes formation and debate of U.S. foreign and defense policies, veterans affairs, and defense spending. (Relations with specific foreign countries are usually found under the region concerned.)*	*Includes business, labor, agriculture, taxation, transportation, consumer affairs, monetary and fiscal policy, natural resources, pollution and industrial accidents.*	*Includes worldwide scientific, medical and technological developments, natural phenomena, U.S. weather and natural disasters.*	*Includes the arts, religion, scholarship, communications media, sports, entertainment, fashions, fads, and social life.*

	World Affairs	Europe	Africa & The Middle East	The Americas	Asia & The Pacific
1927	Aristide Briand and Maxim Litvinov introduce proposals to outlaw war....Three-power arms reduction talks stalemate.	Russia's Communist Party expels Leon Trotsky.	Iraq becomes independent but must allow a British military presence.... Sierra Leone outlaws slavery	Mexico introduces petroleum laws to reduce foreign exploitation, causing tension with the U.S. until the Supreme Court overturns them. ...Mexico begins expropriating church property under its new anti-clerical laws.	Chiang Kai-shek establishes his government at Nanking. Communists challenge his rule.
1928	The Kellogg-Briand Pact outlaws war. Sixty-five nations sign....Norway's Sonja Henie emerges as a skating star at the Winter Olympics....The U.S. dominates a summer games more notable for Germany's return to competition after a 10-year absence and the inclusion of the first women's events.	Joseph Stalin implements the first five-year plan to collectivize agriculture.	Ethiopia signs a 20-year friendship treaty with Italy. The pact lasts until Italy invades Ethiopia.	Herbert Hoover visits Latin America on a Goodwill Tour.	In the Chinese civil war, the Nationalists near victory and, with the subordination of a dozen warlords, unification of China seems feasible....The Indian National Congress calls for dominion status.
1929	Kellogg-Briand becomes effective....The Young Plan replaces Dawes reparations....Revision of the World Court begins.	The Lateran Treaty provides an independent Vatican City within Italy.	Conflicts over access to Jerusalem's Wailing Wall generate the first widespread Arab-Jewish conflict in Palestine.	End comes to Mexico's Cristero War and the longstanding Tacna-Arica dispute between Peru and Chile.... The Chaco War continues, as does instability in Haiti.	Indian nationalists demand independence after Britain announces another study group.

A	B	C	D	E
Includes developments that affect more than one world region, international organizations and important meetings of world leaders.	*Includes all domestic and regional developments in Europe, including the Soviet Union.*	*Includes all domestic and regional developments in Africa and the Middle East.*	*Includes all domestic and regional developments in Latin America, the Caribbean, and Canada.*	*Includes all domestic and regional developments in Asian and Pacific nations (and colonies).*

U.S. Politics & Social Issues	U.S. Foreign Policy & Affairs, Defense	U.S. Economy & Environment	Science, Technology & Nature	Culture, Leisure & Lifestyle	
After extensive appeals and worldwide protests, Massachusetts executes Sacco and Vanzetti.... The Supreme Court rules in *Buck v. Bell* that sterilization of the feebleminded is legal. Indiana passes a new sterilization law.	U.S. Secretary of State Frank Kellogg announces he will negotiate an agreement to outlaw war.	The Holland Tunnel opens, providing an underwater link between New York and New Jersey.... Philadelphia Storage Battery Company (Philco) introduces the first car radio.... General Electric begins regular television broadcasts	Charles Lindbergh becomes the first to fly the Atlantic solo.... The Mississippi River system floods, devastating the South and parts of the Midwest.... Werner Heisenberg, age 26, introduces his uncertainty principle.... Davidson Black discovers "Peking Man."... Georges Lemaitre suggests the "big bang" theory.... Philo Farnsworth introduces all electronic television.	Babe Ruth sets a record with 60 home runs in a season. The Yankees sweep Pittsburgh in the series.... *The Jazz Singer* is the first talking movie.... Dancer Isadora Duncan dies in an automobile accident.... The Academy of Motion Picture Arts and Sciences forms.	1927
Oscar DePriest of Chicago becomes the first black man elected to Congress from a northern state.... Herbert Hoover wins the presidency over Catholic Al Smith.	The Jones-White Merchant Marine Act attempts to restore the competitiveness of the U.S. commercial fleet.... The Flood Control Act of 1928 establishes a long-term project to correct the weaknesses that allow the 1927 devastation.	Ford begins full-scale production of the Model A.... IBM begins using the 80-column punch card.	Richard Byrd begins an Antarctic expedition that lasts until 1930.... Alexander Fleming discovers penicillin. Margaret Mead publishes *Coming of Age in Samoa*.... Amelia Earhart becomes the first woman to fly across the Atlantic.... The Lake Okeechobee flood, caused by a hurricane, kills 2,400 and the Florida land boom.	The Yankees sweep another World Series. Helen Wills and Rene Lacoste win at Wimbledon.... Eugene O'Neill wins another Pulitzer, for *Strange Interlude*.	1928
Chicago is the site of the St. Valentine's Day Massacre, a major gangland slaying.	The U.S. joins the World Court after a year of talks—and with reservations.	The stock market collapses, and the U.S. economy loses $26 billion. The Great Depression follows.... William Paley forms CBS.	Albert Einstein proposes his unified field theory.... Hans Berger develops the electroencephalogram for measuring brain waves.... Richard Byrd, Bernt Balchen, and two others are first to fly over the South Pole.	The Museum of Modern Art opens in New York City.... *Wings* wins the Academy Award for best picture. Thomas Mann wins the Nobel for literature.	1929

F	G	H	I	J
Includes campaigns, elections, federal-state relations, civil rights and liberties, crime, the judiciary, education, healthcare, poverty, urban affairs, and population.	*Includes formation and debate of U.S. foreign and defense policies, veterans affairs, and defense spending. (Relations with specific foreign countries are usually found under the region concerned.)*	*Includes business, labor, agriculture, taxation, transportation, consumer affairs, monetary and fiscal policy, natural resources, pollution and industrial accidents*	*Includes worldwide scientific, medical and technological developments, natural phenomena, U.S. weather and natural disasters.*	*Includes the arts, religion, scholarship, communications media, sports, entertainment, fashions, fads, and social life.*

STORAG

1920

Prohibition begins in 1920: A liquor raid in progress.

	World Affairs	Europe	Africa & The Middle East	The Americas	Asia & The Pacific
Jan.	The League of Nations holds its first meeting. President Wilson presides in the last official U.S. involvement with the League. The League ratifies the Treaty of Versailles. World War I is ended....Holland refuses to turn over Wilhelm II to stand trial. Rather, the Dutch intern him until his 1941 death.	General Kolcak's White Russians surrender at Krasnojarsk....Turkey loses the Ottoman Empire and its non-Turkish possessions....The last Russian Communist troops leave Latvia. The new republic will survive.	Britain assumes mandate for German East Africa. Britain renames the territory Tanganyika and sends German colonists home.		*Shakuntala* is released. This is the first Indian film starring a foreign actor (Dorothy Kingdom.)....Japan concludes a peace treaty with Germany. Japan will later become disenchanted when it realizes the treaty does not recognize its special status in the Far East.
Feb.		Darius Milhaud and Jean Cocteau debut the impressionist ballet, *Le Boeuf sur le toit en.* In Germany, the expressionist film, *Das Kabinett des Doctor Kaligari (The Cabinet of Dr. Caligari)* debuts....Germany's Adolf Hitler enunciates an anti-Semitic program for his NSDAP.		The Royal Canadian Mounted Police come into being as Canada's national police force. The "Mounties" are the merged Northwest Mounted Police and Dominion Police.... Huerta, Calles, and Obregon rise against President Carranza and declare the Republic of Sonora. Mexico is in another civil war.	
Mar.		Sweden establishes a government that manages the economy and provides all Swedes with social welfare coverage. Hjalmar Branting heads the first peacefully-instituted social democratic government.... The monarchist putsch attempt of Wolfgang Kapp fails. He lacks popular support.	Syria declares independence from France. France and Britain recognize Faisal as Syrian monarch.	Bolivia claims that neither Peru nor Chile has a right to Tacna and Arica. Rather, Bolivia has a right to access to the ocean through them.	
Apr.	The League assigns mandates for Palestine and Iraq to Britain. The League requires that Britain establish a Jewish homeland as agreed to in the Balfour Declaration but exempts Transjordan from that requirement.	A German army enters the French-occupied Ruhr to fight the German Spartacists. Germany receives French permission beforehand.... Poland attacks Russia, beginning the Russo-Polish War.	Riots begin in Jerusalem between Jews and Arabs.		In order to keep control of Siberia while avoiding a war with Japan, Russia establishes the Far Eastern Republic....Gandhi becomes president of the All-India Home Rule League.
May	Pope Benedict XV canonizes Joan of Arc as a saint. The 15th century peasant girl is a symbol of French nationalism.	Switzerland holds a referendum on joining the League of Nations	Russian Bolsheviks, having bested the whites, occupy part of Persia. They establish the Soviet Republic of Gilan, which lasts until October 1921.	Obregon captures Mexico City. Carranza is killed. The Mexican civil war is effectively over. Pancho Villa formally surrenders the last government force in July....Canada announces it will send a minister to the U.S.; this recognizes Canada's new autonomy within the empire.	At the Muslim conference in Allahabad, Gandhi wins a resolution supporting *Satyagraha*, his campaign of non-cooperation with the British rulers.
Jun.	The International Labor Organization holds its second meeting. Issues include minimum age for sailors, unemployment compensation for shipwrecked sailors, and conditions of employment for sailors.	Under the Treaty of Trianon, Hungary loses 71 percent of its territory and 63 percent of its people. Minority-dominated territory (with Magyar minorities) went to Yugoslavia, Romania, Czechoslovakia, and Austria.	Britain reorganizes the government of Uganda. The territory has a nominated legislative council.		
Jul.	The Spa Conference sets the formula for German Reparations. France gets 52 percent, Britain 22 percent, Italy 10 percent, and the smaller powers the rest. Germany arranges to ship coal as payment.	Dusseldorf, Germany, bars Roma and Sinti from entering any public recreational or washing facility. The ban includes pools, baths, spas, and parks.	The Arab rising against British rule in Iraq begins. Britain will require six months to quell this nationalist rising against colonial rule....British East Africa becomes the crown colony of Kenya....South Africa establishes a Native Affairs Commission. Issues include reservations and detribalization....France deposes Faisal in Syria.		
Aug.	The 1920 Olympic Games take place. Site is Antwerp, Belgium.	After an Albanian offensive makes the Italian position in Albania untenable, Italy agrees to leave all Albania except the island of Saseno....The last Ottoman sultan signs the Treaty of Sevres ending the empire....Poland counters the Russian offensive and begins a counter-offensive.			India's Ghandi begins his campaign of passive resistance and non-cooperation with the British government.
Sep.	The League convenes a conference on international finance.	Gabriele D'Annunzio declares the free state of Fiume....Adolf Hitler makes his first public political speech in Austria.	France organizes Syria under mandate. It establishes Alaouite, Aleppo, Damascus, and a predominantly Christian and autonomous Greater Lebanon.		The Indian National Congress holds a special session to address wrongs done in Punjab and Khilafat. The INC agrees to use Gandhi's tactics.
	A	B	C	D	E
	Includes developments that affect more than one world region, international organizations and important meetings of world leaders.	*Includes all domestic and regional developments in Europe, including the Soviet Union.*	*Includes all domestic and regional developments in Africa and the Middle East.*	*Includes all domestic and regional developments in Latin America, the Caribbean, and Canada.*	*Includes all domestic and regional developments in Asian and Pacific nations (and colonies).*

U.S. Politics & Social Issues	U.S. Foreign Policy & Affairs, Defense	U.S. Economy & Environment	Science, Technology & Nature	Culture, Leisure & Lifestyle	
Prohibition begins when the Eighteenth Amendment becomes effective. For the 26 states with prohibition already, nothing changes.…The Palmer raids begin. The attorney general nets 650 "reds and anarchists" in the first day. The total arrests top 3,000.	The American Expeditionary Force returns from Europe.…Henry Cabot Lodge backs the irreconcilables rather than compromise on the League treaty. Ratification fails.	The steel workers strike that began in 1919 ends. Strikers win no concessions. A garment workers strike begins in New York City.		The Boston Red Sox sell Babe Ruth to the Yankees for $125,000 and a $350,000 loan. Ruth hits 54 home runs this season.	Jan.
In Chicago, IL, the League of Women Voters comes into being. The LOWV founder is Carrie Chapman Catt of the National American Woman Suffrage Association.		The Oil and Coal Land Leasing Act opens federal lands to private exploitation. This law allows the activities that come to be known as theTeapot Dome scandal.		Emeryville, CA, is the site of the first dog racing track to use an artificial rabbit.…Eugene O'Neill's *Beyond the Horizon* opens. O'Neill's first full length play makes him famous and wins a Pulitzer Prize.…The National Negro Baseball League debuts.	Feb.
	Congress declines for the second time to ratify the Versailles Treaty. In 1921 the U.S. signs the Treaty of Berlin that recognizes peace and reparations but omits mention of the League of Nations.	Radio station WGI in Boston becomes first to provide regularly scheduled broadcasts. The station closes in 1925.		F. Scott Fitzgerald's *This Side of Paradise* is released. Sales are 3,000 copies the first three days.	Mar.
The New York legislature expels five duly elected members. They are Socialists. The Red Scare continues.			Alfred Einstein arrives in New York. He will lecture on relativity at Columbia.	High fashion dictates short skirts. Hemlines are nearer to the knee than to the ankle.	Apr.
Police arrest Nicola Sacco and Bartomeo Vanzetti as suspects in the April 15 Braintree, MA, armed robbery and murder.…The Socialists nominate Eugene Debs for president. He becomes the first candidate to campaign from jail. He gets 3.5 percent of the vote.	The U.S. armed forces begin experimenting with metal airplanes. The first experimental craft are Fokkers purchased from Germany	In Matewan, WV, the UMWA attempts to organize coal miners turn violent. In the town streets UMWA organizers and company detectives wage a gun battle. Twelve company men die.	Kodak reveals the prototype of its Model A 16-mm camera.	The first Negro National League baseball game takes place in Indianapolis, IN.	May
The Democratic Party convention nominates James Cox on a promise to join the League immediately after Cox is sworn in.	Boeing begins building 20 army ground attack airplanes. The contract is cut to 10 planes the next week.			William "Big Bill" Tilden wins Wimbledon. He becomes the first American to win there and goes on to win a total of three titles.	Jun.
	The U.S. Navy establishes standard nomenclature for all vessels, including aircraft. Lighter than aircraft are designated with "Z" while heavier than airplanes are prefixed "V." The navy also designates fleet air detachments as air forces.	Transcontinental air mail service begins. Service is between San Francisco and New York.	Donald Douglas and David Davis form the Davis Douglas aircraft company. Davis Douglas will win its first military contract from the Navy in 1921.		Jul.
With passage of the Nineteenth Amendment, women have the vote.		Detroit's 8MK, later WBL, then WWJ, broadcasts a Jack Dempsey win over Billy Miske in three rounds. WWJ broadcasts the first dance orchestra in September.	A gun show in Ohio is the location of the debut of J.T. Thompson's hand-carried submachine gun. The weapon catches on rapidly with gangsters.	A fastball from the Yankees' Carl May injures Cleveland's Ray Chapman. When Chapman dies, he becomes the only baseball player to die from injury in a major league game.	Aug.
A Wall Street bomb kills 35 and wounds hundreds. The Red Scare fails to revive. Normalcy is under way.	The U.S. agrees to end extraterritoriality in Siam. The Asian country also gets control over its tariffs.	The first radio for home use arrives in the stores. It is a $10 Westinghouse. Joseph Home Company stores in Pittsburgh sells ready-made home wireless for $10.		The American Professional Football Association, led by Jim Thorpe, begins in Canton, OH. The league in 1922 becomes the National Football League.…D.W. Griffith's *Way Down East* premiers. Starring Lillian Gish, it earns $3.9 million, among the best of the 1920s.	Sep.
F *Includes campaigns, elections, federal-state relations, civil rights and liberties, crime, the judiciary, education, healthcare, poverty, urban affairs, and population.*	G *Includes formation and debate of U.S. foreign and defense policies, veterans affairs, and defense spending. (Relations with specific foreign countries are usually found under the region concerned.)*	H *Includes business, labor, agriculture, taxation, transportation, consumer affairs, monetary and fiscal policy, natural resources, pollution and industrial accidents.*	I *Includes worldwide scientific, medical and technological developments, natural phenomena, U.S. weather and natural disasters.*	J *Includes the arts, religion, scholarship, communications media, sports, entertainment, fashions, fads, and social life.*	

	World Affairs	Europe	Africa & The Middle East	The Americas	Asia & The Pacific
Oct.	The League holds a conference on passport and customs rules for international travelers.	The Preliminary Agreement of Riga ends the fighting in the Russo-Polish War. Poland gains more territory than agreed to during the world war peace meetings. . . . Russia recognizes Finland. Russia is now at peace with all Baltic nations.		In Ontario, Canada, Man O' War races Triple Crown winner Sir Barton. Man O' War wins and retires to stud with a record of 20 wins in 21 races.	At Ahmedabad, Ganhi founds the Gujarat Vidyapeeth.
Nov.	The League of Nations assembly holds its first meeting in Geneva, Switzerland. Previous sessions have been of the League council.	Britain bans all wireless broadcasts. They interfere with military communications. . . . The White Russians lose the civil war. Communist Russia becomes the first state to legalize abortion.		The Cuban presidential elections result in fraud allegations. Wilson sends a military observer for new elections. The outcome is the same. . . . The League rejects Bolivia's claim to a stake in Tacna-Arica.	
Dec.		Ireland comes under martial law. In November, IRA bombs kill 14 policemen in Ireland. . . . Turkey and Armenia end their war. . . . Greeks ignore allied objections and vote overwhelmingly for Kin Constantine. The allies forced him to abdicate in 1917 because of his pro-German sympathies.	France and Britain agree to the border between Syria and Palestine. Syria is a French mandate, while Britain holds the Palestinian mandate.		An earthquake and landslide in Gansu Province, China, kills 180,000.

A	B	C	D	E
Includes developments that affect more than one world region, international organizations and important meetings of world leaders.	*Includes all domestic and regional developments in Europe, including the Soviet Union.*	*Includes all domestic and regional developments in Africa and the Middle East.*	*Includes all domestic and regional developments in Latin America, the Caribbean, and Canada.*	*Includes all domestic and regional developments in Asian and Pacific nations (and colonies).*

U.S. Politics & Social Issues	U.S. Foreign Policy & Affairs, Defense	U.S. Economy & Environment	Science, Technology & Nature	Culture, Leisure & Lifestyle	
Charles Ponzi is indicted on multiple fraud counts. He gives his name to a variety of pyramid scams.…A New York judge rules that membership in the Communist Party is grounds for deportation.					Oct.
In the first presidential election in which women vote, Warren Harding defeats James Cox. Statistically, women's votes are the same as men's.		The first licensed station, Westinghouse's Pittsburgh station KDKA, begins broadcasting. Coverage of the presidential election inaugurates commercial broadcasting.	The first scheduled international air service begins. Flights between Havana and Key West take 60 minutes rather than 8 hours by boat.	*The Mask of Zorro* opens. The star is Douglas Fairbanks, Sr. Fairbanks is noted for playing swashbucklers, co-founding United Artists, and marrying Mary Pickford.	Nov.
	Wilson orders arrangements for U.S. withdrawal from the Dominican Republic. Elections must occur first.			Enrico Caruso sings his last performance, *La Juive* at the Metropolitan Opera. He dies in 1921.	Dec.

F	G	H	I	J
Includes campaigns, elections, federal-state relations, civil rights and liberties, crime, the judiciary, education, healthcare, poverty, urban affairs, and population.	*Includes formation and debate of U.S. foreign and defense policies, veterans affairs, and defense spending. (Relations with specific foreign countries are usually found under the region concerned.)*	*Includes business, labor, agriculture, taxation, transportation, consumer affairs, monetary and fiscal policy, natural resources, pollution and industrial accidents.*	*Includes worldwide scientific, medical and technological developments, natural phenomena, U.S. weather and natural disasters.*	*Includes the arts, religion, scholarship, communications media, sports, entertainment, fashions, fads, and social life.*

	World Affairs	Europe	Africa & The Middle East	The Americas	Asia & The Pacific
Jan. 1	Moscow sends a wireless message to the United States forecasting worldwide Soviet authority within the year.			A yellow fever epidemic rages throughout many Mexican cities and towns.	
Jan. 2		Premier Georges Clemenceau urges the repopulation of France through larger families.... The British government outlines plans for an overseas trade offensive.			Students at Tsing-Chau college in Peking go on strike.
Jan. 3		A temporary truce between Estonian and Bolshevik forces goes into effect.... The first German emigrants to leave Europe since before World War I, depart for Brazil.... German President Friedrich Ebert welcomes agents of the American Food Relief organization to Berlin.... Three hundred Sinn Fein volunteers attack a police barracks near Cork City.		Three Bolshevik agents are arrested in Tampico, Mexico.... A third Aztec pyramid is discovered at Teotihuacan, near Mexico City.	Dr. R.A. Shelton, a Christian missionary, is captured by bandits in Laoyakuan, near Yunnan-fu.
Jan. 4	U.S. officials report their cooperation with European agencies in fighting a Bolshevik counterfeit plot.	Bolshevik forces capture Admiral Alexander Kolchak, one of the principal leaders of the counterrevolutionary White forces.... Several German industrial plants are closed due to a coal shortage.... British railway workers reject the government's offer of higher wages, opting instead to continue their strike.			
Jan. 5		Italian Premier Francesco Nitti arrives in London to discuss the Adriatic question with Prime Minister David Lloyd George and other members of the British government.... More than 100 people are killed or injured in antidynastic riots in Sofia, Bulgaria.... Latvian and Polish forces recapture the town of Dvinsk from Soviet forces.		The slain bodies of two U.S. oil workers are discovered near Port Lobos, Mexico.	The Pacific Development company arranges a grant of $5,500,000 to the Chinese government.... Irkutsk passes into the hands of insurgent workers, soldiers, and peasants as the "Political Centre" announces that it has assumed power.
Jan. 6		Forty Sinn Fein prisoners in a jail in Cork, Ireland, begin a hunger strike.			The Indian National Congress calls for the removal of General Reginald Dyer, commander of British forces in the Punjab, for his role in the Amritsar killings.
Jan. 7	The French press appeals to the United States to provide immediate relief to Austria in order to prevent widespread starvation.	The Red Army captures the city of Novocherkassk.... A Hungarian delegation led by Count Albert Apponyi arrives in Paris to receive the peace treaty.... Police and soldiers raid the Sinn Fein headquarters in Dublin.... Strikes and lockouts in Berlin render Germany's political and economic future uncertain.... Heinrich Lammasch, former Premier of Austria, dies.		The December 21 shooting of an American citizen, Gabriel Porter of the Penn-Mex Oil Company, by a Mexican Federal army officer is reported to the State Department.... The strikes of hotel employees, cigar-makers and some other workers end in Jamaica, but the dock workers' strike continues.	Sir Edmund Barton, former Prime Minister of Australia, dies.
Jan. 8	Reports from London warn that Iraq and India are threatened by the advancing Red Army.	British Prime Minister David Lloyd George, Italian Premier Francesco Nitti, and Italian Foreign Minister Vittorio Scialoia depart London for Paris for further conferences on the Adriatic problem.... The situation created by the railroad strike in Germany worsens, especially in the Ruhr district where it becomes impossible to move even emergency food trains.... In Berlin, 10,000 insurance clerks go on strike.	Dispatches from Cairo report serious fighting between French forces and Syrian volunteers along the Syrian-Arabian frontier.		Prohibition is rejected in a referendum in New Zealand.... Reports from Peking indicate that the Bolsheviks have occupied Kiakhta, 170 miles southeast of Irkutsk.
	A	B	C	D	E
	Includes developments that affect more than one world region, international organizations and important meetings of world leaders.	*Includes all domestic and regional developments in Europe, including the Soviet Union.*	*Includes all domestic and regional developments in Africa and the Middle East.*	*Includes all domestic and regional developments in Latin America, the Caribbean, and Canada.*	*Includes all domestic and regional developments in Asian and Pacific nations (and colonies).*

	U.S. Politics & Social Issues	U.S. Foreign Policy & Affairs, Defense	U.S. Economy & Environment	Science, Technology & Nature	Culture, Leisure & Lifestyle
Jan. 1	Over 200 suspected radicals are arrested in Chicago raids.... The Lusk Committee reports a link between the Communist Party of America and the amalgamated textile and garment workers responsible for recent strikes in Utica, NY.		John L. Lewis begins his term as the United Mine Workers of America's ninth president.... Shipping is brought to a standstill at the port of Philadelphia as hundreds of tugboat workers go on strike.	The American Association for the Advancement of Science announces work on a serum to eradicate yellow fever.... Funeral services are held in Oxford for Sir William Osler, noted physician and educator.... Thousands perish in a blizzard in Estonia.	Actress Venita Fitzhugh is killed in an automobile accident.... English poet Cecil Roberts arrives in New York to begin a lecture series.... Andrew Miller, one of the owners of *Life* magazine, dies on the same day as his famous racehorse Roamer.
Jan. 2	Federal officials arrest nearly 2,600 suspected radicals and labor agitators in 33 cities nationwide.... Two hundred convicts in the Chicago county jail are forced to witness a hanging.	The Lusk Committee reports ties between the National Committee of the Socialist Party of America and the Communist International at Moscow.... Captain Karl W. Detzer, court-martialed on charges of cruelty to prisoners in Le Mans, France, concludes testimony on his own behalf.	Members of the Iron League of Steel Erectors threaten to strike if non-Union men are employed.	The Seine River floods, leaving thousands of commuters temporarily stranded.	Musical comedian Elsie Janis suffers a nervous breakdown.
Jan. 3		Senator Hoke Smith of Georgia urges fellow Democrats to break with their party leadership and accept reservations in order to end the deadlock over ratification of the Treaty of Versailles.	Washington State Superior Court Judge R.M. Webster issues a permanent injunction prohibiting membership in the Industrial Workers of the World.... The War Finance Corporation advances loans to U.S. businesses to assist in the reconstruction of war-torn Europe.	A violent earthquake causes widespread panic and loss of life in Mexico.	The National Automobile Show opens in New York.... Pittsburgh heiress Miriam Virginia Hostetter elopes.
Jan. 4	Officials from the Justice Department arrest 280 alleged radicals in Detroit.... The Justice Department announces that more than 4,000 warrants have been issued for aliens suspected of loyalty to the Communist Party.	The New York State Department of the American Legion calls upon Congress to suppress radical newspapers.... Secretary of State Robert Lansing releases a memorandum warning that the Bolshevik regime aims at world domination and cannot be trusted to honor treaties.	The steamship *Pretoria* is damaged in the third mysterious ship fire along the Staten Island shore in three days.... A spokesman for the National Committee for Organizing Iron and Steel Workers reports that steel production is below 50 percent of the normal rate.	Flooding causes extensive damage throughout Holland.	
Jan. 5	The federal government convenes a special board of inquiry on Ellis Island to begin deportation hearings for aliens arrested during the Palmer raids.... The Department of Justice operatives arrest 50 more suspected radicals in New York City, including the Executive Secretary of the New York State Communist Party.	British admiral John Rusworth Jellicoe visits Washington, D.C. and tours the naval yard.	George Otis Smith, Director of the U.S. Geological Survey, calls for American investment in foreign oil fields in order to ensure a future oil supply.		The New York Yankees acquire Babe Ruth from the Boston Red Sox for $125,000.... Track star Eddie Fall retires.... "The Acquittal" by Rita Weiman premiers at the Cohan and Harris Theater in New York.
Jan. 6	In a 5–4 decision, the U.S. Supreme Court upholds the constitutionality of the wartime prohibition sections of the Volstead Act.... Argument begins in the U.S. Supreme Court on the constitutionality of the Farm Loan Act.	A new home for the Navy Club opens on 41st Street in New York.	An international convention of the United Mine Workers of America opens in Columbus.... Rail workers in Detroit threaten to strike if demands for wage increases are not met.		The New York Giants announce the sale of pitcher Jean Dubuc to the Toledo Mud Hens.
Jan. 7	The United Mine Workers of America agree to arbitration by a presidentially-appointed commission.... Five Socialist members elected to the New York State Assembly are barred from taking their seats at the opening meeting of the 1920 session.... Former San Francisco political boss Abe Ruef ends a 14-year prison sentence.		Air mail service between Chicago and Omaha is begun.	Joanna C.S. Mackie, on the staff at the Harvard College Observatory, discovers a new star.	Pitchers Ernie Koob and Wayne Wright of the St. Louis Browns are traded to the Louisville Colonels in exchange for pitcher Dixie Davis.
Jan. 8	San Francisco is selected as the venue for the next Democratic National Convention.... The Democratic National Committee backs President Woodrow's position on the Treaty of Versailles.	President Woodrow Wilson insists that the Senate must not rewrite the Treaty of Versailles.... Brigadier General John H. Sherburne, former commander of the Artillery Brigade of the 92nd Division, blames the General Staff at Chaumont for the needless sacrifice of American lives on November 11.	Three thousand members of the International Brotherhood of Steam Engine Operators and Engineers vote to demand a six-day week, an eight-hour day, and 30 percent wage increase.... The National Committee of Steel Workers' Union officially calls off the steel strike.... William Z. Foster resigns as Secretary-Treasurer of the National Committee of Steel Workers' Union.	The eruption of Cero de San Miguel causes hundreds of deaths in Mexico.... Heavy rains cause floods throughout most of Italy.	Violinist Maud Powell dies.... August Herrmann resigns as Chairman of the National Baseball Commission.... Chicago White Sox shortstop Charles "Swede" Risburg, announces his retirement from baseball.
	F *Includes campaigns, elections, federal-state relations, civil rights and liberties, crime, the judiciary, education, healthcare, poverty, urban affairs, and population.*	G *Includes formation and debate of U.S. foreign and defense policies, veterans affairs, and defense spending. (Relations with specific foreign countries are usually found under the region concerned.)*	H *Includes business, labor, agriculture, taxation, transportation, consumer affairs, monetary and fiscal policy, natural resources, pollution and industrial accidents.*	I *Includes worldwide scientific, medical and technological developments, natural phenomena, U.S. weather and natural disasters.*	J *Includes the arts, religion, scholarship, communications media, sports, entertainment, fashions, fads, and social life.*

	World Affairs	Europe	Africa & The Middle East	The Americas	Asia & The Pacific
Jan. 9	The last of the American Expeditionary Forces leave France.... Baron Eichoff, head of the Austrian peace delegation, appeals to the United States for aid to seven million Austrians who might otherwise die of cold and starvation.	Margaret Lloyd George, wife of the British Prime Minister, takes her seat as the first female magistrate in Wales....Charles Diamond, proprietor of the *London Catholic Herald*, is arraigned on charges of inciting assassinations in Ireland.		Mexican officials compile a list of alleged abuses against Mexican citizens residing in the United States....Seven towns near Jalapa, Mexico, are completely flooded as a result of recent earthquake activity.	Japan's military intelligence department reports that Admiral Aleksandr Kolchak's army has been completely dispersed and Japanese civilians evacuated from Irkutsk.
Jan. 10	The League of Nations formally begins operations....The German and Japanese governments conclude a peace agreement....The Treaty of Versailles officially takes effect.	A Spanish corporal and six soldiers are executed for their part in the Saragossa mutiny....In a lengthy speech before the Cortes, Radical Republican leader Alejandro Lerroux appeals to Spaniards to restore order....The British steamer *Treveal* is shipwrecked near St. Alban's Head and 35 crewmembers drown.	The British government takes over the administration of German East Africa, renaming the territory Tanganyika....The Kionga triangle is ceded from German East Africa to Mozambique, which is under Portuguese control.	Warnings reach the United States that Luis Cabrera, chief of the Mexican Cabinet, has threatened to expel more than 200 Americans for establishing an American Legion post in Tampico....Reports from Ottawa state that an effort to change to a single tax system has been defeated.	
Jan. 11		Elections are held for 240 out of 300 seats in the upper house of the French Parliament....A provisional agreement is reached in the strike of Berlin insurance clerks....The hunger strike of 40 Sinn Fein prisoners in Cork is called off....French authorities investigate several large stores for evidence of profiteering....Italy is invited to participate in the peace alliance with Great Britain and France....More than 500 people are killed when the French passenger ship *Afrique* sinks near La Rochelle.	British forces repulse an attack on Abu Kemal by banks of tribesmen.	A fly infestation destroys nearly the entire crop of citrus fruit on the island of New Providence, Bahamas....Reports from Mexico indicate that Bolshevism is making considerable headway there.	
Jan. 12	U.S. President Woodrow Wilson calls the first meeting of the Council of the League of Nations, to be held at the Quai d'Orsay, Paris, at 10:30 on the morning of January 16.	Bulgaria ratifies the Treaty of Neuilly....Railwaymen in Spain announce a general strike to take effect on January 20....All municipal authorities, including police, strike in Gijon, Spain....The blockade against Germany is lifted in the Baltic....Authorities in Barcelona, Spain, arrest 68 Syndicalist Workers' delegates....The Turkish Sultan declares Smyna inseparable from the Turkish Empire.		Due to the intervention of the Merchants' Association, acting on behalf of U.S. pharmacists, the enforcement of prohibition regulations by Puerto Rico is postponed until February 1....John Barrett, Director General of the Pan American Union, accuses the Allied Powers in Europe of attempting to undermine U.S. trade with Latin American countries.	The U.S. State Department directs the American Legation at Peking to request the cooperation of the French Consul at Yunnan-fu in efforts to secure the release of Rev. Dr. R.A. Shelton.
Jan. 13		British Major-General Charles V.F. Townshend, defender of Kut-el-Amara, tenders his resignation.... Representatives of the Allied nations compile a list of 880 suspected German war criminals....Forty-two people are killed when guards open fire on a crowd of demonstrators outside the German Reichstag.		The subcommittee of the Senate Committee on Foreign Relations charged with investigating the Mexican problem begins hearings in San Antonio....General Pablo Gonzalez accepts the nomination of the Democratic Party for the Mexican Presidency....Reports from Mexico City state that federal forces have killed rebel leader General Alberto Paniagua along with 30 others.	The Japanese government denies any role in the recent supplying of arms to Mexico by a Japanese merchant....Emperor Yoshihito of Japan issues an imperial decree calling on all Japanese subjects to work for the attainment of a lasting peace and to abide by the principle of universal justice.
Jan. 14		Ellis Dresel travels to Berlin to take up his new post as American Commissioner....The Civil Governor in Madrid orders all strikes and lockouts ended within three days....A communication from Greek headquarters reports a victory over Turkish forces in the Odemish sector of Asia Minor.		J.L. Tejada, former Secretary of the Treasury of Bolivia, requests U.S. support in obtaining, for Bolivia, a free outlet to the ocean....Charles E. Magoon, former governor of the Panama Canal Zone and Minister to Panama, and Provisional Governor of Cuba from October 1906 to January 1909, dies in Washington, D.C.	A new Chinese Cabinet is formed with Chin Yun Peng as Prime Minister and Minister of War....Chinese diplomats in the United States are optimistic that peace will soon be restored in China....Australian officials announce their intention to maintain the wartime ban on importing German goods, despite the ratification of the peace treaty.
Jan. 15	Invitations go out to the governments of Great Britain, France, Holland, Switzerland, Denmark, Norway, Sweden, and the United States, as well as to the Reparations Commission and the U.S. Chamber of Commerce, to appoint delegates to an international economic conference to discuss rehabilitating the world's financial and commercial structure.	The first local elections are held in Ireland since the beginning of the Anglo-Irish War....Representatives of the Baltic States hold a conference at Helsingfors to discuss the formation of an alliance....The Supreme Allied Council drafts a note to the Dutch government requesting the extradition of former German Kaiser Wilhelm II.	The spread of Bolshevik propaganda leads the British War Office to anticipate military commitments on a large scale in the Middle East within the next few months.	Agrarian strikers in Argentina use sunglasses to set wheat stacks on fire.	Indian laborers in the Public Works Department of Suva, Fiji, go on strike....Unofficial reports from Tokyo indicate that the U.S. decision to withdraw troops from Siberia will likely result in the resignation or overthrow of the Hara ministry.
	A *Includes developments that affect more than one world region, international organizations and important meetings of world leaders.*	B *Includes all domestic and regional developments in Europe, including the Soviet Union.*	C *Includes all domestic and regional developments in Africa and the Middle East.*	D *Includes all domestic and regional developments in Latin America, the Caribbean, and Canada.*	E *Includes all domestic and regional developments in Asian and Pacific nations (and colonies).*

U.S. Politics & Social Issues	U.S. Foreign Policy & Affairs, Defense	U.S. Economy & Environment	Science, Technology & Nature	Culture, Leisure & Lifestyle	
Jacob Thomsen, president of Thomsen Tea Company, is charged with sugar profiteering.	Soviet agent Ludwig C.A.K. Martens is served with a subpoena to appear before the Senate Foreign Relations Committee.... The U.S. army transport *Buford*, carrying 249 "undesirable aliens," arrives at Kiel, Germany where it docks for repairs before continuing to Estonia.		The U.S. Navy completes construction work in France on the largest and most powerful wireless station in the world.... Inventors from across the United States meet in New York to form the National Laboratory for Invention and Research.	The U.S. Golf Association holds its annual meeting to discuss possible rule changes.	Jan. 9
James B. Reynolds resigns as Secretary of the Republican National Convention.... The House of Representatives for the second time refuses Wisconsin Socialist Victor Berger his seat.... Demonstrations are held in New York to protest the suspension of five Socialist members from the State Assembly.... The U. S. Senate passes the Sterling Sedition Bill.	The U.S. State Department notifies the Germans that, because the United States has not ratified the peace treaty, the armistice signed November 11, 1918, still governs relations between the United States and Germany.... The State Department announces plans to establish an American Legation in Finland.	Henry W. Robinson is elected president of the Coal Strike Settlement Commission.... Heads of oil companies celebrate the 50th anniversary of the incorporation of Standard Oil Company.... Secretary of the Treasury Carter Glass warns Congress not to exceed estimated expenditures or further reduce taxes.	As the San Miguel volcano in western Vera Cruz continues to spurt flames, cracks appear in the sides of an old volcano near Coffre de Perote.	The National Automobile Show in New York City closes with record crowds.... At the opening session of the International Federation of Catholic Alumnae, James Cardinal Gibbons of Baltimore condemns divorce and calls on women to maintain the sanctity of the home.	Jan. 10
Federal agents seize 187 cases of champagne from trucks in Herkimer, NY.... Leaders of the National Women's Party announce that the suffrage campaign is entering the decisive stage, with Oregon about to become the 25th of a necessary 36 states to ratify women's suffrage.... Chicago police round up another 180 suspects in their continued crime raids.	The Social Democratic League of America publicizes statements by leading Americans advocating the ratification of the Versailles Treaty.... Twenty Democratic members of the Senate meet in an informal conference to discuss the possibility of compromise on treaty reservations.... William Jennings Bryan urges ratification of the peace treaty by no later than January 16, the date fixed for the first meeting of the League of Nations Council in Paris.	Secretary of State Robert Lansing informs the American Manufacturers' Export Committee that he has instructed U.S. envoys in Portugal to investigate allegations of trademark piracy by Manuel de Silva Carmo.... The American Economic Association's Committee on Foreign Trade publishes a report advocating loans made to Europe through private channels and not by the U.S. government directly.	The Smithsonian Institute announces that Professor Robert H. Goddard has invented a new type of high-efficiency rocket with the potential to reach beyond the Earth's atmosphere.	American motion picture producer Herbert Brenon is reported missing in Sicily.... Governor William D. Stephens of California announces that he will ask the federal government for help in preventing the proposed world championship boxing match between Jack Dempsey and Georges Carpentier in Tijuana, Mexico.... A committee of horsemen meets to establish a national organization to govern harness racing.	Jan. 11
Renewed federal raids round up a dozen more suspected Communists.... By a vote of 33 to 71, the New York State Assembly refuses to reconsider its decision to suspend five Socialist members.... William Jennings Bryan denies a split with President Woodrow Wilson over the League of Nations covenant.		A presidential commission to investigate wages and prices in the bituminous coal industry holds its first formal session.... The United States Trucking Corporation is formed.... The Pennsylvania Manufacturers' Association blames the high cost of living on inefficient labor.	Alarmed by the unusual prevalence of measles in New York City, Health Commissioner Dr. Royal S. Copeland orders a study of the disease to be undertaken at once.... Fatal avalanches occur throughout the Alps.	Editors Dorothy Parker and Robert Benchley both quit *Vanity Fair*.... David M. Look is appointed temporary president of the new National Racing Organization for harness racers.	Jan. 12
A three-day conference of the New York Urban League opens to discuss problems confronting African Americans.... The Women's Republican Club unanimously endorses the aims of the Women's Equal Opportunity League.... The official call is issued for the Democratic National Convention, to be held in San Francisco beginning June 28.... Oregon ratifies the women's suffrage amendment.	*Les Camarades de Combat*, an organization of French war veterans, proposes affiliation with the American Legion.... The State Department issues a statement that the U.S. government will refuse to accept any part of the indemnity to be paid by Germany for the destruction of the German fleet at Scapa Flow.	The mine operators of the Central Competitive Field accept the award of the Presidential Coal Commission, but stipulate that coal prices cannot be fixed beyond the life of the Lever Act.	Another earthquake in Mexico destroys San Joaquin, a village of 3,000 inhabitants.... Doctors in London are mystified by the outbreak of a new disease, encephalitis lethargica.	Heavy-weight champion Jack Dempsey is barred from any bouts in New Jersey.... American motion picture producer Herbert Brenon is discovered to be safe after he was held for three days by Italian brigands who took his money and camera but released him when they discovered he was an American.	Jan. 13
Two new national organizations, the Constitutional League and the National Board of Fire Underwriters, are launched to combat radicalism.... A senate judiciary subcommittee holds preliminary hearings to consider federal legislation aimed at preventing racial violence.	President Woodrow Wilson nominates Colonel Lansing H. Beach as Chief of Engineers of the U.S. Army.... Assistant Secretary to the Navy Franklin D. Roosevelt finds conditions at the Naval Prison in Portsmouth, N.H., satisfactory, following charges against the prison commander, Lieutenant Commander Thomas Mott Osborne.	The Fair Price Committees of all states report decreases ranging from two to 35 percent on the prices of foodstuffs.... Walker D. Hines, Director General of Railroads, signs an agreement with representatives of the railway clerks' union granting time-and-a-half for overtime and one day off per week.	The Western Union Telegraph Company announces long delays in communications to and from continental Europe due to a general breakdown caused by heavy storms throughout Europe.... Holland is threatened by one of the greatest freshwater floods in its history.	Publisher Frank A. Munsey acquires the *New York Herald*.... Charlie Chaplin and his wife, Mabel Harris Chaplin, along with other independent movie stars, directors, and producers, form the Associated First Pictures, Inc.... Russian violinist Mischa Elman applies for U.S. citizenship.	Jan. 14
Members of the Senate Democratic caucus meet to elect a replacement for the recently deceased Senate Democratic leader Thomas Martin, but the meeting ends in a stalemate.... The Sterling Anti-Sedition Bill is voted down by the House Judiciary Committee and the measure originally proposed by Attorney General Palmer is substituted instead.	Two Americans are reported killed and three others wounded while capturing one of Ataman Gregori Semenoff's armored trains in Siberia.... Bishop Charles H. Brent, Senior Chaplain with the American Expeditionary Forces in France, announces plans to establish and maintain in France an American Field of Honor for soldiers killed overseas.	Department of Justice officials announce that an investigation into the financial transactions of Pacific coast shipbuilders has been ordered.... Plans for an intensive educational campaign in the economic use of natural gas are formulated at a conference of public utility commissioners, geologists, operators of gas properties, and gas appliance manufacturers.	Richard C. McLaurin, president of Massachusetts Institute of Technology, dies of pneumonia.	A special committee meets at the Waldorf Hotel in New York to discuss movie censorship.... An exhibition of the largest collection of photographic and color prints in the country opens in New York.... Thomas J. Hickey is reelected president of baseball's American Association.	Jan. 15
F *Includes campaigns, elections, federal-state relations, civil rights and liberties, crime, the judiciary, education, healthcare, poverty, urban affairs, and population.*	G *Includes formation and debate of U.S. foreign and defense policies, veterans affairs, and defense spending. (Relations with specific foreign countries are usually found under the region concerned.)*	H *Includes business, labor, agriculture, taxation, transportation, consumer affairs, monetary and fiscal policy, natural resources, pollution and industrial accidents.*	I *Includes worldwide scientific, medical and technological developments, natural phenomena, U.S. weather and natural disasters.*	J *Includes the arts, religion, scholarship, communications media, sports, entertainment, fashions, fads, and social life.*	

	World Affairs	Europe	Africa & The Middle East	The Americas	Asia & The Pacific
Jan. 16	The League of Nations Council meets for its first session in Paris.... The Argentine Republic is admitted to the League of Nations....The Supreme Council in Paris announces the Allied Powers' decision to trade with Russia.	Train service is restored in the Rhine and Westphalia regions of Germany as strikers return to work....The miners' strike in Linares, Spain, comes to an end....Count Arco Valley is sentenced to death for the February 1919 assassination of Bavarian Premier Kurt Eisner.... Communications from Warsaw report that Bolshevik forces are retreating east of Dvinsk.		Shipments of paper to American publishers from the Fort Francis Pulp and Paper Company in Canada are stopped at the border because of an embargo against the company.	The Japanese government instructs Yukichi Obata, minister to China, to notify the Peking government that Japan is ready to negotiate for the restoration of Shantung to China.
Jan. 17	The Inter-Allied Military Council meets to consider middle- and near-Eastern questions.	Paul Deschanel defeats Georges Clemenceau in the French presidential elections....A Moscow wireless reports fighting in the streets of Irkutsk....The Allied Supreme Council demands the extradition of former German Kaiser Wilhelm II from Holland.		Due to the shortage of newsprint in Canada, the three daily newspapers in Winnipeg suspend publication.	
Jan. 18		French Premier Georges Clemenceau resigns from office, along with his Cabinet....Viennese authorities respond to a coal shortage by suspending all tramway service and closing theaters, concert halls, and factories....The Serbian Foreign Office announces that complete liberty of transit of goods has been reestablished between Yugoslavia and Rumania.		Secretary of State Robert Lansing approves a proposal for the construction of a canal along the California border in order to free 55,000 settlers of Imperial Valley from dependence on Mexico for irrigation.	Prices continue to soar in the Yokohama raw silk market.
Jan. 19	An agreement reached by the governments of Italy, Britain, and France on Fiume and the Adriatic question is submitted to U.S. President Woodrow Wilson for his approval.	The Dutch government refuses to extradite Kaiser Wilhelm II, the former German emperor, to Allied authorities as a suspected war criminal....The Supreme Allied Council recognizes the independence of Armenia....Fifty thousand spectators watch a replayed English cup tie between Sheffield and Darlington....Dispatches received in Paris indicate that Bolshevik forces occupy all the territory in Siberia west of Krasnoyarsk.	De Beers Consolidated Mines, Ltd., a South African company that controls approximately eighty percent of the world's output of diamonds, offers an issue of 50,000 American shares at $47 each....An American woman breaks precedent by giving a two-hour political address at the Mosque of El Azbar in Cairo.	The Second Pan-American Financial Conference opens in Washington, D.C.	Municipal workers join the strike in Suva, Fiji....Filipino sugar workers, led by Pablo Manlapit, begin a two-month strike in Oahu....The China Society of America appeals to the U.S. Senate to uphold the Shantung reservation to the Paris Peace Treaty....Japan's Diplomatic Advisory Council decides to withdraw Japanese troops from Siberia.
Jan. 20	The Red Cross announces the first general council meeting of the League of Red Cross societies, to be held in Geneva on March 2....Nearly all the powers of Europe, America, and Asia are represented at a banquet honoring foreign diplomats at the Royal Palace in Madrid.	Ernest Daumig, leader of the radical wing of Germany's Independent Socialists, is arrested in Berlin following the Reichstag riots.... Yugoslavia refuses to accept the Adriatic compromise proposed by the Allied Supreme Council, and the council disbands without a settlement.		William McAdoo, former Secretary of the Treasury, appeals to Latin American countries to help relieve Europe....Long caravans of Indians carrying all of their possessions leave the vicinity of the new volcano at San Miguel, in the western Vera Cruz district....The Mexican Foreign Office orders immigration officials to refuse entry to anyone deported from the United States.	
Jan. 21	President Woodrow Wilson reappoints the American members of the Permanent High Tribunal of Arbitration at the Hague.	The Latvian army captures Rezekne from the Soviets....Railroad lines throughout Italy are guarded by troops as the railway strike reportedly assumes a revolutionary character....Wireless communications received in London report Bolshevik successes on all fronts....Germany approves of the Hoover Relief Plan.		The Carranza government grants permission to 46 oil companies to resume drilling operations in Mexico.	Indian sugar workers in Fiji go on strike....In an address at the opening of the Diet in Tokyo, Premier Hara Takashi promises that Japan will strictly carry out every term of the peace treaty.
Jan. 22		Reports from the British War Office indicate that General Anton Denikin's position in southern Russia has improved and that the Bolshevik advance in Siberia has slowed down....Three hundred deputies abstain from a vote of confidence for the newly formed cabinet of French Premier Alexandre Millerand.	A Bolshevik mission is reported to have arrived in Kabul, Afghanistan.	Witness testimony and documentary evidence presented to the Senate subcommittee investigating the Mexican situation suggest that President Carranza and a few of his principal lieutenants were behind a long series of raids on American properties.	Cable advices received from Canton suggest that unification between the northern and southern factions in China is imminent.
	A *Includes developments that affect more than one world region, international organizations and important meetings of world leaders.*	B *Includes all domestic and regional developments in Europe, including the Soviet Union.*	C *Includes all domestic and regional developments in Africa and the Middle East.*	D *Includes all domestic and regional developments in Latin America, the Caribbean, and Canada.*	E *Includes all domestic and regional developments in Asian and Pacific nations (and colonies).*

U.S. Politics & Social Issues	U.S. Foreign Policy & Affairs, Defense	U.S. Economy & Environment	Science, Technology & Nature	Culture, Leisure & Lifestyle	
The Eighteenth Amendment, prohibiting the manufacture, transportation, and sale of alcohol takes effect at midnight.... Indiana becomes the 26th state to ratify women's suffrage.... The U.S. Senate begins discussion of the Kenyon Americanization Bill, designed to combat radicalism through education rather than repression.	The U.S. Senate rejects American participation in the League of Nations.... Army transport *Edellyn* departs for Vladivostok to bring U.S. troops home from Siberia.... U.S. Marines and Haitian gendarmes repel an attack on the Haitian capital by 300 bandits, more than half of whom are killed, wounded, or captured in the exchange.	The International Association of Garment Manufacturers calls for the repeal of the excess profits tax.... The Federal Reserve announces plans to reduce loans to member banks.... The Baltimore Dry Docks and Shipbuilding Company order its supervisors to withdraw from their unions within 30 days.	The temperature in parts of upstate New York reaches 47 below zero.... The development of a new anesthetic is announced in Wilmington, Delaware.	England and Australasia break even in the first round of Davis Cup tennis matches.... The Metropolitan Museum of Art announces its acquisition of the Junius Spencer Morgan collection.... Opera composer Reginald de Koven dies in Chicago.	Jan. 16
The Committee on Arrangements for the Democratic National Convention, which includes women for the first time, holds its preliminary meeting in New York City.... The Inter-Racial Council announces plans for a nationwide educational campaign to combat Bolshevik thinking among foreign-born workers.	Herbert Hoover issues a statement approving the removal of the blockade on Soviet Russia.... The first contingent of American troops is withdrawn from Siberia.	Retailers of gasoline announce a new price of 29 to 30 cents per gallon.... Ice floes in New York Harbor cripple boat traffic. ... National Thrift Week, sponsored by the YMCA, is launched in more than 300 cities nationwide.		Composer Charles Loeffler receives an award from the National Institute of Arts and Letters.	Jan. 17
Vice President Thomas R. Marshall advocates the expulsion of all foreign-born agitators, including naturalized aliens.... The Social Democratic League of America issues an appeal to workers and farmers for support.	The U.S. Army transport *Powhatan* takes on water, but all 500 passengers are rescued.... Major General Leonard Wood, addressing members of the American Legion, advocates a larger navy and pleads for law and order.	The American Federation of Labor goes on record in opposition to the Sterling-Graham Sedition Bill before the House of Representatives.... The worst blizzard in years rages in central and upstate New York.... The buildings of the *Buffalo Evening Times* are destroyed in a fire.	Dr. Robert H. Goddard releases a statement suggesting the possibility of obtaining photographs from space beyond Earth's atmosphere.	Sermons on temperance and prohibition are preached in many churches on "Law and Order Sunday."	Jan. 18
The American Civil Liberties Union receives its charter in New York.... Federal agents round up more than 316 suspected radicals in Seattle.		Trolleys on Staten Island stop running, despite a restraining order prohibiting a cessation of operations.... A four-alarm fire in Harlem forces approximately 200 families from their apartment homes.		Society women serve as boxing judges at a Staten Island tournament for wounded soldiers.	Jan. 19
On his first day as governor of New Jersey, Edward T. Edwards moves to overthrow the prohibition law.... The White House reports steady improvements in President Woodrow Wilson's health.	In a letter to the House Foreign Relations Committee, Secretary of State Robert Lansing requests an additional appropriation in order to enforce wartime legislation necessary to keep Bolsheviks and other "undesirables" from entering the United States.	The State Department announces that Midwest newspapers will be 40 percent short of their paper supply due to a Canadian embargo on shipments of newsprint paper from a supplier in Western Ontario.		Funeral services are held for composer and conductor Reginald de Koven.	Jan. 20
Governor Charles Brough of Arkansas issues requisition papers for the return of Robert L. Hill, under arrest in Topeka, KS. Hill, president of the Progressive Farmers and Household Union, is charged with leading the September race riots near Elaine, AK.... The lower house of the Mississippi legislature rejects the women's suffrage amendment after only 10 minutes of debate.		Figures released by the Department of Agriculture reveal that wholesale prices of staple meats and vegetables have increased despite efforts to lower prices.... The foreign exchange market suffers a record decline.... Attorney General Palmer tells United Mine Workers representatives that the Justice Department will enforce President Wilson's terms for the settlement of the recent coal strike.			Jan. 21
Federal troops are called in to avert a potential race riot in Desha County, AK.	The National Civil Liberties Bureau alleges that conscientious objectors are subject to cruel treatment in military prisons.	Samuel Gompers, president of the American Federation of Labor, appears before the House Rules Committee to oppose antisedition legislation.... A strike by wood heel makers threatens to tie up the shoe industry in Haverhill, MA.	Scientist and African explorer Richard L. Garner dies.	Sir Oliver Lodge delivers a lecture at the Shubert Theater in New York on the structure of the atom.	Jan. 22
F	G	H	I	J	
Includes campaigns, elections, federal-state relations, civil rights and liberties, crime, the judiciary, education, healthcare, poverty, urban affairs, and population.	*Includes formation and debate of U.S. foreign and defense policies, veterans affairs, and defense spending. (Relations with specific foreign countries are usually found under the region concerned.)*	*Includes business, labor, agriculture, taxation, transportation, consumer affairs, monetary and fiscal policy, natural resources, pollution and industrial accidents.*	*Includes worldwide scientific, medical and technological developments, natural phenomena, U.S. weather and natural disasters.*	*Includes the arts, religion, scholarship, communications media, sports, entertainment, fashions, fads, and social life.*	

	World Affairs	Europe	Africa & The Middle East	The Americas	Asia & The Pacific
Jan. 23		Epidemics of influenza and spotted fever plague eastern Europe.... Holland's firm refusal to surrender ex-Kaiser Wilhelm to the Allies is received in Paris....The British and French governments grant Yugoslavia a three-day extension for a final decision on the proposed Adriatic settlement.... Demonstrators in Hungary protest against what many Hungarians perceive as a peace without honor.		The acting Consul General for Mexico reports that General Salvador Alvarado, the former governor of Yucatan who was recently arrested for his political activities, has been released and is en route to the United States.	The Chinese government experiments with a new system of shorthand writing in the hopes of increasing literacy among the Chinese population....The death of O.T. Logan, medical missionary in Hunan, is reported in the American press.
Jan. 24		M. Takeff, former Minister of Public Works and Minister of the Interior in the Malinoff Cabinet, is assassinated in Bulgaria.			
Jan. 25	Five delegates are chosen to represent the United States at the meeting of the General Council of the League of Red Cross Societies, to be held in Geneva beginning March 2.	A mass demonstration is held in Berlin to protest the Allied extradition of Germans wanted for trial.	The South African government prepares to cope with the anticipated rush to Tlaring, a desert nears Tuangs in Bechuanaland, which is expected to follow the opening of Tlaring for diamond digging in March.	U.S. businessmen in La Paz form the American Chamber of Commerce of Bolivia.	Japan offers to speed up the evacuation of Shantung....Japanese silk reaches a record high price.
Jan. 26	The Allied Committee of Ambassadors turns down German requests for revision of the Versailles Treaty	An attempt is made on the life of Matthias Erzberger, German Minister of Finance....Moscow reports that the Bolsheviks have captured Elizabethgrad, northeast of Odessa.	Field Marshal Viscount E.H.H. Allenby, British High Commissioner in Egypt and the Sudan, announces new passport regulations designed to bar "undesirables."		The Chinese Cabinet declines to negotiate with Japan on the retrocession of rights in Shantung.
Jan. 27	Albert Thomas, former French Minister of Munitions, is confirmed as head of the International Labor Bureau of the League of Nations.	French president Raymond Poincaré issues a decree creating a natality division of the Ministry of Health....The Allied Committee of Ambassadors receives a note from the German government asking them not to execute Article 228 of the peace treaty, providing for the delivery of German officers and others guilty of war crimes....Hungary asks for more time to consider the terms of the peace agreement.		The Senate subcommittee investigating conditions in Mexico agrees to provide the Carranza government stenographic reports of testimony in the El Paso hearings....Henry P. Fletcher resigns as U.S. Ambassador to Mexico.... An intense cold wave claims many lives among the poorer classes of Mexico.	The Indian government bars all enemy aliens from entering the country for at least five years.
Jan. 28		Yugoslavia rejects the Adriatic compromise plan proposed by the British and French governments....A six-day strike on the Italian state railways ends at midnight as the result of direct negotiations between Premier Nitti and the union executive....The Turkish parliament adopts the National Pact, rejecting Allied plans for the dismantling of the Ottoman Empire.		Two U.S. Army aviators, en route from Texas to Arizona, make a forced landing in Mexico and are held by Mexican authorities.	
Jan. 29		Yugoslavia attempts to reopen the Adriatic negotiations with France and Britain....French Premier Alexandre Millerand demands an explanation of the surrender of General Alexandre Kolchak to the Siberian revolutionists.			Five thousand dockyard workers in Bombay strike for higher wages.... Representatives of the United States, Great Britain, Japan, and France propose a four-power loan to the Chinese government totaling approximately $25,000,000.
Jan. 30		A new influenza epidemic spreads to Western Europe from eastern and central Europe....Germans take part in disturbances outside the Danish Plebiscite Bureau in Flensburg, Schleswig-Holstein.		At a conference attended by French, Canadian, German, American, and Mexican bankers, the decision is made to establish a clearing house in Mexico City.	Japanese forces thwart a Bolshevik attempt to seize control of Vladivostok....Workers in the Federation of Japanese Labor join the Oahu sugar strike....Telegrams pour into Peking from all parts of China advising against negotiations with the Japanese on the possible return of Shantung.

A	B	C	D	E
Includes developments that affect more than one world region, international organizations and important meetings of world leaders.	*Includes all domestic and regional developments in Europe, including the Soviet Union.*	*Includes all domestic and regional developments in Africa and the Middle East.*	*Includes all domestic and regional developments in Latin America, the Caribbean, and Canada.*	*Includes all domestic and regional developments in Asian and Pacific nations (and colonies).*

U.S. Politics & Social Issues	U.S. Foreign Policy & Affairs, Defense	U.S. Economy & Environment	Science, Technology & Nature	Culture, Leisure & Lifestyle	
Clinton T. Brainard, President and Treasurer of Harper & Bros., is convicted of publishing objectionable material.	The House of Representatives approves a pay increase of approximately 30 percent for enlisted men in the Navy and the Coast Guard.		Three distinct earthquake shocks are felt in the Pacific Northwest.		Jan. 23
The Westchester County Grand Jury orders indictments in connection with alleged fraud in Sing Sing prison.…Police arrest 54 men in raids on alleged gambling halls in New York.	The War Department reports that 21 percent of the Army officers in service when the Armistice was signed have since resigned.…The last troops with the American Expeditionary Force return from France.	Cleveland's industries nearly grind to a halt when storms block shipments of coal.…Secretary of Labor William B. Wilson renders a decision that membership in the Communist Party is grounds for deportation.		The American Academy of Fine Arts reopens in Rome.…Author Cyrus T. Brady dies of pneumonia.	Jan. 24
	The American Defense Society publishes its "War on Bolshevism" report.		Signor Guglielmo Marconi reports that he has received mysterious signals, which he believes might be from outer space, over his wireless equipment.		Jan. 25
Senator Henry Cabot Lodge issues an ultimatum to conferees on the peace treaty that they must agree to the Lodge reservations on Article X and the Monroe Doctrine without change if they wish to continue bipartisan talks.		Four hundred Kansas miners go on strike to protest the passage of the Industrial Courts bill.…New York State Conservation Commissioner George D. Pratt fears the extinction of oysters in New York due to the pollution of Long Island Sound.	French chemists work on perfecting an antigas for military use.…Professor Frederick Soddy of Oxford University claims that physical science can abolish the struggle for food and fuel.	The Pacific Coast League, a new international baseball league, is formed.	Jan. 26
Governor James P. Goodrich of Indiana refuses the use of his name on the Republican ticket for the upcoming primary presidential elections.…President Woodrow Wilson nominates David F. Houston of Missouri to be Secretary of the Treasury and Edwin T. Meredith of Iowa to replace Houston as Secretary of Agriculture.	The Service Pay Bill, which would provide increased pay for members of the armed services, is held up when the lack of a quorum causes the Senate to adjourn.…The bi-partisan conferees on the Peace Treaty agree on a truce until January 29 when talks will resume.	Higher food prices are predicted for 1920.…The Coal Strike Settlement Commission resumes hearings.		Joseph F. Rinn, a former member of the Society for Psychical Research, offers $5,000 to that organization if it can furnish any proof of communication with the spirit world or other supernatural phenomena.	Jan. 27
Federal officials launch an aggressive campaign in New York against violators of the prohibition laws.…Jury selection begins in the trial of Senator Truman H. Newberry and 121 others, charged with conspiracy to gain a Senatorial election in 1918.…A crowd of 3,000 protestors in Madison Square Garden speaks out against the unseating of five Socialists members of the New York Assembly.…South Carolina fails to ratify the women's suffrage amendment.	Senator James Wadsworth, Chairman of the Senate Military Affairs Committee, presents an Army Reorganization Bill to the Senate.	Freight transportation is halted by a strike on two Boston railroads.…William Harding, governor of the Federal Reserve Board, denies that the board has used coercive measures to compel nonmember banks to join the Federal Reserve system.		The Julliard Musical Foundation is established.…Everett McGowan wins the two-mile race and Roy McWhorter the half-mile at the national speed-skating championship in Saranac Lake, NY.	Jan. 28
	A new ruling issued by the Bureau of War Risk Insurance allows former servicemen to reinstate lapsed or cancelled insurance policies anytime before July 1.		Guglielmo Marconi conducts tests to determine the origin, which he believes may be extra-terrestrial, of mysterious signals he received on his wireless.		Jan. 29
A new political party, known as the Land and Labor League, is formed in Oregon.…Responses to a questionnaire sent out by the Post Office Department indicate a widespread spirit of discontent and unrest among the nation's farmers.…The House of Representatives appropriates $1,000,000 to guard the liquor in bonded warehouses throughout the country.	Captain Karl W. Detzer, court-martialed for alleged mistreatment of enlisted men in Le Mans, France, is released from confinement.…The bi-partisan parley of Senators on the Peace Treaty ends in a complete break.…Ludwig C.A.K. Martens, the unofficial representative of the Soviet government in the United States, testifies before a Senate subcommittee investigating Russian propaganda.	The War Department commandeers 72,500 tons of steel rails at the request of the Railroad Administration.	A professor at the University of Bologna is said to have successfully isolated the sleeping sickness germ and is working on a serum to combat the illness.	Art objects valued at more than $500,000 are destroyed in a fire at the American Fine Arts Society galleries in New York. The collection was part of the 35th annual exhibition of the Architectural League.	Jan. 30
F *Includes campaigns, elections, federal-state relations, civil rights and liberties, crime, the judiciary, education, healthcare, poverty, urban affairs, and population.*	G *Includes formation and debate of U.S. foreign and defense policies, veterans affairs, and defense spending. (Relations with specific foreign countries are usually found under the region concerned.)*	H *Includes business, labor, agriculture, taxation, transportation, consumer affairs, monetary and fiscal policy, natural resources, pollution and industrial accidents.*	I *Includes worldwide scientific, medical and technological developments, natural phenomena, U.S. weather and natural disasters.*	J *Includes the arts, religion, scholarship, communications media, sports, entertainment, fashions, fads, and social life.*	

	World Affairs	Europe	Africa & The Middle East	The Americas	Asia & The Pacific
Jan. 31		Holland and Belgium consider a new treaty, not yet ratified, for control of the Scheldt River.…British newspapers criticize the U.S. government's decision against further loans to Europe.…Hungary is given extra time to consider the peace treaty submitted by the Allies.… Nearly 100 leaders and prominent members of Sinn Fein are arrested in Ireland.…The first contingent of Entente troops arrives in Upper Silesia.		Samuel Gompers urges workers in Latin America to form national labor associations for affiliation with the Pan American Federation of Labor.…The Canadian government reports that more than 52,000 people immigrated to Canada from the United States during 1919.… Toronto reports 2,000 new cases of influenza.	The Japanese embassy in Washington is officially informed that the Japanese government has invited China to enter into negotiations for the restoration of rights in Shantung.
Feb. 1	England and France declare that they would accept the U.S. Senate's reservations to the Peace Treaty.	The governments of Latvia and the Soviet Union sign an armistice.…The *Moscow Soviet* reports that a Polish division in Siberia has mutinied and joined the Bolsheviks.…The French government announces drastic measures to conserve coal.	Three American relief workers are murdered in Syria.	Mexican authorities release Lieutenants E.F. Davis and G.E. Grimes, the U.S. aviators who made a forced landing near Guerrero.… The Royal Canadian Mounted Police is established.	
Feb. 2		The Soviet and Estonian governments sign the Treaty of Tartu, recognizing Estonian independence.… The Allied Council of Ambassadors approves a list of German officers and functionaries who must be handed over for trial as war criminals.		San Blas Indians attack police and civilians in Porvenir, Panama.… General Plutarco Elias Calles resigns his post as Mexico's Secretary of Industry, Commerce, and Labor.	
Feb. 3	Indian Privy Councilor Emir Ali warns that attempts to drive the Turks out of Constantinople will cause bitter resentment among Muslims in India and elsewhere.…Egyptian nationalist leader Dr. Abdul Said warns former French Premier Georges Clemenceau not to enter Egypt or his life will be in danger.	Baron von Lerner, chief German peace delegate in Paris, receives the completed list of 890 Germans wanted for war crimes.…The interallied plebiscite commission takes over all administrative functions in Teschen, Silesia.		The El Paso hearings on Mexico begin.…A fresh revolutionary outbreak in Honduras is reported.	
Feb. 4	The premiers and foreign ministers of the Scandinavian countries decide to join the League of Nations.	A wireless dispatch from Odessa reports that the Russian Volunteer Army has driven the Bolshevik forces back across the Don River.…Italian peasants sack the palace of the Duke of Rivona and force the duke to cede his land to them.…The list of suspected German war criminals is made public.…A physical scuffle breaks out in the Italian Chamber between the Socialists and the Catholics.		Socialist members in Argentina's Chamber of Deputies protest against the alleged laxity of capital police in protecting Socialist meetings against radical elements in the party.…Mexican newspapers report the abduction of an American citizen, Joseph E. Askew, by bandits.	
Feb. 5	Exchange rates continue to drop, prompting proposals for an international conference.	Reports reach London that the Czechs have retaken Irkutsk and are turning westward to relieve the Rumanians, Serbs, and Poles.… Armed bands of Slavs attack Italian carabineer outposts near Istria.…Armenians are massacred in Marash.		Business is suspended in Bahia, Brazil, for the third consecutive day due to disorders following the recent presidential elections.	
Feb. 6		British Prime Minister David Lloyd George refuses to entertain the Council of Ambassadors' proposal to modify the allied demand for suspected German war criminals.…Foreigners begin evacuating Odessa as British ships fire over the city.…The French Chamber of Deputies gives the Cabinet a vote of confidence with regard to foreign policy.…Premier Alexandre Millerand asserts that France will execute the terms of the peace treaty fully and will exact from Germany all that is owed.		A sharp decrease in the cost of living is predicted for Canada following the virtual suspension of exports due to the high exchange rate.	Work is resumed following a strike in 55 cotton mills in Bombay, but the Indian Marine Dock Workers' strike continues.
	A *Includes developments that affect more than one world region, international organizations and important meetings of world leaders.*	B *Includes all domestic and regional developments in Europe, including the Soviet Union.*	C *Includes all domestic and regional developments in Africa and the Middle East.*	D *Includes all domestic and regional developments in Latin America, the Caribbean, and Canada.*	E *Includes all domestic and regional developments in Asian and Pacific nations (and colonies).*

U.S. Politics & Social Issues	U.S. Foreign Policy & Affairs, Defense	U.S. Economy & Environment	Science, Technology & Nature	Culture, Leisure & Lifestyle	
Influenza claims 122 lives in Chicago.... A compromise agreement is reached on the Oil Land Leasing Bill.... William H. Sage, former head of the Narcotics Bureau of the Internal Revenue Department, is indicted on charges of violating the Harrison antinarcotic law.... A federal investigation begins of conditions in the U.S. disciplinary barracks at Fort Leavenworth.	Former Captain John L. Lynch is charged with embezzling funds from the U.S. Army.... The Senate Military Committee is divided on an army organization bill that would include compulsory military training.... Two U.S. Army aviators who ran out of fuel and were forced to land their plane near Guerrero, Mexico, are ordered to Monterey for examination by Mexican military authorities.	Twenty people are injured when a train from New York derails near Burlington, VT.... Indictments are returned against 37 members of the Industrial Workers of the World by the special grand jury investigating radical activities.		"Cleopatra's Night" by Henry Hadley premiers at the Metropolitan Opera House in New York.... Two hundred delegates from across the United States meet in Pittsburgh for the National Laymen's Conference, to discuss the role of the Protestant Churches of North America at home and abroad.	Jan. 31
Six alleged Communists are arrested in Newark, NJ.... Miss Helen Todd, Chair of the American Women's Committee, charges that deportees on Ellis Island are not receiving proper medical treatment.... Ohio Governor James M. Cox announces his candidacy for President.	Franklin D. Roosevelt, Assistant Secretary of the Navy, admits that he spent $40,000,000 on guns without first getting the permission of Congress.	The Department of Agriculture denies allegations of profiteering on the part of Iowa farmers.... The first commercial armored car is introduced in St. Paul, Minnesota.	The Aero Club of America announces plans to create an artificial solar eclipse in order to facilitate astronomical observations.... De Forest Laboratories announces advances in wireless technology.	The Architectural League opens its 35th annual exhibition.... The eighth annual convention of the United Synagogues of America opens in Philadelphia.... The International Power Boat Union is formed.... John W. Heisman is appointed head football coach at the University of Pennsylvania.... Anne Spencer's first poem, "Before the Feast of Sushan" is published in *The Crisis*.	Feb. 1
Congress considers a bill to grant statehood to the territory of Hawaii.... Edwin T. Meredith is sworn in as the new Secretary of Agriculture.... Congressional conferees reach agreement on an oil land leasing bill after a three-month deadlock.		Representatives of 300 U.S. firms form the American Commercial Association to promote trade with Russia.... The Federal Reserve Board announces new discount rates.... The coal strike settlement commission resumes consideration of arguments by representatives of coal miners and operators.		Eugene O'Neill's first full-length play, *Beyond the Horizon*, opens at the Morosco Theater.	Feb. 2
Maurice "Moss" Enright, labor leader and alleged chief of Chicago gunmen, is killed.... Alfred Friedlander and Percival McDonough, the "Brooklyn car bandits," are caught while attempting to escape from Sing Sing prison.	Republican House leaders eliminate universal military training from the military bill.... Five civilians and seven soldiers are arrested for allegedly attempting to steal several army motor trucks and $250,000 worth of supplies.	Representatives of more than two million railroad employees meet with Director General Walker D. Hines to discuss wage demands.... Spokesmen for miner workers and operators present their closing arguments before the Coal Strike Settlement Commission.		The National Toy Fair opens in New York.	Feb. 3
Federal agents unload whisky cargo valued at $5 million from the *Yarmouth*.... The Mississippi State Senate unanimously approves women's suffrage.		Edward P. Ripley, chairman and former president of the Santa Fe Railroad, dies.... Director General of the Railroads, Walker D. Hines, issues general orders to Midwest railroads to help ease congested grain elevators.		Actor Leo Delaney dies.	Feb. 4
Former Vermont Governor Horace F. Graham is convicted of embezzling state funds.... Ex-Assemblyman Benjamin Gitlow of New York is convicted of criminal anarchy.... Governors Edward I. Edwards of New Jersey and Alfred E. Smith of New York assail the national prohibition amendment at a Democratic gathering in New York.		Three thousand cutters, operators, and examiners in the petticoat trade are on strike.... Fourteen passengers are injured in an accident involving a Florida express train.		Movie actor Earl Burgess suffers a fatal fall from an airplane.... Actress Edna Hunter dies of pneumonia.	Feb. 5
The Justice Department announces that 895 arrests have been made in the campaign against food profiteers and hoarders.... Four men are arrested in New York on charges of criminal anarchy.... Wayne B. Wheeler, general counsel of the Anti-Saloon League, insists that the work of Americanization must extend beyond aliens.... The Virginia State Senate rejects the Federal Women's Suffrage Amendment.	Naval Secretary Josephus Daniels recommends to Congress the construction of three aviation carriers and four destroyer tenders.	The government accepts a bid for all the unsold houses built by the U.S. Shipping Board near the Hog Island shipyard.... Bankers from 11 states convene in New Orleans and inaugurate a nationwide movement to bring about an amendment to the Federal Reserve Act that would limit the powers of the Federal Reserve Board.	The first delivery of mail by airplane from the United States to foreign territory is made when Aero Ltd., a commercial service in Florida, carries 50 pounds of mail from Miami to Nassau, Bahamas.		Feb. 6
F *Includes campaigns, elections, federal-state relations, civil rights and liberties, crime, the judiciary, education, healthcare, poverty, urban affairs, and population.*	G *Includes formation and debate of U.S. foreign and defense policies, veterans affairs, and defense spending. (Relations with specific foreign countries are usually found under the region concerned.)*	H *Includes business, labor, agriculture, taxation, transportation, consumer affairs, monetary and fiscal policy, natural resources, pollution and industrial accidents.*	I *Includes worldwide scientific, medical and technological developments, natural phenomena, U.S. weather and natural disasters.*	J *Includes the arts, religion, scholarship, communications media, sports, entertainment, fashions, fads, and social life.*	

	World Affairs	Europe	Africa & The Middle East	The Americas	Asia & The Pacific
Feb. 7		Bolsheviks execute Admiral Alexander Kolchak, leader of the counterrevolutionary White forces in Siberia....The forces of Gabriele d'Annunzio, the Italian insurgent leader at Fiume, seize an Italian warship.		Latin American countries considering membership in the League of Nations await a response from President Woodrow Wilson defining the Monroe Doctrine.	
Feb. 8		Moscow reports that Bolshevik troops have successfully entered Odessa.	Madagascar removes an embargo on graphite exports.		
Feb. 9	Arthur J. Balfour, former British Secretary for Foreign Affairs, becomes the British representative on the Executive Council of the League of Nations.	Norway formally annexes the islands of Spitzbergen....The advance guard of a British battalion arrives in Danzig to commence occupation.			
Feb. 10	The Serb-Croat-Slovene state (later Yugoslavia) is admitted to the League of Nations.	Voters in the northern zone of North Schleswig opt by plebiscite for reunion with Denmark....The French garrison at Marash withdraws under cover of night.		Senator John S. McLennan urges the formation of a new national party in Canada.	
Feb. 11	French President-elect Paul Deschanel becomes the honorary president of the Latin Union....The League of Nations Council opens its second session in London.	The League of Nations takes over the administration of the Free State of Danzig from Germany....Moscow reports that General Denikin has retreated to Yalta....Count Apponyi and the members of the Hungarian delegation arrive in Paris.	The American destroyer *Biddle* arrives safely in Constantinople with several Red Cross and Y.M.C.A. workers who aided in the evacuation of Odessa.		
Feb. 12		The British and Russian Soviet governments sign an agreement for the exchange of prisoners....The Allied Commission of Control takes over the administration of Upper Silesia.		Canada protests against the Lenroot reservation to the Peace Treaty, under consideration by the U.S. Senate.	
Feb. 13	The League of Nations recognizes the perpetual neutrality of Switzerland.	An attempt by Socialists to carry a vote of censure against the Polish government during the evening session of the Diet ends in failure.	Jerusalem reports that an unprecedented snowfall of 39 inches has crippled communication and caused considerable distress and hunger.	Mexican bandits kidnap Wilson Welsh Adams, an employee of the American Metal Company, Ltd., and hold him for 50,000 pesos ransom.	
Feb. 14		The Constitutional Commission in Warsaw decides that the Senate and Diet will elect a President of the Republic....The Allied mission in Budapest learns of an alleged plot to return former Emperor Charles to Hungary....Lithuania makes known the terms under which it will be possible to conclude peace with Poland.			
Feb. 15		The Supreme Allied Council agrees to permit the Sultan to maintain his court in Constantinople, but adds that the Allies will keep vigorous military and naval control over the Straits of the Dardanelles....Influenza spreads throughout Germany at an alarming rate.		The Bolivian government formally lays claim to a Pacific port in the disputed province of Arica.	Massive demonstrations are held in Shanghai demanding that the Peking government refuse to negotiate with Japan over Shantung and instead refer the matter to the League of Nations.

A	B	C	D	E
Includes developments that affect more than one world region, international organizations and important meetings of world leaders.	*Includes all domestic and regional developments in Europe, including the Soviet Union.*	*Includes all domestic and regional developments in Africa and the Middle East.*	*Includes all domestic and regional developments in Latin America, the Caribbean, and Canada.*	*Includes all domestic and regional developments in Asian and Pacific nations (and colonies).*

Date	U.S. Politics & Social Issues	U.S. Foreign Policy & Affairs, Defense	U.S. Economy & Environment	Science, Technology & Nature	Culture, Leisure & Lifestyle
Feb. 7	Nevada ratifies the Nineteenth Amendment.…President Wilson delivers a written rebuke to Secretary of State Robert Lansing for holding unauthorized Cabinet meetings.	The Adjutant General announces the final revised figures of American Army casualties during World War I.…Naval Secretary Josephus Daniels testifies before the Senate subcommittee investigating the award of naval decorations.			Pilot Sadi-Joseph Lecointe sets a new air-speed flying record of 171.4 miles per hour.
Feb. 8	The American Federation of Labor announces the appointment of a national nonpartisan political campaign committee to promote the election of candidates sympathetic to labor.				A national baseball conference opens in Chicago.…A national conference of church women is held in Washington.
Feb. 9	Six people are killed in race riots in Lexington, KY.	The Senate votes to reconsider the Versailles Treaty and sends it back to the Foreign Relations Committee.			Baseball's Joint Rules Committee bans all foreign substances or other alterations to the ball by pitchers.
Feb. 10	New Jersey ratifies the Nineteenth Amendment.	The Foreign Relations Committee returns the Versailles Treaty to the Senate with reservations intact.			
Feb. 11	Idaho ratifies the Nineteenth Amendment.	The special committee of the Army, Navy, and Civilian Board of Boxing Control begins its investigation of heavyweight champion Jack Dempsey's wartime activities.	The Kentucky Operators' Association refuses to submit to the jurisdiction of the Coal Strike Settlement Commission.	Thomas Edison celebrates his 73rd birthday.	The price of major league baseball tickets increases to 50 cents for bleacher seats and $1 for the grandstand.
Feb. 12	Arizona and New Mexico ratify the Nineteenth Amendment, but Virginia rejects it.	Brigadier General Peter W. Davison dies.			
Feb. 13	Secretary of State Robert Lansing is forced to resign after holding unauthorized cabinet meetings.		John L. Lewis, president of the United Mine Workers, denies charges that miners oppose the introduction of labor-saving machinery.		Andrew "Rube" Foster launches the Negro National League, the first black baseball league.…Chicago White Sox outfielder Joe Jackson threatens to resign unless his salary demands are met.
Feb. 14	The League of Women Voters is formed in Chicago.…John Barton Payne is nominated to become Secretary of the Interior.…Thirty-seven alleged radicals held in the Youngstown, Ohio county jail demand to be set free or deported.…Department of Justice agents raid suspected radical strongholds in Paterson, New Jersey.				Composer Sol Levy dies.
Feb. 15	Herbert Hoover receives the Civic Federation's Gold Medal of Honor for Distinguished Public Service.…Eleven women are appointed to the Executive Committee of the Democratic National Committee.…Adolph Lewisohn agrees to head a movement to establish a national public works department.…A Senate subcommittee unanimously approves of a national budget measure.	The National Security League makes public the details of an Americanization plan to educate foreign-born adults.	A brewery in Amsterdam, NY receives a federal permit to make beer, which will be sold by prescription only.	A hailstorm hits Atlantic City, NJ.…Guglielmo Marconi predicts that eventually individuals in both hemispheres will be able to communicate through wireless technology.…New Hampshire mountain-climber Charles MacVeagh, Jr., dies in a blizzard on Mt. Monadnock.	A motorcyclist in Daytona, FL, breaks four world records for speed.

F	G	H	I	J
Includes campaigns, elections, federal-state relations, civil rights and liberties, crime, the judiciary, education, healthcare, poverty, urban affairs, and population.	*Includes formation and debate of U.S. foreign and defense policies, veterans affairs, and defense spending. (Relations with specific foreign countries are usually found under the region concerned.)*	*Includes business, labor, agriculture, taxation, transportation, consumer affairs, monetary and fiscal policy, natural resources, pollution and industrial accidents.*	*Includes worldwide scientific, medical and technological developments, natural phenomena, U.S. weather and natural disasters.*	*Includes the arts, religion, scholarship, communications media, sports, entertainment, fashions, fads, and social life.*

	World Affairs	Europe	Africa & The Middle East	The Americas	Asia & The Pacific
Feb. 16	Colombia is admitted to the League of Nations....The Allied Supreme Council debates the borders of Turkey in Asia....Representatives of several neutral nations meet at the Carnegie Peace Palace in the Hague to discuss their nations' participation in the permanent Court of International Justice.	British Prime Minister David Lloyd George informs the Yugoslav Foreign Minister that Yugoslavia must either accept the Adriatic compromise of January 20 or else face the execution of the Treaty of London....The Allies accept the German government's proposal to try suspected war criminals at Leipzig....Gabriele D'Annunzio concedes that the annexation of Fiume to Italy is impossible....Vienna reports 40,000 cases of influenza.			
Feb. 17		The trial of former French premier Joseph Caillaux on charges of high treason begins in Paris....Moscow reports that revolution has broken out in east Siberia.	British and Italian forces use tanks and airplanes to subdue the nationalist forces of Mohammad Abdullah Hassan in Somalia.		
Feb. 18	The reply of the Allied powers to President Wilson's latest Adriatic note reaches the U.S. State Department, but the contents of the letter are not disclosed.	Paul Deschanel takes office as the 10th president of the French republic....The Supreme Allied Council spends the day discussing Turkish boundaries....Germany obtains a concession from the terms of the Versailles Treaty with regard to the rate of demilitarization....Gustav Noske threatens to imprison anyone inciting food strikes in Berlin....Moscow reports fierce fighting between the Bolsheviks and separate enemy groups in the Tiraspol and Odessa regions.		Leon Salinas is named Secretary of Mexico's Department of Industry, Commerce, and Labor.	
Feb. 19		Martial law is declared in the Saar region, which is now occupied by French troops and controlled by an Allied commission.		Wilson Welsh Adams, the kidnapped American employee in Mexico, is released....W.O. Jenkins, U.S. Consular Agent in Mexico City, comes before the Mexican Supreme Court on various charges, including aiding rebel forces.	
Feb. 20		British, French, and Swiss representatives sign an air traffic convention....General A. Niessel, commissioned by the French government to report on the German military situation, alleges a vast conspiracy in Germany to deceive the Allies and avoid fulfilling the peace terms, particularly with regard to the military clauses.		A congress of South American police convenes in Buenos Aires to consider means of suppressing radicalism and enforcing immigration laws....The Carib Syndicate announces that it has gained control of the properties of the Equatorial Oil Company in Colombia.	
Feb. 21	Helen Scott Hay of Savannah, Illinois, is made chief nurse of the American Red Cross Commission to Europe....The Council of Ambassadors authorizes the repatriation of Germans now in Siberia.	The American Chamber of Commerce in London reports that Britain is financially and commercially sound....Former French President Raymond Poincaré joins the Allied Reparations Committee....The Spanish Cabinet resigns, but Premier Manuel Allende Salazar remains as prime minister....Soldiers and anti-Semitic leaders attack a Jewish lecturer in Berlin.		Andres and Concepcion Villegas are arrested in Texas and charged with smuggling ammunition into Mexico.	
Feb. 22		A wheat shortage forces the Italian government to revert to wartime economic measures....Nationalists in Triest stage a demonstration at which President Wilson is denounced..			

A	B	C	D	E
Includes developments that affect more than one world region, international organizations and important meetings of world leaders.	*Includes all domestic and regional developments in Europe, including the Soviet Union.*	*Includes all domestic and regional developments in Africa and the Middle East.*	*Includes all domestic and regional developments in Latin America, the Caribbean, and Canada.*	*Includes all domestic and regional developments in Asian and Pacific nations (and colonies).*

U.S. Politics & Social Issues	U.S. Foreign Policy & Affairs, Defense	U.S. Economy & Environment	Science, Technology & Nature	Culture, Leisure & Lifestyle	
The Central Federated Union, a branch of the Federation of Labor, advocates the formation of an independent political organization.…House and Senate conferees reach agreement on a railroad reorganization bill.…William Grant Webster seeks the Republican nomination as a candidate for the Vice President.…President Wilson names John G. Pollard to the Federal Trade Commission.	The Legislative Committee of the American Legion begins a series of conferences with members of both houses of Congress to urge compulsory training and compensation for servicemen.…The Senate debates the Peace Treaty.…Three units of the Twenty-Seventh Infantry arrive in Vladivostok.	The American Institute of Mining and Metallurgical Engineers inaugurates Herbert Hoover as president of the organization.…The Shipping Board auctions off 30 former German passenger liners taken over by the government during the war.…Railway executives, bankers, and representatives of the Railroad Administration arrange a 15-year trust.		The Federation of Orthodox Synagogues announces the formation of a Jewish Court of Arbitration to handle matters of a religious nature.	Feb. 16
The defense opens its case in the trial of five Socialists ousted from the New York Assembly.…Former Senator Joseph W. Bailey announces his candidacy for the Texas governorship.…President Wilson names Rear Admiral William S. Benson, chief of naval operations during the war, to replace John Barton Payne on the Shipping Board...Maryland rejects the Nineteenth Amendment.	Cross-examination begins in the hearings of Ludwig C.A.K. Martens, Russian Soviet representative in the United States, before a Senate Foreign Relations subcommittee.… The House Education Committee unanimously approves a bill to increase monthly compensation to disabled servicemen.	Colonel Theodore Roosevelt introduces a minimum wage bill in the New York State Assembly.…The Morse Drydock and Repair Company sue the Star Publishing Company for libel.…President Wilson pledges the return by February 29 of all privately owned radio stations seized by the military during the war emergency.		Actor Thomas Commerford dies.… Native American catcher John "Chief" Meyers retires from baseball.	Feb. 17
William G. McAdoo declines to have his name entered in the Georgia primaries.…The Mississippi Senate rejects the Nineteenth Amendment.…Mrs. Rose Pastor Stokes, awaiting trial as a Communist, announces her Congressional candidacy to replace Representative F.H. LaGuardia of New York.…A Baltimore liquor dealer and two former Internal Revenue officials are arrested for an alleged conspiracy to violate prohibition.	Grosvenor B. Clarkson resigns his position as Director of the Council of National Defense, effective March 31.…The Senate confirms the nomination of Robert Underwood Johnson as Ambassador to Italy.… Senate debate on the Peace Treaty is temporarily suspended due to the illness of Republican leader Henry Cabot Lodge.…A unit of the Twenty-Seventh Infantry reaches Manchuria Station.	Merchants from across the United States convene in New York City at the ninth annual convention of the National Retail Dry Goods Association.…The Betts Bill to repeal the daylight savings law is debated in the New York legislature.		Minstrel Lew Benedict, known on stage as "Uncle Lew," dies at age 80.…International ice skating championships begin in Lace Placid, NY.…The American Polo Association's executive committee decides against sending an American polo team to the summer Olympics.	Feb. 18
A Hammond, IN jury acquits Frank Petroni on charges of murder for the fatal shooting of Frank Petrich, after the latter allegedly badmouthed the United States.…New Mexico becomes the 32nd state to ratify the Nineteenth Amendment.	Lieutenant Herbert H. Lowry, former paymaster in the Supply Corps of the Navy, faces a court martial on charges of desertion and embezzlement.…The Senate avoids debate on the Peace Treaty for the second consecutive day and instead waits to see if President Wilson will withdraw the treaty.	Delegates representing 15,000 coal miners in eastern Ohio threaten to strike if their demands for wage increases are not met by April 1.…Reports issued by the Bureau of Labor Statistics show that the wages paid by 11 of the 13 leading manufacturing industries in the United States increased between 25 and 125 percent over last year.	Snowstorms and heavy winds sweep eastern Canada.	Former New York State amateur boxing champion James Tully is denied reinstatement as an amateur in the A.A.U.…Ice skater Joseph Moore is elected president of the International Skaters' Association.…Former world champion bicycle racer Bobby Walthaur seeks a divorce from his wife who, he alleges, tried to kill him.	Feb. 19
One man is arrested in Chicago and others sought in connection with a $1 million dollar swindle involving the manufacture and sail of low-grade imitation spark plugs bearing the name and trademark of an Ohio company.…The National Board of Farm Organizations is established.	Senate and House conferees approve a measure authorizing the sale of three large army camps.	The Shipping Board allocates 63 ships to help relieve the New England coal shortage.	Explorer Robert E. Peary dies.	Benjamin Kauff, former centerfielder for the Giants, is indicted on charges of grand larceny and possession of stolen property.…Everertt McGowan wins the international ice skating championship at Lake Placid.…The 15th Annual Motor Boat Show opens in New York.	Feb. 20
Mayor John Galvin of Cincinnati becomes a candidate for delegate at large to the Republican National Convention.…The House of Representatives approves the Railway bill by a vote of 250 to 150.…F.H. LaGuardia becomes acting mayor of New York City.	Two sailors are killed and several others badly scalded when a steam pipe bursts on the U.S. destroyer *Kilty*.	The New York Federal Reserve Bank's reserves fall below the legal requirements.…The New York Telephone Company agrees to increase the wages of switchboard operators.…The Greater New York Taxi League goes on strike against the Pennsylvania Railroad over alleged discrimination against independent owners and chauffeurs.		Mrs. Kennet Cowan, first wife of the late Harry Harkness, alleges fraud in the probate of her late ex-husband's will.…The Cleveland Indians release pitchers Hi Jasper and George Dickerson.	Feb. 21
More than 8,000 delegates from across the nation meet in Cleveland to discuss educational reform.	The American Legion joins churches, schools, and patriotic societies in celebrating George Washington's birthday.…The French government sends certificates of honor to the families of servicemen who died at the front.	Officers and committees of several railway labor organizations gather in Washington to ask President Wilson to veto the Railroad Bill if it is approved by the Senate.… Samuel Gompers advises against the formation of a separate political party for labor.		A pastoral letter from the Archbishops and Bishops of the United States is read at every Catholic pulpit across the nation.	Feb. 22
F *Includes campaigns, elections, federal-state relations, civil rights and liberties, crime, the judiciary, education, healthcare, poverty, urban affairs, and population.*	G *Includes formation and debate of U.S. foreign and defense policies, veterans affairs, and defense spending. (Relations with specific foreign countries are usually found under the region concerned.)*	H *Includes business, labor, agriculture, taxation, transportation, consumer affairs, monetary and fiscal policy, natural resources, pollution and industrial accidents.*	I *Includes worldwide scientific, medical and technological developments, natural phenomena, U.S. weather and natural disasters.*	J *Includes the arts, religion, scholarship, communications media, sports, entertainment, fashions, fads, and social life.*	

	World Affairs	Europe	Africa & The Middle East	The Americas	Asia & The Pacific
Feb. 23	The Reparation Commission of the Peace Conference meets in Paris.	A midnight curfew goes into effect in Dublin....British Secretary for War, Winston Churchill, announces that conscription will be abolished in Great Britain as of March 31....Hungary objects to the new frontiers determined by the peace conference and instead demands plebiscites in the contested areas....20,000 Welsh miners go on strike.	The Eighth Congress of Karabaghi Armenians meets to consider demands for the incorporation of Karabagh into Azerbaijan....Former French Premier Clemenceau arrives in Khartoum....It is reported from Damascus that 400 French troops have been killed or captured by a force of Turks and Arabs near Houran, Palestine....Lieutenant General Jan Christian Smuts, Prime Minister of South Africa, reports that between 30,000 and 40,000 black natives are on strike.	A new revolutionary party in Mexico, the reorganized government of Mexican free men, is reportedly planning a revolt for May 5.	Siam prohibits the export of rice and rice by-products at least until December 31.
Feb. 24		Adolf Hitler proclaims the National Socialist platform at that party's first large meeting in Munich....The Supreme Allied Council decides to resume trade with Russia.			
Feb. 25	Discussion begins in the Swiss Federal Chamber regarding Switzerland's entry to the League of Nations.	The long-awaited bill for Irish Home Rule is presented in the British House of Commons.			Thirty thousand employees of the Tata Iron and Steel Works go on strike in Jamalpur, India....Korean nationalist Kang Wu Gyu is sentenced to death for his 1919 attempt to assassinate Admiral Saito Makoto, the Japanese Governor-General of Korea.
Feb. 26	Soviet Russia pledges to establish democratic principles in Russia and to call a constituent assembly, if in return Great Britain and the other great powers abandon all intervention in Russian affairs.	French Premier Miller and and British Prime Minister Lloyd George invite President Wilson to join them in issuing a formal proposal to the Italian and Yugoslav governments to renegotiate an agreement on the Adriatic controversy.			The Japanese Diet is dissolved following weeks of agitation for universal male suffrage.
Feb. 27	The British publication *Daily Chronicle* prints an editorial praising U.S. President Woodrow Wilson for his opposition to the U.S. Jones Act, which would severely limit the amount of foreign ships allowed to enter U.S. harbors.				
Feb. 28		Steel workers in South Wales go on strike....The War Criminals Commission draws up a list of 46 men for trial in Leipzig as a test of Germany's good faith....Military experts are called before the Allied Supreme Council to discuss possible responses to the Armenian outrages....Government forces launch a seize of Fiume with a blockade to prevent food and other commodities from reaching the forces of Gabriele D. Annunzio.	Kurds and Turks attack the French garrison at Aleppo; the U.S. Consul at Aleppo requests a squadron of warships to protect the lives of Americans in the region.	Arizona Sheriff R.R. Earhart and his posse cross the Mexican border in pursuit of the two bandits suspected of killing Alexander Frazier and shooting his brother, J.A. Frazier.	Two earthquakes occur in the South Pacific.
Feb. 29	Representatives of Red Cross societies across the globe gather in Geneva, Switzerland, to discuss plans for launching a worldwide health campaign.	Italian Premier Francesco Nitti and Yugoslav Foreign Minister Anton Trumbitch meet in London to resume talks on the Adriatic question....Czechoslovakia's National Assembly approves a constitution establishing a democratic republic....Miklos Horthy overthrows Hungary's Communist government.			
	A *Includes developments that affect more than one world region, international organizations and important meetings of world leaders.*	B *Includes all domestic and regional developments in Europe, including the Soviet Union.*	C *Includes all domestic and regional developments in Africa and the Middle East.*	D *Includes all domestic and regional developments in Latin America, the Caribbean, and Canada.*	E *Includes all domestic and regional developments in Asian and Pacific nations (and colonies).*

U.S. Politics & Social Issues	U.S. Foreign Policy & Affairs, Defense	U.S. Economy & Environment	Science, Technology & Nature	Culture, Leisure & Lifestyle	
Herbert Hoover declines to choose between the two major political parties....The Law and Order Union of New York State, formed to combat radical and revolutionary propaganda, holds its first meeting.	Second Lieutenant Horace M.H. Corey is killed when his airplane bursts into flame and falls 1,200 feet....President Wilson sends a reply to the Adriatic note of Great Britain, France, and Italy in which he adheres to the December plan of settlement and opposes any significant modifications.	The Senate adopts the Railway Bill by a vote of 47 to 17....New York City telephone operators form a union.	The world's first wireless telegraph broadcasting service is transmitted in Chelmsford, England....The body of Rear Admiral Robert E. Peary, discoverer of the North Pole, is buried in Arlington National Cemetery with full naval and military honors.	Helen Keller addresses crowds at the Palace Theater in New York.	Feb. 23
Representative Kraus of Indiana introduces a bill to repeal the Overman Act, which gives the president power to transfer the duties of one government bureau to another....Oregon Senator George E. Chamberlain announces his candidacy for reelection.	President Woodrow Wilson appoints Charles R. Crane as Minister to China, but his confirmation by the Senate is deemed unlikely.	P.F. Richardson, President of the American Federation of Railroad Workers, alleges a conspiracy between the officers of the American Federation of Labor and United States Railroad Administration officers, including Director General Walker D. Hines.	An earthquake destroys several towns and villages near Tiflis, GA.		Feb. 24
President Wilson appeals to the Oklahoma legislature to ratify the federal suffrage amendment....Herbert Hoover asks that his name not be added to the ballot for the Georgia presidential primary....Major General Leonard Wood formally declares his candidacy in the Ohio primaries, where he will compete with U.S. Senator Warren G. Harding for the Republican presidential nomination.	By a bipartisan vote, the House military committee refuses to include universal military training in the army reorganization bill.	The Mineral Leasing Act is passed to govern the leasing of public lands for developing deposits of coal and other natural resources....Secretary of the Interior Franklin K. Lane orders the opening of 360,000 acres in Oregon to homesteaders....Daniel Willard is reelected president of the Baltimore and Ohio Railroad.			Feb. 25
	Two U.S. Army aviators are killed when their plane crashes from a height of 5,000 feet.	Four hundred machinists join the strike at the Baltimore Dry Docks and Shipbuilding Company....A settlement is reached in the financial affairs of Pittsburgh Life and Trust and other concerns affected by the Birdseye conspiracy....The Farmers' National Council, the American Society of Equity, and several railroad unions urge President Wilson to veto the railroad bill.			Feb. 26
Vitto Marriani is arrested on charges of criminal anarchy....Attorney General A. Mitchell Palmer calls for the strengthening of laws against radicals in order to prosecute naturalized citizens who are immune to the present deportation statutes....A Spokane jury finds Chester Brown and seven other alleged members of the Industrial Workers of the World guilty on charges of criminal syndicalism.				World heavyweight champion Jack Dempsey and his manager Jack Kearns are indicted by a federal grand jury on charges of conspiring to have Dempsey avoid the selective draft....A Multatuli Conference is held in the Hague to commemorate the centenary of Eduard Douwes Dekker's birth.	Feb. 27
William Sherman Jennings, former Governor of Florida, dies....John Barton Payne is confirmed as Secretary of the Interior....Oklahoma ratifies the Nineteenth Amendment....John J. Pershing's name is added to the Michigan presidential primary ballot.	The Wright Aeronautical Corporation announces the invention of an airplane cannon motor that automatically fires shells in rapid succession.	Massachusetts Governor Calvin Coolidge telegraphs President Wilson that the fuel shortage in New England has become critical....President Wilson issues executive orders providing for the continuation of the powers of the fuel administration, but dividing them between the director general of railroads and a commission of four....President Wilson signs the railroad bill.	Storm advisories are posted along the Atlantic coast from Norfolk to Boston.		Feb. 28
Secretary of Interior Franklin K. Lane retires from public life after more than 20 years' service, the last seven in the Cabinet.		Several hundred rail employees find themselves out of work as the railroads are returned to private ownership at midnight.			Feb. 29
F *Includes campaigns, elections, federal-state relations, civil rights and liberties, crime, the judiciary, education, healthcare, poverty, urban affairs, and population.*	G *Includes formation and debate of U.S. foreign and defense policies, veterans affairs, and defense spending. (Relations with specific foreign countries are usually found under the region concerned.)*	H *Includes business, labor, agriculture, taxation, transportation, consumer affairs, monetary and fiscal policy, natural resources, pollution and industrial accidents.*	I *Includes worldwide scientific, medical and technological developments, natural phenomena, U.S. weather and natural disasters.*	J *Includes the arts, religion, scholarship, communications media, sports, entertainment, fashions, fads, and social life.*	

	World Affairs	Europe	Africa & The Middle East	The Americas	Asia & The Pacific
Mar. 1		Diplomatic talks between Italy and Yugoslavia are suspended without any resolution to the Adriatic question.... Admiral Miklós Horthy, commander-in-chief of the Hungarian armed forces, is sworn in as Regent of Hungary.	Josef Trumpledor and seven other defenders are killed during an Arab attack on the Jewish settlement of Tel Hai in Palestine.		
Mar. 2	The United States receives formal notification that Argentina, Spain, Paraguay, Chile, and Persia have joined the League of Nations.... The Congress of Red Cross Societies opens in Geneva.	A French railroad strike is called off at midnight.... Schleswig-Holstein declares its independence from Prussia.... An assassination attempt is made on Hungarian Minister of War Stephan Friedrich.... Fifteen hundred French troops sail to Turkey.... Romania signs an armistice with Soviet Russia.			
Mar. 3	Venezuela is admitted to the League of Nations.	William O'Brien, Alderman of Dublin, is arrested during a raid on Liberty Hall.... Moscow reports that Bolshevik forces are advancing rapidly in Caucasus region.... The Turkish Cabinet resigns.		The Ottawa Senators win the National Hockey League championship.	Edwin Cunningham, American Consul General at Shanghai, urges the immediate enactment of the pending federal incorporation law in order to offset trade discrimination in China.
Mar. 4	Denmark and Sweden vote to join the League of Nations.	Coal shortages force the Italian government to suspend the operation of nearly 1,000 trains.... The Turkish Chamber of Deputies requests a U.S. commission to investigate the Marash massacre and conditions in Anatolia.... Peasant strikes disrupt Northern Italy.... Karabaghi Armenians reject demands for incorporation into Azerbaijan.		Gerald Brandon, Mexico City correspondent for the *Los Angeles Times*, is expelled from Mexico.... Passengers on a train from Chihuahua City to Mexico City are robbed at gunpoint by bandits claiming to work for Francisco Villa.	K. Shidehara, Japanese Ambassador to the United States, denies that Japan has aggressive or expansionist intentions.
Mar. 5	The Norwegian Parliament votes to join the League of Nations.	German monarchists form a new National Party.... The German and Latvian governments sign the Treaty of Berlin.... Sir Edward Carson is reelected President of the Ulster Unionist Council.... Mediation ends a multi-industry strike in Sweden.			
Mar. 6	Japan formally recognizes the Armenian Republic.	The Portuguese Cabinet resigns following a vote of no confidence.... The Italo-Yugoslav Conference on Fiume begins.	Reports from Cairo indicate that Egypt is facing a serious food shortage.	Buenos Aires is disturbed by violent street clashes on the eve of congressional elections.	The Philippine Assembly rejects prohibition and women's suffrage bills.
Mar. 7		Prince Joachim Albrecht of Prussia assaults a party of French guests in a Berlin hotel.... Polish forces capture Mozir and Kolenkovitz.... Russia invades Poland.		Argentina holds congressional elections.	The Associated Press reports that warfare has broken out in the Honan region of China.
Mar. 8	Cuba, Denmark, and Switzerland join the League of Nations.... The Interchurch World Movement holds a conference on religious education in the United States.	Moscow reports heavy fighting in the Mozir and Ovrutch regions of Russia.	Syria declares itself an independent state.	The Mexican Foreign Office announces the discovery of a cooperative kidnapping ring made up of both Mexicans and Americans along the border.	The Japanese deny rumors that they bought victory over Russia in 1904–05.... The Council of the All-India Muslim League warns that the campaign to take Constantinople away from the Turks will drive Muslims into desperate action.

	A	B	C	D	E
	Includes developments that affect more than one world region, international organizations and important meetings of world leaders.	*Includes all domestic and regional developments in Europe, including the Soviet Union.*	*Includes all domestic and regional developments in Africa and the Middle East.*	*Includes all domestic and regional developments in Latin America, the Caribbean, and Canada.*	*Includes all domestic and regional developments in Asian and Pacific nations (and colonies).*

Date	U.S. Politics & Social Issues	U.S. Foreign Policy & Affairs, Defense	U.S. Economy & Environment	Science, Technology & Nature	Culture, Leisure & Lifestyle
Mar. 1	New York Supreme Court Justice Philip H. Dugro dies.…U.S. Senator John H. Bankhead from Alabama dies.…Attorney General A. Mitchell Palmer announces his decision to seek the Democratic Party's presidential nomination.	King George honors Captain B.A. Long.	The government restores control of U.S. rail transportation systems to corporate ownership.	Direct commercial wireless communication between the United States and England is reestablished.	
Mar. 2	Governor Edward I. Edwards of New Jersey challenges federal dry laws by signing a bill to permit the manufacture and sale of beverages containing 3.5 percent alcohol.	The U.S. Senate votes to adopt two of the Lodge reservations to the Peace Treaty.…A naval board of inquiry clears Thomas Mott Osborne on charges of misconduct related to his command of the U.S. Naval Prison at Portsmouth, NH.	Nantucket faces a coal shortage.…Senator James A. Reed of Missouri calls for an investigation of the United States Grain Corporation.		Actor and film director Harry Solter dies from a stroke.
Mar. 3	Senator Warren G. Harding of Ohio becomes the first Republican Presidential candidate ever to make a personal campaign appearance in Texas.…Ten alleged anarchists from Paterson, NJ, appear before the Board of Special Inquiry at Ellis Island.…The West Virginia Senate rejects the Federal Suffrage Amendment.…President Woodrow Wilson appears outside of the White House grounds for the first time since October.	The State Department denies reports published abroad that the government has ordered the withdrawal of U.S. representatives placed in Europe to observe the peace process.	A St. Louis judge issues a temporary restraining order forbidding the calling or fostering of strikes.…A train crash near Elizabeth, NJ, kills three people and injures eight others.	A blizzard sweeps the western United States.	Shortstop Larry Kopf signs with the Cincinnati Reds.
Mar. 4	The State of New Jersey files a suit in the U.S. Supreme Court challenging the constitutionality of the Eighteenth Amendment and the Volstead Act.…The House of Representatives rejects a motion to repeal the Volstead Act.…Lester H. Woolsey, Solicitor of the State Department, resigns.	Philadelphia millionaire Grover Cleveland Bergdoll faces a general court-martial on charges of desertion.…President Woodrow Wilson sends his Adriatic reply, the contents of which are not disclosed, to the British and French premiers.	Former Secretary of the Treasury William McAdoo proposes a $1 billion federal tax cut to help businesses.	The blizzard that has been sweeping the western states reaches Chicago, crippling transportation and communication systems.	
Mar. 5	Former Postmaster General Frank H. Hitchcock is made co-manager of General Leonard Wood's campaign to become the Republican presidential candidate.		The Wholesale Coal Association charges Walker D. Hines, Director General of Railroads, with illegally interfering in the distribution of coal.…The United Mine Workers of Ohio amend their constitution to make citizenship compulsory for membership.	The American Chemical Society awards the William H. Nichols gold medal for original research to Dr. Irving Langmuir.…Heavy rain and melting snow causes flooding in New York and eastern Pennsylvania.	Monsignor Bolealaus Puchalski of Brooklyn, NY, is appointed private chamberlain to Pope Benedict XV.…The House of the Kentucky legislature votes to legalize boxing.…Two world records are broken at the Miami Power Boat Regatta.
Mar. 6	Prohibition agents raid cafés and restaurants in New York City.…Police and federal agents in Cleveland discover an underground saloon stocked with $80,000 worth of liquor.	Two members of the American Expeditionary Force are burned to death and two others reported missing when a fire destroys the American barracks at Vladivostok.	New York City's Central Federated Union threatens a rent strike.…The American Railway Express Company in Chicago issues an embargo on all express shipments except newspapers and funeral supplies.	New England is crippled by a major blizzard.…Chicago chemist Angelus Casten is believed kidnapped.…Maryland's eastern shore suffers its worst storm in 30 years.…Storms cause millions of dollars worth of damage in New York City.	The National Catholic Women's Council is formed.…The University of Chicago wins the Western Conference basketball championship.…Eight world records are broken on the final day of the Miami Power Boat Regatta.…The National Aircraft Show opens.
Mar. 7	Returning from a tour of inspection abroad, Surgeon General H.S. Cumming warns of a possible typhus or plague invasion from the Levant.		Chicago tenants organize to fight exorbitant rents.…The captain and crew of the shipwrecked schooner *Eva B. Douglas* are rescued at sea.…The Department of Justice urges consumers to start buying less expensive cuts of meat.	Aeronautical engineer Henry A. Berliner announces the possibility of vertical flight through the use of lifting propellers known as helicopters.	Arabian Sheik Ben Mahomet arrives in the United States to search for his brother's fiancée, who disappeared from Constantinople just after the armistice.…A six-day bicycle race begins at Madison Square Garden.
Mar. 8	The U.S. Supreme Court begins hearings on the constitutionality of the Eighteenth Amendment and the Volstead Act.…Edward E. Clark is elected chairman of the Interstate Commerce Commission.…The Supreme Court rules that stock dividends are not subject to income tax; Dow, Jones & Co. erroneously reports the verdict.	Secretary of the Navy Josephus Daniels appeals to the House Naval Affairs Committee for more naval bases on the Pacific.…Lieutenant Commander Thomas Mott Osborne announces his resignation as commander of the naval prison in Portsmouth, NH.	Henry S. Graves resigns as head of the Federal Forestry Service.		The private collection and studio furnishings of the late Dutch artist Hendrik Willem Mesdag are sold at the American Art Galleries in New York.…Outfielder Armando Marsans signs with the Boston Red Sox.

F	G	H	I	J
Includes campaigns, elections, federal-state relations, civil rights and liberties, crime, the judiciary, education, healthcare, poverty, urban affairs, and population.	*Includes formation and debate of U.S. foreign and defense policies, veterans affairs, and defense spending. (Relations with specific foreign countries are usually found under the region concerned.)*	*Includes business, labor, agriculture, taxation, transportation, consumer affairs, monetary and fiscal policy, natural resources, pollution and industrial accidents.*	*Includes worldwide scientific, medical and technological developments, natural phenomena, U.S. weather and natural disasters.*	*Includes the arts, religion, scholarship, communications media, sports, entertainment, fashions, fads, and social life.*

	World Affairs	Europe	Africa & The Middle East	The Americas	Asia & The Pacific
Mar. 9	Norway, Sweden, and the Netherlands join the League of Nations.			American oil worker Patrick Foley is reported killed by Mexican bandits.…Mexican generals Adolfo de la Huerta, Alvaro Obregon, and Plutarco Elias Calles proclaim the Republic of Sonora, launching another Mexican Civil War.	
Mar. 10	El Salvador is admitted to the League of Nations.	The Red Army under Marshal Mikhail Tukhachevsky begins its Western offensive.…The chief training school for cadets in Prussia is closed in accordance with the Peace Treaty.	General Elections take place throughout the Union of South Africa.…The Egyptian legislative assembly passes a resolution demanding independence from Britain.	The Canadian House of Commons returns a vote of confidence for Premier Robert Borden.	Armenians in Adana close their shops and threaten to send armed forces to the relief of Hadjin, where the Turks are reportedly terrorizing the populace.…Three hundred thousand workers in India go on strike against British rule.…In Jamshedpur, British troops fire on a protesting striker.
Mar. 11		A Russian airplane carrying four emissaries to Germany is forced down by gunfire near Kovno, Lithuania.…Martial law is declared in Teschen.	Feisal, son of the King of the Hedjaz, is proclaimed King of Syria.…The British West African Conference is held in Accra.	N.W. Rowell, President of the Canadian Privy Council, warns that Canada will block the United States from entering the League of Nations if the Lenroot Proviso is accepted.	
Mar. 12	The Executive Council of the League of Nations meets in Paris to discuss sending an investigative committee to Russia.	Free Corps troops march on Berlin during the night and temporarily seize control of the government, installing Wolfgang Kapp in the chancellery.…Repressive measures by President Josef Pulsudski bring a general strike in Warsaw to a quick end.		The U.S. State Department is notified that General Alvaro Obregon, a popular Mexican military figure, has promised not to start a revolution if he is defeated in his candidacy for president.…Mexican federal troops secure the release of kidnapped rancher Peter W. Summers.	
Mar. 13		The Weimar government's press officer publishes a call for a general strike.…Fiume is near famine.…At least four people are killed and 12 injured when an infernal machine explodes in a theater in Sofia, Bulgaria.		A landslide at Cucaracha holds up ships in the Panama Canal.	
Mar. 14	The Allied Supreme Council asks the League of Nations to assume the mandate for Armenia.	The Entente powers announce their intention to impose a blockade if Wolfgang Kapp remains in power in Berlin.…Voters in the southern zone of the North Schleswig plebiscite choose to remain part of Germany.			
Mar. 15		A general strike shuts down transportation and public utilities in Berlin.…Insurgents in Berlin fire shots on the War Office.…Dissident Socialists in France form a new party.		After receiving official notification of attacks on the Peruvian Legation in La Paz, the U.S. government warns Bolivia not to disturb the peace of South America.	
Mar. 16		Allied forces under General Sir George Milne occupy Constantinople.…The Allied Committee of Ambassadors votes to maintain relations with Germany's Ebert government.…Wolfgang Kapp's attempted counterrevolution ends in failure.		The Canadian parliament ratifies the Bulgarian treaty.…Buenos Aires reports growing labor unrest throughout Argentina.…A Canadian caucus rejects proposals for a naval building program.	The Peking government announces its intention to negotiate with Japan on the Shantung question in order to reconcile the North and South factions in China.

A	B	C	D	E
Includes developments that affect more than one world region, international organizations and important meetings of world leaders.	*Includes all domestic and regional developments in Europe, including the Soviet Union.*	*Includes all domestic and regional developments in Africa and the Middle East.*	*Includes all domestic and regional developments in Latin America, the Caribbean, and Canada.*	*Includes all domestic and regional developments in Asian and Pacific nations (and colonies).*

U.S. Politics & Social Issues	U.S. Foreign Policy & Affairs, Defense	U.S. Economy & Environment	Science, Technology & Nature	Culture, Leisure & Lifestyle	
General Leonard Wood wins the New Hampshire primary.... Four individuals, including the editor of *Class Struggle*, are indicted in Chicago on charges of conspiring to overthrow the government by force.	The U.S. Senate votes to adopt Lodge Reservation No. 14, designed to ensure voting equality in the League of Nations Assembly.	.		The Providence, RI, franchise of the Eastern Baseball League is sold to Albany, NY.... Manhattan property accumulated by John Jacob Astor is sold at public auction.	Mar. 9
West Virginia becomes the 34th state to ratify the Federal Suffrage Amendment.... In deciding the Red River oil land dispute, a federal district court judge fixes the south bank of the river as the boundary between Oklahoma and Texas.		The National Coal Association seeks an injunction against the Federal Trade Association's requirement to furnish business reports.			Mar. 10
Will Lockett is executed for the murder of 10-year-old Geneva Hardman.... A secret inquiry is launched following allegations of graft in the New York City police department.... The Committee of Forty-Eight announces its intention to enter a candidate in the forthcoming presidential election.		A federal grand jury indicts 125 miners and operators for an alleged coal price conspiracy.... The Senate orders an investigation of the United States Grain Corporation.	Tornadoes in Missouri kill at least 13 people.	The fourth annual exhibition of the Society of Independent Artists opens in New York.	Mar. 11
Abraham White, known as the "Postage Stamp Bidder," is arrested on a charge of grand larceny.	Secretary of War Newton D. Baker informs the Senate Military Committee that the bodies of approximately 50,000 American soldiers will be returned to the United States, while between 20,000 and 25,000 will remain permanently interred overseas.			Painter and lecturer Alexander T. Van Laer dies in Indianapolis.... American Norman Ross breaks the world speed record for swimming 500 meters.	Mar. 12
The U.S. Senate confirms the nomination of Rear Admiral William S. Benson to succeed John Barton Payne as a member of the Shipping Board.... Seven members of the I.W.W. are found guilty of second degree murder for having killed Warren O. Grimm, one of four former soldiers shot during an Armistice Day parade in Centralia, Washington.	The House of Representatives approves large increases over the prewar strength of the infantry, cavalry, and artillerymen.	More than 7,000 longshoremen, checkers, and stevedores at the Port of New York go on strike.		The Football Rules Committee eliminates the punt-out after a touchdown and introduces new penalties.... The Lotus Club celebrates its 50th anniversary.	Mar. 13
Eugene Debs accepts the Socialist Party's presidential nomination.	The commander and three crew members of the U.S. Submarine *H-1* lose their lives when the craft runs aground at Redondo Point, CA.	Several passengers are killed and many more injured when two trains collide on the Rutland Railroad in Vermont.			Mar. 14
John Barton Payne takes office as Secretary of the Interior.... The U.S. Supreme Court grants the State of New Jersey permission to institute proceedings to test the validity of the Prohibition Amendment and the Volstead Enforcement Act.... General Leonard Wood wins the Minnesota primary.	The House of Representatives passes a bill authorizing the United States Grain Corporation to sell surplus flour to the governments of Armenia, Poland, and Austria.	The unions of Great Lakes sailors, marine firemen, and marine cooks demand a 30 percent wage increase and an eight-hour day.... Financiers, builders, manufacturers, and labor union representatives meet to discuss the housing shortage in New York City.		The women's national indoor tennis championship tournament begins.	Mar. 15
Senator Hiram Johnson runs unopposed in the North Dakota primary.		Masked robbers hold up the Internal Revenue Office in Seattle.	A major blizzard sweeps North and South Dakota.	Ethelda Bleibtrey sets a new world swimming record for the 50-yard backstroke.... American portrait and landscape painter William Henry Lippincott dies.	Mar. 16

F	G	H	I	J
Includes campaigns, elections, federal-state relations, civil rights and liberties, crime, the judiciary, education, healthcare, poverty, urban affairs, and population.	*Includes formation and debate of U.S. foreign and defense policies, veterans affairs, and defense spending. (Relations with specific foreign countries are usually found under the region concerned.)*	*Includes business, labor, agriculture, taxation, transportation, consumer affairs, monetary and fiscal policy, natural resources, pollution and industrial accidents.*	*Includes worldwide scientific, medical and technological developments, natural phenomena, U.S. weather and natural disasters.*	*Includes the arts, religion, scholarship, communications media, sports, entertainment, fashions, fads, and social life.*

	World Affairs	Europe	Africa & The Middle East	The Americas	Asia & The Pacific
Mar. 17		Troops clash with working men in several districts in Germany.... Wolfgang Kapp flees to Sweden.... The Estonian government authorizes the American Red Cross Commission to take any measures necessary to eradicate a typhus epidemic....The Swiss government announces a new commercial treaty with France.			
Mar. 18	The British and French governments refuse to recognize Prince Faisal as King of Syria.	Reports reach London that General Anton Denikin has surrendered to the Bolsheviks....American Red Cross workers report finding Grand Duchess Olga, sister of the late Czar Nicholas of Russia, living in a boxcar near Novorossisk....The German National Assembly opens in Stuttgart.		Under Secretary of State Frank L. Polk appeals to Chilean Ambassador Don Beltran Mathieu for Chile's help in maintaining peace between Peru and Bolivia.	
Mar. 19	The U. S. government issues a strong remonstrance against rulings of the Allied Reparations Commission that the sale of German property in neutral countries can be forced in order to satisfy the initial payment of the German indemnity.	The Spartacists lead a major revolt in the Ruhr, the industrial heartland of Germany....Essen surrenders to armed insurgents....Without awaiting Allied permission, the Ebert government sends troops into the demilitarized Ruhr Valley to quell the uprisings....Political chaos and street fighting continue in Berlin.	At the opening of the Cape Town Parliament, Governor-General Viscount Buxton urges the establishment of an advisory commission and the creation of native councils to assist the South African government.	The Bolivian government apologizes for the attacks on Peruvians in La Paz.	
Mar. 20	British Prime Minister David Lloyd George rejects the pleas of an Indian Caliphate delegation for the restoration to Turkey of prewar territorial status....The Dutch *Communist Tribune* publishes a list of resolutions secretly adopted at a recent meeting of the Communist International.	Thomas MacCurtain, Lord Mayor of Cork, is murdered in his home.... British Prime Minister David Lloyd George rejects the pleas of an Indian Caliphate delegation for the restoration to Turkey of prewar territorial status.			Women vote in the Philippine primaries for the first time....Thomas W. Lamont of J.P. Morgan & Co. arrives in Peking.
Mar. 21		Bulgaria seeks to form a new Balkan Confederation with Yugoslavia and Greece.		C.C. Ballantyne, Canadian Minister of Naval Affairs, orders the demobilization of Canada's naval forces.... The employees of the Great Western Railway in Brazil go on strike....The Panama Canal is temporarily closed due to a landslide in the Cucaracha section of the waterway.	Peking reports news of great social unrest in Japan.
Mar. 22	The governing body of the International Labor Bureau meets in London.	Armenians rise in revolt in Nagorno-Karabagh....A general strike is called in Strasbourg....German Minister of Defense Gustav Noske resigns from the Ebert government....The Russian Soviet government proposes the resumption of relations with Italy....The tension between Estonia and Livonia increases over a boundary dispute, despite British attempts at conciliation.	British Secretary for War Winston Churchill proposes guarding Mesopotamia by air patrol rather than by military forces....Emir Faisal, the newly elected King of Syria, declares a boycott against France and England.		
Mar. 23		Turkish-Azerbaijani troops burn and rob Sushi, the capital of the Nagorno-Karabagh district....Admiral Miklós Horthy declares Hungary a monarchy....Major General Walther von Lüttwitz, the military commander in the Kapp revolt, is placed under arrest....Heavy fighting is reported on the Polish front....The Red Army advances on Wesel....A general strike on the railways of Spain goes into effect at noon.			The Perserikatan Communist of India (PKI) political party is formed.

A	B	C	D	E
Includes developments that affect more than one world region, international organizations and important meetings of world leaders.	*Includes all domestic and regional developments in Europe, including the Soviet Union.*	*Includes all domestic and regional developments in Africa and the Middle East.*	*Includes all domestic and regional developments in Latin America, the Caribbean, and Canada.*	*Includes all domestic and regional developments in Asian and Pacific nations (and colonies).*

U.S. Politics & Social Issues	U.S. Foreign Policy & Affairs, Defense	U.S. Economy & Environment	Science, Technology & Nature	Culture, Leisure & Lifestyle	
President Woodrow Wilson is photographed for the first time since the onset of his illness....President Wilson nominates William Martin Williams to succeed Daniel C. Roper as commissioner of Internal Revenue....The Virginia Republican Convention backs Illinois Governor Frank O. Lowden for the presidential nomination.	The U.S. Senate defeats the Lenroot reservation on foreign policy.	Labor leader Joe Hurley is found murdered in Chicago....General Electric acquires the Remington Arms Company in Bridgeport, CT.	The Harvard College Observatory announces the discovery of a new star by one of its staff members.		Mar. 17
The National Woman's Party appeals to the U.S. Supreme Court in its fight against an Ohio referendum on the Nineteenth Amendment.	Herbert Hoover advocates the immediate ratification of the Peace Treaty with reservations.	West Virginia operators seek an injunction against the Coal Control Act.			Mar. 18
Harry Winitsky, Executive Secretary of the New York Communist Party, appears in court on charges of criminal anarchy.	The U.S. Senate rejects the Versailles Treaty and League Covenant by a vote of 49 to 35.				Mar. 19
Senator Truman H. Newberry (R-MI) is convicted on charges of violating campaign laws....Four St. Louis brewing companies file suits in the U.S. District Court challenging the constitutionality of the Eighteenth Amendment and the validity of the Volstead Act.	The super dreadnought *Maryland* is launched in Newport News, VA.		The first flight from London to South Africa lands safely.	Helene Pollak wins the women's national indoor tennis championship....Book collector and writer William Loring Andrews dies.	Mar. 20
Detectives arrest 88 men during gambling raids in New York....Rival gang leaders shoot each other to death in Newark....Congressman Isaac Siegel announces that several hundred alien radicals will be deported within the next two or three weeks.				The Seventh International Flower Show in New York draws to a close.	Mar. 21
Fugitive "Nicky" Arnstein fails to appear in General Sessions, despite his promise to surrender to authorities....Edward J. McGoldrick is sworn in as a New York State Supreme Court Justice....The U.S. Senate confirms the nomination of Bainbridge Colby as Secretary of State....Washington becomes the 35th state to ratify the Nineteenth Amendment....Abraham White, out on bail following his March 12 arrest, is accused of selling fraudulent stock and is once again arrested.	Senator Henry Cabot Lodge decides against asking the Senate to act on the Knox Resolution to terminate the war with Germany....The Senate confirms the nomination of Charles R. Crane to be Minister to China.	The New York Cotton Exchange reports a sharp rise in the cotton market.	Electrical disturbances accompanying the appearance of the Aurora Borealis wreak havoc with cables, telephone, and telegraph service....Dr. William H. Meyer of New York announces the successful treatment of superficial cancer by X-ray radiation in 50 consecutive cases.	Publisher Horace Liveright is summoned to appear in court for publishing and distributing *The Story of a Lover,* which New York officials consider obscene....Vaudeville agent Tom Jones dies.	Mar. 22
Bainbridge Colby takes office as U.S. Secretary of State....The Hoover Republican League is founded in Boston....Kansas Governor H.J. Allen refuses the extradition petition of Arkansas for the return of Robert Hill, alleged leader of the Elaine insurrection....Christian A. Herter, special attaché to the State Department, resigns to become Herbert Hoover's secretary....General Leonard Wood captures the South Dakota primary.	President Wilson nominates Henry Morgenthau, former Ambassador to Turkey, to be Ambassador to Mexico.	With strong warnings against any attempt at profiteering, President Woodrow Wilson orders the termination of governmental control over bituminous coal prices, effective April 1....President Wilson calls on operators and miners to negotiate a new working agreement based on the Coal Commission's majority report....Three more coal operators and two officials of the United Mine Workers of America are arrested in Indiana following an investigation of the bituminous coal industry.	The worst storm of the winter rages in Colorado.	European heavyweight champion Georges Carpentier arrives in New York....Dr. Theodore Emanuel Schmauk, religious scholar and head of the United Lutheran Churches of the United States, dies in Pennsylvania.	Mar. 23
F *Includes campaigns, elections, federal-state relations, civil rights and liberties, crime, the judiciary, education, healthcare, poverty, urban affairs, and population.*	**G** *Includes formation and debate of U.S. foreign and defense policies, veterans affairs, and defense spending. (Relations with specific foreign countries are usually found under the region concerned.)*	**H** *Includes business, labor, agriculture, taxation, transportation, consumer affairs, monetary and fiscal policy, natural resources, pollution and industrial accidents.*	**I** *Includes worldwide scientific, medical and technological developments, natural phenomena, U.S. weather and natural disasters.*	**J** *Includes the arts, religion, scholarship, communications media, sports, entertainment, fashions, fads, and social life.*	

	World Affairs	Europe	Africa & The Middle East	The Americas	Asia & The Pacific
Mar. 24		Under the Bielefeld Agreement, rebellious workers in the Ruhr agree to hand over their weapons and return to work in exchange for promises of social welfare legislation and retribution against right-wing participants in the Kapp Putsch.	King Feisal orders French troops out of Syria.		The Japanese steamship company Osaka Shosen Kaisha inaugurates a long distance steamship service between Singapore and New York.
Mar. 25		William Cosgrave, Sinn Fein member of the Dáil Éireann and the Dublin Council, is arrested.... Press censorship is abolished in Italy.			
Mar. 26		Dublin magistrate Alan Bell is assassinated.... Thirty-five prominent Sinn Feiners are arrested in Dublin.			
Mar. 27		General Peter Wrangel assumes command of the White forces in southern Russia.... The Polish government demands that Soviet Russia recognize the Polish territorial boundaries of 1772.			
Mar. 28		German workers threaten a massive strike in response to the Weimar Republic's hesitancy in arresting those involved in the defeated Kapp Putsch.			
Mar. 29		Margaret Schlachta becomes the first woman member of the Hungarian National Assembly. The *New York Times* notes that she is "very attractive."		Relations between Peru and Bolivia deteriorate as reports surface indicating that Bolivia is amassing troops along the Peruvian-Bolivian border.	
Mar. 30	Greece joins the League of Nations.				
Mar. 31	U.S. President Woodrow Wilson publicly backs the French Government in their efforts to expel the current administrative leadership in Turkey.	Russian Foreign Minister George Tchitcherin meets with his Polish counterpart to discuss ways to end border clashes on the Polish-Russian border.			
Apr. 1	The Dutch Foreign Minister and American Food Commission representatives agree on amounts each country will contribute to Austrian and Polish Relief. The Dutch tentatively agree to a $10 million commitment.... An Armenian state is created by the League of Nations.... The largest shipments to date of American Red Cross relief goods, including food, medical supplies, and clothing, arrive in Czestochowa, Poland, and Vienna, Austria.	The German Workers Party changes its name to Nationalist Socialist German Worker's Party (also known as the Nazi Party).... Turkey expresses outrage at President Wilson's message urging that Turkish forces should leave Europe.... The Greeks are dismayed at the U.S. lack of support for land claims.	The First South African Aero (airplane) Conference opens in Johannesburg.	The Associated Dress Industries of America announces demand for American-made ready-to-wear clothing is up in Latin America. Moderately priced satin dresses are the most requested item.... Prince of Wales arrives to ecstatic crowds in Panama and views Pacific defenses of the canal.	Bolshevist fighters have control of Kiev even though fierce fighting with Ukrainians continues in the city and surrounding areas.
Apr. 2		The French government fears workers will join with Red Army advancing into the Ruhr Basin to destroy mines.... German troops occupy Red Towns of Duisberg and Ruhrort following extensive street fighting. Workers in the cities urge organized protest to action, including possibility of a general strike.	The mayor of Jerusalem, Musa Kazim al-Husayni, is replaced by Raghib al-Nashashibi. Angry residents rally around the two figures and violence is threatened.	The government of Brazil announces that captured German ships will be purchased by a group of French ship owners.	Chinese troops, under General Tan Keng-beng, mutiny in revolt against Governor Low Hun-sin of the Anhul Province in China.

A	B	C	D	E
Includes developments that affect more than one world region, international organizations and important meetings of world leaders.	*Includes all domestic and regional developments in Europe, including the Soviet Union.*	*Includes all domestic and regional developments in Africa and the Middle East.*	*Includes all domestic and regional developments in Latin America, the Caribbean, and Canada.*	*Includes all domestic and regional developments in Asian and Pacific nations (and colonies).*

U.S. Politics & Social Issues	U.S. Foreign Policy & Affairs, Defense	U.S. Economy & Environment	Science, Technology & Nature	Culture, Leisure & Lifestyle	
William J. Browning, Republican Representative from New Jersey, dies in the U.S. Capitol building.					Mar. 24
Delaware rejects the Nineteenth Amendment.... Edward Reed, Mayor of Glenns Falls, NY, dies in office.			On the Seine River near Paris, a French motorboat records a speed of 75 miles per hour, breaking an all-time record for motorboat speed of 69 miles per hour.	Adeline Gehrig wins the U.S. Women's National Fencing Championship.	Mar. 25
		The Copper Export Association reports that 1919 was the best year on record for worldwide sale of U.S. copper.	The Red Cross reports that a large percentage of the Polish population is currently infected with typhus.	Scribners publishes F. Scott Fitzgerald's first novel, *This Side of Paradise.*	Mar. 26
Senator William Borah publicly alleges that war profiteers are conspiring to fix the results of the Democratic and Republican National Conventions, adding that their activities have resulted in a "saturnalia of corruption."		Speaking before the Industrial Club of America, War Finance Corporation managing director Eugene Meyer declares that "this is America's hour" for economic prosperity.		The 21st annual tournament begins for the national men's indoor lawn tennis championship.... Character actor Sol Aiden dies at 67.	Mar. 27
		The Esch-Cummins Act restores the railroads to private ownership and sets up the Railroad Labor Board.	Thirty tornadoes across eight states claim 153 victims, ranking the Palm Sunday tornado outbreak among the deadliest in U.S. history.	Film stars Douglas Fairbanks and Mary Pickford wed.	Mar. 28
Mississippi rejects the Nineteenth Amendment.			A series of tornadoes rip through Georgia and Alabama, claiming the lives of more than three dozen people and causing property damage in excess of millions of dollars.		Mar. 29
W.D. Nesbit, Chairman of the Alabama State Democratic Executive Committee, rules that African Americans will not be allowed to take part in the state's upcoming Democratic primary.		The U.S. Industrial Alcohol Company releases its annual statement showing that, owing to Prohibition, the company's earnings have dropped from $14,073,102 in 1918 to $4,426,264 in 1919.	Several agricultural groups in New York State band together to formally request that legislators end Daylight Savings Time.		Mar. 30
Edwin Warfield, former governor of Maryland, dies.... Members of the New York City Assembly call for an ousting of five of their fellow members who belong to the Socialist Party of America, which is deemed "a disloyal organization composed exclusively of perpetual traitors." Governor Franklin D. Roosevelt expresses opposition to the proposed ousting.				Oxford University votes to remove the Greek language from its list of required subjects.	Mar. 31
Suffragists are denied ratification of the Nineteenth Amendment by the state legislature of Delaware. They await the thirty-sixth, and last, state to ratify an amendment to give women the right to vote.... Five members of the New York State legislature are expelled because they are members of the Socialist Party.	President Wilson announces that U.S. occupation army is under his control, outweighing conflicting jurisdiction of the Rhineland Commission and Field Marshal Ferdinand Foch, Commander-in-Chief of the Allied Forces [Germany].	Committees of the New State Chamber of Commerce vote to recommend that the government return control of the Erie Canal to private industry and vote to unite against laws mandating employee health insurance.... New York Supreme Court rules publicly funded operation of New York city bus lines is illegal on the grounds that the buses created unfair competition to the city's surface railway car companies.		Journalist and author Howard "H.H." Hinton of *Old Home Journal* dies. Literary critics classified Hinton as the last living author of the classical period of American literature.... French artist Francis Picabia publishes the first issue of *Le Cannibale*, a Paris Dadaist magazine.	Apr. 1
		North American Fruit Exchange charges that a railroad car shortage and problems with restrictions on car movement causes rotting cabbage and vegetables. Problem is acute in southern crop fields.	Scientist Albert Einstein arrives in New York City to lecture on the Theory of Relativity at Columbia University.... Oil speculators rush to buy leases in Oregon.	The Chicago Art Institute is urged to buy and restore Mark Twain's Chicago home to protect it against real estate developers.... Nevada State Attorney General announces that actress Mary Pickford's divorce from Owen Moore will be annulled due to the actress' false residency claim.	Apr. 2

F	G	H	I	J
Includes campaigns, elections, federal-state relations, civil rights and liberties, crime, the judiciary, education, healthcare, poverty, urban affairs, and population.	*Includes formation and debate of U.S. foreign and defense policies, veterans affairs, and defense spending. (Relations with specific foreign countries are usually found under the region concerned.)*	*Includes business, labor, agriculture, taxation, transportation, consumer affairs, monetary and fiscal policy, natural resources, pollution and industrial accidents.*	*Includes worldwide scientific, medical and technological developments, natural phenomena, U.S. weather and natural disasters.*	*Includes the arts, religion, scholarship, communications media, sports, entertainment, fashions, fads, and social life.*

	World Affairs	Europe	Africa & The Middle East	The Americas	Asia & The Pacific
Apr. 3	In an effort to reduce debt and improve the exchange rate, the Bank of France announces it will deflate its bank currency notes.	France announces it will operate alone to assist Germany in halting violence in Ruhr basin....Germany asks for assistance of the Allied Supreme Council, and does not wish France to operate unilaterally.... Military troops reinforce measures to prevent Easter rioting in Dublin, Ireland....The Danish monarch meets with a delegation of town councilors heading a march of more than 40,000 people eager to avoid a general strike of all workers.		Mexican General Alvaro Obregon, candidate for the presidency, tells of assassination attempt.	Japan announces it will delay withdrawing troops from Siberia due to danger from Korea and Manchuria.
Apr. 4		France makes plans to enter Germany in answer to German troop entry into Ruhr Basin to defeat Red Army....Danish Premier Liebe presents his resignation after failure to halt general strike.....The Red Army digs in to fight in outskirts of Essen....A Berlin correspondent for the *Long Times* announces that militarists have taken over German government offices....The U.S. is thought likely to support Armenian people, if a request is made to do more than assist in food supplies....Government troops in Duisburg, Prussia, clear Red troops and attempt to restore civil authority to the city.	King Faisal of Syria sends a message to U.S. President Woodrow Wilson asking him to assist Arabs in their efforts to unify Syria.... Bedouins and Druses oppose government draft policy in Syria.... Fighting between Arab and Jewish residents of Jerusalem causes city leaders to declare a state of siege....British General Louis J. Bols attempts to keep peace between groups during Passover and Nabi Musa celebrations.	Political unrest in the Republic of Guatemala results in rioting and deaths. President Cabrera, fearing for his life, orders student rebels executed. Guatemalan refugees blame the United States for troubles, insisting that Washington's support of Cabrera is creating problems for their country.	England's India Office makes public a report of special commission appointed by the National Congress of India that Baron Cheimsford (Viceroy and Governor General of India) is not capable of carrying out his duties. The committee demands his recall....Roland Morris, U.S. Ambassador to Japan, and Japanese Premier Shibusawa urge the U.S. government to set up a joint commission to decide land issues in the state of California and questions involving Allied action.
Apr. 5		A Danish strike is called off with strikers guaranteed amnesty.... The Danish cabinet is declared temporary, not permanent.... German troops capture the cities of Oberhausen, Dortmund, Luderscheid, and Mulheim and Horst....The French capture the city of Frankfort....Copenhagen police break up crowds around the royal palace in Denmark in fear that Soviet supporters will cause rioting and assist in formulating a general strike.	Easter Day fighting in Jerusalem results in 188 deaths.	Argentina ballots are now totaled and show President Irigoyen's party will continue to hold power. Radical representatives in the Congress will outnumber both Conservative and Democrat Party members....Canada outlaws foreign trapping and hunting in Banks and Victoria Islands, and declares lands reserved for native Eskimos.	Japanese forces make surprise capture of Vladivostok while Red Army celebrates Easter....Japanese Vice-Council Ishida is killed in fighting in eastern Siberia....The Japanese government announces that it will join the United States, Great Britain, and France in loaning money to fund the Chinese railway....Major Dennis P. Quinlan, former Judge Advocate of the Philippines Department, is found innocent of embezzlement charges in Manila today.
Apr. 6	The League of Nations reports the filing of neutral nations, including Netherlands, Salvador, Norway, Denmark, and Switzerland, for membership in the League covenant.... The League of Nations makes an appeal to its members for $1 million to fund its operations....Germans in Berlin are surprised and angry over French occupation of Frankfort, Darmstadt, and Hanau. The French occupation is predicted by German newspapers to slow peace process.	The Soviet Russian government establishes a ruling organization in the Far Eastern Republic in eastern Siberia, with a capital at Chita.... France sends occupation forces to the Ruhr to take control of industrial and economic segments of the cities, including Frankfurt....*The New York Times* reports that residents of Ruhr welcome France due to the large number of munitions and food supplied to the region by the new occupants.	Rioting is reported instigated by Arab leader Haj Amin El Husseini and Aref El Aref in the cities of Jerusalem and Hebron. Many are reported to be killed and injured.	A formal membership announcement is made by the League of Nations claiming membership by all nations of South and Central America. Venezuela was the last Latin American nation to file notification....A bulk of gold shipments arriving in New York from London on the *Carmania* and *Minnekahda* are headed for South America to pay off war debts and allow South American traders to continue supplying goods to England..... Canadian Secretary of State Arthur Lewis Sifton announces that his country's population is nine million.	
Apr. 7	The Supreme Military Council of the Allies give Greek troops permission to enter Asia Minor in preparation for an attack by Mustafa Kemal. Troops enter from their position east of Smyrna.	The evacuation of American troops from Siberia is completed today. The Commander in Chief of the American Expeditionary Forces in Siberia, Brigadier General William S. Graves, and staff arrive in Manila on the *Great Northern* from Vladivostok. Additional troops with war brides arrive a short time later aboard the *South Bend*.			

A	B	C	D	E
Includes developments that affect more than one world region, international organizations and important meetings of world leaders.	*Includes all domestic and regional developments in Europe, including the Soviet Union.*	*Includes all domestic and regional developments in Africa and the Middle East.*	*Includes all domestic and regional developments in Latin America, the Caribbean, and Canada.*	*Includes all domestic and regional developments in Asian and Pacific nations (and colonies).*

U.S. Politics & Social Issues	U.S. Foreign Policy & Affairs, Defense	U.S. Economy & Environment	Science, Technology & Nature	Culture, Leisure & Lifestyle	
Movement is announced to ban Socialists from law school admission. Diplomas will be withheld from student radicals currently attending schools.		The U.S. Department of Justice rules that vaudeville performances do not violate the Sherman Antitrust Act under the Commerce Clause of unfair competition.…The Federal Reserve Board, with President Harding's approval, is given ability to discount rates at each of the 12 Federal Reserve Banks by the U.S. Congress.	Blizzards hit the western U.S. states of Montana, Nebraska, and Colorado.…The recent outbreak of scarlet fever in Rhode Island is traced to infected milk.…Naturalist John Burroughs celebrates his 83rd birthday by announcing he has completed a new book, *The Faith of a Naturalist.* Guests at the party include Thomas A. Edison and Hamlin Garland.	Author F. Scott Fitzgerald and Socialite Zelda Sayre are married in New York City.…The Chicago Art Institute is given charge of the Mrs. W.W. Kimball Collection after estate fears thieves were working to steal collection.…The announcement is made that U.S. skaters Theresa Weld and Nathaniel W. Niles, both of Boston, will represent America at the Belgian Olympics.	Apr. 3
The primary election vote is held in Michigan today.…The Peace Resolution is debated in U.S. Congress.…Herbert Hoover denies that he will run in election as independent.	U.S. Secretary of the Treasury Houston announces plans to guarantee availability of Victory notes (war bonds) in small denominations of $50 and $100.…U.S. politicians are angry over France's unilateral military plan to send troops to occupy Frankfort and additional cities of the Rhine's right bank.	A national labor strike is declared to preserve the eight-hour work day in the United States.…Record profits are reported for the rubber industry in the United States.		Violinist Jascha Heifetz gives the last Carnegie Hall recital of the season.…The New York University Hall of Fame nominates Frederick Douglass, the first black nominated for such a spot.	Apr. 4
The Republican Party calls for reforms to improve the economy at the national convention.…Delaware delays in deciding ratification of the suffrage amendment.…Herbert Hoover's application to file as a Republican in the California primaries is thwarted due to the late arrival of his affidavit of registration from New York.…Indiana State Board of Election Commissioners and Governor James P. Goodrich agree to bar women from voting in the state primary elections on May 4.…Johnson and Hoover are defeated in New York primaries.…Johnson and Hoover are leading in Michigan primary.	Warren G. Harding criticizes Woodrow Wilson's policies and urges Americanism over Internationalism.…The League of Nations bill is readied for resubmission to the U.S. Senate, this time as an amendment.…U.S. Senator William M. Calder voices opposition to the League of Nations in a speech claiming the United States would be required to provide troops to settle boundary disputes. He cites French action as an example.…Congress debates U.S. Constitutional war powers.	A railroad strike is called in Chicago rail yards.…Elevator operators demand an eight-hour day and an increase in salary.…Anthracite coal miners lobby for a 30-hour workweek. Operators oppose but do offer a wage increase. Coal miners strike in Kansas and Illinois. Other workers may join in strike action across the United States.…Head of circus, John Ringling, takes trucks to guarantee food supplies for employees during the New York harbor strike.…The Executive Committee of the National Association of Clothiers sends the decision to advance the clothing seasons (to save on production and shipping costs) to committee for a final determination.	A bill passes in the U.S. House to give the federal government absolute control of the national parks of Yosemite, Sequoia, and General Grant.…The British ship *Furious* reports the first takeoff and landing of an airplane on the deck of a ship. Prior to this, planes landed but did not take off from the same ship deck.…Hundreds of trees are destroyed by storms in Oregon.	The body of Jeanne Anna De Kay, a Hull House Settlement worker, is found after long national search. Suicide is believed to be the cause of death.…The announcement is made that Cornelius Fellowes, President of the International Skating Union and proponent of hockey, will manage American skaters at the Olympics in Antwerp, Belgium this year. Fellowes replaces Roy D. Schooley, who was unable to attend due to family illness.…The head of the Perfume Manufacturers' Association, A.M. Spiehler, denies that the Volstead Act is being circumvented by individuals purchasing perfume as a substitute for alcohol.	Apr. 5
Women vote and work at polls in large numbers during the New York primaries.…Irish women in the United States barred from street protest instead fly over the Embassy in Washington D.C. in an attempt to call attention to the Irish protest.…Julius H. Barnes, President of the United States Grain Corporation, receives commendation for his service providing more than $5 million in food aid to war-torn areas.	Brigadier General W.W. Harts defends his command of the Paris district during the war and claims American prisoners were not treated harshly under his watch.…The New York Milk Fund conducts a benefit to raise money to bring home American war dead.	American Federation of Labor President Samuel Gompers demands employers discontinue menacing representatives of the AFL.…New York state votes to increase pay for teachers and pay bonuses to soldiers.…A New York bank opens in Madrid, Spain.	The Norwegian Geographical Society questions reports that Captain Roald Amundsen has begun final dash to the North Pole, since plans indicate the dash was expected next year.	The Ambassador Hotel on Park Avenue announces plan for a large roof garden.	Apr. 6
Georgia voting issues result in two sets of Republican delegates planning to attend the national convention in Chicago. Wood and Lowden representatives attend a meeting in the Georgia House of Representatives, but only after convention doors are opened by police. Georgia Governor Hugh M. Dorsey rules that the session must be open to all delegates.	Governor William D. Stephens, San Diego Mayor Louis J. Wilde, and Pacific Fleet Vice Admiral Williams meet Edward, Prince of Wales, arriving in San Diego, CA, for a two-day visit. City businesses close at noon to celebrate the visit.	An announcement of a shift in commercial paper production to cotton content.…Unique printed silk is used for hat production.…U.S. Shipping Board Chair W.S. Benson questions the United States Steel Corporation about possible discrimination against the American Merchant Marine (and Shipping Board ships) through utilization of foreign ships in moving steel from Pacific Coast ports.		A New York bill is introduced to establish a corporation to carry out the terms of the will of Henry C. Frick and the plan for display of his vast collection of art.	Apr. 7

F	G	H	I	J
Includes campaigns, elections, federal-state relations, civil rights and liberties, crime, the judiciary, education, healthcare, poverty, urban affairs, and population.	*Includes formation and debate of U.S. foreign and defense policies, veterans affairs, and defense spending. (Relations with specific foreign countries are usually found under the region concerned.)*	*Includes business, labor, agriculture, taxation, transportation, consumer affairs, monetary and fiscal policy, natural resources, pollution and industrial accidents.*	*Includes worldwide scientific, medical and technological developments, natural phenomena, U.S. weather and natural disasters.*	*Includes the arts, religion, scholarship, communications media, sports, entertainment, fashions, fads, and social life.*

	World Affairs	Europe	Africa & The Middle East	The Americas	Asia & The Pacific
Apr. 8	Portugal is admitted to the League of Nations.	General Agapieff, commander of the South Russian forces in Constantinople, and British General Denikin order all navy officers in Constantinople to register under penalty of arrest.		Governor de la Huerta is declared Supreme Power of the Republic of Sonora. Customs houses are seized and goods turned over to the new government.	
Apr. 9	The fourth session of the League of Nations is held in Paris.…The League of Nations refuses to hear Germany's appeal regarding international intervention between the country and France.…The League Council discusses questions of minority protection in Turkey, the Armenian mandate, and the return of Allied prisoners held in Siberia.…Britain announces it may leave the Rhine, if other countries do not join with France.	Belgian Military Mission announces that Belgium will formally join the French occupation of Frankfort.…American writer John Reed is executed in Finland for supporting the violent overthrow of the government as part of the Russian Lenin-Trotzky plan.…Bradford Socialists on the London City Education Committee announce they will open a floating ship as a secondary school.	Prophet Enoch Josiah Mgijima, leader of the Israelites, refuses to pay taxes in Kamastone, South Africa, creating a movement for African independence from colonial powers.	Spanish bankers attempt to take control of the German Electric Company in South America.…Salvador sets up an arbitration court for Latin and American states, but omits any participation by the United States.…The Mexican Sonora state takes over the American-owned Southern Pacific Railroad subsidiary involved in a strike.…Bolivia tells Peru it will continue to seek a Pacific Ocean port in Arica.	Japanese forces capture Ussuri Railroad.
Apr. 10	Huge increases are posted in foreign sales of chewing gum and U.S.-manufactured cigarettes.…France denies claims they will advance further to take more territory on the right bank of the Rhine, but make a stand on the Treaty of San Remo demanding disarmament of Germany and strict enforcement of treaty policy.…France receives the first shipment of German cattle required under Treaty of Versailles. A second shipment is expected tomorrow.	The British are unwilling to intervene in the French occupation of the Ruhr region.…Striking workers end a fight in the Ruhr district and turn over power to local municipal authorities under the terms of the Bielefeld and Munster Peace Agreements.…Russia and Finland agree to meet in Terijoki (on the Finnish and Russian border) to work out a truce.…British Ambassador Sir Auckland Geddes begins his service in Washington.			The Indian Reform Bill is introduced to the Department of Excise in an attempt to outlaw the use of alcohol in India.
Apr. 11		The Turkish government is dissolved by the Ottoman government. The official newspaper *Takvim-I Vekayi* blames former leaders for breaking the peace and working against the Turkish government.		The Mexican government files official protest over five American ships entering Mexico's territorial waters in Magdalena Bay of Lower California. American crews left the ships without official permission from the Mexican government.	
Apr. 12	The League of Nations declares a mandate for Armenia could not be administered due to lack of resources and finances.…France and England come to an agreement on the execution of the San Remo Conference accords with the French supporting the Treaty of Versailles and withdraw troops from Frankfort, Darmstadt, Hanau, Homburg, and Dieburg.	Communist leader Hoelz flees his castle in Falkenstein to Klingenthal, taking millions of marks with him.…Irish labor calls a general strike.…Bavaria refuses to dissolve guard.…Berlin orders the army cut.…Captain d'Annunzio sends word that the situation in Fiume is critical due to labor strikes and shortages of food.		Thirteen Mexican states secede from the union.…Governor Esteban Cantu of Lower California (Baja) announces that secessions are isolated and Baja will remain under the control of the President of Mexico.…General P. Elias Calles takes over the government as Governor Adolfo de la Huerta enters the hospital for appendicitis.…Guatemala City is shelled by Cabrera forces, resulting in numerous deaths.	
Apr. 13	The League of Nations opens the International Health Conference in London.	Sheik-ul-Islam at Constantinople, Deurrizade Abdullah Effendi, dissolves the Turkish government and calls for a Holy War on nationalists and rival Mustafa Kemal.		The Northern Military Commander for Mexican President Carranza tells de la Huerta and General Calles that military measures are planned unless Sonora is turned over to the national government.	
Apr. 14		The French Prime Minister Millerand announces a settlement to the Franco-British incident and occupation of Rhine cities. England agrees to uphold the treaty and France agrees to withdraw most of the troops from the neutral zone. With German troop reduction, France agrees to withdraw from occupied German cities.			Thirty thousand students demonstrate in Shanghai over secret negotiations over Shantung.
	A *Includes developments that affect more than one world region, international organizations and important meetings of world leaders.*	B *Includes all domestic and regional developments in Europe, including the Soviet Union.*	C *Includes all domestic and regional developments in Africa and the Middle East.*	D *Includes all domestic and regional developments in Latin America, the Caribbean, and Canada.*	E *Includes all domestic and regional developments in Asian and Pacific nations (and colonies).*

U.S. Politics & Social Issues	U.S. Foreign Policy & Affairs, Defense	U.S. Economy & Environment	Science, Technology & Nature	Culture, Leisure & Lifestyle	
					Apr. 8
The Senate Elections Committee urges a full investigation into the Michigan voting results.... Presidential candidate Hiram Johnson protests the U.S. entry into the League of Nations and criticizes companies that made a fortune on war, calling them "Patrioteers."... Acting Labor Secretary Louis F. Post rules that only bona fide members of the Communist Party will be deported.... The Tammany Hall political organization announces it supports ending corruption in the police department.... The Appellate Court in Brooklyn supports barring women from serving on juries.	The U.S. Army announces it will train civilian aviators.... The Peace Resolution passes in the U.S. House of Representatives on a 242–150 vote.	The Shipping Board considers the purchase of 29 confiscated former German passenger liners.... Health insurance costs make a huge jump. Insurance companies claim higher costs are related to the large number of influenza cases.... There is strong demand for single-family dwellings in New York.... The Brotherhood of Railroad Trainmen's unauthorized strike spreads west to Portland, Omaha, and Salt Lake City. Chicago strikers announce they may return by the weekend.... Detroit and Kansas City rail yards are empty due to the strike.... A wildcat strike in New York results in a halt to all freight and passenger services.		The School Principals' Report of the National Motion Picture League finds movies are bad influence on students and urges a ban on serial films.... A new law allows sports and outdoor games to be played in public parks in New York City.	Apr. 9
The Anti-Dry Society has a parade in Chicago... Mrs. Herbert Hoover announces she is not in favor of her husband's candidacy and does not support Hoover Clubs on college campuses.... Additional Irish picketers are arrested in Washington, D.C.	Rear Admiral Thomas Washington, Chief of Bureau of Navigation, warns U.S. Senate committee that resignations over the last year are at an alarming level.... Herbert Hoover announces in a campaign speech that he does not favor intervention in the Armenian situation, citing unnecessary risks to American military.	The head of the railroad conductors' union blames President Woodrow Wilson for the strike.... The head of the Railroad Brotherhood asks the U.S. Congress to act to halt "renegade" strikers.... Indianapolis railroad switchmen join the strike.... The Big Four and Pennsylvania Railroad embargo all freight.... the wildcat strike moves to Cleveland, OH.... Toledo, OH announces food shortage due to strike.		Davis Cup tennis officials meet to consider allowing France and Canada to send entries to the matches.... The National Association of Women Painters and Sculptors awards the prize for the best painting to A. Albert Wigand.... Ted Cann of the Detroit Athletic Club sets the world record in the 220-yard event, and the New York Swimming Association sets another record in the 400-yard relay event at a National A.A.U. swim meet in Detroit.	Apr. 10
New York proposes a plan to license automobile operators through a one-time registration and a fee of 50 cents.... Automatic telephone answering systems reduce the need for Hello Girls.	The thwarted German plan to bomb New York with a Super-Zeppelin on Thanksgiving Day, 1918, is disclosed by Colonel William N. Hensley, Jr.	Two thousand rail workers walk out in Milwaukee, forcing the city into food and industry crisis.... Six-thousand railroad clerks strike in Cincinnati, Ohio.... Railroads claim to be baffled as to discovery of new leaders behind strikes, and state that companies will deal only with Railroad Brotherhoods.	Henry Holt & Co. announces American rights to publish Albert Einstein's *Relativity: The Special and General Theory*.... Marie Antoinette Czaplicka, the only woman on anthropological expeditions to Siberia and Caucasus, ends her speaking tour of the United States.	Yale president Dr. Arthur Twining Hadley resigns his post after serving more than 20 years in that position.... The demand for rabbit fur for use in hats and clothing creates shortages.	Apr. 11
New York municipal courts throw out thousands of landlord claims due to their failure to meet new paperwork requirements.... Jay Gould defends his tennis title at the Racquet and Tennis Club contest in New York.... Wide movement is seen in the Democratic Party for Ohio Governor James M. Cox.... New Jersey passes a bonus bill providing $10 a month for every month served fighting in the war.	The U.S. Senate debates proposals for the training of the volunteer army, standing army, and National Guard forces.	President Woodrow Wilson announces he is prepared to act on rail strike.... U.S. Shipping Board announces that all confiscated German cargo ships taken during the war have been sold to private interests.... The rail strike continues in most areas, but the Columbus district sees an opening.... New York is left with only five days of food supplies.			Apr. 12
Newport, RI asks President Woodrow Wilson to make the city the summer capital.... President Wilson appoints members of the Railroad Labor Board and calls for a Cabinet meeting on the rail strike.... Rail strike leaders are arrested in New Orleans on charges of interfering with U.S. mail.	The U.S. House of Representatives asks that materials collected on illegal wartime construction actions be turned over to the U.S. Attorney General for prosecution.... Tentative agreement made by Ways and Means Committee requiring a dollar a day to be paid to men in service during the war.	Outlaw strikers fire on a Staten Island train in New York City.... Labor talks are at a standstill for train workers.		American League President B.B. Johnson announces only 10 pitchers have permission to use a "spitball" this season.	Apr. 13
	The army delivers meat during the shortage by distributing surplus stocks from U.S. War Department.... The U.S. Post Office uses army vehicles to collect and deliver mail delayed by rail strikes.	The Senate Interstate Commerce Committee debates the Poindexter Bill calling for punishment for causing a transportation strike or walkout.	Tornadoes hit the southern United States, killing hundreds. Hardest hit are the states of Alabama and Mississippi.	Today is Opening Day for the baseball season.... Harry Houdini's interview outlining his magic tricks used in his latest movie, *The Terror Island*, is published in *Moving Picture Stories*.... Marion Harris records *St. Louis Blues* and *Homesick Blues* in New York for Columbia Records.	Apr. 14
F *Includes campaigns, elections, federal-state relations, civil rights and liberties, crime, the judiciary, education, healthcare, poverty, urban affairs, and population.*	G *Includes formation and debate of U.S. foreign and defense policies, veterans affairs, and defense spending. (Relations with specific foreign countries are usually found under the region concerned.)*	H *Includes business, labor, agriculture, taxation, transportation, consumer affairs, monetary and fiscal policy, natural resources, pollution and industrial accidents.*	I *Includes worldwide scientific, medical and technological developments, natural phenomena, U.S. weather and natural disasters.*	J *Includes the arts, religion, scholarship, communications media, sports, entertainment, fashions, fads, and social life.*	

	World Affairs	Europe	Africa & The Middle East	The Americas	Asia & The Pacific
Apr. 15		Second Anzavur incident occurs at Yayaköy.		New Canadian one-cent coin is released.	
Apr. 16	Banat Germans request the reestablishment of the Republic of Banatia from Paris Peace Conference officials, but the request is denied.	A resolution is made by Yerevan demonstrators asking the Soviet government to defend Armenian rights in Karabagh.		Compania Edison Hispano Americana, the branch office of Edison products in Buenos Aires, is dissolved.	
Apr. 17					Australian political cartoonist Claude Arthur Marquette drowns in a boating accident.
Apr. 18	The Allied Conference opens in San Remo to discuss territorial questions and overall wording of Turkish peace treaty.…The Treaty of San Remo and the Council of Allied Prime Ministers give France a mandate over Syria.…The British delegation at San Remo, Italy, asks that the Balfour Declaration be incorporated in the Turkish Peace Treaty.				
Apr. 19	The League of Nations disagrees with President Woodrow Wilson on policy toward Turkey and criticizes the U.S. decision not to sign the peace treaty and join the League of Nations.…The League of Nations announces a financial congress to be held in Brussels in May and invites the United States to attend.…The League of Nations informally agrees that it will not follow the recommendations of the Council of Premiers to have a mandate for Armenia.…The British Under Foreign Secretary reaffirms the British government's commitment to the Balfour agreement in establishing a Jewish homeland in Palestine.	The Constituent Assembly of Lithuania elects President Aleksandras Stulginskis.…Ali Fuat Pasha arrives in Bursa.…Large-scale rioting is reported between Unionists and Sinn Feiners in Ireland.…Fierce fighting is reported on the Polish Front by the Russian Soviet government.…Czech troops engage Japanese troops at Khailar, near the Trans-Baikal border.…The Allies let Sultan rule Turkey, and Allied troops occupy Gallipoli.…Resident Socialists in Düsseldorf fear the entry of Reichwehr due to killings that occurred in other occupied cities.…Food stacks up at Irish ports due to an embargo by the Labor Party and Trade Union Congress.		A Chilean coal strike involving more than 10,000 workers over 30 days is settled.…The British and U.S. Embassies in Guatemala declare shell damage in last week's fighting.…Former Guatemalan President Manuel Estrada Cabrera is declared insane by a representative of the American Secret Service after he surrendered to them to avoid capture by troops supporting the new president, Carlos Herrera.…Chihuahua troops are in revolt with Carranza soldiers supporting rebellion.…The plans for the new American Virgin Islands are unveiled, substituting Danish regulations for an American system for taxes and currency.	The Japanese economy is in turmoil.…The Bank of Japan sets a discount rate at 10 percent.…Japanese prices fall on all commodities.
Apr. 20	The seventh modern Olympic games open in Antwerp, Belgium.	The high court building in the State of Andhra Pradesh is opened by Nizam VII Mir Osman Ali Khan.…The discussion over partitioning Turkey leaves French negative and other world leaders in favor of the policy.…A typhus outbreak in the Balkans is widespread.…Berlin soldiers strike for pay.	Palestine is placed under British Mandate.	Argentina verbally attacks New York banking interests after Britain turns down a new loan.	
Apr. 21	The Supreme Allied Council meeting in Copenhagen pauses to consider Russian trade claims.…A U.S. envoy leaves for San Remo Conference to serve as an observer, not as a voting representative.…Allies pressure the Turkish government to accept a treaty to end fighting.…A Belgian delegation asks Herbert Hoover to intercede with other nations for additional loans.	The Germans ask the Allies to keep some forces for defense.…Irish politician Eamonn de Valerra lists grievances against the *English Tyrant*.…Poles are killed in rioting in Petrograd.…The Hudson's Bay Company celebrates its 250th Anniversary.		The committee appointed by the Mexican government rushes to Sonora to mend differences between the government and renegades who have declared Sonora an independent state.	Wu Ting Fang, Administrative Leader and Minister of Foreign Affairs of Southern China, predicts China will reunite soon and Shanghai will host the new parliament.…There are claims that Japanese soldiers fired on American barracks in Manchuria.

A	B	C	D	E
Includes developments that affect more than one world region, international organizations and important meetings of world leaders.	*Includes all domestic and regional developments in Europe, including the Soviet Union.*	*Includes all domestic and regional developments in Africa and the Middle East.*	*Includes all domestic and regional developments in Latin America, the Caribbean, and Canada.*	*Includes all domestic and regional developments in Asian and Pacific nations (and colonies).*

U.S. Politics & Social Issues	U.S. Foreign Policy & Affairs, Defense	U.S. Economy & Environment	Science, Technology & Nature	Culture, Leisure & Lifestyle	
Charles Dirba takes over as Acting Secretary of the Communist Party of America.... Frederick Parmenter and Alessandro Berardelli are killed in South Braintree, MA, for the company payroll.		A federal act is passed authorizing the Secretary of Interior to sell certain lands to school district in Wyoming.	The Under Secretary of State for Aeronautics and Aerial Transport adopts the Standard Atmosphere as the official airplane.... The American Chemical Society meets in St. Louis.	James Joyce publishes the poem "A Mirror at Midnight."... Lyle Bigbee breaks into the major leagues with the Philadelphia Athletics.... Chewing gum heir William Wrigley, Jr's ship *Avalon* sails to Catalina for the first time.	Apr. 15
		The DuPont Fibersilk Company is established in New York.... The Gunboat U.S.S. *Petrel* is sold to Snare and Treest of New York.			Apr. 16
			Tommy Milton sets a land speed record in his Duisenberg at Daytona, Florida Speedway.	The American Professional Football Association (later called NFL) is formed.... Author Edgar Rice Burroughs' last serialized story, *Tarzan and the Valley of Luna*, in *All-Story* is completed.	Apr. 17
Minnesota passes the United States' first anti-lynching law.					Apr. 18
President Woodrow Wilson meets his cabinet today, only the second time since his illness last year.... City investigators charge that Communist sympathizers are behind the rent revolt in New York City.... A black man is lynched by a mob of 1,000 in Pittsburgh, KS.	Sir Auckland Geddes arrives in the United States as the newly appointed envoy of Great Britain.	Judge Elbert H. Gary, Chairman of the U.S. Steel Corporation, denounces the idea of one major labor union.... John Grunau, President of the Chicago Yardmen's Association, was arrested and held without bail for violating the Lever Act.... An outlaw strike still has a significant hold on rail travel and transportation in the United States.... The U.S. Railroad Labor Board refuses to hear strikers unless represented by recognized union following formal rules for hearing.		Greek resident Peter Trivoulidas wins the 24th Boston Marathon.... Denim overalls are worn to work in New York City as a protest of high clothing prices.... The first intercollegiate flying events are announced for a college meet at Mineola Field in New York.... American manufacturers and golfers oppose a British proposal for uniform ball.	Apr. 19
		New Jersey makes plans for a huge pier, ocean terminal, warehouse, and commercial project at Lehigh Valley.	The Grand Canyon National Park is dedicated.... Mary J. Reynolds patents a loading mechanism.	The New Jersey governor signs a bill allowing amateur baseball to be played in county parks on Sunday.	Apr. 20
William Jennings Bryan is chosen to represent Nebraska as a delegate at the Democratic Convention in San Francisco.	The U.S. Navy asks for additional bidding on coal prices, stating current prices are too high.... Ships loaded with groups ordered for deportation for their political stand sit in New York Harbor awaiting a U.S. Congressional order.	Dozens of sugar retailers, manufacturers, and brokers are charged with war profiteering.... The Walton Bill is signed, ending power of parties to withdraw without cause in agreements.... Rail companies order 2,000 freight cars.... The outlaw union Chicago Yardmen's Association leader John Grunau is released from jail and meets with members to plan strategy.... A huge drop in cotton prices creates a market crisis.	Dr. Frederick H. Millener listens for interplanetary messages from his lab in Cedar Creek, NE.... Tornadoes kill 155 in the southern United States with more than $2 million in damages.... The New York Port quarantines the U.S. *Pocahontas* due to a major outbreak of typhus.	John Galsworthy's play *Skin Game* opens on the London stage.... British residents give New York funds to build a peace monument in New York Harbor.... Genre painter Henry Mosler dies.... Lowe's buys six additional movie theaters.	Apr. 21

F	G	H	I	J
Includes campaigns, elections, federal-state relations, civil rights and liberties, crime, the judiciary, education, healthcare, poverty, urban affairs, and population.	*Includes formation and debate of U.S. foreign and defense policies, veterans affairs, and defense spending. (Relations with specific foreign countries are usually found under the region concerned.)*	*Includes business, labor, agriculture, taxation, transportation, consumer affairs, monetary and fiscal policy, natural resources, pollution and industrial accidents.*	*Includes worldwide scientific, medical and technological developments, natural phenomena, U.S. weather and natural disasters.*	*Includes the arts, religion, scholarship, communications media, sports, entertainment, fashions, fads, and social life.*

	World Affairs	Europe	Africa & The Middle East	The Americas	Asia & The Pacific
Apr. 22	The San Remo Conference transfers Asia Minor to the Allies.…The Supreme Council determines Dardanelles will be under the control of two international commissions. One commission will act as an administrative control and the other will provide military defense of the region, ensuring that traffic in the Straits will be free to all nations.…Canada offers to take the mandate for Armenia if Norway defers.	Mustafa Kemal Pasha announces calling a National Assembly to create a new state.…British Prime Minster Chamberlain is firm on support of excess profits levy for Britain.…French soldiers rescue stranded Americans in Aintab.…Rioting occurs in Spain between Basque Provinces and government.…A committee of the House of Commons tables a bill to allow women to vote.…Max Holz is to be tried for treason for crimes he committed prior to his extradition to Germany.			
Apr. 23		The Turkish Grand National Assembly (a provisional government) is established in Ankara (Angora) by the Nationalist faction.		Belgian King Albert, Queen Elizabeth, and family accept an invitation to travel to Brazil.	
Apr. 24	Members of the International Railway Board (excluding Japan) go on record to protest the Japanese military action in Siberia.…An agreement is reached between China and the Soviets at Verkhnie Udinsk, Transbaikalia to open the Russo-Chinese frontier for imports and exports, recognize Soviet control over the Eastern Manchurian Railway, and allow for the Chinese to remove troops along the railroad line. The Chinese government will deny troops of General Semenoff access to the frontier. China will no longer recognize the Russian government in Peking.	The British Mandate over Palestine goes into effect.…Polish troops attack Ukraine.…Vladimir Lenin gives a speech at a meeting of the Moscow Committee of the Revolutionary Communist Party in honor of his 50th birthday.		A duel between Uruguayan President Baltassar Brum and Director of El Pais Dr. Rodriguez Larreta has been called off. Larreta claims government retribution if Brum is killed in the duel.…Canada defeats the United States in the semi-finals of Olympic hockey in Antwerp.	
Apr. 25		An alliance is established between the government of Poland and Simon Petilura's Ukrainian supporters.…France and England turn down a new constitution put forth by Italian Premier Nitti.…Belgium buys freighters built under United States Shipping Board program.	Britain receives the Supreme Council mandates for Palestine and Transjordania and Iraq (Mesopotamia) under the Balfour Declaration.…France receives the Supreme Council declaration regarding Syria.		The Chinese Merchants' Association welcomes trade merchants in San Francisco to the largest event in the Association's history.
Apr. 26	A letter arrives in Washington from Supreme Council of the Allied Powers in conference at San Remo, inviting U.S. President Woodrow Wilson to assist in the decision of the Armenian and Turkish border.…The Armenian mandate is again offered to the United States.…The Allies divide control of Asia Minor.	The 11th Red Army of Soviet Russia begins their attack on Azerbaijan. The Azerbaijani army is weakened by this invasion and by the fighting on a second front against Armenia.…Poland invades Russia.…The first Danish Folketing Election is held.…Britain negotiates terms to ensure that Shell Oil Company interests are not transferred to other countries through sale or trade.			The Anzac day of mourning and celebrations, widespread this year, are held throughout Australia and New Zealand in memory of the bravery and courage shown by the Australian and New Zealand Army Corps during their 1915 invasion on the Gallipoli Peninsula.
Apr. 27		Ukraine declares independence under leader Petloera (Petlyura).…Irish rioters burn military housing in a three-hour fight.		The Canadian War Mission represents the country at a meeting to explore the potential role of teh Canadian Ambassador to the United States.…The United States investigates charges that German war equipment has been shipped to Mexico to fuel an insurrection.	
Apr. 28		The American Commission for Relief in the Near East announces that relief workers are trapped in Aintab, Turkey and fear for their safety against Turkish forces.…Baku is taken by the Red Army as they advance into Caucasus.…The Azerbaijan Republic is taken by the 11th Red Army entering Baku.…White Russians begin an offensive in South Russia.…The Azerbaijan Parliament votes to give up fighting and joins the Soviet Union to avoid additional death and destruction.		Reports indicate that the 62nd Mexican Federal Regiment under Colonel del Arco has joined the revolt in the State of Chihuahua.	

A	B	C	D	E
Includes developments that affect more than one world region, international organizations and important meetings of world leaders.	*Includes all domestic and regional developments in Europe, including the Soviet Union.*	*Includes all domestic and regional developments in Africa and the Middle East.*	*Includes all domestic and regional developments in Latin America, the Caribbean, and Canada.*	*Includes all domestic and regional developments in Asian and Pacific nations (and colonies).*

U.S. Politics & Social Issues	U.S. Foreign Policy & Affairs, Defense	U.S. Economy & Environment	Science, Technology & Nature	Culture, Leisure & Lifestyle	
The New York legislature debates the sale of 3.5 percent alcohol.... The Red Cross begs Americans for assistance in European aid.... A U.S. District court judge halts "Red" deportations on grounds that arrests were made without warrants.	The Service Pay Bill increases pay for military by double figures.... The Bonus Bill for soldiers serving in war is debated in U.S. Congress.... Rear Admiral Carlo B. Brittain commits suicide while on duty with American fleet in Cuban waters.	Minors, represented by the Industrial Workers of the World, strike in Butte, MT.... The U.S. Chamber of Commerce asks Congress for Anti-Strike legislation.... A Detroit judge invalidates a portion of the Lever Act allowing milk price fixing.... Sugar prices soar and the U.S. Justice Department calls refiners to a meeting to explore solutions to the problem.	Explorer Roald Amundsen is thought to have reached Siberia. He has remained frozen on his boat, the *Maud*, hoping the thaw would allow him to drift east cross the ice to the Arctic (New Siberian Islands) and across the North Pole. In case drifting does not work, Amundsen carries two airplanes to take his party to the Pole.... Scientists Millener and Gamer listen without results for sounds from the planet Mars.	American Air Delivery Service begins.... There is a call to celebrate American Day featuring the melting pot of cultures and ethnic groups.	Apr. 22
Fierce fighting in the Anhai region of China kills more than 1,000. Residents of Anhai flee to Amoy to escape.	Los Angeles publisher Harry Chandler charges that Hiram W. Johnson's alliance with San Francisco publisher William Randolph Hearst is unstable.	Attorney General Palmer and the U.S. Department of Justice will seek the return of millions of dollars in illegal transactions and fraudulent war claims.		Frank Jay Gould is sued for divorce on grounds of cruelty and drunkenness.	Apr. 23
				Little Sparks, a nursery comic, is published for the first time.	Apr. 24
					Apr. 25
United States v. Reading Co. is heard by the U.S. Supreme Court charging that owners and railroad carriers have a monopoly on coal.... Warren G. Harding, U.S. Senator, gives a speech at the Lincoln Club in Ohio.		CHX Stock Clearing Corporation is established.... American businesses eye the Orient for expansion programs of the National Foreign Trade Council.	Harlow Shapley of Mount Wilson Observatory and Heber Doust Curtis of Lick Observatory give talks on *The Scale of the Universe* (later called "The Universe Debate") at the Academy of Sciences in Washington, DC.... Emil Racovita, Antarctic explorer, founds the world's first speleology institute in Cluj-Napoca.	Huck Betts first plays for the Philadelphia Phillies in the major leagues.... The Winnipeg Falcons win the 1920 Olympic Gold Medal for Hockey in Antwerp, Belgium.	Apr. 26
The American Olympic hockey team defeats Sweden and will play the Czech team tomorrow night for a second place medal.... Congress debates Bonus Bills in a contentious session.				Igor Stravinsky's *Ragtime for 11 Instruments* is premiered in London.	Apr. 27
Ohio governor James M. Cox and Franklin Delano Roosevelt of New York receive nominations as delegates to Democratic National Convention in San Francisco.				Artist Charles H. Woodbury's show opens at the Cleveland Museum of Art.	Apr. 28

F	G	H	I	J
Includes campaigns, elections, federal-state relations, civil rights and liberties, crime, the judiciary, education, healthcare, poverty, urban affairs, and population.	*Includes formation and debate of U.S. foreign and defense policies, veterans affairs, and defense spending. (Relations with specific foreign countries are usually found under the region concerned.)*	*Includes business, labor, agriculture, taxation, transportation, consumer affairs, monetary and fiscal policy, natural resources, pollution and industrial accidents.*	*Includes worldwide scientific, medical and technological developments, natural phenomena, U.S. weather and natural disasters.*	*Includes the arts, religion, scholarship, communications media, sports, entertainment, fashions, fads, and social life.*

	World Affairs	Europe	Africa & The Middle East	The Americas	Asia & The Pacific
Apr. 29	An American and Canadian Union of Orthodox Jewish Rabbis telegram to President Woodrow Wilson is read at White House, asking the American government to take action to support the restoration of a Palestine state as a home for the Jewish people.…French Premier Alexandre Millerand announces an agreement with the German government to meet to discuss findings of the San Remo sessions of the Supreme Council of the Allies.	The Mussavat Party Government is overthrown in the Republic of Azerbaidjan (the area includes parts of Armenia and Persia). The Azerbaidjan Provisional Military Revolutionary Committee has taken power.…The French announce they will not reduce troops in Frankfort until Germany reduces forces in the Ruhr region.		Soldiers supporting former Mexican President Carranza and revolutionary troops fight Sonoran troops in Chihuahua-Sonora Mountains near Pulpito Pass.…General P. Elias Calles, commander of the northwestern rebel forces, claims that nearly 4,000 troops have joined him in Jiminez, Parral, and Chihuahua City.	The Japanese government pushes the Chinese to return the Province of Shantung.
Apr. 30	French aviator Renaud has gone missing somewhere near Sardinia while on a trans-Mediterranean flight from Monaco to Bizerta, Tunis. Ships and destroyers are sent out to search for his plane.…Industries operating in the Mexican State of Sonora are ordered to pay taxes and customs to a new, unrecognized government.	The British government ends conscription and returns to volunteer forces for defense.…A general strike is called today for May Day in France.…British Olympic athletes delay their departure due to lack of funding.…Khalifate extremists advocate violence in Delhi and Sindh area of India.		Mexican President Venustiano Carranza flees to Mexico City as American warships ready for possible deployment to Vera Cruz to remove U.S. citizens from the country.…Vera Cruz readies for violence.…Rebel forces now hold the State of Chihuahua.…Chinese citizens in Mexico ask the United States for assistance in escaping if lives are threatened.	
May 1	Countries agree to additional terms to the International Convention over Air Navigation in a meeting in Paris.	Three people are killed in a May Day disturbance in Valencia, Spain.…The Belgian-Luxembourg toll tunnel opens.…Warfare breaks between Poland and Czechoslovakian forces in Teschen when Czechoslovaks take over territory.…A new constitution is drafted for Latvia.…Luxembourg and Belgium open trade in a customs union.…Four hundred French are killed in a battle with Kurdish and Turkish fighters.…French workers, including the General Federation, stop all work on May Day. Most workers return after a day, but railroad workers continue striking.		In a May Day riot in Uruguay, citizens fight with police officers	Tokyo banks increase funds to avoid panic.…Tokyo tram workers go on strike.
May 2		Switzerland rejects an eight-hour day for workers.…France supports Polish troops and offers military reinforcements and supplies.…Mustafa Kemal and Turkish Nationals send troops to the Marmora Coast to fight British and Sultan forces.		An historic Canadian merger is announced with nine transportation and natural resources companies merging into British Steel Corporation, with capital totaling more than $500 million.…Mexican rebels will soon attack the capital using a plan that cuts off Tampico Oil Fields and rallies labor to strike.	The Chinese government announces a plan for the 1922 World's Fair in the Temple of Heaven in Peking.…Thousands of Panama residents take to streets in protest against the U.S. purchase of Taboga Island as military fortification for the Panama Canal.
May 3	The Allied High Commissioner Colonel William N. Haskell tells the United States that Baku Armenians face genocide and extermination by Azerbaijan Muslims.	The Russians fail to issue a statement confirming concessions were made in a meeting with China for the recognition of the Russian Soviet government.…A French strike shuts down shipping.…The Prince of Wales tours New Zealand.…A French rail strike is averted at the last minute.…A call goes out for a general strike in France.…Polish and Russian troops are involved in heavy fighting over Kiev.		Juarez is in turmoil while U.S. warships wait in the Gulf.…Obregon and supporting rebels have charge of the Mexican state of Chihuahua and are nearing the capital city. Residents are surrendering without fighting or bloodshed.	Dr. Wu Lien-teh, head of the Anti-Opium Society, warns of a huge increase of opium smuggled into Shanghai and declining prices due to increased production in new poppy fields in Szechwan and Fukien.
May 4	The International Parliamentary Conference of Commerce opens in Paris. Delegates from many countries arrive, but the U.S. sends a formal observer rather than a delegate.…The Supreme Council refuses to consider issues of trade until a guarantee is made on humane treatment of Denikin's Army.…A special advisory committee readies a report for German indemnity payments for the Spa Conference.	The Dublin Corporation passes a resolution recognizing the Republican Parliament as the officially elected representative of the Irish people.…German newspaper owners meet to solve the newsprint shortage.…The French strike oil in northern Morocco and expect to find huge stores.…Poles are nearing the city of Kiev despite strong fighting.…Kiev is in distress fighting Chinese mercenary troops.		The Mexican State of Juarez declares neutrality in fighting.	A.H. Wiggin, Chairman of the Board of Directors of the American Foreign Banking Association, announces the use of a new China-American Bank over opening branches of current banking houses in China.…Doubts are raised that China will officially recognize the new Soviet government.…The Japanese port of Yokohama clogs with ships as banks refuse to make advances on arriving cargoes.

A	B	C	D	E
Includes developments that affect more than one world region, international organizations and important meetings of world leaders.	*Includes all domestic and regional developments in Europe, including the Soviet Union.*	*Includes all domestic and regional developments in Africa and the Middle East.*	*Includes all domestic and regional developments in Latin America, the Caribbean, and Canada.*	*Includes all domestic and regional developments in Asian and Pacific nations (and colonies).*

U.S. Politics & Social Issues	U.S. Foreign Policy & Affairs, Defense	U.S. Economy & Environment	Science, Technology & Nature	Culture, Leisure & Lifestyle	
The U.S. Senate Foreign Relations Committee gives approval to the Knox Peace Resolution that repeals the declaration of war made by the U.S. Congress against Germany and Japan.…Republican leaders in the House of Representatives announce that they will not support retroactive war profits taxation bills.…President Woodrow Wilson takes a long car trip, his second in two days since becoming ill.	William Jennings Bryan encourages the government to pass a peace treaty, claiming that a delay will mean additional deaths in foreign lands and political strife in the United States.…The American Bankers' Association claims retroactive taxes to fund soldiers' bonus pay will be disastrous for the country and urges a sales tax instead for funding.	Railroad switchmen walk out in New York railroad yards in disagreement over recent wage settlement.…Coal miners and anthracite mine owners announce a deadlock, leading U.S. Secretary of Labor William B. Wilson to make an invitation to both parties to meet with him personally in Washington to resolve issue. Both parties in the labor action accepted the invitation.		The First International Art Exhibition since World War I opens today in Pittsburgh at the Carnegie Institute. Abbott H. Thayer of Monadnock, NH takes the gold medal and first place honors for his painting, *Young Women in Olive Plush*. London artist Algernon Talmadge captures second place. Walter Ufer of Chicago, Illinois takes bronze medal for third place.	Apr. 29
The U.S. House Rules Committee hears testimony into investigations and deportations of radicals by Louis F. Post, Assistant Secretary of Labor.…President Woodrow Wilson names F.A. Wallis to head immigration regulation, citing increase in immigration and deportation as a major problem in the United States.	U.S. Department of Justice agents arrest 300 people suspected of being involved with the International Workers of the World (I.W.W), Communist Labor Party, and Communist Party.…U.S. Attorney General Palmer warns of an international plot for May Day that includes bombings and assassinations.	Haircuts in Chicago now cost 75 cents.…U.S. Bankers urge vote on treaty to end the war, claiming the delay is costing America world trade and business.…A committee elected by the Executive Council of the American Bankers' Association is to meet with the Federal Reserve Board regarding deflation of credit to reduce the amount of speculation in the American economy.	Glenn H. Curtiss and the Curtiss Corporation are defeated in a court challenge claiming patent ownership of the hydroplane. Albert S. Janin is declared the owner by the court. Curtiss will appeal the ruling to the Supreme Court.…A seaplane arrives in New York from Miami, FL, in less than a day.	The nominations to the American Academy of Arts and Letters' Hall of Fame are announced, Thomas Paine, Susan B. Anthony, Jefferson Davis, Clark Durant, and Frederick Douglass are largest vote-getters.	Apr. 30
The conviction of Communist supporter Mollie Steimer is supported by the U.S. Supreme Court.	The American government is given a copy of the trade agreement between the Bolshevist and Danish governments.	European state banks discount rates to slow inflation.…A shortage of real capital is announced by National City Bank.…1,000 non-union longshoremen have been hired to unload *Apache*, docking today in New York from Jacksonville, FL, with a load of fruit and vegetables.	Norwegian Artic explorer Roald Amundsen sends a message from the *Maud* that he will make another attempt to the North Pole.	George "Babe Ruth" Herman hits his first home run as a member of the Yankees baseball team at the Polo Grounds.…French artist Francis Picabia publishes the last issue of *Le Cannibale*, a Paris Dadaist magazine.…The *Saturday Evening Post* publishes F. Scott's Fitzgerald's fourth story for the magazine, "Bernice Bobs Her Hair."…Twelve thousand Pittsburgh women march in support of inexpensive staple clothing.	May 1
The American Socialist Party opens its convention in Newark, NJ.…Herbert Hoover and Hiram Johnson work heatedly ahead of the California primary election. State officials call the campaign the dirtiest in California's history.…The Hoover campaign counts on women voters in California to push him to victory there.	The U.S. Fleet arrives in New York Harbor to throngs of spectators.		Tornadoes sweep through Oklahoma, causing injuries and five deaths.…The Bureau of Mines predicts a U.S. oil shortage before summer.…A lunar eclipse is visible in parts of Africa, North and South America, Western Europe, and on the Atlantic, and from certain vantage points in the Indian and Pacific oceans.	Indianapolis hosts the first baseball game of the National Negro Baseball League.…David Brown, former President of the U.S. Board of Commerce, urges people to wear old clothing as a protest against high clothing costs.…The International Power Boat Union agrees to a series of championship contest races.…The Oscar Hammerstein Memorial Concert at the Hippodrome raises $20,000.	May 2
President Woodrow Wilson announces the Peace Resolution will be a campaign issue.…Suffragists begin work in Connecticut for amendment ratification.…Socialist Party supporter James L. Larkin is convicted of attempting to overthrow the U.S. government and is sentenced to five to 10 years in prison.	C.W. Morse is accused of conspiracy, namely selling a ship to Tunis government during the war and later conspiring to sink it.	Sawmills in Wisconsin, Michigan, and Minnesota are closed due to strikes.…Charges that the content in U.S. newspapers is controlled by the International Typographic Union and its local chapters are investigated by the U.S. Senate.…The International Ladies' Garment Workers Union convention decries the action of Attorney General Palmer.…The U.S. Supreme Court refuses to reopen the U.S. Steel Anti-Trust Case.	Tornadoes race through Oklahoma, killing 55 and injuring more than 100 people. The town of Peggs is destroyed.…Sir Ernest Shackelton's most recent Antarctic expedition is the subject of *The Bottom of the World*, opening today at the Rivoli Theater in New York.	The movie *Honey Girl*, starring Lynne Overman, Edna Bates, Louise Meyers, and George McKay, opens to enthusiastic audiences at New York theaters.	May 3
Henry Cabot Lodge is selected as temporary chair of the Republican National Convention.…Anticipating moves to repeal the Volstead Act, The House of Representative Rules Committee outlaws attaching amendments to appropriation bills.	The Knox Resolution is debated.…William H. Hays, chair of the National Committee of Republicans, talks with Bitter Enders and fails to meet with Reservationists in the U.S. Senate.…Sicilian Andrea Salsedo, suspected pamphleteer and Socialist organizer of the June Plot, commits suicide by jumping from the Department of Justice Building on Park Row.	The U.S. Shipping Board announces the sale of 14 cargo ships, many of them former German ships.…The commodities market is quiet with cotton prices leveling off.…A huge rise in freight rates is expected.…Promoted by Henry G. Brunner, the new Bankers' Union for Foreign Commerce and Finance is incorporated.…A freight car shortage is announced.	African American M. Toland, one of few women applying for patents this year and one of a handful of black female applicants, patents a circuit closer that uses a floating device.	Englishman James Moore Hickson conducts a spiritual healing clinic in New York City.…A man sets a record climbing 40 stories of the New York Equitable Building in nine minutes.…Commander Ross wins at Pimlico Race Track.	May 4

F	G	H	I	J
Includes campaigns, elections, federal-state relations, civil rights and liberties, crime, the judiciary, education, healthcare, poverty, urban affairs, and population.	*Includes formation and debate of U.S. foreign and defense policies, veterans affairs, and defense spending. (Relations with specific foreign countries are usually found under the region concerned.)*	*Includes business, labor, agriculture, taxation, transportation, consumer affairs, monetary and fiscal policy, natural resources, pollution and industrial accidents.*	*Includes worldwide scientific, medical and technological developments, natural phenomena, U.S. weather and natural disasters.*	*Includes the arts, religion, scholarship, communications media, sports, entertainment, fashions, fads, and social life.*

	World Affairs	Europe	Africa & The Middle East	The Americas	Asia & The Pacific
May 5	Great Britain agrees to accept the Iraqi mandate from the League of Nations....The Treaty of Berlin is signed between Germany and Latvia....The final text of the Hungarian Treaty is given to the Hungarian delegation at Versailles. This treaty estimates the cost for reparations over a set number of years, rather than giving a fixed sum for payment.	The Polish government announces plans to print 11 million marks.... Bavarians request citizen guards to protect against Communist fighters....The Deutsche-Americanische Petroleum Company, a subsidiary of Standard Oil, announces a 10-year contract with the German government. The contract requires a fixed fee for products sold on a cash-only basis.		Generals demand resignation and order Mexican President Carranza out of Mexico by May 15....The Parliament in Canada heatedly debates a steel merger.	
May 6	Francois Marshal, French Minister of Finance, explains that German war payments are necessary for French recovery, at a speech to English and British newspaper reporters in Paris today.	The Danish army frees northern Slesvig from German control....The Red Army fights west of Kiev....The Ukrainian Minster in Berlin, Dr. Porsch, states his belief that movement was done with Entente's full knowledge in support of an independent Ukraine.		The Mexican government announces an increase in the export duty on oil....Francisco Villa, along with a group of 2,000, joined the revolutionary forces in Chihuahua promising a future force of more than 10,000 men....A split is announced between Mexican General Obregon and Pablo Gonzalez over the strategy in the State of Sonora, with Gonzalez refusing to recognize Obregon's authority. Carlos Green heads the third army involved in the Mexican movement.	
May 7		The Soviet Union recognizes Georgian independence under the Treaty of Moscow....Polish and Soviet troops clash in Kyiv....The Ukrainian People's Republic retakes power....Anarchist rioting is still unchecked in Italy; the Leghorn region is hit with the most severe attacks.		Argentina workers and students wear denim to work to show displeasure with high cost of clothing, citing the U.S. protest as an inspiration in the movement....Venustiano Carranza refuses to resign his office and leaves Mexico City by train with his cabinet to escape revolutionary forces....The army in Sonora begins an invasion of Chihuahua.	
May 8	Britain is asked to publicly declare the amount of influence it has over the Sultan of Turkey prior to completing any international agreement. An article published today indicates Britain signed a secret treaty with the Sultan before the San Remo Conference.	Tiflis has fallen into Bolshevik control. Rear Admiral Harry S. Knapp, commanding the *Pittsburgh* and the *Cole*, has collected American relief workers and is transporting them to Constantinople.	Ibn Rasid, Emir of Hail, is assassinated in tribal warfare.		The illegal sale and transportation of alcohol are organized on a large scale in large American cities by illegal crime syndicates, including La Cosa Nostra.
May 9	Premiers meeting at San Remo push to carry out the Treaty of London.... Yugoslavia gives the delegation at the meeting full powers....Arthur H. Titus, Vice President of the National City Bank, is elected President of the First Federal Foreign Banking Association....The British Commons questions the United States' seizure of the Island of Taboga, a possession of the country of Panama.		Egyptian Minister of Works, Hussein Darwiche, escapes a bomb thrown at his car while on his way home from work.	Mexican General Alvaro Obregon and troops enter Mexico City....The Canadian Soldiers' Settlement Board receives an additional $50 million from the Canadian Parliament to assist former servicemen in purchasing homes and farms.	The Peking-Kalgan-Suiyuan Railroad announces an efficient operation.... San Francisco Chinatown Merchants burn imported goods and urge a boycott of Chinese made products....William Hughes, Premier of Australia, proposes an export ban on all wool before October of this year. Auctions of wool would also be banned from September of this year until May 1921.
May 10	The League of Nations, while awaiting a reply from Russia regarding formal visitation, appointed Lord Emmott as the chief British delegate....J.H. Gundy and G.C. Castles, Manager of the Bank of Montreal, will represent the Canadian government at the financial meeting at the League of Nations in Brussels.	An assassination attempt on Damad Ferid Pasha, the Grand Vizier of Turkey, causes guards to take more severe safety measures....The British House of Commons rejects the Irish Plan for a single Irish Parliament.	Chinese governments deny claims that the country has officially recognized the rights of the Russian Soviet government to control the Eastern Manchurian Railway....The U.S. State Department announces plans for an international consortium to secure loans to China. Banking institutions in United States, France, Japan, and Great Britain will take part in the plan.	Canada is to send a representative to Washington D.C. to represent interests, establishing an independent presence from England in the United States....Former Mexican President Carranza is fleeing to the countryside with rebel troops in hot pursuit....Generals Obregon and Gonzales control Mexico City in an apparent agreement made between the two leaders....Reports from the field indicate Tampico is captured by rebel troops.	
May 11	Pirates on the Black Sea terrorize the crew and rob passengers of a French packet boat.	The Sevres Peace Treaty is given to the Istanbul government....Poles and Ukrainians enter Kiev....The Turkish National Assembly meets in Ankara....Bolshevik troops shell the city of Kiev....Polish troops on the west bank of the Dnieper River take control of land and river traffic.		Canada bans the exportation of mixed grains containing wheat without a permit and restricts the importation of the same without a license....A Canadian envoy to be stationed in the United States will act when British Ambassador is not available to handle Canadian issues.	

A	B	C	D	E
Includes developments that affect more than one world region, international organizations and important meetings of world leaders.	*Includes all domestic and regional developments in Europe, including the Soviet Union.*	*Includes all domestic and regional developments in Africa and the Middle East.*	*Includes all domestic and regional developments in Latin America, the Caribbean, and Canada.*	*Includes all domestic and regional developments in Asian and Pacific nations (and colonies).*

U.S. Politics & Social Issues	U.S. Foreign Policy & Affairs, Defense	U.S. Economy & Environment	Science, Technology & Nature	Culture, Leisure & Lifestyle	
Membership in the Communist Party is declared illegal in the United States, but federal laws do not provide for deportation of party members.…Nicola Sacco and Bartolomeo Vanzetti are arrested on murder charges.…Public debate takes place over the high cost of enforcing Prohibition.…General Wood leads in the primary vote in Indiana with Hiram Johnson in second place.	President Woodrow Wilson meets with his cabinet for an hour today.	Congress announces opposition to raising postal rates.…The Senate examines charges of paper broker fraud and an artificial shortage created by newsprint manufacturers.…Railroad freight companies ask the government for a 28 percent increase in fares. Passenger rates would not be increased.…Chicago strikers urge the creation of a national union representing rail workers.		The New York Symphony, under Conductor Walter Damrosch, begins its first European tour by an American symphony orchestra with performances at the Theatre National de l'Opera in Paris.	May 5
Large cities see an increase in the subdivision of large buildings for apartment dwellings.…The conviction of a Christian Science father who denied his child medical care stirs debate over the role of government.…Secretary Wilson denies Attorney General Palmer deportation plans for Communists, claiming 1918 legislation does not apply. As a result, 100 additional arrest warrants are cancelled.	Six U.S. destroyers and one tender ship head for Mexico with charges to aid Americans there, if help is requested. Ships will be based in Key West.…The U.S. government admits that Carranza's government has fallen.…Mexican Governor Adolfo de la Huerta invites the United States to send a military observer to accompany General P. Elias Calles, Minster of War, and discuss the aims of the new leaders.	Telegraph delivery workers demand increased wages and threaten to strike.…Chicago businessmen begin a collar and shirt strike as a protest against high living costs.… Food prices rise due to a freight car shortage.…Coal mine operators in Cleveland and St. Louis file court papers charging constitutionality of Lever Act.		Broadway groups raise $250,000 for Vaudeville Artists' Fund.… American violinist Jascha Heifetz makes a London debut at Queen's Hall to critical acclaim.…X-rays used to examine vintage paintings to determine the technique of Old Master painters.	May 6
		General Electric workers in New York strike in response of company's refusal to collect union dues.… Representative King from Illinois charges that U.S. Federal Reserve Bank commodity policies contribute to food shortages.…Federal Reserve review stresses the need for stricter control of credit.		Golfer Bobby Jones announces he will compete in the National Open Golf Championship for the first time.…The Metropolitan Museum of Art in New York celebrates its 50th Birthday with guest collections and throngs of famous visitors. Featured exhibits included a gem display.	May 7
		A securities case breaks wide open with the secret testimony of Bill Furey, James Kean, and David Joseph Haines that they conspired to kidnap and succeeded in stealing $2.5 million in securities hiding their actions by burning a yacht last year in Canadian waters.	New York Health Commissioner Dr. R.S. Copeland sails to represent New York City at the Congress of the Royal Institute of Public Health in Brussels and to investigate the programs to prevent disease in European cities.	Paul Jones, with jockey Ted Rice, wins the 46th Kentucky Derby.… Silent picture actress Lillian Gish graces the cover of *Motion Picture* magazine.…American author Sloan Wilson is born in Norwalk, CT.	May 8
The New York Commissioner of Public Welfare, Bird S. Coler, alarmed at the increase in hospitalizations due to alcohol abuse, calls on the state and nation to increase attention to the problem and improve funding for enforcement measures.….Republican Convention speeches accuse Democrats of financial waste in years before the war.	The West Point officer training program is challenged, citing war mistakes made by officers educated at the institution.	William B. Colver, Federal Trade Commissioner, leads attacks against the continuation of the excess profits tax, claiming the goal of meeting needs during an emergency (the war) has passed and maintaining that it increases the cost of goods by four times.…The Director of the New York Bureau of the State Bureau of Farms and Markets, Herschel H. Jones, endorses Grace and Flatbush societies, two farm cooperatives.	The British Consul announces the discovery of 6,200 square miles of chicle gum-producing trees in British Guiana. Investigation is ongoing to determine country of ownership.	The Metropolitan Museum in New York announces a special program of works of the Classical School of painting.…The San Francisco (California) County Board of Supervisors will purchase a plane to carry payroll from the city to the county-owned sawmills in the mountains. They claim that truck traffic is too slow and expensive for the task.	May 9
Oregon residents slow in giving attention to candidates running in the primaries. Small numbers attend speeches and debates.…Flying Squadron suffragists take to the air to promote voting rights for women and to deliver lobbyists to states important to amendment ratification.…Henry Cabot Lodge, Republican Senate Leader, will conduct the Republican National Convention in Chicago.		U.S. Postmaster General Burleson asks Congress to fund an $8 million increase for his office due to rising costs for transportation.…The Belgian envoy, Emile Franqui, visits the United States promoting bond maturity extension for Belgium.… Republican members on the House Ways and Means Committee agree to remove the sales tax provision from the Bonus Act.	Black Rust threatens the grain crop.…Homer Folks, Secretary of the New York State Charities Aid Association, challenges a state law recognizing chiropractic work, questioning the medical foundations of the practice.…U.S. Captain Lowell H. Smith sets a world altitude record for a pilot and three passengers in El Centro, California.	The silent film *Passion's Playground*, directed by J.A. Barry and starring a newcomer Rudolph Valentine (later to become Rudolph Valentino), is released today.…Bishop J.H. Vincent, author and founder of Chautauqua, dies.	May 10
William Jennings Bryan attacks Woodrow Wilson's handling of the peace treaty and disagrees with the decision to make the treaty a campaign issue.…William Howard Taft insists he is not a candidate at this time.	The Select Committee of the House on Shipping Board Operations questions the intention of retrofitting the *Leviathan* and the planned transfer to the International Merchant Marines.…Secretary of the Navy Daniels answers Rear Admiral Sims' challenge that the U.S. Navy relies too much on British advice in planning and strategies.	A legal suit is filed in district courts to force steamships to carry goods during manufacturing and labor strikes.…Paper company officials blame government tariffs for paper shortages.		American author William Dean Howells dies.…National Baseball League President John A. Heydler fines players for behavior, stating he will not tolerate rowdy actions in his league.	May 11
F *Includes campaigns, elections, federal-state relations, civil rights and liberties, crime, the judiciary, education, healthcare, poverty, urban affairs, and population.*	G *Includes formation and debate of U.S. foreign and defense policies, veterans affairs, and defense spending. (Relations with specific foreign countries are usually found under the region concerned.)*	H *Includes business, labor, agriculture, taxation, transportation, consumer affairs, monetary and fiscal policy, natural resources, pollution and industrial accidents.*	I *Includes worldwide scientific, medical and technological developments, natural phenomena, U.S. weather and natural disasters.*	J *Includes the arts, religion, scholarship, communications media, sports, entertainment, fashions, fads, and social life.*	

	World Affairs	Europe	Africa & The Middle East	The Americas	Asia & The Pacific
May 12	There are huge amounts of furs for sale on the international market.... The Allies name 46 German military U-boat personnel, including officers and enlisted men, for war crimes. The group will come before the Leipsic Supreme Court on charges that include the use of torpedos against English hospital ships.			After a request by the Mexican government, the U.S. Court attaches funds after charges are made that Bernardino Mena Brito, former Carranza government Consul General at New Orleans, planned to take money (deposited in his own name) and leave for Europe.	
May 13	British critique plans for extending the Supreme Council....The Supreme Council requests that the United States weigh in on the Polish-Russian conflict....Australia demands immigration regulations if Britain approves the Anglo-Japanese Treaty.	Paris curfews irritate visitors.... Emperor Charles of Austria calls on residents of Prague to support the Hungarian Peace Treaty.		Mexican President Carranza holds on to power at Rinconado, but his forces are outnumbered. Monterey has fallen to revolutionary troops. General Obregon appeals to the United States as a friendly nation....Uruguay urged to ban alcohol in a national campaign.	China's president has given Premier Chin Yun-Peng a week's vacation in exchange for the removal of his letter of resignation.
May 14	The Fifth session of the League of Nations Council opens in Rome.... Red Cross workers report shock at conditions in Moscow and Petrograd and hope for resolution to the war before things become worse.	Herr von Kemnitz, the candidate for the German People's Party in the Reichstag, says he is the author of a message to Mexico giving German support to any military actions against the United States.			
May 15	Record numbers of orders for airplanes are received by manufacturing plants.	Civil war breaks out between British troops and Sinn Fein supporters. Black and Tan troops are sent to end the fighting with fierce battles resulting....Russian Maria Bochkareva is executed by firing squad on the orders of the Omsk Cheka for her part in fighting the Red Army.		Argentina is set to pay war loans floated in 1915....Carranza's troops escape to the mountains....The last border town falls to Mexican revolutionary forces....Indications show Vollarreal is the favored candidate for the new government head.	
May 16	A Swiss referendum favors the country joining the League of Nations.... France asks for specific details on a payment plan from German reparations.	A Soviet representative announces Russian residents support the idea of a buffer state, and the Soviet government has recognized a provisional government in Vladivostok.... Field Marshal Foch orders troops to abandon captured ground in Frankfurt after confirmation that the Germans have retreated from the Neutral Zone in exchange for French hostages....Troops in Georgia stop Tartar advance....French workers end the strike and will return to work....Germans protest the use of Danish money by calling a general strike.			
May 17	The Joint Distribution Committee for All-American Funds for Jewish War Relief authorized $3 million in funds for rehabilitation of war-damaged businesses.	French and Belgian forces leave occupied German countries....The Koninklijke-Luchtvaart-Maatschappij (KLM) Dutch airline takes to the air for the first time.		Textile imports to Argentina increase as yearly sales top $18 million from mills in the United States.	
May 18		The Soviets capture Enzeli and Resht and occupy majority of Gilan....The Bolsheviks set up the Soviet Republic of Gilan.		The Mexican states of Yucatan and Campeche join Obregon forces.	
May 19		French Socialists take over the chamber after a Royalist questions the motives of labor.	U.S. Marine Corps Captain Jesse L. Perkins, Sergeant Albert Adolph Taubert, Sergeant William F. Passmore, and Private Emery L. Entrekin kill bandit leader Benoit Batraville in Gendarmerie d'Haiti.		

A	B	C	D	E
Includes developments that affect more than one world region, international organizations and important meetings of world leaders.	*Includes all domestic and regional developments in Europe, including the Soviet Union.*	*Includes all domestic and regional developments in Africa and the Middle East.*	*Includes all domestic and regional developments in Latin America, the Caribbean, and Canada.*	*Includes all domestic and regional developments in Asian and Pacific nations (and colonies).*

U.S. Politics & Social Issues	U.S. Foreign Policy & Affairs, Defense	U.S. Economy & Environment	Science, Technology & Nature	Culture, Leisure & Lifestyle	
Warren G. Harding is in a dilemma about political options—presidential candidate or run for reelection to U.S. Congress?	Joseph M. Nye, Chief Special Agent of the State Department and organizer of the U.S. Secret Service, has resigned his post to work for Guaranty Trust Corporation of New York.	Gasoline prices up with dramatic increase in wholesale costs.... Republican Senator Borah from Idaho proposes $300 million loan plan to allow farm purchases for former military soldiers.		Dadaist artists stage new play *Vous M'oublierez* in various European locations....Air Mail plane crashes with W.J. McClendliss Superintendent of the Chicago-Omaha division on board. Pilot is injured....Enrico Caruso performs in Havana to full houses as fans shower him with praise on the streets outside the theater.	May 12
William Jennings Bryan attacks choice of Homer S. Cummings as Chair of the Democratic National Convention....Colonel Henry L. Stimson heads campaign to organize a fight against the bonus bills under consideration.		United States contributes well over 80 percent of aid to Europe.... Cotton prices decline.	U.S. oil supply predicted to be exhausted in 20 years.	Dancer Isadora Duncan receives praise for performances in Carnegie Hall....Babe Ruth takes up golf, with success.	May 13
Eugene V. Debs is nominated as presidential candidate for the American Socialist Party....Indiana Model suggested for Peace Plan in U.S. Congress....Republican leaders in the House of Representatives lack the votes necessary to override President Wilson's veto of the appropriations bill that included restrictions on the chief executive.	British admirals defend record, actions, and decisions made by Woodrow Wilson during war.	Buffalo, NY clothiers issue court challenge over regulations of the Lever Act claiming provisions are unconstitutional....Bakers fear shortage of flour.		Baseball's Washington Senator Walter Johnson wins 300th game in a match against Detroit Baseball's Giants are informed that Polo Grounds lease will not be extended beyond 1920....Noted Yiddish actor David Kessler dies in New York City.	May 14
Eugene Debs, Socialist Party presidential candidate, speaks out from federal prison.	British General Sir Charles E. Townsend details how his troops opened the straits of Dardenelles after Allied failure at a meeting of the 1st Division, A.E.F.	North Carolina cotton mills pay huge dividends....Eastern telephone workers leave Electrical Brotherhood Union to form own labor union.	H. Holbrook Curtis, noted laryngolist, dies in Wyoming.	*Pulcinella*, a one-act ballet for solo voices and chamber orchestra written by Igor Stravinsky, is performed for the first time at the Paris Opera....A.G. Curtis takes record for typing 133 words in a minute in London.	May 15
		Railroad Brotherhood states delay in dealing with wage issues may mean future strikes....Food rots on docks as strike continues at ports.	Fires sweep through woods of the Adirondack. New York predicts heavy timber losses.	Martyr Joan of Arc is canonized by the Catholic Church in Rome in lavish ceremony....Spanish bullfighter Joselito is killed in the ring.	May 16
Miss Garrett Hay, Second Vice President of the National Woman Suffrage Association, will fill in as acting president for Carrie Chapman Catt who will attend international meeting in June.			De Havilland, the first double-decker design, takes flight from London to Schiphol.		May 17
Opponents claim enough votes to defeat William G. McAdoo, former Secretary of the Treasury and son-in-law of President Woodrow Wilson, in his bid as presidential candidate.					May 18
Idaho Senator Borah urges U.S. aid to be withheld from Europe until conditions are more stable.		Riots break out in coal region of Matewan, WV....U.S. Justice Department request that women stop buying new suits in an effort to keep prices in check.			May 19

F
Includes campaigns, elections, federal-state relations, civil rights and liberties, crime, the judiciary, education, healthcare, poverty, urban affairs, and population.

G
Includes formation and debate of U.S. foreign and defense policies, veterans affairs, and defense spending. (Relations with specific foreign countries are usually found under the region concerned.)

H
Includes business, labor, agriculture, taxation, transportation, consumer affairs, monetary and fiscal policy, natural resources, pollution and industrial accidents.

I
Includes worldwide scientific, medical and technological developments, natural phenomena, U.S. weather and natural disasters.

J
Includes the arts, religion, scholarship, communications media, sports, entertainment, fashions, fads, and social life.

	World Affairs	Europe	Africa & The Middle East	The Americas	Asia & The Pacific
May 20		The First Danish Folketing Election of 1920 is held on the Faroe Islands.…The Turkish National Assembly meets in Ankara.		Former Mexican president Venustiano Carranza attempts to flee the country through Vera Cruz, but is killed by Rodolfo Herrera as he sleeps at San Antonio, Tlaxcalantongo.	The Japanese government announces it awaits a reply from the Chinese regarding negotiations over Shantung.
May 21					
May 22	The Allies agree to float huge loan, without American assistance, in an effort to prove the countries can stand alone.			American policy in Dominican Republic and Haiti is critiqued at a conference at Clark University in Massachusetts.	
May 23	Catholic Pope Benedictus XV publishes the *Encyclical Pacem Dei*.	A national tribute to Italy is held on the fifth anniversary of the Italian entry into World War I.		Wealthy sugar plantation owner General Rafael Montalvo is nominated as the Conservative Party candidate for the Cuban presidency. There is speculation that Alfredo Zayes will be the vice-presidential candidate.	
May 24				Venustiano Carranza is buried in Mexico City with revolutionary troops arresting members of the mourning party as enemies of the state.…Adolfo de la Huerta is elected Mexico's provisional president.	
May 25		Sir Auckland Geddes, British Ambassador to the United States, denies that the British are attempting to corner the oil market.… A British commission condemns April actions in India, where General Dyer's troops fired on a crowd in Amritsar, killing many.		Venustiano Carranza is buried in a poor village cemetery.…New Mexican President Adolfo de la Huerta is scheduled to take presidential oath on June 1.	
May 26	The German government is to spend $5 million to restore the Louvain Library. Efforts have begun to trace artwork removed from the historic structure. World leaders offer assistance in restoration.	Strikers, students, and police clash in Italian rioting.	Bolshevist troops take over Persia, occupying Resht.	Otto Kohl, a German citizen living in Chile, attempts suicide in his cell awaiting trial on charges of spying.	
May 27	A $50 million Belgian loan is arranged by New York bankers.	Tomas Masaryk is installed as President of Czechoslovakia.… Leonid Krassin, the trade delegate from the Soviet Union, arrives in London.	Bolshevik troops are trapped by the Polish as they attempt to cross Beresina.		
May 28	A financial conference by the League of Nations is held in Brussels.	A warrant is issued for Count Michael Karolyi, former Provisional President of Hungary, by the commander of the military tribunal in Budapest. He is charged with murder and treason.		In the first Guatemala trial for high crimes in 22 years, seven high-ranking supporters of former President Estrada Cabrera have been found guilty of treason and have been sentenced to death in front of a firing squad.	
May 29		New Prime Minister of Czechoslovakia, Vlastimil Tysar, and his cabinet hope for closer relations and possibility for aid from the United States.…England experiences record floods in the Great Horncastle Flood.			
May 30	Memorial Day is celebrated in the United States and is observed by other Allied countries.				

A	B	C	D	E
Includes developments that affect more than one world region, international organizations and important meetings of world leaders.	*Includes all domestic and regional developments in Europe, including the Soviet Union.*	*Includes all domestic and regional developments in Africa and the Middle East.*	*Includes all domestic and regional developments in Latin America, the Caribbean, and Canada.*	*Includes all domestic and regional developments in Asian and Pacific nations (and colonies).*

U.S. Politics & Social Issues	U.S. Foreign Policy & Affairs, Defense	U.S. Economy & Environment	Science, Technology & Nature	Culture, Leisure & Lifestyle	
The U.S. Congress passes a joint resolution ending the war between the United States and Germany, with President Woodrow Wilson vetoing the bill.…Jailed Eugene V. Debs is nominated as the presidential candidate of the Socialist Party.				Police officers, disguised as fans and acting on a tip from the Cubs' baseball management, raid the stands at the park to make arrests for gambling.	May 20
The Minnesota legislature passes an amendment giving women the right to vote.…House Republicans accept the text of the Senate Peace Resolution.		Housewives are asked to avoid sugar as a U.S. boycott begins.…Bank robbers net $12,000 and Liberty Bonds in a midday shootout in Toledo, OH.…Americans purchase a significant number of European hotels.		The American Federation of the Arts is urged to decentralize and establish branch museums.…The New York City Tulip Show is held at the Botanical Gardens.	May 21
Henry Ford's company newspaper, The *Dearborn Independent,* attacks Jews for the first time in an article with circulation of 700,000. E.G. Pipp, the newspaper's editor, resigns in disgust.		The Bank of Commerce chief announces the business slump should not be of any concern, provided transportation is improved and price structuring is addressed.			May 22
			Archeologists work at dig site in a stone quarry (known as Dragon Bone Hill) southwest of Beijing (Zhoukoudian, Chou K'ou Tien region), searching for remains of prehistoric humans.	Crowds attend the official opening of the new Olympic Stadium in Antwerp.	May 23
					May 24
The Texas state Democratic convention is held.…House Republicans are unable to come to an agreement on a plan for military bonuses.…The House agrees to meet to consider President Woodrow Wilson's request for an Armenian mandate.…Pro-Irish supporters are arrested in a Philadelphia protest.	U.S. President Woodrow Wilson vetoes the Knox Peace Resolution.	Airplane pilots' salaries rise to nearly $1,000 for a month of airtime.			May 25
				Festival Dada takes place at the Salle Gaveau in Paris. Jean (Hans) Arp is a featured artist at the festival.	May 26
Republicans meeting at the National Convention in Chicago omit the mention of Prohibition in the platform.…Ths Bonus Army grows in strength as Disabled Veterans and the American Legion join the cause.				Fans call right field bleachers Ruthville in honor of the home run hitter Babe Ruth.…Americans spend $1 billion on candy each year.	May 27
				The Budapest Royal Medical Association begins to expel members making negative public comments. Expulsions include Sandor Ferenczi.	May 28
			A type of snorkel is invented in Greenland.		May 29
The American Federation of Labor announces plans to campaign in 32 states using its Non-Partisan Political Campaign Committee.			Flooding in the English countryside near Louth takes 20 lives.		May 30
F *Includes campaigns, elections, federal-state relations, civil rights and liberties, crime, the judiciary, education, healthcare, poverty, urban affairs, and population.*	G *Includes formation and debate of U.S. foreign and defense policies, veterans affairs, and defense spending. (Relations with specific foreign countries are usually found under the region concerned.)*	H *Includes business, labor, agriculture, taxation, transportation, consumer affairs, monetary and fiscal policy, natural resources, pollution and industrial accidents.*	I *Includes worldwide scientific, medical and technological developments, natural phenomena, U.S. weather and natural disasters.*	J *Includes the arts, religion, scholarship, communications media, sports, entertainment, fashions, fads, and social life.*	

	World Affairs	Europe	Africa & The Middle East	The Americas	Asia & The Pacific
May 31	Fifty nurses from 15 countries receive the Florence Nightingale Medal for Heroism in Geneva, Switzerland.	The British Cabinet discusses the Irish Question today....Workers seize a landlord's land in Dublin.... Prince August William, son of the former leader, awaits the leadership decisions of the New Potsdam Movement while workers in Berlin consider all political factions. The father of former Emperor William Hohenzollern is guarded nearby, awaiting success of a coup to return him to power.		Provisional Mexican President Adolfo de la Huerta promises workers better conditions, industry assistance in developing natural resources, and international relations for all free peoples while hospitalized for appendicitis....Huerta promised the release of Ygnacio Bonilla, former U.S. Ambassador to Mexico....Canada and the West Indies host a meeting to establish closer ties.	
Jun. 1	Carrie Chapman Catt, President of the National Woman Suffrage Association of the United States, and officers and delegates arrive in Paris to attend the Congress of the International Woman Suffrage Alliance in Geneva, Switzerland.... Legal scholar Elihu Root, American member of the International Court, sets out for London to attend the first meeting of the Organizing Committee....$50 million in Belgian bonds are prepared.	General Peter Wrangel begins a military offensive north of the Sea of Azov, capturing most of southern Russia. Red Army troops are diverted by Polish invasion of Ukraine, resulting in less military resistance for Wrangel....Armenia appeals to France for aid in answering attacks by Azerbaijani troops, Mustafa Kemal's Turkish National forces, and Kurdish troops on the south....The Bolshevist movement has taken Alexandropol and has cut lines of communication.		Forest fires burn in New Brunswick, destroying houses and businesses. Nova Scotia is threatened by fires.	
Jun. 2	Ottoman Grand Vizier Damat Ferit Pasha, with other officials, leaves for Paris to discuss the details of the peace treaty.	Polish and Russian troops fight at the Battle of Boryspil near Kiev.		The Mexican government fails to halt looting of former public officials' homes and offices.	Japanese imports total $220 million this year.
Jun. 3	The International Chamber of Commerce makes plans to meet to stabilize the exchange rate and deal with trade and business issues.				
Jun. 4	The Allies sign the Treaty of Trianon with the Hungarians after the evacuation of Romanian troops. The Treaty terms are harsh on Hungary and include the loss of population and territory, and payment of reparations. Future terms include a limit on the army, debt assumption, and delivery of war criminals to Allies.... The Allies vote to control Austria's monetary policy, trade, and finances under a repatriation committee.	The Greek leader Alexander refuses to abdicate....The French make an overt effort to court world visitors, especially Americans....Supporters of French Prime Minister Georges Clemenceau claim at a peace conference that he did not intend to split Germany....Polish troops experience a new round of fierce fighting from Bolshevik forces....The Belgian glass industry rebounds with so many orders that factories are unable to fill requests.	Bolshevik troops deny that they have taken Teheran.	Mexican revolutionary forces deny receiving aid from U.S. oil interests.	
Jun. 5	The Gregorian Congress meets and requests the restoration of chanting....In a first test vote, Congressional analysts believe that the League of Nations, with reservations, will be approved by the U.S. Congress....World governments set rates for sale of bread, some regulating prices only for poor.... U.S. delegates to the International Chamber of Commerce sail for a conference....The Swiss are assured that the League of Nations headquarters will remain in Geneva.	Germany votes in an open election....The French and Turkish Armistice is announced in Asia Minor....New York merchants turn a deaf ear to Bremen, Germany Chamber of Commerce's request for assistance to protest international treaty terms....A clothing shortage is reported in London....German merchants favor one large union for all trades....The German government reimburses Argentina for sinking *Monte Protegido* during the war.	The Ugandan government is reorganized by the British with terms that include a nominated legislative council.	Plague spreads in Vera Cruz, so buildings are burned to halt the spread of the disease....Captured passenger ships will be used as part of a new service of the Munson Line traveling to South America.	China formally objects to any sort of Anglo-Japanese Alliance.

A	B	C	D	E
Includes developments that affect more than one world region, international organizations and important meetings of world leaders.	*Includes all domestic and regional developments in Europe, including the Soviet Union.*	*Includes all domestic and regional developments in Africa and the Middle East.*	*Includes all domestic and regional developments in Latin America, the Caribbean, and Canada.*	*Includes all domestic and regional developments in Asian and Pacific nations (and colonies).*

U.S. Politics & Social Issues	U.S. Foreign Policy & Affairs, Defense	U.S. Economy & Environment	Science, Technology & Nature	Culture, Leisure & Lifestyle	
The Republican Party hears challenges to delegates from the American South and seats delegates from Alabama and Arkansas. Additional cases from delegates from Florida and the District of Columbia were postponed. This has been the first time this group has heard delegate challenges.... Woodrow Wilson, in high spirits, meets with members of the Democratic National Committee to discuss strategy for the convention.	The newly formed Mexican government agrees to commission claims for American losses during revolution....The U.S. Senate votes to decline authorizing a mandate for Armenia.	The Senate reports little chance for a Bonus Bill to pass this session of Congress....A call is issued to former servicemen to pick up lost luggage that has been brought to the Governor's Island in New York. The New York office of the Knights of Columbus group will return hundreds of thousands of pieces using claim information, if petitioners write to their offices to identify baggage.	As a crowd of 125,000 watches, Gaston Chevrolet finishes first at the Indianapolis Speedway 500-mile race....An American record for a six-passenger plane is set by Pilot Leo Mons while flying a Larsen monoplane at the third Pan-American Aeronautic Congress in Atlantic City.	Gene Walker wins a 10-mile motorcycle race in Greeley, Colorado.... The 101st anniversary of the birth of Walt Whitman is celebrated with comments questioning Whitman's position on Communism.... Parades were seen throughout Oyster Bay, NJ today to honor former President and Colonel Theodore Roosevelt. Soldiers march to the gravesite at Young's Memorial Cemetery, and Lieutenant Colonial Theodore Roosevelt lays a wreath at his father's grave.	May 31
Ernestine Rose is appointed librarian of the 135th Street Branch Library in Harlem, NY and begins collecting literature for the library from local writers and essayists....Baby Blakely Coughlin, 13 months, is kidnapped from his crib in Norristown, PA.		The National India Rubber Company in Bristol, RI, reopens with state National Guard assistance after rioting closed the plant several days earlier....John D. Rockefeller, Jr. begins inspection trip of Union Pacific rail lines using a special travel car and a special train for part of the route....Millions made in phony liquor permits force tightening up of permits and wholesale houses....A barbers' strike is spreading throughout New York State.	Charles LaJotte is hired as a U.S. Air Mail Service pilot.	Nearly 65,000 applications await phone installations due to delays of materials and labor for installation.	Jun. 1
Suffragists set up headquarters opposite the Chicago convention headquarters to center their lobbying campaign....Geroid Robinson publishes "The New Negro" in *The Freeman* magazine.				German General von Kluck buys a castle in German Switzerland with profits from his book about his life and war experience. Book profits were paid in pounds and dollars, affording Kluck the opportunity for the purchase.	Jun. 2
Éamon De Valera works to include recognition for Ireland in both political party platforms....Farmers' groups lobby both political parties for platforms at national conventions.		President Wilson appoints three individuals to establish a policy for anthracite coal workers. A panel of an independent operator, mineworker, and college president are given two months to complete the agreement.		The New York Athletic Club hopes the new track meet run at Travers Island will be an annual event.	Jun. 3
Rumors circulate that President Woodrow Wilson may run for a third term of office as President of the United States....An alcohol agent attends dinner where alcohol is served. He claims he thought it was lemonade as the story hits major U.S. papers....Members of the faculty of Yale University send the U.S. Congress the message that they do not think the United States should make a public statement of sympathy for Ireland....A ransom is demanded for the Coughlin baby kidnapped earlier this month.	The authorization is made for the office of Chaplain (Chief) of the U.S. Army....The Army Citizens' Military Camp is authorized.... J.C. Stimson is conferred with the rank of major, the first time in the history of the U.S. Army....The Crow Reservation Act is passed by the U.S. Congress, sponsored by the tribe, prescribing rules to divide the reservation into land tracts that will be allotted to enrolled members of the tribe.	A large counterfeiting operation is discovered in Harlem, NY, where a forger claims he learned his art skills from visiting the public library.... The Federal Reserve Board outlines how loans are made and refuses to make loans directly to borrowers....Builders claim to be put off by higher than normal costs.	The American Ice Company president claims the firm was not involved in profiteering and price fixing....The U.S. Shipping Board announces that the terms for the Longshoreman's Union cannot be met....President Wilson vetoes the budget bill, declaring it is unconstitutional, citing the section stating Congress may appoint a new Controller General as an example. The House is unable to marshal the number of votes necessary to override the veto.	Horn and Hardart announce they will build an Automat Diner in New York City on Greenwich Street.	Jun. 4
Blacks claim representation exclusion at the Republican Convention will cost the party a significant number of votes....The Senate continues an investigation into irregularities in campaign funding. Both parties agree to participate in hearings....Congress adjourns without passing a budget bill due to filibuster action....The Bonus Bill fails due to a pocket veto by President Woodrow Wilson....Attorney General Palmer's campaign chair states that Palmer will receive the presidential nomination at the convention.	The Women's Bureau in the U.S. Department of Labor is organized as a permanent feature of the department.	The Federal Labor Board rushes to make a settlement to avoid a labor strike by train dispatchers....The Gas Company of New York wins a rare case in a rate challenge. An 80-cent increase is delayed....New York Governor Smith works to assist a bond issue for Poland....A Rhode Island mill postpones reopening, as the company is lacking orders to fill....Hardware King manufacturer Charles E. Billings dies....The Longshoremen's strike shuts down West Coast.	Fishmeal is introduced as an additive for pig food....The U.S. Secretary of Agriculture request additional funding to construct forest roads in the western United States.	The United Waist League displays new blouses at the annual fashion show in New York City....The Freelance Artists' Guild develops their own system for placing members' work, with profitable results....French artwork is to be displayed at the New York Metropolitan exhibit....The population of native Hawaiians shrinks on the Hawaiian Island chain....W.E.B. Du Bois receives the Springarn Medal.	Jun. 5

F
Includes campaigns, elections, federal-state relations, civil rights and liberties, crime, the judiciary, education, healthcare, poverty, urban affairs, and population.

G
Includes formation and debate of U.S. foreign and defense policies, veterans affairs, and defense spending. (Relations with specific foreign countries are usually found under the region concerned.)

H
Includes business, labor, agriculture, taxation, transportation, consumer affairs, monetary and fiscal policy, natural resources, pollution and industrial accidents.

I
Includes worldwide scientific, medical and technological developments, natural phenomena, U.S. weather and natural disasters.

J
Includes the arts, religion, scholarship, communications media, sports, entertainment, fashions, fads, and social life.

	World Affairs	Europe	Africa & The Middle East	The Americas	Asia & The Pacific
Jun. 6	The Congress of the International Woman Suffrage Alliance opens in Geneva, Switzerland.…Persia is used as test case for the leadership at the League of Nations. This case will be the first to display international leadership.	National elections are held in Germany to replace the National Assembly. The election reestablishes the regular Reichstag with the Weimar political coalition losing control to the liberal People's Party, Center Party, and the Democrats.…A Socialist mob shouts down speeches regarding the possible secession of the Rhineland.		The countries of Bolivia, Peru, and Chile dispute ownership of Tacna and Arica.…Reports cite large tracts are involved in drilling for oil in Mexico.…Jamaica boasts large numbers of bats that aid in island health by eating mosquitoes.	The Japanese occupy Nikolalevsk.
Jun. 7	French newspapers begin discussing a sliding scale for German war payments.…The Spa Conference may be delayed due to disagreement among Allies.…The Supreme Council of the League of Nations sets their meeting agenda, to include Persia's appeal.	The French crop of wheat fails to meet national demand.…Italian troops shell Alessio.…An Italian fort is destroyed by exploding munitions.…Lenin's plot for world domination is made public. The May Day celebration was to kick off campaign, but his letter exposes the plot.…Polish troops take down the Hindenburg Line quickly on the Beresina Front and take munitions from retreating Bolshevik troops.	The Leader of the Egyptian nationalists, Saad Zaghul Pasha, meets with British Sir Alfred Milner in London to begin talks to establish independence for his country. The British express concern about the safety of the Suez Canal and indicate they wish to remain involved in Egyptian policy making.…The Pope beatifies Ugandan natives as martyrs for Catholicism.	Mexico agrees to consider a U.S. request to return American draft dodgers.…General Roberto Cejudo is unaccounted for after Mexican action.	
Jun. 8	The United States, China, Honduras, and Costa Rica elect not to join the League of Nations.	The Germans are unable to set up a coalition government.			
Jun. 9	Britain refuse to take the mandate for Armenia.…The Allies request U.S. President Woodrow Wilson's advice on boundary questions.…France asks Britain to hold gold cargo from Soviet ships in port, and Britain complies. Sweden announces support for the plan while other countries weigh in on the action.	Italian Premier Nitti, cabinet ministers, and President of the Chamber Signor Orlando resigned today over price restrictions and payments of a government subsidy on bread.…The French regret not accepting Mesopotamia as part of the agreement ending the war.…The German government announces a reduction of troops to meet the treaty agreement.		The Canadian Parliament expresses outrage that the International Labor Convention incorporates support of Irish workers since the meeting is on British soil.	
Jun. 10	The Allied Powers gives The Treaty of Sevres to the Turkish government.	Turkish leader Sultan Mohammed VI is outraged at the Treaty of Sevres and gains additional support within the Nationalist Party over the treaty terms.…Polish Marshal Pilsudski returns to the fighting front from Warsaw after talks to end the fighting against the Bolshevik army.		Residents of Tlaxcaiantango, Mexico claim former Mexican President Carranza offered no defense but was shot 30 times by soldiers.…Jamaica asks Great Britain for a new constitution that would include a simplified form of self-rule. Jamaican politicians form a committee to draft a letter of appeal to King George.	The Japanese and British governments come to agreement on the continuation of the Anglo-Japanese Alliance and bar any additional changes to the document.
Jun. 11	The Allies question the need for the Spa Conference. France cites German elections as the reason. Other nations view the conference as a critical step in arranging European financial politics.	The Red Army introduces a counterattack against the Polish-Ukrainian army.…The Port of Avlona in Italy fears an attack from 15,000 Albanian troops that have already captured the villages of Bestrova, Tepeleni, and Selenitze. The city asks for protection from gunboats in the port.…The Spanish government in Barcelona expels foreign nationals accused of spying.	The British report the massacre and deaths of all officers and government officials at a town near Mosul. Arab insurgents are identified as the killers.	New German Envoy Count Montgelas, appointed by President Ebert, arrives to take on duties of the office in Mexico.…General Murguia Herrero is charged with killing former Mexican President Carranza after he changed his testimony regarding the details of the death at a legal hearing. Herrero originally claimed that Carranza committed suicide, but admitted that he did not witness the event.	
Jun. 12	Damad Ferid Pasha, Turkish Grand Vizier, leaves for Paris for international talks after a public hanging of men convicted of plotting his death.	The British announce that 52 constables have been killed this year alone in Ireland.…Charges circulate that French Prime Minister Clemenceau failed to represent French interests in the division of Middle East and German land.…The Austrian Cabinet is disbanded when Dr. Karl Renner resigns after a debate with the Socialist Democratic Party.…Bolshevik forces are defeated in battle at Beresina.			
	A *Includes developments that affect more than one world region, international organizations and important meetings of world leaders.*	B *Includes all domestic and regional developments in Europe, including the Soviet Union.*	C *Includes all domestic and regional developments in Africa and the Middle East.*	D *Includes all domestic and regional developments in Latin America, the Caribbean, and Canada.*	E *Includes all domestic and regional developments in Asian and Pacific nations (and colonies).*

U.S. Politics & Social Issues	U.S. Foreign Policy & Affairs, Defense	U.S. Economy & Environment	Science, Technology & Nature	Culture, Leisure & Lifestyle	
Hiram Johnson avoids radical terms in an attempt to attract mainstream backing at the convention....Large numbers of Maltese arrive in Detroit....Eight thousand Mennonites from western Canada request to come to the state of Mississippi.	Under State Secretary Norman H. Davis is to take post as presidential advisor.	The Harriman Ship Line takes over travel lines from the Hamburg-American Company; the ships will fly the flag of the United States. Additional ships will be built to join the fleet....Italy refuses to use German dyes, preferring importation of American dyes....The last company involved in cutting whalebones closes in New York....Electric molders strike....A debate opens as to the morality of taxing spinsters.		Chinese handmade batik fabrics with embroidery are all the rage in women's fashions....The Harlem Y.M.C.A. is hailed as one of the finest in the nation....The Knickerbocker Yacht Club Regatta in the New York Harbor is cancelled due to lack of participation....The directors of the Lincoln Highway make plans to build a permanent roadway.	Jun. 6
Oklahoma v. Texas (U.S. Intervener), 253 U.S. 465, is decided by the U.S. Supreme Court, confirming the boundaries between the two states.	The armored Cruiser *South Dakota* is renamed *Huron*; the *North Carolina* is renamed *Charlotte*; and the *Montana* is renamed *Missoula*....Navy leaders critique the new naval bill, claiming that cuts will hurt ship repairs, expansion of air power, expansion for new equipment, and ships and upkeep for Pacific bases.	The Federation of Labor Party meets in Montreal, Canada with Samuel Gompers attending as a representative for the American Federation of Labor....Merchant groups advocate a ban on Russian trade, claiming a boycott would send a message to Lenin.		The population of Los Angeles, CA, surpasses the city of San Francisco and other large cities in the western United States.	Jun. 7
The Chicago Council passes a law for daylight savings time, but labor groups say they will not observe the time change....The U.S. Supreme Court upholds the Volstead Act on the States' Rights Doctrine. The case provides an interpretation of Concurrent Powers.	The U.S. 7th Regiment Officer School expands recruiting efforts for soldiers to take leadership positions.	The 40th Annual Labor Federation meeting in Canada hears a speech by Samuel Gompers calling for impeachment of Attorney General Palmer....Action by telegraph operator unions ends with the prohibition of wireless devices at the Republican National Convention in Chicago.		The manuscript of a Kipling novella fetches $4,000 at auction....Motion Picture Owners of America meeting at the New York Hotel Winton denounce state censorship of movies.	Jun. 8
Idaho Senator Borah threatens to leave the national party convention if the platform includes the endorsement of the League of Nations, even with proposed reservations....Clergy propose a League of Religion that would include all faiths.	The U.S. Department of the Navy sends officers to Peru as advisors.	U.S. garment workers propose a strike.		An investigation of U.S. Census collecting methods finds that many agents used guesswork and faulty assumptions in amassing data. Some cities claim they will conduct their own data collection to check the results of U.S. information.	Jun. 9
The Republican Party reads the official party platform at the National Convention in Chicago....The Republican Party endorses Woman's Suffrage at the national convention....Henry Cabot Lodge becomes the permanent chair of the convention....The American Federation of Labor eliminates the color barrier for workers in a platform statement from the national convention that states black workers must have the same rights and privileges as white workers.		Drug stores (chemists) endorse a sales tax or excess profits levy....Attorney General Palmer arranges talks to begin to set terms to end a coastal port strike....A federal judge rules a portion of the Lever Act unconstitutional.	R.B. Anderson, member of the American Chemical Society, publishes an article in the *Journal of Industry and Engineering Chemistry* outlining the process of obtaining gasoline from natural gas....Lieutenant Henri Roget starts leg one of an around-the-world flight beginning in a Paris to Warsaw air trip.	Architect Chalfin is hired by the Famous Players–Lasky Movie company as the resident architect for sets and design....The Chicago Opera signs an agreement with a Manhattan, NY theater for several years' temporary residency....A huge train accident in New York kills dozens when a Penn Central engineer ignores signs while a fireman jumps from the cab to safety.	Jun. 10
A cabal of Republican bosses select Warren G. Harding as the Republican presidential nominee....A heat wave in Chicago has national political convention delegates questioning early adjournment....The American Labor Party offers to join with the Democratic Party, claiming Republican Party platform differences are too great for cooperation.		The National Sales Association urges the federal government to take over hotels, charging that lodging and meals have reached outrageous prices. Price fixing by hotel owners is suggested....Restaurants are urged to ban sugar bowls from tables in an effort to restrict scarce foodstuff....Los Angeles, CA reports business boom.	The U.S. Shipping Board steamer *Huron* arrives in Buenos Aires from New York in a record time of 19 and a half days.	Big city newspapers feature fashions worn at the national political conventions....The airplane edition of the *New York Times* arrives in Chicago on the date of publication....The English Queen sets new fashion with narrow skirts at the official opening of the Court.	Jun. 11
The Republican convention in Chicago announces the ticket of Harding for president and Calvin Coolidge as running mate....The Farmer Labor Party is established in Chicago.		A group of traders, wholesalers, and merchants are arrested on charges of illegal trading in sugar....The London silver market soars with the help of American bankers' actions.	The Jamaican drought is broken with torrential rains. Several are killed in the flooding....Record heat hits in New York, with several deaths recorded.	Mr. and Mrs. Fairbanks (Mary Pickford and Douglas Fairbanks) leave on their European honeymoon aboard the *Lapland*.	Jun. 12
F *Includes campaigns, elections, federal-state relations, civil rights and liberties, crime, the judiciary, education, healthcare, poverty, urban affairs, and population.*	G *Includes formation and debate of U.S. foreign and defense policies, veterans affairs, and defense spending. (Relations with specific foreign countries are usually found under the region concerned.)*	H *Includes business, labor, agriculture, taxation, transportation, consumer affairs, monetary and fiscal policy, natural resources, pollution and industrial accidents.*	I *Includes worldwide scientific, medical and technological developments, natural phenomena, U.S. weather and natural disasters.*	J *Includes the arts, religion, scholarship, communications media, sports, entertainment, fashions, fads, and social life.*	

	World Affairs	Europe	Africa & The Middle East	The Americas	Asia & The Pacific
Jun. 13	Great Britain announces Palestinian policies, including freedom of religion and economic development.	The Punjab (India) Sub-Committee of the Indian National Congress report asks for arrest to be made for the Spring 1919 riots in Amristar.... Belgian King Albert announces the country will open trade with Brazil.			
Jun. 14	The sixth session of the League of Nations Council meets in London.			Mexican General Jacinto B. Trevino, Minister of Commerce and Industry under the Provisional President Adolfo de la Huerta, announces that Mexico will respect oil companies' legal rights provided they are legitimately created foreign interests.	
Jun. 15	A second session of the International Labor Organization (BIT) in Genoa debates issues related to seamen and sailors....Italian Baron Mayor des Blanches chairs the BIT session.	Control over the northern zone of North Schleswig is taken over by the Danish government....The Red Army captures Kiev....Albanian General Essad Pasha is shot and killed in front of a Paris hotel by a student, Avenic Rustem, who claims the general was a tyrant responsible for the current economic condition in Albania.			
Jun. 16	Delegates to the International Court meet in The Hague....The Interallied Commission of Control announces provisions for limited internationalization of the Port of Constantinople under provisional terms of the Turkish Treaty. The port will also be included in the Zone of Straits....Persia makes an appeal to the League of Nations to aid in a dispute with the Soviet government.	Reports state Americans in Kiev turned over private cars to evacuate wounded soldiers from the city....Turkish Nationalists attack British Indian troops on the Ismid front....A debate takes place in British House of Commons over the Nauru Agreement Bill and the amount of support to be provided to the island nation formerly owned by Germany from Great Britain, Australia, and New Zealand.	The Revolutionary Committee of Persia issues a statement announcing the abolishment of the monarchy and formation of a republic at Resht and all officials appointed to office.	Ygnacio Bonillas, former Mexican Ambassador to the United States and Mexican presidential candidate, maintains he was not deported from Mexico during the recent revolts and maintains he was treated humanly during his incarceration by revolutionary forces after Carranza was killed in Mexico.	
Jun. 17	A.J. Balfour, Lord President of the Council, tells the British House of Commons that the League of Nations is expanding and reminds nations that treaties must be filed with the League of Nations, and open to inspection, before they will be considered binding and enforceable.	American firms Kuhn, Loeb, and Company and the Guaranty Trust Company buy stock in Austrian Bank....New Italian Premier Giovanni Giolitti reinforces the Italian policy of friendship toward France....British troops evacuate Erivan, Armenia.			U.S. State Department officials deny knowledge of San Francisco law challenging Japanese economic interests in California.
Jun. 18	Plans are announced for the Allies to meet in Boulogne. Belgium, France, England, Japan, and Italy will attend....Italian representatives ask for new indemnity agreement and Japan wishes to be paid for ships lost during the war....British Premier Lloyd George meets with delegates from the League to Abolish War. George cites strained finances for the League of Nations as one reason to deny international aid for an international military force, one platform favored by the League to Abolish War.	British Prime Minster Lloyd George asks the British representative in Hungary to investigate charges of Jews and Communists in that country; a special investigation commission is under consideration.... Vienna workers meet to consider a general strike against Hungary for the failure to stop the persecution of workmen....With King Albert conducting the meeting, Belgian Cabinet Council votes to lift the blockade against Soviet Russia.	Bolshevik troops leave Persian Port Enzell.		Emma Goldman gives an interview claiming she sees tyranny in Russia.
Jun. 19	The Conference of Hythe begins with Allied representations discussing conditions in Turkey and problems relating to reparations....The German payment plan of 42 years is set by the Allies.	Air travel is so popular in Europe that reservations are difficult to obtain....German leader Konstantin Fehrenbach fails to form a coalition cabinet in Germany after approaching members of each party....British Prime Minister Lloyd George tells Irish workers to carry trains transporting English soldiers or risk railroad shutdown.			

A	B	C	D	E
Includes developments that affect more than one world region, international organizations and important meetings of world leaders.	*Includes all domestic and regional developments in Europe, including the Soviet Union.*	*Includes all domestic and regional developments in Africa and the Middle East.*	*Includes all domestic and regional developments in Latin America, the Caribbean, and Canada.*	*Includes all domestic and regional developments in Asian and Pacific nations (and colonies).*

U.S. Politics & Social Issues	U.S. Foreign Policy & Affairs, Defense	U.S. Economy & Environment	Science, Technology & Nature	Culture, Leisure & Lifestyle	
The U.S. Post Office declares children may not be sent via parcel post.... The Second Convention of the Communist Party of America opens in New York City....Democratic National Convention delegates admit that candidate division is vast....The Committee of Forty-Eight announces plans to form a political party on the grounds that the Republican National Convention failed to deal with the most serious problems facing the nation.		California raisin manufacturers open a consumer campaign asking buyers to eat one raisin a day. The campaign features the Queen of the Vineyard Domain of the San Joaquin Valley....William Fellows Morgan asks New York Dock Commissioner Murray Hulbert to construct a special fruit pier to ensure that fruit is not damaged during winter weather or spoiled during hot deliveries.		A bomb explodes in a Havana, Cuban hall where singer Caruso performs....The United States withdraws their golf team from the Olympic Games due to lack of interest. Golfers Bobby Jones and Max Marston joined the team, but an eight-person team was required.	Jun. 13
Senator Robert M. La Follette of Wisconsin is reported to be the Progressive presidential candidate for the secessionist Committee of Forty-Eight.		Wholesale grocers agree to cut profits to lower the cost of food for consumers.	The Aero Club of America announces plans to organize an around-the-world air race. Handley-Page, airplane manufacturer, is slated to provide planes and passengers for a test flight for the event.	Promoter Florenz Ziegfeld shows the new Follies at the New Amsterdam Theater.	Jun. 14
At a race riot in Duluth, MN, a white crowd of 5,000 lynches a trio of black men.		Private trucks and cars are used to transport goods in the New York port strike.	The wedding between W.E. Ebert and J.R. Wichman is broadcast from Detroit, MI, the first on radio.		Jun. 15
George C. Coughlin, father of kidnapped baby in Norristown, PA, announces he does not expect the holders of the ransom money to return his child who was kidnapped two weeks ago.		The American Federation of Labor reaffirms their stand for official recognition of the Irish Republic at a rally in Montreal, Canada.	Strong winds hit the eastern coast of the United States; short storms cause massive damage to New York harbor.	Jack Kearns, manager of boxer Jack Dempsey (also known as William Harrison), accepts the challenge of George Carpentier, European boxing champion for a match October 10. Dempsey currently holds the world heavyweight champion belt....Charges against boxer Jack Dempsey for draft evasion are dismissed in federal court in San Francisco, CA.	Jun. 16
The Labor Committee of the Woman's Bureau of the Democratic National Committee drafts a labor plank for the party that includes collective bargaining through recognized labor representatives, approval of National Industrial Councils, condemnation of mandatory injunctions and outlawing the hiring of children under 14 years of age.		The Czechoslovakian government sells a large amount of sugar to the United States. Negotiations are in place for additional sales between the two countries.		The U.S. Olympic rugby team is announced by W. Harry Maloney, President of the California Rugby Union.	Jun. 17
The Committee of Arrangement of the Single Tax Party met to denounce the selection of Wisconsin Senator William La Follette as candidate for a new third party....Political leader, pioneer in profit sharing, philanthropy work, financier, and political advisor to President Theodore Roosevelt, George W. Perkins, dies in Samford, CT....Samuel Gompers is reelected President of the American Federation of Labor, the 39th time he has been elected.	Ludwig C.A.K. Martens is recalled by Soviet authorities from his post as the unofficial Russian Soviet Ambassador to the United States....The U.S. Department of State announces departing alien residents will no longer be required to obtain a foreign permit from the State Department. This is a change from the current law that requires individuals to obtain permits to all countries, with the exception of Europe.	Charles E. Hughes files suit with U.S. Supreme Court Justice William R. Day in Canton, OH to overturn the case of *U.S. v. C.R. Weed and Co.*, a conviction of profiteering by a Buffalo, NY, firm.	The Pacific meeting of the Ecological Society of America in Seattle, WA is held....A Wireless Concert is performed by Dame Melba, using a Marconi Company apparatus in Clemsford and heard up to 1,000 miles away from transmitter....A large earthquake hits Los Angeles, CA, at 2:15 a.m.	Jockey Clarence Kummer rides Man O' War to a win in the Preakness.... Pickering's Ocean Park Amusement Pier in southern California celebrates its grand opening.	Jun. 18
Detroit's population growth ranks it as the fourth fastest growing city in the United States, outranking Boston, Cleveland, Pittsburgh, and Baltimore....President Woodrow Wilson signs the Water Power Bill after 10 years of political debate.	Four of six U.S. destroyers are asked to return from Mexican ports.	Vigo-New York steamship service opens with regular service between the United States and Spanish ports.	Danish scientist Lauge Kosh, who was a part of the earlier Knud Rasmussen expedition, announces plans to reach the north point of Greenland and chart the landscape along the route.	Actor Harold Lloyd is given a contract for $1.5 million for his first year of motion pictures for Associated Exhibitors.	Jun. 19
F *Includes campaigns, elections, federal-state relations, civil rights and liberties, crime, the judiciary, education, healthcare, poverty, urban affairs, and population.*	**G** *Includes formation and debate of U.S. foreign and defense policies, veterans affairs, and defense spending. (Relations with specific foreign countries are usually found under the region concerned.)*	**H** *Includes business, labor, agriculture, taxation, transportation, consumer affairs, monetary and fiscal policy, natural resources, pollution and industrial accidents.*	**I** *Includes worldwide scientific, medical and technological developments, natural phenomena, U.S. weather and natural disasters.*	**J** *Includes the arts, religion, scholarship, communications media, sports, entertainment, fashions, fads, and social life.*	

	World Affairs	Europe	Africa & The Middle East	The Americas	Asia & The Pacific
Jun. 20	The Hythe Conference discusses German reparations, the military situation in Turkey and the draft of a treaty before the Council of Ambassadors in Paris. Greek Premier M. Venizelos is in attendance.	British ships rush to Constantinople to provide military force against Mustafa Kemal and the Nationalist troops.			
Jun. 21	The Supreme Allied Council determines Germany must make 42 annual reparation payments. The majority of moneys will go to France, Britain, Italy, and Belgium.	Konstanin Fehrenbeck becomes Chancellor of Germany....St. Paul's Cathedral in London opens a drive to purchase goods to aid in restoration of the bomb-damaged building.			
Jun. 22	Red Cross reports workers are forced to drive a convoy through a fire zone of fighting from Kiev, but arrive safely in Warsaw today.	The Greek army offensive begins in western Anatolia, with support of British Prime Minister David Lloyd-George....The Second London Court of the Season sees several Americans as sponsored guests.			
Jun. 23				Charges issued against General Francisco Murguia, former Mexican Minister of War, for fraud in using two million pesos to purchase ladies' garments.	
Jun. 24	The British Treasury Department denies claims that repudiation of Allied debt to America was an issue at either the Hythe or Boulogne Conferences.	The Greeks defeat Turkish troops at Alashehr....The Chuvash Autonomous Region is established in RSFSR....The English government sends troops to Mudanya, Turkey.		Charles W. Whittemore, President of the Chamber of Commerce in the United States, announces British traders surpass American manufacturers in the amount of imported goods to Argentina.	Prince Iyesato Tokugawa, President of the House of Peers, attends a formal government ceremony recognizing the troops killed by Russian Bolshevik soldiers in Nikolaievsk. Members of the royal family, government ministry, and Diet attend the event.
Jun. 25	The International Court of Justice to be located in The Hague....The League of Free Nations Association announces U.S. President Woodrow Wilson's Fourteen Points were written as a publicity campaign for citizens of Russia and Germany, rather than a valid policy direction for the United States and governments of the world.				
Jun. 26	The Allies ask U.S. President Wilson to issue a call for the first meeting of the Assembly of the League of Nations. Debate over the meeting location takes place with some countries opting for Geneva, while other favor Brussels....The International Congress of Chambers of Commerce adopts a resolution in favor of the Allies notifying Germany that terms of the Treaty of Versailles must be met without delay....A meeting between the Permanent Committee of the Supreme Economic Council and Russian Soviet Minister of Trade, Leonid Krassin, is held in London, England.	England's King George hosts 350 soldiers at Buckingham Palace to make awards for the Victoria Cross....The arrest of members of the Ulster Volunteers is announced in Londonderry, Ireland....The Irish rail situation become worse with southeastern line trains halted.		Mexican Minster of Finance, General Salvador Alvarado, announces a visit to the United States accompanied by Alberto M. Gonzales, Justice of the Mexican Supreme Court. Both men will discuss the issue of oil production....General strikes expand in all areas of Mexico....The Mexican government announces property rights to be returned to postrevolution owners, except for properties belonging to Victoriano Huerta, Felix Diaz, Francisco Villa, J.W. Maytorena, and Eugenio Paredes. Owners must document rights to the property and sign a waiver for war damages.	Students are arrested on charges of selling war maps featuring Siberian military sites. The maps were sent to General Semenoff, anti-Bolshevik leader in Siberia.
	A *Includes developments that affect more than one world region, international organizations and important meetings of world leaders.*	B *Includes all domestic and regional developments in Europe, including the Soviet Union.*	C *Includes all domestic and regional developments in Africa and the Middle East.*	D *Includes all domestic and regional developments in Latin America, the Caribbean, and Canada.*	E *Includes all domestic and regional developments in Asian and Pacific nations (and colonies).*

U.S. Politics & Social Issues	U.S. Foreign Policy & Affairs, Defense	U.S. Economy & Environment	Science, Technology & Nature	Culture, Leisure & Lifestyle	
Race riots in Chicago, IL injure many and kill two.... The Federal Water Power Act is passed.	The Italian government demands details surrounding the death of Andrea Salsedo, the suspected anarchist who mysteriously jumped from the Secret Service Offices while under supervision of the U.S. government.	Distribution of Victory Medals begins for all men who served in U.S. Army or U.S. Navy.			Jun. 20
The U.S. Anti-Saloon League attacks presidential candidate Governor Cox on ground that he will nullifying Eighteenth Amendment to the U.S. Constitution by allowing sales of alcohol.... A shortage of farm laborers will bring an increase in food costs this year.				The Retail Millinery Association in America announces ostrich feathers for hat trim will be all the rage in fall fashions.	Jun. 21
				American tennis players win all opening matches at the British lawn tennis championship without overt effort.	Jun. 22
The New York City Schools Superintendent makes an appeal to teachers to study over the summer break to advance teaching skills.... The Northern Baptist Convention votes to withdraw from the Interchurch World Movement.				Bathing suit manufacturers ask for clarification of a law banning one-piece bathing suits from public beaches. Combination two-piece suits with a longer skirt may not be included under the regulations.... The New York Metropolitan Museum of Art announces the purchase of an altar piece by Girolamo del Libri from the Church of San Leonardo located near Verona, Italy.	Jun. 23
		Judge A.T. Ayers of Topeka, KS, with the approval of state officials, demands that copies of a court injunction be distributed throughout the state's wheat growing regions warning workers against membership in the International Workers of the World (I.W.W.).... A share distribution plan is announced for American shareholders of Shell Transport and Trading Company.	The introduction of the Typophonia, an invention by Vienna Dr. Max Herz, allows visually challenged people to read through touch and hear phonographic recordings of sound.	French tennis player Andre Gobert is defeated by Zenzo Shimidzu of Japan at the British lawn tennis championship (Wimbledon).... The Olympic Committee rules that athletes from India may run without shoes in contests.... Cherokee Bill, a 123-year-old Native American, celebrates his birthday in Grand Junction, CO.	Jun. 24
The directors of the Permanent Blind Relief War Fund for Soldiers and Sailors of the Allies, Inc. announce the donation of more than 18,000 books to the fund.		The President of the Brotherhood of Railway Trainmen, W.G. Lee, invites walkout delegates to return to the Brotherhood after 15,000 were removed in actions to punish unauthorized strikers.... Western Maryland Railroad places an embargo on all goods due to a switchmen walkout in Hagerstown, MD.... Railroad yardmen are given arrest warrants at a meeting in San Francisco for strike actions in April, citing a violation of the Lever Food Act.... The Cotton Belt Yardmen's Association is disbanded in Pine Bluff, AR, with all yardmen returning to work.	Two Alaskan earthquakes rock an area 100 miles north of Anchorage, the first one at 4:41 p.m.	American film companies announce that more than 75 percent of the films shown in United Kingdom are made by U.S. companies.... Author Daisy Ashford releases a collection of her novels, including *The Young Visitors* and *The Jealous Governess*, represented by the printing firm George H. Doran Company.	Jun. 25
The first woman, A.A. Adams, is appointed as a sub-Cabinet member in the U.S. federal government.... U.S. sponsors announce plans to fund a home for British war orphans.	Rear Admiral Benton C. Decker, commander of the Seventh Naval District in Florida, attacks Secretary of the Navy Daniels and Assistant Secretary of the Navy Roosevelt charging both with failure to listen to advice from Navy officers, and later retaliation against them in appointments and advancement.... The Annapolis Academy will conduct another entrance examination in August. Numbers applying for entrance are usually filled in June, but classes are now in need of 400 students.... Cases of tuberculosis on military bases and training facilities are widespread.	The American Automobile Association announces after inspection that the Lincoln Highway, between New York and Philadelphia, is not fit for auto travel. The AAA recommends motorists avoid the road for any long-distance travel.... Beef prices are near record levels.... The cost of building homes rises to near record levels.... Two million dollars in gold from the Transvaal arrives on the Cunard ship *Mauretania* in port in New York City.	John L. Larsen, a licensed manufacturer responsible for introducing the all-metal airplane to the United States, touts the utility and economy of the planes to withstand weather without the need for hangars.	New York City School of Commerce junior Lou Gehrig receives first national attention for his grand slam home run in the eighth inning today against Lane Tech of Chicago. Scouts sit up and take notice at the Chicago park later to be called Wrigley Field.... The *New York Daily News* is published for the first time.... Ten thousand attend the National Symphony Orchestra opening concert at City College Stadium in New York City.... Designers at New York City Basic Style Show's Blouse Show put on by the United Waist League of America announce the success of the event, and that fall shirt shipments will feature three-quarter and full-length sleeves.	Jun. 26
F *Includes campaigns, elections, federal-state relations, civil rights and liberties, crime, the judiciary, education, healthcare, poverty, urban affairs, and population.*	G *Includes formation and debate of U.S. foreign and defense policies, veterans affairs, and defense spending. (Relations with specific foreign countries are usually found under the region concerned.)*	H *Includes business, labor, agriculture, taxation, transportation, consumer affairs, monetary and fiscal policy, natural resources, pollution and industrial accidents.*	I *Includes worldwide scientific, medical and technological developments, natural phenomena, U.S. weather and natural disasters.*	J *Includes the arts, religion, scholarship, communications media, sports, entertainment, fashions, fads, and social life.*	

	World Affairs	Europe	Africa & The Middle East	The Americas	Asia & The Pacific
Jun. 27		The Commercial Attaché at Madrid reports to the U.S. Department of Commerce that a free port at Bilbao will be opened soon.			Representatives from northern and southern Chinese provinces announce progress in Shanghai negotiations for unification.
Jun. 28		The Irish rail strike spreads to more lines as a troop train from Dublin-to-Cork is left by workers when British troops board.			
Jun. 29	The President of the Executive Council of the League of Nations, Leon Bourgeois, announces the German government would be invited to send delegates to the financial conference held in Brussels on July 23.	Violence escalates in Erivan, Armenia since British troops pulled out on June 17....Italian Premier Giolitti states his country will recognize the independence of Albania, despite his refusal to endorse a Socialist motion demanding the withdrawal of troops from the territory.		The former Mexican Army uniform is deemed comic looking by President de la Huerta, who claims he will personally pay for new, more distinguished, officer uniforms.	Troops capture Yuen Chow, under control of north China forces, after fierce fighting.
Jun. 30	Liberia and Haiti are admitted to the League of Nations....General Commissioner of the American Red Cross Mission in Albania, Colonel Olds, orders members to leave the military zone fearing for the lives of the volunteers....The League Advisory Committee on the High Court of Nations considers the rights of nonmember countries and agrees on five classes of cases that could be submitted.	The Albanian city of Avlona is taken from the Italians by independent Albanian fighters. Italian troops were also taken by insurgents....A bomb explodes in the Valencia offices of the Spanish newspaper *Diario Valencia*....Albanian government officials report the murder of Essad Pasha on June 13 was the result of a family vendetta. Assassin Avni Rustem was the nephew of Minster Nedjati Bey, who purportedly was killed on Essad Pasha's orders five years ago.		The newly organized Mexican government negotiates a settlement with the Yaqui Indian residents after decades of unrest....President-elect of Paraguay, Manuel Gondra, arrives for a visit in New York. Gondra had been the representative from his country in Washington, D.C. The inauguration is planned for August 15....The Mexico City newspaper, *El Democrata*, reports that American capital invested in Mexican oil production totals $600 million....Ship lightermen in Tampico strike, demanding Closed Shop for workers.	
Jul. 1	Don Jaime of Bourbon, son of the late Don Carlos and pretender to the Spanish throne, arrives in Bogota.	Representatives from England, France, and Italy meet in Brussels to discuss German war reparations....Germany delivers the L-71 Zeppelin to the British in compliance with the terms of the Peace Treaty....A women's suffrage bill is defeated in Belgium's Chamber of Deputies.	Sir Herbert Samuel, the first British High Commissioner for Palestine, arrives in Jaffa and proceeds by special train to Jerusalem.	Canadian Prime Minister Sir Robert Borden announces retirement from public life due to ill health....Don Fernando Iglesias Calderon, special commissioner from Mexico, meets with acting U.S. Secretary of State Norman P. Davis to discuss relations between the two governments....The Hawaiian Labor Association calls off the strike of sugar plantation workers on the Hawaiian Islands after nearly six months.	The American Legation at Peking reports that the Chinese Foreign Office has expressed regret for the killing of American missionary Dr. W.A. Reimart by General Chang-Ching-Yao's troops.
Jul. 2	An inter-allied conference is held in Brussels, Belgium, to formulate a program for the upcoming Spa Conference....Delegates from Venezuela and Colombia present reports to the Swiss commission chosen to arbitrate a boundary dispute between the two South American countries.	Allied representatives meeting in Brussels agree on a sum of six billion pounds for German war reparations, but fail to reach agreement on the allotment of reparations....The Ukrainian government relocates from Kamenetz-Podolsk to Lublin, southeast of Warsaw....More Greek troops land at Panderma to assist in the capture of the Panderma-Smyrna Railroad.		Uruguay receives a check for $10 million in gold from the British government as the first installment on debt repayment....The Mexican government announces General Arnulfo R. Gomez's defeat of insurgent forces led by Carlos Osuna.	Part of an Irish regiment stationed in the Punjab, India, mutinies after learning of recent events in Ireland....The Treaty for the Mutual Surrender of Fugitive Criminals, signed by Great Britain and Switzerland in 1880, is extended to the Federated Malay States.
Jul. 3	The International Committee of the Red Cross at Geneva bestows the Florence Nightingale Medal on 41 nurses, including six Americans.	The Allied premiers decide to readmit Germany into the council of the nations of Europe....The Dutch Parliament approves a loan of $80 million to Germany....Switzerland reports a critical housing shortage....Fighting erupts between Italian and Greek troops near Ajasoluk on the Aidin Railroad, southeast of Smyrna.		The Brazilian delegation to the Olympic games sails for Antwerp....Provisional Mexican President Adolfo de la Huerta sends an Independence Day message of cordiality to U.S. President Wilson.	The Japanese government announces its decision to occupy territory in the Saghalien province of Siberia pending a satisfactory settlement for the massacre of 700 Japanese at Nikolaievsk....Chinese President Hsu Shiu Chang nominates Chow-Shumu as premier.
	A *Includes developments that affect more than one world region, international organizations and important meetings of world leaders.*	B *Includes all domestic and regional developments in Europe, including the Soviet Union.*	C *Includes all domestic and regional developments in Africa and the Middle East.*	D *Includes all domestic and regional developments in Latin America, the Caribbean, and Canada.*	E *Includes all domestic and regional developments in Asian and Pacific nations (and colonies).*

U.S. Politics & Social Issues	U.S. Foreign Policy & Affairs, Defense	U.S. Economy & Environment	Science, Technology & Nature	Culture, Leisure & Lifestyle	
Federal prohibition agents of the Treasury Department confiscate 35,000 gallons of liquor worth over $1 million in New England ports.... Go to School drives are planned for summer, encouraging non-English speakers in New York City to learn the English language.		U.S. grain reserves are reported to be $31 million....H.W.A. Deterding, head of the Royal Dutch-Shell group, and American Standard Oil fight to control oil market....The Anglo-Persian Company purchases Scottish-American Oil and Transport Company.	Dr. Charles Norris, Chief Medical Examiner of the City of New York, advocates photographing the retinas of the dead to record the last image for criminal prosecution.	The intercollegiate golf title is won by Jess Sweetser of Yale University.	Jun. 27
The First Democratic National Convention is held in San Francisco, the first in the western United States. The Democratic National Convention agrees to adopt a party platform that includes ratification of the Treaty of Versailles after hearing President Woodrow Wilson's appeal at the convention.					Jun. 28
The Democratic National Convention in San Francisco, CA, ends the second session with the Palmer delegation from Georgia seated and a refusal to admit Senator Reed from Missouri. The decision was also made to ban voting delegates as a unit vote. The greatest change was the ruling that all future state delegations would be composed of one man and one woman from each state. Mrs. Alice Foster McCullough of Fort Wayne, IN proposed the resolution.		Armin W. Riley, Special Assistant to U.S. Attorney General Palmer and head of the Flying Squadron of the Department of Justice, sends agents into Chicago and other cities in the Midwest to investigate charges of sugar speculation by brokers and unscrupulous investors.	After a lengthy investigation by the U.S. District Attorney Leroy W. Ross, a Federal Grand Jury issued indictments for more than 2,000 men who failed to appear for military duty in New York. Additional indictments are expected for three types of offenses: failure to complete a questionnaire, failure to obtain a draft board physical, and failure to report for induction at a draft board. Those in the last category will be turned over for court martial on the grounds of desertion.	The French invite members of the Aero Clubs (Air Clubs) in France and the United States to the government-sponsored unveiling of a monument to American aviator Wilbur Wright in Le Mans, France on July 17.	Jun. 29
Senator Warren G. Harding, presidential candidate for the Republican Party; Governor Calvin Coolidge, vice presidential candidate; and Will H. Hays, Chair of the Republican National Committee, meet for the first time since the national convention to determine strategy. Harding states that their campaign will stress party government over personal gain.	Arrests are made by U.S. Treasury Secret Service agents of workers at the War Risk Insurance Bureau on charges of defrauding disabled soldiers by offering them cash now in exchange for a future split on federal government benefits....U.S. Customs receipts break all records.			Olympic Committee members and the presidents of baseball ask individual ballpark owners to collect funds from fans at games on July 5 to fund the transportation of U.S. Olympic team members to Anterwp.	Jun. 30
Bartolomeo Vanzetti is convicted for his alleged role in the Bridgewater robbery....Louisiana rejects the Nineteenth Amendment....A federal prohibition agent reveals a widespread bootlegging conspiracy surrounding the recently murdered Joseph B. Elwell....Coal miners in Kentucky and West Virginia go on strike.	Benedict Crowell retires as Assistant Secretary of War....Marine Lieutenant Herman H. Hanneken and Corporal William R. Button are awarded Congressional Medals of Honor for their service in Haiti.	The federal grand jury indicts the brokerage firm of Blum, Reynolds, & Co. on charges of defrauding oil investors....Elevator inspectors and electrical engineers join the other 2,000 municipal workers already on strike in Chicago....The 3,000 employees of the New Orleans Railway and Light Company go on strike.	William Dutcher, founder and President of the National Association of Audubon Societies, dies.	Charles S. Garland of Pittsburgh and Richard Norris Williams II of Boston win the semi-finals of the men's doubles competition at Wimbledon.	Jul. 1
After prolonged debate, the Resolutions Committee of the Democratic National Convention decides to omit any definite statement on prohibition from the party platform....New York's acting governor, Harry C. Walker, orders an investigation into alleged gambling in Saratoga Springs.	The War Department announces the appointment of Colonel Jesse McIlvaine Carter as chief of the Militia Bureau.	A federal grand jury indicts Roulston-Beckert & Co., Inc., and its president Andrew Roulston on charges of sugar profiteering.	An earthquake hits Jamaica, but no major damage is reported.	The New York Giants release infielder Edward J. Sicking to the Cincinnati Reds....The Giants trade outfielder Benny Kauff for Toronto's Vernon Spencer....New York journalist William H. Muldoon dies at 73.	Jul. 2
New York's Socialist Party opens its state convention....Police arrest 12 crewmembers in connection with the looting of the steamship *Belgic*....Missouri Republicans ask Jacob L. Babler and W.L. Cole to resign from their respective positions as Republican National Committeeman and Chairman of the Republican State Committee.	Major General William C. Gorgas, former Surgeon General of the U.S. Army, dies in London....Retired Chief of Army Engineers, Brigadier General William L. Marshall, dies.	A train wreck near South Pittston Station in Pennsylvania kills 35 people and injures 60 others....Poor market conditions force shoe factories in Lynn, MA to shut down for two weeks, leaving 4,000 employees temporarily out of work.	A Swiss airplane firm announces the invention of a silencer for airplane engines.	Bill Tilden becomes the first American to win the men's singles title at Wimbledon.... Several prominent U.S. clergymen sail for Europe in an effort to strengthen the ties of international church friendship....Swimmer Ethelda Bleibtrey breaks the world record for 500 yards and the American record for 300 yards.	Jul. 3
F *Includes campaigns, elections, federal-state relations, civil rights and liberties, crime, the judiciary, education, healthcare, poverty, urban affairs, and population.*	G *Includes formation and debate of U.S. foreign and defense policies, veterans affairs, and defense spending. (Relations with specific foreign countries are usually found under the region concerned.)*	H *Includes business, labor, agriculture, taxation, transportation, consumer affairs, monetary and fiscal policy, natural resources, pollution and industrial accidents.*	I *Includes worldwide scientific, medical and technological developments, natural phenomena, U.S. weather and natural disasters.*	J *Includes the arts, religion, scholarship, communications media, sports, entertainment, fashions, fads, and social life.*	

	World Affairs	Europe	Africa & The Middle East	The Americas	Asia & The Pacific
Jul. 4	The Rev. Dr. J.W. Vankirk, originator of the "world's flag" adopted by the Hague and the Peace Conference at Paris, begins his third pilgrimage around the world.	A new 14-member cabinet is formed in Vienna....Spain reduces the requirement for active military service to two years....Rioting takes place in the mining region of Huelva, Spain.	Egyptian nationalist leader Abdel Rahman Fahmi is arrested.	Complete returns for the June Presidential election in Chile show Arturo Alessandri of the Liberal Alliance the victor by a narrow margin....The Mexican Secretary of the Treasury prohibits the exportation of sugar.	General Hsu Chu-cheng is relieved of his posts as Resident Commissioner of Inner Mongolia and commander on the northwestern frontier.
Jul. 5	The sixth Lambeth Conference of the Anglican Church opens in London, with 270 bishops and archbishops from around the globe in attendance.	The Spa Conference to discuss the payment of German war reparations opens in Belgium. The first session is abruptly adjourned, as Germany is unprepared first to discuss disarmament....A general strike is underway in Ancona, Italy, since June 26 is called off....The Schleswig Treaty returning the northern zone in Schleswig to Danish sovereignty is signed....Turkish Nationalist troops occupy Beicos, about 10 miles from Constantinople.	The formation of a new Persian Cabinet under Premier Mochir-ed-Dowleh is announced.	In an effort to discourage emigration, Mexican President de la Huerta promises safeguards to Mexican workers.	
Jul. 6	The Root-Phillmore plan is accepted for the selection of judges for the International Court of Justice.	The Allied representatives at Spa threaten to adjourn the conference unless the German delegates present a definite statement of how Germany will meet the disarmament terms of the treaty.		Provisional Mexican President de la Huerta abolishes movie censorship....Judge Alberto M. Gonzales, an Associate Justice on the Supreme Court of Mexico, arrives in Washington as part of a special mission to pursue U.S. recognition of the new Mexican government.	
Jul. 7	The International Zionist Conference convenes in London....The International Seamen's Conference, meeting in Genoa, adopts an amendment providing for the strict enforcement of a 48-hour week for seamen.			The Hon. Arthur Meighen is chosen to succeed Sir Robert Borden as Canada's Prime Minister....Mexican bandit Francisco Villa offers a conditional surrender....Leon Giuliani, the Belgian Minister to Peru, dies at sea of pneumonia.	Japan's foreign minister announces his government's decision not to negotiate with the Siberian government for the creation of a "buffer state."...At a mass meeting in Hiroshima, a resolution is passed protesting against the anti-Japanese movement in California.
Jul. 8		The Polish National Council of Defense issues a manifesto requesting volunteers for immediate service against the advancing Russian Bolshevik forces....The Allied powers meeting at Spa grant Germany a six-month extension to fulfill the disarmament terms of the Versailles treaty.	Nineteen-year-old Ibrahim Massoud is executed in Cairo for his June 12 attempt to assassinate Egyptian Premier Tewfik Nessim Pasha.	Sir Lomer Gouln resigns as Premier of Quebec....President Hipólito Irigoyen of Argentina limits further exportations of wheat to 500,000 tons.	
Jul. 9	The League of Nations Council opens its seventh session in London....League of Nations representative Fridtjof Nansen arrives in Moscow to negotiate with the Soviet government for the repatriation of foreigners and Russian prisoners abroad.	The northern zone of North Schleswig is officially incorporated into Denmark....Greek forces seize Brusa....Germany and Switzerland sign a commercial treaty....German delegates at the Spa Conference sign a disarmament agreement.	Persia reports new landings of Bolshevik troops at several ports on the Caspian Sea.	The Mexican government rejects the peace proposals of Francisco Villa....Roberto V. Pesquiera is appointed Mexican financial agent to the United States....L.A. Taschereau, Attorney General of Quebec, is sworn in as Premier of that province.	Panic grows in Peking as militarist leaders gain ground....The Diplomatic Corps in Peking warns the government that, in case of an uprising, no fighting must take place in Peking.
Jul. 10	The seamen's convention fails to gain a two-thirds majority at the international labor conference in Genoa.	Professor Israel Friedlander and Rabbi Bernard Cantor, both relief workers with the American Joint Distribution Committee, are killed in Ukraine....A force of 700 Russian prisoners of war escapes from an internment camp near Turnhout, Belgium, and marches upon Antwerp.		The Canadian province of New Brunswick decides by referendum to retain wartime prohibition laws....The Hon. Arthur Meighen is sworn in as Canadian Prime Minister.	An estimated 100 people are drowned and 4,500 houses flooded when the River Han overflows in Seoul, Korea....The Japanese government receives a vote of confidence by a large majority of the House of Representatives.
Jul. 11		Eugénie María de Montijo, the wife of Napoleon III and former Empress of France, dies in Madrid....Plebiscites are held in East Prussia to determine whether the residents of Allenstein and Marienwerder will remain German or become Polish....Soviet troops occupy Minsk.	Diamonds are discovered near Nairobi, British East Africa....A dispatch from Teheran to the *London Times* reports disturbances in Lower Mesopotamia and adds that the Basra-Baghdad line has been cut in three places.	A general strike begins in Tampico, Mexico under the direction of the I.W.W....Guatemala imposes a higher tax on sugar exports....The National Liberal Convention in Cuba nominates General José Miguel Gomez for president of Cuba.... Rebels cut the railway line between Mexico City and Nuevo Laredo at Santa Elena.	Troop movements are reported near Peking. Minor skirmishes occur between military factions on the outskirts, but the city itself remains quiet.

A	B	C	D	E
Includes developments that affect more than one world region, international organizations and important meetings of world leaders.	*Includes all domestic and regional developments in Europe, including the Soviet Union.*	*Includes all domestic and regional developments in Africa and the Middle East.*	*Includes all domestic and regional developments in Latin America, the Caribbean, and Canada.*	*Includes all domestic and regional developments in Asian and Pacific nations (and colonies).*

U.S. Politics & Social Issues	U.S. Foreign Policy & Affairs, Defense	U.S. Economy & Environment	Science, Technology & Nature	Culture, Leisure & Lifestyle	
One man is shot and another stabbed seven times in a Brooklyn race riot....Joseph D. Cannon is nominated as Socialist candidate for Governor of New York.		The Department of Agriculture warns against the use of canning powders....Harry Wilfred Du Puy, President of the Pennsylvania Rubber Company and son of Pittsburgh capitalist Herbert Du Puy, dies.		Golfer R. H. Boyd wins the Governors' Cup....The Boston Red Sox acquire outfielder Benjamin Paschal.	Jul. 4
James Spencer, a black postal clerk charged with stabbing a white coworker, is lynched in Mississippi....In a speech delivered from his front porch in Marion, OH, Senator Warren G. Harding, Republican nominee for President, urges a return to "normality."	Lieutenant Pat Logan is fatally injured when his plane crashes in an exhibition flight.			The Elks Club's National Convention opens in Chicago....The Grand Circuit harness horse-racing season opens at the North Randall racetrack in Ohio....Ethelda Bleibfrey adds the national one-mile title to her list of swimming accolades.	Jul. 5
The Democratic Party nominates James M. Cox for president and Franklin D. Roosevelt for vice president....Irving and Herman Arthur, two black men charged with killing their landlord and his son, are burned at the stake by a Texas mob.				The 15th annual convention of the National League of Masonic Clubs opens in New York City.	Jul. 6
A mob takes Ed Roach, arrested on charges of attacking a 13-year-old white girl, from the county jail in Roxboro, NC, and lynches him in a nearby churchyard....Escaped convict Fred Canafex is shot to death by a mob of white farmers near Centerville, MO.	A radio compass apparatus is used for the first time to guide a naval aircraft to a battleship at sea and then back to base....The U.S. government lifts all restrictions against trade with the Soviets, except for the ban on shipping war materials to Russia.	Employees of the Borderland Coal Company in Mingo County, KY, are fired upon as they attempt to enter the coal mine....Three packing companies and a sugar company are indicted in Boston on charges of food profiteering.	Isolated cases of bubonic plague are reported in Pensacola, FL and Port Arthur, TX.	Play begins in the Masters' chess tournament in Atlantic City....Dr. Lynn Harold Hough resigns as President of Northwestern University.... Classicist Thomas Dwight Goodell of Yale University dies....Babe Ruth escapes injury when his car goes off the road.	Jul. 7
The Louisiana legislature refuses to ratify the Federal Suffrage Amendment....Proceedings are filed in the Kansas Supreme Court against 38 wholesale grocery concerns charged with violating state antitrust laws.		The New England Commissioners of Foreign and Domestic Commerce appoint a committee to appeal to the federal government regarding the coal shortage....Eleven coal mines in Illinois are closed because miners refuse to work at the present wages.	Eleven cases of bubonic plague are reported in Texas.	The Davis Cup tournament begins.	Jul. 8
Herman W. Beyer announces his candidacy for the Republican nomination for Secretary of State....Jury selection is completed in the trial of William Bross Lloyd and nineteen other members of the Communist Labor Party for alleged conspiracy to overthrow the government by force.	Brigadier General Frank T. Hines, chief of the War Department's Bureau of Transportation, is selected to head the Inland and Coastwise Waterways Service established under the new Transportation Act.	The Department of Agriculture forecasts higher than average production in the nation's principal farm crops....The governors of Minnesota, Iowa, Wisconsin, North Dakota, and South Dakota appeal to President Wilson to appoint a federal fuel administration.		The appellate division of the Supreme Court dismisses charges against Harper & Brothers for publishing the novel *Madeleine*....John D. Rockefeller celebrates his 81st birthday.	Jul. 9
The convention of the Committee of Forty-eight, called to form a third party, opens in Chicago.... Prohibition officers arrest 35 people and confiscate about 150 gallons of liquor in Aurora, IL.	General Peyton C. March, Chief of Staff of the U.S. Army, receives the Distinguished Service Cross for an act of bravery performed while in action in the Philippines in 1898.... The Pennsylvania Railroad hands out 2,945 war medals to employees who served in the world war, or to their next of kin.			Competition begins in the national clay court tennis championship tournament in Chicago.	Jul. 10
The New York State Supreme Court reverses a wrongful death verdict against Dr. Arthur N. Bauman, D.D.S. when expert witnesses recant their testimony....Julius Maler, a fugitive from Sing Sing prison for 15 years, is recaptured.		Approximately 3,000 bituminous coal miners go on strike in Johnstown, PA.	Dr. Winthrop J.V. Osterhout joins the Board of Scientific Directors for the Rockefeller Institute for Medical Research.	The nation's leading track and field athletes compete in the Legion Games held at Ebbets Field in Brooklyn....Daredevil Charles Stephens from Bristol, England, perishes while attempting to go over Niagara Falls in a barrel....Cyclist J.D. Freeman of St. Louis sets a new speed record in the final Olympic tryout.	Jul. 11
F *Includes campaigns, elections, federal-state relations, civil rights and liberties, crime, the judiciary, education, healthcare, poverty, urban affairs, and population.*	G *Includes formation and debate of U.S. foreign and defense policies, veterans affairs, and defense spending. (Relations with specific foreign countries are usually found under the region concerned.)*	H *Includes business, labor, agriculture, taxation, transportation, consumer affairs, monetary and fiscal policy, natural resources, pollution and industrial accidents.*	I *Includes worldwide scientific, medical and technological developments, natural phenomena, U.S. weather and natural disasters.*	J *Includes the arts, religion, scholarship, communications media, sports, entertainment, fashions, fads, and social life.*	

	World Affairs	Europe	Africa & The Middle East	The Americas	Asia & The Pacific
Jul. 12		The Soviet government recognizes Lithuanian independence through the Treaty of Moscow, thus ending Lithuania's participation in the Russian Civil War....Bolshevik Minister of Trade and Commerce M. Krassin returns to London....The Allies issue an ultimatum to the German delegates at Spa, demanding the delivery of two million tons of coal per month to the Allies.... Ulster Unionist Sir Edward Carson threatens to reorganize the Ulster Volunteers.		The Panama Canal is formally opened....A coup d'état topples Bolivian President José Gutiérrez Guerra.	
Jul. 13	Great Britain and Japan notify the League of Nations that they have prolonged their treaty alliance for a year.	Following an unsatisfactory German reply to the coal ultimatum, Allied statesmen suspend the Spa Conference and summon military chiefs Marshal Foch and Sir Henry Wilson....Anti-Slav demonstrations in Trieste result in three deaths, scores of injuries, and damage in excess of $1 million.		Canadian Prime Minister Arthur Meighen announces the selection of his Cabinet.	
Jul. 14		The German delegates at Spa accept the Allies' coal terms at the last minute, under the threat of immediate Allied occupation of the Ruhr basin....The flag is stolen from the French embassy in Berlin....British police arrest Bolshevik emissary Santeri Nuorteva and arrange for his deportation.	The French send a 24-hour ultimatum to King Feisal of Syria, demanding his acquiescence in the French mandate for Syria and the adoption of French as the official language.	Forces under General Irene Villareal capture two military barracks before being driven out of Monterey....Ten thousand workers in the petroleum fields around Tampico go on strike....Chile mobilizes approximately 10,000 reserve troops in its northern provinces, but the Chilean War Minister denies any hostile designs.	
Jul. 15	President Wilson issues a call for the first meeting of the Assembly of the League of Nations, to be held in Geneva on November 15.... Associate Justice Louis D. Brandeis, head of the American Zionist delegation, refuses to serve on the executive committee of the Zionist World Conference.	Red Army troops regain control of Vilna from the Lithuanians.... Communication via telegraph, telephone, and mail is cut off between Adrianople and Constantinople.... One American is reported killed and another missing in the battle between the Poles and the Russian Bolsheviks near Minsk....Turkish Nationalists virtually wipe out the Greek village of Fouladjik.	The French open hostilities against Syria, with one column moving against Aleppo and another against Damascus.	The Bolivian Minister to the United States, Ignacio Calderon, resigns his position in protest against the recent coup d'état in Bolivia.... General Pablo Gonzalez is captured near Monterey along with Brigadier Generals Carlos Garcia and José Santos.	Peking informs the U.S. State Department that General Chang Tsolin, Military Inspector of Manchuria, intends to occupy Peking.
Jul. 16	The League of Nations admits China as a member state....The World Y.M.C.A. Congress held in Geneva closes.	The exchange of ratifications of the Treaty of St. Germain, which establishes peace between the Allies and Austria, takes place at the French Foreign Office. ...The Spa Conference ends at 9 p.m., when the Germans sign the Allied coal terms. The question of reparations is referred to a commission.		A special committee is formed under Ernest L. Bogart, Assistant Foreign Trade Advisor of the U.S. State Department, to remedy the acute port congestion in Havana.... Daniel Waters is appointed Trade Commissioner for Lima, Peru.	Fighting occurs between rival factions 30 miles south of Peking.
Jul. 17		The Allied powers threaten to oust Turkey from Europe if the Turks fail to sign the peace treaty and put it into effect within 10 days....IRA gunmen assassinate Commissioner Gerard B. Ferguson Smyth of the Royal Irish Constabulary....Prince Joachim, the youngest son of former Kaiser Wilhelm, commits suicide.	The Bedouin tribes of northern Mesopotamia form a coalition against the French.	Members of the Canadian Railway Board meet with the Interstate Commerce Commission in Washington, DC....The Colombian government sends a group of engineers and laborers to the San Jorge district to exploit the coal mines of that region....Chilean Warships arrive in Arica.	Martial law is proclaimed in Peking....A machine gun battle takes place on the outskirts of Hankow between the Anfu troops of Wu-Kwang-Hsin, recently appointed Military Governor of Honan, and the forces of Wang-Chan-Yuen, Military Governor of Hupeh.
Jul. 18		Two men are killed and 40 injured in street fighting in Cork....Djemal Pasha, Minister of Public Works, and Fahreddine Bey, Minister of Education, both resign from the Turkish Cabinet.	King Feisal of Syria orders a general mobilization in reply to the French ultimatum that he recognize the French mandate of Syria.	The Mexican government recognizes the new Bolivian government.... General Jesus M. Guajardo, who revolted against the de la Huerta government in June, is executed at daybreak....The Democrats and Unionists in Guatemala both select Carlos Herrera as their presidential candidate for the upcoming election.	The Japanese in Nikolsk prepare for an immediate evacuation of Trans-Balkalkia.

A	B	C	D	E
Includes developments that affect more than one world region, international organizations and important meetings of world leaders.	*Includes all domestic and regional developments in Europe, including the Soviet Union.*	*Includes all domestic and regional developments in Africa and the Middle East.*	*Includes all domestic and regional developments in Latin America, the Caribbean, and Canada.*	*Includes all domestic and regional developments in Asian and Pacific nations (and colonies).*

U.S. Politics & Social Issues	U.S. Foreign Policy & Affairs, Defense	U.S. Economy & Environment	Science, Technology & Nature	Culture, Leisure & Lifestyle	
James T. Newton resigns as Commissioner of Patents.... Governor Percival W. Clement of Vermont refuses to call the legislature in special session to make possible the ratification of the suffrage amendment.	The first annual convention and reunion of the 42nd Infantry "Rainbow" Division veterans opens in Birmingham....Colonel George Van Orden, former Commander of Marines at Tours, France, is awarded the French Order of the Black Star.	In New York City, 1,000 longshoremen stage a walkout rather than handle goods delivered to the piers on nonunion trucks....Frank Trumbell, head of the Chesapeake & Ohio Railroad, dies of heart disease.		The final Olympic tryouts for boxing are held New York City....The St. Louis Cardinals acquire pitcher Mike Kircher from Richmond....Novelist Julie Cruger, who wrote under the pen name of Julien Gordon, dies....The Cincinnati Reds acquire first baseman Fred Luderus from the Philadelphia Nationals.	Jul. 12
The Single Tax Party nominates newspaper reporter Bob MacAuley from Pennsylvania for president.		New York City patrolmen and firemen demand a salary increase.	Swarms of grasshoppers invade Traverse City, MI.	Boxers Eddie Eagan and Bill Spengler qualify for the U.S. Olympic team....Pitcher George Lowe joins the Cincinnati Nationals....New York City architecture student P. McLaughlin, Jr., wins the Paris Prize of the Society of Beaux Arts Architects.	Jul. 13
The Single Tax Party nominates Robert C. MacAuley for president....Eleven alleged Communists from points west of Chicago are sent to Ellis Island for deportation....The Third Party adopts its platform.	Government buildings in Washington, DC display the French Tri-Color in recognition of Bastille Day.	Buyers from all over the United States assemble in New York City for the Fall Fashion Fête, hosted by the National Garment Retailers Association....A lifejacket from the *Lusitania* is discovered in the Delaware River....Oil is discovered in southern Alaska.		Final selections are made for the U.S. Olympic team in all sports but track and field....Opera singer Claire Dux is seriously injured in an automobile accident....Victor H. Potachek resigns as publisher of the *Sun* and the *New York Herald*.	Jul. 14
The Farmer-Labor Party nominates Parley Christensen for president and Max Hayes for vice president....Texas Governor W.P. Hobby suspends the board of city commissioners, the city attorney, and the police department of Galveston for alleged neglect of duty in connection with a prolonged strike of dockworkers....Ethelbert Stewart is appointed Commissioner of Labor Statistics.	The Committee for Aid to Disabled Soldiers meets to formulate a plan for the care of 641,900 disabled ex-servicemen....Four army airplanes embark on an expedition to Nome, AK....Veterans of the 3rd Division, A.E.F. convene in Chicago.	Trade in wheat futures reopens after a three-year suspension....Nearly the entire Memphis fire department resigns when a pay raise is refused....The trial begins for the C.A. Weed Company, Buffalo clothiers, charged with 21 counts of profiteering....Three hundred electrical engineers go on strike in Chicago.	Scientists at the College of Technology in Manchester, England, announce the discovery of a new process by which rubber can be vulcanized without being heated....A 50-foot long petrified fish is found incased in the rocks in Garfield county, Utah.	*Shamrock IV* wins the first race in the America's Cup series; *Resolute* fails to finish the race after sustaining damage to her mainsail halyard....Miss Helen Taft, daughter of the former President, marries Frederick Johnson Manning, a history instructor at Yale.	Jul. 15
Bomb plot suspect Roberto Elia is ordered deported.	Major General Amos A. Fries is appointed chief of the U.S. Army's chemical warfare service....Miss Julia C. Stimson of New York City is appointed Superintendent of the Army Nurse Corps....President Wilson appoints seven new Major Generals and 22 new Brigadier Generals for the regular army.	Six thousand mine workers with the Pennsylvania Coal Company go on strike....The Interstate Commerce Commission warns the railroads to refrain from confiscating coal consigned to government departments and other public utilities.	Four earthquakes cause near panic in Los Angeles and the surrounding suburbs....Salvadoran bacteriologist Dr. Peralta Lagos claims to have isolated the microorganism that causes yellow fever.	Babe Ruth becomes the first player to hit 30 home runs in a season.... The United States defeats Australia in five straight matches to win the Davis Cup.	Jul. 16
A "flying squadron" of 25 federal prohibition agents raids 12 saloons in Homestead, PA and confiscates 800 gallons of whisky.			The Society for the Protection of New Hampshire Forests attempts to restock the White Mountain region with beaver.	Olympic tryouts are held in track and field....Famous Cornell rowing coach Charles E. Courtney dies....Chick Evans of Chicago wins the Western Amateur Golf Championship.	Jul. 17
Democratic Presidential nominee James M. Cox meets with President Wilson to discuss the League of Nations and other international affairs....North Carolina Governor Thomas Bickett orders National Guard protection for three prisoners threatened with lynching.	Memorial exercises are held for members of the Third (Marine) Division who died in service.	A 10 percent wage increase takes effect for approximately 3,500 employees of the New York Railways Company....The street car strike in Chicago is called off.	Storms sweep upstate New York, damaging crops and interrupting wire communication.	Eugene Bolden of Chicago wins the 10-mile national swimming championship for the second consecutive year....Roland Roberts wins the National Clay Court Tennis Championship....G.L. Thompson wins the President's Cup in golf.	Jul. 18

F	G	H	I	J
Includes campaigns, elections, federal-state relations, civil rights and liberties, crime, the judiciary, education, healthcare, poverty, urban affairs, and population.	*Includes formation and debate of U.S. foreign and defense policies, veterans affairs, and defense spending. (Relations with specific foreign countries are usually found under the region concerned.)*	*Includes business, labor, agriculture, taxation, transportation, consumer affairs, monetary and fiscal policy, natural resources, pollution and industrial accidents.*	*Includes worldwide scientific, medical and technological developments, natural phenomena, U.S. weather and natural disasters.*	*Includes the arts, religion, scholarship, communications media, sports, entertainment, fashions, fads, and social life.*

	World Affairs	Europe	Africa & The Middle East	The Americas	Asia & The Pacific
Jul. 19	The Second International Communist Congress opens in Petrograd, with representatives from 51 countries in attendance.	The Bolshevik Army advances into Armenia.... Czechoslovakian Foreign Minister Eduard Benes meets with the Allied Council of Ambassadors to discuss the Teschen dispute.... Jurors boycott the Court of Assizes in Cork.... Durrizailde Abdullah Effendi, Minister of Religion, resigns from the Turkish Cabinet.... Railway traffic is interrupted by fighting between the Greeks and Turks in the region of Adrianople.			
Jul. 20	The Executive Committee of the Olympic Games denies Ireland permission to participate in the upcoming Olympics as a separate nation.	Polish delegates appear before the Allied Council of Ambassadors to discuss Teschen.... The Soviet government rejects a British proposal for an armistice with Poland and refuses to send delegates to London for a peace conference.... The British government warns that if the Soviets advance further into Poland all negotiations for trade between Great Britain and the Soviet Union will be broken off.		General Pablo Gonzalez, charged with leading an abortive revolution in Nuevo Leon, is unconditionally released as no longer constituting a threat to the Mexican administration.... All Bolivian Ministers abroad are ordered to turn over the archives of their respective legations to the secretaries of the legations.	Peking estimates the casualties from recent fighting at 6,000.
Jul. 21		A tramway strike is declared in Rome, immediately on the heels of another strike that lasted several weeks.... Riots break out in Belfast shipyards and spread to the rest of the city.... London receives a report that Greeks forces, aided by the British fleet, have occupied Heraclea and Rodosto on the Sea of Marmora.			
Jul. 22		The French government lifts a ban prohibiting the importation of many articles from America, but increases custom duties on luxury items.... Rioting is renewed in the Falls area of West Belfast.... The Turkish Crown Council approves the signing of the peace treaty with the Allied Powers.	The French Foreign Office announces that Emir Faisal has accepted the terms of General Henri Gouraud's ultimatum, which includes recognition of the French mandate in Syria. Gouraud's troops continue to move forward, however, to occupy the main railroad line from Damascus to Aleppo.	Honduras reports that Vicente Mejia Colindres has resigned as Minister of Foreign affairs and will be replaced by Dr. Alberto Ucris.	
Jul. 23	The Zionist Conference in London concludes with the election of U.S. Supreme Court Justice Louis D. Brandeis as honorary President of the Zionist organization.... A wireless dispatch from Moscow reports that the Congress of the Third International at Moscow has appealed to Syria, Turkey, and Arabia to rise against the Allies. ... The U.S. team wins the finals of the Olympic team-trapshooting competition in Antwerp.	Dr. Milenko R. Vesnitch, who resigned earlier in the week as Premier of Serbia, is asked to form a new ministry.... A general strike in Rome is called off, and work resumes in all industries.... Turkish nationalist commander Colonel Jafar Tayar evacuates all noncombatants from Adrianople.... German officials arrest Rhineland Separatist leader Dr. Hans Dorten in the occupied territory, in violation of the Rhineland agreement.	British East Africa is renamed Kenya and its status is changed from protectorate to British crown colony.	A case of smallpox is reported in Jamaica.... Canadian Arnold Love confesses to having murdered his mother in 1912, a crime for which his father was hanged.	
Jul. 24	The United States takes the first five places in the Olympic individual trapshooting.	The Treaty of St. Germain takes effect.... The Soviet government suspends hostilities against Poland and begins negotiations for an armistice.		A general strike is called in Vera Cruz, Mexico, where workers demand a further wage increase of 100 percent.	Fighting ceases near Peking as the Anfu forces retreat and Tuan Chi-jui tenders his resignation as Generalissimo of the army.
Jul. 25	The Boy Scout Association opens its first World Jamboree at Olympia, London.	Greek forces capture Adrianople, the key Turkish fortress in Thrace.... The French, British, and Italian Ministers to Austria present their credentials to President Karl Seitz.... Fire breaks out in a Venice arsenal.... The Turkish Nationalist Congress in Angora denounces the peace terms accepted by the Constantinople government.	French forces occupy Damascus, forcing King Faisal to flee Syria.	Carlos Herrera is sworn in as constitutional President of Guatemala.	In Peking, President Hsu Shih-chang accepts the resignation of Tsang Yuchun, Minister of Communications; Li Shih-hal, Minister of Finance; and Chu-shen, Minister of Justice.... Charges of official corruption involving Ministers Takahashi, Yamamoto, and Nakahanhi, are brought before the Japanese Diet.
	A *Includes developments that affect more than one world region, international organizations and important meetings of world leaders.*	B *Includes all domestic and regional developments in Europe, including the Soviet Union.*	C *Includes all domestic and regional developments in Africa and the Middle East.*	D *Includes all domestic and regional developments in Latin America, the Caribbean, and Canada.*	E *Includes all domestic and regional developments in Asian and Pacific nations (and colonies).*

U.S. Politics & Social Issues	U.S. Foreign Policy & Affairs, Defense	U.S. Economy & Environment	Science, Technology & Nature	Culture, Leisure & Lifestyle	
Four men, including two officers, are killed during prohibition raids in Kentucky....National Guard machine gunners open fire on a crowd outside the jail in Graham, NC, killing one man and injuring two....Dr. Julius Hammer receives a sentence of 3½ to 15 years in prison for performing an illegal abortion that resulted in the death of Marie Oganesoff.		Union carpenters return to work in Pittsburgh after a strike that lasted several months....Employees of seven motion picture studios in Fort Lee, NJ, go on strike....Nine miners are trapped in a shaft explosion in Renton, PA....The Pennsylvania Railroad announces its decision to dismiss approximately 12,000 employees in order to reduce operating costs....The Fidelity Trust Company and the International Bank merge.	The largest and most powerful wireless station in the world is completed near Bordeaux....A sharp earthquake shock is felt in Los Angeles.	Babe Ruth hits his 30th and 31st homeruns of the season in a double-header against the White Sox.	Jul. 19
George White of Ohio becomes the Democratic National Chairman....Former heavyweight champion Jack Johnson, under sentence in Chicago for violating the Mann act, is arrested in San Diego and arraigned on federal charges as a fugitive from justice....New York State Controller Eugene M. Travis withdraws his candidacy for the Republican gubernatorial nomination.		The U.S. Senate Special Committee on Reconstruction and Production holds the first of a series of hearings in New York City....The body of one of the nine miners trapped in the Renton explosion is recovered....Three children and an adult are killed when a New Jersey saloon explodes.	An airline opens between Spring Lake, NJ, and New York City.	*Shamrock IV* wins the second race in the America's Cup series....Frank J. Marshall of New York wins the 10th and final round of the Master's Chess Tournament in Atlantic City....Babe Ruth hits his 32nd home run of the season.	Jul. 20
The Prohibition Party nominates William Jennings Bryan as the party's presidential candidate, despite a message from Bryan that he would decline the nomination....Senator Warren B. Harding promises to support women's suffrage....The People's Union is formed with the object of protecting the general public against strikes.	Lieutenant Colonel John E. Hunt, Commander of Castle Williams Prison, faces a court-martial on Governors Island in connection with the escape of millionaire draft dodger Grover Cleveland Bergdoll....The War Department announces the promotion of 1,599 army officers to higher ranks.	The Department of Justice investigates dealers on the Pacific Coast accused of oil profiteering....A search is conducted for the missing bodies of pilot George H. Hall and his mechanic after their plane plunges into a swamp near West Yarmouth, MA.	Wireless communication is established between Chelmsford, England, and the steamship *Victorian,* 600 miles away, en route to Canada.	*Resolute* defeats *Shamrock IV* in the third race of the America's Cup best of five series....Arthur Jerome Eddy, a leading Chicago lawyer, financier, and author, dies....Roosevelt Day celebrations are held at the Chautauqua Institute, as 20,000 visitors from across the nation honor the memory of the late president.	Jul. 21
William Jennings Bryan declines the Prohibition Party's nomination for president. The party instead nominates Aaron S. Watkins for president and D. Leigh Colvin for vice president....Senator Warren B. Harding accepts the Republican nomination for president.		Former New York Central railroad chairman William K. Vanderbilt dies....Nearly half the coal mines in Illinois are closed down as a result of strikes.	Two photographs of the race between *Resolute* and *Shamrock IV* are transmitted to London by the experimental process of phototelegraphy.	The national A.A.U. gymnastics championship tournament is held in New York....Pitcher Bill Bolden returns to the St. Louis Cardinals....The Thirteenth Annual Congress of the Esperanto Association of North America opens in New York.	Jul. 22
	Assistant Secretary of the Navy Franklin D. Roosevelt announces the appointment of a special board to consider revising the navy yard wage scale.	Strikes involving more than 30,000 coal miners in Southern Illinois threaten to shut down the coal industry in that state....Fire destroys thousands of motion picture films in the vaults of the Famous Players-Lasky and Metro Pictures corporations....Three more bodies are recovered from the Renton mine explosion....Two miners are shot in an attack on a West Virginia mine.		*Resolute* wins the fourth race in the America's Cup series....James Cardinal Gibbons celebrates his 86th birthday.	Jul. 23
William J. Shearer, former superintendent of schools in Elizabeth, NJ, and one-time Congressional candidate, is arrested on charges of land fraud....Department of Justice agents bring 63 "undesirable aliens" to Ellis Island for deportation.	Franklin D. Roosevelt resigns as Assistant Secretary of the Navy....Mrs. Cornelius Vanderbilt, Sr., agrees to head the women's committee to aid the Army and Navy Club.	The Transmarine Transportation Company opens a new canal barge line between Jersey City and Buffalo....Kansas miners prepare for a strike protesting fines levied for refusal to work on Saturdays.	Marconi officials at a wireless station in St. John's, Newfoundland, hear phonograph selections sent from aboard the steamer *Victorian* more than 800 miles away....One player is killed and five others injured when lightning strikes near home plate during a baseball game in Georgia....Lightning kills many cattle and damages crops and orchards in Orange County, NY.	Al Clayton joins the Red Sox pitching staff....Lew McCarty, veteran catcher for the New York Giants, is traded to the St. Louis Cardinals....Featherweight boxer Frankie Mahone dies from a hemorrhage sustained during a bout in Elizabeth, NJ.	Jul. 24
A mob in Fayetteville, WV, takes confessed wife-slayer William Bennet, Jr., from jail and lynches him.		Union street car workers in New Orleans end a 3-week long strike.		Babe Ruth hits his 35th homerun of the season in a victory over the Boston Red Sox.	Jul. 25

F	G	H	I	J
Includes campaigns, elections, federal-state relations, civil rights and liberties, crime, the judiciary, education, healthcare, poverty, urban affairs, and population.	*Includes formation and debate of U.S. foreign and defense policies, veterans affairs, and defense spending. (Relations with specific foreign countries are usually found under the region concerned.)*	*Includes business, labor, agriculture, taxation, transportation, consumer affairs, monetary and fiscal policy, natural resources, pollution and industrial accidents.*	*Includes worldwide scientific, medical and technological developments, natural phenomena, U.S. weather and natural disasters.*	*Includes the arts, religion, scholarship, communications media, sports, entertainment, fashions, fads, and social life.*

	World Affairs	Europe	Africa & The Middle East	The Americas	Asia & The Pacific
Jul. 26		A fifth battalion of troops arrives in Belfast to attempt to restore order.... The Germans release Dr. Hans Dorten in response to threats of Allied reprisals.... Seven Sicilians are killed and several wounded in a riot over the distribution of macaroni.... The Bulgarian Chamber of Deputies ratifies the Treaty of Neuilly.			
Jul. 27		Turkish Nationalists cut off the city of Adana from the outside world.... Italian newspapers report that Italy has decided to abandon Avlona to the Albanians.		Delegates from British newspapers to the Imperial Press conference arrive in Nova Scotia.	The Chinese government announces the formation of a joint Sino-American mining company for the development of silver, tin, and copper deposits in the Yunan Province.... The Japanese House of Peers approves a tax increase, which will allow for army and navy extensions.
Jul. 28		The Allied Council of Ambassadors divides the province of Teschen up between Czechoslovakia and Poland.... Female jurors are empanelled in England for the first time.	The South African government establishes a Native Affairs Commission and extends the native council system.	The War Department in Mexico City receives word that guerilla chief Pancho Villa has surrendered.	Japan's Minister of War informs the Diet that 4,000 Japanese troops have been ordered to complete the occupation of the northern part of Saghalin Island.
Jul. 29		A mob of soldiers storms the Belgium Chamber of Deputies to demand a lump sum payment for every veteran.... The signing of the Turkish treaty is postponed by a dispute between Italy and Greece over the Aegean Islands, Albania, and Asia Minor.... Prince Abdul Medjid Effendt, heir apparent to the Turkish throne, renounces his right to the Sultanate.	The French Foreign Office announces that Emir Faisal has officially been deposed and invited to leave Syria with his family.	Esteban Cantu, Governor of Lower California, raises an army to resist Federal troops.... The Mexican government names Roberto Pesqueira to replace Dr. Alfredo Caturegli as Mexican financial agent in the United States.	
Jul. 30	The Council of the League of Nations meets in San Sebastian, Spain.	Germany frees Bela Kun, former Communist dictator of Hungary, and his Communist companions, who were recently detained at Stettin while en route to Russia.... A force of more than 800 armed and uniformed Hungarians raids Austria's Fürstenfeld Arsenal.			Seven Koreans carrying bombs are arrested and charged with conspiring to assassinate officials and destroy public buildings in Seoul.... A spokesman for General Wu-Pei-fu declares the general's objectives in combating Anfu forces to be the restoration of the union between Northern and Southern China and the establishment of an administration on democratic principles.
Jul. 31	The International Socialist Conference opens in Geneva.	The French Foreign Office reports that Russian War Minister Leon Trotsky has secretly ordered the Red armies to capture Warsaw before armistice negotiations are begun.... The German Reichstag passes a bill to abolish compulsory military service.	The U.S. government receives a copy of a letter in which Turkish Nationalist leader Mustafa Kemal promises to support an uprising against the British in Mesopotamia.		
Aug. 1	The Jewish World Relief Congress opens in Carlsbad.... The Universal Negro Improvement Association's first international convention opens in New York.... The International Congress of Miners convenes in Geneva.	The Russian Soviet army advances to within 75 miles of Warsaw.... German Bolsheviks seize control of Zittau, Saxony.		Congressional elections are held in Mexico.... Carlos Felix Diaz, former Mexican Minister to Bolivia, is shot to death at a hotel in Mexico City.... A new cable is opened between Santa Elena, Ecuador and Lima, Peru.... Dr. Belesario Porras is reelected President of Panama.	
Aug. 2		The Italian government agrees to evacuate troops from Albania with the exception of the island of Saseno.... Rumania issues an ultimatum giving the Soviets three days to withdraw their troops from Rumanian territory or else face a general mobilization.... Sixty thousand businessmen in Vienna protest high municipal business taxes.		Esteban Cantu, governor of the northern territory of Lower California, officially declares a revolt against the Federal Government.... Telephone operators in Puerto Rico go on strike.	
	A *Includes developments that affect more than one world region, international organizations and important meetings of world leaders.*	B *Includes all domestic and regional developments in Europe, including the Soviet Union.*	C *Includes all domestic and regional developments in Africa and the Middle East.*	D *Includes all domestic and regional developments in Latin America, the Caribbean, and Canada.*	E *Includes all domestic and regional developments in Asian and Pacific nations (and colonies).*

U.S. Politics & Social Issues	U.S. Foreign Policy & Affairs, Defense	U.S. Economy & Environment	Science, Technology & Nature	Culture, Leisure & Lifestyle	
A Federal Grand Jury indicts five New York City men in connection with a large ring of automobile thieves.…New York Assemblyman Louis Cuvillier charges in court that a band of Socialists from Finland attacked him on the streets in retaliation for the ousting of Socialists from the New York Assembly.	Two hundred disabled veterans strike to remain at the Home Sanitarium in Saranac Lake rather than transfer to other hospitals.…A conference is held at the State Department to discuss the maintenance of friendly intercourse between Japan and the United States.	Chicago faces a fuel crisis.…Day laborers and drivers in Indiana coal fields begin an unauthorized strike.	A strong earthquake is felt in Santiago, Chile.	Composer Carlos Troyer dies at 83.…U.S. Olympic athletes sail for Antwerp.	Jul. 26
Massachusetts Governor Calvin Coolidge accepts the Republican nomination for vice president.…Judge C.B. Ames, Assistant to the Attorney General, resigns.		Warren B. Harding is reappointed head of the Federal Reserve Board.…Police are called in to break up a clash between film industry strikers and workers in Fort Lee, NJ.…Fifty National Guardsmen are sent to patrol the West Virginia–Kentucky border in order to prevent further shootings of miners.	A Paris newspaper publishes a photograph transmitted by wire from Lyons.…New York State receives one gram of radium to be used in cancer research.…Los Angeles experiences three more earthquake shocks.…Norwegian explorer Roald Amundsen reaches Nome, AK.	*Resolute* defeats *Shamrock IV* in the deciding race to win the America's Cup.…The city of Camden, NJ, purchases Walt Whitman's former home from the poet's heirs for $600.	Jul. 27
Federal prohibition enforcement agent John Whitehead is charged with murder for the shooting death of an Ohio saloon keeper.…Secretary of War Newton D. Baker issues an order prohibiting military officers from taking part in political campaigns.	The War Department announces plans to abandon Camp Zachary Taylor in Louisville and to transfer the 1st Division to Camp Dix, NJ, instead.…Major General Frank Hines, head of the War Department's transportation service, resigns.	Sixty bank clerks at the First National Bank of Cincinnati quit work and walk out.	Another light earthquake shock is felt in Los Angeles.	Chicago boxer Jack Foltine dies following a knockout blow.…St. Louis editor William Marion Reedy dies.	Jul. 28
Federal agents seize $40,000 worth of liquor in New Jersey raids.	William R. Williams is appointed Assistant Secretary of War.…Two torpedo boat destroyers are launched on the Delaware River.…The Navy Department orders six more destroyers and a cruiser dispatched to Turkish waters as a precautionary measure.		A preliminary reconnaissance trip is made to establish a transcontinental air mail route between New York and San Francisco.		Jul. 29
Federal prohibition agents seize the American Sugar Refining Company's steam tanker, on which it is alleged 48 cases of whisky were recently discovered.…Frank Burke, assistant chief of the Department of Justice's Bureau of Investigation, resigns.		A fire that starts in a Philadelphia factory kills eight people and injures four others.	Wireless messages are successfully sent from Chelmsford, England, to Copenhagen.	Paddy Driscoll signs with the New York Giants.	Jul. 30
		Employees of the Brooklyn Rapid Transit Company threaten to strike unless their demands for increased pay and better working conditions are met.…The Interstate Commerce Commission grants rate increases to the railroads.…John L. Lewis, president of the United Mine Workers of America, orders striking mine workers in Indiana and Illinois to return to work.			Jul. 31
Authorities arrest 15 coal operators and brokers in Knoxville on charges of profiteering.…Frank Hanly, ex-governor of Indiana and erstwhile presidential candidate, is killed when a freight train strikes the automobile in which he is a passenger.		Twenty passengers are injured when a trolley car derails in Queens, NY.…One thousand streetcar workers go on strike in Denver.…Standard Oil grants a 10 percent bonus to refinery employees to offset increases in the cost of living.		Gaston Chevrolet sets a new world record by driving 100 miles over a dirt track in 89 minutes and 23 seconds.	Aug. 1
A mob of more than 1,000 men storm the county jail in Center, TX, and lynch Lige Daniels, a black man accused of murdering a white woman.…Millionaire William B. Lloyd and 19 other members of the Communist Labor Party are found guilty of sedition.	The Bureau of War Risk Insurance announces that disabled veterans in need of hospital treatment will be transferred to government-owed hospitals.	Approximately 2,500 laboratory workers in the motion picture industry return to work following a two-week strike.…Discouraged by the low prices offered for their produce, Eastern Long Island farmers go on strike.…Work is resumed in a large number of Illinois mines, pending negotiations.		Babe Ruth hits his 38th home run of the season.…Mildred Harris Chapin files suit for divorce from comedian Charlie Chapin.	Aug. 2
F *Includes campaigns, elections, federal-state relations, civil rights and liberties, crime, the judiciary, education, healthcare, poverty, urban affairs, and population.*	G *Includes formation and debate of U.S. foreign and defense policies, veterans affairs, and defense spending. (Relations with specific foreign countries are usually found under the region concerned.)*	H *Includes business, labor, agriculture, taxation, transportation, consumer affairs, monetary and fiscal policy, natural resources, pollution and industrial accidents.*	I *Includes worldwide scientific, medical and technological developments, natural phenomena, U.S. weather and natural disasters.*	J *Includes the arts, religion, scholarship, communications media, sports, entertainment, fashions, fads, and social life.*	

	World Affairs	Europe	Africa & The Middle East	The Americas	Asia & The Pacific
Aug. 3	The League of Nations' Permanent Advisory Committee on Naval, Military, and Air Questions holds its first meeting in San Sebastian, Spain....Delegates at the International Congress of Miners unanimously adopt resolutions calling for the nationalization or socialization of mines....The International Socialist Congress votes to move its headquarters from Brussels to London.		The War Office in London reports that a British column on the Lower Euphrates has been attacked by tribesmen and sustained 300 casualties.	A new trade agreement between Canada and the British West Indies is made public....The Mexican government mobilizes 3,000 men, under the command of General Abelardo Rodriguez, for the campaign against Estaban Cantu in Lower California....Cantu forces seize the Mexican patrol ship *Tecate* and kill the ship's captain Leonardo Zepeda.	Japan announces plans to increase its garrison forces in Korea by 4,800 men.
Aug. 4		Turkish insurgent leader Colonel Jafar Tayar arrives in Athens under armed guard, having been captured by the Greeks shortly after their occupation of Adrianople....Five men open fire on a carriage in Valencia, gravely wounding the former Governor of Barcelona and his wife, and killing his sister-in-law.			
Aug. 5	The International Socialist Congress, in session in Geneva, formally repudiates Bolshevism.	Hungary formally offers two divisions each of cavalry and infantry to aid the Poles against the Soviets....Rumania concentrates troops on the Russo-Rumanian frontier....The Polish armistice and peace delegation leaves Warsaw for Minsk....The German Reichstag passes the disarmament bill....Turkish Nationalist forces begin an offensive against the Greeks in region northeast of Brussa.	Four columns of Spanish forces under General Fernandez Silvestre overcome native resistance to capture Mount Tafersit and adjoining positions in Morocco.	Dueling is legalized in Uruguay.	
Aug. 6		The Irish Crimes Bill is passed in the British House of Commons after the Nationalist and Labour members walk out....Polish officials report that East Galicia has been completely plundered....Rumania announces its neutrality in the Russo-Polish conflict, but pledges cooperation with the Allies in the event that any joint action becomes necessary.	The U.S. State Department receives news of a Soviet advance in Persia.		General Isouiro Kojima leaves Tokyo to take up his new post as commander of the army garrison for North Saghalin.
Aug. 7		A wireless dispatch from Moscow reports that Soviet Foreign Minister George Tchitcherin has offered to resume peace negotiations with Rumania.... A plot, believed to be of Communist origin and designed to blow up General Army Headquarters, is discovered in Warsaw.		The Press Club of Havana, Cuba, appeals to President Wilson to intervene in the trial by American naval authorities of Dominican poet Fabio Fiallo.	A strike of Filipino employees of American newspapers in Manila is called off.
Aug. 8	The International Miners' Congress in Geneva closes with a pledge that the miners of all European countries will issue an ultimatum, backed by the threat of an international miners' strike, to their respective governments demanding nationalization of the mines.	Nearly 100,000 men, women, and children join in a prayer procession through the streets of Warsaw....The Soviet government rejects Allied proposals for an armistice with Poland....The French government reports that Hungary has agreed to contribute 140,000 men to help fight the Soviets.		Forty-eight cases of typhus are reported in San Pedro de Las Colonias, Mexico....Mexican President de la Huerta orders an end to gambling and games of chance.	
Aug. 9	Nearly 400 delegates from around the world attend the opening ceremonies of an international Esperanto conference held at the Hague.	The Treaty of Neuilly, which established peace terms for Bulgaria, takes effect....The Armenians of Cilicia proclaim their independence under French protection and form a provisional government....The British Parliament passes the Restoration of Order in Ireland Act, also known as the Coercion Act.			

A	B	C	D	E
Includes developments that affect more than one world region, international organizations and important meetings of world leaders.	*Includes all domestic and regional developments in Europe, including the Soviet Union.*	*Includes all domestic and regional developments in Africa and the Middle East.*	*Includes all domestic and regional developments in Latin America, the Caribbean, and Canada.*	*Includes all domestic and regional developments in Asian and Pacific nations (and colonies).*

U.S. Politics & Social Issues	U.S. Foreign Policy & Affairs, Defense	U.S. Economy & Environment	Science, Technology & Nature	Culture, Leisure & Lifestyle	
President Wilson reappoints William S. Culbertson of Kansas as a member of the U.S. Tariff Commission.		A conference of the National Board of Jurisdictional Award opens in Atlantic City to discuss labor disputes in the building trades industry.	State and national health officers meet in Galveston, TX, to consider measures for eradicating the bubonic plague....Two more cases of smallpox are discovered in New York City.	The first public session of the 38th annual Knights of Columbus convention opens in New York....Stunt aviator Lieutenant Omar Locklear and his assistant, Lieutenant Milton Elliott, are killed in a plane crash while filming "The Skywayman."...Writer John P. Ritter dies.	Aug. 3
Annette Adams, the first female Assistant Attorney General of the United States, begins her duties at the Department of Justice....Zachary Saylor and his son Austin are both fatally wounded in a shootout between the Saylors and a posse of officers in the mountains of Harlan County, KY.	A military court fully exonerates Colonel John E. Hunt, who was court-martialed in connection with the escape of draft-dodger Grover Cleveland Bergdoll.		A Massachusetts medical commission reports favorably on a new leprosy treatment involving Chaulmoogra oil, a product of an East Indian fig tree.	The Retail Millinery Association holds its fall fashion show in New York.	Aug. 4
One man is killed and more than 30 injured when a mob of striking streetcar employees in Denver attempts to block the operation of cars by strikebreakers....Troops are called in to restore order when a mob in West Frankfort, IL, begins attacking Italian immigrants and burning their homes....City, county and federal officers arrest 10 alleged members of the I.W.W. near Spokane, WA.	The Rank and File Veterans' Association, a national organization of servicemen, endorses Parley P. Christensen for President and blacklists 260 Congressmen.	Representatives of 80,000 naval yard employees appear before the Navy Yards Wage Board to request substantial wage increases.		Actor John Barrymore marries poet Blanche M. Thomas....Babe Ruth hits his 39th home run of the season.	Aug. 5
Authorities arrest draft-dodger and Communist propagandist John Alexander, alias John La Granche, in Chicago after a three-year search....The Chicago militia is mobilized to avert threatened race riots in Chicago Heights....Prohibition agents from Philadelphia raid nine saloons in Elizabeth, NJ.	President Wilson confers with Bainbridge Colby, Secretary of State, and Norman H. Davis, Under Secretary of State, on the Polish situation.			Actress Ruth Shepley is hospitalized with acute nephritis....Babe Ruth hits his 40th and 41st home runs of the season.	Aug. 6
Federal troops under the command of Colonel C.C. Ballou arrive in Denver to restore order....Rioting resumes in West Frankfort, IL, despite the presence of 720 State Guardsmen and a machine gun platoon....Will H. Hays, Chairman of the Republican National Committee, meets with 33 suffragists from Connecticut and pledges to advocate a special session of the legislature to ratify the suffrage amendment.	The U.S. Army transport *Antigone* arrives from Europe carrying the bodies of 1,575 dead American soldiers....A court martial at Fort Dix sentences Edward J. Ressler to 15 years in federal prison for desertion.	Attendants at the Westchester County penitentiary are granted a salary increase.			Aug. 7
The arrest of a sailor for drunkenness sparks a riot at Revere Beach, MA, when 400 sailors and marines attack the arresting officer and other members of the police force; soldiers from Fort Banks are called in to restore order....Five hundred soldiers from Camp Fenston arrive in Denver to protect strikebreakers operating street cars.		Two people are killed, several injured, and five reported missing when three railroad cars are derailed near Ashland, KY....Six hundred postal workers in Chicago protest the decision of Washington officials to fire 11 clerks who led a publicity campaign to expose alleged unjust working conditions.	Two planes from New York City, sent to blaze a trail for transcontinental air mail service, land in Oakland, CA....Captain Roald Amundsen leaves Nome, AK, to continue exploring the Arctic.		Aug. 8
Franklin D. Roosevelt is officially notified of his nomination for Vice President on the Democratic ticket....An extra session of the Tennessee legislature convenes at noon to consider ratification of the federal suffrage amendment....The Committee of Forty-Eight decides not to put a presidential ticket in the field for the upcoming election.	Franklin D. Roosevelt ends his tenure as Assistant Secretary of the U.S. Navy.	The Nyanza cotton mills in Rhode Island close down for two weeks due to general business depression....The firm of Roulston-Eckert & Co., Inc., is exonerated on charges of sugar profiteering....Work is resumed at all but two Illinois coal mines.		*Ladies Night* by Avery Hopwood and Charlton Andrews opens at the Eltinge 42nd Street Theater....Twenty-two hundred Boy Scouts start camp at Lake Kanohwahke in the Palisades Interstate Park....Three Americans complete a 22-day voyage across the Atlantic in a 35-foot yacht....Author Fannie Hurst undergoes an operation for appendicitis.	Aug. 9
F *Includes campaigns, elections, federal-state relations, civil rights and liberties, crime, the judiciary, education, healthcare, poverty, urban affairs, and population.*	G *Includes formation and debate of U.S. foreign and defense policies, veterans affairs, and defense spending. (Relations with specific foreign countries are usually found under the region concerned.)*	H *Includes business, labor, agriculture, taxation, transportation, consumer affairs, monetary and fiscal policy, natural resources, pollution and industrial accidents.*	I *Includes worldwide scientific, medical and technological developments, natural phenomena, U.S. weather and natural disasters.*	J *Includes the arts, religion, scholarship, communications media, sports, entertainment, fashions, fads, and social life.*	

	World Affairs	Europe	Africa & The Middle East	The Americas	Asia & The Pacific
Aug. 10		France, Great Britain, and Italy sign a tripartite agreement dividing a large part of Turkey into zones of special influence.... The Italian and Greek governments sign an agreement determining the status of territory in the eastern Mediterranean.... Turkish forces under Mustafa Kemal attack Greece and Armenia.... Allied leaders decide to await the result of a Russo-Polish truce parley at Minsk before deciding whether to take action against Russia.	By the Treaty of Sevres, Sultan Mohammed VI recognizes the independence of the Kingdom of the Hejaz; Syria becomes a French mandate, while Mesopotamia and Palestine become British mandates.		Seoul reports 600 deaths from an ongoing cholera epidemic in Korea.
Aug. 11	The World Peace Foundation publishes a statement defining the duties and leading features of the Permanent Court of International Justice.... Anglican bishops issue an appeal to all Christians for church unity.	Soviet Russia recognizes Latvian independence with the signing of the Treaty of Riga.... France announces its recognition of the de facto government of General Peter Wrangel in south Russia.... Russia and Finland agree upon armistice conditions at Dorpat.... Eight people are killed and 100 injured when grenades from a burning powder magazine bombard Florence, Italy.			Peking announces the personnel of a new Chinese Cabinet under Premier and Minister of War General Chin Yun-Peng.
Aug. 12	Delegates from 35 countries assemble in Geneva for the opening of the Faith and Order Congress, a world congress of Christian churches.... The International Seaman's Congress adopts a motion refusing to transport troops and munitions.	Lord Mayor of Cork, Terence MacSweney, is arrested for possession of seditious documents.... Australian Archbishop Daniel Mannix declares his intention to defy an exclusion edict issued by the British government that bars him from visiting Ireland.... The French government advises Poland against accepting the peace terms offered by the Soviets.... Eleutherios Constantine Venizelos, Prime Minister of Greece, narrowly survives an assassination attempt by two former Greek officers in Paris.		The Mexican government sends 5,000 soldiers into Lower California.... Custom House officials in Argentina foil an attempt to smuggle gold into the United States.... Adolph Pauli is appointed German Minister to Argentina.	
Aug. 13	American athlete Dan Ahearn, world record holder in the triple-jump, is ousted from the U.S. Olympic team on charges of insubordination.	News of the attempted assassination of Premier Vinizelos sparks riots in Athens.... Bela Kun, the former Communist dictator of Hungary, arrives in Petrograd.... Organized labor in Britain empowers a Council of Action to pursue whatever steps are necessary to prevent war against Russia.... A preliminary peace treaty is concluded between the Russian Soviet government and Armenia.		Estaban Cantu, the Governor of Lower California, offers to abandon his rebellion against the Mexican government if he is permitted to remain in office until December.... The Mexican Embassy in Washington reports that President de la Huerta will not seek reelection in September.... A bomb explodes at the Palace of Justice in Buenos Aires, where 11 alleged anarchists are on trial for plotting a Communist revolution.	
Aug. 14	Dan Ahearn is allowed to rejoin the U.S. Olympic team after fellow-Olympians petition for his reinstatement.... Opening ceremonies are held for the Olympic Games in Antwerp.	Yugoslavia and the Czechoslovak Republic sign a treaty of alliance.... Supported by French troops, Marshal Josef Pilsudski mounts a vigorous defense of Warsaw.... Gabriele d'Annunzio breaks with the National Council of Fiume and announces plans to establish a free and independent Fiume with extended boundaries.		After initially denying reports, the Mexican Embassy in Washington, DC, admits that a rebellion against the De la Huerta government has started in the State of Jalisco, and that President De la Huerta has dispatched 7,000 troops to restore order.... A new case of bubonic plague is discovered in Tampico, Mexico.	Fighting is resumed in China between the provinces of Fukien and Kwantung.... A group of American Congressmen arrives in Peking.
Aug. 15	The Finnish javelin team makes a clean sweep at Antwerp and shatters all previous records.... The League of Nations purchases the National Hotel in Geneva to house the staffs of the member nations.	A general strike of dockworkers ties up Italian seaports.... Russians hoist the German flag over the Town Hall of Soldau, the first town in the Polish Corridor occupied by the Bolsheviks.... The Austrian government notifies the Reparations Commission of the Peace Conference that Austria cannot fulfill treaty stipulations regarding the delivery of livestock and furniture to Italy, Rumania, and Yugoslavia.	A British force is destroyed during an Arab uprising in Shas Raba, Mesopotamia.	Dr. Manuel Gondra is inaugurated President of Paraguay.... An American-Cuban Commission recommends steps to relieve freight congestion in Havana Harbor.... Yellow fever is reportedly spreading in Vera Cruz.	Japanese Field Marshal Prince Yamagata is closely guarded after he receives a letter threatening his life for interfering in the politics of the empire.... Tokyo announces a death toll of 400 from the recent floods in Saghalin Island.

A	B	C	D	E
Includes developments that affect more than one world region, international organizations and important meetings of world leaders.	*Includes all domestic and regional developments in Europe, including the Soviet Union.*	*Includes all domestic and regional developments in Africa and the Middle East.*	*Includes all domestic and regional developments in Latin America, the Caribbean, and Canada.*	*Includes all domestic and regional developments in Asian and Pacific nations (and colonies).*

U.S. Politics & Social Issues	U.S. Foreign Policy & Affairs, Defense	U.S. Economy & Environment	Science, Technology & Nature	Culture, Leisure & Lifestyle	
The Republican National Committee opens a Southern headquarters in Washington, DC.... Entertainer Al Jolson accepts the presidency of the Harding and Coolidge Theatrical League.	Secretary of State Bainbridge Colby pledges that the United States will employ all available means to preserve Poland's political and territorial integrity.	The 35th annual convention of the United Master Butchers of America opens in New York City.... Eighty thousand employees of the American Railway Express Company are awarded increased wages.... Striking employees of the Denver Tramway Company vote against calling off their strike and returning to work under conditions named by the company.		Actor James O'Neil dies after a prolonged illness.	Aug. 10
The Rev. Aaron S. Watkins and running mate D. Leigh Colvin both formally accept their nominations by the Prohibition Party.... Detectives with the anarchist squad in New York begin searching for agitators who placarded public places with appeals for a general strike in sympathy with Soviet Russia.		The Federal Anthracite Coal Commission and the Anthracite Board of Conciliation instruct striking employees of the Pennsylvania Coal Company to return to work.			Aug. 11
Governor Alfred Smith convenes a special session of the New York legislature to discuss the housing crisis.... Charles Ponzi surrenders to federal authorities and is arrested on charges of using the mail to defraud.... Prison officials in South Trenton capture two escaped convicts from the New Jersey State Prison.	The court martial at Governors Island reaches a decision in the Erwin R. Bergdoll desertion case in under five minutes, but the verdict is not yet released to the public.... The War Department considers a request by Polish Minister Lubomirsky for permission to purchase war materials from the United States.... The War Department announces plans to abandon Count Upton, Long Island.	Potato farmers in Vermont form the Vermont Seed Potato Growers' Association.			Aug. 12
The Universal Negro Improvement Association officially adopts the Declaration of Rights of the Negro Peoples of the World.... The Tennessee Senate ratifies the Suffrage Amendment.... Authorities shut down Charles Ponzi's Old Colony Foreign Exchange Company in Boston.	The War Council created by Congress at its last session is formally organized.	The scale committee of bituminous coal operators and miners meets in Cleveland, as directed by President Wilson, to attempt to settle wage disputes in the mining industry.... At least six people are killed and three injured in an explosion at a Virginia limestone mill.... A lightning bolt destroys the Corning mill of the E. I. du Pont powder plant in New Jersey.... The Central Federated Union votes to form one central labor organization for all of New York City.	Captain W.E. Beaver and his mechanic, W. Burton, fly nonstop from New York to Kentucky.... A collection of 800 birds and 200 other animals for the New York Zoological Garden arrives in New York from London.	Film star Pauline Frederick files for divorce from actor and playwright Willard Mack.	Aug. 13
Gambling clubs in New Orleans are closed down.... Four armed bandits hold up a motor truck loaded with whisky near Fullerton, MD.	First Sergeant Dan Kelly, the recipient of two Congressional Medals of Honor, retires from active service with the Marine Corps.	The entire force of the Manhattan & Queens Traction Corporation goes on strike.		Eighteen motor craft compete in the first race for the cruiser championship of America.... Artist and author George Wharton Edwards is awarded the King Albert medal.... Babe Ruth hits his 42nd home run of the season.... Louise Brownell flips her plane in the air 87 times, shattering the previous world record for women aviators of 25 loops.	Aug. 14
Alleged Bolshevik agents or sympathizers attempt to incite a riot at the Cathedral of St. Nicholas in New York.... At a mass meeting in Madison Square Garden, 15,000 Irish sympathizers protest against the removal by British authorities of Archbishop Mannix of Australia from the liner *Baltic*.... Authorities raid three alleged gambling houses in Saratoga Springs, NY.	Over a million Polish Americans gather in towns and cities across the nation to thank the government for its stance on Poland, as outlined in Secretary Colby's note of August 10.	The Labor Department announces a settlement in the strike of 3,000 Pennsylvania coal miners		The Professional Billiard Players' Fraternity is formed.	Aug. 15

F	G	H	I	J
Includes campaigns, elections, federal-state relations, civil rights and liberties, crime, the judiciary, education, healthcare, poverty, urban affairs, and population.	*Includes formation and debate of U.S. foreign and defense policies, veterans affairs, and defense spending. (Relations with specific foreign countries are usually found under the region concerned.)*	*Includes business, labor, agriculture, taxation, transportation, consumer affairs, monetary and fiscal policy, natural resources, pollution and industrial accidents.*	*Includes worldwide scientific, medical and technological developments, natural phenomena, U.S. weather and natural disasters.*	*Includes the arts, religion, scholarship, communications media, sports, entertainment, fashions, fads, and social life.*

	World Affairs	Europe	Africa & The Middle East	The Americas	Asia & The Pacific
Aug. 16	Frank Loomis of the United States breaks the world record for the 400-meter hurdle race at the Antwerp Olympics.	A successful counter-offensive at Warsaw forces large numbers of Red Army troops to withdraw from Polish territory.…Lord Mayor of Cork Terence MacSweney is sentenced to two years in Brixton Prison and immediately begins a hunger strike.…Polish and Russian peace delegates meet at Minsk to negotiate a possible armistice.	A dispatch from Teheran reports that Persian government troops have begun fighting Bolshevik forces northwest of Teheran and have captured a strongly fortified Bolshevik stronghold at Esmaniabad.	Jamaican police go on strike, as do conductors and engineers on the island railway.…General Ricardo Gonzales, leader of a failed attempt to start an uprising against the Mexican government, is arrested in Piedras Negras.	
Aug. 17	Richmond Landon of the United States sets a new Olympic record for the high jump.	Romania joins the alliance between Yugoslavia and the Czechoslovak Republic.…A settlement is reached through government intervention in the Italian dockworkers' strike.…At least 27 people are killed when French troops clash with the inhabitants of Kattowitz in Upper Silesia.…Seven people are killed in a riot in Abbadia, Italy.…Soviet delegates offer peace terms to the Polish representatives at Minsk.		Cuba ratifies the Treaty of St. Germain.…Soldiers replace striking policemen in Jamaica.	King George V issues a royal decree canceling a proposed visit by the Prince of Wales to India.…Shipping rates from Japanese ports are increased by 20 percent.
Aug. 18	Canadian hurdler Earl Thomson sets a new Olympic record in the 110-meter hurdle race.	Polish delegates at the Minsk Conference refuse to agree to the disarmament of the Polish Army unless the Russians also disarm.…The Belgian State Railway Men's Syndicate votes to prevent the transportation from or through Belgium of troops and munitions intended for Poland.…Fighting and anti-Polish rioting are resumed in Kattowitz.		Taxicab drivers in Havana strike in sympathy with the Havana Electric Street Railway Company's employees, who are already on strike.	Japan reports an alleged Korean plot to kidnap a party of American Congressmen visiting the Far East.
Aug. 19	The World Christian Conference on Faith and Order closes with an appeal to all nations to join the League of Nations.	The Belgian Council of Ministers decides that Belgium will remain neutral in the Russo-Polish conflict until peace negotiations at Minsk have been concluded.…Soviet troops begin to evacuate Vilna, Lithuania.…Polish troops enter Brest Litovsk.…In defending Taraboso from Albanian forces, 220 Serbs are killed and 250 others taken prisoner.…Czechoslovakia and Yugoslavia sign a defensive treaty.		The Mexican Foreign Office dismisses Rafael de Soto, Vice Consul in charge of the Spanish Consulate-General in Mexico City.…Transportation workers in Vera Cruz go on strike.	
Aug. 20	Frank A. Foss of the United States sets a new world record in the pole vault at the Antwerp Olympic Games.…Belgian Foreign Minister Paul Hymans is selected to preside at the first Assembly of the League of Nations in November.	A conference of Baltic states is held at Riga to lay the foundation for a political and economic entente.…Swiss police uncover a plot to assassinate British Prime Minister David Lloyd George, who is visiting Geneva.…Polish troops occupy the entire border district of Upper Silesia.…The Belgian government resumes diplomatic relations with Germany.	Syrian Premier Droubi Pasha and a member of his Cabinet are killed when bandits attack their train en route from Damascus to Haifa.	Orders are issued for the arrest of General Federico Cordova, alleged to have been chiefly responsible for the kidnapping of William O. Jenkins.…Sugar refiners in Argentina threaten to close down their factories, claiming that the purchase price fixed by the government is below the cost of production.	A group of Korean leaders presents Korean grievances against Japanese rule to Senator William J. Harris of Georgia and Representative Stephen B. Porter of Pennsylvania, members of the American Congressional Party touring the Far East.
Aug. 21		Ninety French citizens repatriated from Russia arrive in Paris.…Belgian workers refuse to load munitions aboard an American vessel destined for Poland.…The Soviets threaten to discontinue the evacuation of Lithuania after a Bolshevik Commissioner and some soldiers are killed near the border.…The Austrian government concludes a one-year commercial treaty with Rumania.		Mexican rebel Pedro Zamora demands ransom for a mining party, including five Americans, kidnapped in Jalisco.	Anfu troops from the Chinese province of Fukien invade the loyalist province of Kwantung.
Aug. 22	Finnish runner Hannes Kolehmainen wins the Olympic marathon in just over 2½ hours.	Italian Premier Giovanni Giolitti confers with British Prime Minister David Lloyd George in Lucerne, Switzerland, with the hope of reestablishing cordial Anglo-French relations.…Communists seize the factory town of Coethen, Germany, and declare it a Soviet republic.			

A	B	C	D	E
Includes developments that affect more than one world region, international organizations and important meetings of world leaders.	*Includes all domestic and regional developments in Europe, including the Soviet Union.*	*Includes all domestic and regional developments in Africa and the Middle East.*	*Includes all domestic and regional developments in Latin America, the Caribbean, and Canada.*	*Includes all domestic and regional developments in Asian and Pacific nations (and colonies).*

U.S. Politics & Social Issues	U.S. Foreign Policy & Affairs, Defense	U.S. Economy & Environment	Science, Technology & Nature	Culture, Leisure & Lifestyle	
An armed bandit holds up a trolley car in Atlantic City....A.C. Hatfield dies from gunshot wounds he sustained in an ambush attack in front of his hotel in Matewan, WV....A race riot breaks out in New York City when 50 white striking longshoremen attack a band of twenty-five black strikebreakers returning home from work.	American warships are dispatched to Polish waters in the Baltic as a precautionary measure....The Knights of Columbus appeal to Secretary of State Colby for recognition of the Irish Republic....The body of Major General William Gorgas is buried at Arlington National Cemetery.	Between 1,500 and 2,000 textile workers, on strike since May, return to work under open shop conditions in Cohoes, NY....Twenty-eight passengers are injured when the brakes fail on a Staten Island municipal bus.	Heavy rainfall causes an estimated $500,000-worth of damage to Toledo, OH....English scientist Sir Norman Lockyer dies at 84.	Cleveland Indians shortstop Ray Chapman is hit by a fastball and suffers a skull fracture....Arthur Hammerstein's *Tickle Me* debuts at the Selwyn Theater in New York....Cape Cod residents begin a series of observances to celebrate the tercentenary of the landing of the Pilgrims.	Aug. 16
		Members of the International Longshoremen's Association vote to end a five-month coastwise strike....Employees of the Western Union Telegraph Company in all parts of the country receive a bonus to offset the increased cost of living....The meeting of the joint scale committee of operatives and miners in Cleveland adjourns without having reached any agreement.		Shortstop Ray Chapman dies from his head injuries following an unsuccessful surgery; New York pitcher Carl Mays is exonerated of all blame for the tragedy....Screen actor Owen Moore survives an airplane crash without serious injury.	Aug. 17
Tennessee becomes the 36th state to ratify the suffrage amendment.	The American Relief Administration terminates its work in Latvia....Second Lieutenant Samuel P. MacNeill of the Marine Corps is killed in an airplane crash....Representatives of Polish-Americans call upon Secretary of State Colby to urge American aid for Poland.	The Ohio Public Utilities Commission refuses to permit railroad lines to increase intrastate passenger rates by 20 percent; the railroads will appeal to the Interstate Commerce Commission.	Heavy rains flood 12 towns in New York's southern tier.		Aug. 18
The North Carolina House of Representatives fails to ratify the federal suffrage amendment by a vote of 71 to 41....Charles Ponzi is arraigned on fraud charges.		The National Board of Farm Organizations announces the formation of the Co-operative Farm Borrowers of the United States, with headquarters in Washington, DC.	The Popocatepetl volcano in Mexico shows signs of activity.	A spectator suffers a fatal heart attack while cheering for Babe Ruth's 43rd home run of the season....Artist and sportsman Samuel M. Roosevelt, a cousin of the late Theodore Roosevelt, dies of a brain hemorrhage.	Aug. 19
William White, alias Michael Stanley, is sentenced to 18 months to five years in Sing Sing prison for leading a gang of hotel burglars....Fifty convicts start a riot in the Maryland Penitentiary....All five of the Socialists expelled from the New York State Assembly are nominated for the special elections to be held in September.	The U.S. Army is reorganized into nine corps, each including one regular army, one National Guard, and one reserve division.	Two men are killed and 12 others injured when a 2,000-gallon gasoline reservoir explodes in Syracuse, NY....Twenty-nine crew members of the ore carrier *Superior City* are killed when another ship collides with the freighter, causing the boilers to explode.	A series of violent earthquakes shakes the southern region of Chile.	The Cincinnati Reds purchase pitcher Herb Brenton from Seattle.	Aug. 20
Chicago police arrest seven men involved in an early morning clash between approximately 100 railroad workers and an equal number of strikers....Six people are reported killed in a pitched battle between mine guards and striking miners in Cirtsville, WV.	Secretary of State Colby warns the Polish government against engaging in territorial aggression against Russia....Six U.S. battleships carrying 1,500 midshipmen arrive in Panama on a training trip.	A federal grand jury indicts the officers of the Utah-Idaho Sugar Company and several other Salt Lake City and Ogden businessmen for profiteering in sugar....The Interstate Commerce Commission grants a $2.5 million loan to the Kansas City, Mexico, and Orient Railroad Company.	Secretary of the Navy Josephus Daniels receives the first wireless message sent from the new Lafayette Radio Station in Bordeaux, France.	An estimated 75,000 spectators attend the police field day games in Brooklyn, NY....William M. Johnston and Clarence J. Griffin regain the national tennis crown in doubles.	Aug. 21
The New York Training School for Boys, a farm reformatory in Yorktown, is closed down due to too many prison breaks.		Eight people are killed and seven injured when an electric train hits a bus in a suburb of Philadelphia....Outlaw strikers are blamed for attacks on the employees of New Haven freight yards.		Vice Commodore Critchley's yacht *Mohawk* wins the Commodore's cup.	Aug. 22

F	G	H	I	J
Includes campaigns, elections, federal-state relations, civil rights and liberties, crime, the judiciary, education, healthcare, poverty, urban affairs, and population.	*Includes formation and debate of U.S. foreign and defense policies, veterans affairs, and defense spending. (Relations with specific foreign countries are usually found under the region concerned.)*	*Includes business, labor, agriculture, taxation, transportation, consumer affairs, monetary and fiscal policy, natural resources, pollution and industrial accidents.*	*Includes worldwide scientific, medical and technological developments, natural phenomena, U.S. weather and natural disasters.*	*Includes the arts, religion, scholarship, communications media, sports, entertainment, fashions, fads, and social life.*

	World Affairs	Europe	Africa & The Middle East	The Americas	Asia & The Pacific
Aug. 23	The Olympic track and field events are concluded, with the U.S. team in the lead by a margin of 107 points....The Committee of Jewish Delegations, meeting in Paris, announces a campaign to obtain a seat in the League of Nations for representatives of the Jewish people.	More than 300,000 workers in Scotland take part in a one-day strike to protest against higher rents....Polish delegates at Minsk reject several fundamental terms of the Soviet peace proposal.		The Chilean government purchases a battleship and four light cruisers from Great Britain....Pedro Zamora continues to hold one American and one Briton for ransom, but he releases the other hostages kidnapped in Jalisco....Colonel Salvadore Perez stages a revolt in the State of Campeche, Mexico.	
Aug. 24	The International Olympic Committee selects Brazil to host the intermediate Olympic games of 1922.	Lithuania regains Vilna and the surrounding territory following the evacuation of Soviet troops....John von Berenberg-Gossler is appointed German Ambassador to Rome....A conference of Irish Moderates convenes in Dublin....Belgian Foreign Minister Paul Hymans resigns.	The Persian Cossack Brigade temporarily regains Rasht from the Soviet Russians.		
Aug. 25	Dr. Leo Motzkin is elected president of the new World Jewish Congress.	Poland's war minister announces that four Bolshevik armies, consisting of 250,000 troops, have been completely defeated on the northern Polish front.		Pedro Zamora releases his remaining hostages and offers to surrender....The Mexican government orders the arrest of U.S. military deserters charged with spreading Bolshevik propaganda.	
Aug. 26	American swimmer Ethelda Bleibtrey sets a new Olympic record in a trial heat of the 300-meter free-style race....The Royal Alliance for Promoting International Friendship through Churches opens its sessions in Switzerland.	M. Dombski, President of the Polish-Minsk peace delegation, is recalled to Brest-Litovsk to confer with Polish government representatives....German Nationalists in Breslau storm the Polish and French Consulates and destroy records....Rioting is renewed in Belfast.	A Northern Afghan garrison mutinies and demands soldiers' councils on the soviet model....Palestine reports that a band of Bedouins have killed 150 Christians in Ajlun, a village near Jerusalem....A force of 1,500 rebellious tribesmen launches an attack against Hillah.	Captain Trinidad Sanchez and Sergeant Roman Fernandez, two rebel leaders in the State of Vera Cruz who initiated a revolt a week ago, are captured and executed.	Deputy Commissioner R.W.D. Willoughby is assassinated at his residence in Kheri, India.
Aug. 27	Sweden's Olympic team captures the first three places in the modern pentathlon finals at Antwerp....Colonel Harry Cutler, Chairman of the Jewish Welfare Board, dies in London.	Eleven people are killed and dozens more injured in Belfast street fighting.... Delegates from the National Council of Fiume appeal to Italian Premier Giovanni Giolitti to recognize the independence of Fiume.... The Italian Ministry of Foreign Affairs accuses Serbian soldiers of atrocities against Montenegrins.... Tax riots spread throughout several towns in Germany.		Carlos Herrera is elected President of Guatemala....The Salvadoran National Congress approves plans for a Central American Union.	General Utsunomiya, commander of the Japanese forces in Korea, warns of a potentially serious outbreak among Korean nationalists in Manchuria.
Aug. 28					Dr. Paul S. Reinsch, former American Minister to China, announces his resignation as legal adviser to the Chinese government....Martial law is declared in Canton.
Aug. 29	The U.S. swimming team sets a new world record for the 800-meter relay.	Cardinal Leon Adolphe Amette, Archbishop of Paris, dies....The French government closes its Berlin Consulate pending reparation for the recent attack on the Breslau Consulate....The Soviet government accepts Poland's proposal to transfer peace negotiations from Minsk to Riga, Latvia....Premier Paul Teleky of Hungary suffers from blood poisoning, prompting rumors that he was deliberately poisoned.			
Aug. 30	The Spanish and Rumanian Cabinets resign.	Athens authorities arrest the brother of Apostolos Iserpris, one of the two men who shot and wounded Premier Venizelos....After a fifth day of rioting in Belfast, the death toll reaches 18 and the number of seriously wounded exceeds 200....Dispatches from Constantinople report the massacre of 400 Armenians by Kurds in Anatolia.			Famous Japanese aviator Lieutenant Yamagata is killed in an airplane crash.

A	B	C	D	E
Includes developments that affect more than one world region, international organizations and important meetings of world leaders.	*Includes all domestic and regional developments in Europe, including the Soviet Union.*	*Includes all domestic and regional developments in Africa and the Middle East.*	*Includes all domestic and regional developments in Latin America, the Caribbean, and Canada.*	*Includes all domestic and regional developments in Asian and Pacific nations (and colonies).*

U.S. Politics & Social Issues	U.S. Foreign Policy & Affairs, Defense	U.S. Economy & Environment	Science, Technology & Nature	Culture, Leisure & Lifestyle	
A prohibition agent reports that coffins and hearses are being used in Westchester County for the illegal transportation of whisky.	Herbert Hoover directs the American Relief Administration to spend an additional $500,000 for the care of war refugees in Poland.…The State Department announces that 27 men passed the recent Consular Service exam.	Plans are announced for the International Petroleum Company, a subsidiary of the Standard Oil Company of New Jersey, to take over the Tropical Oil Company.…Attorney General A. Mitchell Palmer issues orders to all United States District Attorneys to investigate potential cases of profiteering in bituminous coal.…More than 1,500 boilermakers and shipbuilders go on strike in Newburgh, NY.	The 24th Annual Convention of the National Dental Association opens in Boston.…Members of the army flying expedition to Nome, AK, reach their destination.	*The Bat* by Mary Roberts Rinehart and Avery Hopwood opens at the Morosco Theater.	Aug. 23
Republican leaders of the 14 Atlantic States convene in New York City to finalize campaign plans.		Indiana coal operators and miners sign a supplemental contract granting a substantial pay increase to miners.	The American Telephone and Telegraph Company purchases a minority interest in the Radio Corporation of America.…Astronomer William H. Pickering discovers a new star in the Cygnus constellation.	Automobile racer Joe Thomas is seriously injured when his car overturns in practice.	Aug. 24
Masked men steal 15 barrels of whisky from the Van Ardsdell distillery near Harrrodsburg, KY.	Alarmed by Central American unrest, the U.S. Navy sends the gunboat *Sacramento* to Honduras to protect American interests.	The New York Federation of Agriculture charges apple dealers in New York City with profiteering.…Increased fares on nearly all railroad and steamship lines take effect at midnight.		Portrait-painter Henry M. Hoyt commits suicide.	Aug. 25
The Nineteenth Amendment, granting women the right to vote, is ratified.…Robert J.B. Wright is arrested for allegedly stealing $10,000 worth of Liberty Bonds from the First National Bank of Poughkeepsie, NY.…John Egan and Frank Kelley are put to death by the electric chair at Sing Sing prison.	President Wilson appoints Gordon Woodbury to replace Franklin D. Roosevelt as Assistant Secretary of the Navy.	Illinois coal miners are granted a wage increase of $1.50 per day.	The Ford Motor Company announces the establishment of an educational department, which will grant degrees in mechanical, electrical, and chemical engineering.	Screen actors Lester Torpey and John Messlein are killed in an automobile accident.…Millionaire Guy L. Brigg commits suicide.…Thousands of Universalists gather in Gloucester, MA, to celebrate the 150th anniversary of the founding of Universalism in the United States.	Aug. 26
The Joint Legislative Committee appointed to investigate New York State's public schools holds its first session.	John W. Davis, Ambassador to Great Britain, meets with Secretary of State Bainbridge Colby in Washington.…After conferring with Secretary of State Colby, Secretary of the Navy Josephus Daniels orders the cruiser *Pittsburgh* to Danzig to protect American interests there.				Aug. 27
Mrs. Ella O'Gorman Stanton is elected president of the Cox-Roosevelt League of Women.…The Catholic Educational Association denounces as unconstitutional the Smith-Towner bill to nationalize schools.	The War Department calls off plans for an army test flight from Alaska to Siberia.	Delegates to the annual convention of the Indiana State Federation of Labor unanimously endorse the Plumb plan for public ownership of the railways.		U.S. polo player James M. Waterbury, Jr., dies.…Marjorie Dodd Letts wins the women's Western golf championship for the third time in six years.	Aug. 28
A New York man is arrested for transporting $5,000 worth of champagne without a federal permit.		The employees of the Brooklyn Rapid Transit Company vote unanimously to strike.…Disturbances are renewed at the Willis Branch Coal Company mines in Raleigh County, WV.…Federal troops arrive in Mingo County, WV, to guard mines in the strike zone.…Anthracite miners threaten to strike if President Wilson does not accept the minority report of the Anthracite Wage Commission within three days.	An earthquake rocks the island of Malta, damaging many buildings in Floriana and the surrounding district.…A preliminary test is successful in electrically piloting vessels into New York Harbor by means of a submerged cable.	Musical conductor and composer Samuel Lehman is hit by a car and killed.	Aug. 29
	A federal grand jury indicts 59 defendants, including 38 steamship lines, for an alleged conspiracy to restrain trade in violation of the Sherman anti-Trust law.	Baggage men with the New York Transfer Company and the Westcott Express Company return to work after a week-long strike.… Workers at Ellis Island threaten to quit unless they receive substantial wage increases.…President Wilson approves the majority report of the Anthracite Wage Commission.	Noted geologist, mining engineer, and inventor Benjamin Smith Lyman dies.	Sculptor George E. Bissell dies.…Envoys from Great Britain, France, and Holland join with Americans in celebrating the Pilgrim tercentenary in Provincetown, MA.	Aug. 30

F	G	H	I	J
Includes campaigns, elections, federal-state relations, civil rights and liberties, crime, the judiciary, education, healthcare, poverty, urban affairs, and population.	*Includes formation and debate of U.S. foreign and defense policies, veterans affairs, and defense spending. (Relations with specific foreign countries are usually found under the region concerned.)*	*Includes business, labor, agriculture, taxation, transportation, consumer affairs, monetary and fiscal policy, natural resources, pollution and industrial accidents.*	*Includes worldwide scientific, medical and technological developments, natural phenomena, U.S. weather and natural disasters.*	*Includes the arts, religion, scholarship, communications media, sports, entertainment, fashions, fads, and social life.*

	World Affairs	Europe	Africa & The Middle East	The Americas	Asia & The Pacific
Aug. 31		A curfew is imposed in Belfast, where 214 buildings have been burned in a week....The Syndicalist Union in Milan orders metal workers throughout Lombardy to take forcible possession of all factories....Polish staff officers petition the Lithuanian government for the right to use Lithuanian territory during upcoming operations against Russia.		Dr. J.L. Tamayo is inaugurated as President of Ecuador.	
Sep. 1		The death toll from Belfast rioting reaches 25....Lithuanian delegates break off negotiations with Polish staff officers, stating that Polish demands would violate the Russian-Lithuanian peace treaty....An eleven-day celebration of the Mayflower tercentenary begins in Plymouth, England....Turkish Nationalists propose an armistice with Armenia until President Wilson defines the Armenian boundaries.		John Barrett retires after 14 years as head of the Pan-American Union; he is succeeded by Dr. L.U. Rowe, former Assistant Secretary of the Treasury....The Mexican government orders the deportation of U.S. draft dodger Lynn E.A. Gale, the editor of an anti-American newspaper, for his alleged involvement in Bolshevik plots in Mexico.	Peking reports that V.K. Wellington Koo, Chinese Minister to the United States, will be transferred to London in order to represent China in the League of Nations and Alfred Sze, Chinese Minister to London, will go to Washington.... Japan grants dissolution of the Chinese-Japanese military compact for combined defense of China's borders.
Sep. 2		The French government denies reports of a commercial treaty with Hungary....The Employers' National Syndicate in Italy proclaims a general lockout in the mechanical and metallurgical trades all over Italy....The Agudath Israel, the most powerful organization of Orthodox Jews in Europe, decides to transfer its headquarters from Zurich to London....Poland's Finance Minister, Ladislas Grabeld, arrives in Paris to negotiate a commercial treaty....Adolph Abramowicz Joffe replaces M. Danishevsky as head of the Russian Bolshevik delegation to negotiate an armistice with Poland.			
Sep. 3	The U.S., British, and Japanese governments engage in informal conversations with respect to the Anglo-Japanese Treaty.	Striking metal workers in Venice seize a military arsenal.... Commercial treaties between Austria and Germany are renewed, with the addition of "favored nations" clauses....Independent Socialists at a Berlin Convention oppose union with Moscow.	General Gouraud, French High Commissioner for Syria, proclaims the new state of Lebanon.	Deserting members of Pedro Zamora's forces report that the Jalisco bandit has threatened to kill hostages W.A. Gardiner and Bertie C. Johnson if he does not receive ransom immediately....Leaders of striking mill workers and tobacco factory employees decide to call off a strike that affected at least 30,000 workers in Mexico City.	The U.S. Congressional Party visiting the Far East is welcomed in Tokyo.
Sep. 4		Reports from Constantinople reveal that French forces have captured Urfa and Greek forces are occupying two towns south of Brusa....Strikers in Milan place machine guns on the roofs of several factories and organize a workers' militia to resist intervention by government troops.... Police escort George Gavan Duffy, Sinn Fein's envoy to Paris, to the Belgian frontier after the French government asks him to leave.	Spanish forces occupy Zautum, Morocco....Persian Minister Sadigh-es-Saltaneh denies reports of a secret treaty purportedly signed between Persia and Great Britain in 1919....Prince Mejid, brother of the Shah of Persia, matriculates at an American school in Turkey and declares his wish to be an American.		The bureau chief of the Japanese Foreign Office is shot in the abdomen and gravely wounded.
Sep. 5		The Spanish government proscribes a planned Communist demonstration in Madrid....Germany's Foreign Minister, Dr. Walter Simon, apologizes to France for the Breslau incident....Britain's Council of Action decides to send two labor delegates to Riga to attend the Russo-Polish conference....Armed bands of Yugoslavs violently interrupt a meeting of Austrian adherents in the southern plebiscite zone of Styria.		General Alvaro Obregon is elected President of Mexico.	In a meeting with visiting American Congressmen, former Japanese premier Marquis Okuma asks that Japan be given a free hand to improve conditions in Korea.
	A *Includes developments that affect more than one world region, international organizations and important meetings of world leaders.*	B *Includes all domestic and regional developments in Europe, including the Soviet Union.*	C *Includes all domestic and regional developments in Africa and the Middle East.*	D *Includes all domestic and regional developments in Latin America, the Caribbean, and Canada.*	E *Includes all domestic and regional developments in Asian and Pacific nations (and colonies).*

Date	U.S. Politics & Social Issues	U.S. Foreign Policy & Affairs, Defense	U.S. Economy & Environment	Science, Technology & Nature	Culture, Leisure & Lifestyle
Aug. 31	The Tennessee House of Representatives reconsiders its position on suffrage and votes 47 to 24 for a motion to nonconcur in the action of the Tennessee Senate in ratifying the federal suffrage amendment.	The headquarters of the American Expeditionary Forces, located in Washington DC, is demobilized and General John J. Pershing becomes the permanent head of the army.	Two people are killed and 16 others injured when a passenger elevator in the Clarendon Building in New York falls 10 stories.…Representatives of New York City painters vote to strike for higher wages and shorter hours.…Forbidden by law to strike, 42 of 67 firemen and engineers in New York City government buildings resign.	Electrical and hail storms in Connecticut kill two people and cause heavy damage to farm buildings and crops.	Shortstop Ray French joins the New York Yankees.…Dr. Bernadotte Perrin, professor emeritus of Greek literature and history at Yale, dies.
Sep. 1	The Massachusetts Republican Committee asks State Treasurer Fred J. Burrell to withdraw his candidacy for renomination at the upcoming primary.…The Indiana Prohibition Party nominates Mrs. Culla J. Vayhinger for the U.S. Senate.…Prohibition enforcement agents seize $75,000 worth of liquor from 50 saloons and restaurants in New York City.	The U.S.S. *S-5* suffers partial flooding during a practice dive off the Delaware Bay.	Three thousand van drivers, chauffeurs, and packers and 2,000 plumbers go on strike in New York City.…Election officials in Mount Vernon, NY, threaten to strike if their salaries are not increased.…John L. Lewis, President of the United Mine Workers of America, orders a general strike in the bituminous coal field in Alabama.…Three thousand men are imported to New York City to break the strike on the B.R.T. lines.	The 24th meeting of the American Astronomical Society opens at Smith and Mount Holyoke Colleges.…U.S. Air Mail aviator Lieutenant Max Miller is killed in a plane crash, along with his mechanic Gustav Rierson.	The Western Golf Association refuses to accept a newly adopted stymie rule.…Film star Robert Harron accidentally shoots himself with a pistol.
Sep. 2	Thirteen detainees at Ellis Island are injured in a brawl over granulated sugar.…One man is killed and 13 people are injured when the driver of a stolen car loses control of the vehicle and runs into a crowd in front of the New York's Hippodrome Theater.…Three women escape from New York's Bedford State Reformatory.	A U.S. destroyer arrives at the port of Danzig to protect Americans there.	The anthracite coal industry nearly comes to a standstill as 125,000 workers, dissatisfied with the wage award approved by President Wilson, stage a peaceful walkout.…B.R.T. strikers stab and beat a 17-year-old boy, apparently mistaking him for a strikebreaker.…In the fifth day of the B.R.T. strike, strikers and their sympathizers continue to hurl stones at elevated and surface cars.…Three thousand longshoremen and dock workers in Brooklyn pledge not to return to work on any British ship until England recognizes the Irish Republic.		Samuel Goldwyn resigns as president of the Goldwyn Pictures Corporation.
Sep. 3	The District of Columbia Supreme Court refuses to grant an injunction to prevent Secretary of State Bainbridge Colby from promulgating the suffrage amendment.…Police in Bridgeport, CT, arrest the alleged leader of an extortion ring and confiscate enough dynamite to blow up a dozen of the city's largest factories.…James W. Gerard, former ambassador to Germany, is appointed Chairman of the Finance Committee of the Democratic National Committee.	The officers and crew of the U.S.S. *S-5* are rescued by the steamship *Alanthus* and later taken aboard the battleship *Ohio*, which attempts to tow the submarine into shallower water.	Longshoremen and freight handlers in Boston leave work as a protest against England's treatment of Ireland.…Massachusetts State Treasurer Fred J. Burrell announces his resignation.…A gang of men, believed to be outlaw strikers, hijacks a freight train in Chicago after beating the crew and throwing them from the train.…Two thousand employees of the Lehigh Valley Coal Company in Pennsylvania vote to return to work.	A slight earthquake is felt in outlying parts of Los Angeles.	Actress Elizabeth McKentry dies of pneumonia.
Sep. 4	Fifty federal prohibition agents seize more than $100,000 worth of liquor during a sensational raid in Atlantic City, NJ.…New York City police are summoned to restore order when striking van drivers stop trucks in several parts of the city and beat the nonunion drivers.	The U.S. Army transport *Princess Matoika* arrives from Antwerp with the bodies of 1,280 dead American soldiers.	The French government awards James Stewart & Co. an $11 million contract to construct a crude oil pipeline from Havre to Paris.…Seeking to avert the strike ordered by John L. Lewis of the United Mine Workers of America, Governor Thomas Kilby of Alabama appoints a commission to adjust miners' grievances.	Scientists at the Department of Agriculture's Arlington experimental farm produce gas from the distillation of straw.	Babe Ruth sets a new home run record by hitting his 45th and 46th home runs in a double-header at Fenway Park.…Man O' War shatters the world record for a mile and five furlongs.
Sep. 5	Officials arrest 11 men and seize $10,000 worth of alcohol at Coney Island.…Department of Justice agents in Springfield, IL, arrest 20 members of the Communist Party of America, five of whom confess participation in a plot to destroy the Diamond Special train of the Illinois Central Railroad.	Representatives of the American Legion attend ceremonies in France commemorating the Battle of the Marne.	The Geological Survey issues a report indicating that the coal output for the year to date is higher than that for the same period in 1919.		Actor Robert Harron dies from self-inflicted gunshot wounds sustained when his pistol accidentally misfired.

	World Affairs	Europe	Africa & The Middle East	The Americas	Asia & The Pacific
Sep. 6		Lithuania announces its readiness to resume negotiations with Poland.... The French government announces plans to repay a $250 million loan to Britain via funds in hand, gold shipments, and a new loan underwritten by J.P. Morgan & Co.		Dr. Belisario Porras, President-elect of Panama, announces the establishment of the Pan-American College of Commerce.	Representatives of the Japanese Chambers of Commerce adopt resolutions opposing American shipping legislation as injurious to the trade interests of other countries.
Sep. 7		Several serious revolts against the Russian Soviet government break out in the neighborhood of Moscow....Poland appeals to the League of Nations for mediation in the dispute with Lithuania.	A dispatch from Guatemala City reports that the Guatemalan and Mexican governments intend to build an international bridge over the Suchiate River.		Japan confers titles of nobility on the members of the Japanese delegation at the Peace Conference of Versailles.
Sep. 8	The opening session of the International Congress of Women is held in Christiana, Norway.	Russian Soviet forces recapture Omsk from peasant insurgents.... An actors' strike closes several Madrid theaters....Five transports of Greek troops arrive at Ismid, 55 miles southeast of Constantinople, to begin replacing British troops.			
Sep. 9		Gabriele d'Annunzio proclaims Fiume an independent state....In a meeting with Sir Robert Horne at the Board of Trade, British coal miners reject all of the government's proposals to avert a strike....The German peace delegation in Paris warns that unrest in Silesia might make it impossible for Germany to carry out its coal delivery obligation.		The Bolivian Legation informs the U.S. State Department that Ismael Montes, former Minister to France, has been replaced by Don Felix Avelino Aramayo.	The Governor General of India appoints Alexander Frederick Whyte as first president of the forthcoming Indian Legislative Assembly....The Philippine Council of State announces plans to deport 3,000 Chinese accused of smuggling large quantities of opium into Mindanao.... Japan's Premier Takashi Hara refuses a peerage, preferring to keep his seat in the House of Representatives as a commoner.
Sep. 10		The General Confederation of Labor convenes in Milan to decide its policy relative to the labor situation in Italy....Customs guards at the French border thwart an attempt to smuggle 900 pounds of silver out of Germany....Workers in Milan seize more than 200 chemical works and immediately hoist red flags and banners bearing the Bolshevik emblems of the hammer and sickle....A Socialist revolt breaks out in Trieste, but Italian troops restore order by nightfall....Finland recognizes Hungary.	British troops occupy Shereban, 60 miles north of Baghdad.	A dynamite explosion, resulting from apparent negligence in handling the explosive, takes the lives of 30 men in Callao Bay, Peru.	
Sep. 11	A large contingent of Olympic athletes returns to the United States and complains bitterly about the treatment they received in Antwerp.			President de la Huerta bans liquor on Saturdays and Sundays in Mexico City.	Tokyo police prohibit anti-California mass meetings scheduled for September 12 by the Constitutional Labor Union.
Sep. 12	A group of 778 Russian refugee children bound ultimately for Petrograd leave New York on the Japanese steamer *Yomei Maru*.	Premier Millerand of France and Premier Giolitti of Italy meet for the first time at Aix-Les-Bains in an effort to promote harmonious feelings between their two countries.... Former French President Raymond Poincaré announces that he will not resume his former office in the event that President Deschanel resigns....Fifteen hundred refugees arrive in Ismid, Asia Minor, from the village of Kirazil.		Peruvian newspapers repudiate claims that an agreement has been reached between Peru and Chile with regard to the Tacna-Arica controversy....Five spectators at an automobile race in Mexico City are killed when a driver loses control of his vehicle and crashes through a fence.	Japanese newspapers report that Japanese troops in Siberia will be reduced from three to two divisions in accordance with the policy of gradual evacuation.

A	B	C	D	E
Includes developments that affect more than one world region, international organizations and important meetings of world leaders.	*Includes all domestic and regional developments in Europe, including the Soviet Union.*	*Includes all domestic and regional developments in Africa and the Middle East.*	*Includes all domestic and regional developments in Latin America, the Caribbean, and Canada.*	*Includes all domestic and regional developments in Asian and Pacific nations (and colonies).*

U.S. Politics & Social Issues	U.S. Foreign Policy & Affairs, Defense	U.S. Economy & Environment	Science, Technology & Nature	Culture, Leisure & Lifestyle	
		Census data for 1920 reveals that one-quarter of the U.S. population lives in 68 cities, with one-tenth of the population in Chicago, New York, and Philadelphia.…Ten passengers are killed and 87 injured when two trolleys collide in a suburb of Denver.…The Federal Trade Commission charges the International Harvester Company with profiteering.	Radio station WWJ in Detroit airs the first radio broadcast of a prizefight.…The Radio Corporation of America purchases the wireless station in Tuckerton, NJ, from the Marconi Company.	World heavyweight champion Jack Dempsey defends his title by knocking out Billy Miske in three rounds.…Aviator stuntman Myron L. Tinney falls to his death before 200,000 spectators at the state fairgrounds in Detroit.…Bill Tilden defeats William Johnston in the finals of the national tennis championship.	Sep. 6
Chicago Mayor William Hale Thompson sues Lieutenant Governor John G. Oglesby for libel.	One hundred refugee boys escape from the Fort Wadsworth military reservation, where they and 860 other Russian refugee children were being held until they could be returned to their homes in Russia.…Fourteen officers of the National Guard and Officers Reserve Corps are added to the army's General Staff.	Four civilian workers at the Edgewood Arsenal in Baltimore die from wood alcohol poisoning, and 11 others are reported seriously ill.…The Federal Reserve Bank announces the dissolution of the Victory Liberty Loan Association.	Flooding causes extensive damage throughout Austria.…Six towns are wiped out and hundreds of people killed when a powerful earthquake hits the greater part of Northern and Central Italy.	A grand jury investigation is ordered to consider allegations that the August 31 game between the Chicago Cubs and Philadelphia Phillies was fixed.	Sep. 7
The brokerage firm of S.P. Orange & Co. sues the United States Cane Sugar Corporation for $3 million for breach of contract.…Prohibition agents seize 2,000 gallons of liquor from a home in Allenhurst, NJ.	The U.S. Navy recalls Rear Admiral Harry S. Knapp to active duty for special service in Haiti.	A pilot and passenger are fatally injured when their hydroplane crashes into a cornfield near Wilkes-Barre, PA.…The anthracite miners' strike begins to crumble as a large number of miners return to work despite a church holiday.	Regular air mail service between New York and San Francisco begins.	Rida Johnson Young's *Little Old New York* opens at the Plymouth Theater in New York.…Professional bouts open to the public are legalized in Boston.…Woodie Platt unseats S. David Herron as national amateur golf champion.	Sep. 8
A crowd of 25 men attack and severely beat a New Jersey prohibition agent as he attempts to make an arrest.…A grand jury in Springfield, IL, indicts the eight leaders of an alleged plot to wreck the Illinois Central Diamond Special.	A soldier at Fort Wadsworth accidentally kills a Russian refugee boy while demonstrating the manual of arms.…An additional 75 Russian refugee boys escape from Fort Wadsworth.…The armored cruiser *Pittsburgh* runs aground on rocks in the Baltic Sea and is reported to be in a dangerous position.	The Justice Department joins the U.S. Army's investigation into the alcohol-related deaths of nine civilian employees at Edgewood Arsenal in Baltimore.…A fire disables telephone connections and some of the news wires at the *Morning Telegraph*.…The U.S. steamer *Siboney* runs aground in the harbor of Vigo, Spain.	Another violent earthquake, the second in a week, occurs in the Emilia district of Italy.…An earthquake is felt in San Jose, CA.…A new flax-pulling machine, which promises to revolutionize the linen industry, is demonstrated in Troy, NY.	Babe Ruth scores his 47th home run.	Sep. 9
Cincinnati police uncover a nationwide baseball lottery scheme headquartered in Pittsburgh.	The second annual American Legion convention opens in Albany.…A court martial on Governor's Island acquits Sergeants John O'Hare and Calvin York on charges of violating the 73rd Article of War in allowing their prisoner, Grover C. Bergdol, to escape.	An open trolley car collides with a sightseeing automobile in New York, injuring 24 passengers.…The amount of coal received at various ports is estimated at only 25 to 30 percent of the normal tonnage.…The Bureau of Internal Revenue publicizes income tax figures for the year.…A federal investigation of coal profiteering begins.…President Wilson refuses to reconvene the Scale Committee of the anthracite coal operators and miners.	An earthquake shock is felt in Riverside, CA, but no major damage is reported.	Scribner's publishes F. Scott Fitzgerald's first collection of short stories, *Flappers and Philosophers*.…Babe Ruth hits his 48th home run of the season.…Movie actress Olive Thomas dies in Paris after accidentally ingesting mercury.	Sep. 10
George D. Pteriotis and five others are charged with a bill of lading forgery scheme that netted at least $250,000 in one month.…The American Civil Liberties Union announces that a $50,000 bail fund has been raised to release 33 members of the Industrial Workers of the World from Leavenworth Prison.	The U.S. armored cruiser *Pittsburgh* is towed into Libau Roads.	British steamship agents in Boston give striking longshoremen two days to return to work or their positions will be filled.…United Mine Workers officials issue a statement advising workers to return to the mines.…One person is crushed to death and 70 others injured when two open trolley cars collide in New York City.	A strong electrical storm causes extensive damage to parks on both the American and Canadian sides of Niagara Falls.	The Gold Cup Regatta opens in Detroit.…Chick Evans defeats Francis Ouimet to regain the national amateur golf title.…The fall racing season opens at Havre De Grace, MD.…U.S. pugilist Billy Shade knocks out Australia's welterweight champion Tommy Aren in the 19th round.	Sep. 11
The Minnesota State Supreme Court rejects both A.J. Volstead and the Rev. O.J. Kvale as potential Republican nominees for Congress for the Seventh District.…The National Conference of Catholic Charities opens in Washington, DC.…Seven thousand Italian-Americans celebrate Fiume Day in New York City.		The results of a survey conducted by the National Industrial Conference Board indicate that the cost of living for U.S. wage earners has increased 104.5 percent in six years.…The engineer and fireman are killed and one passenger is fatally wounded when a landslide strikes a passenger train near De Beque, Colorado.	Frank K. Gardner, President of the General Food Products Company, announces that scientists have invented and perfected a process by which white sugar can be obtained from corn and manufactured for less than four cents per pound.		Sep. 12
F	**G**	**H**	**I**	**J**	
Includes campaigns, elections, federal-state relations, civil rights and liberties, crime, the judiciary, education, healthcare, poverty, urban affairs, and population.	*Includes formation and debate of U.S. foreign and defense policies, veterans affairs, and defense spending. (Relations with specific foreign countries are usually found under the region concerned.)*	*Includes business, labor, agriculture, taxation, transportation, consumer affairs, monetary and fiscal policy, natural resources, pollution and industrial accidents.*	*Includes worldwide scientific, medical and technological developments, natural phenomena, U.S. weather and natural disasters.*	*Includes the arts, religion, scholarship, communications media, sports, entertainment, fashions, fads, and social life.*	

	World Affairs	Europe	Africa & The Middle East	The Americas	Asia & The Pacific
Sep. 13		Belgium accepts the Franco-Belgian defensive military agreement, effective immediately, to apply in the case of unprovoked aggression by Germany.... Rioters drown several Bolshevik commissioners in the Neva River when news of Soviet military defeats reaches Petrograd.		The Empire Trade Congress opens in Toronto.	
Sep. 14	The Congress of the International Council of Women adopts a resolution urging each member state of the League of Nations to send a female delegate to the Assembly.... Rumania joins the League of Nations.	Five thousand unemployed men bearing red flags demonstrate before the office of the Employment Council in Berlin before forcibly removing the council members from the office.... Austria's Constitutional Committee grants consent for Vienna to become a separate Austrian province.... Rumania officially ratifies the Treaty of Versailles.... An Italian Socialist begins a hunger strike in prison.		The International Association of Fire Fighters holds its third annual convention in St. Louis, with delegates from the United States and Canada.	
Sep. 15		M. Konitz, Albanian Minister of Foreign Affairs, appeals to the United States, France, and Britain to compel the withdrawal of Serbian troops from the territory claimed by Albania.... The British members of the Entente Commission in Upper Silesia resign in protest against the alleged intimidation of the German population by the Poles.... Fighting between Polish and Lithuanian forces is resumed in the Suwalki sector, near the German border. Disarmament begins in Berlin in accordance with the demands of the Entente.		Delegates from Central American countries meet to discuss the formation of the Central American Union.... President-elect Carlos Herrera of Guatemala takes the oath of office.... E.W. Speed, a U.S. citizen, is shot and killed on the Mexican border.	The Chinese government decrees an income tax, effective in January.
Sep. 16	The Council of the League of Nations begins a three-day session in Paris.... The legal authorities of the League of Nations decide that Finland has no valid claim to the Aland Islands.	French President Paul Deschanel resigns.... Italian Premier Giovanni Giolitti urges conciliation and moderation in conferences with workmen and employers in Turin.... Spanish newspapers report a serious land crisis in Andalusia and other sections of Spain.	French and Spanish troops launch a joint operation against Moroccan tribesmen in the zone lying between the Spanish and French territories in Morocco.	Felipe Piñeda, leader of a revolt in the state of Chiapas, Mexico, surrenders to General Francisco Cosio Robelo.	The Attorney General launches an investigation into an alleged agreement among Manila banks to regulate interest and exchange rates.
Sep. 17		A bomb explodes at the Stock Exchange in Genoa, but no casualties are reported.		The Prince of Wales arrives in Trinidad on board the battleship *Renown*.... A fire in Tampico, Mexico, destroys 40 buildings and a wharf.	
Sep. 18	Finland and Sweden agree to accept intervention by the League of Nations to settle a dispute over the Aaland Islands.	With the exception of one manufacturing plant controlled by American interests, workmen occupy all the factories in the Italian industrial town of Terni.... The War Office in Warsaw reports that Polish detachments have driven enemy troops across the Stirpa and have captured several towns as well as the Styr and Stockhod Rivers.... Heads of the Polish and Soviet peace delegations meet informally for a two-hour conference in Riga.... Six Hungarians are held in Genoa as suspects in the bombing case there.		Canadian politician Robert Beaven, the former premier of British Columbia, dies.	

A	B	C	D	E
Includes developments that affect more than one world region, international organizations and important meetings of world leaders.	*Includes all domestic and regional developments in Europe, including the Soviet Union.*	*Includes all domestic and regional developments in Africa and the Middle East.*	*Includes all domestic and regional developments in Latin America, the Caribbean, and Canada.*	*Includes all domestic and regional developments in Asian and Pacific nations (and colonies).*

U.S. Politics & Social Issues	U.S. Foreign Policy & Affairs, Defense	U.S. Economy & Environment	Science, Technology & Nature	Culture, Leisure & Lifestyle	
The first chapter of American Indian War Mothers is formed in Fort Yates, ND.…Herbert Stirling, charged with robbing and killing an aged peddler, is arrested in New Jersey following a year-long search.…Republicans win a record victory in the Maine primaries.	The 21st encampment of the Veterans of Foreign Wars opens in Washington.	New York's Governor Alfred E. Smith meets with Samuel Gompers, President of the American Federation of Labor, in an effort to settle the Brooklyn Rapid Transit strike through mediation.…The annual convention of the Institute of American Meat Packers opens in Atlantic City.…The "outlaw" railroad strike in Chicago ends as railway men vote to return to work.	A brief hail and thunder storm with 45-mile-per-hour gales does damage estimated at hundreds of thousands of dollars in New England.…An earthquake tremor is felt in Scotland.	The national women's tennis championship tournament opens in Philadelphia.…European heavyweight boxing champion Georges Carpentier arrives in New York from France.…Babe Ruth hits his 49th home run of the season.	Sep. 13
The West Virginia legislature holds a special session to amend registration and election laws so that women may vote in November.…A federal judge in Michigan upholds the constitutionality of Section 4 of the Lever Food Control Act.…A white man, Alto Windham, is lynched in Alabama for remarks he allegedly made to a woman.…Connecticut becomes the 37th state to ratify the federal suffrage amendment.		Walter Stevens, a pioneer of the air mail service, and Russell Thomas, his mechanic, are burned to death when the gasoline tank of their airplane explodes.…The Commission on the Necessities of Life reports a serious coal shortage in New England and appeals to dealers and consumers to employ conservation measures.		Gar Wood of the Detroit Yacht Club wins the American Powerboat Association's gold challenge cup and sets a new world record for speed when his hydroplane, *Miss America*, reaches 71.43 miles per hour.…Babe Ruth ties the American League record of 147 runs in a season.	Sep. 14
Anti-Saloon League officials hold a national conference in Washington, DC.…Pittsburgh attorney Jacob Margolis is disbarred for alleged revolutionary activity.…Robert G. Meads pleads guilty to manslaughter in the death of Henry E. Maroney, a fellow student at Dartmouth College, and is sentenced to 15 to 20 years hard labor in the New Hampshire State Prison at Concord.…Connecticut's Governor Marcus Holcomb refuses to certify the state legislature's ratification of the suffrage amendment.	Secretary of State Bainbridge Colby begins formal negotiations with Baron K. Shidehara, Japanese Ambassador to the United States, on the subject of proposed anti-Japanese legislation in California.	The Interstate Commerce Commission authorizes the New York Central Railway to issue new collateral trust bonds and mortgage bonds.…Zion National Park opens in Utah.…Fourteen people are injured when a bus collides with a motor truck in Brooklyn.…Five people, including two policemen on strike duty, are treated for shock when two Brooklyn Rapid Transit surface cars collide.…Representatives of ship owners in North Atlantic ports reject the demands of the International Longshoremen's Association for a 25 percent wage increase.		Babe Ruth scores two more home runs in an exhibition game against Toledo.	Sep. 15
A bomb explodes outside J.P. Morgan's Wall Street office building, killing 31 people and injuring several hundred more.…Federal agents are sent from Chicago to apprehend I.W.W. chieftain William "Big Bill" Haywood as a precautionary measure following the explosion in the Wall Street financial district.…All five Socialist assemblymen expelled from the New York legislature in April are reelected.		Nearly 350 B.R.T. strikers return to work.…Thousands of Pennsylvania mine workers in the Scranton district return to work.…Trading on Wall Street is suspended for the day following an explosion outside the J.P. Morgan building.		The Boxing Commission formally restores boxing as a legalized professional sport in New York State.…Missing pilot John L. Eaton is found alive and safe in Nevada.	Sep. 16
The death toll from the Wall Street explosion reaches 33.…A grand jury investigation is launched to determine responsibility for the Wall Street explosion.…Rewards totaling $2,500 are offered for evidence leading to the arrest and conviction of the perpetrators of the Wall Street explosion.…The Republican Party officially opens its speaking campaign.	A fragment of a shell strikes and kills a four-year-old boy during a battle reenactment at Camp Meade.	The Stock Exchange reopens as usual at 10 a.m.…Secretary of Labor William Wilson agrees to meet with the Policy Committee of the United Mine Workers of America.		The American Professional Football Association (later renamed the National Football League) is founded.…A patriotic pageant entitled "We, the People" is performed at Carnegie Hall under the auspices of the Constitutional League of America.	Sep. 17
Presidential hopeful Warren B. Harding addresses from his front porch in Marion, OH, delegations of foreign-born citizens representing 30 different nationalities.…Suspecting that he might be connected to the Wall Street explosion, police arrest Alexander I. Brailovsky as an undesirable alien.…Department of Justice agents seize an Italian stowaway just before a White Star liner leaves New York for Naples.	The Veterans of Foreign Wars vote against admitting women to their organization.	An elevated train catches fire after colliding with another train in Queens, NY.…Approximately 10,000 anthracite mine workers in the Schuylkill region decide to remain on "vacation" until the mine operators reinstate all other workers who quit in sympathy with the miners.…Two additional companies of Alabama troops are ordered to join the five companies already in the coal strike district near Birmingham, where several thousand miners are on strike.		Ralph de Palma sets three new world records for speed in the New York State Fair automobile races.	Sep. 18

F	G	H	I	J
Includes campaigns, elections, federal-state relations, civil rights and liberties, crime, the judiciary, education, healthcare, poverty, urban affairs, and population.	*Includes formation and debate of U.S. foreign and defense policies, veterans affairs, and defense spending. (Relations with specific foreign countries are usually found under the region concerned.)*	*Includes business, labor, agriculture, taxation, transportation, consumer affairs, monetary and fiscal policy, natural resources, pollution and industrial accidents.*	*Includes worldwide scientific, medical and technological developments, natural phenomena, U.S. weather and natural disasters.*	*Includes the arts, religion, scholarship, communications media, sports, entertainment, fashions, fads, and social life.*

	World Affairs	Europe	Africa & The Middle East	The Americas	Asia & The Pacific
Sep. 19		Three members of the Turkish Cabinet resign, necessitating the selection of a new ministry.		King Albert and Queen Elizabeth of Belgium, the first king and queen to visit a South American country, arrive in Brazil....The entire Montreal financial district is carefully guarded as a result of the bomb explosion in New York.	The Federal Ministry of Australia decides to allow limited trade with Germany in exceptional circumstances.
Sep. 20		A massive German nationalist demonstration is held in Vienna....A meeting between Sir Robert Horne and the British coal miners' executive fails to produce a settlement....Poland and Lithuania agree to an immediate suspension of hostilities, pending a settlement of their dispute by the League of nations....Jewish refugees arriving in Vienna report anti-Semitic outrages by Ukrainian troops in East Galicia....Gabriele d'Annunzio appoints a Cabinet for the provisional government of Fiume.			
Sep. 21	The 50th International Congress Against Alcoholism opens in Washington, DC.	The Russo-Polish peace conference opens in Riga, Latvia, with American and other foreign observers in attendance....John Lynch, a republican leader and Sinn Fein judge, is shot dead in a Dublin hotel.		The Canadian ladies' golf championship tournament opens in Toronto.	Two Japanese are sentenced to 10 years in prison for attempting to sell stolen naval plans to Americans....Commercial and banking institutions in Shanghai place a ban upon the latest issue of bonds offered by the Peking government.
Sep. 22	The Socialist congress in session in Montevideo, Uruguay, votes to adhere to the Third International at Moscow.	Metal workers throughout Italy protest the agreement concluded in Rome between the government and the Metal Workers' Union....Nine people are killed and six wounded when workers in Turin battle in the streets with the Royal Guard.			Prince Koudacheff, Russian envoy to China, refuses to suspend the Russian legation.
Sep. 23	The Chinese government issues a mandate suspending all Russian rights in China and requesting the withdrawal of all diplomatic and consular representatives of the former Kerensky government.	Alexandre Millerand succeeds Paul Deschanel as President of the French Republic....British miners reject the government's mediation proposal and refuse to withdraw their strike notices....Italian Premier Giolitti threatens a blockade of Fiume and other reprisals if d'Annunzio refuses to surrender the transatlantic liner *Cogne*, seized at the beginning of September....Three more people are killed in the Turin disorders.		Argentina and Bolivia appoint delegates to the League of Nations Assembly to be held in November.	Twenty-five people are killed during an anti-Japanese riot in Gensan, Korea.
Sep. 24	An international financial conference opens in Brussels.	Adolf Joffe presents the Russian government's armistice terms at Riga, along with an ultimatum that Soviet Russia will begin a winter offensive if an armistice is not arranged within 10 days....President Millerand appoints Georges Leygues to head the cabinet as Premier and Foreign Minister of France....British coal miners agree to suspend for one week the strike scheduled to begin on September 27 and to meet again with coal mine owners.		Police commissioners in Toronto forbid the Self-Determination for Ireland League to hold public meetings....A supposedly miraculous painting of the Blessed Virgin is discovered on a church window in a suburb of Mexico City.	Rioting in Gensan continues.
Sep. 25		France's ex-President Paul Deschanel retires to a sanatorium for treatment of a nervous disorder....Italy's King Victor Emmanuel sees the Vatican for the first time from a dirigible.		The Chamber of Commerce of the United States in Argentina protests against the assessment of the U.S. income and excess profits tax upon U.S. citizens and business firms residing and operating abroad.	

A	B	C	D	E
Includes developments that affect more than one world region, international organizations and important meetings of world leaders.	*Includes all domestic and regional developments in Europe, including the Soviet Union.*	*Includes all domestic and regional developments in Africa and the Middle East.*	*Includes all domestic and regional developments in Latin America, the Caribbean, and Canada.*	*Includes all domestic and regional developments in Asian and Pacific nations (and colonies).*

U.S. Politics & Social Issues	U.S. Foreign Policy & Affairs, Defense	U.S. Economy & Environment	Science, Technology & Nature	Culture, Leisure & Lifestyle	
The police in several U.S. cities take extra precautions to guard churches, public buildings, and the homes of prominent individuals.…Prohibition leaders from the United States, Canada, and England address meetings in 65 Washington, DC churches.		The American Federation adopts resolutions demanding representation in the Cabinet for farmers and stock raisers and opposing government price-fixing of farm products.		*Heading Home*, a silent film starring Babe Ruth as himself, debuts at Madison Square Garden.	Sep. 19
Jules "Nicky" Arnstein is jailed for contempt of court.…Department of Justice agents and members of the police Anarchist Squad raid a newly established printing press in Chicago and arrest two men.…Race riots erupt on Chicago's South Side after Thomas E. Barrett is slain by a black man.…Three arrests are made at a Socialist meeting in Harlem.	Secretary of State Bainbridge Colby issues a statement in defense of the U.S. government's policy in Haiti.…Testimony begins in the trial of Mrs. Emma C. Bergdoll, on charges of aiding her sons in the evasion of military service.		The Sixth National Exposition of Chemical Industries opens in New York's Grand Central Palace.		Sep. 20
The New York State Assembly votes to expel once again three of its five Socialist members.…Michael Kolachuk pleads guilty to charges of placing a bomb near the home of Police Superintendent George M. Beach in Waterbury, CT.…Will H. Hays, Chairman of the Republican National Committee, selects 40 men and women to serve as the Republican Campaign Advisory Committee.	James Weldon Johnson, Secretary of the National Association for the Advancement of Colored People, attacks the policy of the U.S. government in its occupation of Haiti.	William Harding, Governor of the Federal Reserve Board, meets with representatives of various farmers' organizations to discuss credit conditions facing the nation's farmers.…The New York and Jersey Tunnel Commission opens contract bidding for work on the construction of a vehicular tunnel under the Hudson River.…The Ford Motor Company announces a reduction in the price of its cars to the prewar level.		Thirty-six Rhodes scholars sail for Southampton.	Sep. 21
A grand jury investigation begins into allegations of gambling by baseball players in the 1919 World Series and in the August 31 game between the Chicago Cubs and the Philadelphia Phillies.		A train carrying Governor James M. Cox and approximately 50 influential Arizona Democrats is wrecked near Peoria.…At a meeting in Shamokin, PA, the General Mine Workers Committee votes to return to work.		The Coliseum Theater opens in New York City.…Sixty-two bishops and archbishops of the Catholic Church in the United States begin their annual meeting at the Catholic University of America.	Sep. 22
William G. McAdoo begins a speaking campaign in support of the Cox-Roosevelt ticket.…Two bandits hold up a U.S. mail truck in South Bend, IN.…Congestion at Ellis Island causes a temporary halt to immigration.…A New York City policeman discovers a lighted bomb at an elevated train station in Brooklyn and snuffs out the fuses with his fingers.		The H.H. Franklin Manufacturing Company announces price reductions ranging from 17.5 to 21.5 percent on all models of Franklin automobiles.…Sears, Roebuck & Co. and Montgomery Ward & Co. both announce substantial price reductions in many lines of merchandise.		Several thousand Catholic leaders from across the United States assemble in Washington, DC for the laying of the cornerstone of the Monumental Shrine of the Immaculate Conception.…At an annual rules meeting of more than 150 football coaches, officials, solons, and former star players, unnecessary roughness is defined to include clipping from behind.	Sep. 23
Democratic leader Thomas Taggart files a $100,000 libel suit against the *Brooklyn Standard Union*.	The Sons of Veterans adopt the red poppy as the memorial flower of the order.	Taxicab drivers in Boston go on strike when their demand for a $5 per day wage is refused.…The Crow-Elkhart Motor Corporation announces reductions to prewar prices on all models.…The Cleveland Worsted Mills Company announces a 15 to 30 percent price reduction in wools.	Extensive flooding cripples railway traffic and wire communications in the Friuli province of Italy.	Scribner's publishes Edith Wharton's *In Morocco*.…Babe Ruth hits his 50th and 51st home runs of the season.…French automobile racer Leon Duray breaks four world records for speed on the Eastern States Exposition track in Massachusetts.	Sep. 24
Two masked men hold up an Illinois Central train and escape with thousands of dollars worth of registered mail.		The Farmers' National Grain Dealers' Association reports that midwest farmers are holding wheat for higher prices.			Sep. 25
F *Includes campaigns, elections, federal-state relations, civil rights and liberties, crime, the judiciary, education, healthcare, poverty, urban affairs, and population.*	G *Includes formation and debate of U.S. foreign and defense policies, veterans affairs, and defense spending. (Relations with specific foreign countries are usually found under the region concerned.)*	H *Includes business, labor, agriculture, taxation, transportation, consumer affairs, monetary and fiscal policy, natural resources, pollution and industrial accidents.*	I *Includes worldwide scientific, medical and technological developments, natural phenomena, U.S. weather and natural disasters.*	J *Includes the arts, religion, scholarship, communications media, sports, entertainment, fashions, fads, and social life.*	

	World Affairs	Europe	Africa & The Middle East	The Americas	Asia & The Pacific
Sep. 26		The Swiss government decides not to open political or commercial relations with Soviet Russia....In response to an ultimatum threatening action by the French Black Sea fleet, Soviet Foreign Minister M. Tchitcherin agrees to the immediate repatriation of all French prisoners in Russia.		Consul General Frederic Goding reports critical financial conditions in Ecuador....Uruguay wins the South American football championship.	
Sep. 27		The Lithuanian government calls on the people to arm themselves as Polish forces capture Grodno and push on toward the important railway junction of Lida....After a long search, Dublin police capture and arrest Sinn Fein leader Countess Markievicz.		Communist demonstrations are held at several locations in Mexico City.	
Sep. 28		Polish forces capture Lida and Pinsk and continue to advance toward Vilna, the Lithuanian capital.		Both President de la Huerta and President-elect Obregon vow not to tolerate any further Communist demonstrations in Mexico.... Panama's National Assembly elects three vice presidents of the republic: Federico Boyd, Sr., Guillermo Andreve, and Julio Fabrega.	
Sep. 29	Former Italian Premier Vittorio Orlando leaves to visit Brazil on behalf of King Victor Emmanuel, who is unable to leave Italy.	French President Millerand receives Wilhelm Mayer von Kaufheuren, German Ambassador to France, thus restoring diplomatic relations between France and Germany to a prewar basis....Alderman James Roll is elected Lord Mayor of London....The German-American Commercial and Economic League resume activities after a five-year lapse.			Chinese newspapers report the capture of Canton by Constitutionalist troops under General Chen Chung-Ming.
Sep. 30		Louis Franck, Belgian Minister of the Colonies and the last remaining Liberal on the Delacroix Cabinet, resigns his post.		Deputy Raoul Fernandez, a former member of the Brazilian delegation to the peace conference in Paris, is named to represent Brazil at the League of Nations Assembly in November.	
Oct. 1	The U.S. State Department announces that the League of Nations Secretariat in London has issued a communication listing 34 countries as members of the League. The report states that 13 other countries have applied for admission to the League.	The Dutch Parliament passes an eight-hour workday....Relief efforts continue in Catania, Sicily, for victims of major earthquake and aftershocks. Reports indicate that the village of Codadivolpe, near Giarre, was demolished and other villages and cities experienced large-scale devastation....Smuggled Russian jewels belonging to the Romanoff royal family are offered for sale in Berlin, Germany, on the black market. Market speculators state that sales will benefit *Rote Fahne*, the Communist Party newspaper.... Turkish National Forces take back Kagizman.		Training operations of the Canadian Air Force begin at Camp Borden in Ottawa, using equipment donated by the British government.... Published reports claim Los Angeles bankers have lost nearly $6 million in bad loans to the Mexican State of Lower California. The removal of the Governor of Lower California Esteban Cantu by new Mexican President de la Huerta contributed to the forfeiture of the loans.	M. Gandhi founds the Gujarat Vidyapeeth at Ahmedabad.
Oct. 2		The Delibas Revolt begins in Konya, Turkey.			The armed Korean independence movement attacks Hun-ch'un, in eastern Manchuria, and kills Japanese consulate police....The Chinese government issues a mandate removing the official status of Russian consulates and delegates....Japan announces it will supply Chinese famine victims with rice paid for by an international loan.

A	B	C	D	E
Includes developments that affect more than one world region, international organizations and important meetings of world leaders.	*Includes all domestic and regional developments in Europe, including the Soviet Union.*	*Includes all domestic and regional developments in Africa and the Middle East.*	*Includes all domestic and regional developments in Latin America, the Caribbean, and Canada.*	*Includes all domestic and regional developments in Asian and Pacific nations (and colonies).*

	U.S. Politics & Social Issues	U.S. Foreign Policy & Affairs, Defense	U.S. Economy & Environment	Science, Technology & Nature	Culture, Leisure & Lifestyle
Sep. 26	Three Boston policemen are arrested on burglary charges and ousted from the police force.		C.M. Keys, Vice President of the Curtiss Aeroplane and Motor Corporation, purchases control of the company from the Willys-Overland Corporation....Governor Calvin Coolidge of Massachusetts meets with leading Boston bankers to discuss the closing of several banks within a comparatively short time.		Arthur Spencer is crowned the professional bicycle champion of America....The *New York Times* reports that the dice game craps is attaining social prominence.
Sep. 27	Harvard University begins the new academic year with a record enrollment of approximately 6,000 students, including women who are admitted for the first time to a regular department....New York's Governor Smith signs into law several measures designed to remedy the housing shortage.	A three-day convention of the American Legion opens in Cleveland.	The Boston meatpacking company Armour & Co. pleads not guilty in federal court on charges of profiteering.	A violent earthquake in Giarre, Sicily, demolishes the nearby village of Codadivolpe....Inventor Parker H. Bradley demonstrates a method of fireproofing airplanes at New York's Hazlehurst Field.	Babe Ruth hits his 52nd and 53rd home runs of the season.
Sep. 28	Eight White Sox players are indicted on charges of fixing the 1919 World Series....Women vote for the first time in New Jersey at the primary election....President Wilson pardons Howard W. Showalter, a West Virginia banker sentenced to five years in federal prison for misapplication of national bank funds.	A jury in Philadelphia finds Mrs. Emma C. Bergdoll and four of her codefendants guilty of conspiring to aid Edwin and Grover C. Bergdoll in evading the draft.	Governor John J. Cornwell of West Virginia announces that federal troops will be withdrawn form the strike zones of the Mingo coal fields as soon as 1,600 new deputy sheriffs are appointed to help maintain order.		Thirteen-year-old Frederick Santee enrolls as a freshman at Harvard.
Sep. 29	The home of Chicago Alderman John MacAlister is bombed....Thirty-four alleged radicals awaiting deportation are transferred from Ellis Island to Boston's Deer Island....White Sox pitcher Claude "Lefty" Williams confesses his role in the baseball gambling scandal.	J.W. Galbraith, Jr., is elected National Commander of the American Legion.	Deep sea longshoremen affiliated with the International Longshoremen's Association vote to renew their contract, relinquishing union demands for a 25 percent wage increase....Presidential nominee Warren G. Harding's train is derailed on an 80-foot trestle in West Virginia.	The largest wireless sending station in the world is officially dedicated in Nauen, Germany.	Babe Ruth hits his 54th home run of the season.
Sep. 30	Governor Smith approves a measure to provide for the immediate issue of long-term bonds for the erection of new schools in New York City....The 37th victim of the Wall Street explosion dies in a New York hospital.	A navy dirigible crashes into a mountain peak near Hollywood, injuring four of the five crewmembers.	Eight thousand miners with the Pennsylvania Coal Company go on strike again, in part to protest alleged interference by state police....Fire destroys a pier and 3,500 bales of cotton in Galveston, TX.		The Times Square Theater opens on West 42nd Street.
Oct. 1	In a rare political statement, Edith Kermit Roosevelt, widow of Theodore Roosevelt, comes out in support of Ohio Senator Warren G. Harding and Massachusetts Governor Calvin Coolidge....Presidential candidate Governor Cox makes speeches in Kansas today supporting Prohibition and a hands-off policy for the United States in dealing with Russia and Mexico....William H. Cox of St. Louis files in several state primaries as the presidential candidate for the U.S. Socialist Labor Party. August Gillhaus of New York is the vice-presidential candidate on the ticket.	U.S. military forces stationed in Germany will have the aviation unit restored with trained fliers and state-of-the-art U.S. Army airplanes....U.S. General John J. Pershing is awarded the Medaille Militaire, the top French military decoration, by the French government, and French Army General Fayolle for his service during two periods of at least three years and for his exceptional service in the organization of national defense. The award ceremony is held in Washington, DC.	The U.S. Interstate Commerce Commission announces preparation of a plan to merge a number of U.S. railroad companies under Section 407 of the U.S. Transportation Act of 1919....The American Shipbuilding Company reports a profit of nearly $3 million after payment of taxes....Galveston, TX begins cleanup from a waterfront fire that recorded damages of nearly $2 million....New rent laws are put into effect, creating an official Moving Day in New York City for tenants. Rioting breaks out in Brooklyn as a result of landlord and tenant tensions over new rent regulations and fees.	The Midwest is hit by freezing temperatures that destroy most of the remainder of the corn crop....The Atlantic Coast is hit by tropical storms with wind gusts of more than 60 miles per hour that damage Mount Vernon and break glass in Times Square buildings in New York City....U.S. airmail service pilot Bryan McMullen is killed while making a landing attempt in Batavia, IL. McMullen's plane hits a telephone wire and bursts into flames. The pilot was involved in an airplane crash earlier in the week and was flying an older service plane. Both facts are thought to contribute to the disaster.	Chief Justice McDonald announces that the investigation into the charges that eight White Sox baseball players purposely changed the outcome of the 1919 World Series for monetary gain would continue....Brooklyn District Attorney Harry E. Lewis opens investigation into charges that gamblers are involved in a plot to alter the upcoming games between the Brooklyn Robins (later known as the Dodgers) and the Cleveland Indians....The Roosevelt Newsboys' Club of Boston passes a resolution condemning indicted Chicago White Sox baseball players.
Oct. 2					The baseball teams Pirates and Reds play three games in one day, the only tripleheader of the century. The Reds win two games (13–4 and 7–3), while the Pirates win in a shutout 6–0 when the last game is suspended at darkness....James "Cot" Tierney is one of five players to play in all three games of the tripleheader.
	F *Includes campaigns, elections, federal-state relations, civil rights and liberties, crime, the judiciary, education, healthcare, poverty, urban affairs, and population.*	G *Includes formation and debate of U.S. foreign and defense policies, veterans affairs, and defense spending. (Relations with specific foreign countries are usually found under the region concerned.)*	H *Includes business, labor, agriculture, taxation, transportation, consumer affairs, monetary and fiscal policy, natural resources, pollution and industrial accidents.*	I *Includes worldwide scientific, medical and technological developments, natural phenomena, U.S. weather and natural disasters.*	J *Includes the arts, religion, scholarship, communications media, sports, entertainment, fashions, fads, and social life.*

	World Affairs	Europe	Africa & The Middle East	The Americas	Asia & The Pacific
Oct. 3				The South American soccer Championship between Argentina, Chile, and Uruguay wraps up tournament in Valparaiso, Chile.	The Chinese delegation from the conference on the Far Eastern Republic of Siberia sends the United States word that the Chinese government will not tolerate Bolshevist propaganda materials and literature inside China.
Oct. 4		The first Congress of Soviets of the Republic is called to order at Orenburg with 273 delegates in attendance.			
Oct. 5	Pope Benedict XV presents an encyclical.	French newspapers make jest of American reports that Thomas Edison has constructed a device to speak with the dead in the spirit world.	The American University opens in Cairo.		
Oct. 6	All committees of the international financial conference in Brussels announce unanimous agreements on recommendations.... Polish officials report intense fighting with Lithuania on the border in Orany, between Grodno and Vilna.... England's Prime Minister Lloyd George makes a formal statement for *The Lloyd George Liberal Magazine* highlighting the importance of the United States and Germany joining the League of Nations.	Turkish National Forces enter Konya.... Delegates from Yugoslavia and Italy agree to meet at a future date in Venice on details of the Adriatic settlement.... An economic depression hits England with thousands of workers losing their jobs daily. The lack of set prices and specified delivery date of goods are listed as primary causes for the work reductions.... The heads of Polish and Russian delegations meeting in Riga sign an armistice agreement.... The former head of the American Red Cross tells of 30,000 people dying each month of disease and starvation in Petrograd. Workers are unable to fulfill orders for coffins.... The German textile industry posts record gains.	Members of The Vengeance Gang, a purported anti-British society dedicated to political assassinations, are convicted on conspiracy charges. Abdul Rhamen-Bey Fahny, the former provisional governor, is found guilty.	Mexican president-elect Obregon enters El Paso, TX, across the International Bridge from Juarez, officially opening railroad passenger lines between the United States and Mexico. Traffic had been halted for the last eight years.	The American Red Cross gives $500,000 to China for relief in the Chinese famine. The money will be appropriated through the U.S. State Department.... The Yokohama and Tokyo American Associations, representing American business interests in Japan, report they will send E.W. Frazar and John Richard Geary, general manager of the Japanese branch of General Electric Company, to the United States to report to American businesses the impact of California's new legislation regulating Japanese immigration in Japan.
Oct. 7		The *Ceride-I Resmiyre* (Turkish Government Gazette) premieres.... The Republic of Lithuania and the Republic of Poland sign agreement over territorial and boundary claims between the two countries. An agreement is signed at Suwalki.... Prime Minister Lloyd George calls the Irish Republican Army "a real murder gang" in a speech in Carnarvon.			
Oct. 8		The Swiss Socialist Party issues charges that the loan arranged by the Swiss government in the United States was done without consent of the Parliament and at a rate of interest that is not acceptable.... The British government threatens action against Soviet Russia if British prisoners held by the Bolshevist government are not immediately released. Bolshevists react with a statement claiming the British are still holding prisoners in violation of the initial prisoner transfer agreement.			Reverend J.A.L. Singh and his wife begin their visit with the Wolf-Children of Midnapore (India) at the orphanage. Rev. Singh keeps a diary of the journey and observations.
	A *Includes developments that affect more than one world region, international organizations and important meetings of world leaders.*	B *Includes all domestic and regional developments in Europe, including the Soviet Union.*	C *Includes all domestic and regional developments in Africa and the Middle East.*	D *Includes all domestic and regional developments in Latin America, the Caribbean, and Canada.*	E *Includes all domestic and regional developments in Asian and Pacific nations (and colonies).*

U.S. Politics & Social Issues	U.S. Foreign Policy & Affairs, Defense	U.S. Economy & Environment	Science, Technology & Nature	Culture, Leisure & Lifestyle	
The New York Times newspaper publishes an editorial titled, "Why Gambling and Baseball Are Enemies."			The last of eight lectures are given by Rudolf Steiner on *The Boundaries of Natural Science* in Dornach, Switzerland.	American Professional Football Association (later to become the National Football League) plays its first games.…*The Beaver*, the Canadian history magazine, premieres.	Oct. 3
U.S. President and Mrs. Harding take a trip to Spiegel Grove in Fremont, OH, with their son, Scott Russell Hayes.…A bronze memorial plaque is attached to the Rutherford B. Hayes Presidential Center in formal ceremony.		A special session of the Texas state legislature facilitates open shop throughout the state.…Galveston, TX, longshoremen go on strike.…The recommendation is made to the city of Manistique, MI, in Schoolcraft County to float a bond to construct a new pumping station and water storage facility.	Wing Commander Robert Leckie takes off from Dartmouth, Nova Scotia in the first leg of the first air flight across Canada, totaling 4,341 miles.…A meeting of the Philadelphia Academy of Surgery is held.	George Allen and Unwin Ltd. publish John Dos Passos' *One Man's Initiation: 1917* in London.…St. Louis Browns first baseman George Sisler has a record 257th hit in one season.…The National Academy of Arts presents oil painter Robert C. Spencer with a diploma.…Harry Langdon, Frank Fay, and Joe E. Brown open the play *Jim Jam Jems* on Broadway in New York City. This would be the first of 105 performances.	Oct. 4
Chairman of the Columbia County Republican Club of Lake City, FL, B.J. Jones, is abducted and threatened with lynching in a late night kidnapping from his home. Jones is active in organizing black women to register to vote in his county.	President Woodrow Wilson telegraphs Missouri Senator Spenser denying he had made any promises of American military aid to Serbia or Rumania at the Peace Conference in Paris.			The first day of baseball's World Series is played with Cleveland winning 3–1 against the Brooklyn Robins.…A total of 16,624 Cleveland fans are seated for the World Series Baseball game.…F. Scott Fitzgerald and family take an apartment at 38 West 59th Street in New York City.	Oct. 5
Mrs. Helen Grossman of West Newton, MA, requests divorce from her husband on the grounds that she discovered he was an anarchist.…The trial of Isaac E. Ferguson of Chicago and Charles E. Ruthenberg of Cleveland begins on charges of criminal anarchy for their part in the publication of the Communist Manifesto. Six have already been convicted from the 25 listed in the original indictment. Attorney Ferguson is defending himself and Ruthenberg on the charges.…Voter registration of women sets records in New York City.…Anarchists, including Giacomo Carusso, are arrested in New York City for the September 16th Wall Street bombing.	Senator Spencer and Paul D. Cravath make a statement in Congress giving their interpretation of the League of Nations Covenant to read that the U.S. Congress would be required to declare war under the regulations if any member of the League were threatened.…Alfred F. Clegg, Vice President of Kerr Steamship Company, makes a public statement against using U.S.-owned ships to reopen German prewar trade routes of the Hamburg-American Lines, claiming that the economic advantages would favor only Germany.	Fire damage aboard the steamer *Bismarck* is far worse than originally thought, amounting to millions of marks. The German government is held accountable for damages since it purchased the ship from the Hamburg-American Lines last month.…U.S. President Woodrow Wilson is unable to find qualified men to fill openings on the new Shipping Board required under the new Merchant Marine Act.…George Gordon Battle, counsel for the Adelphia Coal Company, pleads innocent to federal charges of profiteering in setting coal prices.…New York apartment tenant problems revolve around huge increases in rents.…New York Brandt and Company asks for the decision of the U.S. Supreme Court in efforts to remove tenants for nonpayment of rent.	Aviator Paul Collins lands at an airstrip at Hazelhurst Field (near Mineola, Long Island) with flaming torches and mirrors attached to the wings of his plane in the first demonstration of a night landing. British and U.S. Army and Navy representatives are present for the event.…The Electrical Show, the 13th annual exhibit, opens in Grand Central Palace in New York City displaying wireless telephones, factory lighting, and use of electricity in the bakery and laundry industries.	Soprano Jenny Lind's 100th birthday anniversary is celebrated at New York City's Carnegie Hall by artists in period costumes.…The Duchess of Marlborough, formerly known as Consuelo Vanderbilt of New York City, petitions for divorce from the British Duke of Marlborough in London.…Brothers Wheeler and Jimmy Johnston are the first brothers to play against each other in the baseball World Series. Wheeler pinch-hits for the Cleveland Indians while brother Jimmy plays third base for the Brooklyn Robins (known later as the Brooklyn Dodgers).…Brooklyn wins the second game of the World Series of Baseball.	Oct. 6
U.S. Captain Emmet Kilpatrick of Alabama, serving with the Red Cross in South Russia, is captured by the Russians and placed in a Moscow prison.	The Smithsonian Museum takes possession of the United State Signal Service building for use in exhibiting aircraft and accessories from World War I.	The Southern Rice Growers' Association announces it will provide funds to establish a national rice advertising campaign to explain the health reasons for adding rice to the American diet.	A perissodactyl fossil is found by a geologist under the hire of the Pure Oil Company on the Huallaga River in Peru, and is donated to the American Museum of Natural History.…B.M. Stewart, air pilot, begins service with the U.S. Airmail at College Park, MD.…Count Arco publishes "Conductor-directed radio telephony" in *Electrotech* magazine.	The Brooklyn, NY Robins baseball team beats the Cleveland Indians 2–1 in the third game of the World Series.…*Life* magazine awards $100 to the individual selecting the best title for a photograph.…A permit is issued to the Silber Amusement Company for a 1,526-seat motion picture theater on the corner of Seventh Avenue and West 145th Street in New York City, to be called the Roosevelt Theater. The theater will be part of a complex with the Odeon and Douglas theaters.	Oct. 7
Senator Warren G. Harding states that President Woodrow Wilson's claim is false and that the League of Nations Covenant does interfere with the Congressional right to declare war.…New U.S. Census results show that more representatives are required in the House.		The Export Managers' Convention of the National Automobile Chamber of Commerce requests lower tariffs on foreign automobiles entering the United States. American made autos have seen increasing export since the close of the war.	The first transcontinental air mail service flight leaves from New York on its way to San Francisco. The flight takes place only during daylight hours with mail transported by train during the evening and night hours.	Dick Williams will not be on the Davis Cup Tennis Team due to business considerations.	Oct. 8

F	G	H	I	J
Includes campaigns, elections, federal-state relations, civil rights and liberties, crime, the judiciary, education, healthcare, poverty, urban affairs, and population.	*Includes formation and debate of U.S. foreign and defense policies, veterans affairs, and defense spending. (Relations with specific foreign countries are usually found under the region concerned.)*	*Includes business, labor, agriculture, taxation, transportation, consumer affairs, monetary and fiscal policy, natural resources, pollution and industrial accidents.*	*Includes worldwide scientific, medical and technological developments, natural phenomena, U.S. weather and natural disasters.*	*Includes the arts, religion, scholarship, communications media, sports, entertainment, fashions, fads, and social life.*

	World Affairs	Europe	Africa & The Middle East	The Americas	Asia & The Pacific
Oct. 9	Lithuanians appeal to the League of Nations for help in Polish takeover of Vilna.	Polish fighters led by General Lucien Zeligowski capture Vilna from Lithuanian troops. Marshal Josef Pilsudski provides secret assistance to the recapture of the province.			
Oct. 10		Residents of Klagenfurt (Carinthia) vote to continue association with Austria over alignment with the Serbs, Croats, and Slovene governments.... Italian government annexes South Tyrol (Alto Adige) into Italy.... Appeal made for food and clothing for Armenian families and orphans.... Barcelona may face striking steel workers but Spanish troops will remain neutral.... German President of General Electric Company, Dr. Walter Rathenau, is denied entry into London for the Fight Famine Conference. Details of the refusal are not known.			Chinese worldwide celebrate the ninth anniversary of the establishment of the Republic of China.
Oct. 11	The first session of the conference of the International Chinese Consortium of bankers from Great Britain, France, Japan, and the United States is held in New York City at the Chamber of Commerce.	Irish prison warden, Thomas Griffin, disappears on his way home from work. No clues have been uncovered. Griffin was listed by protesters as torturing prisoners in the jail by denying them food and water.		Continental Airlines Company announces it will begin an air freight service between Chicago and Cuba next month.... Aeromarine Corporation will operate a freight line between Key West, FL and Havana, Cuba.	
Oct. 12		Armistice signed between the Polish and Soviet Russian governments at Riga that ends the Russo-Polish War. The Makhnovists (The Revolutionary Insurrectionary Army of the Ukraine) will halt insurrection of the masses and join the army of the republic, although keeping a separate internal structure separate from the Red Army.			
Oct. 13		Leon Trotsky writes *Order Number 246, The Southern Front: The Fight Against Wrangel to the Armies of the Southern Front.*			
Oct. 14		Soviet Russians and Finland sign an agreement at Dorpat (Tartu) that recognizes an independent Finland and grant land to Finland between Murmansk and Norway. This strip of land gives Finland an ice-free port in Pechenga and access to the Arctic Ocean.			Yunnan and Szechuan soldiers fight in Chunking after English merchant is killed. British gunboat fires on the city during fighting.
Oct. 15	League of Nations opens the Paris Conference on Passports and Customs Formalities.	Saimbeyli is rescued at the Turkish southern military front.... As ongoing dispute between Armenia and Turkey continues, 1,387 people are killed in nearly 100 villages in and around Bayburt.			
Oct. 16					China and the Governor of Jilin give Japanese permission to send troops to eastern Manchuria.

A	B	C	D	E
Includes developments that affect more than one world region, international organizations and important meetings of world leaders.	*Includes all domestic and regional developments in Europe, including the Soviet Union.*	*Includes all domestic and regional developments in Africa and the Middle East.*	*Includes all domestic and regional developments in Latin America, the Caribbean, and Canada.*	*Includes all domestic and regional developments in Asian and Pacific nations (and colonies).*

U.S. Politics & Social Issues	U.S. Foreign Policy & Affairs, Defense	U.S. Economy & Environment	Science, Technology & Nature	Culture, Leisure & Lifestyle	
		The announcement is made that the British and French $500,000 loan will be repaid on time next Friday.		The Brooklyn Robins are beaten by the Cleveland Indians in the fourth game of the World Series with a score of 5–1....The first radio broadcast of a football game, between Texas A & M and Ohio State University, is aired.	Oct. 9
The New York League of Foreign Born Citizens earns $10,000 in theater benefit to aid Citizenship League in the United States.				Cleveland Indian Elmer Smith hits the first ever baseball World Series grand slam. The Indian's Bill Wambsganss (known fondly as Wamby) completes the World Series' first unassisted triple play....The Cleveland Indians beat the Brooklyn Robins 8–1.	Oct. 10
		New York Public Service Commissioner Lewis Nixon requests further investigation into charges that coal companies routinely obtain priority orders for emergency public use and then turn around and sell coal at speculative profits....Officials of Brooklyn Edison Company are indicted on charges of speculation in coal deals....The British government makes an offer to purchase Direct United States Cable Company.	Wing Commander Robert Leckie arrives in Winnipeg, Manitoba, completing the first flight across Canada. Air Commodore A.K. Tylee, with three other pilots, take off from Winnipeg in the second leg of the journey to Vancouver, British Columbia.	Well-known French astronomer Camille Flammarion is married today in Paris. He is 78 years old....French author Anatole France, age 76, is married today in Tours, France.... The sixth game in the Baseball World Series sees Cleveland win 1–0 over the Brooklyn Robins.	Oct. 11
			The Holland Tunnel opens, connecting New York City and Jersey City, NJ. It is the first twin tube subaqueous vehicular tunnel.	Thoroughbred horse Man O'War retires after a win in Ontario, Canada, beating Sir Barton (a Triple Crown winner) by seven lengths. Big Red, Man O' War, retires after losing only once in his racing career. Jockey Kummer receives $5,000 to ride the horse, the highest fee to date paid to a jockey....The Cleveland Indians take the baseball World Series in a 3–0 win over the Brooklyn Robins.	Oct. 12
The Bureau of the Census announces that the population of the United States living in cities has grown significantly....The press announces Chicago mob boss Laughlin's $30,000 bribe to facilitate trade in illegal alcohol.				Palo Casals, born Pau Carles Salvador sCasals i Defillo, after organizing the Orquesta Pau Casals, conducts the group in concert for the first time in Barcelona....Italian cyclist Franco Giorgetti wins a gold medal at the Olympics.	Oct. 13
				The first college radio station, WRUC at Union College in Schenectady, NY, begins operation.	Oct. 14
				The first licensed college radio station WRUC begins its first series of weekly radio programming.	Oct. 15
The U.S. gunboat *Dolphin* is assigned the duties of the flagship of the Special Service Squadron.	The first woman patent attorney Florence King gives the speech "Suffrage Yesterday and Tomorrow" at the League of Women Voters and was elected Director of the Illinois League of Women Voters.	A Wall Street explosion is blamed on blasting gelatin....*The Electrical Review* publishes a story outlining how the Westinghouse Company is entering the "wireless field."		Publisher D. Appleton publishes Edith Wharton's *The Age of Innocence*....Bishop, author of biography of Theodore Roosevelt, writes his editor that the work is completed.	Oct. 16

F	G	H	I	J
Includes campaigns, elections, federal-state relations, civil rights and liberties, crime, the judiciary, education, healthcare, poverty, urban affairs, and population.	*Includes formation and debate of U.S. foreign and defense policies, veterans affairs, and defense spending. (Relations with specific foreign countries are usually found under the region concerned.)*	*Includes business, labor, agriculture, taxation, transportation, consumer affairs, monetary and fiscal policy, natural resources, pollution and industrial accidents.*	*Includes worldwide scientific, medical and technological developments, natural phenomena, U.S. weather and natural disasters.*	*Includes the arts, religion, scholarship, communications media, sports, entertainment, fashions, fads, and social life.*

	World Affairs	Europe	Africa & The Middle East	The Americas	Asia & The Pacific
Oct. 17		Turkish Damat Ferid Pasha resigns his position in the Grand Vizierate.... The Russian make a formal request for independence for Armenia, but the Turkish Grand National Assembly denies the request....The Turkish National Assembly turns down Soviet demands....In ongoing fighting between Turks and Armenians, 9,287 people are killed in 30 villages near Pasinier....The Communist Party [CPI(M)] is officially formed in India.			
Oct. 18		The Turkish Communist Party is founded.			
Oct. 19	The Passport Conference meeting in Paris comes to an agreement on customs, registered baggage, and exportation of money....Sir Robert William Philip, M.D. is elected president of the International Society of the Prevention for Tuberculosis, a permanent body composed of all members of the League of Nations and the United States. The society is organized at the International Anti-Tuberculosis Conference meeting in Paris today.	In ongoing fighting between Turks and Armenians, 8,439 killings are documented in various neighborhoods of Erzurum.	All nations signing the League of Nations, as well as the United States, attend the International Anti-Tuberculosis Conference in Paris, France. Scottish M.D., Sir Robert William Philip, is elected president of the organization. A second conference is scheduled for next year in London.		
Oct. 20	The League of Nations opens the 10th session of the Council in Brussels....The American Asiatic Association holds its 23rd annual meeting in New York City and elects new officers.	Ottoman and French leaders sign the Treaty of Ankara recognizing th French mandate in Syria....Bombs are discovered in Milan, Italy in a park near the Hotel Cavour....Police in Naples, Italy conduct a citywide search of anarchists and discover a number of homes containing literature in Italian, German, English, and Russian. Many of the individuals hold letters of safe conduct signed by Bela Kun, former leader of Hungary and by Soviet councils.			
Oct. 21	The League of Nations closes the Paris Conference on Passports and Customs Formalities....The Council of Ambassadors issues Serbia a memo that troops in the Klagenfort area must be withdrawn within 48 hours. The document fails to list any consequences if the order is not met....Clergyman James Cardinal Gibbons adds his signature to the list of American religious leaders supporting the U.S. entry into the League of Nations.	Turkish President Tevfik Pasha establishes the last Ottoman government in Istanbul....Turkish Nationalist forces open a military offensive against Armenians....The Self-Determination League reports the Lord Mayor of Cork, Terrance MacSwiney, is in his 70th day of fasting....Armenia rejects Soviet demand to allow Bolshevist soldiers to enter the country to meet up with Turkish Nationalist forces.... The National Union of Railwaymen serves the British government an ultimatum that they would join the coal strikers unless the government agrees to settlement talks....The U.S. State Department claims only 35 American citizens are currently in Russia.		British Columbia votes to allow government sale of alcohol, ending prohibition. Penticton and Nelson vote against government control, but the majority of cities, towns and outlying areas are in favor of ending the prohibition on alcohol.	The Japanese Azuma Detachment begins combat with Korean guerrillas in eastern Manchuria....Former Chinese Minster to the United States, Dr. V.K. Wellington Koo, sails from the United States to assume new duties as Chinese Minster to Great Britain.
Oct. 22	The Tittoni Report and Resolution are presented to the League of Nations by the Minorities Section of the Secretariat.		The Free State Nationalist Congress votes to accept resolutions of a party principles and platform that includes sovereign leadership in the Union of South Africa.		

A	B	C	D	E
Includes developments that affect more than one world region, international organizations and important meetings of world leaders.	*Includes all domestic and regional developments in Europe, including the Soviet Union.*	*Includes all domestic and regional developments in Africa and the Middle East.*	*Includes all domestic and regional developments in Latin America, the Caribbean, and Canada.*	*Includes all domestic and regional developments in Asian and Pacific nations (and colonies).*

U.S. Politics & Social Issues	U.S. Foreign Policy & Affairs, Defense	U.S. Economy & Environment	Science, Technology & Nature	Culture, Leisure & Lifestyle	
			A group of Canadian pilots complete the first flight across Canada in 45 hours and 20 minutes. The flight covers 5,488 km.	U.S. author and social commentator John Reed dies in the Soviet Republic.…The Decatur Stanleys (later to become the Chicago Bears) play (and win) the first game in the National Football League with a score of 7–0.	Oct. 17
			The findings of French medical doctors of a way to avoid the side effects of tetanus and croup vaccinations are presented at a Paris meeting of the Academy of Sciences.	Directors of baseball's National League meet in New York City with four of the owners of the American League teams to hammer out an agreement to be given to Baseball Commissioner Ban Johnson. The suggestion is made that five American League teams will join the National League.	Oct. 18
A New York State judge rules membership in the Communist Party is just cause for deportation from the United States.…Black Atlanta business owner David T. Howard states blacks want better schools, justice in the courts of law, and suitable railroad accommodations for travel, rather than social equality.		Coal exporters claim they are operating at full capacity, despite backorders of millions of tons of coal.…Armed robbers hold up a messenger from the State Commercial and Savings Bank in Chicago in front of numerous rail passengers. The three men escaped by car with more than $70,000.		Connie Mack, co-owner of the Philadelphia American League baseball club, and Frank J. Navin, President of the Detroit American League baseball club, make public statements.…Charles Blasgen of Chicago, IL is taken into custody after testifying before the grand jury about baseball gambling operations.…Twelve-year old Edward Rochie Hardy, Jr. is admitted to Columbia University, the youngest student in the history of the school.	Oct. 19
	Edward J. Lamothe, musician Jelly Roll Mortion's father, is given a passport with occupation listed as "contractor," when in reality he is working as an agent of the U.S. Naval Intelligence Office in Haiti and Santo Domingo.	Roosevelt Family heirs sell business property of Roosevelt & Son on Broadway in New York City. The family had owned the building since 1844.	WWJ in Detroit begins a daily broadcast, becoming one of the first commercial radio station in the United States.	*First Year* starring Frank Craven premiers in New York City.…Runner Allen Woodring wins the 200-meter dash in the Olympics while wearing shoes he borrowed from another runner.	Oct. 20
W. Bourke Cockran speaks at the Chicago Stock Yards Pavilion in favor of the presidential candidate Governor James M. Cox, claiming Senator Warren G. Harding's statement of American neutrality guaranteed long-term violence in Ireland. Members of Sinn Fein threaten violence but instead distribute literature in front of the pavilion.…Governor and presidential candidate Warren G. Harding announces a prize for any person who can present an essay proving any inconsistency or change of position in his formal statements.…Governor Smith states he would support an amendment to the Volstead Act to allow states to set alcohol content of liquor.		U.S. federal agents investigate threats against north Texas paper plants refusing to join the boycott hoping to raise the price of cotton to 30 cents a pound.…The Federal Reserve Board in the Eleventh District states the bank will assist cotton farmers by extending longer credit terms on cotton notes.…The Zeppelin Company of Berlin announces it will not construct any additional new airships and dismisses workmen at Staaken. The company states the profit margin is too small to consider large-scale production of the airship.…Bank robber George "Jiggs" Losteiner is shot in a street battle at a branch of the Cleveland Trust Company in Bedford, OH after attempting to rob the bank.	The Preliminary Communications Conference in New York City demonstrates communications by wires and wireless between Catalina Island and a ship, the *Gloucester*, anchored off the coast in New Jersey. Sea captains on both ends of the line speak for nearly four minutes while dinner guests at the Waldorf Hotel in New York City listen in to the conversation. Delegates also observe an experimental system using a carrier-current telephone circuit that will be in commercial use within the month. The system allows phone and telegraph messages to be sent simultaneously over the circuits within one wire.	The New York District Attorney dismisses charges against Harry C. Toback, who was arrested for the theft of jewels from the East Hampton home of Enrico Caruso last June.	Oct. 21
Yale Professor and Chairman of the Pro-League Independents announces that a jury is needed for an essay contest, offering $25,000 for an essay proving that entry of the United States into the League of Nations would mean war.…William J. Hutchins becomes the fourth president of Berea College in Ohio.	The U.S. destroyer *Peary* is commissioned on the east coast.	Copper prices drop to the lowest levels since 1915.	Delegates to the Preliminary Communications Conference in New York City observes a demonstration of the capture of the electrical pattern of the human heart onto a photographic recording. Western Electric Company and Bell System Research Laboratories presented the machine, called an oscillograph.	British author W.L. George opens his U.S. lecture tour in New York City encouraging American men to try marriage because it is a great alternative to loneliness in old age. He emphasizes that men have nothing to lose, since divorce is easily obtained in the United States.	Oct. 22

	World Affairs	Europe	Africa & The Middle East	The Americas	Asia & The Pacific
Oct. 23	The Council of the League of Nations debates the official language of the permanent International Court. The group fails to decide on French or English as the official language.... The Council agrees to accept guardianship over minorities created by the Bulgarian and Austrian Treaties.	The American Red Cross announces it has given out goods and supplies to the Crimea totaling more than 10 million francs....The Greek government tells Bulgaria it will not try Bulgarian war criminals, a right issued under the Peace Treaty, if Bulgaria agrees it will try the offenders and provide appropriate punishment for the convicted....A mass meeting of the Central Association of German Jews hears non-Jewish clergymen speak of the growing amount of anti-Semitism in the country. They call the actions un-Christian and call for an end to the persecution.	South African poet Nontsizi Mgqwetho, the first female poet to write in Xhosa, publishes her first poem under her clan name Cizama.		
Oct. 24		The Gediz offensive takes place on the Turkish western military front.... Armenian troops begin a counterattack on the Turkish front....A plot to turn the Italian election on November 4 into a military dictatorship is exposed.			
Oct. 25		The conference of the American Jewish Congress meeting in New York City reports massacres, torture, and the murder of Jews in Poland by both soldiers and civilians. The Congress debates action to halt the pogroms....Greek King Alexander I dies at age 27, after being bitten by an ape, creating regency under Queen Olga, Alexander's grandmother.	Italian leaders recognize Sensussi leader Sheikh Sidi Idriss' authority over Kufra and other Libyan settlements.	Canadian citizens vote to continue prohibition of alcohol in Nova Scotia, Manitoba, Alberta, and Saskatchewan.	
Oct. 26	The Council of the League of Nations meets in Brussels over Article 87 of the Treaty of Versailles, also called the Vilna Dispute.	Estonian Minster of War Aleksander Tonisson leaves office after only four months of service....In fighting between Turks and Armenians 10,693 people die in the vicinity of Kars....The State Bank of the Republic of Armenia is established.		The Monument to Newfoundland (Canada) volunteer nurse Ethel Dickenson is dedicated in Cavendish Square. Dickenson died during the Influenza Epidemic of 1918 while treating the ill at the King George V Institute, St. John's....Presidential candidate Alvaro Obregon defeats Alfredo Robles Dominguez (who had backing of the Catholic Church) in the regular Mexican elections.	
Oct. 27	The League of Nations Secretariat relocates to new headquarters in Geneva. The collections, staff of 20 and library reside in the Hotel National on Quai Wilson.	Greeks occupy the Turkish towns of Inegol and Yenisehir....The Turkish Grand National Assembly refuses to recognize any political representatives from the Istanbul Parliament.			
Oct. 28		Romanian control over Bessarabia is recognized in an agreement made by the governments of Japan, Italy, France, and England.			
Oct. 29		The mayor of Pecs Bela Linder claims there is no connection between the ratification of the Treaty of Trianon and the future of the city....The 13th-century *Icon of Kursk* is taken from the city by the Russian White Army and evacuating civilians for protection of the religious icon....The British Parliament approves the Emergency Powers Act allowing the ruler to declare a state of emergency.		E.J. L'Esperance of Montreal is elected as president of the Ontario-Quebec-Maritime district of the Kiwanis at a convention in Ottawa, Canada....Argentina faces a bread shortage unless the government releases part of the wheat stock held. Millers threaten a labor walkout unless foreign wheat supplies purchased with proceeds from the wheat export tax are released to the mills.	India's Jamia Millia Islamia is established at Aligarh Muslim University with Hakim Ajmal Khan as first Chancellor and Maulana Mohammed Ali as first Vice-Chancellor.

A	B	C	D	E
Includes developments that affect more than one world region, international organizations and important meetings of world leaders.	*Includes all domestic and regional developments in Europe, including the Soviet Union.*	*Includes all domestic and regional developments in Africa and the Middle East.*	*Includes all domestic and regional developments in Latin America, the Caribbean, and Canada.*	*Includes all domestic and regional developments in Asian and Pacific nations (and colonies).*

U.S. Politics & Social Issues	U.S. Foreign Policy & Affairs, Defense	U.S. Economy & Environment	Science, Technology & Nature	Culture, Leisure & Lifestyle	
				A Chicago grand jury brings indictments against Abe Attel, featherweight boxing title holder, Hal Chase, and Bill Burns.…Baseball players "Shoeless" Joe Jackson, Lefty Williams, and Happy Felsch (real name Oscar Emil), and Ed Cicotte sign confessions that they were involved in a White Sox gambling incident.…The youngest son of Joseph Pulitzer of New York, Herbert Pulitzer, escapes serious injury when his airplane crashes at le Bourget Field near Paris. The former French army pilot of the plane, the Marquis des Champs de Boishebert, dies of his injuries.… Italian Professor Mario Mazzei is lost on a hunting expedition from a steamer ship in Dakar.	Oct. 23
Franklin D. Roosevelt issues a request for all newspapers to print the full covenant of the League of Nations, without any editorial commentary.					Oct. 24
		John S. Drum, head of the American Bankers' Association, calls the plan for a national foreign trade financing corporation a sound proposal.…The apple crop in the east is so plentiful that is cannot be harvested. Citizens of the state of New York are encouraged to fill their cars with the fruit before it rots.			Oct. 25
			A rare species of fungus [Zythia Resinae (Ehrenb.) Karst] is collected at the Pennsylvania State College greenhouse.…Richard C. Harris of Fallon, NV patents a fastener for mower guard fingers.	Local farmers offer excavation and foundation work to construct the Church of St. Martin of Tours near Cincinnati, OH.…Fire destroys the Commercial Hotel, an historic resort hotel in Ocean Springs, MS.	Oct. 26
	The U.S. small seaplane tender *Hulbert* and destroyer *Pope* are commissioned on the east coast.		The Westinghouse-owned radio station KDKA begins broadcasting in East Pittsburgh.…Albert Einstein presents his lecture, *Ether and the Theory of Relativity*, while holding the position of Extraordinary Professor at the University of Leyden.	The first radio station is licensed in the United States at Pittsburgh, PA.	Oct. 27
				Life magazine features a woman's suffrage centerfold.	Oct. 28
Communist Party members Benjamin Gitlow and I.E. Ferguson are sentenced to 5–10 years in New York's Sing Sing prison as a result of the Lusk Committee raids searching for individuals in violation of New York's anarchy law (passed in 1901 after the assassination of President McKinley). A U.S. Supreme Court appeal in 1925 would later become a landmark decision for American rights to free speech.	The U.S. destroyers *Barry II* and *Williamson* are launched on the east coast.…A concrete hulled freighter sinks after collision with the SS *City of Atlanta* after less than a year of service.		Cyclones are reported on the west coast of Mexico.…The Wireless Society of London meets to discuss superheterodyne. The discovery is necessary to television and radio production; it was invented by E.H. Armstrong and sold to Westinghouse.…The Pathological Society of Philadelphia publishes F.M. Huntoon's presentation, *The Reversal of the Antigen Antibody Reaction.*	Red Sox manager Ed Barrow is signed as the business manager for the New York Yankees baseball team.…An additional 13 people are indicted by a Chicago Grand Jury on their roles in the Black Sox baseball scandal.…African American printmaker Gabrielle DeV. Clements exhibits artwork at Milch Galleries in New York City.…The Operetta *Mountain Lovers* is performed at the Queen's Theater in London.	Oct. 29

F	G	H	I	J
Includes campaigns, elections, federal-state relations, civil rights and liberties, crime, the judiciary, education, healthcare, poverty, urban affairs, and population.	*Includes formation and debate of U.S. foreign and defense policies, veterans affairs, and defense spending. (Relations with specific foreign countries are usually found under the region concerned.)*	*Includes business, labor, agriculture, taxation, transportation, consumer affairs, monetary and fiscal policy, natural resources, pollution and industrial accidents.*	*Includes worldwide scientific, medical and technological developments, natural phenomena, U.S. weather and natural disasters.*	*Includes the arts, religion, scholarship, communications media, sports, entertainment, fashions, fads, and social life.*

	World Affairs	Europe	Africa & The Middle East	The Americas	Asia & The Pacific
Oct. 30		The Turkish Revolutionaries of the Turkish National Movement take back Kars from the Democratic Republic of Armenia (DRA).... American D.J. Theophilatos, speaking on behalf of 105 Greek-American clubs and organizations, sends the exiled Greek King Constantine a letter of support to his residence in Lucerne, Switzerland....La Societe Nationale des Habitations et Lodgements a Bon Marche begins a campaign to bring inexpensive housing to Belgium.		Babe Ruth debuts in Cuba as the New York Giants take a Cuban team in a stadium in Havana. The Giants win the game 4–3.	The Japanese Vocational Supplemental School Teacher Training Center Order is passed, but is scheduled to be implemented on April 1, 1921. The act established a network of education training facilities....The Communist Party of Australia is founded in Sydney by 26 men and women.
Oct. 31		Romania annexes Bessarabia.			Fifty of the largest stores are robbed by troops at Hochien, Chihli Province.
Nov. 1	The Bolivian government requests the League of Nations intervention in sovereignty issue over Tacna-Arica provinces. Bolivia, Peru, and Chile all make claims for provinces and Bolivia claims ocean access point.	The Slutsk uprising breaks out against the Bolsheviks in Belarus. The Belarusian National Republic makes an appeal to the United States and western powers for military assistance to halt the violence....The first Turkish officer candidates graduate from school in Ankara....Michael Collins, member of the Irish Republican Brotherhood (IRA), and Richard Mulcahy plot to assassinate British intelligence agents in and around Dublin.... Teacher and activist John MacLean publishes an article on unemployment riots in Glasgow, Scotland for *The Vanguard* magazine.		Cuba holds a national election with the ticket for the presidency between the Liberal Party ticket of General Jose Miguel Gomez and Miguel Arango, versus the current President of Cuba Menocal. This election is the first under the new laws formulated by U.S. Major General Enoch Crowder, who has served as the Provost Marshal General of the country....Canada claims the second largest wheat crop on record....Cuban elections see eight deaths in fights over closing of electoral offices.	The Central Japanese Railway opens a Kakamigahara City, Gifu rail station....Groups of soldiers (and a few others) attack the Bank of China in Hsu-chang, Honang Province, killing 40 people.
Nov. 2	France announces that the League of Nations will make public treaty between the country and Belgium.	Austrian detectives capture a gang of Valuta money smugglers in Vienna before they can make their way across the frontier to engage in currency speculation....The first hanging takes place in a series of Irish executions.			
Nov. 3	Nicaragua and Honduras are admitted to the League of Nations....The Costa Rican Minster to France announces he will attend the League of Nations meeting on November 15 to request admission of Costa Rica into the League.	Premier Delacroix presents the Belgian King Albert with the resignations of his cabinet today....Albert, King of Belgium, leaves Spain after visiting with King Alfonso....Belgian Premier Delacroix resigns his post due to attacks on his foreign policy....White Russian troop leader General Balakhoviteh and soldiers are set to strike directly at Smolensk and Moscow. Plans to join French General Wrangle are in ruins with Wrangle's defeat.		Cuban presidential election results between Liberal Party candidate General Jose Miguel Gomez and the Coalition candidate Dr. Alfredo Zayas is announced with Zayas given as victor....American Samoan naval governor, Commander Warren Jay Terhune, commits suicide at the official government house.	An immigration and ownership agreement is made with U.S. Japanese Ambassador to avoid tensions after a California referendum passes to limit Japanese nationalists' ownership of land in the state. The agreement awaits approval by the Japanese government and U.S. Senate.
Nov. 4		Turkish government announces change in the executive committee election procedure allowing the president of the Turkish Grand National Assembly to elect candidates....General Wrangel retreats and settles in for the winter on the Perekop isthmus. Some of his troops are leaving on ships in the Sea of Azov.		U.S. Naval Court of Inquiry, conducted by Captain Waldo Evans, investigates the *Mau* (an American Samoan ship) and the official dealings with it from a station aboard the battleship U.S.S. *Kansas*.	

A	B	C	D	E
Includes developments that affect more than one world region, international organizations and important meetings of world leaders.	*Includes all domestic and regional developments in Europe, including the Soviet Union.*	*Includes all domestic and regional developments in Africa and the Middle East.*	*Includes all domestic and regional developments in Latin America, the Caribbean, and Canada.*	*Includes all domestic and regional developments in Asian and Pacific nations (and colonies).*

U.S. Politics & Social Issues	U.S. Foreign Policy & Affairs, Defense	U.S. Economy & Environment	Science, Technology & Nature	Culture, Leisure & Lifestyle	
Margaret Blaine Damrosch attacks *The Woman Republican* for the editorial slant against U.S. entrance into the League of Nations.	The Packard Company of Detroit announces it will reduce the price of its cars from $3,640 to $2,975 to keep employees working on the assembly line.	The *Cape Fear* hits the *City of Atlanta* in an accident that damages both ships.…An empty shrapnel shell is found in the Pennsylvania Rail Station in New York City.…The U.S.S. *Des Moines* crosses the equator.	Dr. Banting writes article supporting the idea of insulin for use in regulation of diabetes.	Conductor Bruno Walter publishes an essay on Beethoven's *Missa solemnis* in *Munchner Neueste Nachrichten*.…*Scientific American Magazine* publishes the thoughts of Thomas Edison in an article titled, "Edison's Views on Life After Death."…Author Edgar Rice Burroughs' book *Thuvia, Maid of Mars* is published as a hardback by A.C. McClurg and Company publishers.	Oct. 30
Los Angeles Police Chief Alexander W. Murray is replaced after serving in the office less than a month.…Mother Seton, founder of the American Sisters of Charity, is canonized as America's first saint by the Catholic Church.			Reports show crows flying further south for the winter.	The Gloucester sailing schooner *Esperanto* defeats Canadian schooner in the first three races of the International Fisherman's Cup held in Halifax, Nova Scotia.	Oct. 31
California ratifies the Nineteenth Amendment to the U.S. Constitution.…A whisper campaign starts in the Chicago area suggesting Verne Miller, a Republican candidate for sheriff of Beadle County, is working with local organized crime in bootlegging operations.…*Popular Science* magazine runs a story on problems with the new mechanical lever voting machine adopted to avoid ballot-stuffing fraud.	Record numbers of men enlist in the U.S. Army during the month of October.	The Chorus Equity votes to combine with Actors Equity. Both groups cooperate, but remain independent.…The Pennsylvania Railroad gives the Pullman Company the right to sell parlor cars.	Aeromarine West Indies Airways makes the inaugural flight of the Santa Maria and the Pinta airplanes, the first regularly scheduled international air passenger and mail operations in the United States. The air service operates between Meacham Field in Key West, FL and the waterfront in Havana, Cuba using FSL aircraft, former U.S. Navy equipment popularly called the "Flying Boat."…A gasoline fraud is exposed. A chemist's claim to extract usable alcohol fuel is proven to be false.	Playwright Eugene O'Neill's *The Emperor Jones* opens at the Neighborhood Playhouse. It later moves to Broadway.…The Special Land Radio Station at Camp Greenbrier at Alderson, WV, begins service at 8YF on the radio dial.…The Gloucester sailing team wins the International Fisherman's Cup sailing the schooner *Esperanto*.…Former baseball player Roger Bresnahan encourages Canadian businesses to support the return of the Montreal team to the International Baseball League. The town has been without a team since 1918.	Nov. 1
Florence Kling DeWolfe Harding votes for her husband in the presidential election.…Eight million American woman vote in the election.…Warren G. Harding is elected as President of the United States and repeats his promise to the American people of a "Return to Normalcy" for the United States.	The California Alien Land Law is adopted, restricting land ownership or transfer in the state to citizens.		Scientists Albert Einstein and Harm Kamerlingh Onnes meet a week after Einstein gave his first lecture as external professor at Leiden.…The first commercial radio broadcast covers the presidential election results.…The first regular radio broadcasts in the United States begin on KDKA station in Pittsburgh. The station is established by the Westinghouse Electric Corporation.…Dick Rose patents the Comptometer Card.		Nov. 2
Arson and fighting are reported in Ocee, FL, (near Orlando) after July Perry attempts to vote in the presidential election. Poll workers had turned him away from the polls claiming he had failed to pay a poll tax. Perry is taken from his car and lynched by whites en route to the jail.…Ohio Governor James M. Cox announces he will tour Europe in January 1921.	The U.S. destroyer *Simpson* is commissioned on the east coast.	One thousand women block sidewalks and store entrances on Fifth Avenue, near the Waldorf Astoria Hotel in New York City, trying to purchase apples at cost. The event is part of the International Apple Shippers' Association's Apple Week, a promotion by the Consumer Food Committee of the New York State Division of Foods and Markets that offers apples at retail price. Shoppers line the streets for blocks waiting to enter the discounted marketplace.		The Cornell University football squad practices at night under artificial lighting.…Author and war cartoonist Captain Bruce Bairnsfather arrives in New York City for a six-week U.S. speaking tour.…Popular bullfighter Raoul Barrios arrives in the United States on his way to Lima, Peru to work for the season.…French pianist Jacques Pintel makes his U.S. debut in Carnegie Hall in New York City.	Nov. 3
Four other blacks are reported killed in Ocoee, FL over the issue of voting rights.…Republican candidate Alice Robertson is elected from Oklahoma, the second woman (after Republican Jeanette Rankin of Montana) to serve in the House of Representatives.	President-elect Warren G. Harding makes the public announcement that a well-equipped merchant marine is essential to U.S. commerce and emphasizes that the Panama Canal should be opened without restriction to U.S. ships.	The coal shortage in the state of New York becomes so severe that state representatives go to Washington to ask for relief for residents.	KDKA (AM) of Montreal, Quebec, Canada, the first commercial radio station in the world, is renamed CFCF-AM.	The American Trapshooting Association annual meeting convenes at the Hotel Astor in New York City and discusses major changes made last year to rules allowing a committee to represent amateurs and changes in the geographical membership representation for the United States and Canada.…Eight-year-old chess prodigy and Polish citizen Samuel Rzeszewski arrives from England on a White Star liner. He defeats numerous players in a series of demonstrations while sailing on the *Olympic* to New York City.	Nov. 4
F *Includes campaigns, elections, federal-state relations, civil rights and liberties, crime, the judiciary, education, healthcare, poverty, urban affairs, and population.*	G *Includes formation and debate of U.S. foreign and defense policies, veterans affairs, and defense spending. (Relations with specific foreign countries are usually found under the region concerned.)*	H *Includes business, labor, agriculture, taxation, transportation, consumer affairs, monetary and fiscal policy, natural resources, pollution and industrial accidents.*	I *Includes worldwide scientific, medical and technological developments, natural phenomena, U.S. weather and natural disasters.*	J *Includes the arts, religion, scholarship, communications media, sports, entertainment, fashions, fads, and social life.*	

	World Affairs	Europe	Africa & The Middle East	The Americas	Asia & The Pacific
Nov. 5	President Woodrow Wilson selects an American representative to the League of Nations to work on the dispute between Sweden and Finland over the ownership of the Aland Islands.				
Nov. 6		Armenians call for a truce on the Turkish eastern military front.…V.I. Lenin delivers a speech at the Joint Plenum of the Moscow Soviet of Workers, Peasants, and Red Army Deputies on the third anniversary of the October Revolution.…French government repeals a law requiring French citizens wearing awards given by foreign countries to first obtain authorization from French officials.			Nine people are killed in a timber train rail accident in Wokalup, Queensland, Australia.
Nov. 7		Turkish military on the eastern front occupy Gumru (Alexandropol).	Lord Robert Cecil, South African delegate to the League of Nations, is protested by the French government on the grounds that he would represent English interests, not those of South Africa. England had previously received six votes in the League Assembly based on the country and the colonies.…American car manufacturers retain their monopoly on car sales despite increased competition from British manufacturers.		
Nov. 8	Denmark enters the League of Nations.	Armenians turn down peace terms offered by the Turkish Grand National Assembly.…Ali Fuat Pasha is sent to Moscow as Turkish Ambassador to the Soviets.…The Turkish and Armenian War continues.…The Swiss Parliament discusses the 300 million franc loan raised in the United States, with the Socialist Party leading the criticism.			
Nov. 9	Danzig, declared a Free State, is admitted to the League of Nations as part of the Treaty of Versailles agreement.	Ismet Bey (Inonu) takes over command of the Turkish northern front, serving as Commander of the Western Front and Chief of the General Staff.…Refet Bey takes command of the Turkish southern sector.			
Nov. 10		In response to a massive letter writing campaign, the coffin of an unidentified soldier, representing the French Unknown Soldier, is first taken to the Pantheon in Paris and then to the Citadel of Verdun. A chapel on the first floor of the Arc d'Triomphe in Paris is the final stop for the French Unknown Soldier.…Austrian reforms, including 8-Studen-Tag (eight-hour workday), Betriebsrategesetz (a council of workers), and a new constitution, go into effect.			Rampaging troops kill nearly 100 people in Kwei-yang, Kweichow Province.
Nov. 11	Coauthor of the League of Nations covenant Lord Robert Cecil announces he will support admission of former enemy states into the League of Nations. Most member nations do not favor admission of Germany and Hungary, but are favorable to admission of Bulgaria and Austria.	Turkish headquarters on the eastern front is moved to Gumru.…The British government inters the coffin of an unknown British soldier, selected by Brigadier General Wyatt from a group of unknown soldiers who had been killed at the Somme, Ypres, Arras, and Aisne, at Westminster Abbey in an elaborate ceremony.			Captain Waldo Evans assumes the office as the 13th American Samoan naval governor.

	A	B	C	D	E
	Includes developments that affect more than one world region, international organizations and important meetings of world leaders.	*Includes all domestic and regional developments in Europe, including the Soviet Union.*	*Includes all domestic and regional developments in Africa and the Middle East.*	*Includes all domestic and regional developments in Latin America, the Caribbean, and Canada.*	*Includes all domestic and regional developments in Asian and Pacific nations (and colonies).*

U.S. Politics & Social Issues	U.S. Foreign Policy & Affairs, Defense	U.S. Economy & Environment	Science, Technology & Nature	Culture, Leisure & Lifestyle	
Maine ratifies the Nineteenth Amendment to the U.S. Constitution.…Members of the Electoral Board of Virginia affirm that they performed their duties legally and stated there were more Republican people of color in the City of Charlottesville than white Republicans.…Indiana Governor James Goodrich proclaims this day the beginning of Girl Scout Week.		Recorded held at member banks at the federal reserve banks is $2,278 million.…The Yosemite Terminal Company files for voluntary dissolution.	The Marcel Benoist Foundation for the promotion of scientific research is founded by the Swiss Federal Council.…The Umatilla National Forest absorbs the Wenaha National Forest in the state of Oregon.	"Fred Fearnot and the Mill Girl" is the featured story in *Work and Win* pulp magazine.…The University of Washington Sun Dodgers play their final game at Denny Field, a loss against Stanford University.…The Masion d'Art in Bucharest holds a private exhibition.	Nov. 5
U.S. President Woodrow Wilson signs an order temporarily withdrawing lands with the Zia Pueblo in New Mexico from settlement, entry, sale or other disposition until 1922, when they may be disposed of according to laws in force at that time.…California ballot proposition Number One, Alien Land Law Initiative, passes restricting transfer of real property to U.S. citizens.	Devils Lake Indian Reserve is formed by President Warren G. Harding from lands withdrawn from settlement, entry, or sale.…U.S. Fort Sherman, Military Reservation on the Republic of Panama is enlarged as part of Executive Order 3352.…The French government gives Vassar University a French war tank as a gesture of thanks for the school's aid through war fundraising and the university nursing unit that numbered more than 100 Vassar graduates.		Westinghouse Electric and Manufacturing Company, and the subsidiary International Radio Telegraph Company, make history in the first transmission of election results by wireless telephone. The results were called into a station at East Pittsburgh, PA.	Musician John Philip Sousa performs at the University of Iowa Homecoming football game at the University Armory.…The University of Georgia is called the "Georgia Bulldogs" for the first time.…*Publisher's Weekly* prints a short summary of Sinclair Lewis' novel *Main Street*.…Famous Players-Lasky opens the Missouri Theater in St. Louis. Famous Players-Lasky produced the majority of movies shown this year.	Nov. 6
		Coal mine guards and strikebreakers are attacked by striking workers at Rawl and Rose Siding, WV.	The U.S. Aerial Mail Service De Havilland DH-4 plane crashes, piloted by John Percy Woodward, in Tie Siding, WY during a snowstorm, killing Woodward. (Woodward Airport in Salt Lake City is later named in his honor).…J.J.R. Macleod and Frederick Grant Banting meet for the first time in London, Ontario to discuss diabetes. This team would later be instrumental in the discovery of insulin.	The Senate of the University of the State of New York, under the direction of Mrs. William Vanamee, elects author Mark Twain (Samuel Langhorne Clemens), Statesmen Patrick Henry, and Roger Williams to the American Immortals in the American Hall of fame. Martha Washington and a former U.S. President fail to win nominations.	Nov. 7
				Actress Edna Lewis Thomas makes her acting debut at the Putnam Theater in Brooklyn, NY.…The new 12-team National Baseball League appoints John Heydler as president and Judge Kenesaw Mountain Landis as chair of new baseball commission.	Nov. 8
				Baseball's St. Louis Cardinals purchase Les Mann from the Boston Braves.…The University of Tulsa has its charter approved by the state of Oklahoma. The college incorporated the University and Henry Kendall College.	Nov. 9
	The U.S. destroyer *Sands* is commissioned on the east coast.…Rhode Island Battery A, 103rd Field Artillery, 26th Division, A.E.F. becomes the Battery A, Field Artillery, R.I.N.G.	A railroad tipple at Thacker, WV, is dynamited by striking coal miners.	A partial solar eclipse, visible in the United States, takes place. The eclipse was visible at sunrise in Montana, Idaho, Wyoming, Washington, and parts of Canada.	Playwright George Bernard Shaw's play *Heartbreak House* premiere opens in New York City.	Nov. 10
	Memorial Day parades are held in cities and towns in the United States, including different boroughs of New York City where different regiments conducted ceremonies.…The Baltimore mayor and city council dedicate land for a War Memorial Plaza In the downtown area with plans to develop a park to complement the war memorial building.	The Pennsylvania Railroad lays off 1,350 men at the Altoona Shops. This is approximately 15 percent of the total work force at the shops.	Thirteen plantations of trees are planted in Owego County, NY.		Nov. 11
F *Includes campaigns, elections, federal-state relations, civil rights and liberties, crime, the judiciary, education, healthcare, poverty, urban affairs, and population.*	G *Includes formation and debate of U.S. foreign and defense policies, veterans affairs, and defense spending. (Relations with specific foreign countries are usually found under the region concerned.)*	H *Includes business, labor, agriculture, taxation, transportation, consumer affairs, monetary and fiscal policy, natural resources, pollution and industrial accidents.*	I *Includes worldwide scientific, medical and technological developments, natural phenomena, U.S. weather and natural disasters.*	J *Includes the arts, religion, scholarship, communications media, sports, entertainment, fashions, fads, and social life.*	

	World Affairs	Europe	Africa & The Middle East	The Americas	Asia & The Pacific
Nov. 12	The Treaty of Rapalio is signed by the Serbs, Croats, Slovenes, and Italians to answer the Fiume Question. Under the terms of the treaty, Fiume becomes a free state and the Italian government relinquishes claims to Dalmatia. Zara and a group to the Dalmatian Islands remain outside the agreement. The Serbs, Croats, and Slovenes are given Susak, and Istria is divided between the treaty countries.	During fighting between the Turks and Armenians, 1,215 people are reported killed....Finland issues an official doctrine on the use of the Finnish national flag....V.I. Lenin signs orders establishing the People's Commissariat for Education after a decree of the Council of People's Commissars is passed.			
Nov. 13		The Red Army captures the city of Simferopol....A/S Norsk Flyveselskap is registered as the first airline company in Norway....The Extraordinary Congress of the people of Dagestan declares the country independent of any outside rule.	*Sierra Leone Weekly News* publishes an article titled, "Marcus Garvey and His African Problems."		
Nov. 14	The League of Nations' Eleventh League Council Session begins in Geneva.				The commander at Ping-kiang, Hunan Province is shot and killed as troops attack the city for money and goods.
Nov. 15	The first League Assembly Session, under the leadership of Belgium's Paul Hymans, begins in Geneva.... The League of Nations Congress in Geneva meets in special conference over the reconciliation between France and Germany....The League of Nations decides to have six commissions with defined topics for duties....Debate at the League over the amount of public information is to be released. A large number of delegates favors secret discussion and votes.	Islahiye is taken by Turkish forces....The Free City of Danzig forms under the protection of the League of Nations....Armenian forces are defeated by the Turks at Dahne.	Libyan Sheik Sunusi arrives in Ankara.		
Nov. 16	The president of the Swiss delegates M. Motta and Lord Robert Cecil make a public appeal to the United States to join the 41 countries at the meetings in progress at the League of Nations.	Russian democratic forces leave Russia, many taking asylum in nearby Czechoslovakia.			
Nov. 17	U.S. President Woodrow Wilson sends a greeting today to Paul Hymans, the President of the League of Nations Assembly in Geneva, stating the session will be productive for peace to the entire civilized world....Owners of the Carnegie Peace Palace will increase the rent when the new League of Nations for the High Court of Justice moves into the building in The Hague.	Turkish Nationalists issue a demand that Georgians turn over the Provinces of Kars, Ardahan, and Batum and allow free use of the Georgian Railway....The Bolsheviks begin government reorganization in the Crimea with committees forming at Sebastopol and Yalta.... Anti-German Czech rioters attack printing companies, businesses, and official offices in protest over the destruction of statutes of Emperor Joseph II, liberator of the Austrian Serbs in the 18th century.		President-elect of Chile Aruturo Alessandri requests that all banquets in his honor forego the use of alcohol. He requests that funds used to buy the liquor instead be donated to working class causes.... The U.S. State Department will refuse to recognize the Mexican government if Article 27 of the Mexican Constitution is interpreted to allow confiscation or be interpreted retroactively.	Troops extort money from merchants and kill more than 100 in Kaoyang, Chihli Province.

A	B	C	D	E
Includes developments that affect more than one world region, international organizations and important meetings of world leaders.	*Includes all domestic and regional developments in Europe, including the Soviet Union.*	*Includes all domestic and regional developments in Africa and the Middle East.*	*Includes all domestic and regional developments in Latin America, the Caribbean, and Canada.*	*Includes all domestic and regional developments in Asian and Pacific nations (and colonies).*

U.S. Politics & Social Issues	U.S. Foreign Policy & Affairs, Defense	U.S. Economy & Environment	Science, Technology & Nature	Culture, Leisure & Lifestyle	
		The *Francis Wilder* (owned by the Cleveland Ship Company) is severely damaged by storms on Lake Superior after leaving the harbor in Duluth, MN. All on board, including a dog, are rescued.... The oil tanker *Falls of Clyde* made the last ocean voyage oil transport from California to Hawaii.		Kennesaw Mountain Landis is elected the commissioner of major league baseball at a meeting where 16 team representatives attend and former head Ban Johnson is barred. The meeting decides that two separate leagues will remain, discarding the idea of incorporation. Judge Landis is given permission to retain his position as federal judge.... The Immaculate Heart of Mary receives its charter from the Commonwealth of Pennsylvania.	Nov. 12
Los Angeles sheriff deputies are arraigned for shooting and beating Arthur Valentine in Santa Monica, with the deputies entering a plea of not guilty.		The *John F. Eddy* is damaged in a storm on Lake Erie.... Bolton & Hay, Inc. open their first restaurant in Iowa (No. 1) on Fifth Street in Des Moines.... *Oceanside Blade* carries a story about the housing problem in southern California.	THe Hudson River freezes at Albany, NY.... A navel radio station sends the first message from Bayboro Harbor, St. Petersburg, FL.... K.W. Wagner publishes "Multiplex Telephony and Telegraphy Using High-Frequency Currents" in the journal *Radio Review*.... A Carnegie Institute telescope records the *Horsehead*, of the Nebular Region No. 25.... The *Literary Digest* advertises UNDARK, a radium product to apply to clock hands, theater seat numbers, watches, and fish bait.	Edith Wharton's story "Traveling by Proxy" is published in the *Independent*.... Florian Slappey, an early black fictional detective by Octavus Roy Cohen, is featured in a short story titled "Bird of Pray" in *The Saturday Evening Post* magazine.... *Publisher's Weekly* prints a full-page advertisement for Sinclair Lewis' book *Main Street*.	Nov. 13
				Philadelphia's *Public Ledger* publishes "The Scarecrow's Overcoat" by Ruth Plymly Thompson.	Nov. 14
The Centre Marshfield, MA, post office is closed.				The Apollo Theater, owned by The Selwyns, opens in New York City on the new Times Square on 42nd Street with a musical comedy *Jimmie*.... Playwright Ernst Toller's play *Massen und Menschen* opens in Neurenberg.	Nov. 15
Labor union member Obe Isenhover is paroled from Leavenworth Penitentiary after serving more than three years for union organizing in Oklahoma.... The Volstead Act takes effect, barring the manufacture and consumption of alcohol in the United States.			Walter Bowes and Arthur Pitney, were introduced by U.S. postal authorities and encouraged to develop a postal meter using inventions by both men. Pitney-Bowes developed, along with Walter Wheeler, Jr., the first postal meter patented in September; it is used for the first time today for commercial purposes.	The first U.S. postage meter is set at Stamford, CT.... The first organizational meeting of the Kansas Health, Physical Education, Recreation, and Dance (KAHPERD) is held.	Nov. 16
August Pascal, confessed abductor of the youth Blakely Coughlin, pleads guilty to second degree murder and kidnapping for extortion in Norristown, PA.	The U.S. Chemical Warfare Service announces that nearly 31 percent of soldiers admitted to overseas hospitals in World War I were gassed while on duty. This figure does not include members serving in the navy and the marines.	The Executive Council of the American Federation of Labor takes steps to halt radicalism and immigration of workers to the United States in an effort to halt the large numbers of unemployed.... An American foreman of the Puerticitos Mine of the Cananea Consolidated Copper Company, Canenea, in Sonora, México is shot by a Mexican resident who escaped by mule.... The 15 shirt factories of George P. Ide and Company, Inc. will close after the remaining orders are filled.... Two large sheeting mills in Utica, NY, will reduce its work week, and the Shenandoah Cotton Mills will close for a month or more due to lack of work.	Buffalo, NY, has been hit with one of the worst storms in history with more than a foot of snow on the ground in less than three hours.... Sixty mile an hour winds blow in New York City.	Fur colors are all the rage and in high demand as an accessory to clothing and coats this season.... Norma and Constance Talmadge sign contracts with Associated First National Pictures for $20 million, making them the highest-price actors in history. The salary covers four films per sister each year. Joseph M. Schenck, producer, is husband of Norma Talmadge and will share in the profits of this arrangement.	Nov. 17

F
Includes campaigns, elections, federal-state relations, civil rights and liberties, crime, the judiciary, education, healthcare, poverty, urban affairs, and population.

G
Includes formation and debate of U.S. foreign and defense policies, veterans affairs, and defense spending. (Relations with specific foreign countries are usually found under the region concerned.)

H
Includes business, labor, agriculture, taxation, transportation, consumer affairs, monetary and fiscal policy, natural resources, pollution and industrial accidents.

I
Includes worldwide scientific, medical and technological developments, natural phenomena, U.S. weather and natural disasters.

J
Includes the arts, religion, scholarship, communications media, sports, entertainment, fashions, fads, and social life.

	World Affairs	Europe	Africa & The Middle East	The Americas	Asia & The Pacific
Nov. 18	The League of Nations' First League Assembly Session and Eleventh League Council Session end in Geneva....Small member nations make a request to increase power in the League of Nations. Argentina and Peru are vocal supporters of the movement.	Turkey and Armenia sign armistice at the last of a series of meetings between the two countries....The Turkish Grand National Assembly issues a statement against imperialism....Soviet Russia hands down a Decree of Abortion, making it the first modern nation to legalize abortion....Troops under the command of S. Petlura leave the Volochysk frontier and retreat to Poland....The Jewish National Council of Warsaw sends a report that a new set of pogroms have taken place in the Ukraine. Bolshevist forces, following General Petlura, have committed the crimes.			Troops extort money from Hwangchow, Hupeh Province governors....The British government creates a report, as part of the Ancient Monument Preservation Act of 1904, claiming that ownership of the Taj Mahal in India is owned by the government and not by any individual or group.
Nov. 19					
Nov. 20	The first formal meeting is held at the new League of Nations headquarters on Palais Wilson, the former five-story Hotel National.	Russian Orthodox Church bishop Partiarch Tikhon and the Sacred Synod form the Russia Church Outside of Russia with the first head Metropolitan Anthony of Kiev and Galich....Greek General Papulas is given command of the Greek forces in Turkey....The Irish Republican Army assassination teams begin the process of killing 35 British intelligence operatives in Dublin, Ireland....North Ossetia becomes an Osetinskyj okrug in the Autonomous Mountains Soviet Republic.		Mexico debates making this a national holiday to honor the Mexican Revolution of 1910 and Francisco I. Madero's legacy.	The Kamioka, Naomi, and Naokawa train stations are opened in Saiki City, Oita....Indian leader Jathedar Jhabbar organizes a group to liberate the Gurdwara Panja Sahib at Hasan Abdal and then take a shrine at Sacha Sauda....Britain begins the process of converting railroad track gauge in India to match the gauges in Malaysia, Burma, and Cambodia.
Nov. 21		Ali Fuat Pasha is appointed the Turkish Ambassador to Moscow....Mussolini supporters begin a crackdown, killing 11 in Bologna, Italy....Members of the Black and Tans, a term used for British auxiliary forces, enter Croke Park during a football game between Dublin and Tipperary citing the need to search for illegal firearms. The event creates an unrest that leaves more than a dozen viewers and members of the sports team dead....Three Republican Army prisoners are shot. Guards report prisoners made an escape attempt.			
Nov. 22	U.S. President Woodrow Wilson presents his recommendations regarding the boundaries of Armenia and Turkey.	Greek Commander-in-Chief General Papulas arrives in Izmir, Turkey....Fourteen military officers and former officers are killed and six wounded in attacks in their homes around Dublin, Ireland in attacks by supporters of Sinn Fein.			Troops break into stores at Chunghsiang....The central Japanese railway stations Matsukawa and Nagano open to the public.
Nov. 23	The countries of Poland and Lithuania are ordered to stop fighting by the League of Nations and the countries comply with the demand.	The British Broadcasting Company, under the authority of the General Post Office, stops radio broadcasts due to reports of interference with military communications.	Somalian resistance leader Mohammed ibn Addoellah, Mad Molla, dies.		Troops continue looting stores in Chung-hsiang.
Nov. 24					The Australian House of Representatives votes to pass a new law outlining seditious behavior....Troops in Tienmen, Hupeh Province rob and burn villages.
Nov. 25	Panama is admitted to the League of Nations.	The Turkish Grand National Assembly votes to outlaw extravagant spending at weddings.			The Australian Senate votes to pass the new sedition law.... Troops at Lin-hsiang, Hunan Province and Yangshing and Fuchikow, Hupeh Province rob and extort money from merchants and government officials.
	A *Includes developments that affect more than one world region, international organizations and important meetings of world leaders.*	B *Includes all domestic and regional developments in Europe, including the Soviet Union.*	C *Includes all domestic and regional developments in Africa and the Middle East.*	D *Includes all domestic and regional developments in Latin America, the Caribbean, and Canada.*	E *Includes all domestic and regional developments in Asian and Pacific nations (and colonies).*

	U.S. Politics & Social Issues	U.S. Foreign Policy & Affairs, Defense	U.S. Economy & Environment	Science, Technology & Nature	Culture, Leisure & Lifestyle
Nov. 18	The Russell Sage Foundation opens a conference on the Babies' Welfare Federation in New York City. Scholarly papers to be read include the role of the foster family and payment of board for foster children.…President Warren Harding is on his way to New Orleans from the Panama Canal. The president has requested to have the ship stop in Vera Cruz, but it is unknown if Harding will make a speech there.	The U.S.S. *Conestoga* leaves Hampton Roads, VA for the Pacific Ocean.	Speyer & Co. requests that all holders of Mexican bonds deposit them in the New York Trust Company in an effort to force the Mexican government into honoring their commitment to pay interest and dividends on the bonds.…Cotton crops are hurt by the unusual cold season with frost creating the worst crop hazard.…Western and southern farmers request that War Finance Corporation be revived to aid them in their plight. Farm organizations ask President Woodrow Wilson for legislation to legalize collective marketing.		The Apollo Theater opens on West 42nd Street in New York City.…*November Woods*, a tone poem for orchestra by Arnold Bax, is performed for the first time in Manchester, England with the Halle Orchestra under the direction of Hamilton Harty.…The Syrian Protestant College changes its name to the American University of Beirut.…The owners of the Shubert Theaters announce that they will open the first of new chain of six theaters. The first theater will be built in New York City.
Nov. 19	Robert E. Crowe is elected Illinois state attorney general, and enforcement of Chicago handbook gambling operations is put as a state priority.				English pianist Katherine Bacon makes her New York debut.…The movie *The Mask of Zorro* premieres with Douglas Fairbanks starring in the title role.…The Daile Theatre in Riga, Latvia opens with *Indulis and Arija*.
Nov. 20	Ninety-six-year old Antoinette Brown Blackwell votes in the first national federal election at El Mora School in Elizabeth, NJ.		Qantus Airlines is formed.…The steel ore freighter *J.H. Sheadle* runs into a reef and sinks in Marquette, MI.…Kansas approves a funding amendment to begin building a centralized state highway system.	An earthquake in Albania kills 36 and wounds 102. Nearly 2,500 homes were destroyed in the quake.… Aviatrix Bessie Coleman leaves for France, where she is scheduled to enter the Ecole d'Aviation des Freres Caudron to fly the Nieuport Type 82 biplane.	Black American Aviatrix Bessie Coleman leaves for France to enter flying school at the Condrau School of Aviation in Le Crotoy, France.…U.S. President Woodrow Wilson is awarded the Noble Peace Prize.…Igor Stravinsky completes work on *Symphonies of Wind Instruments*.…The State of Illinois gives the Chicago Figure Skating Club a charter.…The first African-American baseball league, the Negro National League, is organized in Kansas City, MO.
Nov. 21			The Conference on the Humanitarian Labor Alliance is held in New York City.		Playwright Karel Capek's *Vec Makropulos* makes a premiere performance in Prague.
Nov. 22					The first ringside radio broadcast of a boxing match is aired in New York City.
Nov. 23	The city of Anchorage, AK, is legally incorporated.…African-American resident of Tylertown, MS, Harry Jacobs, is lynched.	The U.S. destroyer *Abel P. Upshur* is commissioned on the east coast.		The inventor and director of the Edison Labs, Thomas Edison, receives a patent for electroplating metal on metal.…A patent is granted for the Glowurm fishing lure.	
Nov. 24					
Nov. 25				The first Pulitzer race is won by a Verville-Packard 600 piloted by Lt. C.C. Mosely at the airfield at Michel Field, NY. Mosely flies 132 miles at the average speed of 156.54 miles per hour.	The first college football game is broadcast on the radio from College Station, TX.…Philadelphia hosts its first of what will become the Thanksgiving Day Parade.
	F *Includes campaigns, elections, federal-state relations, civil rights and liberties, crime, the judiciary, education, healthcare, poverty, urban affairs, and population.*	G *Includes formation and debate of U.S. foreign and defense policies, veterans affairs, and defense spending. (Relations with specific foreign countries are usually found under the region concerned.)*	H *Includes business, labor, agriculture, taxation, transportation, consumer affairs, monetary and fiscal policy, natural resources, pollution and industrial accidents.*	I *Includes worldwide scientific, medical and technological developments, natural phenomena, U.S. weather and natural disasters.*	J *Includes the arts, religion, scholarship, communications media, sports, entertainment, fashions, fads, and social life.*

	World Affairs	Europe	Africa & The Middle East	The Americas	Asia & The Pacific
Nov. 26		The town of Hulyai Pole, located in the center of the Makhnovists, is captured by the Red Army after a surprise attack.			
Nov. 27		Fighting begins in the Slucak region against the Bolshevik forces.			
Nov. 28	Slovenes, Serbs, and Croats hold elections for a constituent assembly in Yugoslavia, but fail to establish a clear majority. Stephen Radich, representing the Croats, does not attend the assembly, citing the failure of the group to base the constitution on a federal model. Nicholas Pasich, representing the Serbian Centralists, takes the lead in directing the language of the new constitution.				
Nov. 29		Turkey passes the Independence Medal Law....The Armenian Ministry of Interior is replaced by the Soviet controlled People's Commissariat of Internal Affairs....Police chiefs meet in London to discuss possible violence from Sinn Fein groups....Armenian forces recapture Kars after defeating Kemal forces. Reports indicate more than 7,000 Turkish troops were unable to evacuate the area and froze to death in the extreme cold....The Socialistic Workmen's Party of Austria was organized in a congress of delegates from throughout the country....Austria fails to meet its credit payment under the reparation system.		Cuban President Menocal signs an extension of the moratorium until December 31....The Mexican government withdraws its plan for an income tax due to large-scale protests....Ministers from Costa Rica, Dr. Octavio Beeche; Guatemala, Dr. Julio Bianchi; and the Dominican Republic, Emilio Joubert, arrive in Washington, DC as diplomats.	Soldiers burn and rob stores and warehouses in Ichang, Hupeh Province....The Chinese Minster of Finance announces that the country will raise its own loan, finding the terms and conditions of the international banking consortium unacceptable.
Nov. 30	The League of Nations received official notification of a treaty signing between Lithuania and troops under command of General Zellgouski at Kovno. The agreement also establishes a neutral zone between the forces and protocol for prisoner transfer....Reports of continued fighting are received from both Poland and Lithuania.	The free state of Prussia passes its constitution....The Universal Postal Convention is held in Madrid, Spain....The government of Azerbaijan recognizes the governments of Nagorno and Karabagh.		Olvaro Obregon is installed as President of Mexico, having defeated Alfredo Robles Dominguez for the office....U.S. President-elect Warren G. Harding makes a stop in Kingston, Jamaica....U.S. Border Patrol agents capture revolutionary materials and falsified government documents in El Paso, Eagle Pass, Laredo, Brownsville, and San Antonio, TX, indicating a plot to overthrow Obregon in Mexico.	Troops at Tayei, Hupeh Province disobey orders and begin robbing local merchants....Municipal Council members resign in Tokyo under suspicion of accepting graft to influence their decisions.
Dec. 1	The Fifth Committee of the First League of Nations refuses to accept the Azerbaijan Democratic Republic into the League based on reports of Armenian deaths by government leaders and territorial quest of the country....The government of Fiume, under leadership of poet Gabriele D'Annunzio, declares war on Italy over the terms of the Treaty of Rapallo....Austria is admitted to the League of Nations.	Demirci Mehmet Efe begins a revolt in Turkey....Nariman Narimanov, President of the Revolutionary Committee of Azerbaijan, reads a declaration of the Revkom granting Karabagh, Zangezur, and Nakhichevan to Armenia....It is the last day of the First Armenian Republic and the beginning of Armenian Soviet Socialists Republic.		The Cuban election pits National League's Dr. Alfredo Zayas against Liberal Party's candidate Jose Gomez. U.S. President Woodrow Wilson sends delegation headed by General Enoch Crowder to investigate charges of election corruption in the Zayas victory....U.S. President Woodrow Wilson orders studies of the Dominican Republic to begin to determine if the country is ready for elections and political independence. This would end U.S. occupation of the island.	Chinese troops in I-chang, a port in Hupeh Province, abandon their commanders, set the city on fire, and loot businesses....The Nagpur Congress of India adopts M. Gandhi's resolution refusing to be subjugated by other nations and declaring the people will work to be free through any and all peaceful means.
	A *Includes developments that affect more than one world region, international organizations and important meetings of world leaders.*	B *Includes all domestic and regional developments in Europe, including the Soviet Union.*	C *Includes all domestic and regional developments in Africa and the Middle East.*	D *Includes all domestic and regional developments in Latin America, the Caribbean, and Canada.*	E *Includes all domestic and regional developments in Asian and Pacific nations (and colonies).*

U.S. Politics & Social Issues	U.S. Foreign Policy & Affairs, Defense	U.S. Economy & Environment	Science, Technology & Nature	Culture, Leisure & Lifestyle	
	U.S. destroyer *Edsall* is commissioned on the east coast.		The Scott Polar Research Institute is founded at the University of Cambridge, England.…This month records unusually warm days, leading to an invasion of Arctic Three-toed Woodpeckers (Pieoides arelieus).…The first formal meeting of the Society of Neurological Surgeons is held in Boston.…The *Elizabeth Hindman* is launched at Midland, Ontario by Midland Shipbuilding Co. Ltd.	The Church of St. Martin of Tours (in Cheviot, OH) excavation begins.…The Maltese community of Detroit will receive a priest, Rev. Michael Borg.…The first trademarked use of "Schweppes" appears in the United Kingdom.…Boy Scout Troop 20 is chartered (one of the oldest troops in Los Angeles).…Italian tenor Beniamino Gigli makes his debut at the Metropolitan Opera in New York City in Boito's *Mefistofele*.	Nov. 26
		West Virginia governor John J. Cornwell declares a state of martial law in Mingo County due to violence surrounding coal strike.…Calvin Coolidge, while presenting a speech, states that civilization and profits go hand-in-hand.	Mitchel Field in New York holds the first National Air Race (Pulitzer Race).	The University of Washington football team moves to the new Husky Stadium with a game that ends with a 28–7 defeat by Dartmouth University.…The National President of the National League of American Pen Women presents the Western New York branch its charter at the first anniversary celebration.	Nov. 27
		West Virginia governor John J. Cornwell sends troops to Mingo County to assist in unrest with striking miners and coalmine operators. This was the third major outbreak of violence in the region. The 19th Infantry, under the director of Colonel Herman Hall, from Camp Sherman, OH, arrives in Mingo County to maintain order.			Nov. 28
Sweet spirits of nitre is now used as a substitute for liquor in a group of drinks called *Nitre Cocktails*. Federal and state officials warn that this fluid is a metal solvent and is extremely hazardous to human health.…Four European liners arrived yesterday at Ellis Island with nearly 2,700 of the 4,000 passengers sailing in steerage. The large number of immigrants slowed processing and two of the ships had to delay allowing passengers to debark.	The U.S. destroyer *Dallas* is commissioned on the east coast.	Jefferson and Eagle Lake Woolen Mills, of Holden, MA, reopen with workers' salaries reduced by 10 percent.…Richmond (Virginia) Cedar Works announces a 25 percent cut in salaries of all employees.…Twenty-four coal companies are indicted by a federal grand jury for violation of the Lever Act by fixing the prices of coal.…The Farmer's National Bank of Sterling, CO, was closed today by the Federal Reserve System citing excessive number of defaults on farm loans.…West Virginia Governor John Cornwell declares martial law in Mingo County due to tensions over coal strike.	William W. Coblentz, a native of Ohio, is awarded the Janssen Medal from the Academy of Sciences. Coblentz was given the award for his discoveries related to measuring ultraviolet and radiant heat from the earth and stars. He is a physicist with the U.S. Bureau of Standards in Washington, DC.	Playwright Eugene O'Neill copyrights his play *Dat Ole Davil*, earlier known as *Anna Christie* (reinterpreted play of *Chris Christopherson*).…Amherst College announced that a fundraising drive beginning today has collected nearly a quarter of their final goal in just one day. Arthur Curtis James, Amherst graduate in 1889, contributed $250,000 to the endowment fund.… American Walter Hill of Chicago paid top auction dollar for an 1833 first edition of Robert Browning's *Pauline*.	Nov. 29
	The U.S. State Department works to gain release for female relief workers arrested on charges of spying by authorities in Lithuania. The State Department requested the British government to make inquiries about the charges.		The Green Section, headed by Charles Vancouver Piper, is established to create green grass golf turf, and develop golf architecture and golf course construction.…The New York Psychoanalytic Society holds meeting on spirit mediums and their manifestations.	Preliminary boxing matches for Amateur Athletic League (AAU) draw more than 5,000 fans in New York City.…The Toronto and District Cricket Association is formed.…Film star Roscoe "Fatty" Arbuckle sails to Europe on the *Aquitania*.	Nov. 30
The state of North Dakota ratifies the Nineteenth Amendment to the U.S. Constitution.…*The Encyclical of Pope Benedict XV* is promulgated.…Miss Harriett Reid is appointed to a position as arbitrator on the Illinois Industrial Commission. She is the first woman in the history of the state to hold the office.		West Virginia governor John J. Cornwell is ordered to remove federal troops in the state by the U.S. Secretary of War Newton D. Baker on the grounds that the order was illegal. Baker sends a letter that state troops are to be used in such situations and refuses the order.…The Southern Pacific Company Board of Directors vote to separate their oil and railroad interests under two separate companies.	The Courtot Expedition begins crossing the Sahara Desert by automobile.	Actors at the Booth Theater in New York celebrate the 85th anniversary of Mark Twain's birth in a performance of *The Prince and the Pauper*.…A New York auction announces a record price paid for a letter signed by Thomas Jefferson. The letter went for $85.	Dec. 1

F	G	H	I	J
Includes campaigns, elections, federal-state relations, civil rights and liberties, crime, the judiciary, education, healthcare, poverty, urban affairs, and population.	*Includes formation and debate of U.S. foreign and defense policies, veterans affairs, and defense spending. (Relations with specific foreign countries are usually found under the region concerned.)*	*Includes business, labor, agriculture, taxation, transportation, consumer affairs, monetary and fiscal policy, natural resources, pollution and industrial accidents.*	*Includes worldwide scientific, medical and technological developments, natural phenomena, U.S. weather and natural disasters.*	*Includes the arts, religion, scholarship, communications media, sports, entertainment, fashions, fads, and social life.*

	World Affairs	Europe	Africa & The Middle East	The Americas	Asia & The Pacific
Dec. 2		Armenia and Turkish Nationals sign a peace treaty at Alexandropol. Armenia troops will turn over the majority of arms to the Turkish leaders and the group will be restricted to the territorial districts of Ervan and Kale Gokcha....The Soviets announce that a government is being organized at Erivan. This body has been given the authority to make agreements with Armenia, Russia, and Azerbaijan....I.V. Lenin sends a telegram to the Chair of the Revolutionary Military Committee of Armenia stating that he sends fraternal solidarity to the working people of Armenia, Turkey, and Azerbaijan.		Ontario, Canada's Conservative Party holds its first leadership convention....The University of Montreal is founded.	
Dec. 3	Heated debate takes place in the League of Nations Assembly over Article X.	Turkey and Armenia sign the Peace Treaty of Gumru ending fighting on the Eastern Front and the Turco-Armenian War. Turkey controls Kars and Ardahan, and Armenia rules Erivan as part of the agreement. Armenians give up nearly half of their pretreaty territory in the Peace of Alexandropol.		The Imperial Oil Company announces they have discovered oil in Fort Norman in the Northwest Territories of Canada....Mexican President Obregon hosts 10,000 people at the National Palace, shaking hands with each visitor.	
Dec. 4		A series of meetings are held between Mustafa Kemal, Ismet Inonu, and Deputy Cerkez Resit in Eskisehir, Turkey....Supporters of Indian independence urge alliance with Germany and Soviet Russia.	French Sudan is established by the French government in the former Upper Senegal-Niger....A Superior Council governing body is established in French West Africa by French government.	The University of Toronto defeats the Toronto Argonauts in the first Grey Cup football match to take place in the city since 1915. The Varsity Blues are the victors.	The Japanese government denounces California alien land law, calling it a regulation against humanity.
Dec. 5		Greek King Constantine is reinstalled by plebiscite as leader of the country. The king was removed in 1917 due to his support of German government....A series of meetings begin in Bilecik, Turkey, with Izzet Furgac, Salih Hulusi Kezrak, and Mustafa Kemal.		Lieutenant Governor of British Columbia, Edward Gawlor Prior, dies in office, the first to do so in the history of the province.	
Dec. 6	The League of Nations announces that the group's goal of mediation between the Kovno government and the new State of Central Lithuania is complete with the negotiated armistice and recent prisoner exchange. An international police force will take charge of order in Vilna....Discussion in the League of Nations centers on the Argentine request to withdraw from the League of Nations. Praise for Argentina is printed in the German newspaper *Vorwärts*.				
Dec. 7	The League of Nations Assembly discusses solutions to end the current typhus and cholera epidemics....Government officials of Japan and Chile formally denounce claims of an alliance between the two countries.	German USPD-KPD political parties merge into the Vereinigte Communist Party of Germany....There are 14,620 reported killed in groups of villages near Kars, Digor in continued fighting between Turkey and Armenia....Great Britain and the Soviets agree to meet to work out the final details of a trade agreement....Sinn Fein member and British House of Commons representative Dr. Richard Hayes is arrested in Dublin....An Italian naval destroyer leaves the blockade and joins military supporters of Gabriele d'Annunzio....The Athens government will not ask the former King Constantine to return home to take power of the country.	The Japanese government announces massive troop losses in fighting on the Siberian front.	Sir Robert Borden, head of the Canadian peace delegation to the League of Nations, claims that Article X is a major deterrent to Canada joining the organization. He states Article X would require Canada to come to the military aid of many countries challenged by sovereignty issues....Colonial Governor of Alaska Territory Thomas Riggs, Jr. requests that the federal government make a formal statement of colonial policy for that area....Washington State Senator Jones introduces a bill to ban the sale of opiates in any territory under the jurisdiction of the United States. The bill's jurisdiction includes consular districts.	Burmese university students begin rioting against British control of the country.

A	B	C	D	E
Includes developments that affect more than one world region, international organizations and important meetings of world leaders.	*Includes all domestic and regional developments in Europe, including the Soviet Union.*	*Includes all domestic and regional developments in Africa and the Middle East.*	*Includes all domestic and regional developments in Latin America, the Caribbean, and Canada.*	*Includes all domestic and regional developments in Asian and Pacific nations (and colonies).*

U.S. Politics & Social Issues	U.S. Foreign Policy & Affairs, Defense	U.S. Economy & Environment	Science, Technology & Nature	Culture, Leisure & Lifestyle	
	The Chief of the U.S. Air Service issues letter stating that all commanding air station officers to consider any officer holding a flying rating to be on regular flying duty, regardless of what the official duty designation might be. This entitled the personnel to a 50 percent increase in pay.	General Chemical, Solvay Process Company, Semet-Solvay, Barrett Company, and National Analine and Chemical announce a merger to be in effect as of the beginning of next year.... Mayor and Corporation Legal Counsel begin preparation of legal suit to be filed in the New York Supreme Court to halt a 10 percent rate increase by the electric companies serving the state.			Dec. 2
					Dec. 3
South Dakota ratifies the Nineteenth Amendment to the U.S. Constitution.					Dec. 4
				The movie *The Mask of Zorro* starring Douglas Fairbanks is premiered.... The featured story about the E.M. Laird Company's Laird Limousine plane is in production. The craft holds five passengers and two pilots.	Dec. 5
				The U.S. Court of Appeals reverses the decision of a lower court and rules that baseball's Baltimore Federal League is not entitled to monetary damages awarded by an earlier judge in the case decided in April 1919. This decision is a landmark by interpreting that baseball is not interstate commerce and cannot be regulated by antitrust laws.	Dec. 6
U.S. President Woodrow Wilson gives his eighth annual message to the U.S. Congress.... NAACP sends U.S. Congressional Representative George H. Tinkham of Massachusetts a telegram of support of the group's request for Congress to investigate charges that blacks had been denied the right to vote in the South. The group claims they have detailed proof of disenfranchisement for use in the investigation.... Solicitor General William L. Frierson announces that he interprets the Eighteenth Amendment to read that ships sailing under American registration may not serve alcohol, even though they may be operating on the high seas or docked in foreign ports.	The U.S. Army pays $10 million to Great Britain for war contracts. This includes munitions and equipment ordered before the armistice. Included in this payment was a note for the North Russian military campaign.	U.S. President-Elect Warren G. Harding will appoint 240,000 jobs under his administration. This is the largest group of patronage appointments in the history of the office.... The North Dakota State Bank Examiner announces another bank closing in that state. This brings the total closure to one national and 23 state banks this month. State bankers hold a conference to discuss solutions to the banking crisis.... David Moffat Myers, a member of the U.S. Fuel Administration, proposes conserving coal by extending war conservation techniques, in a speech before the American Society of Mechanical Engineers in New York City.	A new pass through the mountains of the Andes chain in Colombia is discovered by H. Case Wilcox and climbers employed by the Carib Oil Syndicate. The purpose of the expedition is to find a path for an oil pipeline and supply lines for drilling.	American and Australian lawn tennis teams arrive in Auckland, New Zealand after an ocean voyage to attend matches in the Davis Cup contest.... The American Gallery opens etching exhibit, featuring works by Frank Brangwyn, Axel Hermann Haig, and Seymour Haden.... A. Barton Hepburn, Chair of the Advisory Board of Chase National Bank, endows the chair of economics at Williams College with a gift of $150,000.... Students at St. John's College in Annapolis, MD, disregard agreement against hazing other cadets. Reports claim that a number of freshmen students have left school over the harassment.	Dec. 7

F	G	H	I	J
Includes campaigns, elections, federal-state relations, civil rights and liberties, crime, the judiciary, education, healthcare, poverty, urban affairs, and population.	*Includes formation and debate of U.S. foreign and defense policies, veterans affairs, and defense spending. (Relations with specific foreign countries are usually found under the region concerned.)*	*Includes business, labor, agriculture, taxation, transportation, consumer affairs, monetary and fiscal policy, natural resources, pollution and industrial accidents.*	*Includes worldwide scientific, medical and technological developments, natural phenomena, U.S. weather and natural disasters.*	*Includes the arts, religion, scholarship, communications media, sports, entertainment, fashions, fads, and social life.*

	World Affairs	Europe	Africa & The Middle East	The Americas	Asia & The Pacific
Dec. 8				General Cipriano Castro, former President of Venezuela, arrives in Santiago, Cuba on his way to New York City....The League of Nations representative to Chile and Argentina, Senator Gonzalo Bulnes, makes the statement that all countries must respect the rights of neutrals.	
Dec. 9	Bulgaria announces it will join the League of Nations.	Nurettin Pasha becomes Commander-in-Chief of the Turkish Central Army....Dr. Michael Hainisch, a Socialist writer, is elected Austrian President by the National Assembly.			There is discussion of a bill proposed in the Philippine Territorial Senate mandating residents of the islands to wear long pants in public. Violators could be sentenced to five years in jail under the legislation.
Dec. 10		The office of the Russian Foreign Intelligence Service (SVR) opens for the first time.			
Dec. 11		Turkish troops are sent to Demirci Mehmet Efe....Matko Laginja ends rule of Croatia.			
Dec. 12		Representatives of Hungary and Yugoslavia meet to divide Pecs coalmines and wrap up details of evacuation. A massive number of workers and residents attend the meeting....The Most Rev. Daniel Cohalan, Bishop of Cork, issues a decree of excommunication of people taking place in the Irish violence.			The Nagpur Congress of India adopts M. Gandhi's resolution, refusing to be subjugated by other nations and declaring the people will work to be free through any and all peaceful means.
Dec. 13	The League of Nations establishes the International Court of Justice in The Hague.	The headquarters of the Turkish eastern military front is moved to Kars.			
Dec. 14		During continued fighting between Turks and Armenians, 5,337 people are reported killed in 18 villages in Sarikamis.			The Shiromani Akali Dal is formed as a political party in India.
Dec. 15	Austria is admitted to the League of Nations....The Allies open the reparations conference in Brussels. The conference requires Germany to pay a total of 13.5 billion pounds over 42 years.	The Conference of Ambassadors meets on questions remaining in bilateral agreement between Yugoslavia and Hungary.		Juan Luis Sanfuentes leaves office as the 17th President of Chile.	The Philippine legislature authorizes establishment of a yearly fund of one million pesos to study the costs associated with independence.
Dec. 16	Finland, Bulgaria, Costa Rica, and Luxembourg are admitted to the League of Nations.	Demirci Mehmet Efe falls to Turkish forces.			Australia signs a treaty establishing the Statute of the Permanent Court of International Justice for the League of Nations....An 8.6 earthquake in the Kansu Province of China hits an area totaling 15,000 miles, killing more than 180,000 people.
	A	B	C	D	E
	Includes developments that affect more than one world region, international organizations and important meetings of world leaders.	*Includes all domestic and regional developments in Europe, including the Soviet Union.*	*Includes all domestic and regional developments in Africa and the Middle East.*	*Includes all domestic and regional developments in Latin America, the Caribbean, and Canada.*	*Includes all domestic and regional developments in Asian and Pacific nations (and colonies).*

U.S. Politics & Social Issues	U.S. Foreign Policy & Affairs, Defense	U.S. Economy & Environment	Science, Technology & Nature	Culture, Leisure & Lifestyle	
A new federal bill suspending immigration for two years draws fire from a group in the House of Representatives, claiming authors did not have adequate input from congressional leaders against the legislation.…Jersey City Chief of Police orders all blacks on the streets at night to be detained in local jails. The action draws outrage from black community leaders.		A joint resolution is introduced in the House of Representatives to investigate the causes of growing unemployment and actions, if any, the federal government can take to reduce the number of jobs lost.		U.S. President Woodrow Wilson will be awarded the Nobel Peace Prize on December 10, Swedish and Norwegian newspapers announce.	Dec. 8
Pennsylvania officials increase the reward for capture of arsonists of 12 schools, 19 stores, and five mines in the Fayette-Westmoreland district over the last 14 days. The American Legions vote to offer services of former military to assist in protecting structures against damage.				*Life* magazine features a story on Irish Home Rule.…Baseball great Babe Ruth signs 500 baseballs to be sold by the Indiana Knights of Columbus to benefit orphaned youth living at the Gibault Home in Indianapolis, IN.…The sale of women's neckware is doing well.	Dec. 9
California Governor Stephens gives formal notification that the recently passed Anti-Alien Land Law will go into operation today and that his office will support enforcement of the regulation.…Howard County in Nebraska records its first death by electrocution. Executions prior to this time were by hanging.		American wool and cutlery manufacturers and ask Congress for embargo on foreign imports.		U.S. President Woodrow Wilson and Leon Bourgeois, President of the French Association for the Society of Nations, are awarded the Nobel Peace Prize. Bourgeois was awarded the delayed prize for the year 1919.	Dec. 10
			Mattie Larid's prototype airplane fails in test at its factory site in Wichita, KS.	The Albright Art Gallery in Buffalo, NY, opens the "Exhibition of Paintings by Frederick Carl Frieseke, Maurice Fromkes, Hayley Lever, and Jonas Lie."…Enrico Caruso performs at the Academy of Music in New York City. His mouth begins to bleed and by the time the performance is completed, his towel is filled with his blood.	Dec. 11
	The U.S.S. *Macdonough* is launched from the Bethlehem Shipbuilding of San Francisco and will be placed in commission at Mare Island Navy Yard in California next year.	The western mining town of Courtland, AZ, begins a massive shutdown due to mining failures. The Arizonan Hotel is the first large business to close. The railroad and other businesses soon follow in the closure.		*La Valse, Poeme Choreographique* by Maurice Ravel premiers in Paris, France with Camille Chevillard conducting the Lamoureux Orchestra of Paris.…H.P. Lovecraft's short story *The Picture in the House* is written.…The Art Institute of Chicago ends the "33rd Annual Exhibition of American Oil Paintings and Sculpture."…Actress Greta Garbo stars in the advertising film *Mr. and Mrs. Stockholm* (also known as *From Top to Toe or How Not to Dress*) in Stockholm, Sweden.	Dec. 12
			Astronomers, using F. Pease's interferometer, measure the size of a mixed star for the first time.		Dec. 13
	The first nongraduate of the Army School, C.H. Hodges, takes his teaching post at the West Point, NY, facility.			Boxer Jack Dempsey knocks out Bill Brennan in the 12th round to capture the heavyweight boxing championship title.	Dec. 14
Colorado ratifies the Nineteenth Amendment to the U.S. Constitution.	The U.S. destroyer *Pillsbury* is commissioned on the east coast.			The National Baseball League announces teams used 27,924 baseballs during the last season.	Dec. 15
	The U.S. destroyer *King* is commissioned on the east coast.				Dec. 16

F	G	H	I	J
Includes campaigns, elections, federal-state relations, civil rights and liberties, crime, the judiciary, education, healthcare, poverty, urban affairs, and population.	*Includes formation and debate of U.S. foreign and defense policies, veterans affairs, and defense spending. (Relations with specific foreign countries are usually found under the region concerned.)*	*Includes business, labor, agriculture, taxation, transportation, consumer affairs, monetary and fiscal policy, natural resources, pollution and industrial accidents.*	*Includes worldwide scientific, medical and technological developments, natural phenomena, U.S. weather and natural disasters.*	*Includes the arts, religion, scholarship, communications media, sports, entertainment, fashions, fads, and social life.*

	World Affairs	Europe	Africa & The Middle East	The Americas	Asia & The Pacific
Dec. 17	Albania is admitted to the League of Nations.... A British condominium is established for Nauru.			More than 400 people are killed and injured in a massive earthquake in the Mendoza region of Argentina. A number of structures are also damaged and large-scale flooding is occurring related to the earth tremor.	Japan is given control over Pacific islands north of the equator (including the Marshall Islands, Marianas, Caroline, and Ladrone) by the League of Nations.... The League of Nations establishes an Australian Mandate for German New Guinea and a New Zealand Mandate for German Samoa.
Dec. 18	France and Ireland join the Permanent Court of International Justice as Member States.... The First Ordinary Session of the Assembly of the League of Nations ends in Geneva.... The League of Nations Assembly ratifies annexation of Nagorno Karabagh to Armenia.	Ukrainian Nationalist troops under Symon Petliura leave the Volochysk frontier and retreat to Poland.... A.G. Chervyakov begins service as Chairman of the Central Executive Committee and the Council of People's Commissars of Belorussian SSR.			
Dec. 19		Greek King Constantine returns to Greece meeting thousands of hysterical supporters in Athens, some who rush to kiss the harness of the horses pulling his carriage. He retakes control of government and announces support for the war with Turkey. Allies withdraw support for the Greek government.... American troops will not be withdrawn from the Rhine region, according to American commander Major General Henry T. Allen.		The Canadian government cuts luxury taxes in an effort to increase sales of goods.... U.S. Secretary of State Bainbridge Colby reports from his goodwill trip to South America that he will deliver a message of goodwill omitting any discussion of the League of Nations or the Monroe Doctrine.	China announces it will increase duties on relief goods entering the country to assist in feeding victims of the famine there.... Japanese troops stationed in the Chentao district of the Korean-Manchurian border will not be withdrawn. The Japanese government cites recent Korean attacks as the reason.
Dec. 20		The last remnant of the uprising against the Bolsheviks is halted in the Slucak region.... The Republic of Armenia is annexed to the Soviet Union, becoming the Soviet Republic of Armenia.		Hydroelectric unit No. 2 is opened as part of the Ontario Power Generation plan.... The National Health Department records the last case of yellow fever in the state of Yucatan.	Acting Secretary of State Norman Davis signs a new treaty with Siam (Thailand) that was arranged by President Woodrow Wilson.... Executive Order No. 59 is issued by Governor-General Francis Burton Harrison establishing Currimao, Philippines as a municipality.
Dec. 21		The Constituent Assembly of Latvia passes a second reform bill to distribute expropriated lands.	Religious and Nationalist leader Mohammed Abdullah Hassan (born Maxamed Cabdulle Xasan, Sayyid) dies of influenza in Somalia at the age of 54.	Two destroyers are presented to the Canadian government in Halifax.	A mass meeting is held in Burma (at the front of the Shwedgon pagoda) to make plans to finance national education.
Dec. 22		V.I. Lenin proposes electrification of entire country at the eighth All-Russian Congress of Soviets.		The Crown Game Preserve in Ottawa, Canada, is declared a game sanctuary.	The National Day of the Union of Burma remembers a boycott against passage of the British Rangoon University Act, which limited attendance at the university to only the wealthy British classes. This is later thought to be the start of the National Education Movement in Burma.

A	B	C	D	E
Includes developments that affect more than one world region, international organizations and important meetings of world leaders.	*Includes all domestic and regional developments in Europe, including the Soviet Union.*	*Includes all domestic and regional developments in Africa and the Middle East.*	*Includes all domestic and regional developments in Latin America, the Caribbean, and Canada.*	*Includes all domestic and regional developments in Asian and Pacific nations (and colonies).*

U.S. Politics & Social Issues	U.S. Foreign Policy & Affairs, Defense	U.S. Economy & Environment	Science, Technology & Nature	Culture, Leisure & Lifestyle	
				American League Baseball votes to allow pitchers to use a spitball. The conditions limit use to players who used spitballs in the 1920 season. The new regulations allow 17 designated spitters. Newcomers are barred from using the pitch.	Dec. 17
				Ty Cobb replaces Hughie Jennings as manager of the Detroit Tigers baseball team. He signs a contract worth $32,500.…An arrest warrant is issued for Joe "Shoeless" Jackson on charges of illegal gambling on baseball games.…The Norman Rockwell painting, *Children Looking in a Toy Store Window*, appears on the cover of *The Literary Digest*.	Dec. 18
The Salvation Army cites a shortage of money donated to assist the group in providing food for holiday dinners. Donations are the lowest in years.…A Florida real estate man is tarred and feathered after his letter of German support is printed in the local newspaper. No arrests have been made.		U.S. leaders in Congress claim that continuation of the War Finance Corporation and the creation of a temporary tariff on foreign farm goods will not solve the long-range financial problems plaguing farmers.		The first U.S. indoor curling rink opens in Brookline, MA.…Balboa Park (San Diego, CA) opens the National History Museum.…One hundred friends of biographer Horace Traubel meet for dinner in his honor.	Dec. 19
Customs House officials in Brownsville, TX make an elaborate ceremony of destroying alcohol as part of their enforcement strategy.…Kansas National Guard troops arrive in Independence to put down railroad worker protests and rioting.…Indian homesteads on the Santee Reservation in Nebraska expiring today are extended for 10 additional years.	The U.S.S. *Relief*, a hospital ship, is commissioned by the U.S. War Department with the capacity for 500 patients.…The destroyer U.S.S. *Barry* is commissioned.	The Alaskan mail steamer the SS *Dora* is destroyed in a wreck at Hardy Bay, Vancouver Island.		Speed flier Frank Monroe Hawks takes Amelia Earhart on one of her first plane rides at the Kansas State Fair.…The Abbeydale Cinema is built in Sheffield, England.…Actor Bob Hope becomes an American citizen.…Author and playwright Franz Kafka enters Prague Villa Tatra sanatorium for treatment of tuberculosis.	Dec. 20
			Scientists Robert H. Goddard patents a method and means for producing electrified jets of gas and a second on electrogravitation.…Woodward Field in Salt Lake City, the largest of the fields used by the U.S. Post Office, is dedicated in a naming ceremony for Airmail Pilot John P. Woodward, who was killed attempting to deliver mail in Wyoming.	George Herbert Walker, representing the National Golf Links of America, suggested the idea of international golf team matches and offered to donate an International Challenge Trophy (later called The Walker Cup) for winners of the event.…The musical *Sally* (based on the book by Guy Bolton with music and lyrics by Jerome Kern, Clifford Grey, and P.G. Wodehouse) opens at the New Amsterdam Theater in New York City.	Dec. 21
The state of Massachusetts codifies general laws of the Commonwealth.	The Alabama National Guard is sent to the coalfields in Walker County to keep the peace between United Mine Workers of America and coal mine owners.…A vigilante mob takes the admitted killer of local police officer from his holding cell in a jail in Fort Worth, TX, and shoots, beats, and hangs him from a tree. Mob members are not identified.…The Ajax Dress Company of New York City files for bankruptcy.	Lightship 103 is built in New York and commissioned this day for the U.S. Lighthouse Service.	Calvin B. Coulter publishes a paper in the *Journal of General Physiology* on the equilibrium between hemolytic sensitizer and red blood cells.	*Neighbors* is released, a film directed by Buster Keaton and Eddie Cline and produced by the Comique Film Corporation.…The SS *Niagara* arrives in New York City from Naples after a 21-day voyage.…Bantamweight Joe Lynch defeats Pete Herman for the world championship of boxing.	Dec. 22

F	G	H	I	J
Includes campaigns, elections, federal-state relations, civil rights and liberties, crime, the judiciary, education, healthcare, poverty, urban affairs, and population.	*Includes formation and debate of U.S. foreign and defense policies, veterans affairs, and defense spending. (Relations with specific foreign countries are usually found under the region concerned.)*	*Includes business, labor, agriculture, taxation, transportation, consumer affairs, monetary and fiscal policy, natural resources, pollution and industrial accidents.*	*Includes worldwide scientific, medical and technological developments, natural phenomena, U.S. weather and natural disasters.*	*Includes the arts, religion, scholarship, communications media, sports, entertainment, fashions, fads, and social life.*

	World Affairs	Europe	Africa & The Middle East	The Americas	Asia & The Pacific
Dec. 23		The British Parliament passes the Government of Ireland Act creating two separate parliaments for the country, one representing southern Ireland in Dublin and the other representing northern Ireland in Belfast. The Council of Ireland is set up as a body to represent all of Ireland on common issues.... British King George V signs the Home Rule Act.... The Franco-British Convention is signed outlining the boundary between Syria and Lebanon.	A treaty signed by Britain and France defines political boundaries and Mandates for Syria, Palestine, Lebanon, and Mesopotamia. It included details regarding irrigation of the area.		The famine in China has spread to cover the provinces of Chili, Shantung, and Honan. Large numbers of residents in Shansi and Shensi have also reported food shortages.
Dec. 24		Turkey sends advisors to Cerkez Ethem.... The World Zionist Conference is held in London, England.... The Central Library of the Crimea begins construction.		Artist and architect Francisco Salazar constructs a pavilion in Morazan Park in Costa Rica that is used for speeches and ceremonies.	
Dec. 25		A revolt begins in Cerkez Ethem.			
Dec. 26			Puerto Rican activists rally against the United States for home rule. Antonio R. Barcelo, President of the Puerto Rican Senate and head of the Unionist Party, leaves the country for a meeting with President-Elect Warren G. Harding to discuss the issue.		Vietnam's Ho Chi Minh writes a public letter criticizing French influence in Asia.... The importation of vast quantities of asbestos into Japan creates a market for re-exportation to the United States.
Dec. 27	The Council of Ambassadors refuses to make policy, leaving the plan for disarming the German Bavarian Einwohnerwehr and other anti-Communist groups to the Allied Premiers who will meet in Nice at the beginning of next year.	Fiume is bombed by Italian navy. Government head Gabriele D'Annunzio leaves Fiume, and political debate continues between factions of the nationalists and autonomists.		Dr. Carlos Manuel de Cespedes, Cuban Minister to the United States, refutes claims that Cuba has requested U.S. intervention in domestic unrest.	
Dec. 28		Bolshevik troops take the Ukraine and an alliance treaty is signed between V.I. Lenin and Ukrainian Communist Leader Khristian.		The Law of December 28, 1920 provides the terms to make an agrarian revolution in the country by allowing sales of land to Mexican citizens who had never owned land before.	
Dec. 29		The Eighth All Russia Congress of Soviets is called by V.I. Lenin.... The Communist Party is organized in France.... The special conference of the British Parliamentary Labor Party meets in London to discuss the Irish Question.... Cracow reports that food is depleted and requests aid for goods to feed children from European countries and the United States.... The French government charges that the French treasury lost $3 billion in fraudulent stock purchases from Americans recently.		The U.S. State Department approves a bill to allow small arms to be shipped into Mexico.... Former President William Howard Taft and his wife arrive in Bermuda for a two-month stay.... Two large earthquakes hit Argentina, one at 2:00 a.m. and the other nearly two hours later. No one was killed and little damage to structures is reported. Mendoza Oil Company reports severe damage as a result of the earthquakes.	Four sons of the former President of China, Yuan Shih Kai, arrive in Vermont to join the student body of Middlebury College.
Dec. 30		A group of prominent New York businessmen of Irish heritage meet to collect money to assist starving residents of Ireland.			
Dec. 31		Great Britain announces a new plan for unemployment insurance. Men will receive 15 shillings and women 12 under the new benefit plan.	The Courtot Expedition arrives at Lake Chad after crossing the Sahara Desert by automobile.		

A	B	C	D	E
Includes developments that affect more than one world region, international organizations and important meetings of world leaders.	*Includes all domestic and regional developments in Europe, including the Soviet Union.*	*Includes all domestic and regional developments in Africa and the Middle East.*	*Includes all domestic and regional developments in Latin America, the Caribbean, and Canada.*	*Includes all domestic and regional developments in Asian and Pacific nations (and colonies).*

U.S. Politics & Social Issues	U.S. Foreign Policy & Affairs, Defense	U.S. Economy & Environment	Science, Technology & Nature	Culture, Leisure & Lifestyle	
				New York Times features article on film *Passion,* the first foreign film shown in the United States to achieve large audiences and bring in high box office revenues.... Frank Fredrickson is signed by a free agent by the Victoria (PCHA) hockey team.... Elaborate open-air program is held by the San Diego Elks Club Chanters in Balboa Park, CA.	Dec. 23
Joseph Ventolo is examined by officers investigating the Sacco-Vanzetti Case.			A small tidal wave from an earthquake takes a dozen beach cottages from Sunset Beach in the Quinault and Grays Harbor region of Washington state....The Hawaiian Islands are threatened by storms and flooding.	Enrico Caruso gives his last public performance, as Eleazar in Halevy's *La Juive*, in New York City at the Metropolitan Opera....Miniaturist Charles Bowdish creates a tiny railroad and village in Brookville, PA. He will later give the display to the Carnegie Science Center in Western Pennsylvania.	Dec. 24
				The San Diego City Council announces plans to open the Academy of Fine Arts in the Sacramento Building of Balboa Park after the first of the year.	Dec. 25
Purported mob member Edward "Monk Eastman" Osterman is killed outside his restaurant, The Blue Bird Café in New York City, by a federal bootlegging agent when he attempted to return to bootlegging after serving with honors in the military service in World War I.		New York City union printers receive an increase in salaries after going to arbitration with companies. Increases will be retroactive.		The San Francisco Thistle Football Club plays Scotland at the Seals Ballpark....The female soccer (football) team plays a demonstration game in London in front of a sell-out crowd of nearly 53,000 fans, many more than the men's team attracted.	Dec. 26
The U.S. Socialist Party criticizes President Woodrow Wilson after the government denies a request to allow their jailed leader Eugene V. Debs an opportunity to visit his home for the season holidays.			A New York telephone company announces the installation of automatic dial phones next summer. In place of using a Hello Girl (operator), the person using the phone will use the dial on individual phones to call parties....Telephone number directories are delivered to public libraries.		Dec. 27
California leaders announce a law that will prohibit alien ownership of land in the state, citing the need for protection of oil and coastal tracts. Japan and the U.S. State Department have been included in the discussions.		The New York Stock Exchange announces new rules against trading by stock market clerks and others working in the market, citing investor fear that trading by these groups increases the speculative degree of market investments.	The Society of Economic Geologists, Inc. is established at a meeting with 60 people.	The first U.S. ship designed for use as a hospital and ambulance ship is delivered. *The Relief* is put into service immediately....The Capitol Theater in Ansonia, CT, opens.	Dec. 28
Chicago Prohibition Director Frank D. Richardson asks for an army airplane to lead raids on alcohol production facilities in that geographic area....William H. Moran, head of the Secret Service, announces that crime in the United States is the worst since 1897. Bank robberies are at a record number....The town of Culver, IN, takes on bank robbers in a huge gunfight. Five would-be robbers are captured by townsfolk after emptying the bank drawers of cash.	Idaho Republican Senator Borah announces special meeting of the Foreign Relations Committee to consider his proposal to ask the U.S. President to meet with Great Britain and Japan regarding an agreement to reduce naval armaments. He defined the talks to the three powers named and stated the reduction would include current naval construction underway in the United States.	Two top hotels in Kansas City, MO lower rates for rooms....The Ford Motor Company plant in Highland, MI extends the shutdown until February 1. Slow auto sales are cited as the reason for the extension....Five striking miners and coal company employees are arraigned and charged with a shooting in Thacker, WV, (Mingo) during a strike on December 18.	Eduardo Chavez, a Brazilian pilot, is the first person to complete the 1,100 mile flight from Rio de Janeiro to Buenos Aires.	Coloratura soprano and opera star Selma Kurz begins her American tour with an appearance at the New York Hippodrome with the National Symphony Orchestra....Hollywood starlets hold a double wedding, with movie actress Dorothy Gish's marrying fellow actor James Rennie and Constance Talmadge marrying John Pialoglou, a tobacco importer. The wedding was to be kept a secret until after the first of the year, but the press persuaded the justice of the peace to release the details.	Dec. 29
	The U.S. destroyer *John D. Ford* is commissioned on the east coast.				Dec. 30
The United Shipping Board receives four ships from the German government. After retrofitting, these ships will join the present ocean service between New York, Plymouth, Cherbourg, and Southampton.				Roy Park makes the first ball duck in a match at the Test Cricket Inn against England at the Melbourne Cricket Grounds.	Dec. 31

F	G	H	I	J
Includes campaigns, elections, federal-state relations, civil rights and liberties, crime, the judiciary, education, healthcare, poverty, urban affairs, and population.	*Includes formation and debate of U.S. foreign and defense policies, veterans affairs, and defense spending. (Relations with specific foreign countries are usually found under the region concerned.)*	*Includes business, labor, agriculture, taxation, transportation, consumer affairs, monetary and fiscal policy, natural resources, pollution and industrial accidents.*	*Includes worldwide scientific, medical and technological developments, natural phenomena, U.S. weather and natural disasters.*	*Includes the arts, religion, scholarship, communications media, sports, entertainment, fashions, fads, and social life.*

1921

An American street scene in 1921.

Young Men's Shop"
YOUNG MENS SHOP
"The Young Shop"

	World Affairs	Europe	Africa & The Middle East	The Americas	Asia & The Pacific
Jan.	The Paris Conference begins discussions of reparations. Despite being in economic crisis, Germany agrees to pay 11.3 billion pounds over 42 years.	The Republic of Turkey comes into existence.	France organizes the colony of Mauritania. This is part of a reorganization of French West Africa.... Britain begins withdrawing from Northern Persia (Iran).	The Federation of Central America forms. Members are Costa Rica, Guatemala, Honduras, and El Salvador.	A White Russian army occupies Mongolia and forces the Chinese out of Outer Mongolia.
Feb.		At Kronstadt on the Baltic Sea, the Russian navy rebels in protest of the economic crisis and food shortages. The government crushes the rebellion but institutes reforms.	Russia and Iran sign a treaty whereby Russia withdraws and cancels all claims against the new Iranian government.	Panama occupies territory claimed by Costa Rica.	
Mar.		Lenin implements his New Economic Policy. The NEP is an effort to counter the collapse brought on by the civil war and Allied blockade.... Spanish premier Eduardo Dato dies at the hands of Catalan anarchists. Dato has led the conservatives since 1913, serving as premier three times.... The Polish-Soviet war ends. Russia takes Belarus and Ukraine.	Belgium formally transfers its mandate in Tanganyika to Britain. Belgium retains rights of free transit.... The Cairo Conference convenes to address Iraq and Palestine. Colonial Secretary Winston Churchill is chair.		Russia and Afghanistan sign a treaty of friendship. The Amanullah government is seeking to reduce British influence.... Mongolia begins the struggle that will culminate in independence from China in July. Mongolia establishes a limited monarchy with Russian assistance. In November Mongolia becomes a people's republic.
Apr.	The first general conference on communications and transit meets in Barcelona, Spain. This is a first step in improving world communications.	The Red Army offensive in the Caucasus destabilizes the Armenian government. Bolsheviks establish an Armenian Soviet Republic.... The Austrian Tyrol votes to join Germany. Peace treaties bar such a move, but other Austrian provinces attempt to join Germany.	The Emirate of Transjordan comes into being. Taken from Palestine and exempt from the Balfour declaration, Transjordan is a Hashemite kingdom under British mandate.	A total lunar eclipse is visible in the Americas as well as Australia and parts of Africa and Europe.	
May		Famine begins in Russia.... Sweden ends capital punishment.... Britain's Ministry of Health issues a report on the causes of blindness and eye problems. The film industry changes the type of lights used in its studios.			
Jun.	The international conference on traffic in women and children meets in Geneva.	The Little Entente is finished. Members include Czechoslovakia, Romania, and the Kingdom of the Serbs, Croats and Slovenes.		Guatemala joins the Federation of Central America.	
Jul.		Russia's famine becomes more widespread. As many as 18 million people face starvation.... France provides the first BCG vaccine against tuberculosis in humans. The Bacillus of Calmette and Guerin is a bovine strain first developed in Paris in 1906.	The Communist Party of South Africa adopts its manifesto. The party is an amalgamation of various South African socialist groups and will later affiliate with the Communist International.		At Shanghai, the Chinese Communist Party comes into existence.
Aug.			At the Battle of Annual, Moroccan forces destroy Spanish troops attempting to stifle the Riff rebellion. Spanish losses are 12,000 of their 20,000-man contingent.	The United States intervenes in Panama and forces an end to hostilities between Panama and Costa Rica. Costa Rican forces take the disputed territory after Panamanians withdraw under duress.	Gandhi begins his boycott of foreign cloth. The first symbolic act is burning of imported cloth at Mumbai.
Sep.	The League's Permanent Court of International Justice comes into being.	Germany opens the first stretch of its autobahn, the Avus highway near Berlin. Begun as a test track in 1912, the road is a four-lane undivided toll road.			
Oct.					
Nov.		Hungary exiles King Karl to Madeira. Karl has twice this year sought to reestablish the Habsburg monarchy.			
Dec.	The Eight Power resolution of the Washington Conference requires a reexamination of Chinese law regarding extraterritoriality. The Four Power Pacific Treaty guarantees all signatories' Pacific possessions and ends the Anglo-Japanese treaty of 1902.	The economic downturn in Britain worsens, with two million unemployed.... Britain and Ireland declare the southern part of Ireland to be a British dominion, the Irish Free State. Ratification of the treaty will occur in January 1922.		William Lyon Mackenzie King becomes prime minister of Canada. He will be prime minister for a record 22 years and lead the Liberal Party for nearly 30.	At Ahmendabad, Gandhi takes total control of the Indian National Congress.... Japan opens an institute for film studies. Australia establishes its Commonwealth Cinema and Photographic Branch to expand studies in cinematography.

A	B	C	D	E
Includes developments that affect more than one world region, international organizations and important meetings of world leaders.	*Includes all domestic and regional developments in Europe, including the Soviet Union.*	*Includes all domestic and regional developments in Africa and the Middle East.*	*Includes all domestic and regional developments in Latin America, the Caribbean, and Canada.*	*Includes all domestic and regional developments in Asian and Pacific nations (and colonies).*

U.S. Politics & Social Issues	U.S. Foreign Policy & Affairs, Defense	U.S. Economy & Environment	Science, Technology & Nature	Culture, Leisure & Lifestyle	
		Unemployment totals 3.5 million. Manufacturing, transportation, construction, and mining have a combined rate of 23.1 percent.	Radio station KDKA broadcasts the first religious service, that of Calvary Episcopal Church. It also broadcasts a Hoover speech at the Duquesne Club.		Jan.
	Wilson recalls the American delegation to the reparations commission.	The government reports that the U.S. has nine million automobiles at of the end of 1920.	Etienne Oehmichen of France makes the first helicopter flight.	*The Kid* debuts with Charlie Chaplin and six-year-old Jackie Coogan as its stars. *The Kid* is Chaplin's first full-length movie. Coogan's film debut was in 1917.	Feb.
Sanbury, CT, police mandate that skirts must reach at least four inches below the knee. The effort to stop shortening skirts proves futile.... Thompson submachine guns begin coming off the assembly line.		The Public Health Service completes an aerial ;survey of the Mississippi Valley watershed.	The first family planning clinic opens in London. The operator is Dr. Marie Stopes, a disciple of Margaret Sanger, who opens the first clinic in the U.S. later in the year.	Rudolf Valentino's *Four Horsemen of the Apocalypse* debuts. One of the decades biggest moneymakers, it earns $3.8 million for Metro Pictures.	Mar.
	The U.S. declines to mediate the reparations disagreement. Germany asks for intervention after the commission demands 132 billion gold marks, with one billion due by the end of the month or the allies will occupy the Ruhr.		The first deep sea cable between Havana and Key West begins operation.	The new world's record in the 100 meter dash is 10.4 seconds. Holder is Charley Paddock, Olympic champion in 1920 and 1924 and first to be known as "World's Fastest Human."	Apr.
The Sacco-Vanzetti trial opens.	The Immigration Quota Act goes into effect. The act limits immigration to no more than three percent of the 1910 total for each nationality.	President Harding gives the Interior Department control of government emergency oil reserves, including Teapot Dome, WY. The intent is to prevent adjacent private developers from siphoning oil intended for naval use in emergencies.	A solar storm burns out railroad switches in New York and causes damage in Sweden. Phone, cable, and telegraph service in Europe and part of the U.S. are disrupted.	Modernists Manet, Millet, Degas, and Matisse are featured at an art exhibition at the Metropolitan Museum of Art in New York City.... The New York legislature authorizes censorship of dances.	May
Race riots in Tulsa, OK, kill 60 blacks and 25 whites....Penn State graduates the first woman engineer.	The U.S. Army successfully flies a plane with a pressurized cabin.	The Radio Corporation of America (RCA) forms.	The first Western Electric switching machine office opens in Dallas, TX.	Bessie Coleman receives a pilot's license in France. She is the first licensed black pilot.	Jun.
A jury finds Sacco and Vanzetti guilty....To reduce high maternal and infant mortality rates, Congress passes the Sheppard-Towner Act, establishing maternity and pediatric clinics. The legislation expires in 1929.	General Billy Mitchell leads a 17-bomber flight in a "raid" over New York City.... Airplanes sink a battleship for the first time.	A short but severe depression hits the United States, due to industrial overproduction and cutbacks in defense industries. Unemployment tops 5.7 million in August.	Frederick Banting and Charles Best of Canada produce insulin. This culminates a three-month effort by them, a decades-long effort by the scientific community....The Aeriola Jr. crystal set with headphones, made by Westinghouse appears on the market. It sells for $25 and can receive a signal from 25 miles away.	Dempsey knocks out Georges Carpentier. The fight is the first million dollar fight as well as the first heavyweight championship broadcast over radio.	Jul.
	The U.S. agrees to provide food relief to Russia. By year's end one million Russian children are receiving American food....The U.S. officially ends World War I.	The Federal Trade Commission begins anti-trust action against Famous Players-Lasky for block booking. The practice requires exhibitors to take unwanted films in order to get popular ones.	The first baseball play-by-play is broadcast over KDKA. Harold Arlen calls the Pittsburgh Corsairs victory over Philadelphia....Lee DeForest patents a sound-on-film process.	Enrico Caruso dies in Naples, Italy....The Connecticut barber commission rules that women who bob hair must have barber licenses.	Aug.
Members of the National Women's Party enter the U.S. capitol carrying buckets, soap, and brushes. Their aim is to clean statues of Anthony and Stanton neglected in a storage closet.	The USS *Alabama* ends her career as a bombing target in Chesapeake Bay. She will be raised for scrap in 1922.		Elsinore, UT, experiences an earthquake. Another will follow on October 1. Elsinore is on the Sevier Fault.	The first Miss America pageant takes place in Atlantic City, NJ. First Miss America is Washington, DC's 16-year-old Margaret Gorman, who resembles Mary Pickford.	Sep.
Reportedly the divorce rate has doubled since 1896. Women's liberation is blamed.	Liberia is unable to meet its foreign obligations. The Harding administration and Liberia agree to U.S. economic assistance.			Babe Ruth ends another record setting season, hitting 59 homers for the year.	Oct.
The National Birth Control League of Margaret Sanger and the Voluntary Parenthood League of Mary Ware Dennett combine.	Harding convenes a Washington disarmament conference. The meetings, lasting through February 1922, also deal with the Far East.		The first aerial refueling takes place when an individual steps from the wing of one plane to another and fuels it with a 5-gallon gasoline can.		Nov.
Eugene Debs gets a Christmas present—release from prison.			Westinghouse introduces vacuum tube radios. A dry-battery model sells for $60. A wooden-cabinet console with internal speakers goes for $175.		Dec.

F	G	H	I	J
Includes campaigns, elections, federal-state relations, civil rights and liberties, crime, the judiciary, education, healthcare, poverty, urban affairs, and population.	*Includes formation and debate of U.S. foreign and defense policies, veterans affairs, and defense spending. (Relations with specific foreign countries are usually found under the region concerned.)*	*Includes business, labor, agriculture, taxation, transportation, consumer affairs, monetary and fiscal policy, natural resources, pollution and industrial accidents.*	*Includes worldwide scientific, medical and technological developments, natural phenomena, U.S. weather and natural disasters.*	*Includes the arts, religion, scholarship, communications media, sports, entertainment, fashions, fads, and social life.*

	World Affairs	Europe	Africa & The Middle East	The Americas	Asia & The Pacific
Jan. 1		The British Labor Commission describes the situation in Ireland as a "tragedy," with the government condoning and committing brutality on the population.... Soviet newspaper, *Pravda*, criticizes the increasing bureaucratization of the Soviet government with many Communists holding jobs that are superfluous.	The General Secretary of the Zionist organization in London reports that Jewish immigration to Palestine is drawing in immigrants from all over the world.	Reports from Newfoundland indicate that it has hit a peak of prosperity and that its fishing, timber, and mining are beginning to decline.... An American has been granted a large concession in eastern Peru to begin a colony that will be built by American settlers.	
Jan. 2		German Lloyd announces its intentions to re-enter the shipping trade.... A new book, *The Mysterious Ship*, published in Germany describes for the first time how the German government sent arms to Ireland in an attempt to foster a rebellion there against British rule.... British troops near Cork, Ireland, burn several homes as retaliation for the residents not having warned the British of an ambush.	Records for the 10 months that ended in September 1920, show that more than 8,000 immigrants entered Palestine with another 2,000 entering in October and November.... Reports from Armenia indicate that the area is in a state of anarchy, that the Armenian Army has left the region and that there are Soviet troops there.	The President of Panama announces that the country has a budgetary surplus of more than $2.5 million.... Diego Manuel Chamorro is inaugurated as President of Nicaragua.... The Cuban Liberal Party appeals to the U.S. State department to supervise upcoming elections in Cuba as President Menocal cannot be trusted to hold fair elections.	The American Bureau of Foreign and Domestic Commerce reports that there is a great deal of advertising done in Asia; at least 1,000 newspapers and 1,500 magazine run advertisements.
Jan. 3		New casualty figures for the fighting in Adriatic coastal city of Fiume, which was rebelling against Yugoslavia to become part of Italy, have been issued; 37 were killed and 180 were injured.... Reports from the Soviet Union have led analysts to believe that an attack by the Soviet Red Army on the Baltic nations and Poland is imminent.		Reports from Haiti, which is occupied by American troops, indicate that a Marine officer was killed and eaten by Haitians, while others have been killed and mutilated.	
Jan. 4		Admiral von Tirpitz, states that if Germany is to survive, all Germans in Central Europe, must be united.... The independent military force that has been holding the city of Fiume evacuates the city today; its leader, the poet Gabriele d'Annunzio is the last man to leave the city. The British announce that they are extending martial law in four more counties and Waterford City in southern Ireland.		Representatives of the Cuban-American Telephone and Telegraph company obtain a permit to allow them to install three underwater cables to Cuba.... A general who was part of the Carranza faction in Mexico has escaped from prison; it is feared that he will renew the struggle against President Obregon.... President Wilson has sent General Enoch Crowder to Cuba to assist in solidifying financial and political arrangements; his presence in Cuba is widely interpreted as part of an effort to take Cuba over.	The Australian government announces it would welcome a cooperative arrangement with the Canadian and U.S. navies in the Pacific.
Jan. 5		British politicians are arguing the benefits of a temporary halt in building warships for a period of five years.	Mustafa Kemal, leader of Turkey sends a telegram thanking British Prime Minister Lloyd George for the 40,000 British-manufactured rifles captured by the Turks from Armenian forces.		An editorial in a Japanese newspaper states that Japan should end its alliances with Britain in order to bring about an alliance with the United States.... Japanese troops occupying Siberia are improving their defensive positions in response to reports that Soviet troops will soon be attacking their positions.
Jan. 6			Reports from Turkey indicate that the army is being expanded by a large draft; further reports claim that the troops are being indoctrinated as Communists.		Japan is reported to be spending millions of dollars of steel products from Pittsburgh, PA.
Jan. 7		The American Red Cross ships 31-railroad carloads of goods, valued at $100,000 for relief to the Hungarian population.... In Switzerland there are discussions of bringing the Hapsburg Emperor Karl back from exile to rule in either Austria or Hungary.... The government of Georgia announces that it has successfully suppressed the Communist Party in that country.	The British government announces that it is planning to establish a regular air service between London and Egypt; the route that will probably include Palestine is planned to be operational by the end of the year.	The U.S. Senate Committee on Cuban relations is considering that it may send representatives to observe first hand the current situation in that country and see if American intervention is possible or desirable.	Japan's ambassador to Britain, Baron Hayashi, announces that the Japanese government would be ready to cooperate with the United States on Naval arms limitations.

A	B	C	D	E
Includes developments that affect more than one world region, international organizations and important meetings of world leaders.	*Includes all domestic and regional developments in Europe, including the Soviet Union.*	*Includes all domestic and regional developments in Africa and the Middle East.*	*Includes all domestic and regional developments in Latin America, the Caribbean, and Canada.*	*Includes all domestic and regional developments in Asian and Pacific nations (and colonies).*

U.S. Politics & Social Issues	U.S. Foreign Policy & Affairs, Defense	U.S. Economy & Environment	Science, Technology & Nature	Culture, Leisure & Lifestyle	
According to the Superintendent of the Syracuse State School for Mental Defectives, the prohibition of alcohol in the United States has led to fewer cases of mental illness. . . . The American Red Cross announces that it helped 200 families of people killed or injured in the Wall Street explosion of last year.	The U.S. Navy seaplane *NC-5* sets a new record, flying from San Diego to Panama, a journey of 702 miles in nine hours and 15 minutes.	Herbert Hoover heads up a new American Engineers Council based in a similar organization that existed during the World War; President-elect Harding has promised to help this effort.	British doctors state that experiments being conducted at the Michigan State Penitentiary to cure criminals of their tendencies by surgery will probably not work.		Jan. 1
The U.S. Chamber of Commerce announces that the nation needs 1.25 million homes and that four million people in the country lack adequate housing.	A Naval balloon, the *A-5598*, which has been missing since it left its base in New York on December 13, 1920, has been found in northern Ontario; the crew is safe.	The Federal Reserve Board reports that wholesale prices fell 8.5 percent in December 1920, unemployment has increased, and business activity has continued a declining trend.			Jan. 2
Franklin D. Roosevelt, who ran for Vice-President of the United States in 1920, has accepted a position with the Fidelity and Deposit Company, a bank, in New York City. . . . Federal troops in Merrimack, WV, are fired on by strikers at the White Star Mine; no casualties are reported.	Canadian police are sending a party to find the lost American balloonists. . . . A naval flight of two seaplanes completes a flight from San Diego to Banderas Bay in Mexico.	The U.S. tobacco market is doing very poorly; of 5.5 million pounds offered for sale in Lexington, KY, there are bids for only 100,000 pounds.			Jan. 3
Strikers against clothing manufacturers have threatened to kill a judge in Baltimore if he does not deal leniently with striking workers. . . . Workers in the clothing mills of Lawrence, MA, say they will fight any wage cuts proposed by the mill owners. . . . Senator Borah of Idaho opposes the expenditures being proposed for Harding's inaugural that will take place in March as too costly.					Jan. 4
	The Council of the League of Nations announces that it may send an envoy to President-elect Harding to encourage him to have America participate in the League. . . . The American Atlantic and Pacific fleets have departed their home bases for joint maneuvers to be conducted off the coast of Panama.			Physicians note that tenor Enrico Caruso's health continues to improve.	Jan. 5
Five hundred workers for the Pullman Company, which manufactures railway cars, walk off the job rather than submit to a wage cut.	President-elect Harding announces that he may call an international arms reduction conference in Washington.	U.S. Senators attack British policy of selling oil to America at substantially higher prices than the U.S. charges for oil it sells to Britain.		Broadway actor and manager, George M. Cohan, denies that he has any interest in purchasing a baseball team in the newly proposed Continental Baseball Association.	Jan. 6
Residents of Texas bar a group of Japanese who had arrived by train to establish a community; their possessions are kept from being unloaded by local businessmen and the American Legion. . . . Attorney General Palmer acknowledges that he is studying the possibility of pardoning imprisoned Socialist leader Eugene Debs but that he has not made any promises to do so.	The U.S. government states that based on recent reports, the U.S. Navy is currently half the size of Britain's.	U.S. Congressman Madden states that airmail is not economical and that sending mail by train is faster and cheaper than current airmail.	Archaeologists in Cyrenaica in Italian North Africa, announce that they have found a sculptured head of Venus in the ruins of a temple there.		Jan. 7

F	G	H	I	J
Includes campaigns, elections, federal-state relations, civil rights and liberties, crime, the judiciary, education, healthcare, poverty, urban affairs, and population.	*Includes formation and debate of U.S. foreign and defense policies, veterans affairs, and defense spending. (Relations with specific foreign countries are usually found under the region concerned.)*	*Includes business, labor, agriculture, taxation, transportation, consumer affairs, monetary and fiscal policy, natural resources, pollution and industrial accidents.*	*Includes worldwide scientific, medical and technological developments, natural phenomena, U.S. weather and natural disasters.*	*Includes the arts, religion, scholarship, communications media, sports, entertainment, fashions, fads, and social life.*

	World Affairs	Europe	Africa & The Middle East	The Americas	Asia & The Pacific
Jan. 8		Police in Spain have arrested three radical labor party members for making bombs; the arrested men admit that have been responsible for recent bombings....Police in Lisbon, Portugal raid the offices of a Monarchist newspaper and find bombs and ammunition....British newspapers respond to American attacks concerning inequality in oil prices to be the work of Irish and other anti-British groups and their propaganda.	Raymond Custer, a worker for Near East Relief is arrested and imprisoned for resisting a Turkish policeman.	The Argentine government announces that bandits have taken control of Santa Cruz territory in the southern part of the country....Reports from Newfoundland describe a serious decline in the fishing and timber industries and a movement of men out of the region to find work	The British government sends Lord Reading to India to resolve the issues that have arisen from a nationwide boycott of the British led by Mohandas Gandhi....The former British Governor of Punjab in India states that anti-British sentiment has gone too far and that Britain must respond quickly and forcefully....The American Vice Consul in Bombay, India, note that Indians do not have screens for their windows and that there is an excellent business opportunity for American companies.
Jan. 9		Reports from the Soviet Union state that Lenin may visit Communist leaders in Finland....A Dutch newspaper states that the government wishes that the exiled Kaiser Wilhelm II of Germany and his family would leave the country and go into exile elsewhere.	Turkish troops are reported to have attacked French troops near Turkey's southern border....Reports claim that 200 Soviet officers may be in Turkey to assist the Turks in training their army.	Juan Leguia, chief of the Peruvian Seaplane Service, announces he will be flying from there to the United States before the end of January.	
Jan. 10		The Spanish battleship, *Espana*, which ran aground earlier off the coast of Chile, is refloated with only minimal damage reported....There are currently 500,000 people out of work in France, which is planning several projects to put people to work....The U.S. transport, *Wheaton*, lands in Cherbourg France with 4,300 coffins, which will be used to transport the bodies of Americans killed in the war back to the United States.	Food prices in Palestine are dropping as the government withdraws its prohibitions against importing barley.		The Japanese Foreign Offices denounces recent reports that relations between the United States and Japan have been strained.
Jan. 11		The Rumanian government sends a diplomatic note to the Soviets declining any discussions about the contested area of Bessarabia....British soldiers capture a house used by Sinn Fein fugitives and destroy it.			An American Naval officer, part of the occupying forces in Vladivostok, Russia, is shot and killed by a Japanese sentry.
Jan. 12		Members of Sinn Fein derail and attack a British troop train near Dublin....Austria will send an envoy to President-elect Harding to discuss the possibility of a loan to assist Austrian government finances.			
Jan. 13		Reports claim that the recent illness of Lenin, which required medical attention, was actually the result of an assassination attempt....Members of Sinn Fein attack the British in Country Clare, Dublin, and Ulster; martial law is being further expanded in the island as a result of the increasing conflict.		Six leaders of the fight against the current President of Mexico, Obregon, are captured by Federal troops and executed.	Reports of famine in India by the British India Office state that more than 77,000 people are currently receiving relief.
Jan. 14	The Pan-American Federation of Labor announces its intent to obtain permission of the League of Nations to have a representative to represent labor in all countries.	The Soviet Union announces that it has a new decree that will forbid strikes with imprisonment and loss off food ration cards as punishment....Soviet forces positioned on the border of Georgia are being withdrawn as the Soviets cease their efforts to enter that country....Admiral Horthy, regent and ruler of Hungary announces that he will pardon four Hungarian Communists sentenced to be hanged for murder and counterfeiting.	British authorities in Egypt uncover a plot to assassinate several members of the government.	The Panamanian government protests against what it considers to be seizure of its land by the United States as the Army takes possession of a small hill near the Canal Zone to be used for a fortification.	Soviet agents in Central Asia are said to be preparing to instigate anti-British activity in India.

A	B	C	D	E
Includes developments that affect more than one world region, international organizations and important meetings of world leaders.	*Includes all domestic and regional developments in Europe, including the Soviet Union.*	*Includes all domestic and regional developments in Africa and the Middle East.*	*Includes all domestic and regional developments in Latin America, the Caribbean, and Canada.*	*Includes all domestic and regional developments in Asian and Pacific nations (and colonies).*

U.S. Politics & Social Issues	U.S. Foreign Policy & Affairs, Defense	U.S. Economy & Environment	Science, Technology & Nature	Culture, Leisure & Lifestyle	
The American Red Cross announces that most of its efforts will be directed toward European Relief and that $5 million has been allotted to this task.…It is announced that the formal election of Warren Harding and Calvin Coolidge as President and Vice President, respectively, by the Electoral College will take place on February 9.		Two seats on the New York Stock Exchange are sold, one selling for $89,000 and the other for $90,000.…Prices for lumber continue to drop from their high of March 1920.…The National Board of Fire Underwriters states that the loss in buildings, fire department maintenance, and water due to fires totals $2 million each day.	The High School of Commerce announces that a list of films available for students as a supplement to their class work is available.	The United States Game Wardens announces that there are currently seven million licensed hunters in the United States.	Jan. 8
In Paterson, NJ, 2,000-ribbon weavers state that will not accept a wage cut.…The United Mine Workers raise $1 million to support strikers in Alabama and West Virginia.…President-elect Harding resigns as Senator from Ohio.…After a month of meetings, the incoming Harding Administration claims to have its future policies defined with the exception of a final statement as to who will be on the Cabinet.		Despite the fact that many prices have dropped in the past year, costs for rent, fuel, and electricity have risen in eight cities, including Boston, Detroit, New York, and San Francisco.			Jan. 9
President-Elect Harding announces that he will cancel the inaugural ball and keep the ceremonies simple to reduce expenditures.…Reports indicate that President Wilson, who has been in very poor health, is showing improvement and can now work up to two hours at a time.	Secretary of War Newton Baker states that he thinks efforts should be made to construct another canal in Central America.	A Federal judge signs a decree ordering the Albany Chemical Company to cease applying for the registration of the word "aspirin" be used as their exclusive trademark.	The President of the American Optometric Association recommends that blondes should wear dark glasses to make them less temperamental due to glaring sunlight.…The Royal Alpine Club and Royal Geographical Society announce pans for an expedition to climb Mount Everest.	Grover Cleveland Alexander of the Chicago Cubs holds the record as the best pitcher in the National League.	Jan. 10
The Mayor of New York City sends a letter to the Commissioner of Police stating his opposition to the Ku Klux Klan activities in the city.				The wife of a Princeton Professor, in addressing Wellesley students, states that jazz is the source of present social ills and that lipstick and rouge are "the trademark of the girl of the street."	Jan. 11
		The Federal government defines the term "gross income" for those paying income tax, stating that it means every dollar that they receive during the year although deductions will be allowed.		Judge Kennesaw Mountain Landis accepts the position of first Commissioner of Baseball with absolute power over both major and minor leagues.	Jan. 12
The Census Bureau announces that for the first time in more than 51 percent of Americans live in cities and towns; for the first time the rural population is now the minority.		William C. Durant, founder of General Motors, announces that he is starting a new a new auto company called Durant Motors.			Jan. 13
The Appellate Division of the Supreme Court decides that a child is entitled to receive payment for damages that occurred before birth; the court states that human rights may precede birth.	The U.S. Senate votes to cut the size of the Army to 150,000 men.…President-elect Harding announces that he will not call for an arms reduction conference despite earlier reports.				Jan. 14

F	G	H	I	J
Includes campaigns, elections, federal-state relations, civil rights and liberties, crime, the judiciary, education, healthcare, poverty, urban affairs, and population.	*Includes formation and debate of U.S. foreign and defense policies, veterans affairs, and defense spending. (Relations with specific foreign countries are usually found under the region concerned.)*	*Includes business, labor, agriculture, taxation, transportation, consumer affairs, monetary and fiscal policy, natural resources, pollution and industrial accidents.*	*Includes worldwide scientific, medical and technological developments, natural phenomena, U.S. weather and natural disasters.*	*Includes the arts, religion, scholarship, communications media, sports, entertainment, fashions, fads, and social life.*

	World Affairs	Europe	Africa & The Middle East	The Americas	Asia & The Pacific
Jan. 15		An article published in a London newspaper asserts that the Soviets cannot conduct world trade as they now have nothing to export and that there are shortages in food and almost every other commodity.... The Soviet sixth Army has been moved from the border with Estonia to the interior as a result of several mutinies.... Portugal announces that there are significant price increases in coal, wood, and food.	The Greek offensive in Turkey continues to be successful, advancing from the coast toward the Turkish capital of Ankara.		The British government announces that it has restored order in several districts in India and that rioting has been stopped; several of these riots are blamed on Communist agitators.
Jan. 16		The government of the Belorussian Republic signs a treaty of alliance with the Soviet Union.... German Admiral Scheer states that he sees the U-Boat as an instrument of peace and that the dread of it will prevent nations from going to war.... A large area of Dublin is cordoned off by British soldiers; barbed wire and machine guns are set up as troops and police conduct a house-by-house search of the city.... The Leader of the Italian Communist Party states that the party must seize factories and make its own weapons.	Reports claim that Russian propagandists in Constantinople have succeeded in converting several hundred refugees to Communism, which they will spread throughout Turkey.		
Jan. 17		The Rumanian government announces that it is seeking an alliance with Poland; both nations are concerned about the Soviets and both have issues of contention with Czechoslovakia.... The French government is sending invitations to several prominent Germans to give them tours of parts of France devastated by the World War in order to convince Germans to pay war reparations.			
Jan. 18		King Alfonso XIII of Spain encounters a group of striking civil servants telling them they should do their duty; in response they call the strike off.... Sin Fein conducts two ambushes on British units.... Preparations in Dublin are being made for the "Bloody Sunday" trial; 30 suspects are being held for the murder of several British officers.... The Dutch government denies having asked the exiled Kaiser Wilhelm II to leave the country.	The Premier of Persia, Mochir-ed-Dowleh, withdraws his resignation from the Persian government and announces he will stay; at the same time the Shah of Iran announces he will not abdicate in favor of his brother.		Refugee centers have been set up in the Chinese city of Tientsin to feed approximately 100,000 famine victims.
Jan. 19		The cost of living in Britain has shown signs of decreasing although it is still 165 percent over what prices were before the World War.... The French government states that Germany's claim that it is bankrupt and cannot pay war reparations is untrue.		The government of Chile has authorized negotiations for a $25 million loan, which will be used for the State Railways.... Two dams burst in Mexico, killing 100 and injuring another 200; 1,000 persons are homeless and many of the deaths were caused by the fact that the water held behind the mines was poisoned from chemicals used in mining.	
Jan. 20		France's Premier, Aristide Briand, states that Germany must begin to pay its war reparations and begin to disarm immediately.... In reprisal for an ambush in which six British soldiers are killed, several houses near Cork are blown up; British officials claim that the expanded martial law is working to preserve order.		Heavy rains in several parts of Jamaica have caused heavy losses to various planters as well as the United Fruit Company.... The government of Guatemala will cut its army from 15,000 to 5,000, saving $50,000 a month.	The Council of the Viceroy of India votes to reduce the size of the Indian Army despite fears of the Soviets building up forces near the Afghan frontier.

A	B	C	D	E
Includes developments that affect more than one world region, international organizations and important meetings of world leaders.	*Includes all domestic and regional developments in Europe, including the Soviet Union.*	*Includes all domestic and regional developments in Africa and the Middle East.*	*Includes all domestic and regional developments in Latin America, the Caribbean, and Canada.*	*Includes all domestic and regional developments in Asian and Pacific nations (and colonies).*

U.S. Politics & Social Issues	U.S. Foreign Policy & Affairs, Defense	U.S. Economy & Environment	Science, Technology & Nature	Culture, Leisure & Lifestyle	
The Surgeon General of the United States says that the number of sick and mentally ill soldiers is on the increase and that increased government expenditures for assisting these veterans is needed.... The New York City Bureau of Vital Statistics reports that in the city, the infant mortality rate rose in 1920 with 86 deaths per thousand as opposed to 83 per thousand in 1919.		For the first time since the World War, bread is once again selling for five cents a loaf.			Jan. 15
Three members of the Alabama National Guard are arrested as the result of an investigation into the lynching of William Baaird, a coal miner at Jasper, AL.... Workers at the textile mills in Lawrence, MA, state they will go on strike if they are forced to accept wage reductions.... The home of James A. Joyce of Wilkes-Barre, PA, is blown up; Joyce is a leader of the miners union and has opposed recent strikes.					Jan. 16
The U.S. Treasury Department issues a statement that Prohibition includes all manufacture of alcoholic beverages and that those who brew beer at home could be fined $1,000.	The navy announces that it plans to use catapults on ships to launch aircraft.	New York City is hit by gale force winds of up to 84 miles per hour adding a severe wind chill to temperatures that are 10 degrees above zero.			Jan. 17
Massachusetts schools will begin teaching the rules of the road to children in order to decrease the number accidents; last year 178 children were killed and 2,300 were injured in auto accidents in that state.... Twelve lawyers file a brief with the Senate Judiciary Committee criticizing the "Red" raids conducted nationwide by U.S. Attorney General Palmer last year.				The Brentano Public school in Chicago issues a statement forbidding its students from dancing the "shimmy" and the "toddle."	Jan. 18
The warden of Sing Sing Prison announces that all prisoners must wear official prison uniforms and that silk shirts and ties will no longer be allowed.... A mining camp in West Virginia is fired on by unknown persons; Federal troops are sent to investigate who did it and if it is related to current strikes.	The State Department confirms reports that there are many passport forgeries and there is concern that large numbers of undesirable aliens will enter the country using these forged passports.	At a meeting of the New York Agricultural Society, a speaker declares that of all the businesses that failed in 1920, 84 percent did not do any type of advertising.... The Department of Agriculture reports that the wages of farm hands have doubled in the past 10 years, averaging $65 a month, although in California they were able to make as much as $107 a month.			Jan. 19
A strike has been called for 15,000 construction workers in Boston.	The Senate Committee on Foreign Relations recommends that the Borah naval disarmament resolution be favorably acted on which would call for prompt negotiations between the United States and Britain and Japan.	The United States collected revenues of $337 million on imported goods valued at $2.108 billion in 1920 according to a statement from the Department of Commerce.	A new cave in the Mammoth Cave region of Kentucky is discovered.	An original manuscript of Lord Byron's poem, *Sardanapalus*, is sold for $3,300.	Jan. 20

F	G	H	I	J
Includes campaigns, elections, federal-state relations, civil rights and liberties, crime, the judiciary, education, healthcare, poverty, urban affairs, and population.	*Includes formation and debate of U.S. foreign and defense policies, veterans affairs, and defense spending. (Relations with specific foreign countries are usually found under the region concerned.)*	*Includes business, labor, agriculture, taxation, transportation, consumer affairs, monetary and fiscal policy, natural resources, pollution and industrial accidents.*	*Includes worldwide scientific, medical and technological developments, natural phenomena, U.S. weather and natural disasters.*	*Includes the arts, religion, scholarship, communications media, sports, entertainment, fashions, fads, and social life.*

	World Affairs	Europe	Africa & The Middle East	The Americas	Asia & The Pacific
Jan. 21	Former American ambassador Henry White recommends that there should be a general disarmament conference but reductions in naval forces should be done only by Britain, Japan, and the United States.	Two Serbian political parties, the Radical Party and the Democratic Party, form a new government.... The Italian Communist Party, denied recognition by the Third International in Moscow, splits off from the Italian Socialist Party....At least half a dozen British Police barracks in Ireland are attacked by Sinn Fein.	An attempt to assassinate Mustafa Kemal, Turkey's leader, fails.	A group of 30 American teachers is traveling to Peru in order to assist in a reorganization of the Peruvian educational system.	The United States will call a conference of the Pan-Pacific Union, which will include the United States, Canada, Australia, China, Japan, and several South American nations.
Jan. 22		The French government has had to admit that some French arms manufacturers have been supplying Turkish troops, a situation that causes difficulty because both Britain and France are supposed to be supporting the Greeks against the Turks.	Despite denials by the Greek government, the Greek troops fighting the Turks are suffering a series of defeats.	A treaty creating the Union of Central American Republics is signed by El Salvador, Honduras, Guatemala, and Costa Rica.	Viscount Kato, leader of the opposition to the Japanese government states that Japanese forces in Russia should already have been withdrawn back to Japan by this time.
Jan. 23		Two British constables are found dead in Ireland and there are reports of men being kidnapped from their homes by Sinn Fein and executed....Because of a lack of business orders, Sweden is facing a severe depression in both trade and industry.	French and British troops may once again land in Constantinople and occupy it as they did at the end of the World War due to conflicts between Turkey and Greece.		
Jan. 24		The Soviet government denies rumors that Lenin is dead.... Because of increased unemployment, Switzerland is barring all foreign labor from entering the country....The Rumanian government denies rumors of uprisings and that the Rumanian Army is sufficiently strong enough to defend the country against the Soviets.	British airmen have successfully broken resistance in Somaliland on the Horn of Africa; the force of 200 men and 11 airplanes has managed to break resistance in a period of about three weeks.	The United States has presented a note to the Mexican government demanding an inquiry into invasions of American oil concessions in Mexico.	
Jan. 25		Reports from Latvia indicate that Soviet troops on the border have mutinies and killed several of their commissars; Moscow denies that there have been similar outbreaks in other parts of Russia....There is rioting in several cities in Italy, today including Modena, with Nationalists, Fascists, Communists, and Socialists fighting in the streets....In Dublin a Court-Martial begins to try three men accused of ambushing and killing a British officer.	The British government indicates that it may withdraw its forces from most of Mesopotamia (Iraq) and keep only a small contingent in Basra.		Small-scale riots have broken out and a threatened strike is being called in Bombay in response to the killing of pigeons by two European boys; several people are injured and 17 are arrested.
Jan. 26		Political unrest in Italy takes the form of riots with Fascists and Nationalists fighting Communists with severe riots in Milan and Bologna....Lenin is said to have publicly rebuked Trotsky for spreading dissatisfaction and dissension in the party.			
Jan. 27	Members of Austria's Christian Socialist Party are attempting to promote a movement in which Austria would become a Papal State and be ruled by the Pope.	The Soviet Union defends its actions against individuals that have been described as reprisals because the Soviet Union is defending itself against worldwide counterrevolution....There is severe fighting in several cities in Italy, especially Florence, as Fascists and Communist are clashing....Irish Republican leader Eamon de Valera, whose location has been a mystery, is recent weeks, is located in Paris where he gives an interview stating that there are no divisions among the Irish and that they all want independence.		Representatives of 16 oil companies and the Minister of Mexico's Treasury discuss proposed legislation that would establish a fixed rate of taxation.	The Japanese government announces it will file a protest against the construction of an American wireless station in Shanghai, China.

A	B	C	D	E
Includes developments that affect more than one world region, international organizations and important meetings of world leaders.	*Includes all domestic and regional developments in Europe, including the Soviet Union.*	*Includes all domestic and regional developments in Africa and the Middle East.*	*Includes all domestic and regional developments in Latin America, the Caribbean, and Canada.*	*Includes all domestic and regional developments in Asian and Pacific nations (and colonies).*

U.S. Politics & Social Issues	U.S. Foreign Policy & Affairs, Defense	U.S. Economy & Environment	Science, Technology & Nature	Culture, Leisure & Lifestyle	
Republican Senators Sherman and Fernald attack proposed efforts to regulate the meat packing industry stating private industries should not be subjected to "unwarranted interference."...Republican Senators have formed a group that opposes the appointment by Harding of Charles Evans Hughes as Secretary of State.		Crude oil prices have dropped to 60 cents a barrel.			Jan. 21
		A survey conducted by the State Department of Labor reports that one-quarter of unionized workers in Massachusetts are put out of work, a total of 57,420.			Jan. 22
Mine workers striking in West Virginia accuse the mine owners of hiring men to patrol the mines who are armed.		The Department of Agriculture announces that world wide wheat production has increased over 1919 from 2,571,807,000 bushels to 2,671,488,000 bushels....In the Pittsburgh, PA, region 180,000 men are out of work principally in the iron, steel, and coal industries but all sectors are affected.	Argentine inventor, Peteras Pescara, claims that he has invented a helicopter that can not only rise but hover and fly horizontally.		Jan. 23
Residents of Aroostook County in northern Maine are protesting the refusal of doctors in the area to make house calls in childbirth cases.	Secretary of the Navy, Josephus Daniels denies having insured the U.S. Navy with Lloyd's of London....Woodrow Wilson's proposal that the League of Nations declare that Russia is not to be attacked is coldly received by members of the League.	A million pounds of fresh fish are brought into the port of Boston for sale.		A copy of *Mourt's Relation or Journal of the English Plantation at Plimoth in New England*, the first book ever published in England about Plymouth Colony is sold at auction for $3,800....An unidentified woman in Kittaning, PA, blows up an illegal gambling house in order to stop her husband from gambling; no charges are being pressed.	Jan. 24
	The Senate adopts a resolution to study the feasibility of halting all naval construction for the next six months....The U.S. and Japanese governments complete an agreement that will define the rights of Japanese citizens living in the United States.	Severe earth tremors are reported in the eastern Pennsylvania-Southern New Jersey area....The Senate Post Office committee recommends that transcontinental airplane mail service be continued....Borden's Farm Products announces it will cut the price of milk by one cent a quart.		Concert Pianist Ignace Paderewski arrives in the United States where he will go on to spend several weeks at his ranch in California.	Jan. 25
A fire destroys the Cleveland (Ohio) Greys Armory apparently in retaliation by Communists....Henry Lowery, an African American, accused of a double murder, is burned at the stake by a mob in Nodena, AR.					Jan. 26
	As a result of economy measures, the Coast Guard announces it will put to sea only in cases where it is necessary to save lives....Senator Borah of Idaho states that the United States should disarm and reduce its Navy or to build a Navy so large it could defend the United States against any combination of enemies.	Earth tremors are felt in upstate New York in the Lake George area.			Jan. 27

	World Affairs	Europe	Africa & The Middle East	The Americas	Asia & The Pacific
Jan. 28		Observers are of the opinion that if current negotiations for trade between Britain and the Soviet Union succeed there will be trade between the Soviets and Italy, Holland, and Sweden....Labor exchanges in Britain announce that the number of jobless has increased by 60,000 in the past week....The Allies determine that the war reparations that Germany must pay will be $55.5 billion, which will be paid over a 42-year period.		The Bank of Spain and America suspends operations in Buenos Aries, Argentina, as result of the failure of the Bank of Spain and Paraguay.	The Census Bureau reports that there are currently 109,274 Japanese living in Hawaii, an increase of 33 percent over the past 10 years....The Japanese government is planning a railroad that would run across Asia and join with the rail line in Baghdad that runs to Europe.
Jan. 29	Pope Benedict XV in an encyclical to all Bishops calls for peace in the wake of greed and social and moral unrest.	The Cunard Steamship Company signs a license for all Hungarian immigrant and emigrant transatlantic traffic through the ports of Trieste, Cherbourg, Rotterdam, and Hamburg....British troops successfully break up a Sinn Fein ambush in southern Ireland.			
Jan. 30	The Save-a-Life League reports that the worldwide suicide rate is rising, especially in Germany, Hungary, and China; reasons for the increase are said to be Prohibition, politics, and divorce and they also note the great increase among farmers and veterans.	Lenin tells visiting Socialists from Spain that the dictatorship in the Soviet Union may last another 40 years....American observers report that in Poland at least 500,000 children depend on American relief to eat....The Allies declare that Germany cannot take a loan to pay its war reparations and that it must not delay in its efforts to reduce its military forces.	Turkey's leader, Mustafa Kemal demands to the French, British, and Greeks that Turkey will not participate in any discussions until all foreign troops are withdrawn from Turkish territory.		
Jan. 31		French officials announce that they are planning for anticipated Communist-inspired uprisings to occur on May 1....The Greek Chamber of Deputies breaks out into disorder as many of the members refuse to swear allegiance to King Constantine.			
Feb. 1		The population of Montenegro rises in rebellion against the Yugoslav government; more than 300 have been wounded in the fighting....The Ukrainian National Council asks for recognition from the United States as well as aid for its children....The Irish Nationalist Party states that it will not join with Sinn Fein.		General Enoch Crowder is in Cuba as an envoy of the U.S. government and declares that where elections have been contested, new elections will be conducted.	Japanese politicians declare that Japan should reduce the size of its Navy....New riots break out in India; an estimated 10,000 are involved in disorder in the city of Allahabad.
Feb. 2		Two unrelated explosions occur in Italy when munitions depots in Brescia and Palermo explode....In Ireland, two men are killed and nine injured when a bomb explodes near a British police car....King Constantine of Greece says he will not open discussions with Turkey's Mustafa Kemal, calling him an outlaw....The British government states that it could easily survive an oil embargo from the United States.		The Association of Producers of Petroleum in Mexico deliver a message to Secretary of the Treasury Adolfo de la Huerta protesting the excessive taxation on oil exported from Mexico.	Revolts against the Communists have broken out though all of Turkestan....Some members of the British government are stating that the reports of large deposits of oil in Iraq, which the British are interested in, may be exaggerated.

A	B	C	D	E
Includes developments that affect more than one world region, international organizations and important meetings of world leaders.	*Includes all domestic and regional developments in Europe, including the Soviet Union.*	*Includes all domestic and regional developments in Africa and the Middle East.*	*Includes all domestic and regional developments in Latin America, the Caribbean, and Canada.*	*Includes all domestic and regional developments in Asian and Pacific nations (and colonies).*

U.S. Politics & Social Issues	U.S. Foreign Policy & Affairs, Defense	U.S. Economy & Environment	Science, Technology & Nature	Culture, Leisure & Lifestyle	
The Internal Revenue Department reports that in 1920 9,401 liquor stills were captured in Virginia, North Carolina, South Carolina, Kentucky, and Tennessee and that 5,328 arrests were made.... The U.S. House Commerce Committee reports that being a mother is safer in 17 foreign countries than in the United States and that infant mortality rates in 10 countries are lower than they are in the United States.	Despite the fact that the Commander of the Air Service, General Billy Mitchell has asked for a $60 million appropriation for the air service, only a thirds of that is actually allocated by Congress for the next year's budget.	The U.S. Geological Survey announces that the output for oil production in 1920 was 443.402 million barrels, a gain of 19 percent over 1919.	The Army Chemical Warfare Service in cooperation with the Department of Agriculture is preparing to spray poison gas on cotton fields to remove the boll weevil population; the technique has already been used successfully against rats in seaport cities and locusts in the Philippines.	Sergeiu Rachmaninoff gives a concert at Carnegie Hall with the New York Philharmonic.... The racehorse Man o' War makes his final public appearance at Lexington, KY.	Jan. 28
The American Red Cross announces that in 1920 it spent $780,000 for relief in 57 disasters in the United States.... The British government issues the *Sinn Fein White Book* in which it details the widespread support given in the United States toward Irish rebels.... Mrs. Lulu Simms is running for the position of Alderman in the City Council of Chicago, the first African-American woman to do so.	U.S. Secretary of State Bainbridge Colby states in an interview that the U.S. policy towards the Soviet government has not changed and there is no intent to recognize the Soviet government.... The Navy Department issues a statement that recent experiments at bombing ships from the air have proven that battleships will not be made obsolete by aircraft.	Several auto manufacturers in Detroit announce they will recommence production in the plants that have been closed; these include Ford, Cadillac, Hudson, and Hupp.... Office rents in the area of New York City near Grand Central Station have declined and office space is cheaper than at any time in several years.	The British dirigible R-34, which had successfully crossed the Atlantic in 1919, is caught in a heavy wind storm as it is moored in England and is destroyed as the frame is broken in two.	The New York Yankees baseball club announces that it has selected a site for its own stadium so that it will not have to share the Polo Grounds stadium with the Giants.... The president of Princeton states that he does not oppose the use of cigarettes as long as they are used in moderation.	Jan. 29
				Fishermen off Montauk Point on Long Island catch a naval mine that the Navy had deployed during the World War.	Jan. 30
The International Detective Agency announces that it is still offering a $50,000 reward for the arrest and conviction of those responsible for the Wall Street bombing of 1920.... President Wilson refuses to issue a pardon to Socialist leader Eugene Debs who is scheduled to remain in prison until December 1925.		The Kodak Company withdraws an appeal it had made concerning government suits that it was exercising monopoly rights to include fixing retail prices and prohibiting its dealers from selling any other kind of photo equipment.... The Ford factory in Highland Park, MI, opens after having been closed since December 23; 15,000 men return to work.... Companies in Texas, Kansas, Illinois, and Pennsylvania announce that they are cutting the price of gas.	Viennese doctor Goldknecht reports that his experiments using X-rays have resulted in a younger appearance and a return to youthfulness in about 30 percent of the women he has treated.	Oscar ("Happy") Felsch, one of the Chicago "Black Sox" accused of throwing the 1919 world series surrenders to authorities and will stand trial with the other accused baseball players.	Jan. 31
President Wilson is expected to call, on the request of President-elect Harding, a special session of the new Senate to approve Harding's nominations for the Cabinet.... Former Governor of Louisiana, R. G. Pleasant, proposes a plan that will exclude from voting anyone whose ancestors came from south of the 20th parallel (that is, from Africa).... Socialist Eugene Debs states that it is President Wilson and not he who needs a pardon as Wilson has betrayed his ideals.	U.S. Admirals Coontz and Taylor testify before Congress that battleships should be kept in the Navy's inventory and that there should not be a halt in building new ships.	The textile industry in New England shows signs of revival; more orders have been received in the past three weeks than in the preceding six months.... Sears and Roebuck announce that its sales in January 1920 were sharply below those of January 1919.... A Federal Court dissolves the Kodak Company under the Sherman Anti-Trust Act, ordering the company to sell some of its factories.	John Willheimer of Monmouth, KS, has gathered five groundhogs, which he will observe on February 2, to determine the truth of the animals' weather-predicting skills.	Babe Ruth loses a court case in which he contended that films showing him playing should not be shown.... Two original watercolors by John James Audubon are sold for $680.	Feb. 1
The Omaha, NE, police will begin wearing bulletproof back- and breastplates to protect them from bullets.	U.S. Submarine *L-1* is rammed by the Pilot Boat *Philadelphia* off the Delaware Coast; none of the crew are injured.... It is announced that the U.S. Army will buy the Italian airship, *Roma*.	Despite the fact that Ford Motor Company has reopened, there are still 160,000 unemployed in the Detroit region.			Feb. 2

F	G	H	I	J
Includes campaigns, elections, federal-state relations, civil rights and liberties, crime, the judiciary, education, healthcare, poverty, urban affairs, and population.	*Includes formation and debate of U.S. foreign and defense policies, veterans affairs, and defense spending. (Relations with specific foreign countries are usually found under the region concerned.)*	*Includes business, labor, agriculture, taxation, transportation, consumer affairs, monetary and fiscal policy, natural resources, pollution and industrial accidents.*	*Includes worldwide scientific, medical and technological developments, natural phenomena, U.S. weather and natural disasters.*	*Includes the arts, religion, scholarship, communications media, sports, entertainment, fashions, fads, and social life.*

	World Affairs	Europe	Africa & The Middle East	The Americas	Asia & The Pacific
Feb. 3		Sinn Fein takes credit for having recently sunk the British submarine K-5 by shooting at it from one of their gunboats.…A German Court begins war crimes trials, picking four individuals identified by the Allies as war criminals; the trials are set to begin in March.…British soldiers fight a pitched battle against an estimated 500 members of Sinn Fein.	The commander of French Naval Forces in the Near East threatens to bombard Turkey if French soldiers being held by the Turks are not released.	The government of Chile states that due to its large exports of nitrates, it has been able to significantly reduce its national debt.	The current Japanese budget is estimated to allocate 50 percent of the total toward maintaining the Army and the Navy; a member of the government's opposition predicts that the proportion devoted to the military will rise to 75 percent.…The Chinese government in Canton announces that it will not try to seize customs money for outside goods brought into China.
Feb. 4		Reports from the Soviet Union state that political enemies are being killed at an increased rate; from January 1 to January 10 of this year, 347 opponents of the government have been shot.…The Premier of Greece and the Cabinet that has ruled the Country since last November, resigns; King Constantine must form a new cabinet soon.…Scotland Yard foils an attempt to blow it up; the building has been a recruiting station for the Royal Irish Constabulary (The Black and Tans).	The British government issues a statement defining its League of Nations Mandate in Palestine, which includes providing for a Jewish National Home.	Reports from Mexico City state that Pancho Villa is once again active, this time fighting rebels in opposition to the current Mexican government.…Unemployed workers in Chile attack a nitrate factory and kill the plant manager and 20 soldiers.	The Chinese island of Formosa, which is ruled by Japan, has become the scene of increased unrest.
Feb. 5		Polish troops are supposed to occupy the former Lithuanian city of Vilna as soon as the date for a plebiscite is fixed.…The Soviet government announces that it will open a campaign of violence against internal enemies while targeting and killing opposition figures in other countries.…Telephone lines between Dublin and Belfast have been cut, presumably by Irish rebels.	Opposition statements to Britain talking on the responsibility of the Palestine Mandate begin appearing in several newspapers.	Mexico's Mount Popocatepetl has begun to erupt; there is some speculation that recent earthquakes in the area, which have killed many people, have triggered the eruption.…Mexican railroads, which suffered great losses during the years of the revolutions, are now repairing the damage and purchasing new equipment to make up the losses.	
Feb. 6		General Wrangle, the Russian anti-Bolshevik leader predicts that the Soviets will attempt to invade both Poland and Rumania.…French newspapers are enthusiastic on their reception of the French accord with Poland.…The Zeppelin company is looking for a site outside of Germany where it can manufacture airships without restrictions placed as a result of the Versailles Treaty.	Mustafa Kemal issues a declaration that the Sultan of the Ottoman Empire must recognize that the only Turkish capital is Ankara.…Conflicting reports are received concerning the Greek invasion of Turkey; depending on the account either the Greeks or the Turks are victorious.	The Chilean government is discussing measures that could be put into effect to assist unemployed nitrate workers who have been creating disturbances.	The entire Revolutionary Soviet Committee in Siberia has been tried for secret negotiations with Japan; five are shot and six are sentenced to life in prison.…Japanese women are rallying against a bill that has made it illegal for women to join political associations.
Feb. 7		Reports from Ireland suggest that Sinn Fein has dropped the idea of an Irish Republic and that it is being subdued by the British Army and police.…Lenin states that labor unions put the Soviet state in jeopardy and if they are not crushed, they will place the Soviet state in danger.		Mexico's Ambassador to the United States announces that Mexico is seeking to negotiate loans with American banks.	Soviet War Minister Trotsky states that nothing must be done to harm relations between Japan and the Soviets.
Feb. 8		Sinn Fein wrecks a train carrying British soldiers; in another action, 100 members of Sinn Fein raid a railway yard near Dublin.…Reports from Russia claim that a mutiny has occurred on one of the warships docked in the city of Petrograd; Soviet officials deny the story.…British experiments at determining the damage aerial bombs can inflict on a ship are successful; British planes manage to sink the German battleship, *Baden*.	Emir Faisal, the King of Syria has protested to the British government against the Mandates in Iraq and Palestine, claiming that they were not part of the agreements drawn up during the World War in an effort to get Arab support.	The Canadian government has accepted 12 airships from the British; each of these air ships is 150 feet long.	

A	B	C	D	E
Includes developments that affect more than one world region, international organizations and important meetings of world leaders.	*Includes all domestic and regional developments in Europe, including the Soviet Union.*	*Includes all domestic and regional developments in Africa and the Middle East.*	*Includes all domestic and regional developments in Latin America, the Caribbean, and Canada.*	*Includes all domestic and regional developments in Asian and Pacific nations (and colonies).*

U.S. Politics & Social Issues	U.S. Foreign Policy & Affairs, Defense	U.S. Economy & Environment	Science, Technology & Nature	Culture, Leisure & Lifestyle	
The Employers' Association of Pittsburg, PA announces that it will fight all efforts to impose closed (all-union) shops in the city.…In the state of Missouri, Senator McCoullough introduces a bill making any strikes illegal.	The Secretary of the Navy sends a report to the Senate stating that the United States cannot do without battleships and would be unable to face other navies of the world without them.		An outbreak of sleeping sickness in Boston has claimed five lives; 13 others have been stricken with the disease.…French military officers observe the tests of Pescara's new helicopter and express satisfaction with the results of the trials.	Actress Sarah Bernhardt is made an officer in France's Legion of Honor.	**Feb. 3**
The League of Women's Voters has found that its recent campaign to enroll more women has been assisted by comments of New York's Governor Miller's comments that the League is a "menace."…John L. Lewis is reelected as President of the United Mine Workers.…The state of Nevada will begin to require a six-month residence for all those seeking to obtain a divorce.					**Feb. 4**
	The Coast Guard Cutter *Seneca* is being prepared for duty patrolling the coast of Newfoundland to locate icebergs and radio warnings to ships.…The House of Representatives in a vote of 271 to 16 overrides President Wilson's veto of the Army reduction bill.…A bill is before the Senate that proposes that four aircraft carriers be constructed for the Navy at a cost of $96 million.	Coca Cola's earnings for year ending December 31 are reported as $2,451,062, before taxes.…Prices for eggs, butter, condensed milk, beef, and lamb have shown significant reductions.		The New York Yankees announce that their new stadium will be in the Bronx and will extend from 157th to 161st Streets; the estimated cost is $2 million and will be ready for the 1922 season.…A group of American authors, including Robert Frost and William Allen White, will lecture at the Summer Sessions at Columbia University.	**Feb. 5**
A proposal coming from Franklin Wilcox of the Connecticut State Hospital for the insane that the incurably insane be put to death is receiving favorable consideration from some members of the State General Assembly.	The Army's aviation section is trying to get a series of tests in which aircraft will drop bombs on old battleships to see of it is possible to sink ships from the air.				**Feb. 6**
Building trades' workers in Buffalo, NY, will be forced to take wage reductions from a dollar to 80 or 90 cents an hour.…Vigilantes have been organized in Union County, NJ, to patrol roads after several people were robbed.	A resolution placing the naval plane *NC-4*, which flew around the world, into the Smithsonian Institution is introduced in the House of Representatives.…Navy Secretary Daniels invites the Army Air Corps to use an old captured German battleship to test the effectiveness of aerial bombs.…Naval maneuvers are about to begin pitting the U.S. Navy's Atlantic Fleet against its Pacific Fleet off the coast of Peru.		A typhus outbreak among passengers on ships coming into New York has prompted suggestions of setting up a quarantine camp at Camp Dix, NJ.…Sleeping sickness in Boston has now claimed eight deaths and a further 12 have been stricken.…A French scientist, Theodore Moreaux estimates that the age of the earth is five hundred million years old.		**Feb. 7**
The Illinois Telephone Company announces it will award prizes to operators whose actions save lives or who show bravery in dangerous situations.	The War Department demonstrates the newest tank designs including the Christie Tank, which mounts a 6-inch gun and can travel at 12 miles an hour on broken ground and 30 miles an hour on roads.	The Department of Commerce reports that all world trade except in Belgium and Scandinavia shows little improvement over the past year.			**Feb. 8**

F	G	H	I	J
Includes campaigns, elections, federal-state relations, civil rights and liberties, crime, the judiciary, education, healthcare, poverty, urban affairs, and population.	*Includes formation and debate of U.S. foreign and defense policies, veterans affairs, and defense spending. (Relations with specific foreign countries are usually found under the region concerned.)*	*Includes business, labor, agriculture, taxation, transportation, consumer affairs, monetary and fiscal policy, natural resources, pollution and industrial accidents.*	*Includes worldwide scientific, medical and technological developments, natural phenomena, U.S. weather and natural disasters.*	*Includes the arts, religion, scholarship, communications media, sports, entertainment, fashions, fads, and social life.*

	World Affairs	Europe	Africa & The Middle East	The Americas	Asia & The Pacific
Feb. 9		U.S. Secretary of War Baker tells senators that while France has the largest standing army in the World, Italy has a greater total force....Police in Berlin seize 45 machine guns and 40,000 rounds of ammunition from an organization that referred to itself as a "home guard."		U.S. Marines raid a newspaper in Managua, Nicaragua, and wreck the presses in retaliation for the newspaper printing derogatory stories about some of the Marines....Oil has been discovered near the shores of Lake Nicaragua....Nicaragua states that it will consider joining the Central American union, which now includes Costa Rica, El Salvador, Guatemala, and Honduras....The offices of Brazil's Foreign ministry and the Stock Exchange are bombed by anarchists.	Japan's nationalist Party is continuing its call for large cuts in Japan's Army and Navy....A group British of aviators is schedule to go to Japan to teach members of the Japanese Air Service to fly.
Feb. 10	The Soviet Union states that if the League of Nations sends a military force into the contested Lithuanian city of Vilna that it will consider that to be a hostile act.	Reports claim that there are now 1,000 executions a month in Russia; the death penalty is being handed out for many crimes including drunk and disorderly conduct....Shell and Royal Dutch are negotiating for oil drilling rights in Russia....France's National Committee of the General Confederation of labor expels Communists from the group by a vote of 82 to 31.	General Jan Smuts, leader of the South African Party, presides over a large victory in the South African general election.	Twenty-one American Marines who broke into a newspaper office and smashed the presses have been arrested....The United States recognizes the new government of Bolivia.	Deputies in Japan's legislature reject any cuts in the Navy by a vote of 245 to 38.
Feb. 11		A large number of Czechs are leaving the Catholic Church as a response to the Church's close association with the Austrian dominance of the country for 300 years....The Premier of Greece states that the country's financial condition is desperate and the only hope the country has is if the United States will release credits promised in 1918.			Five U.S. sailors stationed at the Russian city of Vladivostok are fired on; it is suspected that Communists did the shooting.
Feb. 12		The Greek government orders the region of Thrace, which Greece had acquired from Bulgaria, to be under martial law....A new commercial treaty is signed between Italy and Czechoslovakia....In Bantry, Ireland, 300 men, probably Sinn Fein, attack the Police Barracks there....A group of men attack a British troops train leaving Cork, killing and wounding several soldiers....Winston Churchill is named into the new position of Secretary for the Colonies by King George V.		A labor riot in Argentina results in two men killed and several injured....Tomatoes are once again being grown in, and shipped from, the Guaymas Valley in Mexico where Indian raids and fighting between revolutionary factions has prevented this activity for some time.	
Feb. 13		France's General Reynaud predicts that France will be attacked by Germany and Russia and that the United States should have an armed force of four million men to assist in the coming war....France is facing a financial crisis; experts state that one of the reasons for these problems has been the successful evasion of paying taxes by farmers.			
Feb. 14		Lithuania and the Soviet Union sign a peace treaty....British troops blockade the Dingle and Derry area of Ireland; women and children are reported to be near starvation as a result of the blockade.			

A	B	C	D	E
Includes developments that affect more than one world region, international organizations and important meetings of world leaders.	*Includes all domestic and regional developments in Europe, including the Soviet Union.*	*Includes all domestic and regional developments in Africa and the Middle East.*	*Includes all domestic and regional developments in Latin America, the Caribbean, and Canada.*	*Includes all domestic and regional developments in Asian and Pacific nations (and colonies).*

U.S. Politics & Social Issues	U.S. Foreign Policy & Affairs, Defense	U.S. Economy & Environment	Science, Technology & Nature	Culture, Leisure & Lifestyle	
Rioting breaks out in Albany, NY, as a result of the city's Union Traction Company attempting to operate its lines in the face of a strike involving 1,200 employees....The Matewan (WV) Battle trial involving 21 miners accused in killing 10 detectives employed by the mines begins after the jury has been selected....An effort has begun by William Jennings Bryan and his brother Charles to take control of the Democratic Party and change its agenda to aims that are more Progressive.	Secretary of War Baker states that the planned funeral for America's unknown soldier should be the ceremony that would be accorded to a general.			The Westminster Kennel Club begins its 45th annual dog show at Madison Square Garden....A trial date for the members of the White Sox accused of throwing the 1919 World Series is set for March 14....Chicago schools again offer German as a language in high school, a course that had been dropped during the World War.	Feb. 9
William Jennings Bryan states that the voters must reform the Democratic Party.			More cases of sleeping sickness are reported, the most recent in Connecticut is where one more has died.	A new world's record is set by a motor boat, traveling 50 miles in one hour and 18 minutes.	Feb. 10
The War Department refuses the request of West Virginia's Governor to keep Federal troops on strike duty during the Matewan Battle Trial; two of 21 defendants have charges against them dropped.	A benefit ball is given in New York City in honor of the World War's famed "Lost Battalion."	The R.G. Dun Company reports that there were 364 business failures in America over the past week.	In what is the third outbreak of sleeping sickness in three years, the number of cases is growing each day although it is milder than previous outbreaks....British Antarctic expedition, under Commander John Cope, departs from the Falkland Islands.	Charles Gorman of New Brunswick ties the world record for the 440-yard indoor skating race.	Feb. 11
President-elect Harding in a speech in Florida calls Abraham Lincoln "the greatest American and the supreme human being since the days of Calvary."...An unidentified African American man accused of assaulting a Caucasian woman is taken from the jail at Ocala, FL, and lynched....Police in Albany, NY, using mounted troopers, ride down and disperse strikers.					Feb. 12
Striking transit workers in Albany, NY, force a streetcar and a snowplow back to the barns where they are normally kept preventing them from running; two men are arrested and Albany police are patrolling the entire city to prevent disorders....Wilbur Glenn Voliva and 400 members of his Zion City followers will come to "wicked New York" to clean the city of sinners, professors, astronomers, and scientists.	Secretary of the Navy Daniels issues a statement that the United States should be prepared to launch an oil export embargo at any time the President believes that it would serve the interests of the nation.		There are five more deaths due to sleeping sickness in the state of New York; the city of Port Chester, NY, bans public funerals.		Feb. 13
	The House of Representatives approves a $95 million appropriation for the Navy; it will be part of a program that will make the U.S. Navy as large as Britain's.	Demand for oil has decreased in the past week while production has increased by 15,000 barrels....Herbert Hover, who will become Secretary of Commerce, states that part of his program will be to combat waste in American industries....Four shipyards operated by Bethlehem Steel announce they will cut wages by 10 percent.		Wilson's Dance Studio, on 46th Street in New York City, is raided by police; 39 women are arrested on the charge of maintaining a nuisance by immoral and indecent dancing while the patrons are charged with disorderly conduct....Members of the White Sox baseball club accused of throwing the 1919 World series demand the charges against them.	Feb. 14

F	G	H	I	J
Includes campaigns, elections, federal-state relations, civil rights and liberties, crime, the judiciary, education, healthcare, poverty, urban affairs, and population.	*Includes formation and debate of U.S. foreign and defense policies, veterans affairs, and defense spending. (Relations with specific foreign countries are usually found under the region concerned.)*	*Includes business, labor, agriculture, taxation, transportation, consumer affairs, monetary and fiscal policy, natural resources, pollution and industrial accidents.*	*Includes worldwide scientific, medical and technological developments, natural phenomena, U.S. weather and natural disasters.*	*Includes the arts, religion, scholarship, communications media, sports, entertainment, fashions, fads, and social life.*

	World Affairs	Europe	Africa & The Middle East	The Americas	Asia & The Pacific
Feb. 15		The first official census in Czechoslovakia reports a total population of 13,613,172 persons including Czechs, Slovaks, Ruthenians, and Germans....King George V of Britain condemns the increased use of violence in Ireland....Lloyd George, Prime Minister of Britain, claims that conditions in Ireland are improving.			President-elect Harding appoints General Leonard Wood as Governor of the Philippine Islands.
Feb. 16		Soviet troops invade the nation of Georgia; supervision of the occupation is assigned to Josef Stalin.... The Finnish government states that its policy for quarantining all visitors from the Soviet Union will apply to a trade delegation from the Soviet Union; it is expected that this action will cause a breaking off of diplomatic relations between the two nations.		The Argentine government reports that its exchange rate between its peso and the British pound is improving....King Alfonso XIII of Spain will be asked to intervene with the United States to restore full liberty to the country of Dominica.	A Japanese journalist, speaking in New York, criticizes the United States stating that it is the nation that is pushing the naval arms race in the Pacific....At a meeting of Presbyterian Missionaries in Toronto, Japan's widespread killing of Korean civilians is compared to Turkish atrocities against the Armenians.
Feb. 17		Hungary and Austria agree to meet to discuss settling the western border of Hungary and Austria.... In Ireland, a train is ambushed and in fighting four civilians are killed....Because of the spread of typhus, Italy closes its borders and no immigrants will be allowed to depart for United States at the present time....Germans continue to protest the use of African soldiers in French service as part of the Allied occupation of Germany.	Representatives of Greece arrive in London to begin a conference that will discuss peace terms between that country and Turkey; Turkish representatives are expected soon.	According to some observers, the oil wells in Mexico's Tampico region are failing.	
Feb. 18	France Premier Aristide Briand states that no more concessions can be made in terms of restructuring Germany's reparations to the Allies and they must be paid.	Patients in the city of Trieste are reported to be recovering from a typhus outbreak that has hit the Adriatic region....Concert Pianist Jan Ignace Paderewski announces he will leave the concert stage and devote his life to politics in his native Poland....Italy's Minister of Industry states that the country's finances are improving and they would be even better of Italy's war debts were to be cancelled....Britain agrees to give Czechoslovakia credit to ensure that it can buy enough food for the country.	A report issued by Lord Milner recommends that Britain give Egypt total independence....C.D.B. King, the President of Liberia, is in Paris and announces that he will be coming to the United States to seek a loan for his country....Winston Churchill announces he will go to Cairo, Egypt to attend a conference that will determine colonial policies in Britain's colonies and mandates in the Middle East.	Mexico's President Obregon states that U.S. companies have not been granted permits to drill and cannot start any new oil wells.... Standard Oil of New Jersey has cut back its drilling operations in Mexico by about $8 million....The United States begins the process of withdrawing its soldiers from Dominica....Argentina says not will not prevent Germany from sending war materials to that country.... Argentine strikers surrender unconditionally to authorities, turning in their weapons.	
Feb. 19		France and Poland sign a treaty of mutual aid and military cooperation; France promises aid but not troops in the event of an attack.... There are 10 million cases of malaria reported in Russia with a large number of factories in Petrograd closed due to illness....The French government announces that it will mobilize its army and send them into Germany if the Germans do not live up to the reparations payment agreements.	Representatives of the British Dominions state that they are opposed to giving Egypt self-rule....At the London Conference, it is beginning to be observed that the British are favoring the Greeks while Italy and France are favoring Turkey.	An earth tremor hits the city of San Salvador in El Salvador; no damage is reported.	
Feb. 20		Censorship and martial law have been imposed in Hungary as a response to a threatened general strike to be held in that country....Investments in France during 1920 are reported to be five times those made in 1919.			Prince Hirohito, the heir to the Japanese throne, announces that he will wed the Princess Nagako....A prominent Japanese journalist writes an open letter to Japan's Minister of the Interior criticizing Japan's arbitrary policies....Reports from China indicate that famine conditions are improving.

A	B	C	D	E
Includes developments that affect more than one world region, international organizations and important meetings of world leaders.	*Includes all domestic and regional developments in Europe, including the Soviet Union.*	*Includes all domestic and regional developments in Africa and the Middle East.*	*Includes all domestic and regional developments in Latin America, the Caribbean, and Canada.*	*Includes all domestic and regional developments in Asian and Pacific nations (and colonies).*

U.S. Politics & Social Issues	U.S. Foreign Policy & Affairs, Defense	U.S. Economy & Environment	Science, Technology & Nature	Culture, Leisure & Lifestyle	
Three Jewish groups in Detroit attack the recent comments by Henry Ford alleging plots by international Jewish groups, which they call "un-American."...Federal troops leave the town of Williamson, WV, and their place will be taken by West Virginia state troopers who will keep order during the Matewan Battle trial.	The U.S. War Department estimates the Soviets have the largest army in the world with 1.5 million soldiers on duty; China's army is next in size and the United States ranks near the bottom in relative strength of troops to the number of inhabitants.	The Baldwin Locomotive Company announces that its profits for 1920 have decreased despite the fact that sales were up; increased operating costs have kept the profits from being as great as they should be.		Tenor Enrico Caruso's condition has worsened; he is given oxygen and his friends have been called to his bedside.	Feb. 15
Wage cuts are becoming a widespread phenomenon throughout the country; cuts of 10 to 20 percent are being imposed in Massachusetts and Pennsylvania....In the Matewan Battle trial in West Virginia, witnesses provide description of the "battle" that resulted in 10 deaths....A crowd of 5,000 persons seizes John Lee Eberhardt, an African American from the Clarke Country, GA, jail and burns him at the stake....Samuel Gompers, President of the American Federation of Labor states that there is a nationwide attack on the right of unions to organize.	The American Graves Registration Service is expressing its opinion that the Unknown Soldier would not yet be selected because their methods of identifying dead soldiers have become very advanced and a period of time should be allowed so that the one selected for this honor cannot be identified in any way.	Temperatures in New York City set a new record for warmth for this date; the temperature is 63 degrees....The Quaker Oats Company announces that it will reduce the quarterly dividends on its common stock.	A case of Typhus has been reported in a hospital in New York City; there are nine new reported cases of sleeping sickness and one new case of smallpox.	A print by the 18th century Japanese artist, Hiroshige, sells for $105.	Feb. 16
The state of New Hampshire's legislature passes a bill approving the imposition of standard time in the state; railroads will not be allowed to arrange their timetables to conform with the schedules of interstate trains that are operating on daylight-saving time....Senator Borah of Idaho tells his colleagues that he will not remain silent on issues during the coming Harding administration and that he will be as outspoken as he was during the Wilson term of office.				A bill allowing an open season on beaver is being discussed in New York state owing to the damage that the animals are causing to timber....Caruso's doctors say that he is doing better but he is still very ill.	Feb. 17
Attorney General Palmer tells a Senate committee that his widespread raids on suspected Communists were justified....A Grand Jury investigating the Wall Street explosion finds that the explosion was a criminal act and not an accident and that a reward of $50,000 be established to find the perpetrators....The U.S. Attorney General Palmer states that informers who lead Federal authorities to supplies of illegal liquor will be given rewards.		The Savage Arms Company states that its earnings in 1920 were $117,000 compared with $2.032 million in 1919....Standard Oil of Kentucky announces that for 1920 its profits were $7.29 million compared with $4.24 million in the previous year....The Curtiss Aeroplane Company announces that it had serious losses in the year 1920.		A surveying party finds the skeleton of a mastodon 35 miles west of Bisbee, AZ.	Feb. 18
The American Red Cross reports that 20,000 children up to age 14 are killed in accidents each year....A witness at the Matewan Battle trial states that it was the miners and not the detectives working for the mines who fired first.		The United States produced 69 percent of the world's total of oil in 1919 according to a report released by the U.S. Geological Survey.			Feb. 19
The Matewan Battle trial continues, observers are guessing that the trial with all of its testimony could go on for another three weeks.				A piano sonata by composer Ernest Bloch is premiered in New York's Aeolian Hall by Paul Kochanski and Arthur Rubenstein.	Feb. 20

F	G	H	I	J
Includes campaigns, elections, federal-state relations, civil rights and liberties, crime, the judiciary, education, healthcare, poverty, urban affairs, and population.	*Includes formation and debate of U.S. foreign and defense policies, veterans affairs, and defense spending. (Relations with specific foreign countries are usually found under the region concerned.)*	*Includes business, labor, agriculture, taxation, transportation, consumer affairs, monetary and fiscal policy, natural resources, pollution and industrial accidents.*	*Includes worldwide scientific, medical and technological developments, natural phenomena, U.S. weather and natural disasters.*	*Includes the arts, religion, scholarship, communications media, sports, entertainment, fashions, fads, and social life.*

	World Affairs	Europe	Africa & The Middle East	The Americas	Asia & The Pacific
Feb. 21		In elections in the German state of Prussia both Communists and Extreme Nationalists make important gains.... Germany's war minister, in a speech says that he believes that the allies will let a Polish Army of 200,000 enter Germany.... The Touring Club of France announces its plans to set up a chain of stone monuments marking the extent of the battlefront in the World War.		It is announced that the Tijuana racetrack in the United States will close unless the Mexican government rescinds it rule of paying $10 for permanent passports and $2 for temporary passports.	
Feb. 22	The German government complains that the Inter-Allied Commission has been interfering with German shipping delivering goods to the Soviet Union.	The Soviet State Planning Commission, known as GOSPLAN, is formed.... As part of the continuing conflict in Yugoslavia, Montenegrans have declared a holy war against Serbs; Montenegro is currently occupied by at least two Serbian regiments.... Lawyers representing the Austrian government state that they will sue the ex-Emperor Karl in order to take possession of the Crown jewels that Karl took with him into exile.... There is a major fuel crisis in the Soviet Union that has prevented trains from bringing food to urban centers such as Moscow.		Striking railroad workers in Mexcio clash with police with some reports of injuries.... Chile voters to raise its import duties on goods coming into the country by 50 percent.	A Japanese Court Martial returns a finding of Not Guilty for the Japanese sentry who shot and killed an American naval Officer in Vladivostok in January.... Bingen Shoku, a Korean leader, is assassinated in Tokyo; he had been an outspoken advocate of giving Koreans voting rights as Japanese citizens.... The Japanese government's Foreign Office is drawing up a proposal to the League of Nations to make changes to the League's covenant so as to provide special recognition for Japan's place in the Pacific region.
Feb. 23		The Dutch government reiterates that Kaiser Wilhelm II, who is in exile in that country, must live with some restrictions on his personal liberty.... Soviet troops, driving toward the Georgian city of Tblisi have been stopped by the Georgian Army.... French ships in the Black Sea are firing on Soviet military positions.... Sailors who have mutinied against the Soviet government in Petrograd are inviting Soviet army troops to join them.			Reza Khan of Persia, whose troops are occupying Teheran, states that Persia will establish a strong administration loyal to the Shah and will not be bullied by the Communists.... Reports from eastern Siberia indicate that the Soviet Army may be planning an offensive against Japanese positions.
Feb. 24		Railroads in Warsaw are now being operated under martial law; Russian prisoners of war are used as strikebreakers.... The King's Bench in Ireland judges that a state of War exists in Ireland, giving the military a full range of powers under martial law to suppress disorder.... Food revolts are reported to be taking place in the Soviet Union and the mutinous sailors are said to be shelling the city of Petrograd.		Panamanians attack the Costa Rican Consulate at Panama City in response to reports that Costa Rica had invaded Panama.... The Chilean government issues an official denial that it has any agreements or treaties with Japan or Britain.	In Lahore, in northern India, there is rioting between Sikh pilgrims and Sikh merchants; many have been killed or injured.
Feb. 25		A Sinn Fein army of an estimated 300–400 men attacks British police in County Cork.... Serbian forces are reported fighting Montenegrans who have risen against the Yugoslav government.... A representative of the Lithuanian government complains that although a plebiscite has been scheduled to determine if the city of Vilna will go to Poland or Lithuania, Polish troops still have not left the city.... The Hungarian government orders troops to Budapest to prevent disturbances in the streets as a result of threatened strikes.		Thousands of enlistees are said to be seeking to join the Panamanian Army in its efforts to meet and roll back the invasion from Costa Rica.	

A	B	C	D	E
Includes developments that affect more than one world region, international organizations and important meetings of world leaders.	*Includes all domestic and regional developments in Europe, including the Soviet Union.*	*Includes all domestic and regional developments in Africa and the Middle East.*	*Includes all domestic and regional developments in Latin America, the Caribbean, and Canada.*	*Includes all domestic and regional developments in Asian and Pacific nations (and colonies).*

	U.S. Politics & Social Issues	U.S. Foreign Policy & Affairs, Defense	U.S. Economy & Environment	Science, Technology & Nature	Culture, Leisure & Lifestyle
Feb. 21	A.G. Spalding, manufacturer of sporting goods, announces that it will cut wages by 10 percent but will continue to work on a 48-hour week basis.		The price of Pennsylvania crude oil drops 50 cents a barrel, bringing it to $3.25 a barrel.…The American Chicle Company, manufacturer of chewing gum, announces its profits in 1920 were lower than in 1919.		The Syracuse City Council has banned the toddle, the camel walk, the Chicago flop, and all other forms of jazz dance.
Feb. 22	Professor Paul Shorey of the University of Chicago says that America must restrict immigration and continue to be a nation using only one language if the country is to preserve its spiritual unity.…The Pope names Archbishop Dennis Dougherty of Philadelphia to be a Cardinal along with five other archbishops.…Tentative selections for President-elect Harding's cabinet include Charles Evan Hughes as Secretary of State, Andrew Mellon as Secretary of the Treasury, John Weeks as Secretary of War, Albert Fall as Secretary of the Interior, and Herbert Hoover as Secretary of Commerce.		The world's oil input increased in 1920 with a total production of 689 million barrels, a gain of more than 23 percent over 1919.		
Feb. 23				Ten additional cases and two deaths, as a result of sleeping sickness, are reported in New York City; additional cases are reported in upstate New York and Indiana.…An airplane carrying the mail flies from San Francisco to New York in 33 hours and 20 minutes.	Army veteran Fred Williams returns to his home in Lafayette, GA; listed as having been killed in action he finds that there is a grave with a body reportedly his, and that his wife received his insurance and has subsequently remarried.
Feb. 24		Army flying officers will be receiving special training in how to bomb battleships.…The annual Naval appropriation bill drafted by the Senate Naval Committee allows for an additional 20,000 men and additional funding for aviation.…The United States announces it will offer to mediate between Panama and Costa Rica, which have begun to fight.	The system used by Piggly-Wiggly stores for customers to use self-service to get their goods has been patented; that patent's legality and its scope are being tested in a Federal Court case.…Herbert Hoover announces he will accept the post of Secretary of Commerce, but will also keep his job directing European relief efforts.		Violinist Fritz Kreisler plays a concert with the Philharmonic Society at Carnegie Hall.
Feb. 25	Woolen Mills in Bloomfield, NJ, announce they will resume operations on a 48-hour a week basis with the workers taking a 20 percent cut in wages.…The population of African Americans in New York City, according to the 1920 census, is 153,088, an increase of 67 percent over 1910.…A court in Ohio rules that the Pullman Company, which makes railroad cars, is responsible for the safety and security of possessions of those who use the sleeping cars.…Henry Chamberlain, operating director of the Chicago Crime Commission states that at least 10,000 people in Chicago have taken up crime as a profession.	President-elect Harding in a speech states that he would prefer that the United States engage in wide ranging trade as a means of binding with other nations instead of treaties.	Both imports and exports decreased in the month of January according to the Department of Commerce although exports were still greater than imports.…New York legislators are discussing a bill that would prohibit all trucks that weigh more than 7½ tons to prevent damage to highways.		Samuel Goldwyn, President of Goldwyn pictures, states that the United States is in danger of losing the world's film market due to censorship and other restrictive legislation.

F	G	H	I	J
Includes campaigns, elections, federal-state relations, civil rights and liberties, crime, the judiciary, education, healthcare, poverty, urban affairs, and population.	*Includes formation and debate of U.S. foreign and defense policies, veterans affairs, and defense spending. (Relations with specific foreign countries are usually found under the region concerned.)*	*Includes business, labor, agriculture, taxation, transportation, consumer affairs, monetary and fiscal policy, natural resources, pollution and industrial accidents.*	*Includes worldwide scientific, medical and technological developments, natural phenomena, U.S. weather and natural disasters.*	*Includes the arts, religion, scholarship, communications media, sports, entertainment, fashions, fads, and social life.*

	World Affairs	Europe	Africa & The Middle East	The Americas	Asia & The Pacific
Feb. 26		France announces that it will maintain a fleet capable of defeating any German ships in the event Germany does not live up to the provisions of the Versailles treaty.... The French government announces it will dedicate a monument on August 2 to honor Corporal Peugeot, the first French soldier killed in the World War.... British soldiers and police attempt to capture a Sinn Fein unit while Sinn Fein issues a bulletin identifying 28 cases of assassination of Irish civilians by the British Constabulary.... Reports claim that Soviet troops are setting up cannon and machine guns and using them on striking workers.... In Italy clashes are reported between members of the Socialist and the Fascist parties.		The Krupp steelworks announces it will build the largest steel and munitions plant in South America in Chile.... U.S. Marines are sentenced to two years in prison and dishonorable discharges for having wrecked a newspaper office in Managua, Nicaragua.	The Japanese government indicates that it may withdraw its forces that have been occupying Siberia region along Russia's Pacific Coast.... The Chinese Ambassador to the United States arrives and states that he believes the Chinese Republic is making excellent progress in this rough period of transition.
Feb. 27		Romania's Princess Elizabeth marries Crown Prince George of Greece.... Italy's Labor Congress is expected to defeat and marginalize the Communist faction within its organization. .... Former French President Poincarre states that despite Germany's excuses, it can afford to pay all of the war reparations it owes.... General Sir Nevil Macready, commander of British forces in Ireland is wounded in a Sinn Fein ambush.	The full text of the British mandate in Palestine is published; the Zionist Organization is acknowledged as the advisor to the British administration.	Reporters claim that in general the population of Costa Rica does not know that their country is at war with Panama.	Japan states that it has the right to administer the island of Yap in the Pacific under a League of Nations mandate.
Feb. 28		Reports from the Soviet Union claim that the Communists in the city of Petrograd have been overthrown; the Soviet Press denies that there are uprisings in any city.... In reprisal for the execution of six members of Sinn Fein five British soldiers are killed in the Irish city of Cork.... Radio Corporation of America announces that it has a contract to build a large radio station in Warsaw for the Polish government.	The State Department denies that it has been negotiating for naval bases in Liberia.	Three labor leaders in Manitoba, Canada, who were imprisoned for a year are released from jail to assume their seats in the provincial legislature.... Fighting between Costa Rican and Panamanian forces has resulted in the Panamanians capturing a town on the Pacific side of their common border.	Two Filipinos are killed and 10 Chinese stores are destroyed in the Samar islands and Leyte over Chinese merchants refusing to buy the local hemp crop.... The Turkish Army is in position to fight the Society forces near the city of Batum in Central Asia.
Mar. 1		Britain's Prime Minister, David Lloyd George states that Germany's proposals to avoid paying war reparations are unacceptable; the Allies are united in rejecting those proposals.... A Communist uprising in the Italian city of Florence is becoming violent.... In Central Italy, more than 120 have been killed in this latest violence.... The French Army is ready to enter Germany if the reparations are not paid on time; the combined force of Belgian and French troops ready to invade numbers 225,000.... Greece announces that it will not accept any revisions to the Treaty of Sevres that ended the war between the Allies and Turkey.		An extraordinary session of Panama's Assembly meets to plan defense measures against Costa Rica.... The Costa Rican government sends an addition 2,500 soldiers to its border with Panama.... It is expected that there will be significant changes in Mexican President Obregon's cabinet, which will now include more moderate politicians in favor of labor unions.... Striking Mexican railway workers are now returning to their jobs.	The first census of the Japanese Empire has been completed; it reports that the total population is 77,005,112.

A	B	C	D	E
Includes developments that affect more than one world region, international organizations and important meetings of world leaders.	*Includes all domestic and regional developments in Europe, including the Soviet Union.*	*Includes all domestic and regional developments in Africa and the Middle East.*	*Includes all domestic and regional developments in Latin America, the Caribbean, and Canada.*	*Includes all domestic and regional developments in Asian and Pacific nations (and colonies).*

U.S. Politics & Social Issues	U.S. Foreign Policy & Affairs, Defense	U.S. Economy & Environment	Science, Technology & Nature	Culture, Leisure & Lifestyle	
The Joint Congressional Postal Commission reports on its findings to speed mail delivery as well as a recommendation to lock mail trucks in order to prevent theft.…Senator Borah introduces a bill in Congress that would punish any Federal official who tries to curb any individual's free speech.…The Commander of the American Legion criticizes the government for its neglect of wounded and ill veterans.…The government states that it expects to collect $500 million in taxes when they fall due on March 15.				Sergei Rachmaninoff gives an all-Russian concert at Carnegie Hall.…Anna Pavlova and her Russian Ballet Company announce that they will be giving 10 performances in New York starting on March 10.…Tenor Beniamino Gigli is ill and cannot perform in a scheduled performance of *Andre Chenier* at the Metropolitan Opera.	**Feb. 26**
Former President Taft, in comparing unions to Communists, states that when it is considered that they are endangering the public welfare, then strikes should be outlawed.…A meeting of the American Federation of Labor declares that all workers are called upon to fight "Leninism."	The Naval Destroyer, USS *Woolsey*, is sunk when it is rammed by a merchant steamer; one man is dead and 15 are missing.	Pulp wood consumption in the Northeast and the Great Lakes area has increased 17 percent in 1920 over 1918.		John Armstrong Chaloner, self-professed psychic, states at a show in New York City that within five years Jesus Christ will appear with 600,000 bullet-proof soldiers to "clean up the world."…Doctor Henry van Dyke of Princeton, in a speech to educators, describes jazz as "invented by demons for the torture of imbeciles."…Enrico Caruso celebrates his 48th birthday; he is still recuperating from pleurisy.	**Feb. 27**
Five maritime labor unions combine and will strike over a wage reduction that would affect 275,000 workers on the Atlantic and Pacific coasts.…The Supreme Court rules that evidence found by government Revenue agents cannot be used in court unless the raiders have a search warrant.…Annette Abbott Adams, the first woman assistant Attorney General of the United States, says in a speech that men should not try to sidetrack women from meaningful participation in public affairs.	Swiss military observers, after a tour of parts of occupied Germany, praise the American Army for its tact and discipline.				**Feb. 28**
Colorado's Senator Thomas attacks a proposed bill that would provide bonuses and land reclamation for homesteads for veterans to be mercenary and sordid and should not be passed.		The Chandler Motor Car Company states gross profits of $9.440 million for 1920 as opposed to $6.650 million in 1919.…The owners of 45 steam trawlers fishing out of Gloucester and Boston, MA, say they will not be putting out to sea given the high wages and high cost of coal and low prices for fish.	Sir Ernest Shackleton, the Antarctic explorer, states that in April or May he will launch a new expedition to the Arctic.	Tenor Enrico Caruso undergoes surgery for the third time to cure his attack of pleurisy.…The State Attorney of Illinois states that the eight baseball players accused of throwing the 1919 World Series will be accused of operating a confidence game and obtaining money under false pretences.…The dancer, Isadora Duncan is named in a $200,000 alienation suit of the wife of Edward Steichen, the artist.	**Mar. 1**

	World Affairs	Europe	Africa & The Middle East	The Americas	Asia & The Pacific
Mar. 2		Nine persons are wounded in gunfire exchanged between Sinn Fein and the British forces; people in the streets are said to have become used to violence and to pay little attention to it.…Italy states that while it has supported Germany in the past, it cannot tolerate the proposals Germany is making now to make changes to the reparations it is supposed to pay to the Allies.… Britain's Duke of Northumberland states that he believes that current uprising in Ireland is linked with a Communist Conspiracy.	The American Chamber of Commerce for the Levant incorporates and will promote trade between the United States and the Middle East.…France and Turkey conclude a peace agreement and the French will evacuate the Turkish city of Cilicia.	Fighting continues between Costa Rica and Panama; Panama's forces capture a Costa Rican vessel and about 100 men.	Filipino students complain of continued disrespect shown their flag by Mrs. J.F. Oliver, an American teacher working in the islands.
Mar. 3		Poland, Rumania, and Hungary form an alliance to protect them from invasions or other aggression from the Soviet Union.…Reports now indicate that Soviet troops have successfully repressed the revolt by workers and sailors in Petrograd and that Soviet authorities are now in full control.…The German Press indicates surprise that the Allies have stood firm against Germany's proposals to make changes to the reparations payments.		Fighting escalates between Costa Rica and Panama; reports state that the United Fruit Company may be asking the U.S. government to send troops to protect its banana plantations.	In the Japanese national assembly there are arguments concerning the extent of mistreatment of Koreans by Japanese occupation forces.
Mar. 4		Krupp and 12 other German companies agree to sell locomotives to the Soviet Union; transporting the engines through Poland for delivery may have adverse diplomatic affects due to Poland's war with the Soviets.…Three are killed and many wounded in fighting between Sinn Fein and the British Constabulary in Dublin.	Greece has rejected outside proposals for resolving its issues with Turkey over Thrace and Smyrna although the Turks have been receptive to having discussions.	The League of Nations' primary business is to resolve a dispute between Costa Rica and Panama over their border.…The schooner *Tipperary* sailing with a cargo of salt from Portugal is caught in ice flows near Newfoundland and is crushed; the crew escapes by walking over the ice and using a small boat to cross stretches of open water.…Mexican newspapers editorialize that they have great hope in the new U.S. president after the bitter experience Mexico had with outgoing President Wilson.	
Mar. 5		The mutiny of Russian sailors at Kronstadt continues; some reports are now discounting earlier accounts that large portions of the Red Army were rebelling against Lenin and Trotsky.…A British general is reported killed in a Sinn Fein ambush near Killarney, Ireland.	The British government issues a statement that neither Americans nor any other non-British individuals have the same right to open businesses in Iraq as the British do under their Mandate.…The High Commissioner for Palestine announces that public works projects in that area will begin as soon as it has been approved by the League of Nations.	In one of his final acts, President Wilson vetoes a tariff bill that would have raised the cost of Argentine products; the news of the veto is enthusiastically received in Argentina.	
Mar. 6		Fighting breaks out in Silesia, the coal-mining region populated by both Germans and Poles; in the latest rioting more than 100 men have been hospitalized.…The Protestant Synod of Switzerland decrees women can be pastors but only if they are single.…Latest reports describe the Kronstadt sailors as aiming the guns of their ship on the city of Petrograd.	The President of Liberia arrives in the United States to seek a $5 million loan for his country.	Speeches are given in the Spanish Chamber of Deputies demanding that the Spanish government exert itself to improve relations with the countries of Latin America.… Panama announces it will not accept the Costa Rica-Panama border adjustment proposed by U.S. Supreme Court Justice White.	The Japanese government states that it will not withdraw from its position that the former German island of Yap in the Pacific should now be a mandate under Japanese administration.
Mar. 7		British and French troops are now on their way to occupy portions of Germany as a result of payments disagreements between Germany and the victorious allies.…The Mayor of Limerick, Ireland, and an ex-mayor are killed in a reprisal for recent attacks on British officers.…In fighting between the Communists and Fascists in Rome, four people are killed, 12 wounded, and 200 arrested.		Merchants in Montevideo, Uruguay, state that they will not accept Americans goods, which they say arrive damaged because they are so poorly packed.…Costa Rica's troops withdraw from Panamanian territory, stating they will accept the boundary proposed by Justice White.	The American Committee reports that 20 million Chinese are starving.

A
Includes developments that affect more than one world region, international organizations and important meetings of world leaders.

B
Includes all domestic and regional developments in Europe, including the Soviet Union.

C
Includes all domestic and regional developments in Africa and the Middle East.

D
Includes all domestic and regional developments in Latin America, the Caribbean, and Canada.

E
Includes all domestic and regional developments in Asian and Pacific nations (and colonies).

U.S. Politics & Social Issues	U.S. Foreign Policy & Affairs, Defense	U.S. Economy & Environment	Science, Technology & Nature	Culture, Leisure & Lifestyle	
In Sharon, MA, letters have been sent to 150 citizens calling for certain residents to be run out of town; officials believe that the letters were sent out by members of the Sharon Vigilance Committee....U.S. Health Commissioner, Royal Copeland, asks for a Congressional appropriation of $1,291,330 to help fight the outbreak of typhus I the Northeast United States....Leaving his home in Marion, OH, President Elect Harding tells well-wishers that all will be well as he leaves to be inaugurated.		Business failures in the United States in February were greater than those reported in January, a 16 percent gain.			Mar. 2
President Wilson signs bills repealing nearly all wartime measures passed since 1917....Wounded and disabled veterans testify to Congress that they have been neglected and improperly treated by government authorities.	U.S. submarines *O-7* and *O-8* run aground in Long Island sound; there are no casualties in either boat and neither sub is in danger....The U.S. Senate completes enactment of a House resolution calling for the removal of the body of an unidentified soldier in France to be brought back for burial in the United States as the Unknown Solider.	Sear and Roebuck stores announce that starting today they will reduce the pay of between 2,500 and 3,500 employees.		Washington officials report very few tourists in the capital to see the inauguration; most state that the reason is the lack of spectacle that was decided on to save expenses.	Mar. 3
President Warren G. Harding and Vice-President Calvin Coolidge are inaugurated....Harding's inaugural address is well received by the business community....Harding introduces the word "normalcy" to the English language....Among President Harding's first duties is to make about 50,000 appointments in Federal Service (including 15,000 postmasterships) for a total salary of $100 million.	Submarine *O-8* has been refloated; submarine *O-7* is still on the rocks; there are no casualties....The navy is experimenting with a new means to deploy sea mines, dropping them into the water by air.	The Baltimore and Ohio's revenue for January is reported at $1,907,415, greater than the $1,416,016 revenue of January 1920.	The "airplane" edition of The *New York Times* is flown from New York to Washington and distributed to hotels and newsstands where it is sold out within minutes.	The Cleveland Indians baseball club experiments with head guards for batters; a member of the team, Ray Chapman, was killed in the 1920 season from being hit in the head from a pitch.	Mar. 4
Senator Henry Cabot Lodge of Massachusetts is reelected as Majority Leader.	In a report filed with the U.S. Senate, the final cost of the World War for the United States was $41,873,948,225 with the total Allied expenditure estimated to be $139,702,269,225....U.S. submarine O-8 is refloated and returns to New Haven, CT....The War Department begins to make arrangements to transport the body of the Unknown Soldiers from France to the United States.	The New York Central railroad warns that the failure to impose standard or daylight saving time uniformly across the northeast region will create serious rail traffic problems.			Mar. 5
		Illinois game wardens are now using aircraft to locate and run down game law violators, arresting six in their latest sweep.	Cancer deaths in the United States are estimated to have been 90,000 in 1920.		Mar. 6
The New York State Bureau of Municipal Information reports that in 1920 thieves stole 7,005 cars, of which only 3,996 were recovered; total value of the stolen vehicles is estimated at $7 million.	The U.S. Senate ratifies several foreign treaties to include treaties with Portugal, Greece, Argentine, and Britain.			Doctors officially state that Caruso's progress in his convalescence is progressing well.	Mar. 7

F	G	H	I	J
Includes campaigns, elections, federal-state relations, civil rights and liberties, crime, the judiciary, education, healthcare, poverty, urban affairs, and population.	*Includes formation and debate of U.S. foreign and defense policies, veterans affairs, and defense spending. (Relations with specific foreign countries are usually found under the region concerned.)*	*Includes business, labor, agriculture, taxation, transportation, consumer affairs, monetary and fiscal policy, natural resources, pollution and industrial accidents.*	*Includes worldwide scientific, medical and technological developments, natural phenomena, U.S. weather and natural disasters.*	*Includes the arts, religion, scholarship, communications media, sports, entertainment, fashions, fads, and social life.*

	World Affairs	Europe	Africa & The Middle East	The Americas	Asia & The Pacific
Mar. 8		Communists in the Portuguese city of Oporto set off six bombs creating serious damage and killing a railway official....The rebellion in Petrograd is spreading as a result of the successes of the Kronstadt sailors; Soviet troops attacking several rebel locations are forced to retreat....Spain's Premier, Eduardo Dato is attacked and killed....Fighting is reported between Lithuanians and Poles in the Vilna region....German towns on the border with France are quickly occupied by British and French troops.	According to the Guaranty Trust Company, the finances of the Turkish government are near collapse.		
Mar. 9		There are conflicting stories coming out of Petrograd....The Swiss government announces that it may station Army troops along the Swiss-German border as was done during the war because of the recent events with the British and French moving in....Large numbers of Jews are reported planning to leave the Soviet Union in fear of pogroms resulting from the current round of anti-Communist uprisings.		The Argentine government has intervened to prevent an American corporation from boycotting hides.	
Mar. 10		Crown Prince Carol of Romania marries Princess Helen of Greece....Communists are now said to have completely crushed the anti-Communist uprising in Moscow even as rebels in Petrograd and Kronstadt are still holding on....Czechoslovakia and Austria sign an agreement fixing the border between the two countries.	Britain announces that it will be assisting agricultural projects in Palestine.		
Mar. 11		*Soviet Russia,* a magazine published in New York City, carries an editorial stating that "prospective undertakers" from the west should not assume that the Soviet leadership has been overthrown....Rebel sailors from Kronstadt commence shelling Petrograd again....The British government announces it will hang four men in Ireland for ambushing police in January....The Polish government states that it fears that a civil war will break out between ethnic Poles and Germans in Silesia with arms and support being brought across the border from Germany.			
Mar. 12		In exile, Germany's former Kaiser Wilhelm II writes an account of the World War, stating it began because the nations of the world were conspiring against Germany....One Constable and six members of Sinn Fein are killed in an ambush in Tipperary.	Since 1910, and especially since 1915, production of diamonds in the Belgian Congo has increased to 200,000 carats a year....Riots in Alexandria protesting the arrival of Winston Churchill leave 29 injured....Churchill's arrival in Egypt is part of the opening of the Cairo Conference, which will determine British policy in the Middle East, with Churchill, T.E. Lawrence, Gertrude Bell, and others.	The Ecuadorian Congress creates a government monopoly on the following items: alcoholic beverages, tobacco, dynamite, cigarette papers, and matches....The *Blue Nose,* a schooner being built in Lunenburg, Nova Scotia, will be launched on March 26; it may be Canada's representative in the international fishing schooner races.	Zinc mines in Australia close down due to the poor condition of the world metals markets.

A	B	C	D	E
Includes developments that affect more than one world region, international organizations and important meetings of world leaders.	*Includes all domestic and regional developments in Europe, including the Soviet Union.*	*Includes all domestic and regional developments in Africa and the Middle East.*	*Includes all domestic and regional developments in Latin America, the Caribbean, and Canada.*	*Includes all domestic and regional developments in Asian and Pacific nations (and colonies).*

U.S. Politics & Social Issues	U.S. Foreign Policy & Affairs, Defense	U.S. Economy & Environment	Science, Technology & Nature	Culture, Leisure & Lifestyle	
The American Legion is told of neglect and incompetence in the medical treatment and pensions paid out to veterans of the World War.... The American Federation of Labor severs its relationship with the International Federation of Trade Unions because of the latter's ties with the Soviets.	The American Secretary of War states that U.S. troops currently on Occupation duty in Germany will remain there and not be withdrawn soon.		Albert Einstein leaves Europe for a lecture tour in the United States, which he will follow up with a tour of Palestine.	Leopold Stokowski conducts the Philadelphia Orchestra in a performance of the Brahms *German Requiem*.	Mar. 8
		A serious storm hits the northeast; in eastern Pennsylvania roofs have been blown off buildings, many persons have been injured, and 1.3 inches of rain fell in the first five minutes of the storm.... Standard Oil cuts the wholesale price of gasoline by two cents in New Jersey and by one cent in New York.... The Baltimore and Ohio Railroad has now laid off workers, part of a national trend: U.S. railroads have laid off 400,000 workers since October 1920.		It is expected that the trial of several members of the White Sox for throwing the 1919 world series will be delayed.	Mar. 9
A gun battle between guards of a whiskey shipment and bandits near Covington, KY, results in two men killed.... Despite advice from the American Federation of Labor's Samuel Gompers, members of the Detroit Federation of Labor state that they will send a delegate to the Soviet Labor Congress.		The building trade in February shows significant improvement, a gain in February of 32 percent of expenditures over January.			Mar. 10
In what is termed as a "race riot," 14 African Americans have been shot by police and private citizens in Springfield, OH, following the arrest of a man for allegedly assaulting a woman.		The DuPont Company announces that both sales and earnings have dropped, in the wake of the end of the World War, for gunpowder.			Mar. 11
	The U.S. government sees some possibility of the Soviets being overthrown as a result of the recent rebellions near Petrograd.... Concert pianist and former Premier of Poland, Jan Ignace Paderewski, meets with Senator Henry Cabot Lodge.	Secretary of Commerce Hoover says that in the near future the United States will be importing food.		Gray is the fashionable color this season for women's daytime formal wear and the hemlines will remain high.... The Metropolitan Museum of Art announces it will make prints from two wood blocks that were cut by Albrecht Durer in the early 16th century.	Mar. 12

F	G	H	I	J
Includes campaigns, elections, federal-state relations, civil rights and liberties, crime, the judiciary, education, healthcare, poverty, urban affairs, and population.	*Includes formation and debate of U.S. foreign and defense policies, veterans affairs, and defense spending. (Relations with specific foreign countries are usually found under the region concerned.)*	*Includes business, labor, agriculture, taxation, transportation, consumer affairs, monetary and fiscal policy, natural resources, pollution and industrial accidents.*	*Includes worldwide scientific, medical and technological developments, natural phenomena, U.S. weather and natural disasters.*	*Includes the arts, religion, scholarship, communications media, sports, entertainment, fashions, fads, and social life.*

	World Affairs	Europe	Africa & The Middle East	The Americas	Asia & The Pacific
Mar. 13				The Nicaraguan Senate rejects a proposal to ask U.S. troops to leave the country....In the state of Puebla, Mexico, there is danger of an Indian revolt that would threaten the stability of the federal government....President Obregon of Mexico refuses to sign agreements with the United States even though his refusal may keep the United States from extending recognition to his government.	Reports state that the railroads in Manchuria have been captured by anti-Soviet forces and the Soviet government there has been overthrown.
Mar. 14		Leon Trotsky, in command of the forces trying to suppress the mutiny in Kronstadt and the Petrograd area begins a blockade to starve the population....Soviet troops are reported massing on the Polish border....Six members of Sinn Fein are hanged in Dublin by the British....Anti-Soviet Georgians are defeated by the Soviets and retreat from the city of Poti....An Anti-Semitic demonstration in Vienna, numbering between 5,000 and 6,000 participants marches through the streets.	Greece and Turkey exchange accusations about repression conducted by the other against minorities in territories they are occupying.		An anti-Soviet uprising in the Caucasus region is under way.
Mar. 15		Britain's Secretary for War declares to the House of Commons that Britain's Army cannot be reduced in size....The Romanian government announces it will begin registering all inhabitants of the country....Today is the closing session of the Austrian Anti-Semitic Congress in Vienna; among the proposals is a call on the government to expel all alien Jews from Austria....Two hours of street fighting in Dublin result in four killed and several injured; further south a group of British officers are ambushed near Cork.	Talaat Pasha, former Grand Vizier of the Ottoman Empire, is shot and killed by an Armenian student in Berlin....Reports state that the Greek Army may be planning new offensives against the Turks.	Elections for President of Cuba are being held today amid accusations of voter fraud.	
Mar. 16		Lenin institutes the New Economic Plan (NEP), which will, for a few years, provide greater economic freedom....Josef Stalin is elected to the Politburo.		Dr. Alfredo Zayas y Alfonso is elected President of Cuba; there is open question as to whether he can form a government in time for his inauguration scheduled for May 20.	Reports state that Armenians have overthrown the Soviet government there and the Soviets have been driven out.
Mar. 17		A new Polish Constitution, modeled on the French and American systems is adopted....Soviet forces, numbering 60,000, force the surrender of the 16,000 anti-Soviet rebels in Kronstadt....Constables in Ireland are being shot as reprisals for the latest set of hangings performed by the British government....Alexander Kerensky, Premier of the Revolutionary Russian government, overthrown by the Communists, denounces the recent Soviet-Polish treaty....The Allies state that they will defer the war reparations payments to be made by Austria on order that the country can recover economically.		The Mexican government is recognized by the government of France in a diplomatic move that has surprised many observers....American border patrols and soldiers engage in gun battles with Mexicans attempting to cross the border....The opposition in Costa Rica attacks the agreements that the government has made in resolving the border dispute with Panama.	
Mar. 18		The Peace of Riga ends the Polish-Soviet War....Czechoslovakia, Romania, and Poland sign a treaty for common defense....Fires and explosions are creating panic in the streets of Dublin; Sinn Fein is blamed for the disturbances.	An uprising by the natives of the Belgian Congo has resulted in the burning of 50 trading posts.		The Soviet Union is said to have signed a treaty with Afghanistan, which would run counter to many terms in a treaty recently signed between Britain and the Afghans.

A	B	C	D	E
Includes developments that affect more than one world region, international organizations and important meetings of world leaders.	*Includes all domestic and regional developments in Europe, including the Soviet Union.*	*Includes all domestic and regional developments in Africa and the Middle East.*	*Includes all domestic and regional developments in Latin America, the Caribbean, and Canada.*	*Includes all domestic and regional developments in Asian and Pacific nations (and colonies).*

	U.S. Politics & Social Issues	U.S. Foreign Policy & Affairs, Defense	U.S. Economy & Environment	Science, Technology & Nature	Culture, Leisure & Lifestyle
Mar. 13		President Harding states that he believes that having the largest navy would be an incentive for peace, giving additional scope in negotiations with other countries; the result is that plans for a continued naval building program will go on.			
Mar. 14	Dr. James Whitney Hall blames Prohibition for a 25 percent increase in insanity cases.	Secretary of State Charles Evans Hughes states that the United States will seek to build closer and friendlier relations with central and South America.... The transport ship Somme returns 1,609 bodies of American troops killed in France.			
Mar. 15	The national American Council is formed with the purpose of encouraging what is termed "Americanization," to, among other things, combat "un-American and disloyal propaganda."	The U.S. State Department receives a report from the Italian government, which indicates that the financial state of Italy continues to improve.	The Chairman of the American Association of Railway Executives states that the recent incidences of railways cutting wages for workers have all been independent actions and that there has been no collusion among railroads.... The Bureau of Public Roads reports that there are 9,211,295 registered autos in the United States, an increase of 1,645,849 over the previous year.	Experiments are being conducted at the Dunning State Asylum in Illinois, near Chicago to see the effects of music on mentally ill patients.	
Mar. 16	In Ohio 300 men go on strike against Standard Oil Company in response to the company's announcement that wages would be cut and the workday lengthened.	The Harding Administration announces that the Unknown Soldier will be buried on Armistice Day, November 11.			Charles A. Comiskey, owner of the White Sox, states that the players accused of throwing the 1919 World Series have been released from the White Sox baseball club.
Mar. 17	The state of Nevada announces it will use poison gas to for executions replacing hanging and firing squads.	A U.S. Navy balloon with three men aboard at Guantanamo Bay, Cuba, breaks away from its moorings and has drifted out to sea.... The U.S. Submarine, *N-2*, runs aground near Watch Hill, RI.	The American Tobacco Company states that last year it made $18,615,398, a drop from 1919, which had been the largest in the company's history.	A black sea devil catfish, weighing 2,000 pounds is caught off Palm Beach, FL.	The State of New York passes a law making it a felony to "throw" a professional baseball game.... The prosecutor in the case against the baseball players accused of throwing the 1919 world Series refuses to continue the trial because of a failure to gain the delay he requested; he states he will seek a reindictment.
Mar. 18		In both cabinet meetings held by President Harding and in comments made by Senators, there is a visible effort to push international affairs to the back and concentrate on domestic issues.			The Chicago prosecutor states that he has started a second investigation into the alleged throwing of the World Series in 1919 and may indict a greater number of individuals the second time.

	World Affairs	Europe	Africa & The Middle East	The Americas	Asia & The Pacific
Mar. 19		Fighting in Cork, Ireland, has resulted in the death of 15 and several wounded; the British capture 20 members of Sinn Fein....Germany orders the last of the Russian prisoners of war from the World War to leave Germany; currently there are 43,000 left....Germany's Reichstag approves a measure that will cut the size of the army to 100,000 men....Francisca Lasheras of the Spanish village of Calerno is murdered by inhabitants after being accused as a witch.		Panama's objections to the proposed Panama-Costa Rica boundary dispute brokered by the United States are rejected by President Harding.	The U.S. commercial attaché in China reports great success in using films to convince producers of goods such as silk to sell their goods to U.S. merchants....The Yokohama, Japan silk market is reported very firm in light of increased demand for raw silk and increasing pieces.
Mar. 20		A plebiscite in Silesia partitions the province between Germany and Poland....Threats have been made against British officers monitoring the Silesian elections....The Italian volcano, Stromboli, erupts; the smoke can be seen for several miles.			Rebellion against the Soviets continues to grow; reports describe strong efforts against the Soviets in the Lake Baikal region of Siberia.
Mar. 21		King Nikola, deposed king of Montenegro, dies....The results of the Silesian plebiscite seem to indicate that Germany will keep upper Silesia whole Poland will take Lower Silesia....British aircraft are once again providing cross-channel flight to France at lower rates than what had been charged earlier.		Honduras announces that it is prohibiting the importation of all silver coins except for American dollars....The first duel fought under Uruguay's recently legalized dueling law, results in the death of Captain Melo of the Uruguayan Army.	A train wreck in a tunnel in Japan results in 10 killed and 50 injured.
Mar. 22	The League of Nations issues mandates for territories in the Pacific and in Africa to be administered by New Zealand, Australia, and Britain.	Reports state that Communists in Germany have received orders from Moscow to begin strikes and other disorders in Germany....The Soviets are reported to be placing very large orders for tools and farm implements from German factories....The French government announces that will give up its oil monopoly; gas and oil will be sold by private companies....The French government states its belief that the Plebiscite in Silesia justifies giving all mines there to Poland.			The Soviets hold the city of Batum on the Black Sea; all Americans have been evacuated from that city and are now in Constantinople.
Mar. 23	The Allied Commission receives a note from Germany concerning the war reparations owed by Germany; Germany states in its note that it does not owe the reparations and could not pay them even if it did.	The German government announces that in May it will begin trials for men accused of having committed war crimes during the World War....Reports from Latvia state that there may be two additional army mutinies by Soviet troops against the government....There is more violence in Ireland as 63 have been killed and 67 wounded in the past five days....A bomb, supposedly planted by anarchists goes off in a theater in Milan, Italy, killing 20 and injuring many.	The Greek offensive against the Turks is said to have started with King Constantine expected to lead the Army in person.		Pope Benedict XV is heading a subscription effort to relieve the famine in China.
Mar. 24	French government officials state that if Germany does not pay its war reparations it is possible that France may order troops to occupy Berlin.	Sinn Fein attempts to rescue prisoners in Cork who are sentenced to die, but fails in the attempt.... Fighting breaks out between the Lithuanian Army and Polish troops, which have seized a town near the city of Vilna....Two members of the Fascist party challenge the head of the Soviet Mission to a duel after he accused them of being "ill bred."...Another explosion in Milan, this time in reprisal for yesterday's theater bombing, kills 31 and injures 100.	Greece reports dramatic successes as its troops attack Turkish troops advancing up to 19 miles....France declares that it will set up mandates in the former African possessions of Germany, Togoland, and Cameroun, with approval of the League of Nations.	The League of Nations states that it has not received any official word that Nicaragua will leave the League although it knows of that country's complaints about the expense of membership....There is great concern that large numbers of Communists will be arriving in Mexico to assist labor unions there in overthrowing the government.	

A	B	C	D	E
Includes developments that affect more than one world region, international organizations and important meetings of world leaders.	*Includes all domestic and regional developments in Europe, including the Soviet Union.*	*Includes all domestic and regional developments in Africa and the Middle East.*	*Includes all domestic and regional developments in Latin America, the Caribbean, and Canada.*	*Includes all domestic and regional developments in Asian and Pacific nations (and colonies).*

U.S. Politics & Social Issues	U.S. Foreign Policy & Affairs, Defense	U.S. Economy & Environment	Science, Technology & Nature	Culture, Leisure & Lifestyle	
Adolphus Ross, an African American, charged with assaulting a woman is taken from jail by a mob, hanged to a tree, and shot repeatedly in Water Valley, MS.…In Williamson, WV, the jury in the Matewan Battle Trial has not returned a verdict.… The Woman's National Party will begin its campaign for legislation to remove all sex discrimination in laws made by the U.S. Congress.… Governor Kilby of Alabama, as arbitrator in the recent coal strikes in that state, declares against the miners, stating that the coalmine owners and operators have been fair and that they are not bound to recognize unions or reemploy men who have gone out on strike.		A grain elevator in Chicago explodes due to the combustion of grain dust; four are killed and a dozen injured while the financial loss is estimated to be $10 million.…The Department of Agriculture announces that in 1920 Americans ate 154.3 pounds of meat and lard per person, 10 pounds less than in 1918.		The Boston Symphony Orchestra under the direction of Pierre Monteaux presents a concert in New York, featuring music by Liszt and Wagner.…John Philip Sousa announces that he will take his band for a tour of Mexico and other Latin American Countries, starting in August; this is the 29th season that the band has toured.	Mar. 19
The Knights of Columbus report on their Americanization program conducted in 132 schools in which 50,000 are said to be learning about citizenship.					Mar. 20
The total number of Coal Mine deaths in the United States was 2,260 in 1920, 57 less than the preceding year.…The Young Women's Christian Association asks William Jennings Bryan to run for President in 1924.	Secretary of Commerce Herbert Hoover states that he is opposed to negotiating any trade agreement with the Soviet Union.			A survey of marriages in Massachusetts indicates that most women marry between the ages of 27 and 33, while most men are between 30 and 40; the reasons for people waiting are given to be unemployment, housing shortages, and the cost of living.	Mar. 21
Samuel Rea, President of the Pennsylvania Railroad appeals to the employees to stay with the railroad and that there will be no unfair cuts in wages.…The California legislature authorizes the establishment of separate schools for Japanese in the state although these separate schools will not be mandatory.…The Vice President of the Pennsylvania System Railway admits that his railroad used spies to disrupt unions as well as maintaining its own arsenal of weapons to be used against the unions.	A free balloon with a crew of five men takes off from the Naval station at Pensacola.…The superdreadnought battleship, USS *Colorado*, is launched from the New York Shipbuilding Company at Camden, NJ.…American troops on occupation duty have been hit with an influenza epidemic; none are reported to have died so far.…In a recently published book, Admiral Bradley Fiske criticizes the way in which Secretary of War Josephus Daniels managed the Navy in the World War.				Mar. 22
New England railroads lay off 1,700 men.…The State of New York passes a bill requiring all teachers in the public school systems to take an oath of allegiance to the flag and Federal and State Constitutions.		The average American consumed 44 gallons of milk in 1920 according to the Department of Agriculture.	Dr. Nathan Raw of the Tuberculosis Society of Great Britain announces that he believes he has found a vaccine against tuberculosis.…T.S. Casner and Oliver Badger have perfected a self-winding clock that is corrected daily by a wireless message from the Washington Observatory each day at noon.	Ten women at Columbia University have formed a class that will prepare them to assume management positions in banks.…California movie houses will ban all films made by Clara Smith Hamon, despite the fact that she has been acquitted of killing her husband.	Mar. 23
Socialist Leader Eugene Debs confers with Attorney General Daugherty on the possibility of a pardon, which had been refused earlier by the Wilson administration.		Tornadoes strike Tennessee and Kentucky creating damage and killing at least three with 10 seriously injured.…International Harvester Company announces it will reduce wages between 6–20 percent for its workers and will be laying off several thousand of their 45,000-employee workforce.			Mar. 24

	World Affairs	Europe	Africa & The Middle East	The Americas	Asia & The Pacific
Mar. 25		A Sinn Fein arsenal in Dublin is seized by the British; three autos, two motorcycles, as well as guns and bombs are seized....Spain's King Alfonso XIII plans to give pardons as well as including the sentence of death for six men.			The Soviets have been negotiating and signing treaties with Persia, Afghanistan, and Turkey in order to minimize British influence in the area....Thousands are reported dying and nine million are starving in the Chinese famine; American relief work is being sent there.
Mar. 26	The Heads of the National Red Cross Organizations are preparing to meet in Switzerland for the first time since before the World War.	British soldiers and constables wreck a house and several shops in reprisal for the killing of British personnel by Sinn Fein....Several anti-Soviet uprising are now reported along the Volga River, in the Kazan region, and western Russia....Reports in Germany describe increased Communist activity with barricades set up in several cities.	Greek forces continue to make good progress across the Turkish countryside.	African-American leader Marcus Garvey is on a speaking tour in Jamaica where he is being very well received.	Australia reports that its gold production in 1920 was the lowest of any year since 1851.
Mar. 27		The Swiss government extends the workweek from 48 to 52 hours a week to assist the country in its economic recovery....Fascists parade in Rome demonstrating against the most recent attack on a theater in Milan.	A Turkish airbase is bombed as the Greek Army continues to advance across Turkey.		A fire in Tokyo destroys 1,000 buildings resulting in a loss estimated at $12.5 million and leaving thousands homeless.
Mar. 28		Diplomats in Europe state that they believe that Germany may be paying its reparations....A British motor convoy in Silesia is bombed while the French government reports that its troops there have been infiltrated by Communists.	A law is being considered by the Turkish Assembly to make it mandatory for all men 25 years or older to be married....The Greek Army has captured an important junction of the Baghdad Railway in Turkey as it continues to advance.		The Chinese government expresses concerns that the Manchu dynasty is planning a coup to return to power.
Mar. 29		The British government forbids the importation of weapons and explosives into the United Kingdom, this includes Ireland....James Crawford, an American engineer just back from visiting the Soviet Union says that the Soviets are on the brink of losing power....Italian police have discovered an anarchist plot in Florence and in Genoa, police arrest an anarchist with a bomb and ammunition....Former King Charles is said to be in Hungary, conferring with Admiral Horthy and other government officials in an effort to return as King.	The Greek government reports that it is driving the Turkish government eastward and the way is clear to capture Turkey's capital at Ankara.	Panama's President Porras warns the National Assembly that if it refuses to accept the border settlement provided by the United States, that U.S. support for the country may end.	The Chinese government signs a contract by which the Federal Telegraph Company, an American company, will build a radio station in Shanghai.
Mar. 30		Riots and disorders inspired and led by Communists are breaking out all over Germany; Berlin is quiet but there is rioting in the Belgian-occupied regions as well as in Cologne, while one city in eastern Germany reports 50 Communists killed....In the wake of his failed attempt to regain the Hungarian throne, Charles states he may go to Spain.		Mexico's President Obregon criticizes the oil companies, stating the U.S. government campaign against Mexico is backed by the oil companies themselves....The U.S. State Department sends a diplomatic note to Mexico asking the government to take action in the case of three Americans killed there....This year's sugar crop in Cuba is approximately a million tons short of expectations.	
Mar. 31		Six British police are killed when Sinn Fein blows up a barracks near the city of Cork....Eamon de Valera states that Sinn Fein will participate in all of the upcoming elections....It appears that Charles, after having failed to return as Hungary's King, will go back into exile in Switzerland....Czechoslovakia, Romania, and Yugoslavia threaten to invade Hungary if Charles is installed as king.	Winston Churchill tells the Arabs of Palestine that the Balfour agreement giving Jews a homeland must stand.		

U.S. Politics & Social Issues	U.S. Foreign Policy & Affairs, Defense	U.S. Economy & Environment	Science, Technology & Nature	Culture, Leisure & Lifestyle	
Former President William Howard Taft visits President Harding reviving speculation that Taft may be nominated to the Supreme Court.		Because demand for coal has been so low, it is estimated that 100,000 members of the United Mine Workers have not worked since January 1.	Scientists in Pittsburgh, PA, claim to have found the secret behind the aluminum alloy that Germany has used in constructing its dirigibles.		Mar. 25
In Delaware, four African Americans are punished by being publicly whipped and then imprisoned for larceny and highway robbery.				Karl Muck, former conductor of the Boston Symphony Orchestra and imprisoned in the United States during the War, denies all accusations that he was involved in espionage.…The film, *The Four Horsemen of the Apocalypse*, starring Rudolph Valentino, opens in New York.…The Chicago prosecutor has now indicted 18 men for their roles in the 1919 World Series scandal.	Mar. 26
A coroner's jury is investigating the apparent murder of at least 11 African Americans at a plantation owned by John Williams.	The 27th Infantry Division, a New York National Guard unit, will create an aerial unit that will be assigned to the Division.	The Women's Bureau of the Department of Labor reports that women are capable of working in transit jobs as conductors and ticket agents.	The Bureau of Standards reports that an invention to record radio signals has been successfully developed.		Mar. 27
U.S. Senator Penrose, from Pennsylvania, tells a delegation visiting him that he favors a Pennsylvania bill being consider that would give African Americans equal rights.…President Harding watches 50,000 people, mostly children, roll Easter eggs on the White House lawn.					Mar. 28
A warehouse in Chicago, leased by a fireworks company, blows up; the explosion of two tons of gunpowder and fireworks kills eight and injures approximately 75.…Henry Ford's weekly newspaper, *The Dearborn Independent* will not be sold in Cincinnati, OH; the city passes an ordnance that prohibits publications "that hold up to ridicule any race, creed or religion."	A U.S. Army balloon at the Army Balloon School in Arcadia, CA, explodes, injuring nine.	Between 6,000 and 7,000 men will be returning to work at the Willys-Overland company in Toledo, OH, in April; auto tire factories in Akron are also taking new orders.…The Federal Reserve Bank of Minnesota states that the cost of living in the Western United States has decreased by more than 9 percent.		President Harding has been assured of a seat for this year's World Series.	Mar. 29
The Attorney General of Michigan declares that beer is a beverage and not a medicine and is subject to the laws of prohibition.		Oil stocks in the United States increased 7.5 million barrels in February according to the Geological Survey; domestic production is now averaging more than 130,000 barrels a day.			Mar. 30
The Census Bureau reports that according to the 1920 census, illiteracy in the United States is decreasing in the first three states where results have been tabulated.	The Secretary of the Navy announces an investigation will be conducted into the disappearance of the balloon that departed from Pensacola on March 22.…Former Secretary of War Newton Baker is attacked by the Commander of the American Legion for the poor treatment disabled veterans have received from the government.	Tidewater Oil reports its 1920 profits are up from 1919.…New York State Income Tax returns indicate that half of all of those filing had incomes between $1,000 and $2,000 in 1920.		Harvard announces that it will make tests on the Bible a part of the series of exams seniors must pass in order to graduate.…Beniamino Gigli will sing in *La Boheme* at the Metropolitan Opera.	Mar. 31

F	G	H	I	J
Includes campaigns, elections, federal-state relations, civil rights and liberties, crime, the judiciary, education, healthcare, poverty, urban affairs, and population.	*Includes formation and debate of U.S. foreign and defense policies, veterans affairs, and defense spending. (Relations with specific foreign countries are usually found under the region concerned.)*	*Includes business, labor, agriculture, taxation, transportation, consumer affairs, monetary and fiscal policy, natural resources, pollution and industrial accidents.*	*Includes worldwide scientific, medical and technological developments, natural phenomena, U.S. weather and natural disasters.*	*Includes the arts, religion, scholarship, communications media, sports, entertainment, fashions, fads, and social life.*

	World Affairs	Europe	Africa & The Middle East	The Americas	Asia & The Pacific
Apr. 1		A nationwide coal miners strike begins throughout Britain....Lord Edmund Talbot, a Catholic, is chosen to be British Viceroy of Ireland....Switzerland will admit former King Charles of Hungary after his failed attempt to return to rule....Last week's casualties in Ireland were 18 killed and 28 wounded among British personnel....Belgians occupying part of Germany arrest 281 Communists.	Winston Churchill promises Arabs in Palestine that they will keep their rights; he states that Palestine is to be "a" and not "the" national home of the Jews.	The French flier, Adrienne Boland, becomes the first woman to fly over the Andes from Mendoza, Argentina, to Santiago, Chile.... Businessmen in Cuba are expressing concern over a proposed tariff before the U.S. Congress that would raise the import duties on sugar brought into the United States.	
Apr. 2		Despite the fact that he is a Catholic, the appointment of Lord Talbot as Viceroy of Ireland is not well received by the Irish....The Dutch government announces that it will be providing a loan to the German government.		A member of the Cuban Congress, Fernando Quinones, is gunned down in Havana by Ernesto Collado, another member of Congress.	The Japanese government states that its policies are purely defensive and regrets that other nations have received a different impression during recent negotiations about concessions in China.
Apr. 3		Miners in Spain are threatening to go on strike in response to a cut in wages....Ex-King Charles is still in Hungary, although he has been allowed exile in Switzerland; his claims to being ill are not accepted by many within Hungary, both those for and against.	Mustafa Kemal, leader of Turkey announces that in a great battle at Eski-Shehr, the Greek Army has been defeated and is now retreating back to the coast.		
Apr. 4		The Romanian government adopts a law creating a national monopoly on oil in which all drilling operations will be supervised by the government as well as domestic prices....Reports from London claim that Lenin has given orders for Soviet Trade Agents to instigate strikes and unrest....Dutch stocks, with the exception of Royal Dutch Shell and Holland-America, are declining in price.	Prince Andreas, brother of Greece's King Constantine, is reported killed in the retreat from the Turkish Army.	The Mexican Petroleum Company stock is selling at a record low, largely due to the drop in oil prices....The House of Representatives in Cuba has not proclaimed the new President as most members of the Liberal Party have avoided the session.	The Jewish community in the city of Vladivostok is appealing to the Zionist organization in London because of the likelihood of pogroms.
Apr. 5		A group of German mine operators and manufacturers are attempting to boycott all British, French, and Belgian goods in retaliation for the penalties being assessed with Germany's war reparations....Fascists, aided by regular Italian troops, battle Croatians near the city of Trieste; several are killed and at least 100 injured in the fighting that began when the Croats attacked Italian positions....Parcels containing bombs are found throughout Berlin; they are believed to have been planted by the Communists.	Zaghlul Pasha, a very popular nationalist leader returns to Egypt where he is welcomed by large and enthusiastic crowds.	Statements by Mexican Petroleum, directly contradicting those recently made about its value, announces that its gross income for March will equal the largest earnings in its history.	The Persian government announces that it wishes to cancel the treaty it has with Britain and for all foreign troops to be withdrawn.

U.S. Politics & Social Issues	U.S. Foreign Policy & Affairs, Defense	U.S. Economy & Environment	Science, Technology & Nature	Culture, Leisure & Lifestyle	
	The Secretary of War orders 235 additional airplanes for the Army; 200 will be pursuit planes and 35 will be bombers.…The U.S. State Department notifies Panama that there will be no change on its part toward the proposed settlement of the border between Panama and Costa Rica.…President Harding's cabinet upholds the demands of the Allies that Germany pay war reparations.	The Stutz Motor Company, maker of the Bearcat, reports that its profits for 1920 $1,027,385, a drop from 1919.			Apr. 1
New York City police report 21 vehicles were stolen in one day.…Alex Johnson, an African-American bellboy in Dallas, TX, is kidnapped by masked men, whipped, then, with acid, the letters "KKK" are branded on his forehead.		In Salt Lake City, the wage of painters has been reduced from $8.00 a day to $7.20; plumbers' wages are reduced from $9.00 to $8.00 a day.…The Department of Commerce reports that the U.S. exports more copper to Germany than any other country and more cotton than any other country except Britain.…The Airmail Service reports that in the three years that the Service has been operating 49 million letters have been transported by air.		Columbia's summer session will enroll 10,000 students; among the faculty members will be Robert Frost and William Allen White.…The *New York Times* reviews *The Trembling of a Leaf*, the latest book by Somerset Maugham.…According to the American Library Association, the two most popular authors among American soldiers in the Army of Occupation are Julius Caesar and Zane Grey.	Apr. 2
In the House of Representatives, the Republican majority is so great that the leadership is having difficulty in determining committee assignments, 300 republicans to be assigned to 10 committees.	The National Disabled Soldiers' League criticizes the care given to veterans by the government; the organization claims that 70,000 mentally ill veterans have not been cared for.	The United States Corporation announces it is planning a reduction to an eight-hour day for its workers.…In order to save money, the Maine Central Railroad suspends Sunday operations.			Apr. 3
A speaker at the annual Methodist Conference states that Prohibition is winning and that in its first year has been a success.…An anti-Prohibition meeting with more than 1,500 participants rallies to oppose Prohibition.…John Williams of Jasper County, GA, goes on trial today for the murder of 11 of his African-American farmhands.…Sandy Thompson, an African American who allegedly shot and killed a planter, is lynched near Langford, MS.…The number of jobless in Chicago is more than 100,000.	The State Department announces Americans do not have to have their passports to either leave or enter the country.	Six steel mills in Ohio resume operations after having been closed or working at reduced capacity for two months.			Apr. 4
U.S. Senators, as a group, favor a "Monroe Doctrine for all the World" in which the United States will not have alliances but will stand for world peace.	Gold Star Mothers (mothers who have lost sons in the war) testify before Congress along with veterans concerning the poor treatment disabled veterans have received from the government.	The average of prices in the United States has declined by 4 percent in the past month.	Greek archaeologists have discovered a large temple in an excellent state of preservation.	Leopold Stokowski ends his concerts with the Philadelphia Orchestra in New York with an all-Tchaikovsky program.	Apr. 5

F	G	H	I	J
Includes campaigns, elections, federal-state relations, civil rights and liberties, crime, the judiciary, education, healthcare, poverty, urban affairs, and population.	*Includes formation and debate of U.S. foreign and defense policies, veterans affairs, and defense spending. (Relations with specific foreign countries are usually found under the region concerned.)*	*Includes business, labor, agriculture, taxation, transportation, consumer affairs, monetary and fiscal policy, natural resources, pollution and industrial accidents.*	*Includes worldwide scientific, medical and technological developments, natural phenomena, U.S. weather and natural disasters.*	*Includes the arts, religion, scholarship, communications media, sports, entertainment, fashions, fads, and social life.*

	World Affairs	Europe	Africa & The Middle East	The Americas	Asia & The Pacific
Apr. 6		British authorities state they are not seeking to arrest Eamon de Valera because they see him as a moderate who will aid in establishing the peace in Ireland.…Cardinal Bourne of Dublin informs the British Prime Minister that the Black and Tan Constabulary should be withdrawn.…A spokesman for Sinn Fein states that he expects that the Vatican will give the same support to Irish nationalists as was given to Poland during the World War.…Fighting between Italians and Croatians in the region near Trieste continues.	Fighting has diminished somewhat on the Turkish-Greek front.	General Manuel Palaez, former commander of Federal troops in the Tampico region, will visit the United States, Britain, and France on a diplomatic mission.…The Chilean government announces that a consortium of German farmers is seeking to buy 50,000 tons of nitrate.…Jamaican workers traveling to Cuba to harvest sugar cane find that there are few jobs this season and they have all been taken by Cubans.	A fire in Tokyo leaves 1,000 homeless.
Apr. 7		At least eight are killed and two are wounded in street fighting in Dublin between Sinn Fein and the British Constabulary.		Chile's currency falls on both the American and London currency markets, in large part because of the country's economic crisis and the lack of demand for nitrates, Chile's biggest export.	Members of the Japanese Imperial Navy state that their plan for eight battleships could be modified to allow a reduction as Japan is not trying to compete with the U.S. Navy.…Sun Yat-sen is elected as President of China.
Apr. 8		King George V calls up the armed reserves, as a potential strike of 2.5 million workers appears certain in sympathy with the Miners' strike.…Moscow has absorbed the White Russia (Belorussia) region.…Fighting between Fascists and anarchists in the Italian city of Padua has resulted in one killed, several injured, and 39 anarchists arrested.	The League of Nations declares that the British mandate in Iraq will be discussed in June.…The Zionist Organization in Palestine will support raising a number of Jewish regiments to assist the British in maintaining order in the Mandate.…Greek forces continue their retreat, now 25 miles from the Baghdad railway junction they had captured a few days ago.		Reports from the U.S. commercial attaché in China report a large amount of manufactured goods are being imported into China from Germany.
Apr. 9		One person is killed and six are injured in a gunfight between the British and Sinn Fein in Limerick.	Greece still maintains a front that it will win the war against the Turks although most observers are noting the recent successes of Mustafa Kemal in the field.	A delegation from the Mexican government is received by President Harding who expresses hope that the two countries can enjoy closer trade relations.	
Apr. 10		Striking miners in Spain are now commonly seen on the roads begging for food.…British police in Ireland capture 10 truckloads of arms from Sinn Fein; houses in Limerick are destroyed in reprisal for an ambush of British troops.…The Women's Suffrage Convention opens in Athens; King Constantine and Queen Sophia attend.	Forces under Mustafa Kemal counterattack the Greeks and drive them back; the Turks are actively seeking French assistance against Britain, which is supporting Greece.	Observers from the Guaranty Trust Bank state that the current depression in Peru is not serious; even though there are currency and financial problems, there is still a fair level of optimism.	The Chairman of the American Committee for China Famine states that more than $2 million has been sent to aid in the relief effort.
Apr. 11		Soviet officials have determined that gold watches are a luxury and that all gold watches are to be gathered up for foreign trade.…Twelve Soviet officials responsible for food distribution have been sentenced to death for corruption.…The Allied Commission in Silesia uncovers a German plot to seize the region for Germany.		Standard Oil of New Jersey is very close to reaching a deal with the government of Venezuela to develop oil drilling near Lake Maracaibo.	
Apr. 12	The United States receives word that neither the Soviet Union nor Latvia will admit 35 political radicals that the United States is seeking to deport.	A dispatch from Finland claims that there are currently 100,000 political prisoners in the Soviet Union.…The Hungarian government states that Charles is its lawful sovereign and would have allowed him to rule if it had not been for foreign intervention; it then asks Switzerland to grant the ex-king exile in Switzerland.…Anti-Soviet revolts, led principally by General Antonov, are active in southern Russia.	Mustafa Kemal is receiving aid from the Italian government in return for economic concessions.		The Japanese government proposes sending a mission to Washington to discuss the Yap mandate, Japanese immigration to the United States, and arms limitation.
	A	B	C	D	E
	Includes developments that affect more than one world region, international organizations and important meetings of world leaders.	*Includes all domestic and regional developments in Europe, including the Soviet Union.*	*Includes all domestic and regional developments in Africa and the Middle East.*	*Includes all domestic and regional developments in Latin America, the Caribbean, and Canada.*	*Includes all domestic and regional developments in Asian and Pacific nations (and colonies).*

U.S. Politics & Social Issues	U.S. Foreign Policy & Affairs, Defense	U.S. Economy & Environment	Science, Technology & Nature	Culture, Leisure & Lifestyle	
Sheriff John Logan of Polk County, FL, saves Wilmer Collins, an African American, from being lynched by deputizing a mob and charging them with assisting him in transporting the prisoner to Bartow, then speeding away with his prisoner before they can react.…A witness testifies that John Williams chained two of his workers and then threw them off a bridge; they were killed to prevent details of slave-like conditions on the Williams farm, which was being investigated by Federal agents.		Unemployment has increased nationwide in the past month; one exception is in Detroit where the auto industry is beginning to revive.			Apr. 6
John Williams denies murdering his African-American farmhands although he admits the conditions they worked under, saying that on most Georgia farms the conditions are the same.		According to toy manufacturers, sales of dolls in the first quarter of 1921 have been excellent and exceeded sales in the first quarter of 1920.	A French scientist claims that he has been able to develop a means to detect icebergs even in the fog using ultra-red light wave radiation.		Apr. 7
The trial of John Williams for the murder of his farmhands goes to the jury.…President Harding is studying current highway projects throughout the nation and states he is against large Federal outlays of funds that do not take into account maintenance of the roadways.		Petroleum output continues to increase; production for the week ending April 2 shows a daily average of 1,263,370 barrels.	A partial eclipse of the sun is visible from Paris and London.	"Shoeless" Joe Jackson, Charles "Swede" Risberg, and Claude Williams, three former members of the White Sox who have been released because of their alleged activities in the 1919 World Series are forming their own baseball team and will play against independent clubs.…Child actor Jackie Coogan arrives in Chicago on his way to New York to sign a $300,000 a year contract.	Apr. 8
John Williams is convicted of the murder of his farmhands and receives a life sentence.…James Jones, formerly a servant of Confederate President Jefferson Davis dies; he had buried the Great Seal of the Confederate States, and was the only person to know where it was and died without telling anyone.		The National Industrial Conference Board reports that the cost of living in the United States has dropped by 17 percent; at the same time, the unemployment rate in the country has risen.		Enrico Caruso's health continues to improve although he still cannot sing.	Apr. 9
The number of unemployed in Philadelphia is 150,000 and it expected to grow.	The War Department is planning to establish training camps for men in the coming summer on the Plattsburgh model.		Albert Einstein begins the first of three lectures at Columbia University.	The Tupper House in Sandwich, MA, built in 1636, is burned to the ground as the result of arson.	Apr. 10
The Governor of Iowa signs a bill legalizing cigarettes in the state.	The War Department reports on the expenditures of the Air Service during the World War; the cost of the Air Service was $598,090,781 and not the $1 billion that critics had claimed.				Apr. 11
The Commonwealth of Massachusetts may authorize a bill that would allow cities and towns to bottle soft drinks to include beverages containing less than 5 percent alcohol; this law would include root beer, ginger ale, and unfermented grape juice.…The Reverend Nikolai Velimirovic, Bishop of Ochrida, Serbia, speaking in New York criticizes American levity and says that Americans do not understand the world's agony.		The American commercial attaché in Denmark reports that the nations in the Baltic area would be a good place for American businesses to do business.			Apr. 12
F *Includes campaigns, elections, federal-state relations, civil rights and liberties, crime, the judiciary, education, healthcare, poverty, urban affairs, and population.*	G *Includes formation and debate of U.S. foreign and defense policies, veterans affairs, and defense spending. (Relations with specific foreign countries are usually found under the region concerned.)*	H *Includes business, labor, agriculture, taxation, transportation, consumer affairs, monetary and fiscal policy, natural resources, pollution and industrial accidents.*	I *Includes worldwide scientific, medical and technological developments, natural phenomena, U.S. weather and natural disasters.*	J *Includes the arts, religion, scholarship, communications media, sports, entertainment, fashions, fads, and social life.*	

	World Affairs	Europe	Africa & The Middle East	The Americas	Asia & The Pacific
Apr. 13		As a result of the failed attempt to bring Charles back as King of Hungary, the Hungarian government under Pal Teleki falls.…Three Sinn Fein candidates are running for the Ulster Parliament including Eamon de Valera.…Sinn Fein attacks a prison in Cork; using flares, guards armed with machine guns drive back the attack.		Chile's cabinet presents its collective resignations to President Allesandri over the legislature's refusal to approve the nomination of Chile's ambassador to France.	
Apr. 14		Count Istvan Bethlen forms a new government in Hungary.…The Soviet Press reports that American engineers in 1916 proposed a canal connecting the Baltic with the White Sea; the canal was not begun but there are proposals to let Americans dig a canal there now.…Russian miners applaud the British miners for beginning the "class war against the bourgeoisie."…The French government announces plans to increase the size of its Navy.	An attack by 30,000 Turks against the Greeks is reported to have failed; 6,000 prisoners are taken.	The Colombian government denies it is sending weapons to Panama to aid it in its dispute with Costa Rica.	A fire in the city of Hokodate, Japan destroys 4,000 houses.
Apr. 15	France warns the Austrian government that it will cease all aid if the Austrians continue their movement to unite with Germany.	There are 26 British casualties for the past week in fighting in Ireland; military casualties have increased while murders of police officers have decreased; there were 25 ambushes and six attacks on police barracks.…The French government states that it will take the Ruhr Valley if Germany defaults on its payments and tax the industrial activities in that region to get the reparations payments; Germany is attempting to develop alternative proposals.…A split in the Labor Party has effectively removed the chance of a general strike in Britain, leaving the coal miners on their own in their strike.	President King of Liberia is received by President Harding at the White House; negotiations for the hoped for loan of $5 million are progressing.	Cuban sugar manufacturers are rushing their stocks of sugar to the United States as quickly as possible to avoid what seems like an inevitable tariff applied to sugar imported into the United States.…Chile's currency continues to drop in value; Chile's currency problems are due in part to the apparent collapse of the nitrate market, as well as gold speculation that has hurt the value of the currency.	The arrival of General Leonard Wood is looked on with anticipation in the Philippines, as many observers believe he will be able to resolve many of the problems, including the future political status of the islands.
Apr. 16	France states that it may seize and occupy part of the German state of Westphalia; Germany has requested that Czechoslovakia act as an intermediary between Germany and the Allies on the payment issue but Czechoslovakia refuses.	Reports from the Soviet Union describe some of the opposition to Soviet rule including farmers killing Soviet officials who come to requisition food.…The British coalmine strike continues, but there is optimism that it can be resolved.…Lenin states that the New Economic Plan will save the revolution.…According to the U.S. Consul in Naples, Italy, the only limitation on the number of Italian immigrants to the United States will be the number of ships that can carry them.…The Polish Diet ratifies a peace treaty with the Soviets.		Peru bans importation of all firearms by individuals.	
Apr. 17	There is speculation that the German government may pay its reparations by offering to pay the debt that the Allies owe to the United States, paying it directly to the United States on their behalf.	Doctors in Avila, Spain, have gone on general strike.…The streets in Bologna and Mantua have seen street fights and gun battles between Fascists and Communists and Socialists.…Kitty MacCarron, aged 45, is the first woman to be executed by Sinn Fein; a card is left on her body accusing her of being a spy and informer.			
Apr. 18		Construction will soon begin on a wireless radio station in Pisa, Italy; transmissions to the United States are expected to start in 1922.…Fighting in Tuscany, Italy, rages between Fascists and Communists; 14 are killed and 100 are wounded.…German shipping is growing with more competition being given to American shipping companies.		Panama has been warned by the United States not to engage in any fighting with Costa Rica over the border, which has been settled by a U.S. Supreme Court Justice.…The province of Ontario votes again to enforce prohibition within the province, maintaining a law that became effective in 1916.	Japan insists that it has a right to administer the mandate over the island of Yap, which formerly belonged to Germany.…The Japanese army is recalling all Japanese nationals in foreign countries in the Pacific to return home for training.

A	B	C	D	E
Includes developments that affect more than one world region, international organizations and important meetings of world leaders.	*Includes all domestic and regional developments in Europe, including the Soviet Union.*	*Includes all domestic and regional developments in Africa and the Middle East.*	*Includes all domestic and regional developments in Latin America, the Caribbean, and Canada.*	*Includes all domestic and regional developments in Asian and Pacific nations (and colonies).*

U.S. Politics & Social Issues	U.S. Foreign Policy & Affairs, Defense	U.S. Economy & Environment	Science, Technology & Nature	Culture, Leisure & Lifestyle	
	Three Army airplanes leave Mitchell Field, NY, to begin bombing runs near Aberdeen, MD, on captured German ships.	President Harding announces he may call a railroad conference with workers and managers to reach a common agreement on the issue of wages.…The American Association of Advertising Agencies celebrates its 10th anniversary at a banquet at New York's Hotel Commodore.	The Pons-Winnecke comet is photographed by British astronomers.	On Opening Day in New York, the Yankees beat the Philadelphia Athletics 11–1 at the Polo Grounds.…President Harding throws out the first ball of the Senators' season, then watches them beaten by the Boston Red Sox 6–3.…Tenor Enrico Caruso continues to improve and plans a trip to Italy in May.	Apr. 13
A conference of farm and labor organizations meets in Washington to draft a statement defining a program of legislation.…Federal agents have continued their investigations into the Williams Plantation owned by John Williams and have raised the total of murders to 18, including an aged couple who were killed because they were too old to work; workers on the farm were fed and clothed but never paid.	The dirigible ZR-2, which has been under construction in Britain for the U.S. Navy, will be flown to the United States in July.…Secretary of War Weeks states that he wants the Army to be 175,000 and promises other economies so long as that figure can be maintained.…At least 100 wounded veterans have been turned away from the Soldier's Relief department in Boston because there were not enough clerks to handle their applications for assistance.	The income of the American Telephone and Telegraph Company for the first quarter of 1921 was $26,356,000.			Apr. 14
	Officials of the Army and the American Legion deny the accusations of Owen Wister (author of the novel, *The Virginian*) that the bodies of Americans returned from France are unclaimed and being sent to "potter's fields."…The State Department is asking the Congress to authorize legislation that would prohibit the shipment of arms or ammunition from the United States to any country.	Tide Water Motor Oil Company announces a reduction in the price on its Veedol Motor Oils, ranging from 13 percent to 24 percent.		The Black Sox, a team of former members of the 1919 White Sox and other players, has been banned from the Chicago Baseball League.	Apr. 15
Jacob Rubin of Milwaukee, WI, member of the Socialist Democratic Party, returns from a trip to the Soviet Union and declares that after his experience there he will never again participate in any Socialist political organization.	The Army's Chief of Cavalry issues a statement that when the current force reductions go into effect, the Army must keep at least 20,000 cavalry troopers for several tasks to include an effective border patrol.	Estimated per capita consumption of lumber in the United States is 307 board feet; in 1906, it was 515 board feet per person.…The radio market news service, operated by the Bureau of Markets, provides information to farmers by broadcasting news of markets by radio from four locations in the United States.		The Opera season at the Metropolitan is closing with performance of *Carmen*, *Andrea Chenier*, *Aida*, and *La Boheme*.…Composer Percy Grainger will be giving a concert of Tchaikovsky piano pieces.	Apr. 16
Evangelist Billy Sunday accuses anti-Prohibition men of having knocked down his mother's tombstone, torn up the fence around the grave, and then sent pictures around the country as a way of getting back at him.					Apr. 17
William Jennings Bryan pays a visit to President Harding.	Harry J. Boland, secretary to Eamon de Valera, addresses the convention of the American Association for the Recognition of the Irish republic with messages and greeting from de Valera and Michael Collins.				Apr. 18

F	G	H	I	J
Includes campaigns, elections, federal-state relations, civil rights and liberties, crime, the judiciary, education, healthcare, poverty, urban affairs, and population.	*Includes formation and debate of U.S. foreign and defense policies, veterans affairs, and defense spending. (Relations with specific foreign countries are usually found under the region concerned.)*	*Includes business, labor, agriculture, taxation, transportation, consumer affairs, monetary and fiscal policy, natural resources, pollution and industrial accidents.*	*Includes worldwide scientific, medical and technological developments, natural phenomena, U.S. weather and natural disasters.*	*Includes the arts, religion, scholarship, communications media, sports, entertainment, fashions, fads, and social life.*

	World Affairs	Europe	Africa & The Middle East	The Americas	Asia & The Pacific
Apr. 19		British troops attack Sinn Fein bands killing five, wounding two, and capturing six....The Allies declare that Germany must deposit in gold all that it owes as war reparations; refusal will be considered to be a violation of the Treaty of Versailles and will result in an occupation of the Ruhr Valley by the Allies....An alliance has been formed by France, Yugoslavia, and Czechoslovakia to prevent the union of Austria with Germany....The British government announces it is beginning the process that will lead to Irish Home Rule with a high degree of autonomy from Britain....Bands of Fascists roam the streets in several Italian cities looking for Communists.	The Turkish National Assembly chooses Ahmed, Chief of the Senussi as ruler of Iraq as an alternative to Prince Faisal, whom the British are attempting to install.	Bandits hold up a train in northern Mexico; the government sends troops after the raiders.	Japan's House of Peers is investigating the issue of League of Nations mandates in the hope of preserving Japan's hold on various claims in the Pacific; naval disarmament is also discussed.
Apr. 20	Observers describe the new countries carved out of the old Austro-Hungarian Empire as slowly recovering from the effects of the World War; Austria is making slow progress, while Czechoslovakia and Yugoslavia are doing well economically; Romania needs Allied assistance; despite recent attempts at reestablishing the Monarchy, Hungary is quiet and stable.	Italian Socialists demand that they be protected by the government from Fascist violence....The French government reports that for the first quarter of 1921 its exports have exceeded its imports....The Bank of Yugoslavia announces it will open a branch in New York City.	The Greek government, while denying that it was defeated by the Turks at the battle of Maksur, claim they have launched a major counterattack to hold the city of Ushak from the Turks.	The U.S. Secretary of War states that he will cut down the costs of administering the Canal Zone in Panama, which he characterizes as "extravagant."	
Apr. 21		A three-year investigation of Henri Girard by Paris Police has resulted in the arrest of Girard, his wife, and his mistress on charges of murder; Girard is accused of insuring his friends with himself as beneficiary and then poisoning them....Trotsky threatens Poland with a new invasion....The German government formally apologizes for an attack on Americans by a crowd of Germans in Potsdam; apparently the Americans were mistaken for a group of French tourists....British coal miners do not accept a new proposal.			
Apr. 22		Communists in Paris set up posters calling on Frenchmen not to answer the government's recent activation of the Army Reserves....The British government reports that in the past week there have been 29 attacks by Sinn Fein and the Irish Republican Army with 30 casualties....France's Premier Briand promises that France will get from Germany all of the reparations money that it is owed.		Refugees from Peru describe how President Leguia has established a dictatorship....The Argentine government is preparing a message that the United States should give the Dominican Republic its full freedom.	Opposition parties in Japan declare that the nation's foreign policy is disgraceful and that Japan should withdraw its occupation forces currently in Siberia.
Apr. 23		Romania and Czechoslovakia form a treaty to uphold the Treaty of Trianon, imposed on Hungary after the war, and to defend each other in the event of a Hungarian attack....A Sinn Fein attack on a British barracks results in three dead; a train of 34 cars is held up by 200 members of Sinn Fein....American IWW leader Bill Haywood is now in Moscow where he says he will help direct propaganda for Lenin....The French Chamber of Deputies passes an amnesty for French soldiers executed during the World War who had ignored an order to attack without artillery support....Anti-Soviet activity in the Ukraine is increasing; peasants under General Makno are successfully engaging Soviet troops.		Nicaragua withdraws from the League of Nations due to the expense of remaining in that organization.	China's leading imports from the United States are cigarettes, lamp oil, leaf tobacco, and dyes; in addition, the Chinese are also purchasing American locomotives (at least 42 last year) and autos.

A	B	C	D	E
Includes developments that affect more than one world region, international organizations and important meetings of world leaders.	*Includes all domestic and regional developments in Europe, including the Soviet Union.*	*Includes all domestic and regional developments in Africa and the Middle East.*	*Includes all domestic and regional developments in Latin America, the Caribbean, and Canada.*	*Includes all domestic and regional developments in Asian and Pacific nations (and colonies).*

U.S. Politics & Social Issues	U.S. Foreign Policy & Affairs, Defense	U.S. Economy & Environment	Science, Technology & Nature	Culture, Leisure & Lifestyle	
Postal employees will be armed with sawed-off shotguns as well as .45 caliber pistols to guard post offices against robberies.				Frank Zuna of New York wins the Boston Marathon; out of 77 starters, 34 runners finish the course; Zuna's time is two hours, 18 minutes, 57 seconds.…A sculpture by Rodin, entitled *The Kiss,* is sold at an auction in New York for $3,000.	Apr. 19
Mae McDonald, aged 17, is arrested by Chicago police on suspicion of being the "flapper bandit;" she denies the charges.	General John J. Pershing, who commanded American troops in France during the World War, is named to become the next Chief of Staff of the Army.…Professor W. Lee Lewis, inventor of Lewisite, one of the world's deadliest poisonous gases, predicts that future battleships may require a type of "gas mask" to be placed around the entire ship.	Railroad unions accuse the railroad companies of waste and inefficiency and that if these were corrected there would be no need to cut wages.	A total lunar eclipse is predicted that will be visible throughout eastern North and South America.	The New York Giants defeat the Boston Braves and take the lead in the National League.…Babe Ruth is cited for speeding on his way to play against the Boston Red Sox.	Apr. 20
"Professor" E.I. Bagonyer of Milltown, NJ, is arrested on a charge of witchcraft.		Crude oil output in the United States averaged 1,254,840 barrels a day for the week of April 16, a very slight drop from the week before.		George M. Cohan will reprise his play, *The Tavern*, with himself in the leading role.	Apr. 21
Women garment workers on strike in Boston attack a group of strikebreakers; two are arrested.…The Pejepscot Paper Company states it will not join in demands made by other paper companies; it will not cut wages and will not demand a working day longer than eight hours a day.		A broken connection at a N. J. chemical plant in Bound Brook releases a cloud of phosgene gas, killing one and injuring 100.			Apr. 22
The President of the Eastern States Mission of the Church of Latter Day Saints protests against an article in the *Cambridge History of American Literature*, which discusses *The Book of Mormon*.…The Detroit Police Department has installed a wireless radio station that allows it to communicate with any point in the United States.	According to the Commander of the American Legion, the number of mentally ill soldiers is rapidly increasing with 250 new cases in the state of New York alone.…The European Relief Council, directed by Herbert Hoover, has raised $29 million, $4 million short of its goal but reduced food requirements mean that it will still accomplish its goals.	Government figures indicate that American exports in March declined from February's figures as well as those for March 1920.…The American Petroleum Institute reports that gasoline consumption increased in March, especially in the Middle West.		The U.S. Bureau of Education reports that there has been a large increase in the number of American students attending British Universities.…A son is born to reputed con man "Nicky" Arnstein and actress Fanny Brice.…Andrew Corey, the "human fly," falls while climbing the Howard Hotel in Baltimore and dies.	Apr. 23
F *Includes campaigns, elections, federal-state relations, civil rights and liberties, crime, the judiciary, education, healthcare, poverty, urban affairs, and population.*	**G** *Includes formation and debate of U.S. foreign and defense policies, veterans affairs, and defense spending. (Relations with specific foreign countries are usually found under the region concerned.)*	**H** *Includes business, labor, agriculture, taxation, transportation, consumer affairs, monetary and fiscal policy, natural resources, pollution and industrial accidents.*	**I** *Includes worldwide scientific, medical and technological developments, natural phenomena, U.S. weather and natural disasters.*	**J** *Includes the arts, religion, scholarship, communications media, sports, entertainment, fashions, fads, and social life.*	

	World Affairs	Europe	Africa & The Middle East	The Americas	Asia & The Pacific
Apr. 24		Germany's sales to the United States in 1920 totaled $98,836,230, less than half of what Germany was selling to the United States before the World War.... The Tyrol region of Austria has cast ballots with 90 percent stating that they want Austria to be part of Germany.	Reports for 1920 indicate that Near East Relief, an American organization chartered by Congress, spent $13,129,117 to provide food and medial assistance in Turkey, Armenia, Syria, Kurdistan, Palestine, Iraq, and other areas.... Spain and Tangier reach an agreement over the extent of Spanish fishermen's rights.	A new revolution in Mexico has broken out under the leadership of Estaban Cantu who is recruiting out of work miners to his cause.	
Apr. 25				A Brazilian-American Chamber of Commerce is organized to improve trade relations between the two nations.	Although it has been officially denied, representatives of Standard Oil are offering a deal with the Dutch government to drill for oil in Indonesia.
Apr. 26		Serbia will employ 10,000 former members of the anti-Soviet forces to work on railroads and in the forests there; Japan will take on an additional 3,000 men from the same army to labor for the Japanese.... The Soviets are acting very aggressively to sign trading and commercial treaties with European nations.... In many parts of the Yugoslav coast, works of art left by the Italians from the years they occupied the region are destroyed by Slav nationalists.	British police in Constantinople halt rioting there between Jewish and Greek factions.		Japan's Foreign Minister, Viscount Uchida states that Japan has been pictured as a warlike nation but in reality is not.... The U.S. Department of State sends observers to Siberia to report on the state of the so-called Far Eastern Republic.
Apr. 27		At war crimes trials being held in Leipzig, Germany, 47 British witnesses testify against German officers who ran prison camps.... A pogrom in the Gomel region of Russia is said to have claimed several thousand lives with 60,000 survivors driven from their homes.... In the Italian city of Turin, Fascists burn down a building used by labor unions.	The Palestine Mandate budget calls for a budget that will create a Palestinian Defense Force made up of Jews and Arabs.	The Spanish government recognizes the Mexican President Obregon's government.	The Japanese commander at the occupied Russian city of Vladivostok commits suicide; his death is seen as the final act in a sequence of events that began with the shooting death of an American naval officer by a Japanese sentry in January.... The Philippine national Committee states that it wants the islands to be free and not to become an American state.
Apr. 28		Reports from Germany, England, and Sweden allege that large amounts of counterfeit money originating from the Soviet Union are appearing in great amounts.... The British execute four men in Cork for conducting attacks on the British soldiers and constables.... Germany's proposed payment plan for its war reparations is unanimously dismissed by the Allies.		Ten people are killed in the bloodiest payroll hold-up in the history of the Mexican oil fields when the payroll of the Agwi Oil Company in Tampico is taken.... A jury in Deming, NM, acquits a group of 16 Mexicans accused of being part of the Pancho Villa gang that attacked Columbus, NM, in 1916.	Rioting is reported in India; reports are sketchy because telegraph cables have been cut; troops have been sent to suppress the disorder.
Apr. 29		In a new book by Andre Tardieu, *The Peace*, he states that the French government was opposed to occupying the Ruhr Valley in 1919, a step that is seriously contemplated by the French now.... An American engineer, Royal C. Keely, who has been visiting Russia, is sentenced to two years in prison by the Soviets for "circulating false reports." ... The city of Fiume, which is contested by Italians and Croats, has been taken over by a band of fascists who claim to be Italian but are not recognized by the Italian government.			

A	B	C	D	E
Includes developments that affect more than one world region, international organizations and important meetings of world leaders.	*Includes all domestic and regional developments in Europe, including the Soviet Union.*	*Includes all domestic and regional developments in Africa and the Middle East.*	*Includes all domestic and regional developments in Latin America, the Caribbean, and Canada.*	*Includes all domestic and regional developments in Asian and Pacific nations (and colonies).*

U.S. Politics & Social Issues	U.S. Foreign Policy & Affairs, Defense	U.S. Economy & Environment	Science, Technology & Nature	Culture, Leisure & Lifestyle	
The American Defense Society proclaims that May 1 will be "America Day" to counter May Day rallies held by Communists and Socialists.... Talks are in progress between clothing manufacturers and members of the Ladies' Garment Workers Union; the main point of contention is a reduction in wages; if there is no agreement, a general strike will be called....FBI agents report that they have found another farm in Georgia where African Americans were forced to work in conditions similar to slavery where three were killed; the site under investigation is similar to that owned by recently convicted John Williams of Jasper County.					Apr. 24
Eleven members of the International Workers of the World (IWW) leadership are on their way to prison for obstruction of the draft act.		Secretary of Commerce Herbert Hoover will conduct a conference to discuss with business leaders the reorganization of the Commerce Department....A strike will be called to begin on May 1, over wage cuts by the engineers, seamen, and firemen of the Great Lakes ships.			Apr. 25
Tornadoes destroy every building but one in the town of Braxton, MS, killing more than 12 and injuring at least 20....The mother of a six-year old girl, suing for $20,000 in the wrongful death of her daughter, is awarded $800....The American Security League states that the apathy of Americans toward the dangers of May Day demonstrations by Communists and others is an indicator that patriotism needs to be awakened.				George Smiley of the Knoxville Pioneers makes an unassisted triple play, the first time this has ever been accomplished by an outfielder.	Apr. 26
General Pershing urges Americans to visit veterans' hospitals to see the conditions in which wounded veterans are treated....Senator Walsh states that the soldier aid system has broken down and has "failed miserably."				Former Chicago White Sox pitcher, Eddie Cicotte will appear voluntarily in Chicago to answer charges resulting from the 1919 World Series case; "Chick" Gandil, another former member of the team is also going to Chicago.	Apr. 27
Police in New York City are ready to combat any unrest that may break out on May 1 as a result of May Day demonstrations.		The Tennessee Copper and Chemical Corporation annual report for 1920 shows a total income of $6,079,699 compared with $4,236,280 for 1919....Commerce Secretary Hoover describes to the U.S. Chamber of Commerce his plan to have the government provide a wide-ranging statistical bureau to provide market information to businesses.		*The Daily Chronicle* in England criticizes President Harding's misuse of the English language, coining the term "normalcy," and using protesting instead of protecting.... Mrs. Amy Davis Winship, aged 90, is planning to take a course in psychology at the University of Wisconsin; she has attended classes at universities in Ohio, Florida, and Kansas over the past 11 years.	Apr. 28
Federal agents raid a Communist headquarters in New York City; a similar raid is conducted in Chicago.					Apr. 29

	World Affairs	Europe	Africa & The Middle East	The Americas	Asia & The Pacific
Apr. 30		The French government announces its plans call for an occupation of Germany's Ruhr Valley within two days....Sinn Fein planning documents describing a large attack on Ulster have been found by the British....The Italian government announces it is beginning a program to find work for crippled war veterans within the government as well as in privately owned companies....The Soviet Union predicts a large grain harvest later in the year....The French government expects that May Day will be quiet with no major disturbances anticipated.		The Mexican government continues its campaign against rebels seeking to overthrow President Obregon; several captured rebels have been brought before firing squads and executed.	
May 1	The Allies are in near agreement and will soon deliver to Germany conditions and the amount of the reparations payments to be made.	Socialist May Day celebrations in Europe are largely peaceful....Five Post Offices in Waterford Country, Ireland are raided by Sinn Fein....Estonia and Finland are rounding up known Communists with the intention of deporting them....Italy's Socialist party is struggling against the rising tide of the Fascist Party and debating whether it should boycott upcoming elections....British coal miners give no indication that they are ready to end their strike.	May Day demonstrations begin in Jaffa, Palestine.	The first ship of the Bremen-Chile line arrives in Valparaiso, marking the first time a German ship has arrived since the beginning of the World War....Two bombs are thrown during May Day celebrations in Buenos Aries, Argentina; there are no injuries.	Wireless reports from the Soviet Union claim that the British have withdrawn from Persia.
May 2	Germany sends a message to the League of Nations protesting the use of French troops to occupy Germany's Saar Region as a result of the disagreements on reparations payments.	An uprising begins in Silesia among Poles to prevent the area from becoming part of Germany....The Soviet Union announces it will introduce the use of coins in its monetary system in addition to the use of paper money....The Allied Commission begins its efforts to mark out and separate the region of Silesia into German and Polish-controlled regions.	Six U.S. Navy destroyers leave Constantinople, Turkey, to join the U.S. Fleet in the Philippines....Twenty people are killed and 150 wounded in a fight between Arabs and Jews in the city of Jaffa.	The Quebec Central Railway Company reports that its surplus in 1920, after charges, was $469,667, almost $200,000 greater than 1919....The Mexican Petroleum Company announces that it has struck a large well with a 100,000-barrel a day capacity....W.G. Walton, a British Missionary, reports that the scarcity of game in Northern Quebec has turned some of the natives to cannibalism.	Lieutenant General Senba resigns his seat in the Japanese House of Representatives, calling it an "assembly of Hooligans."...Former rebel against American rule in the Philippines, Emiliano Aguinaldo, defends the new American Commission and its recommended future political development in the islands.
May 3	The Allied Commission states that Germany must make a total payment of 135 billion marks in gold or else face the possibility of the Ruhr Valley being occupied by the Allies.	Polish troops invade Upper Silesia....Reported outbreaks of new peasant rebellion against the Soviet government, led by officers of Admiral Kolchak's army, have required sending Soviet troops to western Siberia....The Allied Commission puts Silesia under martial law....Reports from Spain describe how 494 people have been killed in clashes between employers and works....The German cabinet is working on the subject of payments.	Fighting between Arabs and Jews in Jaffa, breaks out again; at least 227 are reported to have been injured....Reports are now stating that many of the Jewish refugees coming into Palestine from Russia are Soviet agents and responsible for beginning the unrest.	A report is made to Canada's House of Commons on the increasing use of aircraft to smuggle drugs into the country.	
May 4		An American observer claims that Lenin has become a figurehead and the Soviet Union is ruled by a small group led by Trotsky....A group of British constables is ambushed by Sinn Fein and seven are killed....British Labor leaders are now stating that the end of the national coal strike in Britain could be over in about a week....Polish troops stop their raids into Lithuania, but are massing troops on the border; currently a Polish Army, which claims it has severed its ties with the Polish government, is holding the city of Vilna against the Lithuanian Army....French troops are moving to German border.	Thus far, 40 have been killed in the Arab-Jewish disturbances in Jaffa, Palestine; 66 from both sides have been arrested.		Reports from Vladivostok, Soviet Union, describe how a form of pneumonia, supposedly more dangerous than Bubonic Plague, has broken out; it is said to be similar to an outbreak that killed 65,000 people in Manchuria 10 years ago....The Soviet newspaper, *Izvestia*, reports that Japan is making military preparations against the Soviets, which will include the use of anti-Soviet Russian troops under General Wrangle.

A	B	C	D	E
Includes developments that affect more than one world region, international organizations and important meetings of world leaders.	*Includes all domestic and regional developments in Europe, including the Soviet Union.*	*Includes all domestic and regional developments in Africa and the Middle East.*	*Includes all domestic and regional developments in Latin America, the Caribbean, and Canada.*	*Includes all domestic and regional developments in Asian and Pacific nations (and colonies).*

	U.S. Politics & Social Issues	U.S. Foreign Policy & Affairs, Defense	U.S. Economy & Environment	Science, Technology & Nature	Culture, Leisure & Lifestyle
Apr. 30	The number of unemployed nationwide is three million with some labor leaders as well as government agencies predicting an increase to five million.…For farm laborers there are more men than jobs available with many farmers that cannot or will not hire additional help; farm wages have drooped sharply since last year.…Governor Hugh M. Dorsey of Georgia has published a book calling for a state constabulary and laws that will prevent abuses of civil rights such as lynching, intimidation, and work conditions that are close to slavery.		Several prices are dropping sharply; chain stores are currently selling butter at 39 cents a pound, the lowest price since before the World War.		
May 1	G.B. Hogan of Dublin, GA, admits that three African Americans had been killed on his plantation but that he is innocent of any wrongdoing; investigation into Hogan's farm is part on an ongoing federal and state investigation of African-American workers forced into peonage and murders of hired hands in Georgia.		The New York Harbor Anti-Pollution Associates, an organization of land owners who are attempting to end pollution in New York Harbor, comes into being.		Austrian composer, Richard Strauss, announces that he will be touring the United States in the Fall.…The Metropolitan Museum of Art in New York begins an exhibition of French Impressionists, to include canvases of Cezanne, Courbet, Manet, Degas, and Renoir.
May 2		President Harding announces he will not send a diplomatic envoy to the Vatican.…U.S. Secretary of State Charles Evans Hughes informs Germany that it must go directly to the Allies and not through the United States to resolve the war reparations payment impasse.			A crash of a Norfolk & Western train in West Virginia leaves six dead and 27 injured.…One of Florenz Ziegfeld's major stars, Billie Burke, will be starring in a series of films produced by Ziegfeld.
May 3	The United Textile Workers of America calls for a strike against textile mills in the South over proposed wage cuts.…Police in Baltimore are having trouble keeping order in the wake of a shipping strike on the waterfront.…Strikes against shipping lines are continuing in Boston, Philadelphia, and Portland, ME.…U.S. Steel announces it will reduce the wages of 150,000 of its workers by 20 percent.		Secretary of Commerce Hoover tells a House Committee that he approves of protective tariffs as being the only way to protect American industry from competition.		
May 4	President Harding selects November 11 as the day to bury the Unknown Solider in Arlington Cemetery.…In Atlanta, a 5,000-person celebration of the Ku Klux Klan begins; more than 1,000 are to be initiated into the Klan.	War Secretary, Weeks, sends a letter to each Senator and Representative encouraging participation in the annual military training camps that are planned for the summer, the Plattsburg camps.…Senator Hiram Johnson of California announces a western Congressional Committee to consider Japanese immigration and land ownership in the western United States.…The U.S. Navy minesweeper, *Falcon*, leaves Philadelphia shipyard to salvage the submarine S-5, which went down in September 1920.…Approximately 500 American soldiers on Occupation duty in the Rhineland, who have married there, are ordered home.	The price of a barrel of oil in Wyoming drops 25 cents a barrel, the lowest price in four years.…Standard Oil of New Jersey lowers its prices by ½ to one cent a gallon.…Railway Express announces it will be reducing wages to its 80,000 employees on June 1.	The Pons-Winnecke Comet is observed at Smith College; it is estimated that the earth will pass through the tail of the comet sometime in June.	

	World Affairs	Europe	Africa & The Middle East	The Americas	Asia & The Pacific
May 5	The Interallied Commission in Silesia states that it will not oppose the formation of German police units to keep order in Silesia.	The London Ultimatum, establishing Germany's total war reparations payments is finalized.…French troops are massed on the border and are ready to enter German territory.…Polish troops and local Poles are currently besieging the cities of Katowice, Beuthen, Gleiwitz, and other cities in Silesia.…Sir James Craig, Premier of Ulster, Northern Ireland meets with Eamon de Valera to exchange views on the future of Ireland.		Mexico's government under President Obregon receives recognition from the British government.	
May 6	The fighting in Silesia continues with soldiers of the Inter-Allied Commission (French, British, and Italian) fighting Polish insurgents.	At least 30 Italian soldiers have been killed and 70 wounded in fighting with the Poles, while the French forces have lost 70 killed and an even greater number wounded.…Polish insurgents are using artillery in their attack on predominantly German cities in Silesia.…Dr. Gregory Zatkovic, former steelworker from Pittsburgh and Governor of the Carpathian Russia portion of Czechoslovakia, resigns his position.…The French forces prepared to invade Germany over the war reparations payment issue now number 50,000.	Spanish troops in Morocco under General Sanjurjo have encountered a number of Moors fighting against Spanish rule in the region; rebels in another part of Morocco have attacked an army convoy, losing three dead and five wounded.		
May 7	German troops are massing on the border of Germany and Poland near Silesia.	British Prime Minister, Lloyd George, states that Poland must disarm and that if Germany complies with Allied requests they will be right in demanding that the Poles disarm.…British Prime Minister George states that the meetings between Sinn Fein and the Northern Irish authorities are a good sign.…Mensheviks are being jailed in large numbers in the Soviet Union to prevent a revolt.…The Latvian government suppresses trade unions to prevent any disorders.	Muslims and Christians in Palestine have formed organizations to protect their rights in the wake of the increased numbers of Jews arriving there.…French and Turkish soldiers are fighting near the city of Cilicia.	C.E. Bacon of the New York Clearing House reports that economic conditions in Cuba are improving.…Brazil is anticipating a large number of immigrants, especially Italians and Germans.…Canada's trade, especially with the United States, has increased significantly in the past year, improving its balance of trade.…Eight railroads in Argentina that are British-owned have showed a profit for the past year.	Japan's Crown Prince Hirohito continues his world tour, arriving in Britain.…China is undergoing a severe drought, which is delaying planting and will require that outside nations send more food assistance.
May 8	The League of Nations will assume the position of receiver for Austria to help it recover its financial stability.…There are now 125,000 French troops ready to enter the Ruhr Valley; they are 12 miles from the German city of Essen; Belgian troops are ready to enter Germany.	The Soviet government announces the defeat of the anti-Communist army of General Antonov, although the General escapes.…Hundreds of British Army Reservists, many of whom are striking miners called on active duty, riot in Alshot, Britain, destroying and looting stores.…German popular opinion is now swinging against paying reparations of any kind to the Allies as Germans assume the Allies will occupy the Ruhr Valley regardless of events.…Continued fighting in the streets of Italian cities between Fascists and Communists has resulted in six dead and 40 injured.		A Haitian delegation visiting the United States says that it wants the U.S. occupation of Haiti to end, that American soldiers have committed many atrocities, and that thousands of prisoners have died while under U.S. captivity.	Governor Leonard Wood of the Philippines is greeted by 7,000 demonstrators, mostly friendly, demanding independence for the islands from the United States.
May 9	According to the League of Nations International Labor Office, 11 nations have 5.5 million men disabled as a result of the World War; France has 1.5 million, Germany has 1.4 million, Britain has 1.17 million, Italy 570,000, and the United States 200,000.	The fighting in Silesia is confusing as British, French, Italian, Polish, and German forces are fighting.…It is widely believed that if German forces enter Silesia, France will immediately invade Germany.…The German government bans a Communist newspaper, the *Red Banner*, which had been encouraging a revolt in Silesia.…The estimated damage for the soldiers' riot in Aldershot, Britain, has now reached the equivalent of $100,000.…Writer Erskine Childers, author of *The Riddle of the Sands*, is arrested in Dublin by British police.		Canada's foreign trade is expanding but it is predicted that its unfavorable trade balance with the United States will continue.…Navy Secretary Denby denies allegations of the Haitian delegation that visited the United States to complain of conditions; he states that U.S. troops should stay there to keep order.	Crown Prince Hirohito of Japan is greeted in London with the first full honors of state accorded any visitor since 1914.
	A *Includes developments that affect more than one world region, international organizations and important meetings of world leaders.*	B *Includes all domestic and regional developments in Europe, including the Soviet Union.*	C *Includes all domestic and regional developments in Africa and the Middle East.*	D *Includes all domestic and regional developments in Latin America, the Caribbean, and Canada.*	E *Includes all domestic and regional developments in Asian and Pacific nations (and colonies).*

U.S. Politics & Social Issues	U.S. Foreign Policy & Affairs, Defense	U.S. Economy & Environment	Science, Technology & Nature	Culture, Leisure & Lifestyle	
Chicago printers end their strike; their demand for a 44-hour week will be met, but they must accept a wage cut.... The Glens Fall, NY, *Evening Times* goes back into operation after its printers agree to a 44-hour workweek.	At least 400 applications have been received to attend the military training camp at Plattsburgh, NY, for the first training camp held there since 1916.	The president of the National Live Stock Exchange testifies before Congress and states that butchers are responsible for the high cost of meat.		President Harding's shoe size is 10D, a fact revealed when Camp Fire Girls ask in order to make him a pair of beaded moccasins with the worlds "Great White Father," written in beads in Camp Fire language.	May 5
E. Mont Reily, an early supporter of the Harding campaign for the Presidency, is named as Governor of Puerto Rico.... The War Department is identifying men called up by the draft during the World War and who evaded military service; investigators are finding that many of the men on the so-called slackers list served in the Army during the war, were decorated for bravery and, in some cases killed in action.... The House of Representative kills a measure by a vote of 285 to 46 that would have investigated why African Americans are being denied the right to vote.				Teachers in New Bedford, MA, cannot use make up, but the length of the skirts is left to the teachers' discretion.... Thomas Alva Edison condemns the primary schools in America for failing to develop young men who are capable of thinking; he claims that using movies instead of reading would be better.	May 6
The National Disabled Soldiers League declares that the week of May 29 will be War Crippled Week.... Several State Commissions state that they fear the regulatory power of the Federal Interstate Commerce Commission, especially in how it has restricted their jurisdiction.... The president of the International Seaman's Union testifies before a U.S. House Committee that the working conditions for sailors have significantly declined in recent years.			American archaeologist, Carl Blegen, has discovered the ruins of an ancient Greek city, located between Corinth and Mycenae in southern Greece.		May 7
A speaker at the Manufacturer's Association of New Jersey condemns the closed shops sought by the unions and compares union goals to trying to impose tyranny on factory owners.... A gathering of 40 New York State Police Chief states that it is becoming impossible to enforce Prohibition.... Women attending the meetings of the Women's League of Voters are accused of smoking at their meetings at Atlantic City based on the evidence of many crushed out cigarettes found in the hallway after each meeting.... The revival of D.W. Griffith's *Birth of a Nation* is picketed by the National Association for the Advancement of Colored People.	General John J. Pershing endorses the idea of summer military training camps.	The price of carnations for Mother's Day is running at one dollar each; florists claim that it is a result of supply and demand, but consumers are accusing them of profiteering; dandelions are being substituted in many cases.... The Head of the U.S. Railway Association states that wage cuts are not the only means being used by railroads to cut costs but that other economies and increased efficiency are being employed as well.		The Manager of the Metropolitan Opera states that he believes that Caruso will return to sing his contracted engagements at the Met.	May 8
I. Sam Ballinger, an African American accused of shooting a local deputy sheriff, is taken from his cell by a mob in Starke, FL, and lynched.	Henry K. Rechert, 33, of New York City dies after his 21st operation to remove shrapnel he received in the fighting in the Argonne in 1918.	The U.S. Department of Agriculture predicts that the winter wheat crop will be the fourth largest on record.... On the commodity markets prices for both wheat and corn decline, while prices for other commodities are unchanged.		Albert Einstein receives an honorary degree from Princeton.	May 9

F	G	H	I	J
Includes campaigns, elections, federal-state relations, civil rights and liberties, crime, the judiciary, education, healthcare, poverty, urban affairs, and population.	*Includes formation and debate of U.S. foreign and defense policies, veterans affairs, and defense spending. (Relations with specific foreign countries are usually found under the region concerned.)*	*Includes business, labor, agriculture, taxation, transportation, consumer affairs, monetary and fiscal policy, natural resources, pollution and industrial accidents.*	*Includes worldwide scientific, medical and technological developments, natural phenomena, U.S. weather and natural disasters.*	*Includes the arts, religion, scholarship, communications media, sports, entertainment, fashions, fads, and social life.*

	World Affairs	Europe	Africa & The Middle East	The Americas	Asia & The Pacific
May 10	The League of Nations General Conference on Communications and Transit, held in Barcelona, closes.	Britain's overseas trade, both exports and imports, has declined in the past month.…By a vote of 221–175, the German Reichstag accepts the terms of reparations payments demanded by the Allies.…Polish Insurgents in Silesia are said to be attempting to install a Soviet-style government.…The Polish government awards medals to 10 U.S. volunteer airmen who flew for Poland in its conflict with the Soviets as the Kosciuscko Squadron.		The Canadian Pacific Railroad denies rumors that it is seeking bank loans from New York.…The Panama Canal is becoming popular as a means of shipping California fruit, as it is takes three days less time to ship from California to Europe than to ship it first by rail to the east coast.…The first discovery of natural gas in Central America takes place in Costa Rica fields.	Herbert Hoover encourages Americans to increase their trade with China.
May 11		Continued problems with the Greek currency may cause the government to suspend its payments to foreign nations.…France states that even though it will not invade Germany, because the payments crisis has passed, that it will still keep its soldiers in readiness until Germany disarms.…Polish and German forces are fighting artillery duels in Silesia as fighting continues although negotiations are continuing to establish a ceasefire.	The Turkish government announces that it has foiled a plot to overthrow Mustafa Kemal and establish a Soviet-style government.	The Peruvian government has exiled former President Benvides and others for plotting against the current government.…Canada's House of Commons is debating a bill that would restrict immigration.…In Mexico, several unions support the demands of striking phone operators and may call for a general strike.…The Austrian government recognizes the government of Mexico's President Obregon.	The Chinese government sends its advisor to the President of the United States in an attempt to warn the United States about the potential effects of an Anglo-Japanese treaty.…Representatives of the Japanese-occupied region known as Korea petition U.S. Secretary of State Hughes for diplomatic recognition.…The U.S. Department of Agriculture reports its opinion that heavy deforestation in China has been responsible for the increased famines there.
May 12		A general strike is declared in the Silesian city of Oppeln.		The Canadian government states that fliers from the United States must have special permits in order to cross the border.…Panama has been notified by U.S. Secretary of State Hughes that it will have more time to consider the proposed border settlement between that country and Costa Rica.…Argentina sends an official communication to the League of Nations, indicating it still considers itself to be a member of the League.	
May 13		Michael Collins is nominated to be a candidate for the Irish Parliament for Armagh in northern Ireland.…Joseph Wirth, Germany's new Chancellor, states that Germany will pay all of the reparations it owes but that Germany also expects fair play over the Silesian issue.…The French commander in Silesia blames Britain in part for the recent disturbances, stating that Britain should have sent troops to reinforce the interallied forces.		Between 10 and 50 people are killed by local troops and police in the city of Morelia as a result of protests against what is considered the Mexican government's policy of desecrating churches.	
May 14		France and Britain come to a serious disagreement over the situation in Silesia; Britain states that Germany can use troops to keep order while the French are opposed to Germany military action. British officers are claiming that the French troops in the area have been assisting the Poles even when firing on British soldiers.…On Germany's western border, French troops are still in position, now at a strength of 100,000 with French Military commanders stating that they want a free hand in dealing with Germany.…The Czechoslovak Communist Party is founded.			

A	B	C	D	E
Includes developments that affect more than one world region, international organizations and important meetings of world leaders.	*Includes all domestic and regional developments in Europe, including the Soviet Union.*	*Includes all domestic and regional developments in Africa and the Middle East.*	*Includes all domestic and regional developments in Latin America, the Caribbean, and Canada.*	*Includes all domestic and regional developments in Asian and Pacific nations (and colonies).*

U.S. Politics & Social Issues	U.S. Foreign Policy & Affairs, Defense	U.S. Economy & Environment	Science, Technology & Nature	Culture, Leisure & Lifestyle	
In Chicago, two union organizers are convicted of hiring individuals to bomb upholstery shops.	The U.S. House votes to limit the number of soldiers in the Army to 150,000.	The heads of the various railroads in the United States join in blaming labor as their greatest cost and not operating expenses.... Testifying before the House Territories Committee Colonel, Alfred Brooks claims that Alaska contains large fields of oil.		*Six Authors in Search of a Character* by Luigi Pirandello premiers.... Thomas Alva Edison asks questions of a group of 25 University of Chicago students; only 35 percent of the men and 28 percent of women answer correctly. The results of the test stir up a controversy as many state that they did not require reasoning but a memorization of a wide variety of facts.... Charlie Chaplain is severely burned when a torch on a movie set ignites his clothing.... The World War epic film, *J'accuse* by Abel Gance is shown in New York.	May 10
	Howard Franklin, 25, of Jersey City, NJ, who lost his sight due to poison gas in the World War commits suicide by turning on the gas in his room.	Illinois reports that unemployment in the state is decreasing.		The Russian bass, Feodor Chaliapin, announces that he will be touring the United States.	May 11
Lydia Southard is arrested in Honolulu for poisoning four of her husbands for life insurance.... The House of Representatives in Massachusetts kills a proposed bill to make voting mandatory.... Democratic candidate for President in 1920, James Cox, declines to criticize President Harding and states that the Administration should have a chance to declare what its policies will be.	A fleet of 70 U.S. Navy destroyers arrives in New York City on its way to Newport, which will be their summer base.... The Senate begins work on the appropriations bill for the U.S. Navy for the coming year.	Crude oil output in the United States is increasing; the daily total for the past week is recorded as 1,308,650 barrels.	A new flight record is set by French aviators flying over the Andes.... Speaking in the United States, Marie Curie states that radium is not the cure for every type of cancer, but that it can be useful in curing many forms of it.	George Bernard Shaw states that Shakespeare would have liked Charlie Chaplin's movies; Shaw is trying unsuccessfully to have films shown in the Shakespeare Memorial Theatre.	May 12
Members of the I.W.W. state that former leader, "Big Bill" Haywood, is now in the Soviet Union because he stole $35,000 of I.W.W. funds.... At least six are known to be killed although the total may be as high as 15 in the fighting in Mingo country, WV.... Women and children are said to be evacuating the towns in Mingo county while Federal troops in Ohio are preparing to move in at the request of the Governors of Kentucky and West Virginia.... Paul Vincent Southard, fifth husband of Lydia Southard who has been arrested for poisoning her previous spouses, states that he believes his wife is innocent.		The Bank of America announces plans to build a headquarters in a 23-story building on Wall Street.	The appearance of the Northern Lights (Aurora Borealis) is severely affecting both telephone and telegraph operations in upstate New York as well as creating interference that affects electrical railroad signals.		May 13
The 1920 census indicates that despite Congressional warnings about waves of immigrants that fewer had entered the country than in 1910.... In a speech to the American Federation of Labor, Samuel L. Gompers, states that the "forces of greed," will be defeated.... Alaska's Caucasian population decreased from 1910 to 1920 from 36,400 to 27,883.... The Republic Iron and Steel Company in Youngstown, OH, has abandoned the practice of the 8-hour day with overtime paid after that; straight time will be paid for 10- and 12-hour days.			New investigations are leading doctors to believe that prolonged exposure to x-rays can be dangerous to health.		May 14

	World Affairs	Europe	Africa & The Middle East	The Americas	Asia & The Pacific
May 15		Italians go to the polls today to select members of the Chamber of Deputies; there is fighting between Socialists and Fascists, as the Socialists lose ground (about 50 seats) in the election and Catholics are expected to lose as well.... Germans in Silesia are reported to have stolen 4,000 rifles to supply their local defense forces.... A peace activist, daughter of Sir Charles Barrington, is killed in Ireland by Sinn Fein.	Turkish Nationalists are raiding towns and cities in the area near Constantinople, which is occupied by the Allies.	Communists in Mexico begin demonstrations against the Obregon government that lead to riots.	Dr. Sun Yat-sen, newly elected President of China, formally asks the United States for recognition of his government.
May 16	The Conference of Ambassadors and Ministers on World Trade, with representatives from 40 nations, begins in New York City.	In two days of fighting in Ireland, 32 have been killed making it the bloodiest two-day period since the violence began.			
May 17		The Czechoslovak Social Democrats vote to become part of the Communist Third International ("Comintern").... Sinn Fein fires on a British Army football game, killing one and injuring several more.		Newly elected President of Cuba, Alfredo Zayas y Alfonso, announces he will be the first President to be inaugurated in public.	
May 18		The Silesian problem is still not resolved; possible solutions include making it a free state independent from both Poland and Germany.... Reports from Britain indicate that a resolution to the coal strike may occur soon.... The leader of the Polish insurrection in Silesia gives orders for his soldiers to surrender their arms; more than 10,000 Polish insurgents have been demobilized.	The British government announces that its determination to administer the mandate of Palestine has not been shaken by the recent violence.	The Canadian Railway Association announces that it will begin negotiations to reduce the wages of its workers.	The city of Omsk in Siberia is reported as having been captured by anti-Communist forces.... Citizens of Hawaii state that they want Japanese immigrants barred from performing work on U.S. Army and Navy projects in the islands.
May 19		Romania's exports during 1920, especially in agricultural products, oil, and timber, were 1,238,550 tons compared with 108,879 tons in 1919.... Election riots break out in Belfast; elsewhere six are killed in various shootings.	Riots in Cairo claim one life with many reported injured as soldiers are brought into the city to restore order.		The Chinese government delivers a protest against the Japanese-British alliance as impairing the dignity of China.
May 20		The British government reduces the tariffs on goods entering from Germany.... Armored cars patrol Belfast as the election nears.... Aristide Briand will not meet with Lloyd George to discuss the Silesian border problem.... Fascists battle workers organizations throughout Italy; two are killed and several injured in fights between fascists and longshoremen.		The Premier of Newfoundland requests the London owners of paper mills, which are not on strike, to consider a settlement; the owners respond the 1,200 men on strike must accept the proposed wage cuts.... Alfredo Zayas y Alfonso is inaugurated as the fourth President of Cuba.	A. Barton Hepburn of the Chase Manhattan Bank returning from a trip to Asia states that Japan is making a rapid business recovery.
	A *Includes developments that affect more than one world region, international organizations and important meetings of world leaders.*	B *Includes all domestic and regional developments in Europe, including the Soviet Union.*	C *Includes all domestic and regional developments in Africa and the Middle East.*	D *Includes all domestic and regional developments in Latin America, the Caribbean, and Canada.*	E *Includes all domestic and regional developments in Asian and Pacific nations (and colonies).*

U.S. Politics & Social Issues	U.S. Foreign Policy & Affairs, Defense	U.S. Economy & Environment	Science, Technology & Nature	Culture, Leisure & Lifestyle	
Addressing the Sunday Afternoon Club in Evanston, IL, William Jennings Bryan states that newspapers do not give facts, but fool the public regularly; Bryan also states that Americans who go to Cuba to avoid Prohibition and drink should not be allowed back into the country....In response to Georgia's Governor Hugh M. Dorsey statements on how African Americans are treated in that state, the Macon branch of the Guardians of Liberty calls for his impeachment.				Thomas Edison states that he would like to find men from college to work for him who were clever enough, but his test proves that they cannot meet his standards; Edison's son takes the test, does well on scientific aspects of it, but flunks the rest.	May 15
New violence breaks out in Mingo County, WV, between miners, local authorities, and the National Guard; the Governor of West Virginia asks for Federal troops and is told by the Secretary of War that none are needed.	The United States received a payment of $17.38 million on its war debt from Britain....Congressman Chandler of New York asks Secretary of State Hughes to recognize the new nations of Latvia, Lithuania, and Estonia....Secretary of State Hughes tells the Senate that the U.S. government must be vigilant in preventing oil concessions agreements being signed anywhere that would be to the detriment of the United States.	An income tax report from the University of Chicago states that the average income of a college graduate, 10 years after graduation is $5,762.51 a year.		Jack Dempsey begins serious training for his upcoming title fight with Georges Carpentier.	May 16
President Harding will not send Federal troops into West Virginia until the Governors of that state and Kentucky have used all their resources.	The House Naval Committee approves a bill to authorize the construction of an aircraft carrier, which will cost $25 million and carry 80 aircraft....Senator Borah succeeds in having his naval disarmament amendment attached to the Naval appropriations bill....The superdreadnought, U.S.S *Tennessee* performs its final tests off the Maine coast.	The 1920 Census reports that the population of the United States is 105,710,620....Speaking over the telephone from Washington, President Harding opens an Orange Show in Anaheim, CA.	Underwater cables are still showing the effects of the electromagnetic disturbances caused by the recent appearance of the Aurora Borealis.	Continuing his travels in the United States, Albert Einstein visits Boston; he is given the "Edison test" and fails.	May 17
A bill that would give veterans preference for Civil Service jobs is opposed by several reform organizations because it would destroy the merit system that has been created....Citizens of Mingo County, WV, begin to mobilize for their own defense; at least 500 have gathered to form this force that will protect local homes against feared violence by miners....Six African Americans are shot in Byromville, GA, in what is reported as a race riot starting over an attempt to collect taxes.	The U.S. State Department reports that 100 Americans are being held by the Soviets; although only eight or nine are in prison, all are forbidden to leave the country....The bodies of 5,212 soldiers who died in the World War are brought from France to New York.			President Harding states that he may use movies to deliver his messages to the nation.	May 18
Congress passes the Emergency Quota Act establishing quotas on a national basis for immigrants coming to the United States....President Harding signs the law that will place restrictions on immigration to the United States....Today is the first anniversary of the Matewan battle in West Virginia; despite this, the day is fairly calm although some mining companies has been dynamited....Former President William Howard Taft is the candidate brought up most often in discussions about who will succeed Justice White.					May 19
Transportation workers in Albany are charged by state and city police during disturbances; the workers throw stones at the streetcars....Martial law has been declared in Mingo County, WV, with the Governor proclaiming that the county is in insurrection; this action is warmly received by the coalmine owners and operator....The United Mine Workers attempt to get a Congressional investigation opened into the events in Mingo County.		The Ford Motor Company will abolish the yearly bonus and instead raise regular wages.	President Harding presents a gram of radium to Marie Curie, a gift paid for by American women.		May 20

F	G	H	I	J
Includes campaigns, elections, federal-state relations, civil rights and liberties, crime, the judiciary, education, healthcare, poverty, urban affairs, and population.	*Includes formation and debate of U.S. foreign and defense policies, veterans affairs, and defense spending. (Relations with specific foreign countries are usually found under the region concerned.)*	*Includes business, labor, agriculture, taxation, transportation, consumer affairs, monetary and fiscal policy, natural resources, pollution and industrial accidents.*	*Includes worldwide scientific, medical and technological developments, natural phenomena, U.S. weather and natural disasters.*	*Includes the arts, religion, scholarship, communications media, sports, entertainment, fashions, fads, and social life.*

	World Affairs	Europe	Africa & The Middle East	The Americas	Asia & The Pacific
May 21		The city of Fiume in the Adriatic has been overrun by bandits; political assassinations number at least five so far; elsewhere in Italy there is fighting in the street between Fascists and Communists.... Observers note that life in Germany is improving economically; politically, most agree that Germany want to have a return of the monarchy but along constitutional lines.	French representatives arrive in Turkey to talk to Mustafa Kemal to negotiate a new alliance with Turkey....Mustafa Kemal forces his cabinet to reign; the national legislature has refused to provide more funds to the war with Greece; Kemal states that since it is the "historic pride of Turkey to wage wars without money," that is exactly what he will do.	A new oil field is discovered in Chihuahua in northern Mexico.... British oil companies are negotiating drilling rights in Chile.	The Japanese Consul General in Canada states that Japan does not expect that the British would aid Japan in a war against the United States....Opinion in Australia generally supports the drafting of new agreements with Japan.
May 22		Fighting between Poles and Germans in Silesia has resulted in a defeat of Polish forces and the loss of machine guns and artillery....Sinn Fein attacks have expanded to Britain....Despite the conflict between Sinn Fein and British forces, the election is Ulster is the quietest in years....Pope Benedict XV has sent a letter to both Irish and British authorities asking them to resolve their issues without violence....Eamon de Valera and Lloyd George are rumored to be engaged in peace talks....Austria and Hungary begin border discussions.		Mexico's President Obregon has been presented with American demands concerning oil-drilling rights before it will receive recognition by the U.S. government.	An article in the *London Daily Chronicle* suggests that the United States should join Britain in an alliance with Japan....Japan announces it will be abandoning its stations in Siberia and will restore Shantung to the Chinese government at the earliest opportunity, as soon as the Chinese government shows that it can control the region and keep order.
May 23		German troops, known as *Freikorps* organizations, attack the Poles at St. Annaberg in Silesia....War Crimes trials begin in Germany for a group of German soldiers....The French government states that if German troops enter Silesia to keep order, it will be considered as an invasion and will result in war between France and Germany; Lloyd George decides to send troops to Silesia.... The British government announces that it will begin to use 16-inch guns on its battleships and will adopt the American system of three guns to a turret.	Rioting in Alexandria, Egypt, results in 37 deaths and more than 150 injured; the rioting is between native Egyptians and Greeks and is eventually subdued by Army troops.	The Mexican Petroleum Company announces that it has drilled a well capable of producing 675,000 barrels daily.	
May 24		The German government bans all *Freikorps* organizations....The commander of Polish forces in Silesia cuts all communications lines so that news of German successes will not demoralize Polish troops....Germany agrees that it will not send troops into Silesia to keep order.	Although the rioting in Alexandria has quieted down; the revised total of casualties is 48 killed and 191 injured.	Rear Admiral Samuel Robison has been named as the Governor of Santo Domingo in Dominica.	
May 25		Sinn Fein burns the Custom House, in Dublin, center of British government....Bulgarian Communists are accused of having thrown a bomb at school children in Sofia, Bulgaria; 18 children have been injured, not all are expected to survive.		Mexico's government charges that 30 armed men from Texas illegally entered Mexico in pursuit of a criminal, then killed him by dragging him behind a horse before returning to the United States.	
May 26		Protests take place in Petrograd with 20,000 said to be on strike protesting economic and general living conditions in the Soviet Union.... Polish forces in Silesia capture the mining city of Katowice....Aristide Briand, Premier of France, brings the conduct of his policies to a vote in the French Chamber of deputies and wins 403–163....Romanian workers are granted the right to form unions.	Field Marshall Viscount Allenby warns Egyptians that continued disorders will result in intervention by Egyptian and British troops.	The U.S. State Department announces it has nearly finalized plans for a withdrawal of U.S. forces from Dominica.	Authorities in Vladivostok are calling on the Japanese to bring in troops to safeguard the city as fighting between Communists and anti-Communists comes closer to the city.

U.S. Politics & Social Issues	U.S. Foreign Policy & Affairs, Defense	U.S. Economy & Environment	Science, Technology & Nature	Culture, Leisure & Lifestyle	
President Harding receives a request from 21 patriotic societies asking him to curb radical agitation.... Martial law has been imposed in the Mingo Mine district in West Virginia; some rifle shots have been fired from the Kentucky side of the Tug River, but no casualties have been reported....Newspapers supporting the mineworkers in Mingo Country have been suppressed....In Haverhill, MA, carpenters, electricians, painters, and sheet metal workers agree to take a 10 percent wage cut.					May 21
Arsonists set one of the main buildings of the Stone Mountain Coal Corporation afire in Mingo County, WV; local firemen refuse to put the fire out....Nonunion workers in Matewan, WV, are ordered to stop working under pain of death and have all quit....Labor unrest and demonstrations in Albany, NY, surrounding the transit strike have calmed down to the extent that the National Guard will not be called in....More immigrants pass through the station at Ellis Island than have ever passed through in one day since 1907: 3,071 are recorded as having passed through.		Boston is suffering from record heat, 93 degrees Fahrenheit with one death and 13 recorded cases of heat prostration.		Georges Carpentier arrives at his training camp in preparation for his title bout with heavyweight champion, Jack Dempsey.	May 22
	American battleships, the U.S.S *Connecticut*, *South Carolina*, and *Michigan* begin their annual practice cruise.			Baseball observers are unanimous in noticing the dramatic increase in home runs; 1920 surpassed all years and all indications are that 1921 will see even more; speculation is that a livelier baseball is being used.	May 23
Sid Hatfield, police chief of Matewan, WV, and supporter of striking miners, responds to a warrant issued for his arrest for having beaten an official of the Stone Mountain Coal Company; Hatfield is released on his own recognizance.	The U.S. Senate refuses to reduce the number of U.S. Navy personnel of 100,000 and instead states that it should be 120,000.	Selling on Wall Street in the past week has resulted in a large number of declining prices, in several instances, record low prices for stocks have been reached.	It is announced that a group of six American scientists will begin an expedition up the Amazon River starting on June 1; they will explore the River of Doubt Region explored by Theodore Roosevelt in 1914.	Finnish Composer Jan Sibelius, scheduled to teach at the Eastman School of Music in Rochester, NY, will not be arriving due to ill health; his place will be taken by Norwegian composer, Christian Sinding.	May 24
Fresh fighting breaks out in Mingo County, WV, with three killed.... Forte Velona, a labor organizer is kidnapped and burned with sulfuric acid during his attempts to help unionize workers at the Ideal Clothing Factory in Binghamton, NY.	The Borah Amendment to the Navy Appropriations Bill passes unanimously and it seems that the House will accept it as well; the Borah Amendment calls for the President to convene a naval disbarment conference among the major powers.			The Dean of Princeton's Graduate School reports that only one student in 40 years has died of overwork.	May 25
An anti-Prohibition march, which may total 200,000 people, is underway to be held in New Jersey....In Mingo County renewed fighting has resulted in two men shot and seven arrested....A shipment of 10,000 cartridges sent from St. Louis to Matewan Police Chief Sid Hatfield has been stopped by state authorities.		The price for a hundred pounds of potatoes is 90 cents, a 90 percent drop from prices of more than $8 in 1920.			May 26

F	G	H	I	J
Includes campaigns, elections, federal-state relations, civil rights and liberties, crime, the judiciary, education, healthcare, poverty, urban affairs, and population.	*Includes formation and debate of U.S. foreign and defense policies, veterans affairs, and defense spending. (Relations with specific foreign countries are usually found under the region concerned.)*	*Includes business, labor, agriculture, taxation, transportation, consumer affairs, monetary and fiscal policy, natural resources, pollution and industrial accidents.*	*Includes worldwide scientific, medical and technological developments, natural phenomena, U.S. weather and natural disasters.*	*Includes the arts, religion, scholarship, communications media, sports, entertainment, fashions, fads, and social life.*

	World Affairs	Europe	Africa & The Middle East	The Americas	Asia & The Pacific
May 27		Germany pays the first installation of its reparations payment, totaling $200 million....Romania announces it will reduce taxes on oil exports....Sinn Fein cuts communications cables between the Queenstown Naval Dockyards and the remainder of Ireland....The casualties in Ireland for the past week have been 25 deaths and 32 injured....British troops arrive in Silesia to assist in keeping order.... Discussion continue to resolve the British mine workers strike.			Afghan is recognized as a sovereign state....Anti-Communist forces capture the port city of Vladivostok.
May 28		After 17 years, France resumes diplomatic relations with the Vatican....The Hungarian government announces its intention to join the League of Nations.... German airplanes bomb Polish positions in Silesia....Striking workers in Christiana, Norway, clash with police; several are arrested....Austria and Hungary cannot reach any kind of agreement over the border between Austria and Western Hungary, which contains many German-speaking residents.	The Turkish government announces it may fire on a British Warship that is currently in Constantinople....A Soviet diplomatic mission has arrived in the Turkish city of Trebizond and the Soviets are said to have supplied both gold and weapons to the Turks.	The economic situation in both Cuba and Colombia is said to be improving....Police in Buenos Aries, Argentina, arrest more than 600 suspected Communists during labor strikes in the city....New York banks offer to make a loan to the government of Uruguay for an undisclosed amount.	
May 29		Fighting breaks out in Paris between Communists and police....The Interallied Commission in Silesia has arranged a truce between Germans and Poles in the region.... The Premier of Poland, submits his resignation to President Pilsudski but the resignation has not been accepted just yet.			Violence breaks out in Vladivostok when anti-Communist troops arrive in the area; Japanese soldiers disarm whatever forces they meet and are attempting to restore order.
May 30		The Austrian city of Salzburg votes to join Austria with Germany; the vote is 67,533 for and 677 against....As part of the justification for the Soviet Union's New Economic Plan, Lenin admits that the country is bankrupt, capitalism must be free to operate, and all exiles are welcome back....The Armistice in Silesia has been broken with Germans and Poles renewing the fighting; 400 are reported killed.	The Turkish government announces a program of reprisals for the 10,000 Turkish citizens they allege were killed by the Greeks. Supporters of former War Minister Enver Pasha have been discovered at Ankara, arrested, and executed.	Canada announces that it will put into effect protective tariffs against U.S. potatoes, wheat, and wheat flour.	
May 31	The Imperial Premiers of the British Empire and as representatives of the Indian government will meet in June to discuss several issues including the proposed Anglo-Japanese Alliance and how much the dominions will pay for the upkeep of the Royal Navy....Several nations complain about the League of Nations accommodations in Geneva, Switzerland, and seek to have League headquarters moved to Belgium or France.	Sinn Fein ambushes a group of British soldiers, in County Cork, killing seven and wounding 20....The British indicate that they expect the Irish Army to soon take the field against them in an escalation of the conflict; six soldiers are killed by a Sinn Fein bomb....Germans successfully defend the city of Annaberg from a Polish attack; 50 Poles and 15 Germans are killed with 175 wounded on both sides....Polish insurgents in Silesia have attacked positions occupied by the Italian occupation troops.		Canada denies that it is imposing a protective tariff against U.S. goods.	Governor Leonard Wood of the Philippines is told by Filipino representatives that they prefer to remain an American protectorate; if the islands became independent, their taxes would triple.
Jun. 1		The French newspaper, *Le Matin*, accuses former Prime Minister Clemenceau of having betrayed Poland by not granting it Silesia outright after the war....Lenin further defines the New Economic Policy, stating that small capitalists will be encouraged although larger enterprises will remain in state control....Five British constables are killed in ambushes set by Sinn Fein.		In Vera Cruz, radicals have begun a strike protesting the Mexican government's deportation of two Communist leaders.	

U.S. Politics & Social Issues	U.S. Foreign Policy & Affairs, Defense	U.S. Economy & Environment	Science, Technology & Nature	Culture, Leisure & Lifestyle	
The U.S. Senate Committee on Labor and Education announces it will investigate the recent disorders in Mingo County, WV.…The sections of Mingo County under martial occupation are quiet.				Enrico Caruso leaves New York City for Italy, sailing on the SS *President Wilson*.	May 27
Authorities in the town of Matewan, WV, appear to have lost the keys to their prison, preventing the National Guard from incarcerating anyone violating martial law; the National Guard commander warns the mayor to find the key in case the jail is needed.…One person has been killed in what appears to be the beginning of an uprising by the Ute Indians in the state of Utah.…Police in Denver, CO, arrest 27 men supposed to be members of the I.W.W. for seizing a Union Pacific train.	The U.S. Ordnance department claims to have developed a .50 caliber machine gun that can fire armor piercing bullets, capable of penetrating tanks.…The United States is withholding its statements of approval for a five-nation compact signed by Nicaragua, Costa Rica, Salvador, Honduras, and Guatemala to form the Central American Federation.…It is planned to conduct bombing tests in June and July with aerial bombs of up to one ton in size being used.	The cost of living is now 65.7 percent over what it was in 1914, although it has been declining since July 1920.		Isadora Duncan announces she will accept an invitation to go to the Soviet Union and will open a dance academy in Moscow.…The *New York Times* reviews *Out of My Life*, the biography of Field Marshall Paul von Hindenburg.	May 28
	A U.S. Army ambulance plane flying near Washington crashes with seven aboard when caught in a severe storm. General Billy Mitchell is caught in the same storm and barely manages to land without mishap.		Emory University receives the mummy of Queen Ti who died in approximately 1420 B.C.E.	In Milwaukee 16 people are injured when an airplane crashes into a grandstand at an air show.	May 29
A group of Confederate and Union veterans meets at the military cemetery in Chattanooga, TN, and leave flowers on 14,000 graves.	The U.S. Navy transfers its Teapot Dome oil reserves to the Department of the Interior.…Former U.S. Senator James Lewis predicts a war between the United States and Japan with the U.S.'s former allies in Europe, backing the Japanese.		Albert Einstein concludes his tour of the United States and sails to Britain stating that his theory of relativity is receiving a sympathetic hearing in the United States.	In the past three days, 36 home runs have been hit in both National and American Leagues.…The crowd at Coney Island, NY, for Memorial Day exceeds 300,000.	May 30
The Tulsa race riots begin, with the attempted mass lynching of Dick Rowland, an African American accused of assaulting a woman in an elevator.…The Northern Paper Mills in Green Bay, WI, are attacked by a "mob of 1,000 moonshine-crazed workers;" the local Sheriff asks for help from the National Guard.…The murder trial of Nicola Sacco and Bartolomeo Vanzetti begins in Dedham, MA.	Secretary of War Weeks orders an investigation into the causes of the airplane crash that killed the pilot and six passengers.…The United States receives its first reparation payment from Germany in the amount of $35,733,000.	The Department of Commerce reports that trade with Europe has been decreasing in the past month.…Studebaker Auto reports that it sold 7,400 cars in May this year as opposed to 4,024 in May 1920.…The price of milk (Grade B) in New York is 14 cents a quart, the lowest price since September, 1918.…The Superintendent of the Chicago Division of the Air Mail Service is fired as the result of inquiries into the deaths of five airmail pilots resulting from inefficiency at air fields.		Film Star Buster Keaton marries movie star Norma Talmadge.	May 31
The section of Tulsa, OK, where the African Americans live is attacked by groups of white citizens; much of that part of town is set on fire.…The National Guard has been sent to keep order in Tulsa; an estimated 85 persons have been killed.	A congressional committee investigating the recent crash of an Army plane that killed the pilot and six passengers finds that the Weather Bureau should inform pilots of approaching storms.	A financier in San Francisco announces that a new bridge will be constructed across San Francisco Bay at a cost of $25 million.…The U.S. Labor Board reports that almost of all of the wage gains made by rail workers in 1920 has been lost in the recent set of proposed and actual pay cuts.…Clothing workers in New York City agree to take a 15 percent wage cut; 30,000 return to work.		Georges Carpentier continues his training regimen, preparing for his fight with Jack Dempsey, scheduled for next month.…Jack Dempsey spends the day quietly, taking a four-mile walk but not spending any time training in the ring.…*Gold*, a brand new play by Eugene O'Neil opens to good reviews in New York City.	Jun. 1

F	G	H	I	J
Includes campaigns, elections, federal-state relations, civil rights and liberties, crime, the judiciary, education, healthcare, poverty, urban affairs, and population.	*Includes formation and debate of U.S. foreign and defense policies, veterans affairs, and defense spending. (Relations with specific foreign countries are usually found under the region concerned.)*	*Includes business, labor, agriculture, taxation, transportation, consumer affairs, monetary and fiscal policy, natural resources, pollution and industrial accidents.*	*Includes worldwide scientific, medical and technological developments, natural phenomena, U.S. weather and natural disasters.*	*Includes the arts, religion, scholarship, communications media, sports, entertainment, fashions, fads, and social life.*

	World Affairs	Europe	Africa & The Middle East	The Americas	Asia & The Pacific
Jun. 2	The Third International of the Communist Party with members from around the world opens today in Moscow.	Austria's postwar stability problems continue with little success held for new attempts to form a new government; the situation is complicated by an increased political movement to join Austria to Germany.…Treason trials in Hungary begin for 11 officers charged with attempting to set up former King Charles as King of Hungary.…Sinn Fein ambushes Black and Tan police unit, killing eight and wounding four.	Britain and France indicate that they will both support Greece in its current conflict with Turkey.	Secretary of State Hughes announces that the United States approves of a proposed union of Central America (Honduras, Guatemala, Costa Rica, and Salvador).…Panama makes another appeal to have the arbitrated border dispute results changed; the United States is not responsive.…The Argentine government arrests several Communists and manages to suppress a General Strike.	Australia notifies the League of Nations that it is assuming responsibilities for the mandate of New Guinea.
Jun. 3	The International Olympic Committee announces that Paris will be the site of the 1924 Olympics and that Amsterdam will be the site of the Olympic Games in 1928.	Sinn Fein raids kill 11; a British munitions factory is attacked and set on fire and a bridge is bombed.…Britain's shipping industry is at its worst state in history; thousands of seamen are unemployed and the value of ships owned by the shipping companies has decreased.…The Austrian town of Styr names one of its streets "Herbert Hoover Strasse" in appreciation for his efforts in leading Austrian relief campaigns.…A British court-martial acquits 18 Black and Tan Constables on a charge of looting.	Saloman Tellirian, who shot and killed former Turkish Grand Vizer Talaat Pasha in Berlin in March, is acquitted; the defense was based on retaliation for the Armenian genocide.	Lord Julian Byng who led Canadian forces at the battle of Vimy Ridge in the World War has been named Governor General of Canada.…The British possessions of Grenada and St. Lucie petition the British government for self-rule.	
Jun. 4		Polish troops occupying portions of Silesia use firing squads to shoot looters as they impose martial law on the sections they control.…Fighting throughout Silesia continues and food is becoming scarce in some areas.…British forces begin a 10-day operation that will attempt to clear part of County Cork of Sinn Fein activity.…Jane Addams of Hull House is scheduled to attend, with 40 delegates, the Convention of the Women's International League in Vienna in July.	The diamond output for South Africa in 1920 exceeded all records with a value 35 percent over 1919.	In April, Mexico exported 16,252,000 barrels of oil.…The Peruvian government announces that it will hold an exposition of American manufacturers concurrent with the celebrations of Peru's independence.…Mexican Police set up security around the U.S. Embassy after threats of bombings by anarchists.	The estimated harvest of wheat in India for 1921 is estimated to be 69.3 percent of the 1920 harvest.…American missionaries in India are increasingly using autos as a means of visiting the various towns.…Japan's increasing population has encouraged an active interest in birth control, a perspective that is coming into conflict with an increasing Japanese desire to fix overcrowding by conquering Asia and putting it under Japanese control.
Jun. 5		Sweden increases the import tariffs on luxury goods such as silks, fruit, gold, and silver goods.…The *New York Times* reports that the city of Geneva, Switzerland, has 88 banks although the city's population is only 135,000 and that Geneva's bankers are "the smartest in the world."…French commentators, in discussing the recent peace proposals and plans put forth by President Harding, state that they do not see the difference between the world association he is proposing and the already existing League of Nations.	Greece's King Constantine states that he appreciates the assistance of Britain in Greece's war against Turkey.	After a lapse of 10 years, the British "colony" in Mexico has revived horseracing on a regular basis.…General Pablo Gonzalez, former Mexican Army Chief of Staff, is executed on the order of President Obregon for plotting against the government.…Guatemala's National Congress votes to close the nation's legations in Cuba, England, and Spain.…The archbishop of Guadalajara's home has been bombed prompting demands from Catholics that the government protect them from Communists.	
Jun. 6		The British government announces that it will send more troops to Ireland.…A state of famine is being reported in Petrograd and peasant uprisings outside the city are also reported.…The Port of Fiume on the Adriatic, once part of the Austro-Hungarian Empire, contested by Italy and Yugoslavia, will be a Free City with its own government, but total access will be given to Italy and Yugoslavia.	A new convention is signed between Britain and Liberia in which wives cannot be purchased for more than five pounds sterling.	Cuba's newly inaugurated President Zayas announces that he hopes to work closely with the United States.	The Siberian city of Omsk has been captured by anti-Communist forces.

A	B	C	D	E
Includes developments that affect more than one world region, international organizations and important meetings of world leaders.	*Includes all domestic and regional developments in Europe, including the Soviet Union.*	*Includes all domestic and regional developments in Africa and the Middle East.*	*Includes all domestic and regional developments in Latin America, the Caribbean, and Canada.*	*Includes all domestic and regional developments in Asian and Pacific nations (and colonies).*

U.S. Politics & Social Issues	U.S. Foreign Policy & Affairs, Defense	U.S. Economy & Environment	Science, Technology & Nature	Culture, Leisure & Lifestyle	
The Labor Department issues a report on the effects of child labor in the United States, which include widespread illiteracy.					Jun. 2
Military forces are withdrawn from Tulsa as civilian police take over; city officials claim that within the past 60 days a secret organization, the "African Blood Brotherhood," may have instigated the unrest....U.S. Attorney General Daugherty orders a Federal inquiry into the Tulsa riots....The National Association for the Advancement of Colored People asks President Harding to issue a statement condemning violence against African Americans....Seven jurors are chosen for the Sacco and Vanzetti trial after running through a pool of 500 prospective jurors....A strike of 54,000 cloak, suit, and skirt manufacturers is avoided when the workers agree to a 25 percent increase in productivity in return for no wage cuts.	The navy prepares for extensive war games, which include aerial bombing attacks on captured German ships; the exercise is planned for June 21 to July 20....Indications are that the U.S. House of representatives wants to expand the disarmament provisions of defense spending that the Senate has thus far approved....The navy awards a contract to the Dayton-Wright aircraft company for designs of aircraft the navy will use; additional contracts for naval aviation are also awarded.				Jun. 3
The presiding judge at the Sacco and Vanzetti trial orders the Sheriff to find 200 people to be interviewed for the jury as the current jury pool has been exhausted....The African Blood Brotherhood releases an announcement that defends the purposes of the organization as a defensive group and denies having started the race riots in Tulsa.		After seven years in developing the Lincoln Highway, which runs from New York City to San Francisco, a total of $31,284,520 has been spent on improvements....The dam holding the Cheyenne Reservoir is reported to have broken with an eight-foot wall of water heading for Pueblo, CO....In the immediate wake of the flood in Pueblo estimates claim that thousands may have died; martial law has been declared with orders for troopers to shoot to kill all looters as there is no time for trials.		Bryn Mawr College is beginning a summer school that will last for eight weeks for woman industrial workers.	Jun. 4
		Accounts of the devastation of the Pueblo, CO, flood describe houses being swept away with their occupants and hundred having been drowned....The American Red Cross is providing an emergency fund of $100,000....The loss of lives is currently estimated at between 500 and 1,000 and property loss may be as high as $15 million.			Jun. 5
Military authorities in Mingo Country arrest 40 miners on the charge of violating martial law....The Court of Appeals in Washington, DC, rules that radical political literature is obscene and cannot be sent through the mails.	Secretary of War Weeks announces he will decrease the number of officers in the Army to remove those who have a record of inefficiency....Lieutenant J.A. Macready establishes a new flying height record, reaching 34,150 feet.	All males in the Pueblo, CO area are being called into service to assist rescue and cleanup efforts; initial estimates of hundreds of casualties are now being revised with the current official death toll at 83. Army troops from San Francisco and San Antonio are being rushed to assist in recovery effort, most military assistance will be doctors, nurses, and field hospitals....Senator Nicholson of Colorado proposes a bill that would create a new federal Department of Mines.			Jun. 6

F	G	H	I	J
Includes campaigns, elections, federal-state relations, civil rights and liberties, crime, the judiciary, education, healthcare, poverty, urban affairs, and population.	*Includes formation and debate of U.S. foreign and defense policies, veterans affairs, and defense spending. (Relations with specific foreign countries are usually found under the region concerned.)*	*Includes business, labor, agriculture, taxation, transportation, consumer affairs, monetary and fiscal policy, natural resources, pollution and industrial accidents.*	*Includes worldwide scientific, medical and technological developments, natural phenomena, U.S. weather and natural disasters.*	*Includes the arts, religion, scholarship, communications media, sports, entertainment, fashions, fads, and social life.*

	World Affairs	Europe	Africa & The Middle East	The Americas	Asia & The Pacific
Jun. 7		Czechoslovakia, Yugoslavia, and Romania sign a treaty bringing the Little Entente into existence.…The continued popularity of the idea of a union between Austria and Germany is causing serious concern among many officials of the League of Nations.…Soldiers of Britain's Black Watch Regiment in a surprise attack capture the Silesian city of Rosenberg from Polish rebels and a neutral zone between Poles and Germans is created.…British forces in Ireland capture 100 members of Sinn Fein in County Cork; additionally, three members of Sinn Fein are executed for anti-British activity.	The British government claims that it has foiled a Turkish-Soviet plot that would have seized Constantinople from British occupation.	Americans may now enter Canada without possessing passports.… U.S. Secretary of State Hughes states that Mexico must bind itself to respect the property rights of foreign corporations before it will receive recognition by the United States.	
Jun. 8		Romania and Yugoslavia sign a treaty to settle their boundary line.…To demonstrate support for a unified Austrian-German state, 5,000 demonstrators from Salzburg cross the German frontier without passports and meet with Bavarian authorities.…The British government announces it will seek to repeal the Agriculture Act that has provided a subsidy to British farmers and will also seek to reduce the amount of money the unemployed are paid.…Sinn Fein cuts 247 telephone, telegraph, and signal lines from Britain to Ireland.	Muslims from the Soviet Union are rumored to be massing near the Armenian border to join Mustafa Kemal; anxiety over their ability to hold Constantinople has led the British to order ships to the region.	Mexico's President Obregon stops a plot that would have overthrown his government; the leaders have been arrested and executed.…Major General George Goethals, who worked on completing the Panama Canal, states that he would be very interested in working on improving the roads in Cuba.	A Japanese newspaper states that the alliance with Britain would be essential to Japan's best interests in light of the advancing of American outposts throughout the Pacific.
Jun. 9		British officials state that in the past week 67 have been killed in the fighting in Ireland, the highest weekly total since 1916.…The British have destroyed a total of 185 houses in Ireland as retaliation for raids and ambushes since January 1.…The British government claims it has found the text of a proposed treaty between the Soviets and the Irish rebels.…Conflicts between French rail workers and rail companies takes a new turn as French authorities are finding evidence of sabotage of tracks and signals.		President Obregon states that he refuses to sign a special treaty with the United States in order to gain recognition of his government.	Rainfall in China, after a long period of drought, continues and will be important in preventing a widespread famine in the coming year.
Jun. 10		The Swedish government announces that it has prevented an attempt by Communists to overthrow the government; similar revolutions are said to have been planned in Norway and Finland.…British and French troops are moving in well-coordinated fashion in Silesia, not only to consolidate efforts at peacekeeping but to show that despite disagreements they are working together.			Reports describe the mutiny of a Communist regiment, which then took control of the city of Blagovestchensk in Siberia from the Communists; a few hours later the Communists retook the town.
Jun. 11	Diplomatic relations are reestablished between France and the Vatican.	The Yugoslav Communist Party withdraws from the Constituent Assembly in protest over a Constitution creating a highly centralized government.…Lenin declares that the Soviets will restore property rights.…A raid on union offices in Paris by moderate factions oust the Communists from their place in the offices and in control of the Union, which now reverts to non-Communist factions.…Italy's Civil Service calls off its planned strike.…The French government is complaining about British foreign policy, blaming it for the seriousness of the situation in Silesia as well as for the war between Greece and Turkey.…Denmark's Foreign Ministers is accused of leaking state secrets to Germany.	King Constantine of Greece departs for the battlefield to lead his troops against the Turks.	The Argentine government declares that the United States has no right to demand a special treaty of Mexico in return for recognition of President Obregon's government.	
	A *Includes developments that affect more than one world region, international organizations and important meetings of world leaders.*	B *Includes all domestic and regional developments in Europe, including the Soviet Union.*	C *Includes all domestic and regional developments in Africa and the Middle East.*	D *Includes all domestic and regional developments in Latin America, the Caribbean, and Canada.*	E *Includes all domestic and regional developments in Asian and Pacific nations (and colonies).*

	U.S. Politics & Social Issues	U.S. Foreign Policy & Affairs, Defense	U.S. Economy & Environment	Science, Technology & Nature	Culture, Leisure & Lifestyle
Jun. 7	The prosecutor's opening remarks are presented at the Sacco and Vanzetti trial....The Oklahoma Attorney General begins an investigation into the Tulsa, OK, race riots while four African Americans are charged with rioting....Chicago meat packing companies petition a Federal Court to reduce the wages of 100,000 workers by five cents an hour.	As part of the annual naval maneuvers conducted, naval vessels fire on and sink the captured German *U-97* in Lake Michigan.			
Jun. 8		In a change from its previous voting, the Senate votes 36–32 to reduce the size of the Army to 150,000 men; the actual effect will be to cut the force down to 120,000.	In Pueblo, CO, the death toll is officially 66, much lower than initial estimates but officials are trying to track down approximately 2,500 missing people.		The Wagner Festival in Bayreuth, Germany, will resume in 1923 not having taken place since 1914.
Jun. 9	Conflicting witnesses in the Sacco and Vanzetti trial testify on whether they could identify the men in the hold up car....Secretary of Labor James Davis warns corporations not to try to smash the unions, as radicals would then fill the vacuum.	Major General Charles T. Menoher, Chief of the Army Air Service, requests that Secretary of War Weeks remove his deputy, Brigadier General Billy Mitchell as Mitchell has caused a great deal of friction within the air service.	The potential toll of the Pueblo flood continues to be revised downward; authorities are now stating that the number of missing is only 127.		The Cleveland Indians lead the American League followed by the Yankees, Senators, Tigers, Red Sox, Browns, White Sox, and Athletics....The first place team in the National League is led by the Pirates, followed by the Giants, Cardinals, Braves, Robins, Cubs, Reds, and Phillies....Jack Dempsey continues his training for the upcoming fight with Georges Carpentier....The Internal Revenue Service estimates that the taxes on the championship bout will be approximately $500,000.
Jun. 10	The Maine State branch of the American Federation of Labor votes in favor of resumption of trade between the United States and the Soviet Union....Nineteen members of the I.W.W. imprisoned for activities against the war effort are released from prison.	A resolution is introduced in the House of Representatives asking President Harding to recognize the Soviet government.	The Maine Forestry Commission reports that in the past month extensive forest fires have burned more than 20,000 acres.		
Jun. 11	Miners in Francisco, IN, force a group of 100 foreigners, who had been working in the local mines, to leave; the men had been brought in to work the mines during a recent strike....The Kansas Supreme Court rules that the Kansas Anti-Syndicalism Law does not bar members of disloyal organizations from entering the state.		Production of oil in the United States continues at a very high rate; the total output for May was 40,039,000 barrels.	The American Bison Society estimates that there are 9,311 bison in the world, of which 3,527 are in the United States.	Dr. Samuel Riddle announces that he may bring back his colt Man o' War to racing, who had been retired last year....Laurence Brown of the University of Pennsylvania breaks the world record for the 1,000 yard run, running the distance in two minutes, 12.2 seconds....*Back to Methuselah* by George Bernard Shaw is reviewed by the *New York Times*....Poet Amy Lowell publishes a new book of poems, *Legends*.

F	G	H	I	J
Includes campaigns, elections, federal-state relations, civil rights and liberties, crime, the judiciary, education, healthcare, poverty, urban affairs, and population.	*Includes formation and debate of U.S. foreign and defense policies, veterans affairs, and defense spending. (Relations with specific foreign countries are usually found under the region concerned.)*	*Includes business, labor, agriculture, taxation, transportation, consumer affairs, monetary and fiscal policy, natural resources, pollution and industrial accidents.*	*Includes worldwide scientific, medical and technological developments, natural phenomena, U.S. weather and natural disasters.*	*Includes the arts, religion, scholarship, communications media, sports, entertainment, fashions, fads, and social life.*

	World Affairs	Europe	Africa & The Middle East	The Americas	Asia & The Pacific
Jun. 12		The Soviet government denies that there has been any attempt to draw up agreements with the Irish rebels against British rule.…Silesia presents a problem that is growing increasingly complex as ethnic Poles and Germans are fighting against each other with an allied force of British, French, and Italians, who do not often agree on a course of action.			
Jun. 13		Italy has now stated that it will provide Britain its full support in keeping the peace in Silesia; British forces move closer to the Polish insurgent front.	The British government states that it will be neutral in the war between Greece and Turkey.…Pope Benedict XV states that the Jews in Palestine have taken advantage of the sufferings of the inhabitants due to the World War and have a "privileged position," which is "dangerous for Christians"; the Pope further states that he hopes that the League of Nations will define exactly what the British Mandate in Palestine will entail.	General Jose Gomez, 66, former President of Cuba dies in New York City; he was in America to seek support in opposing the current Cuban President Zayas.	
Jun. 14		A strike is threatened to begin tomorrow in Britain by 1,500, men in the engineering trades over the issue of wage decreases.…Albert Mere, known as "Albert the Silent," dies at the age of 81; he was a member of Germany's Reichstag for 44 years and made no speech in all of that time.…Members of Sinn Fein manage to keep thousands of workers from entering the British shipyards in Belfast.…Although the Polish Army has now complied with the Allied Commission's demand for withdrawal, German forces refuse to leave Silesia.	Britain announces that it wishes to transfer power in Iraq to King Faisal as early as possible.		The French government announces plans to send it war hero, Marshall Joffre, to begin military discussions between France and Japan.
Jun. 15		The Allies state that they will seize all airplanes in Germany in retaliation for Germany's failure to live up to the aircraft construction provisions of the Versailles Treaty.…French Premier Briand promises that he will take up a bill to allow woman suffrage in France.…A shipment of 600 machine guns intended for Sinn Fein is seized by Federal agents in New York City.…Nikolai Bukharin of the Soviet Union admits that there are serious difficulties in the Soviet Union and that outside aid will be necessary.	The British government issues a statement that any attempt to take Constantinople from the British will mean war.		Canada's Premier states that he is against an Anglo-Japanese alliance as it would be a challenge to the United States.
Jun. 16		Reports from the Soviet Union describe widespread famine in the Ukraine with thousands dying while officials in Moscow are becoming wealthy through corruption.…British miners insist that they will not accept the latest set of terms proposed to bring them back to work.…Hearse drivers in Paris declare that they will not wear Napoleonic style uniforms any longer.	French forces encounter Turkish troops in French-occupied Syria and defeat them.	President Obregon's insistence on not signing a special treaty with the United States in order to gain recognition of his government is very popular with Mexicans.	A Communist newspaper in Latvia reports that Japan has made a decision to definitely withdraw its troops from Siberia.

U.S. Politics & Social Issues	U.S. Foreign Policy & Affairs, Defense	U.S. Economy & Environment	Science, Technology & Nature	Culture, Leisure & Lifestyle	
	President Harding encourages all American young men to attend the Plattsburgh-style military training camps that will commence this summer.			The George Bernard Shaw play, *Arms and the Man*, while playing in Vienna, causes a near riot as Bulgarians attending the play try to disrupt it for what they consider insults to Bulgaria.	Jun. 12
Samuel Gompers of the American Federation of Labor calls for an alliance between workers and farmers; Gompers also states that he is in favor of excluding all Asians from immigrating to the United States.... Governor McCray of Indiana warns local officials that they must prevent vigilantes from driving out foreign strikebreakers as in the recent incident in Gibson County....Fiorello LaGuardia, President of the Board of Aldermen for New York City, states that he will run for mayor of New York City....In Moorestown, NJ, Prosecutor Jonathan Kelsey prevents a mob from lynching an African America, Louis Lively, by promising that he will be charged with first-degree murder so he can be executed by electrocution.				Mrs. Jane Burke of Milton, MA, claims that she has been in communication with philosopher William James, who has been dictating a book to her; Professor James has been dead since 1910.	Jun. 13
		The number of draft horses in New York City has decreased from 128,224 in 1910 to 56,539.	Research into the German patent office reveals that Germany had developed both flamethrowers and poison gas as early as 1908.	Teachers in France give students permission to dance the shimmy so long as it is done decorously.	Jun. 14
In the Sacco and Vanzetti trial, the defense attempts to impeach one witness because of a deal made with the prosecution, but the judge does not allow the defense motion....All telephone and telegraph wires passing through the regions of West Virginia affected by the unrest in Mingo County have been cut.	Former Secretary of the Treasury, William McAdoo, has written to Secretary of State Hughes encouraging him to recognize the new republic of Lithuania, especially as such recognition would curb Poland's aggression against that country.		The number of icebergs in the North Atlantic is greater than at any time since 1912, the year the *Titanic* sank.		Jun. 15
A mob in Autreyville, GA, burns down an African-American church as well as several homes because of the murder of a 12-year-old Caucasian girl earlier in the week.		Pennsylvania crude oil is now selling for $2.50 a barrel, the lowest price since 1916.	While tuberculosis is increasing in Europe, occurrences are declining in the United States leading some experts to believe that the disease may be eradicated in this country....A serum has been developed in France that will provide protection against hoof and mouth disease.	*The Portrait of Mr. W.H.*, a manuscript by Oscar Wilde, which has been lost, has been discovered. ...*The Ziegfeld Follies of 1921*, the 15th such production, opens in Atlantic City where it will play for three nights before moving to New York; this year's cast features Fanny Brice and W.C. Fields.	Jun. 16

F	G	H	I	J
Includes campaigns, elections, federal-state relations, civil rights and liberties, crime, the judiciary, education, healthcare, poverty, urban affairs, and population.	*Includes formation and debate of U.S. foreign and defense policies, veterans affairs, and defense spending. (Relations with specific foreign countries are usually found under the region concerned.)*	*Includes business, labor, agriculture, taxation, transportation, consumer affairs, monetary and fiscal policy, natural resources, pollution and industrial accidents.*	*Includes worldwide scientific, medical and technological developments, natural phenomena, U.S. weather and natural disasters.*	*Includes the arts, religion, scholarship, communications media, sports, entertainment, fashions, fads, and social life.*

	World Affairs	Europe	Africa & The Middle East	The Americas	Asia & The Pacific
Jun. 17	The 13th session of the League of Nations Council begins.	King Peter of Serbia who has been seriously ill is reported as recovering.... British miners vote to continue their strike.... Ex-King Charles, currently in exile in Switzerland, may stay in the country indefinitely because it has been discovered that technically he is a Swiss citizen.... Premier Briand of France and British Foreign Secretary Lord Curzon are discussing how the two nations can contain the conflict between the Greeks and the Turks.... Swiss authorities conclude that many of the deaths that take place on hiking trails are suicides rather than legitimate climbing accidents; in many cases the victims are Russians forced into exile because of the Revolution.		Canadian Railways formally notify their employees that wages will be cut effective July 1; the cut affects 150,000 workers.... Rioting among sugar workers in Cuba seeking payment results in five being killed.	
Jun. 18	There are several new developments on international trade: Italy has banned the importation of synthetic dyes; German toy manufacturers are providing strong competition to Japanese toy companies resulting in layoffs in Japanese plants; British machinery sales are very active in Argentina as indicated by the opening of a new machinery sales office in Buenos Aries; Norway announces a glut on its whale oil market; Mexico announces that it will implement import tariffs on cotton goods.	The League of Nations reports on its findings that the free city of Danzig has become a large-scale weapons sales center.... Visitors returning to the United States from Czechoslovakia comment on the extent to which American business and other methods are being adopted throughout the country.... Former Commander of the Imperial Russian Navy, Admiral Michael Smirnoff, leaves the United States to live in Germany; he states that he will not return to Russia; the Admiral adds he will not miss American prohibition.		The German Immigration Syndicate has signed a contract to furnish 2,000 German families to move to Brazil.... Mexico's President releases several of his political foes from prison.... A shipment of 2.25 million gallons of gasoline arrives in Montreal; gasoline prices in Canada are now expected to drop.	Japan's Baron Kanda arrives in the United States on a tour and states that sending Japanese students to the United States would help the good relations between the two countries.
Jun. 19		Lenin manages to convince many of the wisdom of his New Economic Plan in a meeting of the Soviet leadership, although neither Leon Trotsky nor Felix Dzerzhinsky have been well received by the majority of Soviets in attendance.	The Muslims and Christians of Palestine sign a treaty of friendship against the Jewish population.... The British, French, and Italian governments send a note to the Greek government demanding that it not continue its war with Turkey.	The members of a special commission charged with investigating the civil administration of the Panama Canal arrives from the United States.... The funeral of former President, General Gomez, in Havana results in rioting with three killed and many injured.	Floods in Japan claim more than 130 lives and many homes have been swept away.
Jun. 20		An earthquake strikes Messina, Italy, reports indicate there have been no victims and no damage.... Five British officers are killed by Sinn Fein near Dublin.	King Constantine of Greece has not yet responded to the Allied demand that he halt the war with Turkey; the situation is complicated by the fact that although France and Britain agree on wanting the war to stop, they disagree on nearly every subsidiary issue concerning the Greek-Turkish conflict.		
Jun. 21	At the British Imperial Conference, Jan Smuts of South Africa states that the Empire must turn its attentions to Asia, which will become increasingly important in the future.	Eamon de Valera states that he is opposed to Ireland belonging to the Dominions of the British Empire but wants full independence and complete neutrality.... The Minister of the German state of Prussia declares that Communists are not eligible to hold office.			
Jun. 22	According to reports in Moscow, representation at the Third Communist International from the Middle East and Asia has been very heavy; in addition, there are many woman delegates from around the world.	King George V addresses the first session of Northern Ireland's parliament, asking the Irish to "forgive, forget."		Two Mexican soldiers from the Nuevo Laredo outpost are reported killed in clashes with bandits.	Afghanistan and Persia sign a nonaggression treaty.... The Chinese government publicly states that it is suspicious of Japan's motives in beginning discussions about restoring Chinese authority in Shantung province.

A	B	C	D	E
Includes developments that affect more than one world region, international organizations and important meetings of world leaders.	*Includes all domestic and regional developments in Europe, including the Soviet Union.*	*Includes all domestic and regional developments in Africa and the Middle East.*	*Includes all domestic and regional developments in Latin America, the Caribbean, and Canada.*	*Includes all domestic and regional developments in Asian and Pacific nations (and colonies).*

U.S. Politics & Social Issues	U.S. Foreign Policy & Affairs, Defense	U.S. Economy & Environment	Science, Technology & Nature	Culture, Leisure & Lifestyle	
	Colonel Frederick Folz, commander of the 6th Cavalry, is relieved from command as a result of physically abusing a trooper by keeping him in chains.…The U.S. Fleet is testing a new type of radio compass that provides bearings from shore stations.				Jun. 17
John Henry, an African American convicted of murdering a young girl, is taken from custody of the sheriff in Moultrie, GA, and lynched.…Near Cincinnati, OH, 2,000 new members of the Ku Klux Klan are inducted into the society; members from 22 states attend.…President Harding states that he will not give Civil Service employees in Washington a half day off on Saturdays, as it would not be in the interest of public service.	The Secretary of War announces that there will be no force reductions in Panama or Hawaii.	The National Industrial Conference Board reports that 45 million Americans work for a living. In addition, that 90 percent of all manufacturing plants in the United States have fewer than 500 employees.…Senator Borah states that the government must not put "business in a straitjacket," by legislating excessive regulation.			Jun. 18
In McCormick, SC, Herbert Quarles, an African American accused of assaulting a Caucasian woman, is forced to climb a tree by a mob of 2,000 men, tied to the tree, and then shot.…W.A. Domingo of the African Blood Brotherhood, at a speech in New York City, advises African Americans to retaliate in kind when attacked by whites.					Jun. 19
The General Grievance Committee, an organization of miners, calls a strike of 10,000 anthracite coal miners in Pennsylvania; this is the second time in less than a year that these men have gone out on strike.…The United Mine Workers ask President Harding to investigate the conditions that have led to the unrest in Mingo County, WV.…Police in New York City are asking for a raise from $2,280 to $2,500 a year.	Three U.S. ships have disappeared in recent weeks; there is speculation that they have been seized by pirates or by Soviet agents, perhaps using submarines.	Standard Oil of New Jersey announces it will once again cut prices.…Goodyear Rubber has stopped its policy of retrenchment and is recruiting additional salesmen.	Marie Curie receive an honorary degree from Wellesley College, the first time that college has ever awarded such a degree.		Jun. 20
	U.S. Army Air Corps bomb the captured German warship *Ostfriedland* as part of a demonstration of how air power can make battleships obsolete.…Navy aviators drop 12 bombs on the captured German ship and it goes down in 16 minutes.		For the third time in several years mastodon bones have been found in Newburgh, NY.		Jun. 21
The defense begins presenting its case in the Sacco and Vanzetti trial.…Seven members of the I.W.W. begin their sentences for murder at the so-called Armistice Day shooting in Centralia, WA; their sentences range from 25 to 40 years.	Naval maneuvers continue off the east coast of the United States.…Fliers bomb and sink two more captured German vessels.…U.S. destroyers are using captured German ships as targets from ranges of 2,000 to 3,000 yards.	Today, with the temperature at 93 degrees, is the hottest June 22 in New York City's history.		Three unknown sparring partners appear at the Georges Carpentier training camp, work with the fighter, and then leave as mysteriously as they came.…Reports throughout the country report a flood of counterfeit tickets for the upcoming Dempsey-Carpentier fight.…Charles H. Taylor, who published the *Boston Globe* for 48 years, dies.	Jun. 22

F
Includes campaigns, elections, federal-state relations, civil rights and liberties, crime, the judiciary, education, healthcare, poverty, urban affairs, and population.

G
Includes formation and debate of U.S. foreign and defense policies, veterans affairs, and defense spending. (Relations with specific foreign countries are usually found under the region concerned.)

H
Includes business, labor, agriculture, taxation, transportation, consumer affairs, monetary and fiscal policy, natural resources, pollution and industrial accidents.

I
Includes worldwide scientific, medical and technological developments, natural phenomena, U.S. weather and natural disasters.

J
Includes the arts, religion, scholarship, communications media, sports, entertainment, fashions, fads, and social life.

	World Affairs	Europe	Africa & The Middle East	The Americas	Asia & The Pacific
Jun. 23		Flight Lieutenant Proctor, an air ace and winner of the Victoria Cross in the World War, dies when his plane crashes near Salisbury Plain, England....Sinn Fein blows up a British troop train, killing four soldiers and many horses.	The Greek government indicates that it may accept mediation in halting the fighting with Turkey.	All schools in Argentina have been closed as a result of an outbreak of influenza.	Japanese soldiers in Siberia are fighting Communist troops.
Jun. 24		Norwegian arctic explorer and diplomat, Fridtjof Nansen, attempts to secure the release of Americans currently being held by the Soviets, but has yet to succeed.		Mexico states that it is considering making claims to several islands now claimed by the United States to include Santa Catalina Island.	The Osaka, Japan, Chamber of Congress, issues a statement seeking that Japan lead the disarmament effort.
Jun. 25	A new organization called the Red Shield of David comes into existence to become the Jewish equivalent of the Red Cross and the Red Crescent....The Royal Mail Steam Packet Company reports that the actual shipping tonnage on the world's oceans is 11 million more tons than it was in July 1914....The League of Nations rules that it cannot intervene in a dispute between Albania, Greece, and Yugoslavia, based on an Albanian demand that those nations withdraw from territory claimed by Albania.	A railway accident on the Lille-Paris express kills 23 and injures 43....Lloyd George invites Eamon de Valera to come to London to discuss a peaceful settlement in Ireland....Reports from Moscow indicate that Lenin has appointed Leon Trotsky to take responsibility for world revolution while Lenin will focus on strengthening Soviet control domestically....Greece informs Britain and France that it will not stop its war with Turkey....A severe heat wave in Paris has claimed at least one life; outside the city, the heat is accompanied by a severe drought that will affect the harvest later this year....German exports to, and imports from, America are approaching record amounts.	Italy announces that it will grant limited home rule to tribesmen in Libya.	Observers state that the government of Mexico's President Obregon has done so much to accede to U.S. requests that it will eventually receive full recognition.	The Chinese government expresses concern that the Anglo-Japanese Alliance is not only bad for China but would threaten American interests there.
Jun. 26	Addressing a session of the Communist Third International, Leon Trotsky predicts that the United States and Britain will go to war in 1924, commencing with a great naval war....Albania repeats its plea to the League of Nations to resolve the issue of territory it claims was taken by Greece and Yugoslavia; the League decides to refer the matter to the Council of Ambassadors.	War crimes trials against German soldiers continue; within the week, a case will be brought against a General Stenger for ordering the massacre of French prisoners of War in August 1914....Spanish immigrants who have gone to Brazil and the United States seek to return because they cannot find work....Eamon de Valera agrees to meet with Lloyd George in London.	The South African Reserve Bank is established.		
Jun. 27	At the conference of British Dominion Prime Ministers, Arthur Meighen of Canada states that the nations of the Dominion must have increased influence over the conduct of foreign affairs.	A plan is submitted at the League of Nations to resolve the conflict between Lithuania and Poland over Vilna....A Spanish economic publication predicts that after years of depression, industry in Spain is staging a revival.			The Japanese government is employing a group of 100 men, both current British and former German officers, to help improve Japan's aviation capabilities.
Jun. 28	The 13th session of the League of Nations Council ends.	After three months, the nationwide coal miners strike in Britain comes to an end....The leader of Polish elements in Silesia declares that if a just solution is not brought to Silesia it will turn into "a second Ireland."...The volcano, Stromboli, near the north coast of Sicily, has erupted....Reports in the Soviet Press admit that there may be as many as 25 million Russians in danger of starvation....Poland and Lithuania reject all proposals by the League of Nations over possession of the city of Vilna....The Dublin Parliament is formally opened; a small number attend with many in the lower House, who are Sinn Feiners, refusing to attend.	A representative of Mustafa Kemal denies that there is any kind of Turkish-Soviet alliance.	Mexican antigovernment rebels are active, in some cases attacking villages with American residents who have succeeded in defending themselves against attacks.	

A	B	C	D	E
Includes developments that affect more than one world region, international organizations and important meetings of world leaders.	*Includes all domestic and regional developments in Europe, including the Soviet Union.*	*Includes all domestic and regional developments in Africa and the Middle East.*	*Includes all domestic and regional developments in Latin America, the Caribbean, and Canada.*	*Includes all domestic and regional developments in Asian and Pacific nations (and colonies).*

U.S. Politics & Social Issues	U.S. Foreign Policy & Affairs, Defense	U.S. Economy & Environment	Science, Technology & Nature	Culture, Leisure & Lifestyle	
Four boys in New York City are arrested for taking pennies, placing them on trolley rails to smash them into a larger size, and then using them in postal stamp machines as quarters; the boys have been put into their parents' custody.... President Harding announces that he will rest on July 4 and make no official speeches....The nationwide strike of affiliated Maritime Unions, which began on May 1, ends.	The U.S. Naval Armory at Pearl Harbor, HI, is destroyed by fire, destroying 75 percent of the contents; the fire's cause is unknown.... The Navy's newest battleship, the USS *Maryland*, will be ready next month and will be assigned to the Pacific Fleet....Officers of the navy, who are advocates of battleships, state that they are not yet convinced by the results of the recent successful bombing of captured ships off the U.S. east coast.			Astrologer Professor Gustav Meyer, of Hoboken, NJ, predicts that Jack Dempsey will win the title fight with Georges Carpentier.	Jun. 23
New York City police pour $50,000 of liquor and wine into the gutters of Houston and Sheriff streets; police details on hand try to prevent bystanders from attempting to salvage the liquor.	Secretary of War Weeks writes to Major General Menoher, Chief of Aviation, that greater precautions are to be taken against accidents in the wake of 18 deaths of pilots in the past few weeks.			Jules "Nicky" Arnstein, convicted confidence man and husband of actress Fanny Brice, is sentenced to two years in prison for securities frauds.	Jun. 24
Samuel L. Gompers is reelected to the Presidency of the American Federation of Labor, defeating John L. Lewis of the Miners Unions by a 2–1 margin....The Immigration Bureau reports that 22,240 immigrants arrived in the United States in 1920....The Bureau of the Census reports that New York City has 870,149 alien-born women in New York City, of whom 360,255 have become citizens.	General Pershing announces that when he takes over as Chief of Staff he will initiate a program that will strengthen both the National Guard and the reserves....The Navy reports it has developed a star shell that illuminates wide areas and works better than a searchlight.... Naval and Army aviators are planning their bombing runs on radio controlled ships that will be part of a series of tests in which aviators must find ships at sea, bomb them, and then destroy them.	The heat wave continues in the northeast; one more person dies and three are hospitalized for heat stroke....Petroleum production, according to the government, broke all records in May with 41.92 million barrels....The Bureau of the Census reports that the value of American farms in 1920 was $67,795,965,000, double the reported value for 1910.		Babe Ruth hits his 26th home run for the season, placing him ahead of his 1920 home-run mark....The fraternal group, the Improved Order of Red Men, announces that the Ohio chapter will confer the Warrior and Chief degrees on President Harding....Plymouth Rock, where the Pilgrims are alleged to have landed in 1620 has been restored and the three pieces reassembled; a marble canopy will be built over the rock....A conference of the Northern Baptists condemns dance halls and theaters as a "menace to the moral life of the nation."	Jun. 25
Joseph Laspisa, bodyguard of the late Anthony D'Andrea, a Chicago labor and political leader, is shot and killed.				The trial on fraud charges against those accused of "fixing" the 1919 World Series has the Prosecution confident that it will win the trial quickly....Elsie Janis, famed American entertainer known during the World War as "the Sweetheart of the AEF," closes her successful run at the Apollo Theatre in Paris....A monument to composer Johann Strauss, Jr. is unveiled in the Vienna State Park.	Jun. 26
President Harding sends a message to the Disabled Veterans of America pledging that the government will do its utmost to provide "justice and humane consideration."					Jun. 27
The Socialist National Convention, meeting in Detroit, refuses to eliminate members who are Communists or who support the Third International....A state trooper is killed in the latest fighting in Mingo County, WV; Governor Morgan proclaims that authorities in the region are empowered to make all men in the area liable to military support duty.	Aviators on exercises to test bombing of ships run into difficulties in finding the ships because of heavy cloud cover.		Sir Ernest Shackleton announces that at the end of August he will launch another expedition to the Antarctic.	An organization is formed in Geneva, Switzerland, opposing the increased appearance of short skirts.	Jun. 28
F *Includes campaigns, elections, federal-state relations, civil rights and liberties, crime, the judiciary, education, healthcare, poverty, urban affairs, and population.*	**G** *Includes formation and debate of U.S. foreign and defense policies, veterans affairs, and defense spending. (Relations with specific foreign countries are usually found under the region concerned.)*	**H** *Includes business, labor, agriculture, taxation, transportation, consumer affairs, monetary and fiscal policy, natural resources, pollution and industrial accidents.*	**I** *Includes worldwide scientific, medical and technological developments, natural phenomena, U.S. weather and natural disasters.*	**J** *Includes the arts, religion, scholarship, communications media, sports, entertainment, fashions, fads, and social life.*	

	World Affairs	Europe	Africa & The Middle East	The Americas	Asia & The Pacific
Jun. 29		The Silesian city of Katowice, which is surrounded by Polish insurgents, is being defended by French troops; currently food supplies are so scarce that people are eating rats.…The German government is planning to demand that the Allies pay damages resulting from the recent and continued fighting in Silesia.…Eamon de Valera rejects a plan that would divide Ireland into two distinct entities.…Former Naval Lieutenant Commander Bolt, a U-boat commander who torpedoed a British Hospital ship, begins his trial in Leipzig as a war criminal.		The Cuban Senate defeats a measure that would have given women the vote.	Governor Leonard Wood returns to Manila after an extensive tour of the Philippines.…The Japanese Minister to China will ask the Chinese government to participate in a conference to resolve differences in Japanese rights in the Shantung Province.
Jun. 30	The League of Nations begins its International Congress on the Treatment of Women and Children; 33 nations are represented in this conference including the United States, which has sent an unofficial delegate.	Losses because of the World War and the Revolution have resulted in only a quarter of Russia's prewar railroad capability being in service.…An engineering strike is averted when British engineers accept a provisional offer modifying the original proposed wage cuts.	Turkish successes in the war with Greece are prompting the British to consider courses of action if the Turks advance to capture Constantinople, which has been occupied by the British since the conclusion of the World War.…Fighting in and around Ismid has resulted in charges of atrocities committed by both Greeks and Turks.		Soldiers of the South Chinese Republic have recaptured the city of Wu-chow, about 100 miles west of Canton, cutting off opposing armies from the sea.
Jul. 1		The Ruhr region of Germany expects a French invasion and occupation as eminent despite agreements by Germany to pay the reparations to the Allies.…The heat wave in Switzerland has been temporarily broken by several hailstorms that have caused severe crop damage.…Members of the Fascist party claim to have killed 15 Communists in street fighting.	Reports from Turkey deny that there are either Soviet troops or artillery assisting Mustafa Kemal's forces.…Spanish authorities are considering sending an additional infantry division into Morocco to assist in the fighting against Moorish rebels.…The fighting in Turkey is creating a significant rift between France and Britain.	Today is opening day of the Mexican baseball season; President Obregon throws out the first pitch at a game in Mexico City.…The Peruvian government forbids the export of any antiquities found in the country.	In the Philippines, 77 members of the Constabulary are found guilty of murder in recent riots in which three American members of the force were killed last December.
Jul. 2	The International Federation of Trade Unions, an organization with 25 million members worldwide will not allow any of its organizations to support the Third Communist International or support Communism in general.	In the war crimes trial of German General Stenger, a witness describes the shooting of two wounded French prisoners in August 1914.…In France, there are currently 1.9 million cases of tuberculosis with 20,000 dying a year of that disease.…The Soviet Union claims it has discovered a Polish plot to use dissidents to help overthrow the Soviet government.…Nineteen Hungarian Communists escape in a prison break with the aid of prison guards they had converted to their cause.…A conference is underway to create an alliance among Lithuania, Latvia, and Estonia to be known as the Baltic Triple Union.…Poland's Minister of Finance accuses a group of Austrian and German bankers in plotting to discredit the government of Poland.	American marines land at the Turkish city of Ismid to protect an American mission during the Greek-Turkish fighting in the immediate area; massacres committed by both sides have been reported by several sources.	The Panamanian government has contacted Costa Rica asking to resolve their border dispute without American intervention.	The government of the Far Eastern Republic of Siberia has asked Moscow for assistance in removing Japanese troops from its territory.
Jul. 3		The Communists are still keeping all of then mutinous sailors from the Kronstadt Mutiny in prison.…The British Air Ministry states that it cannot find customers for the air ships that it wants to build and sell.…The French government announces that it will begin construction of dams on the Rhone River to generate electrical power.…With less than a quarter of an inch of rainfall, this is the driest June in Britain in a century.	The Turkish government admits that it has made a deal with the Soviets and there are Soviet troops in the Kars region of eastern Turkey but they are there as a "symbol of brotherhood."	Newfoundland's revenue for this year has fallen to $6 million compared with $8.5 million the previous year.…The Nicaraguan government has made it known that it is anxious to join the Central American Union with Honduras, Salvador, and Costa Rica.…A group described as "Mexican cowboys," kidnaps and kills General Reves Salinas in Piedras Negras, Mexico; the General was the nephew of the late President Carranza.…The Presidential Suite in Peru's government House in Lima has been destroyed by fire.	New Zealand has the lowest infantry mortality rate of any country, according to a report by the U.S. Department of Labor's Children's Bureau.

A	B	C	D	E
Includes developments that affect more than one world region, international organizations and important meetings of world leaders.	*Includes all domestic and regional developments in Europe, including the Soviet Union.*	*Includes all domestic and regional developments in Africa and the Middle East.*	*Includes all domestic and regional developments in Latin America, the Caribbean, and Canada.*	*Includes all domestic and regional developments in Asian and Pacific nations (and colonies).*

U.S. Politics & Social Issues	U.S. Foreign Policy & Affairs, Defense	U.S. Economy & Environment	Science, Technology & Nature	Culture, Leisure & Lifestyle	
Secretary of Labor James Davis states that the Department of Labor could assist in registering all immigrants and guiding them toward citizenship.	The first two phases of the joint Army-Navy aviation exercises have completed with the aviators failing to sink the retired battleship USS *Iowa*, dealing a setback to the claims of aviation proponents; only two hits are made from 80 bombs dropped.…The Borah Amendment, including disarmament discussions as part of the Naval Appropriations Bill, passes in the House 330–4.			The list of people getting tickets for the upcoming Jack Dempsey-Georges Capentier fight is growing; some of the people include the U.S. Attorney General Henry Daugherty, Harry Frazee, George M. Cohan, and Douglas Fairbanks.	Jun. 29
Former President William Howard Taft is nominated as Chief Justice of the Supreme Court.		News on Wall Street is that the recent overproduction of oil and low prices have hurt oil stocks, while rail stocks are doing very well.…Reports on railroad income show that revenues are up significantly since 1920.…R.G. Dun & Co. reports that the number of business failures in June was 1,290 compared with 1,356 in May.		Preparations are being made to describe the Dempsey-Capentier heavyweight fight by telegraph; more than a 100 operators are in place to provide reports of the action as it happens.…Hotels in New York City are completely booked as people arrive to watch the fight.	Jun. 30
Mrs. Kate O'Hare, a Socialist activist, who had recently been released from prison, is kidnapped by an unknown group of men while visiting in Twin Falls, ID.…Crime in Washington, DC, has increased by 20 percent in the first six months of 1921.…An Alabama court rules that 20,000 veterans, who served in the war, are ineligible to vote because they did not pay poll tax while on active duty.	U.S. policy makers are debating if they should withdraw American occupation forces from the Rhineland as a means of cutting expenses.	The United States Commercial Travelers of America pass a resolution asking Congress to authorize special books of tickets at a reduced rate for traveling salesmen on the railroads.		William Burns, a former member of the White Sox, turns state's evidence and testifies against his former teammates in the trial over the fixed 1919 World Series; Burns is the only witness for the state who is also under indictment.	Jul. 1
Union leaders of the rail unions have issued a statement that they are against a strike for the time being and that wages are not the prime issue as they may go back up, but that working conditions are a vital issue.…The first national convention of the American Red Cross is planned to be held in Washington in October.…Because of the great number of holdups on the roads of New Jersey, insurance companies are now equipping fast cars with gun crews to patrol the routes between New York City and Philadelphia.…The cost of running the federal government in the fiscal year just ended was $5,115,927,689.	Newly established Chief of the Army General Staff Pershing calls his personal aids together and asks them to take measures to economize as much as possible.…The Army has announced a program that will allow any soldier to leave the Army during this month as part of an economy program to reduce the numbers of the forces.…The U.S. Transport *Wheaton* arrives in New York with the bodies of 5,824 Americans killed in France in the World War.	President Hoover pledges that he will assist architects and builders in their efforts to devise standards, the lack of which currently adds at least 20 percent to the cost of construction.…The Armour Meat Packing Company reports that foreign orders are on the increase and predicts that this trend will affect other American industries.…Eight coal dealers in upstate New York are indicted for a conspiracy to control coal prices in the region.…The first full train car of fresh figs from California arrives in New York City; the demand for fresh fruit is very high in the city and prices are sharply increasing.	American and Dutch geologists announce that they will launch an expedition in South Africa in 1922 to study the origins of granite.…Commander Donald McMillan of the U.S. Navy departs Boston for Wiscasset, ME, on his way to explore the Baffin Island area in the Arctic.…Madame Curie arrives back in France after her tour of the United States, where she received honorary degrees and a personal gram of radium purchased by the Women of America.	Jack Dempsey beats Georges Carpentier for the heavyweight title.	Jul. 2
		The U.S. Geological Survey estimates that the production of soft coal for the week ending June 25 was 7,869,500 tons, an increase of 1.5 percent more than the previous week.	The U.S. Weather Bureau reports that the increasing practice of ships broadcasting weather conditions to one another has proven to be very helpful.	A common theme of many sermons today is the condemnation of the Dempsey-Carpentier fight.…With hot temperatures, nearly one million people went to the beaches in the New York City area; 400,000 of these visited Coney Island.	Jul. 3
F *Includes campaigns, elections, federal-state relations, civil rights and liberties, crime, the judiciary, education, healthcare, poverty, urban affairs, and population.*	G *Includes formation and debate of U.S. foreign and defense policies, veterans affairs, and defense spending. (Relations with specific foreign countries are usually found under the region concerned.)*	H *Includes business, labor, agriculture, taxation, transportation, consumer affairs, monetary and fiscal policy, natural resources, pollution and industrial accidents.*	I *Includes worldwide scientific, medical and technological developments, natural phenomena, U.S. weather and natural disasters.*	J *Includes the arts, religion, scholarship, communications media, sports, entertainment, fashions, fads, and social life.*	

	World Affairs	Europe	Africa & The Middle East	The Americas	Asia & The Pacific
Jul. 4	Karl Radek, speaking at the assembled Communist Third International urges the members to engage in every possible activity to speed up world revolution.	In Rome, 16 more are killed in street fighting with members of the Fascist Party....In Dublin, Eamon de Valera and other Irish leaders have a successful meeting with British officials about the arrangements of a separation of Ireland from Britain....A French Army Major, a member of the Interallied Forces in Silesia, is killed by a civilian....Technically, British miners are back at work, but until the mines are repaired so they can be worked, many of the miners will stay unemployed.		Five U.S. naval vessels are sighted off Tampico, giving rise to speculation that the United States is planning to invade Mexico....Canada's Prime Minister Meighen unveils a monument to the Canadians who died at Vimy Ridge in France in 1917.	
Jul. 5	The League of Nations International Conference on the Treatment of Women and Children closes.	South Africa's Jan Smuts meets with de Valera and other Irish leaders to facilitate the process where a peaceful separation between Ireland and Britain can be effected....More fighting occurs between Communists and Fascists in Italy, this time in Genoa....British soldiers fire on crowds in Silesia, breaking up riots....The drought in France has caused an 11 percent decrease in the projected harvest compared with 1920.	The Greek Legation charges that Kemal's Turkish troops are committing atrocities against Greeks.... With a force of 300,000, Greece is preparing another offensive against Turkey.	Additional U.S. ships are sent to Tampico to guard Americans if that should prove necessary....Police in Lima, Peru, confirm that the recent fire at the Presidential Suite in Peru's government House in Lima was arson and have made arrests....Three American warships arrive in Lima, Peru, to participate in the country's centennial celebrations.	Japanese forces in Siberia are fighting Koreans near the border with that region inflicting 500 casualties on the Koreans who are said to have joined the Communists against the Japanese.
Jul. 6		Although there is no confirmation, there is a rumor from Moscow that Leon Trotsky has been jailed by Lenin....General Karl Stenger, accused and tried for ordering the execution of French prisoners in August 1914, is acquitted by a German court.	There is great concern among the Allies, particularly the British, that Turkish forces will attempt to seize Constantinople, which is currently garrisoned with 10,000 allied troops.	President Obregon says there is no danger of any unrest in Tampico and claims that reports of disturbances are being spread by the oil companies that do not want to pay the export tax....Standard Oil of New Jersey has begun drilling for oil in the Lake Maracaibo region of Venezuela....The United States announce that it is not going to make any kind of financial intervention in Cuba.	The Mongolian Socialist Republic is established.
Jul. 7		Although Eamon de Valera is scheduled to go to London for discussions with Lloyd George, there are rumors in Dublin that he may not go unless he gets a clear mandate from the Irish people....French opinion is enraged at the not guilty verdict of General Stenger, who is alleged to have murdered French prisoners of war.	Mustafa Kemal, Turkish commander, informs the British that he would like to discuss terms to end the war.		The Japanese government is making active steps to begin disarmament negotiations....The personal representative of China's President Sun Yat-sen is in Washington accusing the Japanese of encouraging, by shipments of arms and men, the Chinese civil war.
Jul. 8		Britain and officials of Sinn Fein sign an agreement to end hostilities....Ethnic Ruthenians in southern Poland revolt against the Polish government....Italy sends 15,000 troops to keep order in the Adriatic city of Fiume.		U.S. warships leave their station three miles off Tampico as the government does not believe that conditions warrant them staying.	
Jul. 9	Several developments have occurred in the world trade markets: the Australian government has placed an embargo on all coal exports; Chinese factories are now manufacturing Panama hats for export; and Japan has exported 27,522 bales of silk to the United States....The French and Italian authorities in the Inter-Allied Commission in Turkey are expressing dissatisfaction with both the direction and attitude of British members of the Commission; both countries are taking an increasingly pro-Turkish view in contrast to the British.	A new government is formed in Italy with the King's assistance that will hold a moderate outlook on most issues but will have a definite anti-Communist stance....Some observers note a revival of the French economy and its trade with the United States is increasing....The Vatican expresses satisfaction over the recent peace between Britain and the Irish population....Railway transportation in Romania is now reported as having almost entirely broken down....A cholera outbreak is reported in the Soviet Union with more than 8,200 cases confirmed so far....As a result of the recent 3-month coal strike, many industries in Britain have converted their burners from coal to oil.	The Moorish rebel chief Raisuli, who is currently having problems in his campaign against the Spanish in Morocco, may be considering a surrender to Spanish authorities....In a speech in Parliament, Colonial Secretary Winston Churchill claims great success in the Middle East as the military occupation of Iraq is to be ended soon....Christian and Muslim residents of Palestine are expressing dissatisfaction with the British government's negative reply to their petition stating grievances against Jewish settlers coming into Palestine....Greek Diplomats in the United States are alleging that the Turks have massacred at least 700,000 Greeks in recent fighting.	Peru instructs its ambassador to leave Ecuador in response to Ecuador not accepting an invitation to attend the Peruvian centennial celebrations....The Argentine Chamber of Deputies passes a law to prevent the formation of trusts, monopolies, and combinations; the bill now goes to the Argentine Senate....Ecuador has signed a contract with an American company to drill for oil....While unemployment in Canada has risen sharply since May 1920, it seems to now be dropping....U.S. battleships, the U.S.S *Arizona*, *Oklahoma*, and *Nevada*, leave New York to sail to Peru as part of that nation's centennial celebration.	Manuel Quezon, a popular leader in the Philippines states that the United States must give the islands their independence within the next 12 years....The Japanese press is taking the view that nothing in the Anglo-Japanese treaty must ever be offensive to the United States....The British penal colony on Andaman Island, off the coast of India, which has been in operation since the Sepoy Mutiny of 1857, will now be closed....Continuing on his tour of Europe after visiting Britain, France, and Holland, Crown Prince Hirohito leaves to visit Italy....Shipyard workers in Kobe, Japan, are on strike and have closed down the Kawasaki dockyard; they are joined by strikers from Nagasaki.

A	B	C	D	E
Includes developments that affect more than one world region, international organizations and important meetings of world leaders.	*Includes all domestic and regional developments in Europe, including the Soviet Union.*	*Includes all domestic and regional developments in Africa and the Middle East.*	*Includes all domestic and regional developments in Latin America, the Caribbean, and Canada.*	*Includes all domestic and regional developments in Asian and Pacific nations (and colonies).*

U.S. Politics & Social Issues	U.S. Foreign Policy & Affairs, Defense	U.S. Economy & Environment	Science, Technology & Nature	Culture, Leisure & Lifestyle	
A posse of sheriff's officers in Kentucky fight with and kill three "mountain men" alleged to have been rumrunners.		The Manufacturers Aircraft Association declares that flying is safe and only 15 people have died during the 3.25 million miles flown in the first six months of 1921.…Bethlehem Steel, in the wake of recent 15 percent wage cuts for its workers, is lowering the price of steel.		In reports about injuries and deaths surrounding the Fourth of July holiday, more people have died from drowning and auto accidents than from fireworks.	Jul. 4
As the Sacco and Vanzetti trial continues in Dedham, MA, Bartolomeo Vanzetti takes the stand in his own defense.…The Pennsylvania Corporation, a coal company, cuts the wages of its workers by 20 percent.…After a three-week furlough, mechanics of the Baltimore and Ohio Railroad are back to work.	The U.S. Congress passes a bill officially terminating the war between the United States and Germany and Austria-Hungary.		A party of scientists and explorers from Columbia University, that will explore the Amazon, has reached La Paz, Bolivia.	There are 20,000 students who have enrolled for summer studies in the city of New York, including 12,000 at Columbia.…Selection of the jury for the trial of the former White Sox players accused of throwing the World Series begins.	Jul. 5
Nicola Sacco takes the stand in his own defense.…Dr. Thomas Salmon, formerly of the Army medical Corps, testifies before Congress that in 1920 four hundred veterans in New York City committed suicide and that most would be alive if they had received proper attention.…Secretary of the Treasury Andrew Mellon states that paying soldiers from the World War any kind of bonuses would ruin the treasury.	U.S. Senator Penrose states that the United States should disarm, regardless of what other nations do.…General Pershing awards Stubby, a Boston Terrier who was mascot of the 26th Division in France, a gold medal; Stubby was present at 17 engagements and wounded once.		A Dutch company is promoting a helicopter invented by German engineers that they claim can travel at 312 miles per hour.		Jul. 6
Nocola Sacco states that when he left the country in 1917 for Mexico, in order to avoid serving in the Army, he did a brave thing because he was opposed to war.…Arthur C. Banta of Great Bend, KS, assigned as prosecutor of the I.W.W. in Kansas, is found shot to death.	A Navy airship, the dirigible *C-3*, explodes in flight near Hampton Roads, VA; there are no casualties as all of the crew manages to escape.	The American Locomotive Company sells 51 engines, valued at $3 million, mostly for China and Mexico.			Jul. 7
The Sacco-Vanzetti trial is temporarily adjourned due to Vanzetti being ill.…The Appellate Branch of the Supreme Court rules that losses from gambling are not tax deductible.		The federal forecast for July shows that bad weather will result in a significantly lower harvest for wheat, potatoes, rice, and apples.			Jul. 8
Nicola Sacco has recovered and the trial in Dedham, MA resumes; the court has not ruled on a motion for separate trials.…Louis H. Capelle, an Ohio prosecutor, states that felonies are increasing and that Prohibition is the major factor behind the greater number of crimes.…The efforts of the United Mine Workers to get a release of 11 of their leaders from prison in Mingo County, WV, fail.…In a speech to the Christian Endeavorers, William Jennings Bryan predicts that President Harding will be as famous as Abraham Lincoln.	The Goodyear Tire and Rubber Company announce that it has been awarded a contract to build three dirigibles for the Army and the Navy and 38 observation balloons.…The War department announces that it will operate nine summer military training camps for young men 16 and older.…The War and Navy departments announces they will establish a uniform method for classifying veterans who are now working for those agencies.…Pershing has been given the rank of General of Armies, which appears on his first official orders as Chief of Staff.…Secretary of War Weeks states that as part of the extensive economy measures, the army may disband some of its regiments.	Steel mill capacity in most Pittsburgh plants is down to 20 percent.…The Forest Service claims that there is sufficient timber in Alaska to provide two million cords a year for paper manufacture; because Canada furnishes the majority of newsprint used in the United States, this capacity could become very important.…The Forest Service announces its largest timber sale ever, 100 million cubic feet of wood to the Alaskan-American Paper Corporation.	The U.S. Revenue Cutter *Bear* has left Nome to the area off the Siberia Coast where arctic explorer Roald Amundsen's vessel, *Maude*, has become frozen in the ice.	In New York City, Mrs. Libby Custer, widow of General George A. Custer who was killed by the Sioux 45 years earlier, receives a delegation of descendants of the Indians who defeated the General; when asked about his most memorable moment on the trip, White Eagle mentions having seen the Dempsey-Carpentier fight.…The Pittsburgh Pirates announce that when baseballs are hit in the stands that fans may keep them and police are not to take them away.…Vice President Calvin Coolidge states that colleges are failing to teach students the fundamentals and that they should not allow radical influences by Communists and "other cults."	Jul. 9

F	G	H	I	J
Includes campaigns, elections, federal-state relations, civil rights and liberties, crime, the judiciary, education, healthcare, poverty, urban affairs, and population.	*Includes formation and debate of U.S. foreign and defense policies, veterans affairs, and defense spending. (Relations with specific foreign countries are usually found under the region concerned.)*	*Includes business, labor, agriculture, taxation, transportation, consumer affairs, monetary and fiscal policy, natural resources, pollution and industrial accidents.*	*Includes worldwide scientific, medical and technological developments, natural phenomena, U.S. weather and natural disasters.*	*Includes the arts, religion, scholarship, communications media, sports, entertainment, fashions, fads, and social life.*

	World Affairs	Europe	Africa & The Middle East	The Americas	Asia & The Pacific
Jul. 10		Bulgaria has suggested an alliance of itself and Yugoslavia with Turkey against Greece....A plot by Communists to kill Yugoslavia's Prince Regent is foiled....Eamon de Valera has been invited to go to London with any of his colleagues to engage in talks with British authorities....Reports from the Soviet Union state that 200 Soviets in the countryside requisitioning supplies have been killed by local peasants or bandits.	Greece launches a major attack on Turkish positions.	The Mexican government is attempting to find work for more than 7,000 additional unemployed by the sudden drop in oil production in Tampico.	China's Foreign Minister Sao-Ke Alfred Sze praises the United States for its stated policies to not allow monopolies of trade in China.
Jul. 11		With temperatures consistently in the 90+-degree range, vast crop damage has been reported in France, Britain, and Holland....The French government states that it is against any type of land disarmament until all safety issues have been resolved, but it is in favor of naval disarmament.			
Jul. 12		The Italian government states that it will support President Harding's proposal for a naval arms conference....Irish Protestants, who today are marching in Northern Ireland to commemorate the British victory at the Battle of the Boyne in the 17th century, state that they will not join with Catholic Ireland to the South.	Spanish troops battling Moorish rebels in Morocco have managed to inflict heavy losses on the tribesmen....The Turks manages to defeat a Greek detachment while elsewhere the Greek Army is successfully advancing.	The Mexican government is sending unemployed workers in the Tampico area to other parts of the country to work on government projects.	The Japanese government announces its support for the Naval disarmament Conference proposed by President Harding.
Jul. 13		The temporary truce is broken in Ulster with riots and at least seven are reported injured.		President Obregon of Mexico announces he will form a board to review all foreign business losses in Mexico since 1910 and will adjudicate compensation.	
Jul. 14		Fighting again breaks out in Belfast; there are gunfights in the streets that the police and Army have not been able to halt, but the streets become quiet after sundown....Eamon de Valera confers with Lloyd George for two hours; there are plans for the conference to resume tomorrow.	News reports describe a 52 year-old woman, Ayesha Hanum, who commands a women's brigade in the Turkish army, known as the Kain Brigade, which is fighting against the Greeks....The Greek Army claims to have advanced 50 miles against the Turks in one day.	Panama and Costa Rica agree to begin discussions to negotiate their boundary; the U.S. stand is that Costa Rica may decide not to accept the U.S. solution, but Panama cannot force Costa Rica to change unless it is willing to do so; the United States wishes to be not involved in the controversy in any case....Argentina's president states that he wants the nation to increase its exports and dramatically decrease its exports to improve its balance of trade.	
Jul. 15		Gregory Zinoviev is again elected as President of the Third Communist International....The Prosecutor, in the trial of two former German naval officers for sinking a hospital ship, asks for four years imprisonment for the convicted officers.		Mexican politicians are blaming American oil companies for the unrest that has occurred in Tampico because the Americans do not want to pay Mexico's tax on exported oil.	
Jul. 16	Jane Addams expresses great satisfaction over the success of the International Woman's Conference being held in Vienna.	Miners in the Ruhr Valley go on strike after failing to negotiate a wage increase with mine owners....British officials state that they believe Ireland will stay in the Empire and that an Irish Republic will not exist, at least for the time being....Gregory Zinoviev is reported to have resigned his position as Governor of Petrograd.	A Greek diplomat visiting the United States says that Russia and Turkey present a grave threat to peace and stability and that the Greek Army is the "real bulwark of Europe."...Greek troops under the command of King Constantine take the city of Kutaia from the Turks....Reports from Moscow indicate that during the meeting of the Communist Third International, Turkish Communists claimed Mustafa Kemal was as bad a ruler as Sultan Abdul Hamid ("the damned").	General Martinez Herrerra surrenders ending his revolt against the Mexican government.	Japan has indicated an interest in participating in the proposed naval disarmament conference, but has not yet formally stated its acceptance....On the Italian stage of his tour, Crown Prince Hirohito visits Pope Benedict XV.
	A *Includes developments that affect more than one world region, international organizations and important meetings of world leaders.*	B *Includes all domestic and regional developments in Europe, including the Soviet Union.*	C *Includes all domestic and regional developments in Africa and the Middle East.*	D *Includes all domestic and regional developments in Latin America, the Caribbean, and Canada.*	E *Includes all domestic and regional developments in Asian and Pacific nations (and colonies).*

U.S. Politics & Social Issues	U.S. Foreign Policy & Affairs, Defense	U.S. Economy & Environment	Science, Technology & Nature	Culture, Leisure & Lifestyle	
					Jul. 10
A crowd of 300 unemployed veterans storm the Welfare Building in Bridgeport, CT, demanding that they be given a share in the $300,000 civic work program.... William Howard Taft takes the oath as Chief Justice of the Supreme Court.		The Federal government reports that in 1920 the United States had a favorable trade balance in overseas trade to the amount of $2.862 billion.			Jul. 11
Harry Olmstead, Chairman of the Executive Committee of the Williamson Coal Operators Association in Mingo County, states that the mine owners have nothing to discuss with the United Mine Workers, that there is no strike and the only problem is lawlessness in the region.... In Beaverdale, PA, five buildings, occupied by foreigners, allegedly members of the Black Hand, are blown up by local residents.		Standard Oil of California announces that it will soon begin exploring Alaska for oil.			Jul. 12
	In a demonstration of the power of aircraft, aircraft under the command of Brigadier Billy Mitchell, drop 40 bombs on a captured German destroyer, score 20 direct hits, and sink the ship in 20 minutes.				Jul. 13
Sacco and Vanzetti are found guilty of first-degree murder; Judge Webster Thayer allows the Defense until November 1 to file an appeal.... A 15-week building trades strike in Lawrence, MA, ends with 3,000 men returning to work after accepting a 15 percent wage cut.	The Navy announces that all Navy Yards and shore stations will go on a five-day week as part of an economy measure.			In Boston children march to the Mayor's office and the Governor's office to protest the high price of ice cream.... The Dutch government receives a newly purchased painting, Jan Vermeer's *The Little Street*, which many had feared would be sent to America; there are now eight of Vermeer's paintings in the country.	Jul. 14
Testifying before a Congressional Committee about the problems in Miogo County, WV, members of the United Mine Workers have agreed to leave West Virginia after the court had refused to release them.		The first two weeks of this month are reported to have been the hottest in Chicago according to all records.		Babe Ruth hits his 35th home run of the season.	Jul. 15
Miners in Mingo County deny that they are using union funds meant for their relief for the purchase of guns as they describe the Battle of Matewan to a U.S. Senate Committee.... Members of the I.W.W. kill a veteran in Wolsey, SD, because he refuses to join the organization; two men of 300, who were riding on the tops of railroads cars when the incident occurred, have been arrested.	Chairman Julius Kahn, Chairman of the House Military Affairs, states that he opposes the selling of military camps that will no longer be used as part of Secretary Weeks' economy measures.	The American Chemical Society states that German scientists are making a concerted effort to keep their wood making processes secret, even preventing the export of books that would provide information on cellulose chemistry.... Officials of the National City Bank in New York state that they believe that trade with the Soviets will soon become sizable; already exports and imports these officials claim, is much greater than is generally supposed.... Federal banks in the United States report a drop of 3.6 percent of volume in the past week.	Dr. P. Weil, a French physician, claims to have found a cure for hemophilia by the use of a serum derived from horses.	Black is the favorite color of the season in Paris fashions with so many black dresses, "they look almost like a national costume."	Jul. 16

F	G	H	I	J
Includes campaigns, elections, federal-state relations, civil rights and liberties, crime, the judiciary, education, healthcare, poverty, urban affairs, and population.	*Includes formation and debate of U.S. foreign and defense policies, veterans affairs, and defense spending. (Relations with specific foreign countries are usually found under the region concerned.)*	*Includes business, labor, agriculture, taxation, transportation, consumer affairs, monetary and fiscal policy, natural resources, pollution and industrial accidents.*	*Includes worldwide scientific, medical and technological developments, natural phenomena, U.S. weather and natural disasters.*	*Includes the arts, religion, scholarship, communications media, sports, entertainment, fashions, fads, and social life.*

	World Affairs	Europe	Africa & The Middle East	The Americas	Asia & The Pacific
Jul. 17		Anti-Communist leader in the Ukraine, General Makno, has been defeated and surrendered to the Communists....France presents three demands to the German government concerning the problems in Silesia: Germany must disarm all ethnic Germans in the region, must take all measures to ensure the Allies do not encounter opposition in Silesia, and Germany must assist the allies in rushing reinforcements to the area.	By a combination of advances along the front and encircling maneuvers, Greek forces are continuing to force the Turkish Army back.	Rebels against the Mexican government in Tampico are now being disarmed by the government.	The South Chinese Republic under Sun Yat-sen, with its capital in Canton, informs Washington that it wishes to represent China at the Far Eastern Conference and that the Beijing government does not truly represent China.
Jul. 18		Romania's production of oil in the first quarter of 1921 is 27 percent greater than its production in the first quarter of 1920....The Polish government issues a plea to the Allies to prevent Lithuania from "bullying" them in the recent border disputes between the two nations....A Christian tribe of Mirdites in heavily Muslim Albania declares their own republic in the northern part of the country.		A bomb explodes outside the capital building in Buenos Aries, seriously injuring a policeman, but casing little damage; Communists are suspected of having left the bomb....Mexico's President Obregon visits the Tampico oil fields to get a personal view of the unrest there.	
Jul. 19	Britain's Prince of Wales announces that he will visit Japan next year after his visit to India.	An anti-Soviet plot is said to have been discovered that would have gone into action next week; more than 100 officers and soldiers have been imprisoned....The Romanian government denies reports that this year's harvest will be considerably smaller than last year's.	Greek forces capture Kutaia in Turkey.		
Jul. 20		The Albanian government responds to the Mirdite insurrection and sends troops into northern Albania....Polish diplomats deny rumors that there has been a coup in Poland....Reports from the Soviet Union describe a serious outbreak of cholera.		Argentine refuses to mediate in the Panama-Costa Rica border dispute.	
Jul. 21		Yugoslavia's anti-Communist Minister of the Interior Milorad Draskovic is assassinated by Communists....Luxembourg and Belgium sign a 50-year Economic Agreement.	Spanish forces sent to suppress an uprising under Abd-el-Krimn in Spanish Morocco are defeated in a battle at Annual.		
Jul. 22		In Italy, 26 are killed in political rioting.	The Greek Army continues to advance with all Turkish escape routes now cut off.		
Jul. 23		Some observers, who have watched developments in the Soviet Union and the Third Communist International, predict a power struggle between Lenin and Trotsky....The Allied powers warn Bulgaria that it must not support unrest in neighboring Thrace....Britain and France are still far apart on their policies in Silesia....Fighting in the area in and around Genoa is brought up in Italy's Chamber of Deputies by Benito Mussolini, head of Italy's Fascist Party, and that while government efforts to pacify the area have been good, more must be done....The Commander of the Irish Army states that his officers have been instructed to stop cooperating with British officers until there is recognition of truce violations.	Fighting in Morocco between Spanish forces and the Moors continues with the general commanding killed in action and Spanish troops forced to retreat from positions they had just captured.	Governor Joy Morrow of the Panama Canal Zone states that the Panama Canal is now profitable, providing a return on the investment mad by the United States....E. Mont Reily, new Governor of Puerto Rico, states that he favors statehood for the island....Francisco "Pancho" Villa has made a singular change attending church on a regular basis and has established a reputation for charity; some observers claim that this is part of a campaign to become President of Mexico....A massive oil well fire in Mexico is now being contained after 4,000 men have been sent to put the flames out....Mexican railways will put a 20 percent wage reduction into effect on August 1; the number of staff will also be reduced.	The Chinese cities of Shanghai and Nanking are to be soon connected by telephone lines.

A	B	C	D	E
Includes developments that affect more than one world region, international organizations and important meetings of world leaders.	*Includes all domestic and regional developments in Europe, including the Soviet Union.*	*Includes all domestic and regional developments in Africa and the Middle East.*	*Includes all domestic and regional developments in Latin America, the Caribbean, and Canada.*	*Includes all domestic and regional developments in Asian and Pacific nations (and colonies).*

U.S. Politics & Social Issues	U.S. Foreign Policy & Affairs, Defense	U.S. Economy & Environment	Science, Technology & Nature	Culture, Leisure & Lifestyle	
	Army and Navy planes are preparing the bomb and sink the German Cruiser *Frankfort* in exercises off the Virginia coast; the ship is sunk after being hit by three bombs.	The Union Pacific Railroad announces that it is taking back 1,500 employees who were laid off.…As an example of a growing trend, the ocean liner *Berengaria* is being converted from a coal burning to an oil burning ship; the increased cost of coal and the increased difficulty in finding men to shovel coal is the reason behind this and other conversions.		Now that preliminary motions have been filed and the jury selected, the trial of alleged gamblers, as well as members of the 1919 Chicago White Sox, begins over the charge of throwing the 1919 World Series.	Jul. 17
Representatives of the mine operators in Mingo County, WV, testify before a Senate Committee they will fight unionization to the end.…Twenty-seven cars are stolen in one day in New York City, a new record.		Workers at the International Paper mills in Ft. Edward, NY, agree to go back to work at the 1919 wage scale.		The Prosecution presents is opening arguments in the trial of individuals accused of having thrown the 1919 World Series.	Jul. 18
Speaking before a convention in Cleveland, the President of Mills College states that there are currently eight million women in the workforce, half of them teachers.				Testimony for the prosecution in the White Sox trial describes the arrangements and the plan for how the games were to be thrown.	Jul. 19
	Attempts by aviators to bomb and sink the captured German ship, *Ostfriedland*, fail.			Film Actress Pearl White gets a divorce from her husband, Wallace McCutcheon.…Bill Burns continuing to testify at the 1919 World Series trial, describes how when the gamblers failed to pay the players, they won games they were supposed to lose.	Jul. 20
	Brigadier General Billy Mitchell dropping bombs from his aircraft and sinks the German battleship *Ostfriedland* as part of combined Army-Navy and aerial exercises off the east coast of the United States.				Jul. 21
				Signed confessions made by some of the White Sox players, which were to have been entered as evidence, are missing.	Jul. 22
In June, 29,901 aliens became U.S. citizens, almost 22 percent of these were German.…Police in New York City continue to make searches for liquor without warrants; additionally, in one case a judge rules that whiskey spilled on a floor and presented as fluid wrung from a sponge is not admissible as evidence.…The political feud in Chicago's 19th ward continues with the death of its ninth victim, John "Two Gun Johnny" Gardino; the killer escapes after succeeding in what was the fourth attempt to kill Gardino.	Herbert Hoover offers assistance to feed starving people in the Soviet Union; the offer is accepted.…Italy's ambassador to the United States and General Pietro Badoglio, Italian Chief of Staff during the World War, visit a New York National Guard regiment in summer training.…Secretary of War Weeks announces further cuts in the Army; six camps are to be closed: Camp Devens, MA, Camp Meade, MD, and four others that have not been named.…Secretary Weeks announces he is canceling the program that would have allowed enlisted men to leave the Army during the month of July as more of them wanted to leave than the Army could afford to lose even with its attempts to economize.	The Secretary of the Interior reports that in June there were 1,066 requests for permits to drill on public land.		The Federal Hill Mansion in Bardstown, KY, the original "My Old Kentucky Home," has been purchased by the state, which will restore it.…State evidence against White Sox baseball players accused of fixing the 1919 World Series has disappeared along with original confessions.…New books published include *Our Common Country* by Warren Harding, *Pan* by Knut Hamsun, and *Out of their Own Mouths* by Samuel Gompers.	Jul. 23
F *Includes campaigns, elections, federal-state relations, civil rights and liberties, crime, the judiciary, education, healthcare, poverty, urban affairs, and population.*	G *Includes formation and debate of U.S. foreign and defense policies, veterans affairs, and defense spending. (Relations with specific foreign countries are usually found under the region concerned.)*	H *Includes business, labor, agriculture, taxation, transportation, consumer affairs, monetary and fiscal policy, natural resources, pollution and industrial accidents.*	I *Includes worldwide scientific, medical and technological developments, natural phenomena, U.S. weather and natural disasters.*	J *Includes the arts, religion, scholarship, communications media, sports, entertainment, fashions, fads, and social life.*	

	World Affairs	Europe	Africa & The Middle East	The Americas	Asia & The Pacific
Jul. 24		So far, the casualty rate of the recent riots in Belfast is 22 killed.... Countess Georgina Markiewicz, member of Sinn Fein is released from prison by the British.	The Turkish army loses 6,000 in a series of unsuccessful attacks against the Greeks....After saving their command from attacks by the Moorish rebels in Spanish Morocco, Spanish General Silvestre and his staff, who had remained behind while their forces retreated to safety, commit suicide.		Japanese trade in the Pacific for the month of July has so far shown a decline.
Jul. 25			Reports state that Spanish forces have landed in Morocco to combat the Moorish rebels, but at the same time other reports describe how the Spanish troops on the line are evacuating their advanced positions.	Former bandit, Francisco Villa has become known as an investor in local oil companies....Venezuela's foreign trade is growing dramatically; in 1919 its imports and exports were 143 percent greater than they had been for 1918.	
Jul. 26	The British government decides that linking the Dominions by airship will be impractical and too expensive to attempt.	The Soviet Union grants powers to a Committee to fight the growing famine; the committee has several members who are not Communists....A general strike begins in Rome; the Army is present in force with machine guns and armored cars....France agrees with Britain on the Silesian issue and there will be no reinforcements sent to Allied troops already there.	The Greek army claims that 75 percent of the Turkish army has been lost so far.	Mexico's President Obregon issues an order cutting the pay of all military and civil government employees by 10 percent.	The British foreign Secretary, Lord Curzon, announces that Britain is not going to continue relations with Persian as the government in Tehran has become so unstable.
Jul. 27		In the general strike in Rome, the Pope has appealed to all parties to stop fighting and Italian troops in the city have kept order....Reports from Poland describe an increase in production and a drop in unemployment....Despite Soviet threats, the nations of Latvia, Lithuania, and Estonia along with Poland are forming a Baltic alliance.			The Japanese Cabinet is discussing whether to attend the proposed Naval disarmament conference held by the Americans; most of the responses are favorable.
Jul. 28		Newspapers in Madrid predict the inevitable fall of the current government as soon as the situation in Morocco has quieted down....The city of Leipzig, Germany, has been overrun with rats....In a speech to Soviet officials in charge of food, Lenin admits that there are significant problems and encourages the implementation of the New Economic Plan to foster small capitalist enterprises.	Greek forces are advancing toward the city of Ismid and it appears as though the Turkish forces there will have to retreat and evacuate the city....There are rumors that the Greek forces are planning an invasion of Turkey's Black Sea Coast.	Crops in Mexico will be very bad this year with the northern states of the country having to import grain; the banana crop in southern Mexico has been lost due to cold weather....Colombia's Minister of Foreign Affairs denies that there is a secret treaty between his country and Peru.	
Jul. 29	At the Conference of Imperial Premiers, it is agreed that each of their respective nations will be responsible for coastal defense while Britain maintains a navy that can fight extended conflicts around the world.	The British government states that it resents the tone of French diplomatic communications over the issues of Silesia and the Middle East....France's Premier Briand states that France has no designs on controlling Silesia.	An American Military observer states that Mustafa Kemal has lost most of his army and cannot possibly cope with the Greek forces now inside Turkey.	Mexican police investigate an alleged attempt to poison President Obregon.	
Jul. 30	The National City Bank reports that world trade in 1920 totaled $100 billion, an increase of $37.5 billion since the World War began in 1914.	French labor unions reject and affiliation with the Communist Party by a vote of 1,572 to 1,325....The German Foreign Office accepts the war claims made by the United States and believes that there is a basis for a formal peace treaty between the two countries....Adolf Hitler becomes President of the Nationalist Socialist German Workers' Party.	Greek reports claim that the Turkish Army has now been reduced to 50,000 men....Turkish Commander Ismail Pasha is said to have been relieved of command....Turkish cities on the coast of the Black Sea are being bombarded by ships of the Greek navy.	Mexico is predicted to be shipping less petroleum due to a new tax recently imposed by the Mexican government....Mexican railway workers are planning to go on strike in response to the proposed wage cuts to take effect on August 1.	While they are interested in discussing disarmament with the western powers, many in Japan see an attempt to destroy the League of Nations in President Harding's proposals for a different world organization.

U.S. Politics & Social Issues	U.S. Foreign Policy & Affairs, Defense	U.S. Economy & Environment	Science, Technology & Nature	Culture, Leisure & Lifestyle	
	In the wake of the recent demonstrations of airpower against ships, leading military and naval strategists are pushing for a greater air capability for the Navy to include a force of up to eight aircraft carriers.			President Harding is on a camping trip with Thomas Edison and Harvey Firestone.	Jul. 24
The National Grange suspends the head of the Grange I Washington State for his remarks in favor of political radicals.	The British government is building an airship for the United States that will carry a wide array of arms to include machine guns and two kinds of bombs.	In Baltimore 2,000 men seek to get 30 jobs; in the ensuing riot, the employment office is wrecked.			Jul. 25
	The U.S. government reports that there are currently 12,000 veterans who are still hospitalized and costing the government an average of $3.68 a day.			The state rests its case in the 1919 World series trial.…The State of New Jersey's receipts from the Dempsey-Carpentier fight is $139,000.…President Harding announces he will vacation in the White Mountains of New Hampshire.…Divorces in San Francisco equal 48.5 percent of the number of marriages.	Jul. 26
	Michael Felix Christoff, an alleged spy for Austria, is arraigned on a charge of enlisting in the Army as a citizen when he was, in fact, an alien; the true purpose of the proceeding is to begin investigation into his involvement with the Black Tom explosion in 1916 in which a U.S. arms warehouse was blown up.	Coca Cola made $14,903,046 for the first six months of 1921 with a net income of $1,804,263.		American composer and conductor Victor Herbert leads an all-Wagner program as part of the Stadium Concerts in New York.…In the 1919 World Series trial, the state drops its case against two of the gamblers accused; it is speculated that the charges against players "Buck" Weaver and "Happy" Felsch may be dropped as well.	Jul. 27
The ex-police chief of Matewan, WV, Sid Hatfield, is arrested for a shooting alleged to have taken place a year ago.	The U.S. Army Air Service puts new rules into effect that prohibit Army fliers from performing any stunt flying.			The Defense rests in the White Sox trial.	Jul. 28
The United States will be visited by Bulgaria's Prime Minister, who states that he wants to deliver a message of friendship and of gratitude for everything the United States has done for his country.	During war exercises an "enemy" air fleet under the command of Brigadier General Billy Mitchell drops 21 tons of "bombs" on New York City and "destroys" it.				Jul. 29
Vermont State Troopers have been sent to Bellows Falls to put an end to disorders, including rifle fire at a lumber camp, where a strike is called against the International Paper Company's proposed wage reductions.…The wages of 40,000 men working for the H.C. Frick Coke Company in Pennsylvania have been cut by 10 percent as of August 1.…The oil industry, like other industries in the United States, is cutting the wages of its workers, in some case from 30 percent to 50 percent.…Six miners are killed in Grand Junction, CO, when their tramway cable car cable slips and the car falls a distance of 2,000 feet.		Oil is reported to have been discovered in Alaska.…The Chicago Board of Trade has received its first application for membership by a Japanese citizen.…In New York State, the average weekly wage for a factory worker is $25.71, a drop of 15 cents since May 15 and a drop of $3.06 since July 1920.	Scientists examine what appears to be an approximately 800 year-old human remains in a cave in Kentucky, but are not sure that the discovery will be of much scientific value.…During the course of campaigning throughout Asia Minor against the Turks, the Greek Army describes several important archaeological finds it has made.…The French aviation company Morane-Saulnier announces that it will build a giant monoplane constructed to carry passengers.	D.W. Griffith, and other movie producers and directors, state that they are very concerned about the effects of censorship as proposed in New York and other states.…Harry Heilmann of the Detroit Tigers leads the American League in batting (.429), while Rogers Hornsby leads the National League with his batting average of .417.…In his closing argument in the White Sox scandal case, the prosecutor asks that the men be found guilty, be given 5-year prison sentences, and be fined $2,000.	Jul. 30

F	G	H	I	J
Includes campaigns, elections, federal-state relations, civil rights and liberties, crime, the judiciary, education, healthcare, poverty, urban affairs, and population.	*Includes formation and debate of U.S. foreign and defense policies, veterans affairs, and defense spending. (Relations with specific foreign countries are usually found under the region concerned.)*	*Includes business, labor, agriculture, taxation, transportation, consumer affairs, monetary and fiscal policy, natural resources, pollution and industrial accidents.*	*Includes worldwide scientific, medical and technological developments, natural phenomena, U.S. weather and natural disasters.*	*Includes the arts, religion, scholarship, communications media, sports, entertainment, fashions, fads, and social life.*

	World Affairs	Europe	Africa & The Middle East	The Americas	Asia & The Pacific
Jul. 31		Reports are reaching London that hundreds of Jews have been killed in a pogrom in the Ukraine.…In Spain, a large vein of coal deposits has been discovered.…The French press is extremely hostile to British Prime Minister Lloyd George as a result of his policies, which have clashed with recent initiatives of France in the Mideast and Silesia.			Japanese forces near the city of Vladivostok provide arms to the local anti-Communist groups to help them defend the city.…At least 50 striking workers in Kobe, Japan, are injured when police are sent in to break up a workers parade.
Aug. 1		A severe earthquake in the Lake Lugano District of Italy results in severe damage; there is no word on the extent of casualties.…Reports from the Soviet Union describe a massive famine that threatens 20 to 40 million people and is resulting in masses of victims moving on cities (in one report six million toward Moscow).		The State Department informs Panama that it will not open discussions with Costa Rica over the Panama-Costa Rica border dispute.	
Aug. 2	The Third Communist International asks the assistance of the workers of the world for famine assistance so that the Soviet Union will not have to accept food from the United States.	The death total of the Italian earthquake in the Lake Lugano region now stands at eight although there are believed to be more bodies yet to be found.…Belgium expresses outrage at the recent acquittals of accused German war criminals.			The Japanese government announces 21 subjects that it wishes to not discuss during the upcoming Disarmament and Far East talks with the western powers; these include the disputed mandate for Yap Island, the Japanese occupation of Siberia, and the status of the Shantung Peninsula in China.
Aug. 3		Serbian police arrest 14,000 suspects to find the extent of a plot to kill Prince Alexander, Yugoslavia's regent.			Airmail service has begun in China and passenger flights between Beijing and Shanghai are expected soon.
Aug. 4	At the British Imperial Conference, one of the agreements is that the Dominions will have a greater influence on the formation and implementation of Britain's foreign policy.	Germany pays another installment, this one of $5 million as part of its war reparations.…In addition to famine, there are now reports of a widespread cholera epidemic, in the Soviet Union.…Yugoslavia expels 14 members of the Communist Party in retaliation for the recent attempt to kill Prince Alexander.	The Moorish tribal leader, Raisulli, offers to put an end to the fighting against the Spanish in Morocco, if he is made Caliph.		There is fighting on a 10-mile front between the forces of the Southern Chinese Republic and soldiers in Hunan province who do not recognize that government.
Aug. 5		Greece states that arms for the Turks are being shipped from the United States.	Spain is suffering a series of disasters in Morocco as its troops come under increased attacks from the Moors; two towns have been captured and stories of massacres of Spanish garrisons are arriving from the front.		A new German Bank is being opened in China, indicative of the aggressive financial and commercial activities of Germany in Asia.
Aug. 6	International trade developments have taken place in a number of different countries across several industries: a Czechoslovak company is establishing the first-ever mirror factory in Yugoslavia; the government of Trinidad, British West Indies, has removed all restrictions on the export of sugar; Norway will now allow the importation of autos, cigarettes, and cheese; the Polish government will allow commerce and transportation through the country for all goods, except sugar and liquor.	According to the Russian National Society, a group of Russian exiles in the United States, the Soviet Union faces ruin with economic chaos and an army that cannot be relied on.…The French government announces that its revenues in July exceeded its expenditures by 18 million francs; a large part of French revenue is based on special taxes on war profits as well as the sales of military surplus.…Tommasso Tittoni, President of the Italian Senate, while visiting in the United States, makes a speech endorsing President Harding's call for a peace conference.…Railroad service in Russia is severely limited; at present there is only one trains a week that runs from Moscow to Kiev.…Hundreds of refugee families in Latvia are living in old fortifications, bunkers, and dugouts that were built in the early days of the World War.…Albanian forces near the city of Mirdita have successfully defended the city against Serbian attacks.	The cotton crop in Egypt this year will be taken from 1,335,055-planted acres, a decrease from 1920 when 1,897,327 acres were planted with cotton.…The Spanish garrison of Zeluan, in Spanish Morocco, is attacked by the Moorish rebels; of 200 men, only nine survive the attack and escape.…Two Greek Army divisions are advancing on the Turkish city of Ismid.…Reports state that part of the Turkish government is beginning to evacuate from the capital at Ankara.	An attempted revolt against the government has been suppressed in Guatemala.…A company in Seville, Spain, has been formed that plans to provide air service from that city to Buenos Aries and New York City.…The Mexican government denies that it was planning to sponsor a fight between Jack Dempsey, current heavyweight champion, and Jack Johnson, former heavyweight champion.…Jamaica is sending a group to meet with Colonial Secretary Winston Churchill to petition for more rights for Jamaicans.…Draft animals have become so scarce in Mexico that it is not uncommon to see men dragging plows.…Costa Rica imposes a tariff on goods imported from France, a measure that causes the French government to register a protest.…Four large Canadian Railroad Brotherhoods state they will contest the proposed wage cuts they have been presented with.	A newspaper article in a Japanese newspaper states that the United States has communicated its desire that the Japanese drop their claims to a special position in China.…A company working under the auspices of the Chinese government has begun to design and build aircraft.…The Afghan government announces that the nature of relations between that country and Britain will depend on the attitude Britain shows toward the Turkish government and that the Afghans will stand by the Turks.

A	B	C	D	E
Includes developments that affect more than one world region, international organizations and important meetings of world leaders.	*Includes all domestic and regional developments in Europe, including the Soviet Union.*	*Includes all domestic and regional developments in Africa and the Middle East.*	*Includes all domestic and regional developments in Latin America, the Caribbean, and Canada.*	*Includes all domestic and regional developments in Asian and Pacific nations (and colonies).*

U.S. Politics & Social Issues	U.S. Foreign Policy & Affairs, Defense	U.S. Economy & Environment	Science, Technology & Nature	Culture, Leisure & Lifestyle	
Former boxing champion Jack Johnson preaches on racial equality in a church in New York City.		The Controller of the Currency of the United States reports that there has been an increase of 4,561 of active national banks for a current total of 8,178 now in operation nationwide.…In Philadelphia, 72 percent of the businesses claim a slight gain in employment.			Jul. 31
Sid Hatfield, former police chief of Matewan, WV, is killed in a gunfight on the court house steps in Welch, WV, by a private detective working for the mine operators.	Herbert Hoover moves to deliver food relief to the Soviet Union, which faces a severe famine; one condition to the aid is stipulated and it is that the Soviets release Americans they currently hold in prisons or other custody.	American businesses doing business in Latin America are voicing concern over what seems to be waves of Belgian and German merchants who are seriously underselling the Americans.		In closing arguments, the defense in the 1919 White Sox trial, asks why Arnold Rothstein, one of the instigators of the "fix" was not indicted; the defense states that the state was trying to make "goats of underpaid ball players."	Aug. 1
The Catholic organization, the Knights of Columbus, announces its intentions to open up a correspondence school for veterans that will handle 100,000 students.…The Prosecuting Attorney in Mingo County, WV, states that the murder of Sid Hatfield was a carefully devised plot.		A grand jury in Baltimore indicts directors of the Coal Exchange for combining to illegally fix coal prices.		Enrico Caruso, world famous tenor, dies at the age of 48 in his native city of Naples. Despite his serious illness, which was treated recently in New York, doctors had expected that he would make a full recovery.	Aug. 2
			Recent archaeological excavations in Ashkelon in Palestine have revealed a statue of Herod the Tetrarch.	"Kid" Gleason, manager of the White Sox, says he will quit if any of the accused players in the 1919 trial ever play in organized baseball again.	Aug. 3
While on his vacation, President Harding speaks to a crowd in Lancaster, NH, and states that America can lead the world to peace and that a new order in the world will be established before the end of his term.	The airship ZR-2, which is being manufactured in Britain for the U.S. Navy, is scheduled to fly from Britain on August 25.	After six weeks of consecutive declines, oil production in the United States is beginning to increase.			Aug. 4
Department of Labor Secretary Davis announces a group of 1,000 Assyrian Christians, part of an original group of 75,000 that fled from Persia, are now on their way to the United States.	Army airplanes are to bomb the obsolete battleship, USS *Alabama*, as a target in their exercises to determine the effectiveness of aircraft against ships.				Aug. 5
In what they see as retaliation, several hundred men from Dixon, IL, run several African-American men out of town after the shooting of a local resident; the men accused of the shooting were already in prison.…Detective C.E. Lively alleges that he shot former Matewan police chief Sid Hatfield in self-defense.…Samuel Gompers, President of the American Federation of Labor publishes a book entitled *Out of their Own Mouths,* a book that attacks Communism.	Military instruction to members of the Reserve Officer Corps will be given for the first time since the conclusion of the World War; the instruction will be conducted at Camp Meade, MD.	A forest fire in Maine is advancing along a 12-mile front causing more than 700 people to flee their homes; several towns are in danger of being destroyed.		The *New York Times* reviews the study, *The American Novel*, by Carl van Doren.	Aug. 6

F	G	H	I	J
Includes campaigns, elections, federal-state relations, civil rights and liberties, crime, the judiciary, education, healthcare, poverty, urban affairs, and population.	*Includes formation and debate of U.S. foreign and defense policies, veterans affairs, and defense spending. (Relations with specific foreign countries are usually found under the region concerned.)*	*Includes business, labor, agriculture, taxation, transportation, consumer affairs, monetary and fiscal policy, natural resources, pollution and industrial accidents.*	*Includes worldwide scientific, medical and technological developments, natural phenomena, U.S. weather and natural disasters.*	*Includes the arts, religion, scholarship, communications media, sports, entertainment, fashions, fads, and social life.*

	World Affairs	Europe	Africa & The Middle East	The Americas	Asia & The Pacific
Aug. 7		Bulgaria announces that it will disband its current army and to develop an all-volunteer force within the 12,000-man limit decreed by the Allies.... Reports indicate that as many as two-thirds of all of the Soviet Union's citizens may be close to starving.		The Costa Rican Senate rejects Costa Rica's membership in the Central American Federation; one result of membership would be that Costa Rica would be closing all its legations in foreign countries.... Delegates from Cuba, visiting the United States, state that the proposed tariffs on sugar in the United States will be disastrous for Korea.	Dr. Syngman Rhee, President of the Provisional Korean Republic, states that Korea's hope of freedom from Japan is stronger than ever.
Aug. 8	Italy and China indicate that they will attend the upcoming Naval Disarmament and Far East conference.	A group of Americans is assembling at the Estonian-Soviet border to meet six Americans who have been released from Soviet prisons.... Relief workers in the Soviet Union are sending back reports that confirm many of the dramatic stories told earlier; at least 2,000 people, many of them crawling, are entering the city of Brest-Litovsk for aid.... The Southern Irish leadership is close to accepting the peace terms offered by the British government after the last of the Sinn Fein members of the new parliament had been released from prison.	Replacing Ismail Pasha, Mustafa Kemal takes direct control of the Armies of Turkey in their fight against Greece.	The government of Mexico's President Obregon is recognized by Germany.... In a café in Mexico City General Jacinto Trevino kills General Allesio Robles in an unplanned duel.	There may be as many as 10 anti-Communist armies in southwestern Siberia mobilizing against the Soviets.
Aug. 9	Japan announces that it will attend the Naval Disarmament and Far East conference.	France and Britain have come to an agreement on Silesia and will partition the region with the more industrialized portion going to Germany; Poland will get more than what the British were willing to give, but less than France wanted Poland to receive.... Poland indicates that it fears great masses of staving Russian refugees will attempt to enter the country.... The Soviets claim that by using 863 public kitchens, feeding six million people a day is possible.	The heat, which has struck North America and Europe with sometimes dire results, has now visited the near east; great forest fires are now reported throughout Asia minor because of the heat wave there.... In response to the dire situation in Morocco, Spain is sending 50,000 troops there to combat the Moorish rebels.	New York banks have reached an agreement where they will furnish a loan of $9 billion for Uruguay.... A threatened railway workers strike in Mexico is prevented while a wage settlement is to be worked out.	Strikes at Japan's Kawasaki shipyard end.
Aug. 10		Spain's cabinet resigns over the crisis in Morocco; King Alfonso summons political leaders with the intention of forming a new government.... Eighteen oil wells in the Russian oil fields of Batum are on fire.	The Allies have effectually negated the Treaty of Sevres, which concluded Turkey's war with the Allies; the decision means that the Greeks and Turks will fight over territory and whichever side wins, can keep what it has captured.... No Allied interference will be placed on any nation that wishes to sell weapons to Turkey.	Baron Byng of Vimy arrives in Canada to begin his tour as Canada's Governor General.... Jamaica protests protective tariffs in the United States that have been placed on Jamaica's exports of bananas and coconuts.	
Aug. 11		Rain falls in Belgium ending an extended drought and bringing about the possibility of salvaging some of the crop.... Hungary receives the text of the American resolution that will become the peace treaty between the two nations officially ending the war between the two nations.... Poland announces that it will give Herbert Hoover the use of railways in order to move food to assist the Soviet Union.	A Holy War has been declared by the King of the Hedjaz (Arabia) to assist the Turks who are now fighting against Greece.... Moorish rebels defeat a Spanish force capturing a general and killing 400 Spanish soldiers.	The Mexican government continues the pay cut for all government employees that went into effect on August 1; the decrease will remain in effect until December 31, 1921.... The month of June saw a record of oil shipments from Tampico in order to send as much oil out as possible before the Mexican export tax went into effect on July 1; on June 17 million barrels of oil were sent to the United States.	The Japanese government is supposed to be strongly against the birth control movement in that country.... A British survey party, which is part of the British expedition to conquer Mount Everest, is currently exploring the area to see if there is a possible route to the summit.
Aug. 12				A Windsor, Ontario, magistrate issues a ruling that will prevent Canada from helping the United States enforce Prohibition.... The estimated wheat harvest for Canada will be 25 million bushels, a substantial increase over the 1920 harvest.	

A	B	C	D	E
Includes developments that affect more than one world region, international organizations and important meetings of world leaders.	*Includes all domestic and regional developments in Europe, including the Soviet Union.*	*Includes all domestic and regional developments in Africa and the Middle East.*	*Includes all domestic and regional developments in Latin America, the Caribbean, and Canada.*	*Includes all domestic and regional developments in Asian and Pacific nations (and colonies).*

	U.S. Politics & Social Issues	U.S. Foreign Policy & Affairs, Defense	U.S. Economy & Environment	Science, Technology & Nature	Culture, Leisure & Lifestyle
Aug. 7	Carpet workers in 23 factories across the country return to work after accepting up to 20 percent wage cuts....In Atlanta, the Ku Klux Klan issues a statement that it will not tolerate acts of lawlessness....Police in Detroit prevent a mob from lynching Sam Griggs, an African American accused of shooting two boys.	In Plattsburgh, NY, for the first time since 1918, a military training camp for young men opens; there are 800 in attendance....Men who served in the U.S. Merchant Marine during the War are asking for a badge or medal to indicate recognition of their wartime service.	The world's largest phone cable has been installed in Detroit that allows up to 600 conversations to be transmitted at once to Windsor, Ontario.		Dr. A.A. Roback of Harvard University states that the Edison test is not useful and that it is more reasonable to know where one can find the answers than to try having them, especially for "useless things."
Aug. 8	Labor Leader Samuel Gompers tells a labor gathering in Quebec that the worst of economic times have passed and that unemployment will decrease.		Standard Oil of California cuts the price of oil; a gallon of gas is two cents less.		William Edmonds and his brother, Reverence Albert Edmonds, are both seriously ill after having been bitten by a copperhead snake during a religious revival at Nauvoo, AL; William is not expected to recover.
Aug. 9	Thirty-five cars are stolen in one day in New York City, a new record, breaking one established only days before....Marshall Field stores state that their women employees cannot wear bobbed hair in public....Interviews for prospective members of the Ku Klux Klan are conducted in Philadelphia; the Klan lists among its objectives the rooting out of the I.W.W., Sinn Fein, and Soviets; members are free to drink, however....U.S. Attorney General Daugherty states he will discuss the possibility of a presidential pardon for Eugene Debs with President Harding....The city of Worcester, MA, begins a plan to put 1,000 unemployed men to work on city improvement projects.				Everett Scott, who has played for the Boston Red Sox for nine years, gets his first home run at home in Boston's Fenway Park.
Aug. 10		The battleship USS *New Mexico* wins the Navy's annual trophy for excellence in gunnery and efficiency.	Westinghouse announces that it has received an order for two electric freight locomotives from the Imperial government of Japan.		Police in Philadelphia fire 800 bullets in an eventually successful attempt to kill a bull that had gotten loose in the streets of the city and injured 15 people....Babe Ruth hits home run number 42 for the season.
Aug. 11		A new battleship, the USS *California*, is commissioned at Mare Island, CA.			
Aug. 12	A survey of orphanages in Delaware shows that only three percent of all the institutionalized children are missing both parents.	Secretary of State Hughes is named to be the chief American delegate at the upcoming arms conference in November....Storms in Britain are delaying the final tests of the British-made airship *ZR-2* before its planned voyage to be delivered to the U.S. Navy.			Former New York Giant pitcher Christy Mathewson celebrates his 41st birthday as he convalesces at Saranac, NY, from tuberculosis, the effect of inhaling poison gas during the World War....Russian poet, Alexander Blok, dies of cancer.

F	G	H	I	J
Includes campaigns, elections, federal-state relations, civil rights and liberties, crime, the judiciary, education, healthcare, poverty, urban affairs, and population.	*Includes formation and debate of U.S. foreign and defense policies, veterans affairs, and defense spending. (Relations with specific foreign countries are usually found under the region concerned.)*	*Includes business, labor, agriculture, taxation, transportation, consumer affairs, monetary and fiscal policy, natural resources, pollution and industrial accidents.*	*Includes worldwide scientific, medical and technological developments, natural phenomena, U.S. weather and natural disasters.*	*Includes the arts, religion, scholarship, communications media, sports, entertainment, fashions, fads, and social life.*

	World Affairs	Europe	Africa & The Middle East	The Americas	Asia & The Pacific
Aug. 13	The British Dominion Premiers attending the Imperial Conference are quite strong in their statements of friendship for the United States and that U.S. considerations should be taken into consideration in Imperial policy.	An American just back from Russia states that starvation has become so bad that people are dying in the streets and that he could see no animals as they had all been eaten....King Peter of Serbia is reported to be ill again....Soviet official Maxim Litvinov accedes to American conditions concerning American supervision of feeding and distribution as defined by Herbert Hoover....The Hungarian Assembly accepts the peace treaty drafted by the United States to end the state of war between the two nations.			Manuel Araullo, ranking Associate Justice of the Supreme Court of the Philippines, has been selected by President Harding to be Chief Justice of that Court....Vice Admiral Kanji Kato has been named to represent his country at the Naval Disarmament and Far Eastern Affairs Conference to be held in Washington in November.
Aug. 14		The British government gives back control it assumed of railroads during the war to the private rail companies....Eamon de Valera states that Ireland must have full independence and not be a British Dominion....Stories of refugees from Russian villages describe how the Communists took all of the grain available, followed by bands of bandits....The Polish government announces it intends to protest the partition of Upper Silesia and the amount of territory awarded to Germany.	Turkish forces have managed to push back Greek patrols.	Testimony is presented to the Senate that native Haitians have been abused by the U.S. Marines occupying their country....Census figures for the city of Lima, Peru, indicate that the population is 280,000.	The pro-Soviet Eastern Siberian Republic is said to have been overthrown by anti-Communist forces.
Aug. 15		H.G. Wells states that the cruelties of American policy have created the famine in the Soviet Union....In France, 40,000 textile workers go on strike protesting against a proposed wage cut....King Peter of Serbia is reported as very ill and near death.	The Greek Army has opened another offensive in Turkey; the Turks are retreating without offering any significant resistance.	Mutinous Peruvian soldiers have broken into a bank in the city of Iquitos and have taken all the cash.	The Soviets will keep an army in the Mongolian Republic until there is no chance of any successes in the region by anti-Communist units.
Aug. 16		King Peter if Serbia dies at the age of 77....The British Army orders all soldiers whose regiments are in Ireland to return from leave to their duty stations....Herbert Hoover states that he will not accept the Communist terms of having total control over food distribution to centers in Russia where famine relief is being distributed; President Harding backs Hoover's stand....Eamon de Valera repeats the policy of Sinn Fein, which is to reject dominion status and to have complete independence.	Earthquakes strike Italian Eritrea in east Africa; the Italian government, which administers the area, is sending aid....In an offensive in Morocco, Spanish troops manage to defeat the Moors.		China's President, Sun Yat-sen thanks the nations of the world for the contributions they have made to alleviate starvation in China. ...Reports describe Japanese preparations to evacuate troops from Siberia completely on a timetable that calls for complete withdrawal before the peace conference in November.
Aug. 17		The Italian government is reported to be very close to concluding a trade treaty with the Soviet Union....Both Poles and Germans ask the Allies to give all of Silesia to either Poland or Germany and not to split the region between the two countries.			
Aug. 18		The League of Nations will discuss the Silesian question on August 29....The Soviet Union accepts Hoover's terms for the administration and distribution of food relief....Former Hungarian Premier Teleki states that undiscovered oil resources in that country may help it return to prosperity.		The port of Montreal is busier than it has ever been before with grain shipments to Europe being the basis for the increased activity.	The Chinese government accepts the invitation of President Harding to the upcoming peace conference....Japan's shipbuilding orders are postponed until the outcome of the peace conferences is known; there is substantial fear in Japan that disarmament could hurt the ship building industry....Prime Minister Lloyd George of Britain is stating that the British Alliance with Japan could be expanded to form a tripartite alliance with the United States, as well to deal with issues in the Pacific.

A	B	C	D	E
Includes developments that affect more than one world region, international organizations and important meetings of world leaders.	*Includes all domestic and regional developments in Europe, including the Soviet Union.*	*Includes all domestic and regional developments in Africa and the Middle East.*	*Includes all domestic and regional developments in Latin America, the Caribbean, and Canada.*	*Includes all domestic and regional developments in Asian and Pacific nations (and colonies).*

U.S. Politics & Social Issues	U.S. Foreign Policy & Affairs, Defense	U.S. Economy & Environment	Science, Technology & Nature	Culture, Leisure & Lifestyle	
In Logan, WV, two state troopers are surrounded by a group of armed men, disarmed, and told to stay out of the area.... The governor of Hawaii is appealing to the U.S. Senate Immigration committee to allow Chinese workers to come in and work in that territory as there is a severe labor shortage.		G. Gennert, a manufacturer of photographic equipment brings a triple damage suit of $6 million against the Eastman Kodak Company; this is only the latest lawsuit against Kodak since the government ruled against it in a monopoly case.... A 300-acre Philadelphia oil facility is on fire after an explosion; of 200 men working at the time of the explosion, many are still unaccounted for.	A four-man air expedition begins aerial mapping of Mount Washington, NH, while flying over the area at heights of 8,000 to 10,000 feet.		Aug. 13
Senator Borah states that the amount of money the United States is spending on armaments and its military exceed the amount of money being paid to this country by German reparations.					Aug. 14
					Aug. 15
Five people are killed and seven are injured in what is described as a race riot in Augusta, GA.... In Trenton, NJ, the chief of police states that if the Ku Klux Klan attempts to organize in that city, members will be jailed or, "if necessary, shot down."... The U.S. Labor Department estimates that there are 5.735 million unemployed in the country.	Senator Henry Cabot Lodge of Massachusetts is named as a delegate to the arms conference, although there is some reservation due to his outspoken anti-League of Nations and anti-British statements in the past.				Aug. 16
New York City police raid an opium den on 49 Mott Street confiscating pipes, lamps, and opium; the owners were said to be charging $2 for a pipe of opium.... The Governor of Puerto Rico states that he will not appoint anyone to an office who is on record for granting independence to the island.				Doctors state that Georges Carpentier may never be able to box again due to internal injuries suffered from his title fight with Jack Dempsey.	Aug. 17
The Army's head of the War Plans Division visits the training center at Plattsburgh, NY.... Police in Wareham, MA, prevent a mob from lynching two African Americans accused of assaulting a girl.				Evelyn Nesbit, former friend of Stanford White and former wife of Pittsburgh industrialist Harry K. Thaw, reports to police that her Specialty Shop has been broken into and robbed.... A light heavyweight fighter, Gene Tunney, from Greenwich Village has defeated Eddie Josephs in a match in Staten Island.	Aug. 18

F	G	H	I	J
Includes campaigns, elections, federal-state relations, civil rights and liberties, crime, the judiciary, education, healthcare, poverty, urban affairs, and population.	*Includes formation and debate of U.S. foreign and defense policies, veterans affairs, and defense spending. (Relations with specific foreign countries are usually found under the region concerned.)*	*Includes business, labor, agriculture, taxation, transportation, consumer affairs, monetary and fiscal policy, natural resources, pollution and industrial accidents.*	*Includes worldwide scientific, medical and technological developments, natural phenomena, U.S. weather and natural disasters.*	*Includes the arts, religion, scholarship, communications media, sports, entertainment, fashions, fads, and social life.*

	World Affairs	Europe	Africa & The Middle East	The Americas	Asia & The Pacific
Aug. 19		A Spanish diplomat is tasked by the League of Nations to investigate the Silesian question; in the meantime, France is sending more troops into the region.			
Aug. 20	The Council of the League of Nations states that it will take part in implementing a solution in Silesia; earlier there had been concern the League would not interfere because the Silesian question was part of the Versailles Peace Treaty.	Czechoslovakia's national sports organization, Sokol, has sent a group to the United States where they will compete in Chicago.…A British financial group announces that it may have a deal with Soviet authorities to obtain a long lease for the Port of Petrograd.…While British and Irish authorities are making progress on issues surrounding the separation of Ireland, one of the major sticking points is the question of whether Ireland will be united or if Northern Ireland will remain separate and be ruled by Britain.	Turkish forces continue to resist the Greek offensive, some reports claiming that there are as many as 60,000 Turks on the front lines.… While Spanish forces are engaged in heavy fighting, authorities in French Morocco report that the do not anticipate similar unrest in French Morocco.	The Mexican government states that it will demand reports from oil companies on the amount of oil they have brought up so that taxation will be accurate.…The Canadian Department of Labor reports that the cost of living in Canada is two and a half times what it was in 1900.	British policy toward Japanese is, according to some observers, based on securing the friendship of Japan while Britain seems to be having troubles in Persia, Afghanistan, and the Middle East.…A New York firm has signed a contract to build a 112-mile power line in Australia.
Aug. 21		Britain refuses admittance to Russian bass player, Feodor Chaliapin, who was scheduled to give several concerts in that country.…American, British, and German companies are competing for contracts to do major rebuilding in the Soviet cities of Petrograd and Odessa.…The Irish convention (the "Dail") meets in secret to discuss a reply to British proposals for terms of separating Ireland from Britain.	Greek forces continue to advance against the Turks; in the latest battle 170 officers and 4,000 men are captured.…The island of Person de Valez, which Spain has held since 1644, is abandoned by Spanish troops as it is fired on by the Moors; the Spanish army is beginning to use aircraft to bomb the insurgents.	U.S. Marines are sent to Panama, to keep order in the recent refusal of Panama to settle its border dispute with Costa Rica, to act as a peacekeeping force between the two countries.…In response to recent revolts, Peru closes its port cities.	The Japanese navy is sending a warship to Brazil on a goodwill tour.
Aug. 22	An international committee is proposing that a radio wave band would be assigned to each country so as to avoid confusion in radio frequencies.	Alexander Karageorgevich, son of the late King Peter of Serbia, proclaims that he will ascend to the throne.…Farmers in Germany, who have received cows from the United States as part of an aid program, state that the American cows yield more milk than native German breeds.…The British census reports that despite losses because of the World War, England and Wales have increased their population by two million.…The town of Oberammergau, which has held a play depicting the Passion of Christ since 1634 at 10-year intervals, announces that it will have its cast chosen by October of this year.	Greece continues to report that its army is making significant progress against Turkish forces.…At least 250 Americans have been recruited to fight for Spain in its war against the Moorish rebels in Morocco; at least half of the men are veterans of the AEF in the World War.	Bolivia and Chile dispute access to the Mauri River for irrigation purposes.…Trade unions in Canada report they are having success in removing Communist sympathizers from the unions.…Panama sends troops into the area that it disputes with Costa Rica; in addition to infantry, machine gun units have been sent in as well.…Police in Havana arrest 11 radicals on suspicion of having exploded a bomb in the streets of the city.	
Aug. 23		The British government reverses its decision and will allow Russian bass player Feodor Chaliapin to enter the country to give benefit concerts for famine relief in the Soviet Union.…More than 3,500 tons of food have been sent so far to relieve the famine in the Soviet Union.	Turks capture two British aviators who have been flying as volunteers with the Greek forces.	Panama states that it is giving up the territory it has disputed with Costa Rica.…A state of war has been declared in five departments in Nicaragua with a state of siege proclaimed in the rest of the country.	
Aug. 24		Germany signs the Peace Treaty with the United States, separate from the Versailles Treaty it signed with the other victorious Allies, thereby ending Germany's war with the United States.…There are 78,000 reported cases of cholera in the Soviet Union.…The Spanish diplomat, asked by the League of Nations to report on Silesia, has declined and a Japanese diplomat has volunteered to do the job; France objects to this substitution as it notes that Japan always takes Britain's side.	Reports from Morocco indicate that the Spanish have made significant advances over the Moors and have captured several positions.	Secretary of State Hughes announces that Sumner Welles will be the State Department Charge d'Affaires for Latin America.	
	A *Includes developments that affect more than one world region, international organizations and important meetings of world leaders.*	B *Includes all domestic and regional developments in Europe, including the Soviet Union.*	C *Includes all domestic and regional developments in Africa and the Middle East.*	D *Includes all domestic and regional developments in Latin America, the Caribbean, and Canada.*	E *Includes all domestic and regional developments in Asian and Pacific nations (and colonies).*

U.S. Politics & Social Issues	U.S. Foreign Policy & Affairs, Defense	U.S. Economy & Environment	Science, Technology & Nature	Culture, Leisure & Lifestyle	
In Knoxville, TN, 3,000 people surround a prison to lynch an African American accused of assaulting a woman; 27 people are injured when deputies guarding the jail fire into the crowd.... In Boston, there are 20,000 veterans who are unemployed.	A Joint Defense Board reports that despite the results of bombing tests, that the battleship is superior to the airplane and still the backbone of the fleet; a concession is made, however, to the fact that effective anti-aircraft armament on ships would be a good idea.	Standard Oil of New Jersey will launch the world's largest tanker, the *John D. Archbold*, with a capacity of 135,000 tons.		The *New York Times* celebrates its 25th anniversary of operating under the current management.... John Weismuller wins the national senior free style AAU swim race in Indianapolis with a time of two minutes, 28 seconds.	Aug. 19
All of Knoxville's police and a company of the National Guard are guarding the prison to avoid a second attempt to lynch an African-American man accused of assault.... A group of 600 miners assemble near Charleston, WV, to march to Mingo County in a demonstration against the imposition of martial law.... The Massachusetts National Guard, armed with machine guns, is sent to Barnstable, MA, to prevent the lynching of three men from Cape Verde who are accused of robbing and assaulting a Caucasian woman.	The Tennessee National Guard activates an air unit, which will function as an air observation squadron.	Wholesale beef prices in the United States have been dropping steadily through the year and are now at the same level as they were in 1913.... The daily demand for June was greater on a daily basis than any other month in 1921.... Oil prices are very low, reaching a point to where they were in 1913; overproduction is seen as the cause for the serious price drop.	In New Jersey, 200 cases of typhoid have been reported.		Aug. 20
A group of 900 men is prepared to march on Logano County, WV, as a demonstration against martial law; the sheriff of Logan County announces that he will not allow armed marchers to go through his county.... Stating that a beast needs only food and shelter but that a worker needs more, American Federation of Labor President Samuel Gompers promises to fight against wage reductions.			Doctors in France blame the increased use of cigarettes and alcohol for the increased frequency of beards and moustaches on women.... John D. Rockefeller gives Harvard University $1,785,000 to establish a public health school.	A fight breaks out in New York City between a man who believes that John McCormick is the greatest tenor ever and two sailors who believe that Caruso was the greatest; the two Caruso fans win with the McCormack fan sent to the hospital with a "badly battered face."	Aug. 21
	The Navy is hoping that the airship it has purchased from Britain, the ZR-2, will be ready for flight by September 5.		Approximately 100 cases of polio have been recently reported in New York State.		Aug. 22
	Referring to the AEF that fought in the World War as the greatest force to have "ever worn shoe leather," General Pershing tells students training at the Plattsburgh camp that they should emulate their predecessors.... The ZR-2, the British dirigible constructed for the U.S. Navy is preparing for its final trial before crossing the Atlantic.			American artist Howard Chandler Christy announces that he will completely quit illustrating magazines and will turn to doing only portraits.	Aug. 23
	The dirigible ZR-2, the largest dirigible ever built, with a crew of 16 Americans and 27 British explodes, breaks into two parts, and crashes into the Humber River; there are only five survivors.... Preliminary inquiries into the ZR-2 disaster mentions the use of hydrogen, but also speculate that the frame of the airship was so thin that it buckled under the strain of bad weather.	In Chicago, the price for a gallon of gas is 17 cents a gallon, a drop of one cent in the previous week.			Aug. 24
F *Includes campaigns, elections, federal-state relations, civil rights and liberties, crime, the judiciary, education, healthcare, poverty, urban affairs, and population.*	G *Includes formation and debate of U.S. foreign and defense policies, veterans affairs, and defense spending. (Relations with specific foreign countries are usually found under the region concerned.)*	H *Includes business, labor, agriculture, taxation, transportation, consumer affairs, monetary and fiscal policy, natural resources, pollution and industrial accidents.*	I *Includes worldwide scientific, medical and technological developments, natural phenomena, U.S. weather and natural disasters.*	J *Includes the arts, religion, scholarship, communications media, sports, entertainment, fashions, fads, and social life.*	

	World Affairs	Europe	Africa & The Middle East	The Americas	Asia & The Pacific
Aug. 25		Germany signs its peace treaty with the United States, which is separate from the Versailles Treaty, but is similar in almost all ways. . . . Sinn Fein, in its discussions with the British government, is not specifically mentioning a Republic but states that it leaves the choice open. . . . Unrest in Moscow has taken the form of arson that has destroyed several hundred houses in Moscow. . . . Observers returning from the Soviet Union report that food is so scarce that people are subsisting on grass and clay.	Six new Turkish divisions go into action against the Greeks.	Three men are arrested in a plot to kill Mexican President Obregon. . . . The president of Panama has ordered that the national flag be flown at half-staff in mourning for the final border dispute results in which Costa Rica now possess territory claimed by Panama.	Hundreds of villages have been destroyed when the Yellow River overflows its banks in Shantung Province. . . . Japanese soldiers fight a band of Communists in Siberia.
Aug. 26		Former German political leader and Armistice negotiator in 1918, Mathias Erzberger, is assassinated. . . . The Trianon treaty ending the state of war between the Allies (minus the United States) and Hungary goes into effect. . . . Hungarian diplomats are preparing the final drafts of the treaty ending the state of war between Hungary and the United States.		Armed groups from Honduras are invading Nicaragua. Nicaraguan troops are being sent to the border to repel them.	British and Indian troops are being called out to handle civil unrest in southern India.
Aug. 27	The United States say that as host it will bear the expenses of hosting the International Conference on Naval Disarmament and the Far East.	Although Germany and Poland are at odds diplomatically, there is still substantial trade in some areas; German electrical products are flooding into Poland and being purchased in great quantities. . . . Muslims in the Yugoslav city of Novipazar have been fighting with Christians, with a death toll of at least 35; the Yugoslav Army is being sent to the city. . . . Prince George, former Crown Prince of Serbia who has renounced his rights, now asserts that he should be king.	The Turks have been defeated in a 10-hour battle.	Reports on business developments in South America note that business is generally healthy with a tendency toward deflation taking place. . . . President Bustillos of Venezuela defends his country's policy of terror as a means to ensure stability and suppress anarchy.	Baron Kato of Japan states that Japan should withdraw its troops from Siberia before the peace conference in November. . . . The British expedition to climb Mount Everest still has yet to identify a viable route to the summit of the mountain. . . . The Malabar region of southern India is now being occupied by British and Indian troops.
Aug. 28	Pope Benedict XV states that he is in agreement with the idea of the forthcoming disarmament conference, but also adds that disarmament should include a pledge to abolish conscription in all countries.	Although Sinn Fein has refused the latest set of British proposals, it is keeping options open and is expected to renew negotiations in the coming week. . . . Mirdite insurgents in Albania rout the Albanian Army, killing more than 100 soldiers in a two-day battle. . . . Communist demonstrations in the German city of Potsdam are broken up when police fire on the crowd, killing two.	Turkish troops in heavy fighting on the Sakaria River defeat the Greeks taking many prisoners and capturing many guns.	The Nicaraguan government reports that it is fighting a group of rebels; the government also announces it is reducing the wages of its civil service by 20 percent and that all public telegraph and telephone service has been discontinued.	Japanese newspapers report that the government of Japan has a great deal of anxiety about a U.S.-British combination that would isolate them. . . . Martial law is being applied in several districts in India as unrest is combining with famine; British authorities have asked Mohandas Gandhi to attempt to pacify the natives.
Aug. 29	The German government announces that it will not ask to join the League of Nations now, but will wait until the Disarmament conference.	Soviet authorities confirm that there are famine conditions brought about by seven years of war as well as drought and plagues of locusts. . . . Clashing in Belfast over whether Northern Ireland will join with southern Ireland has resulted in two killed and six wounded. . . . Reports from the Burgenland region, that area of Hungary that is supposed to be transferred to Austria, describe a coup in which Hungarian terrorists are fighting Austrians.	King Alfonso XIII in a speech to an Army unit, promises vengeance against the Moors in Spanish Morocco.		Fighting in China's Hunan province between soldiers of the Chinese government and rebels continues.
Aug. 30		Germany and Italy sign a trade treaty. . . . Poland is having a serious problem with the refugees entering the country from different parts of the Soviet Union; Poles are driving the refugees back across the border. . . . Fighting between Fascists and Socialists in Italy claims one dead and 10 injured when a bomb is thrown.	More Spanish outposts are captured in Spanish Morocco by Moorish rebels.		

A	B	C	D	E
Includes developments that affect more than one world region, international organizations and important meetings of world leaders.	*Includes all domestic and regional developments in Europe, including the Soviet Union.*	*Includes all domestic and regional developments in Africa and the Middle East.*	*Includes all domestic and regional developments in Latin America, the Caribbean, and Canada.*	*Includes all domestic and regional developments in Asian and Pacific nations (and colonies).*

U.S. Politics & Social Issues	U.S. Foreign Policy & Affairs, Defense	U.S. Economy & Environment	Science, Technology & Nature	Culture, Leisure & Lifestyle	
The average weekly pay of factory workers in New York state fell an average of 45 cents a week during the month of July....Samuel Gompers, President of the American Federation of Labor, states that if employers manage to crush the unions to establish open shops, Communism will be embraced by American workers....A group numbering up to 4,000 men, nearly all armed, are on the march to protest the imposition of martial law in Mingo County, WV; an aircraft scouting the march of the protestors has been fired on....Federal soldiers in Ohio and Indiana are reported to be ready to move into the area.	Investigators who are trying to reconstruct the events that led to the crash of the ZR-2 believe that the frame buckled while the craft was making a high speed turn. Although there were no public statements of doubt concerning the ZR-2, American enlisted crew members called the craft a "lemon."	Members of a capital group that is funding a New York-San Francisco air route using airships states that the ZR-2 tragedy will not stop the development of lighter-than-airships....Wage cuts in the railroad industry are having the desired results as railroads report that their net profits have risen although their gross income is lower than last year....The Sinclair Oil Company announces that it has approximately nine million barrels of oil in storage, contained in 55,000-barrel storage tanks.			Aug. 25
Officials of the United Mine Workers succeed in getting many of the miners to return to their homes....Former Assistant Secretary for the Navy Franklin D. Roosevelt is reported as improving after a serious illness (he would eventually be diagnosed as having contracted polio).		The Commerce secretary states that the drop in foreign trade figures in July is not as bad as it would appear because the total based on monetary value does not really indicate the true value of the international commerce.			Aug. 26
General Bandholz of the West Virginia National Guard reports that the Mingo County crisis is at an end and that order has been restored.	One of the responses to the successful aerial bombings of ships during recent exercises is a call for developing and deploying a greater number of submarines.	The Cloak, Suit, and Skirt Protective Association points out that one of its greatest problems is "style piracy" where their styles are produced by manufacturers who have copied their patterns but use inferior materials.		French composer and conductor, Vincent D'Indy, is scheduled to visit New York and will conduct the New York Philharmonic in December.	Aug. 27
President Harding announces he wishes to open a conference to investigate how unemployment in the country can be reduced....Five miners are killed when they clash with police in Mingo County. National Guard and Miners union officials have been sent to Mingo County to help restore order.					Aug. 28
In light of continuing unrest, West Virginia's Governor asks for Federal troops; President Harding decides not to send Federal troops to Mingo County, WV....A Grand Jury indicts several United Mine Workers officials for murder in disturbances that took place in Mingo County last year....The Ku Klux Klan reports that it has 50 Klans in New Jersey and is growing.	The Plattsburgh military summer training program is such a great success that plans are announced to expand it next year so that three times the participants will be trained.	The U.S. Geological Survey states that oil derived from shale may be a viable alterative to oil taken from wells....The Midwest Refining Company will build a 90-mile gas pipeline that will transport 30 million cubic feet of gas a day.			Aug. 29
				The Boston Braves baseball club announce that this year they have doubled their attendance figures from 1920; the largest attendance at any game was 39,000.	Aug. 30
F	G	H	I	J	
Includes campaigns, elections, federal-state relations, civil rights and liberties, crime, the judiciary, education, healthcare, poverty, urban affairs, and population.	*Includes formation and debate of U.S. foreign and defense policies, veterans affairs, and defense spending. (Relations with specific foreign countries are usually found under the region concerned.)*	*Includes business, labor, agriculture, taxation, transportation, consumer affairs, monetary and fiscal policy, natural resources, pollution and industrial accidents.*	*Includes worldwide scientific, medical and technological developments, natural phenomena, U.S. weather and natural disasters.*	*Includes the arts, religion, scholarship, communications media, sports, entertainment, fashions, fads, and social life.*	

	World Affairs	Europe	Africa & The Middle East	The Americas	Asia & The Pacific
Aug. 31		Riots expand in Belfast; 15 are killed and many injured; some reporters have noticed that there is a religious element to the struggle with Protestants favoring rule of Ulster by Britain and Catholics being opposed....King George V states that he is very hopeful that a peaceful Irish settlement may still come about....Police in Budapest arrest 56 Communists.	Turkish forces are retreating in the wake of a Greek offensive along a 37-mile front....Syrian and Palestinian public figures are presenting to the League of Nations a request for complete independence from the French and the British.	The Panama Canal Commission reports that in the seven years that the canal has been open, 13,416 commercial craft have passed through.	British authorities claim to have uncovered a plot by Sikhs in the Punjab to revolt against British rule....There is rioting in southern India between Muslims and Hindus.
Sept. 1	The world wheat crop is greater than last year's harvests; a survey of 20 nations, including the United States, estimates that the total will be 2,461,430,000 bushels.	There is increased skepticism about famine reports from the Soviet Union; French government officials claim that if observers were to see what was really happening, relief to the Soviets would come to an end....Leon Trotsky claims that eight Soviet leaders in recent months have been killed by French and American agents....British troops have succeeded in restoring order in Belfast.	Moorish rebels successfully manage to rush a Spanish position and capture another outpost in Morocco.	Another attempt to overthrow the Mexican government, this time in Northern Mexico, is detected and prevented.	British troops in southern India, traveling in armored cars, are ambushed by 4,000 rebels; two soldiers are killed....Anti-government disturbances in Madras, India, are now over.
Sept. 2		Food trains leave Riga, Latvia, to bring food aid to the Soviet Union....Former Premier of Russia Alexander Kerensky states that he had asked Britain to provide a haven for the Czar and his family but was refused, leaving them to be captured and killed by the Communists....As shooting resumes in Belfast, another 18 are killed.	Retreating from the Greek Army, Turkish forces are now only 50 miles from their capital at Ankara.	Observers state they are having difficulty in seeing any evidence of the war that Nicaragua claims it is fighting; although a state of war has been declared and the army mobilized, there have been no reports of fighting....The population of Puerto Rico seems united in the desire to have their current governor removed by President Harding.	General Leonard Wood announces he will accept the offer of becoming Governor of the Philippines.
Sept. 3		Revolutionaries issue a manifesto stating their grievances against the current Portuguese government.... In the first three months of 1921, Czechoslovakia has exported more goods than it has imported....The Romanian government orders 200 locomotives from German manufacturers....Despite poor weather this year, the harvest in France will be very good, almost enough to supply all home demand.		The Brazilian government is sending survey parties to investigate the existence of oil and coal deposits in the interior of the country.	British soldiers capture about 40 tribesmen in southern India.
Sept. 4		Reports from Ukraine describe a quiet revolt on the part of Ukrainians who will not allow some 15,000 refugees from other parts of the Soviet Union to enter their towns....Communists are rioting in several cities in Germany.... Although Germany is not a member of the League of Nations, it is still a signatory of the League Convention and for that reason files 20 international treaties with the League.	The Greek Army, in pursuit of the Turks on the way to their capital of Ankara, announce that the city will certainly be captured.	The terms of the export tax on oil from Mexico have been changed to making tax payments on a quarterly basis; with the agreement oil companies are now shipping Mexican oil out of Tampico....Reports coming from South America are indicating that although German companies have been making substantial inroads there, the effect on American business will not be as serious as it was thought to be.	Japanese Crown Prince Hirohito arrives back home after his world tour and, establishing a new precedent, is greeted by large crowds that cheer him....Afghanistan ratifies a treaty of friendship with the Soviet government.

A	B	C	D	E
Includes developments that affect more than one world region, international organizations and important meetings of world leaders.	*Includes all domestic and regional developments in Europe, including the Soviet Union.*	*Includes all domestic and regional developments in Africa and the Middle East.*	*Includes all domestic and regional developments in Latin America, the Caribbean, and Canada.*	*Includes all domestic and regional developments in Asian and Pacific nations (and colonies).*

U.S. Politics & Social Issues	U.S. Foreign Policy & Affairs, Defense	U.S. Economy & Environment	Science, Technology & Nature	Culture, Leisure & Lifestyle	
The Governor of West Virginia and the commander of the National Guard state that the miners of Mingo County are in a state of insurrection....Four men are killed in sniping in Mingo Country.	In yet another aerial disaster, *D-6*, the Navy's newest and largest nonrigid airship explodes and burns along with three other blimps and the hangar in which they were kept; there are no deaths but one man is severely burned.				Aug. 31
General Bandholz requests that Federal troops be sent to Mingo County at once as the miners there have not disbanded in accordance with President Harding's orders. Army aircraft have been sent to scout out the activities of the miners in the effort to prevent them from invading neighboring Logan County. The Chesapeake and Ohio Railroad says it is not making runs through the area after one of its locomotives was allegedly taken by the miners. Samuel Gompers of the American Federation of Labor defends the actions of the miners in Mingo County.	President Harding states that the nation will always need armed forces but the time is coming when the armament burden will be decreased.	The number of business failures in August increased; the total was 1,562 failures, the greatest number since February.	William Marconi, of the Marconi Wireless Telegraph Company, states that he believes that the regularity of signals from Mars is an indication that Martians are attempting to signal to Earth.		Sept. 1
In Logan county, WV, there is a 1,600-man force, combined with the National Guard, prepared to defend Logan county from a force estimated to be approximately 10,000 miners. The government force has been using airplanes to drop bombs on the miners according to some reports. Eighteen miners have been brought in as prisoners. Late in the day, 2,100 Federal troops from Camp Knox and Camp Dix reach Mingo County; the miners state that they will obey Federal troops. In the meantime, although Federal troops are on the scene, the President has not yet taken the step of declaring Federal martial law.			Ernest Shackleton has been asked by the British Admiralty to gather aviation data on his current trip to the Antarctic, which will begin on September 12....At a meeting of the American Astronomy Association, scientists estimate that the width of the universe to be one million light years.		Sept. 2
United Mine Workers officials will request the U.S. Senate Committee investigating the Mingo County situation to include the use of Federal troops as part of the scope of investigation. Federal troops in West Virginia are being deployed into five counties, which have been divided into three military districts. Soldiers moving into the area surround and disarm 400 miners although there is some occasional sniper fire.				In the batting race, Ty Cobb leads the American League with an average of .396 and Rogers Hornsby leads the National League with .412.	Sept. 3
Miners throughout the Mingo-Logan county region are disbanding and returning home....Today is Labor Day; for the first time in many years there will be no Labor Day Parade, because many men are unemployed and those who still have jobs not wanting to spend money on uniforms and bands....Shepherd Urban Ledoux, known as Mr. Zero, gathers 350 unemployed men in Boston Common and provides them with breakfast at his building on Howard Street known as the "Church of the Unemployed."...In a speech, Samuel Gompers claims that U.S. Steel is behind all of the problems that have risen in Mingo County, WV.			Sadi Lecointe, a French aviator, wins the air race at Brescia, flying 300 kilometers in one hour, 13 minutes, nine seconds.	A magazine, the *Review of Reviews*, conducts a survey of how well informed college students are on current events; only 44 percent of 17,500 respondents get the correct answers.	Sept. 4

F	G	H	I	J
Includes campaigns, elections, federal-state relations, civil rights and liberties, crime, the judiciary, education, healthcare, poverty, urban affairs, and population.	*Includes formation and debate of U.S. foreign and defense policies, veterans affairs, and defense spending. (Relations with specific foreign countries are usually found under the region concerned.)*	*Includes business, labor, agriculture, taxation, transportation, consumer affairs, monetary and fiscal policy, natural resources, pollution and industrial accidents.*	*Includes worldwide scientific, medical and technological developments, natural phenomena, U.S. weather and natural disasters.*	*Includes the arts, religion, scholarship, communications media, sports, entertainment, fashions, fads, and social life.*

	World Affairs	Europe	Africa & The Middle East	The Americas	Asia & The Pacific
Sept. 5	The Second League of Nations Assembly Session opens and will be in session until October 5.	The Soviets allege cruel treatment of their prisoners of war at the hands of the Polish authorities.... The Polish government may request assistance from American experts to stabilize its finances.		European companies are in a bidding war to get access to land in Argentina where oil deposits are thought to be located.... Operations in Havana Harbor are stopped when 1,500 men go on strike.	
Sept. 6			Unofficial reports claim that the Greek army has captured the Turkish capital of Ankara.	A revolution in Colombia has resulted in President Saurez being imprisoned, a local bishop, and the Conservative Party candidate for the presidency.	The British have arrested and tried 300 rebels in India, sentencing them to two years at hard labor for each offense of looting or other offenses.
Sept. 7		Britain sends a ship with a 5,650-ton cargo of food to be distributed to Russian children suffering from starvation.... German colleges have a large number of foreign students; currently 7,000 foreigners attend 26 German Universities and technical schools.	The garrison at El Araish, in Spanish Morocco, is attacked by Moorish rebels who are joined by the native troops that were part of the Spanish force; the garrison barely manages to defeat the Moors.	The Hudson Bay Company states that it will be drilling for oil in Canada.... The Nicaraguan government claims to have fought and routed a group of rebels, driving them back into Honduras, while capturing 1,311.	Government opinion in Japan seems to be favoring a limit of Naval weapons and may even be willing to drop two projected battle cruisers from it current building program.
Sept. 8		The American Express Company says that it is impossible to send money to the Soviet Union as the government claims 90 percent of all cash sent there.... Sixty-one people, including 16 women, are shot in Petrograd on the charge of plotting against the Soviets.			In fighting between northern and southern Chinese forces near the Yangtse River, 10,000 are killed and wounded.
Sept. 9		The Allies are prepared to act against Hungary with military intervention probably done by Italy over Hungary's failure to pull terrorists back from Burgenland that is supposed to be turned over to Austria.... Lenin's New Economic Plan seems to be working on the local level; reports from Moscow describe how small scale entrepreneurs are very busy buying and selling goods.... Fifty members of Sinn Fein, held in the Rath Camop prison have burrowed their way to freedom.	The Greek offensive against the Turkish army comes to a halt; the Turks claim that the Greeks have lost 30,000 men thus far; military observers are offering the opinion that the Greek offensive has been a complete failure due to bad generalship, bad transportation, and not enough artillery.	U.S. Treasury Secretary Andrew Mellon is calling for meetings that will be held in Washington and other western hemisphere cities to discuss the international exchange problem.... A new oil well with a 70,000-barrel a day capability has been drilled in the state of Tabasco, Mexico.	The Japanese government announces it will send 200 delegates to the Naval Disarmament and Far East Conference in Washington in November.
Sept. 10		The Soviet government is cracking down on the opposition: 62 anti-Communist officers captured in Siberia are executed, while 400 officers of the Baltic fleet and 180 Army Officers in Kiev are imprisoned.		Bolivia and Brazil are cutting down on their raw rubber output due to the high costs of production and transportation.... Nicaragua demobilizes its soldiers after putting down the rebellion on the Honduras frontier.	Fresh unrest in India, this time 35 miles north of Delhi in Meerut has begun; the rioting may have begun over disputes over food at a time when there are severe food shortages.
Sept. 11		The Burgenland crisis in western Hungary grows worse as Hungarian regular troops have been moved into that region.... In the Armenian section of the Soviet Union a cholera epidemic has combined with famine; it is predicted by some that half a million people will die in the coming winter.... Several American-owned factories in the Soviet Union are taken over by the government; only the plant owned by the Westinghouse Company has been unaffected.		Chile has agreed to submit its border dispute with Bolivia to a special tribunal of the League of Nations.	

A	B	C	D	E
Includes developments that affect more than one world region, international organizations and important meetings of world leaders.	*Includes all domestic and regional developments in Europe, including the Soviet Union.*	*Includes all domestic and regional developments in Africa and the Middle East.*	*Includes all domestic and regional developments in Latin America, the Caribbean, and Canada.*	*Includes all domestic and regional developments in Asian and Pacific nations (and colonies).*

	U.S. Politics & Social Issues	U.S. Foreign Policy & Affairs, Defense	U.S. Economy & Environment	Science, Technology & Nature	Culture, Leisure & Lifestyle
Sept. 5	Federal troops are still in the area, but the miners' demonstration in Mingo and Logan counties seems to be over. A statement by the Mine Owners of Mingo County take issue with Samuel Gompers' accusations of unfair treatment, but also state that the action of the miners bordered on treason against the United States and was not simply a labor action.				Walter Johnson of the Washington Senators throws his 2,291st strikeout, beating the record established by Cy Young.
Sept. 6	While peace has returned to Mingo County, many residents are expressing skepticism that it will last for very long. Secretary of War Weeks orders the 26th Regiment back to Camp Dix and the 88th Bombing Squadron is ordered back to its base although the 19th Infantry will remain in the area.				Mary Pickford's new film, *Little Lord Fauntleroy*, is scheduled to open this week in New York.
Sept. 7	The uneasy peace still holds in Logan and Mingo Counties although observers note that of at least 6,000 miners who were part of the march, only 400 handed in weapons to the Army.…The Matewan murder trial opens with two men accused of murder in the Matewan battle in 1920.…In Illinois, 800 miners are prepared to march on two towns where strikers and mine guards have confronted each other in the past.		The Northern Pacific Railroad reports higher earnings in August, in large part as a result of hauling the large grain harvests.		A play, *Tarzan of the Apes*, based on the character created by Edgar Rice Burroughs opens in New York.
Sept. 8	The state of West Virginia issues 40 arrest warrants for marchers in the recent confrontation between state troops and miners.				Margaret Gorman of Washington, DC, is crowned as the first Miss America in Atlantic City, NJ.
Sept. 9	Mine owners from Mingo County see President Harding and protest that the union is an "autocracy."		The Willys-Morrow Company, maker of Willys-Overland autos, issues a call for 2,000 men to return to work after the plant had been closed for several weeks.		Babe Ruth hits his 54th home run, tying his 1920 record.
Sept. 10	A footbridge in Chester, PA, collapses, causing 34 people to drown.… San Antonio is hit by a flood that has created $3 million in property damage with 40 known dead with perhaps a total death toll of 250.				Police in San Francisco announce that they have actor Roscoe ("Fatty") Arbuckle in custody to question him about the death of actress Virginia Rappe at a party.
Sept. 11	U.S. immigration deports 200 aliens because the quotas for entry of their nationalities had been filled for this month.…The Ku Klux Klan discusses its plan to open a college in Atlanta, which will teach "100 percent Americanism"; the school will accept anyone for admission who subscribes to their principles and not just the sons and daughters of members of the Klan.…The death toll in San Antonio is now at 47 but there are still many people missing.			The week of October 30 to November 5 has been set aside for cancer education programs.	Fatty Arbuckle is jailed on the available evidence that he murdered Virginia Rappe.…Cecil B. DeMille's latest film, *The Affairs of Anatol*, opens in New York City.

F
Includes campaigns, elections, federal-state relations, civil rights and liberties, crime, the judiciary, education, healthcare, poverty, urban affairs, and population.

G
Includes formation and debate of U.S. foreign and defense policies, veterans affairs, and defense spending. (Relations with specific foreign countries are usually found under the region concerned.)

H
Includes business, labor, agriculture, taxation, transportation, consumer affairs, monetary and fiscal policy, natural resources, pollution and industrial accidents.

I
Includes worldwide scientific, medical and technological developments, natural phenomena, U.S. weather and natural disasters.

J
Includes the arts, religion, scholarship, communications media, sports, entertainment, fashions, fads, and social life.

	World Affairs	Europe	Africa & The Middle East	The Americas	Asia & The Pacific
Sept. 12	French Premier Briand announces he will head the French delegation that will attend the Naval Disarmament and Far Eastern Conference to be held in Washington in November.... The agenda and participant list for the major issues are being drawn up for the International Conference; only five nations (United States, Britain, France, Japan, and Italy) will take place in the disarmament discussions although the United States is proposing that Belgium and Holland take part in other discussions as will China.	It is estimated that 900,000 children in Russia will be out of food and that hundred of thousands of others face starvation in the Tartar Republic.... The German Mark is at a new low in international currency exchange.	The American Red Cross announces it will have to stop its operation to assist refugees in Constantinople after October 1 as it is overwhelmed by the job and cannot complete it.		China states that the award of the Shantung Peninsula in that country to Japans as a result of the Treaty of Versailles was illegal and will bring that point up at the upcoming international conference.... Korean insurgents attempt to kill the Japanese governor of Korea with a bomb.
Sept. 13		Police say they have identified the killers of politician Mathias Erzberger; they are two former officers who belong to a reactionary political organization.... Poland and Lithuania tentatively accept a settlement proposed by the League of Nations over their border, the status of the city of Vilna, and relations between the two nations.... Sinn Fein delegates meet with Lloyd George in the latest set of discussions about the details surrounding the eventual separation of Ireland from England; officials throughout Northern Ireland protest against the possibility of a union with the south.	Spanish forces are having success in driving back Moorish rebels in Morocco; as much of the fighting has been near the coast, Spanish troops have received artillery support from Spanish naval guns.... A group of 300 foreign volunteers, including 60 Americans, enlists to fight for Spain in Morocco.		
Sept. 14	The League of Nations elects the bench of judges to the World Court with 11 full members from nations that include Britain, United States, Italy, Spain, Japan, and three from South America.	Observers agree that the peace settlement between Britain and Ireland will come about, but will not be permanent; observers in Ulster report that Protestants there fear a "terror." ... Police in Germany are expanding their search of conspirators in the Erzberger assassination and have arrested another 20 suspects.		Heavy rains in Argentina spoil what would have been a very large wheat crop.	
Sept. 15	Britain has communicated to the United States its concerns about the upcoming International Conference and that if there is not a definite agenda the Conference will fail.... Twenty-six nations have answered an appeal by the League of Nations to not increase their military and naval appropriations; seven nations refuse: South Africa, Brazil, France, Finland, Poland, Greece, and Yugoslavia.	Pope Benedict XV donates one million lira to assist the efforts to relieve starvation in the Soviet Union.... Lithuanian representatives in Washington say there is no basis in fact for the reports that Poland and Lithuania go to war over the Vilnius dispute.... German police capture Arnold Ruge who has operated a secret intelligence center in Silesia aimed at not only ensuring German control in that area but in bringing the monarchy back to Germany.... The World Zionist Conference, which has been in a two-week session in Carlsbad, Czechoslovakia, reelects Chaim Weizman as President and agrees that the headquarters will remain in London.	Greece calls up another "class" of conscripts to participate in the war with Turkey.	Officials in Saskatchewan, Canada, report a serious diphtheria epidemic in that province.... A severe hurricane hits the Caribbean, causing severe damage in Puerto Rico, Dominica, and Bermuda.	The Chinese government expresses serious reservations about Japanese proposals for the Shantung Peninsula, which would result in an expansion and not a decrease of Japanese influence in China.
Sept. 16			Before closing its session, the World Zionist Congress adopts a resolution calling for an "open door" in Palestine and also asks for a confirmation by the League of Nations over Britain's administration of the Mandate in Palestine.		
	A	B	C	D	E
	Includes developments that affect more than one world region, international organizations and important meetings of world leaders.	*Includes all domestic and regional developments in Europe, including the Soviet Union.*	*Includes all domestic and regional developments in Africa and the Middle East.*	*Includes all domestic and regional developments in Latin America, the Caribbean, and Canada.*	*Includes all domestic and regional developments in Asian and Pacific nations (and colonies).*

U.S. Politics & Social Issues	U.S. Foreign Policy & Affairs, Defense	U.S. Economy & Environment	Science, Technology & Nature	Culture, Leisure & Lifestyle	
Two African-American women were taken from a jail and whipped by a crowd of about 150 in Greenwood, SC; the case is being investigated by a judge in that state who is ordering a grand jury to look into the matter and identify who took part.... Although General Bandholz is departing Mingo County, Federal and National Guard troops are staying to keep order.... Bethlehem Steel announces that effective September 16, the wages of its workers will be reduced by eight percent.		International Harvester states that it has received no word as whether its factory in Russia has been seized by the Soviets.		Testimony in the Grand Jury session continues in the Fatty Arbuckle case; many theaters across the United States are banning movies starring Arbuckle.	Sept. 12
Mine operators in Mingo County ask the U.S. Senate to delay its hearings on the recent events there as it might affect the current murder trial.... In addition to 49 who died in the floods in San Antonio, TX, it is estimated that flooding elsewhere in the state claimed 100 to 150 lives.... Mrs. Julia Sidman is sworn in as a member of a grand jury in Hackensack, NJ; she is the first woman to ever sit on a grand jury in New Jersey.	General Billy Mitchell attacks the reported findings of the bombing exercises and the effect of air power and files a dissenting report that states that aircraft can destroy any ship.			Fatty Arbuckle is indicted for manslaughter in the death of Virginia Rappe.... In an experiment, supervisors of the Minneapolis Post Office have been playing phonograph records for the night crew and have found that it increases productivity.	Sept. 13
The United Spanish War Veterans discuss the charges in one of their reports that American history texts are filled with British propaganda; at the same annual meeting the veterans offer a resolution supporting the Ku Klux Klan and making profiteering in wartime a felony.... Franklin Roosevelt leaves his summer home in New Brunswick, Canada, to begin treatment in New York.	The Army General Staff announces it will cut down the number of units in the Army and decrease the number of men customarily assigned to units; this effort is part of the plan to decrease the Army to 150,000 men.				Sept. 14
Today is the first anniversary of the Wall Street bombing, which created serious property damage and killed 39 persons and wounded 200.... Police are patrolling the Wall Street area as a precaution; no suspects have yet been found in this case.... City officials in Louisville, KY, warn citizens that attending Ku Klux Klan meetings will result in their arrest.		The U.S. Department of Agriculture is forming a new board that will regulate the meatpacking industry.		Al Jolson opens a new show, *Bombo*, in New York.... Babe Ruth hits his 55th home run breaking his own record.	Sept. 15
El Paso, TX, bans public gatherings where the participants wear masks, a sample of the kind of regulations being put into place to discourage meetings of the Ku Klux Klan.... Dockworkers have sent their representative to meet with ship owners in New York as to whether or not accept a 22 percent proposed wage cut.	The Army General Staff, working in coordination with the state governors, is reorganizing the National Guard in accordance with a new law that makes the Guard the first reinforcement of the Army in time of war.			San Francisco District Attorney charges Fatty Arbuckle with the murder of Virginia Rappe.... National League batting leader Rogers Hornsby receives a baseball autographed by President Harding.	Sept. 16

F	G	H	I	J
Includes campaigns, elections, federal-state relations, civil rights and liberties, crime, the judiciary, education, healthcare, poverty, urban affairs, and population.	*Includes formation and debate of U.S. foreign and defense policies, veterans affairs, and defense spending. (Relations with specific foreign countries are usually found under the region concerned.)*	*Includes business, labor, agriculture, taxation, transportation, consumer affairs, monetary and fiscal policy, natural resources, pollution and industrial accidents.*	*Includes worldwide scientific, medical and technological developments, natural phenomena, U.S. weather and natural disasters.*	*Includes the arts, religion, scholarship, communications media, sports, entertainment, fashions, fads, and social life.*

	World Affairs	Europe	Africa & The Middle East	The Americas	Asia & The Pacific
Sept. 17		The Soviet Press agency announces that the required amounts of seed have been distributed to the Volga region for planting in the next year....A group of 20 American Relief workers, including doctors and transportation experts, have left London for Riga and from there they will enter the Soviet Union.	After an intense artillery preparation, Spanish troops in Morocco begin a new offensive against the rebellious tribesmen....Greek forces continue to fall back along the line of the Sakaria River; with casualties of 30,000; the political and military collapse of King Constantine is predicted.	Indians in Guatemala are reported near a state of insurrection and have been attacking missionaries....Chilean State Railways is purchasing 10 Mikado locomotives from the Baldwin Company and another 20 from the American Locomotive Company.	Japanese exports and imports for 1921 have declined over what they were at this time last year; Japan still has an unfavorable balance of trade, but the surplus in imports has also decreased in proportion to exports for this year.
Sept. 18			A Palestine Arab delegation cables President Harding to ask him to lend his weight toward an appeal to the League of Nations to grant Palestine a parliamentary government.		Spokesmen from the Southern Chinese Republic insists that they are the party that should be going to the International Conference and not the northern Chinese from Beijing.
Sept. 19		The cost of living has become so high in Paris that many American students are now choosing to go to school in Germany instead.... Hungary Finance Minister quits, aggravating what has been a difficult financial situation in the country since the end of the World War....Lloyd George announces that because of the need to remain in Britain, because of the negotiations over Ireland, he will not be able to personally attend the International Conference in Washington in November.	Spanish troops, now numbering 60,000, are engaged in a new offensive against rebels in Morocco.		The Chinese government selects an American company to build a wireless station....Revolt has broken out in several locations in India with British and Indian troops being sent to several locations to suppress rebellion and keep order.
Sept. 20		Albanian villages are being fired on by the Yugoslav army as it seeks to take areas on the border that it claims are Yugoslav territory.... Hungarians are said to be gathering in the disputed Burgenland region; 30,000-armed men are said to be there and support the restoration of King Charles in addition to setting up an independent state.		The Brazilian government has ordered 50, 5-ton trucks from General Motors Corporation in Detroit, MI.	Lord Curzon, Britain's Foreign Secretary, states that the Soviets have broken faith and are agitating in Afghanistan and India to upset the British control in the area.... Foreign Minister Sze, who will represent China at the International Conference, states that China's main objective is to preserve its national existence.
Sept. 21		Estonia is admitted to the League of Nations....The American Relief administration is said to be feeding 20,000 children in Petrograd....An explosion at a chemical factory in Oppau, Germany, kills more than 550 people with more than 1,500 injured.			
Sept. 22	Latvia and Lithuania are admitted to the League of Nations.	A rail strike in Austria stops all rail traffic in that country and in Hungary....Poland sends a demand to the Soviets stating that the Riga Peace Treaty that ended their war required a payment to Poland of 30 million gold rubles, which have not been paid; Soviet forces are mobilizing on both the Polish and Lithuanian borders....Denmark states it will not be sending anything to the effort to relieve hunger in the Soviet Union.			British and Indian troops are working toward reestablishing order; in one location the rebels have established what they claim is an Islamic republic.
	A *Includes developments that affect more than one world region, international organizations and important meetings of world leaders.*	B *Includes all domestic and regional developments in Europe, including the Soviet Union.*	C *Includes all domestic and regional developments in Africa and the Middle East.*	D *Includes all domestic and regional developments in Latin America, the Caribbean, and Canada.*	E *Includes all domestic and regional developments in Asian and Pacific nations (and colonies).*

U.S. Politics & Social Issues	U.S. Foreign Policy & Affairs, Defense	U.S. Economy & Environment	Science, Technology & Nature	Culture, Leisure & Lifestyle	
A jury in Logan country, WV, indicts 325 miners for murder and also indicts a further 200 for other charges.…The Ku Klux Klan drops its efforts to organize in Louisville, KY, after it has been banned by the city.	Defense experts recommend that the Navy buy an airship constructed by the Zeppelin Company in Germany and also emphasizes the advantages of using helium instead of hydrogen to lift the aircraft.	The National Industrial Conference Board reports that in four major industries (foundries, paper, printing, and meatpacking) a peak was reached in July 1920 and these industries have been in a decline since that date.…American doll manufacturers have lost ground to German competition; in 1918, there were 135 doll manufacturers in the United States and there are only 12 now.	Sir Ernest Shackleton's Antarctic expedition ship, *Quest*, departs from London.…In New York State 269 cases of polio have been reported (to include Franklin Roosevelt who is being treated) of which 53 have died.	Fatty Arbuckle's arraignment for the murder of Virginia Rappe is continued until September 26. He is still being held and will be until he pleads and then gets bail. Although Fatty Arbuckle has not been convicted, he is guilty of murder in the minds of many. Cowboys in the town of Thermopolis, WY, enter the Maverick Theater, grab an Arbuckle film, and burn it in the street outside.…The New York Giants are now in a secure position to capture the National League pennant, providing the team does not collapse in the final days of the season.	Sept. 17
Eastman Kodak will cut the wages of all of its workers by 20 percent due to European competition.…Army intelligence officers in New England have information that members of the Ku Klux Klan are at work in Boston and in Portland, ME.…Two U.S. Senators visit the Lick Creek Tent Colony in Mingo, WV, to hear the miners' side of what has happened in the region; tomorrow they are supposed to talk with the mine operators.…The American Legion reports that between 600,000 and 700,000 veterans are out of work.	Allied experts have estimated that the cost of the United States maintaining occupation forces on the Rhine after the World War has been $278,067,610.	Seventy steel mills in Ohio are scheduled to start production, bringing several thousand men back to work.			Sept. 18
President Harding has completed naming the members of the Committee that he wishes to study unemployment; they will begin their work on September 26.…The Chicago City Council states that the Ku Klux Klan will not be allowed in the city and will assist the police to rid the community of the Klan.					Sept. 19
U.S. Attorney General Daugherty orders an investigation into the activities of the Ku Klux Klan.	Senator Borah states that he will fight ratification of the treaty with Germany although nearly everyone understands that the treaty will be ratified when it is presented to the Senate.…A disabled American submarine, R-27, which sent out a distress call, successfully reaches Guantanamo Bay, Cuba.	The boll weevil is estimated to have caused cotton growers losses of up to $400 million.			Sept. 20
President Harding approves Daugherty's move to investigate the Ku Klux Klan; Post Offices Inspectors are also investigating the Klan's activities.…A Ku Klux Klan parade in Shawnee, OK, 300 in all, kidnap the editor of a local newspaper; he is later released without harm and given a note stating that the Klan is going to keep crime out of the region.	General Mason Patrick is assigned to become the Army's Chief of Aviation, replacing Charles Menoher; General Billy Mitchell will remain as Deputy Chief.			Stories of bands of cowboys in Thermopolis, WY, going into the Maverick Theater and burning the latest Fatty Arbuckle movies prove to have been untrue; it was apparently a publicity stunt by the owner of the theater.	Sept. 21
				It is announced that the World Series will begin on October 5 at the ballpark of the National League team.…The cost of seats will range from $1 to $6; it will be a best of nine game series.	Sept. 22

F	G	H	I	J
Includes campaigns, elections, federal-state relations, civil rights and liberties, crime, the judiciary, education, healthcare, poverty, urban affairs, and population.	*Includes formation and debate of U.S. foreign and defense policies, veterans affairs, and defense spending. (Relations with specific foreign countries are usually found under the region concerned.)*	*Includes business, labor, agriculture, taxation, transportation, consumer affairs, monetary and fiscal policy, natural resources, pollution and industrial accidents.*	*Includes worldwide scientific, medical and technological developments, natural phenomena, U.S. weather and natural disasters.*	*Includes the arts, religion, scholarship, communications media, sports, entertainment, fashions, fads, and social life.*

	World Affairs	Europe	Africa & The Middle East	The Americas	Asia & The Pacific
Sept. 23	The French government announces that it approves the agenda for the upcoming International Conference, but it will insist on safeguards for the provisions of the Versailles Treaty	Rail service will be restored in Austria as the government has agreed to some of the strikers' demands.... When the Vienna stock exchange opened it was attacked by several hundred men, nearly all veterans, and while the destruction in the building seems general, personnel and property attacks seem to focus on Jews.... The Royal Navy has completed its task of clearing the North Sea of antiship mines placed there during the World War.			
Sept. 24		Soviet commentators keep up a running stream of derogatory newspaper articles about the American volunteers to provide famine assistance; they are compared to "the Archduke visiting charcoal miners."... Albanian troops recapture several border towns that had been captured by Yugoslavia.		Financial experts are predicting that the issues that have kept the United States from recognizing the government of Mexico's President Obregon will soon be resolved; they also note that between oil and a resurgence in steel orders, that business in Mexico will be very good.	
Sept. 25		Bombs are thrown in Belfast, killing four and injuring 57.... A report in a London newspaper, presenting evidence to prove that an Interallied Commission will be needed for some time, reports that there is an effort in Germany to build up a 800,000-man army.	Expecting to win a victory in Turkey, Greece announces that it will annex the provinces of Turkey to itself.	President Obregon of Mexico issues an amnesty to all inmates who have served the majority of their sentences as part of the country's centennial celebration.... The government of Chile gives orders that all residents of Santiago are to be vaccinated against smallpox.	It is generally recognized that the upcoming International Disarmament and Far Eastern Conference will redefine the status of China in terms of that country and the other powers that have had commercial and political interests there.
Sept. 26		The French government announces that if the American occupation force in Coblenz, Germany, is withdrawn, it will send its own troops there to occupy the city.... Portugal announces that it would like to be part of the International Conference based on possession of the colony of Macao off the coast of China.... British soldiers are patrolling the streets of Belfast; no assemblies are allowed and troops in armored cars are on patrol throughout the city.... An unsuccessful attempt is made to kill Polish President Pilsudski.			The government of Siam announces that it will be building a plant to make paper, using American equipment.
Sept. 27		Steel workers in Genoa, Italy, are on strike following the announcement of a wage reduction; they have taken over the plant and will destroy offices and equipment if they are opposed.... Reports claim that there are two divisions of the Soviet Army on the border with Turkey ready to help the Turks if they should need it.... In a speech to Soviet soldiers, Leon Trotsky states that the Soviet Union stands for peace but will be willing to go to war with Poland and Romania.			The British government in India will be trying seven Indians for sedition for creating unrest among British troops.
Sept. 28		A mission from the Bulgarian government travels to Turkey to negotiate a political and commercial treaty.... Martial law is proclaimed in the Transylvanian region of Romania due to strikes and other civil disorders.... General Makno, referred to as a "Ukrainian Robin Hood," maintains a large military force and is sought by the Soviets.		The Chilean State Railway places a $7 million order with Westinghouse for railroad equipment.	

A	B	C	D	E
Includes developments that affect more than one world region, international organizations and important meetings of world leaders.	*Includes all domestic and regional developments in Europe, including the Soviet Union.*	*Includes all domestic and regional developments in Africa and the Middle East.*	*Includes all domestic and regional developments in Latin America, the Caribbean, and Canada.*	*Includes all domestic and regional developments in Asian and Pacific nations (and colonies).*

U.S. Politics & Social Issues	U.S. Foreign Policy & Affairs, Defense	U.S. Economy & Environment	Science, Technology & Nature	Culture, Leisure & Lifestyle	
Sixty-two coal mining companies and operators file a suit to prevent the United Mine Workers from organizing in Mingo County, WV, and Pike County, KY; 33 union officials and other miners are indicted for "shooting up" coal mine facilities in Fayette County several months before.…In a meeting of the Congress of Aviators it is proposed that there be a federal system for licensing pilots.					Sept. 23
J.W. McCoy is convicted for murdering Harry Staton during the fighting on the Tug River in Mingo County, WV, last May; this is the first conviction coming out of the fighting in this region.…E.Y. Clarke of Atlanta announces his resignation as Imperial Kleagle of the Knights of the Ku Klux Klan; he added that Mrs. Elizabeth Tyler, his assistant would be leaving her affiliation with the Klan as well, leading to speculation about the relationship between the two and where Klan funds may have gone.	Captain Luke McNamee, commander of the USS *Nevada* of the Atlantic Fleet, is reassigned to become Director of Naval Intelligence.…Army planes drop two 300-pound bombs on the obsolete USS *Alabama* as part of the continuing tests and exercises creating severe damage but not sinking the ship		The lack of autopsies in the United States is seen as an obstacle to making scientific progress and researchers' state that public attitudes toward postmortem examinations must change.		Sept. 24
		In what is the heaviest livestock market since the beginning of the year, hogs in the western United States are selling at the lowest price in six years.			Sept. 25
	In a continuation of the air and naval exercises that have been taking place off the eastern U.S. coast, a 2,000-pound bomb is dropped that sinks the USS *Alabama*.	Passengers arrive in Havana in the first New York to Havana flight, taking 19 hours.	Archaeologists from the University of Pennsylvania discover a habitation in Palestine dating to 2500 B.C.E.	Arc lights are set up on the football field at Penn State to allow night practice.	Sept. 26
At the trial of an African American charged with larceny, in Muscogee, OK, the defense asks two prospective jurors if the are members of the Ku Klux Klan; they admit they are and are not accepted on the jury.	The Army is planning a reserve of four million men who will be organized to reinforce the 150,000 man regular force.…The Navy submarine *R-6* sinks due to the torpedo door opening and goes to the bottom of San Pedro Harbor; two men are drowned and a third man is believed to be on the boat and may still be alive.	American exports in August totaled $209 million compared with $180 million the month before; trade with Latin America has fallen off.			Sept. 27
				Roscoe Arbuckle is allowed bail on the charge of manslaughter.	Sept. 28

F	G	H	I	J
Includes campaigns, elections, federal-state relations, civil rights and liberties, crime, the judiciary, education, healthcare, poverty, urban affairs, and population.	*Includes formation and debate of U.S. foreign and defense policies, veterans affairs, and defense spending. (Relations with specific foreign countries are usually found under the region concerned.)*	*Includes business, labor, agriculture, taxation, transportation, consumer affairs, monetary and fiscal policy, natural resources, pollution and industrial accidents.*	*Includes worldwide scientific, medical and technological developments, natural phenomena, U.S. weather and natural disasters.*	*Includes the arts, religion, scholarship, communications media, sports, entertainment, fashions, fads, and social life.*

	World Affairs	Europe	Africa & The Middle East	The Americas	Asia & The Pacific
Sept. 29				Harry Erwin Bard, Director of Education in Peru, is coming to the United States to engage 20 Americans to teach in that country.	Word from Japan is that the Japanese are adamant that none of the 21 topics that they have listed as not to be discussed will be covered at the forthcoming peace conference, foremost of these is any discussion of the status of Shantung Province.
Sept. 30	The League of Nations defeats a motion to supply a loan to the Soviet government.	German unemployment, despite descriptions of a bad economy, is lower than some analysts had predicted; currently there are 250,000 unemployed German workers.... Relief efforts for the Soviets have now reached a point of great efficiency; 5,000 tons of food have already been sent and it is expected that 1,600 tons a week will be shipped from Riga, Latvia, to the Soviets.... Burgenland, that part of western Hungary contested by Austria and Hungary, has been declared an independent republic.		The U.S. Commerce department reports that the signs of improvement in the Latin American economies appear to be showing a permanent recovery.	
Oct. 1	A resolution calling for Esperanto to be used as an international language is brought to the League of Nations.	Strikers in the port city of Trieste, Italy, threaten to seize and control the city's shipyards.... The Krupp factories in Germany are now producing a locomotive and an 8-car train a day.... The Dutch economy faces serious trouble as many factories have closed due to declining foreign trade.... Hungary is delaying ratification of the peace treaty that would end its war with the United States.... The Yugoslav government is stating that it had no choice but to suppress the Communist Party as it was receiving directions from Moscow.	Blacks outnumber whites in South Africa by a ratio of 5–1; it is expected that soon they will become a political presence in South African politics.... Greek forces have managed to repel the latest Turkish offensive.	Mexico's President Obregon promises to cut Army costs as part of the effort to cut government expenses.... The Canadian Province of Nova Scotia now counts a population of 524,579.	Seven anti-British agitators in India are arrested for supporting revolutionary movements.
Oct. 2	At the upcoming International Conference Britain and France will make a formal invitation to the United States to join the League of Nations.	King Alexander of Yugoslavia is in a car accident in Paris; although there are no details on his condition it seems certain he will not be able to travel to Belgrade for his coronation.... Thirteen workers are killed in a fertilizer factory in Udine, Italy, when a dud artillery shell being emptied for its nitrate explodes.... The Hungarian Cabinet votes to give up Hungarian claims to the western region known as Burgenland and hand it over to Austria.		Guatemala issues a statement in which it says it will formally join in the new Central American Federation.	Lord Northcliffe urges Australia to open up its immigration policies or else the island will be "overrun by Asiatics."... Muslim rebels in India are not only opposing British rule but have seized Hindus to whom they offer conversion to Islam or death.
Oct. 3		At demonstrations in Italy, there are protests against the conviction of Sacco and Vanzetti in Massachusetts for murder.... Reports from Vienna state that 40,000 Hungarian soldiers are currently deployed along the border with Austria.	Spanish forces claim a victory against the rebels in Morocco, stating they have killed at least 1,000 after a 15-hour battle.	Bolivian oil fields comprising 5.32 million acres in Santa Cruz are sold to an American company.	
Oct. 4	Three more nations are invited to the International Conference to discuss Asian issues: Belgium, Holland, and Portugal, but they will not discuss disarmament.				

A	B	C	D	E
Includes developments that affect more than one world region, international organizations and important meetings of world leaders.	*Includes all domestic and regional developments in Europe, including the Soviet Union.*	*Includes all domestic and regional developments in Africa and the Middle East.*	*Includes all domestic and regional developments in Latin America, the Caribbean, and Canada.*	*Includes all domestic and regional developments in Asian and Pacific nations (and colonies).*

U.S. Politics & Social Issues	U.S. Foreign Policy & Affairs, Defense	U.S. Economy & Environment	Science, Technology & Nature	Culture, Leisure & Lifestyle	
The government announces that it will move the original Declaration of Independence and the Constitution from the State Department to the Library of Congress, where they may be seen by the general public.			Earth tremors are felt in the Los Angeles area and as far east as Salt Lake City.	With a victory of the St. Louis Cardinals over the Pittsburgh Pirates and four games to go in the season, the Giants win the pennant.…The Spring Color Card for 1922, issued by the Textile Color Card Association shows the colors that will be considered fashionable next spring; these include browns with names such as "taffy," "Maple sugar," and "fudge," and periwinkle and cornflower blue, bright reds, and different shades of green.	Sept. 29
	The Army Air Corps experiments with a 4,300-pound bomb that is dropped at Aberdeen Proving Grounds, leaving a crater 100 feet in diameter.	The Federal Reserve reports that September has been a month of "distinct encouragement," as the economy in several areas shows signs of distinct improvement.		Sir Harry Lauder, dance hall singer and comedian, knighted for his services to the British troops during the World War, begins a 22-week tour of the United States.	Sept. 30
In Lorena, TX, there is a fight between the Ku Klux Klan marching in a parade and sheriff's deputies; nine are injured.…Because the quota on allowing Greek immigrants to enter the United States was exceeded in July, August, and September, 378 immigrants, who have just arrived, are being deported.…Senator Nelson of Minnesota blames the current economic depression on unions and labor leaders; he states that their refusal to take cuts in wages tends to keep the business world constantly disturbed.		Secretary of Labor Davis reports that there are currently 69 strikes going on in the country right now, the greatest number at any one time since the World War.		Justin Morgan, the first of the line of Morgan horses, is honored by the dedication of a bronze monument in Middlebury, VT.…Mrs. Christian Frederick, in a speech to the Affiliated Advertising Clubs of America, states that the day of the "pretty girl ads" is over and pictures of beautiful women do not sell products any more.…Harry Heilmann of the Detroit Tigers leads the American League in batting (.395) while Rogers Hornsby leads the National League with a .401 average.	Oct. 1
Miners in West Virginia have sent an appeal to President Harding asking protection for the miners being held in state prisons where they are being harassed.	General Pershing, who will soon escort the body of the American Unknown Soldier to the United States, pays homage at the grave of the Unknown Poilu (French soldier) in Paris and leaves the Congressional Medal of Honor on the tomb.			Babe Ruth ends the season with 59 home runs.	Oct. 2
The Michigan Supreme Court rules that if a woman sells bootleg liquor at home without the husband's knowledge, he is still legally liable.					Oct. 3
Congressmen report that their constituents seem to be very critical of their performance and are displeased by their delays in passing legislation on taxation, tariffs, and railroad relief.…A society in Tennessee is undertaking a subscription to pay the mortgage on the farm of Alvin York who had won the Congressional Medal of Honor for his actions in the World War.	President Harding names the American ambassadors to Czechoslovakia, Siam, Finland, Bulgaria, Panama, and Nicaragua.	Copper sales in the United States for September are reported at 100 million pounds showing an increase in domestic demand; copper manufacturers state that they will probably increase their output.			Oct. 4

F	G	H	I	J
Includes campaigns, elections, federal-state relations, civil rights and liberties, crime, the judiciary, education, healthcare, poverty, urban affairs, and population.	*Includes formation and debate of U.S. foreign and defense policies, veterans affairs, and defense spending. (Relations with specific foreign countries are usually found under the region concerned.)*	*Includes business, labor, agriculture, taxation, transportation, consumer affairs, monetary and fiscal policy, natural resources, pollution and industrial accidents.*	*Includes worldwide scientific, medical and technological developments, natural phenomena, U.S. weather and natural disasters.*	*Includes the arts, religion, scholarship, communications media, sports, entertainment, fashions, fads, and social life.*

	World Affairs	Europe	Africa & The Middle East	The Americas	Asia & The Pacific
Oct. 5	The Second League of Nations Assembly Session, which has been in session since September 5, concludes.	Former American diplomat, Charles Sherill, says that he believes that hostilities in the Balkans are very possible, citing mobilization of troops in Romania on its Russian and Hungarian frontiers and Yugoslavia's recent mobilization and deployment of troops on its Albanian frontier.		The Cuban government endows a school for children in the French city of Verdun, scene of some of the war's fiercest fighting; the donation is accepted by Finance Minister, Andre Maginot.	Mohandas Gandhi and 47 other Indian leaders ask Indian soldiers in British service to quit.
Oct. 6		Armed bands of Hungarians are still occupying Burgenland; the Hungarian government denies all responsibility for their presence and says it cannot control them.... Irish delegates leave for more talks in Britain; Eamon de Valera insists that Ireland as a united nation is a "natural unit"	The port city of Haifa, Palestine, will be made into a free port as a result of an agreement between France and England; goods passing onto Syria from the port will be sent duty-free.	New York bankers are offering a $50 million loan to the government of Argentina.	Japan reports that its imports have exceeded its exports.... Japan's emperor Yoshito, who has been ill, is reported to be worsening.... A group of Moros, opposed to the American government in the Philippines, attacks Carl Moore, Governor of the island of Suklu; the Philippine Constabulary saves the governor, killing off the attackers.
Oct. 7	The U.S. government invites participation by members of the British Dominion, but explains that it did not invite them specifically because it was Britain's decision as to who would attend.	The Italian government offers to mediate the conflict between Austria and Hungary in the Burgenland dispute.... Soviet officials announce that they are looking to decentralize the government, reduce bureaucracy, and establish more regional autonomy.			The Chinese government does not accept any proposals offered by Japan for the resolution of control over Shantung Province in China, commenting that the proposals "inadequately prove" Japan's sincerity.
Oct. 8		John McNab has been awarded a 4,000-pound settlement for his "execution" by the Irish Republican Army; he was shot three times as retaliation for being a spy but did not die and managed to get aid.... Food prices in Britain increase because of recent droughts.... British imports have been declining this year as Britain's overall foreign trade increases.		More than 3.5 million fur pelts were produced in Canada this year for a total value of $21,387,000.... To solve the employment problem for its veterans, Canada has spent more than $84 billion in putting 26,000 men on the land as farmers.	
Oct. 9		Premier Briand of France declares that France can never disarm unless it is protected; in general, the French, while they favor naval disarmament are strongly opposed to any reductions in land forces.		The Federation of Honduras, Guatemala, and Salvador, a union modeled on the United States, officially comes into existence with Costa Rica and Nicaragua expected to join in the near future.	The Working Committee of the Indian Natonal Congress calls for a general strike throughout India on the day that the Prince of Wales will arrive in Bombay; a large rebel band in southern India is moving toward the city of Malabar.
Oct. 10		The arbitration of the disposition of the Aaland Islands Conference to determine whether Finland or Sweden gets the islands begins.... Before the upcoming negotiations with the British begin, Eamon de Valera addresses the Irish people saying they must be unified to ensure that they get their rights.			Mohandas Gandhi urges a boycott of non-Indian goods and to demonstrate the point burns clothing that was made in Britain.
Oct. 11		Albania states that it refuses to accept the League of Nations decision concerning the Albanian-Yugoslav border and will not accept a change from the 1913 borders.... Delegates from Hungary and Austria meet in Venice to discuss Burgenland.... King Alexander of Yugoslavia announces that he will not become king, as he prefers to enjoy life in Paris, although an attempted assassination plot against him is said to have affected his decision.... Poland agrees to expel the Russian White Guard, whose presence in Poland has been a point of disagreement between Poland and the Soviets.	Greek General Papoulas claims that at the end of a nine-day battle he has pushed the Turks back in a disorderly retreat.		Soldiers of the Southern Republic of China under President Sun Yat-sen begin their march on the Beijing government, initiating a civil war in China.... Reports from Japan describe secret negotiations between Japan and the Soviets to establish trading relations.... British courts have thus far sentenced more than 2,000 rebellious Indians to prison.

A	B	C	D	E
Includes developments that affect more than one world region, international organizations and important meetings of world leaders.	*Includes all domestic and regional developments in Europe, including the Soviet Union.*	*Includes all domestic and regional developments in Africa and the Middle East.*	*Includes all domestic and regional developments in Latin America, the Caribbean, and Canada.*	*Includes all domestic and regional developments in Asian and Pacific nations (and colonies).*

U.S. Politics & Social Issues	U.S. Foreign Policy & Affairs, Defense	U.S. Economy & Environment	Science, Technology & Nature	Culture, Leisure & Lifestyle	
Chief Justice of the Supreme Court, William Howard Taft, tells senators that there should be more federal judges especially as Prohibition has seriously increased the workload.		The Amoskeag Manufacturing Company, which operates cloth mills in New England, reports that its profits for the year ending May 28 were $1,272,647 as opposed to $4,368,918 for the previous year.	Ernest Shackleton continues on his expedition to the Antarctic, putting into Lisbon, Portugal, for repairs to his ship after a severe storm.	The first game of the World Series between the New York Giants and the New York Yankees takes place today; all games will take place at the Polo Grounds in New York. The Yankees win over the Giants, 3–0.…Frank Dominguez, lawyer for Roscoe Arbuckle in the manslaughter case, quits, stating he cannot devote time to the case being tried in San Francisco, but predicts that the film star will be acquitted.	Oct. 5
The U.S. Attorney General states that he will defer his investigation into the Ku Klux Klan until Congress has taken action; if it does, he will then see if Federal laws have been violated.	The U.S. Navy, in an effort to save money may drop the annual winter maneuvers of the Atlantic and Pacific Fleets; the Navy is also contemplating appealing to Congress to increase the appropriation for fuel oil.	As a sign that the auto industry is recovering, display space at the 1922 Motor Show to take place in New York is oversubscribed.		The second game of the World Series is won by the Yankees over the Giants at 3–0.	Oct. 6
Congressman Upshaw of Michigan calls for a Congressional investigation into all secret societies and not just the Ku Klux Klan.	An investigating committee looking into the ZR-2 airship disaster finds that the design was faulty and was never checked by any kind of competent committee before construction began.		Professor Pickering of Harvard, based on observations made from August 1920 to February 1921, claims there is life on the moon.	The Giants win the third game of the World Series, 13–5; in this game, as in all of the games thus far, reporters comment on the unusually polite crowds.	Oct. 7
President Harding meets with mine union leaders, Secretary of Labor Davis, and Commerce Secretary Hoover to prevent a possible bituminous coal strike in February 1922; the meeting does not produce any agreements.			French aviation engineer Henry Farman predicts that both commercial and military flying will expand greatly with significant technical advances coming in a very short time.	Enrollment at Harvard University is 5,936 students, breaking all previous records.	Oct. 8
				Lloyd Reese, a wing walker, falls to his death at Regina, Saskatchewan, when attempting to pass from one airplane to another using a rope ladder.…The Giants beat the Yankees 4–2.	Oct. 9
A Committee in the U.S. House of Representatives opens an investigation into the activities of the Ku Klux Klan, reviewing evidence presented by U.S. Attorney General Daugherty.	The National Guard in the United States now numbers 126,000 men; the War Department expects that the total number will reach 450,000 by 1924.	Towns in eastern Maine and in the province of New Brunswick are shaken by a slight earthquake.		The New York Yankees win over the New York Giants 3–1; Babe Ruth is injured and probably out of the Series.	Oct. 10
The city off Highland Park, MI, bans all women from civil service positions and all municipal employees will be men.…Wylie McNeely, an African American charged with assaulting an eight-year old girl, is seized by a mob and brought to Leesburg, TX, where he is burned at the stake.			Arctic explorer Roald Amundsen announces he is planning an arctic expedition next year that will use airplanes to reach the North Pole.	The Giants win over the Yankees 8–5, tying the World Series.	Oct. 11

F	G	H	I	J
Includes campaigns, elections, federal-state relations, civil rights and liberties, crime, the judiciary, education, healthcare, poverty, urban affairs, and population.	*Includes formation and debate of U.S. foreign and defense policies, veterans affairs, and defense spending. (Relations with specific foreign countries are usually found under the region concerned.)*	*Includes business, labor, agriculture, taxation, transportation, consumer affairs, monetary and fiscal policy, natural resources, pollution and industrial accidents.*	*Includes worldwide scientific, medical and technological developments, natural phenomena, U.S. weather and natural disasters.*	*Includes the arts, religion, scholarship, communications media, sports, entertainment, fashions, fads, and social life.*

	World Affairs	Europe	Africa & The Middle East	The Americas	Asia & The Pacific
Oct. 12		The League of Nations settles the Upper Silesia dispute, dividing the territory between Germany and Poland.... Hungary and Austria reach an agreement over Burgenland; Hungary will evacuate the disputed area while Austria agrees to a plebiscite in some of the districts in that area.	The French government announces that it plans to establish an auto connection across the Sahara Desert and is experimenting with specially designed autos to begin tests and open routes.		
Oct. 13		At a meeting of the Italian Socialist Congress, a guest speaker from Moscow attacks the Italian party's leadership and succeeds in alienating all Italian Communists from Moscow.... Britain's Chancellor of the Exchequer admits failure in the attempts to develop trade with the Soviets, as there is nothing that they can sell.... The Spanish government announces a six-year program to build an additional 58 ships and gunboats.	France establishes the separate colony of Niger in Africa.... Turkey signs the Treaty of Kars, which recognizes the independence of the Armenian Republic.		
Oct. 14		In Germany dogs are now being slaughtered for food; in the past three months 3,642 carcasses were inspected before sale and the number of horses being used for food is double that before the war.... Germany's dissatisfaction with the Silesian settlement is based on the loss of 86 percent of the anthracite coal deposits and 63 percent of the industries.... Discussions between members of Sinn Fein and British officials are proceeding well.... The Italian government says that it supports the largest arms cuts possible consistent with national security.	Spain claims to have just captured a Moorish stronghold.	Canadian National Railways reports a surplus of earnings over operating expenses with net earnings of $47,231.... A riot of hundreds of unemployed in Santiago, Chile, results in several injuries.	There is a general expectation that because Japan's control of the Shantung Province was brought about by the Versailles Treaty that the Allies will back Japan in this matter against China.
Oct. 15		The Bulgarian government is seen weighing the advantages of invading Greece to occupy territory claimed by Bulgaria while the Greek Army is distracted with its Turkish war.			Chinese Christians support of the Cantonese government under Sun Yat-sen launching its offensive against the Beijing government.
Oct. 16		An agreement has been completed between Soviet authorities and the American relief effort for distribution and payments for food.... Indications in Germany are that the Wirth Cabinet will resign if the League of Nations announces the partition of Upper Silesia.			
Oct. 17		Reports from the Soviet Union state that former General Kuropatkin was poisoned by the Soviets after he refused to accept an assignment to head Communist propaganda in Turkey.... Spanish police kill two peasants and wound several others resisting a tax levy.		In September, Mexico shipped 17,637,179 barrels of oil, almost all of it to Standard Oil of New Jersey.	The Japanese government asks the Chinese government to reconsider its rejection of Japanese proposals for the administration of Shantung Province.

A	B	C	D	E
Includes developments that affect more than one world region, international organizations and important meetings of world leaders.	*Includes all domestic and regional developments in Europe, including the Soviet Union.*	*Includes all domestic and regional developments in Africa and the Middle East.*	*Includes all domestic and regional developments in Latin America, the Caribbean, and Canada.*	*Includes all domestic and regional developments in Asian and Pacific nations (and colonies).*

U.S. Politics & Social Issues	U.S. Foreign Policy & Affairs, Defense	U.S. Economy & Environment	Science, Technology & Nature	Culture, Leisure & Lifestyle	
The City of Detroit bans a planned Ku Klux Klan demonstration in the city planned for Thanksgiving.... Textile workers in the United States plan to create a single union, which will have all 150,000-textile workers in one organization....W.J. Simmons, Imperial Wizard of the Ku Klux Klan, testifies before Congress that the Klan has committed no crimes and that if $^1/_{1000}$ of the charges were true, he would abolish the organization.			Speaking before a medical conference in Chicago, Dr. E. Stillman Bailey claims that exposure to radium prolongs life and cites the experience of miners working in radium mines as proof.	The Giants win the seventh game of the World Series, 2–1, and only need to win one more to win the Series.	Oct. 12
		Standard Oil of New Jersey announces a program that will give work to the unemployed by constructing improvements at three refineries at a cost of $2 million.		Roscoe "Fatty" Arbuckle pleads not guilty to a charge of manslaughter; the trial date is set for November 7....The Giants win the eighth game beating the Yankees 1–0 and the World Series.	Oct. 13
A Federal judge rules that any Mormons who have plural wives who are still living are liable to provide support for them.		The price of crude oil in the United States is up 25 cents a barrel and the price of gas goes up by one cent a gallon....The Rock Island Line has ordered 14 locomotives from the American Locomotive Company.			Oct. 14
The American Red Cross reports that it helped 500,000 Americans in the past year including many jobless veterans and their families as well as immunizing 20,000 children against diphtheria....Governor E. Mont Reily, U.S. Governor of Puerto Rico, attacks the Puerto Rican Independence Movement causing a storm of protest.		The proposed rail strike, which may take place on October 30, may affect 97,238 miles of track on the first day. On the first day of the strike, it is estimated that 750,000 workers will walk out with 1.2 million to follow. Railroad operators assert that the strike will not halt rail service and that many of the workers will stay on the job....Six passengers fly from Mineola, NY, to Providence, RI at a cost of $53.40 for all of them; train tickets for the group would have cost $105.50.	French aviation engineer Henry Juliot writes that the rigid airship is a failure and does not have a bright future and that nonrigid airships are the best possible solution.	The tax paid to the United States for the World Series is $90,023. ...Increased attendance at colleges throughout the United States is seen as a sign of the general prosperity in the country....The most powerful radio station in the world opens at Port Jefferson, Long Island; it is owned and operated by the Radio Corporation of America.	Oct. 15
Court officials in St. Louis state that they believe that increased women's independence has been responsible for the increase in divorces; this year nearly 700 divorce cases were assigned this year in St. Louis alone....Doctors report that the eyesight of Senator Thomas P. Gore of Oklahoma may be improving; he has been blind since childhood.	American Veterans have begun a project to rebuild the French town of Belleau Wood, which was destroyed in the World War and was the scene of fighting by American troops; Marshal Foch of France has agreed to be honorary chairman....The U.S. Navy announces it will begin experiments on using a catapult to launch planes from ships.			Irish tenor John McCormack gives a concert at the Hippodrome in New York in front of an audience of 16,000; 10,000 are turned away from the gate.	Oct. 16
The Congressional inquiry into the Ku Klux Klan ends when the committee terminates the hearing and will not continue unless the Justice Department provides further evidence.	Britain's Victoria Cross has been awarded to the American Unknown Soldier.			Harry ("Bud") Fisher brings a case to the Supreme Court to determine if he has complete copyright protection for his characters "Mutt" and "Jeff" in light of recent infringement by the Hearst papers....The painting *The Blue Boy* by Gainsborough is sold to an American collector and will be transported to the United States from Britain.	Oct. 17

F	G	H	I	J
Includes campaigns, elections, federal-state relations, civil rights and liberties, crime, the judiciary, education, healthcare, poverty, urban affairs, and population.	*Includes formation and debate of U.S. foreign and defense policies, veterans affairs, and defense spending. (Relations with specific foreign countries are usually found under the region concerned.)*	*Includes business, labor, agriculture, taxation, transportation, consumer affairs, monetary and fiscal policy, natural resources, pollution and industrial accidents.*	*Includes worldwide scientific, medical and technological developments, natural phenomena, U.S. weather and natural disasters.*	*Includes the arts, religion, scholarship, communications media, sports, entertainment, fashions, fads, and social life.*

	World Affairs	Europe	Africa & The Middle East	The Americas	Asia & The Pacific
Oct. 18	Five international airlines have been organized that are flying into and out of France.	Among the issues discussed between Sinn Fein Representatives and the British government is whether the Royal Air Force will be able to maintain air bases in Ireland.... Former King Ludwig III of Bavaria, who abdicated in 1918, dies in Hungary.... A member of the American Red Cross estimates that as many as 20 million may have died in Russia since 1914 due to famine and executions.... A volunteer armed force of 100,000 Protestants is said to be raised in Ulster.			Swiss officers are providing training in artillery to the Japanese army.
Oct. 19	Japan indicates that it accepts the agenda of topics for the International Disarmament and Far Eastern Conference.	A military revolt against the Portuguese government is reported to have taken place in Lisbon.			A former Secretary to the Premier of Japan, in speaking to a gathering in Hawaii, predicts that there will eventually be a cultural war between Asia and the west but that Japan and the United States can settle all of their differences amicably.
Oct. 20		The Conference to determine whether Finland or Sweden gets the Aaland Islands ends; the islands are designated as neutral and not belonging to either nation.... The German and Polish governments receive official notification of the League of Nations plan to split Silesia between the two countries; Poland has accepted the terms and it is believed that Germany will do the same.	France agrees to cede the territory of Cilicia near Turkey and will receive economic concessions from Turkey; Turkey further agrees to recognize the French mandate in Syria, which was formerly part of the Ottoman Empire.		
Oct. 21		A bomb thrown at a Communist meeting in Paris injured 20.... Rumors are circulating in Vienna that Prince Alexander was actually wounded in the attempt to kill him with a bomb and that is why he has not left Paris and why he has been claiming to be ill.... Lloyd George announces he will leave Britain for Washington on November 5 and will stay five weeks in America.	Spain relieves the current military commander in Morocco of his command after several reverses in the fight against Moorish rebels.		
Oct. 22		Soviet authorities announce they may free 150,000 political prisoners as part of the celebration of the fourth anniversary of the revolution.... Portuguese troops loyal to the just ousted government are now marching toward Lisbon.... Germany's government, under Chancellor Wirth, has resigned and a new cabinet is expected to be formed by October 27.... Czechoslovakian and Yugoslavian armies mobilize on their borders with Hungary.		The Peruvian House of Deputies approves a bill allowing the government to apply to New York bankers for a $50 million loan.... Costa Rica announces that it plans to build a city on the land recently claimed from Panama.	
Oct. 23		Former King Charles has moved from western Hungary toward Budapest; troops under the command of the current Regent, Admiral Horthy, have either deserted or retreated.... The Allies declare that they will not let Charles rule; the British state that they will take all preventive measures short of sending troops.... Michael Collins consults with Eamon de Valera as Sinn Fein representatives again meet with the British to discuss the disposition of Ulster as well as the definition of terms of "loyalty" to the Crown.... In Portugal, the army is disarming civilians as part of the marital law that has been declared in the past week.		The Cuban government under President Zayas will be deciding the latest measures to decrease government spending.... Former Guatemalan President Manuel Estrada Cabrera is in prison, awaiting execution for his murder of Jose Coronado Aguillar, who was among those killed when Cabrera ordered troops to fire artillery rounds into Guatemala City in April 1920; Cabrera is said to be very depressed.... The government of Nicaragua proclaims a state of war on its border with Honduras and extends the period of martial law.... The first ice has appeared on the Yukon River and navigation is closed for the season.	Governor Leonard Wood of the Philippines states that reports of instability in the islands are untrue and were intended by some parties to discourage American investments.
	A *Includes developments that affect more than one world region, international organizations and important meetings of world leaders.*	B *Includes all domestic and regional developments in Europe, including the Soviet Union.*	C *Includes all domestic and regional developments in Africa and the Middle East.*	D *Includes all domestic and regional developments in Latin America, the Caribbean, and Canada.*	E *Includes all domestic and regional developments in Asian and Pacific nations (and colonies).*

	U.S. Politics & Social Issues	U.S. Foreign Policy & Affairs, Defense	U.S. Economy & Environment	Science, Technology & Nature	Culture, Leisure & Lifestyle
Oct. 18	President Harding declines the offer for the United States to attend the International Monetary Conference to be held in London in December.	The U.S. Senate ratifies the treaties with Germany, Austria, and Hungary ending the state of war between the United States and each of these nations.			Former White Sox third baseman Buck Weaver, one of the alleged "Black Sox" players is suing the Chicago baseball club for $20,000 in salary.
Oct. 19	Mine owners and operators in Indiana are proposing that the 1922 wage scale contain pay cuts for the miners.... Three mine union leaders have been arrested in West Virginia for violating the martial law proclamation by going into mining camps in Mingo County.				
Oct. 20				Astronomers at Greenwich Observatory report that the moon is 12 miles off from its supposed path, a tendency that has been going on for the past 30 years.	A statue of Edgar Allan Poe is unveiled in Baltimore, MD.
Oct. 21					
Oct. 22	While it seems certain that telegraphers will walk out on October 30, at least eight rail unions refuse to go on strike with 600,000 railway shopmen leading the break from the rest of the union. Because the strike does not seem inevitable, railroad companies have ordered cuts in the freight rates for their customers.	Secretary of War Weeks announces that 8,000 American soldiers will return home from occupation duty in Germany, but the remaining 5,600 will stay indefinitely.	The Commerce Department reports that that exports to Germany increased by $97.52 million over the previous year.... The Federal Reserve Board reports that the volume of business in the United States compared to the previous week showed an increase of about 34 percent (in large part because the previous week was only four days long because of Columbus Day).	Frederick Jamke dies at the age of 73; he had been a survivor of the unsuccessful Hall Arctic Expedition, he was one of those left on an ice floe and was rescued after six months.	The following books have just been published: *And Even Now* by Max Beerbohm; *History: Its Theory and Practice* by Benedetto Croce; *The Girls* by Edna Ferber; and *A Treatise on Probability* by John Maynard Keynes.... Sarah Bernhardt has returned to the Parisian stage in a new play written especially for her.... In explaining to reporters the purpose of his test to college students, Thomas Edison states that he believes that memory is better than research.
Oct. 23	It appears that of a potential strike of two million railroad workers, only 400,000 are committed to walking out.	Four coffins containing the remains of unknown American soldiers have been assembled at Chalons-sur-Marne in France, where one of them will be selected by Sergeant Edward S. Younger; the coffin that Sergeant Younger selects will be brought to Arlington National Cemetery and will be buried as the Unknown Soldier.	New England receives its first airmail letters when an airplane lands at Framingham, MA; the pouch contained letters from President Harding, Vice-President Coolidge, and Senator Lodge.	The death rate in the United States is reported as being higher in 1920 than in 1919, which was the lowest year on record since the survey began in 1900.	Scottish comedian and vaudeville star, Sir Harry Lauder, in performing a benefit in New York City, says that disarmament must be successful and refers to his son who was killed in the war; he then leads the audience in a song and comedy routine.

	World Affairs	Europe	Africa & The Middle East	The Americas	Asia & The Pacific
Oct. 24	The third session of the International Labor Conference in Geneva under the auspices of the League of Nations begins.	Italy's King Victor Emmanuelle proclaims an amnesty in honor of his 25th wedding anniversary.... Former King Charles and his wife, Zita, are taken prisoner and will be deported....A battle in which 200 are killed and 1,000 are wounded ends with a defeat of Charles by Admiral Horthy; Austria did not interfere and the general assumption was that if additional military force were needed against Charles it would be provided by the Little Entente. The Little Entente demands that Charles be deposed.		Major General George Barnett, Commandant of the Marine Corps, states that the administration by the Marines has given Haiti its "best government in 100 years."	The American Consortium Group proposes a $20 million credit to the Chinese government....Japan's Naval program is said to be based on the assumption that Japan should be able to defeat any naval incursion into the far east.
Oct. 25	British officials state that they wish the United States were participating in the World Labor Conference.	Poland signs a political and economic treaty with the Free City of Danzig....Switzerland states that it will not allow King Charles or his family back into the country....The Prince of Wales departs Britain on HMS *Renown* to begin his tour of India; he will also visit the Philippines.	British authorities are in the process of drafting a treaty that would end the status of Egypt as a protectorate by the end of the year....After destroying military supplies at the garrison of Arrut in Spanish Morocco, Spanish troops leave the area.		The Chinese government announces that it will propose a plan to the International Conference concerning Japanese control of Shantung Province.
Oct. 26		Germany accepts the partition of Upper Silesia by the League of Nations....An earthquake hits the Tuscany region of Italy with severe damage although there are no reports of casualties.... Premier Gounaris of Greece, on a trip to France to get support for King Constantine and the war with Turkey, is unsuccessful on both counts....The Little Entente demands that Hungary surrender King Charles to them as well as paying financial damages.	The British government designates Alexandria, Egypt, to be a base for the Royal Navy.	The American Consul in Vera Cruz, Mexico, is attacked and seriously wounded....Testifying before a special Senate Committee on the situation in Haiti, Major T.C. Turner states that in the past six years, 2,500 Haitians were killed in fighting, and of these 1,732 were killed between October 1, 1919 and October 1, 1920.	Japan announces it will leave Siberia very soon and will leave its military supplies and artillery there for the use of the Vladivostok government.
Oct. 27		Count Bethlen, Premier of Hungary, states that Charles must abdicate; he and his wife will be kept on a gunboat on the Danube River for the time being.			Japan announces that it is prepared to cut its navy if it is agreeable with the other powers as settled at the upcoming International Conference, but otherwise Japan could easily add to its current fleet.
Oct. 28		The Hungarian government states that although it has not received an ultimatum it expects an invasion by Czechoslovakia, Yugoslavia, and Romania....The French government announces that once current uniform stock runs out, French soldiers will wear khaki and not the horizon blue worn in the World War.	Liberia signs a treaty with the United States, which will provide needed financial assistance for that country.		A transit company, which is planning a new transportation system in Beijing, proposes that the old walls of the city be torn down; the proposal receives strong opposition.
Oct. 29		The Soviets are making additional efforts to obtain recognition from foreign governments and has even made offers to assume the Imperial Russian debts incurred before 1914....Effective January 1, 1922, workers's council will go into effect in every Czechoslovak company that employs 30 or more workers, which will in effect be unions; boards of arbitration will also be set up....Flooding in Naples has caused severe damage after a 12-hour storm and several people are reported drowned.		Rains in western Guatemala have caused floods in which 18 people have died; there has been a great deal of property damage and large parts of the country are still underwater.	Analysts point to the failures of Japan's emigration projects (such as Japanese settlements in the United States) as the basis for its new drive to gaining colonies....China states that it wants an end to "war-made" treaties, a reference to Japan's control of Shantung, which was a result of taking over German concessions after the World War.

A	B	C	D	E
Includes developments that affect more than one world region, international organizations and important meetings of world leaders.	*Includes all domestic and regional developments in Europe, including the Soviet Union.*	*Includes all domestic and regional developments in Africa and the Middle East.*	*Includes all domestic and regional developments in Latin America, the Caribbean, and Canada.*	*Includes all domestic and regional developments in Asian and Pacific nations (and colonies).*

U.S. Politics & Social Issues	U.S. Foreign Policy & Affairs, Defense	U.S. Economy & Environment	Science, Technology & Nature	Culture, Leisure & Lifestyle	
Hearings begin in the U.S. Senate on the events that occurred in the past year in Mingo County, WV.... Ed Kirkland, an African American charged with having killed a man is taken by a mob in Allendale, SC, from the sheriff's custody and shot, then hanged, then burned.	Insurance on the London market gives the chances of war between the United States and Japan in 1922 as 19–1, against.... The body of the Unknown Soldier is being transported to Le Havre where the ship USS *Olympia* is waiting to take it to the United States.		An American archaeological expedition in Palestine finds artifacts dated at 12500 B.C.E.	Charlie Chaplin puts on a show to entertain prisoners at Sing Sing prison.	Oct. 24
U.S. Attorney General Daugherty is making preparation to ensure food supplies and order in the event of a railroad strike; Daugherty says that President Harding has the situation under control and will announce a program of steps to be taken in the event of a nationwide train workers strike.... Mine workers complete their testimony before the Senate Committee investigating the events in the Williamson Coal Field over the past year.	Herbert Hoover is asking the Army to provide surplus supplies, stating that it will save money on the storage of these items and will greatly assist the relief efforts in the Soviet Union.	The Wert Coast of Florida is hit a by a hurricane with extensive damage reported in Tampa.		William Barclay "Bat" Masterson, Deputy Sheriff and Marshall in various western towns and sportswriter for the *New York Morning Telegraph*, dies of a heart attack at the age of 67 while typing his column.	Oct. 25
In a speech in Birmingham, AL, President Harding states that African Americans must have political equality although he does not mean functioning equally on the same social plane. The President's speech is attacked by Senator Watson of Georgia, who states that it is a pity that he should "plant fatal germs in the minds of the black race."... Philadelphia Police receive training in the use of tear gas to control mobs.... Federal agents claim that there is a widespread terrorist plot by radicals to set off bombs in many U.S. cities.	American soldiers being reassigned from Occupation duty on the Rhine River express dismay at having to leave a place where beer can be purchased at two cents a glass.	The death toll stands at five with millions of dollars of damage estimated in the wake of the Florida hurricane.... The Hupp Motor Car Company, manufacturer of the Huppmobile, announces that it will decrease the prices of its cars from $100 to $235 each; this is the second price cut announced by Hupp within the past month.		The cost of tickets to the Army-Navy football game has risen to $6, raising protests on the part of fans; the army and navy each blame the other for the increased price.	Oct. 26
Mine owners in Mingo County, WV, tell a Congressional Committee that they will not deal with the United Mine Workers under any circumstances.... Masked men parading in Enid, OK, warn all African Americans to leave town.... Vigilante committees are being formed in Long Island, NY, to halt a rash of robberies.		The railroad worker unions call off the threatened strike that would have occurred on October 30; the terms of the agreement were not made public.... The reports submitted to the Interstate Commerce Commission indicate that railroad profits were up over August and September 1920.			Oct. 27
A Senate hearing receives testimony that Governor Morgan of West Virginia could have prevented the calling of Federal troops; in addition to living up to his earlier campaign pledges Morgan could also have defused the situation in Mingo County by better handling of the state constabulary.				Henry Ford states that "history is bunk," and that students need only to learn to read, write, and then work out their own ideas.	Oct. 28
	Secretary of State Hughes and Secretary of the Navy Denby are meeting to formulate the American position on naval disarmament that will be taken up as the centerpiece of the International Conference next month.	Coca-Cola announces that its profits for the nine months ending on October 1 exceed the profits for entire year of 1920.			Oct. 29
F *Includes campaigns, elections, federal-state relations, civil rights and liberties, crime, the judiciary, education, healthcare, poverty, urban affairs, and population.*	**G** *Includes formation and debate of U.S. foreign and defense policies, veterans affairs, and defense spending. (Relations with specific foreign countries are usually found under the region concerned.)*	**H** *Includes business, labor, agriculture, taxation, transportation, consumer affairs, monetary and fiscal policy, natural resources, pollution and industrial accidents.*	**I** *Includes worldwide scientific, medical and technological developments, natural phenomena, U.S. weather and natural disasters.*	**J** *Includes the arts, religion, scholarship, communications media, sports, entertainment, fashions, fads, and social life.*	

	World Affairs	Europe	Africa & The Middle East	The Americas	Asia & The Pacific
Oct. 30		The Czechoslovakian army is said to be ready to invade Hungary; demonstrations and strikes have been called protesting the mobilization....The armies of the rest of the Little Entente (Yugoslavia and Romania) are also said to be prepared for war with Hungary....Sinn Fein members resume their discussions with British authorities; whether Ulster will be part of an Irish Free State is now the main point of contention.	France finalizes an agreement with the Turkish government.	A flood in British Columbia completely wipes out a mining settlement killing at least 23 with 13 reported missing....American General Enoch Crowder, American representative in Cuba, is confronted by crowds in Havana demanding justice for Sacco and Vanzetti.	
Oct. 31		Although he is at sea on his way to the International Conference, French Premier Briand is said to be effectively running the country though the use of the ship's radio.			A Chinese commentator states that Japan's overcrowding is a myth and rather than settling its people it is looking to take the wealth of the western powers.
Nov. 1	Delegates are arriving for the International Conference; thus far, members of the British, Italian, Japanese, and Chinese delegations have arrived....All foreign delegations attending the International Conference will be respecting America's Prohibition laws and will not be serving alcoholic beverages at any of their functions.... Leaders of the Third Communist International express their opinions that the International Conference held in Washington will fail; further, they see an attempt by Britain to form an Anglo-Saxon center of power with assistance from America....The world's coal output in the first half of 1921 was 525.3 million tons, the lowest annual rate since 1909.	King Alexander of Yugoslavia arrives in Belgrade from Paris....A bomb explodes at the American Embassy in Lisbon, Portugal, as a protest against the outcome of the Sacco-Vanzetti trial....Italy dedicates the tomb of its Unknown Soldier in Rome; hundreds of thousands attend the ceremonies....The Prince of Wales, beginning his tour of Asia, stops in Malta and opens the Parliament there.	The Turkish National Assembly is sending missions to the United States, France, Britain, and Italy to explain its aims and to negotiate loans.		The Continental and Commercial Trust of Chicago announce that the Chinese government is currently in default for a $5.5 million loan and has asked Washington for assistance in getting the payment.
Nov. 2		Britain's Foreign Secretary Lord Curzon asks the Soviets for clarification on their offer to take on Russia's pre-1914 debts....French journalists report that the German Army under General von Seeckt is preparing to enlarge itself and is not restricting itself to the 100,000-man limit imposed by treaty....The Council of Ambassadors of the League of Nations is requesting that the Hungarian government bar the Habsburgs from succession no later than November 7.		A demonstration in Buenos Aries protests against the results of the Sacco-Vanzetti trial.	Soviet troops evacuate their positions in the Persian city of Enzeli as agreed in a treaty between that country and the Soviets.
Nov. 3	The United States says that it is planning to propose a large cut in the Navies of the world (as well as its own) as part of the International Conference....Many of the sessions of the International Conference will be open to the public as a reaction to secret diplomacy, which has been common in the past; American politicians and newspapers have been strongly advocating this openness.	Inflation has hit Germany very hard; from 1913 to June 1921, prices have risen 1,300 percent....More stories come out of the Soviet Union concerning the results of the famines; children are reported to be living in woods and fields in packs and entire families jump into rivers to drown or parents have been reported as having killed their children....The German Ministry of defense denies that Germany is preparing for another war and states that the poor condition of the country should prove that it cannot build up an army at this time.			Japanese attitudes toward sharing power seem to be edging toward the view that Japan has no quarrel with the United States maintaining a strong presence in the eastern portion of that ocean, but it reserves for itself primacy in the western Pacific region.

A	B	C	D	E
Includes developments that affect more than one world region, international organizations and important meetings of world leaders.	*Includes all domestic and regional developments in Europe, including the Soviet Union.*	*Includes all domestic and regional developments in Africa and the Middle East.*	*Includes all domestic and regional developments in Latin America, the Caribbean, and Canada.*	*Includes all domestic and regional developments in Asian and Pacific nations (and colonies).*

U.S. Politics & Social Issues	U.S. Foreign Policy & Affairs, Defense	U.S. Economy & Environment	Science, Technology & Nature	Culture, Leisure & Lifestyle	
Both mine operators and miners are anxious to hear the ruling of a Federal judge on the status of unions in the Williamson Coal fields in Mingo County, WV.…Nationwide demonstrations are planned for December 1 when the appeal of Sacco and Vanzetti is to be ruled on.		So many turkeys are available on the market that they are selling at below cost.		The state of New York reports that nine people have been killed and nine wounded in hunting accidents since the hunting season began less than a month ago.	Oct. 30
A Federal Judge bans the United Mine Workers from "any and all means" to unionize in the Williamson Coal Field in West Virginia.…President Harding proclaims that November 24 will be Thanksgiving.	President Harding states that he is opposed to any withdrawal of American Occupation forces on the Rhine.	U.S. railroads show a gain of profits being ahead 13.3 percent over 1920 although the gross income is less.…Railroads will be pushing to cut wages for railroad workers within the next 10 days, which will be submitted to the U.S. Railway Labor Board for approval.	A catapult is used to launch an aircraft in Philadelphia; during testing, the catapult manages to thrust the aircraft out at speeds of 48 miles per hour.		Oct. 31
				Opera Baritone Antonio Scotti, famous for his appearances at the Metropolitan Opera and as recording partner with Caruso, returns from a transcontinental tour with his own opera company.	Nov. 1
Margaret Sanger forms the American Birth Control League.…Sixty members of the West Virginia State police are occupying towns in the Mingo County coal fields and will patrol the border between Mingo and Logan Counties; as soon as the West Virginia National Guard has completed its organization and been issued with equipment it will take over for Regular Army troops that will soon be leaving.…The Census Bureau announces that in 1920 approximately 9,000 persons died as the result of auto accidents; while rate of accident fatalities is up slightly from 1919, autos are still not as dangerous as they were when first introduced.	Enlistments fail to offset the number of discharges in the Army and its strength is now falling below the 150,000 man-limit imposed by Congress; the total is now approximately 138,000 men.	Pennsylvania crude oil is now $4 a barrel compared with $2.25 a barrel in June.…Three shoe factories in Lynn, MA, will close due to high wages asked for by the workers; they cannot compete with the shoe factories in other parts of the country.		*Anna Christie*, a play by Eugene O'Neill opens in New York City.…The Connecticut Barber's commission recognizes the existence of bobbed hair and will add that cut to its examination for a barber's license.…The manslaughter trial of Roscoe "Fatty" Arbuckle is being delayed from November 7 to November 14.…President Harding celebrates his 56th birthday.	Nov. 2
A milk strike in New York City has caused riots with drivers and dealers being beaten by crowds and thousands of gallons of milk dumped; there has been one death, two injuries, and 40 arrests.		Railroads in the eastern United States have decided to go ahead with a wage cut; workers will be notified in the next week and the applications for cuts filed with the National Labor Board.			Nov. 3

F	G	H	I	J
Includes campaigns, elections, federal-state relations, civil rights and liberties, crime, the judiciary, education, healthcare, poverty, urban affairs, and population.	*Includes formation and debate of U.S. foreign and defense policies, veterans affairs, and defense spending. (Relations with specific foreign countries are usually found under the region concerned.)*	*Includes business, labor, agriculture, taxation, transportation, consumer affairs, monetary and fiscal policy, natural resources, pollution and industrial accidents.*	*Includes worldwide scientific, medical and technological developments, natural phenomena, U.S. weather and natural disasters.*	*Includes the arts, religion, scholarship, communications media, sports, entertainment, fashions, fads, and social life.*

	World Affairs	Europe	Africa & The Middle East	The Americas	Asia & The Pacific
Nov. 4	The Dutch International Conference delegation arrives in the United States.	The Hungarian National Assembly passes a measure that will prohibit any member of the Habsburg family from ever taking the throne of Hungary....Several members of the Belgian Cabinet resign making it likely that a new government will have to be formed....A British ship is taking King Charles to the island of Madeira in the Atlantic as his place of exile after receiving permission from the Portuguese government.		Earth tremors have been felt in Mexico for the past three days but no damage has been reported.... The Canadian Minister of Lands announces that 1,000 British families will shortly be immigrating to British Columbia, Canada.	Prime Minister Hara Takashi of Japan is assassinated, stabbed to death by a young Korean....Japanese delegates have withheld any comment, but it is believed that the recent assassination of Prime Minister will not affect the International Conference to take place next week....Gandhi's nonviolent plan of revolt is accepted by the Committee of the Pan-India Congress....American officials state that they believe that China's default on its $5.5 million loan to Chicago bankers is a technical issue and that China will make the payments....China has rejected pre-Conference overtures to resolving the Shantung problem that it has just received from Japan.
Nov. 5		King Alexander takes the oath of the new Constitution in Belgrade, Yugoslavia, and is crowned king.... American Dr. Armand Hammer is being investigated by the U.S. government for his business deals with the Soviets to include asbestos concessions in the Urals....Talks in Ireland are breaking down as leaders in Ulster make it clear that they want no union with the South, and Sinn Fein is just as committed to a united Ireland.		Officials of the city of Havana, Cuba, have been indicted for fraud.	
Nov. 6		Czechoslovakia and Poland sign a treaty resolving the Tesin area dispute between the two nations.		Representatives of the Central American Federation (Salvador, Guatemala, and Honduras) are traveling to Washington to explain their Federation to the U.S. government....Panama's Minister of Finance states that the country has a budget surplus of $4 million due largely to the presence of the Canal.	
Nov. 7	French Premier Briand arrives in the United States to attend the International Conference; he states that France and the United States stand together.	Benito Mussolini becomes head of the Italian Fascist Party....A total of 16,000 people are let out of prison by Soviet authorities as part of the celebration of the anniversary of the revolution; many of the Kronstadt mutineers have been released....The mobilization of troops in Austria, Czechoslovakia, Romania, and Yugoslavia, in response to the recent attempt of King Charles to return to Hungary, has cost millions; the defraying of these costs will work a hardship on these countries, not one of which can easily absorb that cost.		The death toll from the hurricane that hit Newfoundland last week is now at eight and several fishing crews are still reported as missing....President Suarez of Colombia announces that he will leave office; the Colombian Congress meets to select a successor.	
Nov. 8	Japanese delegates to the International Conference state that they want an all-around naval reduction and have no desire to exceed or even be equal to the United States or British fleets.	Albania protests to the League of Nations concerning its invasion by Yugoslavia and receives support from Britain....Street battles between Communists and Fascists in northwestern Italy result in several injuries including a Communist deputy who is shot twice.	Italy reaches an agreement with Turkey over the stopping and searching of Italian ships in the Black Sea in September....The British Commission in Palestine lays part of the blame of the Jaffa riots of this past May partly on the Jewish population and warns them to be considerate of the Arab majority in Palestine.	As the result of a revolution, Eusebio Ayala becomes President of Paraguay.	
	A	B	C	D	E
	Includes developments that affect more than one world region, international organizations and important meetings of world leaders.	*Includes all domestic and regional developments in Europe, including the Soviet Union.*	*Includes all domestic and regional developments in Africa and the Middle East.*	*Includes all domestic and regional developments in Latin America, the Caribbean, and Canada.*	*Includes all domestic and regional developments in Asian and Pacific nations (and colonies).*

	U.S. Politics & Social Issues	U.S. Foreign Policy & Affairs, Defense	U.S. Economy & Environment	Science, Technology & Nature	Culture, Leisure & Lifestyle
Nov. 4	Mrs. Lyda Meyer Southard is convicted of murdering Edward Meyer, her fourth husband; her current (fifth) husband who earlier proclaimed her innocence has no comment.... Leaders of the United Mine Workers are freed from jail in Mingo County and then seized and thrown into prison in Kanawha County on charges related to the miners' march in August.... The milk crisis in New York is over, although the strike by 11,000 milk drivers that started it is not. Milk companies will be distributing milk to stores so those whose daily delivery has been interrupted will have a source of milk; the City of New York has declared that it will not have to take over the dairies although guards are being provided for some of the wagons.		Wheat prices are at 98 cents a bushel, the lowest price since 1914.		
Nov. 5	President Harding proclaims that November 11 will be a holiday to commemorate those who "gave their lives in the late World War."... All visitors to the court sessions of the Sacco-Vanzetti trial will be searched for weapons by police due too many threats on both the proceedings and against the judge.... Beer prescriptions for medicinal purposes will still be allowed, but will remain very limited and tightly controlled by the government.... Miners at several coal fields are on strike over the issue of "check-offs" in which employers deduct pay for union dues and pay them directly to the unions instead of the miners paying.		There is concern that the supplies of hickory, used to make 65 million auto wheel spokes a year will run out.... The Commerce Department has received reports that American business in Argentina, Brazil, Chile, Peru, and Mexico is improving.	The yacht, *Carnegie*, which left Washington in 1919 to conduct a magnetic survey of the globe, has just passed through the Panama Canal and is on its way home, after making a journey of 65,000 miles.	French composer Marcel Dupre leaves Paris for a series of concerts he will give in the United States.... The following books have been published: *The Scottish Chiefs* by Jane Porter with illustrations by N.C. Wyeth and *Finding Your Job* by Norman G. Shidle.
Nov. 6	New York City has 343,000 unemployed people, 13.5 percent of the city's population of 2,531,747.... The People's Educational Forum, an African-American organization, passes a resolution criticizing President Harding's recent speech in Birmingham, AL, where he said that political but not social equality was possible for African Americans.				
Nov. 7					A new comedy, *The Perfect Fool*, starring Ed Wynn who also wrote the book and lyrics, opens at the George M. Cohan Theater and is very well received.
Nov. 8	The Defense in the Sacco and Vanzetti Trial moves for a new trial in what is known as the Ripley Motion based on comments by the jury foreman that whether or not the men were guilty, they should hang anyway.... John F. Hylan is reelected as Mayor of New York City.... Many voting violations are reported at polling places in New York.	A resolution in the Senate for full publicity of the activities at the upcoming International Conference for Naval Disarmament and Far Eastern Affairs is adopted.			
	F	G	H	I	J
	Includes campaigns, elections, federal-state relations, civil rights and liberties, crime, the judiciary, education, healthcare, poverty, urban affairs, and population.	*Includes formation and debate of U.S. foreign and defense policies, veterans affairs, and defense spending. (Relations with specific foreign countries are usually found under the region concerned.)*	*Includes business, labor, agriculture, taxation, transportation, consumer affairs, monetary and fiscal policy, natural resources, pollution and industrial accidents.*	*Includes worldwide scientific, medical and technological developments, natural phenomena, U.S. weather and natural disasters.*	*Includes the arts, religion, scholarship, communications media, sports, entertainment, fashions, fads, and social life.*

	World Affairs	Europe	Africa & The Middle East	The Americas	Asia & The Pacific
Nov. 9	The general consensus among delegates at the International Conference is that they are sympathetic to Japan's situation with overcrowding and few resources.	Communists attack a Fascist Convention and call a General Strike....Albania's army succeeds in halting the invasion by Yugoslav forces; Allied ambassadors are pressuring Yugoslavia's government to stop the offensive....The Italian press is expressing alarm at Yugoslavia's invasion of Albania and calls upon the government to take measures to stop it....The possibility of a union with southern Ireland is creating great opposition of Ulster's leadership, which wishes to retain a direct tie with Britain.		Arbitrators approve a maximum 12 percent wage cut for Canadian rail workers.	
Nov. 10	The Italian delegation arrives for the International Conference....In preliminary discussions, some foreign delegates are questioning the American Disarmament formula based on the tonnage of ships and should be based on the number of ships instead.	The Albanian-Yugoslav border is settled by the League of Nations' Council of Ambassadors along the lines of the established border in 1913.			The Soviets claim that British accusations that the Soviets were spreading propaganda in India are false and based on forged documents; the British government produces the documents to prove that the Soviets were agitating in India.
Nov. 11	Today is Armistice day: Large crowds witness the laying of a marble slab over the tomb of Britain's Unknown Solider; a tablet honoring veterans is dedicated in Louisville, KY; the flags of all the Allied nations are at half-staff in Madrid, Spain....Some uncertainty is being expressed in France about the purpose of the International Conference; some observers seem to think that resolving differences between the United States and Japan is being treated as more important than general disarmament.			Street cleaners in Havana are seeking to collect back wages and riot when they do not get them; one man has been killed and a policeman beaten in the disorder....President Obregon of Mexico declares himself very skeptical of the upcoming Conference in Washington, resenting the exclusive nature of the invitations and noting the discussions affect all mankind.	China announces that it has no intention of letting Manchuria be partially ruled by any other country, particularly the Japanese....A group of 900 anti-Government rebels has surrendered to British forces, but the rebellion continues with rebels killing and burning in villages and crowds of refugees seeking to flee from the fighting.
Nov. 12	The Washington Conference for Naval Disarmament and Far East issues opens and will continue until February 6, 1922....President Harding opens the Conference and Secretary of State Hughes is elected Chairman of the proceedings....French Premier Briand states that he is very confident that the International Conference will succeed and if it does not it will not be the fault of America as Secretary Hughes has done an excellent job.	An attempt has been made to kill M. Tchitcherin, the Soviet Foreign Minister; the assailant, identified as a Menshevik has been arrested.		General Jorge Holquin becomes President of Colombia....Revolutionaries have attacked towns in Nicaragua.	
Nov. 13	At the International Conference, U.S. Secretary of State Hughes proposes that Britain stop all future naval construction and scrap much of its fleet, that Japan stop its work on battleships and eliminate some in construction or already existing, and that the United States scrap 15 ships it is building plus 15 it already has in commission.		Visitors report that the oil city of Baku, which was once rich, has fallen on very hard times due to the conflicts in the Soviet Union, and like many cities there has serious shortages of food and clothing.		Initial reception to the Hughes naval disarmament proposal is favorable in Japan....Japan's current naval construction program includes 85 ships.
Nov. 14	Initial responses from delegates to Hughes' proposals at the International Conference include the British who want submarines cut below the Hughes proposal and the Japanese who want to see an increase in the allotment of large war ships but both accept in principle; France and Italy also agree.	The Third Communist International claims that there are currently 2.8 million Communists in Europe....There is a great deal of anxiety in France that with the disarmament talks proceeding on naval limitations that limits on land forces may be next, especially considering the perceived danger of German aggression....German response to the Hughes proposals is mixed even though it does not affect Germany's already reduced naval forces.		Mexicans demonstrate against the American Consulate in Tampico, Mexico, protesting the outcome of the Sacco-Vanzetti trial....Communists are suspected of having bombed and damaged the shrine of Our Lady of Guadeloupe in Mexico.	
	A *Includes developments that affect more than one world region, international organizations and important meetings of world leaders.*	B *Includes all domestic and regional developments in Europe, including the Soviet Union.*	C *Includes all domestic and regional developments in Africa and the Middle East.*	D *Includes all domestic and regional developments in Latin America, the Caribbean, and Canada.*	E *Includes all domestic and regional developments in Asian and Pacific nations (and colonies).*

U.S. Politics & Social Issues	U.S. Foreign Policy & Affairs, Defense	U.S. Economy & Environment	Science, Technology & Nature	Culture, Leisure & Lifestyle	
According to the Bureau of the Census, the number of foreign-born in the country totaled 13,920,692 in 1920, an increase of 3 percent since 1920.	The body of the Unknown Soldier has arrived in Washington from France on the cruiser *Olympia* and is lying in state at the Capitol rotunda.	Meat packing companies request that their employees consider a 10 percent wage cut.		An autographed set of *The Works of Mark Twain* is sold for $610; an autographed volume of writings by Bret Harte goes for $350.	Nov. 9
Workmen at the Laconia (NH) Car Works find explosives in a locker with iron shot that would have been used to make a bomb to be set at either the Armistice Day Parade or the American Legion Ball.	The U.S. Submarine *L-6* has a fire on board while submerged; seven crew members are injured; the craft manages to resurface and return to its base in San Diego....Security for the mail has become such a major issue that U.S. Marines are detailed to escort mail shipments; a detachment of 64 Marines, the first of a unit of 265, begin guarding mail at post offices in New York City.			Irene Castle announces she will dance for the first time in six years in New York; she was best known for dancing with her husband, Vernon, a pilot who was killed in the War....The Nobel Committee announces that Anatole France has won the Nobel Prize for Literature.	Nov. 10
A court injunction prevents striking milk wagon drivers from harassing dealers.	President Harding dedicates the Tomb of the Unknown Solider where a crowd of 100,000 have gathered....The President delivers an address via a local loudspeaker system and by radio telephone that carries his message to large crowds....Commemoration activities are held throughout the country with speeches, doves being released, parades, and mass meetings supporting disarmament....The Treaty between the United States and Germany ending the war goes into effect.	The Treasury Department reports that the country's current gold supply is at an all-time record: $3,504,677,154....Housewives are being advised to stock up on canned goods as they are expected to soon rise in price, in some cases up to 20 percent based on projected shortages.	Walter Nernst of the University of Berlin is named as winner of the Nobel Prize for Chemistry.		Nov. 11
Charles Ponzi, best known for his "get-rich-quick" schemes, is undergoing medical care while serving a prison term for fraud....Two thousand woman march on Fifth Avenue in New York carrying banners in favor of peace and disarmament....Margaret Sanger announces that the first birth control clinic will open in New York.	The U.S. Navy currently has 464 ships compared to 533 in Britain, 99 in Japan, 138 in France, and 86 in Italy.	There is a great deal of argument in manufacturing and business circles as to whether the United States should adopt the metric system.		Russian bass player Feodor Chaliapin gives a concert in the Manhattan Opera House....Wilhelm Backhouse, a German pianist, gives a concert of music by Schumann and Brahms after an 8-year absence from the United States....English writer John Galsworthy writes an article suggesting that Americans should broaden their horizons....Roscoe Arbuckle states that he is ready for the trial, which will begin in a couple of days and he is sure his innocence will be proven.	Nov. 12
Police in New York prevent Margaret Sanger and Mary Wilson from speaking publicly on birth control; reports state that the raid was brought on by pressure from the Archbishop of New York....The state of Kansas warns railroads that they cannot transport medicinal beer through that state.	A Polish gathering at the Cooper Union in New York asks President Harding to look into the outrages Poland is committing against Lithuanians in Vilna and the Lithuanian territories that Poland now occupies....President Harding receives a telegram from Armenians in the territory just evacuated by France (Cilicia) and asks for protection, as they fear a massacre at the hands of the Turks.		Archaeologists from the University of Pennsylvania have found hieroglyphics in the ruins of Beisan in Palestine.	The Rudolph Valentino film, *The Sheik*, opens in New York City.	Nov. 13
The Texas Cherokees and associated tribes have petitioned the Supreme Court to review their claim to more than one million acres in Texas.				The Fatty Arbuckle trial opens today....In the case of Harry ("Bud") Fisher, who brought a case to the Supreme Court to determine his copyright for his characters "Mutt" and "Jeff," is given complete ownership of his creation.	Nov. 14
F *Includes campaigns, elections, federal-state relations, civil rights and liberties, crime, the judiciary, education, healthcare, poverty, urban affairs, and population.*	G *Includes formation and debate of U.S. foreign and defense policies, veterans affairs, and defense spending. (Relations with specific foreign countries are usually found under the region concerned.)*	H *Includes business, labor, agriculture, taxation, transportation, consumer affairs, monetary and fiscal policy, natural resources, pollution and industrial accidents.*	I *Includes worldwide scientific, medical and technological developments, natural phenomena, U.S. weather and natural disasters.*	J *Includes the arts, religion, scholarship, communications media, sports, entertainment, fashions, fads, and social life.*	

	World Affairs	Europe	Africa & The Middle East	The Americas	Asia & The Pacific
Nov. 15	At the International Conference, Britain goes on record as saying it wants all submarines outlawed; if that cannot be done, it wants the smallest number possible allowed.... France and Italy go on record as saying they want larger fleets based on neglect of their navies during the World War.				The recommendations of U.S. Governor Leonard Wood do not recommend independence for the Philippines at this time.
Nov. 16	The League of Nations Council opens its 15th session.... At the International Conference Dr. Sze of China presents proposals for an "open door" policy for China, which would include complete civil and political independence from any outside powers and the ability of the Chinese to regulate tariffs within their country.	The German Supreme Court sentences Berlin Police officials for their part in the unsuccessful Kapp uprising of 1920.... The French Premier once again brings up the importance of France keeping a large land force to defend itself, particularly if it must do so without aid.... Czechoslovakia sends a note to the U.S. government praising the naval disarmament initiative and expressing hopes that the same can be done for land forces.		General Armando Diaz, Italian Chief of Staff on a tour of the United States, is adopted by and made an honorary chief of the Crow Nation.	A British garrison of British-led Gurkha soldiers is attacked by 2,000 Moplah rebels in India; the British hold the fort with four men killed and 34 wounded, while inflicting 700 deaths and many wounded on the Moplahs.
Nov. 17	Japan repeats its proposals that it gets to have a ratio of 70 percent of the allotment of Britain and United States battleships with equality in cruisers.	Anti-Communist forces are reported to have occupied Kiev and 44 Soviet divisions are said to have been disarmed.... The French government is beginning to make plans for hosting the 1924 Olympic Games.... Yugoslavia denies that it has broken any agreements before invading Albania.... The Communist party is being "cleaned up" as a review of its membership in the Soviet Union continues; between ¼ and ½ of the membership has been expelled for associating with the bourgeoisie, drunkenness, or religious fanaticism.		A plague of locusts has infested nearly all of Santa Fe province in Argentina.... France and Italy agree to send missions to Ecuador to help develop aviation in that country.	The Prince of Wales arrives in Bombay as part of his Asian tour; as part of his welcome there is rioting throughout the city.
Nov. 18	The United States and Britain indicate that they will oppose Japan's proposal for a revised proportion of allowed warships.... At the International Conference, the Chinese delegation is stating that it should be granted a charter of general rights that would guarantee its political integrity.	Yugoslavia and Albania state that they have resolved their border dispute and promise the League of Nations Council that they will observe the boundary between the two nations.		Government troops are fighting anti-Government rebels in Mexico's Lower California region; 13 have been killed in a gun battle and four have been executed.	A bank collapse in Beijing is having widespread consequences as Army troops have gone unpaid; it is feared there will be an Army mutiny if they are not paid.... Japan launches a new battleship, the *Kaga*.
Nov. 19	U.S. delegates had originally proposed a ratio of 10 U.S. tons of naval armaments for every five tons allotted to the Japanese; the Japanese are insisting on a 10–7 ratio; in addition to the formal conferences a great deal of discussion is being done on an informal basis.... Reflecting a fear that is worldwide and based on events of the past few years, a newspaper in Buenos Aries criticizes the Washington Conference and fears that secret diplomacy and "old tricks" are taking place.... The place of the new type of ship, aircraft carriers, is being discussed at the International Conference, the main sticking point being whether they are classed as offensive or defensive weapons; the Japanese are expected to ask for the same tonnage as the United States and Britain.	Italian newspapers state the view that Italy should be able to have submarines as a part of its fleet and that its independence depends on having large numbers of these cheaper vessels.... Germany is sending its first accredited diplomat to the United States since the U.S. entry into the World War.... European air service has become a large enterprise and is growing; each business day an average of 116 aircraft are flying 25,000 miles.	A French newspaper has reported that the United States may be sending a destroyer to Cicilia in case the Christians there need to be protected against the Turks who have just occupied the region.	The most used route in traffic on the Panama Canal is between the U.S. east coast and the west coast of South America, which accounts for $^{1}/_{6}$ of the total.... The Canadian government is giving "refresher" training to 10,000 men trained as pilots during the World War.... The price of Cuban sugar has dropped, selling at $3^{15}/_{16}$ cents a pound.	Baron Kato of Japan defines the Japanese view that China should be allowed to control its domestic policy, while Japan will assist it in formulating and implementing foreign policy; the Chinese are not receptive to this proposal.... Mohandas Gandhi is fasting in penance for the violence caused by some of his followers during the visit of the Prince of Wales to Bombay.... Some British commentators are suggesting that the British lend the Naval facilities in Singapore to the United States.

A	B	C	D	E
Includes developments that affect more than one world region, international organizations and important meetings of world leaders.	*Includes all domestic and regional developments in Europe, including the Soviet Union.*	*Includes all domestic and regional developments in Africa and the Middle East.*	*Includes all domestic and regional developments in Latin America, the Caribbean, and Canada.*	*Includes all domestic and regional developments in Asian and Pacific nations (and colonies).*

U.S. Politics & Social Issues	U.S. Foreign Policy & Affairs, Defense	U.S. Economy & Environment	Science, Technology & Nature	Culture, Leisure & Lifestyle	
A New York State Court grants an injunction requested by International Paper that will forbid striking workers from picketing the mills.... Two companies of the Iowa National Guard are sent to keep order at a meat packing plant where rioting has broken out.	Colonel I.N. Lewis, inventor of the Lewis machine gun, states that he wants an end to all war; he would be happy to end all manufacturing of machine guns if the statesmen of the word made that possible.	Estimated losses this year to the cotton crop from the boll weevil will exceed $700 million.			Nov. 15
Anna Elizabeth Niebel of New York City is bringing a lawsuit of $50,000 against Oklahoma Congressman Manuel Herrick for breach of promise to marry her while she was a contestant in a beauty pageant; complicating factors is that Congressman Herrick also allegedly made overtures to 47 other contestants.	President Harding views maneuvers and a mock battle conducted at Camp Benning, GA.	Railroads announce that they will cut the costs of shipping farm goods by 10 percent.			Nov. 16
Colonel Charles Hudson, the Union officer who captured Confederate President Jefferson Davis in 1865, dies.		Western railroads state that there should be no free passage through the Panama Canal, otherwise cities in the Midwest would suffer from the decrease in rail traffic through the region.		The 55-pound turkey selected for President Harding's White House Thanksgiving Dinner leaves Mississippi for its trip to Washington.	Nov. 17
The anti-Beer bill prohibiting beer for medicinal purposes is passed in the Senate 56–22.... The Baltimore and Ohio railroad reports that nationwide 1,500 people were killed and almost 4,500 injured in railway crossing accidents in the past year.... Will Turner, an African American charged with assaulting a Caucasian woman is taken from the Sheriff's custody and shot; after his death he was taken to a city park in Helena, AR, and his body burned.	President Harding issues a proclamation formally declaring the U.S. peace with Austria.	A cyclone hits Arkansas, killing 12 and injuring 30.		The Fatty Arbuckle trial begins in San Francisco; five women are seated on the jury.	Nov. 18
Prohibition has resulted in a large underground industry of home distilleries; Richard Cardulio in New York causes an explosion in his New York City apartment while making liquor that kills him and one of his children and severely burns seven firemen.		Oil prices in the United States are increasing as consumption grows; the price of crude oil had increased 50 to 100 percent in the past two months.		Harvard beats Yale 10–3 in the annual football game.... Harvard and Yale have added each other to their upcoming basketball game schedules.... The Metropolitan Opera presents the premier of an opera entitled *Die Tote Stadt* (*The Dead City*) by a young German composer Erich Korngold.	Nov. 19
F *Includes campaigns, elections, federal-state relations, civil rights and liberties, crime, the judiciary, education, healthcare, poverty, urban affairs, and population.*	G *Includes formation and debate of U.S. foreign and defense policies, veterans affairs, and defense spending. (Relations with specific foreign countries are usually found under the region concerned.)*	H *Includes business, labor, agriculture, taxation, transportation, consumer affairs, monetary and fiscal policy, natural resources, pollution and industrial accidents.*	I *Includes worldwide scientific, medical and technological developments, natural phenomena, U.S. weather and natural disasters.*	J *Includes the arts, religion, scholarship, communications media, sports, entertainment, fashions, fads, and social life.*	

	World Affairs	Europe	Africa & The Middle East	The Americas	Asia & The Pacific
Nov. 20	Attention in the International Conference now turns to the issue of ratios of warships for France and Italy.	The Albanian government sends Colonel Ahmed Zog to the border to deal with Yugoslav rebels inside of Albania's territory....King Alexander of Yugoslavia denies rumors that he is planning to abdicate.			Japan and China are very active in resolving the Shantung issue outside of the formal proceedings of the International Conference; substantial progress is being made in these talks....Riots in Bombay continue with British and Indian troops firing on the rioters; one police station has been burned.
Nov. 21	The third session of the International Labor Conference in Geneva under the auspices of the League of Nations ends....French delegates at the International Conference are seeking to have a navy the same size as Japan in the surface ships category and a number of submarines equal to the British.	Rioting occurs in Berlin as a result of protests against the high cost of living; police believe the riots were a diversion to cover the fact that several expensive shops were broken into and looted....Three people are killed in street fighting in Belfast, while Ulster Loyalists protest in London against Union with southern Ireland.			Britain and Afghanistan sign a treaty that sets the limits on British influence in Afghanistan.
Nov. 22	Chinese delegates at the International Conference state that they are only pursuing major issues, Manchuria and Shantung, and state that if these large issues are resolved, many of the smaller ones will be easily settled.	Further rioting in Belfast claims 13 dead and 50 injured....A near riot breaks out in the French Chamber of Deputies when members of the Communist Party begin to sing the *Internationale* to be met with other Deputies singing *La Marseillaise*.		A majority of the Puerto Rico Assembly cables President Harding asking that E. Mont Reily, the Governor of the island, be removed.	
Nov. 23	The International Conference is not discussing limits on land forces; the agenda is, however, covering the use of aircraft, poison gas, and the laws of war.	The League of Nations sponsors a conference between Poland and Germany to settle the division of Silesia between the two countries....Bela Kun, former Soviet leader of Hungary, predicts that the Soviets will have recovered within the next four to five years....Several people are injured in the Adriatic port city of Trieste in bomb explosions as Fascists and Communists engage in heavy street fighting.		A combined Spanish-German enterprise will initiate air service between Europe and Buenos Aries, Argentine, using zeppelins to carry passengers and freight....Governor Reily of Puerto Rico states that he will not resign despite objections of the island's population.	Britain recognizes Afghanistan's independence in a treaty signed at Kabul, Afghanistan....The Prince of Wales leaves Bombay for the city of Baroda, his next stop.
Nov. 24	Premier Briand returns to France, leaving M. Viviani to head the French delegation. Before leaving, Briand warns against German militarism.	Reports from Ukraine state that the attempted anti-Communist revolt under General Petlura has failed....British Foreign Secretary Lord Curzon tells France that its best hope for security lies in unity with Britain and Italy, otherwise France is heading for disaster.... Army troops in Lisbon, Portugal, are on alert for another possible anti-Government coup.			Mohandas Gandhi says that in recent fighting in Bombay, both Hindis and Muslims should have done a better job of protecting minorities, such as the Parsees.
Nov. 25	The International Conference agrees that by 1923 all foreign post offices will be removed from China....Italy seems to be indicating that it has no objections to reductions in its fleet if the same proportions are applied to France.	U.S. Occupation forces in Coblenz, Germany, begin to return to the United States....Sinn Fein announces that it will not accept an oath to the British crown as one of the conditions of independence....Three trolley cars are bombed in Belfast.			Crown Prince Hirohito becomes Regent of Japan....Japan announces that it will discuss separately with France the possibility of conducting trade agreements between Japan and French Indo-China....The Prince of Wales arrives in Baroda as part of his tour of India.
Nov. 26		General Primo de Rivera is dismissed from the Spanish cabinet when he states that Spanish Morocco is of no strategic value to Spain and ought to be abandoned....The death toll in Belfast in the past few days, as a result of street battles over the question of Union with south Ireland, now stands at 27 dead and 92 injured....The French government is weighing a plan in which its army would number 100,000 men to form the nucleus of a much larger army that could incorporate large numbers of conscripts with this professional core.	The British government has just sent a formal note to France asking for an explanation of the recent French agreements with Turkey.	San Juan, Argentina, is in the midst of a feud in which provincial governors have been killed; the Argentine government is contemplating sending in troops to end the disorder.	India's foreign trade has improved significantly in 1920, although imports are still greater than exports.

A	B	C	D	E
Includes developments that affect more than one world region, international organizations and important meetings of world leaders.	*Includes all domestic and regional developments in Europe, including the Soviet Union.*	*Includes all domestic and regional developments in Africa and the Middle East.*	*Includes all domestic and regional developments in Latin America, the Caribbean, and Canada.*	*Includes all domestic and regional developments in Asian and Pacific nations (and colonies).*

U.S. Politics & Social Issues	U.S. Foreign Policy & Affairs, Defense	U.S. Economy & Environment	Science, Technology & Nature	Culture, Leisure & Lifestyle	
In Chicago, the courts are being asked to decide if the dance, the "shimmy," is illegal after a number of dancing establishments were raided by the police; currently the law provides one year in jail and a $200 fine for immoral dancing.…Archbishop Hayes of New York issues a statement condemning birth control.	Former Governor Cox of Ohio who ran against Harding in 1920 expresses approval of the current International Conference.	In 1921, 40,962 acres of tobacco were planted in New England with 30,509 acres planted in Connecticut.		Ty Cobb is fined $150 dollars for arguing with an umpire in the California Winter League.	Nov. 20
			The Royal Geographic society selects General Charles Bruce to lead the attempt to climb Mount Everest.		Nov. 21
Teachers in New York State protest against a State Department of Education Directive ordering principals to prepare secret reports on the morality and loyalty of teachers.		The best grade of holiday turkeys is selling for 60 cents a pound; turkeys of a lower quality are selling for 20 cents a pound and up.…The production of cigarettes in the first nine months of 1921 was 39,731,263,000.		The State ends its arguments in the Arbuckle case and the defense opens its case.	Nov. 22
President Harding signs into law a bill forbidding doctors from prescribing beer to their patients.	American soldiers are beginning to leave the Rhine as Occupation troops; 900 will leave this month and another 1,000 will return to the United States in December.				Nov. 23
The American Legion protests President Harding's possible pardon of Socialist Eugene Debs.					Nov. 24
William Jennings Bryan, speaking before an audience in Carnegie Hall, criticizes colleges in the United States for their lack of religion.	Some American officials are suggesting that any battleships currently under construction that may have to be scrapped as a result of the International Conference limitations could be turned into ocean liners.…Naval recruiting will stop for a time as it is currently at its authorized strength.				Nov. 25
Immigration quotas for the year ending June 30, 1922 are already exhausted by Greece, Spain, Palestine, Portugal, Africa, Yugoslavia, and Syria.…The way American textbooks describe the history of the United States, especially in light of current views of "Americanism," is sparking a debate among educators, politicians, and publishers.			The jeweler P.C. Cartier of New York states that despite claims made to the contrary, artificially cultured pearls are quite inferior and can be spotted rather easily.…Harvard archaeologists are unearthing the remains of a previously unknown city in Ethiopia.	Navy beats Army in the annual football game 7–0.…The death toll of football players in 1921 is 12, one less than 1920 and five more than 1919; most of the deaths on the field were high school students.	Nov. 26
F *Includes campaigns, elections, federal-state relations, civil rights and liberties, crime, the judiciary, education, healthcare, poverty, urban affairs, and population.*	**G** *Includes formation and debate of U.S. foreign and defense policies, veterans affairs, and defense spending. (Relations with specific foreign countries are usually found under the region concerned.)*	**H** *Includes business, labor, agriculture, taxation, transportation, consumer affairs, monetary and fiscal policy, natural resources, pollution and industrial accidents.*	**I** *Includes worldwide scientific, medical and technological developments, natural phenomena, U.S. weather and natural disasters.*	**J** *Includes the arts, religion, scholarship, communications media, sports, entertainment, fashions, fads, and social life.*	

	World Affairs	Europe	Africa & The Middle East	The Americas	Asia & The Pacific
Nov. 27	The Japanese government sends word to its delegates at the International Conference that it may yield on the naval ratio and accept the 5–5–3 ratio proposed for the United States, Britain, and Japan.	The French government states that it believes that Germany can pay its war reparations without any significant trouble.…London and the rest of southern England report the heaviest fog in several years.	Mustafa Kemal refuses to receive British diplomats to discuss peace efforts with Greece.	Canada reports that its foreign trade, both exports and imports, has declined since 1920 but its gap between exports and imports is more favorable than it was in that year.	Newly established Regent of Japan, Hirohito states that his policy in foreign affairs will be one of friendship abroad.
Nov. 28	At the International Conference, all nations, except Japan, vote to remove all foreign post offices in China as soon as the country is stable.	French Prime Minister Briand asserts that despite recent controversies that he has the greatest esteem for Britain.			Continuing on his tour, the Prince of Wales is now in northern India where he receives an enthusiastic welcome in Rajputana.
Nov. 29	At the International Conference, China states that it wants foreign military and telegraph and wireless systems removed from the country; additionally, a committee is appointed to resolve questions about abolishing the administration of justice by foreign courts in China.…France has indicated that it is agreeable to the Italian Navy being of equal size to the French.…Delegates at the International Convention agree to give China control of courts if an inquiry by international jurists indicates that the courts are competently run; a final decision will be made within a year.…Japan states it will begin withdrawing some of its troops but that none will be taken out of Manchuria.	The American Relief program reports that 500,000 children in the Soviet Union are now being fed regularly as a result of relief efforts and it is anticipated the number will grow to 1.2 million early next year.…German Finance Minister Walter Rathenau meets with the British concerning a possible moratorium of war reparations payments.	A Greek cruiser has intercepted and boarded an Italian ship said to be carrying weapons and airplanes for the Turks.	The city of Buenos Aries, Argentina, has begun preliminary negotiations with New York bankers to get a $25 million loan.	Britain is enforcing the Sedition act in the wake of recent disturbances and has arrested at least 12 natives, including Sardar Singh, former President of the Punjab Legislature.
Nov. 30	At the International Conference, it is agreed that the United States and Britain will mediate the Chinese-Japanese conflict of administering Shantung Province.	The French press is very critical of the meetings that Finance Minister Rathenau has been having with the British, accusing Britain of trying to govern France and take matters into its own hands without consulting its allies.	As part of the treaty agreement between France and Turkey, French troops withdraw from the city of Adana.	The U.S. Commerce Department reports that its attaché reports that economic conditions in Chile are not favorable at the present time.	A Waziri raiding party attacks a British Army unit on India's northwest frontier, killing 22 and capturing many others.
Dec. 1	In the International Conference, Japan's stand that the proportion of ships to be counted in any agreement be only for currently existing ships and not those built or under construction has caused consternation at the conference.…The Dutch government is expressing concern over the possible flood of cheaply made German goods flooding the country.	Reports from Ukraine describe a widespread anti-Communist revolt; Communist soldiers are reported to have killed 217 hostages in one incident.…The Spanish government denies reports that it is planning to intervene in Portugal.…There are claims that the Germans are manufacturing tanks and other war supplies and hiding them in the Black Forest in Bavaria.…Lloyd George proposes to Irish delegates that Ireland be a dominion with Northern Ireland free to choose whether it will join the south or stay under direct British rule.…A demonstration against food shortages in Vienna turns into a large-scale riot with stores and hotels looted; $700,000 of damage is created.	The Turkish legislature removes the privileges of all non-Muslim minorities in the country; American relief workers have been prevented from providing assistance.		The Philippine Legislature sends a request that their views be considered in all U.S. decisions that affect the islands.
Dec. 2	During the International Conference, Chinese delegates attack the Versailles Treaty and say it must be reviewed as its provisions transferred German rights in China directly over to the Japanese.…Italian Delegates at the conference state that they favor the keeping of submarines as part of their naval forces.	The Italian town of San Lorenzo Nuovo, near Rome is shaken by an earthquake.…Sinn Fein is not expected to accept the latest set of proposals offered by the British government.			Japan reports that it is being flooded with cheap Italian and German goods.…British and American oil companies are negotiating for drilling rights with the Persian government.

A	B	C	D	E
Includes developments that affect more than one world region, international organizations and important meetings of world leaders.	*Includes all domestic and regional developments in Europe, including the Soviet Union.*	*Includes all domestic and regional developments in Africa and the Middle East.*	*Includes all domestic and regional developments in Latin America, the Caribbean, and Canada.*	*Includes all domestic and regional developments in Asian and Pacific nations (and colonies).*

U.S. Politics & Social Issues	U.S. Foreign Policy & Affairs, Defense	U.S. Economy & Environment	Science, Technology & Nature	Culture, Leisure & Lifestyle	
Postmaster General Hays announces that any women working for the Postal Service will not suffer any change of status or lose any rights if they marry.			An observatory in Argentina announces that it has discovered a new planet orbiting between Mars and Jupiter.		Nov. 27
	Lieutenant Colonel Charles Whittlesey who commanded the "Lost Battalion" in the World War commits suicide, jumping off a ship sailing in the Caribbean; he had left a note stating he would not return from the trip he was making; he had been a pallbearer for the Unknown Soldier a few days before.	A heavy snowstorm in the northeast wrecks power and telephone lines with more than 5,000 poles down and large sections of New England are without electrical power.		Testifying in his own defense, actor/comedian Roscoe "Fatty" Arbuckle states that he had no part in the death of Virginia Rappe and that she was ill at the party they were attending.... Feodor Chaliapin is to play the title role in *Boris Godunov* at the Metropolitan Opera.	Nov. 28
President Harding sets aside the week of December fourth to December 10 to foster general literacy.... Railroad unions are preparing to fight the latest set of wage cut proposals offered by the railroad companies.	The ship *Toloa* makes a half day search for Charles Whittlesey, but does not find him.			The New American Theater in Brooklyn collapses killing six and injuring 20; first-degree manslaughter charges are being preferred against the owners and builders of the building.	Nov. 29
Robert Murtore, a 15-year-old African American, charged with assaulting a Caucasian girl, is taken by a mob from officers in Ballinger, TX; he is tied to a post and shot several times and killed.				The Fatty Arbuckle case is expected to go to the jury tomorrow.... A special concert is given at the Metropolitan Opera to celebrate the 25th anniversary of Rev. Francis P. Duffy's priesthood; Duffy was known as "Fighting Father Duffy," and chaplain of the 69th New York Regiment when it was mobilized in the World War.	Nov. 30
The United States reestablishes its consulate in Vienna, Austria, for the first time since the War.		The United States had 1,988 business failures in November, the worst monthly total in five years.		The Prosecution begins arguments in the Fatty Arbuckle trial.... French composer and conductor Vincent D'Indy conducts a performance of Puccini's *Tosca*.	Dec. 1
	Naval officers express satisfaction over the test trials of an airship, the C-7, which has been flying using helium instead of hydrogen.... American consuls sent to Germany after the peace treaty have received their recognition and are functioning as they did before the War.	The Department of Commerce reports that in the past nine months 7,912,737 tons of shipping has passed through the Panama Canal.			Dec. 2

F	G	H	I	J
Includes campaigns, elections, federal-state relations, civil rights and liberties, crime, the judiciary, education, healthcare, poverty, urban affairs, and population.	*Includes formation and debate of U.S. foreign and defense policies, veterans affairs, and defense spending. (Relations with specific foreign countries are usually found under the region concerned.)*	*Includes business, labor, agriculture, taxation, transportation, consumer affairs, monetary and fiscal policy, natural resources, pollution and industrial accidents.*	*Includes worldwide scientific, medical and technological developments, natural phenomena, U.S. weather and natural disasters.*	*Includes the arts, religion, scholarship, communications media, sports, entertainment, fashions, fads, and social life.*

	World Affairs	Europe	Africa & The Middle East	The Americas	Asia & The Pacific
Dec. 3	During the International Conference, Japan, Britain, and France agree to withdraw from parts of China; Japan, however, will not leave Manchuria or Port Arthur, which was captured from the Russians in 1905.	Italy states that it agrees with Britain in not drawing up any agreements with Turkey as France has done.	A British proposal to give more freedom to the Egyptian government is turned down by the Egyptians as it would have allow the British to keep a military presence in that country.	Police in Uruguay break up Communist anti-American demonstrations protesting the results of the Sacco–Vanzetti trial.	
Dec. 4	Lloyd George will not be coming to attend the Conference as he is still busy negotiating the Irish question.…Japan states that the resolution of the Naval Disarmament issues will depend on whether the Far Eastern questions are resolved first.…At the Conference, a delegation from the Far Eastern Republic in Siberia requests that the Conference push Japan into evacuating that region, especially Vladivostok.	Sinn Fein rejects the latest British offers, not accepting compromises on the partition of the island.…The German government reports that in the past month its balance of trade has been unfavorable with imports exceeding exports.…King Albert of Belgium asks the Foreign Minister to form a new government.…Germany's President Ebert receives a salary of 300,000 marks; with inflation this equates to $750.			
Dec. 5	Dr. Philip Tyan, Secretary of the Chinese delegation, quits because he says the Conference has slighted China's rights.…Japan agrees to yield some of its rights in Shantung back to the Chinese government, but with conditions.	The Allies announce that they may give Germany a 3-year grace period before making any more reparation payments.…Sinn Fein representatives accept a new set of terms that will be made public later.	A private citizen, paying a ransom of four million pesetas has freed several Spanish hostages held by the Moorish rebels in Morocco.…A famine is reported in the Cape Verde Islands and the Portuguese government is transporting islanders off the island.	Stevedores in Havana are threatening to go on strike in their fight against open shop system in which union membership would not be mandatory.…The United States sells a large supply of arms to the Nicaraguan Army including artillery.	While a fire dance has been put on to entertain the Prince of Wales, there is talk about a new Indian boycott of British goods being called.
Dec. 6	At the International Conference Japan's Baron Nakashima states that growing unrest and instability in China prevent a completely open policy there.	The Hungarian government exiles Charles from Hungary.…In Albania, a new government is formed under Qazim Koculi.…The German government is opening negotiations with British banks for a loan or credits.…The Italian government rejects a proposed treaty with the Soviets on the basis that political matters were inserted with trade issues.…Pope Benedict XV expresses great pleasure over the promised Irish settlement.			Governor Leonard Wood of the Philippines will take up the issue of national defense in the islands after the conclusion of the Disarmament Conference.
Dec. 7	At the International Conference, the United States has offered to negotiate with Japan on the placement and use of bases in the Pacific, although Hawaii will not be discussed.…At the Conference, France is insisting that 75,000 tons of submarines be allowed and that it be allowed a total of 300,000 tons worth of capital ships (battleships) for itself.…China demands that all leases and privileges held by foreign nations be terminated, this affects British and Japanese holdings for the most part, other than Hong Kong.	The Irish Free State is established on the basis of a peace treaty negotiated by Sinn Fein and the British government; the treaty must be ratified by Britain's Parliament and Ireland's Dail.…The Albanian government under Koculi, formed the previous day, resigns and is replaced by a government under Hasan Prishtina.…The Grand Guignol Theater in Paris deletes a guillotine scene, which the public has found too shocking and which caused a riot the night before.	The Uled Setut tribe of Moors has surrendered to Spanish forces in Morocco.	German commercial firms are said to be making great inroads against American merchants in Argentina due to the cheapness of their goods.…A storm off the coast of Newfoundland wrecks several ships with at least 18 lost.…President Herrarra of Guatemala is overthrown and imprisoned with his cabinet in a lightning coup; the unrest in Guatemala may spread now to the other nations that have joined in the Central American Federation.	The South China government of Sun Yat-sen states that it will attack the "hirelings" of North China. …Police in Tokyo have arrested 12 Communists in riots.
Dec. 8	A Four-Power Treaty with the United States, Britain, Japan, and France as the signatories is said to be complete, but the provisions of that treaty have not yet been announced.	Eamon de Valera publicly repudiates the newly signed treaty between Sin Fein and the British.…Discussions on how the Germans will pay the remainder of the reparations they owe to the Allies begin on London.	Adly Pasha resigns as Egypt's premier.	The government of Guatemala recalls all legislation passed during the presidency of President Herrarra, making them null and void; immediately following the coup, the country is very peaceful.	

A	B	C	D	E
Includes developments that affect more than one world region, international organizations and important meetings of world leaders.	*Includes all domestic and regional developments in Europe, including the Soviet Union.*	*Includes all domestic and regional developments in Africa and the Middle East.*	*Includes all domestic and regional developments in Latin America, the Caribbean, and Canada.*	*Includes all domestic and regional developments in Asian and Pacific nations (and colonies).*

	U.S. Politics & Social Issues	U.S. Foreign Policy & Affairs, Defense	U.S. Economy & Environment	Science, Technology & Nature	Culture, Leisure & Lifestyle
Dec. 3				The American Engineering Council reports that since 1909, five years have been added to American life expectancy.	The jury in the Fatty Arbuckle case is deadlocked, 11–1 for acquittal.... The following books have been published: *The Story of Mankind* by Hendrick Willem van Loon, *The Open Sea* by Edgar Lee Masters, *Dreamers* by Knut Hamsun, and *Of All Things!* by Robert Benchley,
Dec. 4	Members of the Ku Klux Klan meet in Philadelphia to start a new order with the same principles of the Klan; the rupture has arisen over the firing of Grand Goblin W.F. Atkin by Imperial Wizard William Simmons.				The jury in the Arbuckle case is dismissed; a new trial is set for January 9, 1922.... Thirty-one American college students have been chosen as Rhodes Scholars to attend Oxford University.
Dec. 5	Two trains crash head on 17 miles from Philadelphia; 21 are killed and 24 are injured.... The Supreme Court holds that picketing is legal but, on occasions, can be stopped by a court injunction.... The first regular session of the 67th Congress begins.... President Harding submits his first budget to Congress.		An organization, called the Adirondack Club, is being formed to improve hiking trails in New York.		
Dec. 6	Citizenship papers are granted by a Federal judge in Philadelphia to 534 aliens, a new record for one day; 200 were Germans whose naturalization was held up by the War.... African Americans in Chicago are opening a First National Bank in Chicago, the first to serve an exclusively African-American clientele.... President Harding issues his annual address (State of the Union) and after his message, the Senate votes to support his proposal to turn surplus war material over to the Russian Relief effort.	The Department of Justice issues a list with the names of 11,000 draft evaders who will be sought and punished.	Secretary of the Interior Fall states that at least $150 billion of resources is contained in the land that is still public domain; coal and oil form the bulk of these resources.		The Metropolitan Museum of Art in New York puts on an exhibition of modern Japanese paintings.
Dec. 7	Imperial Wizard of the Ku Klux Klan, William Simmons, states that he stands by the integrity of Imperial Kleagle Edward Young, who recently resigned and attacks "muckrakers" who seek to discredit the Klan.... A packinghouse strike in Chicago has turned into a riot in which an estimated 100,000 people battle police with nine shot.... Strikes against meat packing plants are on in Albert Lea, MN, Ft. Worth, TX, Omaha, NE, and Kansas City, KS, in addition to the strike in Chicago.				Writer Anatole France who has won the Nobel Prize for Literature is on his way to Stockholm to receive the prize.
Dec. 8	At least 150 are injured as the meat packing strike and riots continue in Chicago.... Attorney General Daugherty states that the Communists are making great inroads into U.S. labor organizations; he asks for more judges and says they should apply conspiracy laws in these cases.	The Commandant of cadets at West Point, General Douglas MacArthur, states that the Corps of Cadets should be expanded from 1,334 to 2,500.... The American Institute of Chemical Engineers goes on the record in favor of using poison gas in warfare, claiming it is a very humane weapon.... U.S. Navy Submarine S-48 goes down off Bridgeport, CT, but all 43 members of the crew manage to escape through the torpedo tube.			

F	G	H	I	J
Includes campaigns, elections, federal-state relations, civil rights and liberties, crime, the judiciary, education, healthcare, poverty, urban affairs, and population.	*Includes formation and debate of U.S. foreign and defense policies, veterans affairs, and defense spending. (Relations with specific foreign countries are usually found under the region concerned.)*	*Includes business, labor, agriculture, taxation, transportation, consumer affairs, monetary and fiscal policy, natural resources, pollution and industrial accidents.*	*Includes worldwide scientific, medical and technological developments, natural phenomena, U.S. weather and natural disasters.*	*Includes the arts, religion, scholarship, communications media, sports, entertainment, fashions, fads, and social life.*

	World Affairs	Europe	Africa & The Middle East	The Americas	Asia & The Pacific
Dec. 9	During the International Conference Japan agrees that it will cede some of its territorial holdings and rights in Shantung Province back to China.	Additional earthquakes in the Rome area have stricken several villages; no deaths have been reported.... It is expected that ratification in Ireland by the Dail will occur; Ulster is not expected to become part of the Irish Free State.		Mexico's President Obregon states that he will not cut the oil export taxes owed by American companies, which now total more than 22 million pesos.	*The Chronicle*, a newspaper published in Bombay, India, suggests that the Viceroy of India, Lord Reading, should take the example of Lloyd George and begin to allow India to become independent.
Dec. 10	Senator Henry Cabot Lodge announces the terms of the Four-Power Agreement that has been constructed at the International Conference.	In Albania, with the faction led by Ahmed Zog threatening a civil war, the Prishtina government resigns.... With the current attempt to restore Charles, the disorders in Burgenland, and economic problems, observers believe that Hungary is very close to a civil war.... A combination of the coal strike this year and the increased use of autos has resulted in Britain importing more petroleum than before; in the first 10 months of 1921 Britain imported 197 million gallons more than it had in 1920.... The remains of Czarist forces in southern Russia under the command of General Siroff have been defeated by the Soviets.	There are 5,000 new refugees in Constantinople, who have fled there from the victorious Communist forces in southern Russia.		Picketing by noncooperationists in Calcutta is in full swing as part of the boycott campaign; in the past two days, 260 picketers have been arrested and those convicted are receiving six months to two year sentences.... Opinion in Japan favors the Four-Power Treaty although many see it as a continuation of the current Anglo-Japanese treaty.
Dec. 11	At the International Conference the United States gets the privileges of being able to use cable and wireless facilities on the island of Yap, which will become a Mandate under Japanese administration.	Hungary ratifies its peace treaty with the United States.... The Allies report that they have disarmed Germany by 95 percent.... British reception to the results of the International Conference has been favorable, in large part because the agreements are seen as a replacement for the Anglo-Japanese treaty, which was not very popular.	The French government finds that the Turks are violating terms of the treaties signed with France and that Christians are being executed or sent into exile; as news of these actions spreads through Europe there is an increased call for the Turks to stop these atrocities.		Japan has relieved its Siberian occupation forces with new troops indicating that it has no intention of leaving that region now.
Dec. 12		The success of the International Conference has caused disappointment in some German circles, which have been looking forward to the possibility of a war between Japan and the United States.	Turkey signs a treaty of friendship with Persia.		The Prince of Wales visits Allahabad, India, where his visit is boycotted by native Indians; 600 agitators against British rule are arrested.... In the negotiations for control over Shantung province, China offers to pay a substantial part of the cost of running the railroad in that region.
Dec. 13	The Four-Power Treaty is signed, which pledges that the United States, France, Japan, and Britain will respect each other's positions in the Pacific.	Lloyd George indicates that he is not in favor of a "two-dominion" solution with Ireland being partitioned.		There are reports that Peru has invaded Chile over a border dispute over the Tacna and Arica provinces.... Marines engage in a gunfight with police in Nicaragua, killing three and wounding four; officials are investigating whether a court-martial will be necessary.... Popocatepetl, the Mexican volcano, is in violent eruption.	A member of the Dominion delegation to the International Conference, Valingmen Sastri, predicts that India will win autonomy in 10 years; he condemns the boycotts and nonviolent opposition that are being adopted now.... On the next stage of his tour in India, the Prince of Wales visits the city of Benares on his way to Nepal to hunt.
Dec. 14	The terms of the Naval Limitations Treaty are announced, which list the number of ships and the tonnage allowed to the signatories (United States, Britain, France, Japan, and Italy).	Albanian political leader Ahmed Zog arrives in the capital city of Tirana with an army and declares a state of martial law.... A plebiscite is held in Burgenland with all of it except a small section choosing to become part of Austria.... A new cabinet has been formed in Belgium.... France and Spain are currently engaged in a trade war with high import duties being imposed on each other's goods; this has particularly affected travelers between the two countries.		Yellow Fever has finally been eradicated in Ecuador; the last case was reported in May 1919.	
	A *Includes developments that affect more than one world region, international organizations and important meetings of world leaders.*	B *Includes all domestic and regional developments in Europe, including the Soviet Union.*	C *Includes all domestic and regional developments in Africa and the Middle East.*	D *Includes all domestic and regional developments in Latin America, the Caribbean, and Canada.*	E *Includes all domestic and regional developments in Asian and Pacific nations (and colonies).*

	U.S. Politics & Social Issues	U.S. Foreign Policy & Affairs, Defense	U.S. Economy & Environment	Science, Technology & Nature	Culture, Leisure & Lifestyle
Dec. 9	Former Ku Klux Klan Grand Goblin W.F. Atkin is formally accused of embezzling $16,000....Anarchist Emma Goldman, who was deported from the United States to Russia in 1919, has left that country and is currently in Latvia seeking to return to the United States.	During a Senate hearing, Senator Watson of Georgia does not like what he perceives as a "look" from one of the officers testifying and suddenly flies into a rage and threatens to hit the officer, later stating that his "Southern blood" had been aroused; the Senator is called to order and rebuked by his colleagues for his bizarre behavior....There are currently 101,941 disabled veterans receiving vocational training from the government.			President William Veeck of the Chicago Cubs announces that the rumors that he plans to resign are untrue....The University of Chicago places notices up in women's dormitories with instructions that women are not allowed to smoke.
Dec. 10	Anthracite coal miners are expected to ask for higher pay when their contracts are up in 1922; plans now are to define the demands at a union meeting to be held on January 17.	Observers believe that despite some opposition, when the Four-Power Treaty is presented to the Senate, it will ratify the treaty.	Corporations in America have begun the practice of insuring the lives of many of their top executives to minimize company losses in the event of their death.	According to American insurance companies, 1921 has been the healthiest year on record for both Canada and the United States with influenza seriously decreasing along with much lower reported cases of tuberculosis and pneumonia; however, deaths from cancer, suicides, homicides, auto accidents, and diphtheria have all increased....Radio engineers expect that it will be possible to transmit a speech by the president to an audience of 50 million people; the President's recent speech at the Tomb of the Unknown Soldier was heard by 100,000 people.	The *New York Times* reviews a new study by Stefan Zweig: *Romain-Rolland: The Man and His Work*....The Nobel Peace Prize has been awarded to Hjalmar Branting of Sweden and Christian L. Lange of Norway....President Harding receives a 135-pound pumpkin grown by children on Staten Island, NY.
Dec. 11			American exports to South America have increased significantly over the amount exported in 1920....Secretary of Agriculture Wallace reports that a gradual improvement in farming conditions is coming, although he is very critical of increased railroad freight rates for transporting harvests.		
Dec. 12		Senator Borah attacks the current International Conference and in particular is critical of the Four-Power Agreement, which he says will commit the United States to force, as well as legalizing, both poison gas and submarines....U.S. General Peyton C. March states that the Army must be kept at 200,000 and predicts danger to the national interest if it is allowed to be set at 150,000.	The Federal government is making arrangements to buy the Cape Cod Canal in Massachusetts for $11.5 million.		
Dec. 13	James Michael Curley is elected Mayor of Boston, defeating the opposition running on a "good government" platform....Miss Sarah Hyams, who teaches cooking in New York Public Schools, is accused of having signed an application to become a member of a left-wing organization; she denies the accusations and states that she has taken the loyalty pledge.	The Brooklyn Navy Yard is told to accept any resignations to decrease the number of Naval staff by 5,000 and is swamped with requests to separate from the service.	The Baltimore and Ohio Railroad announces that it will close its shops and furlough its workers indefinitely over the next few days.		Composer Richard Strauss conducts a program of his own works including *Macbeth* and *Don Quixote*.
Dec. 14		Scrap metal dealers are accepting the Navy's invitation to survey ships slated for decommissioning, which will then be sold for scrap....An Army pilot takes a twin-engined bomber to 25,600 feet, establishing a new record.			
	F *Includes campaigns, elections, federal-state relations, civil rights and liberties, crime, the judiciary, education, healthcare, poverty, urban affairs, and population.*	**G** *Includes formation and debate of U.S. foreign and defense policies, veterans affairs, and defense spending. (Relations with specific foreign countries are usually found under the region concerned.)*	**H** *Includes business, labor, agriculture, taxation, transportation, consumer affairs, monetary and fiscal policy, natural resources, pollution and industrial accidents.*	**I** *Includes worldwide scientific, medical and technological developments, natural phenomena, U.S. weather and natural disasters.*	**J** *Includes the arts, religion, scholarship, communications media, sports, entertainment, fashions, fads, and social life.*

	World Affairs	Europe	Africa & The Middle East	The Americas	Asia & The Pacific
Dec. 15	Japan indicates at the International Conference that it will accept the naval ratios that Secretary of State Hughes has proposed....Japan will give up the Shantung railroad to China for a cash payment.	Cunha Leal is made Premier of Portugal....The British government is reviewing possible cuts in the Armed forces that could save the government 195 million pounds.... The French government repeats its objections to disarmament affecting the size of its army....Germany claims that its next reparations payments cannot be made in full, that efforts to get loans have not been successful and that it needs more time....The Soviet Union begins making its required treaty payments to Poland.			
Dec. 16	At the International Conference there is debate on the quantity of submarines France and Italy will have under the terms of he Treaty	In Britain, the Parliament ratifies the agreement for the Irish Free State by a large majority.		Witnesses testify before a Senate Committee that U.S. Marines committed atrocities on Dominican natives during the U.S. occupation, to include cutting ears off prisoners and pouring salt into open wounds.	The civil war in China is growing as more provinces are declaring their loyalty to the southern Chinese Republic of Sun Yat-sen.
Dec. 17	At the International Conference, there is a general consensus that France's demand for 350,000 tons of capital ships is excessive and that the proposed 175,000 tons is more reasonable; several observers believe, however, that France is pushing this point in order to make a bargain elsewhere, probably in the question of submarine tonnage.	King Ferdinand of Romania dismisses Alexandru Averescu as prime minister to eventually replace him with Take Ionescu....In the Asturias region of Spain, 13,000 miners walk off the job.			Air service will begin this month in China between Beijing and Kansu; the service will be provided by a Chinese company. A recent French proposal to provide air service was refused permission by the Chinese government.
Dec. 18		Czechoslovakia and Austria sign a treaty, pledging to take all future border and other cases to the League of Nations for arbitration.		A political amnesty has been granted in Guatemala that includes nearly everyone except those members of the most recent cabinet who are now in prison....The President of Puerto Rico's Senate denies that the island wishes to secede from the United States....Mexico proclaims that it will impose a tariff of 50 to 100 percent on goods imported after January 1.	The Chinese cabinet resigns over what is considered the unsatisfactory outcome of the negotiations over Shantung....In Tokyo, there are violent protests against Japan's acceptance of the naval warship ratios agreed to at the International Conference.
Dec. 19	French Premier Briand states that France's position on the ratio of ships and type of ships it wants is misunderstood by other nations and that France wants only to maintain a strong defensive navy.			A Conference of the American nations, the Pan-American Conference, will take place in Santiago, Chile in the summer of 1922.	
Dec. 20		Cunha Leal, Premier of Portugal since December 15, is driven from office; new elections are set for January 8 and in the meantime reports indicate that everything is quiet in Lisbon....Krupp industries in Essen, Germany, announce they will begin a profit-sharing plan for its employees.		The Chilean government urges the Peruvian government to accept a plebiscite to resolve the Tacna-Arica dispute, which both nations claim....The municipality of Montevideo, Uruguay, is taking a $6 million loan from American bankers.	
Dec. 21					The Far Eastern Republic in Siberia has declared war on the Republic of Vladivostok and is receiving military assistance from Soviet authorities.

A	B	C	D	E
Includes developments that affect more than one world region, international organizations and important meetings of world leaders.	*Includes all domestic and regional developments in Europe, including the Soviet Union.*	*Includes all domestic and regional developments in Africa and the Middle East.*	*Includes all domestic and regional developments in Latin America, the Caribbean, and Canada.*	*Includes all domestic and regional developments in Asian and Pacific nations (and colonies).*

U.S. Politics & Social Issues	U.S. Foreign Policy & Affairs, Defense	U.S. Economy & Environment	Science, Technology & Nature	Culture, Leisure & Lifestyle	
The House of Representatives is considering a bill that would outlaw lynching....Ben Hooper, Vice Chairman of the U.S. Railroad Labor Board, states that because prosperity is at stake, union workers have no moral right to tie up the railroads by going on strike.		A merger of American Brass with the Anaconda Company is approved by the directors.		The National and American Leagues agree that in future World Series the number of games to be played will be seven; the National League had wanted to keep the nine-game format.	Dec. 15
In Austin, TX, 19 alleged members of the Ku Klux Klan are arrested for murdering a man near a Ku Klux Klan Hall.	The U.S.S *Graham*, a destroyer, is rammed by the liner *Panama* off the Jersey coast.			The Metropolitan opera stages a revival of Wagner's *Die Walkure*.... French composer Camille Saint-Saens dies at the age of 86.... French organist and composer Marcel Dupre gives the last of his American concerts in Philadelphia.	Dec. 16
The government issues revised census figures: the population of the United States is 105,708,711....In a letter to the *St. Paul Pioneer Press and Dispatch*, President Harding states that conditions in the country are improving and that the country is on the way to retuning to "good times."...Agents who have been working to enforce Prohibition state that they doubt if New York will ever be "dry."	Naval officers are being detached to pursue engineering studies at Columbia University....Senator Borah states that Japan is well within its rights to demand a navy as big as Japan has created.... Today is designated as "Forget-Me-Not Day" to honor disabled veterans; forget-me-nots will be sold to raise money for the veterans.		Orville Wright celebrates the 18th anniversary of the first powered flight.	The *New York Times* reviews a timely book this week: *The Influence of the Sea on the Political History of Japan* by G.A. Ballard....Jascha Heifitz presents a violin program for the first time in over a season at Carnegie Hall.	Dec. 17
After receiving an anonymous warning, New York police patrol Wall Street to avoid another bombing, such as the one that occurred in 1920; there is no bomb and police find no suspicious individuals.					Dec. 18
Southern Representatives in Congress are violently opposed to the anti-lynching bill and launch a filibuster to prevent it from passing; it appears, however, that the bill will pass the House.	A House Committee hears testimony how Armenian refugees came to the United States, were deported because of exhausted quotas, and then killed upon their return to Turkey.			The *British Journal of Astrology* predicts that in 1926 there will be a conjunction of Mars and Mercury and that a huge war between the Communists and Muslims on one side and the Anglo-Saxons on the other will be fought, which will end in 1932.	Dec. 19
Paper mills in the United States and Canada announce they will be seeking wage cuts averaging 25 percent.	The Navy announces it will be laying off more employees at the Brooklyn Navy Yard, perhaps as many as 1,000 workers.				Dec. 20
	The 400-foot airship *Roma* is commissioned and put into Army service after taking 5½ hours to arrive in Washington from Langley airfield in Virginia in a storm....Senator Pomorene states that after conducting Senate hearings that the complaints of how Marines treated the natives of Haiti were exaggerated and that with the exception of one officer who killed his prisoners, most of the atrocities seem to have been committed by the natives.			U.S. Postmaster General Will Hayes denies rumors that he will leave government service to head a large combined studio in Hollywood.	Dec. 21

F	G	H	I	J
Includes campaigns, elections, federal-state relations, civil rights and liberties, crime, the judiciary, education, healthcare, poverty, urban affairs, and population.	*Includes formation and debate of U.S. foreign and defense policies, veterans affairs, and defense spending. (Relations with specific foreign countries are usually found under the region concerned.)*	*Includes business, labor, agriculture, taxation, transportation, consumer affairs, monetary and fiscal policy, natural resources, pollution and industrial accidents.*	*Includes worldwide scientific, medical and technological developments, natural phenomena, U.S. weather and natural disasters.*	*Includes the arts, religion, scholarship, communications media, sports, entertainment, fashions, fads, and social life.*

	World Affairs	Europe	Africa & The Middle East	The Americas	Asia & The Pacific
Dec. 22	At the International Conference Britain has been trying unsuccessfully to have a total ban on submarines.	Five are killed and 30 injured when the Orient Express hits another train in northern Italy over the Piave River.	Turkey is negotiating a treaty with the British to recognize the British mandate in Iraq and offer other concessions; observers have noted that Turkey is no longer being supplied with weapons by the Soviets, which may have encouraged Turkey to look elsewhere for diplomatic understanding.	The new Guatemalan government announces that it will remain in the Central American Confederation negotiated by former President Herrerra.	Britain states that it will not take sides in the current fighting in Siberia among pro- and anti-Communist factions and the Japanese, but wishes to be everyone's friend.
Dec. 23		The Soviets are making threats against Finland for its alleged support of anti-Soviet counterrevolutionary activities.	Britain sends warships to Alexandria Egypt; sailors are landed and keep order during increased disturbances.		
Dec. 24	There is a great deal of regret expressed in British newspapers today that the International Conference has not banned submarines completely.	In Albania, a new Supreme Council, heavily influenced by Ahmed Zog, takes power; Zog becomes Minister of the Interior.…In the Bukovina region, which is now part of Romania, the old Habsburg laws forbidding marriages between Catholics and non-Catholics and remarriage after divorce have been repealed.…The Soviets agree to use some $10 million in gold from the old regime to buy food for the population.…Karl Radek of the Soviet government has sent a warning to German Communists not to agitate against the current government of Chancellor Wirth.…A new coalition cabinet is formed in Yugoslavia.	British authorities are sending two regiments from Malta to Egypt to restore order; five have been killed and 20 wounded in rioting in Gizeh and mobs are creating serious damage in Alexandria.…Egypt's cotton exports for this year are predicted to be much smaller than 1920's harvest.	Colombia ratifies a treaty that will end disputes between that country and the United States over Colombian claims to the Canal Zone in Panama; in return, the United States will pay $25 million in five installments.…Argentine soldiers clash with an outlaw band of more than 250; 19 of the bandits are killed and 193 are taken prisoner.	The Siemens Corporation will be opening new plants in China to manufacture electrical supplies.
Dec. 25		Austrians in Burgenland express concern that Hungarians will be invading the region and attempting to seize it as part of Hungary.	British forces occupy Port Said and other strategic locations in Egypt.…British gunboats are sent up the Nile and martial law is declared.	Bolivia has notified Chile that it must be included in any Pacific Conferences among Latin American countries.	The boycott of the Prince of Wales on his visit to India continues; most natives of Calcutta avoid seeing the Prince while he visits that city.
Dec. 26		Italian papers condemn the conviction of Sacco and Vanzetti and predict there will be more disturbances on their behalf.		Chile accepts Peru's proposal to submit the Tacna-Arica dispute to the United States for arbitration.	Crown Prince and Regent Hirohito, in a speech from his throne, praises the results of the International Conference and that Japan's good relations with other nations is increasing.
Dec. 27		King Alfonso XIII of Spain announces he may visit America next year.…The year 1921 has been a bad one for Spain in terms of financial and industrial conditions.	The Spanish government is discussing the possibility of having its men captured by the Moors released; thus far, private payment of ransom has secured the release of some of these prisoners.	President Obregon denies the charge that Mexico is working against the United States in Central America.	British newspapers are predicting that Gandhi will become dictator of India.
Dec. 28		Lithuania rejects the League of Nations shared administration plan for its city of Vilna, which was seized by the Poles.…Further stories from Russia are coming out describing the famine; the first official Soviet report admits that there has been cannibalism in some areas, while children have been left on the steppes to die.…Italy announces it will support the effort to relieve starvation in Russia and will establish 18 medical and food depots.	The British are succeeding in gradually restoring order in Egypt after wide-scale rioting.		The Indian National Congress adopts the Gandhi platform of passive resistance and noncooperation.…A new cabinet has been formed in Australia with William Hughes as Prime Minister and Minister for External Affairs.
	A	B	C	D	E
	Includes developments that affect more than one world region, international organizations and important meetings of world leaders.	*Includes all domestic and regional developments in Europe, including the Soviet Union.*	*Includes all domestic and regional developments in Africa and the Middle East.*	*Includes all domestic and regional developments in Latin America, the Caribbean, and Canada.*	*Includes all domestic and regional developments in Asian and Pacific nations (and colonies).*

U.S. Politics & Social Issues	U.S. Foreign Policy & Affairs, Defense	U.S. Economy & Environment	Science, Technology & Nature	Culture, Leisure & Lifestyle	
	President Harding has received requests for help for Armenians who state that once the French leave Cilicia on January 4, the Turks will massacre all Armenians.…It is estimated that the naval armor plate that will be sold for scrap at the Brooklyn Navy Yard may total $7.5 million in value.			Although there is 40 percent more Christmas mail sent than last year, the post office campaign to "mail early" is having the effect of decreasing the late mailings that are a major problem at this time of year.	Dec. 22
President Harding pardons Eugene Debs and other political prisoners.	Secretary of Labor frees 1,100 aliens held for deportation who will now be allowed to stay in the United States.				Dec. 23
Anthracite coal miners are stating that they are looking for a 20 percent increase, while mine operators are demanding that wages be cut.…Judge Webster Thayer of Massachusetts rules that there will be no new trials for Sacco and Vanzetti.…Construction workers in Philadelphia agree to keep the 1922 pay scale the same as it was in 1921.…A bill is being prepared for introduction in the New York legislature that would make auto insurance compulsory.…The city of Chicago reports that it operated at a $927,228 deficit for 1921.	The Senate Investigating Committee looking into the occupation of Haiti by the Marines advises that the Marines continue their occupation of the island.	Stores report that business has been good, but this year has been unique in that everyone seems to have done their shopping early instead of waiting until the final days before Christmas.…Merchants report that there are few turkeys left this year as twice as many have been sold as there were in 1920.…Cadillac and Buick report that their Spring models will be sold at reduced prices.		The *New York Times* reviews *Sea and Sardinia*, a travel book by D.H. Lawrence.	Dec. 24
					Dec. 25
The city of Chicago reports that 8,000 divorces were granted in the city in 1921.…Eugene Debs, recently released from the Federal Penitentiary in Atlanta, meets with President Harding.…In Key West, FL, Manuel Head is beaten by a group of masked men and in retaliation shot a local man; Head was pulled from his jail cell by a mob, tied to a telephone pole, and shot repeatedly.					Dec. 26
Murders in Chicago for the year ending December 15 total 352, nearly one a day.		Fewer people were killed in railroad accidents in the United States in 1920 than in any year since 1898; in addition to passenger safety, although the numbers of railway employees have increased, the number of railway employees killed in accidents has decreased.…Most railroads indicate that their gross income has dropped by reducing wages and other economies have resulted in higher net profits.	In Alberta, Canada, a new genus of dinosaur has been found that measures 30 feet in length.		Dec. 27
Former President Woodrow Wilson receives more than 1,000 messages on his 65th birthday.…Socialist Eugene Debs, newly released from Federal prison, arrives at his home in Terre Haute, Indiana, where he is greeted by crowds of 50,000.…Unemployment in Chicago is said to be worse in proportion to its population than New York City.			Deaths by tuberculosis were down 10,000 from 1920.	*La Boheme* is performed at the Metropolitan Opera and the Oratorio Society in New York presents Handel's *Messiah*.	Dec. 28

F	G	H	I	J
Includes campaigns, elections, federal-state relations, civil rights and liberties, crime, the judiciary, education, healthcare, poverty, urban affairs, and population.	*Includes formation and debate of U.S. foreign and defense policies, veterans affairs, and defense spending. (Relations with specific foreign countries are usually found under the region concerned.)*	*Includes business, labor, agriculture, taxation, transportation, consumer affairs, monetary and fiscal policy, natural resources, pollution and industrial accidents.*	*Includes worldwide scientific, medical and technological developments, natural phenomena, U.S. weather and natural disasters.*	*Includes the arts, religion, scholarship, communications media, sports, entertainment, fashions, fads, and social life.*

	World Affairs	Europe	Africa & The Middle East	The Americas	Asia & The Pacific
Dec. 29	Claiming that both Japan and Finland are a menace, Leon Trotsky states that the Soviets must have an army larger than their current 1.505 million-man force.	Many local railroad strikes are being called in Germany and there is great anxiety that it could turn into a nationwide strike against the rail companies.... Disorders in Belfast were responsible for 110 deaths and 540 injured.... Actress Ellen Terry has turned down the offer to become a Dame Commander in the Order of the British Empire.... Two people are killed when bombs explode in Lisbon, Portugal.		Peru is proposing that President Harding arbitrate the border dispute with Chile.... Arthur Meighen, Prime Minister of Canada, is succeeded by William Mackenzie King.	Reporters note the increasing influence of Mohandas Gandhi.
Dec. 30	The International Conference establishes the rules that will include aircraft carriers as part of the capital ships included in the Naval Disarmament Treaty provisions.	Soviet Foreign Trade tripled in the past year, exports heavily outweighed by imports.... Allied financial experts are discussing instituting a single currency to be used throughout Eastern Europe.... The French census reports that there are 39,402,739 people in the country, a decline of 397,747 since 1911. ... Bulgaria and Yugoslavia agree to reestablish diplomatic relations for the first time since the War.	Miners in South Africa's Transvaal threaten to go on strike in retaliation of proposals that wages be cut.... French troops have departed from the city off Aintab near the Syrian-Turkish border in conformance to their recent treaty with Turkey; Turkish soldiers entered as the French left.	Rioting breaks out in Mexico City as the Social Democratic party of the Mexican Congress beat the Liberal Constitutionalist Party for the committee that will legislate while Congress is in recess.... Three Marines are convicted in the murder of three Nicaraguan policemen and are sentenced to 10 years in prison.	The Soviets are making rapid progress in capturing towns and cities in Siberia that were held by anti-Communist forces.
Dec. 31		The National Bank of Romania crashes and its Directors are arrested; the President commits suicide.... Irish ratification of the treaty leading to the proposed Irish Free State seems certain to most observers.... Sinn Fein is divided over the terms of the treaty and there is speculation that even if the treaty is accepted that there may be conflict within Sinn Fein.... Vladimir Lenin has been elected without opposition as head of the Soviet government; he is expected to reappoint Leon Trotsky as Minister of War.		In a gunfight in Mexico City between political parties, 11 are injured.	Hazrat Mohani of the All-India Muslim League urges Muslims in India to revolt.

A	B	C	D	E
Includes developments that affect more than one world region, international organizations and important meetings of world leaders.	*Includes all domestic and regional developments in Europe, including the Soviet Union.*	*Includes all domestic and regional developments in Africa and the Middle East.*	*Includes all domestic and regional developments in Latin America, the Caribbean, and Canada.*	*Includes all domestic and regional developments in Asian and Pacific nations (and colonies).*

U.S. Politics & Social Issues	U.S. Foreign Policy & Affairs, Defense	U.S. Economy & Environment	Science, Technology & Nature	Culture, Leisure & Lifestyle	
	Senator King of Utah states that the International Conference has been a failure because it has not banned the use of submarines.	The Erie and Delaware & Hudson Railroads will begin insuring their employees under a group plan with the Aetna and Metropolitan Life Insurance Companies.…The Horse Association of America reports that there are 17 million horses on farms opposed to 246,139 tractors and 134,169 trucks.			Dec. 29
The Defense Attorney in the Sacco and Vanzetti trial moves for a retrial.		President Harding summons a farm conference to discuss agricultural issues and to keep agriculture as a viable entity in the United States.			Dec. 30
Tuskegee Institute reports that there were 64 lynchings in the United States, totaling 4,097 since 1885.…New York City reports that 1921 had the lowest death rate on record with less infant mortality.…A former Grand Jury Foreman, Fred Wurzbach, is organizing a Bronx Vigilance Committee to fight crime.…The death rate in Chicago is reported to have dropped by 4,000 people in 1921.…Supreme Court Justice John M. Kellogg retires from the Supreme Court, where he has served since 1902.	Secretary of State Hughes formally receives the Ambassador of Germany marking a formal resumption of relations, which were broken by the War.	In 1921, there were 19,602 bank failures, more than double the number recorded in 1920.…American copper companies report that they will resume digging operations within the next month.…The Department of Agriculture reports that crop harvests for corn, winter wheat, spring wheat, oats, barley, rye, and cotton were all substantially less than the year before.			Dec. 31

F	G	H	I	J
Includes campaigns, elections, federal-state relations, civil rights and liberties, crime, the judiciary, education, healthcare, poverty, urban affairs, and population.	*Includes formation and debate of U.S. foreign and defense policies, veterans affairs, and defense spending. (Relations with specific foreign countries are usually found under the region concerned.)*	*Includes business, labor, agriculture, taxation, transportation, consumer affairs, monetary and fiscal policy, natural resources, pollution and industrial accidents.*	*Includes worldwide scientific, medical and technological developments, natural phenomena, U.S. weather and natural disasters.*	*Includes the arts, religion, scholarship, communications media, sports, entertainment, fashions, fads, and social life.*

1922

Contestants in a beauty pageant in 1922.

	World Affairs	Europe	Africa & The Middle East	The Americas	Asia & The Pacific
Jan.	Allied governments agree to postpone German reparations temporarily. The Conference of Cannes recognizes that Germany is suffering an economic crisis. . . . Pope Benedict XV dies. He has been pope since 1914. His successor, Pius XI, is elected in February.	Britain establishes the Irish Free State. Michael Collins is first president. Civil war begins between Irish Catholics wanting independence and Protestants preferring to remain British. . . . The Vilna Plebiscite indicates provincial preference for remaining Polish. The Diet votes to remain Polish. Lithuania refuses to accept the results and severs economic ties with Poland, which incorporates Vilna in April.	Britain appoints Hajj Amin al Hussaini as head of the Supreme Muslim Council in Palestine. The council controls all Palestinian Muslim officials.	The Federation of Central America dissolves. A coup in Guatemala is the cause. The result is an ongoing series of border disputes among the Central American states.	Gen. Kim and a Red contingent attack White Russians in Siberia and rout them. Kim becomes head of all Korean and Russian partisan forces in Siberia in July. After the Japanese leave late in the year, Russia disbands all partisans and Kim becomes a schoolteacher.
Feb.	The Permanent Court of International Justice convenes at the Hague. . . . Britain, France, Portugal, Italy, Japan, and the United States sign a pair of treaties that recognize Chinese territorial integrity. The Nine-Power Treaties also recognize the Open Door. The Naval Armaments Treaty binds the U.S., Britain, Japan, Italy, and France to a 5-5-3-1.67-1.67 capital ship ratio. It also mandates a 10-year moratorium on shipbuilding. The Anglo-Japanese alliance lapses.	Britain ends the wartime ban on civilian radio broadcasts. The first station to transmit is 2MT Whittle, Essex, a Marconi Wireless station outside the BBC. It closes in 1923.	Britain declares Egypt independent. The two nations have unresolved issues including defense, security, protection of foreigners, communications, and the status of Sudan.		Indian demonstrations turn violent as nationalists burn to death 22 in a police station. Seeking to stop the violence, Gandhi calls for an end to non-cooperation. . . . Under the Shantung Treaty, Japan agrees to remove its troops from Shantung. Japan also agrees to recognize German interests in Tsingdao and Chinese stake in the Tsinan railway.
Mar.	Pope Pius XI calls for a campaign against women's fashion. He regards the current styles as indecent. . . . A League meeting in Warsaw prepares measures to deal with European epidemics.	Fascists overthrow the government of free Fiume. Italy occupies the city and brings it under Italian sovereignty. . . . Warsaw Conference attendees are Estonia, Finland, Latvia, Poland, and Lithuania. They draw up agreements for dispute arbitration and defense.	The British recognize King Fuad as ruler of independent Egypt.		British authorities arrest Gandhi, charge him with sedition, and quickly sentence him to eight years in prison. Gandhi actually serves two years.
Apr.		Germany and Russia sign the Treaty of Rapollo. Under this agreement the two renounce reparations and agree to work together economically and militarily.			Japan establishes civilian government for its Pacific mandates. The capital is on Koror Island in the Palau Group.
May	The Reparations Commission agrees to allow Germany six months moratorium after the Mark collapses. France protests. . . . The League offers Austria a loan but requires League oversight of Austria's finances.	Italy signs a trade agreement with Russia. This hurts allied efforts to isolate Russia until it agrees to honor tsarist debts.	Italy begins an offensive in Libya. Italy will be engaged in war against Libyan Arabs for eight years.		
Jun.		Germany cedes Upper Silesia to Poland. The area has been the scene of disturbances since the plebiscite.	Kurds rise under the leadership of Sheikh Mahmud. They wage a two-year war for independence against Iraq.	The United States agrees to terminate its military occupation of the Dominican Republic. The republic will first elect a new government.	After Yamagata Aritomo dies, Kato Tomosoburo becomes prime minister of Japan. He dies in August.
Jul.	The League of Nations ratifies the mandate system for administering former colonies of defeated nations.		El-Aziza, Libya, sets a mark for the hottest temperature recorded on Earth. The temperature is 136 degrees Fahrenheit, 58 degrees centigrade. . . . France and Britain receive League recognition of their assumption of mandates in formerly German Togo and Cameroon. France also gets a mandate in Syria and Britain takes Palestine and Transjordan.		The League of Nations gives Togo mandate status. . . The Japanese Communist Party is established in secret.
Aug.	At the London Conference, France rejects the moratorium on German reparations. This after Britain rejects French demands for assets on the left bank of the Rhine and in the Ruhr.	Heavy demands for reparations cause the German mark to devalue sharply. Germany begins a period of hyperinflation. . . . Michael Collins, Irish revolutionary, is assassinated. . . . Czechoslovakia and Yugoslavia reaffirm their alliance. This alliance is the basis for the Little Entente.			The League of Nations sets guidelines for administering the mandate in Palestine.
	A *Includes developments that affect more than one world region, international organizations and important meetings of world leaders.*	B *Includes all domestic and regional developments in Europe, including the Soviet Union.*	C *Includes all domestic and regional developments in Africa and the Middle East.*	D *Includes all domestic and regional developments in Latin America, the Caribbean, and Canada.*	E *Includes all domestic and regional developments in Asian and Pacific nations (and colonies).*

	U.S. Politics & Social Issues	U.S. Foreign Policy & Affairs, Defense	U.S. Economy & Environment	Science, Technology & Nature	Culture, Leisure & Lifestyle
Jan.			AT&T announces that it will enter broadcasting.... Christian Nelson patents the Eskimo Pie.	Insulin is first successfully used in the treatment of diabetes. The initial treatment occurs in Toronto, Canada.	The American Pro Football Association is renamed the National Football League. J.E. Clair gives his Green Bay franchise back to the league.
Feb.	The Conference for Progressive Political Action forms. The organization seeks the election of socialist and labor candidates to Congress.... The Supreme Court rejects a challenge to the constitutionality of the 19th Amendment. Women have the suffrage.		In Washington, DC, the first annual Radio Conference begins. A series of four annual conferences will culminate in the Radio Act of 1927.... Radio stations begin to appear across the United States. Among them are WBAP in Fort Worth, WLW in Cincinnati, WOC in Davenport, IA, and more.	Gugliemo Marconi begins regular radio broadcasts in England.	Expatriate Sylvia Beach's bookstore publishes James Joyce's *Ulysses*. The novel will be banned by England and burned by the U.S. post office this year.... *The Reader's Digest* debuts in the United States. Initial print run is 5,000 copies.
Mar.	The Chicago Federation of Labor raises objections to the American Federation of Labor's preference for craft unionism over organizing both skilled and unskilled workers by industry.		Variety reports that U.S. radio ownership tops one million sets. New stations flood the U.S.: Detroit, Seattle, Denver, Dallas, Honolulu are among those in the deluge.	Philo Taylor Farnsworth tells of his ideas for electronic television. Farnsworth is a 13-year-old Idaho high school student.	F.W. Murnau's *Nosferatu* debuts in Germany. This is the first vampire film.... *The Hairy Ape* by Eugene O'Neill opens on Broadway.
Apr.		Interior Secretary Albert Fall leases the Teapot Dome oilfields.	A strike by coal miners begins as protest against wage reductions and unfavorable business and government policies. The strike will end in September with unionists gaining concessions.	WOI in Ames, IA, becomes the first U.S. licensed educational radio station.	New York University brings back lacrosse.... The Lincoln Memorial opens in Washington, DC. The memorial costs $3 million.
May	The U.S. establishes the Federal Narcotics Control Board to fight drug trafficking. The board has authority to block importation of non-medical narcotics.			Charles Francis Jenkins transmits the first television picture in a laboratory experiment.... Walt Disney incorporates his first company, Laugh-o-Gram Films.	Paris fashion drops skirts below the knee once again.
Jun.	Herrin, IL, miners strike in protest of the use of strikebreakers. The violence kills 26. The strike fails in September.	Henry Berliner demonstrates his helicopter to the U.S. Bureau of Avionics.		Warren Harding becomes the first U.S. president to broadcast live and the first to broadcast from a remote location. His dedication of the Francis Scott Key memorial at Fort McHenry is transmitted over phone lines to a studio then broadcast from there.... David Sarnoff writes the chair of General Electric. He broaches the subject of a broadcast network as a public service. The network will be NBC.	Walter Hagen wins the British Open by one stroke.
Jul.			Railroad shop workers go on strike. Supporting owners, Harding declares the strike to be against the government. The strike fails the next year.	The New York Zoo exhibits the first duck billed platypus in the U.S.	Johnny Weissmuller sets a record. He becomes the first man to swim 100 meters in under a minute.
Aug.			The first known radio commercial airs on station WEAF, New York. A realty company pays $100 for 10 minutes.	Alexander Graham Bell dies.	Curly Lambeau receives the Green Bay NFL franchise.... The Walker Cup golf tournament debuts.

F	G	H	I	J
Includes campaigns, elections, federal-state relations, civil rights and liberties, crime, the judiciary, education, healthcare, poverty, urban affairs, and population.	*Includes formation and debate of U.S. foreign and defense policies, veterans affairs, and defense spending. (Relations with specific foreign countries are usually found under the region concerned.)*	*Includes business, labor, agriculture, taxation, transportation, consumer affairs, monetary and fiscal policy, natural resources, pollution and industrial accidents.*	*Includes worldwide scientific, medical and technological developments, natural phenomena, U.S. weather and natural disasters.*	*Includes the arts, religion, scholarship, communications media, sports, entertainment, fashions, fads, and social life.*

	World Affairs	Europe	Africa & The Middle East	The Americas	Asia & The Pacific
Sep.		Britain and Russia enact a commercial treaty. Britain ignores allied efforts to get Russia to honor its foreign loans....Britain lands in Anatolia to aid Greece in the ongoing war with Turkey.	Britain assumes the Palestinian mandate. Warren Harding signs a call for establishing a Jewish homeland there.		At the Chang Chun conference Japan and Russia fail to agree to the status of Sakhalin Island. Japan retains control.
Oct.		The British Broadcasting Company begins operation....The new fad in Paris is geometric art....Austria agrees to renounce *anschluss*. The allies promise Austria financial aid....Italy and Yugoslavia sign the Treaty of San Margherita. They recognize the independence of Fiume....The March on Rome occurs. The Fascists under Benito Mussolini take the Italian government.	Iraq and Britain sign an alliance. Britain retains a strong role in Iraq while the mandate moves a step closer to independence.	U.S. Marines begin withdrawing from the Dominican Republic. The occupation officially ends.... Through referendum, Southern Rhodesia rejects generous terms from the Smuts government. It votes not to incorporate with the Union of South Africa.	
Nov.	The Conference of Berlin meets. Monetary experts design policies to strengthen the mark and the economy. The first Lausanne Conference meets. Through February 1923 it will work to end the Greco-Turkish war.	Mustafa Kemal announces the end of the Ottoman sultanate. The British evacuate Mohammed VI from Constantinople.	Howard Carter and George Carnarvon discover the tomb of King Tutankhamen in Egypt's Valley of the Kings. They become the first to enter the tomb in over 3,000 years.		After Japan evacuates, the Soviet Union annexes the Far Eastern Republic. This area of Siberia formerly served as a buffer between Japan and Russia.
Dec.	The Reparations Commission once again rules that Germany is in default. Germany fails to deliver timber to France on time....The League forms an intellectual property commission. The commission's work will culminate in the 1926 Paris Conference.	The Bolsheviks having won the civil war, Lenin proclaims the Union of Soviet Socialist Republics. The republics include Russia, White Russia, Ukraine, and Transcaucasia. Capital is Moscow.	Abd-al-Aziz-Ibn Saud of the Nejd agrees with Iraq to recognize their common border and end border raids. The border conflicts will persist for several years more.	The United States hosts the Central American Conference to resolve the Guatemalan-Nicaraguan dispute. Attendees sign agreements on economic, military, and judicial matters.	

A	B	C	D	E
Includes developments that affect more than one world region, international organizations and important meetings of world leaders.	*Includes all domestic and regional developments in Europe, including the Soviet Union.*	*Includes all domestic and regional developments in Africa and the Middle East.*	*Includes all domestic and regional developments in Latin America, the Caribbean, and Canada.*	*Includes all domestic and regional developments in Asian and Pacific nations (and colonies).*

	U.S. Politics & Social Issues	U.S. Foreign Policy & Affairs, Defense	U.S. Economy & Environment	Science, Technology & Nature	Culture, Leisure & Lifestyle
Sep.		The Fordney-McCumber Tariff becomes law. It is highly protective, with the highest rates in U.S. history.		Radio Moscow begins broadcasting at 12 kilowatts. It is the most powerful station of its time.	*Tales of the Jazz Age* is F. Scott Fitzgerald's second book of short stories.... Jazz/blues pianist "Fats" Waller makes his first record. New York's Okeh Records releases "Muscle Shoals Blues."
Oct.	The FBI appoints its first female agent, Alaska Davidson.			Indiana Senator Harry S. New becomes the first candidate to use radio extensively in a campaign. He campaigns over radio for the final five days of his re-election bid. He loses.	Isadora Duncan performs at Carnegie Hall. Duncan is an improvisational or free-form dancer.... Douglas Fairbanks' adventure film, *Robin Hood*, debuts.
Nov.	Minnesota's Farmer-Labor Party wins its first statewide election. It elects a senator.... Georgia appoints Rebecca Latimer Felton to the unexpired term of a deceased Senator. She serves a single day but becomes the first woman U.S. senator.			The first skywriting message is, "Hello, America. Call Vanderbilt 7200." The number receives 47,000 calls.	
Dec.	A filibuster by Southern senators causes the withdrawal of the Dyer Anti-Lynching Bill, which has passed the House of Representatives.... The Motion Picture Producers and Distributors Association establishes a body to oversee content. The Hays Office's goals are to counter public criticism of content and to protect overseas rights.	The United States promises to give Russia $20 million in relief to reduce Russian starvation.	The Dow Jones Industrial Average ends the year at 98.73. The previous year the Dow closed at 81.70. The U.S. is in the early stages of a 7-year business revival led by automobiles.		The first Technicolor film debuts on Broadway. It is *The Toll of the Sea* by Metro Pictures.

F	G	H	I	J
Includes campaigns, elections, federal-state relations, civil rights and liberties, crime, the judiciary, education, healthcare, poverty, urban affairs, and population.	*Includes formation and debate of U.S. foreign and defense policies, veterans affairs, and defense spending. (Relations with specific foreign countries are usually found under the region concerned.)*	*Includes business, labor, agriculture, taxation, transportation, consumer affairs, monetary and fiscal policy, natural resources, pollution and industrial accidents.*	*Includes worldwide scientific, medical and technological developments, natural phenomena, U.S. weather and natural disasters.*	*Includes the arts, religion, scholarship, communications media, sports, entertainment, fashions, fads, and social life.*

	World Affairs	Europe	Africa & The Middle East	The Americas	Asia & The Pacific
Jan. 1	The Allies are divided over how much Germany should pay in reparations for damages done in World War I. The British are content with a payment of 500 million marks this year. The French and Belgians, who suffered far more in World War I, want much higher reparations payments. The question remains as to how much Germany is actually able to pay.	Flemish is given equal status with French as an official language of Belgium. Flemish is the native tongue of three out of five Belgians. Flemish political identity has grown since World War I, when the invading Germans favored Flemish over French....One man is wounded as bombings and scattered shootings rock Belfast in northern Ireland.... Support is widespread for ratification in Ireland of the Anglo-Irish Peace Treaty, recently signed in London.	In this month, Ashot G. Hovannisyan succeeds Sergei L. Lukashin as leader of the Communist Party in the Armenian SSR....In the month of January, the Tripolitanian Republic in western Libya, and the Emirate of Cyrenaica in the east, agree to merge. They elect Idris al-Sanusi, sheikh of the Sanusiyya Dervish Order, which dominates the interior of Libya, as their new leader, and establish a temporary capital at Gharyan, in the mountains south of Tripoli. The Italians, who nominally own Libya as a colony do not recognize the Muslim states as sovereign, but lack the strength to impose controls outside of a few outposts along the Mediterranean shore.	Vancouver, British Columbia, institutes driving on the right hand side of the road....In *Mexico on the Verge*, Dr. E.J. Dillon argues that the United States needs to reach an accommodation with President Obregon's government in Mexico, which the United States currently does not recognize. Obregon is an anti-clerical leader who favors land reform.	Negotiations continue at the Washington Conference on the status of Shantung (Shandong) Province in China. Shandong was the German sphere in China before the Japanese seized it in World War I. China, which declared war on Germany in World War I, wants the German concessions restored to it. Negotiations are proceeding on the issue of fortifications in the Pacific islands, as well as the role of submarine warfare and the numbers of capital ships each power shall have.
Jan. 2	Delegates drift back to the Washington Conference after a New Year's carouse in New York City.	Francisco Cunha Leal, Prime Minister of Portugal, has resigned.... António Maria da Silva, a leader in the Portuguese Republican Party, succeeds as Prime Minister of Portugal....Republican opponents of the peace settlement with Britain begin publishing the newspaper *Poblacht na hÉireann*....Particularly irksome to the Republicans is a provision requiring an oath of allegiance to the British crown.	Coal miners have gone on strike in Witbank, South Africa, in protest against planned wage reductions. The workers, whites, are trying to keep the mining companies from bringing in cheap, black African labor.		Edward, the Prince of Wales, arrived today in Rangoon (Yangon) in British ruled Burma (Myanmar) on a good will visit....It is reported that the recent meeting of the All-India Congress in Ahmadebad has endorsed Mohandas K. Gandhi's Non-Cooperation Movement. Gandhi demands home rule for India within the British Empire as a separate Dominion. Gandhi continues to advocate nonviolent civil disobedience in his confrontations with British authorities.
Jan. 3	M. Sarraut, French delegate at the Washington Conference, has announced his support for an American resolution to strictly ban the use of submarines in attacks on merchant ships and treat violators as pirates. Details remaining are: should merchantmen be armed, and should they be targets for planes and surface ships?...France has rejected as a forgery the text of a treaty between France and Japan. The bogus treaty originated, the French claim, with leaks to the press by Soviet agents in Riga.	The German mark falls to 7,260 to the dollar....The *Dail Eireann*, the extra-legal assembly of the Irish revolutionaries, reconvenes today in Dublin to discuss ratification of the Treaty of London agreed on late last year. Under the terms of the treaty, Ireland will become a Dominion within the British Empire as the Irish Free State. The *Dail* is sharply divided.	The French begin withdrawing from Cilicia, on the southern coast of Asia Minor, as part of their recent settlement with Turks. The French evacuate Mersin today....The French intend to focus on their planned mandate in Syria and Lebanon.		Pundit Madan Mohan Malaviya, editor and founder of Benares Hindu University, has condemned British acts of repression and circulated a call for all parties in India to attend a new conference to iron out differences between them.
Jan. 4	The Supreme Allied Council met in Cannes, France, today, in an emergency session to discuss German reparation payments in light of the current economic crisis in Germany.	The All-Russian Soviet Congress adjourns in Moscow, after reelecting the Presidium under Lenin's leadership.			
Jan. 5			Continuing their evacuation of Cilicia, the French pull out of Adana, Ceyhan, and Tarsus.		In an article in *Young India*, Indian nationalist leader Mohandas K. Gandhi stresses the need for freedom of speech and association.
Jan. 6	The Supreme Allied Council announces plans for a European economic conference to be held in Genoa in March. At British Prime Minister Lloyd George's insistence, the Soviets will be invited.	The Terms of the Anglo-Irish Peace Treaty of London are made public. Under the terms, southern, predominantly Catholic Ireland is to gain sovereignty as a Dominion under the British Crown as the Irish Free State....Republican leader Éamon de Valera, who advocates full independence from Britain, threatens to resign as President of the rebel Irish government in protest.			The *Sydney Daily Mail* begins publication in Australia.
	A *Includes developments that affect more than one world region, international organizations and important meetings of world leaders.*	B *Includes all domestic and regional developments in Europe, including the Soviet Union.*	C *Includes all domestic and regional developments in Africa and the Middle East.*	D *Includes all domestic and regional developments in Latin America, the Caribbean, and Canada.*	E *Includes all domestic and regional developments in Asian and Pacific nations (and colonies).*

U.S. Politics & Social Issues	U.S. Foreign Policy & Affairs, Defense	U.S. Economy & Environment	Science, Technology & Nature	Culture, Leisure & Lifestyle	
	In this month, as the Washington Naval Conference goes on, the United States is secretly monitoring Japanese diplomatic cables. Operating from New York City, M-8, also known as "The Black Chamber," a top-secret section of U.S. Army Intelligence, headed by cryptanalyst Herbert O. Yardley, is deciphering the Japanese diplomatic code. At stake is the ratio of capital ships to be allowed each power. Secret communications from Tokyo have instructed the Japanese delegation in Washington to accept a less favorable 5:3 ratio if pressed. Armed with this information, American negotiators can now press for the most favorable terms for the United States.	H.A. Saks, of Saks & Company, announced that 1921 saw a record year for Christmas sales, reflecting renewed consumer confidence since 1920....W.A. Woods, President of the Automobile Dealers Association of New York, announces that higher labor costs will keep automobile prices from dropping much lower than they have been....New Orleans banker R.S. Hecht encourages Southern farmers to continue efforts to diversify their crops.	General C.G. Bruce is planning a second British expedition to Mt. Everest in the Himalayas. It must set out from Darjeeling in late March to get there before the autumn monsoon. The debate is on over whether the team should carry bottled oxygen, in efforts to climb above 27,950 feet, given the added weight....The American Electric Railway Association announces that electric urban rail lines continue to remain profitable, despite high costs....In this month, Walter Gropius begins transforming the Bauhaus School, focusing on the application of industrial methods to architecture and design.	The eighth annual Rose Bowl, in Pasadena, California, has ended in a tie between the University of California and Washington & Jefferson College. The score: 0–0....Federal agents raid Jimmy Kelly's popular speakeasy on Hester Street in New York City....The custom of giving a New Year's Day reception is undergoing a revival in New York's high society in what is called the liveliest débutante season in years....WDM in Washington, DC, begins broadcasting church services....In this month author, Sherwood Anderson moves to the French Quarter in New Orleans, where his writing is transformed.	Jan. 1
President Warren G. Harding and Mrs. Harding hold a mass reception at the White House for 6,500 visitors. It is the first such reception since William Howard Taft's 1913 celebration.				Debate is rife over the role of the National Collegiate Athletic Association (N.C.A.A.) in regulating the rough and tumble sport of college football. The big East Coast schools—Harvard, Princeton, Cornell, and others—chafe at any regulation of this popular sport....A saloon keeper is shot dead on 2nd Avenue by a United States Customs agent, who demanded a drink in the illegal bar....The musical *Up in the Clouds* opens tonight on Broadway in New York.	Jan. 2
President Warren G. Harding cites progress made at the Washington Conference, rebutting critics who say that not enough is being done to bring about disarmament.				D.W. Griffith's new movie, *Orphans of the Storm*, opens at the Apollo Theater in New York City, it stars Lillian and Dorothy Gish....The United States Golf Association now lists 533 golf clubs active nationwide, up from 476 in 1920.	Jan. 3
In San Francisco, California, Senator Hiram W. Johnson has warned that any four power agreements reached in the Pacific must be carefully studied before approval. He denounces the secrecy of the proceedings at the Washington Conference and warns against strengthening Japan's position in the Far East.	A proposal was made in Congress today, calling on President Harding to support withdrawal of Allied troops, including 9,729 Americans from the Rhineland occupation zones, where they have been stationed since the end of the World War, as a means of lessening the load of reparations on Germany.		New York City has begun testing a system to regulate traffic signals across most of Manhattan, from 14th Street to Harlem, to smooth the flow of traffic.		Jan. 4
	The United States rejects a proposal at the Washington Conference to require signatories to attend an international conference in the event of war between one of the signatories or an outside power.	Under pressure from the Interstate Commerce Commission to prevent interlocking corporate directorships, financiers George F. Baker, Harold S. Vanderbilt, and William Rockefeller have agreed to resign their seats as directors of the Delaware, Lackawanna & Western Railroad.	British Antarctic explorer, Sir Ernest Shackleton, 47, has died of a heart attack on board his ship, the *Quest*, en route to New South Georgia Island, on his fourth expedition to the Antarctic.	A survey by the *Journal of the American Medical Association of Doctors* in 19 states show that a majority reject prescribing liquor, beer or wine as medication. However, two out of five doctors still favor the practice.	Jan. 5
	American Secretary of State Charles Evans Hughes proposes a measure before the Washington Conference, outlawing poison gas in warfare.	Harbor tugboat pilots in New York vote to go on strike if their demands for higher wages are not met.		The Pennsylvania Railroad begins phasing out its old wooden dining cars, replacing them with new, all-steel cars.	Jan. 6
F *Includes campaigns, elections, federal-state relations, civil rights and liberties, crime, the judiciary, education, healthcare, poverty, urban affairs, and population.*	**G** *Includes formation and debate of U.S. foreign and defense policies, veterans affairs, and defense spending. (Relations with specific foreign countries are usually found under the region concerned.)*	**H** *Includes business, labor, agriculture, taxation, transportation, consumer affairs, monetary and fiscal policy, natural resources, pollution and industrial accidents.*	**I** *Includes worldwide scientific, medical and technological developments, natural phenomena, U.S. weather and natural disasters.*	**J** *Includes the arts, religion, scholarship, communications media, sports, entertainment, fashions, fads, and social life.*	

	World Affairs	Europe	Africa & The Middle East	The Americas	Asia & The Pacific
Jan. 7	At the Washington Conference, agreement is reached on an American proposal to outlaw the use of poison gas in warfare. Efforts are being made to wrap up the Washington negotiations. European attention is already moving ahead to the upcoming international conferences in Cannes and Genoa.	The *Dail Eireann* has voted 64–57 to ratify Anglo-Irish Treaty of London. Support for the Treaty is led by Arthur Griffith.	The French evacuation of Cilicia continues, as the French evacuate Osmaniye.		Dogsomyn Bodoo, chairman of the Mongolian People's Revolutionary Party, has been removed from power. Party leaders will meet to choose a new successor. Bodoo has been relatively independent minded. The Soviets will exert pressure on the Mongolians to select a more compliant party leader.
Jan. 8	A delegation from the White Russian Pri-Amur government of President Spiridon Morkujoff, located at Vladivostok, has arrived at the Washington Conference, claiming the entire Pacific coast of Siberia from Vladivostok to the Arctic and demanding that the Japanese withdraw from Siberia.	Polish General Zeligowski, who has established a "Republic of Central Lithuania" with its capital at Vilna (Vilnius), has held a plebiscite. He claims that a majority of the people of Central Lithuania have voted to remain part of Poland. The Vilna Diet has voted to join Poland. The Lithuanian government has denounced the plebiscite as fraudulent and has broken off trade with Poland....The Socialist Youth League is formed in Norway.			The Madras police are reported to be threatening a general strike during the Prince of Wales' upcoming visit unless they receive substantial wage increases....Rioting has been reported in Raynpur, Bengal....The remnants of the rebels in Malabar are reported to be gradually surrendering as fighting dies down in the region.
Jan. 9		Peace treaty opponent Éamon de Valera loses his bid to be reelected as President of the Irish Republic.... The metal workers strike in Rotterdam has ended.			
Jan. 10	The terms of a 10-year Franco-British defensive alliance treaty negotiated at the Cannes Conference were placed before the British cabinet today....The League of Nations opens its 16th Session in Geneva, Switzerland, today.	Arthur Griffith, leader of the delegation that negotiated the Anglo-Irish peace treaty, has been elected President of the Irish *Dail* and head of a new provisional government in Ireland, which will hold power until parliamentary elections are held.... Outgoing President Éamon de Valera and his militant Republican followers walk out in protest.	A strike paralyzes the gold mines in the South African Rand....At the Cannes Conference, the French have agreed to revise their recent settlement with Mustafa Kemal and postpone their evacuation of Cilicia on the southern coast of Anatolia.		
Jan. 11	At Cannes, German Foreign Minister Rathenau announced that the most Germany can pay in reparations is 520 million gold marks. The Allies want 1.75 billion.				
Jan. 12		Premier Aristide Briand has resigned in France....Extreme right wing agitator Adolph Hitler, leader of the National Socialist German Workers' Party, better known as the Nazis, is convicted in Munich for instigating mob violence by his Storm Troopers. He receives a 3-month sentence.			
Jan. 13	The Cannes Conference adjourns, with the Allies agreeing to postpone German reparation payments for the time being.	The British have begun withdrawing their police auxiliaries, the widely hated "Black and Tans," from Dublin....Soviet leader Vladimir I. Lenin announced a reorganization of the Russian cabinet today. Leon Trotsky will be Commissar for War, Joseph Stalin will be Commissar for National Minorities.	The French evacuation of Cilicia is completed, with the French pulling out of Dörtyl into Syria.		Edward, Prince of Wales, has arrived in Madras, India, on a good will visit. Indian nationalists have declared a *hartal*, a general strike, to protest the Prince's arrival....The American Relief Administration has reported that efforts to alleviate the famine in the former Tartar Republic, centered on Kazan in Russia, are breaking down due to a lack of horses and fodder to transport food from the railheads.
Jan. 14	News that reparations are being postponed caused the German mark to recover somewhat, back up to 179 to the dollar from 189.			Guatemala breaks away from the nascent Central American Federation proclaimed last year.... Sugar growers in Jamaica have asked the British government for protective tariffs in the face of competition from Cuba's burgeoning sugar industry....President Obregon of Mexico denounces a recent court ruling in New York that the Mexican government cannot sue in New York courts because it is not recognized by the United States.	The Chinese and Japanese delegations at the Washington Conference reached an agreement on the return of the former German concession at Kiaochow (Jiaozhou) to China....The Chinese also denounce the Twenty One Demands imposed by Japan on China in 1915....Rioting breaks out in Madras, India, on the arrival of the Prince of Wales. This is strongly condemned by Indian nationalist Mohandas Gandhi, who insists upon nonviolent civil disobedience.

A	B	C	D	E
Includes developments that affect more than one world region, international organizations and important meetings of world leaders.	*Includes all domestic and regional developments in Europe, including the Soviet Union.*	*Includes all domestic and regional developments in Africa and the Middle East.*	*Includes all domestic and regional developments in Latin America, the Caribbean, and Canada.*	*Includes all domestic and regional developments in Asian and Pacific nations (and colonies).*

U.S. Politics & Social Issues	U.S. Foreign Policy & Affairs, Defense	U.S. Economy & Environment	Science, Technology & Nature	Culture, Leisure & Lifestyle	
		The American Steamship Owners Association has announced 15–33 percent wage cuts for seamen on ocean going vessels....The United States has broken its all time weekly record for crude oil production, at 1,413, 450 barrels.		The National Automobile Show opens today at Grand Central Palace in New York City. Ninety two makes are on display, ranging in price from the $525 Chevrolet four-door sedan to $11,000.	Jan. 7
Charles R. Young, the first African American to reach the rank of colonel in the U.S. Army, and current United States military attaché to Liberia, has died of a kidney infection while on a reconnaissance mission in Nigeria.	The Federal Council of Churches in Washington, DC called on the United States today to continue to take an active role in international affairs.	A campaign has been started by AAA and other automobile owner's associations to construct a transcontinental highway route suitable for cars, to run from Washington, DC to San Diego.		Eight bootleg liquor stills explode in fires in Brooklyn, injuring five firemen.	Jan. 8
				KQV-AM begins transmissions in Pittsburgh....American expatriate writer Ernest Hemingway makes Paris his home, moving into an apartment on the Rue du Cardinal Lemoine.	Jan. 9
In Washington, DC, President Warren G. Harding has informed the Southern Tariff Association that the proposed Fordney Tariff will provide protection for Southern agricultural interests as well as northern businesses.		Business leaders in 35 states have combined to form the Committee of American Businessmen. It's declared mission to "educate" the public on the need for "sound" taxation of businesses.	*Blitzfunk*, a high-speed wireless messenger service, is opened between Berlin and Hamburg....The Interstate Commerce Commission requires major railways in the United States to begin installing automatic stop or speed controls.		Jan. 10
			A team of researchers at the University of Toronto, Canada, begin treating Leonard Thompson, 14, for diabetes using the newly discovered hormone, known as isletin (mod. insulin).	Ten people have died in the last four days from alcohol poisoning in Hoboken, NJ. The bad hooch is traced to a South American steamship calling in New Jersey.	Jan. 11
					Jan. 12
		The Federal Reserve has reported that the United States imported $691 million in gold in 1921, up from $417 million in 1920. $316 million of the total comes from Europe.		Gene Tunney beats Battling Levinsky in Madison Square Garden in New York, capturing the light-heavyweight title....Buck Weaver, one of the infamous "Black Sox" of the rigged 1919 World Series, applies for reinstatement in the Major Leagues. He is rejected....WHA-AM begins radio transmissions in Madison, WI....An influenza epidemic in Great Britain has claimed the lives of 804 people.	Jan. 13
President Warren G. Harding has issued an appeal to the governors of the states to raise money for a National Victory Memorial Building in Washington, DC, to commemorate American participation in the World War.		Nash Motors announced a $2.2 million profit for fiscal year 1921....Piggly Wiggly Stores, Inc., report profits of $282,000 for the last quarter of 1921.		The National Auto Show closed today in New York City with record crowds. The most popular items are electronic accessories: electric signaling devices and car heaters, which are gaining in popularity.	Jan. 14

F	G	H	I	J
Includes campaigns, elections, federal-state relations, civil rights and liberties, crime, the judiciary, education, healthcare, poverty, urban affairs, and population.	*Includes formation and debate of U.S. foreign and defense policies, veterans affairs, and defense spending. (Relations with specific foreign countries are usually found under the region concerned.)*	*Includes business, labor, agriculture, taxation, transportation, consumer affairs, monetary and fiscal policy, natural resources, pollution and industrial accidents.*	*Includes worldwide scientific, medical and technological developments, natural phenomena, U.S. weather and natural disasters.*	*Includes the arts, religion, scholarship, communications media, sports, entertainment, fashions, fads, and social life.*

	World Affairs	Europe	Africa & The Middle East	The Americas	Asia & The Pacific
Jan. 15		President Arthur Griffith has appointed Michael Collins Chairman of the Irish Provisional government....Raymond Poincaré has succeeded Aristide Briand as Premier of France. Poincaré promises a tougher line on extracting reparations from Germany.			$83,000 were raised at a luncheon in New York as part of an effort to obtain matching funds for a $1 million grant by John D. Rockefeller to endow six women's Christian colleges in India, China, and Japan.... Moderate Sir Sankaran Nair has walked out of the Indian Leadership Conference in Bombay, reflecting deep divisions within the Indian nationalist movement. Gandhi agrees to postpone civil disobedience actions, for now.
Jan. 16		Michael Collins and the Irish Provisional government formally took charge in Ireland today, with out-going British Lord Lieutenant Viscount FitzAlan handing over power at Dublin Castle....The 60,000 British troops remaining in Ireland will begin evacuating in the next few days.			Mohandas Gandhi, leader of the Non-Cooperation Movement, seeking independence for India, met today with a convention of moderate Indian parties in Bombay, and reached an agreement to call for a roundtable conference with British authorities January 31.
Jan. 17	The Washington Conference today voted to approve U.S. Secretary of State Charles Evans Hughes' proposal guaranteeing all nations an "open door" to trade in China.... Japan, Britain, and France combined to block a further proposal to review existing obligations imposed on China.	France is formally invited by the Italian Ambassador to attend the upcoming Genoa Conference on the world economy in March.			A decree by President Millerand of France extending the privileges granted to the Bank of Indochina is made public today. Rumors fly that outgoing Finance Minister Paul Doumer is improperly favoring the Bank over its rival, the Industrial Bank of China.
Jan. 18	In Washington, Secretary of Agriculture Wallace received a report that Europe will continue to require large imports of American grain. Germany alone will need two million tons. Normal grain producing countries cannot make up the lack. Poland, for example, is still recovering from war with Russia and Hungary, and Romania suffers from inefficiency and lack of rail transport.	It was announced that Britain will provide a loan of one million pounds sterling to Ireland to enable its government to begin operating....In Dublin, Michael Collins, head of the new Irish Provisional government, formed a cabinet today with himself as Minister of Finance....Owen O'Duffy succeeds Richard Mulcahy as Chief of Staff of the newly legalized Irish Republican Army. Mulcahy will become Minister of Defense.			The Japanese delegation at the Washington Conference today denied rumors circulating that Japan intends to evacuate Siberia soon. The Japanese insist that Japan will not withdraw without guarantees against Soviet aggression in Korea.
Jan. 19	U.S. Secretary of State Charles Evans Hughes continued to press today at the Washington Conference for a review of commitments imposed upon China by foreign powers. Of particular concern are secret commitments imposed by Japan under the Twenty One Demands of 1915.	Ion I.C. Bratianu has become the new Prime Minister of Romania, succeeding Conservative Democratic Party leader Take Ionescu. Bratianu's National Liberal Party (PNL) seeks a moderate land reform program to limit peasant dissent.			The British release Indian nationalist and renowned scholar Babu Bhagwandas. This is part of a plan by the British to defuse tensions in India, where demands for self-government are growing.
Jan. 20	Japan flatly rejects an American proposal at the Washington Conference to review existing commitments imposed on China.	Pope Benedict XV, now aging and very sick, summons Cardinal Gasparri, Papal Secretary of State, and presents him with his last will and testament. They confer privately.	Mirza Hassan Khan Pirnia has succeeded Shaw as-Saltana as the new Prime Minister of Persia.		The Washington Conference called on China today to reduce the size of provincial armies in the countryside. These armies, effectively under provincial warlords, currently have some 500,000 men under arms and drain off half the country's revenue.
Jan. 21	Delegates at the Washington conference agree to a compromise today under which all treaties made or current with China will be made public.	In the early morning hours, Vatican officials announced that Pope Benedict XV has pneumonia, and was not expected to live. Last rites have been administered. Cardinal Gasparri, Papal Secretary of State, has summoned all Cardinals to Rome....French Premier Raymond Poincaré has appointed Marshal Philippe Petain to be the new inspector general of the French army. The move is widely denounced by Radical and Socialist deputies as militaristic.			
	A *Includes developments that affect more than one world region, international organizations and important meetings of world leaders.*	B *Includes all domestic and regional developments in Europe, including the Soviet Union.*	C *Includes all domestic and regional developments in Africa and the Middle East.*	D *Includes all domestic and regional developments in Latin America, the Caribbean, and Canada.*	E *Includes all domestic and regional developments in Asian and Pacific nations (and colonies).*

U.S. Politics & Social Issues	U.S. Foreign Policy & Affairs, Defense	U.S. Economy & Environment	Science, Technology & Nature	Culture, Leisure & Lifestyle	
First Lady, Mrs. Warren Harding, issues an appeal to the League of Women Voters to throw its support solidly behind the Republican Party for its efforts in achieving women's suffrage.			The New York City Board of Health reports that deaths from alcoholism have dropped in 1921, to 86 from 176 in 1919, the last year before Prohibition. Sixteen of these are from wood alcohol poisoning, down from 54 in 1919....Dr. John Kirk, Scottish botanist and African explorer with David Livingstone, has died. He was 89.	Federal Prohibition Director Ralph A. Day has reported that federal agents are turning up thousands of counterfeit and forged medical prescriptions for liquor. Pads of 100 apiece are selling for $25–50, or $1 to $2 per individual prescription.	Jan. 15
The New York Branch of the National Women's Party will introduce a bill in the New York State Legislature giving women full legal equality with men and outlawing discrimination on the basis of sex. A similar federal constitutional amendment is also discussed.		A United States District Court judge in New York today put the E.D. Dier & Co. brokerage firm in receivership. The firm has failed with excess liabilities approaching $4 million....Communications giant AT&T has announced plans to begin radio broadcasting.		Nicholas Murray Butler, President of Columbia University, today denounced proposals to create a U.S. Department of Education, arguing that they would create waste and bureaucracy.	Jan. 16
	The steamer *Western Maid* sails from Baltimore for Reval, with 7,000 tons of grain for famine relief in Russia....The United States is formally invited to participate in the upcoming Genoa Conference in March.				Jan. 17
	A battalion of American troops parades through the streets before the king and Prime Minister Bonomi in Rome today as the United States presents the Congressional Medal at a monument to Italy's Unknown Soldier.			A. Lawrence Lowell, President of Harvard University, today questioned the value of college football, calling it a "rough and strenuous sport," and one that "has tended to give excessive importance to college athletic contests."	Jan. 18
The American Civil Liberties Union formally appealed to Attorney General Daugherty, calling for the release of Eugene V. Debs and 117 others imprisoned under sedition laws in "wartime hysteria" during World War I.	Republican Senators met in caucus today and struck down all proposals to limit interest rates on the European World War debt.	The Republican Senate caucus reported that discussion of the pending tariff bill remains bogged down.	Success is achieved in the hunt for a cure for diabetes, when Leonard Thompson begins to recover after a second injection of insulin by researchers at the University of Toronto. Diabetics worldwide now have a chance to live....The United States Geological Survey warns that the United States only has enough oil for another 20 years and will eventually have to begin importing oil. It cautions strongly against wasting oil reserves.	Mayor Thompson of Chicago announced that he would institute plans to "clean up" the city, rooting out graft, crime, and corruption regardless of political connections.	Jan. 19
				Police in New York City are accused of police brutality. Reports of such brutality are on the rise....New York Police Commissioner Richard E. Enright denounces such allegations as "pure rot", claiming that they merely "give alibis to the vicious."....Arthur Honegger's ballet, *Skating Rink,* premieres in Paris.	Jan. 20
The United Mine Workers, representing some 43,000 workers in the central Pennsylvania coal mines, call on President Harding for economic relief, citing cases where miners have been reduced to a 1–3 day workweek....Steel production is up in January, averaging 20 million tons a year, versus just 11 million tons in July 1921. Total steel production capacity is up to 52.5 million tons per year, double the capacity existing in 1910.		The Association of Railway Executives meets in Chicago, they discuss plans to reduce railroad workers' wages by 10 percent. The plan has been discussed with Commerce Secretary Herbert Hoover last week. Union representatives have announced that they will oppose the cuts in talks set for February 15.		The first slalom ski race is held in Mürren, Switzerland.	Jan. 21
F *Includes campaigns, elections, federal-state relations, civil rights and liberties, crime, the judiciary, education, healthcare, poverty, urban affairs, and population.*	G *Includes formation and debate of U.S. foreign and defense policies, veterans affairs, and defense spending. (Relations with specific foreign countries are usually found under the region concerned.)*	H *Includes business, labor, agriculture, taxation, transportation, consumer affairs, monetary and fiscal policy, natural resources, pollution and industrial accidents.*	I *Includes worldwide scientific, medical and technological developments, natural phenomena, U.S. weather and natural disasters.*	J *Includes the arts, religion, scholarship, communications media, sports, entertainment, fashions, fads, and social life.*	

	World Affairs	Europe	Africa & The Middle East	The Americas	Asia & The Pacific
Jan. 22		In Rome, Pope Benedict XV died in the early morning hours today, from pneumonia. Considered a liberal pope, the Church is divided over who his successor will be. Papal Secretary of State Cardinal Gasparri will assemble the college of cardinals in 10 days....The Darmstader National Bank has called the recent stock market boom in Germany to be "a sham prosperity" due solely to the current weakness of the German mark.		Giovanni Bonzano, Apostolic Delegate in Washington, DC, has formally summoned all American Cardinals to Rome for the upcoming papal conclave.	
Jan. 23		Preparations for the papal conclave are under way in the Vatican. The Italian Cardinals and the Jesuits are said to favor electing a pope who will be friendly to Germany and the former Central Powers. The French Cardinals, backed by the Polish and Belgian Cardinals, want the new pope to continue avoiding direct relations with Italy.			Baron Shidehara, Japanese envoy at the Washington Conference, has announced that Japan will "respect Russia's territorial integrity" in Siberia. Though it has not set a formal date for evacuating Siberia, the implication is that talks between the Japanese and the Soviet Far Eastern Republic going on in Dairen (Dalian), China, are bearing fruit, and the White Russian Pri-Amur government, centered on Vladivostok, will be abandoned.
Jan. 24		Anti-Bolshevik Karelians have retaken Kilmast-Jaervi in East Karelia, pushing Red Army forces back. The Soviets are rushing troops to the area from other parts of Russia as White volunteers move over the border from Finland....Fighting has been reported at Terijoki and on the Finnish Gulf. The Finnish border station near Kymmene has been shelled, and Soviet planes have probed Finnish air space.	The 24,000 union workers in the South African Industrial Federation have joined the coal miners in their strike in South Africa. South African Prime Minister Jan Christian Smuts is under growing pressure from the National party, who seek to cut ties with the British Commonwealth and who are in contact with the striking miners.		Japan has stalled negotiations at the Washington Conference on the disposition of Shantung (Shandong) Province. The Japanese insist on protection for the 30,000 Japanese workers living in the province.
Jan. 25		Soviet representatives have arrived in Berlin, seeking German assistance for relief efforts. Russia offers raw materials in exchange for help. The Soviets also seek to work through Germany to secure an American loan for Russia.			Yan Huiqing regains his position as Prime Minister of China, succeeding Liang Shiyi.
Jan. 26	At the Washington Conference, progress has been made in resolving the question of fortifications in the Pacific islands. It was agreed that the United states would not further fortify the Philippines or Guam. The Japanese would do the same with Formosa (Taiwan) and the Bonins. The British islands to be included in the building freeze are to be decided.	Walter Breisky succeeds Johann Schober as Austrian Chancellor.	Rioting breaks out in the streets of Cairo in protest against British to establish a Mandate in Palestine under the League of Nations, killing 190 people....The legislative council of Southern Rhodesia has voted to accept a draft constitution. Under the terms of the new constitution, Southern Rhodesia will have limited self-government.		The United States commerce Department warned today that Shanghai produce and bullion exchanges are collapsing. These exchanges have been valued at $100 million in invested capital. A benefit to this will be a revival of Chinese banks as investors seek a safe haven for their money.
Jan. 27	The United States announced that it would not participate in the upcoming world economic conference in Genoa.	The announcement that the United States would not participate in the Genoa conference caused dismay in Germany today. Chancellor Wirth beat down a no-confidence motion by the Communists....Johann Schober resumes his post as Austrian Chancellor, as Austria struggles to form a stable government.			

A	B	C	D	E
Includes developments that affect more than one world region, international organizations and important meetings of world leaders.	*Includes all domestic and regional developments in Europe, including the Soviet Union.*	*Includes all domestic and regional developments in Africa and the Middle East.*	*Includes all domestic and regional developments in Latin America, the Caribbean, and Canada.*	*Includes all domestic and regional developments in Asian and Pacific nations (and colonies).*

U.S. Politics & Social Issues	U.S. Foreign Policy & Affairs, Defense	U.S. Economy & Environment	Science, Technology & Nature	Culture, Leisure & Lifestyle	
The National Child Labor Committee reports that 1.5 million children aged 10–15 are employed in farm work, with inadequate pay, schooling, sanitation, or worker protection. Children as young as 10 or 11 are found to be laboring 10 hours a day in fields for wages averaging a dollar a day....America's total farm population stands now at 38 million, with eight million adult farmers.		President Warren G. Harding opened the National Agriculture Conference in Washington, DC, to discuss the plight of American farmers, reeling from the collapse of farm prices since the end of World War I....The commuter suburb of South Orange, NJ, is in the midst of a building boom, with nearly $3.5 million being spent on new construction in 1921, up more than $1.5 million since 1920....Winton Motor Cars announces price cuts on its six cylinder touring cars, down to $3,400 from $4,600.	Noted French mathematician Camille Jordan has died today. Jordan was known for his pioneering work in group theory.	Chicago's opera company will post a loss of some $800,000 this season. Extravagant spending on productions without adequate monitoring of costs is blamed...."Scantily clad professional dancers" have become commonplace in New York night clubs, with "revelry" going on until 5 or 6 A.M....Reverend Dr. John Roach Stratton denounces Broadway as "captured by greed and commercialism."....Czech writer Franz Kafka begins work on his novel, *The Castle*.	Jan. 22
		The Shipping Board has announced 15–25 percent wage cuts for seamen, effective February 6.	A team of researchers at the University of Toronto, Canada, continues treating Leonard Thompson, 14, for diabetes using a newly discovered hormone, insulin.	Poet Amy Lowell gives a reading of her poetry at the McDowell Club in New York City....The Hotel Plaza in New York now has weekly fashion shows. The war is on between "mannish" trouser suits and more traditionally "feminine" attire....National skating championships begin at Plattsburg, NY, on Lake Champlain today.	Jan. 23
Pittsburgh Director of Public Safety, George W. McCandless, has ordered all police officers above the rank of patrolman to withdraw from the Fraternal Order of Police. A similar order is issued to firemen to leave the Firemen's Protective Association.		Benjamin Schlesinger, President of the International Ladies Garment Workers Union, appealed today to Secretary of Labor Davis and Commerce secretary Herbert Hoover for a nationwide investigation of garment industry profiteering....Railroad workers have rejected new rules approved by the United States Railroad Labor Board, eliminating time-and-a-half pay for overtime work.	The United States government establishes Lehman Caves National Monument in Utah (now part of Great Basin National Park).	Christian K. Nelson of Onawa, IA, has patented a new dessert treat, the Eskimo Pie....The United States Lawn Tennis Association has announced its opposition to exhibition matches in which money is charged for admission....Actress Peggy Wood stars in the title role in the Broadway musical *Marjolaine* opening tonight in New York.	Jan. 24
		Anthracite coal mine operators in Pennsylvania report that meeting coal miners demands for wage increases would raise the price of coal by $1.30 a ton, and that this cost would be borne by consumers.	Robbers in New York City are reported to now be using silencers on pistols.	The Kélékian Collection is on display at the American Art Galleries. Featured are the works of Spanish artist Pablo Picasso, Gauguin, and other Post-Impressionists....The work of Japanese artist Kyohei Inukai is on display at the Arlington Galleries.	Jan. 25
		The National Agricultural Conference adjourned today, rejecting calls for guaranteed minimum prices for farm products. It calls upon the United States government to work to reestablish "parity," whereby farm prices would have an equal exchange value with other products. Prices for farm products have fallen drastically since the end of World War I.		Ralph Vaughan Williams' mystical *Pastoral Symphony* (Symphony No. 3) premieres in London.	Jan. 26
President Warren G. Harding issued an appeal to Federal departments, calling on them to speed up any repair or construction projects they have pending to provide relief for unemployment.		A massive snowstorm blankets the Eastern Seaboard, hitting South Carolina and moving north....Bethlehem Steel reports earnings of $8 million in 1921, although plants are still running at just 30 percent capacity. Bethlehem Steel's Eugene G. Grace warns that production would stay down until workers' wages are cut.		Death of Elizabeth Cochrane Seamon, better known as Nelly Bly, pioneer investigative reporter, at age 54 is reported.	Jan. 27

	World Affairs	Europe	Africa & The Middle East	The Americas	Asia & The Pacific
Jan. 28	In a note to the Allied Reparations Commission, Germany has announced its inability to meet scheduled January and February reparations payments, and asks for a suspension of its 1922 reparations. It further requests that the percentage of payments to be made in kind as opposed to gold, be increased. Germany has cited the danger of capital flight and tax evasion due to increased taxation to pay the debt.		The crisis in South Africa's mines has worsened drastically as South African leaders, under pressure from the powerful Central Mining and Investment Corporation, force a confrontation with striking miners. The government has announced plans to increase the ratio of lower paid Black African workers versus higher paid Whites. Outraged striking miners are backed by South Africa's Nationalist and Labour Parties.		
Jan. 29		Despite high inflation rates, the *Frankfurter Zeitung* reports that German workers' wages have improved since 1913.	The British have announced that they are prepared to revoke their protectorate over Egypt and recognize it as a sovereign state on three conditions: protection of Imperial communications (the Suez Canal), protection of foreigners and religious minorities in Egypt, and that Egypt be safeguarded from foreign incursion.	The revolution that occurred in Guatemala on December 8, 1921, has caused the collapse of the nascent Federation of Central America, established last year between Guatemala, El Salvador, and Honduras.	The American market for raw silk has fallen off, as prices plummet in Japan. Buyers are waiting for newer, lower prices.
Jan. 30	The Permanent World Court began assembling at the Carnegie Peace Palace in the Hague to prepare for formal sessions to begin in February....The first celebration of World Law Day occurs.	The *London Economist* reports the cost of living has increased, with prices of staple commodities in Britain up from 14 percent to as much as 250 percent....The French government is dismissing 50,000 women government employees to cut expenses....Michael Collins begins chairing meetings to draft a constitution for the Irish Free State....Republican opponents of the Treaty of London with Great Britain have been elected in municipal elections in Dublin, Cork, Limerick, and other Irish cities.			
Jan. 31		Walter Rathenau is appointed German foreign minister. A Jewish industrialist, Rathenau favors reaching an accord with the Allies and agreeing to pay at least some of the reparations for World War I. He is bitterly hated by the militant nationalist German right wing.		The Panama Railroad has posted a net loss of $617,000 in the first half of 1921.	The British release more Indian nationalist leaders from prison in an effort to reduce the Indian agitation for self-government.
Feb. 1	Delegates at the Washington Conference have reached an agreement on plans to limit submarine warfare and outlaw the use of poison gas.	The British army has begun handing military installations over to the Irish government as part of the Anglo-Irish Peace Treaty. Today, the British garrison handed over Beggar's Bush Barracks in Dublin....Irish militants fired on a Royal Irish Constabulary convoy at Barnes Gap near Donegal....The Italian, French, and Spanish governments, which have each claimed the unofficial veto power over a pope as the leading Catholic power in Europe, have now quietly informed the Vatican that they will not interfere in the selection of a new pope....Famine has reached such an extent in Russia that cannibalism has been reported in the Orenberg district.	Turkish troops move into Kurdistan. Turkey claims Mosul, which has been allotted to the British mandate in Iraq. Mosul is of special importance as it is a center for oil production....In this month, an emissary from the Emir of Afghanistan has arrived in Ankara, opening negotiations with the Turkish Nationalist government of Mustafa Kemal. The Emir offers friendship and seeks an understanding with the Nationalists, who are also threatened by Britain....In this month British troops move against the rebellious Dinka people of southern Sudan. The Dinka have been in rebellion since 1921, led by Bul Yol, who has taken the name of the Prophet Ariendit.	In this month, the United states has finally completed its evacuation of Cuba, where American troops have been present since 1919. Two companies of infantry are withdrawn from their base at Camaguey.	During the Washington Conference, the British announce that they will return the port of Wei-hai-wei (Weihai) in Shandong Province to China in eight years....Field Marshal Yamagata Aritomo, President of the Privy Council since the Russo-Japanese War, has died in Japan. Yamagata, a former prime minister, though officially retired from the government, has in fact been *genro*, elder statesman of Japan, controlling the selection of prime ministers, for many years. Long wary of Russia, he has sought to prevent a recovery of Russian power in the Far East....Indian nationalist leader Mohandas Gandhi has written a letter to the British Viceroy in Delhi, warning him of mass civil disobedience unless the British unequivocally recognize Indian rights to free speech and assembly.

A	B	C	D	E
Includes developments that affect more than one world region, international organizations and important meetings of world leaders.	*Includes all domestic and regional developments in Europe, including the Soviet Union.*	*Includes all domestic and regional developments in Africa and the Middle East.*	*Includes all domestic and regional developments in Latin America, the Caribbean, and Canada.*	*Includes all domestic and regional developments in Asian and Pacific nations (and colonies).*

U.S. Politics & Social Issues	U.S. Foreign Policy & Affairs, Defense	U.S. Economy & Environment	Science, Technology & Nature	Culture, Leisure & Lifestyle	
Frank O. Owen, former Governor of Illinois, commemorates McKinley Day in Niles, OH, by warning against federal aid to states and municipalities. He condemns federal aid as undermining the power of state and local authorities....Republicans have dropped 150 agents from Prohibition enforcement units in New York City, resulting in hundreds of Prohibition cases being thrown out for lack of witnesses.		Snow blankets Washington, DC, Baltimore, and Philadelphia as the blizzard moves up the East Coast into New Jersey and Delaware. Drifts up to 16 feet in height cover the rails between Philadelphia and Washington. By 6:00 p.m., the Pennsylvania Railroad is blocked south of Philadelphia. Baltimore is hit with a record 16.5 inches of snow. Ninety-eight people have been killed, and 133 injured, as snow from the blizzard causes the flat roof of the Knickerbocker Theater in Washington, DC, to collapse.	The National Automobile Chamber of Commerce reports that in 1921, for the first time, sales of closed cars have surpassed sales of open automobiles....Meteorologist James H. Scarr announces that 1921 was the hottest, driest year for both the United States and the world, since records have been kept. New York's average temperature in 1921: 54.7 degrees, up from the 50 year average of 52 degrees.	The American Pro Football Association has a new name: The National Football League.... Nine University of Illinois athletes have been disqualified from collegiate athletics for taking part a game between rival Illinois towns, Carlinville and Taylorville. Carlinville hired the "ringers" and put them on their town's football team, then betting $50,000 against Taylorville. However, Taylorville residents learned of the scheme, hired ringers of their own from Notre Dame, and beat Carlinville, winning $50,000 in bets in the process....The Green Bay Packers regain their NFL franchise after financial difficulties.	Jan. 28
Miss Alice Fitzgerald, Director of the Department of Nursing of the League of Red Cross Societies, has returned to the United States to study recent progress in the field of nursing in the United States.	Commerce Secretary Herbert Hoover has described Germany's continued payment of its reparations obligations as "vital," but has called on European nations to resolve the reparations question in a manner that will "secure permanent economic and political stability to Germany."	The blizzard finally abates on the East Coast. In Washington, DC, 28 inches of snow have fallen in the last three days.	The feature of the fourth annual Own Your Home Exposition, due to open in April at the 69th Regiment Armory in New York, will be: The Beautiful Home Convenient—a model home equipped with all the latest gas and electric household appliances (for example, incinerators, dryers, gas lighting fixtures, radiators and water heaters).	On New York's Fifth Avenue, the Spring hats are here! *The* fashion this year: hats that set directly over the eyes, allowing the wearer to reveal a glance, or not, as she pleases....*Fortunes Made in Ten Minutes*, a compilation of advertisements for get-rich quick schemes of all sorts has been published.	Jan. 29
			Dr. James A. Hamilton, Commissioner of New York's Department of Corrections, has called for the institution of universal fingerprinting to reduce drug addiction, a growing problem.	Dr. Percy Grant of New York's Episcopal Church of the Ascension has denounced jazz as a retrogression to the "African jungle." Among the evils it encourages are "drunkenness, sex abandonment, domestic destruction, and suicide."	Jan. 30
An alliance of German-American citizens in New York has objected to courts asking whether applicants for American citizenship have purchased Liberty Bonds.			Tremors shake California, Oregon, and Washington as the most powerful earthquake recorded since the San Francisco earthquake of 1906 hits the west coast today. The epicenter of the quake is 300 miles southwest of the Columbia River, in the Pacific off the Oregon coast.	Temperatures in Vermont finally rise above zero today for the first time in eight days. The coldest temperature recorded in this period was 30 degrees below zero.	Jan. 31
Sixteen railway unions have met in Chicago and have proclaimed the establishment of the Conference for Progressive Political Action. The Conference has been proclaimed to assemble support for progressive, pro-union candidates in the face of the Harding administration's hostility to organized labor....The first woman prohibition agent has been appointed. She will operate in Harding's home state of Ohio.	William McAdoo, Director General of the Railroads during World War I, defends the U.S. government's decision to seize the railways during the War today before a Senate Committee. He claims that national control was vital to the war effort.	Commercial radio is becoming big business in this month as more than two dozen licenses are granted to radio stations across the country.... Dodge Brothers Motors has reduced prices on its roadster model to $945.	In this month, a young student drops out of college to become a flight student at the Nebraska Standard Aircraft Corporation. His name is Charles Lindbergh.... Nicholas Murray Butler, President of Columbia University, has written a letter to the president of the University of Kentucky, condemning the Kentucky state legislature's proposed bill to outlaw the teaching of evolution in Kentucky public schools. Butler compares the measure to Communist censorship.... Ships arriving in San Francisco have reported the powerful earthquake in the waters off Trinidad Head in California that occurred at the end of January.	In this month, American expatriate writer Ernest Hemingway meets rising British poet Ezra Pound in a Paris bookstore....Opening tonight in New York are the plays *Needles and Pins* and the *Chauve Souris* revue....A.H. Woods, whose shocking play, *The Demi-Virgin*, has raised talk of censorship of plays and films, has come out in favor of some form of state regulation, preferring that to allowing juries to decide morality issues after a play has already been produced and performed....Roscoe "Fatty" Arbuckle's trial for causing the death of Virginia Rappe, has gone to the jury in San Francisco, with the defense declining to make a final argument.	Feb. 1

	World Affairs	Europe	Africa & The Middle East	The Americas	Asia & The Pacific
Feb. 2		The College of Cardinals has assembled in the Sistine Chapel to select a successor to Pope Benedict XV. The 53 Cardinals of the Papal Conclave will meet in secret, and be kept sequestered until a successor is announced.	Sarkis S. Ambartsumyan has succeeded Aleksandr F. Miasnikyan as chairman of the Communist Party in the Armenian SSR.		
Feb. 3	France has unofficially warned Germany that any attempt by the exiled Hohenzollern crown prince to return to Germany from the Netherlands will result in him being tried as a war criminal....The Soviets are instructing their delegation to the upcoming economic conference in Genoa to make major concessions to secure a loan for Russia. Russia is crippled by a major famine, and is seeking to hold on until harvesting begins in July.	Negotiations between the Provisional Irish government of Michael Collins and the British have broken down over the issue of defining the border between Northern Ireland and the Catholic South. The Protestant North is bitterly opposed to union with Ireland....Black smoke coming from the Vatican chimneys have signaled the failure of the papal conclave to select a pope on the first two ballots. Moderate and conservative factions within the conclave are rumored to be deadlocked....250,000 workers are now on strike in Germany.		The Commerce Department reported generally improved economic conditions across Latin America, with troubled Mexico still stagnant economically.	
Feb. 4				El Salvador has repudiated its membership in the abortive Central American Federation attempted last year. Differences between the Central American countries remain too strong.	At the Washington Conference, the Japanese government announce that they will withdraw their troops from Shantung (Shandong) Province. Under growing international pressure and faced by Chinese consumer boycotts, the Japanese have agreed to restore all the commercial holdings in the province taken from the Germans during World War I to the Chinese, including the port of Tsingdao (Qingdao) and the railway to Jinan.
Feb. 5		Dr. Hainisch, President of Austria, has appealed directly to King George V of Great Britain for a loan of £2.5 million to stabilize Austria's finances.	Prime Minister Smuts has reached an agreement with one of the unions in the ongoing mine strike in South Africa. Remaining unions are growing increasingly militant, calling for a general strike against the government.	After a number of clashes with civilians, the Nicaraguan Congress has received a petition calling for the withdrawal of American marines stationed at Campo Marte, outside of Managua.	
Feb. 6	The Five Power Naval Disarmament Treaty is signed at the Washington Conference today. Representatives of Great Britain, the United States, France, Italy, and Japan, have agreed to a 10-year moratorium on the construction of battleships and battle cruisers. They have also agreed on tonnage ratio for capital ships: five for Britain and the United States, three for Japan, and 1.67 for France and Italy. This is a defeat for Japan, as the Japanese have wanted a 10:7 ratio.	The College of Cardinals has elected a new pope, Cardinal Achille Ratti, Archbishop of Milan, 64, on the 14th ballot, after the longest conclave in many years. He will assume office as Pope Pius XI. Pius XI has given an indication of the more open and active direction his papacy will take. His first act as Pope is to break the tradition, maintained since the Italians overran the Papal State in 1870, that the Pope is a "prisoner" in the Vatican. The new pope walked out onto a balcony over St. Peter's Square and gave his blessing "urbi et orbi," to the city and the world, for the first time in the 20th century.			A Nine-Power Treaty has been reached at the Washington Conference between China, the United States, Great Britain, France, Italy, Japan, Portugal, Belgium, and the Netherlands guaranteeing the independence and territorial integrity of China. The Signatories further agree to the principle of an Open Door, whereby all nations will have equal access to trade with China. However, the treaty does not have provisions for enforcement....The Anglo-Japanese Alliance of 1902 is allowed to lapse....The Four Power Treaty, signed today in Washington limits the building of fortifications in outlying possessions in the Pacific for 10 years.
Feb. 7		King George V opens Parliament today in Westminster, calling for a final resolution of the Irish conflict by the establishment of the Irish Free State.	Striking South African miners march through the streets of Johannesburg in a show of force. The strike has now been taken over by nationalist Afrikaaner militants, who have organized themselves into "commandoes" reminiscent of the Boer War.	Honduras has seceded from the now defunct Central American Federation.	Faced with growing unrest across India, the British issue an ultimatum to Mohandas Gandhi, demanding that he cease his civil disobedience campaign.

A	B	C	D	E
Includes developments that affect more than one world region, international organizations and important meetings of world leaders.	*Includes all domestic and regional developments in Europe, including the Soviet Union.*	*Includes all domestic and regional developments in Africa and the Middle East.*	*Includes all domestic and regional developments in Latin America, the Caribbean, and Canada.*	*Includes all domestic and regional developments in Asian and Pacific nations (and colonies).*

U.S. Politics & Social Issues	U.S. Foreign Policy & Affairs, Defense	U.S. Economy & Environment	Science, Technology & Nature	Culture, Leisure & Lifestyle	
The Haitian delegate to the International Court of Justice in The Hague has condemned American plans to make a $14 million loan to Haiti, claiming that the measure will benefit American banks and push the impoverished Caribbean nation deeper into debt.		The Amoskeag Mill, employing some 14,000 workers in Manchester, NH, has announced that it is cutting wages by 20 percent. This is the start of a massive strike by mill workers. However, it is clear that the New England textile industry is dying, undercut by cheap labor in Southern mills....Striking workers at a plant in Newport, KY, have protested the deployment of tanks by the Kentucky National Guard during the strike.	Massive rockslides have forced the evacuation of the village of Malnon, in the mountainous Clermont-Ferrand region of France....The French government has announced plans for two beacons with a 100-mile radius each, to be put up outside of Paris and Dijon as an aid to growing night air travel....The Soviet War Minister reviews a newly formed tank brigade in Red Square today.	Rejected by major publishing houses, James Joyce has his groundbreaking stream-of-consciousness novel *Ulysses* published in Paris by fellow American expatriate Sylvia Beach. It is Joyce's 40th birthday. The release is a mere 1,000 copies, but it places Joyce and Sylvia Beach's Shakespeare & Company bookstore in the forefront of the literary *avant garde*.	Feb. 2
				A bootlegger's still blows up in an apartment in New York, leaving 200 homeless....*Manon* premiered at the Metropolitan Opera House in new York City.	Feb. 3
		Ford Motors buys the Lincoln Motor Company for $8 million. Henry Ford's son Edsel, 28, will be named the new president. Ford Motors has been suffering from growing competition in the last few years, from such firms as General Motors, which offer a wider range of cars and styles. The purchase of Lincoln Motors is a sign that Ford now intends to diversify his line as well.			Feb. 4
			Greeks are reclaiming archaeological treasures looted by the Bulgarians during World War I, as part of the peace settlement of Neuilly that ended the hostilities between Bulgaria and the Allies.	DeWitt Wallace & Lila Acheson, working in an office over a speakeasy in Greenwich Village, publish Vol.1, No. 1 of *The Readers Digest*. Bargirls from the speakeasy help address and seal the envelopes. It has 1,500 subscribers....William Larned's steel framed tennis racket has undergone its first test.	Feb. 5
	The Washington Naval Treaty forbids all signatories to build capital ships in excess of 35,000 tons, or arm them with larger than 16 inch guns. Each of the five powers is limited to building no more than two aircraft carriers more than 27,000 tons. This clause allows the U.S. Navy to convert two planned battle cruisers to aircraft carriers. The treaty is intended as a means of controlling the spiraling costs of battleship construction.			Opening tonight on Broadway are *The Blushing Bride* and *Frank Fay's Revue*.	Feb. 6
			In Paris, the French Academy of Science has elected Mdm. Marie Curie to its ranks, for her pioneering work in studying radioactivity.	John Willard's *The Cat and the Canary*, opens tonight on Broadway in New York.	Feb. 7

	World Affairs	Europe	Africa & The Middle East	The Americas	Asia & The Pacific
Feb. 8		Irish Republican Army militants have raided across the border into Protestant controlled Northern Ireland, kidnapping prominent Northern Irish Unionists in County Fermanagh and County Tyrone, with militant forces of the IRA seeking a continued struggle with the British. The British have deployed troops and armored cars along the border with Catholic controlled southern Ireland.		A band of marauders has crosses the border near El Paso, burning railroad bridges and trying to rob the Mexico City Express. Northern Mexico is in the grip of serious unrest. It is rumored that oil companies are fomenting the chaos in order to keep the central government weak.	
Feb. 9		IRA militants have attacked British special police forces in Clady, in County Monaghan, along the border with Northern Ireland.... The government of Prime Minister Ivanoe Bonomi has collapsed in Italy. Bonomi's Reform Socialist Party has been unable to control growing unrest in Italy, as Fascists and Communists vie for power.			The British have suspended the government of the Indian city of Ahmadebad in the face of growing civil disobedience.
Feb. 10		The Treaty Bill, ratifying the 1921 Anglo-Irish Peace Treaty of London, has been introduced before the House of Commons today. The measure will dissolve the Irish Parliament and clear the way for elections by the Irish Free State.... Irish militants have gunned down a British officer attached to the Kildare Barracks.			Under pressure from the British government, and faced by rising violence across India, Indian nationalist leader Mohandas Gandhi halts the civil disobedience campaign. Gandhi's stated goals remain: *swaraj*: self-rule, *swadeshi*: economic self-sufficiency.
Feb. 11		IRA militants have struck at British special police at Clones in County Monaghan, killing four and wounding others. At the insistence of the Protestant government in Northern Ireland, the British withdrawal from Ireland has been temporarily halted.		The United States has begun withdrawing its troops from Honduras.	The United States and Japan have reached an accord on equal access to the cable and radio stations on Yap and other islands in the Japanese Pacific mandates.
Feb. 12		Éamon de Valera and other ultranationalist Irish leaders have formally proclaimed the establishment of the Republican Party. De Valera condemns the peace settlement with Great Britain, wherein Britain will retain nominal sovereignty over the Irish free State as a Dominion, as a betrayal of the Irish people and demands that the war of independence continue until Ireland is granted full independence outside the British Commonwealth.	South African Prime Minister Jan Christian Smuts has called on striking mine workers to return to work, as the confrontation with militant Afrikaaner miners continues....The British have decided to support Greek claims to the Aegean coast of Anatolia. This outrages Turkish Nationalists, led by Mustafa Kemal in Ankara.	General Pedro Nel Ospina is elected President of Colombia in elections today, defeating Liberal candidate Gen. Benjamin Herrera by 350,000 votes to 300,000. Ospina's Conservative Party is backed by the military, police, and the powerful Catholic Church.	Mohandas Gandhi has declared a five-day fast for himself, in penance for the massacre at Chauri Chaura.
Feb. 13	Bulgaria has asked for a three-year delay in the payment of World War I reparations. The Reparations commission has received the request favorably, on the condition that Bulgaria pay 10 million gold francs on what she owes now.	Gun battles continued today in scattered street fighting in Belfast....Irish Provisional Government Chairman Michael Collins has warned that an armed coup by militant nationalists is being planned in an attempt to derail the peace settlement with Britain.		A delegation of Canadian businessmen will visit Jamaica, seeking to promote trade between Jamaica and Canada and capture Jamaican business now done with the United States.	30,000 Indians turned out to greet the Prince of Wales on his visit to Agra today. The gathering was peaceful.
Feb. 14		The League of Nations hosts a second conference between Germany and Poland to discuss the status of the disputed area of Upper Silesia.... Finnish Interior Minister Heikki Ritavuori, 41, has been assassinated in his home in Helsinki. Ritavuori had pardoned Red prisoners from the fighting with the Soviets after World War I.		The Canadian government has distributed 25 million trees over the last five years in the prairie provinces of Manitoba, Sakatchewan, and Alberta, to provide windbreaks for crops and shelter for cattle.	In the early morning hours today, Red Army forces marched into Kabarovsk in the Soviet Far Eastern Republic. Khabarovsk has been evacuated by the Japanese troops who were garrisoning it. Without Japanese support, the White Russian remnants holding out in eastern Siberia are rapidly collapsing.

A	B	C	D	E
Includes developments that affect more than one world region, international organizations and important meetings of world leaders.	*Includes all domestic and regional developments in Europe, including the Soviet Union.*	*Includes all domestic and regional developments in Africa and the Middle East.*	*Includes all domestic and regional developments in Latin America, the Caribbean, and Canada.*	*Includes all domestic and regional developments in Asian and Pacific nations (and colonies).*

U.S. Politics & Social Issues	U.S. Foreign Policy & Affairs, Defense	U.S. Economy & Environment	Science, Technology & Nature	Culture, Leisure & Lifestyle	
			President Warren G. Harding installs a radio in the White House.		Feb. 8
	Congress establishes the World War Foreign Debt Commission to try to resolve the problem of unpaid foreign debts from World War I. Great Britain currently owes the United States $4 billion, while the French owe $3 billion, and Italy owes $1.6 billion. The commission is seeking a way to ensure the repayment of most of the debt.				Feb. 9
			Czech chemist Jaroslav Heyrovssky has perfected polarography, designed to accurately measure the amount of ions in a solution.		Feb. 10
				Al Jolson's jazz hit *April Showers* has hit the top of the charts. Jazz is now wildly popular.	Feb. 11
				War has broken out between the Hip Sing and Bing Kong Tongs on the West Coast, with two killed and three wounded in scattered clashes. The rival Tongs have broken off negotiations with each other.	Feb. 12
Three men were arrested in Ft. Worth, TX, for a Ku Klux Klan led lynching in Texarkana, the culmination of four days of raids by KKK groups, in which five White men were flogged and others harassed or warned to leave the area....11 women were admitted to the bar in the District of Columbia today, the largest number in DC yet to do so.	Senator Borah of Idaho attacks the proposed bonus to be paid to veterans of World War I today, arguing that it would cost the United states $75 billion. Borah argued that this money should instead go toward farm relief.			San Francisco Police Chief O'Brien has warned that he will raid all Tong headquarters and deport Tong members en masse to prevent the war between the Hip Sing and Bing Kong Tongs from spreading.	Feb. 13
					Feb. 14

F	G	H	I	J
Includes campaigns, elections, federal-state relations, civil rights and liberties, crime, the judiciary, education, healthcare, poverty, urban affairs, and population.	*Includes formation and debate of U.S. foreign and defense policies, veterans affairs, and defense spending. (Relations with specific foreign countries are usually found under the region concerned.)*	*Includes business, labor, agriculture, taxation, transportation, consumer affairs, monetary and fiscal policy, natural resources, pollution and industrial accidents.*	*Includes worldwide scientific, medical and technological developments, natural phenomena, U.S. weather and natural disasters.*	*Includes the arts, religion, scholarship, communications media, sports, entertainment, fashions, fads, and social life.*

	World Affairs	Europe	Africa & The Middle East	The Americas	Asia & The Pacific
Feb. 15	The Permanent Court of International Justice officially begin proceedings today in The Hague, after an opening ceremony at the Carnegie Peace Palace, attended by Queen Wilhelmina and the Dutch royal family....British famine expert Sir Benjamin Robertson warned today that as many as 25 percent of the people are living in famine stricken areas in Russia without greater relief efforts. The United States has currently contributed $20 million to Russian famine relief.	Winston Churchill, Secretary of the Colonies, in a speech before Parliament, warned that Great Britain would never recognize an Irish Republic. He insisted that the Irish hold elections soon, warning that Ireland is "on trial before the world." Michael Collins, chairman of the Irish Provisional Government, returns to Dublin after conferring with British leaders. Collins has freed 26 men kidnapped along the border with Northern Ireland. Fighting is beginning to die down in Belfast.			Edward, the Prince of Wales, arrives in Delhi today on his goodwill tour of India, in the midst of tight security. A crowd of 60–70,000 throng the parade route. Despite fears of disruptions by Indian nationalists, Prince Edward's arrival is greeted peacefully.
Feb. 16		French Premier Raymond Poincaré admits today that his government has been negotiating secretly with the Soviets by wireless to discuss famine relief....Vytautas Magnus University has been opened in Kaunas, Lithuania. It is to be Lithuania's chief university.	Lord Allenby, hero of World War I in the Middle East, will be dispatched to Egypt with an offer of a British abandonment of her protectorate over Egypt. The British seek to bolster a native pro-British regime in Egypt that will protect British interests in the region.	Troops at Ft. Bliss, TX, have been put on alert amid rumors of a planned rebel attack on Juarez, Mexico, just across the Rio Grande. Among the leaders of the rebellion in Mexico is Esteban Cantu, former Governor of Lower California.	American relief workers in Orenberg have reported appalling scenes of devastation in the famine ravaging the Kirghiz lands of Soviet Russia. Lack of transportation has limited efforts to bring food in or evacuate people from the stricken regions.
Feb. 17	Germany pays the fourth installment of World War I reparations it owes to the Allies: 31 million gold marks....The French have won British support for their plan to bring the members of the pro-French "Little Entente": Czechoslovakia, Yugoslavia, and Romania, along with Poland, to the preliminary discussions at the upcoming Genoa Conference.	More than 100 have been killed or wounded in the last five days in street fighting in Belfast....The British House of Commons has beaten down a measure by Northern Ireland Protestants to prevent any alteration of Ulster's border with Ireland without Northern Ireland's approval....Italian Prime Minister Bonomi has lost a vote of confidence in the Chamber of Deputies, 205 to 107. Any new government must win the support of either the Socialists or the Catholic Party to have a majority.		Uruguay has negotiated a $2.3 million loan from the First National Bank of Boston....The United States has assembled 1,500 cavalry at El Paso, TX, as the confrontation between Obregonistas and rebels continues in Juarez, Mexico, just across the border. Other troops are deployed along the Rio Grande in a show of force.	
Feb. 18	German Foreign Minister Walther Rathenau announces that Germany will submit its own plan for reparations payments at the economic conference slated for March in Genoa.	Rumors are spreading that Russia and Germany have reached a secret economic accord, German and Russian interests converge in opposition to the Franco-British bloc....American Cardinals have formally requested that the Vatican alter the schedule for future papal conclaves to ensure time for the Cardinals to arrive from overseas. The new pope, Pius, is reported to favor the measure.			News has reached the West of serious famine in Jiangsu, Anhui, and Zhejiang Provinces in China, after devastating flooding. As many as six million Chinese could starve. The Chinese government is reported to be pocketing aid money sent to relieve conditions in the stricken provinces, which were already hard hit in 1921....Soviet Far Eastern Republic forces are advancing rapidly as Japanese-equipped White Russian forces are beginning to collapse.
Feb. 19	Nations are stockpiling materials for the production of poison gas. Nations with access to supplies are erecting trade barriers to keep such materials from being exported. It is part of a pattern of growing protectionism as nations struggle to rebuild their economies after World War I.		Three Englishmen, including two officials in the Egyptian government, have been attacked in the last 24 hours by Egyptian nationalists.		
Feb. 20		The Polish controlled Diet of Vilna votes to join Poland....A British convoy has been ambushed outside of Dublin. Two British soldiers have been killed in fighting with Irish nationalists.	The State Department has expressed America's interest in maintaining an "open door" in Turkey and in the Mandates of the former Ottoman Empire in the Middle East. Of particular concern are equal accesses to oil concessions in the region.		

A	B	C	D	E
Includes developments that affect more than one world region, international organizations and important meetings of world leaders.	*Includes all domestic and regional developments in Europe, including the Soviet Union.*	*Includes all domestic and regional developments in Africa and the Middle East.*	*Includes all domestic and regional developments in Latin America, the Caribbean, and Canada.*	*Includes all domestic and regional developments in Asian and Pacific nations (and colonies).*

U.S. Politics & Social Issues	U.S. Foreign Policy & Affairs, Defense	U.S. Economy & Environment	Science, Technology & Nature	Culture, Leisure & Lifestyle	
	Navy Secretary Denby is weighing deep cuts in naval spending as part of the new, reduced "treaty navy." In discussing cutting the appropriations request from $350 million to $250 million, Denby is considering returning the entire Annapolis Academy Class of 1922 to civilian life.		Guglielmo Marconi begins regular commercial radio transmissions in Great Britain.	Ch. Boxwood Barkington, an American Airedale owned by Frederic C. Hodd, of Brookline, MA, is awarded best-in-show at the Westminster Kennel Club dog show.	Feb. 15
Senate Democrats have demanded that the Harding administration release the minutes of the proceedings of the Washington Conference that led to the Four Power Treaty on Pacific bases. The Harding administration has replied, stating that no minutes or memoranda of any kind exist. The Democrats are looking for ways to weaken the Harding administration, portraying it as too soft on Japan.				The President of Yale is among the board of directors of a new corporation formed to provide psychological testing and services to private companies. Psychological testing will help businesses find "the right man for the right job."... Mobsters disguised as Prohibition agents have been shaking down speakeasies and restaurant owners selling liquor under the table, demanding payoffs.	Feb. 16
				France vetoes a measure to include baseball as a sport for the 1924 Olympics, instead selecting canoe racing....The Albuquerque High School Girls League has taken a stand against current problems afflicting American youth, having passed a resolution banning jazz dancing, cigarette smoking, and "petting parties."	Feb. 17
Margaret Sanger and other advocates of birth control have applied to the New York State Supreme Court to be allowed to incorporate The American Birth Control League.		Congress passes the Capper-Volstead Act. This allows farmers' cooperatives to operate free of antitrust regulations. American farmers have been facing hard times since the end of World War I. The measure has been put together by Sen. Arthur Capper of Kansas and representatives of farm bloc states. It will enable farmers to combine to set prices and limit the supply of grain going onto the market.			Feb. 18
Ohio Governor Harry L. Davis insists that Ohio is now making progress in enforcing Prohibition. Ohio has created its own Prohibition Enforcement Department to bolster the limited Federal agencies. Bribery and widespread evasion of the law remain problems.		700,000 American homes and businesses now have radios, with nearly 200,000 having been installed in the last three months. More than 15,000 stations have applied for licenses.	Radio towers on Long Island and elsewhere now enable radio stations in New York City to broadcast across a 10,000 mile radius.	The annual winter exodus of New York's society set to the South or to Europe is now in full swing. The Mediterranean, especially the Riviera, is popular with the American dollar riding high.... Fashion designers are mandating longer, flowing silk dresses in this year's Spring fashions. Capes are out.	Feb. 19
		The Federal Reserve reports that the American economy is on the rise nationwide, as the post-World War slump ends....After rioting in the Pawtucket Valley of Rhode Island, during a strike at textile mills, the Governor of Rhode Island has called out the National Guard to maintain order. Troops deploy in Pontiac, RI, where the worst rioting has occurred.		Marc Connelly and George S. Kaufman's play *To the Ladies* has opened on Broadway in New York City....It is also opening night for *The French Doll* and *For Goodness Sake*. *The French Doll*, a comedy, receives stellar reviews.	Feb. 20

F
Includes campaigns, elections, federal-state relations, civil rights and liberties, crime, the judiciary, education, healthcare, poverty, urban affairs, and population.

G
Includes formation and debate of U.S. foreign and defense policies, veterans affairs, and defense spending. (Relations with specific foreign countries are usually found under the region concerned.)

H
Includes business, labor, agriculture, taxation, transportation, consumer affairs, monetary and fiscal policy, natural resources, pollution and industrial accidents.

I
Includes worldwide scientific, medical and technological developments, natural phenomena, U.S. weather and natural disasters.

J
Includes the arts, religion, scholarship, communications media, sports, entertainment, fashions, fads, and social life.

	World Affairs	Europe	Africa & The Middle East	The Americas	Asia & The Pacific
Feb. 21		Militant Irish Republican leader Eamon De Valera calls the *Ard Fheis*, a convention of the *Sinn Fein*. De Valera is seeking support from the deeply divided convention for continuing the war with Britain. His supporters, though strong, are clearly in the minority.	The Allies have called a diplomatic conference in London to deal with the ongoing unrest in Turkey. Representatives of both Mustafa Kemal's Nationalist government in Ankara and the Ottoman Emperor in Istanbul have been called to the meeting. Kemal's government rejects the Treaty of Sèvres, which neutralizes the Straits and gives much of Thrace and the Aegean coast of Anatolia to Greece.... Britain formally ends it protectorate over the Sultanate of Egypt.		
Feb. 22	The Italian government has issued a formal invitation to the United States to send a representative to the upcoming Genoa Conference on the world's economy in March.	In a compromise between anti-treaty Republicans and pro-Free State forces in Ireland, parliamentary elections and a vote on accepting the London Peace Treaty with Great Britain will be delayed by at least three months. This marks a defeat for Great Britain, which has sought an early resolution of the Irish rebellion. The compromise has avoided, for the time being, an open split in the *Sinn Fein*, the main Irish nationalist party.			
Feb. 23					
Feb. 24		Germany agrees to the extradition of one of the Catalan anarchists responsible for the 1921 murder of Spanish Prime Minister Eduardo Dato Iradier....Pro- and anti-treaty factions in Ireland are busy establishing political parties for the elections that are to be held in Ireland in a few months. The anti-treaty Republicans have established their own newspaper and are busy drumming up support to derail the peace settlement with Britain.			The British Viceroy of India has agreed to a bill lifting repressive measures in an effort to restore calm in India after Mohandas Gandhi's civil disobedience campaign.
Feb. 25		British Prime Minister Lloyd George meets today with French Premier Raymond Poincaré in Boulogne to discuss strategy before the upcoming Genoa Conference....Liberal Luigi Facta, 61, today succeeded Ivanoe Bonomi as Prime Minister of Italy. This is a victory for Liberal Party leader Giovanni Giolitti, who has been Facta's mentor. Facta heads a coalition government that seeks to steer between the rising Fascist movement of Benito Mussolini and Communism.			Edward, Prince of Wales, arrived in Lahore in northwestern India today, amid tight security. The strong Sikh population of the Punjab region, while not supporting Mohandas Gandhi's nationalist movement, is restive....Across India, challenges to British rule are growing, with widespread unrest in Bihar, the United Provinces, and the Calcutta area, where mobs have been attacking *zemindars*, native tax collectors.
Feb. 26	In Boulogne, British and French prime ministers have agreed to extend the alliance between the two countries for 20 years. Lloyd George has assured French Premier Raymond Poincaré that Britain will not accept a revision of the Versailles Treaty at Genoa. The Allies have been under pressure to reduce reparation payments for financially strapped Germany.	The Bank of France is announcing a cut in interest rates on government bonds in an effort to stimulate lagging private investment.... Bombs are thrown at the government palace in the disputed city of Fiume, situated between Italy and the Kingdom of the Serbs, Croats, and Slovenes (Yugoslavia).			Prime Minister Takahashi Korekiyo presented Japan's annual budget to the Diet today, warning of the need to cut expenses by 25 million yen. Takahashi is putting off discussing cuts in the military for the time being, but retrenchment is clearly in the air.

A	B	C	D	E
Includes developments that affect more than one world region, international organizations and important meetings of world leaders.	*Includes all domestic and regional developments in Europe, including the Soviet Union.*	*Includes all domestic and regional developments in Africa and the Middle East.*	*Includes all domestic and regional developments in Latin America, the Caribbean, and Canada.*	*Includes all domestic and regional developments in Asian and Pacific nations (and colonies).*

	U.S. Politics & Social Issues	U.S. Foreign Policy & Affairs, Defense	U.S. Economy & Environment	Science, Technology & Nature	Culture, Leisure & Lifestyle
Feb. 21		An explosion destroys the dirigible *Roma*, when it strikes power lines at Hampton Roads Army Airbase, near Norfolk, VA, killing 34 of the 45 crewmen aboard. The 410 foot airship has only been bought recently by the United States from Italy. Designed to carry 100 passengers, and costing $200,000, the *Roma* has been left vulnerable by the highly flammable hydrogen, which provided the dirigible's lift.	The Rhode Island National Guard has killed one striker, and wounded six other strikers and bystanders, in a melee with striking mill workers at the Jenckes Spinning Company plant in Pawtucket.		*The Lady of the Rose* opens tonight on Broadway....Gainsborough's famous painting: *Blue Boy*, will go on exhibition in the drawing room of the H.E. Huntington estate in San Francisco....The new German film, *The Loves of the Pharaoh*, premiers in New York City tonight. Directed by Ernst Lubitsch, it offers sweeping spectacles, brilliant cinematography and scantily clad slave girls.
Feb. 22		At a meeting of the American Institute of Mining and Metallurgical Engineers in New York today, geologists warned that the United States is in danger of running out of oil, despite reserves in Mexico and the Caribbean. The United States will soon need access to oil fields in the Far East, equally coveted by the Japanese....A Congressional commission has proposed cutting military pay in Fiscal year 1923, to achieve a savings of $28.6 million.	The New York brokerage house of Kardos & Burke has filed for bankruptcy. The partners include John Burke, former United States Treasurer. Liabilities are put at $1.5 million, with remaining assets barely a tenth of that.	A report on the destruction of the R-38 dirigible last August revealed that the design of the airship, built in Britain and bought by the United States as the ZR-2, was fundamentally flawed. The airship's structure was not built to withstand the strains of motion when underway in the air. The report, issued just a day after the destruction of the airship *Roma*, show that the dirigible, though possessing far greater lifting capacity than heavier-than-air aircraft, still face significant problems in service....Congress has been warned that it needs to increase funding for the production of nonflammable helium for airships.	
Feb. 23		Army and Navy ask Congress not to cut appropriations for further development of airships. The Roma disaster and the loss of the R-38 have soured Congress on further funding for vulnerable, hydrogen filled dirigibles.	Five Wall Street brokerage firms have been forced into bankruptcy within 24 hours, after the collapse of the Kardos & Burke brokerage house yesterday.		Bootlegger Jerry "The Wolf" Ruberto has been shot in a gun battle in Lower Manhattan that injures three others. Ruberto's name has been added to the list of 30 slain in this area over bootlegging operations.
Feb. 24					Wedding gifts for Princess Mary have been put on display at Buckingham Palace, the centerpiece is a corsage ornament of diamonds and sapphires worked into a design of roses....Ralph Greenleaf has retained his title as pocket billiard champion in competition with former billiards champion Thomas Hueston....Police discover a moonshine factory in rural New Jersey today. The factories eight stills have a combined capacity of 2,000 gallons a day.
Feb. 25					In Boston, L.T. Brown sets a new world's record for the high jump: 6 feet, 4.75 inches....In Paris, serial killer Henri Désiré Landru, 53, is sent to the guillotine. Landru ran ads in lonely-hearts sections in Parisian newspapers, luring in well-off widows of World War I. Upon gaining access to their assets, he murdered them. He is held responsible for the lives of 10 women, and the child of one of his victims.
Feb. 26				Communications are being restored in northern Michigan after the most severe snow and ice storms in that state's history. Traverse City has just had telegraph connections restored after being cut off for four days.	The increasingly popular sport of skiing has come to the Adirondack Mountains of upstate New York, with a party of skiers descending Haystack Mountain....The American federation of Labor has joined those demanding a revision of the Volstead Act to allow light beers and wines, warning that Prohibition as it stands reduces legitimate jobs and breeds contempt for the law.

F	G	H	I	J
Includes campaigns, elections, federal-state relations, civil rights and liberties, crime, the judiciary, education, healthcare, poverty, urban affairs, and population.	*Includes formation and debate of U.S. foreign and defense policies, veterans affairs, and defense spending. (Relations with specific foreign countries are usually found under the region concerned.)*	*Includes business, labor, agriculture, taxation, transportation, consumer affairs, monetary and fiscal policy, natural resources, pollution and industrial accidents.*	*Includes worldwide scientific, medical and technological developments, natural phenomena, U.S. weather and natural disasters.*	*Includes the arts, religion, scholarship, communications media, sports, entertainment, fashions, fads, and social life.*

	World Affairs	Europe	Africa & The Middle East	The Americas	Asia & The Pacific
Feb. 27		Bombings and shootings again rock Belfast, as sectarian clashes between Catholics and Protestants continue....The Soviet Red Army now has 900,000 men under arms, backed by 200,000 men in the dreaded *Cheka*, the secret police. The Red Army, however, lacks sufficient modern tanks and artillery....The German mark drops to 228 against the dollar as news of Allied unwillingness to grant reductions in World War I reparations.		Canada is facing many of the same economic problems as the United States, including difficulty raising tax revenues to pay for bonuses from World War I....American trade with Mexico stands at more than $221 million as of 1921, despite the unrest there. This is an increase of more than 500 percent since before World War I....American trade with Colombia is up, as Colombia shifts away from her traditional trade with Europe....Police fire on a mob of striking chauffeurs in Mexico City. The protest turns into a riot with two policemen and two strikers killed, and many others wounded.	
Feb. 28	The Allied Reparations Commission has reached a provisional agreement with the German government today. Under the proposal, Germany will pay 720 million gold marks and 1.45 million marks in kind per year.	De Valera's Republican faction has been defeated in the first meeting of the Irish *Dail*. De Valera is finding that he lacks the support to challenge Provisional President Arthur Griffith and government head Michael Collins. The Republicans are anxious to continue the war with Great Britain, even if it means civil war in Ireland....Princess Mary, only daughter of King George V of Great Britain, is married today in a grand ceremony at Westminster Abbey to Viscount Lord Lascelles. Throngs of well wishers cheer the couple in the streets in celebrations lasting far into the night.	Britain formally proclaims an end to its protectorate over Egypt. However, Great Britain will continue to retain control over defense, "Imperial communications," that is, the Suez Canal, and the protection of foreigners and religious minorities in Egypt. The Sudan will remain a joint protectorate of Egypt and Great Britain, with Britain in effective control....The Soviets have installed a permanent Central Executive Committee in the Georgian SSR, under Communist control, in an attempt to increase their control over this turbulent mountain region....Standard Oil of New Jersey has reached an agreement with the Anglo-Persian Oil Company for development of oil fields in Persia (Iran).		
Mar. 1	The Allies are expected to refer the question of the German payment of reparations for damages in World War I to the Reparations Commission. Germany is desperately seeking a reduction in the level of payments to be made.	The Soviet government of Russia has reached a trade accord with Sweden. The Soviets are desperate to break the trade embargo imposed by the West....The British Chancellor of the Exchequer announces plans to reduce government spending by £64 million, less than the £86 million recommended by the Geddes Committee. The British navy will be reduced to 98,000 men, smaller in terms of manpower than that of the United States. The army will be cut by 33,000 men, including 40 percent of the artillery. This will effectively reduce Britain's ability to send troops overseas in the event of an emergency....As part of Lenin's New Economic Policy, allowing some private enterprise to flourish, the Soviets have abolished the government monopoly on the salt trade....Soviet Minister of War Leon Trotsky regards the recent accords between Britain and France at Boulogne as tantamount to an anti-Soviet alliance, and warns that Russia will not continue the plan to reduce the size of its military if it is threatened.	In this month, British forces have finally suppressed the rebellion of the Dinka tribe of southern Sudan. Led by their religious leader, Bul Yol, who has taken the name of the Prophet Ariendit, the Dinka have been in rebellion since 1921....Abdel Khalek Tarwat Pasha is appointed Prime Minister of Egypt, succeeding Adli Yakan Pasha. Egypt is moving rapidly to establish a working government to negotiate more effectively with Britain....British Colonial Secretary, Winston Churchill today rejected Arab demands for independence for Palestine. Churchill did promise that the Arab population of Palestine would be accorded self-government in due time, and that no Jewish homeland would be established in Palestine that would prejudice Arab interests.	The Mexico City newspaper *El Universal* today called upon Mexican President Obregon to reach an accord with the United States in order to win recognition. It condemned Obregon's failure to control state governors who have become virtual warlords, as well as the continuing social unrest in the impoverished states of Michoacan and Vera Cruz. Union leaders are threatening a general strike in Mexico City to force concessions from the Obregon government.	A strike by Chinese seamen in Hong Kong has erupted into a general strike in the British colony, disrupting commerce throughout the Far East. Commercial losses are already estimated at $40 million....Negotiations are going on between the Soviet Far Eastern Republic and the Japanese at Dairen, in Manchuria. Where the Soviets are seeking to negotiate a withdrawal of Japanese forces from Siberia, while the Japanese are insisting that the port of Vladivostok be kept unfortified....The militantly nationalist Tabei Doshi-Kai organization has vowed to protest Baron Tomasaburo Kato, chief Japanese delegate at the Washington Conference, for making excessive concessions to the United States on naval disarmament.
Mar. 2	The Greek government today released a French ship intercepted by the Greek navy en route to the Turkish Nationalists with what the Greeks maintain was contraband of war.	The German military and police are on high alert as bread and coal prices continue to rise. Shortages of food have already been reported. The German mark falls to 239 versus the dollar today as the German economy continues to stagger.	Tensions are rising in Anatolia as Turkish Nationalist forces have begun probing Greek positions near Nazil and Aidin. The Greeks are trying to hold onto the Aegean coast of Asia Minor with its large Greek population.	The United States will mediate a meeting between Peru and Chile in Washington this April in an attempt to resolve the ongoing Tacna-Arica border dispute....The United States and Colombia exchange ratifications today of a treaty paying Colombia $25 million in compensation for the loss of Panama.	

A	B	C	D	E
Includes developments that affect more than one world region, international organizations and important meetings of world leaders.	*Includes all domestic and regional developments in Europe, including the Soviet Union.*	*Includes all domestic and regional developments in Africa and the Middle East.*	*Includes all domestic and regional developments in Latin America, the Caribbean, and Canada.*	*Includes all domestic and regional developments in Asian and Pacific nations (and colonies).*

U.S. Politics & Social Issues	U.S. Foreign Policy & Affairs, Defense	U.S. Economy & Environment	Science, Technology & Nature	Culture, Leisure & Lifestyle	
In *Leser v. Garnett*, the United States Supreme Court has struck down a Maryland court challenge to the Nineteenth Amendment, guaranteeing women the vote. The Court's decision was unanimous. Women's suffrage is here to stay.		Commerce Secretary Herbert Hoover has convened the first National Radio Conference in Washington, DC. Hoover is calling for regulation of the airwaves to maximize the commercial potential of radio by eliminating interference and defining frequencies.	A team of American and French archaeologists plan to excavate the ruins of Carthage in the French protectorate of Tunisia.	George Bernard Shaw's *Back to Methuselah, Parts I and II*, premieres at the Garrick Theater on Broadway in New York....Charitable organizations report that unemployment in New York City has worsened as winter wears on.	Feb. 27
		Department store sales in January were down by 8 percent from the same time in 1921, with clothing sales being maintained by reduced prices, whereas furniture sales remain stagnant, as the economy is still recovering from the post-World War slump.		Mardi Gras celebrations reach their heights in New Orleans, as Lent begins tomorrow.	Feb. 28
The National Association for the Advancement of Colored People (NAACP), at a meeting in New York City, which included W.E.B. DuBois, editor of *The Crisis*, has called on the Congress to pass an anti-lynching bill.		The Interior Secretary today called for a major program of irrigation for California's Imperial Valley. The plan will divert water from the Colorado River and require a major dam at Boulder Canyon near the small Nevada town of Las Vegas....The Pierce-Arrow Motor Car Company has posted losses of $8.76 million for 1921.	Northern Germany is in the grip of the worst winter in 50 years. Temperatures of 12 degrees below zero are reported in Hamburg today, with the Baltic, the Kattegat Straits between Denmark and Norway, and the Kiel Canal all frozen in....An ice mass has broken the Oder Dam in Breslau, Germany....Great Britain has established the Civil Aviation Authority to regulate the booming aviation industry in the United Kingdom.	A new fad has hit aviators in Miami: aerial polo....Lent begins for Catholics and Episcopalians today, ending Mardi Gras merriment in New Orleans....Bootleg liquor is selling well, with a street value of $30 a gallon....The latest fashions from Paris, including long coat dresses, have hit Fifth Avenue in New York City.	Mar. 1
	Congress has voted just half of the $12 million appropriation for fuel for the navy. As modern warships convert from coal to more efficient oil burning engines, the problem of obtaining and stockpiling sufficient supplies of fuel oil has become pressing.		The Kentucky State Legislature introduced a bill today banning the teaching of evolution in Kentucky schools.	Prohibition agents raid a restaurant in New York City's Harlem district, seizing $15,000 worth of bootleg whiskey....In his Lenten sermon, Rev. Dr. A.W. Beaven of Rochester, MA, has warned that jazz is a combination of "nervousness, lawlessness, primitive and savage animalism, and lasciviousness."	Mar. 2

F	G	H	I	J
Includes campaigns, elections, federal-state relations, civil rights and liberties, crime, the judiciary, education, healthcare, poverty, urban affairs, and population.	*Includes formation and debate of U.S. foreign and defense policies, veterans affairs, and defense spending. (Relations with specific foreign countries are usually found under the region concerned.)*	*Includes business, labor, agriculture, taxation, transportation, consumer affairs, monetary and fiscal policy, natural resources, pollution and industrial accidents.*	*Includes worldwide scientific, medical and technological developments, natural phenomena, U.S. weather and natural disasters.*	*Includes the arts, religion, scholarship, communications media, sports, entertainment, fashions, fads, and social life.*

	World Affairs	Europe	Africa & The Middle East	The Americas	Asia & The Pacific
Mar. 3		Fascists staged a coup in Fiume (Rijecka) today and overthrew the Free State government there. The Fascists claim the city, claimed by Yugoslavia, as an integral part of Italy....France's rural population fell to just 15 million, in a country of 37 million people in 1921, just over 40 percent. This is a significant drop since 1896, when there were 23 million rural dwellers out of 38 million people.		Parts of Mexico City were blacked out tonight, in a strike by power company workers. The Mexican military has stationed troops at the main power plant of Necaxa Falls, to prevent sabotage. Workers are demanding that a worker-run commission be put in charge of power and utilities in the capital.	Independence advocate Jawaharlal Nehru and six others were released from Lucknow Jail in a gesture by the British to try to end the campaign of civil disobedience sweeping India....Plans for the Prince of Wales to visit Amritsar are shelved today. Amritsar is the site of the notorious massacre by British troops of Indian protestors in 1919.
Mar. 4		British Prime Minister Lloyd George has beaten down a challenge by Ulster Unionists and discontented Conservatives to force him to step down. This will greatly strengthen Lloyd George's position going into the upcoming Genoa Conference.	The Turkish Nationalist Assembly in Ankara has reelected the World War I hero Mustafa Kemal as head of the Nationalist government.	The British have closed their consulate in Mexico City as the strike by streetcar and power company workers continues.	News arrived today of the murder in February of American missionary Dr. Albert Le Roy Shelton, by Chinese bandits. Shelton had been the first American missionary to reach Tibet.
Mar. 5	In the 10th installment of an ongoing exposé in the *New York Times*, Ray Stannard Baker revealed the details behind secret treaties made by the allies during World War I to redraw the maps of Europe and the Middle East. For Americans sold on involvement in the World War as a "war to end war," such revelations have come as a shock, feeding the growing isolationist sentiment in the United States.	Anti-treaty Republicans seized control of Limerick, Ireland today, as Ireland continues to be torn by violence between Republicans and those loyal to the Provisional government of Michael Collins in Dublin. The 400 rebels have surrounded the police barracks there.		An American working in the Mexican State of Vera Cruz has been gunned down by one of the marauding rebel bands in the countryside....A Manitoba Association of the Unemployed was formed today, demanding reform of the capitalist system and jobs for unemployed workers at union wages.	
Mar. 6	The Italian government has set April 10 for the start of the Genoa Conference on the European economy....A meeting of Allied Foreign Ministers has been set in Paris for March to attempt to resolve the territorial dispute between Turkey and Greece.	Violence has erupted again in the troubled Northern Ireland city of Belfast, with sectarian clashes between Protestants and the Catholic minority, with four dead and 30 wounded in recent days....IRA rebels in Limerick have arrested pro-government police and army officials and have given the government 48 hours to evacuate the police barracks there.			The United States today officially banned the export of arms to China, in response to growing unrest by provincial warlords, challenging the authority of the weak central government in Beijing....Protestors interrupted a speech by the Prince of Wales in Peshawar today, with cries of "Mahatma Gandhi-kijai." Protests in the city have otherwise been peaceful.
Mar. 7		Sigurdur Eggerz has succeeded Jón Magnússon as Prime Minister of Iceland.			
Mar. 8	The United States has announced that it will not participate in the upcoming economic conference in Genoa. This is a harsh blow to German Foreign Minister Rathenau, who is desperately seeking American loans to rebuild the central European economy, and to British Prime Minister Lloyd George, who is trying to stabilize the European economy. President Harding does not want the United states to get "entangled" in European politics, and is also hostile to proposals to invite the Soviets, who the United States do not recognize.	José Sánchez Guerra y Martinez took office as Prime Minister of Spain, succeeding Antonio Maura y Montaner....France is selling its state owned railway system, which this year has seen losses of 100 million francs in its suburban Paris lines in 1921....A bill was introduced in the British House of Commons to give women the vote on the same terms as men.			Gen. Chang Tso-lin, Military Governor of Manchuria, has broken with the Chinese government in Beijing, and is organizing an alliance to seize power. The government in Beijing is in chaos: with the Ministers of Finance and War having resigned and the Prime Minister refusing to perform the duties of office. All payments on foreign loans have ceased and the Beijing government has declared itself bankrupt. In retaliation, the banks have seized the state salt surplus. Chang is trying to oust Gen. Wu Pei-fu, warlord of Hubei and Hunan Provinces, and the real power behind the Beijing government. Chang is backed by Sun Yat-sen's Kuomintang government in Guangzhou (Canton).

A	B	C	D	E
Includes developments that affect more than one world region, international organizations and important meetings of world leaders.	*Includes all domestic and regional developments in Europe, including the Soviet Union.*	*Includes all domestic and regional developments in Africa and the Middle East.*	*Includes all domestic and regional developments in Latin America, the Caribbean, and Canada.*	*Includes all domestic and regional developments in Asian and Pacific nations (and colonies).*

U.S. Politics & Social Issues	U.S. Foreign Policy & Affairs, Defense	U.S. Economy & Environment	Science, Technology & Nature	Culture, Leisure & Lifestyle	
Senator Harris of Georgia introduces a bill calling for a five-year ban on all immigration to the United States....Gov. Harry L. Davis of Ohio announces his opposition to capital punishment, vowing to push for its abolition.				Station WWJ-AM has begun broadcasting in Detroit, WBAP has begun transmitting in Ft. Worth, TX, and WLW is going on the air in Cincinnati. Radio is taking the country by storm.	Mar. 3
		The United Mine Workers claim today that high coal prices are due to mining company profit taking, arguing that labor costs per ton were only $3.92, while coal sold at $12 a ton. The UMW also condemns the 500 deaths in Pennsylvania mines annually, as well as the 20,000 injuries suffered by miners each year.	British portrait artist P. Tennyson Cole warns today that movies are awakening the peoples of the East to a wider world.	Famed African-American comedian Bert Williams died today, at age 46, after a long period of failing health....Chicago fashion experts estimate that it costs a woman $117.70 a year to dress in proper "flapper" style. Essentials include a stylish outfit at $20, two pairs of shoes for $12, five pairs of hose for $6.80, and two hats, costing $10.	Mar. 4
				Murnau's *Nosferatu* premiered today in Berlin. Murnau's Expressionistic masterpiece pushes the boundaries of camera work. It also is the first film to bring the legend of the vampire to the silver screen....Annie Oakley has broken the women's trapshooting record at the Pinehurst Gun Club in North Carolina, shooting 98 of 100 targets. The aging Oakley has come out of retirement in recent years to provide for her family....John Philip Sousa receives a rousing welcome at a "Welcome Home" concert at the Hippodrome in New York after his band's 29th tour.	Mar. 5
Interior Secretary Albert Fall lashed out at criticism by conservationist Gifford Pinchot, who is protesting a decision made recently to transfer forest reserves now managed by the Forest Service under the Department of Agriculture, to Fall's department of the Interior. Fall is known to favor development of the lands, mostly in Alaska, which have been found to have oil and mineral reserves. Fall insists that control of these reserves "should not be divided."	The War Department announced today that of the American soldiers killed in the World War, 44,000 have been brought back to be buried in the United States, while 31,400 will have their final resting place in Europe.	Coal miners today vote overwhelmingly to go on strike nationwide if their demands for improved wages and working conditions are not met.	The British Air Council is announcing a £50,000 prize for a helicopter design that can meet set flight specifications.	Part III and IV of George Bernard Shaw's play, *Back to Methuselah,* premieres on Broadway tonight in New York.	Mar. 6
		Statistics for 1921 show that Germany is now America's number one customer for copper ore. Germany also ranks second in purchasing American cotton, and third for wheat, thus making Germany's economic revival and stability vital to the United States.		Legendary slugger Babe Ruth has signed a three-year contract with the New York Yankees, for the annual sum of $52,000 a year.	Mar. 7
President Harding and his wife are heading south to Florida for a vacation. This is being done during the Senate debate on ratification of last month's Washington Treaties as part of a strategy to show that Harding is not trying to influence the Senate. Among the entourage is Harding's close friend Attorney General Harry Daugherty.	Assistant Aviation Director of the Army Air Corps, Gen. William "Billy" Mitchell, is touring the Netherlands today, visiting the Fokker aircraft factory there, and test flying a Fokker airplane.			A gang of 30 armed men stormed a liquor warehouse outside of Frederick, MD, escaping with 2,100 gallons of whiskey.	Mar. 8

F	G	H	I	J
Includes campaigns, elections, federal-state relations, civil rights and liberties, crime, the judiciary, education, healthcare, poverty, urban affairs, and population.	*Includes formation and debate of U.S. foreign and defense policies, veterans affairs, and defense spending. (Relations with specific foreign countries are usually found under the region concerned.)*	*Includes business, labor, agriculture, taxation, transportation, consumer affairs, monetary and fiscal policy, natural resources, pollution and industrial accidents.*	*Includes worldwide scientific, medical and technological developments, natural phenomena, U.S. weather and natural disasters.*	*Includes the arts, religion, scholarship, communications media, sports, entertainment, fashions, fads, and social life.*

	World Affairs	Europe	Africa & The Middle East	The Americas	Asia & The Pacific
Mar. 9		The resignation of Edmund Montagu, British secretary of state for India, has thrown Lloyd George's coalition government into a state of turmoil.	Edmund Montagu, British secretary of state for India, has resigned from the cabinet, after Montagu leaked a memorandum warning the British government that the Muslim population in India was growing increasingly restive, and that the best way to calm tensions was to reach an accord with the Ottoman Sultan and revise the terms imposed on Turkey by the Treaty of Sèvres.		
Mar. 10		The German Ministry of the Interior has banned all monarchial insignia from public buildings.	Ali Rida al-Riqabi has been appointed Prime Minister of Transjordan, succeeding Muzhir ar-Raslan.... Striking Afrikaaner mineworkers have seized control of much of Johannesburg today, calling for armed rebellion and an overthrow of the South African government.... Jan Christian Smuts, Prime Minister of South Africa, has declared martial law in Johannesburg.		Indian nationalist Mohandas Gandhi has been arrested by British authorities in Ahmedabad. He has been taken to the Sabarmati Jail in Bombay to await trial for sedition. Gandhi has called upon his followers to continue his policy of nonviolent civil disobedience.
Mar. 11		The Engineering & National Employers' Federation began a lockout in Britain today, against some 400,000 members of the Amalgamated Engineering Union, after negotiations broke down last week. Britain's industrial economy, especially her shipbuilding industry, has been battered by increased competition since World War. I	Chaos erupts in South Africa as police and military units attempt to break the mine strike in the Rand by force. Militant Afrikaaner strikers, organized into "commando" groups, have attacked police stations in attempts to obtain weapons.		Indian nationalist Mohandas Gandhi was arraigned today, being formally charged with sedition against the government for his writings in *Young India* and other journals.
Mar. 12	Outrage is growing at American demands to be repaid out of German reparations for the $240 million cost of the American Army of Occupation in the Rhineland. The Allies have warned the United States that they may withhold German reparation payments to the United States if the Americans won't ratify the Versailles Treaty.		South African troops have stormed Brixton Ridge and Vrededorp in the Rand, as fighting goes on against striking miners....The Soviet Republics of Armenia, Georgia, and Azerbaijan are united into a single Transcaucasian SSR, as part of Soviet efforts to bring order to the chaotic ethnic melange of the Caucasus region.		
Mar. 13		Delegates from Estonia, Finland, Latvia, Lithuania, and Poland met in Warsaw today to create a defensive league and provide for arbitration of disputes.			
Mar. 14		Mobs of Fascist thugs, *squadristi*, clash with Socialists in Rome, as Italy verges toward civil war.... The new Parliament of Northern Ireland convenes in Belfast today. Dominated by Protestants, it is committed to maintaining union with Great Britain. Ulster Protestant leader Sir James Craig announces that Gen. Sir Henry Wilson was preparing a plan to "restore order" in Northern Ireland.	South African troops, backed by artillery fire and air power, have stormed Fordsburg, stronghold of striking Afrikaaner miners in the Rand....Harry Thuku, African nationalist leader of the East African Association, has been arrested by British authorities in Nairobi. Thuku is widely popular in Kenya, and his arrest has brought strikes and protests.		
Mar. 15		France and Germany have come to an agreement to modify reparations payments. Until now, France would accept hard currency for reparations. In the revised accord, payments can be made in raw materials.... Former Irish President Eamon de Valera has proclaimed the creation of a Republican Society, vowing to resist the new Irish government and insisting on complete independence from Great Britain....In the face of tightened finances, the British government is calling for reducing the army to 152,000 men, 20,000 less than before World War I. Reserves have already been cut by over 50 percent from their prewar levels.	In a ceremony in Cairo, Sultan Ahmed Fuad Pasha has proclaimed himself King of Egypt. The British government today officially recognizes Fuad I as king. Great Britain and Egypt will continue to share joint sovereignty over the Sudan, and Britain will keep control of the Suez Canal and the defense of Egypt....The South African miners strike has collapsed. There are 214 people that have been killed: 76 strikers, 78 government troops, 30 Black Africans killed by rioting Whites, and 62 civilians. More than 4,700 strikers have been arrested.		Tseren-Ochiryn Dambadorj has been selected as Chairman of the Central Committee of the Mongolian People's Revolutionary Party.

A	B	C	D	E
Includes developments that affect more than one world region, international organizations and important meetings of world leaders.	*Includes all domestic and regional developments in Europe, including the Soviet Union.*	*Includes all domestic and regional developments in Africa and the Middle East.*	*Includes all domestic and regional developments in Latin America, the Caribbean, and Canada.*	*Includes all domestic and regional developments in Asian and Pacific nations (and colonies).*

U.S. Politics & Social Issues	U.S. Foreign Policy & Affairs, Defense	U.S. Economy & Environment	Science, Technology & Nature	Culture, Leisure & Lifestyle	
		The Pittsburgh Coal Company releases its annual earnings statement, showing a loss of $11 million in revenue from 1921 to 1922.		Eugene O'Neill's play, *The Hairy Ape*, opens tonight at the Provincetown Theater in New York....Radio station KJR-AM begins broadcasting in Seattle.	Mar. 9
				KLZ-AM begins broadcasting in Denver.	Mar. 10
				The Vancouver Millionaires have taken the Western Hockey Championship, sweeping the Regina Capitals in two games.	Mar. 11
Will Hays founds the Motion Picture Producers and Directors of America, Inc. "The object for which the corporation is to be created," he says, "is establishing the highest moral and artistic standards."				Plans are unveiled for a $10 million floating "liquor palace," which will be anchored off New York City just outside the three-mile limit. Federal Prohibition Commissioner Haynes has vowed to stop the planned vessel, which is already lining up prospective patrons.	Mar. 12
				Part V of George Bernard Shaw's *Back to Methuselah* premieres tonight in New York....The Ottawa Senators beat down the Toronto St. Pats, 5–4, to capture the NHL Hockey Championship....WRR-AM goes on the air in Dallas, TX.	Mar. 13
				The rush to get on the air continues, with KGU-AM beginning broadcasting from Honolulu, KSD-AM in St. Louis, and WGR-AM in Buffalo, NY.	Mar. 14
A group has been formed in Oklahoma to resist the spread of the Ku Klux Klan in that state.				WSB-AM begins transmissions in Atlanta, GA, bringing the radio phenomenon to the American South.	Mar. 15

F	G	H	I	J
Includes campaigns, elections, federal-state relations, civil rights and liberties, crime, the judiciary, education, healthcare, poverty, urban affairs, and population.	*Includes formation and debate of U.S. foreign and defense policies, veterans affairs, and defense spending. (Relations with specific foreign countries are usually found under the region concerned.)*	*Includes business, labor, agriculture, taxation, transportation, consumer affairs, monetary and fiscal policy, natural resources, pollution and industrial accidents.*	*Includes worldwide scientific, medical and technological developments, natural phenomena, U.S. weather and natural disasters.*	*Includes the arts, religion, scholarship, communications media, sports, entertainment, fashions, fads, and social life.*

	World Affairs	Europe	Africa & The Middle East	The Americas	Asia & The Pacific
Mar. 16		Protestant fanatics in Belfast injure 15 in three bombing attacks around the city today. Two policemen have been killed and another injured in a shootout with Irish Nationalists in Galway....The United states has postponed Austria's debt repayment by 25 years. This will enable Austria to more easily secure short term credit to stabilize its economy.... Italian troops have occupied the free city of Fiume, removing the fascist government installed there by a coup, and have proclaimed the city to be under Italian sovereignty....A naval bill was introduced before the French Senate today, calling for a construction program to modernize the French fleet, particularly cruisers, destroyers, and submarines.	A mass protest shook Nairobi, Kenya, today, as supporters of imprisoned African nationalist Harry Thuku demanded his release. The police suppressed the protest by force, killing 21 protestors. The British are anxious to stabilize Kenya in order to open it to further White settlement....Secretary of State Hughes is backing American oil companies in demanding that the British allow American firms equal opportunities in developing oil concessions in Iraq. The British claim that Britain's own Turkish petroleum Company had been granted sole drilling rights by the Ottoman Empire before the World War.		British forces have reportedly restored order in rural areas of the United Provinces area of India after serious rioting by peasants.
Mar. 17	Soviet Foreign Minister George Chicherin has demanded that Russia be represented at the upcoming Genoa Conference.	Poland and the Baltic states of Lithuania, Latvia, and Estonia have reached an accord, agreeing to neutrality with each other....During the St. Patrick's Day festivities, Irish Free State forces captured the barracks at Castelblayney in County Monaghan from its surprised Republican garrison....A massive typhus epidemic has been reported in the famine stricken Volga region of Russia, as refugees fleeing Russia have slipped into Germany.		Mexican General Felix Diaz has been murdered in Hermosillo in Sonora, as northern Mexico remains in a state of turmoil. Diaz controlled a revolutionary army in the State of Nayarit during the Carranza regime, but had fallen out of favor with the Obregon government in Mexico City.	
Mar. 18		11 people were killed in Belfast as bombings and sectarian gun battles began again after a St. Patrick's Day lull. The Ulster Home Office suppressed five town councils with *Sinn Fein* majorities....The government of Albania has executed Capt. Bajramgiani of the Gendarmerie for his role in an attempted revolt in Durazzo recently....The new government of Luigi Facta passed its first test in Italy today, winning a vote of confidence in the Chamber of Deputies.	Albert Sarraut, French Minister for the colonies, today denied charges that the French military was conscripting native troops in its African Mandates.	Adolfo de la Huerta, Mexican Secretary of the Treasury, will come to New York City to negotiate with American oil and banking interests. The Mexican government of President Alvaro Obregon is desperately seeking diplomatic recognition by the United States....The Dominican Republic is seeking a $6 million loan from New York banks, in a plan supervised by the United States State Department, which is seeking to stabilize the impoverished Caribbean country.	A British judge in Bombay has sentenced Indian nationalist leader Mohandas Gandhi to six years in prison for leading a mass, non-violent civil disobedience campaign against British rule in India....Dr. Wu Ting Fang, Foreign Minister of the Kuomintang government in Guangzhou (Canton) appealed today for American diplomatic recognition, denouncing the Beijing government as illegal and warlord controlled.
Mar. 19	A pre-Genoa conference of neutral nations met in Switzerland today, to discuss issues coming up in the Genoa Economic Conference set for April. Attending were representatives from Sweden, Denmark, Norway, the Netherlands, Spain, and Switzerland.	Thoe Geresh, leader of the Danish Communist Party, has been arrested at Randers, in Jutland, on charges of sedition. Denmark has been in the midst of a general lockout, with 150,000 union workers in the streets. Danish employers are seeking a 20 percent wage cut for Danish workers.	American textiles are selling in Aden, on the Yemeni coast of Arabia, beating out Japanese textiles that sold there when trade was interrupted during World War I.		
Mar. 20		Socialist Revolutionary Party leaders went on trial for treason in Russia today, as Lenin moves to secure the complete control of the Communist Party....British Prime Minister called today on Parliament to support him going into the Genoa Conference. A vote of confidence is scheduled for April 3, a week before the Conference opens.... Danish troops have been called out to maintain order in the continuing labor unrest there.		The United States Congress has appropriated $41 million for an American exhibition at the upcoming Brazilian World's Fair to be held in Rio de Janerio....A shipment of 5,000 rounds of rifle ammunition was intercepted in El Paso, authorities announced today. The shipment was said to be arranged by exiled Mexican General Irenio Villareal, for rebels planning a coup in the Mexican State of Coahuila.	Unrest in India has not abated in the wake of the conviction and sentencing of nationalist leader Mohandas Gandhi for sedition. However, the vast Indian nationalist movement remains without a national leader.
	A *Includes developments that affect more than one world region, international organizations and important meetings of world leaders.*	B *Includes all domestic and regional developments in Europe, including the Soviet Union.*	C *Includes all domestic and regional developments in Africa and the Middle East.*	D *Includes all domestic and regional developments in Latin America, the Caribbean, and Canada.*	E *Includes all domestic and regional developments in Asian and Pacific nations (and colonies).*

U.S. Politics & Social Issues	U.S. Foreign Policy & Affairs, Defense	U.S. Economy & Environment	Science, Technology & Nature	Culture, Leisure & Lifestyle	
A report submitted by Chairman Fordney of the House Ways and Means Committee estimated that payment of the bonus due veterans of World War I will require an outlay of $4 billion dollars over 20 years. The measure is strongly supported by such veterans groups as the American Legion, but debate swirls around how the bonus is to be paid for.				The United States District Attorney's office in Cook County, IL, which contains Chicago, has handed the task of Prohibition enforcement over to Illinois State prosecutors. Prohibition has never been popular with Chicago's large immigrant population, and widespread flouting of the Volstead Act is common....Dr. Lee A. Stone, head of the Chicago Department of Health has informed a conference of concerned health officials that "flappers," independent, uninhibited young women, are not psychologically abnormal, but merely young people revolting against what they see as hypocrisy in dress and manners. Reports of young women smoking, drinking, dancing to jazz music, or attending "petting parties" has caused widespread concern among the older generation.	**Mar. 16**
				The Yale swim team breaks world's records for 400, 500, 600 yard, and mile races in a special meet held with Columbia University at Yale.	**Mar. 17**
	American troops began pulling out of Koblenz today, as America's occupation of the Rhineland draws to a close. Only 4,000 troops remain on the Rhine after today, as troops bound for the United States from where beer is legal marched out to the tune of *How Dry I Am*. 64 German brides are accompanying the troops home.		French inventor Edouard Belin, has developed a system for transmitting fingerprints over telegraph wires.		**Mar. 18**
		Standard Oil is sending geologists out to search for new oil fields for future development. Alaska is reported to be promising, but company officials are calling for a revision of United States conservation policies. Other possible sources include Russia, South America, and Iran.		Lively colors and wide sleeves with elegant lace are "in" as spring and summer fashions arrive en masse from Paris.	**Mar. 19**
President Harding today warns Chairman Fordney of the House Ways and Means Committee that he will not accept additional tax increases to pay for the promised World War veterans' bonus other than a sales tax.	The U.S. Navy has commissioned its first aircraft carrier. Originally, the carrier *Jupiter*, the 11,500 ton USS *Langley*, CV-1, begins her new service at Norfolk, VA. The navy sees aircraft carriers as mainly auxiliaries, providing scouts for the fleet. The value of air power is still the subject of furious debate....President Harding has announced plans for the United States to withdraw the rest of its occupation forces from the Rhineland by next year.	A daily news service for farmers will begin broadcasting from Chicago, in order to provide farmers with up-to-date agricultural and marketing information.	The League of Nations is hosting a meeting of the European Health Conference in Warsaw to determine optimal strategies to deal with epidemics in Europe.	Police reserves were called out to restore order when Federal prohibition agents raided a garage near the "bootlegger's curb market" near Mulberry Street in Manhattan.	**Mar. 20**

F	G	H	I	J
Includes campaigns, elections, federal-state relations, civil rights and liberties, crime, the judiciary, education, healthcare, poverty, urban affairs, and population.	*Includes formation and debate of U.S. foreign and defense policies, veterans affairs, and defense spending. (Relations with specific foreign countries are usually found under the region concerned.)*	*Includes business, labor, agriculture, taxation, transportation, consumer affairs, monetary and fiscal policy, natural resources, pollution and industrial accidents.*	*Includes worldwide scientific, medical and technological developments, natural phenomena, U.S. weather and natural disasters.*	*Includes the arts, religion, scholarship, communications media, sports, entertainment, fashions, fads, and social life.*

	World Affairs	Europe	Africa & The Middle East	The Americas	Asia & The Pacific
Mar. 21	The French government announced today that two French divisions would take over the occupation zone around Koblenz, along the Rhine, which will be evacuated by American troops. France is determined to maintain the Rhineland occupation zones, with their bridgeheads across the Rhine, as a means of coercing Germany into paying reparations owed from World War I....A Chinese student attempted to assassinate Cheng Loh, the Chinese Ambassador to France, in Paris today. It is unclear whether the would-be assassin, Lee Ho-ling, acted alone or at the instigation of either Chinese Communists or the dissident Kuomintang government in southern China, but it underscores the need for security at the upcoming Genoa Conference.	Widespread guerilla warfare has broken out along the border between Northern Ireland and the Catholic South. IRA guerillas have raided deep into the Ulster counties of Tyrone, Derry, and Armagh. The goal of the raiders seems to be to provoke a violent British reaction. In Dublin, Republican militants have called for a Convention of the Army in Ireland, to defy the Provisional government of Arthur Griffith, which intends to make peace with Britain....General de Castelnau, Chairman of the French Army Commission, warned the Chamber of deputies in Paris today that France must have an army three times the size of Germany's "when zero-hour sounds again."...German police raided a late night club frequented by numerous White Russian exiles. Germany is patching up its relations with the Soviets in advance of the Genoa Conference.		141 out of 200 Latin American leaders, sounded out by the United States, have called on America to recognize the government of President Obregon in Mexico, as the best way to promote Pan-American solidarity.	Controversial birth control advocate Margaret Sanger is continuing her tour of Japan. Having left Tokyo after lecturing there, she heads onto Nikko, Osaka, and Kyoto. Although not welcomed by the government here, Mrs. Sanger's visit has been peaceful.
Mar. 22	The United States has insisted on being repaid for the occupation of the Rhineland out of reparations *already* paid to the Allies by Germany. The British and French are angry that the United States has signed a separate peace with Germany, instead of the general Versailles Treaty of 1919....British, French, and Italian foreign ministers began meeting in Paris today to discuss a resolution of the conflict between Greece and Turkey. Particularly divisive are the questions of the Straits and the port of Smyrna in Asia Minor.	The British government warned that it would deploy the army in a border zone to separate Ireland and Protestant Northern Ireland if violence did not cease. Raids and counter-raids along the border have produced a state of near all-out war....An emergency meeting of the Reparations Commission in Paris calls on Germany to immediately cease printing paper money. Germany's inflation is becoming ruinous. The Commission announced a reduced payment schedule for Germany: 720 million gold marks (minus 280 million already paid) and 1.45 million in raw materials in 1922.	The Emir Talal of Transjordan has declared the establishment of the Kingdom of Transjordan, with himself as king.	Standard Oil affiliate Atlantic Refining has organized a subsidiary in Brazil, capitalized at $50,000, to market petroleum products throughout Brazil. This follows Standard Oil of New Jersey's entry into the Argentine market.	
Mar. 23		The British submarine H-42 has been sunk with all hands after being rammed by a destroyer during naval maneuvers off Gibraltar....British Prime Minister Lloyd George called for national support in pulling Britain out of her current economic slump. Lloyd George has warned of the danger of "extremist parties" rising to power in England and elsewhere.		American, British, French, and German companies are negotiating the formation of a consortium to build a single radio tower in Argentina to provide a direct radio link between South America and Europe.	In Australia, Queensland has abolished the Legislative Council, the Upper House of its bicameral legislature.
Mar. 24		The German Mark has fallen to a new low of 329 against the dollar, as the German economy staggers under the need to meet reparations payments....Violence again erupts in Belfast. The British have invited Michael Collins, head of the Irish Provisional Government, and Ulster Protestant leader Sir James Craig to London for talks to try to resolve the issue.		The Swiss Federal Council has settled a long-standing border dispute between Venezuela and Colombia, awarding the disputed territories to the Colombian government.	
Mar. 25	At a meeting of Allied Foreign Ministers in Paris, it is announced that the Allies would give Greece sovereignty over a demilitarized zone on the European side of the Dardanelles Straits. The French had resisted the plan, arguing that it was tantamount to making the Straits a British protectorate, under Britain's Greek ally.	Hysteria is setting in across Germany as the mark continues to plummet in value. Frightened Germans are trying to sell off their marks as quickly as possible, which is causing the value of the mark to fall still further.	The Anglo-Iraqi Military Agreement, giving Britain control over Iraqi defenses, is signed by Iraq and Britain....The British and French Foreign Ministers, meeting in Paris, have decided to hand the problem of Armenia and its displaced population to the League of Nations.		
	A *Includes developments that affect more than one world region, international organizations and important meetings of world leaders.*	B *Includes all domestic and regional developments in Europe, including the Soviet Union.*	C *Includes all domestic and regional developments in Africa and the Middle East.*	D *Includes all domestic and regional developments in Latin America, the Caribbean, and Canada.*	E *Includes all domestic and regional developments in Asian and Pacific nations (and colonies).*

U.S. Politics & Social Issues	U.S. Foreign Policy & Affairs, Defense	U.S. Economy & Environment	Science, Technology & Nature	Culture, Leisure & Lifestyle	
	President Harding, in a split with the Republican controlled Congress, has declared that he will not support further reductions in the army or navy. Pressure is on in the Republican Party to cut taxes and limit government spending....The House of Representatives voted today to reduce the number of army officers from the 13,000 demanded by Harding and recommended by Gen. Pershing, to just 11,000.		Captain Frederick Edward Guest, British Secretary of State for Air, has stated that airplanes, if built in sufficient numbers, could defend the British Isles. Guest believes that in 10 years, navies will be obsolete in the face of air power, and can so be cut drastically.	Threats by organized crime figures in Chicago have forced police to put a 24-hour guard around State's Attorney Robert C. Crowe's home....Automaker Henry Ford stopped in Ft. Pierce, FL, to visit his old friend, inventor Thomas Edison. While crossing the street Ford was nearly run over by one of his own automobiles....Poland has begun national censorship of movies, blaming a crime wave here on youths emulating American "Wild West" films.	Mar. 21
		Gasoline prices are on the rise throughout the Eastern States. Experts predict that prices could reach 30 cents per gallon by the summer.	In a striking demonstration of the new technology, an airplane landed today in front of the United States Capitol building. Weighing just 500 pounds, the mini-plane possess a wing span of just 20 feet.		Mar. 22
Emile Treville Holley has enrolled at Annapolis, becoming the first African-American naval cadet since the Civil War....The House of Representatives overwhelmingly passed a compromise Bonus Bill. The bill will provide for bonuses to be paid to World War I veterans within 25 years.		United Mine Workers (UMW) Union President John L. Lewis leaves New York for Cleveland, where he and other UMW leaders will finalize plans for a massive coal miners' strike set for April 1....United States Attorney general Daugherty today warned miners' unions that violence would not be tolerated during a threatened coal miners' strike. Daugherty went on to insist that the Federal government would not permit a "fuel famine."		An exhibition of modern French art opened at the Sculptor's Gallery in New York City. On display are the works of such masters as Picasso, Rodin, and Matisse.	Mar. 23
The Ku Klux Klan held a mass initiation in Tulsa, OK, today. The KKK has been growing in strength since World War I, amid widespread fear of African Americans, Jews, Catholics, and minorities. Ominously, it is gaining ground outside its traditional territories in the Deep South.	The United States Senate ratifies the Four Power Treaty on Pacific island fortifications today.			Only three out of the 32 horses starting the Grand National at Aintree cross the finish line today.	Mar. 24
			Captain Roald Amundsen, Norwegian arctic explorer and conqueror of the South Pole, announced today that he would fly a newly designed, all metal aircraft from New York to Seattle to test it for an assault on the North Pole in June.	Prohibition agents today dumped 350,000 gallons of captured bootleg wine, beer, and whiskey into the Chicago River today as a public display of the effectiveness of prohibition in Chicago. Chicago's Torrio mob, overseen by "Johnny" Torrio's lieutenant, Al Capone, continues to grow and seek new territories.	Mar. 25

	World Affairs	Europe	Africa & The Middle East	The Americas	Asia & The Pacific
Mar. 26		Republican officers in the Irish Army have repudiated the planned peace treaty with Great Britain and have proclaimed an "Army Executive" under Liam Mellows and Rory O'Connor to take power away from the *Dail*....Some 1.9 million British workers were listed as unemployed in January, though the number is now slowly declining. The prolonged recession in Britain has brought wage cuts and widespread discontent.	The Allied Powers agreed to revise some of the terms of the Sevres Treaty to end the Greco-Turkish War. The Turkish Nationalists have refused to end hostilities until the Greeks have evacuated all of their forces from Anatolia.		
Mar. 27		The Irish Free State Bill, carrying out the provisions of the Treaty of London with the Irish rebels, was passed by the British House of commons today, despite bitter opposition by die-hard Conservatives.			
Mar. 28		Right wing Russian exiles try to assassinate Pavel Milyukov, exiled founder of the Constitutional Democratic (Cadet) Party, today at a conference in Berlin. The attack fails when liberal Russian exile journalist Vladimir D. Nabokov, editor of the *emigré* newspaper *Rul*, "The Rudder," attempts to disarm the gunmen. Nabokov is killed instantly. One of the killers is Piotr Shabelsky-Bork, promoter of the anti-Semitic *Protocols of the Elders of Zion*.			
Mar. 29		The government of Lithuania announces plans for a land reform program. Lithuania has been the home to great landed estates, held by a powerful, German descended landowning class. The Lithuanian government is trying to limit peasant unrest, which can easily be exploited by Lithuania's Soviet neighbors.			
Mar. 30		Irish Provisional Government head Michael Collins and Ulster Protestant leader Sir James Craig have reached an agreement mediated in London to cooperate in bringing the situation in Belfast under control. Irish Republican Army operations will cease, and the Belfast police will be reconstituted to have equal numbers of Catholic and Protestant officers.			
Mar. 31	Soviet Foreign Minister Chicherin signed an accord with Poland, and the Baltic States of Lithuania, Latvia, and Estonia in Riga today, capping a conference in which the signatories agree to partially demilitarize their borders, pulling troops back to leave border zones with border patrols only. The four countries are seeking to resolve their differences before the Genoa Conference. The Soviets in particular want lessened tensions along their borders. Chicherin then left Riga for Berlin, where he will confer with the Germans before the Genoa Conference....A.B. Houghton, the first American ambassador to Germany since World War, I sailed today for Germany from New York City. Houghton hopes to begin "one hundred years of peace and friendship" between Germany and the United States.	The Amsterdam Trade Fair opens today, with Prince Hendrik presiding at the opening ceremonies....King George V of Great Britain signed the bill ratifying the Treaty of London. Ireland, after centuries under British rule, is now a self governing Dominion, the Irish Free State.... Soviet leader Vladimir I. Lenin addressed the Communist Party Congress in Moscow today. Lenin defends his recent concessions to local entrepreneurs forced by the recent famine, in his New Economic Policy (NEP). Lenin counters critics who say that he has departed from Socialism, stating that "the retreat is over."...The condition of deposed Austro-Hungarian Emperor Karl I worsened today. In exile in the Madeira Islands, the ex-emperor, and claimant to the Habsburg crown of Austria and Hungary, is suffering from pneumonia.	Rebels ambush a French column in the Moulenya Valley in Morocco today, killing or wounding 700.		

U.S. Politics & Social Issues	U.S. Foreign Policy & Affairs, Defense	U.S. Economy & Environment	Science, Technology & Nature	Culture, Leisure & Lifestyle	
		Railroad car orders by railroads for the first three months of 1922 have already exceeded orders for all of 1921, indicating a general economic recovery from the post-World War recession is underway.	The British De Haviland firm has unveiled its newest airplane design, the DH 34....France will appropriate 154 million francs this year to encourage commercial aviation. However, it still costs twice as much to fly than to travel by train.	A recent survey of colleges showed that of universities founded since 1870, 70 percent now offer practical, professional training. The old idea of a university as being strictly "cultural" rather than practical, is increasingly coming under fire.	Mar. 26
Reverend John Holmes predicts in a sermon held in New York City that "church religion" will eventually die out and be replaced with a faith embracing the principles of evolutionist Charles Darwin.			Canadian Arctic explorer Stefansson has claimed that in the next 10 years the Arctic will become vital as a direct link between Europe and the Far East using dirigibles or airplanes.		Mar. 27
	The naval subcommittee of the House Appropriations Committee drafts a bill that would reduce the number of Navy seamen personnel to 65,000.		The first microfilm has been developed. Its importance is noted by intelligence agencies around the world.	The Toronto St. Pats (NHL) have beaten the Vancouver Millionaires (PCHA) three games to two to capture the Stanley Cup.	Mar. 28
President Warren Harding calls on Congress to enact funds for the creation of a new "industrial prison," one that would teach valuable trade skills to young prisoners while they remain incarcerated.					Mar. 29
Census officials report that the number of U.S. immigrants who are unable to speak English has risen to encompass over 10 percent of the total foreign-born population.			Two Portuguese pilots, Captains Gago Coutinho and Sacadura Cabral, have left Lisbon in a Fairey III seaplane today, in an attempt to be the first to cross the South Atlantic by air. By nightfall, they reached the Canary Islands, 710 miles the southwest, along the coast of Africa.		Mar. 30
		600,000 coal miners began a nationwide strike today, shutting down mines across the United States. 100,000 nonunion miners may join the walk out.	Coutinho and Sacadura Cabral continued their transatlantic attempt today, leaving the Canaries for the Cape Verde Islands, 816 miles further down the African coast. From there, the two Portuguese pilots will wait until mid-April for a full moon before attempting the most dangerous leg of the flight, across the open South Atlantic to Brazil.... Professor Albert Einstein, of the University of Berlin, delivered a lecture today at the University of Paris. In attendance were famed radiation pioneer Madame Marie Curie and French physicist Daniel Berthelot.		Mar. 31

F	G	H	I	J
Includes campaigns, elections, federal-state relations, civil rights and liberties, crime, the judiciary, education, healthcare, poverty, urban affairs, and population.	*Includes formation and debate of U.S. foreign and defense policies, veterans affairs, and defense spending. (Relations with specific foreign countries are usually found under the region concerned.)*	*Includes business, labor, agriculture, taxation, transportation, consumer affairs, monetary and fiscal policy, natural resources, pollution and industrial accidents.*	*Includes worldwide scientific, medical and technological developments, natural phenomena, U.S. weather and natural disasters.*	*Includes the arts, religion, scholarship, communications media, sports, entertainment, fashions, fads, and social life.*

	World Affairs	Europe	Africa & The Middle East	The Americas	Asia & The Pacific
Apr. 1	French Premier Raymond Poincaré today warned Germany that France would resist all attempts at the Genoa Conference to alter the terms of the Versailles Treaty, particularly in regards to payment of reparations.	Karl I, deposed Habsburg Emperor of Austria-Hungary, has died in exile today on the Portuguese island of Madeira. To his death, he had claimed the throne of both Austria and Hungary. Karl I's son and heir Franz Josef Otto could still claim the throne, but lacks sufficient support....In Austria, the republican government has refused to lower flags to half-mast....The British government has ordered the release of all Irish prisoners in Britain except those held on charges of sedition....Violence again shakes Belfast, as a Protestant policeman and seven Catholics, including three children, are gunned down in sectarian fighting.	The Spanish destroyer *Bustamente* lands supplies to reinforce the Spanish fort on Alhucemas, off Melilla in Spanish Morocco, which has been shelled by Moorish rebels....Armenian leaders today bitterly denounce French and British plans to turn the Armenian question over to the League of Nations, seeing it as tantamount to abandonment of the Armenian people to genocide....President Harding has advised Armenian leaders that there is nothing the United States can do....The South African government reports that the total casualties of the recent rebellion in the Rand came to 810 dead and wounded on both sides.	Federal Prohibition authorities are trying to enlist British help in keeping alcohol from being smuggled into Florida from the Bahamas. Alcohol smuggling has become big business in the British-owned Bahamas and Cuba.	In this month, a rebellion breaks out in the Emirate of Bukhara against Soviet rule. The Soviets have effectively resurrected the Russian empire in central Asia, and are resented by the Muslim inhabitants, especially as the Soviets regard religions, including Islam, as obsolete superstitions....In this month, the Japanese establish civil government for their Pacific island mandates on Korror Island in the Palau Islands.
Apr. 2	The German mark has ceased its plummet as Europeans await the results of the upcoming Genoa Economic Conference.	Republican opponents of the Irish Free State parade through the streets of Dublin in a mass rally....In Dundalk, Republican leader Eamon de Valera has openly denounced both the Irish Free State government in Dublin and the Protestant government loyal to Great Britain in Northern Ireland....Ireland is on the verge of open civil war.		Brazil has been supporting the development of a steel industry of its own through protective tariffs. Iron ore is abundant in the states of Minas Gerais, Sao Paulo, and Parana, but smelting facilities for the ore remain limited.	
Apr. 3	Experts in Paris are drafting proposals for a resolution of Allied differences with Russia before the Genoa Conference. Ideas include recognizing the Soviet regime and a partial cancellation of Russia's debts in exchange for guarantees of protection for foreigners in Russia and abandonment of Soviet claims for damages for Allied support of the Whites in the Russian Civil War.	Lenin appoints Josef V. Stalin as General Secretary of the Communist Party in Russia....British Prime Minister Lloyd George's government beats down a challenge by discontented Conservatives in Parliament, 372 votes to 94. Lloyd George is calling for a cautious recognition of the Soviets, and is prepared to devalue the British Pound to restore economic stability to Britain, whose exports are now overvalued and unable to compete with those of other nations.	Armenian villagers are facing famine, with 49 out of 50 villagers showing signs of malnutrition. War, genocide, and continued instability have paralyzed relief efforts.	Representatives of international banks will meet with Mexican Treasury Secretary Adolfo de la Huerta in New York in early May to try to arrange a settlement on Mexico's foreign debt. Wracked by revolution and unrest, Mexico has been in default since 1914, and currently owes $322 million to foreign banks.	Forces of the Soviet Far Eastern Republic have captured Spasskoye and are pushing south along the Ussuri Railway toward Vladivostok. White Russian forces are rapidly disintegrating in a rout, and are being disarmed by the Japanese guarding Vladivostok.
Apr. 4		A bomb explodes at a dinner for assembled leaders of Hungary's Liberal Party in Budapest, killing six and wounding 30. Liberal Party leader, Karl Rassay, was uninjured. Rassay has recently pulled out of Hungary's coalition government....A split has arisen in Britain's embattled labor movement today, as 47 unions vote to break their alliance with the militant engineers union and reopen negotiations with company owners, who have been engaged in a lock out with unions for weeks.	The Near East Relief Bureau estimates that there are nearly 175,000 war refugees in Constantinople, including 50,000 White Russian refugees from the Russian Civil War.	The Colombian Ministry of War has opened a School of Aviation at Flandes....The state legislature of Nueva Leon today declared Juan M. Garcia, to be removed as governor of the state. In recent weeks, governors have been deposed in the Mexican states of Puebla, Michoacan, Jalisco, and Tabasco.	Japanese troops repulse a column of Red troops near Spasskoye, 100 miles north of Vladivostok.
Apr. 5	The German government today announced that it would reject Allied demands for another $100 million in taxes to pay for reparations....Rumors are rife as Europe prepares for the economic conference in Genoa.	German Chancellor Joseph Wirth today denied that Germany had reached an accord with the Soviets, as German delegates prepared to leave for the Genoa Conference.		Argentine wool exporters are protesting a proposed American tariff on imported wool, arguing that it will make Argentine wool prohibitively expensive.	

A	B	C	D	E
Includes developments that affect more than one world region, international organizations and important meetings of world leaders.	*Includes all domestic and regional developments in Europe, including the Soviet Union.*	*Includes all domestic and regional developments in Africa and the Middle East.*	*Includes all domestic and regional developments in Latin America, the Caribbean, and Canada.*	*Includes all domestic and regional developments in Asian and Pacific nations (and colonies).*

U.S. Politics & Social Issues	U.S. Foreign Policy & Affairs, Defense	U.S. Economy & Environment	Science, Technology & Nature	Culture, Leisure & Lifestyle	
Sen. Charles A. Culberson of Texas today warns his constituents that the Ku Klux Klan has become a menace to the survival of the American Constitution.	As growing unrest wracks northern China, in this month, the United States deploys marines to guard American interests in Tianjin and other Chinese cities.	Coal miners in the United States are now on strike across the country. Two policemen are injured in Benton and Duquoin in clashes with striking miners in the southern Illinois coal country. In two Illinois counties alone, 30,000 men are on strike.	Antarctic explorer Roald Amundsen arrives in New York City today, flying his new all-metal JL.6 monoplane, with which he intends to reach the North Pole....Portuguese aviators Coutinho and Sacadura will leave the Canary Islands tonight for the 910-mile flight south to the Cape Verde Islands, on the next leg of their planned crossing of the South Atlantic to Brazil.	Albanian women are being won over to American women's dresses, after seeing Red Cross nurses working in Tirana.	Apr. 1
	A parade will be held today in Brooklyn to honor the return of the final group of bodies of servicemen killed in World War I.	100,000 American tourists are expected to visit Europe this year, the majority in the summer. The average tourist is expected to spend about $1,500 on the trip. The American dollar has been strong against European currencies weakened by World War I....A Labor department survey of 16 American cities shows that food prices have fallen eight to 16 percent in the last year.	Swiss psychiatrist Hermann Rohrschach, inventor of the famed inkblot personality test named for him, has died....Mexican boll weevils have destroyed between $1.6 and 1.9 billion worth of crops in the Cotton Belt in the last five years. Entomologists are researching chemical pesticides to try to eradicate these pests....The Bureau of the Census reported today that death rates have dropped for all age groups in the United States between 1910 and 1920.	Charlie Chaplin's new film, *Pay Day*, is released today in New York....Act I of Booth Tarkington's new comedy, *The Intimate Strangers*, has come out in magazine form....Public prosecutors in France have been ordered by the Minister of Justice to crack down on dueling, which still goes on there....Hip flasks have become common among "flapper" women, as defiance of Prohibition continues at late night revels....E.M. Forster's novel *The Longest Journey*, appears this week, as does Walter Lippman's nonfiction work, *Public Opinion*.	Apr. 2
	Sen. David Walsh of Massachusetts today proposed the creation of a United States Aeronautical Academy to train officers for the air service, along the lines of West Point or Annapolis....Two Army Air Service pilots are killed in a mid-air collision over Ellington Field, near Houston, TX. The pilots were training in pursuit (fighter) planes, in a simulated dogfight involving 15 aircraft.	John L. Lewis, President of the United Mine Workers (UMW) testifying today before the House of Representatives, has called for nationalization of coal mines in the United States.		Five men, including the architect and construction managers, have been indicted for manslaughter in the collapse in January of the Knickerbocker Theater in Washington, DC, which claimed 98 lives.	Apr. 3
			Dr. George Hale of the Mt. Wilson Observatory is calling on astronomers to work together with physicists in studying cosmic radiation and astrophysics. A scientist in attendance believes that science will soon "Try to knock to pieces the atoms of our elements and see what becomes of them."...Sailors today spot an unexploded naval mine drifting off Canada's Grand Banks. 121 mines, of the thousands laid in the World War, have been spotted between January 1921 and March of this year.	The Student Council at William and Mary University voted today to expel any student found under the influence of alcohol, after a warning. Alcohol has become increasingly prevalent on campus, despite of Prohibition....Bootleggers are using fast cars, with speeds up to 75 mph, along with planes and speedboats to smuggle alcohol into the country. The situation is reported to be particularly bad in Florida and in upstate New York, along the Canadian border.	Apr. 4
	Naval Secretary Edwin Denby today warns that Soviet agents have been trying to spread Communist propaganda among sailors in foreign ports, and warns of the danger of allowing "sinister propaganda" to spread.		Lord Lee of Fareham, First Lord of the Admiralty, in a speech before the Institution of Naval Architects, this evening, assures listeners that the battleship remains the basis of sea power, and dismisses the idea of sinking a battleship by aerial bombing as a "stunt."		Apr. 5
F *Includes campaigns, elections, federal-state relations, civil rights and liberties, crime, the judiciary, education, healthcare, poverty, urban affairs, and population.*	G *Includes formation and debate of U.S. foreign and defense policies, veterans affairs, and defense spending. (Relations with specific foreign countries are usually found under the region concerned.)*	H *Includes business, labor, agriculture, taxation, transportation, consumer affairs, monetary and fiscal policy, natural resources, pollution and industrial accidents.*	I *Includes worldwide scientific, medical and technological developments, natural phenomena, U.S. weather and natural disasters.*	J *Includes the arts, religion, scholarship, communications media, sports, entertainment, fashions, fads, and social life.*	

	World Affairs	Europe	Africa & The Middle East	The Americas	Asia & The Pacific
Apr. 6		In continuing unrest in Ireland, five former police officers are gunned down in County Clare and County Kerry. Republican militants ambush and kill four Ulster policemen along the Irish border....On the Northern Ireland border, Republican militants are enforcing a boycott of goods coming into Ireland from Ulster. Mobs have attacked trains coming into Ireland, dragging out merchandise and burning it. In response to the continuing unrest, Britain today sent a squadron of destroyers to Queenstown, Ireland, to guard government stores against seizure by Republican forces....More than three years after World War I, Belgium is still trying to recover. The ravaged country posted a trade deficit of three billion francs last year, mostly due to the need to import foodstuffs from the United States and Argentina.	Seventeen people are killed in a clash between Palestinian Arab factions near Hebron....An Anglo-American consortium, allied with South African interests and backed by the Morgan group, has established a monopoly on the African diamond trade. The Morgan group recently bought German interests in South-West Africa. Now the Anglo-American group has bought up the output from the Belgian Congo.	President Chamorro of Nicaragua has declared martial law, arresting 34 Liberals in what Chamorro claims is a plot to assassinate him....Two New York mobsters hold up a bootlegger's storehouse on West End Island in the Bahamas today, escaping with $50,000. Crime has been on the rise in the Bahamas, which have been transformed by Prohibition into a major center for smuggling....Boxing heavyweight contender Luis Firpo has become a national hero in his native Argentina after his victories in the United States, with tangoes being written in his honor and stores decorated with his photos.	
Apr. 7	British Prime Minister Lloyd George confers today with French Premier Raymond Poincaré in Paris. The British are eagerly seeking French support in the upcoming Genoa Conference.	Danish unions today vote to accept company terms, ending the 2-month lockout by Danish firms.	Great Britain today issues a concession to Standard Oil, allowing it to drill for oil in the British Mandate of Palestine. Britain has been under pressure from the United States to share development of Middle Eastern oil. By making concessions on Palestine, the British seek to preserve their monopoly on the vast Iraqi oil fields....Brigades commanded by Generals Berenguer and Cabanellas are advancing against Muslim rebels in the Rif Mountains of Spanish Morocco, having captured Chemorra and Laari. The rebels, of the Beni Said tribe, are using guerilla tactics and take advantage of the rugged terrain.		China announces today that it is ending the special reduced tariff that Russia obtained under the Tsars. Russian goods entering the country will now be subject to normal import taxes. The Soviets have accepted this without complaint, seeking an understanding with the Chinese in order to better face Japan and the Western powers.
Apr. 8	The American ambassador to Italy will lead a group of "observers" at the Genoa Conference. American "observers" are in fact drawing regular pay from the State Department for their work. Thus, the "observers" are delegates in all but name. America is in European politics to stay.	Erich von Falkenhayn (62), German General in World War I, has died.... The Soviets have charged Anatoly, Bishop of Irkutsk, and two other Russian Orthodox clergymen, of obstructing government efforts to track down and secure Church treasures, which the government is claiming.		President Obregon of Mexico announces that the government will crack down on unrest, warning radical leaders in Guadalajara in particular.	Zhou Ziqi has succeeded Yen Huiqing as Prime Minister of the Chinese government in Beijing. The Beijing government is rapidly disintegrating amid renewed violence.
Apr. 9	Trade, currency values, the recognition of Soviet Russia, and disarmament are all on the agenda for the upcoming Genoa Conference, which opens tomorrow. Of particular concern are the problems of runaway inflation in Central Europe, especially Germany, and the mutual tariff barriers that have sprung up across Europe, as each nation seeks to keep out foreign competition. Unspoken, but palpable, is the lingering question of the staggering debts owed to the United States.	Responsibility for the bombing attack on the Hungarian Liberal Party in Budapest last week has been fixed on Awakening Magyars, an ultra-right wing, anti-Semitic group in Hungary....20 French soldiers are killed and another 12 wounded when a hidden arms cache exploded in the disputed Silesian region, between Germany and Poland.		Miss Bertha Lutz, the first woman ever to represent Brazil abroad in an official capacity, arrived in the United States today for the upcoming Pan American Congress of Women to be held in Baltimore.... The Brazilian destroyer *Para* has been put on station off Fernando Noronha to assist the Portuguese airmen, who will be attempting the first air crossing of the South Atlantic from the Cape Verde Islands radioing in weather information.	A coalition has been formed between Sun Yat-sen's Kuomintang government in southern China, Chang Tso-lin's Manchurian forces, and a revived "Anfu Clique," led by General Tuan Chi Jui, against General Wu. Pei-fu, the warlord dominating the Beijing government. Chang's forces are moving to cut the Beijing-Tianjin Railway, as panic takes hold in Beijing. Leading Chinese are desperately seeking refuge in the foreign concession in Tianjin. Sun Yat-sen's forces are pushing into Jiangxi Province and threatening Changsha, the capital of Hunan Province....Japanese troops have begun evacuating Shandong, as agreed to in the Washington Treaty.

U.S. Politics & Social Issues	U.S. Foreign Policy & Affairs, Defense	U.S. Economy & Environment	Science, Technology & Nature	Culture, Leisure & Lifestyle	
S.R. Aldredge, Mayor of Dallas, today called on the Ku Klux Klan in the city to disband, stating that the Klan has "brought discord to a peaceful city."		Mine operators in Pittsburgh, Ohio, and Illinois refused today to enter into negotiations with striking coal miners.		Plans are underway to refurbish Pershing Stadium in Paris for the 1924 Olympics. The games are intended to showcase France's recovery after World War I....Police in New York City attribute the city's rising crime rate to unemployment and to the ease with which criminals can steal automobiles to commit crimes. Criminals are becoming more mobile and better armed.	Apr. 6
Interior Secretary Albert B. Fall has leased part of Naval Oil Reserve #7 in Teapot Dome, WY, to the Mammoth Oil Company, owned by Harry Sinclair.		The Controller of the Currency reports today that 365 banks failed in 1921, including 37 national banks, the largest number since 1897. The majority of failures were in the South and on the Great Plains, where farm failures have hurt the local economy....Striking mine workers in Pennsylvania are trying to unionize workers at U.S. Steel and other steel firms, many of which own their own coal mines.	A Daimler Airways DH-18 has collided in mid-air with a Grands Express Farman Goliat over Poix, in France, killing seven. This is the first mid-air collision between commercial aircraft.	Renowned Spanish cellist Pablo Casals makes his debut as a conductor tonight at New York's Carnegie Hall....New Jersey eases handgun restrictions today, allowing anyone to purchase a handgun if they own an automobile or carriage and carry the weapon for "legal purposes."	Apr. 7
Courts in Wichita Falls, TX, and Denver, CO, are taking action to investigate the Ku Klux Klan, as the Klan, formerly confined to the South, seeks to make inroads in the West.	Another contingent of 1,152 troops leave Germany today for the United States, leaving just a token force of 2,600 men in the American occupation zone at Koblenz.		The Chevrolet brothers will install a special two-way radio set in a race car for the upcoming Indianapolis 500 Race, to enable the driver to stay in contact with the pit crew.	Henry E. Huntington has announced that he will donate his estate, including San Marino, his palatial estate near Pasadena, and his world renowned library and art collection. His art collection, valued at $5 million, includes Gainsborough's famous *Blue Boy*, while the $10 million library includes the first book ever printed in the English language, from 1474, and a manuscript copy of Chaucer's *Canterbury Tales*....Rev. G.C. Rarick, of the Methodist Board of Temperance, warned that a lifting of Prohibition would result in a "beer tax" of $5 billion a year on the economy.	Apr. 8
	The National Advisory Committee on Aeronautics (NACA) is planning a series of tests on monoplane airplane wings in an effort to give designers accurate performance data. America's NACA is unmatched worldwide in this kind of systematic aeronautical research.	Automobile production is back up again, with March output surpassing any month since August 1920.	The U.S. Navy Department, in conjunction with the Japanese, British, and Canadian navies and steamship lines, are planning a comprehensive survey of the most heavily traveled routes in the North Pacific, to lay out specific routes for eastbound and westbound traffic to minimize the danger of collisions.	A slow theater season is forcing unemployed New York actors and actresses to seek work in department stores. There are some 32,000 actors and actresses in the United States, and half are predicted to be unemployed through the summer. However, the prospect of earning $250 or even $300 a week on Broadway still draws many...."Eskimo Pies" are earning their inventor, C.K. Nelson, $30,000 a week as the new ice cream sensation sweeps the country....125,000 people pack the entire eight mile length of the Atlantic City Boardwalk today as throngs celebrated Palm Sunday.	Apr. 9

F	G	H	I	J
Includes campaigns, elections, federal-state relations, civil rights and liberties, crime, the judiciary, education, healthcare, poverty, urban affairs, and population.	*Includes formation and debate of U.S. foreign and defense policies, veterans affairs, and defense spending. (Relations with specific foreign countries are usually found under the region concerned.)*	*Includes business, labor, agriculture, taxation, transportation, consumer affairs, monetary and fiscal policy, natural resources, pollution and industrial accidents.*	*Includes worldwide scientific, medical and technological developments, natural phenomena, U.S. weather and natural disasters.*	*Includes the arts, religion, scholarship, communications media, sports, entertainment, fashions, fads, and social life.*

	World Affairs	Europe	Africa & The Middle East	The Americas	Asia & The Pacific
Apr. 10	The Genoa Conference convenes today....Representatives from 34 countries, including Britain, France, Italy, Germany, and Russia will meet to discuss the world economic situation, including the position of Soviet Russia. British prime Minister Lloyd George is struggling to hold the conference together as the French and Soviet delegates have already clashed on the issues of debts and disarmament.	Germany has definitively rejected demands by the Allied Reparations Commission for Allied control of German finances and 60 billion marks in new taxes. France in return, has threatened an occupation of the German Ruhr.		In *Balzac v. Porto Rico*, the U.S. Supreme Court has confirmed the decision of previous "Insular Cases" that Constitutional protections, in this case Sixth Amendment rights to a jury, do not apply in America's overseas possessions.	
Apr. 11		The famine in Russia's Volga Basin is finally being brought under control, as spring opens up communications and river transport routes to the stricken areas.	The Greek army headquarters in Smyrna today categorically refused an armistice with the Turkish Nationalists in Anatolia. The Greeks are dug in on a line from Karahissar to Eski-Shehr.	Louis Borno, former Secretary of State, has been elected President of Haiti, succeeding outgoing president Sudre D'Artiguenave. Borno is said to represent a conservative element capable of working with the American marines, who still occupy the country.	Indian Nationalist Siad Hussein today calls on the British to leave India, saying that Muslims and Hindus now were "one people."
Apr. 12	The French Olympic Committee has decided to hold the 1924 Games at Colombes, outside of Paris. This will cost five million francs less than the original 20 million planned.	In line with Lenin's New Economic Policy (NEP) to encourage private entrepreneurship in some sections of the economy, the Council of Commissars has allowed private individuals to again own cars.... Albania has executed several leaders of a recent revolutionary effort. The Albanian government now controls the major towns, including Scutari and Elbesan, which had previously defied the government.... Major flooding is reported in Latvia, after the army explodes artillery shells on an ice dam on the Dvina River. Eight villages have had to be evacuated.	French President Alexandre Millerand and Marshal Hubert Lyautey, French Commissioner in Morocco, meet with General Berenguer, Spanish High Commissioner in Morocco, today in Mequinez, in the French Zone of Morocco, to confer on suppressing the ongoing Muslim rebellion in the Rif Mountains of Spanish Morocco....Fighting has resumed in Anatolia as the Turkish Nationalist forces Mustafa Kemal begin probing Greek defenses.		Prince Hirohito, Regent of Japan, today welcomed Edward, Prince of Wales to Tokyo today as the Prince continues his tour of Asia.... Japanese troops, backed by artillery and aircraft, drove off Soviet troops of the Far Eastern Republic pursuing Russian White forces in Siberia. The Soviets pull back, losing 30 men, but hold onto the town of Brussifka, which they captured earlier in the day.
Apr. 13	Negotiations continue over Russian recognition in Genoa today, with the Allied powers agreeing to present a common front in dealing with the Soviets.	Catholics and Protestants are sniping at each other from the rooftops in Belfast, Northern Ireland.	Tensions are high in Palestine, with Arab newspapers calling for coordinated attacks on Zionist settlers.		Japanese troops have driven Soviet Far Eastern Republic forces out of the neutral zone protecting the White forces of the Vladivostok government. Japanese troops have driven the Soviets north, capturing Shmakovka, 150 miles north of Vladivostok, and are approaching the Ussuri River. Vladivostok forces have pushed north far more cautiously, securing the town of Olga, but relying on the Japanese for protection.
Apr. 14	France is emerging as a major block to the Genoa Conference. Effectively wielding a veto on whether the Conference will achieve anything, France is determined not to budge on concessions to Germany or Russia.	Irish Republican militants, led by Rory O'Conner, have seized control of the Four Courts building in Dublin, defying the Free State government. The militants, numbering some 200 men, are determined to spark a new war with Britain to achieve a complete break with British rule. Militants also seize Kilmainham Jail in Dublin; Kilmainham is famed as the prison where Irish nationalists were held by the British....Irish Free State leaders Arthur Griffith and Prime Minister Michael Collins meet today with dissident Republican leaders Eamon de Valera and Cathal Brugha in an effort to try to stop the growing bloodshed in Ireland. The meeting breaks up after three hours with no result....Italy's population has continued to boom, reaching 38.8 million in 1921.	General Papoulas, commander of the Greek forces in Anatolia, announces that the Greeks have repulsed Turkish attacks along the Afiun-Karahissar front, where the Greek army is dug in.... Spanish troops today reoccupied Darquebdani in Morocco, where a Spanish garrison under Colonel Araujo had been overrun and massacred last July by rebel Beni Urriaguel tribesmen. Spanish troops find the bodies of more than 1,000 Spanish troops, unburied, but with the bodies looted.	Mexico today announces that it is forbidding the sale of land to foreigners, thus blocking the sale of the six million acre estate of General Luis Terrazas in Chihuahua to an American concern.	Khara Singh, President of the Punjab Congress Committee, has been convicted of sedition in India, over his agitation over the guardianship of Sikh shrines.
	A *Includes developments that affect more than one world region, international organizations and important meetings of world leaders.*	B *Includes all domestic and regional developments in Europe, including the Soviet Union.*	C *Includes all domestic and regional developments in Africa and the Middle East.*	D *Includes all domestic and regional developments in Latin America, the Caribbean, and Canada.*	E *Includes all domestic and regional developments in Asian and Pacific nations (and colonies).*

U.S. Politics & Social Issues	U.S. Foreign Policy & Affairs, Defense	U.S. Economy & Environment	Science, Technology & Nature	Culture, Leisure & Lifestyle	
			Capt. Roald Amundsen, famed polar explorer, is forced to make an emergency landing in his experimental all-metal monoplane, after his engine overheats at 6,000 feet on the first leg of his planned transcontinental flight from New York City to Seattle.		Apr. 10
Miss Maud Younger of the National Women's Party today advocates the passage of an amendment to the Constitution guaranteeing women equal rights. Her idea is immediately denounced by George W. Alger as a "flapper attitude toward legislation."		The National Association of Manufacturers notes today that movies have been found to be particularly effective vehicles for advertising in foreign countries.			Apr. 11
		Beauty parlors are booming as American women rush to improve their looks. Some of the rush is apparently due to Prohibition. The owner of two beauty parlors in Washington, DC, remarks to reporters that: "When men drank, they were not so critical....Now, however, men remained clear-eyed all night and notice wrinkles, pallor, straight hair, and un-sparkling eyes."		President and Mrs. Harding today attend the opening game of the 1922 baseball season at American League Park, to watch the match between the New York Yankees and the Washington Senators. President Harding throws out the first ball before a crowd of on looking dignitaries. The Yankees win, 6–5.... A San Francisco jury today takes just one minute to acquit Roscoe C. "Fatty" Arbuckle of charges in the death of Virginia Rappe at a Labor Day Party in the Hotel St. Francis. This is the third trial of Arbuckle, after two earlier trials ended in hung juries. The sensational trials have ruined Arbuckle's career, and feed Hollywood's growing reputation as morally decadent.	Apr. 12
The State of Massachusetts has opened all public offices in the state to women....Senator Capper of Kansas today lays out the goals of the farm bloc: long-term credits for farmers, reduced railroad rates, tariff protections, and the development of a proposed dam project at Muscle Shoals. American farmers are in increasingly dire economic straits....The coal strike is becoming increasingly bitter in West Virginia, as striking workers complain of evictions from company housing, and mine operators seek protection for nonunion miners who are still working.		A merger is agreed upon today between the Pierce-Arrow Motor Car Company and Lafayette Motors. Charles W. Nash, President of Lafayette and founder of Nash Motors, will head the new corporation. The consolidation will allow for economies of scale, essential in the automobile industry.	Sir Ross Smith, commander of the first flight from Britain to Australia, is killed today, testing an experimental airplane with which he had planned to circumnavigate the globe....The Naval Wireless Station in Virginia will be used to enable President Harding to give speeches and government officials to make announcements over the radio in a 1,500-mile radius.		Apr. 13
The *Wall Street Journal* has reported that Interior Secretary Albert B. Fall leased the naval oil reserve at Teapot Dome, WY, to Harry Sinclair's Mammoth Oil without competitive bidding. Progressive Republican Senator Robert "Fighting Bob" LaFollette is calling for a Senate investigation of the Teapot Dome Scandal after persons unknown ransacked his offices in the Russell Building. Fall has powerful connections, both in the Harding administration and among the corporations that backed Harding's presidency.... Ku Klux Klan members burn three large crosses on Garrett Mountain, overlooking Paterson, NJ, signaling the Klan's intent to spread beyond its origins in the South.	President Harding today asks Congress for funding to send an American delegation to the fifth Pan-American Conference to be held in Santiago, Chile, next year.	Mrs. Edith Rockefeller-McCormick today announces that daily flights between New York and Chicago, with planes carrying as many as 200 people, will begin in a few years.	Captain Sir John Alcock, commander of the first flight across the Atlantic, is killed today, in an air crash in France....The New York Botanical Gardens have recruited Arawak tribesmen to collect botanical specimens for them in the jungles of British Guiana, and have thus far collected thousands of specimens.	A convention of the On Leong Chinese Merchants Association in Philadelphia today decried the spread of "flapper" fashions: bobbed hair and short skirts, among Chinese girls in America, and warning that Chinese women needed to remember "the teachings of their ancestors."	Apr. 14

	World Affairs	Europe	Africa & The Middle East	The Americas	Asia & The Pacific
Apr. 15	Among numerous ideas floated for dealing with the world economy at the Genoa Conference, are proposals to return to a strict gold standard worldwide. This would eliminate political pressure on central banks to inflate the currency, while in effect turning gold into an international currency.	Russia's trade in 1921 stood at a tenth of her prewar trade in 1913. Soviet Russia's largest trading partner now is Britain.			Trade is reviving across the Far East and in India. In China, merchants and businessmen have begun adopting Western methods as China slowly integrates itself with the world economy.
Apr. 16	German Foreign Minister Walther Rathenau has signed an accord with Soviet Foreign Minister Georgi Chicherin. In the Treaty of Rapallo, the two countries have agreed to reestablish diplomatic and trade relations with each other. Both sides renounce all reparations and debts from World War I and have agreed to military and economic cooperation with each other in opposition to the Allied Powers. The German arms manufacturer, Krupp, will produce war material in Russia for the Bolsheviks....In a top secret protocol to the treaty of Rapallo, the Soviets will allow the Germans use of training facilities in Russia to allow the German *Reichswehr* to practice with tanks, planes, artillery, and poison gas, all forbidden to Germany under the terms of the Treaty of Versailles.	Arthur Griffith, President of the Irish *Dail,* has come to Sligo today to speak. Griffith has been warned not to speak in Sligo by Republican militants. Today Griffith defied the threats and addressed the crowds in Sligo without incident....A Republican assassination team attacks Irish Free state leader Michael Collins in Dublin today. Collins returns fire. One of the attackers is captured and is found to have explosives strapped to his body....Bulgaria has barred exiled Russian White General Baron Peter Wrangel, fearing unrest by socialist groups if Wrangel enters the country.	Faced with an armed rebellion, the French have declared martial law in Damascus. The disturbances began with the murder of Assad Bey, Minister of the Interior for Lebanon, which the French are attempting to organize as a separate, Christian dominated mandate.	Secretary of State Charles Evans Hughes today warns Mexican president Alvaro Obregon that confiscations of American property in Mexico are the main barrier to American recognition. The properties include sugar plantations and ranches. American businessmen particularly want security for oil drilling operations before investing in the troubled country....The Mexican War Office today announced that Mexican rebel leaders Manuel Garduno and Jose Delgado, have been "killed while trying to escape" after leading an uprising in the state of Coahuila. Another rebel, Manuel Larrage, continues to lead a guerilla movement against the government in Tamaulipas.	Manchurian warlord General Chang Tsolin has moved 70,000 troops south from Mukden to within 40 miles of Beijing, and now controls the railroad from Beijing to the port of Tianjin. Wu Pei-fu, Inspector General of Hunan and Hubei Provinces, and the warlord who dominates the Beijing government, has marshaled a similar number of troops in Shandong Province and at Chang Sin-Tien, 13 miles south of Beijing on the Hankow Railway. Neither Chang nor Wu want an open bloodbath that could weaken their position. Negotiations and intrigues continue.
Apr. 17	The Allies today bitterly condemn the newly signed Rapallo agreement between Germany and Soviet Russia.	The Belgian National Socialist Party voted today to block a measure that would extend the vote to women in provincial elections. The opposing Catholic Party has favored the idea, believing women to be more willing to adhere to Church doctrine than men....An Italian shipping strike has tied up more than 730,000 tons of shipping in Italian ports.		A new law laying out the rules for expropriation of lands in Mexico by peasant cultivators, is signed into law by President Alvaro Obregon. Mexico's millions of landless peasants have been clamoring for land reform for years, frightening the landed rich who still dominate much of the economy.	Hazrat Mohani, President of the All-India Muslim League, and main Nationalist leader in the Muslim Congress, has been arrested today in Cawnpore, for sedition.
Apr. 18		Poland formally declares the annexation of Vilna. The measure is bitterly condemned by Lithuania, which claims the disputed area.... Sectarian violence erupts again in Belfast today as rival Catholic and Protestant groups clash, using snipers and machine guns....A Serbian munitions train explodes today in the southern Serbian town of Monastir.		Representatives of the Morgan banking interests meet in Paris today with representatives from France, Britain, Switzerland, and the Netherlands to discuss a new loan to Mexico.	
Apr. 19		Irish Free State leaders Arthur Griffith and Michael Collins again meet with Republican leader Eamon de Valera in talks to try to end the fighting in Ireland, but the talks break up after an hour and a half with no results.			The Japanese have broken off negotiations in Dairen in Manchuria with the Soviet Far Eastern Republic. The Japanese army is determined to maintain its position, for now, in Siberia.
Apr. 20	French leaders are weighing the possibility of calling an international conference of its own after the Genoa Conference, including the French-led Little Entente, to deal with the new Russo-German alliance.	German doctors today confirm rumors of Soviet leader Vladimir I. Lenin's ill health, saying that he suffers from overwork. It is an open question as to who among the Soviet leadership will succeed the ailing Lenin....Fighting erupts today in Dublin, as militant Republicans strike at military installations at Wellington Barracks and Beggar's Bush and the telephone exchange.			

A	B	C	D	E
Includes developments that affect more than one world region, international organizations and important meetings of world leaders.	*Includes all domestic and regional developments in Europe, including the Soviet Union.*	*Includes all domestic and regional developments in Africa and the Middle East.*	*Includes all domestic and regional developments in Latin America, the Caribbean, and Canada.*	*Includes all domestic and regional developments in Asian and Pacific nations (and colonies).*

U.S. Politics & Social Issues	U.S. Foreign Policy & Affairs, Defense	U.S. Economy & Environment	Science, Technology & Nature	Culture, Leisure & Lifestyle	
Senator John B. Kendrick of Wyoming (Dem.) has called for Interior Secretary Albert B. Fall to explain the secret lease of the naval oil reserve at Teapot Dome, WY, to Harry F. Sinclair's Mammoth Oil....In a sign of the growing role women are playing in politics, 50 women are listed as candidates for office in Pennsylvania this year, including four candidates for Congress.			Two American athletes, R.H. Anderson and Roy Davis, have succeeded in conquering Mt. Alagheuz in Armenia. The 13,500 peak has defeated climbers for years.	Will H. Hays, addressing members of the National Association of the Motion Picture Industry, states that the best way to handle the problem of censorship is by making movies that do not require it. Hays, who has stepped into the role of unofficial arbiter of movie mores, intends to push for films of high moral quality and educational value.	Apr. 15
	Marshal Joseph "Papa" Joffre, hero of the Battle of the Marne in World War I, visits Chicago today, amid salutes from American Legion veterans and a military honor guard. Joffre and his family are en route back to France from a goodwill visit in Japan.			Christians worldwide throng to churches today, in celebration of Easter. In New York's Central Park, at least 10,000 people gather on the Mall for a sunrise celebration....Annie Oakley has shot 100 clay targets in a row, setting a women's record for marksmanship....Chicago has succeeded in significantly lowering the crime rate through modernization of its police force. Murder, burglary, and armed robbery are all down since 1919....The New England states have agreed to standardize their road signs, adding to the push to standardize signs on roads nationwide.	Apr. 16
	Three marines are killed when their planes collide at 3,000 feet over the Marine Brigade camp, at Quantico, VA.	The nationwide coal strike is beginning to bite, with New York transit companies worried about coal shortages, and mine operators in West Virginia seeking a court injunction to force striking miners to return to work.		Honolulu has banned nude bathing on Waikiki Beach....Prohibition agents continue to try to improve their techniques, focusing recently on using "spotters" to monitor wharves and rail yards. This has led to the capture of greater quantities of bootleg hooch, but few convictions.	Apr. 17
			Portuguese aviators Captains Coutinho and Sacadura arrived safely at St. Paul's Rock, off Fernando da Noronha Island, just above the Equator on the Brazilian coast, having completed the third and most dangerous leg of their pioneer flight across the South Atlantic from the Cape Verde Islands off the African coast.	Despite Roscoe "Fatty" Arbuckle's recent acquittal on murder charges, Will Hays, head of the Motion Picture Producers and Distributors of America (MPPDA) has announced that Arbuckle is banned for working in motion pictures, effectively immediately. The Hays Office, as it is commonly known, is Hollywood's means of policing itself and deflecting government criticism.	Apr. 18
It was revealed today that Interior Secretary Albert B. Fall has also leased access to the Naval Oil Reserve in Elk Hills, CA, to politically well-connected friends.			Charles P. Steinmetz, renowned expert on electricity, today announces that Einstein's Theory of Relativity shows that the concept of invisible "ether" in outer space is no longer necessary to explain the transmission of light and other electromagnetic radiation....The Governor of Arkansas today appeals for federal assistance in protecting towns along the Mississippi from flooding.	Clarence H. DeMar of Melrose, MA, has won the Boston Marathon, setting a new record of two hours, 18 minutes, and 10 seconds.	Apr. 19
	The last of America's 45,000 World War dead to be brought home to the United States are buried with honors today in Arlington National Cemetery.				Apr. 20

F	G	H	I	J
Includes campaigns, elections, federal-state relations, civil rights and liberties, crime, the judiciary, education, healthcare, poverty, urban affairs, and population.	*Includes formation and debate of U.S. foreign and defense policies, veterans affairs, and defense spending. (Relations with specific foreign countries are usually found under the region concerned.)*	*Includes business, labor, agriculture, taxation, transportation, consumer affairs, monetary and fiscal policy, natural resources, pollution and industrial accidents.*	*Includes worldwide scientific, medical and technological developments, natural phenomena, U.S. weather and natural disasters.*	*Includes the arts, religion, scholarship, communications media, sports, entertainment, fashions, fads, and social life.*

	World Affairs	Europe	Africa & The Middle East	The Americas	Asia & The Pacific
Apr. 21		Rescue workers in Serbia are working to rescue survivors of the recent explosion in Monastir. Rescuers are hampered by ruptured gas mains. More than 200 bodies have already been recovered.	The Spanish newspaper *El Liberal* today denounced the government's policy of attempting to garrison Spanish Morocco with small forces deployed in blockhouses, citing the recent massacre of 16 Spanish troops near Tetuan as an example.		Chang Tsolin's troops marched into Beijing and Tianjin today, as General Wu Pei-fu's men retreated south. Wu has established a new headquarters at Paoting Fu, 90 miles south of Beijing, and is preparing to retreat south across the Yangtze River.
Apr. 22	Hope of achieving a larger European settlement out of the Genoa Conference is rapidly fading in the face of growing French outrage at what they see as duplicity and defiance by Germany and Russia, while the Soviets and Germans are less likely to accept compromises with the Western Allies.	Irish Free State leader Michael Collins is prevented by armed Republican militants from speaking in Killarney. Collins later delivers his speech in another part of the town, but tensions remain high in Ireland.	Greek troops have taken over positions formerly held by the Italians in the Meander Valley in Anatolia.		Movies have become a big hit in China, along with electric lighting and motor cars. Chinese have become so enamored with the silver screen that they have begun producing their own movies.
Apr. 23		A one day general strike is called across Ireland today by the Irish Labour Party against a possible coup by Republican elements in the military....Republican militants gun down Irish Brigadier General George Adamson in Athlone.	A Turkish woman, Fatma, has been awarded a combat commission as a lieutenant in the Turkish Nationalist army, during recent fighting in Anatolia. The Turkish Nationalists have created battalions of women soldiers, some of which have fought with great bravery and heavy casualties.	Proposals are being made for a system of modern roads in Argentina. The plan, as laid down by the Touring Club Argentina, proposes building 172,000 kilometers of roads over 15 years.	Sun Yat-sen, leader of the Guomindang government in Guangzhou (Canton), has broken his alliance with Manchurian warlord Chang Tsolin, abandoning plans to attack General Wu Pei-fu in the Yangtze Valley. In the chaos, Britain and the United States have both sent troops to reinforce their legations in Beijing.
Apr. 24		An index of how bad inflation has gotten in Germany can be seen by an announcement today by the Reichsbank, that the cost of printing the astronomical amounts of money in circulation now come to 262 million marks a year in inflated German currency.		In Managua today, President Chamorro of Nicaragua orders the arrest of 300 members of the Nicaraguan Liberal Party for what Chamorro claims is a plot to overthrow the government.	The U.S. Navy today dispatches the USS *Huron* to Chinese waters to safeguard American interests in the growing civil war there....The U.S. government today impounds 15,000 rounds of ammunition and other arms and munitions being smuggled from San Francisco for one of the warring factions in China.
Apr. 25		The British House of Commons reconvenes after its Easter recess today. Being discussed is a proposal to provide £3 million a year to encourage settlement by families currently in Great Britain to the colonies. Of particular interest are Southern Rhodesia and Kenya in Africa.	Sir Herbert Samuel, British High Commissioner for the Palestinian Mandate, has announced that he intends to seek a peaceful settlement with the Arab population of Palestine, seeking to avoid the unrest now engulfing the French in Syria.		Manchurian warlord Chang Tsolin today refused to withdraw from Beijing, reinforcing his troops to 100,000 total south of China's Great Wall. Rail communication with the south has been interrupted, and many in Beijing are fleeing north to Mukden, in Manchuria, for safety.
Apr. 26	British Prime Minister Lloyd George today compares Europe to "seething racial lava," warning that none of the borders in Eastern Europe have been undisputedly accepted, and that the needs of a hungry Russia must be confronted, or else Russia and Germany will stay in an alliance that could bring a second World War.	The British army has been reduced in size to 215,000 men, down from 341,000 last year. This will save Britain £20 million a year....France posts a government of 40 million francs last year, the highest ever....Hungary has announced it will hold general elections in June.			
Apr. 27	Germany and Soviet Russia today resume diplomatic relations, while Russo-German export company has already been capitalized at three million gold rubles. Germany today denies rumors that it has signed a secret military protocol with the Soviets.	Republican militants murdered three Irish Protestants in Dunmanway in West Cork....Soviet officials are continuing their program of "requisitioning" art treasures from churches. The Trinity Cathedral in Petrograd (St. Petersburg) has been stripped. The Kievan Monastery yielded a golden lamp encrusted with 241 diamonds and 207 pearls.	The United States today formally recognizes the independence of Egypt as a sovereign nation, subject to continued extra-territorial protections for Americans in Egypt.	The United States today warns Cuba that it must reform its finances or face renewed intervention by the United States. The United States continues to express its support for President Zayas of Cuba....The Foreign Policy Association of New York today called on President Harding to withdraw American marines from Haiti, where they have been stationed since 1915.	
	A *Includes developments that affect more than one world region, international organizations and important meetings of world leaders.*	B *Includes all domestic and regional developments in Europe, including the Soviet Union.*	C *Includes all domestic and regional developments in Africa and the Middle East.*	D *Includes all domestic and regional developments in Latin America, the Caribbean, and Canada.*	E *Includes all domestic and regional developments in Asian and Pacific nations (and colonies).*

U.S. Politics & Social Issues	U.S. Foreign Policy & Affairs, Defense	U.S. Economy & Environment	Science, Technology & Nature	Culture, Leisure & Lifestyle	
The Teapot Dome scandal continues to heat up in Washington, as Sen. LaFollette of Wisconsin today calls on Interior Secretary Albert B. Fall to explain the suspicious leasing of naval oil reserves to personal friends.			Lee De Forest today announces the invention of motion picture film that can carry a voice track as well as picture. Producers are scrambling to determine the impact of these new "talkies." Will they replace silent films or are they just a fad?		Apr. 21
The American Birth Control League is formally incorporated today, with its headquarters in New York City. Among the incorporators is long-time birth control advocate Margaret Sanger.	The 22nd Battalion of the U.S. 6th Field Artillery start home from Koblenz today, after being deployed in Europe since 1917. The 22nd has been overseas longer than any other American army unit.			Edith Wharton's new novel, *Glimpses of the Moon*, is being serialized in the *Pictorial Review* magazine....Flowing capes, elegant hats, and plenty of silk and taffeta trimmings are the popular women's fashion trends this spring, as heavy overcoats are put away until the fall.	Apr. 22
				Mrs. Owen Kildare, President of the National Opera Club, at a lecture welcoming speakers on psycho-analysis and spiritualism, announces that women should emulate the free-spirited flappers, telling women to "Throw your corsets away."...Bishop George A. Quertin of Manchester, NH, today remarks that the short skirts and low necks prevalent in women's fashions are "Directly responsible for most of the turmoil in the world today."	Apr. 23
			A 10-ton mirror has been built for the Frye Observatory of Seattle, making it the largest telescopic mirror ever made.	Reverend Merton Rice of Detroit today warns that ordinary men and women in America are spending beyond their means.	Apr. 24
	General Pershing, hero of World War I, today tells the Senate Committee on Military Affairs that if America had possessed a strong army in 1914 it might have prevented World War I. Pershing insists that the United States needs a minimum army strength of 150,000 men. However, pressure remains strong to cut costs.	A number of banks have combined to allow payments to be made via wireless to passengers on board large ocean liners, such as the *Mauretania* and the *Aquitania*.	Experiments conducted by the National Advisory Committee on Aviation (NACA) at Langley Field, VA, on engine efficiency and aerodynamic wing design, are beginning to pay off, with improvements being made in the Air Service's workhorse Liberty engine....17 are dead and 3,500 homeless in flooding along the Trinity River in Texas. Ft. Worth has been especially hard hit, with property damage estimated at $1 million....An expedition to recover a plesiosaurus rumored to be living in a lake in Chubut Territory of Argentina returns empty handed today, after expending 11 cases of dynamite in a lake near the town of Esquel.	Brooklyn boxer Lew Brody died today of a cerebral hemorrhage after being knocked out in a bout at the Brooklyn Club last night. The sport of boxing, now more popular than ever, has its toll.	Apr. 25
Lady Astor addresses an overflow crowd at a meeting arranged by the League of Women Voters in Baltimore today. Lady Astor calls on women to get involved in politics and raise the moral tone of political campaigning on both sides of the Atlantic.			The death toll has risen to 62 in the flooding around Ft. Worth, TX, with scores still unaccounted for.	Gas prices continue to climb along the East Coast, hitting 26 cents a gallon in New York....Frederick Van Rensselaer Dey (61), author of the popular Nick Carter detective stories, commits suicide in a New York City hotel early this morning. Dey wrote more than 40 million words, including 1,076 Nick Carter stories.	Apr. 26
The 100th anniversary of the birth of Civil War General Ulysses S. Grant is held today in Washington, DC. Present were Vice President Calvin Coolidge, Secretary of War John Wingate Weeks, and General John Pershing, as a memorial statue was unveiled before a crowd of surviving Civil War veterans.			Major T.W. Blake of the Royal Air Force will take the place of Sir Ross Smith, who was killed in an air crash recently, in an attempt to circumnavigate the world by air. The route planned would go via Southern Europe, Egypt, Iraq, India, China, and Japan. From there, Blake will fly on to the Aleutians, then across North America to return to Scotland via Iceland. Blake intends to start in May. The unprecedented trek will take two months.	Fritz Lang's *Dr. Mabuse, der Spieler (The Gambler)* premieres today in Berlin. Lang's Expressionistic film making is taking cinema to new heights, while his images of a criminal mastermind, manipulating events from behind the scenes, strikes a chord with Germans angered at corruption in the Weimar government....New York City today reduces the speed limit for trucks to 12 mph from 15. Cars in congested areas are held to eight mph.	Apr. 27

F	G	H	I	J
Includes campaigns, elections, federal-state relations, civil rights and liberties, crime, the judiciary, education, healthcare, poverty, urban affairs, and population.	*Includes formation and debate of U.S. foreign and defense policies, veterans affairs, and defense spending. (Relations with specific foreign countries are usually found under the region concerned.)*	*Includes business, labor, agriculture, taxation, transportation, consumer affairs, monetary and fiscal policy, natural resources, pollution and industrial accidents.*	*Includes worldwide scientific, medical and technological developments, natural phenomena, U.S. weather and natural disasters.*	*Includes the arts, religion, scholarship, communications media, sports, entertainment, fashions, fads, and social life.*

	World Affairs	Europe	Africa & The Middle East	The Americas	Asia & The Pacific
Apr. 28		Seven other Irish Protestants have been murdered in and around Dunmanway, in County Cork. Protestant families are fleeing the area in terror. Catholics fear reprisals by Protestants in Northern Ireland....Rumors of a split between Soviet leader Vladimir Lenin and his chief lieutenant, Leon Trotsky, have surfaced in recent days. Trotsky is said to oppose Lenin's New Economic Policy (NEP) tolerating private enterprise.		Banditry has reached such proportions in the Mexican states of Tabsco and Campeche that *campesinos* are fleeing the countryside, abandoning farms wholesale. Some bandit groups have taken up piracy, raiding steamships along the coast of the Gulf of Mexico.	Japan today warns the Soviet Far Eastern Republic that it will send warships to Siberian waters to protect Japanese fishermen.
Apr. 29		Right wing diehards throw a bomb at a group of Soviet officials attempting to remove church treasures from the Tver Cathedral. No one is killed, but much of the cathedral is damaged in the explosion....Crimean guerillas gun down the Soviet Commissar for Education outside of the Crimean resort town of Yalta....Republican leader Eamon de Valera today refuses to submit the Treaty of London establishing the Irish Free State, to a plebiscite.			Fighting has erupted across a hundred mile front today as General Wu Pei-fu's forces launched a counterattack to drive Manchurian warlord Chang Tsolin's troops from the Beijing area. Fighting is raging for control of Marco Polo Bridge and for the Beijing-Hankow Railway. Two cruisers loyal to General Wu are moving north in an attempt to cut the railway from Manchuria to Beijing.
Apr. 30			Arab residents of Mecca have pooled their resources to extend the railroad that currently runs from Constantinople to Medina by adding the 375 miles from Medina to the Muslim holy city of Mecca. This will make the annual hadj easier.		Martial law is declared in Beijing as forces loyal to Manchurian warlord Chang Tso-lin battled the armies of General Wu Pei-fu near Beijing. Chang's men are said to have retaken Changsintien, southwest of the capital. Both sides face serious logistical challenges in trying to maintain their poorly trained armies.
May 1	Dr. Fridtjof Nansen, famed explorer and head of the International Russian Relief Organization, today warns that, while the famine in the Volga region of Russia is receding, starvation continues in the Ukraine, where some five million people are still without food, and deaths may reach as many as 10,000 a day.	Deruluft, German Russian Airlines, begins operation today, as part of the increased open and covert cooperation between Germany and Soviet Russia....The British government submits its annual budget to the House of Commons today, as Lloyd George's government tries to get Britain's massive World War debts under control....Peace talks in Dublin between the Irish Free State and militant Republicans have broken down completely. The Free state government has therefore decided to proceed with elections on its own, which are set for June....Republican rebels have begun holding up banks in Ireland to obtain funds for operations.	In this month, British authorities have finally subdued the Nyala revolt in the Dar Masalit area of western Sudan. The rebellion has been inspired by the messianic prophecies of the dervish, Abdullah al-Sihayni, who was hanged in October 1921....In this month, South African troops move to suppress a tax protest by the Bondelswart people of South West Africa. Supported by machine guns and aircraft, the South Africans have killed some 100 Africans and arrested 150 others.	Senator Borah of Idaho today calls on the United States to withdraw its marines from Haiti and the Dominican Republic, stating that they are being kept there to further American corporate and banking interests....May Day workers' rallies in Mexico City erupt into rioting in clashes with Catholic groups.	
May 2	France and Belgium, Russia's biggest creditors, have withheld their signature from a proposal at the Genoa Conference to recognize Soviet Russia. The Soviets are insisting on a loan of $1.5 billion before making any payments on the debts. Fear is growing that the Soviets will simply seek separate agreements with each creditor nation. Meanwhile Britain's plan for a general settlement on European trade remains stalled.	51 Protestants and 69 Catholics have been killed so far this year in sectarian fighting in Belfast....Free state forces attack Republican strongholds in and around Kilkenny today. The Republicans are holding out in Ormonde Castle and other positions, as fighting rages....Central Ireland is dissolving into anarchy as IRA bands hold up trains and cut rail lines and communications. IRA bank robberies are continuing, with £100,000 having been taken in the last two days.	Rumors abound of negotiations by the Anglo-Dutch Shell Oil Company with the Soviets to develop the rich Baku oil fields of Russia on the Caspian Sea, just north of Iran.	Diamonds have been discovered in British Guiana, on the Mazaruni River, 120 miles inland from the coast....A plot by Mexican General Celso Cepeda to hold up a Mexico City-Vera Cruz train and use the money to start a rebellion, were foiled today when a subordinate of General Cepeda went to the authorities. General Cepeda has fled.	Fighting erupts today on the Hun River, 30 miles south of Beijing, as troops loyal to warlord General Wu Pei-fu tried to drive back the armies of Manchurian warlord Chang Tsolin and cut the Beijing-Tianjin Railroad. Other units loyal to General Wu have been battling Chang's forces at Machang, 100 miles southeast of Beijing, as Chang tries to hold on to his position dominating the approaches to Beijing....Sun Yat-sen, leader of the Guomindang government in Guangzhou (Canton) is said to have reached an accord with Chang, and will support him against General Wu.

A	B	C	D	E
Includes developments that affect more than one world region, international organizations and important meetings of world leaders.	*Includes all domestic and regional developments in Europe, including the Soviet Union.*	*Includes all domestic and regional developments in Africa and the Middle East.*	*Includes all domestic and regional developments in Latin America, the Caribbean, and Canada.*	*Includes all domestic and regional developments in Asian and Pacific nations (and colonies).*

U.S. Politics & Social Issues	U.S. Foreign Policy & Affairs, Defense	U.S. Economy & Environment	Science, Technology & Nature	Culture, Leisure & Lifestyle	
28 members of the United Mine Workers union go on trial today in West Virginia, on treason charges stemming from the labor unrest that erupted in Logan County last year....A sheriff and two deputies are killed in a riot in Beardstown, IL, by Greek railroad workers. 28 of the immigrant workers have been arrested.					Apr. 28
Rioting breaks out today in the mines around Uniontown, PA, as striking miners rushed mines being run by nonunion workers.			Dr. N.L. Britton, Director of the New York Botanical Garden, has returned from Puerto Rico with more than 4,000 samples of Caribbean plant life.	Carl Sandburg's poem *Fins*, is published in *The Measure*....D.H. Lawrence has published a new novel, *Aaron's Rod*.	Apr. 29
			The air show at Curtiss Field on Long Island draws a crowd of 20,000 today as Bert Acosta sets an unofficial speed record of 208 mph in the new Curtiss Wildcat.	Daylight Savings Time goes into effect in New York City and other communities today, moving the clocks ahead by an hour for the summer months. Plans are under way to extend the measure, which saves fuel, across the entire Eastern Time Zone, but the farm bloc remains unanimously opposed to the measure....Debate swirls around the new trend of Expressionism in German art and cinema.	Apr. 30
President Harding met today with Chairman Nolan of the House Labor committee to discuss ways to resolve the nationwide coal miners' strike, which is now a month old.	An American soldier is killed in a May Day protest today in the German city of Mainz. Three other people are injured in the melee.	Police in Cambria County, PA, disperse marches by striking coal miners today, as the month-long coal strike continues.	L.C. Porter, President of the Society of Motion Picture engineers, believes that someday radio waves may be used to carry moving pictures, allowing people to one day watch movies in their own homes.		May 1
		A bridge leading to a coal mine is dynamited today in Listonburg, PA.	Astronomers and geophysicists meet today in Rome for a conference.	Prohibition Field Superintendent C.E. Main reports that Chicago is the "wettest" city in the nation. Main lays the blame on Prohibition agents there, half of whom he says, have degenerated into extortionists, allowing bootleggers to operate for a cut of the profits....In the wake of recent boxing deaths, New Jersey is outlawing "rabbit punches" delivered to the back of the neck and kidney blows.	May 2

	World Affairs	Europe	Africa & The Middle East	The Americas	Asia & The Pacific
May 3		Gangs of armed men attack three police barracks in Northern Ireland today, killing one police officer and wounding two others, while unrest continues in both in Ulster and the Irish Free State.	Lord Allenby, British High Commissioner in Egypt, today repudiates Egyptian claims to sole rule over the Sudan. Allenby announced that Britain will retain the current system of joint rule, wherein Britain effectively stays in control.		Unrest is starting to die down in India, with the rebellion in Malabar over, and revolts in Udaipur and Danta contained. Gurkha troops are being kept on alert around the troubled city of Amritsar, in Punjab.... Chinese General Wu Pei-fu has moved to the front at Machang, to try to steady his unreliable troops in their attacks on rival warlord General Chang's forces. Both sides have depleted their stocks of artillery shells....Political maneuvers continue in China, with General Wu building support among Chinese provincial governors.
May 4	The French government warn today that it is prepared to act unilaterally if the Germans fail in their obligations under the Versailles Treaty to pay reparations for World War I....France and Belgium today announce a full military and diplomatic alliance, allowing for "joint action no matter what circumstances." This is widely taken to include a new invasion of Germany to force the Germans to pay reparations.... The Genoa Conference remains deadlocked with the French refusing to sign any nonaggression pact unless every European power signs it, and that France's right to intervene to enforce the Versailles Treaty be respected. The Germans have in turn flatly rejected French rights to unilateral intervention.	Free State troops stormed Ormonde Castle in Kilkenny, Ireland, capturing 108 Republican rebels. Free state control of Kilkenny is now complete....In Ireland today representatives of the dissident Republican faction, led by Eamon de Valera, met with Irish Free State leaders today at Mansion House in Dublin, and ironed out a three-day truce.... French police have arrested three in what they allege is a Soviet plot to spread subversion and sabotage.			Forces loyal to General Wu Pei-fu have broken through General Chang's lines at three points southeast of Beijing. The gates of Beijing have been shut, as mobs of frightened soldiers are fleeing toward the city. Wu's forces are crossing the Hun River and are trying to cut off the remnants of Chang's Manchurian army from retreating north....The Australian government, under the terms of the Washington Naval agreement, has announced that they will sink the battleship *Australia* in naval exercises off Sydney.
May 5		The Estonian government has executed Communist leader M. Kingiseff for espionage and treason....The German government's Bureau of Engraving and Printing announced today that it cannot print 1,000 mark notes fast enough to keep up with Germany's skyrocketing inflation. The government has arrived at a simple solution: it will start printing 5,000 mark notes.	Near East Relief officials today charge Turkey with planning new efforts to exterminate Armenians and other non-Turkish minorities in Asia Minor. Thousands of Greeks, some from villages where Greeks have lived for centuries, are fleeing Turkish controlled areas en masse.		General Wu Pei-fu's forces have driven Chang Tso-lin's men from Beijing. Chang's men retreat north to his stronghold in Manchuria, leaving 7,000 casualties on both sides. President Hsu Shih-chang has reached an accord with General Wu, who will support the government.
May 6		The British navy today decommissioned the battleship HMS *Erin* and ordered it sold for scrap, as part of the naval reduction clauses in the Washington Treaties.	Reverend Walter H. Overs, Episcopal Bishop of Liberia, today warns of British encroachment on Liberia unless the United States proceedes with a proposed $5 million loan for the Liberian government. Loans are especially needed to build roads to extract resources and develop plantations.	Canada's population jumped by 22 percent in the last 10 years to 8.7 million in 1921, with most of the growth in the western prairie provinces and British Columbia.	China today becomes the first foreign government to ratify the Washington Treaties on the Far East.
May 7		Increased taxation and reduced circumstances are forcing much of the British aristocracy to sell off estates and castles in order to remain financially solvent....Runaway inflation is crippling Germany as the Reichsbank today announced that in the week of April 29 alone the German government has issued eight *trillion* marks! The continued instability of the German economy is putting continued reparation payments in doubt.	King Fuad of Egypt today challenges the British government, asserting Egypt's claim to sole rule over the Sudan.		General Wu Pei-fu has removed the Prime Minister of China, and declared General Chang removed as Inspector General of Manchurian armies. Chang remains in control of Manchuria, while in the south, Sun Yat-sen's Guomindang government is still operating independently.... Despite General Wu's recent success in regaining control of Beijing, popular disgust with the warlords is growing across China. The number of Chinese living in foreign legation zones has nearly doubled in the last 12 years.

A	B	C	D	E
Includes developments that affect more than one world region, international organizations and important meetings of world leaders.	*Includes all domestic and regional developments in Europe, including the Soviet Union.*	*Includes all domestic and regional developments in Africa and the Middle East.*	*Includes all domestic and regional developments in Latin America, the Caribbean, and Canada.*	*Includes all domestic and regional developments in Asian and Pacific nations (and colonies).*

U.S. Politics & Social Issues	U.S. Foreign Policy & Affairs, Defense	U.S. Economy & Environment	Science, Technology & Nature	Culture, Leisure & Lifestyle	
Abraham Cahan, editor of the *Jewish Daily Forward*, warns of Communist subversion in garment industry unions.	Admiral Joseph Strauss, Commander of the American Asiatic Fleet, has ordered the cruiser *USS Wilmington* to Chinese waters from the Philippines, as chaos continues in China....The U.S. Senate today passes a resolution endorsing the establishment of a Jewish national home in Palestine.				May 3
Justice Department agent H.L. Scaife today accuses Attorney General Charles Daugherty of failing to pursue war fraud cases involving well-connected corporations. Scaife went on to accuse Daugherty of using his agents to shadow congressmen seeking to investigate the Attorney General.... Daugherty is also being accused, by Senator Caraway of Arkansas, that he accepted a $25,000 bribe to release a convicted felon from prison.		United Mine Workers' President John L. Lewis meets today at the White House with President Warren Harding and Labor Secretary James Davis in an attempt to resolve the nationwide coal miners' strike, now in its second month.	Lieutenant J.H. "Jimmy" Doolittle and L.I. Andrews have completed a flight from San Antonio to San Diego, a distance of 1,800 miles, in 12 hours and 30 minutes.		May 4
			C.S. Franklin of the Marconi Company announces today that it is possible to provide point-to-point radio beam transmissions that can not be listened in on, over a 100 mile radius....Radio inventor Guglielmo Marconi today announces that he will be monitoring Mars next month when the planet makes its closest approach to Earth to listen for any radio signals from the Red Planet.	Construction has begun on Yankee Stadium in the Bronx....A Shakespeare folio is sold in New York for $9,500....A New York City bus company has installed a radio on a passenger bus. It is believed that it may soon become common to hear radio music even while traveling by bus or train....Movie star Mary Pickford announces the creation of a club of motion picture actresses whose purpose is to protect their good names from scandal mongers.	May 5
	Senator James Wadsworth, Chairman of the Senate Committee on Military Affairs, today warns that the Harding administration's planned cuts in the National Guard will make it impossible to retain the Guard as a balanced force with modern weapons and training.	The American Engineering Council today calls for the closing of marginally profitable mines, and the reduction of the labor force in mining, warning that union calls for nationalization of the mines will be counterproductive.		Pellegrino Scaglia, a prominent leader of the Colorado crime syndicate, has been gunned down by rival mobsters. Colorado and Kansas City mob leaders will meet in New York to try to work out territorial disputes....Gelett Burgess has been credited with inventing the term "blurb" for the lines of gushing praise put on book jackets by publishers to increase book sales.	May 6
A split is developing between President Harding and Congressional Republicans. Harding has warned that he will veto any Bonus Bill for World War veterans that does not contain a sales tax to pay for the $4 billion outlay. Congress is eager to pass the popular Bonus Bill before the November elections.... Questions are growing, even in the Republican Party, about the competence of some of President Harding appointees, after the removal of the Governor of Puerto Rico for incompetence and the appointment of IRS revenue collectors tied to the St. Louis political machine.		Automobile production reaches an all time high in April, with factories now working at full capacity.	The U.S. Department of Agriculture today warns that over-hunting, including the use of poison to meet the demand for furs, is leading to a serious depletion of fur-bearing animals in Alaska.	The "Prohibition Navy" patrolling the Atlantic and Great Lakes has cut deep into liquor smuggling, with good quality Scotch practically unavailable in New York City. However, bootleg beer has become very plentiful, so much so that street prices have fallen to 25 cents a bottle...Sir Arthur Conan Doyle addresses an audience in Carnegie Hall today on spiritualism, displaying photos of what he claims are spirits. Such photos, hotly debated, depicting spirits or "ectoplasm" are the current rage.	May 7

F	G	H	I	J
Includes campaigns, elections, federal-state relations, civil rights and liberties, crime, the judiciary, education, healthcare, poverty, urban affairs, and population.	*Includes formation and debate of U.S. foreign and defense policies, veterans affairs, and defense spending. (Relations with specific foreign countries are usually found under the region concerned.)*	*Includes business, labor, agriculture, taxation, transportation, consumer affairs, monetary and fiscal policy, natural resources, pollution and industrial accidents.*	*Includes worldwide scientific, medical and technological developments, natural phenomena, U.S. weather and natural disasters.*	*Includes the arts, religion, scholarship, communications media, sports, entertainment, fashions, fads, and social life.*

	World Affairs	Europe	Africa & The Middle East	The Americas	Asia & The Pacific
May 8	Prime Minister Lloyd George of Britain, backed by German Chancellor Joseph Wirth and Italian Prime Minister Luigi Facta, today appeal to the Soviets to reach an accord on the repayment of pre-World War debts still owed. This is seen as the last chance Lloyd George has to salvage something from the Genoa Conference.	The fragile truce in Ireland, between the government and rebel Republicans, has been extended, as a committee appointed by the Irish *Dail*, or Assembly, seeks to reach an accord....British shipyard workers finally end a bitter 6-week-old strike today, after failing to achieve a continuation of war-time bonus pay....The Soviets have sentenced eight priests and three others to death for resisting the "requisitioning" of church treasures....The Italian town of Marostica is evacuated today as a stockpile of large caliber gas shells in the town exploded.			The last of General Chang's forces in Tianjin have surrendered to General Wu Pei-fu. Chang has suffered from rumors of his secret connections with the hated Japanese, who are eager to gain a foothold in Manchuria....Wu's forces are now trying to secure control of southern China, having clashed with the forces of General Chao Ti, warlord of Henan Province.
May 9	Britain is negotiating an accord with Italy whereby the status quo in the Mediterranean will be maintained.		The government of Egypt has issued a decree establishing government monopolies over trade in opium, cocaine, morphine, and hashish....The United States and Britain have reached an agreement whereby Americans in Palestine will continue to enjoy extra-territorial rights and protections granted under the Ottoman Empire.		
May 10		Soviet delegates in Genoa have reached an accord with Papal representatives on the status of the Catholic Church in Russia....Negotiations in Ireland have broken down, with no settlement between government and Republican forces....Denmark is reducing its military spending from 65 million crowns a year to just 43 million.			Banks have closed in Guangzhou, capital of Sun Yat-sen's Guomindang government in southern China, as business support for Sun's government crumbles. Sun has tried to play off rival northern warlords against each other. Now General Wu, having defeated his northern rival, is pressing Sun.
May 11		King George V of Great Britain begins a pilgrimage today to the battlefields and cemeteries of the Western Front.		Bolivia is negotiating with a consortium of New York banks for a $24 million loan, to be secured by a lien on the Bolivian national railroad.	Forces loyal to Chinese warlord General Wu Pei-fu have advanced to Tongshan, 60 miles north of Tianjin.
May 12		A proposed bill by the Labour Party to allow the Minister of Labour to regulate labor conditions and hours is voted down by Parliament in Great Britain today....Irish Free State Prime Minister Michael Collins today reassures Irish Protestants that Ireland would continue to protect religious liberty....IRA militants have destroyed the British Naval radio station at Bunbeg, Donegal.		The Mexican government has proclaimed the expropriation of 1.9 million acres, as part of a program of land reform.	American marines have been deployed near Tongshan, in an attempt to keep open the Mukden Railroad to and from Manchuria.
May 13		The German dominated Free City of Danzig is resisting a plan by the Polish government to establish a transshipment center for munitions in the harbor. Danzig has a majority German population, but is Poland's sole port on the Baltic.	The lingering post-World War depression, particularly in Europe, leads to a sharp decline in diamond sales in 1921, which has affected the South African economy in particular.	Canada has formally claimed Wrangel Island, off the Arctic coast of Siberia. An expedition is being organized to occupy the island, which is also claimed by Soviet Russia....The Provincial Government of Alberta has established its own telephone system, allowing farmers in even the most remote areas of the province to have telephone service.	

A	B	C	D	E
Includes developments that affect more than one world region, international organizations and important meetings of world leaders.	*Includes all domestic and regional developments in Europe, including the Soviet Union.*	*Includes all domestic and regional developments in Africa and the Middle East.*	*Includes all domestic and regional developments in Latin America, the Caribbean, and Canada.*	*Includes all domestic and regional developments in Asian and Pacific nations (and colonies).*

	U.S. Politics & Social Issues	U.S. Foreign Policy & Affairs, Defense	U.S. Economy & Environment	Science, Technology & Nature	Culture, Leisure & Lifestyle
May 8	At the convention in Chicago of the Amalgamated Clothing Workers of America, which has 350,000 members, delegates sing *The Hymn of Free Russia*, and raised $200,000 for Russian famine relief. Sympathy for the embattled Marxist regime runs high among many trade unionists....Four African Americans have been lynched in the last three days near Kirvin, TX, after the recent murder of a 17-year-old white girl. Whether the four men were in fact involved in the killing is unknown....The Ku Klux Klan is holding its national congress, an "Imperial Klonvocation" (sic) in Atlanta, celebrating the seventh anniversary of its refounding in 1915. It will be chaired by "Imperial Wizard" William J. Simmons.			Owen Young, Chairman of the Radio Corporation of America, states today that the reason why Europe lags in adopting radio commercially is that they fear it will be used to spread propaganda by neighboring nations.	Vincenzo Terranova, half-brother of Morello crime family crime boss Ciro Terranova, has been shot dead outside his home. Evidence points to Morello lieutenant Rocco Valenti. The Morello mob, based in East Harlem, is the strongest in New York City....Six people are shot in a gun battle in broad daylight between two rival Manhattan bootlegging gangs. One of the shooters, arrested at the scene, is Joe Masseria (35). Masseria isn't talking, but police tie the battle to the shooting of Terranova....Demands are growing on the British government to stem the sale of artworks outside of the country. With the dollar strong, and many old European aristocratic families under financial strain, American collectors have descended on Europe en masse to build collections in the United States.
May 9	Embattled Attorney General Harry Daugherty today blames the Wilson administration for failing to prosecute cases of fraud in procurement during World War I. Daugherty has been under fire for failing to investigate these cases.	Chief of Naval Operations Admiral Robert E. Coontz today denounced charges that a large navy would encourage a new world war. Coontz argued that the $3 billion spent on the navy was worth it to protect $8 billion a year in overseas trade.		Great Britain is working on a plan to link the Empire by radio, with stations in Egypt, East and South Africa, and Australia.	As many as 100,000 Americans are expected to visit England this summer, as the strong dollar encourages American tourism....Reverend Dr. S. Patterson Todd of Milwaukee today calls for federal regulation of the motion picture industry.
May 10	Two policemen are killed in labor riots in Chicago. The city has been in turmoil over a battle to unionize glass making factories. In response, police arrest 200 labor leaders in Chicago for complicity in the murders and in the bombing of a factory.			General John T. Thompson today gives a demonstration of his new, hand carried Thompson submachine gun. Thompson believes this will give police the edge they need when battling modern bank robbers and bootleggers.	At the Longchamps races today in Paris, long skirts are back in style.
May 11	The senate Judiciary Committee today hears charges that the motion picture industry is controlled by a clique of five top producers. The movie industry is also coming under fire because the major producers are foreign born.		The two largest independent steel makers in America, Bethlehem Steel and the Lackawanna Steel Company, announce today that they will merge in a $60 million deal.		3,300 people appealed for treatment at the City Hospital in Boston last year for sickness due to alcohol poisoning from drinking bad hooch. Mayor Curley warns that such patients will, henceforth, be sent to the state hospital.
May 12	The Immigration Bureau today deports Marxist union agitator Nikolai Mansevich, who had attempted to organize a "worker's soviet" at the Ford plant in Detroit.			A hard winter and a cold spring will lead to a short harvest this year in Europe. France and Germany have been especially hard hit, but a bumper crop in Romania is expected to partially offset this....A 20-ton meteorite has fallen near Blackstone, VA, causing a colossal explosion and leaving a 500 square foot hole in the earth.	
May 13	The Harding administration is holding firm to its refusal to recognize Soviet Russia until provisions are made for the repayment of prewar debts.	The new ambassador from Germany, Otto L. Wiedfeldt, has arrived in New York City, marking the restoration of full diplomatic relations between the United States and Germany.	Bootleggers are rushing to buy fast, ocean-going motor boats, causing prices for certain craft to rise all along the east coast.		Morvich, ridden by Albert Johnson, has won the Kentucky Derby....*Ben Hur*, by Lew Wallace, has become the best selling book in America, with more than a million copies sold....*McClure's Magazine* will begin serializing Henry Ford's *My Life and Work*....Professor John Dewey has published a new article on *The American Intellectual Frontier*.

	World Affairs	Europe	Africa & The Middle East	The Americas	Asia & The Pacific
May 14	British Prime Minister Lloyd George convinces the Allied governments to call another diplomatic conference at The Hague in June. Its purpose is to try to iron out a settlement of the debt dispute with Soviet Russia. Lloyd George is urging the United States to participate.	14 people were wounded, and two children have been killed,in renewed sectarian fighting in Belfast....A police patrol is ambushed by IRA guerillas in Armagh in Northern Ireland. Four policemen are injured....Benito Mussolini's Fascist party is organizing 30,000 unemployed workers in Ferrara, demanding jobs on public works projects. Mussolini's power in Italian politics is growing.		Mexico has so far expropriated 1.9 million acres of land around the country from great estates. The largest number of expropriations came in the states of Morelos and Durango....General Felix Diaz, nephew of deposed Mexican dictator Profirio Diaz, has sailed from Galveston with arms and ammunition for the rebels under General Aleman operating in the jungles of Vera Cruz.	British pressure has compelled Manchurian warlord Chang Tsolin to withdraw the rest of his troops from Zhili Province, which contains Beijing. The British have substantial mining interests around Kaiping, which Chang has just evacuated. Chang is said to be digging in at Lwanchow, further to the north, and intends to make Manchuria a separate nation.
May 15	The Harding administration today declined the offer to participate in the upcoming Hague Conference on Soviet Russia. The United States will not consider recognition of the Soviets until the debts are paid.	At the insistence of the Allies, the Germans have agreed to hand over the disputed area of Upper Silesia to Poland, even though a plebiscite in the area went in Germany's favor.... Eight people are killed in continuing violence in Belfast.	A report on the systematic massacre of Armenians and Greeks by the Turks is submitted to the British Parliament today. The Turks are reported to be deliberately driving the Armenians out of their homes in hopes of starving them to death. The Turks are desperate to assert their claim to the Turkish core of the Ottoman Empire against the Greeks, and see the Armenians as traitors.	Louis Borno takes office today as President of Haiti, succeeding outgoing President Philippe Sudre D'Artiguenave, after elections supervised by American marines.... President Harding welcomes representatives from Peru and Chile to Washington, in an attempt to mediate the 40-year-old dispute over the Tacna-Arica region.	
May 16	Commerce Secretary Herbert Hoover today lays out a five point plan for European economic recovery, including arms reduction, balanced budgets, and a settlement of German reparations.	Nikolaos A. Stratos today succeeded Dimitrios Gounaris as Prime Minister of Greece. Stratos, an opponent of Greece's involvement in World War I, will act as interim prime minister for now....Two former colonels in the Russian White forces have been arrested by the Bulgarian government for plotting war against the Soviet Union from Bulgarian soil. A number of other White Russian officers have been forced to leave the country, as Bulgaria returns to its traditional friendship with Russia, Soviet or not.	The Harding administration has declined British offers for a joint investigation of the massacre of Christian minorities by the Turkish Nationalists.	Bolivia is insisting on her right to access to the Pacific, as discussions between Peru and Chile progress. Chile took Bolivia's seacoast in the War of the Pacific in 1879, and the loss of the coast has been a sore point with Bolivians ever since.	
May 17	The League of Nations Council, in Geneva today, appoints former Swiss President Dr. Felix Calonder to head an arbitration tribunal to decide the status of the disputed Silesian region claimed by both Germany and Poland.	Fascists Blackshirts clash with workers in street fighting in the heart of Rome today. Prime Minister Luigi Facta is facing increasing unrest, both by Mussolini's Fascists and the Communists.	The United States and France have reached an agreement whereby the United States will support the establishment of French-run League of Nations Mandates in Syria, and in the former German African colonies of Cameroon and Togoland. Americans will have opportunities to participate in trade and investment as Frenchmen....Egypt is in the middle of the worst drought on record. Officials are trying to save the all-important cotton crop, but water is already scarce as the hottest months begin.		
May 18	Diplomats at the Genoa Conference express their dismay that the United States will not participate in the upcoming Hague Conference. As now the world's strongest economy America, like it or not, shapes the world diplomatic agenda.	Today the last British troops are pulled out of the Irish Free State, as the British haul down the Union Jack over their barracks in the city of Cork. British officers expressed their resentment by cutting down the flagpole before leaving. Irish troops then march in to cheering crowds and hoisted the flag over the gate....A policeman is killed, and another wounded today when IRA gunmen raided the central police station in downtown Belfast in broad daylight.		Chilean and Peruvian negotiators meeting in Washington, DC, to resolve the Tacna-Arica dispute have agreed not to consider Bolivia's claims to the region. Bolivia lost much of the disputed territory, including its only seaport, to Chile in 1879.	
May 19	The Genoa Conference breaks up today when the French government insists that Russia repay its prewar debts. British Prime Minister Lloyd George warns Soviet leaders that they must make some concessions on debts to win diplomatic recognition....The League of Nations reports today that there are still one million more men under arms in Europe than there were at the start of World War I.	The Soviets have established a new, Soviet-controlled nationwide youth organization, the Young Pioneers. The Soviets are eager to inculcate their ideology into the young people of Russia, with the goal of ultimately creating a new, Communist society....Italy and Yugoslavia have reached an accord on the disputed Adriatic seaports of Zara and Fiume.	The Turkish Nationalist government in Ankara today agreed to permit an investigation of the killing of Greeks and Armenians in Asia Minor, but only on certain conditions, including an investigation into the killing of Turks in Greek controlled areas.	Canadian Prime Minister William Mackenzie King today endorses the League of Nations, calling it the only "effective and available" hope for peace.	Korean nationalist activist Son Byong-Hi has died in Seoul after a long imprisonment by Japanese authorities.
	A *Includes developments that affect more than one world region, international organizations and important meetings of world leaders.*	B *Includes all domestic and regional developments in Europe, including the Soviet Union.*	C *Includes all domestic and regional developments in Africa and the Middle East.*	D *Includes all domestic and regional developments in Latin America, the Caribbean, and Canada.*	E *Includes all domestic and regional developments in Asian and Pacific nations (and colonies).*

U.S. Politics & Social Issues	U.S. Foreign Policy & Affairs, Defense	U.S. Economy & Environment	Science, Technology & Nature	Culture, Leisure & Lifestyle	
			The U.S. Navy is installing improved radio equipment on 50 submarines. This will increase their effective communications radius from 50 miles to 500 miles.	A record 175,000 visit Coney Island today, as crowds flocked to the seaside to enjoy the spring weather.	May 14
In *Bailey v. Drexel Furniture*, the Supreme Court has struck down a 1919 Federal law imposing taxes on businesses that use child labor. The result is a bitter setback to opponents of child labor, which is entrenched in large parts of the country, particularly in the South....The Order of Railway Telegraphers union voted today in St. Louis to join the coal miners in their nationwide strike.					May 15
	Naval Secretary Denby today urges Congress to subsidize America's Merchant Marines to enable her to maintain a shipping fleet in time of war.				May 16
Samuel Untermeyer, counsel to the Senate Committee investigating Attorney General Harry Daugherty, today called Daugherty "wholly unfit for office" and "a connecting link between the Administration and Big Business."...Chicago police are on high alert after the fire-bombing of a 72 apartment buildings nearing construction by labor racketeers. Mobsters who can get control of construction unions can extort large sums from builders hurrying to complete projects.					May 17
Illinois mine operators call on the United Mine Workers today to end their nationwide coal strike...In Georgia, an African-American youth has been tortured and burnt alive for allegedly killing a white woman....The Southern Baptist Convention in Jacksonville, FL, votes today to admit women to its Executive Board. One conservative opponent of the measure condemns the decision warning that if such measures continue, "the time will come when a woman will preside over this convention."			Nobel Prize winning French physician, Charles Louis Alphonse Laveran, discoverer of the protozoa responsible for transmitting malaria, has died....Scientists addressing a conference at the American Museum of Natural History in New York today warn that the popularity of furs in high society may cause the extinction of whole species in the foreseeable future.		May 18
			Charles Francis Jenkins achieves the first successful laboratory transmission of television signals.		May 19

F	G	H	I	J
Includes campaigns, elections, federal-state relations, civil rights and liberties, crime, the judiciary, education, healthcare, poverty, urban affairs, and population.	*Includes formation and debate of U.S. foreign and defense policies, veterans affairs, and defense spending. (Relations with specific foreign countries are usually found under the region concerned.)*	*Includes business, labor, agriculture, taxation, transportation, consumer affairs, monetary and fiscal policy, natural resources, pollution and industrial accidents.*	*Includes worldwide scientific, medical and technological developments, natural phenomena, U.S. weather and natural disasters.*	*Includes the arts, religion, scholarship, communications media, sports, entertainment, fashions, fads, and social life.*

	World Affairs	Europe	Africa & The Middle East	The Americas	Asia & The Pacific
May 20		In Ireland, Republican leader Éamon de Valera and Michael Collins, chairman of the Provisional government, have agreed to avoid an open split over the peace treaty with Great Britain in the general elections set for June. Pro- and anti-Treaty *Sinn Féin* candidates will run on a single list. This will allow elections to take place, but the basic issues between the government and the Republicans remain unresolved.			Forces loyal to Manchurian warlord Chang Tsolin have withdrawn north behind the Great Wall, after being threatened with a flanking maneuver by Beijing warlord General Wu Pei-fu.
May 21		Communists in Bulgaria today protest the continued presence of 20,000 Russian White soldiers remaining after the Russian Civil War. Pressure is growing on the Bulgarian government to disarm or expel them.		The Haiti-Santo Domingo Independence Society is calling for a civil disobedience movement modeled on Mohandas Gandhi's program in India to force the United States to withdraw its marine garrison from Haiti....500 rebels seized the La Loma fortress in Nicaragua in an attempt to overthrow the government.	Sun Yat-sen's Southern Army is pushing north against General Chen Kuang-yuan, warlord of Jiangxi Province. Gen Chen is an ally of Beijing warlord General Wu Pei-fu and has appealed to him for help.
May 22		In Northern Ireland today Unionist MP William Twadell is ambushed and gunned down by IRA assassins....A new government has been formed in Greece by Petros Protopapadakis, succeeding interim prime minister Nikolaos Stratos.	Italian forces in Libya began an offensive against the Arabs in the interior.	In Nicaragua, revolutionaries have agreed to evacuate the La Loma fortress and hand it over to U.S. Marines. The rebellion has speedily collapsed due to a lack of popular support.	
May 23		Austrian Chancellor Johan Schober today resigns in protest after the Parliament reduces funding requested by Schober for government operations....Mobs rampage through the streets of Belfast tonight after terrorists bomb a streetcar, injuring 10. Four others are killed in scattered fighting throughout Northern Ireland.	Egyptian nationalist gunmen assassinate the British Assistant Commissioner of Police in Cairo.	Nicaraguan authorities arrest 40 in connection with the recent attempted rebellion there.	
May 24		Italy has signed a commercial treaty with the Soviets, breaking with Britain and France, who have wanted to force the Bolsheviks to recognize foreign debts incurred under the tsarist regime....Fascist gunmen battle Socialists in street fighting in Rome today that leaves 21 wounded.		Nicaragua today announces an amnesty for the perpetrators of the recent seizure of the La Loma fortress....Uruguay is arranging a $6 million loan from New York and Boston banks....Mexican authorities today seize a shipload of armaments bound for rebels operating in the Gulf state of Tabasco under Carlos Greene.	The Chamber of Commerce in the Philippines is calling for a reform of the American administration there and the establishment of a territorial government with a regular elected assembly.
May 25		British Prime Minister Lloyd George addresses Parliament today on the results of the Genoa Conference. Lloyd George stresses that the most important issue is with the Soviets, with which Britain still does not have formal diplomatic relations.			
May 26		British Colonial Secretary Winston Churchill meets with Irish leaders today as rioting continues across Ireland....Soviet leader Vladimir I. Lenin suffers a stroke today. Paralyzed, Lenin will be incapable of working for some time. The door is open to a serious succession crisis in Russia, with Defense Minister Leon Trotsky as a major claimant.		The Commerce Department today reported that the economy of Central America is improving, especially in Guatemala and Costa Rica.	

U.S. Politics & Social Issues	U.S. Foreign Policy & Affairs, Defense	U.S. Economy & Environment	Science, Technology & Nature	Culture, Leisure & Lifestyle	
		Samuel Gompers, President of the American Federation of Labor, announces today that the AFL will hold its annual convention in Cincinnati in June. The AFL will discuss admitting unions with Communist affiliations....Coal miners today reject proposals for a 21 percent wage cut.	The Second British Everest Expedition, under Brigadier General C.G. Bruce begins its ascent of Mt. Everest today.	Screen star Rudolph Valentino is arrested today in Los Angeles on charges of bigamy. Valentino, already wed, is said to have gone to Mexico to marry Winifred Hudnut. Hudnut declares today that she will never leave Rudolph....The General Assembly of the Presbyterian Church today narrowly rejects a resolution calling on ministers to "discourage" the increasingly popular American habit of driving on Sundays.	May 20
Vice President Calvin Coolidge today addresses the General Assembly of the Presbyterian Church meeting in Des Moines, IA. Coolidge extolls the value of religion and states that he believes education should rely on religion for teaching moral values.				Eugene O'Neill has been awarded the Pulitzer Prize for drama for his *Anna Christie*. Other Pulitzer Prize winners include Edwin Arlington Robinson's *Collected Poems*, and Booth Tarkington's *Alice Adams* for fiction.....Police have ordered dance halls at Coney Island to ban "The Shimmy" as too suggestive. One piece bathing suits are also banned.	May 21
			George Mallory, Edward Norton, and Howard Somervell, of the British Everest Expedition reach 26,800 feet (8,170 meters) on the North Ridge before being halted by nightfall and severe weather. They are just 3,200 feet from the summit, breaking the 1910 record of 24,583 feet (7,494 meters).		May 22
African-American Colbert Wilson is whipped to death by a white mob for cattle theft in Bryan, TX. Wilson is the ninth African American to be murdered by mob violence in Texas since May 6.		A young artist named Walt Disney has incorporated a firm he calls Laugh-O-gram Films. Disney intends to make money by producing animated cartoon features for the movies....A firm has been incorporated to make films in Japanese targeted for the West Coast's growing Japanese-American population.	On Mt. Everest, using oxygen this time, George Finch and Geoffrey Bruce ascended the North Ridge and Face, reaching a height 27,300 feet (8,320 meters).	Anne Nichols' play *Abie's Irish Rose* opens tonight at the Fulton Theater in New York. This romantic tale of a young Jewish man and his Irish sweetheart is wildly popular.... The Los Angeles District Attorney's Office today banned the book *The Sins of Hollywood* as "too scurrilous."	May 23
The Ku Klux Klan is ordering a shakeup in its California organization after growing protests against Klan violence there. The KKK is seeking to build a nationwide power base for itself.			Paris records the hottest May day in 116 years, with temperatures hitting 91 degrees in the shade, as a record breaking heat wave sweeping Western Europe enters its fifth day.		May 24
				In a Yankees-Senators game today, slugger Babe Ruth explodes in a tirade. Suspended for one day and fined $200, Ruth is being forced out as team captain of the Yankees.	May 25
Debate is rife in Washington as politicians pore over primary election results. A crucial question is voting patterns by women: Are women using their newly-won power voting differently than their husbands?		Statisticians today noted that at current growth rates, Chicago will surpass Paris as the third largest city in the world by 1924.		F.M. Head today advises the annual convention of the California Pharmaceutical Association that men now form a large and growing market for toiletries, including such novelties as scented shaving cream.	May 26

F	G	H	I	J
Includes campaigns, elections, federal-state relations, civil rights and liberties, crime, the judiciary, education, healthcare, poverty, urban affairs, and population.	*Includes formation and debate of U.S. foreign and defense policies, veterans affairs, and defense spending. (Relations with specific foreign countries are usually found under the region concerned.)*	*Includes business, labor, agriculture, taxation, transportation, consumer affairs, monetary and fiscal policy, natural resources, pollution and industrial accidents.*	*Includes worldwide scientific, medical and technological developments, natural phenomena, U.S. weather and natural disasters.*	*Includes the arts, religion, scholarship, communications media, sports, entertainment, fashions, fads, and social life.*

	World Affairs	Europe	Africa & The Middle East	The Americas	Asia & The Pacific
May 27			The United States and Great Britain reached an accord today in Washington on Palestine. Britain will guarantee the rights of Americans living in Palestine, including equal access to business opportunities and natural resources....The Vatican has issued a statement condemning the proposed British mandate in Palestine as giving preferential treatment to the Jews.	Rebel Mexican General Arcadio Sosa Jurado is captured today in Chachalacas in Vera Cruz. He is immediately court-martialed and will be shot.	
May 28		Elections for the new National Assembly began today in Hungary, where parties loyal to Regent Admiral Horthy are expected to win.		Mexican forces have reportedly defeated rebels under Carlos Greene in the Gulf state of Tabasco. Meanwhile Mexican authorities are monitoring the Rio Grande to guard against an incursion by Mexican rebels over the border into Tamalipas.	
May 29	Pope Pius XI received cheering throngs today as he appeared before 60,000 pilgrims at the Eucharistic Congress in Rome.	British Liberal MP Horatio Bottomley has been convicted of fraud and sentenced to seven years in prison.			The Chinese government of warlord General Wu Pei-fu is under severe financial stress, with Wu issuing a call to provincial governors to produce $5 million by June 1 to meet government payrolls....Sun Yat-sen's Southern Army has captured Tayling in Jiangxi Province, and is advancing on Kanchow.
May 30					
May 31	The Reparations Commission grant Germany a six-month moratorium on reparations payments due to the collapse of the mark and Germans' inability to pay. The French government protested the decision....Bulgarian Prime Minister Stambulisky today addressed assembled delegates of the Peasant's Congress in Sofia, representing agrarian parties from across Eastern Europe. Stambulisky today warned the ruling classes that peasant demands for land reform had to be met.	65,000 Fascist Blackshirts have seized control of Bologna today, attacking anti-fascist newspapers and the Socialist party headquarters. Italy is rapidly drifting toward chaos....The Austrian government has received an international loan guaranteed by the League of Nations to stabilize its finances. A League commissioner will be appointed to supervise Austrian finances....Ignaz Seipel, leader of the Christian Socialist Party, today succeeded Johan Schober as Chancellor of Austria.		Chile is proposing a general disarmament plan for South America for consideration at the Pan-American Congress meeting set for 1923. Of particular concern is the ongoing naval arms race between Chile and Argentina.	Missionaries report today that famine is devastating Hunan Province, with six million of a population of 27 million facing starvation.
Jun. 1		Benitio Mussolini addresses a mass rally today of 50,000 Fascists in Bologna. He has vowed an armed revolution if government continues to support "anti-Fascist reaction."... The Fascists have forced Prefect Mori to flee the city....The British have established the Royal Ulster Constabulary to keep order in the predominantly Protestant northern part of Ireland....Soviet leader Vladimir I. Lenin has suffered a stroke.		Mexican Finance Minister de la Huerta today met with New York City bankers in an attempt to negotiate a settlement on Mexico's foreign debt. Mexico desperately is seeking American diplomatic recognition....American "flapper" fashions have shocked conservative Mexicans with the arrival of ballet companies from New York.	Red Army forces have defeated the Basmachi Muslim rebels under Enver Pasha in Turkestan.
Jun. 2		Aimo Kaarlo Cajandar has succeeded Juho Heikki Vennola as prime minister of Finland....47 British unions have voted to accept the employers' conditions for ending the long-running industrial lockout. The Amalgamated Engineering Union, the most militant of the unions, is now isolated.		Two American pilots are arrested in Jalapa, Vera Cruz, on charges of attempting to transfer arms and airplanes to Mexican rebels.	The Japanese government today ratifies the Shantung Treaty, agreeing to withdraw from the former German dominated Province of Shandong....Zhou Ziqi has succeeded Xu Shichang as President of the Beijing government in China. Xu has been forced out by pressure from the military. Zhou, Prime Minister, is intended as an interim figure.
	A *Includes developments that affect more than one world region, international organizations and important meetings of world leaders.*	B *Includes all domestic and regional developments in Europe, including the Soviet Union.*	C *Includes all domestic and regional developments in Africa and the Middle East.*	D *Includes all domestic and regional developments in Latin America, the Caribbean, and Canada.*	E *Includes all domestic and regional developments in Asian and Pacific nations (and colonies).*

U.S. Politics & Social Issues	U.S. Foreign Policy & Affairs, Defense	U.S. Economy & Environment	Science, Technology & Nature	Culture, Leisure & Lifestyle	
					May 27
		American bankers in a survey cited today declare stability of currency rates to be the most pressing need for the world economy at present.	The Women's Engineering Society meets today, and notes the value in developing electric powered labor saving devices for the home. The Society also calls for the establishment of a universal voltage to facilitate the introduction of new appliances.		May 28
President Warren G. Harding has signed a bill establishing the Federal Narcotics Control Board.		In *Federal Baseball Club v. National League*, the U.S. Supreme Court has declared that since baseball is a sport, not a business, the Major Leagues are not a monopoly, and are exempt from federal anti-trust legislation.			May 29
The Lincoln Memorial is dedicated today in Washington, DC, by former President William Howard Taft. The cost of the building is $3 million.	British and French officials join Americans in honoring the American dead of World War I on Memorial Day today. Feelings between the wartime allies remain strong. The American ambassador lays a wreath at the French Tomb of the Unknown Soldier in Paris, while General Harbord, addressing veterans and families at Belleau Wood, said: "Who can weigh the debt which the whole world owes to France?"			Jimmy Murphy has won the 10th annual Indianapolis 500, with a record-setting average speed of 94.48 mph.	May 30
			Polar explorer Roald Amundsen today announces that the object of his planned flight north from Seattle to the north Pole is to seek an undiscovered Arctic continent among the polar wastes.	Former presidential candidate William Jennings Bryan, in an address at Asbury College in Kentucky, accuses institutions of higher learning of teaching "materialistic doctrines that destroy religious faith in young students."	May 31
The Western States Agricultural Conference meeting in Sacramento today condemns Japanese American farmers as the reason for a "lower standard of living" among farmers in the West. Dismay is spreading among farmers, as prices have not recovered from their historic highs in World War I....Student leaders denounce plans by Harvard University to restrict enrollment, claiming that the intention is to put limits on the number of Jews accepted at the university.	An association of the Army of the United States is forming nationwide to encourage military preparedness.			Columbia University has renewed its annual senior prom, suspended since World War I.	June 1
President Warren Harding today stood by his appointees, who have been coming under increasing fire for corruption in both the press and Congress. Harding feels that the press has been unfair in attacking his cabinet members.	King Albert of Belgium sends President Warren Harding a letter of thanks honoring the sacrifices on the American AEF in liberating Belgium in World War I.				June 2

F
Includes campaigns, elections, federal-state relations, civil rights and liberties, crime, the judiciary, education, healthcare, poverty, urban affairs, and population.

G
Includes formation and debate of U.S. foreign and defense policies, veterans affairs, and defense spending. (Relations with specific foreign countries are usually found under the region concerned.)

H
Includes business, labor, agriculture, taxation, transportation, consumer affairs, monetary and fiscal policy, natural resources, pollution and industrial accidents.

I
Includes worldwide scientific, medical and technological developments, natural phenomena, U.S. weather and natural disasters.

J
Includes the arts, religion, scholarship, communications media, sports, entertainment, fashions, fads, and social life.

	World Affairs	Europe	Africa & The Middle East	The Americas	Asia & The Pacific
Jun. 3		Austria's railway system is staggering under a 52 million crown annual operating deficit, as the Austrian government struggles to remain solvent....Britain is rushing troops to Ulster to guard against growing raids by IRA fanatics.	Under pressure from Christian missionaries, American Secretary of State Charles Evans Hughes today announces that the United States will participate in an international investigation of Turkey's treatment of minorities.		
Jun. 4	French President Raymond Poincaré today warns Soviet leaders in advance that there will be no recognition of the Soviets at the upcoming Hague Conference unless the Soviet government reaches a settlement on the repayment of pre-World War debts. France is Russia's biggest creditor.	Socialists have won a number of seats in parliamentary elections in Hungary. As many as 20 will take their place in the new parliament....British troops have stormed and taken the village of Pettigo in Northern Ireland, killing seven IRA rebels and capturing 16....The British have seized an American steamer in Tralee Bay on the west coast of Ireland with a large quantity of arms for the Irish Republicans.		Talks in Washington between Peru and Chile over the disputed Tacna-Arica region remain deadlocked, with public sentiment in Chile running against giving back the lands taken by Chile in the 1879 war.	The Department of Commerce reported today that demand for beef is growing in China, as a generation grows up in contact with the West.
Jun. 5		German Socialist leader Philipp Scheidemann is attacked today while on holiday near Wilhelmshohe by a right wing extremist, who throws acid in Scheidemann's face. Former Chancellor Scheidemann is hated by monarchists and conservatives for proclaiming the Weimar Republic in 1918.	Rumors are rife that the French have signed a secret treaty with Ibn Saud's Arab kingdom of Nejd to provide arms against the British. True or not, the French are angry at British moves to secure the oil rich Iraq territory and are casting about for ways to counter British influence in the region.		Beijing warlord Wu Pei-fu's armies are pushing north into Manchuria, having reached near Chinchowfu, some 150 miles southwest of rival General Chang Tsolin's headquarters at Mukden.
Jun. 6		French financiers and economists meet today in Paris to discuss the status of the French economy and the European economic scene.... The National Feminist Congress met today in Clermont-Ferrand, and demands votes for French women.			
Jun. 7		Irish Free State President Arthur Griffith reopens negotiations today with the British over the draft Free State constitution.			The newly founded Philippine Democratic Party makes a good showing in today's general elections, winning one senate position and two seats in the lower house. The Philippines are still under American rule, but are clearly being groomed for self-government.
Jun. 8	Germany has invited the United States to name two of the three members of joint committee to adjudicate outstanding claims between the two countries stemming from World War I. The Germans are eager for American loans and want to eliminate any diplomatic obstacles....The International Olympic Committee in Paris today announced that the 1928 Olympics will be held in Amsterdam, beating out an effort by Los Angeles. The Committee also extended its support to holding international games for Latin America in Brazil in 1923.	The cost of living in Berlin has gone up 9 percent in the month of May alone, as Germany remains in the grip of rampant inflation....British troops supported by artillery and armored cars drive IRA militants from the Northern Ireland border village of Belleek in heavy fighting.... The Greek government has warned the League of Nations that it will send troops into southern Albania if persecution of ethnic Greeks in Albanian controlled Northern Epirus do not cease.			Manchurian warlord Chang Tsolin continues to retreat as forces loyal to Beijing overlord Wu Pei-fu push north. Wu's troops today have occupied Chingwangtao, the main port for the export of Manchurian coal. Wu now only has to subdue Sun Yat-sen's government in southern China....Sun Yat-sen's Guomindang troops advancing north have driven the military governor from Jiangxi Province.
Jun. 9	Yugoslavia is threatening to occupy parts of Bulgarian territory, claiming that Bulgaria is stirring up revolutionary movements in bordering Yugoslav territories.	Panic is growing in Austria as inflation spirals out of control. Bread that sold for half a *kronen* before World War I now sells for 1,000 *kronen*. Socialists are threatening armed rebellion, while extreme right wing groups are calling for union with Germany....A major show trial of Socialist Revolutionaries begins today in Moscow, as the Soviets crack down on all dissidents within Soviet Russia, even among fellow socialists.			General Feng Yu Hsiang, known as the "Christian General," warlord of Hunan Province, has banned the binding of women's feet in his territories.

A	B	C	D	E
Includes developments that affect more than one world region, international organizations and important meetings of world leaders.	*Includes all domestic and regional developments in Europe, including the Soviet Union.*	*Includes all domestic and regional developments in Africa and the Middle East.*	*Includes all domestic and regional developments in Latin America, the Caribbean, and Canada.*	*Includes all domestic and regional developments in Asian and Pacific nations (and colonies).*

U.S. Politics & Social Issues	U.S. Foreign Policy & Affairs, Defense	U.S. Economy & Environment	Science, Technology & Nature	Culture, Leisure & Lifestyle	
		Henry Ford wins approval today in the House Military Affairs Committee for development of the power and nitrate processing plant planned for Muscle Shoals, AL. The plan still faces strong opposition in the House....Barley, once used in breweries, is now being used as hog feed.	Arctic explorer Roald Amundsen's ship the *Maud*, sails today from Seattle for Nome, AK. On board are two all-metal monoplanes with which Amundsen will attempt to reach the North Pole.	Federal Prohibition agents reported today that the difficulty in obtaining steady liquor supplies is forcing most smaller bootleg operators out. Larger, better-organized mobs that can afford the planes, high-speed boats, and fast cars needed for rum running, are taking over.	June 3
President Harding today laid a wreath at the graves of Confederate dead at Arlington National Cemetery, announcing that sectionalism has "ended." Harding's Republican Party is trying hard to break into the solidly Democratic South....President Lowell of Harvard today announces that the faculty of Harvard has voted not to extend the power of the Admission Board to restrict admissions, which has been denounced as a ploy to limit the number of Jews coming into Harvard.	The War Department announces today that a token force of 1,000 men will stay in the U.S. Occupation Zone in the Rhineland....American Ambassador Myron T. Herrick today presented the Congressional Medal of Honor on behalf of the American people to the French city of Verdun, for their heroism in World War I. Verdun is the only community thus far to be so honored by the United States.			*Harper's Magazine* will begin serializing Stephen Vincent Benet's new novel, *Young People's Pride*....The Episcopal Church of the Beloved Disciple in New York City has announced that it is moving summer services forward to 10:00 a.m. to allow men more time to play golf.	June 4
			British inventor Louis Brennen, in London, has announced the invention of a machine that can take off vertically from the ground. This "helicopter" has drawn the attention of the British military.		June 5
In an attempt to deflect rising criticism, Attorney General Harry Daugherty today announced the creation of a special Accounting Division to investigate war fraud.				Famed actress Lillian Russell has died, after returning from Europe on a fact-finding mission for President Harding. A tireless recruiter for the military, she will be buried with full military honors.	June 6
	Faced with tightening postwar budgets, the U.S. Army is concentrating all of its artillery schools at Ft. Sill, OK, and its flight and air combat training around San Antonio, TX.		British mountaineer George Mallory makes a third attempt on Everest. A devastating avalanche below the North Col kills seven Sherpa guides, forcing an end to the attempt....Professor Albert Einstein has agreed to serve on the League of Nations Committee on Intellectual Cooperation.	J.F. Hatfield, of the famed Hatfield clan of West Virginia, has been found shot to death near Moundsville, WV, by assailants unknown.	June 7
President Warren Harding today approves Interior Secretary Albert Fall's lease of naval oil reserves at Teapot Dome and Elk Hills to private interests. Harding is backing his appointees in what is fast becoming a major political scandal....The Atlanta school board today votes 5–2 to override Commissioner Carl Hutcheson's efforts to remove all Catholic teachers from the Atlanta school system.		Thomas B. McAdams, President of the American Bankers Association cautions against "paternalistic" government action in trying to help America's troubled farmers. Anger and resentment have been building among farmers as prices have tumbled since World War I.	A French company has begun regular night air flights from Paris to Croyden Field, outside of London. Night flying is still risky, but the growing demand for air service is leading budding airlines to attempt it....Herr Borr, of the Zeppelin works at Friedrichshafen, Germany, has announced plans to launch an airship of 100,000 cubic meters, able to travel from Munich to Chicago in 24 hours. Borr has stated that it will soon be possible for Americans to receive European newspapers within three days of publication.		June 8
Three top union officials in Chicago will be put on trial this month as accessories to the murder of two policemen in labor violence....Governor Thomas W. Hardwick of Georgia today denounces charges by civil rights activists that Georgia leads the nation in lynchings of African Americans.			Archaeologists from Chicago's Oriental Institute have discovered artwork in the ruined Roman fortress of Salihiyah in Iraq. The paintings on the walls reveal the Eastern roots of what later evolved into Byzantine artwork.		June 9
F *Includes campaigns, elections, federal-state relations, civil rights and liberties, crime, the judiciary, education, healthcare, poverty, urban affairs, and population.*	G *Includes formation and debate of U.S. foreign and defense policies, veterans affairs, and defense spending. (Relations with specific foreign countries are usually found under the region concerned.)*	H *Includes business, labor, agriculture, taxation, transportation, consumer affairs, monetary and fiscal policy, natural resources, pollution and industrial accidents.*	I *Includes worldwide scientific, medical and technological developments, natural phenomena, U.S. weather and natural disasters.*	J *Includes the arts, religion, scholarship, communications media, sports, entertainment, fashions, fads, and social life.*	

	World Affairs	Europe	Africa & The Middle East	The Americas	Asia & The Pacific
Jun. 10	The Bankers' Committee of the Reparations Commission, which has been meeting in Paris since May, has refused to support an international loan for Germany. The French are blocking the agreement until they get relief from some of their debts to England and the United States, though they are holding out the possibility of a smaller loan to prevent total economic collapse in Germany.	Colonel William Haskell, head of the American Relief Administration in Russia, reports today that the Volga famine has finally ended, stating that American relief supplies have saved the lives of eight million people....Fascist gunmen attempt to assassinate the Yugoslav Consul-General in Milan, after Yugoslavian agitators arrested a Fascist agitator for attempting an attack on the former President in the disputed city of Fiume.		Officials in Washington today admitt that Cuba is facing a growing financial crisis, but deny rumors that the United States will intervene militarily in Cuba if President Zayas fails to restore fiscal stability.	Agitation is growing in China against the 1.375 million Christians in the country. While Communist agitators are blamed, suspicion of Western Christianity runs high among Chinese traditionalists as well.
Jun. 11	France has paid out some 80 billion francs in restoring regions devastated by the fighting in World War I. France has been counting on German reparations to cover a portion of these costs....Britain today rejects French calls for presenting an ultimatum to the Soviets at the upcoming Hague Conference	Fascist Blackshirts today clash with striking socialist dockworkers on the waterfront in the disputed port of Trieste. Fascist gunmen have grown increasingly bold as Mussolini's power grows in Italy.	Greek warships today have bombarded the Turkish Black Sea port of Samsun, destroying the Standard Oil dumps there. An American destroyer is monitoring the situation off the coast....Falling gold prices are making some gold mines in South Africa unprofitable, forcing miners, especially whites, to accept lower wages, adding to racial hostility toward lower paid African miners.		Li Yuanhong, backed by General Cao Kun, has succeeded Zhou Ziqi as President of China, while Yuan Huiqing has taken over Zhou's post as Prime Minister. Li seeks to reunite China and end warlord rule, but is powerless in the face of the warlord generals who control Beijing.
Jun. 12	Bulgaria, one of the defeated Central Powers from World War I, has refused Allied pressure to surrender control of its finances. The Bulgarian government further called for a three-year moratorium on reparations payments, stating that they are beyond Bulgaria's capacity to pay at present.	The Austrian *krone* fell to 21,000 against the dollar today as inflation spirals out of control. The Austrian government closes the Vienna Boerse, or stock exchange, in an effort to quell the panic....German President Friedrich Ebert pays his first state visit to Bavaria today since assuming office, touring Munich under heavy security. Bavaria is a hotbed of ultra-right wing extremist groups, such as Adolf Hitler's small, but vocal National Socialist Workers Party.	12 British soldiers have been captured and executed by forces loyal to Mustafa Kemal's Nationalist government in a clash near the Dardanelles.	Negotiations in Washington between Peru and Chile over the disputed Tacna-Arica region remain deadlocked today in the face of strong Chilean public opinion against handing back the territories, seized in the last century....The government of President Alfredo Zayas in Cuba agreed to American demands presented by General Enoch Crowder, President Warren Harding's personal representative in Cuba. The United States is demanding a clean up of graft and corruption. The Zayas government has agreed to a cabinet shakeup and controls on spending.	In Japan, Admiral Baron Tomasaburo Kato has been made Prime Minister, succeeding Korekiyo Takahashi. Takahashi has been unable to control factional infighting within his Rikken Seiyukai Party. Baron Kato was Japan's chief negotiator at the Washington Conference, and this appointment is in recognition of his success. Baron Kato tends to favor the aristocracy and the imperial bureaucracy over the military, and favors a withdrawal of Japanese troops from Shandong and Siberia.
Jun. 13		The Amalgamated Engineering Union has voted to accept the employer's terms, ending the long lock out in Britain.			Wealthy Chinese and Western missionaries are fleeing Nanchang, the capital of Jiangxi Province in China, as Sun Yat-sen's Guomindang troops advance north. The American gunboat USS *Isabel* is standing by on the Yangtze, as are British and Japanese gunboats, to protect their nationals....Manchurian warlord Chang Tsolin counterattacked forces loyal to Beijing warlord Wu Peifu at Chingwangtao, but are repulsed in heavy fighting as Wu's forces continue to push north.
Jun. 14		In Russia, Bolshevik leader Vladimir I. Lenin announces that he will take a six-month rest to regain his health after his stroke in May. Lev Kamenev, Grigory Zinoviev, and Josef Stalin will manage the government in his absence....Stalin is said to be using his patronage power as General Secretary of the Communist Party, to support a three-man *troika* to limit the power of Leon Trotsky.		Benson & Hedges is lowering the price of its leading Virginia brand cigarettes in Canada from 18 to 15 cents a pack. With falling tobacco prices, it is believed that the "nickel cigar" will be re-instituted.	A delegation of Filipino nationalists led by Manuel L. Quezon, President of the Insular Senate, arrives in Washington, DC, today to meet with President Harding to demand full independence for the Philippines.

A	B	C	D	E
Includes developments that affect more than one world region, international organizations and important meetings of world leaders.	*Includes all domestic and regional developments in Europe, including the Soviet Union.*	*Includes all domestic and regional developments in Africa and the Middle East.*	*Includes all domestic and regional developments in Latin America, the Caribbean, and Canada.*	*Includes all domestic and regional developments in Asian and Pacific nations (and colonies).*

U.S. Politics & Social Issues	U.S. Foreign Policy & Affairs, Defense	U.S. Economy & Environment	Science, Technology & Nature	Culture, Leisure & Lifestyle	
A crowd of 300 striking miners marches on a coal mine near Terre Haute, IN, and demands that it be shut down, injuring two mine employees. Tensions are rising as the nationwide coal strike heads toward its third month.			Guglielmo Marconi of Italy states that an apparatus can be designed to transmit radio waves from one ship in any desired direction and pick up reflections from another ship in a receiver, a device that would "thereby immediately reveal the presence and bearing of the other ship in fog or thick weather."...The Bureau of Mines is researching techniques to condense petroleum from vapors at refineries. This could potentially produce another 120 million gallons of gas a year....Dr. C.G. Abbott of the Smithsonian Institution is testing a solar cooker, which will use polished aluminum to focus the suns rays to cook food without fuel.	Pillory, winner of the Preakness in May, has won the Belmont Stakes, ridden by jockey L. Morris....Tensions are growing between Fundamentalists and so-called Radicals among Baptists churches as the Northern Baptist Convention prepares to open in Indianapolis.	June 10
				Robert Flaherty's groundbreaking film documentary *Nanook of the North*, debuts in New York City today. *Nanook* is the first feature length documentary, shot on location in arctic Quebec....A group of prominent citizens has formed The American League. Its purpose is to outlaw "immodest" dances such as the "shimmy" and the "toddle."...Drug dealer Ralph Lattore is slain in a gun battle in New York's Chinatown today with rival mobsters. Drugs, while nowhere near as popular as bootleg liquor, are becoming a growing inner city problem.	June 11
	Captain A.W. Stevens (USAS) makes a record parachute jump from 24,200 feet from a supercharged Martin bomber over McCook Field.		A bill has been introduced in Congress to allow the government to restrict flying over major cities as aerobatic stunt flying by amateur pilots becomes more popular.		June 12
Democratic Senator Harrison today openly denounces President Harding, accusing him of appointing "crooks," citing Harding's attempted appointment of Missouri political crony Nat Goldstein to become IRS Collector for St. Louis.			American archaeologists excavating in the ruins of Sardis in Turkey have uncovered Lydian gold coins dating back 2,500 years. These are the oldest known coins in existence.	William Jennings Bryan addresses a convention of 11,000 Northern Baptists at Indianapolis today, calling on Christians to stand by the "fundamentals of the Christian faith."...King George V presides over a flock of notables at the opening of the Royal Ascot Meet today, as society ladies turn out in their finest, despite pouring rains.	June 13
Wilbur D. Foulke, Acting President of the National Civil Service Reform League today condemns federal Prohibition agents as a "gang of mercenary freebooters, who violate the law, cram their pockets with ill-gotten gains, and demoralize the country with their corrupt rapacity." Prohibition agents in some areas earn less than garbage collectors, opening the door to corruption.		Striking miners fire on a train carrying strike breaking coalminers to work at Jacobs, UT, killing a company guard and injuring two mine employees. The governor of Utah has declared a state of martial law, as the nationwide coal strike becomes violent. In Terre Haute, IN, striking miners have vowed to shut down every mine in the area, by force if necessary.		President Warren G. Harding's dedication of the Francis Scott Key Memorial in Baltimore is broadcast by Baltimore station WEAR today, making Harding the first American President to be heard on the radio....Charles Hoffner has won the PGA golf tournament....A movie version of the famous book *Ben Hur* will begin filming soon, with some of the dramatic scenes to be filmed around the Mediterranean.	June 14

F	G	H	I	J
Includes campaigns, elections, federal-state relations, civil rights and liberties, crime, the judiciary, education, healthcare, poverty, urban affairs, and population.	*Includes formation and debate of U.S. foreign and defense policies, veterans affairs, and defense spending. (Relations with specific foreign countries are usually found under the region concerned.)*	*Includes business, labor, agriculture, taxation, transportation, consumer affairs, monetary and fiscal policy, natural resources, pollution and industrial accidents.*	*Includes worldwide scientific, medical and technological developments, natural phenomena, U.S. weather and natural disasters.*	*Includes the arts, religion, scholarship, communications media, sports, entertainment, fashions, fads, and social life.*

	World Affairs	Europe	Africa & The Middle East	The Americas	Asia & The Pacific
Jun. 15		The draft of the proposed Irish Free State Constitution, hammered out in negotiations in London, has been published, just before general elections are scheduled....Britain is putting Daylight Savings Time into effect.		Chile is putting into effect legislation that would require all coastal trade to be done in Chilean ships. This is aimed at regaining control of coastal shipping from the British. Peru is contemplating similar legislation....General Enoch Crowder, American special envoy in Cuba, pronounces himself satisfied with the reorganization of the Cuban cabinet as announced today. America has been pressing Cuba to reform its corrupt government for some time, and possesses a great deal of leverage over the Cuban economy.	Lord Winterton, Under Secretary for Indian Affairs, today issues a report to parliament on the situation in India, claiming that the arrest of independence agitator Mohandas Gandhi had helped quell unrest in India. Winterton also warned that sectarian strife between Hindus and Muslims will only delay Indian self-government....General Wu's Beijing forces have captured Chaoyang and are closing in on Shanhaikwan as Manchurian warlord Chang Tsolin's forces are driven back.
Jun. 16	Delegates at the international conference at The Hague today rejected efforts to come to an agreement in advance of opening negotiations with the Soviets on diplomatic recognition. This underscores the basic divisions between the British and the antirecognition French.	Germany officially begins ceding control of the disputed Upper Silesia region to Poland after Allied threats....In Ireland, national elections have gone overwhelmingly to the Nationalist faction of *Sinn Féin*, who support the creation of the Irish Free State within the British Commonwealth as laid down in the Treaty of London.		Portuguese pilots Captains Gago Coutinho and Sacadura Cabral have arrived in Brazil, being the first to cross the South Atlantic by air.	
Jun. 17	The Soviets are proposing a disarmament conference for Poland and the Baltic States, with the aim of reducing tensions over military spending. The Soviets are also seeking a settlement with Romania over the status of Bessarabia.	Flags are flown at half-mast in Germany today marking the loss of German territory in Upper Silesia to Poland.			Forces loyal to General Chen Chiung-ming, former governor of Guangdong Province, have taken Guangzhou (Canton), capital of Sun Yat-sen's Guomindang government. Sun has fled aboard a gunboat to Whampoa, where Guomindang forces are still holding out. General Chen had been loyal to Sun, but has worked out a deal with Beijing warlord Wu Peifu.
Jun. 18	The Dutch are busily preparing for the upcoming international conference at The Hague. The Dutch are eager to broker a settlement with the Soviets. Dutch bankers hold more than one billion florins in Russian state and railway securities from before World War I, and Royal Dutch Shell is eager to acquire a foothold in the rich Baku oil fields on the Caspian.	Continued inflation is ruining the German middle class. A 70 square meter house that cost 1,584 marks on the eve of the World War now costs nearly 88,000 marks....Fanatics on both sides in the sectarian conflict in Belfast are turning to a deadly weapon—arson, with eight fires being set around the city in one night....Mussolini's Fascist Blackshirts are also using arson—they burned the Labor Exchange in Reggio today.	The Kurds, under Sheikh Mahmud, have rebelled against British rule in Iraq, demanding independence or autonomy.	Americans have done a great deal to eliminate yellow fever in the Panama Canal Zone. Success has been due to rigorous efforts to eliminate pools of standing water where the yellow fever carrying mosquito breeds.	Fighting continues to rage in Guangzhou and in Jiangxi Province, between Sun Yat-sen's Guomindang and Guangdong Province warlord General Chen.
Jun. 19			The heirs of the late Ottoman Sultan Abdul Hamid have sold properties in the Mosul oil fields to the British for $5 million. The Turkish Nationalist government in Ankara has denounced the sale as illegal.		
Jun. 20		50,000 people turned out to cheer the return aboard the HMS *Renown* of Edward, Prince of Wales, after his round the world journey....Prince George, exiled Crown Prince of Yugoslavia, now in Paris, has sent letters threatening the life of King Alexander and Prime Minister Pasitch. George is widely regarded to be half-mad.			The American Consul in Guangzhou is asking for support from the American Asiatic Fleet after gunboats loyal to the defeated Guomindang government, operating from Whampoa, bombarded the Guangzhou waterfront, damaging American property.

A	B	C	D	E
Includes developments that affect more than one world region, international organizations and important meetings of world leaders.	*Includes all domestic and regional developments in Europe, including the Soviet Union.*	*Includes all domestic and regional developments in Africa and the Middle East.*	*Includes all domestic and regional developments in Latin America, the Caribbean, and Canada.*	*Includes all domestic and regional developments in Asian and Pacific nations (and colonies).*

U.S. Politics & Social Issues	U.S. Foreign Policy & Affairs, Defense	U.S. Economy & Environment	Science, Technology & Nature	Culture, Leisure & Lifestyle	
A delegation of Arkansas farmers, most owning less than 100 acres of land, appeals to President Harding for relief as America's farm crisis worsens.				The Fox River Valley Baseball League has expelled former members of Chicago "Black Sox" of 1919. Former "Black Sox" players are already barred from the Major Leagues and have tried to find work in the minors under assumed names....Fire sweeps through Arverne, Long Island today, burning 400 homes and leaving 10,000 homeless.	June 15
	Maj. Gen Henry Allen, Commander of the American Army of Occupation on the Rhineland in Germany, today states that the use of African-American troops in the occupation was "undesirable." General Allen stating that their "lower civilization" made them unwelcome.		Henry Berliner demonstrated helicopter flight to the U.S. Army at College Park, MD. Berliner is using a modified World War Nieuport biplane, fitted with a helicopter propeller.	Northern Baptists meeting in Indianapolis today reject a proposed fundamentalist creed, stating that the New Testament is enough. Still, fundamentalist sentiment runs high among this widespread denomination.	June 16
				Popular fiction books this summer include: F. Scott Fitzgerald's *The Beautiful and the Damned*, D.H. Lawrence's *Aaron's Rod*, John Galsworthy's *The Forsythe Saga*, Edith Wharton's *Glimpses of the Moon*, and Rupert Hughes' *Souls for Sale*. Nonfiction works include: Harold Speakman's *Beyond Shanghai*, Walter Lippmann's *Public Opinion*, Vilhlalmur Stefansson's *The Friendly Arctic*, and Charles S. Chaplin's *My Trip Abroad*.	June 17
			Dutch astronomer Jacobus C. Kapteyn, whose studies of the Milky Way brought the first evidence that galaxies rotate, has died. He was 61....Johns Hopkins University biochemist, Dr. E.V. McCollum, has identified a new vitamin, which researchers are calling vitamin D. Lack of vitamin D has been found by McCollum's experiments to be the cause of the dreaded bone disease, rickets.	The government reports that Prohibition has cut the death rate from alcohol consumption by 21 percent.	June 18
Senate Republicans vote 27–11 to postpone discussion of the veterans' Bonus Bill until after passage of the Fordney-McCumber Tariff Bill, aimed at protecting American businesses from foreign competition. The Bonus Bill is popular with veterans groups, but debate swirls around how the bonus, due veterans of World War I, will be paid for.				The convention of Northern Baptists meeting in Indianapolis has agreed to standardize the requirements for Baptists ministers....Mobsters are trying to infiltrate the Chicago police force. A recent call for 200 applicants revealed 42 with criminal records, including one man wanted for a robbery where $12,000 was stolen.	June 19
President Warren Harding, under fire in the Congress and facing an election year for congressional and gubernatorial seats, is cancelling his planned summer vacation trip to Alaska.		House Republicans today denounce Henry Ford's recent bid to construct a dam and nitrate production plant at Muscle Shoals, AL, accusing Ford of making extravagant promises to end unemployment in the region, and hiding true costs.	A report to the House of Commons today by RAF Major General Seely today warns that Britain's civil aviation industry is seriously lagging behind that of other countries, thus endangering national security.		June 20

	World Affairs	Europe	Africa & The Middle East	The Americas	Asia & The Pacific
Jun. 21	Czechoslovakia today announced that it will provide a loan of $9.5 million to Austria. The Czechs fear that if Austria slips into chaos all of Central Europe will follow.		In Britain, the House of Lords debates the proposed British mandate for Palestine, and blocks efforts to postpone the imposition of the Mandate. Opponents fear that Britain is siding too closely with the Zionists, which will lead to repercussions in the Middle East.		
Jun. 22		Two IRA fanatics gun down British Field Marshal Henry Wilson, Protestant and member of Parliament for Ulster, in the Belgravia section of London after unveiling a war memorial at the Liverpool Street Station. The men are said to have acted in retaliation for the killing of Catholics in Protestant Northern Ireland. Two policemen were shot in the melee before the gunmen were apprehended.			
Jun. 23		French police have broken up a French and Belgian ring that has been smuggling arms to Soviet Russia. Some 25 tons of arms have been shipped since February 1921.	The French Chamber of Deputies has slashed funding for the French occupation of Syria. President Raymond Poincaré only blocked further cuts by threatening to make them take a vote of confidence on the government. The 107 million francs finally agreed on will maintain French troops levels in the troubled Mandate at 35,000 men.		
Jun. 24		Foreign Minister Walther Rathenau of Germany has been assassinated outside his house in Berlin by the militant right wing nationalist Organization Consul, led by Captain Hermann Ehrhardt. A prominent Jewish industrialist, Rathenau had enraged paramilitary fanatics for advocating a settlement with the Allies, and payment of reparations....Hundreds of thousands of workers take to the streets of Berlin in massed protests against the killings....In the Reichstag, Chancellor Joseph Wirth denounces the killing, shouting: "The enemy stands on the Right!."...Right wing militant Adolph Hitler begins serving a one-month jail sentence in Munich today for paramilitary agitation in the southern German state of Bavaria.	The burgeoning town of Tel Aviv has become a symbol for the growing Jewish community in Palestine. Founded just 12 years ago by 60 families, it now has a population of 12,000 people. However, the question of whether Palestine will be the location of a permanent Jewish homeland is still bitterly debated.	Juan Vicente Gómez Chacón has succeeded Victorino Márquez Bustillos as President of Venezuela. Gómez Chacón has been the real ruler of Venezuela since seizing power in 1908. He has focused on bringing economic stability to Venezuela by granting concessions to foreign oil companies, and as such is popular with the United States and European investors. Gómez has also enriched himself, taking bribes and kickbacks. Gómez ostensibly stepped aside in 1914, leaving the presidency to his protégé, Márquez Bustillos. Now Gómez feels strong enough to put pretense aside and rule openly again.	
Jun. 25	Security is tight at The Hague as the Dutch prepare for the arrival of the Soviet delegation to the international conference this week. The assassination of German Foreign Minister Walther Rathenau by right wing fanatics just yesterday has everyone on edge....Crucial to the upcoming conference is the status of the 2.2 billion rubles worth of property and investments held by foreigners in Russia in 1917. The French still claim by far the most: 684 million gold rubles.	The German mark has now fallen to 348.5 to the dollar as Germany appears to be headed toward chaos....200,000 demonstrate in the streets of Berlin today in support of the Republic, as socialists and trade unions united to back President Friedrich Ebert.		A. Bruce Bielaski, former chief of the FBI, has been kidnapped by bandits near Cuernavaca and held for $10,000 ransom. Mexican authorities are sending in cavalry from the states of Morelos and Guerrero to look for Bielaski.	Soldiers of Sun Yat-sen's government in Jiangxi Province have fallen into disorder and are looting as the Guomindang disintegrates.
Jun. 26	French and English Communists meet with Dutch Marxists in The Hague as the city welcomed the Soviet delegation to the Hague Conference today.	The government of Germany has invoked Article 48 of the Weimar Constitution, voting itself emergency powers to deal with the crisis created by the falling German mark. German police have arrested dozens across Germany in connection with the murder of Foreign Minister Walther Rathenau....Albert I, Prince of Monaco, has died, after reigning since 1889.			

A	B	C	D	E
Includes developments that affect more than one world region, international organizations and important meetings of world leaders.	*Includes all domestic and regional developments in Europe, including the Soviet Union.*	*Includes all domestic and regional developments in Africa and the Middle East.*	*Includes all domestic and regional developments in Latin America, the Caribbean, and Canada.*	*Includes all domestic and regional developments in Asian and Pacific nations (and colonies).*

U.S. Politics & Social Issues	U.S. Foreign Policy & Affairs, Defense	U.S. Economy & Environment	Science, Technology & Nature	Culture, Leisure & Lifestyle	
		Striking coalminers beat a mine security guard at Uniontown, PA. 1,000 miners and their families have been evicted in the county as the nationwide strike nears its third month.		The United Confederate Veterans, meeting in Richmond, VA, today, denounce Abraham Lincoln as having "forced the war upon the South." The UCV has called for history textbooks nationwide to be rewritten so as to "fairly teach the magnificent history of the Southern states."	June 21
At least 14 people have been killed as a mob of 5,000 striking coalminers stormed a stockade near Herrin, IL, held by strike breaking workers. The Governor of Illinois has mobilized 1,000 National Guard troops to maintain order. The strike has hit the impoverished coal country of southern Illinois hard. The Harding administration today declined to force an end to the nearly three-month long nationwide coal strike.				An investigation by the Hartford Council of Women's Clubs blames parties thrown by the "better class" for "degrading" dancing. The report also states that it is common in hotels and cabarets to see women smoking cigarettes and people mixing liquor with their drinks.	June 22
		The Horn & Hardart Corporation, owners of the increasingly popular chain of Automat restaurants, are seeking to increase their capitalization from $5 million to $20 million as business booms.			June 23
		Chicago is in the grip of a runaway building boom, with more than 11,000 homes either planned or under construction. A six bedroom apartment in the suburbs goes for $100.		Walter Hagen has won the British Open Golf Cup for the United States, with a victory by one stroke....Carrier pigeons are being used to smuggle cocaine from Germany into France. One "snow bird" is found with 15 grams of the powder.	June 24
Socialist and Farm-Labor Party leaders meet in New York today and voted to field a unified slate of candidates for the November elections.					June 25
A bill has been introduced in the House of Representatives today to reduce the numbers of resident aliens to be allowed in the United States, and barring Asians from permanent residency.	Hundreds watch as an Air Service pilot pulls out of a death dive after his plane's engine stalls at 3,000 feet over the Aberdeen Proving Grounds. The pilot manages to glide to safety.		Arctic explorer Roald Amundsen has chosen Spitzbergen as his target to attempt a flight to the North Pole from Alaska.		June 26
F *Includes campaigns, elections, federal-state relations, civil rights and liberties, crime, the judiciary, education, healthcare, poverty, urban affairs, and population.*	**G** *Includes formation and debate of U.S. foreign and defense policies, veterans affairs, and defense spending. (Relations with specific foreign countries are usually found under the region concerned.)*	**H** *Includes business, labor, agriculture, taxation, transportation, consumer affairs, monetary and fiscal policy, natural resources, pollution and industrial accidents.*	**I** *Includes worldwide scientific, medical and technological developments, natural phenomena, U.S. weather and natural disasters.*	**J** *Includes the arts, religion, scholarship, communications media, sports, entertainment, fashions, fads, and social life.*	

	World Affairs	Europe	Africa & The Middle East	The Americas	Asia & The Pacific
Jun. 27		Republican troops holding Four Courts in Dublin today kidnapped Irish free State General J.J. O'Connell. The Republicans are becoming more and more a direct challenge to Free State control, which today issued an ultimatum to dissident republicans to surrender.		40 Americans have been kidnapped and held for ransom near Tampico, Mexico, by the forces of rebel General Gorozave. Opponents of President Alvaro Obregon are trying to discredit the Mexican government and block recognition by the United States.	British residents of Guangzhou (Canton) are arming as fighting goes on between the Guomindang forces Sun Yat-sen, and troops loyal to the Beijing government....A Naval Intelligence report states that Japan is aggressively building light cruisers, destroyers, and submarines, all categories of ships with no restrictions. While the U.S. Navy officially is not preparing for war, unofficially Japan is seen as the most likely opponent in another war.
Jun. 28		Government forces in Dublin have opened fire on Republican militants holding out in the Four Courts Building, besieging them inside.... Ireland is now in a state of open civil war. Irish Free State leader Michael Collins has resisted a showdown with the militants who seized the building in April. However, continued provocations by the militants, led by Rory O'Conner, have forced Collins to ask the British for artillery to suppress the rebels.	The French have established the Union of Syrian States in Damascus, with Subhi Bey Barakat al-Khalidi as titular head of state. The union comprises the states of Damascus, Aleppo, the Jebel Druze, for the Druze sect, and a state for the Alawite Shi'ite sect. The French will in fact remain in control of the country.	Former FBI chief A. Bruce Bielaski, who was kidnapped by bandits near Cuernavaca has escaped and has been recovered safely. The bandits, who are apparently amateurs, are still at large....The United States has opened direct cable communications with Costa Rica, as the isolation of much of Latin America is slowly lessening.	
Jun. 29		Free State troops are closing in on the anti-Treaty rebels holed up in the Four Courts Building. Irish Free State leader Michael Collins has resisted British offers of air support to prevent the loss of life. The IRA's First Dublin Brigade under Oscar Traynor has seized points along O'Connel Street to help the embattled Four Courts garrison. Telegraph communications between Dublin Castle and London have been cut.... Republicans disarmed a Free state garrison in Listowel in County Kerry, as the civil war spreads to the countryside.			Sun Yat-sen, has resigned as President of the Guomindang government of Guangzhou (Canton), China. Sun has sought democratic reforms for years, but has never had sufficient military support, and is now fleeing southern China for exile in Shanghai.
Jun. 30	Polish irregulars attack the town of Hindenburg in Upper Silesia today, but are driven off by German "self protection" forces. French troops, who are occupying the region under League of Nations auspices as it is being handed over to Poland, clashed with the German forces. One French soldier was killed, and three others wounded, while German casualties came to 17 killed and 17 injured. The mostly German speaking region does not want to become part of Poland.	In the bombardment of Four Courts, a stray shell has hit the Irish Public Records Office, which is being used as an ammo dump by besieged anti-Treaty rebels. The ensuing explosion has incinerated 1,000 years of Irish state and religious archives. Republican militants in the Four Courts Building in Dublin have surrendered to government forces.... Rory O'Connor and 130 of his men have surrendered....Fighting continues in Dublin as some 500 anti-Treaty militants under Oscar Traynor remain at large in Dublin, many holed up in a stronghold at the northeast end of O'Connell Street.		The United States has agreed to end the marine occupation of the Dominican Republic.	
Jul. 1		Irish Free State troops are wiping out Republican pockets south of Dublin, while closing in on Republicans holding out on O'Connell Street, as the savage civil war continues in Ireland....As of July, Mussolini's Fascist Party now has 700,000 members, and is angling for supreme power....In this month, the two IRA gunmen who murdered Field Marshal Sir Henry Wilson last month, Reginald Dunne and Joseph O'Sullivan, are convicted of murder and sentenced to hang....In inflation wracked Germany, food that cost 100 marks in 1914 now costs 6,073 marks.	Members of the American Relief commission in Turkey have claimed that the Greek army has been destroying villages and crops as it retreats amid increasingly bitter fighting in Anatolia....American made aluminum cooking ware is replacing the more expensive Indian made copper ware in the bazaars of Arabia....The Vatican has expressed its opposition to the British allowing further Jewish settlement in Palestine, fearing for the position of Catholic minorities in the Mandate.	Mexican rebel General Larraga has approached the Penn-Mexican oil field at Paolo Blanco, 30 miles west of Tuxpan and demanded 10,000 pesos in ransom. Troops loyal to President Alvaro Obregon have been deployed to the region to counter what is feared to be the opening moves of an all out effort to overthrow the Mexican government.	In this month, Soviet forces are cutting rail links with Vladivostok. This will hurt Russia's Siberian export trade, which passes through the Pacific port, but the Soviets are determined to bring down the Japanese controlled White Russian enclave there.
	A *Includes developments that affect more than one world region, international organizations and important meetings of world leaders.*	B *Includes all domestic and regional developments in Europe, including the Soviet Union.*	C *Includes all domestic and regional developments in Africa and the Middle East.*	D *Includes all domestic and regional developments in Latin America, the Caribbean, and Canada.*	E *Includes all domestic and regional developments in Asian and Pacific nations (and colonies).*

	U.S. Politics & Social Issues	U.S. Foreign Policy & Affairs, Defense	U.S. Economy & Environment	Science, Technology & Nature	Culture, Leisure & Lifestyle
June 27				Spanish archaeologists have unearthed the ruins of an acropolis built by the ancient Iberian peoples of the peninsula, near the town of Vera in Saragossa.	The first Newberry Award for outstanding children's literature is awarded today to Hendrik van Loon for *The Story of Mankind*, a history of the world written for children.
June 28	Senate Democrats are dropping their opposition to the proposed Fordney-McCumber Tariff, which is now expected to pass within a few weeks. Measures raising tariffs on foreign beef and livestock have helped make the measure acceptable to the farm bloc.	Three air service cadets are killed today when their plane crashes shortly after takeoff at Brooks Field near San Antonio, TX.		The bones of famed Renaissance painter Giovanni Boccaccio are believed to have been found at the house in Certaldo where he lived.	
June 29	Embattled Attorney General Harry Daugherty came under fire again today when Ohio Representative accused Daugherty of pressuring federal employees in Ohio to campaign for Carmi Thompson, close ally of Daugherty and President Warren Harding and now candidate for governor of Ohio. Harding is an Ohio political veteran. Consequently, these accusations threaten Harding's political base and open the doors to attacks on the President himself.		President Warren Harding is calling a meeting of representatives of striking coalminers and mine operators in an effort to mediate the 3-month long strike. Suggestions include the creation of a nonpartisan commission to review conditions in the coal industry and make recommendations to Congress. Some experts consider the industry overextended, with as many as 30 percent of mines only marginally profitable, while miners insist that they are paid substandard wages for dangerous working conditions.		Men's fashions, while not changing as quickly as women's, are evolving. At a convention of the International Association of Clothing Designers in Philadelphia, the word is that knickerbockers are no longer just for the golf course, and that the new look in men's suits will be "conservative jazz."...World heavyweight boxing champ Jack Dempsey has accepted a bout with African-American heavyweight contender Harry Wills in New York City.
June 30	The Dyer Anti-Lynching Bill, which will allow the Federal government to prosecute lynchings that states fail to prosecute, has been approved by the Senate Judiciary Committee after passage by the House of Representatives. However, it is generally understood that the bill will be killed in a vote by the whole Senate, where entrenched segregationist sentiment is very strong.			Famed Norwegian polar explorer Roald Amundsen has sailed with his expedition from Nome, AK. Amundsen and his team will establish a base at Point Barrow and then attempt to fly across the Pole to Spitzbergen.	It was reported today that deaths from automobile accidents reached 12,500 in 1921, one death every 42 minutes, with 300,000 injured. Insurance companies are calling for better roads and driver education programs to deal with the problem....The Central Conference of American Rabbis voted overwhelmingly in its convention at Cape May, NJ, to ordain women as rabbis. Speaking of the role of women, the statement declares: "Our sages have always recognized her as the preserver of Israel."...Immigration from the British Isles and Germany to the United States has fallen dramatically between 1910 and 1920. In this same period, immigration from Italy jumped by 57 percent to 3.3 million.
July 1		The U.S. Navy has begun converting the still unfinished battle cruisers USS *Lexington* and USS *Saratoga* into aircraft carriers.	The six-mile stretch of highway between Elizabethtown and Rahway, NJ, is being described as a model for modern highway construction. At 29-feet-wide, the road, costing $85,000 to construct, is meant to handle modern truck traffic between New York and Philadelphia....The St. Louis Federal reserve reported today that the economy is improving all across the MIdwest after a long slump.		Chicago golfer Chick Evans has won the Western Golf Association tournament at the Hillcrest Course in Kansas City, easily defeating rival George Von Elm.

F	G	H	I	J
Includes campaigns, elections, federal-state relations, civil rights and liberties, crime, the judiciary, education, healthcare, poverty, urban affairs, and population.	*Includes formation and debate of U.S. foreign and defense policies, veterans affairs, and defense spending. (Relations with specific foreign countries are usually found under the region concerned.)*	*Includes business, labor, agriculture, taxation, transportation, consumer affairs, monetary and fiscal policy, natural resources, pollution and industrial accidents.*	*Includes worldwide scientific, medical and technological developments, natural phenomena, U.S. weather and natural disasters.*	*Includes the arts, religion, scholarship, communications media, sports, entertainment, fashions, fads, and social life.*

	World Affairs	Europe	Africa & The Middle East	The Americas	Asia & The Pacific
Jul. 2	W.G. Cove, President of the National Union of Teachers of England and Wales, today calls on teachers to work for peace, "banishing from the schools nationalism that does not find its highest expression in service to humanity."	Inflation continues to ravage Austria, where essentials that cost 100 kronen in January 1921, cost 2,028 as of May of this year.	American oil interests will join with British and French firms in developing lands belonging to the Ottoman Sultan in Iraq. The Sultan's family, in dire financial straits since World War I, have opened their holdings, valued at $200 million, across the former Ottoman empire. The Sultan's family seeks to derive a regular annual income of $1 million from oil revenues.		
Jul. 3		The League of Nations is hosting an Intergovernmental Conference on Identity Certificates for Russian Refugees in London. Russian refugees currently are stateless persons. Steps are being proposed to create identity certificates for Russian expatriates to allow them to travel freely....Republican forces attacked a Free State outpost at Boyle in County Roscommon, as fighting continues to spread across Ireland.	Palestinian activists today issue appeals to the Muslim leaders of the Middle East, calling on them to denounce proposed plans to establish a Jewish homeland in the British Palestinian Mandate.	President Epitacio Pessoa of Brazil has officially invited the United States to send a mission to Brazil's coming centenary celebration in September. Germany has already been invited, but has declined due to budgetary concerns in its current economic crisis, much to the dismay of Brazil's 800,000 citizens of German descent.	Rumors of a counterattack by forces still loyal to Sun Yat-sen's Guomindang are flying in Guangzhou (Canton), Sun's former capital. Guomindang troops, backed by a flotilla of six warships, are still holding out at Whampoa on the river near Guangzhou.
Jul. 4	Lord Robert Cecil unveils a plan for international disarmament under the auspices of the League of Nations. The plan is similar to the model developed for the Washington Naval Treaties earlier this year, in that nations will maintain armies in proportional relationship to each other, for example: Belgium 2, Czechoslovakia 3, France 6, etc. The French have expressed an interest in the plan, but insist on maintaining larger forces until Germany has paid its reparations.	American occupation troops on the Rhine celebrates the Fourth of July today with fireworks, parades, and pie eating contests....Fascist Blackshirts have seized control of the town of Andria in southern Italy, after a Blackshirt was shot and killed by Communists there.		President Jose Orellana of Guatemala today announces a general amnesty of all political prisoners in celebration of the victory of the Liberals in the civil war of 1871.	A report has surfaced that Japan allows virtually unrestricted sales of opium in territories under its control in Shandong Province. Profits from the sale of the addictive narcotic go to fund covert operations in China by Japan's intelligence services.
Jul. 5	French occupation forces clash with German guerillas in Peiskretscham in disputed Upper Silesia today, killing six.	Irish Free State troops have smashed the last Republican pocket in Dublin. Republican commander Cathal Brugha has been killed. Remnants of the Republicans Dublin Brigade under Oscar Traynor have fled, leaving Free State forces in full control of the capital. In the fighting 65 soldiers on both sides have been killed, as well as more than 250 civilians. Fighting continues as remnants of the Republican forces regroup in Blessington, 30 kilometers southwest of the city. Anti-Treaty IRA militants have advanced from Tipperary, raiding Enniscorthy and Carlow, but are retreating as stronger Free State forces advance.	The Portuguese Socialist Party today accused the Portuguese government of allowing trafficking in what are effectively slaves from Portugal's Mozambique colony to South African mines.	Cost cutting efforts by the War Department have resulted in a renewed spread of malaria in the Panama Canal Zone, as mosquito abatement programs are cut back due to budgetary concerns.	
Jul. 6		Free State troops have pushed the Republicans back from Boyle, as Free State numbers and firepower begin to have an effect....Soviet security forces have arrested former White Russian Colonel Mikhail Dionysiov and 90 others for plotting an armed rebellion in the Crimea.... The struggle for power during Lenin's convalescence is continuing in Soviet Russia, with Moscow Party leader Lev Kamenev being mentioned as a possible successor.			The Japanese government has formally ratified the Washington Treaty and has begun cutting back the number of capital ships it has in accordance with the treaty.

A	B	C	D	E
Includes developments that affect more than one world region, international organizations and important meetings of world leaders.	*Includes all domestic and regional developments in Europe, including the Soviet Union.*	*Includes all domestic and regional developments in Africa and the Middle East.*	*Includes all domestic and regional developments in Latin America, the Caribbean, and Canada.*	*Includes all domestic and regional developments in Asian and Pacific nations (and colonies).*

U.S. Politics & Social Issues	U.S. Foreign Policy & Affairs, Defense	U.S. Economy & Environment	Science, Technology & Nature	Culture, Leisure & Lifestyle	
	Naval Secretary Charles Denby arrives in Yokohama today aboard the destroyer USS *Henderson* on a goodwill tour, celebrating 68 years of peaceful relations between the the United States and Japan.	Steel production in the first half of 1922 is up, at 16 million tons versus just nine million tons for the same period in 1921.			July 2
		A wildcat strike by New York railroad workers is condemned by rail executives today, who announce that any workers striking will be fired and will have to be rehired as new workers.			July 3
Ohio Republican Congressman S.D. Fess, now a candidate for the Senate, calls for legislation today to prohibit "aliens from verbally assaulting our government."...Ku Klux Klansmen burned a cross on Garret Mountain, visible across Paterson, NJ, as the Klan seeks to expand its footholds outside of the South.		*Bradstreet's* trade journal reported today that business failures were down in June to their lowest level since October 1921, as signs of a robust economy grow.	Native Sherpa guides maintain today that the failure of the recent British expedition to Mt. Everest was not due, as expedition members have claimed, to an early monsoon, but rather to haste by expedition leaders in failing to wait out a passing storm. The mountain remains unconquered.		July 4
			Icebergs remain a concern in the North Atlantic, even in the summer months. The Naval Hydrographic Office is refusing to lift its warning against ships sailing along the northerly, but more dangerous route, between America and Europe. Icebergs, monitored by the international ice patrol, are particularly thick off Canada's Grand Banks right now.		July 5
			French Lieutenant Pelletier Doisy has flown 1,000 miles from Tunis to Paris in just under 12 hours of continuous flying.		July 6

	World Affairs	Europe	Africa & The Middle East	The Americas	Asia & The Pacific
Jul. 7	The Austrian government, staggering under runaway inflation, has asked the Allied Reparations Commission to allow the use of Austrian revenues from customs, mining, and state monopolies as collateral for obtaining an international loan to stabilize her finances....Alarm is spreading in financial circles as the British government received secret reports from intelligence sources in Berlin that Germany is on the brink of collapse and civil war. Prime Minister Lloyd George is meeting with Italian Foreign Minister Carlo Schanzer to discuss plans for Allied action should Germany disintegrate into anarchy.	Free State forces have captured Galway, while Republican remnants under Traynor have pulled back from Blessington....Polish police suppressed renewed anti-Jewish rioting in Vilna today.... The Bavarian Minister of Justice in Munich is openly defying the German government, refusing to order the arrest of anyone wanted on charges of sedition, even for murder, without approving it first. Concerned Socialist and left leaning party leaders are meeting with German President Friedrich Ebert in Freudenstadt, Thuringia, as rumors grow of a royalist revolt in Bavaria.		Paraguayan troops have captured Villarica and are advancing on the headquarters of rebel forces at Paraguari.	
Jul. 8			Petitioners from the Young Kavirondo Association (YKA), headed by Africans educated in missionary schools, confront the governor of Uganda with petitions demanding reform of the colonial administration. African leaders are beginning to grow in education, and are challenging colonial rule with sophistication.	40,000 American automobiles will visit Quebec this summer. American tourism is opening up rural Quebec to fresh commercial life....An attempted military coup by former Brazilian President Marshal Hermes Fonseca, has failed, with an attempted rebellion at the Copacabana Fortress near Rio de Janerio solidly defeated. Fonseca has been captured and is being held aboard the Brazilian cruiser *Floriano*....Chile and Peru have agreed to allow the United States to resolve the Tacna-Arica border dispute if a plebiscite cannot be organized in the region.	The Japanese have warned the Chinese government that they will not tolerate continuing raids by what they term "bandits" on the border of Manchuria and Japanese controlled Korea. The "bandits" are believed to be in fact Korean guerillas, resisting Japanese rule. The Chinese government in Beijing states that Japanese claims of being raided are a "pretext" to prepare world opinion for a Japanese occupation of Manchuria.
Jul. 9	French newspapers are saying that the French are likely to pull out of talks with the Soviets at The Hague, as the French try to put pressure on the British to take a firm line with the Soviets on the repayment of prewar debts, most of which are owed to France. The British are taking a more flexible approach with the Soviets, angling for oil and mining concessions in the Urals.	The French city of Vichy has banned bullfights as cruel and inhumane. Bullfights are becoming confined to Spain and parts of Latin America.... Protestants parade through the streets of Belfast today, celebrating the anniversary of the Battle of the Boyne, which secured Protestant English rule over Ireland.	The French have brought 27 African chiefs from various parts of the French empire in Africa to Paris for a conference. Prominent among them are Chief Baloum Naba, who fought for the French in World War I, and Adadji Abdoukane of Senegal, who recruited soldiers for the French. The conference is part of France's "civilizing mission" in its colonies, with the goal of spreading the French language and culture to its possessions.	Argentina celebrates its independence day today, while large numbers of Argentines take to the streets to call for mandatory old-age pensions.	Major General Haraguchi, Japanese military attaché in Washington, has reported the theft of a large collection of diplomatic correspondence, one more move, in a continuing shadow game of espionage between the United States and Japan.
Jul. 10	The German government, increasingly pressed by runaway inflation and rising violence, has agreed to virtually all Allied demands for financial control of its economy. The Germans are desperately seeking a $1 billion loan from the Morgan banking combine to stabilize its economy....The Soviets seek a loan of three billion gold rubles from the Western Allies to develop their ravaged economy. The Soviets are particularly interested in refurbishing 15,000 miles of trunk railroad lines.		Muhammad V an-Nasir, Husseinid Bey of Tunisia, has died. He will be succeeded by Muhammad VI al-Habib. While the Husseinid Beys retain their throne, the real power in Tunisia lies with the French, who have protectorate over the country.		
Jul. 11	The British Admiralty announced today that it was continuing plans to build two large battleships, incorporating the latest in naval technology. These ships, said to be impervious to aerial or submarine attack, will cost some £8 million each, but will allow the scrapping of four obsolescent pre-Jutland battleships. Ships developed on modern lines, incorporating the lessons learned from the Battle of Jutland in World War I, have become the new hallmark of naval power.				

A	B	C	D	E
Includes developments that affect more than one world region, international organizations and important meetings of world leaders.	*Includes all domestic and regional developments in Europe, including the Soviet Union.*	*Includes all domestic and regional developments in Africa and the Middle East.*	*Includes all domestic and regional developments in Latin America, the Caribbean, and Canada.*	*Includes all domestic and regional developments in Asian and Pacific nations (and colonies).*

U.S. Politics & Social Issues	U.S. Foreign Policy & Affairs, Defense	U.S. Economy & Environment	Science, Technology & Nature	Culture, Leisure & Lifestyle	
	Naval Secretary Edwin Denby is wrapping up a goodwill tour of Japan, dedicating the planting of a tree brought from America at Kurihama, where Admiral Matthew C. Perry came ashore in 1853. Viscount Kaneko, speaking on behalf of the Japanese government said: "As long as the tree stands we will respect and love America."...Rear Admiral William Sims defended the use of poison gas today, arguing that an analysis of American casualties in World War I shows that gas only caused .5 percent of battlefield deaths. Sims advocated the study of tear gases to further reduce casualties from artillery and rifle fire.			The Vatican has placed Nobel Prize winning French author and Legion of Honor winner Anatole France's works on the index of forbidden books. France's works have mocked conventional morality and expressed contempt for sacred things....Movie theaters in Chicago are abandoning pricing movie tickets as high as $1.50 or $2.00. Henceforth, movie house owners will hold the line to 50 cents for admissions.	July 7
President and Mrs. Warren Harding return to Washington after a motor trip to Marion, OH. En route back to Washington, the Hardings meet with Major General John A. Lejeune, Commandant of the Marines, and Brigadier General Smedley Butler, commander of a marine force training near Gettysburg, PA.	J. Matthew Wainwright, Acting Secretary of War, announces that the War department, backed by former World War commander General John Pershing, will work actively to combat pacifism and "internationalist tendencies" that threaten to undermine military preparedness.			The Commerce Department reports that the American dessert, ice cream, is starting to catch on in England, and the demand for lemonade and root beer is growing there. American style soda fountains are appearing in London, though the English habit of taking tea militates against the introduction of new foods and beverages between meals....Suzanne Lenglen has won the Wimbledon women's tennis championship, defeating long time rival, Mrs. Mallory.... Robert C. Benchley is said to be working on a novel, *Love Conquers All*, which is due out in autumn.	July 8
Mine operators and striking coalminers renew negotiations in Washington, DC, as both sides looked to President Warren Harding for mediation to end the bitter strike, now in its 14th week.... Marcus Garvey addresses a cheering crowd of 4,000 African Americans in new York City today, denouncing the Ku Klux Klan as the invisible government in America. Garvey called for a "black race master of its own civilization" and "Africa for Africans."		Joseph Peter DiCarlo, founder of the Buffalo crime syndicate, has died of natural causes. He will be succeeded by his lieutenant, Sicilian born Stefano Magaddino. Prohibition has made Buffalo a particularly important point, along with Detroit. Both cities are major trans-shipment points for bootleg hooch being smuggle in from Canada. Buffalo in particular serves the gigantic New York City market....Direct air service opens between Detroit and Cleveland today, using flying boats operating on the Great Lakes.			July 9
Attorney General Harry Daugherty today announced that the United States government would take steps to ensure the delivery of the federal mails as sporadic strikes continue to disrupt rail service in the Northeast.	An American, Henry Mason Day, President of the International Barnsdall Corporation, has reached an agreement in The Hague with the Soviets for joint development of oil reserves in the Baku region.... Acting Naval Secretary Franklin D. Roosevelt has ordered the closing of the Charleston Navy Yards as the U.S. Navy continues to wrestle with tight peacetime budgets.	The National Industrial Conference Board reported today that some 1.25 million workers are now either on strike or idle due to strikes across the United States, meaning the loss of nearly 10 million work hours a week....City trolley buses are being moved under armed guard in Buffalo, as strikebreakers drive the trolleys past mobs of jeering strikers.			July 10
Vice President Calvin Coolidge addresses business leaders at the Ellicott Club in Buffalo, praising the role businessmen have had in restoring stability to the American economy. Coolidge warns that further cuts in wages for railroad workers and miners are likely if business conditions are to continue to improve....Three striking coalminers are killed in clashes with police near Uniontown, PA, as 65 families a day are evicted for inability to pay rent as the bitter nationwide coal strike continues.				The Cardinal presiding at the Church of San Marco in Rome is refusing communion to women who he does not consider "suitably attired."	July 11

F	G	H	I	J
Includes campaigns, elections, federal-state relations, civil rights and liberties, crime, the judiciary, education, healthcare, poverty, urban affairs, and population.	*Includes formation and debate of U.S. foreign and defense policies, veterans affairs, and defense spending. (Relations with specific foreign countries are usually found under the region concerned.)*	*Includes business, labor, agriculture, taxation, transportation, consumer affairs, monetary and fiscal policy, natural resources, pollution and industrial accidents.*	*Includes worldwide scientific, medical and technological developments, natural phenomena, U.S. weather and natural disasters.*	*Includes the arts, religion, scholarship, communications media, sports, entertainment, fashions, fads, and social life.*

	World Affairs	Europe	Africa & The Middle East	The Americas	Asia & The Pacific
Jul. 12	With inflation raging out of control, the German government appeals to the Reparations Commission for a postponement of the payments due for 1922, and a reduction in monthly payments for prewar claims by 75 percent to £500,000.	After three days of seesaw fighting, Free State troops have driven Republican forces from most of Limerick, while a Republican garrison is still holding out in Strand Barracks and King John's Castle.		Canadian Prime Minister William Lyon Mackenzie King visits Washington, DC, today, seeking an expansion of the Rush-Bagot Treaty of 1817 limiting warships on the Great Lakes to encompass the entire 3,000 mile frontier. The Prime Minister also advocated development of a proposed St. Lawrence Seaway to bring ocean-going commerce to the Great Lakes.	A British court in Ahmedabad today acquitted Hazrat Mohani, president of the all-India Muslim League, of charges of inciting violence against the British crown.
Jul. 13		Bulgarian guerillas raiding across the Yugoslav border are repulsed today in a pitched battle at Kratovo with Yugoslav border patrols, which leaving 10 guerillas dead.		Canada announces that it will send an expedition to occupy islands north of Labrador and west of Greenland in an effort to assert Canadian claims to the region once and for all.	There is opposition to Christian mission schools growing across China. The movement, which began at Beijing University, has spread to Amoy, Tsinan, Shanghai, and other major cities. While Western technical expertise is valued, Chinese are fearful of the erosion of traditional values by foreign religious ideas.... The Governor of Zhejiang province seizes control of telegraph lines in the province.
Jul. 14	The Hague Conference on the Soviet debt is hopelessly deadlocked, with neither the Soviets nor the Western Allies willing to offer further concessions.	The Chancellor of the Exchequer reports today that Britain currently owes the United States £938 million. While it is generally accepted that the debt must be paid, it is not clear how the money will be raised....An assassination attempt against French President Alexandre Millerand failed when the would-be assassin, anarchist Gustave Charles Bouvet (23), fired at the carriage of the Prefect of Police by mistake, as the President's procession returned to the Champs Eylsées after the Bastille Day military review at Longchamps.	The Turkish Nationalist government in Ankara is blocking an international investigation of atrocities committed against Christians in territory under its control, refusing to admit international investigators.... King Alfonso of Spain has appointed General Burguette to command Spanish forces in Morocco, replacing General Berenguer.	An attempted revolt by General Fonseca in Brazil's Mato Grosso region has ended, with Fonseca and all officers involved surrendering peacefully.	
Jul. 15		The Camorra, a Neapolitan secret society and organized crime group similar to the Sicilian Mafia, continues to frustrate efforts by the Italian police and authorities to control it. Its leader, Don Ciro Vitozzi, has amassed influence extending into the highest ranks of Neapolitan society.	Arabs nationalists in Palestine and Transjordan have ended a two-day strike in protest against the establishment of a British Mandate in Palestine. Arab leaders fear that the British will allow increased Jewish immigration to Palestine.		
Jul. 16	Britain is urging an international loan to Germany to stave off financial collapse there. Even the French are now considering giving Germany a breathing space before demanding more reparations.	Christian Democrat Wojciech Korfanty, has succeeded Artur Sliwinski as Prime Minister of Poland. Sliwinski was brought down by a coalition of groups loyal to former Prime Minister Ponikowski, which now seeks to get full control of the government. Korfanty has long been a militant advocate of the annexation of Upper Silesia.		Bolivia's tin mining industry is reported to be recovering after a severe postwar slump....Canada is cutting railroad workers' wages to 40 cents a day.	

A	B	C	D	E
Includes developments that affect more than one world region, international organizations and important meetings of world leaders.	*Includes all domestic and regional developments in Europe, including the Soviet Union.*	*Includes all domestic and regional developments in Africa and the Middle East.*	*Includes all domestic and regional developments in Latin America, the Caribbean, and Canada.*	*Includes all domestic and regional developments in Asian and Pacific nations (and colonies).*

	U.S. Politics & Social Issues	U.S. Foreign Policy & Affairs, Defense	U.S. Economy & Environment	Science, Technology & Nature	Culture, Leisure & Lifestyle
July 12	Owners of the anthracite coalmines of Pennsylvania express support for proposals by the Harding administration to end the nationwide coal strike. United Mine Workers President John L. Lewis announces that his union will study the plan.... The War Department announced today that it would deploy the army if necessary to protect the mails as a rail strike continues to snarl service across the Northeast and mobs clashed with railroad company guards in New Jersey.			Major W.T. Blake has embarked from Ziza, Palestine, for Baghdad on the first leg of a planned circumnavigation of the earth by air. Blake's RAF plane is forced down in the desert due to engine trouble, but Blake has vowed to continue the flight.	Chinese leaders from 14 cities came to New York City today to mark the funeral of Dr. Fong Foo Leung, leader of the powerful Hip Sing Tong. In 1914, Leung was instrumental in ending the bloody war between the Hip Sings and the rival On Leong Tong. 600 Hip Sing members turn out to march in the procession.
July 13					A judge in Chicago dismisses charges against 40 men arrested for gambling at Cubs Park yesterday, when police failed to specifically identify the men. Cubs President William L. Veeck announced that the war against "tin-horn" gamblers operating on the premises will continue.
July 14	President Warren Harding calls in United Mine Workers President John L. Lewis today and warns him that the federal government will take over the coalmines if the nationwide coal strike is not ended.... Samuel Gompers, President of the American Federation of Labor, denounces President Harding and the Railroad Labor Board, attacking them for allowing the reduction of wages for "thousands of employees to below $800 a year."		The Chicago brokerage firm of Nash & Company has failed, leaving liabilities of $6 million. The firm overextended credit to customers in an effort to capture business.		A Franz Hals portrait dating from 1650 sold for £6,510 at Christies today as numerous aristocratic families in Europe liquidate portions of their art collections for cash.
July 15				The first live duck-billed platypus to be seen in captivity in the United States is put on display today at a zoo in New York City.... The Reconstruction Hospital today warned women against going barefoot too long while at the beach or on vacation, cautioning that this can lead to flat feet and fallen arches. The hospital advises women to wear high-heeled pumps while at the beach.	Lionel Barrymore will play the role of Blackie Dawson in the upcoming feature film *The Face in the Fog*, based on one of Jack Boyle's popular Boston Blackie stories....Harry W. Mager, former IRS Collector for Chicago, and Benjamin M. Mitchell, a member of the Illinois State Legislature, are arrested today on charges of graft, extortion, and "fixing" Prohibition cases involving as much as a half a million dollars in bribes. A prominent Illinois brewer is said to have been forced to pay $5 for every barrel of "near beer" with "a kick" put in it.
July 16				Emile Berliner's experimental helicopter is tested today before military observers at College Park, MD. The craft rises 12 feet and hovers successfully. The problem now remaining is stable horizontal flight....Airplanes are slowly becoming more reliable. The U.S. Post Office today celebrated a year of delivering airmail without a fatality.	In a straw poll conducted by the *Literary Digest* of 100,000 readers, just 32,000 were in favor of continuing strict enforcement of Prohibition as it is now. While only 22,000 favor outright Repeal, nearly 40,000 wanted substantial changes in the law as it now stands.

	World Affairs	Europe	Africa & The Middle East	The Americas	Asia & The Pacific
Jul. 17	Poland has begun taking control of the portions of Upper Silesia assigned to it by the Allied Control Commission. These include some villages with a German majority that have voted against incorporation into Poland. German opponents of the Treaty of Versailles claim that the system of plebiscites mandated by the Allies to determine the fate of disputed territories only functions against German claims, fueling increased resentment toward the Treaty in Germany.	Free State troops, backed by artillery and armored cars, are closing in on the Republican holdouts in Limerick. British Home Secretary Edwared Shortt announces that American anarchist Emma Goldman would not be admitted to Great Britain, as her presence is "undesirable."... The Soviet government is allowing peasants to sell their produce freely as part of Lenin's New Economic Policy (NEP) to alleviate Russia's chronic food shortage.			
Jul. 18	Bulgaria appeals to the League of Nations today, stating that its army, limited by the Treaty of Neuilly, which ended its role in World War I, was too small to control numerous bands of guerillas who have been raiding into Romania, Yugoslavia, and Greece. This brought angry denunciations by these three countries, each of whom gained territory from Bulgaria under the Treaty of Neuilly, claiming that the Bulgarians are instigating the violence.	Viscount Curzon reported today that the British Royal Navy has only nine serviceable aircraft, as opposed to 85 operated by the United States. Meanwhile debate swirls in Parliament over the results of tests using torpedo planes against warships.	The League of Nations today confirms the establishment of Mandates under British and French administration in the former German African colonies of Togo and Cameroon. The British and Belgians will also hold Mandates over the former German East Africa. The Mandates are granted after negotiations with the United States guaranteeing Americans the opportunity to conduct business there and maintain missionaries. Britain and France have reached similar agreements with the United States regarding the proposed Mandates in Palestine and Syria.	The United Farmers of Manitoba have swept provincial elections in Manitoba, capturing 28 of 55 seats, and delivering a stunning rebuke to both Conservative and Liberal Parties. It is an index of the discontent among farmers who have been hurt by falling prices for agricultural goods since the end of the World War....Mexican Finance Minister Adolfo de la Huerta meets with President Warren Harding and Secretary of State Charles Eveans Hughes in Washington today, after extensive consultations with banking interests in New York City. De la Huerta is seeking a loan to stabilize Mexico's finances and international recognition for the Obregon government.	
Jul. 19	The Hague Conference on the Soviet debt situation has broken up without any agreement being reached. The Soviets remain essentially locked out of the Western European economy, except for its agreements with Weimar Germany.	After eight days of fighting, Free State forces have secured control of Limerick, with Republican remnants slipping out of the city into the countryside....The Austrian Parliament approves plans today for a forced loan of 400 billion crowns from Austrian citizens of means. The government is also stopping all private trading in foreign currency, as it frantically seeks to regain control of the nation's runaway inflation.	The Medical Director of Middle Eastern Relief today reports that the cholera epidemic in the Caucasus and Armenia is now under control, thanks to the distribution of two million doses of cholera vaccine by the American Vaccine Laboratories in Tiflis in the last month.	One hundred small children storm City Hall in Juarez, Mexico, demanding that schools, which have been closed for two months due to lack of funds, be opened.	
Jul. 20	The French have dropped their opposition to a moratorium on the repayment of German reparations. In exchange the Germans have agreed to provide accurate statistics and information on hidden assets, as well as supervision of Germany's state budget.	Free State forces have captured Waterford after three days of heavy fighting in which artillery was used at close range. With the fall of Limerick and Waterford, Republicans are pinned down in an area south of these two cities, which they are calling the Munster Republic. The Republicans are desperate to force a continued war with the British to secure complete independence for Ireland, but cannot match Free State firepower....Anarchists in Rome kidnapped and flogged a lawyer, who they accused of taking money from the French government.			
Jul. 21	The Reparations Commission has agreed to allow Austria to use state revenues slated for reparations payments as security for an international loan to stabilize her finances.				The American Bible Society announces that it is shipping 187,000 Bibles to Beijing.
	A *Includes developments that affect more than one world region, international organizations and important meetings of world leaders.*	B *Includes all domestic and regional developments in Europe, including the Soviet Union.*	C *Includes all domestic and regional developments in Africa and the Middle East.*	D *Includes all domestic and regional developments in Latin America, the Caribbean, and Canada.*	E *Includes all domestic and regional developments in Asian and Pacific nations (and colonies).*

U.S. Politics & Social Issues	U.S. Foreign Policy & Affairs, Defense	U.S. Economy & Environment	Science, Technology & Nature	Culture, Leisure & Lifestyle	
Federal marshals mobilized hundreds of agents across the Northeast as the rail strike that has blocked mail delivery in the region continues. Workers on the New York Central and the Pennsylvania Railroad are discussing joining the walkout. Mob violence against African American strikebreakers has been reported in Grafton, NJ, while police broke up rioting mobs in New Durham, NJ....Eugene V. Debs, leader of the Pullman railroad strike of 1894, today called on striking railroad workers to "Strike together, vote together, and fight together."		A melee erupted at a mine near Cliftonville, WV, when a mob of 300 striking coal miners attacked a mine being operated by non-union strikebreakers. The sheriff of Brooke County, and six others are reported dead, and more than two dozen people were wounded in the hour and a half long gun battle. Police arrest 20 people, but snipers have impeded a pursuit of the mob, which dispersed into the woods.	The Anchor liner *Columbia* arrived 10-hours late in New York City today after being delayed by an enormous iceberg 900 feet long and 100 high, en route from Great Britain.		July 17
				Two firemen are killed while battling a blaze at the seven-storey Manufacturers Transit Company warehouse in New York City's Greenwich Village, when flames ignite a series of explosions in what newspapers are calling the "Greenwich Village Volcano."...Swedish author Miss Esther Nordstrom, condemns the treatment of Swedish immigrants at Ellis Island today, stating that they were being treated "as if they were animals."	July 18
	Naval Secretary Edwin Denby, on a goodwill tour of the Far East is forced to make an emergency landing when his plane stalls at 4,000 feet while surveying the Great Wall of China. Denby is unhurt, but the Chinese government plane is demolished.	New York City is nearing a coal famine as the long lasting coal strike, now nearing its fourth month, finally begins to take its toll on coal reserves.	Typhus and cholera are reported to be running rampant in Russia, with cases being reported in Mediterranean ports where ships from the region call.	Swarthmore College is sending hundreds of letters out to the parents of women who will be attending the university this fall, advising them of the need to send their daughters wearing simple and modest attire. The letter reads in part: "Extremes or eccentricities in style of the dress and of the coiffure are not indicative of the good taste which college women should preserve."...A report by the Episcopal Church is calling for an explicit condemnation of birth control, and the barring from marriage of "the criminal, feeble-minded, and vicious."	July 19
The governors of Ohio and Pennsylvania have called out National Guard troops to protect mining operations in the bitter nationwide coal strike.		Cleveland's power utility is down to a three-day supply of coal as the coal strike's impact grows.	Noted Russian mathematician Andrei Markov, has died at the age of 66. Markov is known for his groundbreaking theory of stochastic processes, now known as Markov chains.	Paris police have foiled a plan to flood the market with fake works of art. A large stock of paintings, done in the style of Cezanne, Monet, Degas, Pissaro, and other painters are recovered from a Montmartre art gallery.	July 20
		Attorney General Harry Daugherty announces that the government will not pursue anti-trust actions against steel firms seeking to merge. This applies most importantly to Bethlehem Steel's planned merger with Lackawanna Steel of Buffalo.	British aviator Major Morgan is mapping out a route for a flight from San Francisco to Sydney, Australia, for a prize of £10,000 offered by Thomas Ince of Los Angeles. The projected 7,000 mile flight will require two jumps of more than 2,000 miles each, via Honolulu and Samoa.	Edith Wharton's new novel of the New York social scene, *Glimpses of the Moon*, is published today.	July 21

	World Affairs	Europe	Africa & The Middle East	The Americas	Asia & The Pacific
Jul. 22		Bavarian troops have been recalled from maneuvers to be on the alert against a possible revolt by the state's numerous monarchists, as a federal law safeguarding the German Republic is set to go into effect nationwide....The Dutch cabinet headed by Prime Minister C.J.M. Ruys de Beerenbrouck, resigns today, as De Beerenbrouck is called upon to form a new government.			Australian leader William Hughes announces today that Australia will not allow the Germans to establish consulates there. The Australians fear that doing so will stimulate German trade....General Chen Chiung-ming, Guangdong Province warlord, is driving the remnants of Sun Yat-sen's Guomindang forces north around Shiuchow, with Sun's forces reportedly taking heavy casualties from Chen's better equipped forces.
Jul. 23	The Soviets today denounce the Greek government for allowing Greek warships through the Straits into the Black Sea. The Greeks, bombarding Turkish ports in Anatolia, are disrupting Russian shipping.	Free State troops have driven the Republicans in pitched battles from Bruff and Kilmallock in County Limerick as Michael Collins' Free State forces battle to expand their areas of control across southern Ireland....The German Center Party is breaking with the Catholic coalition, and has announced that it is throwing its support behind sustaining the German Republic against monarchist reactionaries.	British High Commissioner General Lord Allenby warned the Egyptian government that it must get control of militant groups who are harassing British citizens in Egypt, or Britain will be compelled to intervene with force.		
Jul. 24		Free State troops have landed at Clew Bay in County Mayo, and have taken Westport, linking up with a Free State column advancing from Castlebar....The pro-monarchist Bavarian government is refusing to accept the applicability of a new German federal law protecting the republic. The loyalty of *Reichswehr* forces in Bavaria is in doubt....The Italian king, Victor Emmanuel, today called on Signor Bonomi to form a new government after former Prime Minister Vittorio Orlando failed to do so. Italy has been without an effective government since the fall of Luigi Facta's cabinet on the 19th.	The League of Nations today approved the creation of a French administered mandate over the Syrian states and British mandates over Palestine and Transjordan, on lands taken from the Ottoman Empire in World War I. The British Empire is now at its greatest territorial extent.		
Jul. 25	The French Olympic Executive Committee, in charge of the Olympics to be held in Paris in 1924, has voted to institute competitions in architecture, literature, music, painting, and sculpture to coincide with the athletic competitions.	Fascist Party leader Benito Mussolini has declined an invitation by former Prime Minister Bonomi to join a coalition government in Italy, as Italy's cabinet crisis continues....Civil war looms in Germany as the Bavarian government continues to defy the central government in Berlin.	Egyptian police arrest three members of the Executive Committee of the nationalist Zaglouist Party in Cairo today, after the Zaglouist Party criticized the Egyptian government as being too pro-British....Exiled Turkish leader Ahmed Djemal Pasha has been assassinated in Tbilisi, Georgia, by Armenian militants, for Djemal's role in the Armenian genocide of World War I....The British Governor of the Sudan has announced that British banks will provide £7 million loans to develop irrigation in the arid region.		Soviet partisans are advancing near Vladivostok and have attacked Nikolak-Ussurisk, north of the city. Partisan forces are disrupting rail communications and have surrounded the Suchan coal mines, as the Japanese prepare to withdraw from Eastern Siberia and the White Russian government in Vladivostok loses support.
Jul. 26		The Bavarian government suppressed the Nazi newspaper *Volkische Beobachter* along with another extreme right wing paper, as the southern German state teeters on the verge of civil war....Fascist Party leader Benito Mussolini today demands that general elections be held in Italy. 10 people are killed and 30 wounded as Fascist Blackshirts rampaged through the streets of Ravenna today.		The Bolivian government today approved the sale of 2.4 million acres of land in the Santa Cruz region to Standard Oil of New Jersey, adding to the eight million acres acquired in 1921.	

A	B	C	D	E
Includes developments that affect more than one world region, international organizations and important meetings of world leaders.	*Includes all domestic and regional developments in Europe, including the Soviet Union.*	*Includes all domestic and regional developments in Africa and the Middle East.*	*Includes all domestic and regional developments in Latin America, the Caribbean, and Canada.*	*Includes all domestic and regional developments in Asian and Pacific nations (and colonies).*

U.S. Politics & Social Issues	U.S. Foreign Policy & Affairs, Defense	U.S. Economy & Environment	Science, Technology & Nature	Culture, Leisure & Lifestyle	
				Author Rafael Sabatini is due to come out with a new swashbuckling thriller next month: *Captain Blood*....The Commerce Department reports that the American style ice cream soda is catching on in Great Britain.	July 22
			A Danish oceanographic expedition has traced the spawning grounds of eels to a section of the Atlantic between Bermuda and the Leeward Islands. Furthermore, the expedition finds that there are two distinct eel species, one that lives off the American coast, and another variety that migrates regularly to Europe....Dr. J.S. Plaskett, Director of Canada's Astro-Physical Observatory in British Columbia, has reported the discovery of twin stars 5,000 light years from the Earth.	Baptist Reverend Dr. George W. McPherson today denounces evolutionists as "baboon boosters" and says that churchmen who believe in evolution should form a "Church for the Descendants of Apes."	July 23
		W.C. Durant of Durant Motors announces that they will begin producing a new car, an improvement upon the popular Chevrolet. It is to be called the Flint.			July 24
Top Ku Klux Klan leaders are summoned before a Fulton County Superior Court in Atlanta, on charges of defying a court injunction against making changes in its staffing until a suit involving former Grand Goblin Harry B. Terr is resolved.			British Major W.T. Blake, crashes while attempting to circumnavigate the world by air. Blake's plane goes down at Sibi, outside of Quetta in British Baluchistan. Blake is unhurt, but the undercarriage of his plane is smashed....Cities in England and Scotland are the dirtiest in Europe, it is reported today, with 300 tons of soot falling per year on every square mile of London, enough to build a pyramid four times as tall as the tower of Big Ben over the Houses of Parliament.		July 25
Police clash with striking railroad workers today in Chicago, Detroit, Toledo, and Creston, IA.	The United States Army Air Service dirigible *C-2* circles the city of New York in night maneuvers in a flight from the Aberdeen Proving Grounds in Maryland. Preparations are being made for the *C-2* to attempt a transcontinental flight.		Joseph J. Thompson of Cambridge University, discoverer of the electron, is awarded the Franklin Medal today in honor of his scientific achievements....French airman Chanteloup has made a close approach to erupting Mt. Bromo, 70 miles southeast of Surabaya, in eastern Java.	Atlantic City Mayor Edward L. Bader refuses to respond to charges that he was lax in enforcing vice laws in this popular seaside resort.	July 26

	World Affairs	Europe	Africa & The Middle East	The Americas	Asia & The Pacific
Jul. 27		The United States today extends diplomatic recognition to the Republic of Lithuania....Republican guerillas have stormed Dundalk, Ireland, dynamiting a prison wall there and freeing Republican prisoners. While the Republicans are losing territory, they retain pockets of determined support in the Irish countryside....Republican commander Oscar Traynor has been captured in Dublin.		Argentina is seeking a loan of $165 million dollars from New York City banking interests to shore up its ailing finances....Britain has edged out America as Canada's best customer for exports, with $301.8 million in exports going to Britain, as opposed to $295.3 million to the United States as of June 1922.	The Australian Senate today ratified the Washington Treaties on Pacific arms and fortifications....Fighting resumed today at Shiuchow, 130 miles north of Guangzhou, as forces loyal to deposed Guomindang President Sun Yat-sen continued to hold out against Guangdong Province warlord General Chen.
Jul. 28		It was announced today that Britain would spend £6 million over the next two years installing radio broadcasting and receiving equipment....Mass protest marches by leftist unions clogged the streets of Rome as Fascist Blackshirts seized the Socialist Party headquarters and burned labor union offices in Ravenna.			
Jul. 29	Alan H. Muhr, Secretary of the International Olympic Committee announced today that as many as 60 nations, a record, will compete in the 1924 Olympics in Paris.	The suburbs of London are growing, with a new house being erected each day in the suburb of Feltham....The German mark has fallen to new lows on the international exchanges. In New York, one mark fetched just over 15 hundredths of a cent.	The Allies today warned the Greeks not to try to occupy Constantinople (Istanbul). The Greeks revere Constantinople as the former capital of the famed Byzantine (or Eastern Roman) Empire, which fell to the Turks in 1453. However, the Greeks know they cannot fight both the Turks and the Allies. The Greek army is therefore halting.		The Chinese government in Beijing has refused to enter into negotiations with the Soviets, who are seeking to secure their Far Eastern flank.
Jul. 30	French Premier Raymond Poincaré dedicates a memorial to the American, French, and Italian war dead at the Argonne battlefield today, and warns that Germany must pay its World War reparations either peacefully or "under compulsion."	Free State forces push their way into Bruree in County Limerick against heavy opposition....Mobs stormed stores in Berlin as panic buying sets in as Germans fear yet another drop in the value of the collapsing mark.			Manchurian warlord Chang Tsolin is massing forces to renew operations against the Beijing government.
Jul. 31	The World Court in The Hague reaches its first decision today, ruling that the Dutch government, not the Dutch unions, had the final say in sending a delegate to an international labor conference.	Free State troops are moving against the Republican stronghold of Tipperary. By now Free State forces have secured key points across central Ireland, while bitter guerilla fighting continues....Harry Boland, Irish nationalist and revolutionary, has been shot and mortally wounded fighting Irish Free State forces in fighting in Skerries, near Dublin.....The German mark has now fallen to where it takes 670 *reichsmarks* to buy one dollar....Britain is considering strengthening its air defense forces by 15 to 20 squadrons.			
Aug. 1	The British government has issued the Balfour Note, offering to give up reparations owed by the former Central Powers if the United States will give up demands for repayment of war debts. The United States continues to maintain that the payment of debts from World War I and German war reparations are two different issues....Representatives of the Austrian government are in Paris seeking Allied approval for a loan of £15 million to stabilize her currency.	The Italian Alianza del Lavoro has declared a nationwide general strike in Italy....Chaos ensues as Fascists clash with Socialists in cities across Italy....Fascists have deposed the Socialist government of Milan, and attacked Socialist party headquarters in Genoa and Livorno....The Italian government has massed troops at key points across Rome as tensions rise. Fascist leader Benito Mussolini has issued an ultimatum to the Italian government to crush the strike in 48 hours, or he will have his Blackshirts do it....Liberal Luigi Facta this evening announced the formation of a government in an attempt to stabilize the situation.	In this month, the Eastern Orthodox Patriarch of Constantinople has recognized the Autocephalous Albanian Orthodox Church....Sir Herbert Samuel, British High Commissioner for Palestine, left to confer with Abdullah, pro-British Emir of Transjordan, at Kerak, in effort to prevent the unrest that is sweeping Iraq from spreading to Jordan and Palestine.		The Chinese Parliament has convened for the first time since 1917 after it was dissolved by hostile warlords. Deep divisions remain between northern and southern factions. Sun Yat-sen's deposed Guomindang government remains popular among southerners....Fighting continues between Sun's followers and pro-Beijing warlord General Chen Chiung-ming between Shiuchow and Guangzhou in the south....Manchurian warlord Chang Tsolin has declared independence from the Beijing government.

U.S. Politics & Social Issues	U.S. Foreign Policy & Affairs, Defense	U.S. Economy & Environment	Science, Technology & Nature	Culture, Leisure & Lifestyle	
	The Army Air Service blimp *A-4* has completed a flight of 1,100 miles from Langley Field, VA, to its new station at Scott Field near Belleville, IL. The flight is a distance record for an army dirigible.				July 27
Denison, TX, is placed under martial law as violence connected with the rail strike spreads....An African-American worker is lynched in Hope, AR, after a quarrel with a white foreman over a drinking cup.					July 28
		The Department of Labor reports today that there are now 113 African-American owned newspapers and 14 magazines in operation around the country.	Polar explorer Roald Amundsen has abandoned his attempt to fly over the North Pole from Point Barrow, AK, after his ship, the *Maud*, failed to reach Point Barrow in time to set up an airstrip before the Arctic winter sets in again.	Atlantic City Mayor Edward L. Bader refuses to respond to charges that he was lax in enforcing vice laws in this popular seaside resort.	July 29
					July 30
			Herr Anthony Fokker, German aircraft designer, warns today that in a new world conflict, poison gas could be used in conjunction with explosives and fire bombs to wreak untold devastation on populated cities. Fokker warns that only an air fleet can defeat an air fleet. Fokker concludes: "Britain is no longer isolated at all."	World champion chess master Jose R. Capablanca defeats Dutch challenger M. Euwe in the first round of the world's chess championship in London.	July 31
		General Motors is slashing prices on its lower priced line of cars, which range from $510 to $2,555. GM is trying to combat competition by Studebaker and Durant. A Chevy roadster now sells for just $510. Buick's popular four-door sedan is still retailing at $1,520, while the deluxe Oldsmobile sedan goes for $2,145.	In this month, the British Air Ministry will issue requirements for a special purpose night fighter.		Aug. 1

F	G	H	I	J
Includes campaigns, elections, federal-state relations, civil rights and liberties, crime, the judiciary, education, healthcare, poverty, urban affairs, and population.	*Includes formation and debate of U.S. foreign and defense policies, veterans affairs, and defense spending. (Relations with specific foreign countries are usually found under the region concerned.)*	*Includes business, labor, agriculture, taxation, transportation, consumer affairs, monetary and fiscal policy, natural resources, pollution and industrial accidents.*	*Includes worldwide scientific, medical and technological developments, natural phenomena, U.S. weather and natural disasters.*	*Includes the arts, religion, scholarship, communications media, sports, entertainment, fashions, fads, and social life.*

	World Affairs	Europe	Africa & The Middle East	The Americas	Asia & The Pacific
Aug. 2	The issue of international access to the Kiel Canal is being referred to the International Court of Justice in the Hague by the Allied Council of Ambassadors.	Fighting continues to rage across Ireland today, as Free State forces occupy Tipperary and land on the western coast of County Kerry.... In another sign of the rapprochement between Germany and Soviet Russia, the German government today orders the demolition of the old Russian Orthodox chapel at the Russian embassy. Berlin's Russian exile community, now numbering several hundred thousand, will be without a place of worship.	The British have reinforced the Allied garrison in Constantinople to 10,000, making a threatened advance on the city by the Greek army unlikely....Mustafa Kemal's Nationalist government in Ankara has denounced the Greek proclamation of Smyrna as an autonomous zone, setting the stage for renewed fighting.	The Allies have warned the Bolivian government that they will not tolerate the reestablishment of the Military Council, which was staffed by German officers, and abolished during World War I....The Chilean cabinet resigned today amid popular opposition by Chileans against restoring the disputed Tacna-Arica territories to Peru.	General Chen's forces are driving north from Guangzhou, pushing the remnants of Sun Yat-sen's Guomindang army into the interior.
Aug. 3		With Prime Minister Luigi Facta's government paralyzed in the face of a general strike, Mussolini has ordered Fascist Blackshirt units to take control of essential services.... Irish Free State forces have taken Carrick on Suir....British Prime Minister Lloyd George announces today that Britain will create a force of 500 fighter planes for air defense. The proposed plan will cost £2 million a year to equip the 20 new squadrons needed....The Dutch are concerned that they will lose top aircraft designer Anthony Fokker to the United States.	The government of Persia has recruited American Mills Paul to be Director General of Finances for five years. The Persian government is trying to modernize its government and economy to resist European encroachment.		
Aug. 4	The British have formally announced a new diplomatic conference, to be held in London, to discuss reparations and war debts.	With Fascist Blackshirts in control of essential services, the general strike in Italy has collapsed....Mussolini's power has now vastly increased.... A Communist group has blown up a power line near Naples.... Republican troops have been driven from Cashel in County Tipperary, while Irish Free State forces continued their advance in County Kerry.... The Austrian crown has fallen again, to the point where it takes 52,000 to equal $1.			Ismail Enver Pasha, exiled Ottoman commander, and a leader of the Basmachi Muslim rebels in Turkestan, is killed in a clash with Red Army forces today at Baldzhuan, Turkestan (in mod. Tajikistan).... The Japanese Finance Department reports today that in July Japan ran a trade surplus for the first time since November 1920.
Aug. 5		Acting on intelligence, Free State forces have smashed the main underground Republican cell in Dublin, arresting 104....King Alfonso XIII of Spain in a ceremony today in Barcelona bestows the ancient title of Count of Barcelona on his second son, Don Jaime. In doing so, King Alfonso is trying to defuse separatist agitation in this Catalan-speaking metropolis....Belgians today commemorate the eighth anniversary of the German invasion in 1914.	British and French troops reinforce their positions opposite the Greek army on the Tchatalja Line in a show of force to keep the Greeks from attempting to seize Constantinople in a *coup de main*....Violence exploded on the Haifa waterfront between Arab and Jewish dockworkers, with five Jewish workmen wounded in the melee....Christians in Anatolia are mobilizing to help the Greeks resist the expected offensive by Turkish Nationalists. Some 35,000 Anatolian Christians, mostly Greeks and Armenians, have been recruited into the Greek army thus far, with a gendarmerie of 25,000 acting as a reserve.	American films are becoming increasingly popular in Chile, with seats going for as little as 13 cents. However, European film companies are moving in quickly to try to capture the growing market for films in Latin America.	Wang Chonghui has succeeded Yan Huiqing as Prime Minister of China....Lack of a standardized currency is still a serious problem in China with notes issued by various governments competing with a dozen different bank notes. The prized currency is Mexican silver dollars.
Aug. 6	French Premier Raymond Poincaré arrives in London this evening, meeting with British Prime Minister Lloyd George.	28 people have been wounded in fighting in Genoa, where a mob of 200 Fascist Blackshirts sack the offices of the Socialist newspaper *Lavoro*, while the Italian government has now extended martial law to Brescia and five other Italian provinces.	Greek troops are pulling back two miles from British and French positions outside of Constantinople. The Greeks are dependent on British support and do not want to risk a clash.	American demands put before the Zayas government in Cuba are leaked to the press today. United States special envoy General Enoch Crowder has warned the financially strapped Cuban government that it must control spending and reduce fraud if it is to continue to receive American support....A Japanese naval training squadron paid a call at Panama today.	Mutinous soldiers go on a rampage through the streets of Jiujiang in Jiangxi Province, smashing up shops and doing some $3 million in damages....Platinum ore of 69 percent purity has been found at the Liangas mines in the Philippines.

A	B	C	D	E
Includes developments that affect more than one world region, international organizations and important meetings of world leaders.	*Includes all domestic and regional developments in Europe, including the Soviet Union.*	*Includes all domestic and regional developments in Africa and the Middle East.*	*Includes all domestic and regional developments in Latin America, the Caribbean, and Canada.*	*Includes all domestic and regional developments in Asian and Pacific nations (and colonies).*

U.S. Politics & Social Issues	U.S. Foreign Policy & Affairs, Defense	U.S. Economy & Environment	Science, Technology & Nature	Culture, Leisure & Lifestyle	
Governor Warren McCray of Indiana declared martial law in and around Staunton, IN, sending in 800 National Guard troops to protect strikebreaking workers as the nationwide coal strike continues and fuel shortages loom.... Prohibition Commissioner Roy Asa Haynes announces today that since Prohibition has been instituted, 22 Federal agents have been killed in the line of duty enforcing the law. The most violent state in this respect has been Texas, where four agents have been killed since 1919.	An unofficial three-man altitude record of 23,350 feet was set today at McCook Field, Dayton, OH, by Lieutenant. L. Wade, Captain A. W. Stevens, and Sergeant Longham in a supercharged Air Service bomber.... Polar explorer Roald Amundsen's expedition, in the schooner *Maud*, has reached the vicinity of Wrangell Island in the Siberian Arctic.		Typhoons hit Swatow (mod. Shantou) on the China coast this evening at 10:00 P.M. Winds are measured at 100 mph. Then a tidal wave hit the Swatow area, devastating 75 towns and villages. Eight-foot floods swept low-lying coastal regions, uprooting trees and destroying buildings. Sampans were found beached, driven 200 feet inland. As many as 60,000 people have been killed....Alexander Graham Bell, famed inventor of the telephone, and cofounder of the National Geographic Society, has died in Nova Scotia. He was 75....German pilot Herr Gotte has completed the first nonstop flight between Berlin and Moscow in just 10 hours and 40 minutes.	High priced handbags with silk and novel trimmings are all the rage this year as fall fashions start to appear.	Aug. 2
Striking miners are calling for President Warren Harding to pressure mine operators to return to the bargaining table, as the strike continues. The National Guard has now been called out in 12 states as sporadic violence continues in the coal fields.	Major General Edwards, addressing a gathering of 3,300 New England youths at Camp Deven, MA, today denounced peace advocates in the United States, warning "This is a period of disturbances both at home and abroad." Edwards cautions that America must be "Well prepared to meet any exigencies that may arise therefrom."		New equipment is being installed in New York City that will allow callers to "dial" numbers directly without being connected by an operator.... Beacon Hill in South Seattle has been selected as the site for a new observatory, which will have a lens 120 inches in diameter and weighing five tons....Commerce Secretary Herbert Hoover warns of the continuing danger of epidemics in Soviet Russia, describing Russia as "a cesspool of infectious diseases." As of May 20, some 837,000 cases of typhus have been reported.	WGY in Schenectady has begun using sound effects on the radio, knocking wooden blocks together to imitate the sound of a door slamming.	Aug. 3
	Lieutenant Clayton Bissell has made the first night flight between Washington, DC, and New York City, completing the flight in five hours and 15 minutes in a DH4-B biplane.			Sixty-five cases of Scotch seized by New York City police from a rum runner have disappeared. The missing hooch is valued at $7,800.	Aug. 4
		President Warren Harding meets with railroad union leaders in an effort to resolve the strike afflicting large portions of the Northeast.... The National Automobile Dealers Association claims that oil companies are forming a combination to raise gas prices, citing wide differences in prices in 28 cities.	The First International Experimental Congress of Motorless airplanes opened today at Clermont Ferrand in France, with 22 gliders on display from around the world. Of interest is the use of wing flaps to turn the gliders and help them control their flight.	The National Association of Book Publishers denounced calls for prepublication censorship of manuscripts by the Society for the Suppression of Vice. Warning against the establishment of a "pooh bah," the Association cited Shakespeare and Byron as being among those threatened with censorship.	Aug. 5
Atlanta Police Chief James Beavers, running for mayor, has called on his rival Walter Sims to come clean about his ties to the Ku Klux Klan. Beavers vows, if elected, to uphold the rule of law and to resist any attempt by the Klan to get control of the city or state administration.		Chicago is in the midst of the greatest building boom in its history, with permits being issued for $127.7 million in housing in the first seven months of the year. The total may reach $175 million by the end of the year.	Army Lieutenant James Doolittle's attempted cross-country flight from Florida to California suffers a disastrous setback today when his specially designed De Haviland 4 biplane crashes upon takeoff at Jacksonville, FL. Doolittle himself is unhurt, but his plane will require extensive repairs before he can attempt the flight again.	Old Orchard, ME, today warned 300 visiting tourists not to use their cars as changing rooms at the beaches here. The town council also announced that it would not tolerate immodest bathing attire that was "too frank for the state of Maine."...The National Merchandise Fair opened today in New York City with Ziegfield's Follies entertaining visitors at the more than 800 exhibits of the latest fashions.	Aug. 6
F *Includes campaigns, elections, federal-state relations, civil rights and liberties, crime, the judiciary, education, healthcare, poverty, urban affairs, and population.*	G *Includes formation and debate of U.S. foreign and defense policies, veterans affairs, and defense spending. (Relations with specific foreign countries are usually found under the region concerned.)*	H *Includes business, labor, agriculture, taxation, transportation, consumer affairs, monetary and fiscal policy, natural resources, pollution and industrial accidents.*	I *Includes worldwide scientific, medical and technological developments, natural phenomena, U.S. weather and natural disasters.*	J *Includes the arts, religion, scholarship, communications media, sports, entertainment, fashions, fads, and social life.*	

	World Affairs	Europe	Africa & The Middle East	The Americas	Asia & The Pacific
Aug. 7	As the London Conference opens today, the French government demands the confiscation of German property and capital on the left bank of the Rhine and expropriation of the state mines in the Ruhr. The British government is rejecting the French demands. The French are refusing to grant a moratorium on reparations payments.	In the Irish Civil War, the IRA has cut the telegraph cable linking the United States and Europe at the Waterville Station....Germany's economy remains in free fall, with her floating debt having increased by 7.5 *billion* marks in just 10 days in July....The Soviet Central Committee today rejects death sentences for Petrograd Metropolitan Benjamin and three other Russian Orthodox prelates, for interfering with the seizure of Church treasures by state authorities.		General Pedro Nel Ospina has succeeded fellow Conservative General Jorge Holguin as President of Colombia.	
Aug. 8		Irish Free State forces have landed in County Cork and are advancing toward the city of Cork amidst heavy fighting....Prices have increased in Austria by 94 percent in just one month, with restaurants closing in Vienna due to prohibitive food costs. Meanwhile the Austrian government has appealed to the Allies to expedite a proposed loan, warning that Austria may enter bankruptcy otherwise.		A bomb explodes in Mexico City University while the president of the university is speaking, injuring several.	Britain and Australia are considering the opening of airship service between the two countries via Marseilles, Cairo, Baghdad, Bombay, and Singapore. The proposed service would improve imperial defense and be cheaper then steamship fares by $150....Japan is preparing to open negotiations with the Soviet Far Eastern Republic to discuss the withdrawal of Japanese troops from the Siberian Far East.
Aug. 9	Five United States Senators and a number of Congressional Representatives will attend the meeting of the Interparliamentary Union in Vienna later this month, to discuss the promotion of world peace.	The Italian Chamber of Deputies gives its support to Liberal Prime Minister Luigi Facta today, as order returns to Rome after days of clashes between Fascists and Socialists. The Italian army is keeping troops on alert in the town of Anzio, 33 miles from the city, in case of renewed violence.			
Aug. 10	The World for International Friendship Through the Churches, at their meeting in Copenhagen, today call for arbitration of international disputes to prevent a new world war.	Reginald Dunne and Joseph O'Sullivan, the English-born IRA gunmen who murdered General Henry Wilson in June, are executed today for murder....King George V of Great Britain formally signed the Washington Conference treaties....Republican troops are abandoning their positions in Cork as the rebels' situation in southern Ireland worsens....A general strike in Lisbon, Portugal, is settled today, with the Portuguese government cutting bread prices. Martial law remains in effect for the moment, however.	An Egyptian military court hands down judgment against seven men accused of issuing a nationalist manifesto. The verdict is not disclosed but it is believed that the men are found guilty. British High Commissioner Allenby will have the final say in their case.		
Aug. 11		The Republicans have abandoned Fermoy, their last stronghold, as the rebels switch from trying to hold populated areas to guerilla warfare in the countryside....Fire has left the Irish city of Cork devastated, with £2 million worth of fire damage done in the wake of the retreat of Irish Republican forces....France is deporting 500 German "undesirables" from Alsace as part of efforts to force continued German payment of reimbursement to French holders of German securities.			
Aug. 12	The split between Great Britain and France on the subject of German reparations widens today at the London Conference as British Prime Minister Lloyd George today calls for cancellation of Germany's annual two billion gold mark payments and rely solely on a 26 percent assessment on German exports to pay reparations costs. France and Italy want to continue to force the Germans to pay.	Arthur Griffith, President of the Irish *Dáil Éireann*, has died of a heart attack. His death, though of natural causes, adds to the mounting instability in Ireland. He will be succeeded by William Cosgrave.			
	A *Includes developments that affect more than one world region, international organizations and important meetings of world leaders.*	B *Includes all domestic and regional developments in Europe, including the Soviet Union.*	C *Includes all domestic and regional developments in Africa and the Middle East.*	D *Includes all domestic and regional developments in Latin America, the Caribbean, and Canada.*	E *Includes all domestic and regional developments in Asian and Pacific nations (and colonies).*

U.S. Politics & Social Issues	U.S. Foreign Policy & Affairs, Defense	U.S. Economy & Environment	Science, Technology & Nature	Culture, Leisure & Lifestyle	
			Two Americans participate in the Gordon Bennett Balloon Race landed today near Choeroetnik, Hungary, 480 miles from their start in Geneva, Switzerland; while an Italian pilot made a stunning 20,000 foot descent in nine minutes over Vienna.	Chess champion José R. Capablanca defeated Russian challenger M. Bogoljubow as the international chess tournament in London continues....Rival tong leaders in San Francisco's Chinatown have signed a peace treaty, ending 17 months of continuing violence....Ko Low, National President of the Hip Sing Tong, is murdered today in New York City's Chinatown.	Aug. 7
		Bumper crops are now predicted across the United States, thanks to favorable weather conditions in July, with hay and sweet potatoes expected to set records.	Edmund Allen of the American Aeronautical Engineering Society has taken the lead in the third day of international glider competition in Clermont Ferrand, France, staying aloft a total of three minutes and 19 seconds in four flights....Authorities in Swatow, China, are racing to bury the thousands of bodies found in the wake of the typhoon that devastated this port city earlier this month. The British in Hong Kong have sent relief supplies to combat widespread hunger, while packs of looters have been fought off by the police.	Hot new trumpeter Louis Armstrong has left New Orleans to join Joe "King" Oliver's Creole Jazz Band at the Lincoln Gardens in Chicago.... The civil war in the Morello crime family of New York continues. Mobster Joe Masseria has narrowly escapes an assassination attempt by rival Morello crime family lieutenant Rocco Valenti, which killed two of Masseria's bodyguards in a 2nd Avenue shop. Eight bystanders are injured in the melee.	Aug. 8
	The War Department is taking action to find the persons responsible for distributing Communist circulars among army, navy, and marine personnel urging them not to shoot workers if called on to suppress continuing coal and rail strikes.		Lieutenant R.B. Thomas makes the first airplane landing inside the Grand Canyon today, coming down 3,000 feet below the canyon rim.		Aug. 9
The Anthracite Coal operators' Association is calling on President Warren Harding to force a separate settlement with anthracite coalminers, concentrated mainly in Pennsylvania, as the nationwide coal strike drags on....Attorney General Harry Daugherty today called on the American Bar Association, meeting in San Francisco, to help combat the spread of "foreign doctrines" that run counter to American institutions.	The battleship *USS California* has been awarded a letter of commendation for excellence in shipboard engineering.		H.C. Baird, flying a Supermarine Sealion, has won the Schneider Trophy race at Naples, Italy. The only non-Italian contestant, Baird reached speeds of 145.7 mph.		Aug. 10
Authorities in Pennsylvania are asking for the extradition of 90 men from West Virginia involved in ongoing violence in the Allegheny coal country....Bombs are set off on railroad property in Roseville and San Bernardino as unrest continues in the Santa Fe rail strike.		President Warren Harding and his cabinet discuss the continuing rail strike, and its effect on the delivery of the federal mails, as the strike has now spread to the sprawling Santa Fe rail system....The Census Bureau reports today that more than a million children ages 10–15 are employed in wage-earning work. This amounts to 11.3 percent of boys and 5.6 percent of girls.	M. DeMuyter of Belgium has won the Gordon Bennett Balloon Race, having flown 1,300 kilometers, landing in Oenitza, Romania.	Joe Masseria has struck back at rival Rocco Valenti, in the civil war that has gripped the Morello crime family of New York. After being lured to a peace conference, Valenti is gunned down outside of a 12th Street restaurant in an assault that wounds one bystander and kills an eight-year-old girl. The assailant: Charles "Lucky" Luciano.	Aug. 11
The home of famed civil-rights activist Frederick Douglass, in Washington, DC, is dedicated as a memorial today.			Captain Angus Buchanan's explorations in the desolate Air region of the Sahara will be chronicled in the upcoming book *Out of the World*. Buchanan has collected more than 3,000 specimens of birds, animals, and insects. Princeton University will publish German physicist Albert Einstein's *The Theory of Relativity*.	Police in New York City seize 25 bottles of heroin from drug smugglers after being tipped off by an addict.	Aug. 12
F *Includes campaigns, elections, federal-state relations, civil rights and liberties, crime, the judiciary, education, healthcare, poverty, urban affairs, and population.*	**G** *Includes formation and debate of U.S. foreign and defense policies, veterans affairs, and defense spending. (Relations with specific foreign countries are usually found under the region concerned.)*	**H** *Includes business, labor, agriculture, taxation, transportation, consumer affairs, monetary and fiscal policy, natural resources, pollution and industrial accidents.*	**I** *Includes worldwide scientific, medical and technological developments, natural phenomena, U.S. weather and natural disasters.*	**J** *Includes the arts, religion, scholarship, communications media, sports, entertainment, fashions, fads, and social life.*	

	World Affairs	Europe	Africa & The Middle East	The Americas	Asia & The Pacific
Aug. 13	In a compromise, the Allies at the London Conference today agree to delay one German reparations payment of 50 million gold marks....Since the end of World War I, Belgium has spent 16 billion francs on reconstruction, while having received just four billion from Germany in reparations.	In a report to the Minister of the Interior in Rome, the Prefect of Milan has warned the government that the army cannot be counted on to stop the Fascists....Mussolini now has some 200,000 armed *squadristi* in his Blackshirt units....Britain's birth rate rose sharply in 1920, while Britain's death rate has dropped to the lowest point since 1862.	Egyptian nationalists are pressing the British to allow the return of exiled Egyptian nationalist leader Saad Zaghul from exile in the Seychelles Islands. Meanwhile a split is growing between Egyptian King Fuad and Prime Minister Abdel Sarwat over the Constitution being debated for the new kingdom of Egypt.	Argentine President-elect Don Marcello de Alvear arrives in Paris today from Belgium. Argentina continues to maintain its strong tradition of European ties....Brazilians are trying to develop a steel industry. Brazil has reserves of between 6–12 billion tons of high grade iron ore available for development....France's pavilion at the upcoming Brazilian centennial exposition in Rio de Janerio will be modeled on the palace of Petit Trianon. On display will be Gobelin tapestries and Sèvres vases.	
Aug. 14	The London Conference breaks up without agreement today, as French Premier Raymond Poincaré returned to France. The French have refused any further concessions to Germany on reparations without further liens on German assets.			At a conference with General Enoch Crowder, Warren Harding's personal envoy, Cuban President Alfredo Zayas agreed to ask the Cuban Congress to approve a $50 million loan from American banks to stabilize Cuba's finances....Coalminers in the Cape Breton district of Nova Scotia have gone on strike, demanding a restoration of their 1921 wages.	Filipino nationalist Emilio Aguinaldo, who led resistance to American forces after the Spanish American War, today addressed surviving veterans of the Philippine Insurrection at Olympic Stadium in Manila, in commemoration of the 24th anniversary of the American occupation of Manila....Peace talks opened today in Shanghai between representatives of Beijing warlord Wu Peifu, Manchurian warlord Chang Tsolin, Sun Yat-sen's exiled Guomindang government, and other Chinese leaders.
Aug. 15	The German government has proposed a plan to pay 25 percent of the total reparations demanded, after paying only £5 million of the £25 million due for this month.	American engineers will help construct a railroad linking Belgrade with Yugoslavia's Adriatic coast.		Brazil is blocking plans to set up an alternate telegraph cable route from Europe to Barbados and Miami via Pernambuco. Brazil is demanding that the cable also service South American businesses. The recent destruction of cable lines by Irish guerillas make alternate telegraph routes between Europe and America imperative.	
Aug. 16		Cholera is ravaging the Crimean Peninsula in Russia, as the long famine there has left people too weak to resist the plague.		The Canadian Minister of Defense has ordered troops into the troubled coal mining districts of Nova Scotia as the United Mine Workers' strike continues....Cuba is protesting the tariff bill as it is being written in Congress, claiming that duties on sugar will hurt its economy.	
Aug. 17					
Aug. 18	The upcoming League of Nations conference in September will focus on the admission of Hungary to the League and a proposal by Uruguay to extend the Washington Naval Disarmament accords to the nations of South America.				Australia is cutting its income taxes by 10 percent, and reducing other levies, in the wake of defense budget cuts as laid down in the Washington Disarmament Treaties earlier this year.
Aug. 19		The Soviet Central Executive Committee is re-instituting the Tsarist punishment of internal banishment for political dissent.			The Soviet newspaper *Izvestia*, reflecting official policy, is calling for Soviet support of China's territorial integrity. The Soviets are eager to exploit Chinese fear of European and Japanese encroachment to gain a foothold there.

A	B	C	D	E
Includes developments that affect more than one world region, international organizations and important meetings of world leaders.	*Includes all domestic and regional developments in Europe, including the Soviet Union.*	*Includes all domestic and regional developments in Africa and the Middle East.*	*Includes all domestic and regional developments in Latin America, the Caribbean, and Canada.*	*Includes all domestic and regional developments in Asian and Pacific nations (and colonies).*

U.S. Politics & Social Issues	U.S. Foreign Policy & Affairs, Defense	U.S. Economy & Environment	Science, Technology & Nature	Culture, Leisure & Lifestyle	
		Railroad unions have rejected a plan offered by President Warren Harding, to end the strike....Two bombs exploded aboard a West Shore train near Weehawken, NJ, injuring some 20 passengers, while arson destroyed 15 engine cars in Portland, ME. A 400 foot railroad bridge was dynamited 15 miles northwest of Springfield, MO.	The Rockefeller Foundation is using fish to devour mosquito eggs and larvae in efforts to reduce yellow fever outbreaks in Ecuador and Peru. The Foundation is also redoubling efforts to reduce hookworm disease. Some 900 million of the Earth's 1.7 billion people live in areas where hookworm is endemic.	Chess champion José R. Capablanca defeated challenger Victor Wahltuch of Manchester today, as the world chess championship tourney in London continues....Ko Low, murdered head of the Hip Sing Tong, is buried today after a mass procession through the streets of New York City's Chinatown. The procession, which includes flowers sent by the rival On Leong Tong, draws 100,000 onlookers.	Aug. 13
			The bones of a 40,000 year old horse are found by well-diggers near Santa Monica, CA.	Alfred Harmsworth, Lord Northcliffe, owner of the *London Times* and the *London Daily Mail*, has died of heart disease. He built these and other newspapers into popular journals with society pages, women's columns, and gossip columns....An open Tong war is averted today after representatives of the rival On Leong and Hip Sing Tongs met in New York City to resolve their differences. The On Loengs vigorously deny involvement in the recent slaying of Hip Sing leader Ko Low.	Aug. 14
A bomb explodes in a rail yard in Evansville, IN. No one is injured, but all nonunion workers at the yard have quit. Unrest erupts on the St. Paul line near Channing, MI, between strikers and nonstriking rail workers....Attorney General Harry Daugherty today announced "The I.W.W. are quite active in connection with the railway strikes."		West Coast fruit growers warn today that the continuing rail strike is endangering $25 million worth of crops.			Aug. 15
				WEAF goes on the air today in New York City.	Aug. 16
	The U.S. State Department has approved a plan by the Western Union Telegraph Company to construct a telegraph cable from Germany to the United States via the Azores.			Cover Garden, the world's largest dance hall, opens today in New York City....The federal government has announced that it will crack down on restaurants and dance halls that let customers defy Prohibition by "bringing their own" in hip flasks.	Aug. 17
In a speech in Tacoma, WA, Vice President Calvin Coolidge today cited the continuing coal and rail strikes as a sign of the underlying health of the economy. He remarks, "There are no strikes when conditions are bad."	The War Department is buying three experimental aircraft from Dutch designer Anthony Fokker. The specifications call for planes using the Curtiss D-12 cylinder engine, which can reach speeds of 140 miles per hour, with a service ceiling of 21,000 feet.	Commerce Secretary Herbert Hoover today warns that distributors have begun profiteering from the shortage of coal as the nearly five-month long mine strike continues.	A German sailplane piloted by Arthur Martens sets the record for the longest glider flight: two hours and 10 seconds, at the Wasserkuppe plateau in Hesse. Under the terms of the Versailles Treaty, the German military is forbidden to use or develop military aircraft, but the Treaty makes no mention of gliders, which consequently are avidly studied by the Germans as a way of giving potential pilots some air experience.	Comedian Al Jolson, popular for his blackface roles, is getting married. The lucky bride is actress Alma Osborne....World chess champion José R. Capablanca of Cuba has again won the chess championship, trouncing his opponents in the London tournament with 13 points. Capablanca will receive a £250 prize.	Aug. 18
			A British airship advocate is calling for the construction of dirigibles with five million cubic feet capacity, carrying 207 passengers and 10 tons of cargo, and distances up to 3,000 miles without refueling. Objections include the vulnerability of flammable hydrogen, while helium remains prohibitively expensive.	Norwegian born Molla Bjurstedt Mallory has won the U.S. Lawn Tennis Association's women's singles championship for the third straight time.	Aug. 19
F *Includes campaigns, elections, federal-state relations, civil rights and liberties, crime, the judiciary, education, healthcare, poverty, urban affairs, and population.*	**G** *Includes formation and debate of U.S. foreign and defense policies, veterans affairs, and defense spending. (Relations with specific foreign countries are usually found under the region concerned.)*	**H** *Includes business, labor, agriculture, taxation, transportation, consumer affairs, monetary and fiscal policy, natural resources, pollution and industrial accidents.*	**I** *Includes worldwide scientific, medical and technological developments, natural phenomena, U.S. weather and natural disasters.*	**J** *Includes the arts, religion, scholarship, communications media, sports, entertainment, fashions, fads, and social life.*	

	World Affairs	Europe	Africa & The Middle East	The Americas	Asia & The Pacific
Aug. 20			South Africa's gold output stands at £37 million, at £4.24773 per ounce in 1921.		
Aug. 21		Two men are killed and eight wounded in a clash between Fascists and Communists at San Vito, near Rome.			Manchurian warlord General Chang Tsolin has issued a warning to the British, insisting that they deal with him as a sovereign power or face a boycott and the withdrawal of protection from British interests. Chang is still angry at the support the British showed to Beijing warlord General Wu Pei-fu during their recent conflict.
Aug. 22	The American congressional delegation, en route to the Interparliamentary Union meeting in Vienna, met today with leaders in Berlin. The delegates seek to lessen formalities in acquiring passports, and to increase the scope and usage of the International Court in The Hague.	Michael Collins, chairman of the Irish Free State Government, has been gunned down in a Republican ambush near Bandon in rural west County Cork. He was 31 years old. Collins was a hero of the war against the British, who later aroused hatred from ardent Republicans for seeking a compromise settlement that kept Ireland in the British Empire as a self-governing Dominion....Fascist Blackshirts have seized control of the Naples waterfront, driving out Communists and labor unions.	The Iraqi cabinet has resigned in protest against the planned Anglo-Iraq Treaty, which will confirm Iraq's status as a British protectorate.	385 Chinese workers, recruited as contract labor, en route via Panama, may be forbidden to disembark in Jamaica, where they were hired to do farm work. British authorities insist that there is no labor shortage on the island.	
Aug. 23			Rif Berbers have renewed their rebellion against Spanish rule in Morocco....An Arab Congress at Nablus has condemned the British mandate over Palestine, demanding the creation of an independent Arab state. The Congress will send delegations to the United States and Great Britain in an effort to raise support for their cause.	The American delegation to the Brazilian Centennial Exposition arrived in Buenos Aires today for a goodwill visit before continuing on to Rio de Janerio....Mexico announces that it will reduce its export tax on petroleum by 60 percent. The increased volume of exports likely to result is expected to yield $2 million a month, which Mexico has earmarked for reduction of its foreign debt.	
Aug. 24		Former Crown Prince Wilhelm, son of exiled Kaiser Wilhelm II, now living in the Netherlands, has ruled out any attempt to return to Germany to try to restore the monarchy. The German mark fluctuated wildly on the Berlin Exchange today, bottoming out at 2,600 at the dollar before restabilizing at 2,000. The fluctuations were due to desperate efforts by the Reichsbank to dump dollars and other hard currencies in an effort to stem the collapse of the mark. Police reserves were called out in Berlin as Communists led protests marches when the price of bread shot up 40 percent in a matter of hours.		A wing of the Portuguese pavilion at the Brazilian Centennial Exposition collapsed today, injuring five, as work continues to meet the fair's September 7 opening.	
Aug. 25					

A	B	C	D	E
Includes developments that affect more than one world region, international organizations and important meetings of world leaders.	*Includes all domestic and regional developments in Europe, including the Soviet Union.*	*Includes all domestic and regional developments in Africa and the Middle East.*	*Includes all domestic and regional developments in Latin America, the Caribbean, and Canada.*	*Includes all domestic and regional developments in Asian and Pacific nations (and colonies).*

U.S. Politics & Social Issues	U.S. Foreign Policy & Affairs, Defense	U.S. Economy & Environment	Science, Technology & Nature	Culture, Leisure & Lifestyle	
In a dramatic demonstration of the growing reach of the Ku Klux Klan, 4,650 new members are initiated in a mass rally attended by 25,000 people outside of Chicago. 18 Klan chapters from the city, and 12 others from other parts of Illinois, are present.			Archaeologists from the National Museum of Mexico have uncovered a ruined city four miles long by three miles wide, at the foot of volcanic Mt. Ixtaccihuatl. 28 pyramids as tall as 100 feet, surrounded by stone walls of up to 20 feet in thickness have been reported.	The International Association of Feminine Athletes' unofficial Women's Olympic Games in Paris, has drawn teams from five nations. The British team has performed the best, winning 50 points overall, with the American team of 15 women winning 31 points.	Aug. 20
		The Santa Fe rail system reports today that it now has all its trains rolling, despite continued work stoppages.		The National Football League has granted a franchise to a rising local team, the Green Bay Packers.	Aug. 21
Senate candidate James E. Ferguson, former governor of Texas, today openly denounced the Ku Klux Klan in a speech in Houston, reportedly a Klan stronghold in Texas. Some 250 people in the audience walked out, jeering and booing, but Ferguson finished his speech as supporters came in to fill the vacated seats.... The Senate begins discussion of the Bonus Bill for veterans of World War I. The bill, which will cost between 4.5 and $5 billion, has been fiercely debated, especially as to how it will be financed.		U.S. Steel announced that it is increasing wages by 20 percent.	The British aircraft firm, Vickers, has unveiled its latest model, the Vickers Victoria.	Federal agents arrest 16-year-old William Behm in New York City today, the youngest person on record to be arrested for bootlegging. Behm promises to get undercover agents as much as 250 cases of whiskey for $29.25 a gallon, considered a bargain price.... Grain alcohol is selling for $7.75 a gallon.	Aug. 22
		A bomb goes off in the Chicago & Alton roundhouse in Venice, IL, as discussions to end the ongoing rail strike continue.			Aug. 23
President Warren Harding is expected to veto the McCumber Bonus Bill as it is currently written in the Senate, and it is clear Harding has the votes to sustain his veto. The cost of the measure will exceed that spent on the entire American Civil War.				Kate Douglas Wiggin, author of *Rebecca of Sunnybrook Farm* and founder of the first free kindergarten in the United States, in San Francisco, has died. She was 66....The Chicago Cubs and the Philadelphia Phillies together scored 49 runs today, setting a new world's record for a single baseball game, while the number of hits, 51, also broke records. The Cubs finally won, 26–23.	Aug. 24
			The round-the-world flight attempt by British Captains Norman MacMillan and Geoffrey Mallins has ended in failure when their Fairey III plane's engine malfunctions over the Bay of Bengal. MacMillan and Mallins survive the crash and have been rescued.		Aug. 25
F *Includes campaigns, elections, federal-state relations, civil rights and liberties, crime, the judiciary, education, healthcare, poverty, urban affairs, and population.*	G *Includes formation and debate of U.S. foreign and defense policies, veterans affairs, and defense spending. (Relations with specific foreign countries are usually found under the region concerned.)*	H *Includes business, labor, agriculture, taxation, transportation, consumer affairs, monetary and fiscal policy, natural resources, pollution and industrial accidents.*	I *Includes worldwide scientific, medical and technological developments, natural phenomena, U.S. weather and natural disasters.*	J *Includes the arts, religion, scholarship, communications media, sports, entertainment, fashions, fads, and social life.*	

	World Affairs	Europe	Africa & The Middle East	The Americas	Asia & The Pacific
Aug. 26	Austrian Assistant Finance minister Dr. Schuler arrived in Rome today, to ask for a 70 million lire loan to stabilize Austria's finances....In accordance with the Washington Naval Disarmament Treaty, the French navy today sank the battleship *France* off Quiberon Bay. The measure eliminates France's naval superiority over Italy.	King Alexander and Prime Minister Nikola Pachitch of Yugoslavia met with Czech Prime Minister Eduard Benes today at Marienbad, agreeing to strengthen the political and economic cooperation between the two pro-French Little Entente countries....Three people are killed and 50 others wounded as troops battled striking metal workers in the French port of Le Havre. One French regiment refused to march against the strikers, prompting the government to call for reinforcements from elsewhere in the country.	This morning, Turkish Nationalist forces under Mustafa Kemal launched a massive counterattack on Greek forces in Anatolia. The assault fell upon the southern flank of Greek positions around Afyonkarahisar. The Greeks have been dug into defensive positions since the failure of their offensive last year. Only one railroad links the Greeks with the coast. Kemal has been gradually building up Turkish forces, while breaking the Allied coalition that supported the Greeks.		The Japanese cruiser *Niitaka*, 3,420 tons, sinks off the coast of Kamchatka today in a typhoon. Virtually its entire crew of 300 has been lost.
Aug. 27		Sweden has voted down a measure that would have introduced Prohibition. The referendum was defeated 51 to 49 percent.... Yugoslavia is reported to be massing troops along the border with Austria, with the aim of occupying the Klagenfurt Basin should the chaos in Austria present an opportunity. While unlikely, it underscores the weakness of Austria in its current economic crisis.... A wholesale purge of intellectuals connected with the outlawed Socialist Revolutionary movement is underway in Soviet Russia, with 200 professors, authors, and journalists arrested and banished to *gulags* in Siberia, particularly in the Arctic islands of Novy Zemlya.	Turkish forces have broken through the Greek lines around Afyonkarahisar, capturing the 5,000 foot Erkmentepe commanding the Greek lines of communications, while Turkish cavalry have broken through into the Greek rear. The Greeks are retreating toward the strategic railhead of Dumlupinar in what is rapidly becoming a rout.		
Aug. 28		Yugoslavia today denied rumors that it had mobilized troops along the border with Austria, calling it "Italian propaganda."			The Japanese have agreed to begin withdrawing their troops from Siberia.
Aug. 29	Condemning recent trials of war criminals in German courts as being too lenient, the Allies today warn Germany that they reserve the right, under the Treaty of Versailles to try war criminals themselves.	Michael Cardinal Faulhaber of Munich today attacks the Weimar Republic, condemning the overthrow of the Kaiser as "treason" and the "Jewish" press, before a mass rally of Bavarian Catholics.		A new government has been formed in Chile, replacing the one that resigned in protest recently over the planned accord with Peru. The new Prime Minister will be Antonio Huneua.	
Aug. 30	Germany today rejected French demands for further gold deposits or liens on resources as surety for reparations payments.	Irish Republicans attacked Bantry in County Cork, but were driven off by Irish Free State forces, who are slowly tightening their grip on the countryside.	Turkish forces under Mustafa Kemal have cut off the retreat of Greek forces around Dumlupinar. The Greek army in Anatolia is now in a state of complete collapse as the Turks pour west toward the Greek occupied Aegean coast.	The United Mine Workers in Nova Scotia have accepted a settlement, ending the coalmine strike there.	
Aug. 31	The Reparations Commission has adopted a Belgian plan for German payment of reparations....The League of Nations Council held its 20th session in Geneva today to consider issues involving the Class A mandates. Also up for discussion is the situation in Austria.	Czechoslovakia and the Kingdom of Serbs, Croats, and Slovenes (Yugoslavia) have renewed their defensive alliance in Marienbad. This alliance is the lynchpin of the French sponsored Little Entenete in Eastern Europe.	Tractors provided by Near East Relief are greatly improving the yields of Armenian farmers. A model farm set up by the agency is producing twice as much using tractors as with men and oxen.	American special envoy General Enoch Crowder issued an ultimatum to the Cuban government to put in effect measures to clean up corruption in the administration within 10 days. While no formal threat of intervention was made, it is clear that the United States will intervene if its demands are not met.	

A	B	C	D	E
Includes developments that affect more than one world region, international organizations and important meetings of world leaders.	*Includes all domestic and regional developments in Europe, including the Soviet Union.*	*Includes all domestic and regional developments in Africa and the Middle East.*	*Includes all domestic and regional developments in Latin America, the Caribbean, and Canada.*	*Includes all domestic and regional developments in Asian and Pacific nations (and colonies).*

U.S. Politics & Social Issues	U.S. Foreign Policy & Affairs, Defense	U.S. Economy & Environment	Science, Technology & Nature	Culture, Leisure & Lifestyle	
Earle B. Mayfield, who has been backed by the Ku Klux Klan, holds an early lead over rival James E. Ferguson in the Democratic primary race in Texas for the United States Senate.		Ford Motor Company has announced that it will begin closing down its plants and laying off workers if the coal shortage due to the strike continues.			Aug. 26
Texas Senatorial candidate James E. Ferguson finally concedes defeat in a bitter Democratic primary election. Ferguson's opponent, Earle B. Mayfield, is backed by both the Ku Klux Klan and by "Dry" forces in the state.	The War Department has completed a reduction in force of 100,000 men for the U.S. Army, down to the 125,000 man force mandated by Congress. The army is keeping the 2nd Division intact at Ft. Travis, TX, to monitor the troubled situation in Mexico, while coast defense forces have been drastically reduced.		Dutch aircraft designer Anthony Fokker has set a new record for a two-man glider flight, staying aloft over Fulda, Germany for 13 minutes. Germany today handed out a 50,000 mark prize to glider designer Herr Hentzen of the Hanover technical School, for his design's successful performance in tests last year. The German military, denied an air force by the terms of the Versailles Treaty, is acutely interested in gliders as a means of giving a cadre of pilots air experience.	Film censorship advocate Canon Chase is calling for federal action to regulate the film industry. Dr. Chase argues, "The motion picture has publicity power greater than the press." And that there must be restraints on "A few producers who will dictate what pictures the people shall see."... A record 220,000 people, including 18,239 Americans, attended the Oberammergau Passion Play in Germany.	Aug. 27
		The Coca Cola Company today announces a quarterly dividend of $1 per share, with second quarter profits of $2.755 million.	The Amundsen Polar expedition is abandoning its efforts to overfly the North Pole this season. Amundsen will fly from Wainwright, near Point Barrow, in order to attempt the flight next year.	WEAF in New York broadcast the first commercial over the radio today, an ad for Hawthorne Court apartments in Jackson Heights, Queens....The Walker Cup international golf team tournament has begun in Southampton, NY, between the United States and Great Britain....Judges have decided to ban perfume, scented flowers, and face powder at the upcoming Miss America pageant.	Aug. 28
			As part of its £2 million plan to upgrade its air forces with all-metal planes, the British government today orders the development of a troop transport plane that can carry up to 25 men with their equipment....Excavation of the Ancient Roman city of Lanuvium, now Civita Lavinia, by the Diocletian Museum of Rome, has revealed the ruins of a Roman theater.		Aug. 29
			Passengers traveling by air from Paris to Geneva will begin having music piped in by radio while in flight. This procedure is now expected to become standard on longer flights....Dr. E.J. Maguire of Warren, OH, demonstrates that an adult male can maintain his normal weight on 50 cents a day worth of food.		Aug. 30
The Senate today passes the House's $4 billion Bonus Bill for World War I veterans. However, the measure is certain to face a presidential veto.				The Davis Cup international tennis tournament has begun. Facing off this year are the United States and Australia....Two Manhattan real estate brokers have been arrested by Federal prohibition agents in the disappearance of $500,000 worth of whiskey and champagne, in what is alleged to be "one of the biggest bootleg gangs in the country."	Aug. 31
F	G	H	I	J	
Includes campaigns, elections, federal-state relations, civil rights and liberties, crime, the judiciary, education, healthcare, poverty, urban affairs, and population.	*Includes formation and debate of U.S. foreign and defense policies, veterans affairs, and defense spending. (Relations with specific foreign countries are usually found under the region concerned.)*	*Includes business, labor, agriculture, taxation, transportation, consumer affairs, monetary and fiscal policy, natural resources, pollution and industrial accidents.*	*Includes worldwide scientific, medical and technological developments, natural phenomena, U.S. weather and natural disasters.*	*Includes the arts, religion, scholarship, communications media, sports, entertainment, fashions, fads, and social life.*	

	World Affairs	Europe	Africa & The Middle East	The Americas	Asia & The Pacific
Sep. 1	A consortium of American banks is prepared to advance a loan to the struggling Austrian government, if the Allies will guarantee the loan.	A loaf of bread that cost half a crown before World War I now costs 6,000 crowns in Austria....The runaway inflation wracking Germany continues, with so much money having been printed that new notes are in short supply. The largest denomination, a 10,000-mark note, is worth just under $8.00. The *Reichsbank* is working on a solution: designing 50 and 100,000 mark notes....One person is dead and 20 injured in bread riots in the streets of Eberswalde, near Berlin.	Greek troops have confirmed that they have pulled out of Eski-Shehr, to avoid being cut off by Turkish forces advancing around their northern flank. The three Greek divisions leaving Eski-Shehr are retreating to join a force of eight Greek divisions at Kiutayali....In a letter to Prime Minister Lloyd George on the British occupation of Iraq, Colonial Secretary Winston Churchill writes: "At present we are paying eight million a year for the privilege of living on an ungrateful volcano out of which we can in no circumstance get anything worth having."	In this month, the French, in a gesture of gratitude, have granted the land around Vimy Ridge to Canada as a cemetery and memorial.	
Sep. 2					
Sep. 3		Prices in Germany have nearly doubled in August, with no end in sight.	The Turkish Nationalists today announced that they have "annihilated" the northern wing of the Greek army in Anatolia. Turkish forces are advancing using tanks and French "75s," rapid firing artillery. The Greeks are concentrating their navy at Smyrna, where 4,000 Greek wounded have been moved in recent days. The British battleship *King George V* has left Constantinople for Smyrna at top speed.	A projectionists' strike has closed all movie houses in Mexico City in a dispute over higher wages.	
Sep. 4	The League of Nations opens its third Assembly Session today in Geneva. The Session will be chaired by Agustin Edwards of Chile.	German industrialists have agreed to contribute to payments for reparations.		The International Committee of Bankers on Mexico made public the terms of its recent agreement with the Mexican government. Under the terms of the agreement, Mexico will resume payments on its foreign debt, setting aside operating revenues from the national railroads. The measure is expected to greatly improve the chances of the Obregon government for diplomatic recognition.	Japanese troops have begun withdrawing from Far Eastern Siberia, being followed cautiously by advancing Soviet forces. The Soviets have occupied Sanchung, 100 miles north of Vladivostok. Soviet forces are massing at Khabarovsk, 150 miles from Vladivostok, to secure the rest of the area as the Japanese pull out. The rump White Russian government of Merkulov in Vladivostok is expected to collapse quickly when the Japanese pull out. American business interests are already eyeing the Siberian Far East for timber and mining concessions.
Sep. 5		Irish Republican rebels attack Free State forces at Waterford and Carrick Barracks near County Monaghan, while sporadic ambushes and sabotage continues....55 people have been sentenced to death in southern Russia for "counterrevolutionary activities." This includes 48 members of Simon Petlyura's Cossacks, who rebelled recently against Soviet rule in the Ukraine.	Allied commanders in Constantinople have concluded that the Greek army in Anatolia is in a state of complete collapse and are preparing to land troops in Smyrna to protect the lives and property of their nationals. Tens of thousands of panic-stricken Anatolian Christians are streaming toward the coast. Refugees from Mudania have already begun arriving in Greece.		Two bank managers in Japan have been indicted for making improperly secured loans totaling 70 million yen to stock swindler Ishii, who recently declared bankruptcy....Deposed Chinese boy emperor Suen Tong, also known as Puyi, has hired an English tutor, and has expressed a desire to cut his Manchu pigtail and enter the world as a private citizen. The Chinese Republic has promised to provide the former imperial household with $4 million a year in living expenses, but these subsidies have not been sent regularly.

A	B	C	D	E
Includes developments that affect more than one world region, international organizations and important meetings of world leaders.	*Includes all domestic and regional developments in Europe, including the Soviet Union.*	*Includes all domestic and regional developments in Africa and the Middle East.*	*Includes all domestic and regional developments in Latin America, the Caribbean, and Canada.*	*Includes all domestic and regional developments in Asian and Pacific nations (and colonies).*

	U.S. Politics & Social Issues	U.S. Foreign Policy & Affairs, Defense	U.S. Economy & Environment	Science, Technology & Nature	Culture, Leisure & Lifestyle
Sept. 1	Federal Judge James H. Wilkerson, in Chicago, has issued a broad injunction, at the behest of Attorney General Harry Daugherty, mandating an end to the widespread railroad strike in the United States. 300,000 railroad shopmen are currently on strike.	The United States today refused to ratify the St. Germain Convention restricting private trafficking in arms and ammunition. The major arms manufacturing states: Britain, France, Italy, Japan, Poland, Canada, and Czechoslovakia, are each waiting to see who will ratify the treaty first.	The federal government has issued an injunction against striking rail workers.		New York City passed an ordinance today requiring all pool halls to change their name to "billiard" halls....*Molly Darling* opens tonight on Broadway in New York City...."Babe" Ruth of the New York Yankees has been suspended for the third time this season, this time for three days, for his use of foul language to an umpire in a recent game.
Sept. 2	The Justice Department is sending out 5,500 Federal Marshals to enforce yesterday's court injunction compelling an end to the rail strike....Former presidential candidate William Jennings Bryan announced today that radio would aid the Democratic Party in mobilizing public support and will help put a Democrat in the White House in 1924.		Under pressure from President Warren Harding's administration, Pennsylvania mine operators have reached a settlement with striking coal miners, ending the nationwide strike.	Boll weevils devoured 6.277 million bales of cotton in 1921, the worst ever, and an 87 percent increase since 1920.	The *Better Times* revue opens tonight on Broadway....Chicago's new municipal stadium, now under construction, will hold 100,000 spectators and be one of the largest in the country....The Chinese game Mah Jongg is catching on in America, after an American entrepreneur in the Shanghai Club, adapted it, using Western numerals to replace Chinese characters.
Sept. 3		Senator Joseph Freylinghausen praised Secretary of State Hughes' success at winning limitations on the size of battleships. Freylinghausen noted that if larger battleships were built they would be too big for the Panama Canal, thus necessitating a two-ocean navy by the United States....The newest American battleships, of the *Colorado* and *West Virginia* class, will have auxiliary diesel engines to provide electrical power. The navy is seeking to phase out its less efficient coal-fired engines and replace them with modern diesels.		A league of California citizens is calling for the establishment of a national park to protect giant redwood trees in danger of destruction by logging interests. The trees are the largest and oldest known organisms, have existed as a species since Mesozoic times....Sherman M. Fairchild, inventor of a camera for aerial mapping, is seeking to utilize gyroscopes to stabilize cameras aboard planes to improve aerial photography.	
Sept. 4	In a Labor Day Manifesto, the Communist Party of America denounces violence in strikes, denying that it is an "underground" organization. The Party does call for an expansion of the recent railroad strike to create a general strike to "destroy the whole building of capitalist society and not the building of some railway station."			Lieutenant J.H. Doolittle of the U.S. Army Air Service has made the first transcontinental flight within a single day. Flying in a specially modified DH-4B Liberty 400, he flew 2,163 miles from Pablo Beach, FL, to Rockwell Field, in San Diego, in 21 hours and 20 minutes....King Alfonso of Spain welcomes the Odontological Congress to Madrid, where the latest advances in dentistry will be discussed.	*Sally, Irene and Mary* opens tonight on Broadway.
Sept. 5		The U.S. Navy has ordered Admiral Mark L. Bristol, American High Commissioner, to send a naval force to Smyrna to deal with the growing refugee crisis there.	A heat wave has killed three people in Chicago along with numerous cases of heat exhaustion, as temperatures soar to 94 degrees.		
	F *Includes campaigns, elections, federal-state relations, civil rights and liberties, crime, the judiciary, education, healthcare, poverty, urban affairs, and population.*	G *Includes formation and debate of U.S. foreign and defense policies, veterans affairs, and defense spending. (Relations with specific foreign countries are usually found under the region concerned.)*	H *Includes business, labor, agriculture, taxation, transportation, consumer affairs, monetary and fiscal policy, natural resources, pollution and industrial accidents.*	I *Includes worldwide scientific, medical and technological developments, natural phenomena, U.S. weather and natural disasters.*	J *Includes the arts, religion, scholarship, communications media, sports, entertainment, fashions, fads, and social life.*

	World Affairs	Europe	Africa & The Middle East	The Americas	Asia & The Pacific
Sep. 6		In just one week at the end of August, the German Reichsbank issued a record 22.978 billion marks.	The Egyptian government is encouraging American and European investors to open manufacturing enterprises in Egypt. Except for cigarette manufacturing, Egypt has no industries, and labor is cheap....150,000 refugees have jammed into Smyrna as Turkish troops, under the personal command of Mustafa Kemal, continue to advance.		Japanese and Russian representatives will meet today in Changchun. The conference will discuss Japanese withdrawal from northern Sakhalin, occupied by Japan since the Russian Revolution.
Sep. 7	Pressure is growing in the League of Nations Council, for the League to take a wider role in preserving world order, and supplanting the current system of domination by the concert of the Allied Powers.... The Irish Free State and the Turkish Nationalist government in Ankara have appealed to join the League of Nations....Several hundred former Austro-Hungarian noblemen are combining to appeal to the World Court for protection of their lands in Czechoslovakia against what they term confiscatory Czech land laws.		The Turks are now just 25 miles from Smyrna, where the number of refugees has swollen to 200,000. The Southern Greek Army is reported to have been surrounded. Greek casualties thus far stand at 50,000, with 15,000 having been taken prisoner. Turkish cavalry have reached the Aegean, and the Turkish army reports having captured 700 artillery pieces, 950 trucks, 11 planes, and vast quantities of small arms. French, Italian, and British marines have landed in Smyrna, and British forces have secured the banks and gas works. Italy is sending a battleship to protect the 20,000 Italian residents of Smyrna.	Brazil celebrated its 100th anniversary of independence today with the opening of a Centennial Exposition in Rio de Janerio, as 100,000 throng the streets of Rio in a mass parade down the Avenida Rio Branco. The battleships USS *Maryland* and USS *Nevada* are in Rio harbor as part of a goodwill visit.	
Sep. 8			The Greek army, now in full rout, has evacuated Smyrna, leaving chaos in its wake. The Greek cabinet has resigned. King Constantine has called on Nikolaos Kalogeropoulos to create a new government.		Forces loyal to Guangzhou warlord General Chen Chiungming have been seizing and destroying American mission property in Kaying, in Guangdong Province.... Manchurian warlord General Chang Tsolin now has 100,000 men under arms and is reportedly planning a new advance against the Beijing government dominated by warlord General Wu Peifu.
Sep. 9		William T. Cosgrave has been elected by the *Dail* as the President of the Irish Free State, to replace Arthur Griffith, who died August 12....The amount of Polish marks in circulation has increased by more than 277 percent since August 1921. The amount of Austrian marks in circulation has increased by 1,632 percent in the same time period....The Vatican has placed the works of Anatole France on its Index Expurgatorius of books not to be read by Catholics. *The Red Lily*, *Thais*, and *The Revolt of the Angels,* are the titles most harshly condemned by the Church. These books have since become the most in demand.	Turkish Nationalist forces marched into Smyrna today. In the chaos, the Greek Metropolitan, Chrysostomos, is killed by a Turkish mob.		
Sep. 10	Bolivia formally announces its withdrawal from the League of Nations, and Peru announces that it would not attend the upcoming session of League in protest against Chilean Agustin Edwards being named League president....British Prime Minister Lloyd George has accepted an invitation to speak to the League of Nations' assembly in Geneva next week....Lloyd George is expected to call for an extension of individual national accords, along the lines of this year's Washington Disarmament Conference, to reduce the risks of war.	Great Britain has signed an agreement opening up trade with Soviet Russia, even though the Soviets still refuse to recognize foreign debt claims....Germany is asking the Belgians to accept German treasury bonds maturing over a period of 18 months as reparations, rather than in gold....Germany has emerged as a major conduit for Western goods to Soviet Russia. In August, Germany shipped the Soviets 198 locomotives, and will ship 150 more by year's end. 67 percent of the manufactured goods entering Russia are from Germany.... Meanwhile Russia's New Economic Policy is encouraging agricultural production again.	Nikolaos Kalogeropoulos has failed to form a government in Greece, as popular outrage over the debacle in Asia Minor grows. Nikolaos Triantaphyllakos, former Greek High Commissioner in Constantinople, has succeeded in forming a government....Flushed with victory, the Turkish Nationalist government has laid claims to the Straits and all its prewar holdings in Eastern Thrace. Meanwhile the French and the British have announced that they are in agreement that Turkey will *not* be allowed to control the Straits.		

A	B	C	D	E
Includes developments that affect more than one world region, international organizations and important meetings of world leaders.	*Includes all domestic and regional developments in Europe, including the Soviet Union.*	*Includes all domestic and regional developments in Africa and the Middle East.*	*Includes all domestic and regional developments in Latin America, the Caribbean, and Canada.*	*Includes all domestic and regional developments in Asian and Pacific nations (and colonies).*

	U.S. Politics & Social Issues	U.S. Foreign Policy & Affairs, Defense	U.S. Economy & Environment	Science, Technology & Nature	Culture, Leisure & Lifestyle
Sept. 6				Lieutenant Ernest de Muyter of Belgium is officially declared the winner of the James Gordon Bennett international balloon race. American Captain H.E. Honeywell came in second....The Fairey Aviation Company of Great Britain is designing a long range, all-metal aircraft with an engine approaching 3,000 horsepower.	The Atlantic City Fall Pageant opened today, with 57 cities represented in the beauty pageant. 50,000 dollars are being spent on the pageant, which is expected to draw 250,000 visitors.
Sept. 7	The executive Council of the American Federation of Labor (AFL) meeting in Atlantic City today voted down calls for a general strike in support of striking railroad workers, who are trying to keep their strike going in the face of a federal court injunction.			In a report to the American Chemical Society today, sea kelp has been found to carry iodine, and has been useful in treating goiter.	
Sept. 8	Ku Klux Klan Imperial Wizard pro-temp Edward Clarke, posts a $2,000 bond in an Indianapolis court today after being indicted on bootlegging charges.	Four battleships and 15 destroyers of the Atlantic Fleet arrive in New York City today after summer maneuvers off Hampton Roads, VA. The 20,000 sailors in the force will visit for a week....The San Pedro, CA, Chamber of Commerce has warned the War Department that a Japanese firm has taken out a long-term lease for property adjacent to Ft. MacArthur. Suspicion of Asians, including Japanese, runs high on the West Coast.			Miss Mary Campbell, age 16, of Columbus, OH, has won the Miss America title in Atlantic City....Willa Cather's new novel, *One of Ours*, is published today in New York City.
Sept. 9	Anthracite miners meeting Wilkes-Barre, PA, voted to end their long strike. 155,000 miners will return to work tomorrow. United Mine Workers' President John L. Lewis, near collapse, announces that the UMW will continue to struggle for an eight-hour day.		Hundreds of families in the Fayette County coke fields of Pennsylvania have been evicted, as the mining companies turn strikers out of company housing. A total of 3,500 eviction notices have been served since the coal strike began in April.	Chicago is again scorched by record-breaking heat for this time of year, with temperatures reaching 96.4 degrees....25,000 chemists are in New York City for the annual Chemical Exposition. Topics most in vogue include the manufacturing of alcohol for industrial uses and the use of gases to control insect infestations.	The two top earning professions in the world are lawyers and movie stars, both of which can earn incomes of $1 million a year or more. Charlie Chaplin, Douglas Fairbanks, and Mary Pickford are the top earners in the movies. The third ranking profession is prize-fighter, with Jack Dempsey and Benny Leonard earning more than $500,000 a year. Belmonte, the popular Spanish matador, also earns $500,000 a year, while Enrico Caruso earns $300,000, and Irving Berlin $250,000. A New York brain surgeon earns as much as $300,000 a year. The best-paid playwright is Avery Hopgood, earning as much as $56,000 a week in 1920.
Sept. 10		New York Congressman Walter M. Chandler calls on the United States to defend the Jewish population in Palestine by force, if necessary, against the Arabs and Turks.	American automobile manufacturers in the first eight months of 1922 have already surpassed the number of cars produced in 1921, and are expected to top the 2.265 million cars produced in 1920.		

F	G	H	I	J
Includes campaigns, elections, federal-state relations, civil rights and liberties, crime, the judiciary, education, healthcare, poverty, urban affairs, and population.	*Includes formation and debate of U.S. foreign and defense policies, veterans affairs, and defense spending. (Relations with specific foreign countries are usually found under the region concerned.)*	*Includes business, labor, agriculture, taxation, transportation, consumer affairs, monetary and fiscal policy, natural resources, pollution and industrial accidents.*	*Includes worldwide scientific, medical and technological developments, natural phenomena, U.S. weather and natural disasters.*	*Includes the arts, religion, scholarship, communications media, sports, entertainment, fashions, fads, and social life.*

	World Affairs	Europe	Africa & The Middle East	The Americas	Asia & The Pacific
Sep. 11	The Financial Committee of the League of Nations is calling on Austria to drastically reduce the size of its government bureaucracy, especially in the railroads. The number of officeholders in Austria is almost equivalent to the size of the bureaucracy in the old Austro-Hungarian Empire.	A Catholic Party rally in Rome degenerated into a three-way brawl involving Fascists and Socialists, as political violence continues in Italy.	The British today formally proclaimed their Mandate over Palestine....Great Britain is shifting to a greater emphasis on air power to control Iraq in order to cut occupation costs. Eight squadrons of aircraft will assume the primary role in policing the country. This will cut costs to 20 percent of their current levels, with King Faisal's native Iraqi army to provide ground support as needed....Greek troops are evacuating the Aegean coast of Anatolia. The Greek army headquarters has been moved to the island of Chios.		
Sep. 12	The Belgian government is demanding that Germany deposit 100 million in gold marks in Belgian banks to provide security for the remaining 270 million due in reparations payments this year....British and French representatives in Geneva announce that they have accepted a plan drawn up by Lord Cecil of Great Britain to establish a system of interlocking bi- and trilateral pacts to guarantee the peace. It was also announced that the Allied Supreme Council will meet next week in Geneva, where British, French, and Italian representatives are expected to work out the details of the first pact.	The divided region of Upper Silesia is rapidly degenerating into chaos. Rioting, which included anti-Semitic violence, has caused 100 million marks worth of damage in Katowice, the capital of the Polish sector. Nine people have been killed and many others wounded. The violence is spilling over into the inflation-wracked German sector.	The 700,000 people of Smyrna, including 30,000 refugees, are without food, as relief agencies and the Turkish occupying forces struggle to restore the flow of food supplies.		The Soviet Far Eastern Republic has granted concessions to American companies for fur trapping and gold mining, and to the Sinclair Company for oil drilling in Sakhalin.
Sep. 13		France and Poland today sign a 10-year military convention. It commits both parties to resist any change in the Versailles border settlement.	A massive fire has broken out in Smyrna. In the confusion following the Greek evacuation on the 8th, the fire is raging out of control....The Soviets today condemn the Allied occupation of Constantinople. The Soviets are trying to ingratiate themselves with the Turkish Nationalists, who are now clearly in the ascendancy in Asia Minor.		
Sep. 14		Irish Free State forces have retaken Kenmare, in County Kerry, which was seized by Republican rebels last week. Meanwhile sporadic raids and ambushes continue in Dublin and in the countryside.	Turkish forces have driven the Greeks from the southern portion of the Zone of the Straits. This area has been set aside as a neutral, international zone by the Treaty of Sèvres. The Turks want to regain full control of Constantinople (Istanbul), where the British, French, and Italians maintain garrisons....The British have only 1000 men to hold the Straits at Chanak, but they are backed by the British warship HMS *Ajax*....Sir Herbert Samuel, British High Commissioner in Palestine, paid a surprise visit to the Arab Congress meeting in Jerusalem, to refute attacks on the British Mandate for the region.	Sports of all kinds are growing increasingly popular in Brazil, including tennis, rowing, and basketball. However, the supreme mania sweeping the cities is soccer.	
Sep. 15	The British cabinet met in an emergency meeting today. It was agreed to draft a joint note with France and Italy warning Mustafa Kemal's Turkish Nationalists from crossing into Europe.	The Allies are considering calling a wider conference to include Yugoslavia and Romania in discussions of the final settlement with Turkey.	The fire that has devastated Smyrna has finally died down. The Christian quarters of the city have been totally destroyed. More than $200 million in damage has been done, with more than 300,000 made homeless. In the past few days, 100,000 people have been killed in the chaos. Reports of wholesale massacres of Armenians and Greeks reported. British forces have evacuated some 180,000 Greek and Armenian refugees....Britain has ordered its naval forces in the Mediterranean to block any attempt by Turkish forces to cross the Straits into Europe.		

A	B	C	D	E
Includes developments that affect more than one world region, international organizations and important meetings of world leaders.	*Includes all domestic and regional developments in Europe, including the Soviet Union.*	*Includes all domestic and regional developments in Africa and the Middle East.*	*Includes all domestic and regional developments in Latin America, the Caribbean, and Canada.*	*Includes all domestic and regional developments in Asian and Pacific nations (and colonies).*

U.S. Politics & Social Issues	U.S. Foreign Policy & Affairs, Defense	U.S. Economy & Environment	Science, Technology & Nature	Culture, Leisure & Lifestyle	
	Under pressure from South Carolina's senators, President Warren Harding has countermanded Navy Department orders closing the Charleston Navy Yard.	The American Petroleum Institute has reported that the amount of oil produced in American between 1920 and June 1922, is equal to the amount of oil produced between 1859 and 1906. The chief reason for this increase is the increased use of the automobile.		*A Fantastic Fricassee* opens tonight on Broadway....200,000 turn out for the crowning of the Coney Island Mardi Gras king and queen in New York City this evening.	Sept. 11
The Protestant Episcopal Church's House of Bishops has voted at its annual convention in Portland to delete the word *obey* from the marriage service. The vote is 36–27. It also voted to allow the substitution of grape juice for wine in communion.	The War Department has determined that the ownership of a tract of land adjacent to Ft. MacArthur in southern California is not a threat to national security.		The British Air Ministry will begin testing a new aircraft design, the Cubaroo, which will serve as a "winged destroyer." Armed with bombs and torpedoes, it will be able to threaten battleships as far as 1,000 miles distant....German geologists are speculating that the continents drift over millions of years. This drift is said to amount to no more than a mile in 9,000 years.	A new edition of *The Greenwich Village Follies* opens tonight at the Schubert Theater in New York.... A New York City judge has struck down a suit by the Society for the Suppression of Vice, to ban three books, including D.H. Lawrence's *Women in Love*.	Sept. 12
	Bishop Cannon, of the Southern Methodist Advisory Committee of the American Near Eastern Relief, today calls upon the United States and the Western Allies to prevent "the annihilation of the Christians in the Near East."...The Army Air Service dirigible *C-2* leaves Langley Field, VA, on a transcontinental flight to California via Scott Field in Belleville, IL. Its purpose is to map a viable coast-to-coast airship route.	In Chicago, the railroad shop workers' General Conference Committee voted to authorize an end to the bitter rail strike that has snarled communications in many parts of the country.	The hottest weather temperature ever recorded is noted today in El Azizia, in the Italian colony of Libya. It reaches 136.4 degrees Fahrenheit (57.8 Celsius).	The Baltimore Orioles have won the International League Pennant, beating the Newark Bears in a double header, 6–3 and 15–10....Paavo Nurmi of Finland has broken the world's record for the 5,000-meter race, with a time of 34 minutes 35.6 seconds, in the Stockholm Stadium. Nurmi also broke the record for the three-mile run, with a time of 14 minutes 17.6 seconds.	Sept. 13
The Senate voted today to authorize a $5 million loan to Liberia. The bill was only passed by adding on a rider by Senator Borah of Idaho, to provide $20 million for Western land reclamation projects.	The American sub chaser No. 96 arrived off Mudania harbor today, evacuating 16 American nationals....The army dirigible *C-2* arrived in Akron today, after an 11-hour flight from Virginia. Its ultimate goal is Los Angeles.		The race is on between German developers of "acoustic films" and Lee De Forest's "phonofilm." The German developers of acoustic films are demonstrating it in New York City today. However, De Forest is en route from Great Britain to demonstrate his version of "talkies."	Federal Prohibition agents seize a British registered rumrunner off Long Island today. The sloop had already unloaded all but 65 cases of the 2,000 cases listed in its cargo manifest, which contains the names of numerous New York and Atlantic City hotel operators. The British consul-general may protest however, as the ship was seized seven miles out, well outside the three-mile limit of American waters.	Sept. 14
The Senate approves a revised version of the Bonus Bill today, by a vote of 36–17, though it now goes to President Warren Harding for his approval.	1,000 American nationals have been rescued from Smyrna. American marines and bluejackets remain on patrol in the city.	Film producer Adolph Zukor is suing actor Rudolf Valentino, claiming that the famed film star is trying to evade his $1,250 a week contract. Zukor's attorneys point out that Zukor's corporation has invested $40 million in its film enterprises, with $7.5 million being spent on advertising alone. They assert that this advertising is what helped Valentino rise from being a virtual unknown in 1920, to his current meteoric fame.	Horace E. Dodge's hydroplane has set a world's record of 62.3 mph as an average speed in the International Power Boat regatta in Buffalo....New York City Police Commissioner Enright addressed a convention of police commissioners today, calling radio the most efficient means of coordinating police operations. Enright predicted that within a few years most major police departments would be equipped with radios.	400,000 throng Coney Island this evening for the celebration of the Mardi Gras Revue....The Episcopalian bishops' conference in Portland today condemned "lax morality" and condemned the practice of birth control.	Sept. 15

F	G	H	I	J
Includes campaigns, elections, federal-state relations, civil rights and liberties, crime, the judiciary, education, healthcare, poverty, urban affairs, and population.	*Includes formation and debate of U.S. foreign and defense policies, veterans affairs, and defense spending. (Relations with specific foreign countries are usually found under the region concerned.)*	*Includes business, labor, agriculture, taxation, transportation, consumer affairs, monetary and fiscal policy, natural resources, pollution and industrial accidents.*	*Includes worldwide scientific, medical and technological developments, natural phenomena, U.S. weather and natural disasters.*	*Includes the arts, religion, scholarship, communications media, sports, entertainment, fashions, fads, and social life.*

	World Affairs	Europe	Africa & The Middle East	The Americas	Asia & The Pacific
Sep. 16		Mussolini's Fascist Party is growing in popularity with wealthy and middle class Italians, who see its Blackshirts as an armed defense force against Socialism.... Bullfighting is coming under fire in France, with campaigns growing to abolish the sport, which is still popular in the south of France, particularly in Toulouse and Avignon.	With Nationalist Turkish forces on the march in Anatolia, the British government appeals to the Dominions for troops to support the collapsing Greek armies. British troops are digging in on the Dardanelles, backed by heavy artillery.		
Sep. 17		The use of foreign currencies in Germany is increasing, with payments being either made in dollars or other hard currencies, or denominated in foreign currencies with provisions to pay in the equivalent number of marks. Discussion is growing of entirely repudiating the German mark, and issuing a new currency.	Eighteen hundred Armenian immigrants have arrived safely in Beirut after a grueling 500-mile journey across wild and mountainous country. The children were protected by a notorious bandit chief, Sherif Agha, who decided to protect the children.	Argentina has triumphed in the Latin American Olympic Games held in Rio de Janerio as part of Brazil's Centennial Exposition. The Argentines captured 94 points, beating out Chile with 85 points and Brazil with 56.	
Sep. 18	Hungary has been admitted to the League of Nations.	Public opinion in Britain is divided over "a new war" against Turkey. Concern is evident in both Britain and France, as both nations have significant colonial holdings with large Muslim populations....Britain is sending its entire Atlantic Fleet to reinforce its squadron in the Dardanelles.	Mustafa Kemal's Turkish forces have advanced to confront the 1,000 British troops at Chanak.... French and Italian troops are evacuated from the Asian shore of the Straits....General Pellé, French High Commissioner in Constantinople, has left the city for Smyrna to conduct direct negotiations with the Kemalists....Australia and New Zealand have agreed to send troops to support Great Britain in the Dardanelles....Only 20,000 Greek troops remain as an organized fighting force of an initial force totaling 250,000. The last Greek forces are concentrated in Eastern Thrace.		
Sep. 19		Former German Kaiser Wilhelm II, in exile in Doorn in the Netherlands, announced that he would remarry, contracting a marriage with Princess von Schoeniach-Carolath.	The Kemalist government's representatives in Smyrna informed the French today that Turkey will respect the neutrality of the Straits in exchange for the restoration of Eastern Thrace....Prime Minister Hughes of Australia warned today that while Australia will support keeping the Straits open, Australia will not fight another war to protect Greek interests....Health officials warned today that there is a real danger of plague breaking out in Smyrna. Currently only the American Red Cross staff there is prepared to deal with such an epidemic.		
Sep. 20	Allied representatives meeting in Paris have agreed to call a new international peace conference on Turkey. Britain, France, Italy, Greece, Turkey, Yugoslavia, Romania, and even Japan will be represented. However, Bulgaria, as a former Turkish ally, and Soviet Russia will not be invited.....The Canadian, Australian, and New Zealand governments today call on the British to use the League of Nations to resolve the dispute with Turkey.	Benito Mussolini addresses a mass Fascist rally in Udine, today, vowing to strengthen Italy by eliminating democratic government and establish a Fascist state.	In Paris, French Premier Raymond Poincaré has warned the British Foreign Minister that France will not support efforts to stop Turkish Nationalist forces from crossing the Straits into Europe....Britain now has some 16,000 troops in Constantinople and the Straits area, backed by strong naval forces. The British plan to increase their forces to 100,000 ground troops.	Bolivia today appeals to the League of Nations to mediate its long-standing boundary dispute with Chile. Chile's control of the Tacna-Arica region since 1879 has left Bolivia without a seacoast.	
Sep. 21			H.C. Jaquith of Near East Relief today warned that there are still 100,000 Christian refugees in and around Smyrna, and calls on the Allies to take steps to get them out.		The Federal Labour Party of Australia has come out against Australian involvement in a war with Turkey.

A	B	C	D	E
Includes developments that affect more than one world region, international organizations and important meetings of world leaders.	*Includes all domestic and regional developments in Europe, including the Soviet Union.*	*Includes all domestic and regional developments in Africa and the Middle East.*	*Includes all domestic and regional developments in Latin America, the Caribbean, and Canada.*	*Includes all domestic and regional developments in Asian and Pacific nations (and colonies).*

U.S. Politics & Social Issues	U.S. Foreign Policy & Affairs, Defense	U.S. Economy & Environment	Science, Technology & Nature	Culture, Leisure & Lifestyle	
The former King Kleagle of North Carolina is being arraigned today in Bryson City, NC, on charges of embezzling $17,000 in Ku Klux Klan funds....The new Fordney-McCumber Tariff bill contains a number of inexplicable duty free items among its numerous provisions. Ice, for example, can be imported tax free, as can volcanic lava, if it is shipped in unaltered form after an eruption.		The Executive Committee of the American Federation of Labor, in its meeting in Atlantic City, today advised its member unions that the AFL does not have the authority to call a general strike, as has been demanded by some labor leaders....Bootlegging has brought a wave of prosperity to little towns along both sides of the Canadian border, with many young men able to find work in smuggling. However, fast cars racing down back roads at night have made driving more hazardous.	Aeromarine Airways has set a new American record for carrying passengers, transporting 574 passengers last week.	A team of American yachtsmen has recaptured the Americas Cup held by Britain, after triumphing in the six-meter category, 111–104.	Sept. 16
	The army dirigible *C-2* landed safely in San Antonio today after flying 850 miles from St. Louis in 16 hours and 20 minutes. The dirigible narrowly escaped crashing into a peak of the Ozark Mountains whose altitude was improperly listed on existing maps.		German physicist Albert Einstein is now deeply involved in studying quantum theory....A mid-ocean heat wave prevails, with temperatures being reported as high as 78 degrees Fahrenheit as far out as 1,500 miles to sea in the North Atlantic. The Gulf Stream is traveling farther north, with types of tropical fish being found at unusually high latitudes.	Artists are complaining that bootleggers are monopolizing studio apartments, particularly in the Greenwich Village and Columbus Circle areas, making it difficult for bona fide artists and sculptors to secure workspaces.	Sept. 17
A study of the laws of New York State by a group of women lawyers reveals that women still lack equality with men, particularly in regards to their ability to keep their own wages and dispose of property freely.				As bootleggers and speakeasies drive up rents in Greenwich Village, artists are beginning to seek out lofts in waterfront warehouses for space to work in.	Sept. 18
President Warren Harding today vetoes the Bonus Bill that would give cash bonuses to veterans.		The United States passes the Fordney-McCumber Tariff Act. It is the highest tariff in the history of the United States. The Harding administration favors American business and assesses duties on the value of imported goods. The announced goal is to equalize the cost of American and foreign production.	Forest fires are sweeping parts of California, with eight blazes currently being fought. 70,000 acres have been burned so far, as firefighters struggle to contain the blazes.	The new play, *Orange Blossoms*, opens tonight on Broadway.	Sept. 19
The Senate failed today, by just four votes, to override President Warren Harding's veto of the Veterans' Bonus Bill. Harding's veto is expected to effectively kill any Bonus measure for the remainder of Harding's term.	The American Committee for Armenian Independence appeals to the State Department today to take active steps to press for the creation of an independent Armenian state.	A company has been formed to tint films using a process developed by Daniel Frost Comstock of the Massachusetts Institute of Technology. The process is being demonstrated today in New York City.	Sadi Lecointe of France has become the first man to fly faster than 200 mph. Lecointe set his record in a Nieuport-Delage NiD 29.	The American team has captured the Argentine Cup in international rifle shooting competition in Milan. This is the second year the American team has won, in a sport previously dominated by Switzerland.	Sept. 20
	President Warren Harding signs a joint resolution of Congress advocating a Jewish national homeland in Palestine....The army begins maneuvers on Long Island today, including coordinating air power with artillery.			President E.M. Hopkins of Dartmouth University today warned, "too many men are going to college." Hopkins called for restricting college to "an aristocracy of brains" rather than have college be a "social club."	Sept. 21

F	G	H	I	J
Includes campaigns, elections, federal-state relations, civil rights and liberties, crime, the judiciary, education, healthcare, poverty, urban affairs, and population.	*Includes formation and debate of U.S. foreign and defense policies, veterans affairs, and defense spending. (Relations with specific foreign countries are usually found under the region concerned.)*	*Includes business, labor, agriculture, taxation, transportation, consumer affairs, monetary and fiscal policy, natural resources, pollution and industrial accidents.*	*Includes worldwide scientific, medical and technological developments, natural phenomena, U.S. weather and natural disasters.*	*Includes the arts, religion, scholarship, communications media, sports, entertainment, fashions, fads, and social life.*

	World Affairs	Europe	Africa & The Middle East	The Americas	Asia & The Pacific
Sep. 22	The British Dominions, Canada, Australia, and New Zealand, today voted with the majority of League states to call on the Allies to turn the situation with Turkey over to the League of Nations for resolution, breaking with Great Britain, which wants to keep the League out of the dispute.	The devaluation of the German mark has forced many Germans to revert to barter. Schools are accepting tuition payments in rye, a power company is accepting eggs, flour, or potatoes in payment, and doctors are accepting payments in bread and butter.	Arabs are boycotting elections for the Palestinian Legislative Council....British troops are being sent into Transjordan to suppress guerilla resistance there....Turkish troops are reported to be deporting Christian refugees in Smyrna into the interior, where their fate is uncertain....The Soviets have moved two divisions of troops to Batum near the Turkish border to be ready for "all eventualities."		
Sep. 23	Rumors are flying of a possible Franco-Turkish alliance. Such an alliance would secure France's foothold in Syria and Lebanon, while increasing the isolation of Soviet Russia.	The Polish Parliament has enacted a scheme to build a seaport at Gdynia on the Baltic coast. This will enable the Poles to bypass the port of Danzig, with its mostly German population....More than 160,000 new houses have been constructed in Great Britain under a new program of subsidized housing.	Raymond Poincaré, Prime Minister of France, has issued the Paris Note with British Foreign Minister Lord Curzon and Italian Ambassador Count Sforza. The Paris Note is a peace offering to Mustafa Kemal, offering to support the Nationalists' claims to Greek controlled Eastern Thrace and withdraw allied troops from Constantinople....The Near East Relief Committee reports that the fighting in Anatolia has produced a half a million refugees, including 15,000 orphans.		An American oil company has been granted a drilling concession on 300 acres around Baku. The Soviets are trying to bring in American capital to boost their oil production.
Sep. 24		Bulgaria will hold a national referendum to decide the fate of cabinet ministers who supported the disastrous decision to go to war with Serbia and Greece in 1913.			The Changchun Conference has broken up, with the Japanese refusing to withdraw from the northern part of the island of Sakhalin.
Sep. 25			The Greek government is appealing to exiled Prime Minister Venizelos to intercede with the Allies to get them to continue to support Greek claims to Eastern Thrace.	Matanzas, Cuba, has become a center for the smuggling of alcohol, drugs, and illegal aliens into the United States, with some 7,000 aliens in Cuba seeking entry into the United States....Canada is planning a trade exhibition in Shanghai to garner a greater percentage of the growing trade with China.	
Sep. 26		The Salonika garrison of 8,000 men has mutinied in Greece, demanding the abdication of King Constantine and the arrest of former prime ministers Gounaris and Stratos, weakened by the disastrous defeat of the Greek army in Turkey. Martial law has been declared in Athens as garrisons on Mytilene, Chios, and Crete have joined the rebellion. Colonels Plastiras and Gonatas have formed a Revolutionary Committee, which has been joined by the crews of warships in Mytilene and Piraeus.	American trade with South Africa is growing, with imports from the United States surpassing trade with Great Britain in certain areas, such as printed matter and canned meats....The British have begun preparations to begin evacuating their nationals from Constantinople as war with the Turkish Nationalists looms. Meanwhile the Grand Vizier and the Foreign Minister of the Ottoman Sultan's rump government in Constantinople have resigned. Turkey's disastrous defeat in World War I has undermined confidence in the centuries old Ottoman Empire, which now only survives in Constantinople under Allied protection.		Japan today denied rumors that it is secretly supplying arms to White Russian General Dieterichs in Siberia and Manchurian warlord General Chang Tsolin. General Chang and the White Russians are said to be working together against the spread of Soviet influence.
Sep. 27		King Constantine of Greece has abdicated in the wake of mass popular rebellion. The cabinet has also resigned. Crown Prince George will succeed as King George II.	Horace Rumbold, British High Commissioner in Constantinople, opens direct talks today with Mustafa Kemal's Nationalist government, as British troops continue to arrive in Chanak....British authorities are monitoring the situation on the Northwest Frontier of India carefully, as Muslim unrest on both sides of the Afghan border grows. Sympathy for Turkey runs high among British India's millions of Muslim subjects.		

A	B	C	D	E
Includes developments that affect more than one world region, international organizations and important meetings of world leaders.	*Includes all domestic and regional developments in Europe, including the Soviet Union.*	*Includes all domestic and regional developments in Africa and the Middle East.*	*Includes all domestic and regional developments in Latin America, the Caribbean, and Canada.*	*Includes all domestic and regional developments in Asian and Pacific nations (and colonies).*

U.S. Politics & Social Issues	U.S. Foreign Policy & Affairs, Defense	U.S. Economy & Environment	Science, Technology & Nature	Culture, Leisure & Lifestyle	
President Warren Harding has signed the Cable Act: American women will no longer automatically lose their citizenship when marrying a foreign citizen, unless she lives abroad with him for two years. In addition, women marrying American citizens do not automatically gain citizenship. However, women who marry aliens "ineligible for citizenship," particularly Asians, will lose their citizenship.				Daylight Savings Time ends tonight in the United States....College football season starts today, with favorite Yale playing Bates, and promising Penn State facing St. Bonaventure.	Sept. 22
An Illinois grand jury today handed down 214 indictments in connection with the massacre of nonunion workers at a mine near Herrin, IL. Six men, including two union officials, have been indicted for murder.		The United States Supreme Court has upheld the injunction against striking rail workers.		Bertold Brecht's new play, *Drummers in the Night*, opens in Munich....An automobile exhibition of enclosed cars opened today in New York City. Fully enclosed vehicles are increasing in popularity. Dark, conservative colors are in. A Hudson coach retails for $1,770. Standard equipment on the popular Studebaker line now includes front and rear bumpers, trunk racks, and nickel-plated radiator shells.	Sept. 23
		Demand is growing for fast speedboats, preferably 75–100 footers. The reason: bootleggers are stocking up for lucrative winter runs from Cuba and the Bahamas to Florida.	An expedition en route to resupply the Canadian scientific party on Wrangell Island in the Siberian Arctic has become marooned in the Arctic ice. A rescue expedition on sledges may be able to make the 800-mile trek from Alaska, but not before February.	Secret Service agents in Chicago have broken up the largest counterfeiting ring in the country, seizing $200,000 in bogus notes.	Sept. 24
			The League of Nations has convened a Serological Conference in Geneva, with the goal of standardizing medical procedures....Roy C. Andrews, leader of the American Museum of Natural History's third Asiatic expedition, has reported finding "vast fossil fields" with rich Cretaceous and Tertiary deposits in the Mongolian interior.	Co-eds at Northwestern University in Illinois have pledged not to date men on Mondays, Tuesdays, and Thursdays in the coming academic year. The purpose is so that campus athletes will have enough time to train for upcoming games.	Sept. 25
Georgia Senator Thomas E. Watson, has died. Watson, a populist, was also a member of the Ku Klux Klan.					Sept. 26
	The U.S. Navy has carried out its first test of large scale torpedo bombing off the Virginia Capes. In maneuvers, a squadron of 18 torpedo planes attack three battleships, and score eight hits in just 25 minutes, theoretically "sinking" the battleship USS *Arkansas*. Debate is bitter between advocates of big gun battleships, and proponents of aviation. Battleship proponents retort that the attack was made under ideal weather conditions and that the ships were not using anti-aircraft guns.		Archaeologists have reported finding the ruins of Native American copper mines, and a substantial town, on Isle Royale in Lake Superior. The ruins date back as far as 2,000 to 3,000 years ago.	New York's Society for the suppression of Vice loses another legal battle today, failing to stop the publication of Petronius' *Satyricon*. The judge noted that the law is not intended "to destroy literature or anathematize all historical manners and morals different from our own or to close the treasure house of the past."	Sept. 27

F	G	H	I	J
Includes campaigns, elections, federal-state relations, civil rights and liberties, crime, the judiciary, education, healthcare, poverty, urban affairs, and population.	*Includes formation and debate of U.S. foreign and defense policies, veterans affairs, and defense spending. (Relations with specific foreign countries are usually found under the region concerned.)*	*Includes business, labor, agriculture, taxation, transportation, consumer affairs, monetary and fiscal policy, natural resources, pollution and industrial accidents.*	*Includes worldwide scientific, medical and technological developments, natural phenomena, U.S. weather and natural disasters.*	*Includes the arts, religion, scholarship, communications media, sports, entertainment, fashions, fads, and social life.*

	World Affairs	Europe	Africa & The Middle East	The Americas	Asia & The Pacific
Sep. 28		Revolutionary forces, under Colonels Plastiras and Gonatas have entered Athens to cheering crowds. The Revolutionary Committee has ordered King Constantine and Queen Sophia to leave the country, along with Constantine's brothers, Prince Andrew and Prince Nicholas, while arresting top military commanders responsible for the defeat in Anatolia.	Raisuli, the leader of the Moroccan rebels in the western part of Spanish Morocco, has surrendered to Spanish authorities....British Prime Minister Lloyd George informed Horace Rumbold, British High Commissioner in Constantinople, that the British government will support war against Kemal, if necessary.	Canada is requesting the return of some of the 19,000 Canadian boxcars, one-eighth of Canada's rolling stock, by American railroads. The cars have accumulated in the United States during the recent long rail strike.	
Sep. 29		Benito Mussolini has won the support of the Pope and of King Victor Emmanuel III, as a bulwark against Socialism.	Mustafa Kemal reinforces Turkish forces confronting the British at Chanak to 4,500 men....The British have intercepted a top secret cable from the Soviets to Mustafa Kemal, urging him to attack the Allies.... The British government has sent High Commissioner Rumbold an ultimatum to give to Kemal, demanding Turkish withdrawal from the Chanak area.		
Sep. 30		Former King Constantine of Greece has left the country with his wife and brothers for exile in Italy. Sotior Krokidas has been appointed the new prime minister of Greece by the Revolutionary Committee.... The Soviet government in Russia has instituted conscription....Benito Mussolini has Blackshirt units take control of Bolzano and Trent.	High Commissioner Rumbold receives a message from Mustafa Kemal, offering a settlement and agreeing not to let his troops before Chanak provoke an incident....Rumbold decides, on his own authority, not to deliver the British ultimatum....Kemal has cabled Rumbold, offering to meet with the British at Mudania on the Asiatic coast of the Sea of Marmora to discuss a settlement.		It is confirmed today that Japanese officers in Siberia have been secretly supplying arms to Manchurian warlord General Chang Tsolin, via White Russian forces in Siberia. 32 truckloads of arms, including many left by the Czech Legion in its retreat through Siberia in 1920, have found their way into General Chang's hands.
Oct. 1		The Czech government announces that it will continue its policy of reducing the amount of currency in circulation, in an effort to control rising prices....Colonel Gonatas, leader of the new military junta in Greece, declares that Greece's new goal is the defense of Eastern Thrace from the Turks....The Austrian krone now has fallen to where 74,600 kronen are needed to equal $1. Meat sells for 50,000 kronen a pound, and taxi fares are multiplied at 9,000 times the meter reading.	British troops continue to reinforce Chanak, commanding the Dardanelles Straits, backed by planes from the aircraft carrier HMS *Argus*....The RAF officially takes charge of British operations in Iraq. The British hope to use air power, in conjunction with King Faisal's ground troops, to police the troubled Mandate.		
Oct. 2		Tomaso Tittoni, President of the Italian Senate, warned today that the Italian government, running an annual deficit of 2.2 billion lire, must control its spending....Britain today recognized the new Greek government.	Dr. Esther Lovejoy, of the American Women's Hospital, warns today that several hundred thousand Christians remained trapped in Smyrna, and that Turkish atrocities there are continuing....Turkish Nationalist leader Mustafa Kemal has offered to accept a cease-fire, if the Greeks will hand over Eastern Thrace to Turkish control.	American Federation of Labor leader Samuel Gompers today denounced America's policy of nonrecognition of the Obregon government in Mexico, at a Pan-American conference of labor leaders. Gompers maintains that nonrecognition only adds to instability in Mexico, while numerous exile groups in El Paso, San Antonio, and Havana continue to plot revolution.	
Oct. 3		The Irish Free State government is offering an amnesty to all Republican rebels who surrender and recognize the authority of the Free State government.	Horace Rumbold, British High Commissioner in Constantinople, and representatives of the Allies met with Ismet Pasha, commander of the Turkish Nationalists in western Anatolia, at Mudania today, on the coast of the Sea of Marmora, to negotiate a settlement to the continuing military and diplomatic stand-off between the two countries. In this, the British are bowing to pressure by the French and Italians who want a settlement with Kemal....France has reduced its army of occupation in Syria to 35,000 men, from 70,000. The French are also appointing Syrian officials to help administer the country and cut costs.	Chilean Senator Rivera today denounced proposals to hold a plebiscite in the disputed Tacna Arica region. Rivera warns that plebiscite will result in Chile losing the area to Peru.	

A	B	C	D	E
Includes developments that affect more than one world region, international organizations and important meetings of world leaders.	*Includes all domestic and regional developments in Europe, including the Soviet Union.*	*Includes all domestic and regional developments in Africa and the Middle East.*	*Includes all domestic and regional developments in Latin America, the Caribbean, and Canada.*	*Includes all domestic and regional developments in Asian and Pacific nations (and colonies).*

U.S. Politics & Social Issues	U.S. Foreign Policy & Affairs, Defense	U.S. Economy & Environment	Science, Technology & Nature	Culture, Leisure & Lifestyle	
			A relief expedition sent to rescue a party of Arctic explorers trapped in the sea ice en route to Wrangell Island in the Siberian Arctic, has turned back in defeat. A new relief expedition will have to wait until possibly July of next year.		Sept. 28
	Two U.S. Army Air Service pilots are preparing to attempt the first nonstop transcontinental flight, from San Diego to New York City. The planned flight will take 32 hours, and require a specially built craft, with a capacity of carrying 725 gallons of fuel.		11 richly illustrated sheets of parchment, containing two cantos of Dante's *Divine Comedy*, have been found in the archives of Chiavari.	D.W. Griffith's film *Two Orphans* debuts today....Josiah H. Penniman, acting provost of the University of Pennsylvania, today called on colleges to open their door to the masses, asserting that the right to an education is fundamental....College football season gets underway in earnest today as Harvard, Princeton, Dartmouth, Columbia, and other schools begin play today.	Sept. 29
	Army Air Service pilots are testing an enormous new three engine bomber, The Owl, with a 107-foot wing span.		The U.S. Bureau of Fisheries is releasing 1,500 bottles to drift in the North Atlantic to study the flow of ocean currents.		Sept. 30
American Federation of Labor President Samuel Gompers denounces Attorney General Harry Daugherty for getting a court injunction to stop the recent nationwide railroad strike. Gompers and other labor leaders are calling for Daugherty's impeachment.		The American Bankers' Association convention opens in New York City today, with some 10,000 bankers expected from around the country.		Dr. John Grier Hibben, President of Princeton University, in his opening address to students there, cautions against students frequently attending movies, calling them "an anaesthetic to the intellect" that saps mental energies....Pittsburgh Police report that there are some 5,000 narcotics addicts on the streets of Pittsburgh, with an average of $35,000 a day being spent on drugs.	Oct. 1
An African American is lynched today when a mob of 1,000 people descended on the County Jail at Union Springs, AL, seeking another African American who was accused of shooting two White men. The accused African American had already been taken from the scene.	The U.S. Navy today dispatches a flotilla of 12 destroyers from Norfolk, VA, to the Middle East to protect American lives and property there.	The New York and Amsterdam Stock Exchanges are now directly linked by cable, allowing swift arbitrage. Businessmen can now take advantage of price differentials in securities, currencies, and commodities between Europe and the United States more quickly than ever.	Polar explorer Roald Amundsen is wintering at Wainwright, AK, readying for a flight across the North Pole to Spitzbergen in one jump. The flight is planned for May or June 1923....The French Museum of Natural History is sending a major expedition, under Dr. Millet Horain, to French West Africa.	Famed dancer Isadora Duncan is finally admitted to the United States today after being delayed by immigration. The reason for the delay being Ms. Duncan's lengthy stay in Soviet Russia....*The Yankee Princess* and *The Lady in Ermine*, two Broadway musicals, open tonight in New York City.	Oct. 2
Rebecca L. Felton, (D-GA) has been appointed by Governor Thomas W. Hardwick of Georgia to the U.S. Senate. At age 87, Ms. Felton will serve out the term of Senator Thomas E. Watson, becoming the first woman ever to serve as a U.S. Senator.	The Army Air Service is planning a nonstop flight from the Mexican border to Canada. The flight will be commanded by veteran airman Lieutenant Leland S. Andrews.		Charles Francis Jenkins has made the first public demonstration of fax and television technology. He transmitted photographs via telephone wire from Washington, DC, to U.S. Naval radio station NOF at Anacostia. NOF then broadcast the photographs over the air back to the post office in Washington.		Oct. 3

F	G	H	I	J
Includes campaigns, elections, federal-state relations, civil rights and liberties, crime, the judiciary, education, healthcare, poverty, urban affairs, and population.	*Includes formation and debate of U.S. foreign and defense policies, veterans affairs, and defense spending. (Relations with specific foreign countries are usually found under the region concerned.)*	*Includes business, labor, agriculture, taxation, transportation, consumer affairs, monetary and fiscal policy, natural resources, pollution and industrial accidents.*	*Includes worldwide scientific, medical and technological developments, natural phenomena, U.S. weather and natural disasters.*	*Includes the arts, religion, scholarship, communications media, sports, entertainment, fashions, fads, and social life.*

	World Affairs	Europe	Africa & The Middle East	The Americas	Asia & The Pacific
Oct. 4	A French business mission is in Moscow today. The Soviets have been seeking a rapprochement with France, offering to recognize the validity of prewar French loans to Russia, in exchange for a diplomatic settlement, effectively renewing the pre-World War *entente*.	Austria today negotiated the Geneva Protocol with the Allies. Austria will receive a major loan to stabilize its economy. In exchange, Austria renounces any plans to unite with Germany....A new government was organized in Czechoslovakia today, with Agrarian Party leader Antonin Svehla becoming the new prime minister. The out-going premier, Dr. Eduard Benes, will remain as Minister of Foreign Affairs.		The Canadian Cabinet Council today announced the merger of the Grand Trunk Railway and the Canadian Northern to form the Canadian National Railways....Forest fires rage through northern Ontario today, destroying three mining settlements and cutting rail and telegraph communication with a wide area.	
Oct. 5		Fascist leader Benito Mussolini today demands that Italy hold general elections, adding that the party that wins a majority should automatically be given three-fifths of the seats in the Chamber of Deputies. Presently the Fascists, while growing in numbers and belligerence, control just 46 of the 535 seats in the Chamber....The Province of Trent, ceded to Italy by Austria after World War I and still retaining a large German-speaking minority, was put under military control today after 5,000 Fascists paraded into the region, demanding that "Italian dignity" be upheld by the government.			White Russian troops clash with forces of the Soviet Far Eastern republic at Khabarovsk, as the Soviets continue to push closer to Vladivostok.
Oct. 6	British Foreign Minister Lord Curzon arrived in Paris this evening, beginning discussions with French Premier Poincaré about the current situation in the Near East, as the Allies struggle to adopt a common front to the Turks.	Fascist leader Benito Mussolini met with his top leaders today, to discuss plans for a March on Rome....Bulgaria today announced that it would remain neutral in the struggle between Greece and Turkey, calling for a neutralized Eastern Thrace as a buffer zone....Former King Constantine of Greece is settling into exile at Palermo, Sicily.	The British walk out of negotiations at Mudania today in the face of Turkish demands to occupy Eastern Thrace. France and Italy favor a settlement with the Turks.		
Oct. 7	Britain and France today reach an agreement in Paris, to offer the Turks Eastern Thrace if they will uphold the neutrality of the Straits.		Prominent Conservative leader Andrew Bonar Law has broken with Lloyd George's government, stating openly that Britain should only try to stop Kemal from occupying Eastern Thrace if backed by the Allies and the United States. Lloyd George is finding himself increasingly isolated on the issue of the defense of the Straits....The British battleship HMS *Benbow* is en route from Malta for Constantinople to reinforce the British squadron there.		
Oct. 8		Italy denounces its prior agreement with the government of Greece over the Dodecanese Islands in the Aegean. Italy was to have handed the islands over to Greece in exchange for a portion of southwestern Anatolia. However, this plan has been made obsolete by the defeat of the Greek army in Asia Minor and the rise of the Turkish Nationalists under Mustafa Kemal. Therefore, the Italians insist, despite British protests, on holding onto the islands....Antonin Svehla has succeeded Edvard Benes as Prime Minister of Czechosolovakia.	The Allies reopened negotiations with the Turks at Mudania today....Mobs thronged the streets of Cairo, cheering the wife of Egyptian nationalist leader Saad Zaghlul as she joins him in exile in Gibraltar....200 artillery pieces now defend British positions at Chanak, backed by air patrols and naval support. Two Turkish corps stand by near Chanak, but are maintaining their distance.		
Oct. 9		Sir William Horwood, Commissioner of the London Metropolitan Police, has been poisoned by arsenic-laced chocolates....The Labour Party has called on British Prime Minister Lloyd George to resign, as resistance to Lloyd George's continued push toward renewed war with Turkey.			

A	B	C	D	E
Includes developments that affect more than one world region, international organizations and important meetings of world leaders.	*Includes all domestic and regional developments in Europe, including the Soviet Union.*	*Includes all domestic and regional developments in Africa and the Middle East.*	*Includes all domestic and regional developments in Latin America, the Caribbean, and Canada.*	*Includes all domestic and regional developments in Asian and Pacific nations (and colonies).*

U.S. Politics & Social Issues	U.S. Foreign Policy & Affairs, Defense	U.S. Economy & Environment	Science, Technology & Nature	Culture, Leisure & Lifestyle	
Edward Young Clarke is resigning as Imperial Wizard of the Ku Klux Klan, claiming to be the victim of "persecution" by his enemies. Former Imperial Wizard Colonel William J. Stevens will resume the post.		30,000 seals were taken in the Bering Sea this summer, up from 26,500 last year. 820 whales were also taken, yielding 30,000 barrels of oil.		The World Series begins today between the New York Giants (NL) and the New York Yankees (AL), with Grantland Rice's play-by-play coverage being broadcast live from the Polo Grounds in New York by WJZ of Newark, NJ. Three other radio stations will also cover the World Series.	Oct. 4
A group of Czech settlers in Texas is asking the Mexican government for terms for setting up a colony in Mexico after continuing persecution by the Ku Klux Klan in Texas.	Church leaders, while divided on whether the United States should involve itself militarily in the Near East to protect Christians there, are united in wanting the United States to be an active participant in any new international conference to determine the status of the region, claims Reverend Charles Macfarland of the Federal Council of Churches in a speech today.	Draft horses are still in heavy demand in many parts of the country, despite the growing popularity of cars and trucks. Breeders of prized Percherons and Clydesdales can still command respectable prices.	General Electric engineers in Pittsfield, MA, have developed transformers that can produce 1.5 million volts, a new record. Just this year engineers developed transformers that can produce one million volts.	The second game of the World Series ends in a 3–3 tie with the game finally being called on account of darkness after 10 innings....*The Revue Russe* opens tonight in New York City.	Oct. 5
			American pilots Lieutenants John Macready and Oakely Kelley have set a new air endurance record, with a flight of 35 hours 18 minutes in a Fokker T-2.	The U.S. government has banned liquor on all ships entering American ports....Co-eds at the University of Wisconsin are protesting a recent ordinance classifying the Junior Promenade and the Military Ball, the high points of student social life, as "public dances," to which female students are forbidden to attend on penalty of expulsion.	Oct. 6
	The convention of bankers has adjourned in New York, with agreement being reached among the body of its membership to support an American policy of settlement of international debts, rather than trying to collect them in full from war ravaged countries.			A definitive edition of Mark Twain's works, in 35 volumes, is being published.	Oct. 7
			An analysis of the test flight of the new Army-Curtiss Racer No. 2, by Lieutenant R.L. Maughan on Long Island, shows that the test pilot has set a new world's speed record, of 220 miles per hour.	The New York Giants have won the World Series, defeating the American League New York Yankees in four of five games.	Oct. 8
			Chicago is enveloped in thick clouds as a temperature inversion, pollution, and a lack of wind combine to make city smog enshroud the metropolis in darkness.	Czech writer Karel Capek's play *R.U.R.* (Rossum's Universal Robots) opens tonight at the Garrick Theater in New York City. This is the first use of the term *robot* in the English language.	Oct. 9

F	G	H	I	J
Includes campaigns, elections, federal-state relations, civil rights and liberties, crime, the judiciary, education, healthcare, poverty, urban affairs, and population.	*Includes formation and debate of U.S. foreign and defense policies, veterans affairs, and defense spending. (Relations with specific foreign countries are usually found under the region concerned.)*	*Includes business, labor, agriculture, taxation, transportation, consumer affairs, monetary and fiscal policy, natural resources, pollution and industrial accidents.*	*Includes worldwide scientific, medical and technological developments, natural phenomena, U.S. weather and natural disasters.*	*Includes the arts, religion, scholarship, communications media, sports, entertainment, fashions, fads, and social life.*

	World Affairs	Europe	Africa & The Middle East	The Americas	Asia & The Pacific
Oct. 10		The Catholic Bishops of Ireland have declared their support for the Irish Free State as the legitimate government of Ireland, and denying communion to any Republican rebels who continue to resist.	Defeated, Greece today signed an armistice with the Turks. Greece plans to secure the Aegean coast after World War I have ended in total defeat....Britain signed an alliance with the kingdom of Iraq. Under the terms of the alliance, the British will retain bases in Iraq, and the right to transport troops through the country. Iraq will eventually receive full independence.		
Oct. 11		Benito Mussolini addresses a mass rally of Fascists in Cremona, Italy, today, the mob chanting: "To Rome!"...German Chancellor Wirth cut short his vacation today, returning to Berlin to deal with the continuing decline of the German mark. Germans are increasingly rejecting their own currency, demanding payment, wherever possible, in hard foreign currency....Bombs go off in Dublin today, igniting sporadic fighting that continues on into the night.	The Allies conclude the Convention of Mudania with the Turkish Nationalists. The Allies will return Eastern Thrace and Adrianople to Turkish control. Greek troops will be withdrawn. The Allies will evacuate Constantinople on conclusion of a new peace treaty with Turkey. Turkey in exchange will accept the neutralization of the Straits under international supervision. Britain is still demanding payment for £100 million in occupation costs, which the Kemal government refuses to pay.	American investors are growing interested in real estate development in Jamaica, where tourism is showing new potential.	
Oct. 12			Turkish troops push forward today near Chanak and Ismid.	Maximo de Alvear Pachecho has succeeded fellow UCR party member Juan Yrigoyen Alem as President of Argentina....American Supreme Court Chief Justice William Howard Taft will arbitrate a dispute between Britain and Costa Rica over control of oil field concessions.	Forces loyal to warlord General Hsu Tung-chi, have captured Fuzhou, the capital of Fujian Province, forcing the governor to flee.
Oct. 13		Albania announces that a constituent assembly will be called to write a constitution for the struggling Balkan country....French War Minister Andre Maginot warned today that France needs an army of at least 660,000 men, including six divisions in the occupied Rhineland zone, in order to defend the homeland. Currently the entire French army, including troops stationed in colonies, come to 660,000....The city of Berlin is bankrupt, with her debt increasing by one billion marks in just three months.	Meletios, Greek Orthodox Patriarch of Constantinople, today warned that as many as 1.25 million Christians could be forced to flee Asia Minor, Constantinople, and Eastern Thrace. Meletios indicated that to deal with this exodus, only about $1 million has been raised in relief funds. American diplomats in Greece warned that there are 80,000 refugees in the port of Mytilene alone, their state, with the oncoming winter, uncertain.		
Oct. 14	The British government announces a plan to offer Germany a 2- to 4-year moratorium on her reparations payments. Britain is concerned that the fragile German economy will collapse, leading to a Communist revolution there. The French are expected to propose seizing more German assets while continuing to put pressure on Germany to pay. The British plan also includes inviting the United States into a revised debt commission.		Turkish Nationalist leader Mustafa Kemal makes a triumphal entry into the ancient Turkish capital of Brusa today, as mobs thronged the parade route. Turkey has been the only one of the former Central Powers of World War I to be able to force a revision of the terms of peace in her favor.		American cars are sweeping the growing Shanghai market, with 178 being imported in the first six months of the year. America's closest competitor is Germany, with 47 cars. American cars are competitive in price and quality.
Oct. 15		Mobs rampage through the streets as thousands of armed Communists disrupt a meeting of the ultranationalist Union for Freedom and Order in Berlin, leaving four dead....Ferdinand, King of Romania, and his wife Queen Marie are crowned rulers of Transylvania today at Alba Julia.	Greek troops have begun retreating from Eastern Thrace.		The Appellate Court of Osaka today issued a ruling emancipating geisha girls from contracts binding them to servitude signed by their parents.
	A *Includes developments that affect more than one world region, international organizations and important meetings of world leaders.*	B *Includes all domestic and regional developments in Europe, including the Soviet Union.*	C *Includes all domestic and regional developments in Africa and the Middle East.*	D *Includes all domestic and regional developments in Latin America, the Caribbean, and Canada.*	E *Includes all domestic and regional developments in Asian and Pacific nations (and colonies).*

U.S. Politics & Social Issues	U.S. Foreign Policy & Affairs, Defense	U.S. Economy & Environment	Science, Technology & Nature	Culture, Leisure & Lifestyle	
		The Actors' Equity Association is pressing film censorship czar Will Hays to redress grievances by actors, which include being forced to work in dangerous conditions and at night.		Losses by the Hamilton County Bank in Cincinnati are revealed today, after the September 28 robbery. Five gunmen made off with $222,000 in cash and bonds.... Britain is refusing American requests to search ships beyond the three-mile limit of American waters. Rumrunners operating from British possessions in the Bahamas and Bermuda are raking in enormous profits shipping in illicit "hooch."... The new musical *Queen O' Hearts* opens tonight in New York City.	Oct. 10
	The army dirigible *C-2* arrived in El Paso today en route back to Langley Field, VA, from California.	Efforts are being made to establish a professional association of baseball players to fight for player rights and better wages and working conditions. Baseball team owners, however, are hostile to the proposed plan....Coal production is back up to 1920 levels, despite a long and bitter mine strike this year.			Oct. 11
			A heavy Martin transport took top honors at the *Detroit News* trophy race for multi-engine planes at Mount Clemens, MI, today, with an average speed of 105.1 miles per hour....A study by Harvard University, in conjunction with Stanford and the University of California has proved that botulism can be killed by sufficient heat....French scientist and churchman Abbe Estines of Toulouse has invented a device that uses the principal of radioactivity to locate deposits of oil.	The *Resolute* arrived in New York City today, becoming the first liner affected by Attorney General Harry Daugherty's instructions that American ships are subject to American Prohibition laws. The ships band played *How Dry I Am* and *Sahara* as she pulled into dock. The news of the liquor ban came is mid-voyage and bartenders were forced to seal the ships ample liquor supply.	Oct. 12
			The American Curtiss Aviation Company unveiled its Curtiss R-6 model today.		Oct. 13
	A flotilla of 12 American destroyers arrived at Gibraltar today en route to Turkish waters. Sailors are practicing battle drills if landing shore parties proves necessary in the chaotic region.		Bronislaw Malinowski's *Argonauts of the Western Pacific*, his anthropological study of Melanesian cultures, is being published....The newly organized American Society for the Control of Cancer is declaring the week of November 12 National Cancer Week, in an effort to draw attention to the causes of the dreaded disease.	The first automated telephone switchboard is installed at the Pennsylvania Exchange in New York City. 9,000 phone users on the Exchange will now be dialing numbers directly instead of relying on an operator....Britain is building the world's largest sports stadium in London. Set to open in 1924, it will have a seating capacity of 125,000, 50,000 more than the Yale Bowl.... Archibald Marshall has published a new novel, *Pippin*.	Oct. 14
A study of death row inmates in New York's Sing Sing Prison shows that most people convicted of capital crimes are poor. The 26 men on death row had an average wealth of $15 per person.	American inventors Lester Barlow and Glenn Martin today revealed that the U.S. military had drawn up plans to make a bombing attack on Berlin in World War I. The long range raid, until now classified top secret, was interrupted by the signing of the Armistice.		The French Air Force is testing a new, all-metal night bomber, capable of carrying several tons of bombs. Despite weight considerations, the trend toward all-metal aircraft is growing as speeds and engine power increase.		Oct. 15

F	G	H	I	J
Includes campaigns, elections, federal-state relations, civil rights and liberties, crime, the judiciary, education, healthcare, poverty, urban affairs, and population.	*Includes formation and debate of U.S. foreign and defense policies, veterans affairs, and defense spending. (Relations with specific foreign countries are usually found under the region concerned.)*	*Includes business, labor, agriculture, taxation, transportation, consumer affairs, monetary and fiscal policy, natural resources, pollution and industrial accidents.*	*Includes worldwide scientific, medical and technological developments, natural phenomena, U.S. weather and natural disasters.*	*Includes the arts, religion, scholarship, communications media, sports, entertainment, fashions, fads, and social life.*

	World Affairs	Europe	Africa & The Middle East	The Americas	Asia & The Pacific
Oct. 16	The Allies are discussing the details of a peace conference to settle outstanding disputes with Turkey. It is agreed to hold the conference in neutral Switzerland, probably at Lausanne. The question of how the Soviets will be represented without formal diplomatic recognition is still under debate.	Mussolini meets with his chief lieutenants in Milan today....The Blackshirts now have a headquarters established at Perugia, controlling units around Rome....Blackshirt units are in position at Civitavecchia, Monterotonda, Tivoli, and Foligno.... French Premier Raymond Poincaré is expected to press the French Parliament to ratify the Washington Naval accords. Opposition to the accords, which reduces France's navy down to the size of Italy's, is unpopular, but are financially necessary.		Britain is allowing Canada to negotiate a new naval treaty for the Great Lakes directly with the United States.	
Oct. 17	Britain today called on Italy to restore the Dodecanese Islands off the coast of Turkey to Greece. The British fear that they will be handed over to Turkey.	Unemployed workers leave Glasgow today in a mass hunger march on London in protest against Lloyd George's government....Berlin police raid the headquarters of the Communist newspaper *Red Flag*, in a massive crackdown on dissidents in Germany.			
Oct. 18	The Fourth Session of the International Labor Conference convenes in Geneva today, chaired by Viscount Burnham of Great Britain. One issue to be decided is the creation of statistics on immigration and emigration.		The Allies today refused to admit Turkish gendarmes, destined for Eastern Thrace, to pass through Constantinople. Meanwhile vast numbers of Christians are fleeing Eastern Thrace as the Greek army pulls out of the region.	The United States and Canada have reached a preliminary agreement to complete the disarmament of the Great Lakes, phasing out the last warships in operation on them and replacing them with revenue cutters.	
Oct. 19		Lloyd George's government, in power since 1915, collapses in Britain today, as Conservative Members of Parliament meet at the Carleton House and voted to leave the coalition....Fascist leader Benito Mussolini signs an alliance with ultra-nationalist Italian poet Gabriele d'Annunzio, vowing to combine forces. Meanwhile, in Milan, Communists have begun organizing a force of Red Guards, as Italy slips nearer to civil war.			
Oct. 20	The French are calling for a new international conference to discuss war debts. The French propose imposing rigorous controls over all aspects of the German economy, to put its finances on a sound basis and extract the greatest possible sums for reparations payments. This runs counter to British proposals for a debt moratorium and a more lenient schedule of reparations payments.	A. Bonar Law is busy working to put together a new Conservative government, lining up support within his party along the way. Stanley Baldwin, will be made Chancellor of the Exchequer, while Lord Curzon will continue as Foreign Minister.... The German mark has fallen to the point where 40 marks are worth just one cent in American money, as the financially strapped German government continues to pour more paper money into circulation.	The Greek exodus from Eastern Thrace is leaving Adrianople and other major towns nearly empty, as throngs flee before the Turks can assume control.		British troops and American marines came ashore in Vladivostok, as the Japanese at long last begin their pull out from the Far Eastern Siberian port. Soviet troops have advanced to within 15 miles of Vladivostok, but have agreed not to enter the city until the Japanese complete their evacuation.
Oct. 21		Living costs in France have shot up by 300 percent since 1911. Art students on Paris' Left Bank, are feeling the pinch. The average cost of living for an artist on the *Rive Gauche* is 7,560 francs a year, or $4,460.... Dissent is growing among radical-minded enlisted men in the German Reichswehr, and their monarchist officers. Of the 14 generals in the post-World War German army, 11 are titled aristocrats.		The United States formally ends its administration of the Dominican Republic today, and will begin withdrawing its marine garrison, as Juan Bautista Vicini Burgos takes office as Provisional President. The Provisional government will rule until elections can be held.	

A	B	C	D	E
Includes developments that affect more than one world region, international organizations and important meetings of world leaders.	*Includes all domestic and regional developments in Europe, including the Soviet Union.*	*Includes all domestic and regional developments in Africa and the Middle East.*	*Includes all domestic and regional developments in Latin America, the Caribbean, and Canada.*	*Includes all domestic and regional developments in Asian and Pacific nations (and colonies).*

U.S. Politics & Social Issues	U.S. Foreign Policy & Affairs, Defense	U.S. Economy & Environment	Science, Technology & Nature	Culture, Leisure & Lifestyle	
The mayor of Liberty, KS, is assaulted by a mob and flogged with bull-whips after denouncing the Ku Klux Klan....President Warren Harding is granting conditional pardons to six radical union leaders convicted of violating wartime offenses. A total of 67 men are still being held at Ft. Leavenworth for resisting the draft and related offenses, though pressure continues to release them.	Rear Admiral William S. Sims, tireless advocate of naval reform since 1897, and until now President of the Naval War College, retired today.... Commerce Secretary Herbert Hoover, in a speech in Toledo, OH, today, stated that Europe can, and should, pay its wartime debts to the United States.	The New York Phone Company installed a record 261,000 new telephones last year, with 11 new switchboards. Some $61 million will be devoted to improving the system by 1922.	Army Air Service pilot Lieutenant R.L. Maughan broke all speed records today, flying at 248.5 miles per hour at Seldridge Field in Michigan.		Oct. 16
	U.S. Navy Lieutenant Virgil C. Griffin, in a Vought VE-7SF, makes the first take-off from an aircraft carrier from the USS *Langley* while moored on the York River in Virginia.... The army Air Service dirigible *C-2* explodes today in a massive fireball as it was being taken from a hanger at Brooks Field, TX, injuring seven of the eight crewmen aboard. The fault has been laid to the highly volatile hydrogen gas used aboard the dirigible. Experts are calling for the use of helium instead.	Standard Oil's recent payment of a 400 percent stock dividend is prompting calls for an investigation of the gigantic oil company for tax evasion. The Rockefeller family, which controls the firm, has a reputed income of $1 million a day....Ford Motors is slashing prices on its line of cars. Factory prices for a top line sedan is $593.			Oct. 17
	Army Air Service Brigadier General William H. Mitchell, in a Curtiss R-6, breaks the world air speed record, flying 222.97 miles per hour over Selfridge Field, MI....The United States is increasing "unofficial" cooperation with the League of Nations, having agreed to work with the League to stop the spread of anthrax, and reduce the trafficking in opium and "white slaves."		Famed inventor Thomas Edison makes his first visit to the General Electric labs in Schenectady, NY, in 25 years, seeing displayed technology that has grown out of his inventions, including vacuum tubes and equipment for making motion pictures with sound, "talkies."	Little Orphan Annie makes her debut appearance in American newspaper comic strips today.... A new corporation has been formed in Great Britain to develop radio broadcasting: the British Broadcasting Company (BBC).	Oct. 18
	Rear Admiral Donald K. Bullard, in a speech today, stated that radio would augment, but not replace, undersea telegraph cables in the event of a new war.			The French are building the first mosque in Paris, as a concession to the many French colonial subjects who are Muslim.	Oct. 19
Police in Portland have expelled 16 I.W.W. members from the city, after arresting them in connection with a recent longshoremen's strike.	Lieutenant Harold Harris becomes the founding member of the Caterpillar Club, those whose lives have been saved by parachutes. Harris' Loening PW-2 developed engine trouble over Dayton, OH, but Harris parachuted to safety.... The practice of "hazing" is coming under fire at the Naval Academy at Annapolis, after a midshipman, Walter H. McGregor, ends up on crutches after a particularly violent hazing episode. The Superintendent, Rear Admiral Henry B. Wilson, has vowed to eliminate the practice.	Nine people are killed when a gas pocket exploded in a coal mine near McCurtain, OK.		A Federal investigation of the U.S. District Attorney's office in Chicago reveals that Federal prosecutors there have been allowing a "systematic and protected" bootleg traffic to flourish in the city....Champion prizefighter Jack Johnson will star in a new production of *Othello*....A jury in the murder of Hip Sing Tong National President Ko Low ended in a hung jury today. The murder is still considered unsolved.	Oct. 20
		American coalmines are reported to be the most productive in the world, with output in 1920 at 743 tons per man.	Today, on the 50th anniversary of the invention of the telephone, 14 million telephones are in the United States, 65 percent of the world's total, with Europe accounting for another 25 percent.	In *The Coming of the Fairies*, acclaimed writer Sir Arthur Conan Doyle, who has come to believe in spiritualism, argues that fairies are real, and appear to people in the countryside....The elegant but practical costume suit has become the rage in women's fashions. Long, stylish, and flowing, it is versatile enough for most occasions.	Oct. 21

F	G	H	I	J
Includes campaigns, elections, federal-state relations, civil rights and liberties, crime, the judiciary, education, healthcare, poverty, urban affairs, and population.	*Includes formation and debate of U.S. foreign and defense policies, veterans affairs, and defense spending. (Relations with specific foreign countries are usually found under the region concerned.)*	*Includes business, labor, agriculture, taxation, transportation, consumer affairs, monetary and fiscal policy, natural resources, pollution and industrial accidents.*	*Includes worldwide scientific, medical and technological developments, natural phenomena, U.S. weather and natural disasters.*	*Includes the arts, religion, scholarship, communications media, sports, entertainment, fashions, fads, and social life.*

	World Affairs	Europe	Africa & The Middle East	The Americas	Asia & The Pacific
Oct. 22		Fascist candidates have swept the elections in the Italian province of Reggio Emilia, indicating strong support for Fascist leader Benito Mussolini....France will be forced to import 2.4 million tons of wheat this year to meet shortfalls in grain production.		Bullfighting season opened today in Mexico City, despite heavy rains, as 15,000 come out to view toreadors in the corrida....Brazil defeated Paraguay 3–0 in the final game of the South American soccer championship....German trade with Chile is growing, for example in the sale of steel rails, but Chileans are still wary of relying on uncertain supplies from Germany.	
Oct. 23		A. Bonar Law, a Conservative, has succeeded Liberal Lloyd George as Prime Minister of Great Britain, while general elections are set for November 15....Italian and Yugoslav representatives have signed the Treaty of Santa Margherita, confirming the independence of Fiume (Rijeka) as agreed on in the 1920 Treaty of Rapallo....German Chancellor Karl Joseph Wirth proposes today that Germany declare bankruptcy. The mark is now down to 4,000 to one American dollar. The price of bread has doubled in one month.		American Secretary of State Charles E. Hughes is calling the five Central American republics together for a disarmament conference in Washington in December, in an effort to reduce tensions in the region.	
Oct. 24	The Allied Reparations Commission will go to Berlin to meet with German leaders there in an effort to stem Germany's rampant inflationary spiral. German Chancellor Wirth is welcoming the economic experts, who include Britain's John Maynard Keynes.	The Irish *Dail* has ratified the new constitution for the Irish Free State....Friedrich Ebert has been re-elected Reich President of Germany....Mussolini addresses 40,000 Fascists today, at a Congress of the Fascist Party in Naples, warning them that a "March on Rome" could take place "in days, perhaps hours."			
Oct. 25		Benito Mussolini has left Naples for Milan. His parting words to the Fascist Congress are, "The government of the country must be given peacefully to the Fascisti or we will take it by force." Still fearing the collapse of his plans, Mussolini wants to be near the Swiss border in case an attempt is made to arrest him....Continuing his defiance of the Free State government in Dublin, Irish Republican leader Eamon de Valera today proclaims himself President of Ireland, denying all continued allegiance to the British crown.		The United States is now Canada's best customer, supplanting Great Britain.	
Oct. 26	The Allies are calling an international conference at Lausanne in November to discuss the state of the Near East. The United States has been invited, as have the Turkish Nationalists, in an effort to resolve the crucial question of the Straits....The question of access to the Kiel Canal will go before the World Court. Germany maintains that it does not have to grant full access to all ships, even in time of war.	The Fascist Party Congress in Naples has issued a Fascist Manifesto, calling for a March on Rome....Prime Minister Luigi Facta is trying desperately to form a new government with Fascist participation....Republican guerillas clash with Irish Free State troops at Upper Bridge, in Ballina in County Mayo, in continuing unrest in Ireland....The British Admiralty has issued orders for the construction of two new 35,000-ton battleships, as provided for in the Washington Naval Accords.			The last Japanese troops evacuate the port of Vladivostok, in eastern Siberia, where they have been stationed since the Russian Revolution, at a cost of 1.5 billion yen. They are being joined by the last remnants of the White Russian forces that have resisted Soviet rule since World War I. The Soviets are now free to openly annex the Far Eastern Republic, completing their control of Siberia....The Japanese Imperial Cabinet voted today to ask the Diet for funding for a new cable to speed communications between Japan and the United States.
Oct. 27		Former Italian Prime Minister Antonio Salandra has invited Mussolini to Rome to form a coalition government. Mussolini, in Milan, has refused, demanding full powers....25,000 squadristi, Mussolini's Blackshirt thugs, advance on Rome as Mussolini calls for a March on Rome....Fascist forces have seized control of Perugia....All over Italy, Fascists are seizing control of towns and cities.	Voters in Southern Rhodesia have voted down a referendum incorporating Southern Rhodesia with the Union of South Africa, in favor of achieving self-government as a separate colony, by a margin of 59 to 41 percent. Southern Rhodesia's White settlers are overwhelmingly British, and do not want to belong to an Afrikaaner dominated Union of South Africa.		

A	B	C	D	E
Includes developments that affect more than one world region, international organizations and important meetings of world leaders.	*Includes all domestic and regional developments in Europe, including the Soviet Union.*	*Includes all domestic and regional developments in Africa and the Middle East.*	*Includes all domestic and regional developments in Latin America, the Caribbean, and Canada.*	*Includes all domestic and regional developments in Asian and Pacific nations (and colonies).*

U.S. Politics & Social Issues	U.S. Foreign Policy & Affairs, Defense	U.S. Economy & Environment	Science, Technology & Nature	Culture, Leisure & Lifestyle	
	The American cruiser *Sacramento* arrives in Vladivostok to safeguard American interests.		A German firm has developed the first silent wristwatch, with a synchronized, oscillating motor.... France is establishing a large preserve in West Africa to breed chimpanzees and other large primates for scientific experimentation.		Oct. 22
	The Army Air Service is making plans for a squadron of planes to circumnavigate the globe, possibly via Iceland, Europe, and Siberia.		Lilian Gatlin has become the first woman pilot to fly across the United States. Her time is 27 hours and 11 minutes.	Mayor Curley of Boston announced that he would bar controversial modern dance artist Isadora Duncan from performing in Boston. Miss Duncan denounced the proposed ban, calling her dance a symbol of the freedom of women, and decried "Puritan vulgarity."	Oct. 23
					Oct. 24
			The post office sets a new record for air mail delivery, carrying mail 431 miles in just two hours and 48 minutes.	An angry mob assaults Prohibition agents making a raid in the Bronx, pelting the agents with rocks from the rooftops as authorities seize 4,500 bottles of whisky.	Oct. 25
	U.S. Navy Lieutenant Commander Godfrey Chevalier, in an Aeromarine 39-B, makes the first successful landing on the deck of an aircraft carrier, on the USS *Langley* off Cape Henry.		Portuguese aviators, Captains Sacadura and Coutinho, received a hero's welcome upon their return to Lisbon from Rio de Janerio by steamer after completing the first transatlantic flight over the South Atlantic....British scientist Sir William Bragg announces today that through the use of X-rays, the molecular structure of crystals can be more precisely studied, opening the door to unlocking the secrets of the structure of the atom.	Federal Marshals are arresting ticket scalpers operating at University of Chicago football games. Two men are arrested for selling tickets to the Chicago-Princeton game for the outrageous price of $15 a ticket....The new musical *Springtime of Youth* opens on Broadway tonight....After an appeal by anti-evolution spokesman William Jennings Bryan, Protestant ministers in St. Paul, MN, have voted to call a statewide meeting of pastors to oppose the teaching of evolution in the state.	Oct. 26
	The United States begins the annual celebration of Navy Day today.				Oct. 27

F	G	H	I	J
Includes campaigns, elections, federal-state relations, civil rights and liberties, crime, the judiciary, education, healthcare, poverty, urban affairs, and population.	*Includes formation and debate of U.S. foreign and defense policies, veterans affairs, and defense spending. (Relations with specific foreign countries are usually found under the region concerned.)*	*Includes business, labor, agriculture, taxation, transportation, consumer affairs, monetary and fiscal policy, natural resources, pollution and industrial accidents.*	*Includes worldwide scientific, medical and technological developments, natural phenomena, U.S. weather and natural disasters.*	*Includes the arts, religion, scholarship, communications media, sports, entertainment, fashions, fads, and social life.*

	World Affairs	Europe	Africa & The Middle East	The Americas	Asia & The Pacific
Oct. 28		Liberal Prime Minister Luigi Facta's cabinet resigns. King Vittorio Emanuele III has refused to sign a decree by Facta declaring a state of siege....The king has invited Benito Mussolini to Rome, offering him a position within a coalition government. Mussolini refuses, demanding that he head the new government.			The Soviet Red Army has occupied Vladivostok as the last Japanese troops have withdrawn.
Oct. 29		Former Italian Prime Minister Antonio Salandra meets with the king this morning, telling him that he cannot form a government without Benito Mussolini....At noon, the king telegraphed Mussolini in Milan, offering to make him Prime Minister....Mussolini left Milan by train for Rome in the evening.... Republican forces have captured the town of Clifden in County Galway, capturing 80 Free State troops.... Prices in Austria are finally starting to decline after a long period of runaway inflation. Flour still costs 8,000 crowns per kilo, down from 14,000.			
Oct. 30		Benito Mussolini has arrived in Rome. He presents his proposed cabinet to the king. Fascists will hold seven seats in the new cabinet, with allied nationalists holding five others....Mussolini today proclaims his friendship with America, but denounced America's system of immigration quotas, whereby Italian immigration is limited to just 42,000 a year....Scattered clashes with Socialists continued throughout Italy as Mussolini tightens his grip on the country. The Communist Party in Italy is officially disbanding, effectively going underground.			The Philippine Legislature today passes a resolution calling on the United States to allow the writing of constitution for full independence.... An army of renegades loyal to Zhao Zhi, brother of the late governor of Henan Province, have cut the Beijing-Hankow Railway and are plundering towns in the province.... Now that the last foreign troops have withdrawn from Siberia, the United States is following the Allies in relinquishing its control of the Chinese Eastern Railway, which the United States took part in occupying during the Russian Civil War. The railway will be returned to Chinese control.
Oct. 31	The United States is negotiating to obtain a seat on the International Court of Justice in The Hague, without joining the League of Nations.	Benito Mussolini is sworn in as Prime Minister and Minister of the Interior, while 100,000 Blackshirts parade through the streets. At 39, Mussolini is the youngest Prime Minister in Italy's history....253 people have been killed, and 753 wounded in political unrest by Unionists in Barcelona since 1918.... A plot by Irish Republican dissidents to detonate mines beneath the criminal investigations building in Dublin was foiled. Meanwhile Republican guerillas burn a railway station at Mallow in southern Ireland.	The Turkish Nationalist government in Ankara today passes death sentences in absentia on the members of the Ottoman Sultan's government who signed the Treaty of Sevres yielding portions of what it considers the Turkish homeland to the Allies after World War I....The Russians have agreed to renounce all claims to extra-territorial rights in Turkey, as the Soviets move to consolidate their partnership with the Turkish Nationalists.		
Nov. 1		At Brockagh Fahy, in County Mayo today, Irish Free State forces maul a column of Irish Republican rebels, killing, wounding, or capturing eight out of 20 men....The Fascist government of Italy has arrested the Communist deputy from Parma, while Fascist Blackshirts attacked the offices of the Socialist newspaper *Avanti* in Milan, along with 15 other "subversive" clubs.	The Turkish Grand National Assembly in Angora (Ankara) has declared the Ottoman Sultanate abolished, proclaiming a Turkish Republic....In Constantinople (Istanbul) Sultan Mehmed VI Vahdettin has abdicated. His cousin will succeed him Abdul Mejid II as Sultan, but the real power in Turkey now lies in the hands of Mustafa Kemal....The Turkish government will appoint a new Caliph as spiritual leader of the Muslim world, but he will have no secular powers.	313 ships will pass through the Panama Canal in October, setting a new record....The Liberal Party has swept local elections in Cuba, capturing six provincial governorships and the mayoralty of Havana. The Liberals may capture control of the lower house of Congress as well.	Renewed fighting has broken out between warlord factions in China.

A	B	C	D	E
Includes developments that affect more than one world region, international organizations and important meetings of world leaders.	*Includes all domestic and regional developments in Europe, including the Soviet Union.*	*Includes all domestic and regional developments in Africa and the Middle East.*	*Includes all domestic and regional developments in Latin America, the Caribbean, and Canada.*	*Includes all domestic and regional developments in Asian and Pacific nations (and colonies).*

U.S. Politics & Social Issues	U.S. Foreign Policy & Affairs, Defense	U.S. Economy & Environment	Science, Technology & Nature	Culture, Leisure & Lifestyle	
			Expeditions to obtain specimens for zoos and museums are rapidly depleting numerous species of large animals. A tiger or lion can be worth as much as $5,000, with a giraffe worth up to $14,000.	AT&T's WEAF in New York City transmits the first nationwide broadcast of a college football game. Princeton plays the University of Chicago at Stagg Field in Chicago, and wins 21–18. Commercial advertising on radio has also begun, when the Queensboro Realty Company advertises apartments in Jackson Heights during the game, paying $100 for 10 minutes of air time.	Oct. 28
Governor Henry J. Allen of Kansas today openly denounced the Ku Klux Klan as a force for "chaos and hatred," and ordered the Kansas Attorney General to expel all known Klan officers from the state.	Army Air Service test pilot Lieutenant Harold Harris, has become the first member of the "Caterpillar Club," people who's lives have been saved by a parachute, after making an emergency parachute jump from his plane over McCook Field, in Dayton, OH.		The University of Indiana is reporting the sighting of a new comet, in the vicinity of Cygnus.		Oct. 29
Two men ae killed when masked gunmen tried to kidnap the leader of a local anti-Ku Klux Klan organization in Henrietta, OK....Birth control advocate Margaret Sanger addresses a meeting of the Birth Control League at Carnegie Hall, in New York City. Mrs. Sanger spoke about her recent visit to China and Japan. Sanger states that overpopulation in Japan breeds "militarism" and "famine and disease" in China.		Gas prices have been reduced in the Midwest, down to 20 cents a gallon in Chicago.	Chicago continues in the grip of Indian Summer with temperatures today still hitting 75 degrees....The Yukon River is reporting the latest ice free season on record so far.	Austin Strong's play *Seventh Heaven* opens at the Booth Theater in New York. In addition, opening in New York City tonight is Italian playwright Luigi Pirandello's *Six Characters in Search of an Author*, at the Princess Theater....Karl and Josef Kapek's play, *The World We Live In*, premieres tonight in New York City....Cincinnati police have halted performances of *The Rubicon*, a French sex farce, as indecent.	Oct. 30
President Warren Harding announces that the improved American economy will allow the United States to wipe out its current $670 million deficit by next fiscal year.				According to an indictment handed down today, a single group of Cleveland bootleggers was able to turn $480,000 worth of alcohol purchased fraudulently from government stocks, into diluted hooch selling for $64 a gallon, for a net profit of $14.88 million.	Oct. 31
			Dr. Edward Oohaner of Chicago is advancing a new theory of fatigue, stating that chronic exhaustion is due to the accumulation of toxins within the body.		Nov. 1

F — *Includes campaigns, elections, federal-state relations, civil rights and liberties, crime, the judiciary, education, healthcare, poverty, urban affairs, and population.*

G — *Includes formation and debate of U.S. foreign and defense policies, veterans affairs, and defense spending. (Relations with specific foreign countries are usually found under the region concerned.)*

H — *Includes business, labor, agriculture, taxation, transportation, consumer affairs, monetary and fiscal policy, natural resources, pollution and industrial accidents.*

I — *Includes worldwide scientific, medical and technological developments, natural phenomena, U.S. weather and natural disasters.*

J — *Includes the arts, religion, scholarship, communications media, sports, entertainment, fashions, fads, and social life.*

	World Affairs	Europe	Africa & The Middle East	The Americas	Asia & The Pacific
Nov. 2		In Berlin, a conference of monetary experts has been called to draw up plans to reorganize Germany's currency, as the German mark falls to 4,500 to the dollar. The Reparations Commission, headed by Louis Barthou of France, is insisting that Germany provide specific economic data in order to make a rational assessment of Germany's ability to pay reparations....As the general election approaches, British political parties are being forced to provide additional funding to members of parliament in order to allow them to campaign for office and still maintain a respectable level of income in Britain's troubled post-World War economy.	An American relief worker has been hospitalized in Beirut, after he and four other Americans are ambushed by Turkish irregulars as they were leading a group of Greek and Armenian refugees to safety in Aleppo. One American is killed in the ambush....The entire Christian population of Anatolia, estimated by the League of Nations at 1.5 million, is now being forced to move by the Turkish Nationalist government in Ankara.	In Mexico, rebel General Francisco Murguia is executed today....The United States is sending a new governor, Colonel Jay Morrow, to take command of the Panama Canal Zone....The Chilean government today accepted a bid by the National City Company of New York, for an $18 million loan, with a 7 percent interest rate. National City Company outbid the Rothschilds in providing the loan.	The Queensland and Northern Territory Air Service, QANTAS, opened regular passenger service today with a flight from Charleville to Cloncurry, Queensland. It is Australia's first airline.
Nov. 3		East Mayo Irish Republican rebels are captured at Ballinrobe, County Mayo....The German mark falls precipitously today, to a new record low of 6,500 to the dollar, as confidence in the German economy, and the Reparations Commission also reach new lows....Benito Mussolini is disbanding the 117,000 Fascist followers in occupation of Rome, as Mussolini's new Fascist regime tightens its grip on the country.	It has been revealed that instead of the 8,000 gendarmes it is entitled to have in Eastern Thrace under the terms of the Convention of Mudania, the Turks now have 30,000, outnumbering the Allied troops in the region by four or five to one. The evacuation of some 500,000 Greek refugees from Eastern Thrace is nearly complete. The refugees are taking everything portable, including livestock and vehicles of all types, before the Turks can take over the area.		Thousands of White Russian refugees have fled Vladivostok in the wake of the Soviet take over of Far Eastern Siberia, and are now trying to find aid in Manchuria....The Soviet government in Vladivostok has banned gambling, cocaine, and opium, all of which flourished under Japanese and White Russian control....The Japanese warship *Kasuga* has left Vladivostok harbor. One last Japanese warship, the *Niishin*, will remain on station in the harbor through the winter.
Nov. 4		Ernie O'Malley, Irish Republican rebel commander in Dublin, is captured in a gun battle today in the Donnybrook section of the city....In a speech today in Leeds, British Conservative leader Bonar Law outlined his party's positions on major issues. Bonar Law has vowed to uphold the Anglo-Irish Peace Treaty, and will continue to support the League of Nations and cooperate with France and Italy. He warned Labour opponents that improved prosperity could only come from renewed trade.		The American State Department has approved a $50 million loan to Cuba to bolster the country's finances.	The Chinese summer resort town of Paitaiho is now linked to Beijing, 200 miles away, by air service. The cost is $70 round trip.
Nov. 5	The French government is claiming that the recent decline of the French franc is due to Britain selling off its stocks of francs in exchange for dollars. Britain denies this, and blames France's budget deficit.	Party leaders in Great Britain are debating which way women will vote in the upcoming general election. Women have strong economic concerns, but in general are very favorable to the monarchy and King George....Republican guerillas have torched the main post office in Dublin.	The Allies have flatly refused demands by the Turkish government that they evacuate Constantinople....General Gouraud, French High Commissioner in Syria, has resigned in protest after the French government reduced troop strengths in Syria to the point where Gouraud believes it is too weak to defend the region.		
Nov. 6	French Premier Raymond Poincaré is backing British Foreign Minister Lord Curzon's note the Turkish government, warning them not to advance on Constantinople.	Irish Republican guerillas attack the barracks at Glanmire in County Cork. One civilian is wounded in the melee....Irish Republican leader Eamon de Valera defies Free State authorities today, refusing to surrender and vowing that the rebels would accept extermination before compromise.			
Nov. 7	Word is out that the meeting of the Reparations Commission, with its staff of economic experts, in Berlin, has effectively ended in failure, with no agreement between Germany and the Allies in sight....The German mark continues its plummet. Opening today at 7,200 to the dollar, by this evening it had fallen to 9,000 to the dollar.	Gun battles returned to Dublin today as Irish Republican raiders struck at military installations in the Irish capital.	Allied representatives in Constantinople today issued an ultimatum to the Turkish Nationalist Governor of the city, giving him 48 hours to release the editor of an opposition newspaper arrested by Nationalist authorities....Muslims in Egypt's Al-Azhar University are divided over the Kemalists recent move to reduce the Caliphate, long associated with the Ottoman Sultanate, to figurehead status.		A bandit army, some 10,000 strong, have kidnapped eight foreigners, including five missionaries, in Hunan Province, in what is an attempt to put pressure on the central government.
	A *Includes developments that affect more than one world region, international organizations and important meetings of world leaders.*	B *Includes all domestic and regional developments in Europe, including the Soviet Union.*	C *Includes all domestic and regional developments in Africa and the Middle East.*	D *Includes all domestic and regional developments in Latin America, the Caribbean, and Canada.*	E *Includes all domestic and regional developments in Asian and Pacific nations (and colonies).*

U.S. Politics & Social Issues	U.S. Foreign Policy & Affairs, Defense	U.S. Economy & Environment	Science, Technology & Nature	Culture, Leisure & Lifestyle	
		Automobile production was up in October, with 244,000 cars and trucks being produced, an increase of 20 percent from September's figures. The rapid increase is due to the renewed availability of coal after the nationwide coal strike. The October figures are a significant advance over the previous October record, in 1919....Automobiles are also killing record numbers of Americans, 10,168 in 1921. This is an increase of 28 percent since 1917. New York City, followed by Chicago were the worst cities for fatalities, but it is the fast growing state of California that has the highest fatality rate in proportion to its population.			Nov. 2
		A mine explosion near Scranton, PA, has killed four men and injured four others.	The American Consul General at Smyrna has arrived in the United States with a set of 30 gold staters, dating to the reign of King Croesus of Lydia in the 6th century B.C.E. The coins, found in the ruins of Sardis by American archaeologists, are believed to be the oldest coins in existence.	An exhibition by the Taos Society of artists is being put on at the Howard Young gallery in New York City. Taos is gaining a growing reputation as a center for innovative art....In France, the Société des Auteurs et Compositeurs is proclaiming itself the defender of the works of composers who have been dead for more than 50 years.	Nov. 3
Vice President Calvin Coolidge, in a speech in Chicago today, blamed elopements and murders by women on prosperity and the misuse of money, saying, "People have too much money and use it wrongly." Coolidge believes the cure is religion.			British Egyptologist Howard Carter has unearthed steps leading to the tomb of King Tutankhamen in the Valley of the Kings. He wired his mentor, George Herbert, Lord Carnarvon, today with the news.	The United States Postmaster General has mandated the use of mailboxes. Homes that do not have mailboxes will no longer receive mail....Bertrand Russell has published a new book: *The Problem of China*....Passenger traffic in New York City has increased by 20 percent since 1919, to 500 million people a year.	Nov. 4
		Racecar drivers are forming a protective association, the Association of Automobile Aces, to protect their interests in dealing with track owners. Former race car champion Barney Oldfield is favored to head the association....Milk prices in Chicago are being cut by 20 percent to 10 cents a quart.	Scientist Dr. Charles P. Steinmetz, in a speech at a Unitarian Church in Schenectady, denies that science and religion are incompatible, calling them separate activities of the human mind.	Convicted murderer Raymond Collins of Brooklyn has become the champion checkers player on Sing Sing's death row. On death row, the players, isolated in separate cells move not only their pieces, but their opponents, according to instructions shouted to them by the other player.	Nov. 5
The General Federation of Women's Clubs is calling for national marriage and divorce regulations to protect the rights of women....A Chicago alderman's house is bombed in an early morning explosion. The alderman, unhurt, blamed "political opponents."	The United States Blind Veterans of the World War will hold its first annual convention in Baltimore today.	100,000 barrels of crude oil have leaked out of earthen reservoirs ruptured in recent rains in Eldorado, AR. The oil flowed into a nearby creek, which then caught fire, causing a massive inferno that blazed out of control for several miles.	The German aviation firm of Dornier, although denied military contracts, has produced a new model, the Dornier Do J.	Utica textile magnate Arthur Hind has become the foremost stamp collector in the world, having bought up the famed collection of Count Ferrari of Austria at auctions in Paris. The most prized item in his possession are 1 and 2 pence post office stamps from Mauritius, for which Hind paid $50,000.	Nov. 6
In today's elections, Republicans have lost 77 seats in the House of Representatives, but retain their control of both Houses of Congress. Most tellingly, the Democrats picked up significant numbers of seats in the crucial states of Ohio and New York....In the Senate, the Republicans will hold a 51–43 majority, after losing five seats to the Democrats....The Republican Party has been battered by factional infighting between progressive and conservative wings.	Brigadier General William "Billy" Mitchell, assistant chief of the Army Air Service, today asserted that recent simulated bombing attacks on naval targets off Hampton Roads show that airplanes are now the key to defense of America's shores. Mitchell asserts that "a couple of pursuit groups of aircraft" in New Jersey could defend the entire Atlantic coast from Chesapeake Bay to Boston.			Famed pioneer baseball star, Big Sam Thompson, long second only to Roger Connor in number of home runs, has died. He was 63.	Nov. 7
F *Includes campaigns, elections, federal-state relations, civil rights and liberties, crime, the judiciary, education, healthcare, poverty, urban affairs, and population.*	G *Includes formation and debate of U.S. foreign and defense policies, veterans affairs, and defense spending. (Relations with specific foreign countries are usually found under the region concerned.)*	H *Includes business, labor, agriculture, taxation, transportation, consumer affairs, monetary and fiscal policy, natural resources, pollution and industrial accidents.*	I *Includes worldwide scientific, medical and technological developments, natural phenomena, U.S. weather and natural disasters.*	J *Includes the arts, religion, scholarship, communications media, sports, entertainment, fashions, fads, and social life.*	

	World Affairs	Europe	Africa & The Middle East	The Americas	Asia & The Pacific
Nov. 8		The French franc has fallen to its lowest point ever against the British pound. The weakness of the franc is ironically linked to the weakness of the German mark, as the collapse of that currency makes it clear that France will only see a fraction of the reparations money due it.	Tensions remained high in Constantinople as the Kemalist government renewed demands that the allies evacuate the city.		
Nov. 9	The Reparations Commission has left Berlin to return to Paris, with negotiations with Germany deadlocked. German Chancellor Wirth is insisting on a complete moratorium on reparations payments....French Premier Raymond Poincaré warned that if the issue of reparations is not resolved soon France will act unilaterally to force Germany to meet its reparations payments.	Fighting has died down in Dublin after three days of gun battles in the city between Irish Republicans and Irish Free State forces....Britain's public debt now stands at £7.7 billion, or $34 billion. This is down somewhat from Britain's postwar high of £7.8 billion.			
Nov. 10		Bulgarian authorities are arresting hundreds of White Russian exiles, the remnants of General Wrangel's defeated army, which fled to Bulgaria after the Russian Civil War. The arrests were prompted by the recent shootings of two Soviet Red Cross delegates there. Bulgaria is moving to patch up relations with its traditional ally, Russia....Two Communist deputies are elected to the Diet in Poland today. The Communists have been calling for greater attention to the country's war wounded.	The Bishop of Smyrna reported today that 4,000 Armenians in Smyrna were killed during the recent Turkish conquest, with property losses of $118 million....Belgium is floating a $20 million bond issue to fund improvements such as railroads in the Belgian Congo.		Two hundred people are killed when fire breaks out on a crowded riverboat on the Yangtze River, near Shanghai.
Nov. 11		Fascist Prime Minister Benito Mussolini addresses the Italian Chamber of Deputies today, demanding full powers....Irish Free State forces have captured Robert Erskine Childers, Irish Republican head of propaganda, in County Wicklow....A fire broke out in the harbor of Naples when flaming naphtha was spilled into the water. The flames have destroyed two Italian navy gunboats and done 10 million lire in damages.			The Manchurian port city of Dairen is enjoying a boom, as Japanese interests pull out of Shandong.
Nov. 12	Tensions remain high in Constantinople, as the British High Commissioner Harrington seeks to avert a direct confrontation with the Turkish Nationalists. The British have gotten the French to delay the peace conference with the Turks in Lausanne to November 20, but Turkish pressure for the allies to leave Constantinople is growing.	Berlin police are beginning a crackdown on the swarms of foreigners in the country illegally, arresting 60 people without passports and deporting them....The bicycle industry is booming in France, with one in eight Frenchmen, nearly five million, owning a bicycle. This is a major jump since 1914, when there were just 1.29 million bicycles on the roads.	As part of his new, forward foreign policy, Benito Mussolini's government proclaims the annexation of Tripolitania in Libya today. Italy has maintained garrisons in towns on the Libyan coast since before World War I, but now Mussolini intends to make Italian control effective throughout Libya....The Black Sea port of Samsun has nearly 50,000 Christian refugees either in it or en route to it. As many as one million Christians may yet reach the ports, fleeing Turkish persecution....Turkish Nationalists executed eight Turks associated with the Ottoman regime for treason.		The first scheduled airmail service in Japan begins today, with flights between Sakai, Osaka, and Tokushima....Japan is tightening censorship restrictions on American movies in order to stimulate its own nascent film industry.
Nov. 13		Some 70,000 fewer children were born in France than last year, as France still reels from the demographic effects of its losses during World War I.			One American missionary being held captive by bandits in China's Hunan Province has been rescued. A Swede, two Frenchmen, and a British subject, all missionaries, are still being held.

A	B	C	D	E
Includes developments that affect more than one world region, international organizations and important meetings of world leaders.	*Includes all domestic and regional developments in Europe, including the Soviet Union.*	*Includes all domestic and regional developments in Africa and the Middle East.*	*Includes all domestic and regional developments in Latin America, the Caribbean, and Canada.*	*Includes all domestic and regional developments in Asian and Pacific nations (and colonies).*

U.S. Politics & Social Issues	U.S. Foreign Policy & Affairs, Defense	U.S. Economy & Environment	Science, Technology & Nature	Culture, Leisure & Lifestyle	
With results in from yesterday's elections, the Democrats are now once again in complete political control of "the Solid South." Nine former Confederate states have elected solidly Democratic congressional delegations, as well as Democratic senators and governors.				Thieves broke into the Viareggio Hotel in Turin today, making off with eight million lire in jewels.... William L. Veeck, President of the Chicago Cubs, announced that the club would expand its ballpark to 32,000 seats, from the current 17,000, making it one of the largest ballparks in the country.	Nov. 8
"Wet" candidates were elected in a number of states in the recent election, but mainly in areas where Prohibition has never been popular. America is dividing into pro-wet urban areas and dry rural and small towns.	Naval Secretary Edwin Denby today called for passage of a bill subsidizing American Merchant Marine shipping. Denby believes that a large merchant fleet will be important as an auxiliary of the fleet in the event of another World War.	In light of America's growing prosperity, Treasury Secretary Mellon is calling for measures to allow increased immigration to prevent labor shortages.			Nov. 9
Former Ku Klux Klan Grand Goblin Harry B. Terrell filed suit in Atlanta's Fulton County Court today to place the assets of the Knights of the Ku Klux Klan in receivership. Terrell charges KKK Imperial Wizard William J. Simmons with incompetence, and diverting KKK funds for private purposes....A committee of women appealed to President Harding today to address "sex prejudice" in federal hiring and employment practices.	The Women's Overseas Service League has compiled a list of 161 "gold star women," who were killed overseas in World War I, and plans a perpetual memorial. Most fell in France, but women were killed in action in England, China, Armenia, and Siberia, as well.		The New York Anti-Vivisection Society is calling for state legislation to prevent experimentation on dogs for medical purposes.		Nov. 10
A group is being formed by prominent Chicagoans to resist the Ku Klux Klan, which claims some 50,000 active members in and around the city. Noted bankers and businessmen are refusing to do business with known Klan members. Chicago is home to 110,000 African Americans, 125,000 Jews, and 1.2 million Roman Catholics, all of whom have come under attack by the Klan.	On Armistice Day today, ceremonies were held at the eight war American cemeteries in Britain, France, and Belgium, where 30,363 American soldiers, sailors, and marines who fell in World War I are buried.		French pilot Etienne Oehmichen has successfully flown a helicopter prototype 525 miles. Problems of stability in flight still afflict helicopter designs.	A Yale literature post-graduate student is collaborating with a Columbia literary major to compile a list of famed works of literature, including Voltaire's *Candide* and some of Shakespeare's sonnets, that would meet with the wrath of censors today.	Nov. 11
	Three Civil War veterans, fed up after waiting 58 years for bonus money promised to them when they enlisted, are now filing suit in Rye, NH, for $12,000 in bonus money and accumulated interest.		At least 1,000 people are dead, and many other injured, in a massive earthquake, accompanied by a tidal wave that struck the Chilean coast. The worst damage was done in the town of Vallenar, which is almost entirely destroyed. The wave's effects were felt over 1200 miles of coastline, from Antofagosta to Valdivia. The epicenter of the quake, which was between eight and nine on the Richter scale, was 200 kilometers from Santiago. The tidal wave in some places caused the coastline to recede for 300 yards before rushing in. The wave that swept in was estimated at 50 meters in height.	The National Horse Show opens today in New York City.... Archbishop Michael J. Curley of Baltimore today condemned the "divorce evil," which he cites as one of the major problems America faces. Archbishop Curley also condemns Scottish Rite Masons and the Ku Klux Klan.	Nov. 12
			The death toll in the Chielan quake has risen to at least 1,200, with many remote villages still completely cut off in the provinces of Coquimbo and Atacama. The port city of Antofagosta is still completely cut off, as Chilean naval and land forces rush to reach the stricken areas.	George M. Cohan's new musical, *Little Nellie Kelly*, premieres tonight on Broadway in New York City....The Chicago Civic Opera kicks off its opening season, the first in Chicago history, with a performance of *Aida* today.	Nov. 13

F	G	H	I	J
Includes campaigns, elections, federal-state relations, civil rights and liberties, crime, the judiciary, education, healthcare, poverty, urban affairs, and population.	*Includes formation and debate of U.S. foreign and defense policies, veterans affairs, and defense spending. (Relations with specific foreign countries are usually found under the region concerned.)*	*Includes business, labor, agriculture, taxation, transportation, consumer affairs, monetary and fiscal policy, natural resources, pollution and industrial accidents.*	*Includes worldwide scientific, medical and technological developments, natural phenomena, U.S. weather and natural disasters.*	*Includes the arts, religion, scholarship, communications media, sports, entertainment, fashions, fads, and social life.*

	World Affairs	Europe	Africa & The Middle East	The Americas	Asia & The Pacific
Nov. 14		A general strike has paralyzed Dusseldorf....Rioting has broken out in Cologne....Kyosti Kallio has succeeded Aimo Kaarlo Cajandar as Prime Minister of Finland.			The Soviet Far Eastern Republic voted today to join Soviet Russia.
Nov. 15	As the Lausanne Conference approaches, the Turkish Nationalist government is demanding a plebiscite to determine the status of Western Thrace, revision of the border with French-controlled Syria, and the abolition of capitulations giving Westerners extra-territorial rights in Turkey....The British are calling for limitations on the Turkish military in Europe, with continued demilitarization of the Straits.	In Great Britain, Conservatives, led by A. Bonar Law, have won the general election, taking 344 seats in Parliament. However, the Labour Party has won 138 seats, and will replace Liberals, down to 117 seats, as His Majesty's loyal opposition. The Liberals have been badly split between factions led by David Lloyd George and Herbert Asquith. The openly working class Labour Party is now gaining in strength. Despite the new voting power of women, only two women were elected to seats in Parliament.	The newly formed Constitutional Liberal Party in Egypt is calling for the restoration of the Sudan to full Egyptian control and abolition of extra-territorial rights for Westerners.	Artur da Silva Bernardes has succeeded fellow PRM party member Epitacio da Silva Pessoa as President of Brazil....A Fascist Party is being formed in Jalapa in the Mexican State of Vera Cruz. It is pledged to fight the spread of "Bolshevism."	
Nov. 16	British Foreign Secretary Lord Curzon will leave tomorrow for Paris, to confer with French Premier Raymond Poincaré before the Lausanne Conference, as Britain and France work to present a united front in dealing with the Turks....The United States will not officially participate in the Lausanne Conference, but will have "observers" in attendance.	Wilhelm Cuno, Director of the Hamburg-American Steamship Line, today was commissioned by German President Friedrich Ebert to form a new coalition government....A proposed agreement between France and the Vatican to modify a 1905 French law limiting the powers of the Church is set to be put before Pope Pius XI, who is now studying the measure.			
Nov. 17		The Italian Chamber of Deputies has given Benito Mussolini a strong vote of confidence, overriding opposition by Socialist groups 306–116.	Deposed Ottoman Sultan Mehmed VI Vahdettin has fled Constantinople (Istanbul) aboard the British battleship *Malaya* for exile in Malta....King Hussein of the Hejaz has offered the deposed Sultan refuge in Mecca....Three ringleaders of the Rand Mine Revolt that shook South Africa earlier this year are executed in Pretoria for murder today.		An American Lutheran missionary has been kidnapped in China's Hunan Province. A bandit army there is growing, having looted more than a dozen towns and endangering foreigners throughout the province....The British are phasing out their mail service in China, handing it over to Chinese control as agreed on at the Washington Conference earlier this year.
Nov. 18	British Foreign Minister Lord Curzon announced that the Allies were in complete accord in being determined to limit Turkish efforts to rewrite the terms of World War I peace settlement. However, the allies have to make some concessions to the Turks, fearing a "Turco-Bolshevik" alliance might result otherwise.	A poor harvest in Italy this year will force the Italians to import grain on a large scale to make up the shortfall.			
Nov. 19	Issues that will be serious matters on contention at Lausanne will include the status of Constantinople and the Straits, Turkish supervision of foreign schools, removal of extra-territorial rights, and revision of the Iraqi and Syrian borders.	President Raymond Poincaré of France and British Foreign Minister Lord Curzon met privately with Benito Mussolini at Teriter, before the opening of the Lausanne Conference. They have agreed to treat Mussolini as an equal partner during negotiations.	Abdul Mejid II, Crown Prince of the Ottoman Empire, has been elected to the strictly symbolic position of Caliph, titular religious leader of Islam....The Belgian mining colony of Elizabethville, in the Belgian Congo, has grown to 3,000 Europeans, as efforts are made to open up the Congo's mineral riches, which include coal, copper, silver, tin, and radium.	Chile is requesting American aid in rebuilding hospitals and clinics in the wake of the recent earthquake and typhoon there.	Russia has announced the annexation of the Soviet Far Eastern Republic. The Soviets were already in control in the Far Eastern Republic, but now that the Japanese have evacuated eastern Siberia, the Soviets can drop any pretense and absorb the area openly....The last American marines have evacuated Russian Island in the Bay of Vladivostok.
Nov. 20		King George of Great Britain opens Parliament today in a grand ceremony before assembled dignitaries.	A peace conference convenes today in Lausanne. President Raymond Poincaré of France, British Foreign Minister Lord Curzon, and Italian Prime Minister Benito Mussolini seek an end to the fighting between Turkey and Greece, and settlement of outstanding issues in Asia Minor. A particular question is the status of the oil rich area of Mosul.		Two are killed and three wounded when Chinese pirates, disguised as passengers seized a British steamer leaving Macao. The captain of the pirates was wounded in the melee, but the pirates make good their escape.
	A *Includes developments that affect more than one world region, international organizations and important meetings of world leaders.*	B *Includes all domestic and regional developments in Europe, including the Soviet Union.*	C *Includes all domestic and regional developments in Africa and the Middle East.*	D *Includes all domestic and regional developments in Latin America, the Caribbean, and Canada.*	E *Includes all domestic and regional developments in Asian and Pacific nations (and colonies).*

U.S. Politics & Social Issues	U.S. Foreign Policy & Affairs, Defense	U.S. Economy & Environment	Science, Technology & Nature	Culture, Leisure & Lifestyle	
The National Association for the Advancement of Colored People appealed to the governor of New York to take action against the Klan, which has been trying to get a foothold in Buffalo and western New York state.			The British Broadcasting Corporation (BBC) has begun the first regular radio broadcasts from the Marconi House on the Strand, in London.... The French Air Ministry unveiled a new four-engine, all metal aircraft, equipped with a 75-millimeter cannon, for night bombardment.	Babe Ruth, slugger for the New York Yankees, today made a public promise to stay off alcohol "until the middle of next October." Ruth has been the subject of controversy this season, getting suspended six times, throwing dust on an umpire, and chasing a fan into the stands.	Nov. 14
			Dr. Alexis Carrel, of the Rockefeller Institute, has announced the discovery of white corpuscles. These leukocytes protect the body from infection....The Museum of the American Indian opened today in New York City....A special meeting of the Russian Communist Party has condemned Einstein's Theory of Relativity as "reactionary of nature, furnishing support for counterrevolutionary ideas" and "the product of the bourgeois class in decomposition."	The Sorbonne is endowing a new chair for the History of World War I. In its first year, research will focus on the causes of the war.	Nov. 15
The National Association for the Advancement of Colored People made an urgent appeal to President Warren Harding to provide federal protection to African Americans in Breckinridge, TX, after recent lynchings of African Americans and Mexicans there....A railroad worker, Edward Fisher, is kidnapped, beaten, branded on the cheek, and left in a field by Ku Klux Klansmen, near Hagerstown, MD.	The American cruiser USS *Pittsburgh*, arrived in Constantinople today, carrying Vice Admiral Andrew T. Long, commander of American naval forces in European waters.			The American All-Star baseball team is touring Japan. Today it defeats Meiji University 11–0.	Nov. 16
The Kentucky General Association of Baptists, representing some 270,000 Baptists, today passed a resolution condemning the teaching of the Theory of Evolution in state public schools.			Famed inventor Thomas Edison, in an interview in the *Daily Princetonian* today, voiced his disappointment with modern college graduates, saying that they object to getting their hands dirty and "expect to be appointed foreman" in short order.	Radio broadcasts of college football games is becoming standard, with live coverage of the Princeton-Yale and Columbia-Dartmouth games today....Federal authorities in the New York City metropolitan area are expected to remove between 30 and 50 Prohibition agents, in a general shake up to try to remove corruption and inefficiency.	Nov. 17
	U.S. Navy Lieutenant Commander Kenneth Whiting, in a Consolidated PT floatplane, has made the first successful launch from a catapult on an aircraft carrier from the USS *Langley* (CV-1).	American cars are growing in popularity at the London auto show, despite a 33.3 percent tariff on American automobile imports in Britain. Smaller cars are popular. The Dodge Coupe, selling for £395, is particularly popular.	The French aviation firm Dewoitine has unveiled its latest model, the Dewoitine D.1....French aircraft designer Captain Charles Nungesser is hard at work on a radical new swept-wing monoplane design. Equipped with a 700 horsepower engine, it is intended to fly up to 250 miles per hour.	French author Marcel Proust died today in Paris. He was 51. His *Recherche du Tempes Perdu, (Remembrance of Things Past)*, survives as his literary masterwork.... An unpublished manuscript by Balzac, *Les Fantaisies de la Gina*, has been released at last in Paris.	Nov. 18
Dr. Nicholas Murray Butler, President of Columbia University, today denounces the Ku Klux Klan while dedicating a memorial to the men of Harlem who fell fighting for the United States in World War I.		Raids around Hot Springs, AR, have resulted in the destruction of dozens of moonshine stills and dozens of arrests. The town has become a center for illicit liquor trade in that part of the country.		The Germanistic Society of Cincinnati, devoted to the study of German culture, has reopened its doors for the first time since World War I.	Nov. 19
Congress opens in special session today to discuss President Warren Harding's ship Subsidy bill. President Harding faces a growing rift in his party between conservatives and reformers, led by Wisconsin Senator "Fighting Bob" La Follette....Governor Parker of Louisiana is in Washington, DC, to confer with President Harding directly on the best methods for combating the rising power of the Ku Klux Klan.			A freak tide in the mouth of the Colorado river causes a 20-foot wave that sinks a Mexican steamer, killing seven people.		Nov. 20
F *Includes campaigns, elections, federal-state relations, civil rights and liberties, crime, the judiciary, education, healthcare, poverty, urban affairs, and population.*	G *Includes formation and debate of U.S. foreign and defense policies, veterans affairs, and defense spending. (Relations with specific foreign countries are usually found under the region concerned.)*	H *Includes business, labor, agriculture, taxation, transportation, consumer affairs, monetary and fiscal policy, natural resources, pollution and industrial accidents.*	I *Includes worldwide scientific, medical and technological developments, natural phenomena, U.S. weather and natural disasters.*	J *Includes the arts, religion, scholarship, communications media, sports, entertainment, fashions, fads, and social life.*	

	World Affairs	Europe	Africa & The Middle East	The Americas	Asia & The Pacific
Nov. 21		The British Labour Party has chosen Ramsay MacDonald to head the Labour members of the House of Commons....The British government is concerned about leaks of confidential information in the poisoning of London Police Commissioner Sir William Horwood. Measures are under discussion to check the spread of unauthorized government information to the press.	Deposed Ottoman Sultan Mehmed VI is setting up a household in exile on Malta. Mehmed has fled Turkey with $500,000, an antique gold dinner set worth $250,000, and several hundred thousand dollars' worth of jewels. Mehmed was not able to take his favorite wife, a Circassian woman who was the daughter of the palace gardener.	Canadian ministers in Paris are working out the final details of a treaty of commerce between France and Canada, a move that is expected to increase mutual trade.	The bandit army in China's Hunan Province has grown to nearly 30,000 men, mostly demobilized soldiers. The bandits are ravaging and burning every village in their path, creating a swath six miles wide through the province. Government troops that tried to stop them have been driven off at Chumatien, and foreigners are fleeing the affected area....The Chinese parliament has voted down a proposed £6 million loan by German and Austrian banks, and has impeached Finance Minister Lo Wen-kan for taking bribes to push the loan through.
Nov. 22		Wilhelm Cuno has succeeded Catholic Center Party leader Joseph Wirth as Chancellor of Germany, taking office with his coalition cabinet today....Juhan Kukk has succeeded Konstantin Pats as Head of State in Estonia....Russian monarchists met in Paris today, choosing Grand Duke Nikolai to be the official successor-in-exile of the murdered Tsar Nicholas II. The Russian monarchists also voted to move the center of their operations permanently to Paris from Berlin, as Germany is now growing friendlier to the Soviets.	The infant mortality rate among Greek refugees in the Piraeus refugee camps has reached appalling proportions, with 180 infants dying in a single day.		
Nov. 23	Secretary of State Hughes announced that he would send a representative to Paris to meet with the Allies to discuss payment of the cost of occupying the Rhineland. The cost of maintaining the American occupation forces on the Rhine since the end of World War I has been put at $300 million.	Irish Free State forces have retaken Newport in County Mayo. Free State forces then pursued the republicans into the countryside, hoping to break up their rural strongholds.... A British officer is injured when Allied officers were assaulted by a mob of German citizens when they tried to inspect an ammunition dump near Ingolstadt, Bavaria, today....German Chancellor Wilhelm Cuno's new coalition government is now complete, with nonpolitical Baron von Rosenberg coming on as Foreign Minister.		The United States has been invited to participate in the upcoming Isthmian Conference between the five Central American nations. The United States is eager to see differences resolved in the region and recently held preliminary talks between the presidents of Nicaragua, El Salvador, and Honduras aboard the USS *Tacoma*.	
Nov. 24	German Chancellor Wilhelm Cuno today called for a moratorium on reparations payments by Germany, and insisted on a loan of 500 million marks to stabilize the country's finances.	Author and militant Republican Erskine Childers is executed today at Beggar's Bush army barracks in Dublin for armed rebellion against the Irish Free State. The rebels in retaliation launched attacks on barracks and government buildings across Dublin.	Abdul Medjid Effendi has been invested as Caliph of the Muslims today in Constantinople. For the first time the daily prayers were recited in Turkish, instead of Arabic, reflecting Turkey's new nationalist sentiment.		
Nov. 25	The American delegation to the Lausanne Conference today announced its opposition to any secret treaties giving special privileges to the Allies in Turkey, and insisted on an "Open Door" for trade with the Near and Middle East.	The Italian Chamber of Deputies, by a 275 to 90 vote margin, has granted Benito Mussolini dictatorial powers for one year.			
Nov. 26		France is weighing cutting arms expenditures. An army of 630,000 has been budgeted for, of which 99,000 are stationed on German soil, keeping costs up....Austria is rushing to meet the demands of the allies for financial reforms, in hopes of obtaining a loan to stabilize its finances.			
	A *Includes developments that affect more than one world region, international organizations and important meetings of world leaders.*	B *Includes all domestic and regional developments in Europe, including the Soviet Union.*	C *Includes all domestic and regional developments in Africa and the Middle East.*	D *Includes all domestic and regional developments in Latin America, the Caribbean, and Canada.*	E *Includes all domestic and regional developments in Asian and Pacific nations (and colonies).*

U.S. Politics & Social Issues	U.S. Foreign Policy & Affairs, Defense	U.S. Economy & Environment	Science, Technology & Nature	Culture, Leisure & Lifestyle	
Rebecca L. Felton, of Georgia, is sworn in today as the first woman ever to serve as United States Senator.			French electrical engineer Maurice Bocquet, who is blind, has devised a typewriter for the blind, which prints out letters in Braille.	The National Council of Catholic Women opened its second annual convention in Washington, DC, today.	Nov. 21
The Independent Order of B'rith Abraham, with 200,000 members nationwide, is mobilizing to oppose the spread of the Ku Klux Klan wherever it finds it.	The American Federation of Labor today rejected plans to attend an anti-war conference in The Hague, and refused to support a measure calling for a general strike in the event of another world war....The Army Air Service today was able to successfully take on passengers from the ground onto the dirigible *A-4* and resume flight in a test near Scott Field in Illinois.		The final death toll for the Chilean earthquake and tidal wave has been put at 600, with as many as 1,500 injured. Total property damages come to 50 million pesos.	Polish pianist and composer Ignace Paderewski performs at Carnegie Hall in New York City today.... Elevator magnate A.B. See said today that all women's colleges should be "burnt to the ground." See believes that education has produced such evils among women as cigarette smoking, high heels, lipstick, and the use of slang.... Willie Hoppe today was awarded a prize of $6,680 for his victory in the world billiards championship in New York City....Baseball slugger Ty Cobb, now manager of the Detroit Americans, was awarded a disputed hit in the 1922 season today, putting him above a .400 batting average for the third season in a row.	Nov. 22
In *Takao Ozawa v. United States*, the Supreme Court, in a unanimous decision, has upheld the Cable Act, ruling that Asians are ineligible for naturalized citizenship, even if they marry an American. This decision reflects the rising sentiment against immigration, especially on the West Coast, where Asian immigration is a hot issue.		Cadillac is slashing prices on its touring cars. A new Cadillac now goes for $2,885....Eighty-four are dead after a coal dust explosion in a mine near Birmingham, AL.			Nov. 23
			The British aviation firm Vickers has unveiled its new Vickers Virginia model....British physician Dr. Bernard Hollander, argues that there is a specific center in the brain for the calculation and expression of figures, thus explaining feats of calculation among "mentally deficient" children....A sawfish 29 feet long and weighing 2¼ tons is caught in the Bay of Panama today.	A poll of 750,000 Methodist youths shows that Thomas Edison is considered number one on a list of great men of history, followed in order by Theodore Roosevelt, Longfellow, Tennyson, Commerce Secretary Herbert Hoover, Charles Dickens, and General John Pershing, with Congressman Andrew Volstead coming in last.	Nov. 24
				The 25th annual Army-Navy football game is held today at Franklin Field in Philadelphia today before Vice President Calvin Coolidge, General John Pershing, and 55,000 fans. Army won 17–14....E.M. Forster's *A Room with a View* is set to be published in January.	Nov. 25
			Howard Carter, with Lord Carnarvon, cuts a hole into the sealed tomb of the Pharaoh Tutankhamen, revealing gold and ebony treasures. It is the first intact pharaonic tomb ever found. Asked if he could see anything, Carter replied: "Yes, wonderful things."		Nov. 26

F	G	H	I	J
Includes campaigns, elections, federal-state relations, civil rights and liberties, crime, the judiciary, education, healthcare, poverty, urban affairs, and population.	*Includes formation and debate of U.S. foreign and defense policies, veterans affairs, and defense spending. (Relations with specific foreign countries are usually found under the region concerned.)*	*Includes business, labor, agriculture, taxation, transportation, consumer affairs, monetary and fiscal policy, natural resources, pollution and industrial accidents.*	*Includes worldwide scientific, medical and technological developments, natural phenomena, U.S. weather and natural disasters.*	*Includes the arts, religion, scholarship, communications media, sports, entertainment, fashions, fads, and social life.*

	World Affairs	Europe	Africa & The Middle East	The Americas	Asia & The Pacific
Nov. 27	The Allies today refuse to admit a Soviet delegation to the Lausanne Peace Conference on the status of the Middle East.	Stilianos Gounatas has succeeded Sotirios Krokidas as Prime Minister of Greece. Revolutionary Court has sentenced to death former Prime Minister Dimitrios Gounaris and members of his cabinet and high command to death in Greece.... The violently anti-Semitic National Socialist Party is gaining ground in Bavaria, where its leader, Adolf Hitler, is calling for a right-wing revolution....Anti-Semitic rioting broke out today in colleges and universities in Vienna.	As many as 250,000 Christian refugees are heading for ports on the Black Sea coast, far outstripping efforts to evacuate them.		
Nov. 28		Five former cabinet ministers, including deposed Prime Minister Gounaris Stratou and former Army Commander in Chief General Hadjianesti, have been executed by firing squad in Greece. Their crime, Greece's catastrophic defeat in its war with Turkey.			
Nov. 29		King George of Greece being is held under house arrest in the palace in Athens by the Gonatas government.	Three battalions of Turkish gendarmerie are poised on the Maritza River in Eastern Thrace, but for now are being barred from crossing by the Allies while the Greeks can reorganize....The Egyptian government has resigned in protest against continued British occupation of the Sudan.		Wang Daxie has succeeded Wang Chonghui as Prime Minister of the Beijing government in China. Wang was forced to resign for his part in a scandal involving taking bribes to approve foreign loans.
Nov. 30	A British newspaper has revealed that 500 German officers are in Soviet Russia, helping to reorganize the Soviet rail system and munitions works. It is rumored that the Germans and the Soviets are planning an alliance to renew war with the Western Allies and partition Poland among them.	Violent right wing agitator Adolf Hitler addresses a rally of 50,000 National Socialists (Nazis) today in Munich. Hitler openly calls for defiance of the Versailles Treaty....The last British soldiers in Ireland are preparing to complete their withdrawal from the country. All British troops are to be gone by January 5, 1923....German police are claiming that Communists are responsible for a wave of factory sabotage around Dusseldorf and Cologne.	Muhammad Tawfiq Nasim Pasha has succeeded Abdel Khaleq Tarwat Pasha as Prime Minister of Egypt.		
Dec. 1	The Allies have demanded that the Bavarian cities of Passau and Ingolstadt pay 500,000 each for recent assaults on Allied arms inspectors.	Josef Pilsudski has resigned as President of Poland.	Mustafa Kemal's government has ordered the banishment of one million Greeks living now in Turkey.		
Dec. 2		British Prime Minister Bonar Law meets with mineworkers today. Law claims to sympathize with the miners' plight, but warns them, "he saw no way to alleviate them by government intervention."	An agreement has been reached between Abd al-Aziz ibn Saud, the Sultan of Nejd, and the British-controlled kingdom of Iraq, defining the borders of Iraq, Kuwait, and the Nejd, which will include two neutral zones. The Uqair Protocol, as the agreement is called, requires ibn Saud to cease raiding Iraq and Kuwait, while ceding Kuwait's al-Hasa region to Nejd.	Oaxacan rebel leader Mario Ferrer has been killed in a clash with government troops near Coxoatlan, Mexico.	17-year old deposed Manchu emperor Hsuan Tung, also known as Puyi, today married Manchu princess Kuo Chin-si in an elaborate ceremony in Beijing's Forbidden City.
Dec. 3		Efforts by Chancellor Joseph Wirth to alleviate Germany's runaway inflation by a forced loan from wealthy Germans have failed, as growing pressure from Germany's business community derailed the measure.			

A	B	C	D	E
Includes developments that affect more than one world region, international organizations and important meetings of world leaders.	*Includes all domestic and regional developments in Europe, including the Soviet Union.*	*Includes all domestic and regional developments in Africa and the Middle East.*	*Includes all domestic and regional developments in Latin America, the Caribbean, and Canada.*	*Includes all domestic and regional developments in Asian and Pacific nations (and colonies).*

U.S. Politics & Social Issues	U.S. Foreign Policy & Affairs, Defense	U.S. Economy & Environment	Science, Technology & Nature	Culture, Leisure & Lifestyle	
				In retaliation for elevator magnate A.B. See's recent "archaic" comments about women's education, Adelphi College for women in Brooklyn received an anonymous donation of $5,000.	Nov. 27
			British airplane manufacturer Fairey has unveiled its new Fairey Flycatcher design....The French government is considering using a system of underground cables to transmit signals to guide aircraft in flights across the Sahara....The Dutch are starting a new air route from Amsterdam to Paris.	Captain Cyril Turner, of the RAF, today introduces skywriting to the United States. His plane spells out the message: "Hello USA. Call Vanderbilt 7200" over New York's Time Square. Some 47,000 people called the number, revealing the potential for mass advertising....Police raid Dinty Moore's Restaurant on 46th Street, a popular theatrical hangout, and seize $10,000 worth of bootleg alcohol.	Nov. 28
					Nov. 29
			Aviator C.O. Prest, whose effort to fly from Buffalo, NY, to Siberia failed when his plane crashed in Alaska, is planning to make the attempt. The big challenge is to face the headwinds over the Bering Strait....British chemists have succeeded in using light to produce sugars from carbon dioxide. This helps explain how plants utilize photosynthesis to process carbon dioxide.		Nov. 30
Representative Oscar Keller of Minnesota today presented a list of 14 charges against United States Attorney General Harry Daugherty before the House Judiciary Committee in Washington, DC, and Keller is calling for Daugherty's impeachment for favoritism to powerful business cronies.	Army Secretary John Weeks warns today that America's current army of 137,000 men is too small, and that further cuts by Congress would endanger America's national security.		French inventor Edouard Belin at the Sorbonne today demonstrates a process by which flashes of light on a selenium element can be used to produce sound waves that can in turn be transmitted by radio waves to an identical apparatus, which can then reproduce the light flashes. This "tele-vision" as Belin calls it, shows promise for the future.	Federal narcotics investigators arrest seven members of the Hip Sing Tong in New York City's Chinatown today, seizing large quantities of opium and arms. The Hip Sings have been planning a retaliatory raid against the rival On Leong Tong for the murder of Hip Sing leader Ko Low in August.	Dec. 1
	Idaho Senator William E. Borah warns that a new World War was likely, due to the situation in the Middle East. Borah called for recognition of Soviet Russia as a way to lessen international tensions.				Dec. 2
The U.S. Congress resumes its regular session today, after being called into special session over the disputed ship Subsidy Bill. Opposition to President Harding's plan is widely considered the opening salvo of the 1924 presidential campaign.	Naval Secretary Edwin Denby calls for a wide expansion of America's navy, with the construction of destroyers, cruisers, and submarines to produce a "navy second to none."		The National Advisory Committee on Aeronautics (NACA) today approved designs for the new ZR-1 dirigible. Modeled on German Zeppelins, the ZR-1 will be 680-feet long, 78 feet in diameter, and will have 20 separate gasbags inside its frame.		Dec. 3

F	G	H	I	J
Includes campaigns, elections, federal-state relations, civil rights and liberties, crime, the judiciary, education, healthcare, poverty, urban affairs, and population.	*Includes formation and debate of U.S. foreign and defense policies, veterans affairs, and defense spending. (Relations with specific foreign countries are usually found under the region concerned.)*	*Includes business, labor, agriculture, taxation, transportation, consumer affairs, monetary and fiscal policy, natural resources, pollution and industrial accidents.*	*Includes worldwide scientific, medical and technological developments, natural phenomena, U.S. weather and natural disasters.*	*Includes the arts, religion, scholarship, communications media, sports, entertainment, fashions, fads, and social life.*

	World Affairs	Europe	Africa & The Middle East	The Americas	Asia & The Pacific
Dec. 4	The British government is undecided over whether to build two 35,000-ton battleships allowed it under the Washington Naval accords. The Royal Navy must start work on the ships by December 21 or forfeit its right to build them, as agreed upon in the Washington Treaty.	A rebellion has broken out in Bulgaria. Todor Alexandrov has led his followers in an armed uprising against the Bulgarian government. His announced aim is taking Macedonia from Serbia and Greece and annexing it to Bulgaria by force....Irish Free State forces, backed by aircraft, have routed a Republican rebel column in the Dunmanway district of West Cork.		The United States opens a meeting of the representatives of the Central American republics in Washington, DC, in an effort to resolve the Nicaraguan-Honduran dispute. Central America has been torn by unrest in the wake of the collapse of the planned Central American Federation earlier this year. The Hondurans are calling for a new federation, but face widespread opposition.	
Dec. 5		The British Parliament has approved the new Irish Free State constitution....Bavarian Prime Minister Dr. Von Knilling warned that any effort to make the towns of Ingolstadt and Passau pay the one million gold marks demanded by the Allies for attacks on arms inspectors could lead to a widespread nationalist revolt in Bavaria....Count Michael Karolyi, former President of the Hungarian National Council, has been put on trial for treason in Budapest for aiding the rise of the short-lived Hungarian Communist government of Bela Kun after World War I.		A series of fires has strike prominent Catholic churches and institutions in Canada, with five incidents occurring in the last few weeks. The Ku Klux Klan has been blamed for the attacks, but denies responsibility....El Salvadoran delegates at the Washington conference of Central American republics have seconded Honduras' proposal for a new Central American Federation, but Costa Rica has declared itself opposed to the new union.	
Dec. 6	At the Lausanne Conference, the United States is calling for complete demilitarization of the Dardanelles Straits, with an international commission including American, Russian, and Turkish members to oversee the Straits. The Turks however, want to be able to close the Straits in times of war.	The 26 primarily Catholic counties of southern Ireland officially gained Dominion status as the Irish Free State today as the new Irish constitution goes into effect. George V is still officially monarch of the Irish Free State, with Tim Healy as Governor General and William Cosgrave as head of the government. The remaining six counties of Ulster, where Protestants hold sway, will not accept this agreement.			An American team composed of Major League baseball players has left Japan after a successful tour and is headed for Shanghai.
Dec. 7	The United States today backed the Allies in insisting that the Turks not expel the 200,000 Greeks now living in Constantinople.	The Parliament of Northern Ireland has voted to remain under Great Britain, rejecting union with the Irish Free State....*Dail Eireann* deputy Sean Hales has been killed by Irish Republicans in front of Leinster House in Dublin....Manuel García Prieto has formed a new government in Spain....Rebel forces capture the Irish Free State barracks at Ballymakeera, killing one, wounding 15, and capturing 90 Free State soldiers.		France has ceded several acres of Vimy Ridge to Canada to be the site of a perpetual memorial to the Canadian soldiers who fell taking it in World War I.	The Reform Party has come out ahead in the general elections held in New Zealand today, capturing 37 of 80 seats. The Liberal Party took 22 seats and the Labour Party won 17.
Dec. 8	The Turkish government has announced its willingness to enter into a compromise agreement with the Allies at Lausanne, allowing defenses for Constantinople and limiting the size of naval forces that can pass the Straits, but guaranteeing their absolute freedom for merchant ships in peace or war.	Republican commander Rory O'Connor and three other Republican rebels are executed in Ireland today, in retaliation for the shooting of Sean Hales.			Unrest is growing in and around the Shandong port of Qingdao (Tsingdao) as the Japanese prepare to pull out. The American destroyer USS *Asheville* is en route to the city, with a force of marines to land if American interests should be threatened.
Dec. 9	A second conference of Allied Prime Ministers meets today in London to discuss the ongoing problems of war debts and reparations. The British are renewing their proposal to cancel war debts by other Allied nations in exchange for a reduction in the amount of reparations to be demanded of Germany. America has no official representative at the conference, but the American ambassadors from London and Berlin are in unofficial attendance.	The Polish *Sejm*, or Parliament, has elected Gabriel Narutowicz, Minister of Foreign Affairs, to become President of Poland. Narutowicz is supported by a coalition of liberal and moderate groups, but is hated by the right wing National Democrats, who denounce Narutowicz as "President of the Jews."...A meeting of the Baltic states, along with Poland, Finland, and the Soviets, is proceeding in Moscow, with most territorial issues being settled.		An American oil worker is killed by guerillas, as violence continues to plague the southern Mexican state of Vera Cruz.	
	A	B	C	D	E
	Includes developments that affect more than one world region, international organizations and important meetings of world leaders.	*Includes all domestic and regional developments in Europe, including the Soviet Union.*	*Includes all domestic and regional developments in Africa and the Middle East.*	*Includes all domestic and regional developments in Latin America, the Caribbean, and Canada.*	*Includes all domestic and regional developments in Asian and Pacific nations (and colonies).*

U.S. Politics & Social Issues	U.S. Foreign Policy & Affairs, Defense	U.S. Economy & Environment	Science, Technology & Nature	Culture, Leisure & Lifestyle	
				The new musical *Our Nell* opens tonight in New York City.... Businessman Henry J. Fleischauer has claimed to be New Jersey's champion commuter, having commuted from Cape May to Philadelphia every day since 1900, logging more than a million commuter miles.	Dec. 4
			Prof. J.B. Shackleford, of the American Museum of Natural History, is returning from Mongolia via San Francisco with the bones of a Baluchitherium mastodon he unearthed in Central Asia.	Union racketeer Benjamin Levinski has been gunned down in New York by rival mobster William Lipshitz.	Dec. 5
The Allied Patriotic Societies, with a membership of more than six million, is calling for legislation barring any party "that subscribes to principles subversive to the Constitution of the United States" from appearing on a ballot.... Republican Representative Ryan of New York is calling for the House of Representatives to investigate the rising power of the Ku Klux Klan.				An unpublished manuscript by Rudyard Kipling is being put on sale in London for £840.	Dec. 6
	The International Lyceum and Chautauqua Society open a three-day conference in Washington, DC, on public opinion and world peace. President Warren Harding sends the body a letter hailing their intellectual leadership....In an economy measure, the Atlantic and Pacific Fleets will be consolidated into a single United States Fleet under Admiral H.P. Jones.			The new musical *The Last Waltz* opens in London tonight.	Dec. 7
President Warren Harding gives his annual address to Congress today. In his speech, Harding calls for a new "nonpartisan tribunal" within the Interstate Commerce Commission, which would have the power to prevent strikes on the railroads. In this, Harding is putting himself in direct opposition to the Progressive bloc of the Republican Party, led by Wisconsin Senator Bob Lafollette.		Senator Arthur Capper, leader of the farm bloc, today called on the Interstate Commerce Commission to investigate profiteering by railroads.	A massive fire sweeps through downtown Astoria, OR, early today, destroying 30 city blocks and doing $15 million in damage before being stopped by dynamiting houses in its path. The National Guard has been called in to maintain order.	The musical *The Battling Butler* opens in London tonight.	Dec. 8
		Speculation by buyers is driving up grain prices to new highs, especially corn and oats.		Author Robert C. Benchley is publishing a new volume of humor.	Dec. 9

	World Affairs	Europe	Africa & The Middle East	The Americas	Asia & The Pacific
Dec. 10		The Reichsbank is reported having issued record-breaking amounts of marks into the inflation-ridden German economy, 110 million for the week of November 15.... Czechoslovakia is reducing tariffs by 25–50 percent, in marked contrast to most Eastern European states, which are increasing theirs.	Mustafa Kemal's Turkish Nationalist government has announced that Ankara will remain the capital of Turkey. Constantinople, the former Ottoman capital, is considered too vulnerable to bombardment by Western warships.		The Japanese have evacuated the port of Qingdao (Tsingdao) in Shandong Province, restoring it to Chinese rule as agreed on at the Washington Conference in February.
Dec. 11	The Second London Conference has ended in failure. The French have rejected Britain's offer to cancel French war debts owed them in exchange for a reduction in German reparation payments. France, along with Belgium, has suffered the most of the Western Allies from the ravages of World War I, and will have the most reparations coming to it from the Germans.	Gabriel Narutowicz is inaugurated today as President of Poland.... France announces the construction of nine new submarines.			Prime Minister Wang Daxie has resigned in China. He will be succeeded by Wang Zhengting.
Dec. 12		The University of Vienna is barring Jewish professors from teaching there.	The United States is appealing for territorial refuges for religious minorities in Turkey. Only some 130,000 of the three million Armenians living in Turkey before the World War are still there.... Zavene, the Armenian Patriarch in Constantinople, has fled to Bulgaria, fearing Turkish attempts to impose controls on the Armenian Church.	Argentina has rejected a proposed disarmament conference of the ABC nations of South America. Argentine naval rivalry with Chile and Brazil continues, with the three nations spending $145 million a year on arms.	
Dec. 13	At the Lausanne Conference, the British have demanded that the Turks give guarantees to religious minorities, threatening to walk out of the conference and risk a renewed war....Theodore E. Burton, an American representative on the World War Debt Commission, today warns against any moves to cancel war debts, but is in favor of reducing the amount of reparations owed by Germany. Above all, Burton calls for an end to "militaristic antagonisms" in Europe.	The Irish Parliament opens today for the first time, with an address by Irish Free State Governor-General Tim Healy....Republican guerillas raided Carrick on Suir in Ireland today.		Chile is inviting all the nations of the Western Hemisphere to a Pan-American Conference in Santiago in March 1923, to discuss general disarmament measures for the region. Latin American countries spend $235 million annually on defense, out of a combined income of $970 million a year. Other topics would include tariff reduction and currency stabilization.	
Dec. 14	British Prime Minister Bonar Law warns against French plans to occupy portions of the Ruhr to force German payment of reparations.	The President of Poland, Gabriel Narutowicz, has been assassinated by militant National Democrat Eligiusz Niewiadomski. The attack takes place as Narutowicz was attending an exhibition at the Zachta Art Gallery in Warsaw.... Free State garrisons in Thomastown and Mullinavat in County Kilkenny deserted to the republicans en masse today.		Gustavo Sainz de Sicilia, leader of the newly established Mexican Fascist movement, claims that his organization now has 100,000 members.	
Dec. 15	The Harding administration is discussing arranging an international loan to help stabilize Germany's finances, but has definitely ruled out canceling Germany's reparations payments.	Standard Oil has abandoned plans to develop oil resources in Czechoslovakia, citing differences with the Czech government over the composition of the board of the Czech company to be in charge of operations....Republican rebels overran Free State barracks in Cavan, Thomastown, and Mullinavat in southern County Kilkenny today.		France and Canada have reached a trade agreement.	In Afghanistan, construction is under way for a railroad between Kabul and King Amanullah's planned new capital at Darulamun, six miles away.
Dec. 16		Daskaloff, the Bulgarian Minister of the Interior, survives a bombing attempt today as he was leaving the Sobranje building of Sofia. Daskaloff claims the plot is the work of the fanatic Anti-Agrarian Party, but no arrests have yet been made.		Bootlegging has brought a revival of Nassau in the Bahamas as a pirate hideout, with all manner of wanted men flocking there. 2,000 cases of "hooch" passed through Nassau last year. Now the total is closer to 50,000.	In Australia, elections have resulted in Labor winning 29 seats in Parliament, the Nationalists have 26, and the Country Party trails with 14 seats. The election has forced Nationalist Prime Minister Billy Hughes to resign. Hughes will be succeeded by fellow Nationalist Stanley Bruce, who will form a coalition government with the Country Party.

A	B	C	D	E
Includes developments that affect more than one world region, international organizations and important meetings of world leaders.	*Includes all domestic and regional developments in Europe, including the Soviet Union.*	*Includes all domestic and regional developments in Africa and the Middle East.*	*Includes all domestic and regional developments in Latin America, the Caribbean, and Canada.*	*Includes all domestic and regional developments in Asian and Pacific nations (and colonies).*

U.S. Politics & Social Issues	U.S. Foreign Policy & Affairs, Defense	U.S. Economy & Environment	Science, Technology & Nature	Culture, Leisure & Lifestyle	
In a new book, Commerce Secretary Herbert Hoover has called individualism vital to the continued success and prosperity of the United States, warning of the dangers of following the Soviet model of state controls.			Danish physicist Niels Bohr has been awarded the Nobel Prize in physics today, for using his theory of quantum mechanics to explain the structure of the atom.	Polar explorer Dr. Fridtjof Nansen is awarded the Nobel Peace Prize today for his work in providing relief to refugees in Turkey and Soviet Russia.	Dec. 10
Without competitive bidding, Interior Secretary Albert Fall has leased the Elk Hills Naval Petroleum Reserve to his friend Edward Doheny's Pan American company.			New shocks are felt near Illapel and Ovalle, Chile, today, interrupting communications and spreading fear, as Chile struggles to recover from the devastating effects of the earthquakes of earlier this year.		Dec. 11
Impeachment proceedings involving corruption and political favoritism were begun against Attorney General Harry Daugherty today before the House Judiciary Committee.	Mason Mitchell, American Consul on Malta, has been wounded in an assassination attempt. Authorities on Malta are holding two men, including a Maltese man dishonorably discharged from the American army in World War I.	John Wanamaker, millionaire and founder of the Philadelphia-based store chain, has died. Born in 1838, Wanamaker pioneered the department store and introduced such practices as price tags and putting advertisements in newspapers.		The New York Public Library is exhibiting a large collection of rare Bibles, including the Gutenberg Bible, the first Bible printed in America, in the Natick Indian dialect, and manuscripts going back to the 9th century....15 people are killed and 40 injured in a train wreck outside Houston, TX.	Dec. 12
	The House Appropriations Committee warned President Harding today that America needs to extend the 5–5–3 naval ratio for battleships to include cruisers, aircraft carriers, and fleet submarines, if it is to avoid an expensive arms race in these categories of ships, particularly with Japan.			Western Union today paid tribute to "T.B." Brennan, America's longest serving telegraph operator. Brennan began working for Western union in 1861....The New York City Police department is beginning a concerted effort to "dry up" Broadway, cracking down on clubs and restaurants that serve alcohol, in advance of this year's New Year's Eve celebrations.	Dec. 13
			In an address before the Illinois Manufacturers' Association, New York City Police Commissioner Richard E. Enright, warns that elevated "L" lines need to be turned into subways, warning that they cause congestion and deterioration of property values along the routes they take.	Rail investigators place the final death toll in the rail crash near Houston, TX, at 17, mostly African Americans, who were scalded to death by steam when a locomotive struck a loose car that had slipped onto the main track.	Dec. 14
		Only 25 percent of the Victory bonds issued in World War I are being redeemed as they mature, as most individual bondholders have only small amounts of money coming to them....50 billion cigarettes were sold in the Fiscal Year ending June 30, yielding $270 million to the government in taxes.	Runaway inflation in Germany is causing German science to stagnate, as researchers cannot afford the skyrocketing prices of books and equipment, or even afford to publish their findings....Charles P. Titus, of the American Microscopical, society reports that cigarette smoking does not endanger your health, as most of the nicotine is burnt off as ash.		Dec. 15
	The American destroyer USS *Bainbridge* rescues 400 people from a burning French hospital ship off the Turkish coast. An explosion aboard the *Vinh-Long* leave five dead and 10 missing.		In Nome, AK, today, Arctic explorer Roald Amundsen announces plans to attempt a new flight to the North Pole in May of next year.	Avante garde Russian playwright Nicholas Evreinov has produced a new play, *The Chief Thing*, which delves into the theme that illusion forms the major part of peoples' lives....Previously unpublished works by Dostoyevsky are being printed in London as *Stavrogin's Confession and The Life of a Great Sinner*....Willa Cather is publishing a new book entitled *April Twilights*.	Dec. 16

F	G	H	I	J
Includes campaigns, elections, federal-state relations, civil rights and liberties, crime, the judiciary, education, healthcare, poverty, urban affairs, and population.	*Includes formation and debate of U.S. foreign and defense policies, veterans affairs, and defense spending. (Relations with specific foreign countries are usually found under the region concerned.)*	*Includes business, labor, agriculture, taxation, transportation, consumer affairs, monetary and fiscal policy, natural resources, pollution and industrial accidents.*	*Includes worldwide scientific, medical and technological developments, natural phenomena, U.S. weather and natural disasters.*	*Includes the arts, religion, scholarship, communications media, sports, entertainment, fashions, fads, and social life.*

	World Affairs	Europe	Africa & The Middle East	The Americas	Asia & The Pacific
Dec. 17		The last British troops leave Dublin today as cheering crowds thronged the streets. All British troops have left the Irish Free State in accordance with the peace treaty reached last year....General Sikorski has been made Prime Minister of Poland in the wake of the assassination of President Narutowicz.			Chinese soldiers fire on the car of the Italian Chief of Police in Tianjin today, riddling it with 52 bullets.
Dec. 18		Irish Republican rebel leader Eamon de Valera narrowly escapes arrest today when he attends mass at Catholic University Church in St. Stephen's Green, Dublin. De Valera is recognized by several parishioners, who notify the authorities. De Valera managed to escape into the crowd before he could be apprehended....The Irish Parliament votes its first official act today since it was dissolved in Ireland's union with Great Britain in 1801.	Under pressure from the Allies and the United States, Turkey today lifted the ban on emigration by Christian minorities from its ports.... The Belgian government is asking hunter and explorer Carl E. Akeley to lay out plans for a vast nature reserve for gorillas in the eastern part of the Belgian Congo.	In a concession to the United States in the ongoing controversy over bootlegging, Canada announces today that it will join Britain in curbing the false registration of ships under the Canadian flag.... A proposed new Central American Federation plan has been shelved until at least 1926, with representatives of the five Central American republics in Washington unable to resolve their differences.	
Dec. 19		A parade by Romanian Jews protesting recent outbreaks of anti-Semitic rioting was attacked today by a mob of students in the Romanian city of Jassy. Violent riots and protests against Jews have spread to Bucharest, Czernowitz, and Klausenberg....It is reported that an American automobile manufacturer is providing large sums of money to violent Bavarian anti-Semitic leader Adolf Hitler.			
Dec. 20	The Turks have agreed to the main points of the Allied plan for control of the Straits at Lausanne. The Turks have decided to reach a settlement, dropping their common front with the Soviets, who are now finding themselves isolated.	Pope Pius is preparing an encyclical, outlining his plans for the Catholic church in coming years.... Benito Mussolini announces plans to incorporate his Fascist Blackshirt militia into a national militia of 70,000 men personally loyal to him. Meanwhile Italian nationalist Gabriel d'Annunzio has announced the disbanding of his own personal militia.			The American All-Star Baseball team is beginning a tour of the Philippines today, arriving in Manila from Japan. The team will then go on to Hong Kong....The Maharajah of Cooch Behar, age 36, has died. He leaves two small sons and a fortune in pearls and precious stones in his Indian kingdom of 600,000.
Dec. 21	French Premier Raymond Poincaré reiterated France's position that Germany must pay the Reparations she owes under the Treaty of Versailles, rejecting any discussion of a moratorium on payments until guarantees for payment are made by the German government.			President Chamorro of Nicaragua today reiterates his support for the American marine force stationed in his country, arguing that it helps maintain the peace. Opposition leaders consider the marines an occupying force.	
Dec. 22		Soviet leader Vladimir I. Lenin has written a Letter to the Party Congress. In this, his Testament, Lenin warns of a clash between Trotsky and Stalin. He suggests that they find a way to remove Stalin from his post as General Secretary of the Communist Party. Lenin does not make his Testament public.			
Dec. 23		Berlin police are moonlighting as private security guards to make ends meet, with private firms hiring some 6,000. The cost of such private security: 15,000 marks a month. However, it is worth it: Berlin reported 28,000 burglaries in 1920, and the figures have since risen.	An American destroyer is on station at Jaffa to help keep the peace during the Holy Week. A small number of Americans and British citizens are visiting Jerusalem and other sites in the Holy Land this year.	A consortium of Los Angeles businessmen have negotiated oil concessions on 11 million acres of land in the Tampico and Tuxpam districts on Mexico....The American Embassy exhibition opened at the Brazilian Centennial Exposition in Rio today.	

	U.S. Politics & Social Issues	U.S. Foreign Policy & Affairs, Defense	U.S. Economy & Environment	Science, Technology & Nature	Culture, Leisure & Lifestyle
Dec. 17	American Federation of Labor President Samuel Gompers today denounces President Harding's appointment of Pierce Butler to the Supreme Court, condemning Butler as pro-railroad.	Isolationist Senator William E. Borah today denounces "Allied militarism," seeing it as a greater threat to the peace than Germany's failure to pay reparations.		Ophthalmologists are noticing numerous cases of conjunctivitis, inflammation, and reddening if the eyes, among film actors. The reason is the large amounts of dust kicked up in movie studios by shifting scenery and the cranking of the cameras.	WHN Radio on Long Island will begin broadcasting Christmas appeals for charity tonight.
Dec. 18	President Warren Harding received 16 state governors at the White House today, in an attempt to coordinate enforcement of Prohibition. Governor Ritchie of Maryland warned though that his constituents believe that the Volstead Act is unenforceable and an infringement on their rights. Governor Allen of Kansas was the staunchest defender among the governors of the "dry position," calling for rigorous enforcement and an end to jokes in newspapers disparaging enforcement efforts.	The House passes a naval appropriations bill today. The measure includes a section calling on President Warren Harding to convene a new five-power conference to set limits on submarines, aircraft carriers, and other types of warships not covered in the limitations on battleships agreed to in Washington earlier this year.	Some nine million barrels of oil a year will be transported by tanker ships from fields in southern California to feed the growing demand on the East Coast....It is estimated that the two million golfers in the United States will spend more than $1.3 billion on their hobby this year. This figure includes $25 million for golf courses, $15 million for clubhouses, another $5 million for club furnishings, as well as $30 million for golf balls, $15 million for golf clubs, $50 million for golf apparel, and $40 million for caddies.	A Director of the Carnegie Institute of Technology, addressing a conference of foremen, superintendent, and plant managers in Brooklyn today, reports that psychological testing of employees is being adopted by growing numbers of major corporations. Intelligence tests are of particular interest to employers....The British Ministry of Agriculture is working with rural communities to develop wind power as a means of providing power in the countryside.	A gang of bank robbers, led by Harvey Bailey, has robbed an armored car in front of the United States Federal Reserve in Denver, shooting a guard and making off with $200,000 in five dollar bills.... A special task force of 130 picked Prohibition agents has arrived in Chicago under the command of Colonel L.G. Nutt. The agents, which include women, intend to infiltrate clubs and cabarets where illegal liquor is served and give Chicago a "dry Christmas."
Dec. 19			Thomas W. Lamont, speaking for the Morgan interests, warns today that American banks are not prepared to float loans for Germany to meet her reparations payments.	American Egyptologist, Professor Breasted, visited the newly opened tomb of King Tutankhamen in the Valley of the Kings today, pronouncing it "an astonishing revelation of the beauty and refinement of Egyptian art." It is now clear that the tomb is not a mere cache, and that it has been virtually undisturbed. Professor Harold Carter, in charge of the excavation, is now preparing the findings for transport to the Cairo Museum.	
Dec. 20				American Egyptologists in Thebes have been invited by Lord Caernarvon, sponsor of the Tutankhamen dig, to participate in further excavations in the Valley of the Kings.	The city of Detroit has ordered sanity tests for speeders. Three out of 23 are found to be of "inferior intelligence." One could not distinguish between "Stop" and "Go" signs.
Dec. 21	The United States Senate has confirmed Pierce Butler, President Harding's choice for Supreme Court Justice, by a vote of 61 to 8. A threatened filibuster move collapsed, but 26 senators avoided voting on the confirmation. Butler has come under fire from Wisconsin progressive Bob LaFollette for his ties to railroads and corporate interests.	The bodies of two Army Air Service men are found on the Papago Indian Reservation 75 miles west of Tucson. The two men, Colonel Francis N. Marshall and Lieutenant Charles Webber, were killed when their plane crashed during a flight from San Diego to Ft. Huachuca, near Tucson, December 7.	Ticket prices in New York City's movie theaters are going up, with some houses charging as much as 50 cents per seat....Automobile manufacturer Henry Ford is planning a new $6 million factory in Chicago. The proposed plant will employ some 16,000 people.		The Intercollegiate Basketball League is modifying the rules on fouls and free throws in an effort to speed up the pace of the game.... The season of debutante balls is in full swing, as wealthy families introduce their daughters to society with lavish parties. Today in New York City, it was the turn of the Brokaws, the Roeslers, the McCalls, the Cawthras, and the Arendts.
Dec. 22		Senator William Borah is calling for a new naval and military disarmament conference. Borah warns that the continuing race to build and maintain military forces is bankrupting the major powers, which are now all together $250 billion in debt.	Christmas turkeys are going for 50 to 60 cents per pound this season, with ducks at 40 cents and roasting chickens available for 30 cents a pound. The market in Christmas trees is slack, with lots going unsold despite distress sale prices.		The new musical *Lilac Time* opens in London tonight....West side Irishman Joe Lynch retains his world's bantamweight title, beating down challenger Midget Smith in Madison Square Garden, taking 10 of 15 rounds.
Dec. 23			The price of eggs has dropped, with a dozen available for from 34 to 69 cents.	Argentine Captain Pedro Zanni, announces plans to fly around the world, from Rome to Tokyo, then on to Alaska, San Francisco, Nova Scotia, and back to Europe.	English writer Joseph Conrad, now 65, is completing a new novel, *The Rover*, set in the Napoleonic era. It is due out in the new year.... German author Thomas Mann's new novel *Buddenbrooks*, will be published here in the coming year.

F	G	H	I	J
Includes campaigns, elections, federal-state relations, civil rights and liberties, crime, the judiciary, education, healthcare, poverty, urban affairs, and population.	*Includes formation and debate of U.S. foreign and defense policies, veterans affairs, and defense spending. (Relations with specific foreign countries are usually found under the region concerned.)*	*Includes business, labor, agriculture, taxation, transportation, consumer affairs, monetary and fiscal policy, natural resources, pollution and industrial accidents.*	*Includes worldwide scientific, medical and technological developments, natural phenomena, U.S. weather and natural disasters.*	*Includes the arts, religion, scholarship, communications media, sports, entertainment, fashions, fads, and social life.*

	World Affairs	Europe	Africa & The Middle East	The Americas	Asia & The Pacific
Dec. 24					
Dec. 25	The Lausanne Conference is in recess for Christmas today, with the Turks and the British still at loggerheads over the oil rich Mosul territory. The British claim Mosul as part of Iraq, but the Turks are insisting on a plebiscite, believing the regions Kurdish majority to be more sympathetic to Turkish rule than the Arab population of Iraq.	The French government of Premier Raymond Poincaré is preparing for a conference of the Allied prime ministers in Paris January 2. The French are drawing up plans for the seizure of German assets in the Rhineland should Germany continue to fall behind in her Reparations payments.			Philippine Governor General Leonard Wood sees off America's All-Star baseball team, which has just finished a tour of the Philippines, and is returning to the United States from Manila.
Dec. 26	The Reparations Commission, overriding Britain's objections, has again declared Germany to be in voluntary default of its reparations payments. A shipment of timber owed to France has not been delivered.	Mobs riot against Jews in Galatz on the Danube in Romania, looting shops and assaulting Jews returning from a meeting on the streets.	A delegation of Egyptian Nationalists, led by Yusuf Razi Bey, arrived in Ankara today to confer with Turkish Nationalist leaders, seeking support for Egyptian independence from Britain.	The Mexican Chamber of Deputies has approved a measure by President Alvaro Obregon granting amnesty to all political prisoners.	
Dec. 27	Stanley Baldwin, Chancellor of the Exchequer, and Montagu Norman, Governor of the Bank of England, sail for Washington, DC, today to try to negotiate American funding for Britain's World War debts. Baldwin is concerned that interest payments on the enormous sums owed are dragging down the British economy.		The Turkish government is allowing Greek ships, escorted by American destroyers, to evacuate Greek and Armenian Christian refugees from the Black Sea ports of Anatolia.		The Imperial Japanese Navy has commissioned its first aircraft carrier, the INS *Hosho*.
Dec. 28		The Belgian Senate today ratifies the Far Eastern treaty signed in Washington this year.	The British Mediterranean Fleet, visiting Malta, has been ordered back to Turkish waters as a show of force against Mustafa Kemal's Nationalist government.		
Dec. 29	In London, American peace activist Jane Addams of the Women's International League for Peace and Freedom, issued a renewed call for America to take part in the League of Nations, to alleviate the economic distress in Europe. Addams is also calling for lifting immigration restrictions on southeastern Europe, to allow children from impoverished regions to come to the United States.	Soviet representatives of Russia, the Ukraine, Belorussia, and Transcaucasia have agreed to unite to form the Union of Soviet Socialist Republics (USSR)....Irish Free State leader William Cosgrave defended a harsh new crackdown on supporters of the republican rebels, claiming that leniency is being mistaken for weakness. Men held on charges of murder or armed robbery have until recently simply been interned in hopes of ending the fighting quickly. Now the Irish *Dail* is authorizing the use of court martials and summary executions to deal with the rebel resistance.		Mexico City officials today institute new, tightened traffic regulations. This has brought a protest by hundreds of car and truck drivers, which snarled city traffic today. Traffic regulations are still not uniform in Mexico, and drivers are not used to the rules.	The Chinese Senate has approved the appointment of General Chang Shao-tseng as Prime Minister. Chang is a protégé of Beijing warlord General Cao Kun, whose forces or those of his allies now dominate 16 provinces of China. Chang will succeed outgoing Prime Minister Wang Tahsieh.
Dec. 30		At a meeting of the First Congress of Soviets in Moscow, Vladimir I. Lenin has proclaimed the creation a new state, the Union of Soviet Socialist Republics, uniting Russia, the Ukraine, Belorussia, and the Trans-Caucasian Republic. While each republic retains some autonomy, real power remains in the hand of Lenin's Politburo in Moscow.		Bluejackets from the battleship USS *Nevada*, on station in Rio since September, have introduced baseball as a popular sport in Brazil.	
Dec. 31		The French Chamber of Deputies and Senate officially extended 1922 by three hours this evening, in order to resolve debate over a budget issue by midnight. The French legislators stop the clock while debate continues before finally resolving the issue.			

A	B	C	D	E
Includes developments that affect more than one world region, international organizations and important meetings of world leaders.	*Includes all domestic and regional developments in Europe, including the Soviet Union.*	*Includes all domestic and regional developments in Africa and the Middle East.*	*Includes all domestic and regional developments in Latin America, the Caribbean, and Canada.*	*Includes all domestic and regional developments in Asian and Pacific nations (and colonies).*

U.S. Politics & Social Issues	U.S. Foreign Policy & Affairs, Defense	U.S. Economy & Environment	Science, Technology & Nature	Culture, Leisure & Lifestyle	
A Catholic parish house is burned today in Woburn, MA, in what is believed to be arson.			Signals by amateur ham radio operators in Manchester and London, are being picked up by American radio operators on the East Coast.	The BBC has opened a radio station broadcasting from Newcastle-on-Tyne....More than 100,000 visitors thronged the streets of Atlantic City today, as the sun shined and temperatures rose to 50 degrees. New Yorkers have overtaken Philadelphians in the number of visitors.	**Dec. 24**
15 members of the New Britain, CT, police force are under investigation for attending a recent Ku Klux Klan meeting....Klan Imperial Wizard H.W. Evans insisted today that the Klan does not condone violence, and is not involved in politics.			Weather in the North Atlantic is at its worst in years, with liners delayed by heavy seas and skippers reporting 120-mile-per-hour winds.	Two new musicals, *The Clinging Vine* and *Glory* open tonight in New York City....Across Europe and the Western Hemisphere, crowds gathered in churches to celebrate Christmas.	**Dec. 25**
Rumors are sweeping Washington, DC, that Interior Secretary Albert Fall may resign soon in the face of the growing Teapot Dome oil field scandal. The White House denies the rumor, stating that President Warren Harding has no information on any such move.		A new Massachusetts state law requiring all automobiles to have rear lights, including a light illuminating the license plate, will be considered as a model for a national standard by the Society of Automotive Engineers.	An association of city planners reports that one day Greater Chicago will extend from Milwaukee to Michigan City, and will have a population of 50 million people....American archaeologists have been denied permission to dig at Carthage in what is now French-controlled Tunisia.	Automobile crashes have become the leading cause of death in Chicago, with 641 fatalities reported at the end of the fiscal year on October 31.	**Dec. 26**
		December is usually a slow month for construction, but this December has been a record breaker for Chicago real estate. Permits for more than $217 million in construction were issued in the Windy City this year.	President Warren Harding, former President Woodrow Wilson, and Supreme Court Chief Justice William Howard Taft were among the many honoring the 100th anniversary of the birth of Louis Pasteur in Philadelphia today. Frenchmen honored Pasteur's memory throughout the country.		**Dec. 27**
		Five railroads operating in the Northeast and Midwest will merge into the consolidated New York, Chicago, and St. Louis line.	Dr. H.E. Wetherell of Philadelphia today demonstrates a pocket typewriter for the American Association for the Advancement of Science. The device can type 17 words a minute and is almost noiseless.	The American Library Association today announces that it is introducing a new annual award, the Newberry Medal, for outstanding authors of children's literature.	**Dec. 28**
	The Harding administration admits today, under questioning by Senator William Borah of Idaho, that it was sending out feelers to European leaders about American participation in a possible economic conference in Brussels some time next year. The American government is officially aloof from European involvement, but concern in business circles about chronic economic instability in Europe remains.	The year 1922 brought a record number of business failures in the Greater New York area: 2,710, though gross liabilities involved were not as bad as in the 2,355 failures in 1921.	An earthquake strikes Avezzano, in the southern Italian province of Apulia this afternoon, sending panicked residents into the street. Citizens of Avezzano fear a repeat of the earthquake of 1915, which killed 8,000 people in the town.	Gunmen stage a daring holdup in New York City's fur district, making off with $10,000 in fine furs.	**Dec. 29**
			The Aeronautical Chamber of Commerce reports that the United States forged ahead decisively in aviation in 1922, with 1.75 million miles of airmail delivery being flown and 49 million letters delivered, without a single fatality.	The Louvre has added two new masterpieces to its collection: a self-portrait by Albrecht Dürer from 1493 and work by French Impressionist Berthe Morisot.	**Dec. 30**
		The year 1922 has been a record year for the American construction industry. Of the $3 billion spent on construction in the first nine months of the year, $1 billion was spent on building homes.	Preliminary work for a tunnel under the Hudson River that can carry automobile traffic between Manhattan and New Jersey has been completed. The tunnel is slated to be finished in three years.	Reverend Charles D. Williams, Bishop of Michigan, today denounced "jazzitis," seeing it as typical of a "modern paganism" that treats life like a "picnic" instead of "a solemn march between eternities."	**Dec. 31**
F *Includes campaigns, elections, federal-state relations, civil rights and liberties, crime, the judiciary, education, healthcare, poverty, urban affairs, and population.*	**G** *Includes formation and debate of U.S. foreign and defense policies, veterans affairs, and defense spending. (Relations with specific foreign countries are usually found under the region concerned.)*	**H** *Includes business, labor, agriculture, taxation, transportation, consumer affairs, monetary and fiscal policy, natural resources, pollution and industrial accidents.*	**I** *Includes worldwide scientific, medical and technological developments, natural phenomena, U.S. weather and natural disasters.*	**J** *Includes the arts, religion, scholarship, communications media, sports, entertainment, fashions, fads, and social life.*	

1923

Funeral procession of President Warren G. Harding in 1923.

	World Affairs	Europe	Africa & The Middle East	The Americas	Asia & The Pacific
Jan.	The political testament of V.I. Lenin says that Joseph Stalin must leave the government of the Soviet Union.	The Soviet Union officially comes into being....Britain and Italy establish reparations arrangements to keep Germany from defaulting again. France objects. Germany defaults on coal shipments. France and Belgium occupy the Ruhr and seize mines and railroads. Germany begins passive resistance. In Munich the Nazi Party holds its first party conference.			The Dutch East Indies receive their first radio telegraph communication from the Netherlands.
Feb.		The Council of Ambassadors gives Lithuania control of an autonomous Memel. The French left Memel in January after a Lithuanian rising and occupation.	Howard Carter breaks the seal on the tomb of King Tutankhamen.	Central American countries and the United States sign a treaty of friendship.	
Mar.		Lithuania accepts Memel, Bulgaria accepts allied reparations terms, and Poland accepts Vilna and Eastern Galacia....Switzerland and Lichtenstein establish a customs union. Effective in June, the Swiss run Lichtenstein's postal and telegraph systems and foreign interests.	France severs the Sanjak of Alexandretta from Syria. The separated region becomes autonomous under France.	The Fourth Pan American Conference meets in Santiago, Chile. It sets procedures for document publication, regulation of trademarks, and regulation of education and health. It prescribes use of commissions to resolve international disputes.	
Apr.		At the Second Lausanne Conference, the allies and Turkey begin peace negotiations. The talks will culminate in July in Turkey's agreeing to cede all non-Turkish territory, and neutralize the straits of Gibraltar. Turkey will pay no reparations.... The Irish civil war ends.	Britain and Iraq sign a protocol to their 1922 agreement. Iraq will become independent on joining the League four years after signing a peace with Turkey.	Mexico nationalizes subsoil resources. It agrees to honor all pre-1917 oil concessions.	Construction begins on Sydney Harbor Bridge. Opened in 1932 it becomes the main route for rail, auto, and pedestrian traffic across the harbor. It holds records for widest long span and largest steel arch bridge. It is Sydney's tallest structure until 1967.
May	In Paris the Allies agree that Germany will have to pay $1 billion to support the Allied occupation army.	A Swiss citizen assassinates the Soviet delegate to the Lausanne Conference. Russia severs diplomatic relations with Switzerland....Greece grants the Kingdom of the Serbs, Croats, and Slovenes access to the sea through Saloniki. The 50-year agreement is effective in 1925.	France and Britain agree that children born of foreign parents in Tunisia can choose their citizenship. Their children will be French citizens....Under Emir Abdullah ibn Hussein, the British mandate of Transjordania comes into being.	The Pan American Treaty establishes procedures for settling disputes peacefully in the Western Hemisphere.	
Jun.	New Zealand claims the Antarctic Ross Dependency.				
Jul.		Italy begins the Italianization of the Tyrol, formerly Austrian territory....The Soviet constitution of 1922 becomes effective....Turkey signs the Treaty of Lausanne, agreed to in April. Turkey also begins exchanging nationals with Greece. By 1930, 1.25 million Greeks will leave Asia Minor with League assistance.	The London Conference on Morocco begins. It continues into October but proves fruitless as Spain, France, and Britain are unable to agree to Morocco's future....Britain assumes control of Southern Rhodesia. It agrees to pay claims of the South African Company as called for in the Cave Report.	Francisco "Pancho" Villa is assassinated in Parral.	
Aug.	The International Conference on Repression of Obscene Publications convenes in Geneva. It ends on 12 September. The United States is among the signatories.	Assassins kill Italian General Enrico Tellini of the Albanian-Greek border commission and several members of his staff. Italy sends a strong note to Greece, then bombs Corfu in early September. Greece accepts League terms for ending the crisis.		The United States recognizes Obregon as Mexico's legitimate leader. In return Obregon agrees to recognize pre-revolution American land titles in Mexico.	
Sep.	The Draft Treaty of Mutual Assistance attempts to define "aggressor" and set up terms for mutual assistance under a series of local alliances. The treaty fails as Britain and the dominions find it too regional.	Germany ends passive resistance and Britain and the United States work to stave off European economic collapse. German hyperinflation has damaged the value of the French franc and caused a general European depression.	Britain assumes the Palestinian mandate....With support from Italy and France, Ethiopia joins the League. Ethiopia eases British concerns about arms trafficking and slavery.		An 8.3 magnitude earthquake rocks Tokyo and Yokohama. Dead number 140,000–200,000; injured exceed 800,000.

A	B	C	D	E
Includes developments that affect more than one world region, international organizations and important meetings of world leaders.	*Includes all domestic and regional developments in Europe, including the Soviet Union.*	*Includes all domestic and regional developments in Africa and the Middle East.*	*Includes all domestic and regional developments in Latin America, the Caribbean, and Canada.*	*Includes all domestic and regional developments in Asian and Pacific nations (and colonies).*

	U.S. Politics & Social Issues	U.S. Foreign Policy & Affairs, Defense	U.S. Economy & Environment	Science, Technology & Nature	Culture, Leisure & Lifestyle
Jan.	The KKK attacks the black community of Rosewood, FL, killing 8 and lynching Sam Carter. Compensation comes only in 1995.	The United States begins withdrawing troops from the Rhineland.			Station KHJ makes the first Rose Bowl broadcast. Another first is the first wireless telephone call from the United States to London.
Feb.	"Renaissance" debuts as the first professional black basketball team.…Mass raids in the U.S. take in large numbers of Mafia.	Secretary of State Charles E. Hughes urges President Harding to have the United States join the world court. He advises that court membership would not entail involvement with the League. Coolidge in three annual messages calls for court membership	Dayton, OH, is the first market for ethyl gasoline.…The first successful chinchilla farm opens in Los Angeles.		Bessie Smith records her first Columbia sides. Smith is the "empress of the blues."
Mar.	Nevada and Montana become the first states to establish old age pensions.…Harding becomes the first president to file and pay income taxes.	The United States and Canada sign a treaty protecting the Pacific halibut fisheries from exhaustion	Struggling to avoid bankruptcy, Columbia Gramophone sells Dictaphone for $1 million.	In New York City, Lee De Forest demonstrates Phonofilm. His process allows the inclusion of sound on film. In coming theaters from coast to coast and in Britain will install it.	Time magazine debuts. Publishers are Briton Hadden and Henry Luce.…Jean Cocteau's *Antigone* debuts in Paris. Picasso designs the sets, Honegger creates the music, and Gabrielle Chanel designs the costumes.
Apr.			Col. Jacob Schick patents his razor.…New York City is hurt by the onset of a general harbor strike.	The first brain tumor operation using a local anesthetic occurs at New York's Beth Israel Hospital. K. Winfield Ney is the surgeon.	Dance marathons begin sweeping the nation...Harold Lloyd's *Safety Last* premieres. The comedy becomes a classic.
May	Ordered to reveal its membership lists, the KKK refuses.		The United States says that unemployment is virtually nonexistent.	The first transcontinental airplane flight occurs between New York and San Diego. It takes 26 hours and 50 minutes.	The Attorney General rules that women can wear pants virtually anywhere.
Jun.	Marcus Garvey receives a 5-year sentence for mail fraud.	British and the United States sign an agreement formally defining British war debt obligations to the United States.		At Anacostia, MD, Charles Francis Jenkins transmits from the naval station facility. His broadcast is the first true demonstration of television.	Okeh releases *The Little Old Log Cabin* by Fiddlin' John Carson. This is the first country recording. Two Carson releases later this year become million sellers.…In Chicago Jelly Roll Morton begins recording for Paramount Records.
Jul.	Harding becomes the first sitting president to visit Alaska.		AT&T joins Boston's WMAF and New York's WEAF to create the first radio network in the U.S.…Kodak releases its model a camera and Kodascope projector. This is the first 16 mm system.	The League Conference for the Standardization of Biological Remedies meets in Edinburgh. The goal is to establish standard treatments for a variety of diseases.	Jelly Roll Morton and the New Orleans Rhythm Kings record Mr. Jelly Lord for Gennett Co of Richmond, IN. This is the first mixed-race recording.
Aug.	Harding has a stroke and dies in San Francisco. Coolidge becomes president.	The United States recognizes the government of Gen. Alvaro Obregon. The general's government has agreed to adjustments to U.S. claims and recognition of pre-1917 oil company land titles. The U.S. and Mexico resume diplomatic relations in September.	Proctor and Gamble guarantees that its employees will have work at least 48 weeks in a year. At the request of Harding, U.S. Steel offers an eight-hour day. Carnegie Steel begins the eight-hour day.		Henry Sullivan swims the English Channel. His time is 28 hours.
Sep.		The U.S.S. *Shenandoah* takes its maiden flight. *Shenandoah* is the first American dirigible, the first of a series of four. Its design comes from a crashed World War zeppelin.		The world's largest dirigible, ZR-1, flies over New York's tallest building, the Woolworth Tower.	

F	G	H	I	J
Includes campaigns, elections, federal-state relations, civil rights and liberties, crime, the judiciary, education, healthcare, poverty, urban affairs, and population.	*Includes formation and debate of U.S. foreign and defense policies, veterans affairs, and defense spending. (Relations with specific foreign countries are usually found under the region concerned.)*	*Includes business, labor, agriculture, taxation, transportation, consumer affairs, monetary and fiscal policy, natural resources, pollution and industrial accidents.*	*Includes worldwide scientific, medical and technological developments, natural phenomena, U.S. weather and natural disasters.*	*Includes the arts, religion, scholarship, communications media, sports, entertainment, fashions, fads, and social life.*

	World Affairs	Europe	Africa & The Middle East	The Americas	Asia & The Pacific
Oct.	The London Imperial Conference begins. It continues into November and at its end the dominions have the right to make foreign treaties.	Turkish forces return to Constantinople. Later, the Turks move their capital to Ankara....At Aachen, with Italian and French support, separatists declare a republic.	Britain places Togoland under the government of the Gold Coast.		Bukhara adopts a new constitution and flag. Independent only since 1917 and a communist state since the overthrow of the emir, Bukhara becomes a Soviet Socialist Republic in 1924.
Nov.	The League of Nations holds its second general conference on communications and transit.	Hjalmar Schacht heads the Rentenbank, which implements harsh anti-inflation policies in Germany. The middle class loses its savings as a dollar equals 7,000 marks in December. Radical movements rise....Hitler attempts his "Beer Halll Putsch." It fails and he receives a five-year term....A Swiss court finds the alleged assassin of the Soviet delegate to Lausanne not guilty. Swiss-Russian relations are tenser.		Mexican Gen. Romulo Figueroa revolts in Guerrero.	
Dec.		The League establishes an economic recovery program for Hungary. A similar program proves successful for Austria....The BBC first broadcasts Big Ben's chimes. The BBC has grown from four to 177 employees this year.	The Tangier Commission establishes that a sultan will rule Tangier. Britain, Spain, and France will have oversight, with France taking the lead role.	Canadian National Railways begins broadcasting from its radio stations to its moving trains. Broadcasts continue until 1931.	An assassination attempt against Japanese Emperor Hirohito fails. Yamamoto resigns to acknowledge responsibility.

A	B	C	D	E
Includes developments that affect more than one world region, international organizations and important meetings of world leaders.	*Includes all domestic and regional developments in Europe, including the Soviet Union.*	*Includes all domestic and regional developments in Africa and the Middle East.*	*Includes all domestic and regional developments in Latin America, the Caribbean, and Canada.*	*Includes all domestic and regional developments in Asian and Pacific nations (and colonies).*

	U.S. Politics & Social Issues	U.S. Foreign Policy & Affairs, Defense	U.S. Economy & Environment	Science, Technology & Nature	Culture, Leisure & Lifestyle
Oct.			The Walt Disney Company begins operations.…With assets of $19 million and debts of $21 million, Columbia Gramophone is unable to avoid bankruptcy. It falls victim to consumer preference for wireless sets.	In Copenhagen, Axel Petersen and Arnold Poulsen demonstrate system that uses two machines—one for sound and another for picture. Companies in France, Britain, and Germany later use this system.	Against the Phillies, Ernie Padgett of the Braves completes the National League's first unassisted triple play
Nov.		The USS *Louisiana* goes for scrap. Idle for three years, the destroyer is a remnant of Teddy Roosevelt's Great White Fleet and a veteran of the Vera Cruz landing and World War I.			
Dec.		The United States signs a commercial treaty with Germany.	Bell & Howell produces its first 16 mm camera. It rejects flammable nitrate 17.5 mm film for the safer, non-combustible Eastman Kodak film.…The Southern Transcontinental Long Distance Telephone Line offers service between Chicago and Los Angeles by way of links in Denver, El Paso, Tucson, and Phoenix.	Vladimir Zworykin seeks a patent for the iconoscope. His device is a tube for an electronic television camera.…A transatlantic voice transmission takes place. Pittsburgh sends; Manchester receives.	

	World Affairs	Europe	Africa & The Middle East	The Americas	Asia & The Pacific
Jan. 1		The Archbishop of Canterbury, in a New Year's Message, expresses support for the League of Nations and urged listeners to learn from the war....In Italy, fascists march through the streets of Rome and pledge allegiance to Benito Mussolini....The Soviet press calls for another attempt to confiscate gold and silver from Russian churches....The Union of Soviet Socialist Republics is officially established under the new constitution.	The head of the Union of South Africa Trade Mission calls for the adoption of a trade agreement between Kenya and South Africa.		The National Congress at Gaya, India, adopts a resolution calling on workers to complete their preparations for civil disobedience and to take immediate steps to secure money and 50,000 volunteers....The Premier of South Australia states that his government is expanding its efforts to persuade skilled British construction workers to immigrate.
Jan. 2		King Alfonso of Spain issues a decree prohibiting Spanish churches from selling artistic treasures and imposing penalties for disobedience.		The International Bankers Committee agreed to make no immediate demand for the payment of loans made to the Mexican government.	
Jan. 3	England plans to increase the production of cotton in Egypt in view of a threatened shortfall of American cotton needed by England's textile industry.	Austria reports that its economy is improving, with the cost of living dropping, savings deposits in banks increasing, and the money supply remaining stable....Roman Catholic authorities in Spain object to the ban on art sales on the grounds that it deprived churches of ownership rights.	Indians leaders in Kenya recommend that the Indians should not pay taxes in light of the absence of any arrangement for Indian participation in the March elections.	Argentina accepts an invitation from Chile to be represented at the Pan-American Congress to be held in Santiago, Chile....The entire Chilean cabinet, headed by President Rivas Vicuna, resigns as the result of differences over the appointment of Braulio Moreno as President of the Supreme Court.	In the Chinese Civil War, the provinces of Yunnan and Kwangsi have formed an alliance with the supporters of Sun Yat-sen in Kwantung.
Jan. 4		The British government promises to consider construction of a Mid-Scotland Ship Canal that would begin at Grangemouth and conclude at the Firth of Clyde....The housing shortage in Germany forces the compulsory housing of tenants with landlords who do not want them.		In a show of support for Edmonton coalminers arrested during a labor dispute, about 150 women surrounded the police station where they are held and pelted it with snowballs for five hours.	
Jan. 5		The Spanish government is taking steps to halt gambling.		British and American diplomats in Mexico City filed official complaints with the Mexican government about the plans of the state of Durango to confiscate 200,000 acres of farm land owned by British and American citizens....Senator James Reed of Missouri introduced a bill to authorize negotiations with France and Great Britain for cession to the United States of their possessions in the West Indies.	
Jan. 6	The American Red Cross appropriated $25,000 for the relief of suffering among German children, at the request of the German Red Cross....The task of taking care of more than 5,000 Russian refugees at Gensan, Korea, has been assumed by the Executive Council of the American Association of Tokyo.	Turkey refused to listen to further Allied pleas for an Armenian homeland at the peace conference in Lausanne, Switzerland....French troops in the American zone in Germany are ordered confined to barracks in order to prevent clashes between them and the Germans....The unemployment is situation in Sweden is improving, but there are fears that winter will worsen the number of jobless.			The Premier of Victoria in Australia is traveling to England to arrange for the immigration of 2,000 heads of families per year to Australia.
Jan. 7	The International Socialist Committee called for the removal of the occupying military forces from the Ruhr in Germany as soon as possible because of the cost of the occupation and the bitterness created among Rhinelanders.	The Prime Minister of Belgium agreed to remain in office after threatening to resign over the removal of French and substitution of Flemish as the language used in the University of Ghent....Forty naval and mining engineers left Paris for Dusseldorf to await instructions designating the different coalmines in the Ruhr that will be under their control.		Great Britain has requested a full report from the Mexican government about the murder of two British citizens by Mexican soldiers.	

A	B	C	D	E
Includes developments that affect more than one world region, international organizations and important meetings of world leaders.	*Includes all domestic and regional developments in Europe, including the Soviet Union.*	*Includes all domestic and regional developments in Africa and the Middle East.*	*Includes all domestic and regional developments in Latin America, the Caribbean, and Canada.*	*Includes all domestic and regional developments in Asian and Pacific nations (and colonies).*

	U.S. Politics & Social Issues	U.S. Foreign Policy & Affairs, Defense	U.S. Economy & Environment	Science, Technology & Nature	Culture, Leisure & Lifestyle
Jan. 1	Two men are shot, a woman is injured, and a barrage of chairs, glassware, plates, knives, and forks are hurled during a riot at the fashionable Hotel Chase in St. Louis, MO, that begins when Prohibition enforcement agents raid a New Year's Day party in a fruitless search for liquor.		The National Association of Manufacturers blames the three percent immigration quota for severely reducing the labor supply.	The Academy of Medicine's Public Health Committee declines to oppose French hypnotist Emile Coue, because his autosuggestions do not involve the prescription of drugs....Dr. C.G. Estabrook, a Brooklyn physician famous for his care of the poor, dies of "smoker's cancer" or cancer of the throat and tongue that had failed to respond to radium treatment.	Wee Willie Keeler, a baseball player and future member of the Hall of Fame, dies.
Jan. 2		The War and Navy Departments protested a provision of the Kellogg-White Federal Radio Control bill that would require military radio operators to be licensed by the Commerce Department.	The Commerce Department voiced support for regulation of all radio broadcasts during hearings on the Kellogg-White Federal Radio Control bill.	Researchers at the University of California discovered a new vitamin in green leafy vegetables that promotes fertility.	Cora Scott Tappan, spiritualist and founder of the National Spiritualists Association, dies.
Jan. 3	Newly appointed U.S. Supreme Court Justice Pierce Butler takes his seat on the Court....The Chicago Coroner's Office reported that it had become overwhelmed by the increasing number of deaths related to the drinking of moonshine whiskey.			The Radio Society of Great Britain announced that it had completed experiments showing that it was possible to conduct wireless communication between Britain and the United States on a far shorter wavelength, smaller aerial, and with less power than had previously been demonstrated.	The State Film Censorship Department of Ohio banned showings of films by comedian and accused rapist Roscoe (Fatty) Arbuckle....The International Aeronautical Federation officially credited American William Mitchell with a world record of 224.05 miles per hour in a flight in a Curtis R-6 over Selfridge Field, MI.
Jan. 4	Izzy Einstein and Moe Smith, Federal prohibition agents, seize 250 cases and 10 barrels of whiskey, imported from the Bahamas, at a garage in New York City....In Shreveport, LA, Leslie Legett, a black man, was lynched for associating with white women.	President Warren Harding vetoes a bill that would have given pension increases to veterans and the wives of veterans of the Mexican-American and Civil Wars....When white vigilantes attack blacks in Rosewood, FL, most of the surviving black residents of the town flee into the swamps and a black church is burned.	The National Association of Hosiery and Underwear Manufacturers announce that one of its members is selling women's hosiery door-to-door on the installment plan.		The Commission on Public Relations, formed by Will H. Hays to advise him on moving-picture problems, decides to ban the showing of Fatty Arbuckle films to protect American youth.
Jan. 5	The U.S. Senate debates the merits of peyote during discussion of a proposed Department of Interior plan, subsequently voted down, to curb peyote use among Native Americans.	About 200 to 300 whites from surrounding areas converge on Rosewood, FL, and the governor is notified of the trouble in progress.	Rodman Wanamaker succeeds his late father as president of John Wanamaker in Philadelphia.		A survey of chewing gum dealers reveals that the advent of prohibition has considerably reduced the sale of chewing gum to men, but more women are chewing to cover up the smell from smoking....Juste François Joseph Thoret of France sets a new world gliding record by remaining in the air for seven hours and three minutes at Biskra, Algeria.
Jan. 6	A train evacuates black residents of Rosewood, FL, to Gainesville.	A shortage of army officers under the reduced strength limits imposed by Congress has led to the removal of officers from the Veterans Bureau and their return to military service.	The 1923 edition of Ocean Records, the pocket handbook for travel abroad, has published for the first time a complete schedule of European commercial flights.	The Russian Academy of Science inducts Albert Einstein....The new treatment of insulin for diabetes has now been tested on 50 patients with promising results.	The Amateur Athletic Union announces that John Weissmuller set 33 official world records in swimming in 1922, according to recently submitted documentation....Light-weight boxer Mercy Montes knocked out Johnny Dundee to take the championship in a fifty-one-round fight that set a world record for rounds under the Queensbury rules.
Jan. 7	A mob of 100 to 150 whites in Rosewood, FL, burned the 12 remaining houses in the black part of town.	The Senate votes to recall American troops from the Rhine.			Emil Hirsh, the best known Reform Judaism rabbi and an influential educator, dies in Chicago.

F	G	H	I	J
Includes campaigns, elections, federal-state relations, civil rights and liberties, crime, the judiciary, education, healthcare, poverty, urban affairs, and population.	*Includes formation and debate of U.S. foreign and defense policies, veterans affairs, and defense spending. (Relations with specific foreign countries are usually found under the region concerned.)*	*Includes business, labor, agriculture, taxation, transportation, consumer affairs, monetary and fiscal policy, natural resources, pollution and industrial accidents.*	*Includes worldwide scientific, medical and technological developments, natural phenomena, U.S. weather and natural disasters.*	*Includes the arts, religion, scholarship, communications media, sports, entertainment, fashions, fads, and social life.*

	World Affairs	Europe	Africa & The Middle East	The Americas	Asia & The Pacific
Jan. 8	The League of Nations met to discuss measures to limit the traffic in opium and other dangerous drugs.…The Permanent Court of International Justice held its second (extraordinary) session in the Hague.	At the Lausanne peace conference, the Allies agreed to accept Turkey's refusal to grant a homeland to the Armenians.…French drivers who break the motoring rules will be warned immediately by whistles that have been issued to 40,000 road police.	The Union Defense Department in South Africa is reorganizing the commando and rifle systems, with mounted infantry to serve as the backbone of the new force.		Admiral Baron Hayao Shima Mura, chief of the General Naval Staff of Japan, dies in Tokyo.…Police protection has been established for several Hindu shrines in Lahore in India following reports of another attempt by Sikhs to seize them.
Jan. 9	The All-India Caliphate Conference warns the Indian government that in the event of a European attack upon Turkey, the Muslims of India would immediately launch a civil disobedience campaign.…The German government declares its inability to export coal to pay its reparations installment.	Folke Cronhold, a Swedish Consul-General in Mexico City who lost his job in the wake of allegations that he had acted as an intermediary between the German Foreign Office and Mexican President Carranza for the delivery Zimmermann Note, is negotiating for reinstatement.		Small earthquakes rock El Salvador with the center of the disturbances about 70 miles from the city.	
Jan. 10	Germany notifies the United States that it would not make reparations to the countries that have occupied the Ruhr.…U.S. officials express anger at French actions in the Ruhr.	Germany recalls her ambassadors to France and Belgium in response to the French occupation of the Ruhr.…France continues to send troops to the Rhine via rail.…Germany announces that coal deliveries to Italy will continue.	A large crowd near the tomb of King Tutankhamen in Luxor, Egypt, sees archaeologists bring out chariots with wheels studded with gems, an ebony chair inlaid with ivory, and hair apparently from the head of Tutankhamen's queen.		One-hundred and seventy-two prisoners are found guilty of murder, arson, and dacoity, and sentenced to death for an attack on a police station in the Hindu village at Chauri Chaura in India.
Jan. 11	Lithuania is attempting to seize Memel.…The Polish Consul has asked France to protect Polish interests in Memel.…Allied warships arrive in Memel while the Allied commissioner in the region has declared that he will resist Lithuania with all means at his disposal.	Ex-King Constantine of Greece dies of heart failure in a hotel in Sicily.		Higher education throughout Cuba was virtually suspended as a result of the general student strike called by the Students' Federation of Havana University to enforce demands for administrative and pedagogic reforms.…Governor Madrazo in the Mexican state of Guanajuato ordered Federal troops to prohibit Catholic ceremonies in the open.	The Filipino Senate voted to establish hospitals in every province.…Martial law has been declared around Canton, China, while many Chinese flee to Hong Kong and Macao.
Jan. 12		The political police in Siberia discover a plot by counterrevolutionaries to establish a Siberian autonomous republic.…The Southern Irish Loyalists' Relief Association has found employment for more than 1,000 refugees and housing for 1,500.	The British Colonial Office publishes the Palestine census showing 589,564 Muslims, 83,794 Jews, 73,026 Christians, and 7028 Druses.	The refusal of the United States to recognize the Mexican government results in a decision by the Mexicans to boycott the Fifth Pan-American Congress in Santiago, Chile.…Brazilian officers involved in the July revolution have been freed from prison by order of a judge.	
Jan. 13		On the motion of Premier Mussolini, the Grand Council of the Fascista organization adopts a resolution affirming loyal devotion to the monarchy as a way of maintaining the unity of the country.		Dr. Harry Roberts is consecrated as the new Episcopal Bishop of Haiti.	An American destroyer is been detailed to watch for the arrival of Russian refugees who sailed from Shanghai and are expected off Manila Bay.
Jan. 14		Germany notifies the Reparation Commission that it intends to suspend payments of money and in kind because of the occupation of Ruhr, which it considers a violation of the Versailles Treaty.…Alexandre Ribot, a former Prime Minister of France, dies.	Items removed from the tomb of King Tutankhamen include an ebony stool inlaid with ivory, wooden bows, and a large egg filled with meats.	Peru refuses to attend the Pan-American conference because of alleged abuses of Peruvian citizens in Peruvian territory occupied by Chile.…President Obregon expels Ernesto Filippi, a Catholic priest, for participating in religious ceremonies contrary to Federal law.	
Jan. 15		Irregular forces in Dublin, Ireland launched attacks on several strategic points throughout the city and, although driven off by Free State troops, they continued intermittent firing throughout the night.…The unsettlement caused by the French advance into the Ruhr is blamed for a new fall of the German mark.			It has been decided to revert to the prewar practice of limiting the appointment of officers in the Gurkha, Garwhali, Kumaon, and Burma battalions to those not over 5-feet, 10-inches in height.

A	B	C	D	E
Includes developments that affect more than one world region, international organizations and important meetings of world leaders.	*Includes all domestic and regional developments in Europe, including the Soviet Union.*	*Includes all domestic and regional developments in Africa and the Middle East.*	*Includes all domestic and regional developments in Latin America, the Caribbean, and Canada.*	*Includes all domestic and regional developments in Asian and Pacific nations (and colonies).*

U.S. Politics & Social Issues	U.S. Foreign Policy & Affairs, Defense	U.S. Economy & Environment	Science, Technology & Nature	Culture, Leisure & Lifestyle	
Methodist ministers in Chicago condemn the ban on members of the Ku Klux Klan serving on juries that is issued by the Chief Justice of the Chicago Criminal Court.... Liquor control agents complain that much of the illicit liquor in the Washington, DC, area came into the United States under consignment to the foreign embassies.	Bench warrants are issued for six of the seven men indicted by the Special War Funds Grand Jury for alleged frauds connected to contracts for the erection of cantonments during and after the World War.		Kodak introduces a 16mm-film motion picture camera that can be used by amateurs.	The Wertheimer family portraits by John S. Sargent are displayed for the first time in their new home in the National Gallery in London.... Opera was broadcast by radio from London for the first time.	Jan. 8
		Motor highway competition and electric transportation service results in cutbacks on the Pennsylvania Railroad system throughout the Midwest.		Barnard College recommends a 10-hour day and 6-day week for college girls....British journalist and fiction author Cyril Gull dies in London....Eddie Foy, a comedian who stars in his family's vaudeville show, marries for the fourth time to Marie Combs.	Jan. 9
A large delegation of women from various organizations appeared before a Senate Judiciary committee to urge the submission of a constitutional amendment giving the Federal government jurisdiction over child labor....The Ku Klux Klan in Atlantic City, NJ, warned bootleggers to stop selling liquor.	President Harding recalls American troops from the Rhine.	Bison have increased their numbers in the United States by 2583 since 1903 according to the American Bison Society.... The Producing Managers' Association declined to halt block purchase of seats by brokers as a prelude to the installation of a central ticket office.	A large lake has been discovered in central Australia near the Lander River.	Conrad Stanislavsky, director of the Moscow Art Theatre, makes his first American appearance on stage in New York City.	Jan. 10
Harvard University President A. Lawrence Lowell declared that it is the policy of the university to bar African Americans from freshman dormitories....Several notable graduates of Harvard issued a letter protesting the policy.			The American Museum of Natural History announced that fossils prove that a broad land connection existed between North America and Asia....An investigation of the teeth of children in New York City schools shows that 96.5 percent of the children have dental problems with an average of seven cavities per child.	The National Committee for Better Films, affiliated with the National Board of Review, declared against the exhibition of films by Fatty Arbuckle.	Jan. 11
Congressman Upshaw of Georgia charged that there is a U.S. House bootlegger who has been plying his trade in the House office building.	The New York Guard, organized during the World War, for the protection of the state during the absence of the National Guard, was abolished.	Radio standardization was approved by 40 radio trade associations and national engineering and scientific societies.		Marion McLaren, a member of a vaudeville musical troupe known as the Five McLarens, was shot to death by an angry ex-fiancé.	Jan. 12
Five hundred citizens of Goose Creek protested the actions of 15 masked men, possible Ku Klux Klan members, who flogged a woman and a male caller to her home.	Senator James W. Wadsworth, Jr. warned in a speech about the dangers of pacifism and unpreparedness for war.	At the national motor car exhibition, automobile manufacturers introduced the air-cooled engine and displayed various accessories that signaled a driver's intention to turn or stop.	The Board of Managers of the New York Botanical Library has recommended that the institution acquire a Photostat to make facsimile reproductions of rare books in its collection.	Edward McKnight Brawley, an African-American author and Baptist minister dies.	Jan. 13
A fleet of schooners believed to be carrying whiskey was spotted off the New Jersey coast.			Wireless radio communication occurred for the first time between New York and London, although only New York had the ability to transmit voices.	Bad liquor is believed to have suddenly killed three men in a saloon in New Jersey.	Jan. 14
			Scientists at Abbott Laboratories in Chicago have discovered butyn, a substitute for cocaine in dental and other minor surgeries.	Benjamin Tucker Tanner, an African Methodist Episcopal bishop and ecumenist, dies....All of those accused of participating in fixing the heavyweight championship boxing match between Battling Siki and Georges Carpentier were declared innocent in a report submitted to the French Boxing Federation....The Duke of York announced his engagement to Lady Elizabeth Bowes-Lyon.	Jan. 15

F	G	H	I	J
Includes campaigns, elections, federal-state relations, civil rights and liberties, crime, the judiciary, education, healthcare, poverty, urban affairs, and population.	*Includes formation and debate of U.S. foreign and defense policies, veterans affairs, and defense spending. (Relations with specific foreign countries are usually found under the region concerned.)*	*Includes business, labor, agriculture, taxation, transportation, consumer affairs, monetary and fiscal policy, natural resources, pollution and industrial accidents.*	*Includes worldwide scientific, medical and technological developments, natural phenomena, U.S. weather and natural disasters.*	*Includes the arts, religion, scholarship, communications media, sports, entertainment, fashions, fads, and social life.*

	World Affairs	Europe	Africa & The Middle East	The Americas	Asia & The Pacific
Jan. 16		Epidemics of typhus, smallpox, and cholera have reached such alarming proportions in the refugee centers throughout Greece that the government bars the admission of more refugees from Asia Minor.			
Jan. 17	Canada seeks to withdraw from the League of Nations.	Greece has decided to admit no more refugees to the country unless private relief agencies provide for them.…The Near East Relief is feeding 35,000 refugees awaiting embarkation at Black Sea ports, but fears that these people will be deported to the interior by the Turks, with consequent heavy death and suffering.…Germany formally protested to France that its extension of the Franco-Belgian military occupation had gone beyond the neutral zone established by the Versailles Treaty.	Several Jews are severely beaten in Jaffa, Palestine, by Arabs in a funeral procession for a police commissioner murdered by unidentified persons.	The Canadian Minister of the Interior stations 10 mounted police on the Six Nations Reserve.…Chief Deskaheh states that the police are attempting to crush the Indians and he wants justice or thousands of Indians will immigrate to the United States.	Sun Yat-sen and his forces take control of Canton, China.
Jan. 18		The Lithuanian government announces that it had nothing to do with the events at Memel and blamed the violence on volunteers.…The government of Georgia denies Soviet claims that Georgia has been re-annexed to Russia.			The British Overseas Settlement Board is sending boys between 14- and 15-years of age to apprentice on farms in Ontario, Canada.
Jan. 19		French and Belgian nationals will be barred from lodging accommodations at any of the leading hotels of Berlin in accordance with a resolution ratified unanimously by the Berline Hotelmen's Association.… Anti-Jewish riots broke out in Moldavia and martial law has been declared in parts of the country.	Howard Carter removes more items from the tomb of King Tutankhamen, including a throne that depicts Horus in solid gold.		
Jan. 20			Interest in the tomb of King Tutankhamen is diverted by the discovery by American archeologists of the body of a 4,000-year-old Egyptian princess.		Holland no longer will be entirely cut off from its Dutch East Indian possessions with the completion of receiving and transmitting wireless telegraph station at Kootwyk, especially for communication with the colonies.
Jan. 21		In Berlin, German theaters agree to stop rehearsals of any French plays and to replace any French plays currently playing as soon as possible.…Some German shops also stop selling French perfumes while Bavarian middle schools have stopped teaching the French language.			
Jan. 22		Eight Greek men are hanged by Turkey for giving money to Greek patriotic societies.…In Paris, an anarchist, Germaine Berthon, shoots and kills Marius Plateau, a newspaper official and leader of a royalist propaganda group, instead of the intended target, Leon Daudet, leader of the French Royalist Party.…Max Nordau, a Zionist leader, dies in Paris.	Indians in Kenya express fears that they will be the targets of violence at the hands of Europeans.…Elders of the Mtawara tribe in Rhodesia hold a human sacrifice to end a drought and poor crop production.		
Jan. 23				Prince Edward Island in Canada decided to prohibit the importation of liquor for export purposes.	Nine Sikhs in Attock Goal in Lahore, India were flogged for refusing to wear prison clothes.

A	B	C	D	E
Includes developments that affect more than one world region, international organizations and important meetings of world leaders.	*Includes all domestic and regional developments in Europe, including the Soviet Union.*	*Includes all domestic and regional developments in Africa and the Middle East.*	*Includes all domestic and regional developments in Latin America, the Caribbean, and Canada.*	*Includes all domestic and regional developments in Asian and Pacific nations (and colonies).*

U.S. Politics & Social Issues	U.S. Foreign Policy & Affairs, Defense	U.S. Economy & Environment	Science, Technology & Nature	Culture, Leisure & Lifestyle	
The Massachusetts House of Representatives unanimously passed a resolution terming the Ku Klux Klan dangerous to American rights.					Jan. 16
A black man in Newberry, FL, charged with stealing cattle, is removed from his jail cell by whites and lynched.	Henry Ford announced that he plans to expand his automobile production worldwide with the aim of making people so prosperous that they will be too happy and too prosperous to make war.			The Riverside Hospital Nurses' Training School in Paducah, KY, temporarily suspended five student nurses for bobbing their hair.	Jan. 17
The Prohibition Enforcement Convention, held under the auspices of the New Jersey Anti-Saloon League, adopted a resolution urging that the army and navy be utilized to establish a blockade to prevent liquor smuggling.			The U.S. Army Air Service tested a new air sextant developed for aerial navigation that permits an aviator to determine his location in the air with respect to the ground over which he is passing.	Alexander Pearson set a new flight record by flying between Dayton, OH, and New York City in four hours and four minutes at 140 miles per hour.…Princeton University sent a letter to the parents of all undergraduates warning that automobiles hinder success in all endeavors.	Jan. 18
African Americans began leaving Blanford, IN, following a warning issued by white residents that they be out by 7 o'clock at night if they were unable to produce the black man charged with assaulting a white girl.	The United States has proposed that Great Britain pay off its debt at reduced rates of three percent interest for the first 10 years, 3½ for the remainder of the period, and a sinking fund charge of ½ percent over the whole term.			Tennessee Claflin Cook, an American spiritualist and stock broker, dies.	Jan. 19
Marcus Garvey, president of the Universal Negro Improvement Association, denied charges by the New Orleans police that his group was anarchistic and contemplated an overthrow of the government.		More people are employed in Detroit today than ever before in its history, according to figures given out by the Employers Association.…The government announced the Colorado River Project to turn hundreds of thousands of acres of arid land in Wyoming, Utah, Nevada, Arizona, New Mexico, and Colorado into fertile farms, while hydroelectric plants will distribute power.	The Charente Steel Works in France cast a 70-foot long gun capable of firing a shell weighing 528 pounds a distance of about 56 miles. It is designed for shore defense.	President Ban Johnson of the American League completed his staff of umpires for the 1923 baseball season.…Johnson also approved of licensure for baseball players with licenses revoked for misconduct on or off the field.…Thousands of people participated in funeral services for actor Wallace Reid in Los Angeles.	Jan. 20
		In an effort to improve efficiency and reduce time spent on telephone lines, the New York Telephone Company offers advice on how to dial a phone and how to property answer one.		The Director of Public Safety of Jersey City, NJ, was charged with failing to close the motion picture theaters on Sundays in compliance with the Blue Law.	Jan. 21
A Massachusetts Communist was arrested for attempting to bomb a shoe factory.…Eight officials and three former officials of Gary, IN, were arrested on warrants charging them with conspiracy to violate the prohibition law.…Benedict Crowell, wartime Assistant Secretary of War, pleaded not guilty of conspiracy to defraud the government in the construction of army cantonments.			The lens of a pig's eye was substituted for the destroyed cornea of a youth in an attempt to restore his sight.		Jan. 22
Margaret Sanger, head of the birth control movement, was prevented from speaking in Albany, NY, because of a protest from religious and civic organizations.			A French scientist, Dr. Magnan, invented an anemometer to detect wind speed for the use by sailors.		Jan. 23

F	G	H	I	J
Includes campaigns, elections, federal-state relations, civil rights and liberties, crime, the judiciary, education, healthcare, poverty, urban affairs, and population.	*Includes formation and debate of U.S. foreign and defense policies, veterans affairs, and defense spending. (Relations with specific foreign countries are usually found under the region concerned.)*	*Includes business, labor, agriculture, taxation, transportation, consumer affairs, monetary and fiscal policy, natural resources, pollution and industrial accidents.*	*Includes worldwide scientific, medical and technological developments, natural phenomena, U.S. weather and natural disasters.*	*Includes the arts, religion, scholarship, communications media, sports, entertainment, fashions, fads, and social life.*

	World Affairs	Europe	Africa & The Middle East	The Americas	Asia & The Pacific
Jan. 24		France declares that it demands respect from conquered Germany and the application of the treaties.			The Inspector-General of Chinese Maritime Customs suggests in a speech to the International Anti-Opium Association of Peking that China consider introducing a temporary opium monopoly in China.
Jan. 25		The French announce that they plan to hold the Ruhr for at least two years even if the Germans accept the reparations plan.... The Italian cabinet has decided not to legalize games of chance on the grounds that such games are inconsistent with Italian dignity and that towns should not depend on returns from gambling for revenue.		Lieutenant Colonel Hector B. Varela, who commanded the Argentine forces that put down an insurrection of ranch laborers in Patagonia, is assassinated by Kurt G. Wilckens, a Dutch anarchist.	
Jan. 26		Adolf Hitler, leader of the National Socialists in Germany, declares that nothing will deprive him any longer of opening an attack on the enemies of November 9, 1918, the men who proclaimed the German Republic.			Masano Hanihara, newly appointed Japanese Ambassador to the United States will resume negotiations with the American government over Japanese immigration.
Jan. 27					The Chinese government issues a statement that the Inspector-General of Chinese Maritime Customs was misunderstood and that China has every intention of fulfilling the provisions of the Opium Convention.
Jan. 28	The peace conference at Lausanne ends.... Turkey refuses to agree to the preservation of the entire Anzac zone and claim the right to reduce the size of six cemeteries elsewhere, much to the anger of the British.	About 100,000 Belgians protest in support of the University of Ghent remaining a French-language institution.... The Chamber of Deputies in France agree to restore the palace at Versailles.		The Constant Spring Hotel, the largest hotel in Jamaica, was destroyed by fire.	
Jan. 29	The Council of the League of Nations devotes its meeting to financial and administrative questions.... The Cologne, Germany, newspaper reports that circulation of the paper has been stopped by the French for nine days although no order has been received by the Inter-Allied Commission.	The Soviet State Political Department announces that more than 10,000 people have been exiled from Russia and Siberia without trial and half of these exiles were Moderate Socialists.... The Soviet government also announces that there are 48,500 people confined in prisons and concentration camps with about 28,000 of these awaiting trial.	The South African Parliament engages in a heated debate over industrial development and the matter of uncontrolled immigration of natives into urban areas.... South African legislators express fears that natives are being exposed to undesirable elements in cities.	The grain growers of Saskatchewan, Canada, approve a resolution in favor of a compulsory wheat board rather than a voluntary pool of growers.	Cantonese refugees flee to Hong Kong.
Jan. 30	The International Labor Office of the League of Nations meets to consider questions affecting war-disabled men.... The Council of the League of Nations debated the future of Mosul in Iraq and invited Turkey to become a temporary member. It also finds that Poland has no right to impose its will upon the Free State of Danzig.	Martial law is declared in the Ruhr.... The political situation led to falls in the currencies of Germany, France, Belgium, Poland, and Hungary.... The Central Railway Station in Milan, Italy, is totally destroyed by fire.... New records for depreciation are set as the currencies of Continental European nations suffer from deflation.	Indians in Kenya are offered a common electoral franchise with Europeans along with property and education qualifications that would allow about 10 percent of Indian adults to vote.... About 20,000 Turks mass in Constantinople in readiness to forcibly resist the Lausanne Treaty.		The Legislative Assembly of India defeats a bill to amend the Criminal Code Procedure Act to reduce the power of the police. It passes the Indian Mines Act Amendment Bill, but a provision limiting the working hours of miners is defeated on the grounds that most miners are farmers who work only part-time in mines.
Jan. 31	The Council of the League of Nations receives a report on the Reduction of Armaments.... The French armored cruiser *Voltaire* arrives in Memel waters, while Memel insurgents use Lithuanian and German currency to buy military supplies for their newly-established military depot.	Poland executes art professor Eligiusz Niewadomski for the assassination of President Gabriel Narutowicz.... Great Britain authorizes 20 women police, known as woman constables, to join the Metropolitan Police.... The Soviet State Political Department announces that more than 10,000 people were exiled from Russia and Siberia without trial.		Several hundred Mexican tramway strikers, accompanied by members of other unions, parade through the main streets in protest against interference by the government in the strike.... The Canadian Parliament opens with the Prime Minister noting the economic condition of the country, the absence of unemployment, and the signs of revival of trade and industry.	The Prime Minister of New Zealand declares that the financial situation of the railways compare favorably with other parts of the British Empire and New Zealand's grading of dairy herds is far ahead of the United Kingdom.... The New Zealand Alliance of Labor authorizes a strike by 50,000 workers, but does not call for an immediate work stoppage.

A	B	C	D	E
Includes developments that affect more than one world region, international organizations and important meetings of world leaders.	*Includes all domestic and regional developments in Europe, including the Soviet Union.*	*Includes all domestic and regional developments in Africa and the Middle East.*	*Includes all domestic and regional developments in Latin America, the Caribbean, and Canada.*	*Includes all domestic and regional developments in Asian and Pacific nations (and colonies).*

U.S. Politics & Social Issues	U.S. Foreign Policy & Affairs, Defense	U.S. Economy & Environment	Science, Technology & Nature	Culture, Leisure & Lifestyle	
Jewish leaders at a meeting of the Union of American Hebrew Congregations recommended that Jews stop using wine and stop speaking Yiddish to become Americanized.... The Commissioner of Immigration declared that people of Northern and Western Europe are not taking advantage of permission to immigrate to the United States.	Paul Reinsch, U.S. Ambassador to China under President Woodrow Wilson and a founder of the American Political Science Association, dies.		The National Canners Association announced that an effective means had been discovered to eliminate the oxygen from cans containing food products.		Jan. 24
Fifty druggists in Buffalo, NY, were charged with selling liquor without the required prescriptions.	The last of the American army of occupation left Europe when the *St. Mihile* sailed from Antwerp, Belgium.		A youth who received a portion of the eye of a pig can distinguish light and darkness.		Jan. 25
For the third time since Congress proposed the Prohibition Amendment to the Federal Constitution, the Connecticut legislature refused to ratify it.			The U.S. Bureau of Mines is operating a plant that is producing helium for the first time in the United States.... The Army Air Service wants to fill an air ship with helium and send it to the North Pole.	Film actor Douglas Fairbanks attacked Will Hays as merely the official fixer of films rather than an uplifter of movies.	Jan. 26
				The new spring styles for clothes feature longer skirts and higher hats.	Jan. 27
					Jan. 28
The United States deported 51 Armenians who claimed the right of admission to the United States on the ground that they were fleeing from Turkish territory under religious persecution.			The Institute of Industrial Psychology in Great Britain found that increased output in coalmines was achieved by using six times the ordinary strength of illumination.	In London, radio is used for the first time to provide music for a large ball.	Jan. 29
	The Secretary of the Treasury, Andrew Mellon, notifies the Senate Finance Committee that a proposal to give the German government a loan to purchase food from American farmers is in contravention to the Treasury's policy that foreign government seeking aid should appeal to the investing public instead of the U.S. government.				Jan. 30
The U.S. government declines to pursue pending espionage charges against Socialist Congressman-elect Victor Berger of Wisconsin for his opposition to the World War.... In a speech on the Senate floor, Senator McKellar, a Democrat from Tennessee, condemns the Debt Funding Commission for selling out the United States by refusing to push the British for payments.		Banker Henry Clews, who sold bonds so successfully during the Civil War that President Ulysses Grant appointed him in 1877 to secure foreign loans for the United States, dies in New York City.	Aviator Walter Hinton, attempting to make the first flight from North America to South America, arrives in Brazil.... Frenchman Emile Coué, father of the autosuggestion movement, takes credit for strengthening the voice of opera star Mary Garden.		Jan. 31

F	G	H	I	J
Includes campaigns, elections, federal-state relations, civil rights and liberties, crime, the judiciary, education, healthcare, poverty, urban affairs, and population.	*Includes formation and debate of U.S. foreign and defense policies, veterans affairs, and defense spending. (Relations with specific foreign countries are usually found under the region concerned.)*	*Includes business, labor, agriculture, taxation, transportation, consumer affairs, monetary and fiscal policy, natural resources, pollution and industrial accidents.*	*Includes worldwide scientific, medical and technological developments, natural phenomena, U.S. weather and natural disasters.*	*Includes the arts, religion, scholarship, communications media, sports, entertainment, fashions, fads, and social life.*

	World Affairs	Europe	Africa & The Middle East	The Americas	Asia & The Pacific
Feb. 1	German union leaders issue an appeal to the U.S. Congress to save Europe and the world from ultimate disaster by blocking the Ruhr occupation that threatens the economic well-being of Germany.…The Allies send Lithuania an ultimatum to withdraw from Memel by February 8.	A large number of Jewish students are injured in an anti-Semitic riot that breaks out in Bucharest.…The University of Bucharest remains closed until February 8 because of the riots.… Many Jewish shops in Bucharest close in fear of possible attacks.…France cuts off shipments of coal from the Ruhr to Germany.…The British government accepts American terms for the funding of British war debt.	In Luxor, Egypt, a crowd of spectators watches as a five-foot tall gilded wooden couch is removed from King Tutankhamen's tomb.…The government of South Africa reaches an agreement with the Marconi Company to erect and operate a high-power wireless station.	More than 1,000 fans of Argentine heavyweight boxer Luis Firpo cheer him as he sails from Buenos Aires for a fight with Bill Brennan in New York City.…Fourteen men die and 30 are wounded in a fight between striking trolley workers and Mexican soldiers guarding street cars.	William Morris Hughes, Premier of Australia, resigns.…Stanley Bruce has been asked by the Governor-General of Australia to form a new government.…Sikhs in India threaten civil disobedience if a statue of Lord Lawrence of Arabia is not removed from Lahore.
Feb. 2	The League of Nations discussed the protection of German minorities in Poland.…The League of Nations representative in Greece reports that there are 100,000 refugees in camps around Athens with new refugees arriving daily.…The Greek government is seeking loans to provide for refugee relief.	French music hall artists vote unanimously to ban German attractions from appearing in France for the next four years.…More than 100 people in Berlin, Germany become ill after eating horse meat.… Crowds of people in the Ruhr violate the French curfew by remaining on the streets between 10 p.m. and 6 a.m.	The Indian Congress in Kenya asks for electoral representation of Indians on the same basis that Europeans enjoy.…The Europeans in Kenya refuse to discuss the proposal for fear of pledging future generations.… Italian forces in Tripoli, Libya kill 300 Arabs in the first day of fighting after Italy attempted to extend its occupation.	Bolivia opens direct negotiations with Chile in hopes of obtaining a seaport on the Pacific Ocean.… Chile is seeking a settlement that gives it possession of part of the coast line along its northern border.…Mexico has readied 7000 troops in Mexico City to quell the trolley strike.	Australia announces that it is developing radio feeder stations to link its major cities with the main radio sending stations.…The government of India is modifying the Indian Code of Criminal Procedure to remove racial distinctions that give privileges to Europeans.
Feb. 3	The Imperial War Graves Commission announces that it is no longer able to return wooden crosses from cemeteries on the Western Front to the relatives of the dead.… The Fren-ch government informs Premier Benito Mussolini of Italy that France will not extend its occupation activities in the Ruhr.	The rapid rise in the cost of foodstuffs caused by the collapse of the mark is dominating discussion in Germany.…Germans speculate that soon 100,000 marks will equal one dollar.			
Feb. 4	The Red Cross requests donations to relieve the destitution and sickness among the refugees in Greece, who have fled from Asia Minor.…The Reparations Committee in Paris rejects German pleas for a moratorium on the payment of war damages.… French troops occupy the west bank of the Rhein including Offenburg and Appenweier.	The closing of public dancing places in Berlin leads to police raids and the arrests of hundreds of patrons of illegal dance halls.…Lithuania has threatened to declare war on Poland over a border dispute.…M. Ernest Judet, former editor of a Paris newspaper, is sentenced to life in prison for aiding the enemy during the war.	A skirmish occurs between a group of armed Arabs and a party of British officers in Iraq.…Ismet Pasha of Turkey declares that the failure of the Lausanne Conference is due to the demand of the Allies that the present Turkish government should recognize all contracts and concessions made by previous Turkish governments.	The government of Ontario in Canada announces a plan to encourage immigration by single men and women for farm work.… Any Ontario farmer who will build a home on his land for a family from the British Isles will receive financial assistance from the Overseas Settlement Board.	Count Tamemoto Kuroki, a Japanese general famed for his actions during the Sino-Japanese War in 1894 and the Russo-Japanese War in 1904, dies.…The Chinese government is deeply in debt and unable to meet its financial obligations.
Feb. 5	The Soviet government demands payment from the United States and Britain for use of ships of the Russian Volunteer Fleet.	Massive avalanches and severe flooding caused by melting snow in Austria threatens villages, shuts down railroads, and prompts evacuations.… Irish nationalists set off bombs in Dublin.		A petition signed by 51,000 Canadians seeking a referendum on the liquor question is presented to the government.…Manitoba, Canada will vote in June on whether to continue the "bone dry" liquor control system.	The British government announces a plan to send 500 British boys, aged between 14 and 18 years, per month to settle in Queensland and South Australia to support agriculture and replace the Australian men killed in the war.
Feb. 6	Switzerland gives the League of Nations several buildings in Geneva.…The British Cabinet meets to discuss the ramifications of the Turkish refusal to sign the Lausanne agreement while the French government seeks to persuade Turkey to sign.	Walter Hannington, leader of the British Unemployed Marchers, was charged with stealing 23 jars of jam from a government workhouse to feed the jobless.…The Nice Chamber of Commerce formally protests a French government proposal to ban the acquisition of real estate by foreigners.…The Danube floods in Austria.…A bomb is thrown by an anarchist at the Bulgarian Prime Minister.	Several members of the Egyptian cabinet resign.	The government of British Columbia in Canada advises naturalization judges not to discriminate against Asians applying for citizenship.	Japan is refusing to scrap battleships until France and Italy ratify the Washington Disarmament Treaty.… Recurring strife in Kwangtung, China has badly damaged merchants and made it virtually impossible to celebrate the Chinese New Year.…The people of Canton, China express support for Sun Yat-Sen.
Feb. 7	The government of Turkey notifies the Allied Powers that foreign warships above 1,000 tons will no longer be allowed in Smyrna and orders all foreign warships to leave by sunset.…No warships leave.	Crowds of men in Austria boo the train of German General Erich Ludendorff.…Ludendorff is called a "murderer" by Austrian Socialists as his speech in a Vienna suburb is concluded with a riot between pan-Germans and Socialists.…The King of England approves permanent instructions to the army regarding the observance of Armistice Day on November 11.			The British demand the abolition of the "mui tsai" system in Hong Kong that they view as being akin to slavery.…Royal assent is giving for a Queensland, Australia law that gives equality to both sexes in divorce proceedings and provides lunacy as an additional ground for divorce.

A	B	C	D	E
Includes developments that affect more than one world region, international organizations and important meetings of world leaders.	*Includes all domestic and regional developments in Europe, including the Soviet Union.*	*Includes all domestic and regional developments in Africa and the Middle East.*	*Includes all domestic and regional developments in Latin America, the Caribbean, and Canada.*	*Includes all domestic and regional developments in Asian and Pacific nations (and colonies).*

	U.S. Politics & Social Issues	U.S. Foreign Policy & Affairs, Defense	U.S. Economy & Environment	Science, Technology & Nature	Culture, Leisure & Lifestyle
Feb. 1	The administration of the Veterans' Bureau is under investigation after many charges of impropriety gained the attention of the White House and Congress.... Colonel Charles R. Forbes, the bureau director, is on his way to Europe for a rest.		Motion picture producer Joseph M. Schenck became principal owner of the United Studios and moved his actors and staff to Los Angeles from New York.		The new Spring and Summer styles by leading French fashion houses feature Balkan, Greek, Turkish, and Near Eastern themes.... Narrow, tight skirts with slits to permit walking are the sensation of the season.... Douglas Fairbanks' photoplay *Robin Hood* extends its run for a second week in New York City.
Feb. 2	Frederick A. Cook, former Arctic explorer who once claimed to have discovered the North Pole, is arrested in Fort Worth, Texas for illegal possession of whiskey.	The War Department exhumed the body of James Jones, an American seaman, to determine whether smuggled Russian Crown Jewels were buried with the body.		An English chemist, Alexander Scott, isolates the element hafnium.... Hafnium is expected to be placed in the 72nd position on the atomic table of elements.	A promoter for the upcoming heavyweight boxing match featuring Jack Dempsey withdraws under pressure from the New York State Athletic Commission for giving the sport a bad image.... The New York Yankees baseball team placed 28 players under contract including Babe Ruth.
Feb. 3		A British government representative meets with the American Debt Commission to arrange a settlement of British war debt.		French bacteriologists offer the theory that bacteria can be attacked and killed by other bacteria.... Other French bacteriologists suggest that bacteria may die when they become unwell and develop fatal chemical poisons within their bodies.... An earthquake strikes the South Pacific.	Samuel Parsons, Jr., an American landscape architect and designer of parks, dies.
Feb. 4	The Carnegie Corporation issues a report that declares public giving to colleges has led to an overemphasis on higher education and prompted young men and women to attend college although they may be happier in other vocations.... President Harding confers with Congress to assure passage of a bill that settles British war debt.	Americans have opened the first Young Men's Christian Association in Bulgaria to teach trades to Russian and Bulgarian men who will then help reconstruct Russia and the Balkans.	Hawaii is struck by an earthquake and a tidal wave but reports only a few deaths, mostly of fishermen.	The Peugeot firm in France successfully tested a car designed to run on less expensive heavy oil rather than gasoline.... American bacteriologists Frederick Gates and Peter Olitsky isolate the influenza germ.	The opening of King Tutankhamen's tomb has influenced Paris fashions, with dress designers copying styles shown on ancient Egyptian frescoes.... A chariot covered with embossed gold and inlaid with precious jewels is brought out of Tutankhamen's tomb.
Feb. 5	The House of Representatives Immigration Committee approves a new immigration bill that restricts immigration to two percent of nationalities resident in the United States, according to the 1890 census.				
Feb. 6	The State Department objects to the Congressional proposal to ban virtually all immigration from Asia.... The Chairman of the House of Representatives Committee on Immigration responds that Congress is merely writing the "gentlemen's agreement" into law.	Japan is carrying out the terms of the Washington Disarmament Treaty to the satisfaction of American authorities.... The Japanese ambassador to the United States and the American ambassador to Japan express satisfaction with the "gentlemen's agreement" restricting Japanese immigration to the United States	Bernhard Fernow, a pioneer in American forestry conservation, dies.	Edward Barnard, an American astronomer and telescope creator, who discovered the faint Barnard's star in 1916, dies.... The French government authorizes the production of synthetic ammonia with a German process.... Germany complains that France is trying to monopolize ammonia production.	Fragments reported to be of the "True Cross" are found in a box of antiques in New York City.
Feb. 7	President Harding delivers his State of the Union Address and pushes Congress to approve a settlement of war debt with Great Britain.	The United States announces that it has been negotiating with Nicaragua to build a new interoceanic canal.		The British government reports that there were no reports of influenza in January 1923, with the death rate for that month half of what it was in January 1922.... Scarlet fever, tuberculosis, and diphtheria are the most heavily reported deadly diseases in Great Britain.	Winston Churchill's memoirs of World War I begin to appear in serialized form in The Times of London to be following by the publication of a book.... Crowds welcome Brazilian Pinto Martins and American Walter Hinton after they complete their New York City to Rio de Janeiro flight in 125 hours.

F	G	H	I	J
Includes campaigns, elections, federal-state relations, civil rights and liberties, crime, the judiciary, education, healthcare, poverty, urban affairs, and population.	*Includes formation and debate of U.S. foreign and defense policies, veterans affairs, and defense spending. (Relations with specific foreign countries are usually found under the region concerned.)*	*Includes business, labor, agriculture, taxation, transportation, consumer affairs, monetary and fiscal policy, natural resources, pollution and industrial accidents.*	*Includes worldwide scientific, medical and technological developments, natural phenomena, U.S. weather and natural disasters.*	*Includes the arts, religion, scholarship, communications media, sports, entertainment, fashions, fads, and social life.*

	World Affairs	Europe	Africa & The Middle East	The Americas	Asia & The Pacific
Feb. 8	The British government formally demands that Turkey release two British airmen captured after a forced landing in December....The Turks agree to release them upon receipt of a written document promising no more British flights over the line of demarcation....The Allied High Commission announces that it will not accept Turkish restrictions on warships.	The government of the Irish Free State offers general amnesty to all those in arms against the state who surrender their weapons before February 18....All executions of Irregulars have been suspended pending possible surrender....The French close German shops and a theatre in the Ruhr in retaliation for their ban on French troops.	Europeans in Kenya try to prevent trading between Indians and Europeans in country areas.... Indian storekeepers on European-owned farms have been warned to leave within two days.	A fire at St. Boniface College in Toronto that killed 10 people in November is officially attributed to careless smoking, while a note that credited the Ku Klux Klan is labeled a children's prank.	The governor of South Australia is seeking British ex-servicemen to immigrate and develop orchards.... A piracy commission in Hong Kong warns that attacks on shipping cannot be stopped until public order is established in neighboring China.
Feb. 9	The Disarmament Commission of the League of Nations met at Geneva.	The daily production of paper money in Germany is increased from 37,000 millions of marks to 45,000 millions of marks, with an increase to 75,000 millions expected to be announced next week....60,000 Greek soldiers are concentrated on the right bank of the Maritza as rumors rage that an invasion of the Turkish city of Adrianople is imminent.	Germany changes its foreign exchange regulations to prevent speculation on the Stock Exchange....Archbishop Georg, leader of the Russian Orthodox Church in Poland is assassinated by an abbot who opposed the independence of the Polish church from the Moscow Patriarchate.	A gas explosion in a Vancouver Island, Canada coal mine kills 45 men.	The Central Caliphate Committee in India calls upon all Indian Muslims to oppose the Lausanne Treaty and prepare themselves for the final struggle between right and wrong.
Feb. 10	Japan refuses to negotiate with the Soviet Union until the Soviets apologize for the massacre at Nikolaievsk.	Unemployed marchers converge on London to demand better food provisions from Parliament....A shortage of hops threatens the English beer brewing industry.	Iraqis protest Turkish tyranny in Iraq and vow to fight to the death rather than allow Turkey to claim Mosul....Indians in Kenya issue a vote of no confidence in the government during a mass meeting....The Turkish and Afghan governments sign a military alliance.	Mexico institutes a 10 percent income tax on all except manual workers.... Mexicans protest the tax....American citizens in Mexico complain that are forced to pay income tax to both the United States and Mexico.	Britain refuses to allow New Zealand to send a representative to London to facilitate consultation on British Empire foreign policy matters affecting New Zealand.
Feb. 11	Lithuania is granted the right to control Memel by the League of Nations provided that it allow other countries to use the port for transit....The Allies guarantee that Poland will not interfere in Memel....11 British, four French, three Italian, and four American warship anchor outside of Smyrna and train their guns on the city.... Allied searchlights illuminate Smyrna at night.	Ten of the 15 Greek newspapers cease publishing to protest government censorship methods.... Mussolini of Italy affirms that he has no intention of interfering with the eight-hour day and defends the recent arrests of Communists.... Irregular forces in Ireland fire on soldiers leaving church....Republican forces in Ireland resolve to continue to fight until they receive independence.			
Feb. 12	The Turks mine Smyrna Harbour and extinguish all nearby navigation lights.	The French complain that German sabotage is halting coal trains in the Ruhr....The police in the Ruhr continue to refuse to salute French officers despite a French threat that they will be court-martialed for this failure.	A bomb is thrown in Cairo, Egypt in an apparent attempt to murder a British railway employee....An armed rebellion in Dahomey in French West Africa is quickly put down by French authorities.	The government takes action to demand payment from thousands of bachelors in Montreal, Canada who have refused to pay a special income tax.	
Feb. 13	The Inter-Allied Commission receives orders form the Conference of Ambassadors to demand that Bulgaria shall guarantee its reparations payments with Customs receipts.	The British Overseas Settlement Commission warns that overpopulation in Great Britain threatens the well-being of the nation.		The Argentine naval station at Bahia Blanca is partially destroyed by fire....A bill to give the government control over the sale of liquor is defeated in the Manitoba legislature in Canada.	Calcutta Muslims protest a Hindu amendment to a bill giving the Indian government the power to restrict the killing of cows.
Feb. 14	At the Conference of Jurists in The Hague, France proposes that international law permit one belligerent state to declare an aerial blockade against another state.	The organized unemployed in Great Britain return to London to push for a meeting with the Prime Minister after recruiting class-conscious men throughout the countryside....The Fascist party in Italy asks Italian fascists who are also freemasons to choose between the two because there is only one loyalty for fascists.	The Orange Free State in South Africa has received the heaviest amount of rain in 40 years and a bumper crop is predicted....In Dahomey, French West Africa rebels with rifles drive native police from their posts after police and soldiers disperse strikers.	The Bishop of New Westminster in Vancouver, Canada issues a warning against the admission of more Asians into Canada, which should remain "white, British, and Christian."	The Indian Assembly declines to amend the Indian Criminal Code to allow police statements to be handed over to the defense.... Private companies are permitted to engage in broadcasting under public control.
Feb. 15	Labor Party members in Great Britain vow to oppose the policy of juvenile emigration to the dominions as an exploitation of workers and disruption of family life....In accordance with a League of Nations decision, Poland begins sending civilian officials and Customs guards to establish Polish administration in the neutral Vilna zone assigned to Poland.	The British Education Committee in London affirmed that all women teachers are required to resign their positions upon marriage....The British Prime Minister states that France is afraid of a Germany strong enough to pay reparations....A 90-mile stretch of French rails has been electrified and electric trains are expected to begin operating shortly.	An Abyssinian raiding party is reported to have crossed the northern border of Kenya and is advancing toward a British settlement at Moyale....Two newspapers in Iran are suspended and their editors exiled for publishing articles libelous to the Shah....The legislative session in Kenya has been extended to settle the question of Indian voting.	The Upper Canada Bible Society reports that the Bible has been issued in 49 languages in Canada.... The president of the Navy League of Canada lamented the immigration of people from Southern and Eastern Europe while requesting greater British immigration to keep Canada within the British Empire.	The Chinese railroads are on the verge of financial collapse because revenue has dwindled and the government is finding it difficult to obtain loans.
	A *Includes developments that affect more than one world region, international organizations and important meetings of world leaders.*	B *Includes all domestic and regional developments in Europe, including the Soviet Union.*	C *Includes all domestic and regional developments in Africa and the Middle East.*	D *Includes all domestic and regional developments in Latin America, the Caribbean, and Canada.*	E *Includes all domestic and regional developments in Asian and Pacific nations (and colonies).*

U.S. Politics & Social Issues	U.S. Foreign Policy & Affairs, Defense	U.S. Economy & Environment	Science, Technology & Nature	Culture, Leisure & Lifestyle	
Bills to settle war debt with Great Britain are introduced in both the House and the Senate.		An explosion in a New Mexico coal mine entombs 122 miners about 5,000 feet from the entrance to the mine.	Albert Einstein lectures on the theory of relativity at Hebrew University in Jerusalem.…Socialists in Germany protest the French production of ammonia with a German process and accuse capitalists of betraying Germany.		Feb. 8
U.S. revenue officers investigate the disappearance of 4000 cases of liquor from a British schooner that sailed between New York and New Brunswick, Canada.…The ship is known to have sailed in the whiskey armada off the New Jersey shore, just outside of the territorial waters of the United States.…The bill approving the British Debt Settlement passes the House of Representatives on a vote of 201 to 44.	The United States signs an agreement to consult with Costa Rica if a canal is built along the Nicaragua-Costa Rican border.…The canal, estimated to cost more than $20 million, will be 35 feet deep and 150 feet wide.…Honduras and El Salvador protest American plans to fortify islands in Fonseca Bay		The Amachinsky volcano in Kamchatka, Soviet Union has begun to erupt accompanied by tremors that shake the earth every 20 minutes.	With his 101st show, actor John Barrymore breaks the New York record for consecutive performances of Hamlet that had been held by Edwin Booth.	Feb. 9
					Feb. 10
A grand jury convenes to investigate possible criminal charges in the race riot that occurred last month in Rosewood, FL.	American public opinion appears to be firmly on the side of the French in the dispute with Germany over the Ruhr.	The American Investigating Commission plans to construct four Zeppelin airships for service between New York and Chicago as well as New York and San Francisco.…Johann Schuette, German designer of many Zeppelins, declares that American construction improvements have resolved the problems that led to a spectacular airship crash in 1921.	Physicist Wilhelm Konrad von Rontgen of Germany, the discover of x-rays, dies.…The Army Air Service announces that its researchers have successfully made rain with electronically-charged sand dropped from airplanes into clouds.	Joseph DeCamp, an American Impressionist painter who founded the group Ten American Painters, dies.	Feb. 11
The U.S. Senate passed a bill to send a constitutional amendment to the states that would change the meeting of Congress to the first Monday in January each year and the inauguration of the president to the third Monday in January.	The Italian government protests proposed immigration restrictions that would limit Italian immigration and require Italian immigrants to become naturalized to gain admittance to the United States.	The Federal Trade Commission issues a report that questions the effectiveness of the anti-trust laws in preventing Royal Dutch Shell from taking control of American oil fields.	British researchers conclude that minerals are more important than vitamins in the diets of farm animals and there is little reason for farmers to pay for foodstuffs rich in vitamins.		Feb. 12
				The National Institute for the Blind issues a manual for musical notation in Braille for blind musicians.	Feb. 13
	The House of Representatives authorizes payment to Norway for ships requisitioned by the United States during the war.…The Senate concludes debate on the Ship Subsidy Bill to focus on the British Debt Settlement bill.		Charles Turner, one of the first African American researchers into animal behavior and a noted biologist, dies.	A five-foot long, gold-covered couch with lion decorations is removed from the tomb of King Tutankhamen.	Feb. 14
An all-white grand jury finds insufficient evidence to prosecute any whites connected to the Rosewood race riot.… A fire at the Manhattan State Asylum for the Insane traps 450 inmates and their nurses inside a building that houses the violently insane and burns at least 25 people to death.	The Senate removes a provision from the British Debt Settlement bill that would have permitted the president to approve debt settlements with other nations.…Senator Henry Cabot Lodge gives a speech in which he declares the maintenance of British credit is as importance for the United States as it is for Great Britain.	Catholina Lambert, millionaire founder of the silk industry of Paterson, NJ, dies.		French aviator Sadi Lecointe breaks the world record for speed by traveling 112 miles per hour in Marseilles, France.…British boxer Roland Todd wins the middleweight championship of Europe in a 20-round fight with Kid Lewis.	Feb. 15
F *Includes campaigns, elections, federal-state relations, civil rights and liberties, crime, the judiciary, education, healthcare, poverty, urban affairs, and population.*	G *Includes formation and debate of U.S. foreign and defense policies, veterans affairs, and defense spending. (Relations with specific foreign countries are usually found under the region concerned.)*	H *Includes business, labor, agriculture, taxation, transportation, consumer affairs, monetary and fiscal policy, natural resources, pollution and industrial accidents.*	I *Includes worldwide scientific, medical and technological developments, natural phenomena, U.S. weather and natural disasters.*	J *Includes the arts, religion, scholarship, communications media, sports, entertainment, fashions, fads, and social life.*	

	World Affairs	Europe	Africa & The Middle East	The Americas	Asia & The Pacific
Feb. 16	The Conference of Ambassadors settled the Memel problem by placing the territory under the control of Lithuania although Memel retains autonomy.	The return of the last Polish refugees now living in Russia, estimated at 350,000, is expected to be completed by the end of July.... Budapest, Hungary authorities have banned children from cafes at night....Belgian industries are suffering because they are unable to purchase inexpensive German coal and are forced to buy pricier British coal.		A bill is introduced into the Upper House of the Canadian Parliament to prohibit any single woman under 30 from voting....A Toronto newspaper suggests that Britain solve its unemployment problem by sending British workers to farming camps in Canada....The Canadian government sends the head of the Soldiers' Settlement Board to England to recruit British ex-soldiers to settle in Canada.	It is rumored that the government of Japan has agreed to send 500,000 Japanese laborers to cultivate rise and fruit in Brazil....The Hong Kong Council denounces the mui-tsai bill as a libelous attack on the Chinese by the British Parliament.
Feb. 17	Iraqis fear that Soviet support of Turkey's plans to control Mosul will lead to the introduction of Bolshevism and atheism in the country....There is increasing sentiment that continued British rule will protect Islam from the disruptive forces of Communism.	Several British merchants and confectioners are fined for carrying, harboring, and dealing saccharin without paying customs duties.... The new Austria census forms will ask for race in a change that is being condemned as anti-Semitic.	The German East Africa Line announces that it is resuming shipping service and will make complete tours around Africa.	The former head of the Quebec Bar Association warns that Canada will be annexed to the United States if a tremendous number of immigrants do not arrive in the next few years.	Sikhs in India issue a statement ordering the custodians of a shrine in Lahore to turn it over or they will take it....Lord Rawlinson, the Commander-in-Chief of India, issues a plan to permit Indians to lead units of the Indian army....Gandhi Day attracts 60 people who discuss the virtues of homespun cloth.
Feb. 18	The Canadian delegate to the League of Nations declares that he is confident that it will be a barrier to war in the future and that the United States will eventually join.	Alois Rasin, the Minister of Finance for Czechoslovakia, dies of injuries suffered when he was shot by an anarchist six weeks ago.			
Feb. 19		Hopes of Irish peace are dashed by continuing violence....The Ballina railroad station on the border of Limerick is destroyed by arson.... Williss Bridge near Blarney is blown up....The house of a member of Dail Eireann is blown up....The mail train from Dublin to Galway is derailed by armed men.	South Africa receives a German order for 4,000 tons of coal....The Kenya Defense Force bill, which would provide for compulsory military service by all Europeans, meets with strong opposition from Europeans who do not want to give strong powers to the government.	A member of the Canadian parliament introduces a resolution to urging Canada to withdraw from the League of Nations....Trinidad is seeking to persuade the Imperial Government to increase the rate of preference given to British-grown sugar.	Sun Yat-Sen, traveling to Canton, proposes to disband half of the Chinese troops, organize an efficient provincial army, and use the disbanded soldiers to build roads.
Feb. 20		All German Customs officials in occupied territory are dismissed and invited to reapply for jobs under the French and Belgians....Yugoslavia removes its ban on mail and telegraph communication to the Soviet Union....25,000 Belgian coal miners go on strike.	The white community in Nairobi, Kenya seeks immediate restrictions on the immigration of Indians.		The Australian government solicits bids for the construction of high-power wireless stations in Australia and England designed for direct, simultaneous commercial communication between the two countries 24 hours a day.
Feb. 21	Representatives of Memel and Lithuania are invited to sign an agreement giving sovereignty over Memel to Lithuania.	Bands of Irish newboys protest a reduction in their pay by seizing and tearing up newspapers in Dublin.... A bill is introduced to temporarily ban the importation of boots and shoes into Holland....The Roman amphitheater at Arles in Provence, France will be preserved by the demolition of private homes just outside the circle of the theatre.... A Vatican Cardinal commends Mussolini for restoring Italy to the greatness of her civil and religious traditions.	An ancient temple in the Chaldean city of Ur, near the junction of the Euphrates and Tigris rivers, is discovered by a joint expedition of the British Museum and the University of Pennsylvania.... A fine is levied on the section of Cairo where a bomb was thrown that injured two British soldiers and killed a Greek shopkeeper.... Khama, the chief of the Bamangwato, dies at Bechuanaland.	The price of Argentine wheat and corn options drops while linseed advances....The government of Jamaica states that there is no common demand for constitutional changes that would give Jamaicans a degree of representative government.	
Feb. 22	Lithuania declares that the decision of the Ambassadors' Conference is unacceptable because it endangers Lithuania's sovereignty over Memel....Robert Cecil, chairman of the Executive Committee of the League of Nations requested that the question of reparations be brought before the League.	The German mark continues to recover, sparked by the continuing efforts of the German government to stabilize the mark by floating a gold loan....The British Home Secretary is asked to support legislation to keep the unsavory details of divorces out of the newspapers....The Leipzig Hotel Owners' Association in Germany passes a resolution to give no accommodations to French or Belgian visitors....France and the Soviet Union begin negotiations for the direct exchange of mail and telegraph messages.	In Cairo, Egypt, the government closes the headquarters of the Wafd or Zaghlulist Delegation and arrests many opponents of the government....Strikes and demonstrations take place throughout Cairo.	In response to a recent spate of fires, insurance companies have cancelled all policies held by churches, schools, and religious institutions in Canada and have instructed their agents to renew policies at new rates representing increases of ranging from 32 to 50 percent....The Argentine government seeks to consolidate its debt of over 1,000 million pesos.	The Legislative Assembly of India unanimously passed a resolution expressing its dissatisfaction with the situation of Indians in Kenya, demanding the equality of Indians and Europeans, and calling for the protection of Indians against violence.

A	B	C	D	E
Includes developments that affect more than one world region, international organizations and important meetings of world leaders.	*Includes all domestic and regional developments in Europe, including the Soviet Union.*	*Includes all domestic and regional developments in Africa and the Middle East.*	*Includes all domestic and regional developments in Latin America, the Caribbean, and Canada.*	*Includes all domestic and regional developments in Asian and Pacific nations (and colonies).*

U.S. Politics & Social Issues	U.S. Foreign Policy & Affairs, Defense	U.S. Economy & Environment	Science, Technology & Nature	Culture, Leisure & Lifestyle	
	The U.S. destroyer *Farquhar* is rammed by a battleship during battle practice off Panama.…The Senate approves the British Debt Settlement bill by a vote of 70 to 13.		Two audiences of electrical engineers in Chicago and New York are brought together by telephone in the first display of simultaneous communication in opposite directions.	An American company has completed a film, The Kaiser in Exile, that shows the daily life of the former German leader.…The discovery of King Tutankhamen's tomb dominates discussion in the United States, particularly since the pharaoh is rumored to be the one whose armies perished in the Red Sea.…Jewelers, hairdressers, and ceramic makers are copying Egyptian designs.	Feb. 16
	Secretary of State Charles E. Hughes urges U.S. membership in the World Court, with the clear understanding that U.S. participation in the court would not involve any legal relations with the League of Nations.				Feb. 17
			John Trowbridge, an American physicist who advocated teaching physics through laboratory work instead of memorization, dies.		Feb. 18
In *Moore v. Dempsey*, the U.S. Supreme Court rules that a trial for murder in a state court in which the accused are hurried to conviction by the threat of a mob-led lynching is without due process of law and is absolutely void.…The Supreme Court rules that Indians are ineligible for American citizenship because a high caste Hindu is not a free, white person within the meaning of the naturalization laws.	Czechoslovakia sends delegates to the United States to negotiate the payment of its war debt.			Katherine Pearson Woods, an American fiction writer, dies.	Feb. 19
The New York State Assembly passes a resolution requesting that the U.S. Congress modify the Volstead Act to permit the drinking of beer and wine.	The U.S. Fleet in Atlantic and Pacific waters is concentrated for joint maneuvers in Panamanian waters for the next six weeks.…The fleet consists of 18 battleship and 120 other vessels.…The U.S. Navy intends to test the defenses of the Panama Canal.		Insulin, the new cure for diabetes, is being used at several hospitals in England and every effort is being expended to increase the supply of insulin so that it can be readily available for general practice.		Feb. 20
Leaders of industry appear before the Senate Committee on Immigration to warn that a reduction of immigrant laborers will lead to economic disaster.…The committee is holding hearings on the Colt Amendment which would permit the Secretary of Labor to authorize the immigration of workers in excess of the national quotas when there is a shortage of workers of a particular type or class.		The Federal Reserve announces an increase in the bank rate from four percent to 4½ percent.…The increase is attributed to a desire to check inflation and the rise in total stock market borrowings.…A prolonged period of easy money is not expected, according to an announcement by the National Bank of Commerce, because the government needs to refinance loans.			Feb. 21
	The House of Representatives approves the British Debt Settlement bill.	Europe's inability to buy and the drop in the exchange rate with South American countries has led to losses for the five major meat-packing companies in the United States, including Swift and Company.		Lord Carnarvon announced that King Tutankhamen will remain in the sarcophagus where he has lain for 3,000 years.	Feb. 22
F *Includes campaigns, elections, federal-state relations, civil rights and liberties, crime, the judiciary, education, healthcare, poverty, urban affairs, and population.*	G *Includes formation and debate of U.S. foreign and defense policies, veterans affairs, and defense spending. (Relations with specific foreign countries are usually found under the region concerned.)*	H *Includes business, labor, agriculture, taxation, transportation, consumer affairs, monetary and fiscal policy, natural resources, pollution and industrial accidents.*	I *Includes worldwide scientific, medical and technological developments, natural phenomena, U.S. weather and natural disasters.*	J *Includes the arts, religion, scholarship, communications media, sports, entertainment, fashions, fads, and social life.*	

	World Affairs	Europe	Africa & The Middle East	The Americas	Asia & The Pacific
Feb. 23	Italy declares that there are no plans for Franco-Italian economic alliance....Italian troops in Tripoli advance as the Italians extend their occupation to the towns of Slitan and Musurata, which were abandoned in 1915....14,000 Americans meet in Madison Square Garden in New York City to protest the French occupation of the Ruhr.	In response to a rabies outbreak in Ireland, England institutes a six-month quarantine for imported dogs....The High Court of Justice in London hears a libel case brought by Marie Stopes, an advocate of birth control, against James Sutherland, who has accused her of exposing the poor to dangerous experiments....An Irish Republican Army commander is captured in Dublin by British forces....Lord Bessborough's house is burned to the ground by armed men in Piltown, Ireland.	An airport is scheduled to be built near Tunis....The Fish and Orange rivers are in flood stage after heavy rains in Southwest Africa....Sitaram Achariar, the editor of a small Indian weekly newspaper in Kenya, is arrested for printing articles that disparage the character of European women in Kenya....Indians in Kenya state that they will make no more concessions to Europeans.	Jamaican legislators complain that Great Britain's fiscal policies have been disastrous to the West Indies and that Great Britain is attempting to keep its colonies in a state of economic slavery.... Jamaican leaders warn that their people should be expected to remain loyal to Great Britain when they live in a state of poverty.... The Uruguayan Senate ratifies the election of José Serrato as President of the Republic.	Attacks on the Secretary of State for India are so mild in the Legislative Assembly that one member objects that the other members are not replying to the British.... The Premier of Victoria, Australia laments the lack of knowledge of Australia and declares that Australians are still part of the British family....The annual demonstration to extend the vote to all men in Japan is carried out peacefully by thousands of marchers.
Feb. 24	The General Council of the Trade Union Congress in Great Britain issues an appeal to all its affiliated unions to support the fund that is being promoted in all countries by the International Federation of Trade Unions to relieve distress among the women, children, and dependents of German trade unionists in the Ruhr.	The Retail Bespoke Tailoring Trade Board in Great Britain confirms that the minimum wages for male workers have been reduced effective March 1....600 Welsh coal miners protest against the use of non-union miners....Other coal companies in Wales are in the midst of work stoppages by union miners angered by the use of non-unionists.			The Japanese Diet debates whether the grant of manhood suffrage would cure the ills of government....Some speakers contend that the restriction of the vote to the moneyed classes stimulates the Socialist and radical elements to resist the state....Yukio Ozaki, a former political leader, declares that on his tours of rural Japan he has noticed that young men no longer regard military service as the only honorable career.
Feb. 25	Yugoslavia abolishes the sequestration of property belonging to Austrian subjects and agrees to sign a commercial treaty with Austria.... Yugoslavia does not agree to pay for Austrian ships sunk in the Danube after the Armistice.	The strike of Amsterdam, Holland taxicab drivers continues and threatens to turn into a general strike.... A gang of masked bandits known as "monks" for the monk's cowls that they wear as headdresses are arrested in France.	The Zambezi river is flooding and part of the Central African Railroad is under water....The flooding has led to calls for a Zambezi bridge so that traffic is not disrupted by future flooding.		
Feb. 26	Relief agencies in the Near East issue an appeal for funds to help refugees in Greece.	The leaders of the Miners' Association meet with the British Prime Minister to demand that the government assume responsibility for the reorganization of both the production and distribution of coal....The Swiss reject woman suffrage by a large majority for the third time.	Excavations begin at the site of the ancient Sumerian city of Kish, present-day Oheimer, near Babylon.	Several people are killed and seriously injured when a train in the state of Pueblo goes off the rails and plunges 20 feet into a gorge.	The Indian Assembly accepts the League of Nations' recommendation to fix the age of consent for females at 16 in an attempt to reduce the sexual abuse of girls.
Feb. 27	Enthusiasm for a Franco-Italian Alliance or Latin Union has waned as French newspapers drop the topic....British newspapers report that such an alliance would weaken the Franco-British Entente.	The Miners' Federation asks the British Prime Minister to inquire into the organization of the coal industry because miners are receiving poor wages despite a rise in demand for coal....Italy captures the city of Misurata after a fierce fight and now has control over the whole of Tripoli....The famed Paris Morgue, in operation since 1864, is scheduled to close on March 1 and its site will become an open space.	Mail sent to Anatolia is being censored by Turkish authorities. The Postmaster-General warns that communications should be written in English, Turkish, French, or Italian and should be as short as possible....A convention of Europeans in Kenya requests that the King of Great Britain should refuse to sanction any policy that is disastrous to future white colonization of Africa.	The Canadian government grants permission to the Marconi Company to establish a wireless station at Vancouver with a range of 7000 miles for the purpose of maintaining communication between Canada, Australia, and Japan.	
Feb. 28		The French Cabinet Council decides to present a bill to permanently establish "summer time" [daylight savings time] to the Chamber of Deputies.... French troops use a bayonet charge to clear the streets of Oberstein in the Ruhr.	The Turkish government postpones the introduction of a bill that would establish a prohibition on the consumption of alcohol because local governments have had trouble enforcing local bans.		The Legislative Assembly of India begins debate on the state management of railroads....The Indian government proposes to take over the East Indian and Great Indian Peninsula railroads....The Australian Parliament opens.
Mar. 1	In a speech to the Angora Assembly in Turkey, Mustafa Kemal declares that peace is in the hands of the Allies and that the Turks would not accept a treaty that does not recognize the financial, economic, and judicial independence of the Turks.	The French disarm, arrest, and expel German police from the Ruhr.... British judicial officials discuss abolishing the law that a wife who commits a crime in the presence of her husband is acting under his coercion and, consequently, cannot be independently convicted....The Swiss are asked by Liechtenstein to run its Customs Service.	In Cairo, Egypt, the Wafd or Zaghlulist organization issues a manifesto calling for abolition of martial law, the release of political prisoners, and a declaration that the Sudan is inherently Egyptian.... British Provisional Government in Iraq is scheduled to end with passage of the Anglo-Iraq Treaty.	The Bishop of Dijon sends to French Canadians, at their request, a packet of wheat grown on the graves of Canadian soldiers buried in France....José Serrato takes office as President of Uruguay....A statue of General Artigas, fighter for Uruguayan independence, is unveiled in Montevideo before huge crowds.	A severe drought in Queensland, Australia, causes increasing anxiety....The government of India is condemned by Sastri, an Indian leader, for its unwillingness to trust Indians although he rejoices that the British are finally taking note of the color bar against which Indians have protested for a century.
	A *Includes developments that affect more than one world region, international organizations and important meetings of world leaders.*	B *Includes all domestic and regional developments in Europe, including the Soviet Union.*	C *Includes all domestic and regional developments in Africa and the Middle East.*	D *Includes all domestic and regional developments in Latin America, the Caribbean, and Canada.*	E *Includes all domestic and regional developments in Asian and Pacific nations (and colonies).*

U.S. Politics & Social Issues	U.S. Foreign Policy & Affairs, Defense	U.S. Economy & Environment	Science, Technology & Nature	Culture, Leisure & Lifestyle	
The attorney general of California announces that the Supreme Court decision banning a Hindu from citizenship places Hindu residents under the anti-alien law and affects large tracts of land owned or leased by them in California....A filibuster against the Ship Subsidy Bill continues in the U.S. Senate....Supporters of the bill are weakening....No measure giving a cash subsidy to the U.S. Merchant Marine is expected to pass this session of Congress.		Treasury Department agents arrested 28 people and smashed an international counterfeiting ring that printed U.S., Italian, and Austrian paper money, postage, and revenue stamps and coined fake U.S. gold coins.	Edward Morley, an American chemist who created the Michelson-Morley experiment to determine whether light travels through ether, dies.		Feb. 23
					Feb. 24
					Feb. 25
The Carnegie Foundation issues a report that the free public school system is in danger of disappearing because the cost of education is becoming prohibitively expensive....President Harding's proposal that the United States become a member of the International Court of Justice organized by the League of Nations is postponed indefinitely by the Senate without discussion.	The Shipping Board, with the approval of President Harding, offers for sale all idle ships owned by the federal government and plans to scrap those that cannot be sold....The American Relief Administration's food stores at Simbirsk in Russia burn down.	The Secretary of Agriculture serves a formal complaint to Chicago meat packers Armour & Company and Morris & Company requiring them to show cause why they should not be penalized for attempting to merge after the proposed merger was declared unlawful in December....Herbert Hoover, the Secretary of Commerce expresses his support for amending legislation to permit additional imports of rubber if the United States experiences a shortage of rubber.		Elihu Vedder, an American Symbolist painter and book illustrator, dies....Work begins to close the tomb of King Tutankhamen in Luxor....John D. Rockefeller, Jr displays the La Rochefoucauld tapestries in his New York City home after paying an estimated $100,000 for them in Paris.	Feb. 26
Joseph R. Burton, a former U.S. Senator from Kansas and bitter opponent of President Theodore Roosevelt, dies.	The U.S. government pays Norway $12 million awarded by The Hague Arbitration Tribunal as compensation for the seizure of Norwegian ships during the war....The U.S. Navy enters three seaplanes in competition for the Jacques Schneider Marine Aviation Trophy to be awarded at Cowes, England next September. .	Reports from Western states that a commercial building boom is in progress prompts a spate of buying on the New York Stock Exchange.	Camille Flammarion, a French astronomer, reports that a star of the second magnitude, Beta Ceti, in the constellation of the whale, has suddenly become a star of the first magnitude with a brightness surpassing that of Aldebaran.		Feb. 27
The White House announces that Albert Fall, Secretary of the Interior, will be replaced by William Work, Postmaster-General....The Senate decides to postpone a discussion of U.S. membership in the International Court of Justice until the next session of Congress.			Franz Boas of the Columbia University Anthropology Department reports that a fossilized human skull has been found in Patagonia and the skull may be 500,000 years older than the skull of *Pithecanthropus Erectus*, which is 500,000 years old.	Henry Phelps Johnston, an American historian, dies....Andrea Sbarboro, an Italian-born banker who helped establish the California wine industry, dies.	Feb. 28
The Senate kills the Ship Subsidy Bill....President Harding signs the British Debt Settlement bill....Senator Harry New is appointed Postmaster-General....Bourke Cochran, a famed Irish-American orator and politician, dies.	By Executive Order, President Harding sets aside an oil reserve in northwestern Alaska for the U.S. Navy....Six sailors burn to death in an explosion on board the destroyer USS *Humbert* in Manila harbor in the Philippines.		Relics of Native Americans, previously unknown to archeologists, are discovered in caves in the Ozark Mountains of Missouri and Arkansas. The discoveries include an atlatl, a stick for throwing spear-heads, which has never before been found so far East.	Maude Royden, a lay preacher as well as a popular author, speaks to great acclaim in a church in Illinois as part of her tour of the United States.	Mar. 1
F *Includes campaigns, elections, federal-state relations, civil rights and liberties, crime, the judiciary, education, healthcare, poverty, urban affairs, and population.*	G *Includes formation and debate of U.S. foreign and defense policies, veterans affairs, and defense spending. (Relations with specific foreign countries are usually found under the region concerned.)*	H *Includes business, labor, agriculture, taxation, transportation, consumer affairs, monetary and fiscal policy, natural resources, pollution and industrial accidents.*	I *Includes worldwide scientific, medical and technological developments, natural phenomena, U.S. weather and natural disasters.*	J *Includes the arts, religion, scholarship, communications media, sports, entertainment, fashions, fads, and social life.*	

	World Affairs	Europe	Africa & The Middle East	The Americas	Asia & The Pacific
Mar. 2	German taxes collected in the Ruhr and the Rhineland by the French will be handed over to the Reparations Committee and will be for the profit of all the Allies.	Epidemics of spotted fever and dysentery rage throughout the Ukraine....A bill is introduced in the British Parliament to legitimize children born out of wedlock if their parents subsequently marry as long as no adultery is involved....Armed men in Ireland derail the Galway to Dublin mail train.	France increases the size of its army in Syria.	The Canadian House of Commons rejects a bill banning gambling on racecourses....Ruy Barbosa, a Brazilian lawyer who helped found the republic and write its constitution, dies....A resolution is presented in the Jamaica Legislative Council to express dissatisfaction with the economic situation in Jamaica, because Great Britain does not give greater preference and secure a home market for Jamaican produce.	The Inchape Report is published, which proposes a cut in the British military budget for India.
Mar. 3	The Spanish edition of the *Munich* (Germany) *Gazette* condemns the brutalities of the Allies toward the Germans in the Ruhr.	Denmark is short of coal because of the occupation of the Ruhr and importers begin to purchase American coal....Holland votes to abolish "summer time" at the request of an Agrarian member of Parliament....Refugees from the Ruhr continue to arrive in Bavaria.	The Angora Assembly met to consider the Turkish government's counterproposals to the Lausanne Treaty.	The Executive Committee of the Communists' International in Russia advises, in a message to Canadian workers, that Great Britain is dependent upon Canada for success in its imperialist plans.	The Punjab government in India disbands the police reserves to save money against the advice of the Inspector-General of Police who warns about increasing lawlessness.
Mar. 4		King Alfonso of Spain denies that he has any plans to abdicate....French troops seize the harbor and customs offices at Mannheim, Germany.	A bomb is thrown into a Cairo, Egypt, fish shop filled with British soldiers. Six soldiers are injured and one Egyptian civilian is killed....The French separated the Sanjak of Alexandretta from Syria and gave the region autonomy.	Large crowds attend the funeral of Ruy Barbosa in Rio de Janeiro, Brazil.	
Mar. 5	British merchants in occupied Germany complain that their businesses are being heavily damaged by a 10 percent tax levied by the French and a German refusal to load goods licensed by the French.... Benito Mussolini, Prime Minister of Italy, agrees to serve as the honorary president of the International Woman Suffrage Congress.	Fishermen in Aberdeen, Scotland, strike to prevent German ships from stopping with fish caught in the North Sea and Icelandic waters.... Floods occur throughout Paris as the Seine River overflows its banks.... The Danish government announces that it will send a delegation to the Soviet Union to negotiate a resumption of trade....A new Norwegian government is formed.	Festivities mark the conclusion of the visit of the Afghan Court to Jelalabad....Persia begins negotiations with the Soviet Union for a Soviet-Persian trade agreement.... The excavations at the temple of the Moon God at Ur near Baghdad have closed for the season.		
Mar. 6	A Baltic economic conference between Estonia, Finland, Lithuania, and Poland begins....Britain announces that it has no plans to interfere in the Ruhr, because such an action would be regarded as hostile by France.	France adopts the French Army Bill to require 18 months of service....In Dublin, armed men stop a passenger train, force out the passengers, and set the train on fire.			
Mar. 7	The Italian government protests to the German government about the abusive treatment of Italian workers who were passing through Germany to work in Belgium....The National Union of Societies for Equal Citizenship issues a demand that the British government pass legislation giving the vote to women on the same basis and at the same age as men.	The German government announces that the number of unemployed in Germany rose from 85,000 in January to 144,000 in February.... The Swiss Federal Tribunal rules that qualified women lawyers are entitled to practice before the Bar....The British Ministry of Transport hears Devon County's attempt to ban automobiles from 70 rural roads.	The Angora National Assembly declares that the Lausanne Treaty is unacceptable....The Assembly disclaims responsibility if the Allied Powers insist on the acceptance of the treaty....The Turkish government is authorized by the Assembly to settle financial, economic, and administrative questions in accordance with the complete independence of the nation....Turkey also wants the Mosul question to be settled as quickly as possible.	The Canadian government announces that it has discovered that a great proportion of the whiskey cleared through Canadian Customs for shipment to the United States is being smuggled back into Ontario where it is sold by bootleggers.	The Chinese government announces that an American company will build and operate a chain of 2000 film theaters throughout the country....The Japanese government announces plans to open an office in Geneva to facilitate work with the International Labor Organization.... The emigration of Indian unskilled workers to Mauritius resumes for one year with the number of immigrants not to exceed 1500.
Mar. 8	Turks resent criticisms by the Soviet Union of Turkey's objections to the Lausanne Treaty.	The Central Committee of the Russian Railway Union formally complains to the Soviet Commissariat about the poor state of the railroads and suggests that the government decentralize the management of the railroads.	A state of siege in Dahomey, French West Africa, ends as the French restore peace by capturing and disarming the rebels.	Mexico reports that an epidemic of spinal meningitis is spreading from Oaxaca to Puebla and is fast approaching the capital city. The Mexican Sanitary Department will receive assistance in combating the epidemic from the Rockefeller Institute.	Wu Pei-fu demands political appointments in the Fukien and Kwantung Provinces that would effectively destroy the position of Sun Yat-sen in these areas and prevent unification of China....India passes the White Slave Traffic Bill, raising the age of consent.
Mar. 9	France states that it withdrew black troops from Guadeloupe and Martinique used in the occupation of the Ruhr because of the poor public relations involved and would have preferred not to use the men at all.	The House of Commons voted to raise the age at which young persons can be served intoxicating beverages to 18 from 16....Arrests are made in connection with a revolutionary plot or *Putsch* in Munich, suspected to have been led by Adolf Hitler, that attempted to overthrow the Bavarian government.	A mass meeting of Indians in Kenya decides to send representatives to Great Britain, India, and Uganda to demand equality in every respect.	Canada refuses to permit the Russian Trade Mission to enter the country....A conference begins in Canada to decide on ways to free Canada from dependence on U.S. coal....Rebels in Paraguay capture the city of Villa Rica.	A new gold field is discovered in Australia near Perth.

A	B	C	D	E
Includes developments that affect more than one world region, international organizations and important meetings of world leaders.	*Includes all domestic and regional developments in Europe, including the Soviet Union.*	*Includes all domestic and regional developments in Africa and the Middle East.*	*Includes all domestic and regional developments in Latin America, the Caribbean, and Canada.*	*Includes all domestic and regional developments in Asian and Pacific nations (and colonies).*

	U.S. Politics & Social Issues	U.S. Foreign Policy & Affairs, Defense	U.S. Economy & Environment	Science, Technology & Nature	Culture, Leisure & Lifestyle
Mar. 2				A new island is discovered about 60 miles from the coast of Annam in the Pacific Ocean. The result of a volcanic eruption, it is circular, 400 yards in diameter, and 110 feet high.	The Metropolitan Museum of Art in New York City receives relics of Sardis, covering the Hittite to the Byzantine period, that were saved during the burning of Smryna.
Mar. 3	With the return of milder weather, the rum running fleet anchored just outside the Port of New York is joined by 11 steamships, including a small liner.				An Italian necropolis of the Vollanovo Apo type has been discovered, together with a sarcophagus and a quantity of bones, paintings, bronze, and terra cotta vase in the region of Montalto di Castro
Mar. 4	The Sixty-seventh Congress concludes its session. A large number of bills are rushed through at the last minute.				A group of scientists from the Carnegie Institute joined by members of the Yucatan Archeological Institute of New York arrives in Mexico to study Mayan ruins at Uxmal, Chichenitza, Ake, and Motul.
Mar. 5	The Department of Labor proposes to take a census of foreign workers in the United States with the aim of persuading them to become U.S. citizens.		Francis Wayland Ayer, a pioneer in advertising, dies.	The discovery of a new fat-soluble vitamin, similar to Vitamin A, is announced.	Irish playwright William Boyle dies.
Mar. 6			American Telephone and Telegraph seeks permission from its shareholders to increase its stock capitalization, which will make it the largest corporation in the United States ahead of U.S. Steel.		
Mar. 7				The International Labor Conference, meeting in Paris, passes resolutions for the abolition of the use of white lead in all paint.	
Mar. 8				Examinations of the tomb of Seti II in Luxor, Egypt, disclose an ornamented, gilt-covered box that apparently contains clothing, including a leopard skin garment.	American filmmaker D.W. Griffith announces that he will begin making movies in Great Britain.... The sale of the late opera singer Enrico Caruso's art collection ends with total proceeds exceeding $151,147.
Mar. 9	A bill by Socialists to abolish the state militia is defeated in the Wisconsin legislature.... Armed robbers, or liquor pirates, board a British ship in New York City and carry away most of her supply of liquors and wines.		The Commerce Department invites the Automobile Chamber of Commerce and the Rubber Association of America to collaborate with the government to investigate the possibility of growing rubber in the Philippines.		Jane Addams, the social worker and founder of Hull House in Chicago, arrives in Rangoon, Burma, as part of a world tour.... Renoir's painting "Les Baigneuses" has been given to the Louvre in Paris by his sons.... A Paris, France, newspaper is fined for changing a cartoonist's caption without his permission.
	F	G	H	I	J
	Includes campaigns, elections, federal-state relations, civil rights and liberties, crime, the judiciary, education, healthcare, poverty, urban affairs, and population.	*Includes formation and debate of U.S. foreign and defense policies, veterans affairs, and defense spending. (Relations with specific foreign countries are usually found under the region concerned.)*	*Includes business, labor, agriculture, taxation, transportation, consumer affairs, monetary and fiscal policy, natural resources, pollution and industrial accidents.*	*Includes worldwide scientific, medical and technological developments, natural phenomena, U.S. weather and natural disasters.*	*Includes the arts, religion, scholarship, communications media, sports, entertainment, fashions, fads, and social life.*

	World Affairs	Europe	Africa & The Middle East	The Americas	Asia & The Pacific
Mar. 10		The British government announces that 400 marriages have taken place between German women and members of the British army of the Rhine between the Armistice and December 1922.		Rebels in Paraguay flee Villa Rica as government forces arrive.…Train service in Paraguay is temporarily suspended because of the political troubles.	Britain attempts to negotiate a settlement in China between Wu Pei-fu and Sun Yat-sen.…The British request that Japan immediately enter negotiation to revise the Chinese-Japanese treaties of 1915.…The Chinese Cabinet resigns to protest Wu Pei-fu's demands.
Mar. 11	Belgium and Switzerland sign a treaty providing for Swiss citizens to settle in the Congo.	Switzerland agrees to a request from Liechtenstein for the Swiss ambassador in Austria to also represent Liechtenstein.…Spanish labor leader Salvador Segui is murdered along with his secretary, apparently by men from a rival labor group.			The Indian government in accordance with recommendations from the Inchcape Committee proposes to abolish the Public Health Commissioner, Director of Medical Research, Trade Commissioner in London, Inspector-General of Irrigation, and Commissioner of Education.
Mar. 12	Lithuania notifies the Allies that it is ready to discuss details for the future government of Memel.…The Salvation Army launches a plan to solve the problem of idle youth by sending 10,000 British boys between 14 and 16 to work on farms in various parts of the British Empire.…The Vatican sends a representative to Eastern Galicia to investigate charges that the Polish government is persecuting Ruthenes who refuse to change from the Oriental to the Latin rite.	The action of the British Home Secretary in ordering the arrest and deportation to Ireland of Irish persons in resident in England and Scotland is challenged in the House of Commons.…English police arrest 33 people of Irish descent in London, including the president of the Irish Self-Determination League, and confiscate both papers and revolvers.	An ex-soldier discovers gold coins and gold bars belonging to the Republican government of South Africa that was buried in the Transvaa; during the flight of President Kruger to the coast.…The Sultanate of Kuwait becomes the latest addition to the postage stamp-issuing dependencies of the British Empire.…New stamps for the French colony of Cameroon will illustrate the local timber and rubber industries.	The designs of stamps for use in the British West Indies are changed to an oblong shape with two medallions in the center, for the King's head and an element from the colony's seal.…Peru begins using automatic postal franking machines to arrange for postage prepayment.	Japan refuses China's request to open negotiations on the China-Japanese Treaty of 1915.
Mar. 13	The Spanish government complains that the Turks are providing rebels in Morocco with arms and ammunition…A Spanish newspaper reports that the weapons are being purchased with the ransom paid for Spanish prisoners to Rif chief Abd el Krim.	Budapest, Hungary, proposes to hold a rat-killing day to persuade the entire population to kill rats.…Bombs in Lisbon, Portugal, thrown at three bakeries partially destroy two of them and injure several employees.			It is announced that the All-India Trade Union Congress will be held at Lahore later this month under the presidency of C.R. Das, the Bengali Congress leader.
Mar. 14	The Allied governments assign Vilna and Eastern Galacia to Poland.	The Italian visa for British passports is abolished.		William L. Higgett, of the Ku Klux Klan, claims that the group has been established in Canada.	The Indian Legislative Assembly defeats government proposals to cut railroads.
Mar. 15	The Reichsbank transfers 48 million marks to the Bank of England to meet its Belgian reparations payment.…A Persian military mission arrives in Moscow to work on a joint military pact.	The Soviet Executive Council temporarily appoints a committee to direct Soviet policy in light of the health woes of Vladimir Lenin.…The Republicans in Ireland adopt categories of people who may be shot on sight, including army officers, all members of the Free State Parliament who support the British, and hostile reporters.	The Duke of Devonshire, the Colonial Secretary for Kenya, confirms that he intends to reserve the Highlands for white settlement.…Spanish gunboats and airplanes in Melilla, Morocco, disperse Moor sailing ships that were attempting to load and move artillery and ammunition.	The President of Peru instructs the Peruvian Consul-General in New York to inform the promoters of the proposed American Rubber Producing Corporation that vast areas of rubber producing territory will be available to them if sufficient sums are invested in the industry.	The Australian government invites geological experts to test the Northern Territories for deposits of oil.
Mar. 16	The Union of Protestant Evangelical Churches of Belgium and the Belgian Christian Missionary Church send a letter of protest to the Archbishop of Uppsala [Sweden], who accused French and Belgian troops of cruelty in the Ruhr.…The Belgian government denies that it will send more troops to the Ruhr.	Scottish Labour Members of Parliament have made applications to visit interned men and women in Dublin, but the British government refuses them permission to visit unless they are friends of the accused.…Queen Milena of Montenegro, who is the mother of the Queen of Italy, dies.… Sarajevo, Yugoslavia, is shaken by a moderate earthquake.	A Soviet university opens in Tiflis for students from Turkey, Afghanistan, India, Persia, Khiva, and Bokhara.…A new Egyptian Cabinet takes office without stating its program.	The mayor of London, Ontario, Canada, states that Canadians do not need the Ku Klux Klan and that he will use all means at his disposal to keep "verminous missionaries" who seek to terrorize citizens who differ from them in race, color, or religion out of London.	The Premier of South Australia announces that the government will aid British ex-servicemen and their families by providing 40,000 acres of farmland in the Murray Valley.
Mar. 17	German hopes of British intervention in the Ruhr evaporate in the face of British denials.…Greece and Turkey begin exchanging prisoners of war and civilian prisoners under the supervision of a commission of the International Red Cross.…The Third Moscow International opens negotiations with the Second International with the aim of united action in opposing the French occupation of the Ruhr.	Physicians treating Lenin of the Soviet Union report that the leader has lost his power of speech and is paralyzed on his right side.…The Soviets announce that they will deal with Communists who lead lives of luxury by depriving them of their official positions, removing them from party membership, and bringing them before the Revolutionary Tribunal for discrediting the Soviet Authority.		The Canadian Senate passes legislation legalizing a marriage between a woman and her deceased husband's brother or her deceased husband's brother's son.…Two hundred leaders from Quebec visited Toronto as the guests of the Ontario government in an attempt to reduce tensions between English and French speakers.	A Wellington, New Zealand, judge fines a British sailor for bringing Communist newspapers and printed matter into New Zealand contrary to the War Regulations Continuance Act.…The Government of Burma announces that slavery and human sacrifice continue in the Naga Hills of Assam, with no fewer than six boys and 10 girls killed annually.

A	B	C	D	E
Includes developments that affect more than one world region, international organizations and important meetings of world leaders.	*Includes all domestic and regional developments in Europe, including the Soviet Union.*	*Includes all domestic and regional developments in Africa and the Middle East.*	*Includes all domestic and regional developments in Latin America, the Caribbean, and Canada.*	*Includes all domestic and regional developments in Asian and Pacific nations (and colonies).*

U.S. Politics & Social Issues	U.S. Foreign Policy & Affairs, Defense	U.S. Economy & Environment	Science, Technology & Nature	Culture, Leisure & Lifestyle	
	The Debt Funding Commission reaches a tentative agreement with Finland for the Finnish debt to be paid over the next 62 years at a three percent rate of interest for the first 10 years and 3.5 percent for the remaining years.		Remains of a Stone Age dwelling as well as flint tools and fragments of earthenware are discovered at Horgen at the Lake of Zurich in Switzerland.... The Amundsen Expedition to the Arctic reports that the men remain on board ship and continue to move through the ice.	A new system of stage lighting, the Schwabe-Hasalt style, designed in Germany has been introduced in the United States by the General Electric Company.	Mar. 10
			Arpad Gerster, an American surgeon and medical educator, dies.		Mar. 11
		A violent storm strikes Tennessee, Missouri, Illinois, and Wisconsin, killing at least 22 people.... Sixty-eight 80-year oak trees were uprooted by windstorms at The Hermitage, former home of President Andrew Jackson in Tennessee.... Cadillac introduces a new model car with an eight-cylindered, V-shaped engine; a cigarette lighter; a tire pump; and an adjustable foot rest.	The National Geographic Society reports that archeologists are using aerial photographs to reveal earthworks and ploughed land invisible to the observer on the ground.		Mar. 12
			A French farmer digging on his land near an old Roman road discovers a number of stone coffins that are apparently Roman in origin.	Gramophone Records issues several new releases including symphony recordings of Strauss' Don Juan and Rimsky-Korsakov's opera Sadko.	Mar. 13
			G. Frank Lydston, an American surgeon and urologist, dies.		Mar. 14
The Connecticut Senate passes a bill declaring that the deaths of a husband and wife in a common accident to be simultaneous events except where there is clear evidence that one died first. The legislation overrules the assumption in common law that the woman, being the weaker one, is the first to die in a joint accident.	Senator William Borah declares that if Republicans do not take action on the French occupation of the Ruhr, the Democrats will take control of the government in the elections of 1924.		The members of the Citroen Expedition, which crossed the Sahara in custom-built caterpillar automobiles, returns to Paris with a native of Timbuktu.... Expedition members report that it is possible to travel more than 600 miles in the desert before reaching a military post and that more posts are needed to make trans-Saharan travel possible.	During a meeting of Italian composers, impresarios, agents, and lyrical agents called to discuss methods of furthering Italian music abroad, two impresarios engage in a fistfight and schedule a duel.	Mar. 15
A grand jury in Morehouse, LA, announced that it is unable to issue any indictments in the deaths of T.F. Richard and Watt Daniels, who were kidnapped, killed, and mutilated. Ten members of the jury are reported to be members of the Ku Klux Klan and the Attorney General is seeking a change of venue.	The British government pays $4,128,085 to the New York Federal Reserve Bank, reducing British debt to the United States to $4.6 billion.		Physicians at a medical conference in London debate whether sleeping sickness, *encephalitis lethargica*, is a form of influenza.	Four theatrical trade unions in England protest the appearance of black performers, most of whom are foreigners, in West End theatrical productions.... The Theatrical Managers' Association unanimously recommends that its members give no facilities for broadcasting.	Mar. 16
The U.S. Commission on International Justice and Good Will, with the approval of the Federal Council of Churches, declares that the United States should accept its full share of responsibility for settling international problems and that American participation is critical to the solution of European economic and political problems.					Mar. 17

F	G	H	I	J
Includes campaigns, elections, federal-state relations, civil rights and liberties, crime, the judiciary, education, healthcare, poverty, urban affairs, and population.	*Includes formation and debate of U.S. foreign and defense policies, veterans affairs, and defense spending. (Relations with specific foreign countries are usually found under the region concerned.)*	*Includes business, labor, agriculture, taxation, transportation, consumer affairs, monetary and fiscal policy, natural resources, pollution and industrial accidents.*	*Includes worldwide scientific, medical and technological developments, natural phenomena, U.S. weather and natural disasters.*	*Includes the arts, religion, scholarship, communications media, sports, entertainment, fashions, fads, and social life.*

	World Affairs	Europe	Africa & The Middle East	The Americas	Asia & The Pacific
Mar. 18	The Inter-Allied Military Commission is notified by the German government that the Germans will not be responsible for the safety of French and Belgian officers.…The Prussian Ministry of Welfare decides that French and Belgian troops will not be provided with housing accommodations use accorded to diplomatic and consular officers.…The Ruhr occupation has increased global prices for coal by 15 percent.	According to official reports, Lenin's condition is unchanged but a Soviet official privately acknowledged that he is dying.…Rumors declare that the Soviets will appoint a temporary leader of Russian or Ukrainian background to act as a figurehead because growing anti-Semitism among the peasantry prevents the appointment of Leon Trotsky or several other leading officials.…The German government announces that the attempt to overthrow the Bavarian government was launched by the French.	The Turkish government begins collecting income taxes from foreigners.…Several foreign insurance companies announce plans to close rather than comply with the new Companies Act in Turkey which restricts deposits for each type of insurance in a transaction.…The Wafd in Egypt declares that the agreement of Yehia Pasha to become Prime Minister is against the nation's interests and only support's Great Britain's imperialistic aims.	The British ambassador to the United States acknowledges that Canada has the right to sign a separate treaty with the United States in regard to fishing rights.…An oil well yielding 120,000 barrels a day is discovered in Laroa, Venezuela.	The captain of the British steamer *Neuralia* refuses to give an English orphan to her adoptive family in Madras, India, because the family is Eurasian with dark complexions.… Members of the Indian National Congress observe a day of mourning in response to the imprisonment of Mohandas Gandhi.
Mar. 19	The Commission of Intellectual Cooperation of the League of Nations meets in Brussels, Belgium, to consider the international organization of scientific documents and inter-university relations.… Communists from Bulgaria, Rumania, Greece, Serbia, and Turkey meet in Sofia, Bulgaria.	Nottingham, England, lace makers present a petition to Parliament seeking protection for the lace trade from imports, particularly those from France.…The Soviet Union reports that wolves destroyed 40,000 cattle in five provinces of Russia in 1922.…The cost of living in France has increased by 27 percent in the first two months of 1923.	The number of dhows used in East African shipping is dropping as newly released figures show that 4774 dhows entered the port of Zanzibar in 1922 versus 5126 entering in 1921, while the number of steamers increased from 409 to 521.	The Canadian government proposes to take action to prevent the employment of Japanese crews on fishing boats operating with seine licenses in the Pacific. All fishing crews will have to be licensed and no licenses will be granted to Japanese.	The Queensland government in Australia dissolves and new elections are set for May 12.…The Japanese government announces that it will use 44 million yen from the Boxer Rebellion indemnity to promote Japanese relations with China.…The Legislative Assembly of India adjourns briefly to find some way to deal with the budget deficit without doubling the tax on salt.
Mar. 20	Allied discussions on the Turkish counter-proposals for the Lausanne Treaty begin.…The American Blind Relief War Fund announces plans to build the largest Braille printing press in Paris for the publication and distribution of printed literature for blinded sailors and soldiers of the Allied Forces.	The Norwegian Odelsting adopts a bill that would end the prohibition on heavy wines. The bill proceeds to the Lagting, where it is expected to pass.…The British Museum accepts the stuffed remains of the dog of Nurse Cavell, who was executed during the war.…The Soviet Union announces that Lenin's health is improving.	Lord Carnarvon, who was instrumental in opening King Tutankhamen's tomb, is seriously ill in Cairo, Egypt, with streptococci infection, the result of a mosquito bite to the face.…The Pungwe River in Rhodesia breaks through dams and causing flooding while the waters of the Zambezi River approaches dangerous levels.	The government of Saskatchewan announces that it refuses to reconsider Prohibition, despite receiving a petition with 65,000 signatures.…The Canadian House of Commons defeats a bill by a vote of 121 to 14 that would have allowed Canadians to accept decorations but not titles for achievements in art, literature, and science.	The Indian Legislative Assembly continues to debate the budget and votes to reject an increase in the salt tax.
Mar. 21	The Inter-Allied Commission considers the Turkish counter-proposals to the Lausanne Treaty.…The Hungarian Chamber of Commerce urge the adoption of Esperanto as the language of international business.	The British House of Lords discusses the aerial weaknesses of British defensive forces with fears expressed about the trend of events in Europe…The printing plant used for the publication of the Republican newspaper, *Daily Bulletin*, is discovered by Criminal Investigation Department officers in Dublin, Ireland, and 14 women are arrested at the site.	The Undersecretary for the British Colonies states that of the 35 senior posts in Palestine, 33 are held by Christians and the remaining two are filled by Jews.…The High Commissioner of Angola in West Africa orders all schools that do not teach the Portuguese language to close.		Four-thousand workers at the Yenang-yaung oil field in Rangoon, Burma, go on strike without warning.…Six million acres of land in New South Wales, Australia, are infested with prickly pear and the government has introduced a bill to combat the pest.
Mar. 22	American delegates to the Congress of the International Chamber of Commerce suggest that the reparations problem be solved by American banks paying France the amount that the country claims in cash on condition that France should permanently withdraw from the question of reparations.…Albert Einstein resigns from the League of Nations' Commission on Intellectual Cooperation.	Germany announces that it has a financial deficit of 7.1 trillion marks. In September 1922, it had a deficit of 843 billion marks.…The collapse of the German economy is blamed by the German government on the French occupation of the Ruhr.…Romania passes the Romanian Constitution Reform Bill, which nationalizes the subsoil and the sources of energy.	The arrest of a noncommissioned officer leads to a fight between Egyptian police and soldiers of the Egyptian Fourth Infantry Regiment in which 30 police officers are injured.		Wu Pei-fu's demands are accepted for the appointment of his nominees to government posts in China.…The Indian government announces its intention to increase the salt tax despite the Legislative Assembly's rejection of the proposal.
Mar. 23	A group of U.S. banks led by the National City Bank has arranged a loan of $20 million for the Oriental Development Company of Tokyo to develop Korea.	The British War Office announces plans to save money by discontinuing the daily firing of time guns at 1 and 8 o'clock in garrison towns.	The new flag of the Syrian Federation is hoisted at the inauguration of the federation in Beirut.…The government of the Sudan approves a balanced budget for 1923–24 that is smaller than previous budgets because of a depression.	An Indian politician visiting Canada declares that he doubts British Columbia will give the right to vote to Indian residents because of the economic rivalry between the white and nonwhite races.	
Mar. 24	The League of Nations Committee for the Suppression of the White Slave Trade issues a resolution requesting a halt to the employment of foreign women in licensed houses of prostitution.…The Congress of the International Chamber of Commerce approves a resolution on reparations by a unanimous vote and then adjourns until next year.	The Moscow Supreme Military Tribunal sentences five Latvians to death for espionage and executes two Estonians convicted of espionage.…France complains that French waiters are being expelled from England.	Europeans in Kenya send a delegation to London to persuade the British government to refuse to give the vote to Indians in Kenya and to block uncontrolled immigration of Asians.…Indians in Kenya send a delegation, on the same ship as the European delegation, to persuade the British to extend full rights to Indians in Kenya.	Canada agricultural officials announce that a greater acreage of wheat will be sown than ever before despite the fact that farmers still hold large stocks of grain and the price for wheat is low.	
	A *Includes developments that affect more than one world region, international organizations and important meetings of world leaders.*	B *Includes all domestic and regional developments in Europe, including the Soviet Union.*	C *Includes all domestic and regional developments in Africa and the Middle East.*	D *Includes all domestic and regional developments in Latin America, the Caribbean, and Canada.*	E *Includes all domestic and regional developments in Asian and Pacific nations (and colonies).*

U.S. Politics & Social Issues	U.S. Foreign Policy & Affairs, Defense	U.S. Economy & Environment	Science, Technology & Nature	Culture, Leisure & Lifestyle	
			A blizzard that is reported to be the worst since 1888 sweeps across the Northwest and Midwest. Wyoming, Colorado, Nebraska, Wisconsin, and Iowa all suffer very cold weather and high winds.		Mar. 18
William Z. Foster of the American Communist Party goes on trial for criminal conspiracy before a federal court in St. Joseph, Michigan.... Testimony reveals that American Communists are acting under the direction of the Third International and that the Secret Service had infiltrated the Party.	Bernard Baruch, one of the economic advisers to the American Peace Delegation and chief American member of the Reparations Committee, states that Germany should end the Ruhr situation by paying $12.5 billion more in reparations.		Milwaukee has 12-foot snow drifts, while Chicago has come to a virtual standstill because of the blizzard.... Fires in Chicago during the blizzard destroy a city block of apartments and leave 40 families homeless.	Mr. Jimmy, a dancing teacher, claims to have established a world record by dancing for 24 hours, four minutes, and five seconds without interruption.	Mar. 19
	The Secretary of State, Charles Evans Hughes, and the Acting Secretary of the Navy, Franklin D. Roosevelt, issue statements that Great Britain is adhering to the terms of the Washington Naval Treaty and is not modernizing its ships.		American agriculturalist John McLaren McBryde dies.... The Nobel Prize Committee announces that it will award prizes worth 114,935 kronar each.... Violent storms in France expose fossilized remains of large trees on the Breton coast.	Henry Krehbiel, a noted American music critic, dies.	Mar. 20
		Western Union Telegrams may now be sent to Canada, Cuba, or Great Britain at night and on the weekend without any additional charge.			Mar. 21
	The USS *Iowa*, famous for service in the Battle of Santiago during the Spanish-American War, is sunk as a practice target by the guns of the USS *Mississippi* in Pacific Fleet maneuvers.... The U.S. Fleet in the Pacific tests the possibility of wireless transmission in naval warfare by steering the USS *Iowa* by radio from another warship several thousand yards away.	Clarence Saunders, president of the Piggly Wiggly grocery chain made almost $4 million on the New York Stock Exchange by demanding that short sellers pay to settle their debts after he caused the company's stock price to rise by buying all outstanding shares.... Saunders announced his intent to take Piggly Wiggly off the New York Stock Exchange because he does not like the ways of the stock market.	The government of the Falkland Islands purchases a ship to conduct research into whaling in South Georgia and the Shetland Islands. The whale researchers will determine the geographical limits of the whales, trace their migrations, count their numbers, and determine their rate of reproduction with the aim of controlling the whaling industry to prevent depletion of stock.		Mar. 22
	The American Consulate in Smyrna is completely destroyed by fire.	The pace of business recovery leads several bankers to issue warnings about the risk of inflation.... The Brooklyn Rapid Transit Company begins to exit receivership as a plan of reorganization is approved.	A type of breathing device, the Blackett's Aerophor Brown-Mills Apparatus, is approved by the government for use at naval rescue stations and mines.		Mar. 23
	The U.S. Navy rates the Japanese and British navies as stronger than the U.S. Navy and urges the modernization of the American fleet.... The navy seeks to extend the range of American batteries to the 24,000 yards claimed by British forces.	Aeromarine Airways announces plans to establish flying-boat routes throughout the United States.... An Aeromarine Advisory Board of aeronautical, banking, and industrial experts has been formed to lobby the U.S. government to support flying boats.	Diphtheria carriers are being treated with a new method of disinfection that uses other bacteria to kill diphtheria bacteria.		Mar. 24
F *Includes campaigns, elections, federal-state relations, civil rights and liberties, crime, the judiciary, education, healthcare, poverty, urban affairs, and population.*	G *Includes formation and debate of U.S. foreign and defense policies, veterans affairs, and defense spending. (Relations with specific foreign countries are usually found under the region concerned.)*	H *Includes business, labor, agriculture, taxation, transportation, consumer affairs, monetary and fiscal policy, natural resources, pollution and industrial accidents.*	I *Includes worldwide scientific, medical and technological developments, natural phenomena, U.S. weather and natural disasters.*	J *Includes the arts, religion, scholarship, communications media, sports, entertainment, fashions, fads, and social life.*	

	World Affairs	Europe	Africa & The Middle East	The Americas	Asia & The Pacific
Mar. 25	Greece demands that Turkey send ships to remove Turks from Greece. The homes of the Turks will be given to Greek refugees. Greece also requests Anglo-American loans to solve the refugee problem.	To resolve the conflict over "summer time," the French government proposes to substitute Strasbourg time, which is 35 minutes ahead of Greenwich time.…In response to an attack on a French Army officer, all restaurants in the district of Ottweiler in Germany are ordered to close at 8:30 p.m., all public meetings are banned, and all assemblies on the street of more than three persons is forbidden.	The waters of the Zambezi River begin to recede but 25 percent of the Nyasaland tobacco crop is estimated to be lost to the continuous rains.	The Minister of Justice in Canada introduces a bill prohibiting newspapers from publishing racing tips, selections, odds, and the amounts paid on horses.…The Fifth Pan-American Conference opens in Santiago, Chile.…The money order service between Great Britain and Brazil, which is operated by the post offices, is suspended.	
Mar. 26	France indicates that it will not give the League of Nations the responsibility for demilitarization of the Rhine.…The Bulgarian government protests to the Great Powers about the treatment of Bulgarians in Western Thrace by the Greek authorities.	Archbishop Cieplak of the Catholic Church has been sentenced to death in Moscow.…Yugoslavia and Bulgaria sign a treaty to suppress lawlessness on the Macedonian frontier.…A Belgian pays a few francs to a second-hand shop in Paris for a painting by Rembrandt.	At the request of the new Prime Minister of Egypt, legal proceedings have been suspended against the Zaghlulist rebels who were arrested after the last bomb attack.		The Australian government announces plans to develop the Northern Territory by developing a port at the mouth of the McArthur River and encouraging industry.
Mar. 27		To celebrate the fixing of the eastern borders of Poland, the government grants amnesty to persons convicted or accused of crimes connected with religious or political motives between November 1918 and March 1923.…Belgian troops receive orders to seize coke from a German factory in the Rhein-Baden State Mine.	Hostilities between the Imam Yehia of Saana in and the Idrissi resume in Yemen, with the Imam's forces suffering heavy losses in fighting at Jebel Milhan.		Kormara Thangal, the Moplah rebel leader, is sentenced to be hanged for waging war against the King, arson, murder, and forcible conversion.…The government of India decides to return the English orphan adopted by a Eurasian family to England.
Mar. 28		The French government protests the pending execution of Catholic officials by the Soviet Union.…The Polish government also protests the executions.		Various companies are organizing in expectation of a gold rush to Labrador, Canada, in the spring.	
Mar. 29	Officers of the Allied Commission of Control face an angry mob in Keczkemet, near Budapest, Hungary, when they attempt to enter the room of a Hungarian lieutenant.	A Presbyterian minister in Glasgow, Scotland, gives a speech in which he declares that the Roman Catholic Irish in Glasgow are three times as likely to commit crimes as the rest of the population.			
Mar. 30	France announces that it will not leave Germany until all reparations are paid.…The All Russian Congress of Soviets passes a resolution to send workers from Moscow and Petrograd to the Ruhr with 10,000 tons of grain.…The Belgian government urges the Allied governments to appoint representatives to fight the death sentences given to Catholic leaders in Moscow.	The German government fails to obtain a loan of 50 million gold marks.…The German Admiralty announces that the *Sussex*, sunk during the war, was attacked by U-Boat 29 under Captain Pustkuchen, who later went down with U-66.…The death sentence given to Archbishop Ciepliak in Moscow is commuted and he is sentenced to 10-years imprisonment.			A notornis, a rare bird the size of a goose, is seen at Dusky Sound in the South Island Fiord district of New Zealand.
Mar. 31		No new hard-wood road paving has been laid in the past year in London, according to the newly-issued annual report of the Metropolitan Committee on Materials and Means of Paving the Streets of London.			
Apr. 1	The American destroyer, USS *McFarland* arrives at Brindisi from Constantinople to take an investigating commission back to Constantinople.…The Allies send a note to Turkey expressing surprise that various questions that were identified as closed by Ismet Pasha in February letters are now being reopened.…The Allies express desire for a just and lasting peace between Turkey and the High Contracting Powers.	Berlin Communists break up a meeting of Italian merchants in the mistaken belief that the Italians are Fascists.…The Danes are warned that German scam artists are trying to sell them worthless shares of German industrial firms…Four coffins believed to date from the 4th century are unearthed in the Boulevard St. Marcel in Paris.…A French bill to fix the period of service in the French army at 18 months becomes law.…Three dancers are arrested in Paris for breaking a new law by offending the public morality.	Omari bin Mohammed, the Sultan of Witu in East Africa, dies.…Turkey announces that it will hold a general election.…A Bedouin chief of Damascus, Emir Nuri Esh Shalaan, goes to Amman to confer with the Emir Abdullah about Wahabite violence in the region.	A strike of steel workers in Nova Scotia, Canada, continues with the workers alleging that a organization formed by the Sydney Board of Trade to maintain law and order is an attempt to create imitation Fascists.…The Canadian Council of Agriculture calls on the government to provide long-term loans to farmers since the system of rural credits is inadequate.…Seven people die during a blizzard in Newfoundland, Canada.	The Muslim League opens its session in Lucknow, India, by attacking British foreign policy.…League President Bhurgri declares that, in view of the aggression in Europe against Asia and Africa, a league of Oriental nations should be formed in the future.…The majority of 55,000 workers employed at mills in Ahmedabad, India, go on strike to protest a reduction of wages.…The Indian Trade Union at Ahmedabad promises nonviolence and enlists volunteers to maintain order.
	A *Includes developments that affect more than one world region, international organizations and important meetings of world leaders.*	B *Includes all domestic and regional developments in Europe, including the Soviet Union.*	C *Includes all domestic and regional developments in Africa and the Middle East.*	D *Includes all domestic and regional developments in Latin America, the Caribbean, and Canada.*	E *Includes all domestic and regional developments in Asian and Pacific nations (and colonies).*

U.S. Politics & Social Issues	U.S. Foreign Policy & Affairs, Defense	U.S. Economy & Environment	Science, Technology & Nature	Culture, Leisure & Lifestyle	
					Mar. 25
	The State Department announces that American oil companies are free to do business in Burma and that a previous statement to the contrary issued in 1920 was incorrect.			Actress Sarah Bernhardt dies in Paris from uremic poisoning after months of poor health.	Mar. 26
At the trial of William Z. Foster, testimony reveals that Communists have been holding meetings in New York, where they discussed the advisability of coming into the open with their activities.... The British quota of emigrants to the United States is met with 77,342 people and no more immigrants will be admitted.					Mar. 27
	The State Department officially protests, through the American Ambassador in Berlin, the scheduled executions of Catholic leaders by the Soviet Union.				Mar. 28
		A fire destroys most of Paragon Park, an amusement park on Nantucket Beach in Massachusetts.			Mar. 29
		John D. Rockefeller, Jr. displaces his father John, Sr. as the richest man in the world.		Vast crowds estimated at 600,000 line the route of actress Sarah Bernhardt's funeral procession in Paris.	Mar. 30
			Frederick Mott, an English pathologist who determined that some cases of shell shock during the World War were actually small hemorrhages in the brain, retires.		Mar. 31
In response to a crime wave, every police officer and detective in New York City is ordered into active service. The New York Police Commissioner blames recent armed robberies on an influx of criminals from all over the country. Jewelry and tobacco shops are typically targeted but paymasters are also being followed from banks and held up even in the midst of crowds.... A group of 16 Ku Klux Klansmen who enter a Pittsburgh Episcopal church are asked by the minister to remove their disguises before an usher pulls the hoods off the heads of six of the men.	The U.S. Army Air Corps makes arrangements to build a semi-rigid dirigible airship at Akron, OH, for use as a mother ship in the transportation of airplanes.		Dr. A. Rollier publishes a book, *Heliotherapy*, arguing that tuberculosis can be treated by sunlight since dark skin pigmentation is closely associated with resistance to other diseases.	The U.S. Shipping Board announces that travelers on its liner Leviathan will be compensated for the lack of liquor by theater productions.	Apr. 1
F *Includes campaigns, elections, federal-state relations, civil rights and liberties, crime, the judiciary, education, healthcare, poverty, urban affairs, and population.*	G *Includes formation and debate of U.S. foreign and defense policies, veterans affairs, and defense spending. (Relations with specific foreign countries are usually found under the region concerned.)*	H *Includes business, labor, agriculture, taxation, transportation, consumer affairs, monetary and fiscal policy, natural resources, pollution and industrial accidents.*	I *Includes worldwide scientific, medical and technological developments, natural phenomena, U.S. weather and natural disasters.*	J *Includes the arts, religion, scholarship, communications media, sports, entertainment, fashions, fads, and social life.*	

	World Affairs	Europe	Africa & The Middle East	The Americas	Asia & The Pacific
Apr. 2	Epidemic disease is sweeping through the 15,000 Near Eastern refugees housed at Corfu and there is no means of separating the sick from the well.…Lord Robert Cecil, in a New York City speech, asks the United States to join the League of Nations because no nation can build a wall around its frontiers.	Officers from the Belgian Exhumation Service arrive in England to supervise the disinterment of Belgian soldiers who died in English hospitals during the war.… A group of fishermen in Aberdeen, Scotland, cause considerable damage by stoning German trawlers at the harbor entrance.…Norway and Portugal sign a treaty permitting the free trade of wine.	The Union of South Africa signs the Mozambique Convention regulating the conditions under which native laborers are recruited in Portuguese territory to work in Rand mines.	The Canadian Minister of the Interior insists that the first objective of the government in immigration policy is to obtain British settlers to maintain the British element and strengthen the fabric of the British Empire.	China sends a second note to Japan requesting to revise the China-Japan Treaty of 1915 with the aim of acquiring Port Arthur and Dalny.… Asutosh Mookerjee, the retiring Vice Chancellor of Calcutta University, announces that he has worked to prevent the government from taking a radically wrong course and will not agree to terms of reappointment that require him to wholehearted support the government's actions.
Apr. 3	A German newspaper suggests that the best solutions to the reparations problem would be the formation of a coalition government of Socialists and the German People's Party (Industrialists) since the Socialists is the only political group with enough goodwill to make reparations while the Industrialists have the means to do so.	The Spanish Cabinet debate granting privileges to people who are not Catholics.…A Irish Free State Customs building on the border with Northern Ireland is burned to the ground by Republicans.… Turkish leader Zaghul Pasha sets sail for France after seven months as a political prisoner at Gibraltar.		A proposal to establish representative government in Jamaica is rejected by the legislature.…A petition requesting the introduction of an electoral system in Dominica is presented to the British Colonial Office by the Governor of the Leeward Islands.	The Rajah of Akalot, one of the youngest Indian princes to serve in the Great War, dies apparently of poisoning in Bombay, India.
Apr. 4	Turkish authorities order the discontinuance of rations provided to 23,000 Christian refugees in Constantinople by the American Near East Relief organization.	The Catholic Church in Spain secures the resignation of the Minister of Finance over a dispute about the designation of a state religion.…British traders demand that the British zone in Germany be freed from Franco-Belgian economic sanctions.…The Bulgarian government repeats its complaints to the Greek government about the expulsion of Bulgarians from Thrace.	The French military makes flights of 800 miles over French West Africa to demonstrate the importance of air services in the development of French colonies and protectorates.	President Zayas of Cuba requests that all members of the Cabinet resign so that he may appoint people more agreeable to his political policies.…The Canadian National Education Conference recommends that French and English be taught in all elementary schools and that Ontario should create a Deputy Minister of Education for the French minority.	The Queensland government in Australia designates 750,000 acres of freehold and pastoral leasehold land for the purpose of establishing settlers to engage in wheat growing alone or wheat and wool growing combined.
Apr. 5	The Archbishop of Cologne arrives in Rome to discuss the situation in the Ruhr with the Pope. The Pope is expected to express a wish for peace and avoid taking a political stance.	Soviet newspapers, in reaction to the sentences imposed on Roman Catholic officials, complain about the unwarranted foreign interferences in the purely domestic affairs of the Soviet Union.	Fifteen Egyptians, mostly students, go on trial for conspiring to murder British soldiers, British civilians, and witnesses to various criminal acts.	Thirty employees of the Canadian Pacific on the Western section are fired with charges expected soon in connection with a ticket-stealing conspiracy centered in Winnipeg.	The Black Plague, which killed 632 people in Bombay, India, last year has returned to the city and is causing deaths. Bombay authorities are reconsidering the notion that the plague would disappear through rats becoming immune.
Apr. 6		Physicians state that Lenin is suffering from incurable paralysis and that he may die soon or linger indefinitely.…Members of the German Aero Club, German aeronautical associations, and German industrial aircraft firms issue a joint statement insisting on Germany's right to freedom in the air.…The Soviet Union hears reports from London that Leon Trotsky has been poisoned, while the Soviet Legation in England neither confirms nor denies the reports.	Roman ruins are found near Bizerta, Tunisia, during digging operations for an oil reservoir.	The first group for this year of 176 British male and female orphans between 12 and 16 years from Dr. Barnardo's Homes boards a ship for settlement on farms in Canada.… The Salvation Army sends 40 British boys to Canada today after they complete a short course on agricultural management.…Canada begins using airplanes in surveying and in efforts to halt forest fires.	The Aga Khan expresses regret that the Indian Muslim League has been almost entirely dissolved and hopes that a new organization will be formed to influence Muslim ideas of civilization. He considers the proposal that Indians should consent to become second-class citizens of Kenya as unfair and derogatory to their self-respect.
Apr. 7		Lord Coke of England is fined for not reporting the presence of an alien, an Italian nursery maid, in his home.…The British Agricultural Tribunal of Investigation advises that the import of flour be prohibited to increase the price of flour in Great Britain.		Of the 1200 people who boarded the Canada Pacific liner, *Montclare*, in Liverpool, England, 700 are farmers or farm workers.…The Canadian Trade Ministry announces that 3500 cattle will be imported to Great Britain every week from Canada, thereby dropping the price of beef in the British market.	The Prime Minister of Australia agrees that the Commonwealth should be represented in London by a Resident Minister but he does not think that it is practical. The Australian Cabinet has not discussed the question of such representation.
Apr. 8	Two squadrons of Lithuanian Hussars with four tanks arrive in Memel.		Turkey sends Ismet Pasha, Riza Nur Bey, and Hassan Fehmi Bey as delegates to the Lausanne Conference. Adnan Bey will serve as a substitute.…Turkey controversially grants mineral rights under and near railways to the Ottoman Development Company, an American-owned firm that builds railroads.	The Canadian government sends a former Arctic explorer, Stefansson, as its representative to London to begin negotiations over Canada's claim to Wrangel Island in the Arctic Ocean.	Two British soldiers from the Seaforth Highlanders die instantaneously in the evening from shots fired in Simla, India, near the Khyber Pass by two men who are presumed to be Shinwaria. Indian troops immediately respond to the shootings. Indian officials regard the murders as the result of a typical Pathan blood feud since the assailants are believed to be relatives of the famous outlaw Multan, who was executed in 1909.

A	B	C	D	E
Includes developments that affect more than one world region, international organizations and important meetings of world leaders.	*Includes all domestic and regional developments in Europe, including the Soviet Union.*	*Includes all domestic and regional developments in Africa and the Middle East.*	*Includes all domestic and regional developments in Latin America, the Caribbean, and Canada.*	*Includes all domestic and regional developments in Asian and Pacific nations (and colonies).*

	U.S. Politics & Social Issues	U.S. Foreign Policy & Affairs, Defense	U.S. Economy & Environment	Science, Technology & Nature	Culture, Leisure & Lifestyle
Apr. 2	William Joseph Simmons, founder of the Ku Klux Klan, and Imperial Wizard Evans present their cases in Georgia Superior Court for control of the Klan.... The sheriff of Fulton County evicts Evans and his supporters from the Emperor's Palace in Atlanta, GA, while ownership of the building is settled by the courts.	Charles Evans Hughes, the Secretary of State, announces that the American Red Cross will bring its emergency relief work in Greece to an end on June 30.			
Apr. 3	Judge William Emmet Dever is elected mayor of Chicago, partly on a platform of municipal ownership of street railways.	In a speech made after consultation with President Harding, Nicholas Murray Butler, president of Columbia University, states that American adhesion to the protocol of the International Court of Justice is sound Republican doctrine.			
Apr. 4	Warrants are issued for the treasurer and chief investigator of the Atlanta, GA, Ku Klux Klan on charges of embezzlement.... Horace Boies, the former governor of Iowa, dies.		A tornado strikes Pineville, LA, killing 14 people and injuring 50.... In Wendell, NC, a tornado injures 25 people and wrecks 50 buildings.... Torrential rains, hail storms, swollen streams, floods, and interrupted train service plagues people in Mississippi and Louisiana.		
Apr. 5	The Federal Census Bureau estimates that the population of New York City will reach 5,927,625 by July 1. This will be a gain in three years of 307,577.			Several aviators state that recent advances in aviation mean that motorless planes, or gliders, will be able to travel 100 miles on a gallon of fuel.	
Apr. 6	The Appellate Division of the New York Supreme Court unanimously rules that the state law exempting new buildings from taxation is constitutional, thereby reversing a lower court decision. The decision ends turmoil in the New York real estate market because buyers refused to take titles on the grounds that doing so would force them to pay taxes in violation of their agreement with the sellers.... The William Z. Foster jury is unable to reach a decision and is dismissed.	Rear Admiral Henry Knapp, who commanded U.S. naval forces in Europe during the war, dies in Hartford, CT.	A shortage of workers created by immigration restrictions has combined with a trade boom to bring about such a shortage of labor that railroads express fears that they will be unable to vouch for the safety of their lines.... Other American employers note that clerks and similar workers are turning to manual labor because it pays better.... Some manufacturers express fears that the high cost of labor will reduce the competitive power of American products in foreign markets.	A British physician warns that food manufacturers are using drugs as food preservatives to mask spoilage and that these drugs may harm consumers.	Alice Cunningham Fletcher, an American anthropologist, dies.
Apr. 7					
Apr. 8			The U.S. Steel Corporation increases wages by 11 percent.		

F	G	H	I	J
Includes campaigns, elections, federal-state relations, civil rights and liberties, crime, the judiciary, education, healthcare, poverty, urban affairs, and population.	*Includes formation and debate of U.S. foreign and defense policies, veterans affairs, and defense spending. (Relations with specific foreign countries are usually found under the region concerned.)*	*Includes business, labor, agriculture, taxation, transportation, consumer affairs, monetary and fiscal policy, natural resources, pollution and industrial accidents.*	*Includes worldwide scientific, medical and technological developments, natural phenomena, U.S. weather and natural disasters.*	*Includes the arts, religion, scholarship, communications media, sports, entertainment, fashions, fads, and social life.*

	World Affairs	Europe	Africa & The Middle East	The Americas	Asia & The Pacific
Apr. 9		An earthquake shakes Majorca, Spain.... The publication of Communist newspapers in Berlin has been suspended for two weeks.... The Hessian State Museum in Germany announces that it is selling its collection of medieval coins dating from the time of Moritz the Learned who ruled in Hesse from 1592 to 1627.		The Canadian Millers' Association asks the Canadian government to modify regulations that mandate that exporters must send 25 percent of wheat offal with 75 percent of flour.	China and Japan appoint a joint commission to discover the sources of morphine consignments that are smuggled through China to Japan.... The continuance of the Commonwealth subsidy for beef shipments is blocked in Australia by shipping companies that are required, as part of the proposal, to reduce their freight charges.
Apr. 10	The German Consul-General protests about the destruction of German statues and the Lithuanian government promises to make repairs.... The situation in Memel is reported to be calmer today.... The Canadian Soldier Settlement Board proposes establishing a training farm in India for the vocational training of British soldiers whose enlistments are about to expire. The Board hopes that the men will be easily able to work on farms in Canada and thus will be more likely to settle in Canada.	At the Belfast Assizes, the Lord Chief Justice states that crime in the city is practically nil compared with this time last year.... A Protestant crowd in Albert Hall in London protests the proposed visit of King George to the Pope.... Representatives of the Lancashire Cotton Manufacturers and Spinners Association along with members of the Northern Counties Textile Association complain that unemployment is worse than anticipated and express pessimism about the future of the trade in Great Britain.			The government entomologist finds boll weevil worms and lesser cotton pests firmly established at Perth, Australia. The native hibiscus serves as hosts for the larvae, making eradication impossible and control very difficult. Entomologists assume that the pests were introduced many years ago before there was a quarantine for seeds.
Apr. 11	The Conference of Abbazia for the determination of the boundary of Fiume begins to meet.	Grand Duke Alexander of Russia calls on Americans of all faiths to support him in his efforts to prevent the Soviet government from persecuting people of religious faith in Russia.			
Apr. 12					Civil forces in Allahabad in India are aided by Sikh villagers in suppressing outlaws who operate along the Indian border.
Apr. 13	The Franco-Belgian Conference begins in Paris with both countries agreeing on the technical measures that should be adopted in order to strengthen the pressure that is being put on Germany.... The Cardinals of the Catholic Church initiate a call for the canonization of Pope Pius X.	Reports in British newspapers indicate that Vladivostok in the Soviet Union has been captured from the Bolshevists by White forces.... Soviet Union plans to reconstruct the state administration meet with opposition from the nationalists of the federated republics, who complain that the All-Russian Central Committee overwhelmingly represents Great Russian and ignores smaller national interests.	General Smuts of South Africa delivers a speech in which he attacks the nationalist aims of the Republicans and attacks the honesty of a Nationalist-Labour alliance in the Transvaal Provincial Council.	Canadian shippers are seeking to charter British steamers to send cattle to Great Britain in greater numbers that are currently accommodated.	Fighting continues in the Peshawar district between a gang of outlaws and Sikh villagers.
Apr. 14		Members of the Berlin City Council propose a measure that would levy heavy taxes upon any shops in Berlin that feature foreign language signs on their windows.			Troops and police take control of Amritsar in India following fighting between Hindus and Muslims that sends 70 people to hospitals but leaves no one dead.
Apr. 15		Eamon De Valera memorializes a dead Irregular soldier in Ireland by declaring that it is better to die nobly as Liam Lynch did than live as a slave.			
Apr. 16	The League of Nations opens its 24th session in Geneva.... The League is expected to address the Polish-Lithuanian dispute, the expropriation in Bulgaria of property held by Hungarians, and the reduction of armaments.	Prime Minister Stanley Baldwin of Great Britain introduces a budget that reduces income and beer taxes while anticipating expenditures of 800 million pounds for the coming financial year.			
Apr. 17	A conference of delegates from British, French, Dutch, and Belgian railroads continues to deliberate in Brussels on the regulation of railroad timetables upon the establishment of summertime in Belgium on April 21. The delegates have decided that all international trains for France will leave Belgium one-hour later while the Dover-Ostend mail boats will keep their present times.				
	A *Includes developments that affect more than one world region, international organizations and important meetings of world leaders.*	B *Includes all domestic and regional developments in Europe, including the Soviet Union.*	C *Includes all domestic and regional developments in Africa and the Middle East.*	D *Includes all domestic and regional developments in Latin America, the Caribbean, and Canada.*	E *Includes all domestic and regional developments in Asian and Pacific nations (and colonies).*

	U.S. Politics & Social Issues	U.S. Foreign Policy & Affairs, Defense	U.S. Economy & Environment	Science, Technology & Nature	Culture, Leisure & Lifestyle
Apr. 9	The U.S. Supreme Court rules 5–3 that Congress acted unconstitutionally in fixing the minimum wages paid to women and girls in the District of Columbia. The court decides that freedom of contract, guaranteed by the Fifth Amendment, prevents Congress from establishing either a minimum or a maximum wage.		Other large steel manufacturers match U.S. Steel by increasing the wages that they pay.	A new method of brine freezing that uses concentrated solutions of salt that remain liquid at temperatures of 0 Fahrenheit has been developed to preserve fish.	
Apr. 10			Stuyvesant Fish, a banker and railroad magnate, dies.... The *New York Herald* introduces a miniature newspaper in its regular edition, with the news condensed for the busy reader.		
Apr. 11					
Apr. 12				George Lincoln Goodale, an American botanist and educator, dies.	
Apr. 13				Researchers seek to determine the precise causes of corrosion in order to save industry from enormous losses due to wastage. The researchers are working on producing household articles, known as stainless silver, that do not require daily cleaning.	
Apr. 14					
Apr. 15			The U.S. Shipping Board is ordered by President Harding to immediately pursue the consolidation of foreign trade lines and then offer the lines and ships for sale.		
Apr. 16		The United States is requested by Lord Robert Cecil to advise the League of Nations about its willingness to cooperate with other nations on the control of traffic in arms and the private manufacture of arms.			
Apr. 17					The 21st season of Major League Baseball begins.

F	G	H	I	J
Includes campaigns, elections, federal-state relations, civil rights and liberties, crime, the judiciary, education, healthcare, poverty, urban affairs, and population.	*Includes formation and debate of U.S. foreign and defense policies, veterans affairs, and defense spending. (Relations with specific foreign countries are usually found under the region concerned.)*	*Includes business, labor, agriculture, taxation, transportation, consumer affairs, monetary and fiscal policy, natural resources, pollution and industrial accidents.*	*Includes worldwide scientific, medical and technological developments, natural phenomena, U.S. weather and natural disasters.*	*Includes the arts, religion, scholarship, communications media, sports, entertainment, fashions, fads, and social life.*

	World Affairs	Europe	Africa & The Middle East	The Americas	Asia & The Pacific
Apr. 18		The German mark begins to drop quickly. The Reichsbank declines to take action to stop the slide and stabilize the currency.			
Apr. 19					
Apr. 20	The British Colonial Office states that families should migrate together to form overseas counties.	The Scottish Trades Union Congress protests against the formation of the Fascist movement in Scotland.... The County of Kent in England forms a migration committee to help people leave Kent. County leaders deny that they are trying to dump people abroad and insist that no one will be forced to leave Kent.			
Apr. 21	The Chamber of Shipping, which includes members from 11 nations, issues regulations regarding load lines for vessels carrying light wood and heavy wood goods on deck.	By a vote of 236 to 14, the British House of Commons rejects a bill that would prohibit alcohol consumption nationwide.			
Apr. 22	The Anglo-Austrian Tribunal requests to hear further cases before deciding whether an English firm deserves compensation from the Austrian government for expenses related to an exceptional war measures decree.	The English Place-Names Society forms to publish the results of a 15-month British Academy survey of place names, which have historical, linguistic, and cultural significance.			
Apr. 23	The League of Nations closes its 24th session in Geneva.... The upcoming international police conference in New York City is expected to devise means for the prompt circulation of information about the movements of criminals known to be international in their operations.	Two mothers from Brighton, England, are charged by the National Society for the Prevention of Cruelty to Children for racing their infants in baby carriages.... The castles of Seaham Hall and Brancepath in England are offered by their owners as hospitals.			
Apr. 24	Speaking in Hartford, Connecticut, Vice Preisdent Calvin Coolidge lends his support to the U.S.'s proposed entry into the Permanent Court of International Justice.				
Apr. 25					The eighth anniversary of the landing of the Australian and New Zealand troops on the Gallipoli Peninsula is celebrated on Anzac Day.

A	B	C	D	E
Includes developments that affect more than one world region, international organizations and important meetings of world leaders.	*Includes all domestic and regional developments in Europe, including the Soviet Union.*	*Includes all domestic and regional developments in Africa and the Middle East.*	*Includes all domestic and regional developments in Latin America, the Caribbean, and Canada.*	*Includes all domestic and regional developments in Asian and Pacific nations (and colonies).*

U.S. Politics & Social Issues	U.S. Foreign Policy & Affairs, Defense	U.S. Economy & Environment	Science, Technology & Nature	Culture, Leisure & Lifestyle	
Nine men, all American citizens, are charged with grand larceny in New York City. As representatives of the Soviet Autonomous Industrial Colony at Kuznetsk, Siberia, they presented Kuznetsk as a sort of industrial utopia. The men, who include Communist sociologist Roger Baldwin, were charged after two disgruntled families returned to the United States from Siberia.					Apr. 18
		The United Fruit Company purchases three electric ships with speeds of 14 knots and lengths of 325 feet. The ships are powered by diesel engines directly coupled to generators supplying a continuous current. They will carry bananas.		Arthur Klein sets the world record for dancing endurance by "fox-trotting and waltzing" for 82 consecutive hours, breaking the previous record of 75 hours set by Magdelene Wolfe.	Apr. 19
Social worker and journalist Louis Levin dies.					Apr. 20
			Medical researchers at the Rockefeller Institute in New York City succeed in isolating an organism, *Bacillus Pneumosyntes*, that they believe is responsible for influenza and successfully vaccinate rabbits.		Apr. 21
					Apr. 22
		The Department of Commerce reports that the month of March saw a record total of 64,000 cars and trucks produced.			Apr. 23
The New York State Assembly passes a bill to establish a New York State Department of Public Works.					Apr. 24
Aiming to disrupt the activities of the Klu Klux Klan, the Michigan House of Representatives passes a bill prohibiting organizations from wearing masks in public.					Apr. 25

F	G	H	I	J
Includes campaigns, elections, federal-state relations, civil rights and liberties, crime, the judiciary, education, healthcare, poverty, urban affairs, and population.	*Includes formation and debate of U.S. foreign and defense policies, veterans affairs, and defense spending. (Relations with specific foreign countries are usually found under the region concerned.)*	*Includes business, labor, agriculture, taxation, transportation, consumer affairs, monetary and fiscal policy, natural resources, pollution and industrial accidents.*	*Includes worldwide scientific, medical and technological developments, natural phenomena, U.S. weather and natural disasters.*	*Includes the arts, religion, scholarship, communications media, sports, entertainment, fashions, fads, and social life.*

	World Affairs	Europe	Africa & The Middle East	The Americas	Asia & The Pacific
Apr. 26	U.S. Senator Robert La Follette publicly argues against the U.S.'s proposed entry into the Permanent Court of International Justice, denouncing the proposal as "sinister and subversive."				
Apr. 27	Canadian economists report that Canada's export trade increased by $191,986,763 from the previous year.				
Apr. 28					
Apr. 29	The German mark stands at 30,000 to the dollar with a strong upward trend.	The prisons of the Soviet Union are reported to hold more than 2000 Russian Orthodox priests and more than 3000 lay and clerical leaders of other denominations.... The British government announces plans to appeal to the House of Lords if the Court of Appeal decides against it in the deportation of Art O'Brien to the Irish Free State.... The British government is inquiring into the prices of vegetables and fruit to be followed by inquiries into the prices charged for meat, cereals, and bread.	British government sources, including Sir Percy Cox, state that British responsibility in Iraq may come to an end in four years. The British government declines to make a formal statement about Iraq.... The Europeans of Kenya send delegates to South Africa and Australia to represent their case about Indians in Kenya.		
Apr. 30	The Federal Premiers of Germany meet briefly before sending a simultaneous note to Paris, Brussels, Rome, and London offering a settlement of the reparations question.... The advocates of the proposal hold that if Germany is to pay anything, the French must evacuate the Ruhr. Other Germans doubt that the French will do that and argue that a stronger attempt should be made to raise definite sums.		Prime Minister Bonar Law in communications to the British House of Commons declares that it is the desire of the British government to reduce British forces in Iraq as soon as possible.		A British man and three Chinese men, who are employed by the British-American Tobacco Company, are kidnapped while traveling in a mountainous region of the interior of Hong Kong and a ransom is demanded.
May 1		Three rioters are wounded by civil guards at La Linea, Spain, in a disturbance following the completion of the Spanish General Election.... At a May Day celebration in Latvia, a procession of Latvian Fascist youths prevents Socialists from speaking by throwing stones and stink bombs.	General Gabriel Haddad Pasha, a political refugee from Turkey who rose in Egypt to become Director of Public Security and a diplomat, dies.... Trials begin in Cairo, Egypt, for a number of people charged with conspiracy to murder British officers, soldiers, and civilians.		

A	B	C	D	E
Includes developments that affect more than one world region, international organizations and important meetings of world leaders.	*Includes all domestic and regional developments in Europe, including the Soviet Union.*	*Includes all domestic and regional developments in Africa and the Middle East.*	*Includes all domestic and regional developments in Latin America, the Caribbean, and Canada.*	*Includes all domestic and regional developments in Asian and Pacific nations (and colonies).*

U.S. Politics & Social Issues	U.S. Foreign Policy & Affairs, Defense	U.S. Economy & Environment	Science, Technology & Nature	Culture, Leisure & Lifestyle	
1923, April 26 (U.S. Politics & Social Issues): U.S. economists report that a total of over 5,000 unskilled African-American laborers have migrated out of the state of North Carolina in the past month.					Apr. 26
					Apr. 27
Knute Nelson, U.S. Senator and former governor of Minnesota, dies.		Representatives of the American tobacco industry report that the number of cigarettes sold in March was 30 percent higher than in March of 1922.			Apr. 28
		The Federal Trade Commission launches a formal complaint against Eastman Kodak and George Eastman as well as a number of other film manufacturers for conspiracy to monopolize the manufacture and sale of cinematograph film. The government alleges that Eastman Kodak has fixed the price of film, has discriminated against companies importing film, and has threatened to undersell these companies if they persist.	Aaron McDuffie Moore, an American physician, dies.		Apr. 29
The U.S. Supreme Court rules that neither American nor foreign ships may carry intoxicating beverages into American waters or American ports.…A black man is lynched in Columbia, MO. James Scott, a janitor for the University of Missouri, had been accused of attacking the 14-year-old daughter of a professor. Despite the professor's pleas, Scott was taken from jail in a two-hour long attack in which the mob used acetylene torches to cut the inner jail doors. The president of the university issues a statement denying that any students played a role in the lynching.				American fiction author Emerson Hough dies.…George Willis Cooke, a Unitarian minister and lecturer, dies.	Apr. 30
Citizens in Bound Brook, NJ, violently break up a meeting of the Pillar of Fire branch of the Ku Klux Klan. The New Jersey State Police are called out to rescue the Klan members.	The Army Medical Corps announces that it has demonstrated the usefulness of poison gases for the treatment of certain diseases ranging from simple colds to peresis. The experiments followed from the accidental discovery during the war that workers in the Edgewood Arsenal, near Baltimore, were immune from influenza in rooms in which chlorine gas was made.		Newly invented stereoscopic film is shown to the press at The Hague. The new film, when projected, gives a picture somewhat similar to a handheld stereoscope but not as good. The inventors, van den Hoek and Rotteveel, use a method of electrical reproduction on a wet screen kept in contact with water automatically.		May 1

	World Affairs	Europe	Africa & The Middle East	The Americas	Asia & The Pacific
May 2		The German government in a semi-official announcement discloses that the production of coke has been stopped in those cookeries under occupation in the Ruhr.	The Council of Ministers in Iraq authorizes space in the new building of the Ministry of Communications and Works for such antiquities as are now available from Ur and elsewhere.	Two Italians, including a woman Mrs. Florence Lassandra, are hanged at Fort Saskatchewan Gaol in Canada for shooting a provincial policeman. It is the first time in 20 years that Canada has executed a woman.... The editor of the Montreal *Star* declares that China cannot be insulted forever with impunity and that Canada must consider the question of Chinese immigration.	
May 3	The Belgian government decides to save money by abolishing the military guard for the Belgian Legation in Peking, China. The guard has cost 300,000 francs annually.			The Cuban government announces that the Cuban Legation in Washington, DC, will be elevated to an embassy.	
May 4		The Salvation Army in Great Britain commissions 500 men and women cadets as probationary officers.... The British Parliament debates amending the Merchandise Marks Act by requiring each imported egg to be marked with its country of origin. The measure would succeed in raising prices without the use of a protective tariff.			
May 5				New Brunswick, Canada, suffers flooding to the extent that trains stop running.	
May 6			Forest fires sweep the hills opposite Constantinople in Turkey.		At the request of the Japanese government, the Danish government announces that it has selected three well-known farmers willing to immigrate to Japan. The farmers and their families will establish farming operations along Danish lines.
May 7		A husband and wife are charged with willfully ill-treating, neglecting, and exposing their 4-month-old son in a manner likely to cause unnecessary suffering and injury to health. The family participated in a baby carriage race from London to Brighton, England.	Three natives are executed in Bulawayo, Rhodesia, for committing an outrage on a European woman on the Bulawayo golf links on November 7.	The legislature in Manitoba, Canada, votes to abolish the grand jury system.	Foreigners protest Sun Yat-sen's action in taking over the supervision of the Salt Inspectorate at Canton in China. The foreign District Inspectors refuses to transfer his seal of office to Sun's nominee.... The Australian drought is broken to some extent by rains that fell in Victoria.
May 8		Work is completed on the old German armored carrier, *Frithjof*, to convert it into a merchant ship to transport locomotives to the Soviet Union. This is the third German vessel of this type to be reconstructed, following the *Aegir* and the *Odin*.			Rioting between Hindus and Muslims at Amritsar, India, leaves 50 people injured.
May 9	Bulgarians continue to be expelled from Thrace by the Greeks. The Bulgarian government announces that it may be forced to take corresponding measures. Observers believe that this means that the Bulgarians will start expelling Greeks from Bulgaria.	A Passenger Vessel Bill is introduced in the British House of Commons to provide for a supply of liquor on all vessels carrying passengers in British waters. The bill is viewed as a rejoinder to an American ban on liquor in foreign ships.			
May 10	Negotiations continue to provide Greece with a loan to help it handle the refugee problem.... The Russian delegate to the Lausanne Conference, V.V. Varonsky, is murdered by a Swiss citizen who had suffered under Soviet rule. The Soviet Union breaks off diplomatic relations with Switzerland.	The Greek government grants a small free zone in Saloniki to the Kingdom of the Serbs, Croats, and Slovenes for 50 years. The free zone began operations in 1925 and provided the Serb-Croat-Slovenes access to the Aegean Sea.			

A	B	C	D	E
Includes developments that affect more than one world region, international organizations and important meetings of world leaders.	*Includes all domestic and regional developments in Europe, including the Soviet Union.*	*Includes all domestic and regional developments in Africa and the Middle East.*	*Includes all domestic and regional developments in Latin America, the Caribbean, and Canada.*	*Includes all domestic and regional developments in Asian and Pacific nations (and colonies).*

U.S. Politics & Social Issues	U.S. Foreign Policy & Affairs, Defense	U.S. Economy & Environment	Science, Technology & Nature	Culture, Leisure & Lifestyle	
An armed Assyrian silk worker is arrested in front of the residence of John D. Rockefeller, Jr. Armed with a stiletto and two long weaver's needles, the man is clubbed into submission by the police after threatening Rockefeller's life.... The Ku Klux Klan in Northern New Jersey initiates 1500 new members before a crowd estimated to be 12,000 strong.			Remains of a previously unknown civilization are discovered in the densely wooded region of Eastern Honduras and Northern Nicaragua by an expedition sent out by the Peabody Museum and Harvard University. Archeologists state that the ruins and relics represent the missing link in the chain of civilization along the Mosquito Coast.	Pitcher Walter "Big Train" Johnson of the Washington Senators gets his 100th shutout, and New York Yankees shortstop Everett Scott gets a gold medal from the American League for playing in his 1,000th consecutive game. Scott's run began on June 20, 1916. The Senators defeat the Yankees 3–0 at Griffith Stadium in Washington, DC, as Johnson allows just three hits.	May 2
		A landslide in Woodside, UT, wrecks a train and kills eight passengers, the engine driver, and a fireman.	U.S. Army Air Lieutenants Oakley Kelly and John MacReady flew nonstop across the United States. The flight was made in a Fokker T–2. It took 26 hours and 50 minutes to make the trip that started on Long Island and ended in San Diego.		May 3
					May 4
					May 5
	Four U.S. battleships are expected to visit Copenhagen, Denmark, next month and festivities are being planned. The ships are the *Florida*, *Delaware*, *Arkansas*, and *North Dakota*.		The Chicago Field Museum expedition to Argentina discovers the fossil remains of a Jurassic era dinosaur at Lake Cardiel. The reconstructed skeleton is expected to measure more than 60 feet.		May 6
The U.S. Supreme Court rules that the United States can compel captains of vessels arriving at American ports to submit manifests declaring all articles on board. The decision involved the *Sisco*, which claimed that it was unnecessary to report the presence of opium on board because that drug was prohibited.				The Little Theater Tournament begins at the Bayes Theater in New York City. It is a national competition of community theaters. A committee of five judges will select the three best plays and award prizes of $100 to each of the winners. Twenty theater groups within a 100-mile radius of New York City are participating.	May 7
					May 8
The Federal District Court in New York rules unconstitutional a section of the Volstead Act that forbids physicians to provide more than one pint of alcoholic liquor for the same patient within 10 days.			A storm that comes down from Alaska into the north central states brings snow to Minnesota, North Dakota, and Wisconsin. Illinois, Kansas, and Iowa receive both snow and sleet. The late season storm is causing anxiety about the fruit crop.		May 9
					May 10

F
Includes campaigns, elections, federal-state relations, civil rights and liberties, crime, the judiciary, education, healthcare, poverty, urban affairs, and population.

G
Includes formation and debate of U.S. foreign and defense policies, veterans affairs, and defense spending. (Relations with specific foreign countries are usually found under the region concerned.)

H
Includes business, labor, agriculture, taxation, transportation, consumer affairs, monetary and fiscal policy, natural resources, pollution and industrial accidents.

I
Includes worldwide scientific, medical and technological developments, natural phenomena, U.S. weather and natural disasters.

J
Includes the arts, religion, scholarship, communications media, sports, entertainment, fashions, fads, and social life.

	World Affairs	Europe	Africa & The Middle East	The Americas	Asia & The Pacific
May 11	The Conference of Ambassadors sends a note of protest to Lithuania for granting autonomy to the territory of Memel without previous consultation with the Allied Powers.	The Bavarian government in Germany issues an ordinance prohibiting public meetings and establishing press censorship, with imprisonment for criticisms of the Bavarian government. The government also empowers itself to imprison anyone for life for giving information to a foreign power in occupation of German territory.	Kabarega, the ex-King of Bunyoros dies. Captured two decades ago by the British, while engaged in hostilities against the new Uganda Protectorate, he went into exile in Seychelles. He returned to his homeland earlier this year.	A fire destroys the Bay of St. Paul Insane Asylum at Quebec. All 250 patients are removed without incident.	
May 12	The International Woman Suffrage Alliance opens its meeting in Rome with representatives from 30 countries present. The alliance intends to discuss all aspects of equality between the sexes including equal pay, equal moral standards, the nationality of married women, and maintenance of illegitimate children.	The Soviet Press reports that peasants killed 112 Communists between January and March.	A government committee advises Rhodesia to invite meat-packing companies to visit the country with a view towards establishing local works for export....Malaria has killed numerous people in the Bushveld of South Africa. Sickness among horses has led to a breakdown of transportation that is making it difficult to provide medical care to some regions.	The Ottawa Progressives decide to oppose the proposed Canadian government budget unless the tariff is further reduced. The budget is categorized as purely protectionist and unacceptable to the West.	The Melbourne, Australia, government announces that canned fruit will not be allowed to be exported unless it conforms to prescribed standards of grading, packing, and labeling. Such measures will enable Australian canned fruit to compete with California products.
May 13		Charlotte Garrigue Masaryk, the Brooklyn, NY-born First Lady of Czechoslovakia, dies....Pope Pius XI improves relations with the French government after a long-term disruption in relations....The last of the revolving Zeppelin sheds is being demolished at Nordholz in Germany. This shed is 800 feet long, 136 feet high, and 320 feet wide.	Several members of the Wafd (Nationalist Party) imprisoned at Almaza are released by the Egyptian government.	The Canadian government indicates its intention to cancel an agreement, in place since 1888 that permitted American fishing vessels to use Canadian ports on the Atlantic to land their catches and dispatch them without hindrance to U.S. markets. The United States granted similar rights to Canadian fishermen in 1918, but the privilege expired without renewal.	New Zealand invites the British Immigration Commission to investigate the conditions of British immigrants to New Zealand with the aim of increasing immigration....New Zealand states that it has no report of any case of unemployment among immigrants....About 1,000 bandits from Hunan, China, demand $150,000 from the city of Hankow for their departure.
May 14	The Court of the Hague finds William Nevens, manager of the Holland News Agency, guilty of acting in bad faith. He intercepted and sold news reports sent by radio by the Trans-Ocean News Agency in Berlin and destined for the Vaz Dias News Agency at Amsterdam.	Customs officials at Cadiz seize a large amount of opium that had been shipped as red pepper on a Spanish ship bound for Cuba.			Narayan Chandavarkar, President of the Bombay Legislature, dies of heart failure in Bombay, India.
May 15	The government of Argentina decides to ask Congress to approve the payment of Argentina's overdue contributions to the League of Nations and to ratify the country's membership in the League.	Sir Robert Newman introduces a bill in the British Parliament to allow married women to file for separation on grounds of cruelty or neglect even though she continues to live with her husband....Charles de Freycinet, a three time premier of France, dies....Rome is shaken by earthquakes....France and Czechoslovakia reach an agreement to send Czech agricultural workers to France. Czech workers are already employed in French oilfields.		The government of Jamaica refuses to contribute toward the maintenance of an agricultural college in Trinidad. Legislators argue that Jamaica needs its own college to serve the Bahamas and British Honduras.	An attempt is made in Lahore, India, to remove the Lawrence of Arabia statue from the mall. The attempt was led by Sirdar Amrit Singh, a member of the Congress Party.... Henry Barwell, the Premier of South Australia, said that his government will not consent to a federal plan to construct big railroads within South Australia until they had observed the legal and moral agreement to build a trans-continental railroad.
May 16	The League of Nations hosts its final conference in Geneva on the exchange of medical personnel between member states....All of the Polish political parties call upon the government to use all legal, political, and economic means to bring to an end Danzig's disregard of Polish rights in Danzig and to establish in full all rights conferred on Poland by the Versailles Treaty.	The joint efforts of the Reichsbank and the Finance Ministry to support the German mark have been abandoned....The Italian Chamber of Deputies opens its session. Political observers do not expect it to do much, although protectionist legislators may argue against commercial treaties made with other countries.	The British government informs Emir Abdullah that it will recognize an independent government of Transjordania, provided that such a government is constitutional.	Nova Scotia police raid the United Mine Workers headquarters in Glace Bay as well as the homes of its leaders. The union literature will be examined to see if it constitutes seditious and Communistic propaganda. The Nova Scotia government is determined to prevent the establishment of a Communist foothold in Cape Breton, Canada.	
May 17	The German government fails to win its objection to the jurisdiction of the Anglo-German Mixed Arbitral Tribunal to consider compensation for the seizure of an Irish ship by Germany in the Lower Elbe on August 3, 1914. The ship's crew was interned for six weeks. Germany used the ship for trade in the Baltic Sea until running it aground and wrecking it in 1916.	A bomb on a train in Dusseldorf derails the engine and several coaches. No lives are lost.... Romania pays tribute to the soldiers who died in the Great War. The body of an Unknown Soldier is laid to rest on a hilltop in Carol Park, overlooking the War Museum.		The Canadian legislature suspends a debate on protecting the rights of Canada to Wrangel Island pending the outcome of a decision by the Imperial government.	India places a number of Indian Bolshevists on trial who were reportedly trained at a propaganda school in Moscow to distribute anti-British propaganda throughout India.

A	B	C	D	E
Includes developments that affect more than one world region, international organizations and important meetings of world leaders.	*Includes all domestic and regional developments in Europe, including the Soviet Union.*	*Includes all domestic and regional developments in Africa and the Middle East.*	*Includes all domestic and regional developments in Latin America, the Caribbean, and Canada.*	*Includes all domestic and regional developments in Asian and Pacific nations (and colonies).*

U.S. Politics & Social Issues	U.S. Foreign Policy & Affairs, Defense	U.S. Economy & Environment	Science, Technology & Nature	Culture, Leisure & Lifestyle	
	Military engineer Henry Martyn Robert dies.	An explosion in a new oil well in Corsicana, TX, burns to death at least 12 men.			May 11
					May 12
New York City police arrest Noah Lerner, a 23-year-old Russian Communist, on the charge of causing the Wall Street explosion of September 1920 that left 34 people dead and injured hundreds more. Lerner recently returned to the United States from Russia with the aim of furthering the interests of the Kuzbuz Colony in Siberia. He is an electrician.				A previously unknown painting by German 16th-century artist Hans Holbein is discovered in the picture gallery of the Hohenzollern Castle at Sigmaringen. The painting shows the judgment by King Solomon.	May 13
	Two American attorneys arrive in Dublin, Ireland, to take evidence in a case that is being litigated in the United States. The case involves the ownership of $2.5 million collected some years ago in an Irish Republican fundraising drive in the United States.		A tornado that strikes Colorado City, TX, mows a path that is 25 miles long. The dead number 50 while the injured are estimated at 100. Serious damage has been done to crops and property.	Led by New York Yankee Wally Pipp's grand slam, the Yankees score eight runs in the 12th inning against the Tigers, to secure victory. Detroit comes back with three runs in the bottom of the inning to set an American League record for most runs in that inning. The Yankees win 16–11 at Tiger Stadium.	May 14
			American physicist Arthur Webster dies.... The resort town of Hot Springs, AR, is flooded by a cloudburst that sends a wall of water 5-feet high through the main street. The business center is isolated and many fires break out.		May 15
President Harding warns state governments that a serious situation would arise if some of the states persist in their intention to repeal their laws for the enforcement of Prohibition. He warns that the federal government might have to enter state territory to set up police and judicial systems to enforce Prohibition.		Financier Jay Gould dies.			May 16
Alva B. Adams, a Democrat, is appointed U.S. Senator for Colorado by Governor Sweet. The new senator is a son of a former governor of the state. He favors having the United States represented in a world court and supports the maintenance of a line of a defense that would leave the United States better prepared for war than in 1917.			Archeologists discover human remains in Hungary that date to the era of the migration. The remains are apparently that of a race that lived largely on horseback, as the lower bones of the leg are slightly curved.	Spain appoints a curator to restore and maintain the Alhambra, one of the most famous sites in the country. The Alhambra (meaning "red") is a palace and fortress of the Moorish monarchs of Granada. Constructed in the 13th century, it is noted for its Islamic architecture and art.	May 17

F	G	H	I	J
Includes campaigns, elections, federal-state relations, civil rights and liberties, crime, the judiciary, education, healthcare, poverty, urban affairs, and population.	*Includes formation and debate of U.S. foreign and defense policies, veterans affairs, and defense spending. (Relations with specific foreign countries are usually found under the region concerned.)*	*Includes business, labor, agriculture, taxation, transportation, consumer affairs, monetary and fiscal policy, natural resources, pollution and industrial accidents.*	*Includes worldwide scientific, medical and technological developments, natural phenomena, U.S. weather and natural disasters.*	*Includes the arts, religion, scholarship, communications media, sports, entertainment, fashions, fads, and social life.*

	World Affairs	Europe	Africa & The Middle East	The Americas	Asia & The Pacific
May 18	Turkey wants the Allies to agree to a black list of 150 Muslims who will not be allowed to remain in or return to Turkey. The dispute is deadlocking negotiations over the Treaty of Lausanne.			Jamaica objects to Canada's plans to repeal the tariff on the dumping of sugar. The Jamaican Chamber of Commerce argues that the admission of American sugar into Canada in large quantities will damage the Caribbean colonies and is contrary to the spirit of inter-Empire trade.... An earthquake at Quito, Ecuador, kills two people and injures many more.	The majority of workers employed at the Yenang-Yenang oilfield in Burma go on strike without warning. The cause is the discharge of a number of employees.... The Prime Minister of New Zealand announces that the country's finances are improving to the point where there may be an early reduction of railroad rates, the reinstatement of penny postage, and tax reductions.
May 19		Three thousand Greek refugees arrive in Athens from Constantinople.... Andrew Bonar Law resigns as Prime Minister of Great Britain because of poor health. His administration lasted 209 days, making it one of the shortest in British history.	Exceptionally heavy rains that have fallen in Kenya over the past two months have left all the rivers in a state of flood and many bridges have been damaged.		Police in Calcutta, India, search a number of houses and seize a quantity of Bolshevist literature.
May 20	The governing commission of the Saar in Germany decides to introduce the French franc as legal tender on June 1. The measure is an attempt to stop speculation in the mark.			The Canadian Pacific and the National Railway systems agree to contribute $50,000 annually to the Canada Colonization Association. The federal government is expected to contribute $100,000 annually and a similar amount may be received from the Overseas Settlement Board in the future.	A gang of 35 Sikhs, believed to be Baba Akailis, armed with pistols and kirpans (short daggers) attack a local official in the Punjab and kill him. The police arrest 200 people in a search for the killers.
May 21	W. Rufus Day, a former U.S. Supreme Court justice, resigns the post of Umpire of the Mixed Claims Commission established to fix war German liability. Day pleads that the work is too arduous for a 74-year-old man.	The Barcelona bullfight is cancelled because of transport workers strike.... Georges Clemenceau, French Prime Minister during the war, declines to run for another political office on the grounds that he is too old.... The Bavarian National Socialist Workers' Party continue to hold frequent rallies in Munich under the guidance of Adolf Hitler.	The Egyptian government announces that it imports enough flax seed from Belgium to plant 5000 feddans (a feddan is a little over an acre).The government has also arranged for the Nile Flax Company to purchase the resulting crop. Experiments at spinning flax are being made at Alexandria. This is an attempt to revive an industry that existed in ancient Egypt.		An epidemic thought to be dengue fever has been sweeping through Bombay, India, over the last two months. A medical expert brought in by the government now declares the prevalent fever to be influenza of a mild type without the complication of broncho-pneumonia, which caused the 1918 calamity.
May 22	The International Agricultural Congress opens in Paris to discuss the world shortage of food and the changes in the sources of supply that have occurred since the war.... The French Minister of Agriculture says that the tendency is to reduce the price paid to the farmer but such a policy will result in people leaving farms for cities with disastrous results.	A farmer plowing his field at Bancourt, France, discovers the bodies of 16 French soldiers who had been buried near the roadside during the war.... The German mark hits a new low as the government announces a large increase in the bread subsidy. As a result of this, the price of bread is to be doubled. Observers expect the prices of other foodstuffs to rise in reaction.	Turkey blows up a large stone bridge over the Maritza River connecting Adrianople with the road leading to Karagatch. The explosion is apparently accidental. Turkey had mined the bridge in readiness for emergency. A lightning strike during a thunderstorm set off the explosives.	Under an agreement with the Denmark government, 500 to 2,000 Danish families will immigrate to Nicaragua to settle in the central districts.... A Canadian passenger liner, *Marvale*, sinks off Newfoundland in seven fathoms of water when fog covers St. Shotts Bay. The ship strikes a rock. All of the passengers are safely transferred to other ships.	The Australian Director of Education receives permission from the British government to recruit more young male teachers. The plan is viewed as an excellent avenue for importing the latest ideas.
May 23		Suzanne Perriet, a French woman who dressed as a man to obtain farm employment, reveals her true identity upon receiving an inheritance. She states that she first donned male clothing in 1914 to join a regiment.... A dockworkers strike in Lisbon, Portugal, paralyzes shipping.	The Belgian Minister for the Colonies reports that there are 700 Roman Catholic missionaries and religious workers in the Belgian Congo. Most of these are of Belgian nationality. There are about the same number of Protestant missionaries, mainly of British, American, Scandinavian, or Swiss birth.		Britain announces plans to improve the port of Hong Kong. It will reclaim 48 acres of Hunghorn Bay, erect six jetties to provide 18 to 20 berths for large ships, and make extensive renovations to accommodate junks and barges.
May 24		A bomb goes off at Warsaw University in Poland, killing a professor. The bomb exploded during a meeting regarding the expulsion of Communist students.... Italy celebrates its entry into the war. Premier Benito Mussolini spends the day among 4,000 disabled ex-soldiers assembled from all parts of Italy.... Communists violently take over the German town of Gelsenkirchen in the Ruhr. They demand a 50 percent increase in the wages paid to workers and a further rise to keep pace with the cost of living as well as strict control of prices.	The French and British governments agreed that children born of foreign parents in Tunisia may choose their nationality but their children would receive French citizenship.... The murder trial of seven Rhodesians concludes in Salisbury. The men are accused of burning alive a man named Manduza in a remote part of the Mount Darwin district as a sacrifice to the Rain Goddess. The Rain Goddess, a young girl, did not give evidence. Six of the men are found guilty and sentenced to death with a recommendation for mercy.	Canada observes Empire Day with parades. Messages from the King and Queen are spoken from a gramophone to the marching thousands in Toronto.	Australia and Hong Kong observe Empire Day quietly with messages from the King and Queen read in schools and at several patriotic gatherings.... A large fire at Sandown meat works near Parramatta in Australia destroys much machinery, thousands of carcasses of mutton, and enormous quantities of tallow and hides.

A	B	C	D	E
Includes developments that affect more than one world region, international organizations and important meetings of world leaders.	*Includes all domestic and regional developments in Europe, including the Soviet Union.*	*Includes all domestic and regional developments in Africa and the Middle East.*	*Includes all domestic and regional developments in Latin America, the Caribbean, and Canada.*	*Includes all domestic and regional developments in Asian and Pacific nations (and colonies).*

U.S. Politics & Social Issues	U.S. Foreign Policy & Affairs, Defense	U.S. Economy & Environment	Science, Technology & Nature	Culture, Leisure & Lifestyle	
A paraffin lamp explodes in the upper story of a schoolhouse in Cleveland, SC, while 300 men, women, and children attend a graduation ceremony. The audience rushes for a stairway that is the only exit from the building but jams against the doors. The dead number 71 with more bodies likely trapped in the rubble. Most of the survivors are suffering from burns.					May 18
	The United States holds meetings in Mexico City with Mexican officials to define the rights of Americans and to settle claims growing out of the Vera Cruz occupation of 1914, the Pershing Expedition of 1916, and the continued American occupation of Chamezal, now part of El Paso.	The Cunard Line announces that it will strictly obey Prohibition. Its ships will be dry on westward voyages and wet on eastward trips as far as the three-mile limit.		Zev, a three-year-old colt owned by John E. Madden of Rancocas Stables and ridden by Earl Sande, defeats Martingale to win the 49th Kentucky Derby in 2:05.4.... The U.S. team defeats the British team to win the Walker Cup in golf at St. Andrews in Scotland. It is the third successive win for the Americans.	May 19
		The New York State Commissioner announces that $16 million of road work planned for this summer and autumn is being indefinitely postponed because of the shortage of materials and the high cost of labor. He blames the immigration laws for the lack of workers.		With the Polo Grounds stadium newly expanded, the New York Giants set a National League attendance record with more than 42,000 fans at their baseball game. The Giants defeat the St. Louis Cardinals, 14–4, on 20 hits.	May 20
		Formal transfer of T.L. Huston's interest in the New York Yankees baseball club to Jake Ruppert is completed for $1.5 million.... The U.S. Treasury revokes a decision made two weeks ago to exempt from income taxes any corporation dividends distributed out of profits earned before March 1, 1913. If the original order had not been changed, the Treasury would have been forced to refund many millions in taxes.		The Geneva, Switzerland, Protestant Church holds a special service to commemorate the acceptance of the principles of the Reformation by the people of Geneva on May 21, 1536.	May 21
The bodies of 32 people are found in the Rio Grande, near Laredo. They are believed to be Italians who were robbed and murdered on May 5 while attempting to enter the United States clandestinely.	Curly, a Crow Indian and the sole survivor on the U.S. side of the defeat of General George Armstrong Custer at the Battle of Little Big Horn, dies.				May 22
Eugene Debs is elected to lead the Socialist Party.... The Presbyterian Church of America passes a resolution at its General Assembly in Indianapolis that requires every Presbyterian minister, church official, church member, and student in denominational schools to sign a pledge of total abstinence from alcoholic liquors.	Egbert Ingersoll, the last surviving U.S. Secret Service operative on duty during the Civil War and a personal messenger for President Abraham Lincoln, dies.	George H. Mackay, the president of the American Postal-Telegraph-Commercial Cables System announces plans to lay a new cable for direct communication between New York City and London. The cable will be the largest ever laid in the Atlantic Ocean and the first laid in the Atlantic between the United States and Europe since 1910.			May 23
			A demonstration of the Peachey process for the cold vulcanization of rubber is given at the laboratories of the company that owns the British patent. The process consists of exposing the material to sulphur dioxide for a few minutes and then to sulphuretted hydrogen for about six minutes. Both gases are at ordinary atmospheric pressure. The two gases diffuse into the material and interact with the diffusion of sulfur, thereby bringing about vulcanization.		May 24

F	G	H	I	J
Includes campaigns, elections, federal-state relations, civil rights and liberties, crime, the judiciary, education, healthcare, poverty, urban affairs, and population.	*Includes formation and debate of U.S. foreign and defense policies, veterans affairs, and defense spending. (Relations with specific foreign countries are usually found under the region concerned.)*	*Includes business, labor, agriculture, taxation, transportation, consumer affairs, monetary and fiscal policy, natural resources, pollution and industrial accidents.*	*Includes worldwide scientific, medical and technological developments, natural phenomena, U.S. weather and natural disasters.*	*Includes the arts, religion, scholarship, communications media, sports, entertainment, fashions, fads, and social life.*

	World Affairs	Europe	Africa & The Middle East	The Americas	Asia & The Pacific
May 25	The Congress of the Second International concludes in Hamburg, Germany, with a declaration that the imperialism of the capitalist ruling classes is driving humanity into new wars, which could only end with the extinction of civilization.... The League of Red Cross Societies passes a resolution urging that the giving of spirits to children under 15 should be declared a criminal offense and that the child concerned should be removed to a healthier atmosphere.... An Inter-Allied agreement for the payment of the costs of the American Army of Occupation in the Rhineland is signed in Paris.	Scotland Yard issues new police orders for saluting... The Bulgarian government plans to try the Gueshoff, Danoff, and Malinoff Cabinets at Sofia for treason for not putting an end to the Balkan War at the right moment, for not making peace before September 20, 1918, and for refusing to surrender to mutinous soldiers who marched on Sofia.... Adolf Hitler's newspaper in Germany is suspended from publication for five days for publishing an abusive article entitled "The Increase in Prices and Parliamentary Incompetence."	The Euphrates River bursts through a dam and covers 45,000 acres of cultivated land to the northwest of Baghdad.... Sir Herbert Samuel, the High Commissioner in Palestine, speaking on behalf of the British government, proclaims the independence of the Trans-Jordan government.	The Panama Canal experiences a record day with 25 ships passing through and paying tolls in the amount of $136,000.	
May 26		The Polish Cabinet resigns after the provisional budget is rejected by the Sojm.... A majority of striking miners in the Ruhr returns to work as Communists in the region engage in bloody clashes with special constables.... The French execute a German shopkeeper, Albert Schlageter, for sabotaging a railway. The execution is causing horror among the German people who did not think that Schlageter would be executed for what they regard as a political offense.	A bridge over the Tigris, connecting the two parts of Baghdad, is broken by flooding. The only other bridge over the Tigris, the Maude pontoon bridge, was destroyed by floods several months ago.		Sikhs of the radical sect, Baba Akali, ransack a house and kill two male members of the household in the Hoshiarpur district of India.
May 27	A conference on reparations between France and Belgium that was to have begun today is indefinitely postponed... Turkey announces that it intends to follow The Hague Convention regulations on opium and that it desires admittance to the League of Nations.... The King of the Hejaz approves a treaty with Great Britain. The British agree to recognize and support the independence of the Arab people in Iraq, Transjordania, and the Arabian peninsula with the exception of Aden.	A Canadian Pacific ocean liner with 11,000 passengers, mostly emigrants, collides with a cargo ship on the Clyde in Scotland. The liner has to return to Glasgow.... During a soccer match at Barcelona, Spain, eight men with revolvers exit a car and execute two volunteer policemen who had been selected as victims by the Syndicalist organization. The killers get back into their car and drive away.	An earthquake strikes Persia at Turbat-i-Haidari, killing about 4,000 people and completely destroying six villages.		
May 28	The League of Nations seeks a compromise on the dispute between Hungary and Romania over control of Transylvania.... The League of Nations Health Committee receives a report on the anti-epidemic campaign being conducted among the refugees in Greece. More than 1.5 million inoculations have been given against typhoid, cholera, smallpox, and other diseases.	The first concrete bridge over the Seine River in France is scheduled to be built. The Pont de la Tournelle bridge will replace the present wooden structure between the left bank of the river and Ile St. Louis.... The Paris Municipal Council discusses municipal house building on a large scale. It is considering building 10,000 apartments within the next three years.... Stanley Baldwin is elected as Leader of the Conservative and Unionist Party in Great Britain.			The Prime Minister of Nepal announces that the government has allocated 21 lakhs of rupees to a fund for lowering the cost of food and grains. He also announces plans to improve communications within the country, including the building of a railroad and a ropeway.
May 29	The Pan-Orthodox Congress in Constantinople, Turkey, decides to harmonize the Old Style with the Gregorian Calendar by making the next Julian October 1 into October 14.... The Opium Commission of the League of Nations continues hearings into opium in the Far East.	The Belgian government issues an announcement that it intends to amend the military law to increase the term of service by four months while the occupation of the Ruhr continues.... The French government decides to require a declaration of fitness from all candidates standing for election.	Heavy rains and the first flooding of the Lahej in 12 years leads to hopes of good crops in Aden.... South Africa ships cattle to Germany... Great Britain, through an Order in Council, declares the elections in Palestine to be null and void.	Malcolm Bruce, sought by the government of Nova Scotia in Canada for sedition, surrenders and is released on bail.	The Commonwealth of Australia agrees to relinquish all income taxation except the tax on companies in an attempt to halt dual taxation by the various states.
May 30	The Austrian government begins negotiations with the Morgan banking group in England about underwriting the American issue of the League of Nations loan to Austria.	Observers in Germany doubt that the new wage increase for miners to 19,000 marks per day will reduce labor strife since two pounds of margarine cost 22,000 marks and two pounds of meat cost 24,000 marks.	The cession of Karagatch to Turkey creates a panic in the city. Most of the 50,000 residents are refugees from Eastern Thrace. They are expected to leave, further increasing the refugee problem.	The Swiss Association for Colonization announces plans to send Swiss girls to Canada.	
	A *Includes developments that affect more than one world region, international organizations and important meetings of world leaders.*	B *Includes all domestic and regional developments in Europe, including the Soviet Union.*	C *Includes all domestic and regional developments in Africa and the Middle East.*	D *Includes all domestic and regional developments in Latin America, the Caribbean, and Canada.*	E *Includes all domestic and regional developments in Asian and Pacific nations (and colonies).*

U.S. Politics & Social Issues	U.S. Foreign Policy & Affairs, Defense	U.S. Economy & Environment	Science, Technology & Nature	Culture, Leisure & Lifestyle	
At the request of President Harding, the Republican National Committee withdraws a statement charging England and the European Powers with attempted to take advantage of the United States in connection with the expenses of the American army in Germany.	The British send a Note to the United States complaining about the prohibition of sealed liquor stores in foreign vessels entering American ports.... The French government protests that observance of Prohibition would necessitate a material violation of the contracts between many shipping companies and crews.... American newspapers suggest that the Europeans consider treating liquor rations to crews as medical stores.	The American Iron and Steel Institute, by a unanimous vote, opposes he abolition of the 12-hour day in the steel industry. Opponents of the eight-hour day sought by steelworkers argue that there is insufficient labor in the country to provide three working shifts within 24 hours while maintaining the current rate of production.	As a result of the poor supply of flowers last summer and the severe winter, about 100,000 hives of cultivated bees in Hungary have died in the past few months. The estimated loss to Hungarian agriculture is four million gold crowns.		May 25
William Randolph Hearst promises to support Henry Ford if he runs for president.	The British Embassy denies that Great Britain has challenged the jurisdiction of American port authorities.		Lieutenant Harrison G. Crocker establishes a new record for a nonstop flight. He flies alone in a De Havilland biplane from the Gulf of Mexico to Canada, a distance of 1400 miles in 11 hours and 54 minutes.	F.J. Marshall defeats Edward Lasker to retain the U.S. Chess Championship. Marshall wins five games to four with nine games drawn to keep the title that he has held for 14 years.	May 26
	President Harding and Secretary of State Hughes express gratification at the arrangement to pay the United States for the cost of her army of occupation.	The *New York Globe* is sold to Frank Munsey, who plans to merge the newspaper with the *New York Sun.*	Hunting rights are available for a 10 or 20 years lease on the island of Jan Mayen. The island is north of Iceland and is uninhabited except for a small experimental radio station. Blue fox and polar bear are reported to be numerous.	Russian dramatist Maxim Gorki completes his memoirs, which will be published in three volumes. Gorki also announces that he is under contract to write the script for a Russian historical film.	May 27
The New York Ku Klux Klan defies the legislature to enforce a measure that requires secret societies to make their membership public. The animosity of the Klan is particularly directed against Governor Al Smith, a Roman Catholic, who signed the so-called Walker Bill. The Klan argues that Smith is attempting to deliver the United States to Rome.		In New York City, the carpenters force the builders to sign a wage scale giving them a basic pay of $10 a day for the next six months.... The bricklayers in New York are striking for $12 a day and a 2-year agreement.... Twenty-thousand other construction workers vote to authorize a strike on June 1 for a rise of a dollar a day.... The New York Stock Exchange sees a large volume of trading, led by railroad stocks, while oil stocks benefited from a growing belief that the decline in crude oil prices is over.			May 28
Six British first-class passengers are refused permission to disembark at New York City because England's immigration quota is filled. All the passengers are taken to Ellis Island where a special Board of Inquiry will decide whether they can ultimately stay.		Detroit is enjoying such an economic boom that city does not have enough houses for all of workers in the automobile industry. Tent camps have been set up in the suburbs of Detroit to house workers.	American wireless messages are being received at an experimental station in Munchentuchsee in Berne, Switzerland. The success of the experiment will lead to the opening of regular service on June 1.... France announces that it has direct communication via underwater cables with North America (three cables).	A part of the Palazzo Pretoria, a 13th-century palace in Italy, that was constructed by Arnolfo di Lapo by order of the Florentine Republic, collapses. Other parts of the building are threatened. The dangerous points have been supported.	May 29
			Ship captains report that the ice conditions in the North Atlantic are worse and more dangerous than they have been in 20 years. Ships are getting stuck in ice floes for days at a time, with the ice acres estimated to be 40 feet deep in places.	Furs are among the most popular of women's dress accessories at the moment, with red fox furs being sold as soon as they can be mounted.... Work is proceeding on the restoration of the Doric Temple of Heracles at Girgenti in Sicily.	May 30
F *Includes campaigns, elections, federal-state relations, civil rights and liberties, crime, the judiciary, education, healthcare, poverty, urban affairs, and population.*	**G** *Includes formation and debate of U.S. foreign and defense policies, veterans affairs, and defense spending. (Relations with specific foreign countries are usually found under the region concerned.)*	**H** *Includes business, labor, agriculture, taxation, transportation, consumer affairs, monetary and fiscal policy, natural resources, pollution and industrial accidents.*	**I** *Includes worldwide scientific, medical and technological developments, natural phenomena, U.S. weather and natural disasters.*	**J** *Includes the arts, religion, scholarship, communications media, sports, entertainment, fashions, fads, and social life.*	

	World Affairs	Europe	Africa & The Middle East	The Americas	Asia & The Pacific
May 31	Turks express reluctance to accept 33 square miles of land subject to flooding by the Mantza in lieu of vast sums of reparations to which the Turks consider themselves due.	*Pravda*, a Russian newspaper calls on the Soviet Union to obtain airplanes for defense as a weapon against bourgeois armaments.... The Italian government adopts a budget that gives full powers to the government.			
Jun. 1	Armenian refugee children in Corfu are scheduled to be sent to Canada to be distributed among farmers.	All work at Barcelona harbor in Spain is at a standstill because of a transport worker's strike. ...Extensive deposits of potash have been discovered at Klein Kuhren on the Elbe during experimental borings for petroleum....The Rhine-Ruhr Civil Servants' Committee, formed to guide government employees in passive resistance, warns of the dangers of attacking Communists.	Five of the colleagues arrested and sent into exile with Egyptian Zaghlal Pasha are released from prison in the Seychelles.	Leo Rogers, an escaped prisoner who killed a police officer, is shot to death by police in Toronto, Canada.	
Jun. 2		In France, Marshal Foch unveils a monument at Abbeville in memory of inhabitants of the town who were killed in the war. After the ceremony, a pilgrimage is made to the Anglo-French Cemetery. Eric Phipps of the British Embassy in Paris, makes a speech in French in which he says that the sign of such a vast army of British soldiers' graves close to those of their French brothers-in-arms should impel the two peoples toward a wider understanding of each other.	The Arab Council at Palestine issues a proclamation attacking the government for reviving the Advisory Council in place of the elected Legislative Council. The government is being charged with introducing, by illegal methods, the Palestine Constitution that was rejected by Arab nations. Arabs nominated to the Advisory Council are urged to refuse to serve.		
Jun. 3		Italian Premier Benito Mussolini completes his tour of Venetia. He concludes his visit with a speech stating that there is no distinction between Mussolini and Fascism.			Akbara, a Muslim leader, who has been defying the government of the Philippines for several months, is routed by federal troops and local militia on the island of Patu, Sulu Archipelago. Akbara loses 53 men while 800 of his supporters surrender. Government forces report negligible casualties.
Jun. 4		In the Spanish Senate, Colonel Mortera attacks the policy of the government in Morocco, especially the agreement with an enemy of the Kalifa in the Spanish zone. He argues that the Spanish Commander-in-Chief will resign if Moors are placed in high authority.	In fighting in Morocco, Spain reports that it has killed 600 Moors. The military success is believed by military experts to have broken the enemy, which has withdrawn from Melilla.		
Jun. 5		The German mark continues to fall. As a result, trade unions state that the burdens placed on Germany cannot be met solely by revenue from the Reich and the federal states.			The Anglican Synod in Brisbane, Australia, votes to reject a motion for local autonomy. The motion had been offered by the laity.
Jun. 6	The Bulgarian government ratifies the reparations agreement.	The Petrograd, Soviet Union Executive Committee devotes 200,000 gold rubles toward building airplanes. Leon Trotsky, the force behind the plan, declares that a Soviet Air Force will protect Soviet liberty as well as helping the colonies of the world to liberate themselves.			The Chinese Cabinet collapses. Its disappearance is attributed to the difficulty of meeting any of the government's financial obligations.

A	B	C	D	E
Includes developments that affect more than one world region, international organizations and important meetings of world leaders.	*Includes all domestic and regional developments in Europe, including the Soviet Union.*	*Includes all domestic and regional developments in Africa and the Middle East.*	*Includes all domestic and regional developments in Latin America, the Caribbean, and Canada.*	*Includes all domestic and regional developments in Asian and Pacific nations (and colonies).*

U.S. Politics & Social Issues	U.S. Foreign Policy & Affairs, Defense	U.S. Economy & Environment	Science, Technology & Nature	Culture, Leisure & Lifestyle	
Claude Kitchen, majority leader of the U.S. House of Representatives during the World War, dies in North Carolina.	American Jews contribute $1.8 million in cash and pledges for the Palestine Foundation Fund or Keren Hayesod, the fundraising division of the World Zionist Organization. Keren Hayesod is the major agency financing Jewish immigration and settlement in Palestine as private Jewish enterprise.		The Norwegian government requests that all Norwegian ships sailing in Spitsbergen waters make preparations for radio connection with the Polar explorer Roald Amundsen during his upcoming expedition.	The Syracuse University lacrosse team, champions of the United States, begins playing a series of matches in England against English teams. . . . New York Yankees baseball team owner Jake Ruppert buys two more sets of uniforms so his players can wear a clean outfit every day, an unprecedented move.	May 31
The United States arrests several British citizens and detain them at Ellis Island for exceeding the British immigration quota. . . . Governor Al Smith of New York signs the bill repealing New York State's Prohibition Enforcement Act.	The U.S. Embassy in London issues a statement that if any foreign vessel having on board liquor for beverage purposes shall leave a foreign port prior to June 10 bound for U.S. territorial waters, then its liquor will not be seized by Treasury officials.	The Associated Advertising Clubs of the World Convention begins at Atlantic City, NJ. The European delegations are the largest ever sent to the United States.			Jun. 1
Governor Al Smith is being deluged with telegrams praising and condemning his decision to sign a bill repealing New York's Prohibition legislation.					Jun. 2
					Jun. 3
Yale University first-year students celebrating the end of their freshman days with rioting and cause damage to the town of New Haven, CT.					Jun. 4
					Jun. 5
Yale University authorities, unable to find anyone who would admit to have participated in the riots on Monday night, announce that the annual Yale-Harvard freshman crew race will not proceed unless the culprits announce themselves.		The Electric Light Association, a convention of electric producers, introduces a plan for electrifying every industry of any size in the United States. A system of 220,000-volt transmission lines a few hundred miles apart, spreading over the entire United States is proposed.			Jun. 6

F	G	H	I	J
Includes campaigns, elections, federal-state relations, civil rights and liberties, crime, the judiciary, education, healthcare, poverty, urban affairs, and population.	*Includes formation and debate of U.S. foreign and defense policies, veterans affairs, and defense spending. (Relations with specific foreign countries are usually found under the region concerned.)*	*Includes business, labor, agriculture, taxation, transportation, consumer affairs, monetary and fiscal policy, natural resources, pollution and industrial accidents.*	*Includes worldwide scientific, medical and technological developments, natural phenomena, U.S. weather and natural disasters.*	*Includes the arts, religion, scholarship, communications media, sports, entertainment, fashions, fads, and social life.*

	World Affairs	Europe	Africa & The Middle East	The Americas	Asia & The Pacific
Jun. 7	The German government rejects the reparations offer made by the Allied governments. In a note, Germany states that it will accept the decision of an impartial international body on the amount and payment of reparations. Germany repeats its claim that it lacks the capacity to make the current amount of payments. Germany is ready to substitute a plan of annuities.	The Estonian Parliament opens and Joenission is elected president. A member of the Democratic Premier, he is a former premier of Estonia.... Italians propose to place a plaque to the memory of Antonio Meucci in his birthplace of Florence. Meucci immigrated to the United States and took out patents for a telephone before Alexander Graham Bell did so.			The Indian government agrees to the resumption of emigration to Mauritius. As a result, 1,500 laborers, including men, women, and children, are being recruited to work on sugar estates and to build government works.
Jun. 8	Fernand Cerf, a French subject who has been imprisoned in Leipzig on charges of denouncing Germans to the French authorities in the Ruhr is released. In consequence, Herr Hollein, the Socialist member of the German Reichstag, who was arrested in Paris some months ago, will shortly be released from a French jail and expelled from France.... The Prime Minister of Greece, Colonel Gonatas, denies that Greece and Turkey will sign a separate peace.	Several coaches that are part of a railroad traveling in Brussels, Belgium, derail and overturn because of an error in shifting the points. Three passengers are killed and scores are injured...The German Opera Festival announces its program as well as plans to charge foreigners four times the price charged to native operagoers.			The funeral of Prince Kitashirakawa, brother-in-law of the Emperor of Japan, takes place with full military honors in Tokyo. Kitashirakawa died in an automobile accident in Bernay, France, in April...A lifeboat from a missing British steamship, *Trevassa*, that sent out an S.O.S. is discovered capsized and empty off the coast of Perth, Australia.
Jun. 9		The Bulgarian government is overthrown by military forces.... Supporters of the deposed Agrarian government engage in fighting with forces from the new government.			
Jun. 10		The customs union between Switzerland and Liechtenstein officially goes into effect....Sporadic strikes occur throughout Upper Silesia in Germany because of the high cost of living....Benito Mussolini of Italy begins a 2two-day visit to Sardinia. He is met by enthusiastic expressions of patriotism as he travels, including peasant women who raise their babies for Mussolini to kiss.	British immigrants to Palestine are filling the ranks of the police force that formed in March 1922. However, it remains an extremely small force....British reports from Kenya indicate that Africans are resentful of any material concessions that may be made to Indians. The anti-Indian feeling in Kenya is said to be a new development.	The Chilean government issues new regulations for visas. Foreign nationals must provide fingerprints, a certificate of good conduct issued by a justice of the peace, a judicial certificate stating that the applicant has never been convicted of a crime, and a medical certificate proving the absence of contagious diseases.	
Jun. 11		Representatives of the Swiss watch making industry adopt a resolution inviting employers and public authorities to meet the workers to examine measures for the improvement of the industrial situation....The French government is being urged by agricultural leaders to grant a national credit to enable France to develop and make greater use of water power and thereby reduce reliance on coal.	Afghan authorities arrest two Hangu-Khel-Shinwaris accused of murdering two British officers from the Seaforth Highlanders on April 9....The French forces in Morocco are finding success. Today, they attack the heights held by the hostile tribes in the Taza region. All objectives are taken despite the fierce resistance of the 3,000 Moroccans, who suffer heavy losses.	The Presbyterian General Assembly in Canada votes by 426 ballots to 129 to approve a resolution in favor of a union with the Methodist and Congregational Churches. It defeats a measure to delay the decision by one year. It is expected that the chief opponent of union will attempt to organize an independent Presbyterian body. This decision ends a 20-year debate over union.	A Hindu newspaper editor in Lahore, India, is ordered to pay 20,000 rupees on account of having published an article that is likely to wound the religious susceptibilities of Muslims....A typhoon on the island of Samar in the Philippines kills 13 people. It is estimated that 95 percent of the houses on Samar have been demolished and famine is feared.
Jun. 12	A group of 50 Armenian boys under the supervision of the Armenian Refugees Fund leaves Corfu for Canada. A farm has been prepared for their reception....The Allies reach a stalemate with Turkey over concessions that may be outstanding after the peace is concluded.	The French government decides to give a state funeral to writer Pierre Loti. The body will be taken from Rochefort in a torpedo boat to the burial site at Saint Denis d'Oléron, France....Georges Boussenot, deputy for Réunion and reporter to the French Chamber of Deputies on the state of French coastal defenses, completes his examination. He concludes that France needs to establish a strong base for airplanes and seaplanes, a powerful mobile defense force of torpedo boats and submarines, defense by land torpedo tubes and floating mines supplemented by submarine chasers, and coastal artillery. Boussenot points out that his plan will require the additional construction of airplanes, seaplanes, and submarines.	Bandits attack the British gendarmerie in Safed, near Jerusalem. The robbers stop a car to rob the passengers when they realize that it contains police. The robbers then fire upon the police, fatally wounding one man. Another police officer is captured, and then returned wounded. There is no trace of the bandits....The Egyptian government considers turning Albert Nyanza in Uganda into a reservoir, thereby making a reserve of water available to raise the level of the Nile River to the normal height at times when it is very low. The Nile has been unusually low for the past two years. The project would also require the simultaneous canalization of the Sudd area.	The Canadian Merchant Marine has decided to fit up eight ships to carry cattle between Montreal and Cardiff....The Canadian Department of Agriculture reports that the export of cattle to Great Britain is steadily increasing....The Manitoba, Canada, government denies that it is experiences a crisis. The Premier of Manitoba, John Bracken, declares that the Lieutenant-Governor J.A.M. Aikens is not interfering unduly with the government....The Canadian government demands an increase in the protectionist tariff and opposes the extension of preference in favor of British goods except for return preference.	The monsoon season has begun in India with a steady rain falling in Bombay, India....All of the captives who were kidnapped by Chinese bandits in the recent Pukow-Tientsin mail train outrage have now been released. The attack, on May 6, killed one British man and left a score of other foreigners in captivity. All but two British men have already been freed.

	A	B	C	D	E
	Includes developments that affect more than one world region, international organizations and important meetings of world leaders.	*Includes all domestic and regional developments in Europe, including the Soviet Union.*	*Includes all domestic and regional developments in Africa and the Middle East.*	*Includes all domestic and regional developments in Latin America, the Caribbean, and Canada.*	*Includes all domestic and regional developments in Asian and Pacific nations (and colonies).*

U.S. Politics & Social Issues	U.S. Foreign Policy & Affairs, Defense	U.S. Economy & Environment	Science, Technology & Nature	Culture, Leisure & Lifestyle	
The Wisconsin House of Representatives passes a resolution, by 47 votes to 43, in favor of the repeal of the state Prohibition Enforcement Law. The supporters of Prohibition claim that they will defeat the resolution when it comes up for vote in the Wisconsin Senate.			Angus Buchanan, accompanied by his cinema operator, arrives in Algiers. The two British men completed a geographical and zoological survey of the Sahara Desert. They return with birds and animals unknown to Europeans as well as 30,000 feet of film.		Jun. 7
The publisher of the Boston *Transcript* is fined $100 for refusing to print as a paid advertisement a report of the Massachusetts Minimum Wage Commission criticizing a Boston department store for underpaying its employees. The publisher feared that he would subject his newspaper to civil damages from the store. He intends to appeal to the U.S. Supreme Court as a constitutional question.				After St. Louis Browns catcher Pat Collins leaves the game after pinch-running in the second inning, Philadelphia Athletics's manager Connie Mack gives permission for him to return as a pinch hitter for pitcher Ray Kolp in the ninth inning. Collins walks. The Athletics beat the Browns by 6–5.	Jun. 8
					Jun. 9
					Jun. 10
	Charles Daugherty, the Attorney General, meets with the Lomer Gouin, the Canadian Minister of Justice, to discuss a dispute over the ownership of alien enemy property seized during the war.		Flooding in Kansas, Oklahoma, and Texas kills five people and leaves thousands homeless. In Kansas, every watercourse in the state is reported to have overflowed its banks. About a quarter of the Kansas wheat crop is estimated to be ruined. Much of the livestock in the three states has also been lost. The Trinity River in Texas is reported to be rising at the rate of seven inches per hour. It has already risen 27 feet.	British middleweight boxer Roland Todd defeats New Yorker Augie Ratner at Holland Park Rink in London for the English championship.…Siegfried Wagner, son of famed German composer Richard Wagner and the subject of his father's "Siegfried Idyll," has been invited by the director of the Chicago Opera Company to tour the United States to raise funds to resume the Bayreuth Festival. The festival is famed for producing the senior Wagner's Teutonic operas.	Jun. 11
Floods in Arkansas leave many miles of crops under water. The Arkansas River reaches the highest level in recorded history with the waters expected to continue rising for the next day. The inhabitants of towns along the river are strengthening the levees with thousands of sandbags.…Flooding in Tulsa, OK, leaves 4,000 people homeless. More than 1,000 are driven from their homes in West Tulsa, where some of the largest oil refineries in the United States are located.	The Japanese steamer, *Africa Maru*, landed its liquor supplies at Vancouver, Canada, before proceeding to Seattle in order to comply with U.S. Prohibition laws. The ship will then return to Vancouver to collect its liquor for its outward voyage back to Japan. This is expected to be the procedure adopted by all ships bound for Seattle.		The Carnegie Institute commissions a Stanford University geologist, Bailly Willis, to study and report on the origin and consequences of the November 10, 1922 earthquake in Chile.…The Great Dolomite road through the Italian mountains is now open for motor traffic for the summer season. It is anticipated that the Stelvio Pass, the highest road in Europe, will be free of snow during the first week of July. It will open to automobiles at that time.…The Italian Parliament passes legislation to protect insectivorous songbirds. The birds, mostly red stars, warblers, chaffinches, and the like, are taken in vast numbers for consumption and other purposes. The new law bans the use of vertical nets, prohibits snares, and imposes limitation on the use of other capture devices.	The sale of possessions from French actress Sarah Bernhardt's estate brings 79,685 francs. The three pieces of sculpture created by Bernhardt, entitled "After the Storm" brought 5,100 francs. The death mask of her husband, Jacques Damala sold for 500 francs.	Jun. 12

F	G	H	I	J
Includes campaigns, elections, federal-state relations, civil rights and liberties, crime, the judiciary, education, healthcare, poverty, urban affairs, and population.	*Includes formation and debate of U.S. foreign and defense policies, veterans affairs, and defense spending. (Relations with specific foreign countries are usually found under the region concerned.)*	*Includes business, labor, agriculture, taxation, transportation, consumer affairs, monetary and fiscal policy, natural resources, pollution and industrial accidents.*	*Includes worldwide scientific, medical and technological developments, natural phenomena, U.S. weather and natural disasters.*	*Includes the arts, religion, scholarship, communications media, sports, entertainment, fashions, fads, and social life.*

	World Affairs	Europe	Africa & The Middle East	The Americas	Asia & The Pacific
Jun. 13		For the first time since 1864, a slight earthquake strikes the island of St. Helena.... The Norwegian printers strike ends.... Antwerp, Belgium, tugboat operators go on strike.... More fighting continues in the Ruhr as hundreds of Germans who violate a curfew are fired upon by French patrols, who remain angry about the recent murder of two French soldiers. Many of Germans flee in terror into nearby houses where they remain until tomorrow morning.	The Arab members of the Palestine Advisory Council resign to protest against the current Constitution. Eight Muslims had been appointed by the British High Commissioner to serve on the Council, which was expected to meet for the first time on June 19.		The Australian Parliament begins its session. It is expected to address the sound financial position of the country and deal with the breaks of gauge on the railroads.... Li Yush-hung, President of the Chinese Republic leaves Peking along with his family for Tientsin. The Garrison Commander has assumed responsibility for the protection of Peking. The flight of the president is attributed to pressure from militarists of the Chihli Party. It is assumed that Tsau Kun will be elected as the new president.
Jun. 14		The Norwegian Employers' Association begins a lockout of 14,000 engineers and cabinet-makers.			
Jun. 15	The Permanent Court of International Justice holds its third session in The Hague.... The government of the Soviet Union protests the proposed sale of Russian ships given to the French government by General Wrangel. The Soviets claim title to the ships, which France proposes to sell to other governments including Romania.	The Belgian legislature adjourns until the political crisis over the Flemish University can be resolved.... Stambulinsky, the leader of the overthrown Agrarian government of Bulgaria, is shot by the military after surrendering to government forces and then getting rescued by his friends.		The official list of candidates for the Ontario, Canada, general election lists 103 Conservatives, 77 Liberals, 75 Progressives, and 33 Labour candidates.	
Jun. 16					The India Legislature tables for balloting a number of anti-colonial measures. Among other ideas, Indians propose to refusale admission to Indian ports ofto any ships crewed and registered in the British Colonies and a doubling of the customs duties on colonial produce.
Jun. 17	The Soviet Transcaucasion Commissariat for Foreign Trade declares absolute freedom of trade for all goods of Russian and Persian origin across the Persian-Soviet frontier.	Three sailors from H.M.S. *Centurion*, docked in Malta, dance around a fire while dressed as Native Americans. The costume of one catches on fire and two of his comrades are also badly burned before the fire is put out. The men are taken to the hospital and the festivities are halted.... General Stanislav Bulak Balahovitch, a noted anti-Bolshevist leader is shot to death while driving a wagon from Brest to Bialystock. Balahovitch led the White forces until his brutal methods cost him his command.			An Italian priest is captured by Chinese bandits at Yingchen, about 100 miles from Hankow. The bandits surround the church of Father Malotto and carried him off, along with 600 children, to the hills. They demand either $1 million or 1,000 rifles or the priest will be executed.... David Henessey, five times Lord Mayor of Melbourne, Australia, dies.
Jun. 18		The further dramatic collapse of the German mark has increased labor discontent in Germany. Workers read the dollar exchange as a barometer of their daily expenditures.... The eruption of Mt. Etna shows no signs of slowing down, with destroyed vineyards and submerged towns.			
Jun. 19	The British and U.S. governments sign an agreement, the Anglo-American War Debt Convention, formalizing Britain's war debt obligations to the United States.				
	A *Includes developments that affect more than one world region, international organizations and important meetings of world leaders.*	B *Includes all domestic and regional developments in Europe, including the Soviet Union.*	C *Includes all domestic and regional developments in Africa and the Middle East.*	D *Includes all domestic and regional developments in Latin America, the Caribbean, and Canada.*	E *Includes all domestic and regional developments in Asian and Pacific nations (and colonies).*

U.S. Politics & Social Issues	U.S. Foreign Policy & Affairs, Defense	U.S. Economy & Environment	Science, Technology & Nature	Culture, Leisure & Lifestyle	
Two British women are detained at Ellis Island because the British immigration quota has been met. Both women state that they have no intention of immigrating. They are simply visiting relatives.	A steamship that arrives in Pennsylvania from Havana, Cuba, reports that nine Cubans attempted to stow away in reserve coal bunkers. Five of the nine men perished from suffocation and were buried at sea.... The U.nited S.tates makes a proposal to the leading maritime powers regarding Prohibition. The U.nited S.tates will permit the carrying of liquor under seal within the three-mile limit if the countries concerned will grant the U.nited S.tates the right to search for and seize contraband articles in ships entering the American 12-mile limit.	The International Cotton Conference, meeting at Washington, D.C., decides to adopt American standards as regards grade and color, but is less definite as regards staple. The present agreement will endure for one year.	British explorers Mr. and Mrs. Scoresby Routledge return from Easter Island in the Pacific Ocean. They report that the mystery of the remarkable statues of a vanished race remains unsolved. However, they have acquired a mass of information about the ways, manner of life, customs, and habits of the people of the Gambier Islands.		Jun. 13
	Colonel Edward M. House, a diplomat in the administration of Woodrow Wilson, predicts that America will yet come to the aid of Europe.... House declares that the only way to solve the reparations problem is to guarantee France against German aggression while fixing a sum for reparations that Germany is able to pay.				Jun. 14
					Jun. 15
		The Holland-Amerikka Line protests against Henry Ford's attempt to complete the technical staff of his works in Detroit with seagoing employees of the leading steamship lines. Apparently, when liners arrive in the United States, men on the engineering staff are offered high wages to induce them to desert.			Jun. 16
					Jun. 17
				Francisco "Pancho Villa" Guilledo beats Jimmy Wilde to become the world flyweight- boxing champion. Despite his nickname, Guilledo is of Filipino descent.	Jun. 18
					Jun. 19

F
Includes campaigns, elections, federal-state relations, civil rights and liberties, crime, the judiciary, education, healthcare, poverty, urban affairs, and population.

G
Includes formation and debate of U.S. foreign and defense policies, veterans affairs, and defense spending. (Relations with specific foreign countries are usually found under the region concerned.)

H
Includes business, labor, agriculture, taxation, transportation, consumer affairs, monetary and fiscal policy, natural resources, pollution and industrial accidents.

I
Includes worldwide scientific, medical and technological developments, natural phenomena, U.S. weather and natural disasters.

J
Includes the arts, religion, scholarship, communications media, sports, entertainment, fashions, fads, and social life.

	World Affairs	Europe	Africa & The Middle East	The Americas	Asia & The Pacific
Jun. 20		The lava coming from Mt. Etna in Sicily has divided into two main branches that are heading toward the towns of Giarre and Linguaglossa. The residents of the towns bring out images of patron saints from the churches and implore for holy intercession.	Turkey closes the Bolshevist office in Angora and is refusing to allow ships flying a Bolshevist flag to unload cargo at Turkish ports.	Quebec, Canada, courts are again considering the case of Father Delorme, the Montreal priest. Delorme went on trial in June 1922 for shooting his half-brother through the head on January 7, 1922. Delorme was found to be insane at the time of the murder and went to an insane asylum. He was released and is now to be tried again for murder. Delorme's legal council is expected to again raise an insanity defense.	
Jun. 21	The Russians and the Japanese begin discussions over Japanese fishing rights in Siberia.... The Belgian government declines to change its policies in the Ruhr in a response to a British Memorandum on the abandonment of passive resistance in the Ruhr.				
Jun. 22		The directors of the local Fascist organization in Turin send a letter to the Municipal Council inviting them to resign on the grounds that they no longer represent politically the views of the voters.		Canadian officials report that the number of divorces in Canada has grown by more than ten times over the past decade, owing largely to disorder caused by World War I.	
Jun. 23		Some 50,000 Austrian government workers engage in a "passive resistance campaign" protesting low wages.			
Jun. 24	Great Britain and the Irish Free State engage in negotiations on the question of payment of compensation to loyalists in Southern Ireland whose property has been destroyed.	Mt. Etna erupts with one branch of the lava stream advancing slowly and covering orchards of hazel nut trees. Hundreds of people come from all over Sicily to watch the lava flow.... The British government British Disposal and Liquidation Committee begins to remove huts in Regent's Park that housed airplane parts.... The British government announces plans to raise naval pay.			
Jun. 25	Great Britain and France formally discuss the deteriorating situation in Germany.... In the House of Lords in Great Britain, the government asks what steps the government plans to take with respect to the removal from British ships in American waters of alcohol officially sealed by British customs.	The Antwerp, Belgium, police arrest a number of men engaged in cocaine trafficking to Belgian soldiers in the Ruhr.... The Turin Municipal Council resigns and a royal councilor is appointed to carry on government administration until a new election takes place.... Smallpox breaks out in the West Country of England. There have been 520 cases of smallpox in the country so far this year.			Robbers attack a train at Shihliho, on the South Manchurian Railway. The passengers are robbed at gunpoint, with the Japanese conductor and a Chinese passenger injured.
Jun. 26	A demonstration is held in London to support the constitutional movement in India towards Dominion status.... Great Britain and France continue negotiations over passive resistance in Germany.	A former German soldier is beaten to death at Parchim, Germany, by other ex-soldiers for reportedly being a Communist sent to spy on the other men.... The Yugoslav government blocks a demonstration by the Republican Party in Croatia.... The eruption of Mt. Etna is officially considered finished.	Egypt adopts a riot act to that prevents the entry into Egypt of refugees and people without means of support.	The Farmer's Party is defeated in the Ontario general elections and the Conservatives are returned to power.	More than 30 Muslim boys in Calcutta, India, die when their two-story orphanage collapses.... China announces that all of the Chinese captives seized by bandits at Lincheng on an attack on a railroad have been released.
Jun. 27	The annual meeting of the Native Races and the Liquor Traffic United Committee is held in London to discuss the increased importation of liquor to areas of Africa under British control.... The Belgian government releases a report that shows 300 to 500 Belgian workers settled in France during each week of 1922, while thousands simply crossed the border daily in search of work.	The former editor of a Paris newspaper, the *Éclair*, begins trial for treasonable practices during the war.... The Master Cotton Spinners' Association in Great Britain considers reducing the working hours of mills in the American section of the cotton trade in response to the continued depression of trade and unsold stock.... A British man who applies for a vaccination exemption certificate on the grounds of conscientious objection is refused permission to do by a magistrate.		A tornado strikes four counties in Ontario, Canada, and kills four people. More than 100 barns have been wrecked by the storm, with orchards destroyed.... The Canadian government gives a grant to Dr. Banting, the discoverer of insulin, to allow him to continue his work.... The Canadian Parliament debates a halibut treaty with the United States. Some legislators and the Canadian government argue that Britain should not sign the treaty out of respect to Canada.	An exhibition of Australian paintings in Sydney, Australia, is marred by a rejection of some of the artworks that were scheduled to be shown in Great Britain. Many of artists involved are now refusing to send any of their works to Britain, while officials have begun packing accepted artworks for shipment.

A	B	C	D	E
Includes developments that affect more than one world region, international organizations and important meetings of world leaders.	*Includes all domestic and regional developments in Europe, including the Soviet Union.*	*Includes all domestic and regional developments in Africa and the Middle East.*	*Includes all domestic and regional developments in Latin America, the Caribbean, and Canada.*	*Includes all domestic and regional developments in Asian and Pacific nations (and colonies).*

	U.S. Politics & Social Issues	U.S. Foreign Policy & Affairs, Defense	U.S. Economy & Environment	Science, Technology & Nature	Culture, Leisure & Lifestyle
Jun. 20					
Jun. 21	President Warren Harding embarks on a "Voyage of Understanding" nationwide tour designed to enlighten the American public on his policies. Harding becomes the first President to visit the state of Alaska, but dies on the tour after suffering a massive stroke.				
Jun. 22					
Jun. 23		The British American Association conducts a memorial service in honor of R.A.F. personnel who died while in training at Fort Worth, TX.			
Jun. 24	U.S. officials seize sealed liquor in two ships, the *Baltic* and the *Berengaria*, in New York port.		The United States experience a heat wave with the temperature more than 90 degrees Fahrenheit on consecutive days.		Sarah Bernhardt's books go on sale in Paris.
Jun. 25	The U.S. Treasury reissues orders to enforce to the letter the regulations in regard to liquor carried in foreign ships.…The liquor seized from the *Berengaria* is sent to bonded warehouse under the direction of the Prohibition Bureau.…Treasury agents examine six other foreign ships in port.				
Jun. 26	The *Baltic* and the *Berengaria* leave American waters with only enough liquor to serve as medical supplies.		The Hamburg-America ocean liner, *Dinteldyk*, catches on fire in the Pacific Ocean and races to reach a Panama port.…The Brotherhood of Railroad Trainmen and the Order of Railway Conductors call a meeting in Chicago for July 9 to consider inaugurating a movement for increased compensation.		
Jun. 27	The Anti-Saloon League opens a conference in Westerville, OH, to plan steps to stop the "nullification of infection" in Massachusetts, New Jersey, Wisconsin, Illinois, Connecticut, and Rhode Island.…The movement to nominate Henry Ford as a presidential candidate continues to gain steam as "Ford for President" clubs announce plans to hold a convention in Dearborn, MI, to form a third party.	The U.S. Army Ordnance Department announces that is has successfully tested a rifle that fires 60 shots per minute. It is similar to the 1903 Springfield and weighs less than the modified Enfield used in high quantities during the war. The weapon is semi-automatic and, while it has some qualities of a machine gun, the trigger must be pulled for every shot.	The New York City death rate from the heat wave averages four people per day.…Plainfield and Elizabeth, NJ, are threatened with a water shortage because of a lack of rain and the excessive use of water.…The farmer bloc in the U.S. Congress seeks to persuade the government to impound a large quantity of wheat to increase wheat prices.	A report on the Eskimo by Canadian Knud Rasmussen is released. He reports that the Eskimo living to the west and north of Hudson Bay have been greatly influenced in their daily lives by whalers. Mission work has had limited success and the Canadian Eskimo do not suffer from tuberculosis as the Greenland Eskimo do.	

	World Affairs	Europe	Africa & The Middle East	The Americas	Asia & The Pacific
Jun. 28	The Allies are unable to reach agreement on Lausanne and await further instructions from their respective governments.	The trial of three members of a Royalist organization charged with assaulting members of the Chamber of Deputies in Paris ends. The men receive sentences of several months' imprisonment and fines....People near Mt. Etna in Sicily are planning a festival to celebrate the end of the eruption. The Italian peasants attribute their safety to a miracle worked by St. Egidius.	The Iraq government arrests a Shiite leader, Sheikh Mahdi al Kahlisis and makes preparations to deport him under the Immigration Law to Persia.	The new West Indian Agricultural College in Trinidad opens to students from every part of the British Empire....Farmers in Alberta, Canada, organize a voluntary grain pool....The Canadian Parliament recommends a conference of colliery owners and transport owners with the Dominion and Provincial governments to discuss methods of establishing a coal supply independent of the United States.	The House of Representatives in New Zealand defeats two no-confidence motions. The Prime Minister of New Zealand declares that the obstruction of business in the House is leading to dissolution of the government.... Japanese residents in Manchuria petition the Japanese government to continue keeping Japanese police on Chinese railroads.
Jun. 29					
Jun. 30		Mt. Etna continues to erupt.	The Holy Carpet begins its annual journey from Calcutta to Mecca.		
Jul. 1	Great Britain sends a warship, HM *Wisteria* to Nova Scotia in connection with the strikes there.	Hungary announces plans to cut 20,000 government officials....In response to a bomb on a train in the Rhine that killed 10 Belgian soldiers, the Belgian government is placing hostages on all trains passing through the Belgian zone. The hostages will be chosen from among German officials who are hostile to the occupying authorities....A blockade of the Rhine is established by the occupying powers.	Turkey passes legislation that requires all foreigners, except for British, French, and Italians to obtain special permission to enter the country....The French Senate passes legislation ratifying the agreement of September 12, 1919 that fixes the frontier between Tripoli and the French possessions in North Africa....Iraq takes ownership of all Iraqi railways.	The U.S. tank steamer *John D. Archbold*, bound for Los Angeles with 20,000 tons of oil, runs aground at Bona Island in the Gulf of Panama.	The bodies of the captain and the chief officer of the Australian steamer *Sumatra* are found on the beach at Port Macquarie, New South Wales. The ship appears to be a casualty of a heavy gale that has raged along the Australian coast for three days.
Jul. 2	David Hunter Miller, one of the framers of the League of Nations, declares that President Harding's proposed changes to a World Court of Justice precludes all possibility of American involvement....Allied representatives at the League of Nations await final instructions from their governments before concluding the Lausanne conference....The Pope sends a letter to the German government requesting an end to resistance in the occupied territories.... The China Consortium, consisting of British, French, American, and Japanese representatives, discusses a proposed consolidation of China's loans.	Ten French military airplanes are carrying out maneuvers above the Valley of the Meuse when a corporal falls out of one of the machines and is killed in a 1200 feet fall into an orchard....The Franco-Austrian Commercial Agreement is signed today, restoring the prewar commercial relations of the two countries....Jews, who are inhabitants of the Old Kingdom of Romania and who have failed to make applications for citizenship during the period prescribed by the decree of August 12, 1918, are invited to apply through the embassies and legations of the countries that they are residing in.	Turkey bans a party of American engineers from entering the country on the grounds that they did not have special permission to do so.	A large group of strikers attacks the British Empire Steel Corporation at Sydney, Cape Breton, Nova Scotia. Mounted police charge the mob and many of the rioters are injured.	In Peking, China, the chief eunuch and seven of his assistants are arrested on suspicion of arson in connection with the recent fire at the Emperor's residence....The Bengal Legislative Council has rejected the government bill to authorize preventive officers to conduct searches in cases of suspected illicit manufacture of salt without the presence of police officers.
Jul. 3	The Turkish Council of Ministers orders the Turkish representative at the Lausanne conference to refuse to permit an extension of the Allied occupation of Turkish territory.	The Prime Minister of Great Britain expresses his gratitude to the American Debt Commission for making Britain's payments as easy and convenient as possible....The Finance Commission of the French Chamber of Deputies states that sums budgeted for the occupation of Germany are no longer sufficient because of the expenses associated with the occupation of the Ruhr.	The Turkish government signs an agreement with the British-owned Smyrna-Aidin Railway to compensate the railroad for the seizure and working of its system during the war....Two of latest two-seater fighting airplanes of the British Air Force fly to Persia on tour at the request of the Persian government.	Leaders of Paraguayan rebels are captured by government forces.... The miners of the Cape Breton district in Canada announce plans to strike at midnight in sympathy with the steel workers unless the federal troops are immediately withdrawn.	
Jul. 4	French politicians state that they want Germany to take the first step in settling the Ruhr problem by ending passive resistance.	The British Parliament passes a bill permitting a wife to divorce her husband on grounds of adultery.... The Bishop of Gloucester calls for more arguments in support of vaccination to counter the anti-vaccination propaganda that he holds responsible for another smallpox outbreak....Dublin, Ireland, shipping companies reduce the wages of dockers and a strike is expected as a result....Belgium announces that of the 78,000 houses destroyed and 22,000 rendered uninhabitable at the Armistice, 71,383 have been rebuilt or restored.	Turkish authorities arrest Basil Novikoff, a Bolshevist, and charge him with trying to spy on the inquiries of the Turkish police into Communist plots....Jewish labor organizations clash when the Poel Mizrachi, a Zionist and Orthodox Jewish worker's group receives a contract to build a house in Tel Aviv. The much larger Council of Jaffa Workmen sends 250 men to interrupt construction and a riot erupts.	Eight-thousand miners join striking employees of the British Empire Steel Corporation in Nova Scotia.... The Canadian government blames a decrease in farm exports to the United States on the Fordney tariff.	The Indian Legislative Assembly approves a resolution urging the British Cabinet to open the commissioned ranks in the gunners and sappers of the army as well as the Royal Air Force to Indians....Rain in Bombay makes it virtually the only place in India where an excess over the normal rainfall for the year is reported.

A	B	C	D	E
Includes developments that affect more than one world region, international organizations and important meetings of world leaders.	*Includes all domestic and regional developments in Europe, including the Soviet Union.*	*Includes all domestic and regional developments in Africa and the Middle East.*	*Includes all domestic and regional developments in Latin America, the Caribbean, and Canada.*	*Includes all domestic and regional developments in Asian and Pacific nations (and colonies).*

U.S. Politics & Social Issues	U.S. Foreign Policy & Affairs, Defense	U.S. Economy & Environment	Science, Technology & Nature	Culture, Leisure & Lifestyle	
New immigration quotas are released by the Labor Department reduces the numbers of immigrants permitted to enter from Austria but increases the numbers allowed from Hungary, Turkey, Greece, and Poland. The numbers permitted from Germany, Italy, and Great Britain remains unchanged.			Wireless experts demonstrate an invention designed to separate wireless messages from conflicting transmissions.		Jun. 28
					Jun. 29
					Jun. 30
Twelve ships carrying about 10,000 immigrants are admitted to quarantine after waiting in international waters for the first moment of the new fiscal year. To lessen the congestion in New York, several of the ships go to Boston and Philadelphia.					Jul. 1
A large number of Americans are reported to be traveling to Europe on Canadian ships, despite a train journey of several hours from the United States to Canadian ports. Observers believe that the change is a commentary on the prohibition of alcoholic beverages in ships leaving from American ports.	Edward Bok, publisher of *Ladies' Home Journal*, offers a prize of $100,000 to any American who can devise a practical plan by which the United States may cooperate with other nations to secure world peace.			The Leviathan's passenger list is closed after 1700 people book passage on its maiden voyage from New York City to Southampton, England. Passengers include Vincent Astor, T. Coleman DuPont, Mrs. W. Borden Harriman, Nicholas Longworth, and a U.S. Supreme Court Justice. The ship was the largest American troop ship during the war.... The Gutenberg Bible, bought in London by Philip H. Rosenbach, will be brought to the United States. It will be the only perfect copy of first binding in America.	Jul. 2
Emperor William Joseph Simmons of the Ku Klux Klan discusses the extension of the Klan to England and all the other white English-speaking people at a meeting in San Antonio, TX.		The Illinois Mine Workers' Union purchases the Lester strip coalmine at Herrin for $726,000. The mine was the scene of riots last year.			Jul. 3
	The British Embassy asks for a response to the problem facing the Cunard Line ship *Tuscania*. It sails between Italy and New York and is obliged by Italian law to provide wine rations for the crew.... The Army and Navy Joint Board announce plans to ask Congress for double last year's appropriations for the air service. The United States does not aim to have an air force equal to that of England or France, but simply needs a much larger force for the defense of large cities along the Atlantic Coast.			Jack Dempsey wins the World's Heavyweight Championship in Shelby, MT, on points.... Two new zoological gardens in Chicago and St. Louis are being stocked by the Hagenbeck brothers of Germany. During the war, the British and Americans took over the business of supplying wild animals, but the Germans have recovered the trade.... For the first time in history, British sailors participate in a Fourth of July parade. The officers and men of three British warships took part in the parade before President Harding at Portland, OR.	Jul. 4
F *Includes campaigns, elections, federal-state relations, civil rights and liberties, crime, the judiciary, education, healthcare, poverty, urban affairs, and population.*	G *Includes formation and debate of U.S. foreign and defense policies, veterans affairs, and defense spending. (Relations with specific foreign countries are usually found under the region concerned.)*	H *Includes business, labor, agriculture, taxation, transportation, consumer affairs, monetary and fiscal policy, natural resources, pollution and industrial accidents.*	I *Includes worldwide scientific, medical and technological developments, natural phenomena, U.S. weather and natural disasters.*	J *Includes the arts, religion, scholarship, communications media, sports, entertainment, fashions, fads, and social life.*	

	World Affairs	Europe	Africa & The Middle East	The Americas	Asia & The Pacific
Jul. 5		The Germans announce that, as long as the Franco-Belgian closure of the frontier continues, no tickets will be issued or luggage registered for travel from Germany to other countries.... The Soviet Union agrees to sell 310,000 tons of grain to Germany by the end of November.	About 300 political prisoners in Egypt receive amnesties because of the abolition of martial law.... The King of Belgium signs a royal decree changing the capitol of the Belgian Congo to Kinshasa from Boma. The name of Kinshasa is also changed to Leopoldville.		The Ceylon budget, introduced today, shows a surplus. While some of the funds will be held in reserve, part will be sent as war contributions to the British Imperial Government and the remainder will pay war gratuities to returned Ceylon soldiers.
Jul. 6		The Constitution of 1922 for the Soviet Union officially comes into force.... The dock strike at the Port of London spread with about 22,000 men now idle.... Great Britain continues the suspension of ordinary passes for travel within British occupied territory in the Rhine, but begins issuing special passes to everyone who has a reasonable reason for traveling.	The Nairobi, Kenya, trial of 13 Masai men charged with murder and with waging war against Great Britain ends. Seven of the men are found guilty and sentenced to death with the remaining men sentenced to transportation for life.... Turkey announces that foreigners no longer have to obtain special permission to travel through the country. However, the exemption does not apply to citizens of Greece, Bulgaria, Albania, Russia, Georgia, or Azerbaijan.	Barbados appoints a government committee to consider an All-British cable route for the West Indies.... Trinidad accepts the proposal for a cable route. It is planned that a spur of the proposed line will go from Barbados to Trinidad while another goes to Demerara, thus bringing the three colonies in direct contact with Jamaica and Bermuda via the Turk Islands.	New Zealand suffers its worst railroad accident when the Auckland-Wellington express train strikes a landslide at Taumaranui before dawn. The train is derailed before catching fire. Fourteen passengers are killed and 30 people are injured.
Jul. 7		Several farm laborers die in Holland from heat prostration in 90 degree Fahrenheit temperatures.... Delegates from the federated Soviet republics ratify the new Soviet constitution for the Union of Soviet Socialist Republics.		The government of Nova Scotia, Canada, arrests the leaders of the United Mine Workers in an attempt to end the strike in Cape Breton.	The Maharajah of Nabha abdicates in favor of his four-year-old son as the result of a disagreement with the government of India over the administration of the state of Nabha.
Jul. 8	The French Chamber of Deputies ratifies the Washington Treaty for the limitations of naval armaments.... Denmark informs the League of Nations that it will not agree to a defensive military alliance between all members of the League.	French troops occupy the Hoch Iron and Steel Works in Dortmund, Germany.... Adolf Hitler announces that three men sentenced to death by the French are members of the Bavarian Fascist Party. Hitler demands that the German government arrest all French subjects in Germany and hold them as hostages until the death sentences are repealed.	Nineteen Greek villagers from the Upper Bosporus, who were charged with aiding Greek troops in persecuting the Turkish inhabitants of Beikos, are sentenced to death.	The Young Canadians' Forest League is formed to train 140,000 schoolboys to watch for and prevent forest fires.	More than 100 bandits attack a Canton-Kowloon Railway train, kill two soldiers, and capture 90 Chinese hostages that are held for ransom.
Jul. 9	Romania and Yugoslavia renew the Treaty of Defensive Alliance for another three years. The treaty provides for military assistance and for joint policy toward Bulgaria and Hungary.... The Conference of the Baltic States opens. Latvia, Poland, Estonia, and Finland are represented. Lithuania does not send a representative.... The Lausanne Conference concludes.	All the mines in the Bilbao basin of Spain are inactive as Communist workers strike.... The Germans complain that the blockade of the Rhine has led to a food shortage.... The French announce that they will arrest one prominent German every other day in retaliation for the arrest of a French citizen, M. Schuldes in Mannheim last May and his continuing detention until trial.... In Paris, Ernest Judet is acquitted of treasonable communication with the enemy during the war.	British troops engage in a skirmish with a band of bandits at Gaza in Palestine.... Heavy fighting occurs in Transjordania when 500 men of the Huweitat tribe attack a Saradiyah tribe caravan of camels bearing salt. The Huweitat capture the caravan after 100 men are killed.... Syrians demand that France permit a union of Syria and Lebanon, elections to form a constitutional administration, amnesty for political prisoners, freedom of the press, burning of all reports of spies, and cancellation of the Syrian part of the Ottoman war debt.		
Jul. 10	Britain, France, and Spain send representatives to London to discuss the future of Tangier.	The president of the Rhine Province in Germany issues a denunciation of sabotage on the railways that has led to the loss of life and property.... A German diplomat in Belgium is assaulted by an ex-officer of the Belgian army in Brussels, Belgium.... An earthquake shakes the south of France.			The Central Mine in Broken Hill, New South Wales, in Australia catches fire at the 400-foot level. All miners are safety evacuated but dense smoke and gases hamper efforts to extinguish the blaze.... Chinese troops pursuing a group of bandits who kidnapped 90 passengers from a Canton-Kowloon Railway train, kill 20 of the bandits. Most of the bandits escape with their captives.
Jul. 11		Torrential rains damage crops throughout most of Spain.		Voters in Manitoba, Canada, refuse to approve a referendum to allow the sale of beer and light wines with meals served in hotels.	The Indian Legislative Assembly defeats a motion to release Mahatma Gandhi from prison.

A	B	C	D	E
Includes developments that affect more than one world region, international organizations and important meetings of world leaders.	*Includes all domestic and regional developments in Europe, including the Soviet Union.*	*Includes all domestic and regional developments in Africa and the Middle East.*	*Includes all domestic and regional developments in Latin America, the Caribbean, and Canada.*	*Includes all domestic and regional developments in Asian and Pacific nations (and colonies).*

	U.S. Politics & Social Issues	U.S. Foreign Policy & Affairs, Defense	U.S. Economy & Environment	Science, Technology & Nature	Culture, Leisure & Lifestyle
Jul. 5	Communists seize control of the Farmer Labor Party convention in Chicago when non-Communists withdraw. They establish a Federated Farmer Labor Party.... The U.S. government announces that the immigration quotas for Egypt, Turkey, Palestine, Syria, Albania, and Africa have been exhausted for July.	The British government makes the last payment on its war debt to the United States.			
Jul. 6			A committee of the Massachusetts Legislature reports that a stoppage of coalmining in Pennsylvania will likely take place on August 31 when the miners' wage agreement expires....The head of U.S. Steel states that the steel industry will soon abolish the 12-hour day. The change will require an additional 60,000 employees and will increase the cost of finished steel products by 15 percent....A fire fueled by high winds sweeps through a gold camp at Goldfield, NV. Attempts to use dynamite to halt the flames fail and hundreds of residents flee with their belongings.		
Jul. 7			Boston purchases 2,000 tons of Welsh coal for city schools.	The Canadian ship, *Arctic*, sails from Quebec to the Arctic Circle to investigate the resources of the Canadian Far North.	
Jul. 8	President Harding and his family arrive in Ketchikan, AK.	The Treasury Department rules, in response to a British request, that the liquor allowance shall be in accordance with the laws of the country with which the ships are trading and not those of the country of registry. This means that ships may carry liquor in accordance with Italian laws.			
Jul. 9			The Brotherhood of Railroad Trainmen and the Order of Railway Conductors, two of the four leading organizations for railroad workers, meet in Chicago to get better wages....A presidential commission investigating the anthracite coal strike of 1921 issues its report. The commission opposes government ownership of coalmines unless a serious suspension of mining occurs.	Lieutenant Russell Maugham fails in his attempt to fly a Curtiss pursuit airplane across the United States between dusk and dawn. He is forced to land at St. Joseph, MO, at 3:30 p.m. after setting out from Mineola, NY, at 4:58 a.m.	
Jul. 10		In response to a threat by Canada to halt the export of wood pulp, the U.S. government is considering retaliatory measures. American paper manufacturers fear that the Canadian action would close American mills even when Americans own Canadian forests.	The Interstate Commerce Commission orders an investigation into all rates for the transport of anthracite coal in the United States and in the foreign anthracite trade.		
Jul. 11	The U.S. Shipping Board decides that commanders of ships are powerless to interfere with passengers who openly drink their own liquors on board ships.	New York Post Office officials admit that mail for Europe is often delayed by up to 24 hours so that it may be carried on American ships.			
	F *Includes campaigns, elections, federal-state relations, civil rights and liberties, crime, the judiciary, education, healthcare, poverty, urban affairs, and population.*	G *Includes formation and debate of U.S. foreign and defense policies, veterans affairs, and defense spending. (Relations with specific foreign countries are usually found under the region concerned.)*	H *Includes business, labor, agriculture, taxation, transportation, consumer affairs, monetary and fiscal policy, natural resources, pollution and industrial accidents.*	I *Includes worldwide scientific, medical and technological developments, natural phenomena, U.S. weather and natural disasters.*	J *Includes the arts, religion, scholarship, communications media, sports, entertainment, fashions, fads, and social life.*

	World Affairs	Europe	Africa & The Middle East	The Americas	Asia & The Pacific
Jul. 12		The Italian Cabinet approves a decree that permits newspapers to be punished for publishing articles, comments, headings, illustrations, or cartoons that incite disobedience of established laws or offend state institutions.... The French Parliament adjourns.			The Australian House of Representatives resolves by a 37 to 12 vote that the next Parliament shall meet at Canberra, the new federal capital.
Jul. 13	The Norwegian Foreign Minister formally invites Denmark to open negotiations on control of Greenland.	The British government condemns the occupation of the Ruhr as a way of forcing reparations from Germany.... Captain Ehrhardt, who has been held in prison at Leipzig, Germany while awaiting trial for the Kapp *Putsch*, escapes through a hole in the roof.... Mt. Etna in Sicily shows signs of resuming activity.... The first woman barrister in Scotland, Margaret Henderson Kidd, is admitted to the Faculty of Advocates in Edinburgh.	Mustafa Kemal Pasha issues an Order of the Day to the Turkish army warning the troops that the conclusion of peace with the Allies at Lausanne is not certain and they may be required to defend their country again.	The Canadian Minister of the Interior announces that no more troops will be sent to the Cape Breton strike area. The Canadian Minister of Labor, who has denounced the troops as an attempt to intimidate workers, states that he is hopeful that all of the troops will be withdrawn. The Premier of Nova Scotia confers with the leaders of the Cape Breton strikers.	
Jul. 14		During celebrations of Bastille Day, Jesse Curely, the French High Commissioner, reminds Turkey that France should be paid reparations.		Five people are killed and many poor people are left homeless when heavy storms strike Montevideo, Uruguay.	Sir Henry Barwell, the Premier of South Australia, recommends that a direct transcontinental railroad be built as soon as possible to take advantage of the riches of the Northern Territory.
Jul. 15	The Soviet Union announces that the adoption of a constitution means that all the representative offices in foreign countries of the separate states in the union will be abolished.	There is rioting in the Ruhr with unemployed workers attacking shops and stripping the stores of all of their goods.... Three Germans are sentenced to death by the French for sabotage.... France declares that it has won in the Ruhr because French industrial power is rising while Germany has been forced into submission.... The government of Malta recommends that Maltese emigrate to Argentina in light of American immigration quotas and the Canadian limitation on the admittance of farmers only.	Wahabi raiders attack a large caravan of Yemeni pilgrims in Egypt on their way to Mecca and kill all but 80 of them.		A Chinese steamer on the Yang-tse-Kiang River just below Chungking is fired upon heavily by bandits and two passengers are wounded.... A fire in the Central Mine in New South Wales, Australia, is extinguished after burning since July 10.... The government of Assam warns about the wide extent and deadly nature of kala azar, or black sickness, and announces an investigation of the illness.
Jul. 16		France announces that the ban on movement between occupied and unoccupied territory in Germany will be continued for another 10 days. The French give no reason for the extension.... Some Germans suspect that France is seeking to establish a Rhineland Republic under French protection.	King Hussein of Egypt criticizes Egyptians for seeking a constitution because they do not need anything more than the Koran and God's laws.	Venezuela and Bolivia conclude a general arbitration treaty.... The state of health of Empress Charlotte, widow of Emperor Maximilian of Mexico, is causing concern.	The Chinese superintendent of the Chinese Telegraph Administration is shot and slightly wounded in Hong Kong by an unknown assailant. The superintendent returned fire.
Jul. 17	The Executive Committee of the Third International, a Communist group, calls on all workers in Bulgaria and other Balkan countries to overthrow the new Bulgarian government.	The Spanish government dismisses the Civil Governor of Palencia for publicly taking part in a bullfight, in which he killed a bull.... The older democratic newspaper in Italy, *Il Secolo*, is purchased by Fascists.... The Soviet government reports that the harvest for Eastern Russia is expected to be poor because of inclement weather.	Egypt's Holy Carpet is returned to Suez.	The miners' strike in Nova Scotia continues as the government's military patrol system is extended to prevent sabotage.	General Leonard Wood, Governor-General of the Philippines, accepts the resignations of the Filipino member of the Council of State and the Cabinet of the Philippines.
Jul. 18	The Reparation Commission, meeting in Paris, considers whether Germany is liable under the Treaty of Versailles to deliver sugar as part of the reparations in kind. France and Italy are demanding sugar.... Turks residing in Crete and Macedonia petition the Greek government to be exempt from the forthcoming compulsory exchange of civil populations required in the Treaty of Lausanne.	Some members of the British House of Lords express concerns that the government has not taken steps to protect the food supply in the event of another war that disrupts trans-Atlantic shipping.... The Paris Municipal Council authorizes 250 cycle-car taxicabs, which carry one passenger and charge less than regular cabs, to operate in the city.... New bells are cast for the town of St. Quentin, Belgium, to replace bells that were carted off by the Germans during the war.	The wheat crop in Algeria is expected to be 2½ times greater than last year's harvest.... A judge sentences rioters involved in a Jewish labor dispute in Tel Aviv earlier this month to a week's imprisonment.... The Congress of Arab Orthodox Laymen resolves to introduce Arab priests and bishops in Palestine.... Jews meet in Jerusalem to establish a Farmer's Federation that will be independent of financial contributions from Jews in the Diaspora and the Zionist Organization in Palestine.	The Grenada Legislative Council votes to join the West Indian All-British cable plan.... Fifty-thousand workers are needed to harvest the Canadian wheat crop.	The Prime Minister of New Zealand attributes the country's recovery from depression to hard work by farmers.... The agricultural situation in western India improves considerably as rains continue to fall.... The State Minister of Lands in Victoria, Australia, announces that the government intends to purchase large estates to provide land for settlers.

A	B	C	D	E
Includes developments that affect more than one world region, international organizations and important meetings of world leaders.	*Includes all domestic and regional developments in Europe, including the Soviet Union.*	*Includes all domestic and regional developments in Africa and the Middle East.*	*Includes all domestic and regional developments in Latin America, the Caribbean, and Canada.*	*Includes all domestic and regional developments in Asian and Pacific nations (and colonies).*

	U.S. Politics & Social Issues	U.S. Foreign Policy & Affairs, Defense	U.S. Economy & Environment	Science, Technology & Nature	Culture, Leisure & Lifestyle
Jul. 12	Albert Lasker, the retiring chairman of the U.S. Shipping Board, states that no greater harm can come to the American Merchant Marine than when foreign ships cannot bring liquor as stores in U.S. waters. He expresses fears that American ships will be the targets of reprisals.				
Jul. 13	William Dillingham, Republican U.S. Senator from Vermont and former governor of the state, dies.		A federal commission on agriculture advises farmers to decrease their wheat acreage because of Europe's declining purchasing power.		Boxer Luis Angel Firpo of Argentina defeats Jess Willard of the United States with an eighth round knockout in Jersey City, NJ, to win the heavyweight championship of the world.
Jul. 14			A fire in the mining town of Mace, ID, results in $1 million damage, 1,200 people left homeless, and the destruction of the business section of the neighboring town of Burke.		
Jul. 15	The Coast Guard notifies the Treasury Department that it needs $10 million to end rum running on the Atlantic coast.				Golfer Bobby Jones wins the U.S. Open Championship on the Inwood Course, Long Island, NY.
Jul. 16	Upon arriving in New York Harbor, 482 British immigrants are detained at Ellis Island because the British immigration quota for the month of July is filled.…More British immigrants are expected to arrive this week but they will not be admitted.…The immigration barrier will be up until August 1.				
Jul. 17	President Harding's itinerary in Alaska is changed to a less arduous schedule, raising fears about the possible worsening health of the First Lady.…The state of California obtains a temporary injunction to make membership in the International Workers of the World contempt of court, punishable by six months imprisonment.	Manuel Quezon, President of the Philippine Senate, telegraphs President Harding to accuse General Wood of violating the rights of Filipinos by breaking the Organic Act of the Philippines and triggering a political deadlock in the nation.			
Jul. 18	Henry Curran, the Commissioner General of Immigration, goes to Ellis Island to try to resolve the situation of the 482 British immigrants who are detained because of the exhaustion of Great Britain's July immigration quota.…Curran suggests that allotments be made at foreign ports instead of American ones.…Representatives of trans-Atlantic steamship companies consider the proposal but reject it until they have received legal advice.		Several New York City construction firms announce plans to resume activity after a two-month suspension of work. The companies state that labor costs have stabilized.	The International Surgical Congress, discussing the lessons learned during the war, recommends that the preliminary cleansing of a wound should include an examination of the state of nerves and blood vessels in the affected area.	

	World Affairs	Europe	Africa & The Middle East	The Americas	Asia & The Pacific
Jul. 19	In an effort to standardize treatments for a wide range of diseases, the League of Nations hosts the Conference for the Standardization of Biological Remedies in Edinburgh.…The Reparations Commission listens to arguments from Germany about why it should not be forced to provide sugar under the terms of the Treaty of Versailles.	The leaders of the Associated Trade Unions of the Ruhr condemn efforts to establish a separate Rhenish state.…The unionists encourage Germans to continue the policy of passive resistance as a solution to the reparations problem.…Great Britain announces that there are about 300,000 ex-military men under 30-years-of-age who are unemployed. The government recommends that the men who are fit to immigrate do so.	The Egyptian government announces that it has no objection to the return of Zaghlul Pasha.…An attempted uprising against the Russians by Turkmen in Turkestan fails and the tribesmen take refuge in northern Afghanistan.	John Lewis, leader of the United Mine Workers of America, cancels the charter of the Glace Bay, Nova Scotia, Canada, chapter for refusing to call off a strike of miners.	The Immigration Department in New Zealand announces that immigration could double if current restrictions were removed and a more open policy adopted.
Jul. 20	The Permanent Mandates Commission of the League of Nations begins meeting to determine the administration of territories under League control.	The British House of Commons refuses to order Cambridge University to admit women.…In response to Russian complaints that Romanians are firing at the Soviet Frontier Guards, the Romanian government states that the Soviets fired first. Romania suggests a meeting of military commanders to resolve the conflict.	In preparation for the final elections to the National Assembly, 500 elections officials in Baghdad chose a committee to examine electoral rolls.	Francisco "Pancho" Villa is shot to death in Chihuahua, Mexico, in an ambush on his estate. Mexican President Miguel Obregon orders that Villa's body be buried with full military honors.…The Saskatchewan Grain Growers Association in Canada decides to use a voluntary wheat pool for this year's crop.	The Ceylon Legislative Council by a vote of 19 to 14 decides to exclude Germans from the colony for another year, beginning August 29.…The Australian Prime Minister states that the further subdivision of Australia is inevitable.…Babar Akalis in the Punjab section of India assault a man with *chavis*, a type of halberd, for cooperating with the police. The man survives his wounds.…The Privy Council in London refuses to hear the appeal of 14 Indians sentenced to transportation for life for unlawfully assembling and rioting.
Jul. 21	The Baptist World Alliance opens in Stockholm, Sweden.				Although the Chinese Parliament is in session, there are no meetings and a quorum has not been obtained because of the unsettled situation in the country.…All sources of revenue in China have dried up and legislators express reluctance to face the unsatisfied demands of police and troops.
Jul. 22	The Soviet Union agrees to sign the Straits Convention because Turkey has agreed to sign it. However, the Soviets reserve the right to propose future alterations and to declare the treaty cancelled if the safety of the Russian coast is threatened.…The International Chamber of Commerce condemns the practice of various countries to prevent foreign firms from doing business.	Bulgaria expels the Soviet Red Cross Mission for engaging in Communist propaganda.	General Smuts of South Africa encourages the various industries in the country to help build a European civilization by hiring whites rather than blacks.	France is using airplanes and balloons to search for coal stacks hidden by the Germans in the Ruhr.	Settlers in southern central Australia petition to leave Northern Territory and be restored to South Australia on the grounds that the federal administrators of Northern Territory are inefficient and incompetent.…Japan states that it has no opposition to a British base at Singapore because it regards such a base as an internal British matter.…Australia complains that Great Britain is sending over unsuitable immigrants, as nine immigrants are caught trying to stowaway on a ship bound from England. The ship had previously discovered 15 stowaways.
Jul. 23	Poland and Turkey sign a treaty of amity and a commercial agreement at Lausanne.	For humanitarian reasons, the French in the Ruhr issue orders to stop the expulsion of women in the last two months of pregnancy, invalids, and persons aged over 60 years.	General Smuts of South Africa warns of the danger of attempting to build up a white civilization as a mere superstructure upon a basis of black labor.	The strikers in Cape Breton, Canada, pass a resolution to return to work tomorrow.…John McDonald, a member of the Communist Worker's Party in Canada, is arrested for seditious utterances and disrespect to the British flag.	Muslims attack a Hindu procession at Ajmer in Rajputana. The troops protecting the Hindus are fired upon, with one soldier killed. The soldiers returned fire, killing 12 people and restoring order.
Jul. 24	Turkey signs the Lausanne Treaty. The Turkish government surrenders all of its claims on non-Turkish territory lost during the World War and regains Eastern Thrace, Karagach, and the islands of Imbros and Tenedos in the Aegean. Greece gains the remainder of the Aegean Islands, Italy retains the Dodecanese, and Britain continues to govern Cyprus. The Allies abolish the Capitulations in return for Turkish judicial reforms and Turkey accepts treaties to protect minorities. Unlike the other Central Empire allies, Turkey does not have to pay reparations.	The German government has apparently dropped its policy of exchange control as one dollar now equals 414,000 marks with the rate of exchange steadily rising.…Damages for breach of promise are awarded for the first time in France. The couple had been engaged for four years when the parents of the would-be groom pressured him to break off the marriage because he was too young. The parents were ordered to pay damages to the woman.	Large Turkish crowds celebrate the peace agreement as the streets are decorated and parades are held.…The British South Africa Company agrees to a plan to relinquish control of Southern Rhodesia.	The cabinet of Sir Richard Squires resigns, leaving Newfoundland, Canada, without a government. The crisis arose over the lavish expenditures of the Department of Agriculture and Mines.	The Philippine Independence Commission passes a resolution demanding the immediate removal of General Leonard Wood and the appointment of a Filipino Governor-General pending the independence of the country.…The abdication of the Maharajah of Nabha is being used by Sikhs in the Punjab to drum up anti-British sentiment.…A British steamer and an American steamer, both being escorted by the American gunboat, *Monocacy*, are fired upon on the Yangtze River near Chungking, China. The *Monocacy* returns fire.

A	B	C	D	E
Includes developments that affect more than one world region, international organizations and important meetings of world leaders.	*Includes all domestic and regional developments in Europe, including the Soviet Union.*	*Includes all domestic and regional developments in Africa and the Middle East.*	*Includes all domestic and regional developments in Latin America, the Caribbean, and Canada.*	*Includes all domestic and regional developments in Asian and Pacific nations (and colonies).*

U.S. Politics & Social Issues	U.S. Foreign Policy & Affairs, Defense	U.S. Economy & Environment	Science, Technology & Nature	Culture, Leisure & Lifestyle	
William H. Anderson, New York State leader of the Anti-Saloon League, is indicted for grand larceny and forgery. Anderson is accused of stealing money from the League.... The British ship, *Kadusak*, is free after its captain posts bail and promises to return for trial in August.... All of the British immigrants being held at Ellis Island are admitted to the United States after a reexamination of the quota shows that 512 more British citizens can enter the country.	Rear Admiral Charles Sigsbee, commander of the USS *Maine* when it blew up in Havana harbor to start the Spanish American War, dies.		The International Surgical Congress discusses the formation of artificial joints. Surgeons note that artificial elbow joints are usually successfully created but attempts to create a lost knee or hip frequently fail.		Jul. 19
Suspected rumrunners fleeing police in an automobile discharge mustard gas from the exhaust in a successful bid to escape.... The attorney for the captain of the *Kadusak* protests to the British Consul-General about the seizure of the ship.... James M. Cox, Democratic candidate for the presidency, states that there must be an immediate end to the American policy of isolation and economic self-sufficiency. Cox fears that the policy will renew international warfare and bring hardship to Americans.	The United States renews an arbitration treaty with France for another five years.		Afghanistan and France sign a treaty giving France rights of archeological investigation.		Jul. 20
Samuel Gompers, head of the American Federation of Labor, expresses anger at the attempts of Communists to tamper with labor organizations in the United States.					Jul. 21
Immigration officials at Ellis Island refuse to allow the week-old child of Polish immigrants to enter the United States. The child, Baby Przygon, was born on the steamer *Lapland*, which flies the British flag. Officials argue that the child is British and the British quota has been exceeded for the month.... Republican leaders warn that the election of Farmer Labor candidate, Magnus Johnson, to the U.S. Senate shows that the third party movement is too infectious to be stopped.			Two Italian scientists, Giovanni di Cristina and Giuseppi Carolia, announce that they have identified the specific germ that causes scarlet fever.		Jul. 22
	Charles Evans Hughes, the Secretary of State, reiterates that the United States will not recognize the Soviet Union because of Russia's disregard of her obligations and the avowed goal of Bolshevists to promote world revolution.	Southern California and Arizona are rocked by an earthquake, with property damage but no loss of life.			Jul. 23
The U.S. Secretary of Labor, Davies, meets with Prime Minister Benito Mussolini to discuss Italian immigration to the United States but no change in American policy is expected.	The Harding Administration refuses to consider the removal of Wood from the Philippines and views the majority of Filipinos as indifferent to independence.... The United States request that Turkey provide a special administration to protect the rights of American citizens in Turkey. Turkey refuses on the grounds that such rules resemble the capitulations that the Lausanne Treaty abolished.	Fifteen-hundred longshoremen go on strike on the New Jersey side of New York harbor. The strikers, members of the Marine Transport Workers' Union, a division of the International Workers of the World, act in defiance of the International Longshoremen's Association, which is affiliated with American Federation of Labor. The strikers seek a dollar an hour more, an eight-hour day, a 44-hour week, and time and a half for overtime.			Jul. 24
F *Includes campaigns, elections, federal-state relations, civil rights and liberties, crime, the judiciary, education, healthcare, poverty, urban affairs, and population.*	G *Includes formation and debate of U.S. foreign and defense policies, veterans affairs, and defense spending. (Relations with specific foreign countries are usually found under the region concerned.)*	H *Includes business, labor, agriculture, taxation, transportation, consumer affairs, monetary and fiscal policy, natural resources, pollution and industrial accidents.*	I *Includes worldwide scientific, medical and technological developments, natural phenomena, U.S. weather and natural disasters.*	J *Includes the arts, religion, scholarship, communications media, sports, entertainment, fashions, fads, and social life.*	

	World Affairs	Europe	Africa & The Middle East	The Americas	Asia & The Pacific
Jul. 25	The Allies continue to debate German war reparations, with Belgium opposed to any reduction of the debt that does not also reduce Belgium's debt to the other Allied countries....Germany formally protests to Belgium and France against the new ordinance of the Rhineland Commission that penalizes people who contest the legality of the commission's rulings or promote resistance to the commission.	While the British House of Commons agrees to permit a British woman who marries a foreigner to retain her British nationality, the House of Lords refuses to allow it....According to newly released official statistics, the population of Belgium increased from 7,482,133 at the end of 1921 to 7,539,568 at the end of 1922....The Soviets arrest workers on suspicion of organizing anti-Bolshevist secret societies in Petrograd.	Great Britain withdraws troops from Turkey as a result of the peace agreement....Britain also reduces its garrison in Palestine and considers ending its policy of subsidizing Arab rulers, particularly Ibn Saud....General Smuts, Prime Minister of South Africa, justifies the compulsory segregation of Indians and Europeans on the grounds that India has a caste system that allows Indians to practice segregation in their native country.	Eight to 10 robbers attack and shoot a dozen armed bank messengers who are traveling on foot and in cars in Toronto. Three messengers are wounded and $16,400 is stolen....Canadian immigration returns for the second quarter of 1923 show 40,952 immigrants, an increase of 63 percent over the same quarter of 1922. British immigrants numbered 22,553 while immigrants from the United States numbers 6,373.	The Australian government estimates that locks being constructed on the Murray River will make enough land available for the settlement of 100,000 people....Wang Ko-ming, appointed Minister of Finance for China on July 11 resigns from office.
Jul. 26		The British government considers reducing army pay, which is still at wartime levels despite a reduction in the cost of living....The Soviet Union announces that the Russian harvest is expected to be 10 percent less than in 1922.	Several Presbyterian branches in South Africa united to form the Bantu Presbyterian Church of South Africa....The Conciliation Board in Johannesburg, South Africa, rejects the request of the Crown Mines mechanics for a 30 percent wage increase.	A schooner arriving at Prince Rupert, British Columbia, Canada, reports a world record catch of 38,000 pounds of halibut.	More than 700 Russian refugees are reported to be starving on a ship off the coast of Chungking, China. The ship is out of coal and it is not allowed to dock at Shanghai because the 1,500 foreign residents in this city are already struggling to support 5,500 refugees.
Jul. 27	France refuses to evacuate the Ruhr until Germany makes reparations payments....Belgium indicates that it is willing to make concessions on the matter of reparations.... The Mandates Commission of the League of Nations discusses customs duties on liquor imports in mandated territory. Liquor smuggling is encouraged by taxes in mandated countries that are sometimes lower than in neighboring regions.	The food situation in Berlin continues to worsen, with people comparing it to the effect produced by the blockade during the later stages of the war. There are large lines outside of food stores in Germany with increasing numbers of stores closing because they are out of stock or do not want to sell at current prices....France is using poison gas to kill field mice that are causing crop damage....Muslims in Greece will not be permitted to vote in the upcoming election because they are expected to leave the country soon.	The Anglo-German Mixed Arbitral Tribunal agrees with the German government's contention that the Cameroon Protectorate possessed an independent legal entity separate from the German Empire before the war and that, therefore, Germany is not responsible for its debts. ....Portugal forms a tobacco syndicate to grow tobacco in its colony of Angola to supply Portugal and other European countries.	A special session of the Manitoba Legislature in Canada passes a law for government control and sale of liquor in the province....In the general election at Prince Edward Island in Canada, Conservatives take power, reversing the political makeup of the Legislative Assembly.	Charlton, the leader of the Labour Party in the Australian House of Representatives, declares that Japan poses no threat to Australia because Japan's destiny is in Manchuria. He opposes the construction of a naval base at Singapore and does not want Australia to contribute to any defense projects outside of Australia....The New Zealand House of Representatives passes a law giving statutory recognition to the Native Council of Western Samoa.
Jul. 28	The Sinaia Conference, expected to help the Little Entente reach agreement in regard to reparations and the general attitude toward Hungary, opens....The Intellectual Cooperation Commission of the League of Nations submits to the Assembly of the League a proposal for the protection of scientific discoveries that would establish copyrights.	The Azerbaijan Soviet government announces plans to erect a monument to the 26 Communists killed by the British during their occupation of Baku.	Iraq and Syria sign a treaty that settles the disputes about the nomadic tribes on the frontier and arranges for the security of traffic between the two countries.	In an address today, the President of Peru complains about Chilean incursions into Peruvian territory in Tacna and Arica. He notes that Peru is on a sound financial basis with a balanced budget.	The Prince Regent of Japan becomes the first member of the royal family to climb Fujiyama, the highest mountain in Japan.
Jul. 29		The value of the Hungarian crown continues to drop, with the Minister of Finance attributing the loss of value partly to speculation and mostly to a trade imbalance and budget deficit.			
Jul. 30	Belgium notifies the Allied governments that it will not negotiate with Germany until passive resistance has ceased. Belgium will only agree to evacuate the Ruhr progressively in proportion to Germany's payment of reparations.				
Jul. 31	The League of Nations Commission on Intellectual Cooperation refuses to recommend the use of Esperanto.	The Red International of Labor Unions in Moscow announces plans to organize an Anti-Fascist Day....The captain of a Spanish steamer is convicted by the Spanish Naval Court of Seville and sentenced to two-years imprisonment for scuttling his ship with bombs in November 1921.			The New Zealand government introduces legislation to suspend rent and mortgage interest owed to the government for a decade without penalty. The legislation is an attempt to help settlers recover from the agricultural depression. ...Great Britain gives administration of its Antarctic territories to New Zealand....Li Yuan-Hung, the president of the Chinese republic, attempts suicide by shooting himself with a revolver. His condition is reported as very serious.

A	B	C	D	E
Includes developments that affect more than one world region, international organizations and important meetings of world leaders.	*Includes all domestic and regional developments in Europe, including the Soviet Union.*	*Includes all domestic and regional developments in Africa and the Middle East.*	*Includes all domestic and regional developments in Latin America, the Caribbean, and Canada.*	*Includes all domestic and regional developments in Asian and Pacific nations (and colonies).*

U.S. Politics & Social Issues	U.S. Foreign Policy & Affairs, Defense	U.S. Economy & Environment	Science, Technology & Nature	Culture, Leisure & Lifestyle	
		Western Union Telegraph Company signs an agreement with the Italian Submarine Cable Company to lay cables between New York, the Azores, and Rome.	Walter E. Elliott, Under-Secretary of Health for Scotland notes, in welcoming the International Physiological Congress to Edinburgh, that the war taught politicians to fear scientists because science could determine military success.	Stormfield, the house at Redding, CT, where writer Mark Twain spent the last years of his life is destroyed by fire.	Jul. 25
	President Harding arrives in Vancouver, Canada, and delivers a speech before a crowd estimated to be 40,000 people. It is Harding's first speech before a foreign audience.	Angry at the lack of mailbags delivered to American ships at British ports, the Postmaster General Harry New charges Britain and France with deliberately courting a trans-Atlantic postal war.			Jul. 26
	The USS *Henderson* rams a destroyer in Puget Sound while carrying President Harding.	The crew of the schooner, *Iskum*, under arrest at East Cape, Siberia, on charges of violating the Soviet commercial law, return to Nome, AK, after overpowering their guards.... A general strike of coalminers is possible for September 1 when the anthracite industry wage contract expires because talks between mine owners and labor leaders break off without any date set for resumption of talks.... The New York Stock Exchange is the scene of increased selling, which is attributed to the weakness of the German mark and the uncertainness of the German situation.			Jul. 27
	A number of British subjects rejected by U.S. immigration authorities, because Great Britain had exceeded its immigration quota, arrive in Southampton, England, and share stories of hardship with the British press....Many of the would-be immigrants complain that they were treated "worse than animals."				Jul. 28
					Jul. 29
President Harding's physicians announce that the president is suffering from pneumonia in his right lung and that his condition is grave, but he is temperamentally suited to make a strong fight.					Jul. 30
President Harding's physicians announce that he had 6½ hours of sleep and seems to be recovering....Henry Ford announces that he is not a candidate for president and does not want political office in an interview in *Collier's Weekly*. ...About 15,000 immigrants arrive at New York City but delay their entrance into American waters until just after midnight when the new immigration quotas open.	The Soviet authorities at East Cape, Siberia, warn an American expedition to Wrangel Island that its ship will be confiscated unless it obtains proper clearance papers and transports a contingent of Red Guards to the island.				Jul. 31

F	G	H	I	J
Includes campaigns, elections, federal-state relations, civil rights and liberties, crime, the judiciary, education, healthcare, poverty, urban affairs, and population.	*Includes formation and debate of U.S. foreign and defense policies, veterans affairs, and defense spending. (Relations with specific foreign countries are usually found under the region concerned.)*	*Includes business, labor, agriculture, taxation, transportation, consumer affairs, monetary and fiscal policy, natural resources, pollution and industrial accidents.*	*Includes worldwide scientific, medical and technological developments, natural phenomena, U.S. weather and natural disasters.*	*Includes the arts, religion, scholarship, communications media, sports, entertainment, fashions, fads, and social life.*

	World Affairs	Europe	Africa & The Middle East	The Americas	Asia & The Pacific
Aug. 1	The European cotton exchanges agree to accept the new cotton standards proposed by the U.S. Department of Agriculture.	The Italian government warns Empress Zita that it intends to block any attempted sale of objects belonging to the Crown of Tuscany, including the Florentine diamond, that were transported to Vienna in the 18th century. The public is also warned against purchasing any jewelry belonging to Empress Zita.... The strike of Silesian metalworkers ends.... The British Royal Air Force conducts bombing practice on the wireless-controlled Agamemnon, an old battle cruiser.	The Egyptian government announces that it will help cotton growers by entering the cotton market as a purchaser. The move comes in response to lobbying by the Cotton Growers' Syndicate.... The body of a Tunisian worker who apparently fell asleep on a pile of grain and was buried alive is discovered during the unloading of a ship in Belgium when the pneumatic tube jams.	The steelworkers at Cape Breton vote to return to work.... During July, Canada exported 4150 head of cattle to Great Britain.... British subjects in Honduras request protection from the government of British Honduras because of maltreatment by some Honduran police and other officials.... The Barbados House of Assembly recommends the establishment of a school that would take up education at the point reached by the highest grade in the existing primary system.	Fighting is reported in Amoy, on the Chinese coast, between the occupying forces of Sun Yat-sen and the opposition forces of Chen Chiung-ming. No one is allowed to enter or leave the city and business is at a standstill.
Aug. 2	Hungary expects that its financial position will worsen unless it is permitted to get aid from the Finance Committee of the League of Nations. The Hungarian exchange has dropped from 45,000 kronen to nearly 100,000 kronen to the pound.... The British Armenian Societies request that the League of Nations consider the plight of Armenian refugees, who were left out of the Lausanne agreement.... Italian and Yugoslav diplomats continue to discuss the settlement of Fiume.	The Soviet newspaper *Izvestia* reports that since June 14 a special Soviet commission has liberated 2,522 persons from Moscow prisons and has banished 824. The majority of the liberated were aged between 18 and 25.... German tobacconists strike to protest the government's heavy taxation of tobacco.... The Belgian government has prohibited the export of coal.... Communists in the Ukraine capture an entire company of insurgents commanded by Skrinchenko, alias Bogdan the Second, the liberator of the Ukraine. Skrinchenko commits suicide.	The Egyptian government has warned newspapers against publishing any more violently worded manifestos from the Wafd.... Indian students in Kenya denounce the Kenyan agreement as favoring native Africans at the expense of immigrants. They warn that the agreement has led to an increase in desire for self-government in India.	Four-hundred Englishmen leave Southampton for Western Canada to assist in gathering the harvest.	Building inspectors and poor construction are blamed during an inquest into the June deaths of 39 boys who died when a Calcutta orphanage collapsed. Residents of the city fear subsequent tragedies because of heavy motor traffic along narrow streets bordered by ramshackle houses built on insecure foundations.... The ex-Maharajah of Nabha dissociates himself from any agitation against his abdication and argues that the movement is disloyal to the British government.
Aug. 3	The French Ministry of Foreign Affairs issues a statement rebuking U.S. visitors for violently showing their disapproval when they have found men of color from French colonies sitting near them in public places.	A Norwegian torpedo boat torpedoed and sank a German liquor smuggling boat in Christiana Fiord, Norway.... Finland and Iceland sign a most-favored nation treaty on the same day that Finland and Denmark sign a similar commercial treaty.	Afghanistan celebrates its annual coronation day despite some violence blamed on reforms by a more liberal government.		
Aug. 4	The Mixed Committee of the League of Nations approved parts of the Treaty of Mutual Guarantee.... The Soviet Union sends a delegation to China to settle Chinese-Russian relations, particularly questions connected with the Eastern Chinese Railway, still held by the White Army.	Relations between the government and the Communists in Bulgaria worsen as the Communists issue an appeal to the workers to collaborate against the present regime.... The government of Finland halts publication of all Communist newspapers, closes party offices, and arrests about 100 leading Communists.... A bomb in the Ruhr wounds three French soldiers and seven German civilians.			The city of Amoy in China is quiet after a British cruiser and an American warship arrive. British marines occupy the British Concession.
Aug. 5		During the performance of a show at the Opera Comique, leaflets are thrown from the gallery calling for the release of the anarchist who attempted to assassinate French President Clemenceau during the Peace Conference.			Calcutta, India, is suffering a severe epidemic of dengue fever and there is a demand to revive the "mosquito brigades" that were abolished as an economy measure.... The Otira Tunnel in New Zealand, the longest tunnel in the British Empire at five miles, is opened.
Aug. 6	The International Labor Commission submits a report on slavery in mandated territories to the Permanent Mandate Commission of the League of Nations. It declares that slavery is widespread in Southwest Africa and New Guinea.... The New York Fund, established by John D. Rockefeller, reports that it has spent more than $9 million dollars to relieve starvation and disease in Europe and China.... Two Japanese scientists visiting Sydney declare that it is altogether ridiculous to claim that Japan has hostile ambitions toward Australia.	The German Reichstag begins an emergency session to address the situation in the Ruhr.... France is threatening to reimpose a travel ban in the wake of the Saturday Ruhr bombing.... The annual Congress of the Irish Labour Party in Dublin is disrupted when the delegates are verbally and physically attacked by a crowd of demonstrators.... Portugal elects Texeira Gomes as its new president over Bernardino Machado.	Morocco holds a *kermasse* to raise funds for memorials to be erected at Rheims and Bamako in honor of the colored troops who fought for France in the war.	The Cunard liner *Laconia*, sailing to New York, will make a special stop in Halifax, Canada, to unload 1,000 passengers, mostly harvesters. All of the British passenger liners report enormous demand for passages to Canada. Britain expects to send 6,000 workers to Canada for the harvest.	The Japanese Home Department has designated funds to encourage emigration.... The postmaster at a Calcutta post office is shot dead by a Bengali robber, who is subsequently captured. In response to the killing, police search a number of houses and discover large quantities of Sinn Fein and Bolshevist literature.

U.S. Politics & Social Issues	U.S. Foreign Policy & Affairs, Defense	U.S. Economy & Environment	Science, Technology & Nature	Culture, Leisure & Lifestyle	
The U.S. Coast Guard seizes the British ship Pessaquid off Cape Hatteras and within the 3-mile limit with 1700 cases of whiskey on board.…An official bulletin on President Harding's health announces that his temperature is 100, pulse 120, and respiration regular. Laboratory findings indicate that the poison is leaving his system. The president's personal physician adds that the crisis is over and Harding is well on his way to recovery.	Relations are strained between the United States and Cuba by the Cuban legislature's adoption of a resolution condemning U.S. interference in Cuban affairs. …Newspapers publish a speech that President Harding intended to give at San Francisco in which he reiterates his advocacy of a World Court.		American Roy Chapman Andrews reports the discovery of a large fossil field in Mongolia. The Natural History Museum of New York, sponsor of the trip, speculates that the find indicates that the dinosaurs of Europe and the United States spread out from some northern paleoarctic regions.	Norwegian explorer Roald Amundsen states that he plans to fly across the North Pole next year. He explains that his expected flight this year could not be made because the machine was not of sufficient power to lift two men and the fuel necessary for the journey.	Aug. 1
Senator Oscar Underwood of Alabama expressed his willingness to accept a Democratic presidential nomination and advocated greater U.S. participation in European affairs.…President Harding dies of apoplexy in his hotel in San Francisco. Calvin Coolidge takes the oath as President of the United States.	At Gibraltar, a memorial tablet is unveiled to the officers and men of the U.S. destroyer *Chauncey*, who lost their lives in a collision while patrolling the Straits of Gibraltar.… Chinese soldiers board an American steamer, *Alice Dollar*, in the Yangtze river and become violent after being refused accommodations and transportation up-river. A squad of American bluejackets from a nearby gunboat arrests 15 Chinese soldiers.… The French Ministry of Foreign Affairs issues a statement rebuking U.S. visitors for violently showing their disapproval when they have found men of color from French colonies sitting near them in public places.		Patients dependent on insulin seek to give themselves injections rather than make bi-weekly visits to a physician or hospital.	Hans Bubendey, a German playwright, completes a play entitled Stinnes, a Grotesque in which the German industrialist of the title is the leading character.	Aug. 2
					Aug. 3
Harding's funeral train begins its journey from San Francisco to Washington, D.C.…About 150 Ku Klux Klansmen gather in Harding's hometown of Marion, OH, to light a fire at midnight and say a prayer for the late president. …Coolidge urges all members of the cabinet and other appointees not to resign.				Captain Finch, Captain Forster, and Mr. Peto make the first ascent of the Dent d'Hérens (13,715 feet.) by the north face in the Pennine Alps in Italy.	Aug. 4
					Aug. 5
All U.S. government business, except routine work and funeral arrangements, is suspended by order of President Coolidge until August 11.…Former presidents Taft and Wilson announce plans to attend Harding's funeral.	The United States signs an extradition treaty with Turkey.			American female swimmer Clemington Corson attempts to swim the English Channel.… American swimmer Henry Sullivan, on his seventh attempt, swims the English Channel from Dover to Calais. It is a length of 56 miles. Sullivan is the third man to swim the channel.	Aug. 6

F	G	H	I	J
Includes campaigns, elections, federal-state relations, civil rights and liberties, crime, the judiciary, education, healthcare, poverty, urban affairs, and population.	*Includes formation and debate of U.S. foreign and defense policies, veterans affairs, and defense spending. (Relations with specific foreign countries are usually found under the region concerned.)*	*Includes business, labor, agriculture, taxation, transportation, consumer affairs, monetary and fiscal policy, natural resources, pollution and industrial accidents.*	*Includes worldwide scientific, medical and technological developments, natural phenomena, U.S. weather and natural disasters.*	*Includes the arts, religion, scholarship, communications media, sports, entertainment, fashions, fads, and social life.*

	World Affairs	Europe	Africa & The Middle East	The Americas	Asia & The Pacific
Aug. 7	The Chinese government at Peking sends an official apology to the British for firing on a British Consular boat at Amoy.…The Princes Georges Tovalou and Marc Tovalou, the sons of the former King of Dahomey, bring proceedings for assault against the proprietor a dance hall in Montmartre, France, from which they were violently ejected because American tourists resented the presence of men of color.	The German mark reaches a new low at 16 million to the pound sterling. Holders of foreign exchange cannot not be induced to sell for marks, which for all practical purposes have ceased to have value.… The women of Bilbao, Spain, send a petition to the Spanish government protesting proposed military operations in Morocco on the grounds that an attack would claim too many of their sons.	J.W. Jolly, Quarantine Superintendent at Haifa, Palestine, is found murdered on the beach by persons unknown.		Government forces attack the main Moro stronghold in the Philippines and breakup a Moro uprising.… An earthquake of moderate intensity strikes Japan.
Aug. 8	The Mixed Commission of the League of Nations on Disarmament approves the text of the draft Treaty for Mutual Guarantees, which will be submitted to the Assembly of the League next month. Italy and France have put their reservations in writing.	Fabrizio, Prince Colonna, Vice-President of the Italian Senate dies at Rome after an operation.… Continual rains are seriously damaging the crops in central Russia and threatening the autumn harvest.			The Wellington, New Zealand, Chamber of Commerce recommends that New Zealand products should be granted a preference by the United Kingdom. The Chamber argues that the Dominions should be assisted to overcome freight handicaps, thus encouraging production and settlement, which would extend the markets for British manufacture.
Aug. 9		Pope Pius XI presents a gold chalice to Catholics in Norway through a visiting cardinal.…The Hamburg, Germany, shipbuilding firm of Blohm and Voss close their yards and lock out employees because of Communist agitation and interference with the running of their works.…A lightning strike breaks out among harbor workers in Danzig who object to being paid in marks and seek dollars instead.	Rhodesia cancels plans to hold an election under the new constitution because of technical difficulties and reschedules them for next April or May.…A white Kenyan man is sentenced to two years in prison for flogging a black African to death for riding a pregnant mare.…A fire in Johannesburg, South African, destroys a block that includes the municipal offices.	A Canadian Pacific Railway train with 400 passengers, mostly harvesters, derails near Warren with two serious injuries.	Australia suspends development of its land, sea, and air forces pending the holding of the Imperial Conference.…The Legislative Council of the Central Provinces in India passes a resolution protesting a magistrate's ban on pro-Gandhi marches at Nagpur.…Burma announces plans to begin aerial surveys of its forests.
Aug. 10	The British government tells the German government that it wants to stabilize the mark, balance the German budget, and impose some form of international control of German financial administration as part of the reparations settlement. Britain also wants Germany to pay as large an amount of reparations payments as is possible according to an estimate by impartial experts.… The Inter-Allied High Commission orders the seizure of mines in the occupied territory because Germany is required to deliver fuel as part of reparations.	Belgium prohibits all exchange operations except for the payments of debts resulting from commerce.…Belgium prohibits the export of potatoes without a license.…The strike in Hamburg, Germany, spreads as three more shipbuilding firms shut down. Crowds of strikers are dispersed by police. Many firms are unable to pay wages while the food shortage is acute and prices rise.… Banknote printers in Berlin go on a lightning strike for a few hours.	Three cases of plague are reported in Syria.…A cholera outbreak is reported in Basra.…The Persian Crown Prince is appointed Governor-General of Azerbaijan.… A new broad-gauge railroad leading from the phosphate deposits in Morocco to the sea opens.… Persian police block demonstrators with black flags from approaching the British Legation in Teheran to protest the expulsion of Shiah Mujtahids from Iraq by King Faisal's government.		The Legislative Council of the Central Provinces in India passes a resolution recommending the abandonment of prosecution of the men arrested in the Home Rule flag dispute.…A representative of the British government declares that the resolution means that the Council endorses civil disobedience.
Aug. 11	As a measure of redress for the Dahomey princes who were expelled from a dancing establishment, Paris police have prohibited the place from opening at night.…George Barthélemy, a Colonial Deputy, announces plans to raise the question of the treatment of French men of color by foreign visitors in the Chamber of Deputies.	Rays of sunshine trigger an explosion at Dannes-Caniers in Paris, one of the principal ammunition bases of the British army during the war.…The Soviet government demands that Bulgaria expel all counterrevolutionary Russian refugees who have taken action against Soviets.…North Sea, Elbe, Weser, and Kaiser Wilhelm Canal pilots go on strike in Germany.			
Aug. 12	The South African *Cape Times* editorializes that the British Dominions are being hurt by trade stagnation caused by the reparations issue. The newspaper wants citizens in the colonies to be consulted on a reparations agreement to which the entire British Empire will be committed.	Thirteen people are killed in a clash between police and strikers in Beslau, Germany…In Silesia, Germany, four strikers are killed in a clash with police that leaves 30 injured and a number of shops plundered.…Food riots occur in Hanover, Germany.…French newspapers report that French banks will prop up the Belgian franc by buying Belgian Treasury Bonds.…Hamburg, Germany, pilots go on strike.…The Cuno government in Germany falls because of the economic situation.	The European Advisory Council of the Bechuanaland Protectorate unanimously requests that the Union of South Africa state the conditions on which the protectorate would be admitted to the union.	The Peru Congress ratifies a constitutional amendment making it possible to reelect a president for a second term.	

A	B	C	D	E
Includes developments that affect more than one world region, international organizations and important meetings of world leaders.	*Includes all domestic and regional developments in Europe, including the Soviet Union.*	*Includes all domestic and regional developments in Africa and the Middle East.*	*Includes all domestic and regional developments in Latin America, the Caribbean, and Canada.*	*Includes all domestic and regional developments in Asian and Pacific nations (and colonies).*

U.S. Politics & Social Issues	U.S. Foreign Policy & Affairs, Defense	U.S. Economy & Environment	Science, Technology & Nature	Culture, Leisure & Lifestyle	
President Harding's funeral train moves slowly through crowds of people in Chicago, with some persons in danger of being forced under the wheels of the train. Movement has been further hampered by young boys who place coins under the wheels to obtain souvenirs.			The Australian Chief Inspector of Fisheries reports that pearls of unusual size and quality are being found, including a 102-grain double button pearl.		Aug. 7
Harding's funeral is held in Washington, D.C. American ships at sea remain motionless during the ceremony.	The U.S. Navy begins a series of maneuvers off the Atlantic coast in the largest assembly of naval aircraft since the close of the war. The maneuvers will continue for a month.				Aug. 8
Harding is buried and all work ceases for two minutes in tribute beginning at five o'clock, the time of the burial.				Clara B. Spence, head of New York City's Spence School for Girls, one of the most famous schools in the United States, dies.	Aug. 9
A day of national mourning is observed for President Harding. He is buried in Marion, OH.…Hotel guests in Long Beach, NY, seize more than 200 cases of liquor that wash ashore. The liquor is rumored to have come from a rumrunner that threw the boxes overboard as it was approached by a Coast Guard cutter or it was hidden at sea and washed loose.…Henry Cabot Lodge and other U.S. Senators from New England announce their support for Calvin Coolidge's presidential nomination.	The United States sign a treaty recognizing Mexico. Out of respect to the late President Harding, negotiations had been suspended until today.				Aug. 10
The Ku Klux Klan holds meetings in Jefferson County, OH, with arrows painted on the roadway to guide KKK members to the meetings.				Argentine swimmer Sebastian Tiraboschi becomes the first to swim the English Channel from the French to the English side, from Calais to Dover.	Aug. 11
The Ku Klux Klan of Oklahoma officially denies involvement with lawlessness. The Klan erects electric fiery crosses in 260 locations throughout the state as a signal of its drive against lawlessness.		Arthur Capper, U.S. Senator from Kansas, tells President Coolidge that the farmers recognize the necessity of diversified farming, are prepared to solve their own problems, and do not seek legislation.…The Department of Agriculture estimates that the value of all farm crops this year will exceed 1922 by $1 billion despite low prices for wheat.		Spanish painter Joaquin Sorolla dies.	Aug. 12

F	G	H	I	J
Includes campaigns, elections, federal-state relations, civil rights and liberties, crime, the judiciary, education, healthcare, poverty, urban affairs, and population.	*Includes formation and debate of U.S. foreign and defense policies, veterans affairs, and defense spending. (Relations with specific foreign countries are usually found under the region concerned.)*	*Includes business, labor, agriculture, taxation, transportation, consumer affairs, monetary and fiscal policy, natural resources, pollution and industrial accidents.*	*Includes worldwide scientific, medical and technological developments, natural phenomena, U.S. weather and natural disasters.*	*Includes the arts, religion, scholarship, communications media, sports, entertainment, fashions, fads, and social life.*

	World Affairs	Europe	Africa & The Middle East	The Americas	Asia & The Pacific
Aug. 13	The Reparations Commission receives a note from the German government that it intends to stop sending deliveries in kind to countries that did not participate in the Ruhr invasion in order to avoid a complete breakdown of the German economic and financial system.	The Reichstag in Germany postpones a scheduled meeting to meet the new cabinet of new chancellor Gustav Stresemann....The Danzig strike over marks ends with workers agreeing to accept marks....Bands of Communists block workers from entering shipyards in Hamburg, Germany....Turkestan notifies the Soviet Government that 387,000 people in Ferghana are expected to starve to death this year....Malaria is also wiping out entire villages throughout the Soviet Union.			
Aug. 14	Greece transports 16,000 Greek refugees from a camp in Constantinople to camps in Salonika and Kavalla. Refugees remain in other towns on the Black Sea....The Persian government complains that the Soviet Union has not turned over the port of Enzeli on the Caspian Sea as stipulated by the Russo-Persian Treaty of 1921.	The Italian government reports that the number of unemployed has dropped from 381,968 on January 1 to 216,590 on June 30....The Italian navy, in its first full-strength assembly since the end of the war, conducts maneuvers near Taranto. Airplanes, seaplanes, and submarines are also participating in the exercises....Violence in the British zone in Germany breaks out at the Bayer dye works as Communist workers blockade entrances to the factory and German police forcibly remove the protesters.	Ghazi Mustafa Kemal Pasha is elected president of the Grand National Assembly in Turkey.		The All-India Congress proclaims a day of mourning in consequence of the recent Kenya decision....The Australian House of Representatives provides funds to help settlers buy wire-netting to help them cope with the rabbit pest....The Madras Legislature in India enacts a Hindu Religious Endowments law that aims to prevent poor administration of temple endowments. Surplus funds will be diverted to support public works.
Aug. 15	The International Maritime Committee discusses the civil immunity granted to government-owned ships....The Anti-Slavery and Aborigines' Protection Society states that slavery today involves more than one million slaves in Abyssinia, Southwest Africa, and Tanganyika. The Society seeks to influence the upcoming League of Nations' investigation into slavery....The last members of the American Relief Committee leave Russia.	Orestias, the new locality designated for the former inhabitants of Karagatch, opposite Adrianople, who are to be displaced as a result of the Treaty of Lausanne, is inaugurated....France launches a light cruiser as part of its plan to reconstitute the French navy by using light cruisers, destroyers, and torpedo boats to scout for battleships....Eamon de Valera, Irish Republican leader, is arrested in Ennis, Ireland.	General Jan Smuts of South Africa appeals to South Africans to stand together with Great Britain in its efforts to save Europe from destruction.	Canadian newspapers voice support for a plan to unite the Allies on a common reparations policy.	A new government has formed in Tasmania, Australia, with Walter Lee as Premier....Tidal waves in northwest Korea sweep away hundreds of houses with the number of dead estimated at more than 1,000.... New Zealand reduces its income tax by 20 percent.
Aug. 16	The Reparations Commission warns the German government against issuing a new gold loan because Germany must pay reparations before it can make any interest payments....The Women's League for Peace and Freedom opens its conference in Prague, Czechoslovakia, with delegates from 20 countries.	The report on the inspection of Ellis Island by Auckland Geddes, British Ambassador to the United States is published as a White Paper. Geddes describes the buildings, ventilation, and sanitation for immigrants as unsuitable. He largely blames immigrants for the dirty situation....The Rhineland High Commission has decided to prolong indefinitely the travel barrier separating occupied from unoccupied Germany.	Afghan raiders damage the Persian telegraph line near Seistan and kill one linesman. Persian camelry are in pursuit.... In retaliation for the dismissal of all Iraq-born officials from Persian governmental posts, Iraqi newspapers urge the Iraq government to dismiss all officials of Persian origin.	At a conference of representatives from industry and business, Jamaicans resolve that the future of the island hinges on an adequate means of sea transportation for the export of Jamaican products and the import of commodities of other countries.	
Aug. 17	The government of Hungary publicly expresses fears about the continued failure of the Allied Powers and the Reparation Committee to reach a decision that would enable Hungary to negotiate a loan through the League of Nations.	The cost of living in Germany rises 190 percent in one week....The German government plans a large increase in all postal, telegraph, and telephone rates....The Hamburg shipyard workers strike ends....Portugal ratifies the Geneva Convention of 1921 dealing with the traffic in women and children....The floating dock delivered to Greece by Germany on account of reparations arrives in Athens.	The Zionist Congress resolves by a large majority to extend the Jewish Agency for Palestine by the inclusion of representatives of Jewish communities from various countries. The Congress also adopts a budget providing funds for the colonization of Palestine....The Khedive of Egypt purchases the yacht, *Meteor*, which had been owned by Kaiser Wilhelm of Germany....Platinum is discovered in the Waterberg of the Transvaal.	Representatives of the United States and Mexico sign a treaty providing for a claims commission to settle claims of Maricans against Mexico and Mexicans against the United States. The Mexican claims largely involve the occupation of Vera Cruz and the Pershing Expedition. American claims involve the expropriation of lands. The Hague Court is asked to provide a judge for claims. Petroleum rights acquired before the adoption of the new Mexican Constitution are confirmed.	The New Zealand Naval Defense Report calls for the expansion of the sea-going squadron to three light cruisers, an oil tanker, and a submarine unit....Flooding in Burma leaves about 12,000 people homeless....Bandits in Tsaoshih, China, set fire to the London Mission hospital, the foreign quarters, and the Catholic church before looting the town....Sailors on German steamships in Australian waters complain that the collapse of the mark has left them with only a few cents in Australian money per month.
Aug. 18		Romanian and Soviet military representative meet to discuss measures for preventing clashes between their respective border guards.... Soviet authorities in Riga report that Vladimir Lenin's physical condition has improved, but his speech and nervous condition continue to cause anxiety.			The government of India publishes a White Paper on the Kenya situation that supports the British position, but expresses regret over restrictions on Indian immigration....A typhoon strikes Hong Kong, uprooting trees, snapping telegraph poles, and leaving debris scattered through the streets.

A	B	C	D	E
Includes developments that affect more than one world region, international organizations and important meetings of world leaders.	*Includes all domestic and regional developments in Europe, including the Soviet Union.*	*Includes all domestic and regional developments in Africa and the Middle East.*	*Includes all domestic and regional developments in Latin America, the Caribbean, and Canada.*	*Includes all domestic and regional developments in Asian and Pacific nations (and colonies).*

	U.S. Politics & Social Issues	U.S. Foreign Policy & Affairs, Defense	U.S. Economy & Environment	Science, Technology & Nature	Culture, Leisure & Lifestyle
Aug. 13	Pirates posing as bootleggers attempt to seize a 70-ton schooner carrying champagne and whiskey off Long Island, NY.	The Secretary of the Navy approves a 20-year plan to improve naval bases in the Philippines, Guam, and Samoa. The plan sets $2 million aside for improvements at Pearl Harbor in Hawaii.	A head-on collision between two passenger trains in Pueblo, CO, kills nine railroad employees but no passengers.	A Dutch firm investigates the possibility of using the new element hafnium in the manufacture of audion lamps in wireless telegraphy.…The Pan-Pacific Scientific Congress, in which 14 countries are participating, opens in Australia.…Reports from the Greenland sealing grounds state that several ships have catches of more than 2,000 seals, but the weather has hampered hunting.	Five tourists are killed while attempting to climb mountains in the Alps between Switzerland and Austria.…Cardinal Gasparri issues a circular letter to the Bishops of Italy calling on them to take energetic steps for the proper preservation of historical and artistic works in the possession of the Catholic Church and warning them against frequent attempts of art dealers to acquire such works.
Aug. 14	James Davis, the U.S. Secretary of Labor, states that he supports selective immigration. He also reports that he has heard rumors of 1,000 aliens per week entering the U.S. illegally.…Tulsa County in Oklahoma is placed under martial law by the governor because of continued violence by the Ku Klux Klan.		An explosion at Kemmerer, WY, kills 135 coalminers.….In response to protests about the high price of gasoline, Standard Oil of Indiana drops the price of a gallon to 16.4 cents in its Midwest territory.…The governor of Nebraska, C.W. Bryan, threatens private-owned corporations in his state with competition from state-owned gas stations unless the price of fuel is reduced immediately. Bryan also asks the federal government to prosecute the oil companies for violating the Anti-Trust Law.		President Harding's estate is estimated at $750,000 with his wife as the chief beneficiary.
Aug. 15		President Coolidge declares that he will respond to any request for aid in Europe as long as it does not involve the United States in controversy or impose obligations.…Coolidge also supports the formation of a commission of disinterested experts to determine Germany's ability to pay reparations.			
Aug. 16	The police in Macon, GA, capture three men who were flogging two African Americans. Georgia police have formed a motorcycle squad to pursue floggers, while the governor of Georgia has threatened to impose martial law if the floggings continue.	Canadian authorities seize the U.S. gunboat *Gopher* for damaging a lock in the Welland Canal. The ship carried naval reservists on an instruction cruise through the Great Lakes.	The Department of Agriculture announces a quarantine as of November 1 on all imports of fruits and vegetables except those arriving from Canada. The restriction is aimed at keeping fruit and melon flies out of the country.		
Aug. 17	President Coolidge appoints C. Bascom Sharp as his secretary. Sharp, a member of the Republican National Committee of Virginia, spent 14 years in the U.S. House of Representatives.…The Russian General Alexander Loukomsky, who arrived in New York with his family, is admitted to the United States after initially being refused because the Russian quota had been filled.		An underground tank with a capacity of 500,000 barrels that is owned by the General Petroleum Company in San Pedro, CA, explodes as a result of spontaneous combustion and shakes the entire city. The resulting fire has prompted hundreds of people to flee their homes.		
Aug. 18					

F	G	H	I	J
Includes campaigns, elections, federal-state relations, civil rights and liberties, crime, the judiciary, education, healthcare, poverty, urban affairs, and population.	*Includes formation and debate of U.S. foreign and defense policies, veterans affairs, and defense spending. (Relations with specific foreign countries are usually found under the region concerned.)*	*Includes business, labor, agriculture, taxation, transportation, consumer affairs, monetary and fiscal policy, natural resources, pollution and industrial accidents.*	*Includes worldwide scientific, medical and technological developments, natural phenomena, U.S. weather and natural disasters.*	*Includes the arts, religion, scholarship, communications media, sports, entertainment, fashions, fads, and social life.*

	World Affairs	Europe	Africa & The Middle East	The Americas	Asia & The Pacific
Aug. 19	The Stresemann government in Germany expects that no help will be forthcoming from the Allies in the wake of disagreements between Britain and France over Ruhr policy.	Germany opens an agricultural bank to finance potato growers....The general absence of butter, margarine, and fats in Germany is reported to be easing....France is battling a huge forest fire just outside of Paris....The British dock strike ends.	Spain suffers heavy casualties on the Melilla front in Morocco as Moors attack and kills 155 Spanish soldiers.	President Obregon of Mexico asserts that recent negotiations with the United States have not altered Mexican law nor diminished the rights of Mexicans.	A procession with Gandhi flags is allowed to march through Nagpur, India, after a compromise between the government and leaders of the noncooperation movement.
Aug. 20	An international Anti-Alcohol Congress opens in Copenhagen, Denmark.... The American Steel Company attempts to use the Treaty of Versailles to collect a claim from a German shipbuilding company. The Greek government, which hired the German company to build the still-unfinished armored cruiser, seeks the return of its money on the grounds that the Treaty of Versailles prohibits the manufacture of war material in Germany and its exportation abroad.	The Spanish Treasury begins an aerial photographic survey of the country as a basis for an effective system of land taxation....Italian Communists are reported to have received funding from the Soviet Union....The Communist International Committee decides to grant the German proletariat one million gold marks and issues a declaration that all the world's workmen will help the Germans....The French forest fire continues to rage with many villages destroyed.	Fighting in Morocco between Spanish and Moorish forces is reported to be hand-to-hand. A Spanish column is ambushed by Moors, with women shouting encouragement to the Moorish men. The Moors are reported to have lost 500 men while Spanish losses are estimated at 250.... Persia is struck by earthquakes.	A fire at the Wawa Hotel on the Lake of Bays, Ontario, leaves nine people burned to death and many injured.	Australia declares plans to dismantle HMA *Australia*. The 18,800-ton battleship, launched in 1911, is being scrapped under the Washington Agreement...An anti-Soviet Muslim uprising in Central Asia prompts the Soviet administration in Azerbaijan to order Muslim religious leaders to issue proclamations calling on all Muslims to defend the Soviet government....The Congress Working Committee in India states that it recognizes the government's right to regulate processions.
Aug. 21	Poland decides not to join the Little Entente because of a possible conflict of interest with the country's commitments under the Treaty of Versailles and a treaty with Russia....The Belgian government announces that it will publish a Gray Book containing all the correspondence exchanged between Belgium and the Allied countries on the subject of reparations.	All newspapers in Athens, Greece, suspend publication because of a strike of printers and news vendors....The Soviet Union announces plans to establish a Ukrainian National Army composed of men of various ages to serve only in the Ukraine....The Minister of Education in Malta resigns after failing to pass legislation in which English and Italian would be the languages of instruction in elementary schools....Leipzig Fair authorities in Germany have been empowered to issue emergency currency to facilitate monetary transactions at the fair.	Fighting continues in Morocco between Spanish and Moorish forces. The Moors have opened a second front, in the West....France sends army detachments and a camel corps to the frontier between Syria and Turkey to stop raids by Turkish Kurds on Syrian Bedouins....A railroad is completed in South Africa connecting Belmont, on the main Cape Town to Kimberly line, with Douglas, the oldest town on the Transvaal. Requests for extension of the railroad across the Vaal have already been made.	The Canadian-Pacific Company's liner *Empress of Scotland* strikes submerged drifting wreckage during her voyage from Hamburg, Germany, to Southampton, England. The ship is escorted under her own steam by five tugs to port but is unable to sail until repairs are made....Canadian cattle exporters object to British branding regulations on the grounds of unnecessary cruelty.	A Japanese submarine, number 77, on its trial run sinks in a heavy sea off Awaji Island in 160 feet of water. Only five of the 88 men on board, including the commander are saved....The government geologist of Tasmania, Australia, estimates that the oil shale reserves situated in five separate fields in Tasmania are rich enough to supply Australia with oil for 20 years.
Aug. 22	Muslims from Tashkend, Afghanistan, Egypt, Algeria, Bombay, Peking, and several other locations urge all Muslims to adopt a common language. They suggest Turkish as that language because Turkey is the champion of Islam. They call for a conference of Muslims to be held at Angora, Turkey, to discuss the language question.	France completes a loan of five million francs to Belgium. The loan will be repaid by installments over a 20-year period....The lock-out of miners in the Ruhr continues....Irish Republican rebels stop a prison van in the streets of Dublin and free 15 prisoners being transported from one jail to another....Russia announces plans to rebuild the Russo-Persian telegraph line.	The Spanish garrison in Morocco is relieved after the men had run out of water. The rebelling Moors retreat in the face of an attack by 20,000 Spaniards. Airplanes and seaplanes drop bombs on the Moors.	The Canadian Colonization Association holds a meeting to consider ways of retaining British harvesters in Canada. The association has 1,200 parcels of land available for purchase on a 32-year payment plan.	The government of India reduces the maximum age limit for military officers to attend Staff College. The age limit drops from 35 years to 33 years to secure able, young men.
Aug. 23	France declares that the occupation of the Ruhr is legal and within the terms of the Versailles Treaty. The French government argues that resistance in the Ruhr does not come from the population but from the government of Germany. France further states that Germany can quickly pay the reparations that are due and that it will not leave the Ruhr until payments are made.	The Berlin Town Council suspends tram service in Berlin until it can be reorganized to stop massive losses....The Soviet Union is conscripting men between the ages of 23 and 26 for service in the Territorial Army. The War Revolutionary Council has the power to recruit younger men if necessary.			
Aug. 24	The United States accept an offer to send representatives to the next assembly of the League of Nations....China declares that it intends to demand from the Great Powers a statement of the conditions under which they would grant China complete independence and would abandon the principle of extra-territoriality.	Spain begins transporting 20,000 soldiers to Morocco to stop the rebellion by the Moors.... Coalminers in the Ruhr return to work after agreeing to an interim payment of 16 million marks....The first torpedo airplane is delivered to France after completing trials. It is a Levasseur machine with a 1,540-pound torpedo suspended under the fuselage. The airplane can attain a height of 9,000 feet in 35 minutes....The Soviet Union sends a note to Great Britain reiterating its claim to Wrangel Island and asserting that the raising of the British flag is a violation of Russian sovereign rights.	A continent of native soldiers from Mozambique, who fought in South Angola during the war, arrives in Lisbon, Portugal, to witness the decoration of their regiment's flag.	Three-hundred Russian immigrants arrive in Montreal on their way to western Canada. They are the advance guard of thousands of Russian who are expected before winter. The Russians had first immigrated to Germany before heading to Canada.	Admiral Baron Kato, Prime Minister of Japan, dies. Count Uchida, the Foreign Minister, is chosen by the Cabinet to act as Prime Minister.... Bandits set fire to the Italian Catholic Church at Tzeho, China and attempt to seize the priest. The Italian ambassador makes a strong protest and states that he holds the Chinese government responsible for this offense.... The New Zealand House of Representatives passes a Dairy Produce Export Control Act that establishes a pool of dairy products for export and creates a board to regulate dairy exports.
	A *Includes developments that affect more than one world region, international organizations and important meetings of world leaders.*	B *Includes all domestic and regional developments in Europe, including the Soviet Union.*	C *Includes all domestic and regional developments in Africa and the Middle East.*	D *Includes all domestic and regional developments in Latin America, the Caribbean, and Canada.*	E *Includes all domestic and regional developments in Asian and Pacific nations (and colonies).*

U.S. Politics & Social Issues	U.S. Foreign Policy & Affairs, Defense	U.S. Economy & Environment	Science, Technology & Nature	Culture, Leisure & Lifestyle	
	In accord with the provisions of the Washington Disarmament Conference agreement, the Secretary of the Navy begins scrapping 28 naval ships, including 11 under construction. The public is offered the opportunity to buy scraps.				Aug. 19
A large Ku Klux Klan demonstration is held in Toms River, NJ. Eight-hundred men and women parade while accompanied by a brass band and a group of men holding a fiery cross. The demonstration concludes with a service at a Methodist Church.	The army holds an aircraft demonstration along 800 miles of the Atlantic coast to demonstrate to the public the necessity of maintaining a large air fleet.		Two mounds of hard earth at Melhus, Norway, that are believed to date from the 4th century are opened. Ashes and charred human bones are discovered. Red earthenware utensils are found in one mound.	French authorities ban D.W. Griffith's *Birth of a Nation.* The American film is prohibited because of its depiction of men of color. The Prefecture of Police states that the ban is for the good of the people.	Aug. 20
	Secretary of the Treasury Andrew Mellon tells President Coolidge that it is impossible to see how the United States can help improve the reparations situation and that any attempt to do so should be resisted.	A delegation of bankers and businessmen urges Coolidge to find some method, official or unofficial, of improving the European situation. They state that American prosperity, especially the prosperity of American agriculture, is inextricably interwoven with the welfare of Europe. They do not offer any concrete suggestions.	The Eastern Telegraph Company, at work on a cable off the coast of South Africa, reports that the ocean bed has risen from three miles to ¾ of a mile. The increase suggests an earthquake.…The largest reinforced concrete bridge in the world opens across the Seine at St. Pierre-du-Vauvray, France. The bridge is about 400 feet long and 25 feet wide.	Mrs. Andre Hahn, an American, agrees to place her "La Belle Ferronnière," a painting by Leonardo da Vinci beside the canvas of the same title in the collection of the Louvre museum in Paris. Art experts will determine which canvas is the original work. Hahn has sued an art expert for damages for declaring that her painting is not the original.	Aug. 21
	President Coolidge declares that he sees no need to alter the present U.S. policy of aloofness toward Europe. He perceives no practical method of rendering aid to Europe.…Coolidge also states that he supports a reorganization of the Merchant Marine.…The naval ship *Gopher* sinks in the Gulf of St. Lawrence in a gale while being towed from Montreal to Boston.	A 900-ton whaler with auxiliary engines in additional to her sails is being built in San Francisco. It will be fitted out especially for trade with the Eskimo of the Canadian Arctic.	Inventor Thomas Edison is reported to have fallen ill after a camping trip, but his condition is not regarded as serious.	The Boy Scouts announce plans to hold a world congress of scouts in Copenhagen, Denmark, next year.	Aug. 22
			The world's largest airplane, the Barling Bomber, is tested at Dayton, OH. Walter Barling of England designed the 20-ton ship with six 400 horsepower Liberty motors. It can ascend to 2500 feet and reach a speed of 93 miles per hour.		Aug. 23
Senator Underwood, expected to be a candidate for the Democratic presidential nomination, declares that Europe needs the strong hand of a strong government standing for peace. He urges the United States to help restore order in Europe and advises that American industry is too mature to need the protection offered by tariffs.		Miners in the anthracite coal country of Pennsylvania announce plans to strike on September 1. The Miner's Union will permit 4,000 miners to operate pumps and carry on the work necessary to keep the mines from flooding during the suspension of normal work.		The New York State Athletic Commission grants a license for the boxing match between Jack Dempsey and Luis Firpo on September 14.	Aug. 24
F *Includes campaigns, elections, federal-state relations, civil rights and liberties, crime, the judiciary, education, healthcare, poverty, urban affairs, and population.*	G *Includes formation and debate of U.S. foreign and defense policies, veterans affairs, and defense spending. (Relations with specific foreign countries are usually found under the region concerned.)*	H *Includes business, labor, agriculture, taxation, transportation, consumer affairs, monetary and fiscal policy, natural resources, pollution and industrial accidents.*	I *Includes worldwide scientific, medical and technological developments, natural phenomena, U.S. weather and natural disasters.*	J *Includes the arts, religion, scholarship, communications media, sports, entertainment, fashions, fads, and social life.*	

	World Affairs	Europe	Africa & The Middle East	The Americas	Asia & The Pacific
Aug. 25	Chancellor Stresemann denies that Germany deliberately brought about the collapse of the mark. He adds that such an act would be a crime against the German people.	Spanish soldiers at Malaga, scheduled to embark for Morocco, mutiny. One officer is killed and several mutineers are injured.... Czechoslovakia announces plans to build a memorial to the nation's emancipation in 1918.		The government of Quebec, Canada, decides to establish a school for printers.	Japan has begun scrapping war ships under the provisions of the Washington Treaty. It has flattened the turrets of two battleship and two battle-cruisers. The number of officers, noncommissioned officers, and men has also been reduced.
Aug. 26		The Port of London Corporation announces that 50,063 rats were destroyed in vessels and building at the port in 1922. Since the corporation began systematic extermination in 1901, 1,260,483 rats have been killed....An English man is fined for selling milk containing 6.9 percent water and told to leave the profession of milk selling.			The Japanese Cabinet formally resigns in accord with convention. Count Uchida remains in office pending the appointment of a new prime minister.
Aug. 27		The first airplane built entirely in Romania lands at the Bucarest airport....The German ex-Crown Prince announces in an interview with a Dutch journalist that he intends to ask the German government for permission to return to Germany and live in Silesia.	The Turkish government cancels all decorations awarded by former regimes and will grant no more recognitions to foreigners....Cholera is slowly abating in Iraq. Only isolated cases are reported in Baghdad.	British harvesters in Canada complain that at a protest meeting in Winnipeg that they had been misled and have been unable to secure employment because of their inexperience.	The Japanese government announces that its sunken submarine, number 77, has still not been raised and that 88 bodies remain on board. It is likely that a month will lapse before the ship is salved.
Aug. 28	France tells Germany that it will stay in the Ruhr unless it is paid....British troops evacuate from Constantinople, Turkey.	Spanish police discover 100 bottles of cocaine in a Madrid apartment.	Zaghlul Pasha announces that he will sail from France to Egypt on September 12.	Immigration to Canada in July was 80 percent more than in July 1922. Most of the immigrants have come from the United Kingdom....The Alberta, Canada wheat crop is expected to double the yield obtained in 1922.	
Aug. 29		Norway announces plans to reorganize its military forces. The Defense Commission states that the air branches of the army and navy will be united while a construction department will be established.... Eamonn de Valera, currently under British arrest, is elected as the representative for Clare in Irish elections.		The U.S. government acknowledges that it is has examined cable messages from Cubans in the United States.	General Wu Pei-fu tells the Chinese government that he desires to organize a special force for the suppression of bandits in the Yangtze provinces....Admiral Count Yamamoto of the Satsuma clan is chosen to head the Japanese government.
Aug. 30	The League of Nations proposes to address the international traffic in obscene publications.	The French rigid airship, *Dixmude*, a Zeppelin surrendered by Germany, embarks on a voyage of 6,000 miles to Dakar in Africa....Norway agrees to sell 4,000 tons of cured fish to Russia.		The Academy of Brazil decides to cooperate in the compilation of a Portuguese dictionary and to give assistance in preserving the uniformity of the language spoken in Portugal and Brazil.	The government of South Australia demands the construction of a north-south railroad through Australia. The South Australian Premier Henry Barwell said that is impossible to develop the territory without a railroad going straight through it.
Aug. 31	Bavarian newspapers object to Germany's entrance into the League of Nations.	A German Communist in Moscow, Russia, states that Communism is rapidly growing stronger in Germany and will seize power next spring.		The Chinese Consul-General for Canada is recalled to report on the amendments to the Canadian Immigration Bill that limit Chinese immigration. This action is not regarded as a break of relations between Canada and China, according to representative of both governments.	
Sep. 1	The League of Nations considers membership applications from Abyssinia and Ireland....The Chairman of the International Red Cross denies a request by two Irish delegates to investigate the treatment of Irish war prisoners in prisons and internment camps.... Italy bombards and invades Corfu. Most of the 15 people killed in the attack are reported to be Greek and Armenian refugees. Surviving refugees have scattered in a panic throughout the city. Greek authorities surrendered immediately.	Four miners are killed in an explosion in a Belgian coalmine....The Metropolitan of Athens resigns because of differences with the Greek Minister of Religion....Miners in Cologne, Germany, continue to strike and attempt to persuade other miners to join them....The Bishop of Kherson, who resisted Soviet efforts to confiscate church valuables, is put on trial for counter-revolutionary activity in Russia.	Turkey sends the Persian ambassador back to Persia because his letters of credit referred to the Ottoman Empire. He will be allowed to return with fresh letters....The Turkish Minister of Instruction publishes a circular banning the title "Sultanic" from schools.... Rhodesia seeks a British loan to pay off its liabilities....The Italian government sends plainclothes police to Tangier, Morocco, to protect the Italian Legation.	A fire at Camp Borden in Saskatchewan, Canada, destroys airplanes, hangars, and other property....The Canadian government authorizes the slaughter of 2,000 buffalo (American bison) in order to reduce the herd in the Wainwright National Park in Alberta.	A major earthquake strikes Japan.

A	B	C	D	E
Includes developments that affect more than one world region, international organizations and important meetings of world leaders.	*Includes all domestic and regional developments in Europe, including the Soviet Union.*	*Includes all domestic and regional developments in Africa and the Middle East.*	*Includes all domestic and regional developments in Latin America, the Caribbean, and Canada.*	*Includes all domestic and regional developments in Asian and Pacific nations (and colonies).*

U.S. Politics & Social Issues	U.S. Foreign Policy & Affairs, Defense	U.S. Economy & Environment	Science, Technology & Nature	Culture, Leisure & Lifestyle	
					Aug. 25
	About 10,000 Ku Klux Klan members gather in the hills above Pittsburgh, PA, in the afternoon. At midnight, they begin to march toward the city but are met by hundreds of people at Glendale Bridge who have blocked the bridge with automobiles. The Klansmen try to force a passage, shots are fired, and one Klansman is killed.				Aug. 26
					Aug. 27
			A British medical commission observes that cases of cancer have tripled in two generations. The physicians state that no evidence shows a food or hereditary link to cancer. The cause is believed to be continued irritation, such as that of a clay pipe on the lip or a jagged tooth rubbing against the cheek.		Aug. 28
				Louvre officials block the disputed da Vinci painting owned by Mrs. Andre Hahn from being displayed in the museum. Only national property can be displayed in a national museum.	Aug. 29
			The bodies of British mountaineer Henry Hayden and his two guides are discovered at the foot of the Agassizhorn in Switzerland.		Aug. 30
Sixteen ships are racing across the Atlantic Ocean in an effort to land their passengers in time to be included in the September immigration quotas. The ships contain 10,000 prospective immigrants.	The United States formally recognize Mexico after a hiatus in diplomatic relations of nine years and four months.				Aug. 31
The United States has refused admission to 1,800 immigrants because the four steamers that carried them entered American waters a few minutes too early for the September quota. The immigrants fall under the August quota, which has already been filled. The ships were maneuvering for favorable positions when a strong tide pulled them over the limit into U.S. waters.... Immigration Commissioner Curran states that the law cannot be relaxed to aid the unfortunate immigrants. He blames the captains for being hasty.	The American Bar Association approves a proposal that the United States should participate in the membership of the Permanent Court of International Justice at The Hague.... Charles Evans Hughes, Secretary of State, gives a speech on the Monroe Doctrine at Minneapolis. He justifies the actions of the United States in Cuba, Santo Domingo, and Haiti and states that the United States has no interest in establishing a protectorate.			A fashion exhibition in New York City shows that tubular lines in dresses remain in style. Embroidered coats in new patterns, in both colors and metal, and without fur collars are introduced by designers.	Sep. 1

F	G	H	I	J
Includes campaigns, elections, federal-state relations, civil rights and liberties, crime, the judiciary, education, healthcare, poverty, urban affairs, and population.	*Includes formation and debate of U.S. foreign and defense policies, veterans affairs, and defense spending. (Relations with specific foreign countries are usually found under the region concerned.)*	*Includes business, labor, agriculture, taxation, transportation, consumer affairs, monetary and fiscal policy, natural resources, pollution and industrial accidents.*	*Includes worldwide scientific, medical and technological developments, natural phenomena, U.S. weather and natural disasters.*	*Includes the arts, religion, scholarship, communications media, sports, entertainment, fashions, fads, and social life.*

	World Affairs	Europe	Africa & The Middle East	The Americas	Asia & The Pacific
Sep. 2	Greece appeals to the League of Nations for help in Corfu. It also protests against the expulsion of all Greek newspaper correspondents from Italy....The Conference of Ambassadors sends the Greek government a note protesting against the murders of Italian General Tellini and his companions who are widely presumed to have been killed by Greeks.	Hundreds of Danish fishermen are reported to be missing and many small vessels are lost after what is reported as the worst hurricane to strike Denmark since 1909....Norwegian Customs captures a large, black-painted nameless ship near Bergen. No people were on board and only some German cans containing liquor were found below deck.		Charles Fitzpatrick, Lieutenant Governor of the Province of Quebec, is elected a chief of the Huron tribe in recognition of the great interest that he has always taken in the welfare of the Indians.	An earthquake strikes Turkestan in the Soviet Union and destroys several villages.
Sep. 3	The League of Nations Assembly opens in Geneva with de la Torriente of Cuba chosen as president over a Swiss candidate....The Prime Minister of Australia, Stanley Bruce, states that crisis between Italy and Greece is regarded as very serious since both are members of the League of Nations and one had taken direct action. Bruce fears that a deathblow will be struck at the League.	A British Member of Parliament, J.H. Thomas, declares in a speech that the drums of war are beating again. He argues that all the elements that contributed to the last war are manifest in the current crisis.			Persia passes legislation removing all foreigners from government posts.
Sep. 4	Portugal submits a report to the League of Nations denying that blacks in St. Thomas' Island and Prince's Island are held in slavery.		Kurds attack a French garrison in northern Syria. After five hours of fighting, the French surrender and are beheaded by the Kurds.		Iraq suffers an earthquake at Sinjar....The press in Iraq is seeking the removal of all Indians from government posts.
Sep. 5	The International Police Congress discusses a common language for the purpose of international police discourse and a common code for the transmission of police requisitions and descriptions of subjects. Latin is rejected as a language with English, French, or German expected to be the final choice. The final creation of a code is left to the International Police Bureau, while international telegraphic code will be used until a standard is established.				Japanese officials announce that the recent 7.9-magnitude earthquake that rocked their country on September 1 has resulted in property damages exceeding billions of dollars.
Sep. 6	The Turkish Evacuation Commission takes possession of the islands of Imbros and Tendos, which Greece is evacuating in accord with the Treaty of Lausanne.	German economists report that the recent influx of American dollars arriving in Germany has been sufficiently large enough for Germany to establish a new currency.			
Sep. 7	U.S. General Henry Allen publicly warns Americans that an attempt at economic isolation will only backfire and result in the troubles of other nations arriving at the U.S.'s shores. He adds, "It is unthinkable that we should pursue a policy of aloofness."	At the start of this week, the exchange rate between the German mark and the British pound sterling was 47 million. Today, the exchange rate is 240 million....The German government estimates the number of unemployed at nearly half a million. A bill for unemployment insurance is stalled in the Reichstag, which is in recess. Relief works on a large scale are being discussed by the government.			
Sep. 8		German economists report that the number of paper marks in circulation has increased from 116 trillion to 273 trillion in a single week.			The U.S. dispatches three additional diplomats to Japan to assist in reconstruction efforts following the country's 7.9-magnitude earthquake.

A	B	C	D	E
Includes developments that affect more than one world region, international organizations and important meetings of world leaders.	*Includes all domestic and regional developments in Europe, including the Soviet Union.*	*Includes all domestic and regional developments in Africa and the Middle East.*	*Includes all domestic and regional developments in Latin America, the Caribbean, and Canada.*	*Includes all domestic and regional developments in Asian and Pacific nations (and colonies).*

U.S. Politics & Social Issues	U.S. Foreign Policy & Affairs, Defense	U.S. Economy & Environment	Science, Technology & Nature	Culture, Leisure & Lifestyle	
William McAdoo's bid for the Democratic presidential nomination is reported to be gaining strength.	Senator Oscar Underwood declares his support for the World Court with the League of Nations. He argues that the Court would be ineffective without the League.	Following the rejection of several compromises, 158,000 anthracite miners go on strike in New York.		Tennis star "Big Bill" Tilden and R.N. Williams of the United States defeat J.O. Anderson and J.B. Hawkes of Australia to win the Davis Cup at Forest Hills, NY.	Sep. 2
		A survey of broadcasting stations reveals that there are 581 listed as active. Many of these stations have ceased to operate, however, with only 450 in working order. Most of the closed stations suffered from financial problems but some fell to more popular competitors.			Sep. 3
	The United States support the demands of the Diplomatic Corps at Peking for damages from the Chinese government. The government trusts the various legations to determine the compensation that is appropriate.			Sevid Abbas, Imam of Mecca, arrives in Jerusalem with 12,500 guineas that have been given by the pilgrims to Mecca for the restoration of the Dome of the Rock (Qubbet-es Sakhra) and the Aksa Mosque in the Sacred Enclosure.	Sep. 4
				The American Consul in Paris hears evidence about the authenticity of the Leonardo da Vinci painting "La Belle Ferroniere" owned by Mrs. Hahn of Kansas City. Hahn hopes to obtain evidence to be used in a court case against an American art expert who proclaimed her da Vinci to be a forgery.	Sep. 5
		Snow strikes Northern Michigan and Minnesota, while frost strikes North Dakota, Wyoming, and Montana.			Sep. 6
A military court in Tulsa County, OK, hears testimony concerning the activity of masked bands of men from the Ku Klux Klan who beat anyone who displeases them.					Sep. 7
Governor John C. Walton of Oklahoma announces his intentions to impose martial law if lawless elements of the local Klu Klux Klan chapter continue to run rampant. N.W. Jewett, Grand Dragon of the Oklahoma Realm of the Klan, had earlier stated that Walton could never "break the power of the Klu Klux Klan in Oklahoma."					Sep. 8

	World Affairs	Europe	Africa & The Middle East	The Americas	Asia & The Pacific
Sep. 9		One of the detachments of troops from the Political Department guarding government buildings in Moscow mutinies. The trouble apparently began because commanding officers prevent the men from communicating with relatives who are not members of the Communist Party.			Stories continue to emerge from Japan about the earthquake. In the Sonjo district of Tokyo, a crowd of about 1,000 people sought safety in a large open space surrounded by flames. The heat became terrific and sparks set fire to the clothing of scores of people. These people set others in the group on fire. Only about 200 survivors of the fire are reported.
Sep. 10		The Union of Soviet Socialist Republics introduces arms that place the hammer and scythe around a globe that is surrounded by the Soviet star. The slogan, printed on a wreath, calls upon the world's proletariat to unite in Russian, Ukrainian, Tartar, Georgian, Armenian, and White Russian.		A tidal wave destroys the Mexican fishing town of San José de Cabo on the southern coast of Lower California.	
Sep. 11	The government of Italy announces that it will remain in possession of Corfu until Greece executes the men who killed Italian diplomats near Janima. Italy states that it believes only the presence of troops will make the Greeks carry out their obligations. Reparation of Corfu was expected to occur on September 12.... The Conference of Ambassadors meets to discuss the Italian evacuation of Corfu.	France begins its first grand military maneuvers since the end of the war in the Rhone Valley. Four army corps are engaged. For the first time, cavalry squadrons will use attached motorized machine guns. There will also be squadrons of caterpillar-track automobiles, machine gun battalions, and divisional reconnaissance groups.	Six men are killed in a clash between Greek and Turkish frontier guards on an island in the Maritza. The Greeks successfully repulse a Turkish attempt to occupy the island.		
Sep. 12		Germany has begun fixing wages every Wednesday at the Ministry of Finance on the basis of an index calculated by the Reich Statistical Office. However, wages may depreciate to a tenth of their value by the time that they are spent because of the continuing fall of the mark.... The Bulgarian government arrests leaders of the Communist and Agrarian parties because of rumors that they were planning to attack the government.	More British troops leave Turkey.... The Egyptian government explains that it sent medical doctors and stores to the Hejaz to help with an outbreak of cholera. It did not intend to trigger a confrontation with the government of Hejaz.		The foreign consuls at Kobe, Japan, meet to organize mail distribution to earthquake refugees. The Emperor of Japan issues an edict appealing to official and private persons to cooperate in the effort to reconstruct the devastated areas and restore national pride....By order of the police, Peking, China, is covered in flags to celebrate the attempt by Parliament to hold a national election.
Sep. 13					Epidemics of dysentery, typhus, and scarlet fever are spreading throughout Tokyo, Japan.
Sep. 14		Yugoslavia sends a note to Bulgaria threatening to invade if the Yugoslavia border is crossed by any of the *komitadji* bands alleged to be making preparations in Bulgarian territory.			
Sep. 15	Greece turns over the city of Karagach to Turkey.	A Norwegian sailing vessel wrecks near Spitzbergen with a catch of over 200 seals and 14 polar bears. The crew is rescued.... Yugoslavia informs the government of Bulgaria that large numbers of *komitadji* bands have been formed on Bulgarian territory and are preparing to invade Yugoslavia. Such an invasion would be considered an act of war and Yugoslavia would occupy strategic places in Bulgaria.... Germans riot over food in Sorau, a small industrial town near the Silesian border.		The Ontario government will cooperate with the federal government to help British settlers immigrate to Canada. Ontario has a great demand for domestic servants and agricultural laborers. The province will make a special attempt to attract men with families.	

A	B	C	D	E
Includes developments that affect more than one world region, international organizations and important meetings of world leaders.	*Includes all domestic and regional developments in Europe, including the Soviet Union.*	*Includes all domestic and regional developments in Africa and the Middle East.*	*Includes all domestic and regional developments in Latin America, the Caribbean, and Canada.*	*Includes all domestic and regional developments in Asian and Pacific nations (and colonies).*

U.S. Politics & Social Issues	U.S. Foreign Policy & Affairs, Defense	U.S. Economy & Environment	Science, Technology & Nature	Culture, Leisure & Lifestyle	
					Sep. 9
			Most of the scientific expeditions to California and Mexico to photograph today's solar eclipse were disappointed by clouds that obscured the view. However, a party from the Massachusetts Institute of Technology captured the sun's corona.		Sep. 10
	The Secretary of the Navy states that he is mystified about the cause of the crash of destroyers off Santa Barbara, CA. Seven destroyers crashed upon the rocks with 22 men missing, two killed, and 13 injured.		Improvements in instantaneous photography allow newspapers to preserve the atmosphere of a scene while registering natural movements. Newspaper photographic departments expect that flash powder will soon become obsolete.		Sep. 11
The British yacht *Frontiersman* is boarded by a Prohibition officer in San Pedro harbor, CA, who removes 65 bottles of Scotch whiskey. The ship is then attached by a Customs officer because a Los Angeles shipbuilder claims that its bill has not been paid. The captain of the ship denies that he was trying to evade Prohibition.	With 178 destroyers out of the commission, the navy does not expect to replace the lost destroyers at an early date.		Adolf Hoel of Norway reports that he succeeded in surveying the entire coast of the Arctic from South Cape to Cross Bay. He discovered a passage navigable for small ships between the coast and the South Cape Isles.		Sep. 12
A report by the Attorney General to President Coolidge categorizes Prohibition as a tragic epoch in U.S. history. He reports that prosecutions have averaged 73 daily since the enactment of the law, down from 111 daily last year.					Sep. 13
				American Jack Dempsey retains his boxing title by defeating Argentine Luis Firpo at the New York Polo Grounds. Dempsey knocked out Firpo during the first minute of the second round.	Sep. 14
				"Big Bill" Tilden advances to the finals of the U.S. National Tennis Championships in Philadelphia. He will play William M. Johnston, also known as "Little Bill," who is famous for his top spin forehand drive with a western grip. The two men met in the championships last year with Johnston losing in five sets.…Boxer Jack Dempsey is spotted walking the sidewalks of New York with a discolored eye. Firpo is mobbed after visiting a restaurant. Dempsey share of the match's proceeds is estimated at $450,000, while Firpo reportedly made $150,000.…Eleanor Goss wins the Middle States Lawn Tennis Championship in Philadelphia.	Sep. 15

F	G	H	I	J
Includes campaigns, elections, federal-state relations, civil rights and liberties, crime, the judiciary, education, healthcare, poverty, urban affairs, and population.	*Includes formation and debate of U.S. foreign and defense policies, veterans affairs, and defense spending. (Relations with specific foreign countries are usually found under the region concerned.)*	*Includes business, labor, agriculture, taxation, transportation, consumer affairs, monetary and fiscal policy, natural resources, pollution and industrial accidents.*	*Includes worldwide scientific, medical and technological developments, natural phenomena, U.S. weather and natural disasters.*	*Includes the arts, religion, scholarship, communications media, sports, entertainment, fashions, fads, and social life.*

	World Affairs	Europe	Africa & The Middle East	The Americas	Asia & The Pacific
Sep. 16	The provisional government of Fiume resigns because of the long delay between Italy and Yugoslavia in reaching agreement over the territory. The people of Fiume are reported to be exasperated while unemployment is rising.	A crowd of Swiss Socialists at Lugano, Switzerland, scuffles with a group of Italian Communists who attempt to land after traveling on a ship from Porlezza.... Between 50,000 and 80,000 Fascists demonstrate in Bavaria against the republic of Germany. Adolf Hitler takes the salute as the protesters march past him.... Boulgone, France, celebrates the end of Fish Week with representatives from every fishing quarter of Brittany wearing their distinctive lace caps and unique colors.	Fighting breaks out between British forces and the Adwan tribe in Transjordania.	Officers of the Federal Department of Colonization, representatives of the colonization departments of railroads, and the agents of the Canada Colonization Association collaborate to find ways to keep as many British harvesters as possible in Canada. They vow to use every endeavor to secure permanent farm work for those who have no capital and desirable homesteads for those who are able to acquire holdings in districts approved by the colonization agents.	A large haul of smuggled cocaine is discovered by Customs officials at Calcutta on board a steamer from Hong Kong. Officers searched the steamer for five days and sifted through 300 tons of coal before discovering the drugs. They were in 24 containers with 25 ounces each of cocaine that had been hidden in the engine room.... The last of the foreign survivors of the Japanese earthquake are transported from Yokohama to Kobe.
Sep. 17	Italy declares that it has no objection to permitting the League of Nations to decide on the future of Corfu, currently occupied by Italy.	A Belfast man is fined for selling liquor on Sunday contrary to the laws of the Northern Ireland Intoxicating Liquor Act.... Bulgaria tells Yugoslavia that its intentions are strictly peaceful. Since it is disarmed and powerless in the military, it is no menace to any country. Bulgaria further adds that it hopes Yugoslavia will withdraw its troops from the border.... King Alfonso of Spain dissolves the Cortes and the Marquis de Estella is proceeding with the task of reorganization.	The Popular (Kemalist) party of Turkey discusses changes in the Constitution that would extend terms in the Assembly to four years and establish a special administration for Constantinople.... Assin Bey, the new Director of Police in Constantinople, issues orders that all police must shave at least twice a week and must not wear their *kalpaks* (hats) cocked on one side of their heads in an unseemly manner.	English and Canadian survivors of the Japanese earthquake arrive in Vancouver. Some of the survivors are destitute. They are being cared for by the Canadian government until they can proceed to their destinations or find employment.	Australian Prime Minister Stanley Bruce states that a naval base at Singapore is a vital necessity.... Financial experts connected with the Japanese Commission to the United States estimate that Japan sustained losses in the earthquake of two percent of its total wealth of 1.865 billion yen. In the devastated area, the building losses are estimated at 60 percent of the total wealth in buildings.
Sep. 18	Bulgaria requests assistance from the League of Nations to reduce tensions between it and Yugoslavia.... Abyssinia's application to join the League of Nations is being blocked by the requirement that it halt slavery. The importation of arms into Africa is forbidden by the 1919 St. Germain treaty, but Abyssinia needs arms to suppress slavery.	German industrialists publicly object to the Ruhr policies of the Cuno and Stresemann governments. They blame trade unionists for the trouble in the region.... An earthquake strikes Malta.... Great Britain reports a small outbreak of smallpox.... Queen Wilhelmina of the Netherlands opens the session of the States-General. In her speech, she states that the financial and economic situation of the country is disquieting with unemployment on the rise. The government plans to place a limit on support of social reforms as a result of the budget shortfall.	Zaghul Pasha arrives in Cairo, Egypt. Dense crowds line the streets to greet him.... A tax collector in Palestine is murdered and robbed on the main road from Hebron to Jerusalem.		The Indian National Congress approves a plan to boycott British Empire goods as a protest against the Kenya decision.... Every foreign ship entering the port at Changsha in the Chinese province of Hunan is fired upon. A Japanese steamer is looted and ransom of $1 million is demanded by the Chinese kidnappers of two Japanese naval officers.... Japan sends the first silk shipment of the season to the United States.... Of Yokohama, Japan's 93,000 buildings, the Japanese government estimates that 68,000 have been destroyed by the earthquake.
Sep. 19	Italy sends 3,000 National Militia members, also known as Black Shirts, to Libya to protect Italian prestige and honor.	The University of Samara in Russia closes due to lack of funds.... The Prime Ministers of Great Britain and France meet in Paris to discuss the Ruhr matter and other subject of mutual interest.... Riots break out in Baden, Germany, in response to the latest rise in the cost of living and the increasing demands for the payment of wages on a gold basis.... Yugoslavia sends a note to Bulgaria stating that it has only peaceful intentions.	An outbreak of yellow fever is reported on the Gold Coast in Africa.... The rule of the Chartered Company in Rhodesia comes to an end with the departure of the Administrator, Drummond Chaplin.... Turkey and Persia threaten each other at Bulak-Bashi in a dispute over the boundaries of the Persian frontier.	Harold Noice, a Canadian explorer, reports that the people of Wrangel Island refused to render him any assistance as they regard the island as belonging to the United States and not Great Britain.	On account of the tragedy of the earthquake that struck Japan, the marriage of the Prince Regent to Princess Nagako is postponed.... Tan Yen-kai drives Chao Heng-ti from Hunan, China, in light fighting.
Sep. 20	Japan ordered the Soviet Union steamer *Lenin* to leave the port of Kobe because it is suspected to be carrying Communist propaganda. The ship traveled to Japan to provide assistance to victims of the recent earthquake. Japanese authorities block another Soviet ship from landing.... The Political Commission of the League of Nations recommends the admission of Abyssinia provided that the Abyssinian government follow the League's advice about the suppression of slavery.	A Portuguese gunboat seizes a Spanish sardine boat within Portugal's three-mile territorial limit.... Bands of Bulgarian Communists attack police stations and barracks with the object of liberating their jailed comrades. Troops called out to quell the trouble kill six Communists.... The British government has appointed a committee to look into the collapse of the lace industry.	The Mozambique Company announces plans to construct a new deep-water harbor at Beira. The company plans to ask the Portuguese government to open up all of Mozambique to trade by constructing roads, building wireless stations at points not served by telegraph stations, and providing pipe-borne water to Beira.	The Mormon settlement at Cardston, Southern Alberta, Canada, completes the first Mormon temple to be built outside of the United States.... Cubans demanding government reform are arrested by the government for sedition but released a few hours later. The Cuban protestors, led by General Garcia Velez, declare that they must have reform or revolution.	Bombay, India, is flooded by torrential rains. Tramway and suburban railroad services have been suspended.... The Japanese navy estimates its losses in the earthquake. About half of the crude oil store at the Yokosuka Naval Base was destroyed by fire, but the sea bottom at the base has not changed. A damaged light cruiser can be repaired and salvage work on a sunken submarine will resume shortly.... General Gregory Semenoff, a Siberian anti-Soviet leader, is reported to have perished in the Japanese earthquake.... The Chinese government announces that it has always been anxious for the safety of foreigners and will protect foreigners from bandits. The government tells local authorities to take immediate steps to fight bandits.
	A	B	C	D	E
	Includes developments that affect more than one world region, international organizations and important meetings of world leaders.	*Includes all domestic and regional developments in Europe, including the Soviet Union.*	*Includes all domestic and regional developments in Africa and the Middle East.*	*Includes all domestic and regional developments in Latin America, the Caribbean, and Canada.*	*Includes all domestic and regional developments in Asian and Pacific nations (and colonies).*

U.S. Politics & Social Issues	U.S. Foreign Policy & Affairs, Defense	U.S. Economy & Environment	Science, Technology & Nature	Culture, Leisure & Lifestyle	
Oklahoma is placed under martial law by the governor in answer to a challenge by the Grand Dragon of the Ku Klux Klan. The Grand Dragon declared that state authorities would never be able to break up the power of his organization. The governor alleges that hundreds of men and women have been beaten in Oklahoma. He accuses police, sheriffs, and some judges of being members of the Klan.	The Secretary of the Navy orders a Court of Inquiry into the naval accident in the Pacific Ocean. The naval authority responsible for fleet repairs states that two more destroyers were slightly damaged, thus making a total of nine damaged vessels.		Wolverines in Norway are ravaging sheep flocks to an extent not seen in generations.	American explorer and big-game hunter Paul J. Rainey dies while crossing the Atlantic and is buried at sea.…Tilden wins the U.S. National Tennis Singles Championship by three sets to none.…Art experts examine Leonardo da Vinci's "La Belle Ferronniere" held by the Louvre and by Mrs. Hahn of Kansas City. The experts decide that the Louvre version is authentic. The Hahn version is faulted for being anatomically poor while the Louvre one is more complex in its psychology and expression.	Sep. 16
	The American Red Cross raises $8 million for the relief of survivors of the Japanese earthquake with funds continuing to be received.	No newspapers in New York City are published today because of a strike by 2,500 printers employed by 18 of the principal daily newspapers.…A fire in Berkeley, CA, burns 600 houses with the loss of property estimated at $10 million. The fire is one of many that has struck California in recent days as the state suffers from lack of rain and high winds.		The Harvard University Graduate School announces that it will award a gold medal and $8,500 for the best periodical advertising in the United States. The prize is a gift of magazine publisher Edward W. Bok. He states that it is time to recognize the artist in advertising as conspicuously as the artist in literature.	Sep. 17
		The anthracite coal strike ends when the Miner's Convention at Scranton, PA, approves the negotiated agreement.…The New York City newspaper strike continues.	The British Ministry of Health opens an investigation into the possible dangers posed by preservatives and coloring agents in food.		Sep. 18
	The battleship *Arkansas* and the destroyer *McFarland* collide during night maneuvers. The destroyer, struck forward on the port side and with a seriously damaged bridge, is proceeding under escort to Boston.…Great Britain refuses to give the United States the right to search ships and seize contraband articles at any point within 12 miles of the shore.		A ship traveling through the North Atlantic reports sighting an iceberg that is 110 feet high by 260 feet long. The position of the iceberg is radioed to other ships.	The libretto of Verdi's opera *Rigoletto* is confiscated at the Paris Opera at the request of the executor of Victor Hugo's estate. Hugo had sought a new libretto during his lifetime.	Sep. 19
				Sculptures from the 13th century are discovered in the dungeon of the castle at Romont, France.	Sep. 20

F	G	H	I	J
Includes campaigns, elections, federal-state relations, civil rights and liberties, crime, the judiciary, education, healthcare, poverty, urban affairs, and population.	*Includes formation and debate of U.S. foreign and defense policies, veterans affairs, and defense spending. (Relations with specific foreign countries are usually found under the region concerned.)*	*Includes business, labor, agriculture, taxation, transportation, consumer affairs, monetary and fiscal policy, natural resources, pollution and industrial accidents.*	*Includes worldwide scientific, medical and technological developments, natural phenomena, U.S. weather and natural disasters.*	*Includes the arts, religion, scholarship, communications media, sports, entertainment, fashions, fads, and social life.*

	World Affairs	Europe	Africa & The Middle East	The Americas	Asia & The Pacific
Sep. 21	A Syrian delegation to the League of Nations protests against the occupation of Syria and requests that Syria be admitted to the League.…The Belgian government denies a German report that it has tried to persuade the French government not to impose unacceptable conditions on Germany for the evacuation of the Ruhr. The Belgian government maintains its demand that as a preliminary to any agreement with Germany, there should be passive resistance in the Ruhr.	The British Ministry of Agriculture announces that it destroyed 2,780 animals who were infected or exposed to foot and mouth disease during the week ending September 15.…Practically no food is available in Dusseldorf, Germany…In Mors, in the Belgian zone of Germany, miners plunder the fields in the countryside for food.…Trial by jury is suppressed in Spain because so many juries have been intimidated by criminals.…The Spanish Directory begins a campaign against dishonest food dealers by fining butchers and grocers who sell meat and sugar at exorbitant prices.	Egypt passes from British to Egyptian control. In Cairo, Egypt, Zaghlul Pasha condemns the independence of Egypt as a sham. He states that Egypt is a British protectorate.	Petitions with 80,000 signatures are presented to the Saskatchewan, Canada, government requesting a referendum on a proposal to substitute a system of wine and beer licenses for Prohibition.…Louis Philippe Brodeur resigns from the Supreme Court of Canada.	Japanese insurance companies propose that the government loan them money to fully pay claims up to 10,000 yen and a percentage on those claims of higher amounts. The government loan should be long term at low interest.…The government of Japan states that insurance companies are under a moral but not legal obligation to pay claims relating to the earthquake… . The Inspector-General of the Australian Military Forces states that the nation is only training between 30,000 and 40,000 men instead of 120,000 because of the expense of training.
Sep. 22		Animals are being transferred from the Berlin Zoo to other countries because of the difficulty in feeding them.…Greece postpones its general elections until December 2 because of difficulties created by the failure to form a reconciliation party. The elections will likely involve the Venizelists and Metaxists, who are unable to work together.…Bulgaria declares martial law because of attacks by Communists.	Zaghlul Pasha issues a manifesto calling upon Egyptians to make further efforts to achieve complete independence.	The Cuban Senate passes legislation prohibiting the establishment of new sub-ports for sugar export.	Yokohama residents protest against a rumored relocation of the destroyed city. The silk merchants, in a meeting, bind themselves by resolution to refuse to use another port.
Sep. 23	Germany and France break off negotiations over the Ruhr.…Paris newspapers unite in denouncing the German idea that cessation of passive resistance should depend on any way upon such conditions as the amnesty and return of persons who have been deported.	The German National Socialists publish a manifesto warning the Premier of Bavaria that they intend to take steps for their own protection against Marxist organizations.…The German government proposes a new currency to replace the mark.…Another Englishman succumbs to smallpox in London.…Two convicted robbers are strangled to death by *garrotte* in Barcelona, in accord with Spanish law.	An earthquake strikes Egypt and Persia.	The General Board of the Methodist Church of Canada announces that approximately 1500 congregations entered into local unions with Presbyterians preparatory to the general church union, which is now planned.	A Madras and Southern Mahratta Railway Company train crashes as the result of sabotage with several people killed and injured. The Madras government had previously warned villagers that refusal to assist the authorities in the capture of saboteurs would be punished. Villagers in the Chittur, Chingleput, and North Arcot districts are now told that if they continue to refuse to cooperate, police will be quartered on them.…Jawaharlal Nehru is arrested in India for visiting Jaito in contravention of government orders.
Sep. 24	The League of Nations Fifth Assembly hears a presentation on the refugee problem in the Near East.…Russian troops attack and kill a six-man Persian garrison at Beliasuvar, on the border between Russian and Persia.…Italy and Yugoslavia reach agreement over Fiume. Italy will annex the area with compensation given to Yugoslavia.	The leaders of the National Socialists are rumored to have begun planning a *putsch* in Bavaria.…A military government takes control in Spain and suspends the Constitution. The Spanish Cortes is dissolved. The post of Prime Minister and all Cabinet positions are abolished. General Primo de Rivera, Marquis de Estella leads the coup d'etat.…Fighting continues in Bulgaria with the Communists losing ground to the government.		The Hungarian government has authorized the Canadian Pacific Railway Company to transport emigrants to Canada. Hungarians have not been allowed to emigrate to the United States for some time because of the restrictions on ex-enemy aliens.	The Chief Commissioner on the administration of the border of the North-West Frontier Province states that Hindustani fanatics are disseminating Communist propaganda to tribes on the Dir and Hazara border.…Chinese bandits kidnap two women missionaries in the province of Hunan.
Sep. 25	In spite of Persian protests, Bolshevists occupy Enzeli in contravention of the Russo-Persian Agreement of 1921. The Russian government is reported to seek fishery concessions abandoned to Persia through the treaty.…Denmark and Norway begin negotiations over the future of Greenland.…The German government announces that it has ceased passive resistance in the Ruhr for reasons of internal policy, including financial grounds. The federal government also declares its firm determination to preserve and defend the unity of the Reich against any attempt to violate it.	About 600 members of the Bund Oberland armed with rifles, machine guns, automatic pistols, and hand grenades attempt to charter a train to take them to Kochel, Germany, to quell an alleged Communist uprising. When the railroad personnel refuse to run the train, the Bund Oberland riots. Troops restore order.…Striking miners in Bilbao, Spain, return to work after protesting since July.…A coal pit near Falkirk, Scotland, floods and traps 75 men. While three miners are brought up dead, 21 are rescued. The remaining miners are still trapped and are presumed dead due to drowning or suffocation.…German newspapers discuss the possibility of civil war.		The government of Canada appoints a Royal Commission to inquire into the causes of unrest among steelworkers at Cape Breton and the calling out of the militia during the recent strike at Sydney.…The British Columbia Electric Company tramway employees in Vancouver, Canada, call a strike to get wages of 65 cents an hour for motormen and conductors. The company offered 60 cents.	The New South Wales Legislative Assembly in Australia adopts a resolution declaring that the granting of titles to be contrary to the sentiments of the citizens of the state.

A	B	C	D	E
Includes developments that affect more than one world region, international organizations and important meetings of world leaders.	*Includes all domestic and regional developments in Europe, including the Soviet Union.*	*Includes all domestic and regional developments in Africa and the Middle East.*	*Includes all domestic and regional developments in Latin America, the Caribbean, and Canada.*	*Includes all domestic and regional developments in Asian and Pacific nations (and colonies).*

U.S. Politics & Social Issues	U.S. Foreign Policy & Affairs, Defense	U.S. Economy & Environment	Science, Technology & Nature	Culture, Leisure & Lifestyle	
The Assistant Secretary of the Treasury recommends that the Departments of Labor and Treasury request an appropriation to cover the cost of additional buildings at Ellis Island. He recommends that a penalty of $1,000 to $2,000 be imposed on any steamship company seeking to land an immigrant whose condition obviously did not meet the health requirements of the Immigration Law.	The Attorney General rules that the Lasker plan to break up the Merchant Marine is illegal. The plan would have allowed the government to operate the ships under subsidiary companies incorporated under the laws of various states.... The navy is considering establishing an air route between the United States and Europe via Greenland to England. The Danish government has given permission for the use of Greenland.		Prehistoric burial sites are discovered by archeologists in Corsica. The sites are in an ancient Roman town that is also being excavated.... Limonite is discovered in Wales. All previous known deposits of the mineral are in the United States. Limonite is used in the manufacture of paint, linoleum, tile, and for glazing.		Sep. 21
					Sep. 22
An armed launch flying the Dutch flag is stopped in Brussels, Belgium. The ship, destined for the United States, is carrying a cargo of champagne, other wines, and liquor worth 100,000 francs. Several machine guns are found on board and each of the 10-man crew is armed with a pistol. The captain and second officer are arrested.		The New York newspaper strike turns violent after the publication of an order by the International Union outlawing the striking union of machinists. A strikebreaking press worker is bludgeoned to death while at work and a reporter is severely beaten.		Three balloonists are killed in the Gordon-Bennett Balloon Race in Brussels, Belgium, when thunderstorms set two balloons on fire. The Gordon-Bennett cup is awarded to the aeronaut who travels the farthest.	Sep. 23
Calvin Coolidge delivers his first speech as president. At the annual meeting of the American Red Cross, he declares that faith in things spiritual tempered by common sense is the kind of practical idealism reflected in American history.				Two of the famous "Seven Cities of Cibola" are reported to have been discovered in New Mexico during an archeological expedition. Representatives of the American Indian Heye Foundation in New York are leading the dig.	Sep. 24
Governor Walton of Oklahoma orders the Adjutant-General of the state to employ all of the state's military forces to prevent the meeting tomorrow of the Oklahoma House of Representatives. The legislature intends to impeach the governor because of his insistence in keeping the state under martial law. The governor claims that he is trying to overthrow the power of the Ku Klux Klan, which purportedly pervades every level of state government. Walton says that the troops are empowered to shoot to kill. Walton also asks President Coolidge to block the legislators from using federal buildings.		The Department of Commerce states that reports from 181 manufacturers show that automobile production in the first eight months of 1923 exceeded that of either of the two preceding years. The output for this year has been 2,431,063 passenger cars and 258,774 commercial vehicles.		The Wright American seaplane, entered in the international Schneider Cup, is wrecked when a blade of the propeller flies off and knocks away one of the floats. The seaplane falls into the water with its pilot and mechanic. The men are rescued and the plane is towed to shore....A Swiss alpine club builds a hut in the Val Soja to facilitate ascent of the 11,150 feet Rheinwaldhorn and neighboring peaks.	Sep. 25

F	G	H	I	J
Includes campaigns, elections, federal-state relations, civil rights and liberties, crime, the judiciary, education, healthcare, poverty, urban affairs, and population.	*Includes formation and debate of U.S. foreign and defense policies, veterans affairs, and defense spending. (Relations with specific foreign countries are usually found under the region concerned.)*	*Includes business, labor, agriculture, taxation, transportation, consumer affairs, monetary and fiscal policy, natural resources, pollution and industrial accidents.*	*Includes worldwide scientific, medical and technological developments, natural phenomena, U.S. weather and natural disasters.*	*Includes the arts, religion, scholarship, communications media, sports, entertainment, fashions, fads, and social life.*

	World Affairs	Europe	Africa & The Middle East	The Americas	Asia & The Pacific
Sep. 26	The League of Nations debates a Canadian amendment that would remove the requirement for member states to go to war without first obtaining the approval of their national legislatures. The amendment is designed to get the United States into the League by removing one of the major objections to American participation... .The Conference of Ambassadors unanimously decides to request that Greece pay damages for neglect that permitted the assassination of Italian diplomats and allowed the killers to remain undetected.	The Bulgarian government arrests about 500 local Communists after learning about rumors of an uprising....Spectators at a bullfight in Spain attempt to set fire to the buildings in the paddock and stone an official after a replacement bull is not provided for a fight that went badly....The Spanish government proposes to reduce the period of military service from three to two years.	Egyptians vote in primary elections but the turnout is relatively light. The Zaghlulists are competing with the Nationalists and Liberal Constitutionalists.	The Imperial War Graves Commission announces that it will send Canada two barrels of soil from the battlefields at Vimy Ridge and Ypres. The earth will be mingled with the soil of Canada under the Cross of Sacrifice at Quebec....The British Columbia, Canada, tramway workers strike is settled with the men accepting 63 cents per hour, representing a five percent increase in pay.	The Japanese government releases official figures showing that as of September 13, the losses from the earthquake in Tokyo alone are 72,600 deaths, 298,455 houses burned, and 36,158 houses collapsed. The high number of casualties is attributed to the fact that residents were unable to escape from low-lying, densely crowded riverside districts. Six wards are almost completely destroyed....Waziristani raiders near Simla, India, carry off 100 cattle but the animals are recaptured after a fight at Girdao with a pursuit party of the Mandokhel tribe.
Sep. 27	The League of Nations debate over the Canadian amendment ends with an inconclusive vote....The premier of Bavaria calls for the German government to declare that the Versailles Treaty is broken and that therefore all payments should cease until the sovereignty of the Reich over occupied territory is restored....The League of Nations discusses the opium problem and agrees to hold a conference to fix limits on the importation of raw opium for smoking into Far Eastern territories....The German government publishes a decree canceling all regulations and orders that were passed with the object of supporting the Ruhr resistance.	Some parts of the French submarine *Curie*, which was lost trying to enter the Austrian port of Cattaro during the war, are discovered in an Italian arsenal. Italy promises to return the objects to the Ministry of Marine in Paris for preservation....Parisian milliners, who are mostly women, receive an increase of wages of 337 francs to 450 francs per month after a 3-day strike....A Soviet commissar who headed the Soviet Frontier Commission is murdered while returning to Russia from Finland and the Soviet government blames White Finns....Germany declares a state of martial law.	Severe earthquake shocks are felt in Persia....The French High Commission for Syria, General Weygand, orders a commission to investigate the possibility of utilizing the water power of the Nair Ibrahim, which enters the sea about 12 miles northwest of Beirut.		The Postmaster-General of Australia announces plans to establish wireless telegraphy in North-Western Australia to enable the farmers and ranchers in the area to communication with the people of the coasts....A gathering of about 2,000 Sikhs listens to fiery anti-British speeches and anti-British poems read by young boys at Amritsar, India....Great Britain proposes to turn over all of its land, buildings, improvements, cable and telegraph connections, telephone system and ferry service in Weihaiwei as a free gift to the Chinese government. In exchange, the British fleet shall enjoy free use of the port for the next 10 years while certain buildings are lent to the navy free of charge.
Sep. 28	British, French, and Spanish officials meet to discuss the future status of Tangier port....The League of Nations unanimously admits Abyssinia to much applause from the public galleries.	The statistician of the Medical Research Council in London announces that deaths from influenza are rising....The Gibraltar war memorial, consisting of marble figures of a sailor and a soldier unfurling a Union Jack, is unveiled....The Swiss National Council votes to electrify the federal railroads....Police in Switzerland stop a man in possession of Austrian, Polish, and Russian passports. They discover papers in his car trunk, leading to speculation that the man is a Bolshevist agent....Italy completes its evacuation from Corfu but the Italian squadron remains offshore in Greek waters until Greece pays 50 million lire.	The British Colonial Office suspends plans for a railroad in Nyasaland, Africa, from Luchenza to Lake Nyasa because of criticism that the chosen route runs through low-lying and sparsely populated territory. As a consequence, the railroad would have carry little traffic for many years....Mozambique and South Africa sign a treaty.	The Canadian government announces that immigration for the five months ending in August amounted to 80,161 persons, an increase of 103 percent over the same period last year. Most of the immigrants came from Great Britain and the United States, although American immigration decreased by 16 percent.	Construction begins in Australia on a new railroad between New South Wales and Victoria amid much fanfare. The railroad is expected to make a million and a half acres available for production. It will run from Moama on the Murray River to Balranald on the Murrumbidgee River....New South Wales coalminers go on strike and shut down eight mines.
Sep. 29	The League of Nations Assembly discusses the poor public image of the organization. Most of the delegates express regret that the League is not yet as powerful an instrument of justice as they had thought it would be or as it will be in the future.	Mailbags left on the Caroline Islands in August 1914 by a German cruiser squadron are discovered. The contents of the bags will be distributed by the German government.		Three men who escaped from prison rob a bank in Nova Scotia, Canada, with revolvers and assault the bank manager before escaping by automobile....The Canadian Manufacturers Association states that Canada should increase its export trade by making preferential tariff arrangements based on the principle of bargaining with other countries. The association declares that the British preference has failed because it has not increased the percentage of Canadian purchases from the United Kingdom nor decreased the percentage of Canadian purchases from other countries.	Trains are now running from Tokyo to Yokohama, Japan, but the train stations remain in rubble. The debris has been cleared from most streets in Yokohama but the changed landscape makes it difficult for visitors to find streets. Bodies continue to be removed from the wreckage of buildings.
Sep. 30	The Portuguese Academy of Science offers proof that 15th century explorer Christopher Columbus was born in Portugal, a statement that disputes the widely accepted theory that Columbus' birthplace was Italy.			Seventeen English women embark from an ocean liner at Montreal. They are traveling to the Western prairies, where they will be married upon arrival.	
	A *Includes developments that affect more than one world region, international organizations and important meetings of world leaders.*	B *Includes all domestic and regional developments in Europe, including the Soviet Union.*	C *Includes all domestic and regional developments in Africa and the Middle East.*	D *Includes all domestic and regional developments in Latin America, the Caribbean, and Canada.*	E *Includes all domestic and regional developments in Asian and Pacific nations (and colonies).*

U.S. Politics & Social Issues	U.S. Foreign Policy & Affairs, Defense	U.S. Economy & Environment	Science, Technology & Nature	Culture, Leisure & Lifestyle	
The Oklahoma militia prevents the legislature from meeting without any violence. The legislators enter the state building in ones and twos but are barred from entering the legislative chambers. The legislators now plan to work through the courts to abolish martial law in the state.		The American Bankers Conference in Atlantic City considers a proposal to cancel the Allies' war debt to the United States. Proponents argue that cancellation would be repaid through the profits of reestablished commerce.…The New York newspaper strike ends. The Publishers' Association promises that newspapers will return to their full size and have all their usual features in a day or two.…Banker Allen Boyd Forbes dies.			Sep. 26
Armed militia from various parts of Oklahoma are moving towards the state capital in response to the dispute over the Ku Klux Klan.	The American Bankers; Association passes resolutions at its annual conference that demands the U.S. government abandon its policy of isolation from European affairs and assume a place of responsibility upon the Reparations Commission.			The United States wins the Schneider International Seaplane Race when Lieutenant David Rittenhouse of the U.S. Navy pilots a Curtiss Racer type CR.3 fitted with a 465 horsepower Curtiss D-12 engine along the 186 nautical mile (214 land mile) race course in one hour, 12 minutes, and 26 seconds at an average speed of 177.38 miles per hour.	Sep. 27
To stop the dangerous race of ocean liners carrying immigrants into New York Harbor at midnight at the end of every month, the U.S. government requires each vessel to pick up a pilot at the Ambrose Channel lightship. In the order of arrival, ships will be assigned times at intervals of 10 minutes to go up to quarantine. The measure is expected to limit racing to the open ocean, where there is room to avoid collision, rather than in the crowded confines of a harbor. The first ship in each month's procession will arrive in quarantine at five minutes after midnight.	Secretary of State Charles Evans Hughes states that the United States refusal to ratify the Arms Traffic Convention of the League of Nations does not indicate that the United States has no interest in controlling the traffic in arms.…Hughes declines to answer questions from reporters about the situation in the Ruhr and in Germany.			The White Star Line announces that its ocean liner, Majestic, arrived at Cherbourg, France, from New York City in a record time of five days, five hours, and 25 minutes at an average speed of 24.76 knots.	Sep. 28
Eleven ships are reported to be hurrying to New York Harbor with about 10,000 immigrants seeking admission under the October quota.				Patriarch Tikhon of the Russian Orthodox Church announces that the church accepts the decisions about the calendar that were adopted by the Ecumenical Conference in Constantinople. The Gregorian calendar (new style) will come into effect October 1.…The first football game at night is played in Cincinnati between the University of Cincinnati and Kentucky Wesleyan University. The event drew a record crowd to Carson Field. Cincinnati defeats Kentucky Wesleyan 17–0. The game featured ordinary footballs instead of whitened ones because of the excellence of the Cincinnati lights.	Sep. 29
					Sep. 30
F *Includes campaigns, elections, federal-state relations, civil rights and liberties, crime, the judiciary, education, healthcare, poverty, urban affairs, and population.*	G *Includes formation and debate of U.S. foreign and defense policies, veterans affairs, and defense spending. (Relations with specific foreign countries are usually found under the region concerned.)*	H *Includes business, labor, agriculture, taxation, transportation, consumer affairs, monetary and fiscal policy, natural resources, pollution and industrial accidents.*	I *Includes worldwide scientific, medical and technological developments, natural phenomena, U.S. weather and natural disasters.*	J *Includes the arts, religion, scholarship, communications media, sports, entertainment, fashions, fads, and social life.*	

	World Affairs	Europe	Africa & The Middle East	The Americas	Asia & The Pacific
Oct. 1	The League of Nations arranges for a loan to help Greece with the one million refugees that it has received from Asia Minor.... The Bulgarian government pays the first installment of its Reparations obligations.... The League of Nations has registered 500 treaties and agreements since June 28, 1919.	Diamond cutters in Antwerp, Belgium, strike for better pay.... New taxicabs are introduced in Paris. These cabs are driven by a four-cylinder, 10 horsepower engine instead of the old two-cylinder, 8-horsepower engine. Brakes are fitted to all four wheels and the cabin is lit by electricity.... The Political Bureau in the Soviet Union appoints an Extraordinary Three leadership team consisting of Josef Stalin, Leon Trotsky, and Felix Dzerzhinksky.	Rhodesia inaugurates self-government with celebrations throughout the country.... The Allies evacuate from Constantinople, leaving the city in the hands of Turkey.	President Obregon of Mexico removes ministers with Communist affiliations from his cabinet.	Chinese Customs revenue is down for the year, with part of the blame for the drop attributed to a continuing boycott of Japanese goods.... The Jahore causeway opens joining Singapore with the Malaysian mainland.
Oct. 2	The Imperial Economic Conference meets in London to consider financial cooperation between Great Britain and the Dominions particularly means of improving inter-Imperial trade.	The government of Bavaria, Germany, bans all strikes under penalty of imprisonment and fines.... Health officials in Paris tout the advantages of inoculation against typhoid.... Paris police step up surveillance of foreigners in the city in the wake of crimes committed by foreigners. Any visitor who remains in the city for more than two months must obtain an identity card.		The Royal Canadian Academy argues that the trustees of the National Gallery in England have no right to select Canadian pictures for the upcoming British Empire Committee. The Canadians demand to be able to choose representative paintings from their country.	The Japanese government announces plans to obtain loans in the United States and Great Britain to aid in rebuilding after the earthquake disaster.
Oct. 3		The Antwerp diamond cutters strike fails and the cutters return to work.... The Berlin Motor Show opens. Mercedes and Daimler, with factories in occupied territories, have been prevented from exhibiting.	The first session of the Legislative Council of the new colony of Southern Rhodesia opens.	A hurricane that strikes Newfoundland and the Maritime Provinces in Canada destroys more than 250,000 barrels of apples.	
Oct. 4	The Italian government gives four million lire to help Greek refugees in Corfu.	The French Ministry of Education makes Latin a requirement for the Baccalaureate.... The Stresemann government of Germany resigns after the Social Democratic Party withdraws from the government. ...*Paris Soir*, a new leftwing newspaper, makes it first appearance.... A Dutch savings bank with more than 100,000 accounts ceases operation.			Tokyo, Yokohama, and other cities and towns in the Kanto District of Japan are glutted and unable to absorb the vast quantities of supplies of all sorts sent as earthquake relief.... The State Arbitration Court in Perth, Australia, reduces the workweek of government employees from 44 to 40 hours.
Oct. 5	The Federation of Ukrainian Jews votes to send a representative to Romania to investigate the situation of the 4,000 refugees in Bessarabia, who were arrested on the Jewish Day of Atonement.... The Reparations Commission issues a table showing the distribution of payments from Germany up to June 30.	Bulgaria ends the state of siege that had been declared throughout most of the country because of the Agrarian Communist uprising. ...Five miners trapped in the Redding Pit are rescued. The men chewed on coal to fight off hunger during the nine days that they were entombed.		The Argentine Congress authorizes the government to fix maximum and minimum rates for the sale of all meats.... Teixeira Gomes is installed as the new president of Portugal.... An attempt to overthrow the Peruvian government is uncovered with Colonel Bustamante of the General staff placed under arrest.	The Indian government considers posting police in every village in Kaira district because of continuing lawlessness by members of the Dharalas.... Marshal Tsao Kun is elected as President of the Republic of China.
Oct. 6	Greece cedes to the Kingdom of the Serbs, Croats, and Slovenes about six acres of territory at Salonika for a period of 50 years. The land will remain under Greek sovereignty but will be administered by Yugoslav officials.	France announces that the airship *Dixmude* will undertake a journey of 6,000 miles across Morocco, the Sahara, and Algeria at the end of November.	The High Commissioner of Angola, General Norton de Mattos, declares that the chief need of the country is for immigrants.... Drunken mobs in Constantinople, Turkey, smash shop windows and tear any headgear that is not a fez or kalpak from the head of its wearer.	Rear Admiral John Pitka of the Estonian navy leaves for Canada to select a site to which Estonians can immigrate.... Officials of the Ontario License Commission declare that 75 percent of the liquor confiscated in Ontario comes from Quebec. They also assert that the flow of liquor into the United States from Quebec is even greater than the flow into Ontario.	
Oct. 7		The Belgian lightship *Wandelaar* has been set adrift by a heavy storm off Brussels. It is flying a flag of distress and a tug has been dispatched to try to take the lightship in tow.... Political instability continues in Greece as the efforts of the revolutionary leaders to form a coalition fail. The Democrat and Agrarian parties plan to stand alone.	Turkey imposes a prohibition on alcohol. The move has been widely expected.	British men are deported from Canada because they are unable to find employment and likely to become a public charge. The men complain that Canadian farmers had refused to pay them the $4 a day that had been promised before they immigrated. Some complain that they received $1 while others allege that they only received room and board.	The Japanese government tells the Soviet Union that the steamer *Lenin* was not allowed to remain in Japanese waters because the Soviet representative demanded the right to distribute the goods brought for the victims of the earthquake and to give aid only to "proletarians." He also began opening making Communist speeches.

A	B	C	D	E
Includes developments that affect more than one world region, international organizations and important meetings of world leaders.	*Includes all domestic and regional developments in Europe, including the Soviet Union.*	*Includes all domestic and regional developments in Africa and the Middle East.*	*Includes all domestic and regional developments in Latin America, the Caribbean, and Canada.*	*Includes all domestic and regional developments in Asian and Pacific nations (and colonies).*

U.S. Politics & Social Issues	U.S. Foreign Policy & Affairs, Defense	U.S. Economy & Environment	Science, Technology & Nature	Culture, Leisure & Lifestyle	
Governor J.C. Walton of Oklahoma mobilizes the state militia to prevent bloodshed during a special election that will be held tomorrow. The mobilization affects 5,000 National Guardsmen, 75,000 Militia Volunteers, and 25 special secret service men.				George Carpentier beats Joe Beckett in 20 seconds of the first round to win the heavyweight-boxing championship of Great Britain.	Oct. 1
Governor Gifford Pinchot of Pennsylvania cracks down on the illegal consumption of alcohol by serving 1,300 saloons in Philadelphia with notices to shut down within 48 hours.…For eight hours, 100,000-armed men in Oklahoma face each other at the polls as vigilantes meet state militia forces. No shots are fired. Out of 450,000 votes cast, 250,000 are in favor of amending the Constitution to permit the Legislature to meet of its own will at any time.			A new fishing bank is discovered 80 miles off the coast of Labrador in Canada. The bank, with a depth of 75 feet, is filled with cod and halibut.	In a 7–5 Detroit Tigers win over the Chicago White Sox, Harry Heilmann goes two for two to put his average over .400. He will win the batting title with a .403 average. Ty Cobb helps in the win with a steal of home in the seventh inning, his first steal of home in more than three years.	Oct. 2
Four convicts in a state penitentiary at Eddyville, KY, shoot and kill two guards while wounding three others.…The Oklahoma State Court issues an injunction restraining the election board from certifying yesterday's election.			The International Council for the Exploration of the Sea plans to organize an investigation of the seas between Iceland and Norway.		Oct. 3
	George Harvey, Ambassador to Great Britain, and Richard Washburn Child, Ambassador to France, resign.				Oct. 4
The Governor of Indiana is placed under investigation for improperly diverting to his own use $155,000 in funds belonging to the state Board of Agriculture.	President Coolidge opposes any plan to cancel debts owed by European countries to the United States.…The scout cruiser *Marblehead* is launched. The ship will be equipped to carry airplanes and lay mines. It has a speed of 35 knots and main armament of 12-inch guns.				Oct. 5
In order to avoid complications at the Port of New York, ships from the White Star have been disembarking immigrants at Halifax, Canada. The passengers then take special Canadian National Railroad trains from the port into the United States within 24 hours of disembarking.	An unofficial American mission to Russia, headed by Senator King, returns to the United States. King declares that he found better economic conditions than he expected and some political advancement. However, Russia needs more capital and more liberty. King blames nationalism for the troubles in Europe.			In his first college football game, University of Illinois running back Harold "Red" Grange helps lead the Illini to a 24–7 victory over the University of Nebraska with touchdown runs of 50, 35, and 12 yards.	Oct. 6
				The Atlanta Symphony Orchestra makes its premiere performance.	Oct. 7
F *Includes campaigns, elections, federal-state relations, civil rights and liberties, crime, the judiciary, education, healthcare, poverty, urban affairs, and population.*	**G** *Includes formation and debate of U.S. foreign and defense policies, veterans affairs, and defense spending. (Relations with specific foreign countries are usually found under the region concerned.)*	**H** *Includes business, labor, agriculture, taxation, transportation, consumer affairs, monetary and fiscal policy, natural resources, pollution and industrial accidents.*	**I** *Includes worldwide scientific, medical and technological developments, natural phenomena, U.S. weather and natural disasters.*	**J** *Includes the arts, religion, scholarship, communications media, sports, entertainment, fashions, fads, and social life.*	

	World Affairs	Europe	Africa & The Middle East	The Americas	Asia & The Pacific
Oct. 8		The British Ministry of Agriculture fixes November 8 as a "Rat Week" because the is when the rodents make their general move from the countryside to winter quarters in the towns and farmsteads.…Many Scottish shipbuilding companies seek tax reductions at the Glasgow Valuation Court because of the depressed state of the industry.	The former Grand Vizier of the Ottoman Empire, Damad Ferid Pasha, dies. He became Grand Vizier in 1919, briefly resigned when the Greeks occupied Smyrna, and finally left office in 1922.	More than 10,000 people greet former British Prime Minister David Lloyd George in Montreal, Canada. He pays tribute to Canada's part in the war.	The Home Minister proposes that the Japanese Diet give the vote to all males aged 25 or older with a six months residential qualification and without any tax limitation. The measure will also make monks, schoolteachers, and priests available for election.
Oct. 9	The first meeting of the International Commission for the Exchange of Populations is held with the Greek member announcing that Turks from Mytilene were already being taken to Aivali. The commission orders Greece and Turkey to report on the exchange.	The British Medical Association declares that the amount of payment to physicians under the National Health Insurance system is inadequate and will drive experienced family doctors into private practice.	A punitive force sent in pursuit of the cattle raiders, who attacked a section of the French Camel Corps in Dakar, recovers the lost booty. The raiders, about 300 of them, killed 60 French soldiers in a 7-hour battle near Timbuktu.	Former British Prime Minister Lloyd George is greeted by large crowds upon his arrival in Ottawa, Canada.…The Canadian government advertises 7,876 job openings for British harvesters willing to emigrate. The jobs are chiefly for farm, lumbering, and bush work.	The Congress of Australian Manufacturers criticizes the restriction of immigration plans to agriculture. It urges the importation of skilled artisans, because Australian industries are suffering from a lack of such workers.…Australia has accepted 50,000 settlers this year, with 17,633 of the settlers choosing Victoria.
Oct. 10	Germany asks Belgium and France if they are prepared to enter into negotiations for the resumption of work in the Ruhr.…German industrialists in the Ruhr demand compensation for the coal confiscated by the French since the occupation, the removal of a coal tax, a lengthening of working hours, and the right to negotiate directly with the authorities in control of occupied territories.	Saxony, Germany, forms a new government when the Communists decide to unite with the Socialists. …Fewer ships are being built in Great Britain and Ireland than in any time in the past 14 years.….The Norwegian navy decides to sell several out-of-date vessels.	A fight between two groups of Bedouins, the Khawaled and Beshakem, sends many men to a hospital in Hama, in French Syria.… Official returns show that 58 percent of Egyptians voted in the primary elections. The highest percentage was in Benisuef Province with the lowest at Alexandria.…Turkana tribesmen on the northeast frontier of Uganda engage in raiding attacks.	The Canadian Board of Railway Commissioners orders a reduction of 10 percent in the railway rates on grain from Edmonton to Vancouver, a distance of 640 miles. The reduction is likely to increase the volume of grain going to Europe through Vancouver and the Panama Canal.	The Netherlands announces plans to construct a fleet for the defense of the Dutch East Indies.…China installs its new president.…Admiral Dudly Rawson Stratford de Chair is appointed to be governor of New South Wales, Australia.…A Japanese army officer argues that he killed an anarchist, his wife, and his nephew out of patriotism.
Oct. 11	David Lloyd George, the former Prime Minister of Great Britain, describes the British Empire as the one effective League of Nations in the world. He considers an international effort to curb militarism as futile. Lloyd George is making a series of speeches throughout Canada.	Food riots occur in Cologne, Germany.…The German mark declines to the point that is has virtually no value.…Benito Mussolini announces that he will ask the Italian legislature to renew the special powers granted to him last year to reform the finances and bureaucracy of Italy. This announcement also means that elections are indefinitely postponed.	Great Britain places sovereignty over British Togoland under the Gold Coast colonial government.… Poland produces more potatoes per person than any other country in the world, with 2750 pounds per inhabitant… .Britain proposes the creation of an Arab Agency in Palestine to represent the interests of Arabs as the Jewish Agency represents Jews. The idea is received unfavorably by Arab extremists.	Diego Manuel Chamorro, President of Nicaragua, dies at San Juan del Sur, Nicaragua.	A recent escapee from the Geelong jail in Victoria, Australia, is arrested for robbing and wounding the manager of a bank in Melbourne.…The Air Force bombs Mahsud villages in Simla, India, to quiet the region.
Oct. 12	At the Bulgaro-Yugslav Conference in Sofia, Bulgaria agrees to pay for requisitions made during the war.	An explosion in Moscow, Russia, completely levels a three-story house. The explosion is blamed on an illegal ammunition depot on the first floor of the building.…The partial recovery of the German mark causes prices to drop by half but still leaving them out of proportion to workers' earnings. Many German shops are sold out because of panic buying and many farmers refuse to bring their goods to market.…The German government requires back taxes to be paid in gold.		Northern Saskatchewan expects to have 2700-winter jobs for British harvesters. Of these vacancies, 1700 are industrial with the remainder connected with farming.…The Canadian Bankers' Association refuses to take any responsibility for the recent collapse of the Home Bank.	The Japanese submarine, No. 70, that recently sunk is successfully towed toward the coast and now lies in 24 fathoms. Four bodies out of the 85 missing have been recovered.…The Australian government announces a bounty for fruit growers and canners for the 1923–24 season only. The Australian Prime Minister states that the industry must rely upon itself and must develop the Australian market. Australians only consume 104 pounds of fruit per person per year compared to 400 pounds in the United States.
Oct. 13	Poland informs British and American Relief Societies in the country that they must cease their activities by January 1 unless they obtain a Polish charter. Poland states that there is no further need in the country for relief organizations enjoying special privileges.	Rioters in Dusseldorf, Germany, smash windows and loot stores. French police arrest a number of looters. Similar disorders occur in the other cities in the French sector, including Weisbaden, Oberhausen, and Hochst-am-Rhein.…A fort in Warsaw, Poland, that stored explosives blows up. More than 2,000 tons of explosives are destroyed with 200 people dead and about 500 people wounded. Windows throughout Warsaw shatter.	Mozambique objects to a Portuguese proposal to administer a railroad and port at Delagoa Bay. Mozambiquans object both to Portuguese control and to any plan for joint South African control.	The Cuban Secretary of the Treasury, Hernandez Cartaya, resigns because Congress passes laws without providing funds for their fulfillment.… Canada sends a representative from the Ministry of the Interior to China to supervise the emigration of Chinese to Canada.	Sun Yat-sen objects to the presidency of Tsao Kun on the grounds that he is illiterate, uneducated, and responsible for attacks on foreigners. Sun Yat-sen further adds that the election was marked by illegality and corruption that make it an outrage to any civilized nation.…The branch of the Royal Mint at Sydney, New South Wales, Australia, will close as of January 1 because of the great drop in gold production within Australia.

A	B	C	D	E
Includes developments that affect more than one world region, international organizations and important meetings of world leaders.	*Includes all domestic and regional developments in Europe, including the Soviet Union.*	*Includes all domestic and regional developments in Africa and the Middle East.*	*Includes all domestic and regional developments in Latin America, the Caribbean, and Canada.*	*Includes all domestic and regional developments in Asian and Pacific nations (and colonies).*

U.S. Politics & Social Issues	U.S. Foreign Policy & Affairs, Defense	U.S. Economy & Environment	Science, Technology & Nature	Culture, Leisure & Lifestyle	
				A painting by Van de Hoeck that belongs to the Pierpont Morgan Gallery in New York City is discovered by Belgian police who arrest a Greek man. The man, who recently left the United States, is arrested on the advice of New York police officials.	Oct. 8
	The delivery of a zeppelin from Germany to the United States is delayed because of difficulties in the construction of a motor. Delivery is now scheduled for next spring.			Paticycles are reported to be the latest craze among French children. The devices are miniature cycle wheels, with rubber tires strapped to the legs and boots of the users. They are sometimes used in conjunction with ski sticks.	Oct. 9
President Harding's estate is valued at $487,000, excluding the value of shares in his newspaper.... In a sensational robbery in the heart of New York City's shopping district, four armed men shoot and kill the escort of a bank clerk before escaping in an automobile. The clerk loses $12,500, but the escort manages to kill one robber.				The New York Yankees and New York Giant begin Game 1 of the World Series at Yankee Stadium. Casey Stengel of the Giants hits a home run and the Giants win by a score of 5–4. The National Broadcasting Company becomes the first radio network to broadcast the World Series.	Oct. 10
A school bus crowded with children is struck by a passenger train near Williamsport, PA. Seven children are killed and a number are injured.... A passenger train is robbed in Redding, CA, as it emerges from a tunnel. The robbers blow open the mail wagon with dynamite and kill a mail clerk in the process. No passengers are injured.	A hydrogen gas explosion in the submarine *S-37* off the coast of California kills three sailors and injures six other men.	American business leaders express concerns about contemplated changes in British tariffs and the extension of the scope of Imperial preferences. California fruit growers, however, assert that the quality of their fruit will offset any tariff advantage given to Australian growers.		Game 2 of the World Series is played at the Polo Grounds. The Yankees beat the Giants by a score of 4–2 before a crowd of 40,400. Babe Ruth hits two home runs.... The remains of James Oglethorpe, founder of Georgia, are discovered in an English church at Cranham.	Oct. 11
Samuel Gompers is unanimously reelected as president of the American Federation of Labor.... Henry Ford makes no objection when his name is offered as Progressive Party candidate for president.		Henry Ford attacks Secretary of War John Weeks for supposedly plotting to prevent the acceptance of his bid for a nitrate plant at Muscle Shoals, AL. The plant would have produced power and fertilizer. Ford argues that Weeks wants high prices for fertilizer to make millions for himself and his friends.	French surgeons report that they have grafted chimpanzee testicular glands onto humans suffering from old age or disability. The vigor of the chimpanzees is believed to be transferred to humans. The operation is reported to be especially helpful to men suffering from nervous breakdowns due to overwork.	Game 3 of the World Series is held at Yankee Stadium. The Giants win 1–0, with Casey Stengel homering, before a crowd of 62,430.... Swiss painter Paul Robert dies.... C.R. Morrison, a Philadelphian attempting to walk around the world, is drowned when his boat capsizes near Cairo, Egypt. Morrison began his walk in 1921 in Maine as a bet.	Oct. 12
Henry Ford announces his intention to pay all of his war profits to the U.S. government. Ford's company made $7 million in net profits. His 51 percent share, minus war taxes, is estimated at $1.75 million. Auditors from the War Department, who have been working on the automobile company's books, have just completed their accounting.			Two Danish engineers demonstrate a new invention that solves the problem of a "speaking film." The human voice is recorded on a separate film, which is not connected with the picture film. Thus, the voice film can be handled separately, but on the same apparatus that accommodates picture film.	Game 4 of the World Series is held at the Polo Grounds. The Yankees win by a score of 8–4.	Oct. 13

	World Affairs	Europe	Africa & The Middle East	The Americas	Asia & The Pacific
Oct. 14		Some French veterans propose to keep an oil lamp burning all night long under the Arc de Triomphe in Paris, where the Unknown Warrior lies in his tomb. The light will begin burning on Armistice Day....A large gathering in Malta, estimated at 12,000 people, pledges loyalty to the British government....Press censorship in Greece is abolished. However, new restrictions are imposed that ban any comment on the revolutionary leaders.	The chief of police at Constantinople, Turkey, apologizes for the recent vandalism at the British Crimean cemetery at Scutari. The cemetery contains remains of British soldiers killed during the Crimean War.... The Khedivah Mother arrives in Alexandria, Egypt, after nine years in exile. The Princess is the mother of the ex-Khedive and the sister-in-law of King Faud.	During the summer months, Quebec received 10,917 immigrants. Most of the immigrants came from England, France, Ireland, Scotland, Belgium, and the United States....Peruvian refugees arrive at Mollendo, on the Peruvian coast, after being expelled from Arica by Chilean authorities.	Moros attack a schoolhouse on Mindanao in the Philippines and kill 13 persons.
Oct. 15	To promote international trade and travel, the League of Nations opens a conference on the unification of customs....Belgium claims that its occupation of the Ruhr has been a success because Germany has ceased resistance and agreed to pay reparations. It opposes the formation of an international committee, proposed by Great Britain, to investigate Germany's capacity to pay reparations.	The German government announces plans for currency reform. The paper mark will remain legal tender, a secured currency will also be issued, and a German Annuity Bank (Deutsche Rentenbank) will be established. The currency will gradually be based upon gold.... The Irish Deportees Compensation Tribunal meets to consider damages for people arrested in England and deported to the Irish Free State.			Fruit canners in Melbourne reject the bounties offered by the Australian government. They argue that only the removal of the embargo on sugar imports will solve the financial problems of fruit growers and canners.
Oct. 16		Food riots occur all over Germany.... A large group of unemployed workers march to Town Hall in Berlin and tried to force entry. Police manage to bar the doors. A small group of workers is then admitted. They demand 10 million marks, two loaves of bread, two pounds of fat, firewood, and coal for each man as well as a reopening of food kitchens.	The Khedivah Mother brings suit against the Egyptian government for the recovery of rents that are in arrears. The rents went into arrears during her exile in Constantinople.	The Cuban Senate confirms the first Cuban Ambassador to the United States, Cosme de la Torrient y Peraza.	The government of India considers creating an Indian Bar.
Oct. 17		The British Ministry of Transport issues a letter to local authorities warning that gasoline pumps on curbs constitute an obstruction. As a result, owners of these pumps are being notified that they must remove them within 12 months.... Rioting continues in Mannheim, Germany.	A bus overturns on the Casablanca-Rabat road in Morocco. Fifteen passengers are killed and 11 are injured, all Moors.	The Canadian National Millers' Association adopts a resolution recommended that if Britain places a duty on imported flour, then Canada should retaliate with a corresponding duty on wheat.... Jamaica complains that Canadian shipping services are inadequate.	
Oct. 18		An English trawler is arrested for illegal fishing in Norwegian waters....French authorities announce that they will permit all Germans to enter Alsace-Lorraine on All Saints' Day to visit the graves of their relatives.			
Oct. 19	Costa Rica wins in arbitration against Great Britain. The dispute involved Costa Rica's refusal to recognize an oil concession granted during the revolutionary dictatorship.	Finland begins an organized sweeping of Gulf of Finland because of the number of mines discovered in the area....An Italian steamer strikes a mine and sinks in 10 minutes in the Gulf of Ismid. The ship was bound to Genoa from Constantinople.... Berlin stockbrokers go on strike because they can be held liable in the event of the failure of clients for which they had executed orders.		Canada establishes additional reservations in the Northwest Territories for the Native American residents of the district that are in danger of suffering want and starvation because of insufficient protected areas for hunting and trapping.	Melbourne, Australia, theaters go dark because of a strike of electricians, mechanics, and property men. The strikers object to an arbitration award that makes their jobs interchangeable....New Zealand dairy producers approve a government plan to establish a pool of dairy produce for export, controlled by a representative of the government, the producers, and a London agency.
Oct. 20	The Italian government seeks an increase in the Italian quota of reparations since the debts of all the ex-enemy countries have been consolidated.	Groups of Fascist and Communist students brawl in Copenhagen, Denmark. The police make several arrests.		The Canadian Minister of Agriculture encourages Canadians to show a friendly attitude toward newcomers and to guide settlers with money so that they would not become victims. Such measures might help promote immigration and help Canada to acquire the agricultural workers that it needs.	India is being flooded with Europeans seeking employment. The Indian Statute book contains no prohibition against landing without means of support. Unemployed men drift to a Salvation Army home or similar establishments before being declared vagrant and being shipped back to their countries of origin at government expense.

A	B	C	D	E
Includes developments that affect more than one world region, international organizations and important meetings of world leaders.	*Includes all domestic and regional developments in Europe, including the Soviet Union.*	*Includes all domestic and regional developments in Africa and the Middle East.*	*Includes all domestic and regional developments in Latin America, the Caribbean, and Canada.*	*Includes all domestic and regional developments in Asian and Pacific nations (and colonies).*

U.S. Politics & Social Issues	U.S. Foreign Policy & Affairs, Defense	U.S. Economy & Environment	Science, Technology & Nature	Culture, Leisure & Lifestyle	
A crash between a passenger train and a car at a level crossing kills nine members of the same family in Fairland, IN, as they return from church.				Game 5 of the World Series is won by the Yankees at Yankee Stadium by a score of 8–1.	Oct. 14
The British quota for immigration into the United States is exhausted. As a result, 700 people arriving on a steamship are denied entrance. They are appealing on the grounds that a collision at sea delayed their arrival past the time for entrance.	U.S. Senator Smoot of Utah, a member of the American Debt Funding Commission, advises that the United States should appoint a commission to visit Germany and report upon that country's capacity to pay reparations.... The American Jewish Congress opens its meeting in New York City. Israel Zangwill, the opening speaker, declares that political Zionism is dead and that Jews must abandon their hopes for Palestine. If they do not, Anglo-French friction will kindle another world war.		Representatives from Great Britain, Italy, Czechoslovakia, Greece, Romania, Yugoslavia, and Poland meet to consider the general adoption of the Westinghouse brake as a standard for cargo trains. The brake comes automatically into action when an out-of-control train runs down a slope.	The Yankees win the World Series by beating the Giants 6–4 at the Polo Grounds. The star of the series is Babe Ruth, who scored eight runs, hit three home runs, and had a batting average of .368 throughout the games.... Dancer and future silent film star Louise Brooks makes her first appearance with the famed Denishawn Dance Company at the Apollo Theater in Atlantic City, NJ.... The Episcopalian Bishop of Georgia objects to the removal of the remains of James Oglethorpe from his English grave to the state capitol of Georgia.	Oct. 15
Flooding in Oklahoma City leaves 15,000 people homeless as the whole south side of the city is put underwater. Sandbag levees gave way before the waters of the North Canadian River, which is 25 feet above its normal level.			American surgeon Max Thorek of Chicago announces that he has transferred chimpanzee testicles to hundreds of men and women. He operates through the lumbar region, inserting the new organ through the small of the patient's back. This substitution of animal glands for aged human glands has resulted in the restoration of mental and physical strength.	Soon after Babe Ruth receives his World Series winner's share of $6160.46, insurance agent Harry Heilman, who beat Ruth for the batting title by 10 points, sells him a $50,000 life insurance policy. Beneficiaries are Mrs. Ruth and adopted daughter, Dorothy.... The Archbishop of Canterbury announces that James Oglethorpe's remains will stay in England.	Oct. 16
				The Maryland State Fair promises to pay the trainers of racehorses Zev and Papyrus $50,000 to have the winner of Saturday's race at Belmont Park to meet Admiral Grayson's My Own in a special race over the fairgrounds course. Papyrus is the favorite to win at Belmont.	Oct. 17
				The octet for wind instruments, Igor Stravinsky's latest composition premieres at the Paris Opera. The work is scored for flute, clarinet, two bassoons, two trumpets, and two trombones.	Oct. 18
	Frank Lowden, the former governor of Illinois, declines the position of Ambassador to Great Britain.			Citing the unsavory characters associated with the sport, American League president Ban Johnson persuades AL owners to prohibit boxing matches in their baseball parks. The National League declines to go along with the plan.	Oct. 19
The governors of 37 states confer with President Coolidge about enforcement of Prohibition. The meeting ends with an agreement to adopt whatever means are practicable to cause respect for the law.... The President informs the governors that the Labor Department estimates that 100,000 unauthorized aliens enter the country yearly.	The American Debt Funding Commission approves a report stating that a sum of $6 billion remains due from foreign countries with accumulating interest of $1 billion.				Oct. 20

F	G	H	I	J
Includes campaigns, elections, federal-state relations, civil rights and liberties, crime, the judiciary, education, healthcare, poverty, urban affairs, and population.	*Includes formation and debate of U.S. foreign and defense policies, veterans affairs, and defense spending. (Relations with specific foreign countries are usually found under the region concerned.)*	*Includes business, labor, agriculture, taxation, transportation, consumer affairs, monetary and fiscal policy, natural resources, pollution and industrial accidents.*	*Includes worldwide scientific, medical and technological developments, natural phenomena, U.S. weather and natural disasters.*	*Includes the arts, religion, scholarship, communications media, sports, entertainment, fashions, fads, and social life.*

	World Affairs	Europe	Africa & The Middle East	The Americas	Asia & The Pacific
Oct. 21		A Rhine Republic is proclaimed by separatists, at Aachen. Belgium is maintaining neutrality. It intends to intervene only when it is necessary to discuss the reparation question in relation to the new political situation.…Crown Prince Peter of Yugoslavia is christened.		The former Secretary of the Treasury in Mexico alleges that the government wasted 10 million pesos, mostly by paying the salaries of fictitious persons. As a result, Mexico cannot comply with the conditions of a debt agreement with the United States.	The Australian Labour Party votes to expel all Communist members.… The Perth Diocesan Synod unanimously passes a resolution in favor of the autonomy of the Anglican Church in Australia.
Oct. 22	The International Labor Organization opens its fifth session in Geneva under the chairmanship of Mineichiro Adatei of Japan. The primary issue at this session to be discussed is the inspection of labor protection.	A Greek counterrevolution begins with the demand that the Revolutionary government immediately dissolve. Several thousand copies of this demand are dropped by airplane over Athens. The government invites the insurgents to surrender and sends out troops.…The Rhineland Separatist movement spread through the Belgian and French zones.…A French duke and a manager of a French theater duel with swords on the outskirts of Paris. The duke is wounded. He had objected to paying tax on his complimentary admission.	Feizi Bey, the Minister of Public Works for Turkey, declares that foreign companies must only employ Turkish Muslims. Companies that fail to comply will have their charters cancelled in violation of the terms of the minority clauses in the Treaty of Lausanne.…Turkey blames Russia for encouraging Armenian violence against Turks.	A steamer belonging to the United Fruit Company grounds on Providence Island, near Panama.… An attack upon a parade of the Calles faction leaves five people dead and 20 wounded in Mexico City.	The government of Australia advocates a railroad from Western Australia through Northern Territory to Queensland as a means of promoting settlement. The Northern Territory has a diminishing population, with farms moribund and rich mining areas that have been abandoned.
Oct. 23	Germany informs the Reparations Commission that it is not in a position to meet the cost of deliveries in kind, although it is willing in principle to make deliveries.…General Smuts of South Africa calls for a conference of powers interested in the reparations question. The United States should take an active part and bear their full weight.	German Communists storm the police stations in Hamburg and Altona. By nightfall, most of the stations are reoccupied by police. Food shops in the cities are also plundered.…The German Senate announces plans to control the price of bread. Starting tomorrow, a loaf will cost 4.2 billion marks.…Henri Barbusse, author of the well-known war book, *Le Feu*, appears before a Paris court on a charge of provoking military insubordination.	Turkey increases the pay of the army.…An Armenian mob at Erivan tears down the flag of the Turkish Legation. Turkey is considering sending troops to punish the Armenians.	The directors of the failed Home Bank in Canada are reported to have owned an interest in a steamship that engaged in rum running.…The Panama Canal closes because of heavy rains and debris from flooding. The level of water in the locks is beyond manageable conditions.	Mismanagement of the state of Nabha in India has meant that the few resources have been applied to ordinary public services. As a result, the state is in serious financial and administrative difficulty.…The Prime Minister of New Zealand, W.F. Massey, states that his country is attempting to end the depression in Great Britain by buying more British goods and by recruiting British immigrants.
Oct. 24	A collection box supposed to contain from 10,000 to 15,000 francs is stolen from the League of Nations at Geneva. It had been placed in the lobby to collect donations for Japanese earthquake relief.	Two Gobelins tapestries are stolen from the chateau of Versailles in France. The Versailles magistrate declares that the guards are guilty of negligence of duty. None of the guards entered the building after six o'clock.…The Greek counterrevolution is spreading as army regiments join the uprising. Government forces fire on revolutionaries at Kalamaki.…Bavaria declares that the establishment of a Rhineland Republic is treasonous.	Robert Coryndon, the Governor of Kenya Colony, offers a literacy test to Indians seeking to vote. The test only measures the ability to read and write a language in common usage in the colony.…The Khalifa of the Spanish zone of Morocco dies suddenly.…The Prime Minister of Persia, Mirza Hassan Khan, offers his resignation to the Shah.	Normal traffic resumes on the Panama Canal.	Chinese pirates attack and loot a steamship near Hong Kong. The 60 pirates boarded the ship as passengers, took possession of the engine room and bridge while at sea, and forced everyone below. They spent the night filling the ship's boats with bounty, including the ship's armory.
Oct. 25		Polish railroad workers go on strike over the depreciation of the Polmark and the high cost of living.…The Communist uprising in Hamburg, Germany, is put down.			A Sikh sets off a bomb on his body that kills him as well as five policemen in Lahore, India. The police had just taken a revolver from the man and handcuffed him when the bomb exploded.
Oct. 26		The Bavarian government announces that it will apply the death penalty in extreme cases of profiteering and speculating.… A prominent Jewish art dealer is expelled from Bavaria as a troublesome person. The deportation campaign against troublesome people is largely directed at Jews and foreigners.			
Oct. 27		Italy celebrates Mass throughout the country for the Fascists who died in the revolution. The event is a celebration of the Fascist March on Rome that took place on October 27, 1922.…The government of Germany demands that the government of Saxony resign. Communists in the state government are alleged to be provoking the Saxon populace to violence.			

A	B	C	D	E
Includes developments that affect more than one world region, international organizations and important meetings of world leaders.	*Includes all domestic and regional developments in Europe, including the Soviet Union.*	*Includes all domestic and regional developments in Africa and the Middle East.*	*Includes all domestic and regional developments in Latin America, the Caribbean, and Canada.*	*Includes all domestic and regional developments in Asian and Pacific nations (and colonies).*

U.S. Politics & Social Issues	U.S. Foreign Policy & Affairs, Defense	U.S. Economy & Environment	Science, Technology & Nature	Culture, Leisure & Lifestyle	
				Kentucky Derby winner Papyrus loses to Zev at Belmont Park in New York before a crowd of 50,000. The race took place on a very muddy track with Papyrus slipping on the course. The purse was $100,000 with Zev getting $80,000.	Oct. 21
	German Americans in New York who gather to celebrate German Day are urged to rally to the aid of Germany before it is overwhelmed by internal trouble and engulfed by French troops.		Three skeletons of mammoths are discovered in Warsaw while digging a tunnel.…Work resumes on Tutankhamen's tomb in Egypt.		Oct. 22
Would-be immigrants taken through Ellis Island before being sent home to Great Britain complain about being housed in cages in filthy and crowded conditions.					Oct. 23
Governor Walton of Oklahoma is suspended from office by the state senate pending his impeachment trial. Only one senator voted against suspension. Among the charges that Walton faces is an allegation that he pardoned scores of prisoners from the state penitentiary for his own profit.		In Olympia, WA, the Pacific Highway is dedicated in a series of ceremonies marking the hard-surfacing of the highway from Canada to California. After the ceremonies, participants drive to the Interstate Bridge at Vancouver where "Old Man Detour" was hung in effigy amidst the acclaim of thousands of spectators.	It is announced that the fossil remains of an unknown bear-like animal have been discovered in Central Africa. The creature had the general appearance of a horse, but with claws instead of hooves.		Oct. 24
			The Nobel Prize for Medicine is awarded to Drs. Banting and Macleod of Toronto for the discovery of insulin.		Oct. 25
Two Texas men in Freestone County duel to the death. Standing toe to toe with their left hands clasped, they fired at each other with revolvers.			Charles Steinmetz, a pioneer in electrical engineering, dies. Steinmetz invented a successful alternating current motor and held over 200 patents.	*Oedipus Rex* is presented for the first time in America at the Century Theater in New York City.…The birthplace of Theodore Roosevelt, at 28 East 20th Street in New York City, is formally dedicated as a patriotic shrine.	Oct. 26
					Oct. 27

F	G	H	I	J
Includes campaigns, elections, federal-state relations, civil rights and liberties, crime, the judiciary, education, healthcare, poverty, urban affairs, and population.	*Includes formation and debate of U.S. foreign and defense policies, veterans affairs, and defense spending. (Relations with specific foreign countries are usually found under the region concerned.)*	*Includes business, labor, agriculture, taxation, transportation, consumer affairs, monetary and fiscal policy, natural resources, pollution and industrial accidents.*	*Includes worldwide scientific, medical and technological developments, natural phenomena, U.S. weather and natural disasters.*	*Includes the arts, religion, scholarship, communications media, sports, entertainment, fashions, fads, and social life.*

	World Affairs	Europe	Africa & The Middle East	The Americas	Asia & The Pacific
Oct. 28		The Soviet Union refuses to accept 14 Russian refugees who were once wealthy merchants in St. Petersburg and Moscow. They are now stricken by poverty.			
Oct. 29	As the result of the admission of new states to the League of Nations and a resulting redistribution of expenses, the organization reduces the contributions required from Romania, Greece, Portugal, and Hungary. These countries are the most overburdened according to the new method of distribution.	The Saxon government refuses to resign on the grounds that there is no political justification for the demand and no legal grounds for one.…Germany announces that it will appoint an Imperial Commissary for the Free State of Saxony to replace the current state government.	The Earl of Athlone is appointed to be Governor-General of South Africa.	The directors of the failed Home Bank of Canada are formally charged with fraud and conspiracy. The prosecution is in the hands of the government of Ontario. The provincial government lost $1.25 million that it had on deposit at the bank.	Japanese submarine No. 26 sinks during a memorial service for the men who died when No. 70 sank. The crew is saved by another submarine.
Oct. 30	The Swedish Foreign Minister emphasizes that Sweden will go to the aid of Finland if the country is menaced by the Soviet Union.… Russia protests the entrance of Japanese ships into Russian ports without permission.	Andrew Bonar Law, former Prime Minister of Great Britain, dies.	The Legislative Council for the Colony and the Southern Provinces of the Protectorate of Nigeria meets for the first time. The council was established in November 1922 as an effort to establish popular representation and participation in the practical work of government.		
Oct. 31		The Separatists in the Rhine destroy all official documents, including the Criminal Register and the Rogues Photograph Gallery.…France bans the export of cheese and eggs throughout the winter to avoid a further rise in the cost of living.…The government of Portugal resigns.	The Governor-General of French West Africa issues a decree forbidding the capture, detention, sale, or exportation of live chimpanzees, except at the request of scientific or medical authorities.…The draft of the new Iraq Constitution is published.		Melbourne, Australia, police announce plans to strike if supervisors appointed by the Police Commissioner are not removed. The police view the supervisors as spies.
Nov. 1		Prime Minister Stanley Baldwin advocates protectionism for British industries. He aims to tax imported manufactured goods that cause the greatest amount of British unemployment and give substantial preferences to the colonies.			
Nov. 2	Britain tells Greece that it would view with grave concern any movement resulting in the overthrow of the monarchy.…France objects to the creation of a Committee of Experts to consider Germany's ability to pay reparations. France wants the means by which Germany will pay to also be considered.	Ex-Crown Prince Wilhelm receives permission to return to Germany from the Netherlands. He has been in exile for five years.…Britain announces plans to establish a straw rope-making industry to solve the long-standing problem of surplus straw.		The Canadian Department of Agriculture bans all dogs other than lap dogs or dogs less than 20 pounds from entering the country from the United Kingdom under the Animals Contagious Diseases Act.	Guam is struck by an earthquake that is recorded in Canada. The tremors are reported to equal those of the recent Japanese earthquake.
Nov. 3		The British Commission on Compensation for Suffering and Damage by Enemy Action reported that almost all claims for loss of life, injury to health, maltreatment during internment, and loss of personal effects at sea have been paid. The Commission is now engaged in examining property claims.		Fifty British harvesters returning to Britain engage in a fight with 200 longshoremen at Montreal. It took the harbor police 20 minutes to quell the disturbance but there were no serious injuries. The fight reportedly began when a harvester made an anti-French remark.	
Nov. 4		An observatory in Milan, Italy, detects an earthquake that lasts more than three hours and has an epicenter in the Far East.…Italy celebrates the fifth anniversary of the signing of the Armistice with Austria.… Funeral services are held for Andrew Bonar Law, former Prime Minister of Great Britain, in Westminster Abbey.…Greek officers post a manifesto stating that the king of Greece is implicated in the recent insurrection and that he has expressed support for the rebels. They demand an immediate vote on the future of the monarchy.			A band of toughs takes control of the central sector of Melbourne, Australia, in the wake of a police strike. Drunks batter peaceful citizens over the heads with beer bottles, plate-glass windows of shops are shattered, and rioters loot jewelry and clothing shops. Street traffic is paralyzed. Women as well as men participate in the looting. A Citizens Safety Committee is attempting to stop the disturbances.
	A *Includes developments that affect more than one world region, international organizations and important meetings of world leaders.*	B *Includes all domestic and regional developments in Europe, including the Soviet Union.*	C *Includes all domestic and regional developments in Africa and the Middle East.*	D *Includes all domestic and regional developments in Latin America, the Caribbean, and Canada.*	E *Includes all domestic and regional developments in Asian and Pacific nations (and colonies).*

U.S. Politics & Social Issues	U.S. Foreign Policy & Affairs, Defense	U.S. Economy & Environment	Science, Technology & Nature	Culture, Leisure & Lifestyle	
	The submarine O-5 sinks in Limon Bay in the Panama Canal zone after a collision with a steamer. Five of the crew members are missing.		Spanish men fishing in the Huerva River, a tributary of the Ebro, catch a dogfish from the Mediterranean that had traveled 150 miles upstream.		Oct. 28
Prohibition agents report that foreign ships are violating the order against bringing liquor into U.S. waters. As evidence, they state that ships open their bars as soon as they reach the three-mile international limit while outbound. Accordingly, they must have liquor when they are in American territory. Treasury officials announce plans to seize the vessels if enough evidence can be found.	Great Britain accepts a U.S. proposal for the establishment of a 12-mile limit for the purpose of extending the right of search for contraband.... A sunken U.S. submarine is raised and two men are discovered to be alive after 31 hours confinement.		A Smithsonian expedition in Southern California discovers two skulls near Santa Barbara. The skulls are from men who existed before the Neanderthals. The mouth of one skull measured seven inches from jaw to jaw, indicating a mouth cavity larger than that of modern man. Crude implements, including pestles and barbless fishhooks, were found with the skulls.		Oct. 29
	The U.S. government plans to send an expedition to Haiti to show motion picture films in villages. The expedition, organized by Theodore Roosevelt, will be led by navy and marine officers.		Limestone caves are discovered in New Zealand, a few hours by automobile from Auckland.		Oct. 30
Russian refugees from Constantinople who are now in Cherbourg, France, had been waiting for a steamer to take them to New York. They are informed that the quota for Russian immigrants has been met. As a result, they cannot emigrate before June 1924 and arrangements are being made for their return to Constantinople.					Oct. 31
					Nov. 1
		The Goodyear Tire & Rubber Company purchases all patents and rights to manufacture Zeppelin airships and their accessories. The company will bring a staff of experienced Zeppelin builders and designers from Germany. Five types of airship will be built to fit the various needs of the army, navy, Post Office, and private industry.			Nov. 2
		The Chevrolet Company intends to make Copenhagen, Denmark, its center for the sale of cars to Scandinavia and Northern Europe. It purchases a large factory. Ford Motor Company already has a large factory in Copenhagen.			Nov. 3
The *Leviathan* arrives in New York with 1359 British immigrants, nearly all of whom will have to be returned to England because the British quota is exhausted. There are 600 Britons in other ships and in other ports who will be similarly disbarred from entrance into the United States. The *Leviathan* may face a fine of $200 for each immigrant plus refunds of the passage money, which averages $100 per person.... There are also 1,921 Russians facing exclusion, their quota of 700 being exhausted.	David Lloyd George, former British Prime Minister, speaks to an audience at the Metropolitan Opera House. His route to the speech is lined by 2,000 police officers in response to announced plans by Irish Republicans to attack. No one without a ticket was permitted within a block of the Opera House.				Nov. 4

F	G	H	I	J
Includes campaigns, elections, federal-state relations, civil rights and liberties, crime, the judiciary, education, healthcare, poverty, urban affairs, and population.	*Includes formation and debate of U.S. foreign and defense policies, veterans affairs, and defense spending. (Relations with specific foreign countries are usually found under the region concerned.)*	*Includes business, labor, agriculture, taxation, transportation, consumer affairs, monetary and fiscal policy, natural resources, pollution and industrial accidents.*	*Includes worldwide scientific, medical and technological developments, natural phenomena, U.S. weather and natural disasters.*	*Includes the arts, religion, scholarship, communications media, sports, entertainment, fashions, fads, and social life.*

	World Affairs	Europe	Africa & The Middle East	The Americas	Asia & The Pacific
Nov. 5	The Mixed Commission upholds United States claims of $22.6 million against Germany for the loss of lives, personal injuries, and loss of property resulting from the sinking of the *Lusitania.*	"Rat Week" begins in Great Britain as the public is encouraged to destroy the vermin. About 80 rat clubs are formed in Kent to kill the creatures. Members use dogs, ferrets, sticks, and shot guns to win prizes donated by farmers and others suffering from rat damage....A mass meeting of 5,000 people in favor of republicanism is held in Athens, Greece....A steamship steward is fined by a British court for smuggling four bottles of eau de Cologne.			The government of Melbourne, Australia, swears in 2,000 special police officers and declares that it is prepared to swear in 3,000 more men. People are obeying the warning not to enter the city at night. State government troops are held in readiness if they should be wanted.
Nov. 6		A British snuff mill ceases operation after two centuries because of a loss of business resulting from the decline of the snuff habit....The hunger strike in the Irish Free State prisons continues with 600 people continuing to fast.		Alberta voters decide to end Prohibition by a 25,000-vote majority out of the 200,000 ballots cast.	
Nov. 7		The Soviet Union celebrates the sixth anniversary of the Bolshevist revolution....Several thousand tons of Russian grain is shipped for the use of the German proletariat.			Melbourne, Australia, declares a state of emergency because of a strike by police. The declaration is good for one month. The opposition Labour Party charges that the government is responsible for the rioting in Melbourne.
Nov. 8	A committee of representatives from the Italian metallurgical, mechanical, and chemical industries joins the Ministry of Foreign Affairs to examine the present position of the Ruhr in regard to the economic condition of Italy.	Britain bans the import of all cattle from Ireland because of the discovery of foot-and-mouth disease....An Italian fort near Genoa blows up when workmen drop a box of explosives. Debris is flung more than two miles into the sea. Nine people are killed as a fire rages all day long.		A large party of single women leaves Scotland for Canada.	
Nov. 9	The British Imperial Conference concludes its meeting. It states that the European situation can only be solved with the help of the United States and that U.S. failure to help will damage the peace and economic recovery of the world. It also opposes the separation of Germany.	Adolf Hitler attempts his Beer Hall Putsch, an attempt to seize the government of Bavaria. Nazi police enter Jewish-owned stores, arrest the proprietors, and hold them in a beer hall for several hours....The German government issues an order that some sugar may be exported provided that the profits from foreign exchange are handed over to the government.	The British Colonial Secretary advises Herbert Samuel, High Commissioner for Palestine, that it is useless to continue to attempt to involve Arabs in the governing of Palestine. Arabs boycotted a proposed legislative council, forcing the plan to be abandoned.	Canada seeks a preference for salmon and apples shipped to Great Britain. The Canadian salmon industry has lost considerable business in recent years to Siberian and American competition.	The government of Victoria, Australia, reaffirms its refusal to re-employ striking police officers. Melbourne is now policed by men who did not go on strike, special constables, and men from the country. Traffic in the street has resumed, restaurants have reopened, and street barricades are being removed. The government bans the exportation of film of the disturbances.
Nov. 10		Britain holds "Poppy Day" today because the anniversary of the Armistice falls on a Sunday. More than 25 million Flanders poppies are on sale to raise money for a fund for disabled and distressed ex-servicemen. All ranks of the army are permitted to wear a poppy in their caps when not on duty.		Henry Ford states that Ford Motor Company will spend more than $5 million in plant extensions, garages, and offices throughout Canada next year.	
Nov. 11		Armistice Day is celebrated in Belgium with a parade of 15,000 disabled men. The blind and those unable to walk followed the procession in a long line of automobiles....The Flame of Remembrance is lit for the first time at the Tomb of the Unknown Soldier in Paris....Adolf Hitler is arrested at Essing, 40 miles from Munich.		The National Association of Veterans and Patriots for the Purification of the Cuban Administration chooses a committee of five to direct the organization....Armistice Day is celebrated throughout Canada.	

A	B	C	D	E
Includes developments that affect more than one world region, international organizations and important meetings of world leaders.	*Includes all domestic and regional developments in Europe, including the Soviet Union.*	*Includes all domestic and regional developments in Africa and the Middle East.*	*Includes all domestic and regional developments in Latin America, the Caribbean, and Canada.*	*Includes all domestic and regional developments in Asian and Pacific nations (and colonies).*

	U.S. Politics & Social Issues	U.S. Foreign Policy & Affairs, Defense	U.S. Economy & Environment	Science, Technology & Nature	Culture, Leisure & Lifestyle
Nov. 5		The U.S. Navy places guards on American steamships in the Yangtze River in China. The guards have orders to reply when fired upon and the commanders of U.S. gunboats have orders to beat off all hazards, any attacks by Chinese bandits or military units. All of the leading military and civil authorities in the provinces concerned have been notified of the role assigned to U.S. forces. The orders come in response to continued attacks upon foreigners in China.	Admiral Moffat of the U.S. Navy states that the navy believes that its decision to build airships, after Germany was stopped by the peace treaty and Britain and France hesitated, contributed materially to the advance of the airship industry in the United States. The U.S. government intends to make public all information about the operating costs of military airships with the aim of aiding commercial interests.	Great Britain announces plans to open the country's first automatic telephone exchange. It announces these plans as what is presumably the last manual exchange open in London. The system to be adopted resembles the one in New York. The full capacity of the exchange will be 9,000 lines. The exchanges will use a four-digit system with three letters preceding the numbers to distinguish the exchange, for example ABC-1234.	
Nov. 6	Federal agents seize a British schooner off the Florida coast, near South Pablo Beach, with a cargo of 3,000 cases of liquor after a 3-mile chase. The crew declares that they fled because they thought that the Customs agents were pirates.		The strongest earthquake in years strikes the Imperial Valley in California. Buildings are dislodged from their foundations, walls are cracked, and windows break. No casualties are reported.... A coalmine explosion at the Glen Rogers mine in Beckley, WV, kills 27 men.		
Nov. 7	The election results from today's voting do not substantially change the situation in Congress. The Republicans elected one senator and three representatives, while the Democrats elect four representatives. Accordingly, the Senate will have 51 Republicans, 43 Democrats, and two Farmer-Laborites, while the House will have 225 Republicans, 207 Democrats, one Socialist, one Farmer-Laborite, and one Independent.		The Goodyear Tire Company is organizing a separate firm for the manufacture of airships. The Zeppelin interests will receive a minority of holding stock in this corporation. No cash is involved.		
Nov. 8		General John Pershing, commander of U.S. forces during the war, visits American cemeteries in France.			Milton Hersey, the millionaire chocolate maker, gives his entire fortune to an industrial school for boys that he founded 14 years ago. The actual transfer was made in 1918, but kept secret until today at Hershey's request. The school is near the town of Hershey, PA.
Nov. 9		A White House spokesman declares that if the proposed inquiry into Germany's ability to pay reparations were limited to its present capacity or capacity up to 1930, then it would be wholly futile and useless.	Five directors of the Ottoman American Development Company resign in a protest to the firm's decision to sell stock to the public. The directors declare that the company no longer controls many concessions in Turkey.... Herbert Hoover, the Secretary of Commerce, recommends that the number of American merchants abroad be increased to build up the American Merchant Marine.		
Nov. 10			The premature explosion of flashlight powder fatally injures a photographer taking pictures of people arriving in the *Aquitania* at New York Harbor.... A worker at an air carnival in Long Island is killed when he is carried into the air by an airship and then falls from 50 feet.		
Nov. 11	Armistice Day is celebrated throughout the United States. Two minutes of silence is observed at 11 o'clock.				

F	G	H	I	J
Includes campaigns, elections, federal-state relations, civil rights and liberties, crime, the judiciary, education, healthcare, poverty, urban affairs, and population.	*Includes formation and debate of U.S. foreign and defense policies, veterans affairs, and defense spending. (Relations with specific foreign countries are usually found under the region concerned.)*	*Includes business, labor, agriculture, taxation, transportation, consumer affairs, monetary and fiscal policy, natural resources, pollution and industrial accidents.*	*Includes worldwide scientific, medical and technological developments, natural phenomena, U.S. weather and natural disasters.*	*Includes the arts, religion, scholarship, communications media, sports, entertainment, fashions, fads, and social life.*

	World Affairs	Europe	Africa & The Middle East	The Americas	Asia & The Pacific
Nov. 12	The Conference of Ambassadors meets to consider the return of the former Crown Prince to Germany and the German refusal to permit the Allies to resume their investigations into military control of Germany.	The Soviet newspaper *Izvestia* reports that homeless children are continually arriving in Moscow from all parts of Russia. The children are in a pitiable state, having lost their parents and every means of livelihood.... Munich University students pass a vote of no confidence in the Bavarian government.	In a meeting of the Turkish Assembly, legislators demand reprisals against Greeks for alleged atrocities against Muslims in Macedonia.... The National Arab Party holds its first meeting in Jerusalem. Some 150 Arabs from Palestine assemble to consider solutions to the Palestinian problem.	A model sugar factory is being established at Trinidad to train scientists and technologists to aid in the development of the sugar industry of the British Empire.	The Japanese government reports that almost all documents in the Japanese Patent Office were destroyed in the recent earthquake.
Nov. 13		The British government advises King George of Greece to pay no attention to suggestions that he should voluntarily leave Greece.... Three insurgent Greek officers are sentenced to death and three others receive imprisonment for life.... Germany announces that two million people in occupied territories are unemployed and 700,000 people in unoccupied lands are unemployed.	A Syrian automobile is stopped in Jerusalem and its passengers robbed by men in British uniform who claim to be acting officially. The robbers advise the passengers to claim their money from the District Governor of Jerusalem.		The Emperor of Japan calls an emergency session of the Diet to discuss the restoration of the towns and districts laid waste by the earthquake.
Nov. 14		Statistics show that the production of cigars in Switzerland has dropped by 500 million pieces or 47 percent since 1914. Tobacco industrials request that the government reduce import duties on raw tobacco.... The director of the political section of the Ukrainian Soviet warns that anti-Semitism is growing in the army while Communist influence is diminishing.	The Supreme Court of South Africa declares that the color bar in the Transvaal is repugnant to the general law of the land.		The Government of India appoints a committee to consider the creation of an Indian Bar.
Nov. 15		Ginestal Machado becomes Prime Minister of Portugal, succeeding Maria da Silva.... A Jewish man is shot and killed in the Jewish section of Dublin, Ireland. He was asked if he was a Jew prior to the attack. It is the second attack on Jews in two weeks.... General von Steeckt, the German Reich dictator, authorizes local military commanders to confiscate, if it is considered necessary, dance halls, bars, and similar establishments that cater purely to luxurious needs and turn them into kitchens for the relief of the suffering populace.	Persia forms a Red Lion and Sun Society to cooperate with the International Red Cross.... The Customs agreement signed in 1890 between the Ottoman Empire and Egypt is no longer applicable between Palestine and Egypt. Imports from Egypt are liable to the same duties imposed on goods from other foreign countries.	Canada announces a new immigration policy that lowers the bars to admit people of all nationalities who are able and willing to work.	
Nov. 16	The government of Turkey complains to the League of Nations about Greek mistreatment of Muslims in Macedonia and Crete.... Mussolini of Italy declares that he will consent to no further occupation of Germany.	The Canton of Zurich, Switzerland, imposes fines on 600 persons who evaded mandatory vaccination during the recent smallpox epidemic.... Ex-Kaiser Wilhelm of Germany states that the ex-Crown Prince made the decision to return to Germany without consulting him. Had he been consulted, the Kaiser states, he would have objected.	A bi-weekly 30-hour train service between Cape Town and Johannesburg, South Africa, begins. This is a savings of 15 hours compared with ordinary daily service.... People in Baluchistan kill large numbers of fowls in the belief that they contain snakes and their eggs contain scorpions. The rumor is scotched by authorities.	A plan to overthrow the government of Peru is uncovered. The conspirators, led by German Leguia Martinez, a member of the Supreme Court and former Prime Minister, planned to bombard the presidential palace and assassinate the president. Authorities seize bombs, 50 boxes of munitions, money, and compromising documents as they arrest the conspirators.	Japan ends martial law, imposed after the earthquake.
Nov. 17	The Greek government protests to the Powers, to Turkey, and to the League of Nations against the treatment of the remaining Greek hostages and prisoners of war in Asia Minor.				
Nov. 18	The Bulgarian and Yugoslavian Commission agreed upon details for reparations to Serbia for requisitions during the war. Bulgaria will pay 150 million levas in four annual payments.	Foot-and-mouth disease spreads for the first time in 50 years to the north of Scotland.... The Soviet Union exiles 120 students to Siberia for agitating against the government.... The German government denies that the Bavarian monarchy will be restored.		An explosion in a cartridge factory in Santiago de Chile destroys three workshops and injures about 100 people.	A number of Muslim centers, especially those in India celebrate a new holiday. The Arab Countries Day is marked by speeches that urge Muslims to secure the freedom of the Holy Places.
	A *Includes developments that affect more than one world region, international organizations and important meetings of world leaders.*	B *Includes all domestic and regional developments in Europe, including the Soviet Union.*	C *Includes all domestic and regional developments in Africa and the Middle East.*	D *Includes all domestic and regional developments in Latin America, the Caribbean, and Canada.*	E *Includes all domestic and regional developments in Asian and Pacific nations (and colonies).*

U.S. Politics & Social Issues	U.S. Foreign Policy & Affairs, Defense	U.S. Economy & Environment	Science, Technology & Nature	Culture, Leisure & Lifestyle	
The Secretary of the Treasury proposes to reduce income tax receipts by $323 million per year. Andrew Mellon says that a reduction would free business from interference and encourage a more healthy development of productive enterprise. He advises that the reduction is possible only if Congress rejects the proposal for the soldiers' bonuses.			The United States offer the airship *Shenandoah* to Roald Amundsen as an emergency auxiliary ship for his next expedition to the North Pole.	Pope Pius XI issues an Encyclical Letter urging members of the Greek Orthodox Church to return to the bosom of the Church of Rome.... The United States may not defend its rowing championship at the next Olympic Games at Antwerp in 1920 unless the French Olympic Committee consents to alter the dates already fixed for the event. The July dates conflict with the race between Yale and Harvard Universities.	Nov. 12
			Robert A. Millikan of California is awarded the Nobel Prize for Physics for his work on the elementary charge of electricity and on the photoelectric effect. Fritz Pregl of the University of Graz wins the Nobel Prize for Chemistry for his invention of the method of microanalysis of organic substances.	Faith healer and clairvoyant Frederick L. Rawson dies in New York City from pneumonia. Hundreds of his followers, unaware of his death, had flocked to a hall where he was scheduled to speak. They are shocked to learn of his death.	Nov. 13
A volunteer aerial policeman, after chasing two airmen in another airplane at Akron, OH, arrests them after they land. The men are charged with stunt flying over the city, contrary to an ordinance recently passed by the city council.... Two youths in New York City shoot and kill two bank messengers. They seize $43,000 and escape in an automobile.	A total of 22,165 peace plans are submitted for the Edward W. Bok prize of $100,000 before the contest closes today. They come from 10 countries plus the United States. Most are bulky manuscripts but some are telegrams and others are cabled summaries of schemes. The contest is for the best practical plan by which the United States can promote world peace.		France sends a big gun, modeled along the lines of Germany's wartime "Big Bertha" to the Experimental Commission for testing. The gun has a length of 69 feet and weighs more than 87 tons. The projectile weight is 914 pounds and has a range of 60 miles.	Two men are arrested in London for willfully exposing to view an indecent exhibition. The men admitted adults only to see a number of anatomical specimens preserved in alcohol as well as waxwork figures of human bodies with some parts of the framework removed to show internal organs.	Nov. 14
Senator Hiram Johnson of California announces that he is seeking the Republican nomination for the presidency of the United States.	The U.S. Social Hygiene Bureau notifies the League of Nations that it will contribute more than $30,000 to combat the white slave trade.			The House of Bishops of the Episcopal Church unanimously adopts a Pastoral Letter at its Dallas, TX, meeting. The letter says that it is irreconcilable with his vows for a minister to deny or suggest doubt as to the faith or the truths declared in the Apostles' Creed.	Nov. 15
					Nov. 16
President Coolidge approves a Treasury plan for the expansion of the Coast Guard for the prevention of rum smuggling. An expenditure of $20 million for new craft and new personnel is anticipated.				A letter written by Scottish poet Robert Burns fetches $2,460 at a New York auction of autographed letters and manuscripts by European and American authors.	Nov. 17
	A statue of President Warren Harding is dedicated in Peking, China, in the presence of 10,000 people and the U.S. Ambassador to China.				Nov. 18
F	G	H	I	J	
Includes campaigns, elections, federal-state relations, civil rights and liberties, crime, the judiciary, education, healthcare, poverty, urban affairs, and population.	*Includes formation and debate of U.S. foreign and defense policies, veterans affairs, and defense spending. (Relations with specific foreign countries are usually found under the region concerned.)*	*Includes business, labor, agriculture, taxation, transportation, consumer affairs, monetary and fiscal policy, natural resources, pollution and industrial accidents.*	*Includes worldwide scientific, medical and technological developments, natural phenomena, U.S. weather and natural disasters.*	*Includes the arts, religion, scholarship, communications media, sports, entertainment, fashions, fads, and social life.*	

	World Affairs	Europe	Africa & The Middle East	The Americas	Asia & The Pacific
Nov. 19	The Conference of Ambassadors decides that no immediate territorial sanctions will be taken to enforce the resumption of Allied military control in Germany.	King Alfonso of Spain publicly asks the Pope to admit Spaniards to the Noble Guard, make more appointments of Spaniards, and increase the number of South American Cardinals....Vienna University in Austria is closed until further notice owing to serious anti-Semitic demonstrations, which culminated in attacks on Jewish students by youths of the German Party.		James Lyons, Minister of Lands and Forests for Ontario, Canada, advocates the construction of a highway from Sault Ste. Marie to Winnipeg. Canadian engineers will soon survey a road around the north shore of Lake Superior. The road will be one of the most scenic in the world and will attract thousands annually.	The Reconstruction Budget Committee in Japan plans to spread the work of repairs after the earthquake across six years in order to avoid seeking foreign loans. The estimate of 705 million yen covers the cost of roads, canals, parks as well as subsidies for assisting industries, rebuilding public buildings, and interest on long-term municipal loans.
Nov. 20		The Minister of Foreign Affairs in Belgium states that the return of the ex-Crown Prince to Germany indicates that there is no division of opinion in that country. He says that there is only one Germany, the one that made the war and tortured Belgium....Textile workers in Russia refuse to give three percent of their wages to help German Communists struggle against the German government.	The Kenya Uasin Gishu Railroad will be extended to Uganda. The extension, paid for with an imperial loan for colonial development, will open up an important cotton area and become the main artery to Uganda.		W.M. McPherson, the treasurer of Victoria, Australia, resigns because the state cabinet decides to spend more money than is available as surplus. The money will be spent to increase the pay of police and civil servants.
Nov. 21	The German Charge d'Affairs in Paris handed the French government a note protesting strongly against the action of the French authorities in assisting the Separatists in the Palantinato and hindering German officials in combating seditious and revolutionary elements.				In response to a Papal decree regarding the validity of marriages between Catholics and Protestants, the New South Wales, Australia, legislature proposes the Amending Marriage Bill that would provide a fine, imprisonment, or both for alleging that persons lawfully married are not truly married.
Nov. 22	King Albert of Belgium opens the Colonial University by giving a speech stating that public officials have rallied to the cause of colonization. He says that a great duty to the world has to be fulfilled by developing the riches left profitless by primitive tribes. The university will train colonial officials, with 70 men in the first class.	Socialists in the Belgian Chamber of Deputies fail to get approval of a motion supporting the government policy of strict neutrality in the occupation of the Rhine and opening an inquiry into the manner of strict neutrality....Dutch military authorities discover that maps and documents relating to the Dutch defense system were sold to foreign countries. Four Dutch officers are arrested....Serious rioting occurs in the Ruhr as Communists demonstrate.		Canadian Customs officers have been instructed to search vessels bound for the United States to see that the laws of a friendly nation are not violated. The officials will search for liquor.	The South Australian government seeks legislative authority to help the immigration of girls between 16 and 20 for domestic work on farms selected by the government of Australia....An Australian shipping firm is fined for allowing eight Chinese, prohibited immigrants, to land in Sydney.
Nov. 23		The Irish Republican hunger strike ends in prisons and internment camps. About 200 men and women were fasting....Four cases of anthrax are reported among workers at an English tannery. The men worked on hides imported from China....Greek elections are postponed until December....The Soviet newspaper *Pravda* reports that a number of American communes in the Soviet Union have collapsed with American immigrants left destitute.		The Ontario, Canada, government arranges with the Rockefeller Foundation to make tryparsamide available in the province. The drug treats general paralysis.	Rinderpest is detected for the first time in Australia. It causes heavy mortality among dairy cattle. ...Japan announces that it has discharged 10,700 employees at the various naval arsenals and factories under the terms of the Washington Disarmament Treaty.
Nov. 24					

A	B	C	D	E
Includes developments that affect more than one world region, international organizations and important meetings of world leaders.	*Includes all domestic and regional developments in Europe, including the Soviet Union.*	*Includes all domestic and regional developments in Africa and the Middle East.*	*Includes all domestic and regional developments in Latin America, the Caribbean, and Canada.*	*Includes all domestic and regional developments in Asian and Pacific nations (and colonies).*

U.S. Politics & Social Issues	U.S. Foreign Policy & Affairs, Defense	U.S. Economy & Environment	Science, Technology & Nature	Culture, Leisure & Lifestyle	
The conviction of Charles T. Craig, chief financial officer of New York City, for contempt of court is confirmed by the U.S. Supreme Court. Craig was sentenced to 60 days imprisonment in 1919 for writing a letter to one of the Public Service Commissioners criticizing a decision of a federal judge that opened the way for public ownership of New York City's railroads.... The Supreme Court rules that aliens, ineligible for citizenship, cannot own stock in a land-owning corporation according to the provisions of the Alien Land Laws.	The Secretary of War and the State Department approve a projected around the world flight by a naval air squadron. The flight is expected to give important information regarding transoceanic air communication.				Nov. 19
The Governor of Oklahoma, James C. Walton, is removed from office by the State Senate sitting as an Impeachment Court. He is convicted of abusing his powers to parole and pardon prisoners as well as padding the state payroll, suspending the habeas corpus act, obstructing a special election, collecting excess campaign funds, and incompetence among other charges.					Nov. 20
The Department of Labor issues orders permitting students to temporarily enter the United States, even if the monthly or annual quota of immigrants has been exceeded.... F.A. Cook, an Arctic explorer who claims to have discovered the North Pole and who was found guilty of using the mails with intent to defraud investors, is sentenced to 14 years imprisonment.					Nov. 21
A special grand jury in Connecticut investigates the grant of licenses to 40 or more bogus physicians, who purportedly graduated from a St. Louis, MO, medical school. The physicians bought their degrees and have little medical knowledge.... A warrant is issued for one of the physicians, Sutcliffe, for manslaughter in connection with the death of a factory worker with a crushed finger. Sutcliffe is a former newspaper photographer.					Nov. 22
New York begins an inquiry about bogus physicians. The New York Board of Health estimates that there are between 1,500 and 2,000 imposters practicing medicine in New York City without a license. Some "naturopaths" claim to be able to heal any and all sickness and disease; restore all parts removed by accident or surgery; and restore the recent and long-time dead.	The United States and Bulgaria sign a naturalization treaty. It is the first treaty between the two countries.	The Ford Motor Company is building, at a cost of $110 million, new plants and extensions that will increase the output within four months to 10,000 automobiles and trucks per day.... Two miners are killed in an explosion in a coalmine in Benton, IL.... The laying of a new transatlantic cable between the United States and France is almost complete and expected to be operational within a few days.		Director Cecil B. DeMille's silent film *Ten Commandments* is released by Paramount Pictures. It is one of the first films to use color.... Charles "Red" Wolverton becomes the first rider to go over the two-mile-per-minute mark in a 42 horsepower, four-cylinder Ace Motorcyle. The event is witnessed by hundreds of spectators lined along a concrete highway just outside of Philadelphia, PA.	Nov. 23
	In Texas, a schooner with 865 cases of whiskey and two barrels of beer on board is captured off Galveston Island. The ship hails from the Grand Cayman Islands in the British West Indies.... The Italian and Spanish Consulates in Philadelphia are bombed. The police blame alien Communists angry about an agreement between Italy and Spain to take action against anti-Fascists.			Frederick Dixon, editor of the *Christian Science Monitor*, dies.... Yale University defeats Harvard University in their annual football game by a score of 13–0. The game, played before 55,000 people who sat through a three-hour downpour at Harvard's Soldier Field, marked the first time that Yale beat Harvard since 1916.	Nov. 24
F	G	H	I	J	
Includes campaigns, elections, federal-state relations, civil rights and liberties, crime, the judiciary, education, healthcare, poverty, urban affairs, and population.	*Includes formation and debate of U.S. foreign and defense policies, veterans affairs, and defense spending. (Relations with specific foreign countries are usually found under the region concerned.)*	*Includes business, labor, agriculture, taxation, transportation, consumer affairs, monetary and fiscal policy, natural resources, pollution and industrial accidents.*	*Includes worldwide scientific, medical and technological developments, natural phenomena, U.S. weather and natural disasters.*	*Includes the arts, religion, scholarship, communications media, sports, entertainment, fashions, fads, and social life.*	

	World Affairs	Europe	Africa & The Middle East	The Americas	Asia & The Pacific
Nov. 25		Baron and Baronne Gaston de Montigny of France are found shot to death on the grave of their son, who was killed by a bomb in 1918 while serving with the Engineers.... Heavy fog prevents many ocean liners from sailing from Southampton, England, including the Cunard liner *Aquitania*, bound for New York.		The Royal Commission appointed by the Dominion and Ontario governments to investigate the claims of the Chippewa and Mississauga Indians for the loss of hunting and fishing grounds in Central and Northern Ontario, has awarded $500,00 to the Indians.	The New South Wales government asks the Australian Minister for Migration and Settlement for 200 prospective settlers from Britain with small capital and agricultural experience to take up farms in the state.
Nov. 26	The Tangier Conference recognizes that Tangier and its zone will continue to form an integral part of Morocco, under the control of the Sultan. The district will be known as the Tangier Zone of Morocco and the Sultan will provide a government for it. Tangier will have a large amount of Home Rule. France, Britain, and Spain will retain a degree of administration that will keep Tangier neutral in time of war.	The French airship *Dixmude* reports troubles with its engines. It drifts towards the Italian coast for some time until repairs are made....Austria announces plans to introduce silver coinage as an incentive to frugality and saving....A woman who dies in London is reported to have never spoken to or recognized anyone since her soldier son was reported missing in France in 1916....The President of the Supreme Court in Germany complains that Bavarian authorities are refusing to surrender for trial of the people implicated in the Hitler *Putsch*.	Serious disturbances occur in Kandahar City, Afghanistan, because of the enforcement of compulsory military service. One man in eight is affected by the order.	The Canadian Minister of the Interior denies that Canada has made a request to the United States for a greater supply of water for power purposes under the treaty regulating the diversion of water from the Niagara River.	
Nov. 27	Irish Republicans in Paris ask the Soviet government to assist the Irish Republicans who are suffering under the mandate of the Irish Free State.	Portugal announces plans to sell ex-German steamships to Portuguese citizens and companies. Portugal will retain three of the ships for its colonies and two to serve as transports....Vienna University reopens....The Jewish Academicians adopts a resolution declaring that Jewish students and professors must have unrestricted freedom to teach or learn at Austrian seats of learning.		Arthur Meighen, leader of the Progressive Party, urges an increase of the Canadian navy and a larger contribution by Canada to the defense of the British Empire. He declares that the Canadian defenses on the water are a joke and scarcely sufficient to maintain order in Canada.	A branch of the Ku Klux Klan is founded in New South Wales, Australia, under the name of the Anglo-Saxon Clan.
Nov. 28	The Reparations Commission is considering reducing its personnel and the salaries of its staff in order to meet the financial crisis created by the suspension of German contributions to its funds.	The League of Communist Youth in Russia sends out instructions to its local branches for a Communist Christmas. The branches are advised to present a series of lanternslide lectures on the part played by religion in the history of mankind.			The Australian Natives Association seeks assistance from the Minister of Education to induce University of Melbourne authorities to include Australian literature and history in the Arts course. The present subjects are described as being suitable for Oxford and Cambridge, but not Australia.
Nov. 29	The Conference of Ambassadors drafts a note to Germany protesting the arrests of a Belgian officer of the Inter-Allied Commission of Control and a French noncommissioned officer. Although Germany has expressed a willingness to apologize to the Conference, the ambassadors demand that the apology be directed to the Commission.	The skeletons of 100 German soldiers are discovered in a tunnel built during the war at Mort Homme, near Verdun, France. ...German fascist leader Adolf Hitler is reported to be suffering from an acute nervous breakdown following his arrest....Leon Trotsky calls for the Soviet Union to create a fighting navy because the British and Norwegians had plundered the northern coasts of fish and game, while the Japanese do what they want in Russian territorial waters.		A fire at Tampico, Mexico, destroys six blocks of buildings in the most important part of the city. More damage is expected as the fire is being fanned by strong winds blowing from the Gulf....John Mackay, a pioneer missionary in Saskatchewan, Canada, dies....The Finnish Consulate in Montreal reports that the number of Finnish immigrants to Canada between July and September amounted to 3,187.	
Nov. 30	The Reparations Committee formed two committees today. One committee will deal with the budgetary and monetary situation in Germany while the other will address the capital exported by Germany....The Finance Committee of the League of Nations completes its discussions on the financial reconstruction of Hungary.	A Warsaw tribunal acquits Makhno, a Ukrainian leader of irregulars, of plotting to separate Eastern Galicia from Poland....Ruhr miners and their employers agree to extend their working day by one hour for the next three months....French Captain d'Armont is arrested by German authorities on the German-Swiss frontier on a charge of military espionage. The officer is a member of the French General Staff and has been attached to the French General Consulate at Basle since 1921....The list of members of the new German Cabinet is presented by Dr. Marx to President Ebert.	The South African Supreme Court dismisses an appeal by Jacobus Christian of his conviction for high treason for taking a leading part in the Bondelswart revolt in Southwest Africa.	The Premier of Saskatchewan receives a petition with 80,000 names seeking a change in the present liquor prohibition legislation...The final returns of the Alberta, Canada, referendum show a majority of 32,039 supporting government control of the sale of liquor instead of the continuation of prohibitions....For want of labor, the sugar cane acreage in British Guiana has been reduced from 78,000 acres in 1918 to 54,000 acres. The Planters' Association invites the governor to persuade at least 1,500 families from India to emigrate.	A British political officer, Major H.C. Finnis, is shot and killed by a gang of Waziris while driving near Manikhwa, Baluchistan, India. All the passes in the area are blocked and pursuit parties have been sent out.

U.S. Politics & Social Issues	U.S. Foreign Policy & Affairs, Defense	U.S. Economy & Environment	Science, Technology & Nature	Culture, Leisure & Lifestyle	
	A British two-masted schooner is captured by the Coast Guard off New Jersey. Two shots are fired across its bow before the ship stops. Two hundred cases of whiskey are on board and the crew of nine is detained along with a smuggler found with $60,000 in the ship's hold.				Nov. 25
	President Coolidge says that he believes in the withdrawal of the United States from the Philippines as soon as the country is deemed to be fit for self-government.		A British Broadcasting Company radio broadcast is sent at 10:10 p.m. EST to the United States, a time when every American broadcasting station is stilled. At 10:25, a piano solo is tried although none of the listeners could identify the melody. Wireless broadcasters in Chicago and San Antonio broke in without waiting for the end of the agreed upon 30 minutes silence and drowned out the rest of the program.	A number of Saxon relics are discovered under the floor of an old English church during renovations.…Australian artists in Europe protest about being taxed on work that they send back to Australia. Many Australians go to Paris or London to study art and ship their paintings home. Until recently, all painting by Commonwealth artists were admitted free of duty, provided that the artists had not been absent from home for more than seven years.	Nov. 26
	A number of politically well-connected Americans, including Mr. Gerard the former Ambassador to Germany, are reported to be lobbying against the ratification of the Treaty of Lausanne by the Senate. They object to the treaty because it makes American missionaries subject to Turkish law and ignores American promises to Armenia.			Heavy snows in Switzerland prompt the start of the winter sports season.	Nov. 27
The New York State Legislature holds an inquiry into the exploitation of immigrants. It is stated that a ring of real estate swindlers had, in the last few years, swindled immigrants out of $12 million by selling them lots that are under water, the Brooklyn Bridge, the post office, and various other public buildings.	A number of U.S. and Canadian Customs and legal officials meet in Ottawa today to discuss the prevention of liquor smuggling across the border. U.S. officials are reported to be demanding the refusal of clearances to vessels with liquor cargoes for the United States, the right of search in inland waters, and legislation making bootlegging an extraditable offense.		The American Museum of Natural History prices dinosaur eggs at $2,000 each. The eggs, recently brought by Roy Chapman from Mongolia, are really priceless but surplus eggs are sold to other museums. None of the eggs will be sold until the museum's experts complete their examination of them. X-ray photographs will soon be made.	Residents at Lake Como in Italy protest the government's treatment of the 17th-century Villa Carlotta that is a local historic landmark. The home, which belonged to a subject of the Central Empire, went to Italy in the peace agreement. Italy removed all the artworks and magnificent plants from the villa and is now planning to sell it.	Nov. 28
	Richard Washburn Child, the U.S. Ambassador to Italy, declares that it is insulting to say that the United States is pursuing a foreign policy of isolation. He argues that those abroad want America to intervene as a cats paw for one nation or another. The United States has contributed billions of dollars to Europe and will never pledge its army and navy to settle the hatreds of other nations.		A tomb with objects bearing the name of Amenemhat IV (1800 to 1792 B.C.E.) is unearthed in Syria. The tomb consists of a pit hewn in the rock and ending in a chamber.…The International Council for the Exploration of the Sea decided to carry out a scientific investigation of the fisheries of Iceland and the Faroe Islands.	Two men are killed in a Thanksgiving Day crash at a motor race in Los Angeles. The accident occurs when a race car, moving about 90 miles-per-hour, crashes into a group of newspaper photographers and some other men standing on the track but hidden from view of the driver.	Nov. 29
The governor of Indiana, McCray, is indicted by the Marion County Grand Jury on eight charges ranging from embezzlement to forgery. His bail is fixed at $25,000.	Negotiations continue between the United States and Great Britain on the subject of allowing revenue officers to search suspected smugglers outside of a 12-mile limit. Revenue officers may be allowed to pursue contraband ships that are actually observed to be transferring liquor just outside of territorial waters.		The second statue of King Tutankhamen is transported to the laboratory in the Valley of the Kings, Egypt. The preparatory work inside the tomb is now complete and everything is ready for the demolition of the partition wall, the first step in solving the mystery of the shrines.…Pescara makes a record flight in his helicopter outside of Paris. He remains in the air for five minutes and 44 seconds. In his last trial, he flew in a horizontal direction for 270 yards, landed, and after a 30-minute interval returned to his starting point.	The Oberammergau Passion Players leave Germany for New York where they will present plays and carvings to American audiences.… Restoration begins at Versailles, France. A 6-ton horse of the Char d'Appolon is removed for repair. The entire chariot with horses weighs more than 100 tons.	Nov. 30

	World Affairs	Europe	Africa & The Middle East	The Americas	Asia & The Pacific
Dec. 1	The International Conference on Liquor Smuggling between Canada and the United States ends. No statement is released as to the conclusions reached.	Poland announces that it has obtained a loan of 200 million Swiss francs secured on a lease of the tobacco monopoly for 45 years. It did not name the supplier of the loan, presumed to be a French firm....A Swedish steamer bound for England strikes a mine and sinks. The crew are saved....At a mass meeting of Roman fascists, a resolution is passed stating that the age of Italian cowardice and misery will never return and that the Black Shirts are ready to resume their advance.	The new cabinet of Iraq is completed and it announces a nationalist program. The Iraqi government vows to promote patriotism, suppress foreign intrigue, obtain a strong northern frontier, establish friendly relations with neighboring states, especially in Arabia, submit the Anglo-Iraqi Treaty, and send the draft constitution to the assembly for ratification.		
Dec. 2	Norway and Denmark resume negotiations over Greenland.	The Soviet Union continues to export grain via Baltic ports despite reports of famine within the country....Although strenuously opposed by the Labour Party, Britain passes a bill for the introduction of English domestic servants to South Australia.	A new Advisory Council consisted solely of government officials are appointed for Palestine. This action follows the refusal of the Arab inhabitants to take a share in the government of Palestine.		The Swaraj Party gains victories in Bombay and Bengal. Surendra Nath Banerjee of Bengal and many other well-known Liberals have lost their seats. The Swaraj Party is expected to oppose every measure of the Indian government with the object of compelling it to dissolve the Assembly.
Dec. 3	Numerous floating mines are reported in the Baltic, especially between Estonia and Finland. The mines are believed to be Russian ones that broke loose in the Kronstadt region.	Winston Churchill is mobbed by a large, angry crowd after leaving a political meeting. A man smashes one of the windows of Churchill's car. Many people spit on the car as it drives away....The Bavarian cabinet are unable to agree on matters of policy during a meeting. Munich, in Bavaria, gains the distinction of being the most expensive city in Germany.			
Dec. 4	The German-Polish Mixed Arbitration Tribunal sitting in Paris hears a case relating to war damages in occupied territory. The Hirzburg and Wilezyuski Company of Lodz, Poland, seek payment for requisitions of its property during the war. The German government responds that the Treaty of Versailles applies only to citizens of Allied States existing before the war and, therefore, the plaintiff has no standing. Judgment is reserved.	A Corsican politician and a French newspaper editor fight a duel with swords near Paris. The duel is stopped when the editor is wounded in the arm....The strike in the cigar industry in Ghent, Belgium, ends after six weeks. Wages are increased by 12 percent as against the 15 percent demanded by the workers.		One of the biggest nuggets of silver ever discovered in Ontario is found by a prospector a few miles from Cobalt. It weighed 2,005 pounds and is about three-quarters silver.	The New South Wales Legislative Assembly passes a bill preventing monopolies.
Dec. 5	The Pope announces that he does not intend to create any foreign Cardinals during the upcoming Consistory. He will only create Italian Cardinals The statement comes in response to a remark by King Alfonso of Spain that Spain and South America should have a larger representation in the Sacred College.	The Executive Committee of the Italian Communist Party invited Signor Bombacci, the well-known Communist leader, to resign his seat in the legislature after praising fascist leader Benito Mussolini....The Soviet government purchases aircraft in France. It has previously purchased aircraft in England, Holland, Germany, and Italy.		The Canadian government releases statistics showing that that there are 1,768,129 dwellings in the country. Of these, 85 percent are single houses and eight percent are semi-detached. Only 35,095 or two percent are apartment houses....The University of Toronto announces plans to establish a research bureau to investigate medical and industrial problems.	The murderers of British Major H.C. Finnis are arrested in India....Sun Yat-sen threatens to seize the Customs House at Canton, China, and appropriate the revenues unless he is granted a share of the Customs surplus.
Dec. 6		Winston Churchill loses his election bid for M.P. from West Leicester in Great Britain....The Swiss National Council votes to abolish Sunday postal delivery....René Dezar Ley is sentenced to seven years imprisonment in a fortress by the Assize Court of the Bas-Rhin for founding that Executive Committee of Alsace and Lorraine at Baden-Baden in 1919 with the object of conspiring against the current government....The Soviet Union informs the Estonian Foreign Office that it has not been able to sweep its part of the Gulf of Finland for mines because of stormy weather. Sweeping is expected to be completed next autumn.		A revolt against the government of Mexico breaks out in Vera Cruz under the leadership of General Guadalupe Sanchez. Nine states join in the rebellion including San Luis Potosi, Chihuahua, Michoacan, Tamsulipas, Jalisco, Sinaloa, Sonora, and Tepic. There are reports of uprising in Oaxaca and Guerrero against the Obregon government. The military forces in the eastern seaboard states have gone over to faction of Adolfo de la Huerta. He is the Cooperatista candidate for the presidency in opposition to General Plutarco Elias Calles, Obregon's choice.	Marines under the command of the Allied Powers land at Canton to take possession of the Customs House....The Afghan government announces that most of the Alizai tribe in Zamindawar district will be removed to Turkestan. The tribe rebelled last summer because of taxation and forced conscription....The annual report of the Australian Viniculturalists' Association shows that the year's wine yield for Australia totals 8,653,579 gallons, a record.

A	B	C	D	E
Includes developments that affect more than one world region, international organizations and important meetings of world leaders.	*Includes all domestic and regional developments in Europe, including the Soviet Union.*	*Includes all domestic and regional developments in Africa and the Middle East.*	*Includes all domestic and regional developments in Latin America, the Caribbean, and Canada.*	*Includes all domestic and regional developments in Asian and Pacific nations (and colonies).*

U.S. Politics & Social Issues	U.S. Foreign Policy & Affairs, Defense	U.S. Economy & Environment	Science, Technology & Nature	Culture, Leisure & Lifestyle	
	The Secretary of War warns against the slighting cutting of the army budget in his annual report to Congress. The secretary recommends that the strength of the regular army should be increased from its present limit of 12,000 officers and 125,000 men to 13,000 officers and 150,000 men. The War and Navy Department costs are roughly 14 percent of the federal budget with only six percent going to purely military activities.…The battleship *West Virginia* is commissioned at the Norfolk, VA, Navy Yard.		Demolition of the partition in the tomb of King Tutankhamen begins in the Valley of the Kings, Egypt.… *Science* magazine publishes the findings of Russian Nobel Prize winner Ivan P. Pavlov on the training of instincts. Pavlov used dogs and mice to detect a so-called "Pavlovian response" to stimulations of the senses of sight and smell.		Dec. 1
A gang cuts through the door of a safe in a newsstand in the Pennsylvania Railroad Station, one of the busiest places in New York City. They steal about $1200.	The Shipping Board declares that preferential tariffs or a subsidy remain the only methods of ensuring the maintenance of a U.S. Merchant Marine.	The Postmaster General, Harry S. New, issues his annual report to President Coolidge. New wants to promote the usage of American ships by assigning them U.S. mail to carry abroad whenever possible.	Mount Vesuvius erupts in Naples, Italy. The lava stream is estimated to be 30 feet deep. A bright glow is visible for miles around at night. The cone is enveloped in a thick mist.		Dec. 2
Congress opens its session. It is expected to consider taxation, land and sea transportation, soldiers' bonus, the coal industry, immigration, Prohibition, public works, and foreign affairs. The matter of the League of Nations is not expected to be raised by either party.…President Coolidge grants executive clemency to Charles T. Craig, the chief financial officer of New York City who had been sentenced to 60 days imprisonment for contempt of court.			Guglielmo Marconi, speaking before a meeting of shareholders of Marconi's Wireless Telegraph Company, discloses an entirely new system of long-distance communication. Electric waves that carry messages are projected in one direction only instead of being allowed to spread around in all directions. Only stations inside a certain restricted angle are able to receive, thus increasing the privacy and secrecy of communication.		Dec. 3
The New York Police Department requests that the grand juries bring indictments as quickly as possible because of a wave of crimes of violence in the city.…Two men wearing army gas masks enter the shop of an Italian boot maker in Brooklyn. They killed the man with a blow to the head, knock his wife unconscious, and spray the air in the shop with chloroform, which stupefies two children.			A French diver attempting to attach a cable to the wreck of the battleship *Liberté* off Toulon is attacked by a large octopus. The diver gives the alarm after a struggle. He is brought to the surface still in the grip of the animal, which is hacked to pieces to free the man.…A great bed of iron ore is reported to have been discovered in southern Russia. It is believed to be the richest bed of magnetic iron ore in the world.		Dec. 4
A New York City jury convicts the so-called "king of the bootleggers" Emanuel Kessler of various offenses of the Prohibition law. Kessler is estimated to have a fortune of $5 to $10 million and had managed to avoid any convictions to this point. His conviction is expected the open the way to a considerable number of other prosecutions.	The State Department declares its support for a German loan to be devoted to the purchase of foodstuffs. About half of the loan would be offered on the U.S. market.	In a test at Erie, PA, an electric locomotive sets a new railroad speed record at 105 miles per hour. General Electric built the locomotive for the Paris-Orleans line in France. According to the provisions of the contract, the locomotive had to attain a speed of 81 miles per hour. Engineers estimate that with a longer track, the train can reach 125 miles per hour.	The partition wall in King Tutankhamen's tomb is completely demolished.…An ancient Greek temple is discovered while the foundations of a church are being dug at Doiran in Southern Macedonia.	The Nobel Prize Committee in Sweden decide that no Peace Prize will be awarded this year.	Dec. 5
Millions of Americans listen on the radio as President Coolidge delivers his Message to Congress. In New York City, people heard Coolidge's voice coming from the open doorways and transoms in scores of shops, transmitted from Washington and made audible by amplifiers. Receivers were set up in restaurants across the nation so people could hear the speech while they ate lunch.…Coolidge pays tribute to Warren Harding before discussing foreign affairs. He declares that tax reduction is the major service that Congress can render to the country. The speech is received well by Republicans.	Senator Irvine Lenroot of Wisconsin introduced a bill to appropriate $20 million for relief work in Germany with the money to be expended under the direction of President Coolidge.…In his Message to Congress, Coolidge states that the main problems of the United States are domestic and that he does not plan any European ventures. He says that Europe must save itself.		For the first time, an airplane is refueled in the air by another airplane Officers of the French 34th Aviation Regiment perform the maneuver after practicing for several days. American pilots have refueled airplanes in flight but not from a supply provided by another airplane. The maneuver helps in establishing duration records for flights.	Gregory, Metropolitan of Kadikeuy, is elected Ecumenical Patriarch of the Greek Orthodox Church. The Turkish authorities had intimidated that the new Patriarch needed to be a Turkish citizen. Gregorios VII is a citizen of Crete. The leader of the Turkish Orthodox in Anatolia attempted to enter the Synod during its session but was prevented.	Dec. 6
F *Includes campaigns, elections, federal-state relations, civil rights and liberties, crime, the judiciary, education, healthcare, poverty, urban affairs, and population.*	G *Includes formation and debate of U.S. foreign and defense policies, veterans affairs, and defense spending. (Relations with specific foreign countries are usually found under the region concerned.)*	H *Includes business, labor, agriculture, taxation, transportation, consumer affairs, monetary and fiscal policy, natural resources, pollution and industrial accidents.*	I *Includes worldwide scientific, medical and technological developments, natural phenomena, U.S. weather and natural disasters.*	J *Includes the arts, religion, scholarship, communications media, sports, entertainment, fashions, fads, and social life.*	

	World Affairs	Europe	Africa & The Middle East	The Americas	Asia & The Pacific
Dec. 7	The annual meeting of the Council for the Representation of Women in the League of Nations is held in London. It passes a resolution in favor of the League continuing in its efforts to stop the traffic in women and children in all mandated territories.…The joint commission of the International Red Cross and League of Red Cross Societies issues an appeal asking for help on behalf of the Germans affected by the economic crisis. The Save the Children Fund sends a delegate to Berlin to establish a kitchen to feed 4,000 children.	The Soviet authorities send instructions to all the branches of the League of Communist Youth to limit this year's anti-religious Christmas festivities to scientific atheistic propaganda.…The Soviet State Publishing Department plans to publish a world atlas containing 160 maps and diagrams representing the geographical, economic, and political state of the world according to a Marxist historical interpretation. Vladimir Lenin first proposed the idea.		Mexican federal troops defeat rebel soldiers at a battle at Maltrata on the railroad line between Vera Cruz and Mexico City. The casualties are reported to be slight. The Mexican government has sent 28,000 troops to Vera Cruz while the strength of the rebels in the state is estimated at 22,000.…General Enrique Estrada defects from the federal government with several thousand of his men.…The Mexican government stops all coded telegraph messages sent in either direction and strictly censors others transmitted from Galveston, TX. Galveston is the channel for most communications between the United States and Mexico.	An emergency issue of postage stamps is produced at Osaka, Japan, by private contractors. The Imperial Printing Bureau together with the plant and reserve stock of postage stamps was destroyed in the earthquake.…The Japanese government asks the United States for help in reorganizing its government printing bureau, which used similar equipment to that employed by the U.S. Bureau of Engraving and Printing.
Dec. 8		The Soviet government expels 12 men from the Communist Party for joining the Russian Communist Party, which was formed by a man expelled from the party last year after leading a revolt against the Moscow Central Committee.…The leader of the Spanish Military Directory reminds the officers of the army of the need for unity in governing the country.	Spain declares that the situation in Morocco is gradually improving with the military contingents in the protectorate gradually being reduced.		The Premier of Victoria in Australia sends a telegram to Great Britain stating that his government is unable to accept a British offer to pay part of the interest on a five-year loan for English materials to be used in development works. The policy of the Victorian government is to give preference to Australian manufactures.
Dec. 9		Italy abandons a plan to divert the waters of the Adige after heavy protests from the residents of Verona. The citizens viewed the project as a threat to the artistic attractions of their city. If the project had been completed, the Adige would not flow through Verona for several months each year.…Eight people are killed in a Royalist demonstration in Athens, Greece. About 100,000 people met in front of the Temple of the Olympian Zeus to express their loyalty to the monarchy.	Persia appoints Romaine A. Philpot, a New York financier, as director of Persian financial affairs. Philpot's appointment is conditional on his success at obtaining a $40 million loan in the United States.…The Kenyan government takes over the Voi-Taveta-Kahe railroad and proceeds immediately with the construction of a new branch. The railroad connects Kenya with Uganda. It was built as a military line during the war.		A strike of butchers halts Adelaide, Australia's supply of meat. The butchers want better wages for men employed in slaughterhouses.
Dec. 10	At the request of Albania, the League of Nations is examining the situation of Muslim Albanians living in Greece.…France opposes the participation of Italy in the Tangiers Conference because Italy's request for participation arrived too late.…The League of Nations Commission of Intellectual Cooperation vows to use every effort to reconstitute the foreign collections of the library of the Imperial University of Tokyo.	Benito Mussolini informs the Italian Cabinet that he does not intend to ask Parliament to prolong his plenary powers, in spite of the fact that all the various legislative groups had already expressed their willingness to grant such an extension.…Leon Trotsky is reported to be suffering from an illness diagnosed as either ulcers or cancer in Moscow.…The Austrian government refuses to extend the wage increase already granted to railroad workers and other officials. A strike of postal, telegraph, and telephone employees begins.	The Counter-Revolutionary Court arrives in Constantinople. The Turkish government does not want to declare martial law and has instead formed the court to deal with suspected anti-Republican organizations. The court has orders to make a rapid inquiry and punish conspirators.	The Canadian government announces plans to appoint a customs officer at New York to facilitate the transport of Canadian produce and manufactures from Eastern to Western Canada via the Panama Canal. At present, such goods are shipped at New York and categorized as foreign upon their arrival in Vancouver or Victoria.…Fighting continues in Mexico as the revolutionaries capture Jalapa, the capital of the state of Vera Cruz with a loss of 300 lives on both sides.	Sun Yat-sen of China states that he has been unable to carry out reconstruction in consequence of the disorders and invasions organized by the Chihli party, who are financed with the surplus national revenues released through Peking by the foreign powers. He therefore intends to get control of the Chinese Customs House.
Dec. 11	Italy denounces as untrue France's claim that its request to participate in the Tangiers Conference arrived late. It believes that a Mediterranean Power should be allowed to join in discussions on the fate of the key to that sea.	A Women's Suffrage Bill is introduced in the French legislature. The bill would give the vote and the right to be elected to the Chamber of Deputies to women over the age of 25. A similar bill passed the Chamber in 1919 but the Senate refused to consider it. A counter-proposal is made for a family vote. Such a vote would give a vote to women and privilege parents over the unmarried or married without children. It is proposed to increase the birth rate. The French Cabinet supports the family vote since it regards the birth rate as a matter of extreme gravity.		The Chilean government resigns.…Tepic, the capital of Nayarit, is been taken by Mexican revolutionaries as fighting continues across the country. An attack on Tampico by the revolutionaries is reported to be imminent.…The National Railways hold a conference at Montreal to discuss immigration. The organization intends to make a special effort to bring boys and girls from 15 to 18 years to homes in the rural districts of Canada where they will learn Canadian agricultural methods.	Elections for the Indian legislature in the Central Provinces, United Provinces, and Berar result in a near-complete victory for the Swarajists. The Swaraj Party is pledged to refuse all cooperation with the Indian government until the demands of the Indian Congress have been satisfied by the British parliament.

A	B	C	D	E
Includes developments that affect more than one world region, international organizations and important meetings of world leaders.	*Includes all domestic and regional developments in Europe, including the Soviet Union.*	*Includes all domestic and regional developments in Africa and the Middle East.*	*Includes all domestic and regional developments in Latin America, the Caribbean, and Canada.*	*Includes all domestic and regional developments in Asian and Pacific nations (and colonies).*

U.S. Politics & Social Issues	U.S. Foreign Policy & Affairs, Defense	U.S. Economy & Environment	Science, Technology & Nature	Culture, Leisure & Lifestyle	
The U.S. Senate and House of Representatives adjourn until Monday as a mark of respect for the late President Harding.	The U.S. Air Service abandons plans to develop a helicopter. The hangar used to house the helicopter at McCook Field will be converted into a swimming pool while the machine is being sent to the Air Service Technical Museum.				Dec. 7
The Coast Guard seizes a Dutch schooner off Fire Island, south of Long Island in New York, on a charge of rum running. A search of the ship turned up 7,500 cases of champagne as well as other liquors of value.			The keel and stem planks of a wooden ship that is believed to predate the Vikings is found in a peat bog by a Norwegian farmer.…The doors of the outer shrine at the tomb of King Tutankhamen are removed in Egypt. The archeologists state that no physical or radiological examination of the king's body will be attempted this season.		Dec. 8
	The State Department announces that a new commercial treaty has been signed with Germany to replace one that was abrogated when war was declared.…Instructions have been sent to the American delegation at The Hague to begin negotiations with the Dutch government for a similar treaty.	Two sections of the Twentieth Century Limited, the New York Central fast train to Chicago, collide in a thick fog at Forsythe, NY. One section is stopped following a crash with an automobile when it is struck by another section traveling at 60 miles per hour. Nine persons are killed and a large number of others are injured. Emergency calls go to Erie, PA, and Buffalo, NY, requesting every available physician be sent to Forsythe.	A new remedy for sleeping sickness, the Bayer 205, is being tested in East Africa. Bayer 205, discovered in the Bayer Dyeworks in Germany, is reported to be more effective than atoxyl with relapses occurring in only two of 95 cases. In both cases, the third stage of the disease in which the nervous system is attacked had been reached.	France and Germany compete in a soccer match for the first time since 1914. France wins by five goals to none. There will be a return match.	Dec. 9
The Senate and the House of Representatives focus on the membership of committees. This session of Congress is expected to focus on tax reduction before adjourning early for campaigning in the primary and presidential elections of 1924.…President Coolidge announces that he is a candidate for the Republican presidential nomination.…Frank B. Kellogg is nominated to serve as the U.S. Ambassador to Great Britain. Kellogg, a Republican U.S. Senator from Minnesota, lost his reelection bid in 1922.	Secretary of Commerce Herbert Hoover issues a statement on the food situation in Germany. He finds that Germany has three major difficulties: the breakdown of the currency, the inability of German merchants to finance imports to make up for the deficit in domestic production, and widespread unemployment. Farmers are growing less food because they refuse to accept a worthless currency. Hoover suggests the creation of a foreign commercial credit for food supplied.			W.B. Yeats is awarded the Nobel Prize for literature.	Dec. 10
	Myron Herrick, the U.S. Ambassador to France, attends the unveiling of a memorial to American soldiers killed in France during the war.				Dec. 11

F	G	H	I	J
Includes campaigns, elections, federal-state relations, civil rights and liberties, crime, the judiciary, education, healthcare, poverty, urban affairs, and population.	*Includes formation and debate of U.S. foreign and defense policies, veterans affairs, and defense spending. (Relations with specific foreign countries are usually found under the region concerned.)*	*Includes business, labor, agriculture, taxation, transportation, consumer affairs, monetary and fiscal policy, natural resources, pollution and industrial accidents.*	*Includes worldwide scientific, medical and technological developments, natural phenomena, U.S. weather and natural disasters.*	*Includes the arts, religion, scholarship, communications media, sports, entertainment, fashions, fads, and social life.*

	World Affairs	Europe	Africa & The Middle East	The Americas	Asia & The Pacific
Dec. 12	The League of Nations debates a loan to Hungary.	The failure of the potato crop in western Scotland has led to fears of widespread starvation. There is already widespread destitution because of a lack of work and heavy rains that have ruined the hay.... Countess Louis Esterhazy, aged 24, a member of the famous Hungarian family, is arrested in Slovakia on the charge of spying for the Hungarian government.	Turkey arrests three editors in Constantinople on the grounds that their publications are treasonous and calculated to provoke sedition.	Wiiliam Mackenzie King, Prime Minister of Canada, states that in the future the Canada government would have the same power as the Imperial government to determine whether correspondence involving Canada will be published. The relations between a Prime Minister of a Dominion and the Governor-General will be the same as the relations between the Prime Minister of Great Britain and the Sovereign.	Rinderpest is detected in dairy cattle in Western Australia....A Japanese merchant is convicted in London for violating the Dangerous Drugs Acts by unlawfully procuring 500 pounds of morphine hydrochloride for a Japanese firm. He is sentenced to three years in prison. The man is suspected to be part of a ring of smugglers that has sent drugs into India and China from Japan.
Dec. 13	Armenian merchants win a verdict in France against a Russian trading organization, Optorg. The Armenians sued for the return of number of bales of silk. Optorg pleaded in defense that it bought the silk from the Soviet government. The French court holds that the requisition by the Soviet government constituted acts of fraudulent usurpation.	Seven tons of hay and a barn disappear into a large hole that suddenly appears in Lithuania. The pit is 100 feet wide and of unknown depth, although a heavy object tossed down produces a splash. The size of the pit is steadily increasing.... Ginestal Machado, Prime Minister of Portugal, announces the resignation of his government following a vote of no confidence....The French Inter-Ministerial Commission restricts Russian ships to the ports of Dunkirk, Havre, and Marseilles.... A French airman and French author duel with pistols until the airman is severely wounded in the shoulder.	The governor of Tanganyika Territory, Horace Byatt, announces that the Colonial Office has approved the extension of the Tanga railroad towards Arusha as far as the Sanga River. Tanganyika is also exporting greater numbers of European and native crops.	A provisional government is established at Vera Cruz, Mexico, under de la Huerta. The revolutionaries notify all Mexican diplomatic and consular officers in the United States that they constitute the de facto government of Mexico and demand obedience to their orders....President Obregon has left Mexico City and is rumored to be taking the field at the head of the government army in the West....The Mexican legislature gives Obregon extraordinary power to deal with the revolution.	A bill making women eligible to serve in the Victorian Parliament in Australia passes both houses....The Acting Prime Minister of Australia, Dr. Page, and his Minister of Customs are cited by a police officer for smoking in a public hall at a political meeting in New South Wales....The Japanese Restoration Board tentatively plans to budget 750 million yen to build and repair bridges, improve canals and the port of Tokyo, survey land, and improve communications between Tokyo and Yokohama. The question of insurance payments remains unsettled.
Dec. 14		The government of Saxony in Germany resigns. Several ministers were under attack for being Socialists....The German government states that it intends to stop making payments that are being used for the maintenance of the armies of occupation. It does not indicate a date of stoppage, rumored to be January 1....The German Cabinet discusses raising the excess profits duty, rental tax, and tax on mortgage interest income.	The governor of Tanganyika Territory announces that there are no plans to make extensive improvements at Dar es Salaam harbor since the port at Tanga handles most of Tanganyika's exports. He plans to add cranes and other minor facilities to Tanga to restore the port to its prewar position. It was damaged in fighting in 1914.	Fighting is reported to be widespread in Mexico as a large battle takes place in the state of Vera Cruz between the Mexican revolutionaries under General Sanchez and the federal troops barring the way to Mexico City. The battle is reported to be centered in the city of Puebla, which has been evacuated by the federals before the fighting began....The Canadian Parliament is asked to provide legislation permitting the union of the Presbyterian, Methodist, and Congregational Churches to form the United Church of Canada.	The Government of India appoints a committee to investigate the management of the forests of India and Burma with a view to making commercial use of the woods....Dame Nellie Melba, the famed Australian soprano, is having difficulties with the opera chorus in Melbourne. The chorus is incensed at plans to supplement it with specially imported Italians.
Dec. 15	The German government asks the Reparation Commission for a credit for the purchase of wheat and fats. Germany declares that the purchase of wheat abroad for the purpose of its timely import and distribution in the country cannot be delayed until the internal supplies of wheat are exhausted.	A second telephone cable will be laid between England and Holland....Danzig merchants protest against an order of the Polish Finance Ministry that import duties on luxury goods must be paid in actual gold.	The Court of Appeal in Nairobi, Kenya, quashes the conviction of several Masai men implicated in unrest against the British....The Indian Congress of East Africa instructs the members of the Kenya Executive and Legislative Councils to resign immediately on the ground that the policy of the government is anti-Indian.	The government of British Columbia introduces amendments to the Liquor Control Act calling for a plebiscite on the question of permitting the sale of beer on licensed premises....Bolshevik activity is alleged to be occurring among Central Europeans in Western Canada....Two towns in Colombia are destroyed by an earthquake. The roads are obstructed by great landslides, making it difficult to determine the full extent of the damage.	The South Australian Parliament passes legislation to extend the term of the Agent-General beyond the six-year limit provided by law. Edward Lucas, the Agent-General, accepted the extension of his appointment.
Dec. 16	The International Chamber of Commerce Rail Transport Committee recommends that an international conference be held to work out improvements in the examination of passenger luggage and goods when crossing a border.	In appreciation of Italy's recognition of the Soviet Union, the latter has granted a 30-year concession for oilfields to a group of Italian industrialists. The oilfields are in Georgia....The Polish Cabinet resigns....Greece holds general elections.	South Africa celebrates Dingaan's Day with parades and thanksgiving services. The celebration is held in memory of the defeat by the Dutch of the Zulu Army of Dingaan at the Blood River in December 1838. The defeat struck a fatal blow to Zulu power in the Natal.	Earthquake shocks continue in Colombia....The revolt in Rio Grande do Sul, Brazil, ends. Through the intervention of General Setembrine Carvalho, Minister of War in the Federal Cabinet, the opposing groups signed a formal peace treaty. The trouble began when Borges de Medeiros, who had been president of Rio Grande do Sul for 25 years, announced his reelection bid. Disaffected groups took up arms in favor of a rival candidate.	The government of Bengal, India, resigns and C.R. Das, the leader of the Swarajist opposition, is invited to form a new government....The naval concentration of foreign ships at the port of Canton stands at 15 vessels, with warships from the United States, Britain, France, Portugal, and Italy.

A	B	C	D	E
Includes developments that affect more than one world region, international organizations and important meetings of world leaders.	*Includes all domestic and regional developments in Europe, including the Soviet Union.*	*Includes all domestic and regional developments in Africa and the Middle East.*	*Includes all domestic and regional developments in Latin America, the Caribbean, and Canada.*	*Includes all domestic and regional developments in Asian and Pacific nations (and colonies).*

	U.S. Politics & Social Issues	U.S. Foreign Policy & Affairs, Defense	U.S. Economy & Environment	Science, Technology & Nature	Culture, Leisure & Lifestyle
Dec. 12	Senator Hiram Johnson of California, a candidate for the Democratic presidential nomination, states that the United States should establish relations with the Soviet Union because it is the recognized government of Russia. It is no affair of the American people as to what form of government the Russians choose.	The Navy Department announces that it will ask Congress to support a five-year program for naval aviation. Secretary of the Navy Denby declares that only 12 aviators have been added to the rolls in the last year and the equipment is practically obsolete.…Six destroyers are sent to Hong Kong to cooperate with the Allied flotilla in Canton, China, waters.	Hiram Johnson declares that the people of California are anxious to resume trade with Siberia and hope that some agreement can be reached with the Soviet Union.		Rutgers Presbyterian Church in Manhattan, New York City, announces plans to solve the difficulty of maintaining its position in an expensive location by razing its current building. In its place, a five-story combination church and bank will be erected with a large electric sign projecting into the street.
Dec. 13	The Republican National Committee decides to hold its annual convention at Cleveland on June 10, 1924.…The smuggling of liquor from Canada and off the coast of New Jersey into the United States has increased dramatically with the approach of the holidays. There are now 22 ships in "Rum-runners Row" off New Jersey with cargoes of liquor estimated to be worth $5 million. The Indians on the St. Regis reservation are reported to be particularly active bootleggers, using boats on the St. Lawrence river at night to bring Canadian liquor to the United States.	The White House announces that it encourages American experts to join the two committees established by the Reparations Commission. The committees will attempt to balance the German budget and stabilize the German currency.		A new German cipher machine is tested. It is claimed that the machine will prevent an unauthorized receiver from deciphering messages dispatched on the machine. There is no loss of time in transmission.	Visitors are arriving in great numbers at Luxor, Egypt, to see King Tutankhamen's tomb.
Dec. 14	The New York State Police report that bootleggers moving from Canada through the Adirondack mountains to the Hudson River have established a series of concealed repair stations for damaged blockade-runners. The stations have tools and gasoline.			Sections of the Great Shrine in the tomb of King Tutankhamen are examined and protected in preparation to dismantling.…A royal tomb is discovered at Jeibel, near Beirut by a French archaeologist, Montet. It is composed of several chambers that include an intact sarcophagus.	British Brigadier-General C.G. Bruce announces plans for a third attempt to reach the summit of Mount Everest. Bruce led the 1922 attempt.
Dec. 15		Charles G. Dawes, former Director of the Budget, and Owen Young, a banker and president of General Electric, are invited to join the Reparations Commission committees on the German budget and currency.			
Dec. 16	Ned Ryan, alias Norman Slade, is captured at Minneapolis, MN, in a gunfight in front of the Minneapolis Post Office. Ryan escaped with three associates from Kingston Penitentiary in Ontario, Canada, some months ago. He has been tracked through Michigan, Illinois, South Dakota, and Wisconsin. It is not known if he will be extradited to Canada or face trial in the United States for numerous robberies.				Dr. Leighton Parks of St. Bartholomew's in New York City publicly proclaims his disbelief in the doctrine of the Virgin Birth and challenges Bishop Manning of New York to try him for heresy. At the same time, he announces that 500 clergy within the Episcopal Church have formed a Modern Churchmen's Union to support the interpretation of the Bible in light of modern science.

F
Includes campaigns, elections, federal-state relations, civil rights and liberties, crime, the judiciary, education, healthcare, poverty, urban affairs, and population.

G
Includes formation and debate of U.S. foreign and defense policies, veterans affairs, and defense spending. (Relations with specific foreign countries are usually found under the region concerned.)

H
Includes business, labor, agriculture, taxation, transportation, consumer affairs, monetary and fiscal policy, natural resources, pollution and industrial accidents.

I
Includes worldwide scientific, medical and technological developments, natural phenomena, U.S. weather and natural disasters.

J
Includes the arts, religion, scholarship, communications media, sports, entertainment, fashions, fads, and social life.

	World Affairs	Europe	Africa & The Middle East	The Americas	Asia & The Pacific
Dec. 17		Finland and Great Britain sign a commercial treaty promising not to place higher duties on articles imported from the other than it charges on similar commodities imported from any other source.... Dusseldorf, Germany, police go on trial for manslaughter, abetting manslaughter, assault, and battery for violently breaking up a Separatist demonstration on September 30.		Merida, Mexico, falls to the revolutionaries. General Lariga, who was arrested there at the outbreak of the revolution and then released when he promised to support President Obregon, went over to the rebel cause. He took the entire garrison at Merida with him.	The Peking, China, Diplomatic Corps tells Sun Yat-sen that it has no power to concede or refuse his request to take over the Canton Customs House. The reply further states that under the Protocol of 1901, the Diplomatic Body has the right to assure priority of payment of interest.
Dec. 18	The Soviet Union states that it has not changed its position on the League of Nations. However, it is willing to send a representative to discuss the proposed extension of the Washington Naval Agreement to states other than those that originally signed it.	The German government has adopted a draft ordinance for regulation of the hours of labor. Eight hours a day will be recognized as the legal duration of a day's work.... The trial of anarchist Germaine Berton for assassinating Marius Plateau, the leader of the French Royalist Party, begins. Berton blames Plateau for the French occupation of the Ruhr.		General Cavazos, the Federal Chief of Staff, is reported to have been killed in Mexico.... The Canadian Department of Marine and Fisheries has received a protest from the Venezuelan Consul in Montreal against vessels being given clearance papers at Niagara for Venezuela. Apparently, bootleggers are making Venezuela the nominal destination of their liquor shipments.	A committee of the Delhi (India) Congress recommends an immediate boycott of British goods. An uphill fight is expected since many Indian manufacturers use British machinery that requires British spare parts.
Dec. 19		The British Drug Houses announce that they are making a further reduction in the price of insulin.... The Bavarian Diet rejects the Financial Powers Bill, which would have given wide powers for the carrying out of important measures of financial reform. The President of the Bavarian People's Party says that he will seek the dissolution of the Diet.... The King and Queen of Greece leave the country at the request of the revolutionary government. The tears of King George II are apparent as he boards a ship at Athens.	The Responsible Government Party elects to change its name to the Rhodesian Party. It will also enter negotiations for a union with the Rhodesian Labour Party.	The port of Tampico, Mexico, is closed from sunset to sunrise until further notice. Vessels entering after closing will be liable to be fired upon.... Canadian Naval Volunteers will be given the opportunity for voluntary service in the battleships *Hood* and *Repulse*, which embark at Vancouver and sail to the West Indies and eastern Canadian ports.	
Dec. 20		Ten Spanish fishing boats are seized by Portugal for fishing in territorial waters.... The civil tribunal of the Seine Department in France rejects the claim of the Marquis de Ponteves for 550,000-franc damages against the Comtesse de Beaurepaire for breach of promise.			
Dec. 21	Great Britain and Nepal sign a treaty releasing Nepalese goods from duties upon import to India.... The Soviet newspaper *Izvestia* declares that Great Britain intends to apply a spark to Afghanistan, which may plunge the whole of humanity into war and chaos.	In the Soviet Union, Josef Stalin publishes an essay accusing Leon Trotsky of duplicity for playing a lone hand and then joining the Bolshevists after the success of the revolution.	Turkish authorities propose to remove from trams the thick red curtains that have separated the seats of Muslim women travelers from the rest of the car on the grounds that the curtains carry disease. The two front rows of seats will be reserved for women.... The Rhodesian Party fails to reach an agreement with the Labour Party for an allocation of seats in the Rhodesian Parliament.		One of the most disastrous droughts in the history of Queensland, Australia, is broken by rain.
Dec. 22					Sun Yat-sen issues a statement that if the Inspector-General does not comply with his command regarding Customs duties, he will appoint and install new officials. He contends that the foreign powers have no treaty right to interfere in any such act of the Chinese government.
	A *Includes developments that affect more than one world region, international organizations and important meetings of world leaders.*	B *Includes all domestic and regional developments in Europe, including the Soviet Union.*	C *Includes all domestic and regional developments in Africa and the Middle East.*	D *Includes all domestic and regional developments in Latin America, the Caribbean, and Canada.*	E *Includes all domestic and regional developments in Asian and Pacific nations (and colonies).*

U.S. Politics & Social Issues	U.S. Foreign Policy & Affairs, Defense	U.S. Economy & Environment	Science, Technology & Nature	Culture, Leisure & Lifestyle	
			The Curator of Reptiles at the New York Zoo announces that the zoo held conferences with some drug laboratories and found that snake anti-venom could not be produced on a commercial basis. The zoo also concludes that the danger to the general public from snakebites remains comparatively small despite the rise in the number of bites. The zoo proposes to send the venom of North American snakes to a Brazilian laboratory for the preparation of suitable anti-venom serums.	Modernists in the Episcopal Church rebel against the attitude of the House of Bishops. They object to the Pastoral Letter unanimously adopted by the Bishops at Dallas in November that declared the truth of the Virgin Birth and Christ's divinity. Dr. Leighton Parks of St. Bartholomew's publicly proclaims his disbelief in the doctrine of the Virgin Birth and challenged the Bishop Manning to try him for heresy. At the same time, he announces that 500 clergy within the Episcopal Church had formed	Dec. 17
Liquor warehouses on the Canadian side of the Detroit River are reported to be closing because they cannot compete with the prices of European liquor in Detroit. So much smuggled liquor comes into Detroit from the Atlantic coast that the best brands of whiskey can be cheaply acquired. Scotch whisky can be bought in Detroit for $50 to $70 a case compared to $70 to $85 a case for Canadian whisky and $90 to $100 a case for Scotch whisky from Canadian warehouses.		The port of Progreso in Mexico is expected to be in rebel hands shortly. Sisal is shipped to the United States from this port, raising fears about disruptions in the supply.			Dec. 18
Henry Ford announces that he will never consider becoming a candidate for the presidency on any ticket against President Coolidge. He states that 90 percent of the American people feel safe with Coolidge and that the president should not have to devote any of his time or strength to political campaigning.... President Coolidge orders the release of all persons who are still in prison as a result of contravening war regulations. The order affects about 30 people.	Secretary of State Charles Evans Hughes says that he sees no reason for negotiations with the Soviet Union and that the United States has no intention of bartering away its principles.... The State Department publishes intercepted instructions from the Soviet government to the Workers' Party of America giving detailed plans for a proletarian revolution in the United States. The Department of Justice has assured the Secretary of State of the authenticity of these instructions.	The New York *Evening Post* is purchased by Cyrus H.K. Curtis of Philadelphia. He is the owner of the *Saturday Evening Post* and *Public Ledger* of Philadelphia.	The French Chamber of Deputies votes a pension of 40,000 francs to Marie Curie, the discoverer of radium.... The Kozloff Tibet Expedition has entered Eastern Mongolia. However, it has stalled because Chinese authorities fear that Colonel P. Kozloff will engage in Bolshevist propaganda. The team of 22 Soviets plans a three-year journey to Tibet and adjacent regions.		Dec. 19
			The wreckage of a British ship that carried gold for the British forces during the Crimean War is discovered in the Black Sea. The prospects of finding and raising the gold are considered to be good.	France authorizes a special postage stamp to be issued on the occasion of the Olympic Games in Paris next year.... Pope Pius XI elevates two Italians, Aurelio Galli and Evaristo Lucidi, to Cardinals.	Dec. 20
Congress adjourns for the Christmas and New Year holidays having accomplished nothing.		Christmas shopping is reported to be strong, causing prices to move up on the New York Stock Exchange. ...The ocean liner *Leviathan*, famed during the war as a troop transport and the pride of the U.S. Merchant Marines, runs aground on a mudbank in New York harbor. A dozen Shipping Board tugs are quickly on the scene, but they were unable to shift the 900-ton vessel as the tide moved out. The ship is refloated in the late afternoon.	The ancient site of Millo is apparently found in Jerusalem. Millo appears to have been an ornamental portico. It is referred to in the Books of Samuel and of Kings.		Dec. 21
					Dec. 22

F	G	H	I	J
Includes campaigns, elections, federal-state relations, civil rights and liberties, crime, the judiciary, education, healthcare, poverty, urban affairs, and population.	*Includes formation and debate of U.S. foreign and defense policies, veterans affairs, and defense spending. (Relations with specific foreign countries are usually found under the region concerned.)*	*Includes business, labor, agriculture, taxation, transportation, consumer affairs, monetary and fiscal policy, natural resources, pollution and industrial accidents.*	*Includes worldwide scientific, medical and technological developments, natural phenomena, U.S. weather and natural disasters.*	*Includes the arts, religion, scholarship, communications media, sports, entertainment, fashions, fads, and social life.*

	World Affairs	Europe	Africa & The Middle East	The Americas	Asia & The Pacific
Dec. 23		In the Soviet Union, venomous articles and speeches are directed against Leon Trotsky, who is blamed for seeking a dictatorship. Three men have been appointed to carry on the Commissariat of War until Trotsky's health permits him to return to his post.…The Free State of Ireland Department of Agriculture issues an order banning the import of all animals and poultry from areas in Great Britain affected by foot-and-mouth disease. To date, England has slaughtered 49,238 cattle, 21,355 sheep, 25,824 pigs, and 38 goats that have been exposed to the disease or infected by it.	Afghan troops occupy Mandatai in an effort to track down the gang responsible for a series of murders of British officers and British women. The gang has not yet been located.… The French naval airship *Dixmude* is adrift without fuel over Algeria. It is one of the German airships surrendered to France under the Treaty of Versailles. The ship has a crew of 30. All available naval vessels in Algerian and Tunisian waters are searching for it.	The government of Brazil announces an end to the state of siege in the Federal District and Rio de Janeiro that has existed since the revolution of July 1922.	The High Commissioner of Australia is asked by the Commonwealth Government to use the Quarantine Act to prohibit the importation of cattle, sheep, swine, and goats from Great Britain and Ireland. Foot-and-mouth disease is raging in England.
Dec. 24		Two Germans are sentenced to prison at Cologne for supplying a British soldier in uniform with opium.		Canadian opinion about a U.S. plan to deepen the St. Lawrence waterway remains divided. As a result, the Canadian government is blocking the project from proceeding.	
Dec. 25		Denmark has a white Christmas for the first time in many years.		President Rafael Gutierrez of Honduras orders the imposition of martial law following a Presidential election between three candidates that failed to produce clear results.	Kenjiro Den resigns as Japanese Minister of Agriculture after receiving criticism for failing to properly lead disaster reconstruction efforts.
Dec. 26				Under the new liquor system in Alberta, Canada, the sale of beer by bottle or glass for consumption on the premises will be permitted. Wine and spirits may be purchased in sealed packages on presentation of a permit.	
Dec. 27	The International Red Cross sends a telegram to all national Red Crosses requesting that money, food, and clothing be sent immediately to the German Red Cross. The British Red Cross declines to help because of the large amount of unemployment and distress in England arising out of the economic situation.	A bomb at a Jewish dance in Hungary kills one person and injures 17 others.		Mexican revolutionary forces claim to have annihilated a column of 2,000 Federal troops near Irapuato, Guanajuato.	An attempt is made on the life of the Japanese Regent.
Dec. 28		French troops leave Luxembourg. They have been stationed in the Grand Duchy since the Armistice.… The Battersea coroner blames the death of a man knocked down by a car on a "road hog" who dashed about the streets without a care for others.			The largest locomotives ever sent to India are lowered into the hold of a Norwegian steamer. The 12 locomotives weigh 120 tons each.…A British steamer is attacked by pirates 3 hours after leaving Hong Kong.
Dec. 29		The unrecognizable body of the commander of the missing French airship *Dixmude* is found floating off Sicily. A search of the area discloses no other trace of the ship or her crew.			The India National Congress debates some way of overcoming tensions between Hindus and Muslims. The National Pact, proposed by Bengalis, is strongly opposed by Hindus across the country on the grounds that it is too favorable to Muslims.
Dec. 30		The Seine River floods in France, sending water into the underground railway. Train services have not been interrupted.…The French Ministry of Marine announces that the airship *Dixmude* is officially lost.		Canada reduces the tax on newsprint by 50 percent. The rate will be three instead of six percent.	
Dec. 31		Portugal bans the import of any British animals, which can contract foot-and-mouth disease.…Germany sends its sympathy to France on the loss of the *Dixmude*.		De la Huerta, leader of the revolutionary forces in Mexico, states that as soon as his troops are in control of the oil zone, the duties on oil production must be paid to his government.	The Yamamoto Cabinet resigns, in spite of the Regent's request that they continue, owing to their responsibility in connection with the attack on the Regent.

A	B	C	D	E
Includes developments that affect more than one world region, international organizations and important meetings of world leaders.	*Includes all domestic and regional developments in Europe, including the Soviet Union.*	*Includes all domestic and regional developments in Africa and the Middle East.*	*Includes all domestic and regional developments in Latin America, the Caribbean, and Canada.*	*Includes all domestic and regional developments in Asian and Pacific nations (and colonies).*

	U.S. Politics & Social Issues	U.S. Foreign Policy & Affairs, Defense	U.S. Economy & Environment	Science, Technology & Nature	Culture, Leisure & Lifestyle
Dec. 23					
Dec. 24					Frank Jay Gould, an American millionaire, obtains an injunction from the French courts to prevent his divorced wife from appearing as a dancer under the name of Edith Kelly Gould.
Dec. 25	The American Medical Association asks Congress to pass a law forbidding the sale and usage of heroin, and claims that over 95 percent of the drug addicts in New York City are addicted to heroin.				
Dec. 26				The 25th anniversary of the discovery of radium by Pierre and Marie Curie is celebrated at the Sorbonne in Paris.	
Dec. 27					
Dec. 28					George Bernard Shaw's play *Saint Joan* is performed publicly for the first time at the Garrick Theater in New York City.
Dec. 29					Critics fault George Bernard Shaw's new play *Saint Joan* for being overly long at four hours but also characterize it as his greatest achievement.
Dec. 30		The U.S. government announces plans to sell rifles and other military supplies to federal forces in Mexico.			
Dec. 31					

F
Includes campaigns, elections, federal-state relations, civil rights and liberties, crime, the judiciary, education, healthcare, poverty, urban affairs, and population.

G
Includes formation and debate of U.S. foreign and defense policies, veterans affairs, and defense spending. (Relations with specific foreign countries are usually found under the region concerned.)

H
Includes business, labor, agriculture, taxation, transportation, consumer affairs, monetary and fiscal policy, natural resources, pollution and industrial accidents.

I
Includes worldwide scientific, medical and technological developments, natural phenomena, U.S. weather and natural disasters.

J
Includes the arts, religion, scholarship, communications media, sports, entertainment, fashions, fads, and social life.

1924

A crowd in the stands at the 1924 baseball World Series between the Washington Senators and New York Giants.

	World Affairs	Europe	Africa & The Middle East	The Americas	Asia & The Pacific
Jan.	The Semaine Internationale des Sports d'Hiver begins at Chamonix, France. Later the International Week of Winter Sports will be labeled the inaugural winter Olympic games.	A great fire occurs in London Harbor. A British submarine sinks in the English channel with loss of 43 lives.…Lenin dies. Stalin begins eliminating rivals.…Ramsay MacDonald becomes British prime minister. He is the first prime minister from the Labour Party.…France allows the Catholic Church to retake its property under the "diocesan associations" system. Relations with the Vatican improve.…Assassins kill Heinz, president of the Rheinland Republic. The Republic collapses.	Britain and France agree to the border between French and Anglo-Egyptian Sudan.	Canada mandates use of the red flag on government buildings. This is the first official authorization of what is a long-standing practice.	Gopinath Saha attempts to shoot Calcutta Police commissioner Charles A. Tegart, but shoots the wrong man. Authorities arrest Saha quickly.…The Australian Loans Council holds its inaugural meeting.…The first Kuomintang meeting takes place with Sun Yat Sen presiding. The meeting allows Communists and Russian advisors, particularly Michael Borodin.
Feb.	The International Ski Federation is founded.	Britain recognizes the Soviet government.	Spain, France, and Britain agree that Tangier will be neutral into perpetuity. Government will be by international commission.	After Rafael Lopez Gutierrez establishes a leftwing dictatorship, conservatives rebel. The United States refuses to recognize Lopez Gutierrez, and Honduras enters civil war, and the United States sends troops. After Gutierrez dies in March the war ends in May.	Mohandas Gandhi receives early release from prison. His health is frail.
Mar.		In a Bavarian prison, Adolf Hitler begins dictating Mein Kampf. With the deposing of Abdul Mejid II, the 1,400-year-old Ottoman caliphate is history. In its place is the Turkey of Kemal Pasha Ataturk.…Italy incorporates Fiume.	King Hussein appoints himself caliph of the Hejaz.	Santiago, Chile, establishes its first Rotary Club. This is Latin America's ninth Rotary. The organization debuted in Latin America in 1918.	Japan agrees to cede its tariff and extraterritorial rights in Siam.
Apr.	The Dawes Plan establishes German reparations at one billion marks a year, rising slowly to two billion marks. The plan provides a loan of 800 million marks to stabilize Germany. Germany accepts.…The League agrees to intervene in Hungary to stabilize the economy.	Hitler receives a five-year sentence for his role in the Beer Hall Putsch. He will serve only nine months.…Sabena Airlines, the Belgian carrier, makes its first flight.…Fascists win a two-thirds majority in Italy.	Syrian Alawites kill Christian nuns. French troops pursue them. Alawites are Sunni Muslims. They have their own nation from 1925 until 1930.	The Royal Canadian Air Force comes into existence.	
May	The 1924 Summer Olympics open in Paris.	Gottlieb Daimler and Karl Benz merge their automobile companies into Daimler-Benz.			Russia gives up extraterritoriality in China and returns the remainder of the Boxer indemnity. China agrees to Russian control of the Chinese Eastern Railroad. China has violated an agreement with Japan not to build railroads in Manchuria.
Jun.		Italian Fascists kidnap and murder Socialist leader Giacomo Matteotti, an outspoken foe of fascism. One escapes. Authorities arrest five and convict three. Victor Emmanuel III amnesties them after two months.	Iraq ratifies an agreement with Britain to change the mandate to an alliance. Rioting against Britain is widespread in Egypt.…The Riff rise again against Spain in Morocco.	Peru and Ecuador sign an agreement to negotiate border disputes. Failure to do so will trigger outside binding arbitration.	Noel Odell reports that teammates George Mallory and Andrew Irvine are heading for the top of Mount Everest. This is Mallory's third ascent. The two disappear and Mallory's body is not found until 1999.
Jul.	The World Chess Federation forms in Paris as the 8th Olympic Games close in the same city.	*Sovetsky Sport* debuts. This is a Soviet sports newspaper.	Britain quells Kurdish rioting in Iraq.	After supervised elections result in victory for Horacio Vasquez, the Dominican Republic is in compliance with U.S. expectations. The withdrawal of the marines follows.	The Commonwealth Electoral Act of 1924 passes. Effective in October, it makes voting compulsory in Australian federal elections and provides punishment for failure to do so.
Aug.		Georgia rises against the Soviet Union. The effort fails with several thousand dead.…France begins withdrawing troops from Germany.			
	A *Includes developments that affect more than one world region, international organizations and important meetings of world leaders.*	B *Includes all domestic and regional developments in Europe, including the Soviet Union.*	C *Includes all domestic and regional developments in Africa and the Middle East.*	D *Includes all domestic and regional developments in Latin America, the Caribbean, and Canada.*	E *Includes all domestic and regional developments in Asian and Pacific nations (and colonies).*

U.S. Politics & Social Issues	U.S. Foreign Policy & Affairs, Defense	U.S. Economy & Environment	Science, Technology & Nature	Culture, Leisure & Lifestyle	
The Agriculture Department revises "Milk and its Uses in the Home," which advocates, in order, milk from women, cows, and goats. The pamphlet also cautions against commercial baby foods.	The U.S. Navy establishes a radio intelligence office.	Ford stock totals $1 billion.	President Coolidge decides not to permit an arctic expedition.	Carl Taylor of Cleveland patents an ice cream cone rolling machine.	Jan.
Nevada becomes the first state to use gas in an execution. The state replaced hanging and shooting in 1921. First to die is Chinese-born Gee Jong.…The Castle Gate mine disaster in Utah kills 172 coal miners. The mine reopens in a few months and officially shuts down in 1960.		Herman Hollerith's Tabulating Machine Company merges with other companies. The result is IBM.…U.S. dockworkers go on strike.…The National Carbon Company sponsors The Eveready Hour, becoming the first company to put its brand on a radio show.	Calvin Coolidge is the first president to broadcast from the White House. Listeners total five million.…John Joseph Carthy of Bell Laboratories makes the first coast-to-coast radio broadcast. Audience is an estimated 50 million.	Woodrow Wilson dies.…George Gershwin premiers "Rhapsody in Blue." Paul Whiteman's orchestra backs him.…Jazz cornetist Bix Biederbecke of the Wolverines makes his first recordings for Gennett.	Feb.
	The Canadian-American Liquor Treaty goes into effect. The treaty is a response to American prohibition.…In an attempt to fly around the world, four Douglas biplanes leave Seattle. Two of the army planes complete the 51-stop, 357-hour trip.	A Castle Gate, UT, coal mine explosion kills 171.	Army personnel at Wright Field, OH, develop a technique for spraying chemicals from an airplane.	Douglas Fairbanks' *The Thief of Baghdad* opens. It earns United Artists $3 million.	Mar.
	Japanese begin anti-U.S. demonstrations and a boycott. They are responding to unilateral U.S. abrogation of the 1907 Gentlemen's Agreement and total exclusion of Japanese immigrants.	Metro Pictures, Goldwyn Pictures, and the Louis B. Mayer Company merge into Metro-Goldwyn-Mayer (MGM.)	The Soviet Union establishes an organization to study rocketry.	Radio station WLS premiers the Chicago Barn Dance, later the National Barn Dance, the first country and western radio show. WLS is owned by Sears (World's Largest Store.)	Apr.
Richard Loeb and Nathan Leopold, Jr., students at the University of Chicago, murder 14-year-old Bobby Franks in a thrill killing.…J. Edgar Hoover becomes acting head of the Bureau of Investigation. In December the job becomes permanent.	Coolidge signs the 1924 immigration act that sets quotas of two percent of the 1890 census, provides a 150,000 ceiling in 1927, and excludes Asians.…The United States returns the remainder of the Boxer indemnity to China. Purpose is financing of the China Foundation for the Promotion of Education and Culture.	Western Electric begins marketing its sound on disk film format. Only Warner and Fox show interest.	Bell Laboratories engineers publicly demonstrate the transmission of pictures over a telephone line.		May
Coolidge signs the Indian Citizenship Act. Indians born in the United States are citizens.…NBC broadcasts the Republican National Convention.	Army test pilot Russell Maughan flies coast to coast in a Curtiss pursuit plane. His time from New York to San Francisco is 21 hours, 48 minutes. This is his third attempt this month to fly coast-to-coast dawn-to-dusk.	Firestone Rubber agrees with Liberia to lease a million acres for 99 years in return for a $5 million loan over 40 years at seven percent.…Columbia Pictures Corporation incorporates.	Ernst Alexanderson sends the first facsimile across the ocean. Recipient is his father in Sweden. Alexanderson totals 345 patents, many in radio and television.	Will Rogers returns to the Ziegfeld Follies. He first performed in the follies in 1915. In the 1920s he tries movies but has little success until the advent of the talkies.	Jun.
		The Post Office begins continuous night and day coast-to-coast airmail service. The initial effort of 1920 failed to succeed.			Jul.
An ailing Samuel Gompers asks labor to back the independent presidential candidacy of Robert LaFollette. The candidate wins only Wisconsin and the effort to create a Labor Party dies.				John Ford's *Iron Horse* premiers. Ford's debut film introduces many of the themes that mark his talking westerns.	Aug.

F	G	H	I	J
Includes campaigns, elections, federal-state relations, civil rights and liberties, crime, the judiciary, education, healthcare, poverty, urban affairs, and population.	*Includes formation and debate of U.S. foreign and defense policies, veterans affairs, and defense spending. (Relations with specific foreign countries are usually found under the region concerned.)*	*Includes business, labor, agriculture, taxation, transportation, consumer affairs, monetary and fiscal policy, natural resources, pollution and industrial accidents.*	*Includes worldwide scientific, medical and technological developments, natural phenomena, U.S. weather and natural disasters.*	*Includes the arts, religion, scholarship, communications media, sports, entertainment, fashions, fads, and social life.*

	World Affairs	Europe	Africa & The Middle East	The Americas	Asia & The Pacific
Sep.	The Dawes Plan goes into effect after August ratification by the Reichstag.	Belgium implements the eight-hour day. The demand comes from the General Christian Workers Union.	Abd-al-Aziz ibn Saud captures Taif in the Hejaz. The Wahhabis control the region.	The last marines leave the Dominican Republic. The League accepts the Dominican Republic as a member.	Kauai police kill 16 striking Filipino sugar workers in the Hanapepe Massacre. The workers want $2 a day for an eight-hour day. Authorities arrest 101, try 76 and convict 60 for violating anti-syndicalism laws.…In Kohat, India, anti-Hindu riots kill 155 Sikhs and Hindus. Gandhi and other Indian leaders intervene to calm the crisis after the area's Hindus and Sikhs flee.
Oct.	To strengthen the League in the absence of Germany, Russia, and the United States, members adopt the Geneva Protocol to settle international disputes peacefully. Arbitration is compulsory; failure to arbitrate brands a nation an aggressor.	Britain reveals the Zinoviev letter, which calls for a workers' revolution in Britain. The conservatives win the elections four days later.…The Uzbek SSR joins the Soviet Union.… Dixie Dean scores a hat trick for the Tranmere Rovers, becoming the youngest to score a hat trick in English football. Dean is the most prolific scorer in the game.… France recognizes Russia.	The Nejd capture Mecca. Abdul Aziz declares that he is protector of Mecca's holy places.…Persia defeats the last of the Bakhtiari chieftains in the southwest. With aid from the British government and Anglo-Persian Petroleum, the Bakhtiari had nearly won independence.…Ruanda and Urundi become Belgian protectorate. They are parts of the former German East Africa.	An explosion on a train near Ferron, BC, kills three Sikhs and Doukhobor leader Peter Verigin. Suspects in the unsolved murders range from a jealous wife to the Soviets to the KKK.	
Nov.	The League convenes an opium conference that will continue into Februay 1925. The United States has a delegation.	France and Belgium are completely out of the Ruhr. The region is in German control again.…The new British Conservative government repudiates the Labour-signed commercial treaties with Russia.	After Egyptians assassinate Sir Lee Stack, Britain demands apologies, suppression of demonstrations, and withdrawal from the Sudan. Egypt initially refuses to leave the Sudan but accepts the other terms. By month's end Egypt is out of the Sudan.	Gerardo Machado wins the Cuban election. The liberal wins 5 of 6 provinces on a platform of "Water, Roads, and Schools."	The Philippine legislature demands independence.
Dec.		Communists fail to take over in Estonia. The republic's conservative government has tensions with Russia.…Ahmed Zog leads a successful counterrevolution in Albania. He ousts Bishop Fan Noli with aid from the Kingdom of the Serbs, Croats, and Slovenes. Fan Noli finds refuge in Italy.	After defeats in the interior, Spain withdraws to the coast of Morocco.		

A	B	C	D	E
Includes developments that affect more than one world region, international organizations and important meetings of world leaders.	*Includes all domestic and regional developments in Europe, including the Soviet Union.*	*Includes all domestic and regional developments in Africa and the Middle East.*	*Includes all domestic and regional developments in Latin America, the Caribbean, and Canada.*	*Includes all domestic and regional developments in Asian and Pacific nations (and colonies).*

	U.S. Politics & Social Issues	U.S. Foreign Policy & Affairs, Defense	U.S. Economy & Environment	Science, Technology & Nature	Culture, Leisure & Lifestyle
Sep.		On the first National Defense Test Day, the military and broadcasters combine to demonstrate the usefulness of radio in a national emergency.		Army flyers return to Seattle after they complete the first round-the-world, first trans-Pacific, and first westbound Atlantic crossing flight. The 175 day, 26,345 flight totals 363 air hours between April and September.	
Oct.	Toastmasters begins when Ralph Smedley forms a club at the Santa Ana, CA, YMCA. His goal is to make public speakers that are more effective.			The German built dirigible ZR-3, later renamed *Los Angeles,* arrives in the U.S. The craft is part of German reparations to the U.S.	
Nov.	Nellie Tayloe Ross becomes Wyoming's governor. She is the first woman governor.…The American Federation of Labor convention declares Sacco and Vanzetti victims of class and race prejudice.…Railroad union officials reject a third party.		The stock market hits a five-year high. November 7 sees 2.33 million shares trade.	The first trans-Atlantic transmission of a radio facsimile occurs.	The first Macy's Thanksgiving Day Parade takes place in New York City. The parade features Macy's employees in costume, floats and bands, Central Park Zoo animals, and Santa Claus. The parade replaces the one by Bamburger's of Newark.
Dec.	Congress receives a civil aeronautics act. The act proposes establishment of a Civil Aeronautics Bureau in the Commerce Department.			The first diesel locomotive enters service—in the Bronx.…William Einthoven wins the Nobel Prize for medicine.…Edwin Hubble announces the existence of distant galazies.	Charlie Chaplin causes a scandal when the press discovers that he is married to 16-year-old Lita Gray.…Knute Rockne and the Four Horsemen of Notre Dame finish the season undefeated.

F	G	H	I	J
Includes campaigns, elections, federal-state relations, civil rights and liberties, crime, the judiciary, education, healthcare, poverty, urban affairs, and population.	*Includes formation and debate of U.S. foreign and defense policies, veterans affairs, and defense spending. (Relations with specific foreign countries are usually found under the region concerned.)*	*Includes business, labor, agriculture, taxation, transportation, consumer affairs, monetary and fiscal policy, natural resources, pollution and industrial accidents.*	*Includes worldwide scientific, medical and technological developments, natural phenomena, U.S. weather and natural disasters.*	*Includes the arts, religion, scholarship, communications media, sports, entertainment, fashions, fads, and social life.*

	World Affairs	Europe	Africa & The Middle East	The Americas	Asia & The Pacific
Jan. 1		More than a week of constant snowfall paralyzes Austria and Switzerland.... Former Greek premier Eleftherios Venizelos calls upon Greeks to vote whether or not Greece should adopt a monarchical or republican form of government.		In response to a growth in robbery and looting by revolutionary forces in parts of Mexico, hundreds of farmers and laborers flock to join the Mexican army.... Officials of Adolfo de la Huerta's revolutionary government announce that they will collect taxes from all petroleum companies operating within rebel-held territory in Mexico.	Prince Regent Hirohito calls upon Viscount Kiego Kiyoura to become the new prime minister of Japan.
Jan. 2		The dollar value of both the British pound and the French franc declines by nearly five cents.... Italy's Adriatic coast experiences earthquake tremors.... The Greek National Assembly meets for the first time in nearly a year and a half.... The Soviet Union outlaws private schools and forbids punishment of students in public schools.			
Jan. 3	Boston department store president Edward A. Filene will donate money to be awarded to the English, French, and Italian essayist who best proposes a workable peace plan for the world.	Seven regiments of the French army have departed the Ruhr valley. More will follow.... German industrialist Arnold Rechberg suggests that France accept shares in German companies as reparations. ...Wreckage of the missing French dirigible the *Dixmude* is sighted off the coast of San Marco, Sicily, and Bizerta.	Archaeologist Howard Carter finds the sarcophagus of Egyptian pharaoh Tutankhamen.	Mexican revolutionaries warn American, British, French, and German merchants that they must pay import duties to the rebels or lose property seized at the port of Vera Cruz. The governor of Vera Cruz warns that they will be fined if they give money to the rebels.... The new Chilean cabinet, composed of political liberals, takes office. It intends to combat the actions of Chile's conservative Senate.	
Jan. 4		German laborers in the Ruhr valley refuse to work 10-hour days. As a result, many metal works shut down.	South Africa's Labor Party restates its intentions to combine with the country's Nationalist Party to remove Prime Minister Jan Smuts from office.	Resident Commissioner Felix Cordova Davila requests that Puerto Rico be given broader powers to govern itself and insists that Puerto Ricans receive the benefits of federal aid programs.	The U.S. Army denies that it is distributing anti-independence propaganda in the Filipino province of Mindanao
Jan. 5		German teachers denounce government plans to fire 25 percent of the teaching staff at Prussian schools in order to save money.... Eleftherios Venizelos is elected President of the National Assembly of Greece.	Persia plans to sell state treasures, including the crown jewels, in order to raise funds to build rail lines.	Guatemala prohibits the sale of weapons to Mexico.... Interruptions in rail service caused by the revolution forces factories near Mexico City to cease production.	Bombs are thrown at the Imperial Palace in Tokyo, but no damage is done.
Jan. 6		Berlin will use revenues derived from a tax levied on dancers in restaurants and cabarets to feed the poor.... German unemployment declines.... Swedish financier Arthur Wallenberg buys land in anticipation of founding a Swedish colony in Guatemala.	The Egyptian government plans to close Tutankhamen's tomb at the end of January.		
Jan. 7	General Charles G. Dawes and Owen D. Young arrive in Paris. They are the American representatives on the first of two committees of experts charged by the International Reparations Commission with formulating a plan by which Germany will be able to pay damages to those countries to which they are owed. The first committee, of which Dawes and Young are a part, is charged with assessing Germany's financial strength.	Russians celebrate a traditional Christmas despite threats from the government that those not reporting to work would suffer pay cuts.... An attempt is made to kill Turkish president Mustafa Kemal. He is not hurt, but his wife is injured by a hand grenade.			The United Christian Missionary Society reports that American missionaries in China were not harmed when Tibetan bandits captured the town of Batang in Szechwan province.
	A *Includes developments that affect more than one world region, international organizations and important meetings of world leaders.*	B *Includes all domestic and regional developments in Europe, including the Soviet Union.*	C *Includes all domestic and regional developments in Africa and the Middle East.*	D *Includes all domestic and regional developments in Latin America, the Caribbean, and Canada.*	E *Includes all domestic and regional developments in Asian and Pacific nations (and colonies).*

U.S. Politics & Social Issues	U.S. Foreign Policy & Affairs, Defense	U.S. Economy & Environment	Science, Technology & Nature	Culture, Leisure & Lifestyle	
The Brooklyn Bureau of Charities encourages New York City teachers to undergo regular physical examinations in order to prevent disease and to serve as a role model for students.		The Lago Petroleum Company announces that it will drill for oil in Venezuela.	Britain claims to have developed a method of using radio waves to stop the engines of aircraft while they are in flight.... Psychology professor B.B. Breese and Dr. Louis A. Laturie announce that, when given to children, secretions from the pituitary gland can alleviate mental retardation and growth disorders.	The soccer team from the passenger liner *Aquitania* defeats the *Leviathan's* team in a match played in New York City.... Violinist Jascha Heifetz performs at Carnegie Hall.... California oilman Courtland S. Dines is shot by actress Mabel Normand's chauffeur. Mabel Normand and actress Edna Purviance are present at the time.	Jan. 1
	U.S. Navy battleships leave San Francisco to take part in war games in the Caribbean and in Panama.... Representative Benjamin L. Fairchild prepares a joint resolution to be presented Congress that would prohibit the U.S. government from selling arms to foreign countries.	Democrats in the House of Representatives meet to discuss their opposition to the income tax bill proposed by Secretary of the Treasury Andrew Mellon.	Temperatures in California fall to record lows. Thermometers in Los Angeles register 37 degrees.... A beacon that emits a 180-degree arc of light extending for more than a mile is demonstrated at Mitchel Field, Long Island. The beacon will improve the safety of night flying and make night baseball possible.	The World Series-winning New York Yankees will receive gold watches from baseball commissioner Kenesaw Mountain Landis.	Jan. 2
Representative Louis Marshall of New York denounces a proposed bill that would limit the number of immigrants from a given country who are allowed to enter the United States each year to two percent of the total number of immigrants from that country living in the United States in 1890. Marshall notes that the plan would discriminate against those not from northern Europe.		Cotton prices rise by one cent per pound.... An explosion at a starch plant in Illinois leaves 40 men either dead or missing.	Moscow reports that a Russian surgeon has successfully operated on a hypnotized but conscious patient.	Memphis, TN, bans the showing of all movies featuring actress Mabel Normand, who was involved in the shooting of Courtland S. Dines on January 1.... Bishop Harry T. Moore decides that the Reverend Lee W. Heaton will not be tried for heresy for suggesting that members of the Episcopal Church do not need to believe in the virgin birth of Jesus.	Jan. 3
Attorney General Harry M. Daugherty defends the actions of the federal government in imprisoning opponents of the World War.... The People's Progressive Party and Ford-for-President clubs unite and call for a national convention to nominate a presidential candidate.	Secretary of War John W. Weeks confirms the sale of rifles, airplanes, and ammunition to the government of Mexico by the government of the United States.	The White House announces that President Calvin Coolidge will reject proposed changes to the Mellon tax bill.	Experiments conducted in the Hudson River tunnel prove that radio waves can penetrate earth and water. Radios can be used to contact people underground in case of an emergency.... The U.S. Army announces the names of pilots selected for a fight around the globe.		Jan. 4
	Representative Henry Lee Jost of Missouri calls on Congress to delay granting bonuses to the World War veterans until a pension plan is created.	Four hundred new models are revealed at national auto show in the Bronx.... Sinclair Consolidated Oil Corporation refuses to discuss reports from the Soviet Union that the Soviet government is rethinking its leasing of oil lands in the Baku region to the company.	Dr. Lee De Forest demonstrates his invention of the phonophone, a device that records both sound and moving images on film.... Extreme cold causes deaths and interferes with business and transportation in several states.		Jan. 5
The prize-winning Bok Peace Plan, written by Charles H. Levermore, is announced.	U.S. senators who oppose U.S. membership in the League of Nations declare that the recently announced Bok Peace Plan will not affect their position on the matter.				Jan. 6
A national referendum begins in the United States on the Bok Peace Plan. The referendum, which will end in February, will gauge public interest in implementing the plan's suggestions.	Speaking before the Senate, Henry Cabot Lodge, Chairman of the Senate Committee on Foreign relations maintains that the United States should not recognize the government of the Soviet Union. Senator William E. Borah disagrees.	The U.S. Supreme Court declares that provisions in the Transportation Act that allow Congress to divert the profits of larger railroads to smaller railroads are constitutional.	Six deaths in Georgia are blamed on unusually low temperatures. Atlanta reports a temperature of 16 degrees. Temperatures reach 80 degrees in Los Angeles.	The United States Lawn Tennis Association names William T. Tilden number one men's player and Helen Wills number one women's player.... Vassar College gives its teachers freedom of speech provided they do not violate state or federal laws.	Jan. 7
F *Includes campaigns, elections, federal-state relations, civil rights and liberties, crime, the judiciary, education, healthcare, poverty, urban affairs, and population.*	G *Includes formation and debate of U.S. foreign and defense policies, veterans affairs, and defense spending. (Relations with specific foreign countries are usually found under the region concerned.)*	H *Includes business, labor, agriculture, taxation, transportation, consumer affairs, monetary and fiscal policy, natural resources, pollution and industrial accidents.*	I *Includes worldwide scientific, medical and technological developments, natural phenomena, U.S. weather and natural disasters.*	J *Includes the arts, religion, scholarship, communications media, sports, entertainment, fashions, fads, and social life.*	

	World Affairs	Europe	Africa & The Middle East	The Americas	Asia & The Pacific
Jan. 8		British Labor Party leader Ramsay Macdonald, at a celebration of the party's victory at the polls, calls for greater use of the League of Nations and for recognition of the Soviet Union.			
Jan. 9	The French announce a competition and award for the best European peace plan. Italy and England will hold similar competitions.	Franz Josef Heinz, the leader of the Separatist movement in the Rhenish Palatinate, which advocates secession from Germany, is assassinated.…Throughout Germany, unemployed and striking workers clash with strikebreakers and the police.…The Berlin premiere of Eugene O'Neill's *The Emperor Jones* is derided in the conservative press for its supposed attack on monarchy.…The government of Switzerland calls for a 52-hour workweek.		The Mexican army gathers in preparation for attacks on rebel forces in Guadalajara and Vera Cruz.	Filipino political leaders charge Major General Leonard Wood, Governor General of the Philippines, with having misused his authority and ask for Philippine independence.
Jan. 10		Severe storms batter the coasts of France, Spain, and Portugal.…A meeting of representatives of the Little Entente (Romania, Yugoslavia, and Czechoslovakia) begins in Belgrade.…Hungary is in need of a loan from the League of Nations but fears foreign interference with its economic development.	Arabs in Amman await the arrival of Arab nationalist King Hussein of the Hedjaz. Many wish for Hussein to proclaim himself the caliph of Islam.…A 35-foot tidal wave floods the port of Rabat.	Troops of the Mexican army begin their march on Vera Cruz, headquarters of the rebel movement.	The value of the Japanese yen falls sharply.
Jan. 11		An avalanche in the Swiss Alps buries 30 men.…Former Greek prime minister Eleftherios Venizelos agrees to head the Greek government when Greek Liberals fail to unite.	Troops of the Persian government defeat a group of Lur rebels. The Lur are an ethnic minority from western Persia.	Mexican federal troops capture the city of Pachuca.	
Jan. 12			Egypt's nationalist Zaghloulist Party wins 80 percent of seats in the Egyptian legislature.		A Bengali revolutionary kills a European merchant in the streets of Calcutta. The police believe that the merchant was mistaken for the police commissioner.
Jan. 13	Italian and Belgian members of Charles G. Dawes's Committee of Experts arrive in Paris.	The celebration of "German Day" begins in Berlin and in the rest of Germany. The festivities honor the founding of the German Empire in 1871.…Germans from the Ruhr valley immigrate to Brazil, where they plan to work in factories as machinists.	Prince Kamel Eddine Hussein departs Cairo on an expedition into the Libyan desert. The prince is searching for both an old caravan route and a bottle, containing stolen documents that was left in the desert 50 years ago.	Mexican Indians attack Oaxaca. Rebel forces abandon the town of La Piedad.	Professor Bernard Hoff, a Lutheran missionary from the United States, dies from injuries inflicted by Chinese bandits who attacked Hoff's mission.
Jan. 14	General Charles G. Dawes's Committee of Experts holds its first meeting.…Woodrow Wilson's Under-Secretary of State, Norman H. Davis, becomes head of League of Nations commission to determine the fate of Memel, a Baltic city claimed by both Lithuania and Poland.			Delegates from Puerto Rico accompanied by the governor of Puerto Rico, Horace M. Towner, arrive in New York City. The delegates intend to ask Congress to allow more self-government for the island.…Mexican revolutionaries led by General Martinez Herrera seize control of Cerro Azul and Zacamixtle and interrupt the shipment of oil.…Three Mexican army fliers are killed or captured by rebel forces.	
	A *Includes developments that affect more than one world region, international organizations and important meetings of world leaders.*	B *Includes all domestic and regional developments in Europe, including the Soviet Union.*	C *Includes all domestic and regional developments in Africa and the Middle East.*	D *Includes all domestic and regional developments in Latin America, the Caribbean, and Canada.*	E *Includes all domestic and regional developments in Asian and Pacific nations (and colonies).*

	U.S. Politics & Social Issues	U.S. Foreign Policy & Affairs, Defense	U.S. Economy & Environment	Science, Technology & Nature	Culture, Leisure & Lifestyle
Jan. 8	The Italian Ministers' Association states that new immigration plans should not include literacy tests because illiterate people make the best workers.	President Calvin Coolidge places restrictions on the sale of arms to Mexico. The Mexican government will still be able to buy weapons and ammunition in the United States, but Adolfo de la Huerta's revolutionary forces will not.	The price of Pennsylvania crude oil rises to $3.40 per barrel.... Representative George P. Darrow introduces a petition calling for tax relief for farmers.	A 10 million year old dinosaur egg found in the Gobi Desert is auctioned off by the Museum of Natural History in New York.	
Jan. 9	Federal authorities demand that liquor raids in Illinois's Williamson County led by prohibitionist and Ku Klux Klansman Glenn Young come to a halt....Senator Earle Mayfield of Texas refutes charges that he is either funded by the Ku Klux Klan or has used the Klan to intimidate voters....More than 20,000 ballots either accepting or rejecting the Bok Peace Plan have been received at the headquarters of the Policy Committee of the American Peace Award. A million other ballots have been sent to those requesting them.		Representative John J. O'Connor of New York proposes that parents be encouraged to produce more citizens by giving them a $400 federal tax credit for their first child and $500 for their second, with a $100 increase in the sum for each subsequent child....The Department of Labor foresees no unemployment problem in 1924....The Department of Agriculture reports that nearly nine percent of farmers in the northern Great Plains have lost their farms since the beginning of the decade.		The president of Roanoake College, Charles J. Smith, criticizes the drinking, smoking, and sexual openness of female college students.
Jan. 10	West Virginia Democrats give their support to fellow West Virginian John W. Davis, former ambassador to Britain, as Democratic nominee for president.		Production of crude oil in the western states decreases....Price of cotton falls.		Golf officials ban from tournament play a ball capable of flying 50 yards beyond the range of balls in current use....Unless Bishop William T. Manning allows New York City's St. Mark's-in-the-Bouwerie to include dancing in its services, the church will remove itself from the Protestant Episcopal Diocese of New York.
Jan. 11	Frank Hendrick, an entrant in the contest to win the Bok Peace Plan award, asserts that contestants were referred to the League of Nations Non-Partisan Association. This, Hendrick asserts, indicates that the Peace Plan prize committee intended to select a plan favoring the League of Nations.	President Calvin Coolidge intends to veto any bill that calls for payment of a bonus to veterans.			
Jan. 12	Requests for copies of the Bok Peace Plan award continue to arrive at the American Peace Award headquarters....Representative William Larsen of Georgia criticizes Attorney General Harry M. Daugherty for not arresting Charles R. Forbes, former head of the Veterans Bureau, on charges of fraud.	Brigadier General Hugh H. Drum and Admiral W.M. Moffett describe the present state of America's military forces as inadequate and call for the construction of more airplanes, gun ships, and cruisers.		Large numbers of whales are spotted off the coast of New Jersey.	
Jan. 13			Phillipe Bunau Varrilla, who sold the Panama Canal Company to the United States, suggests that the United States widen the canal and transform it from a lock canal into a sea-level strait.	French inventor Edouard Belin proclaims that in less than a year he will have invented television, which will allow the transmission of images of the human face.	Protestant Episcopal minister Dr. Percy Stickney Grant defends the rights of Episcopal Modernists to remain within the church and calls upon other members of the church to respect their beliefs....Fundamentalist minister John Roach Stratton compares Protestant Modernists to cuckoo birds and criticizes them for using Baptist schools to spread destructive religious propaganda.
Jan. 14			Senator Kenneth McKellar of Tennessee advises the Senate to reject the offer of a group of power companies to purchase the federally owned power plant at Muscle Shoals, AL. McKellar states that the majority of stock in the Alabama Power Company is owned by the British and this would make the United States dependent on another nation. McKellar urges that Muscle Shoals be sold to Henry Ford.		The U.S. Post Office states that the January issue of the arts magazine *Broom* cannot be mailed. Formerly published in Italy and Germany, the magazine has featured the works of Amy Lowell, Gertrude Stein, and Sherwood Andersen. The current issue contains an article by William Carlos Williams and poetry by E.E. Cummings....Underwear manufacturers discuss the possibility that the popularity of mah jongg will lead to new complementary underwear styles.

F	G	H	I	J
Includes campaigns, elections, federal-state relations, civil rights and liberties, crime, the judiciary, education, healthcare, poverty, urban affairs, and population.	*Includes formation and debate of U.S. foreign and defense policies, veterans affairs, and defense spending. (Relations with specific foreign countries are usually found under the region concerned.)*	*Includes business, labor, agriculture, taxation, transportation, consumer affairs, monetary and fiscal policy, natural resources, pollution and industrial accidents.*	*Includes worldwide scientific, medical and technological developments, natural phenomena, U.S. weather and natural disasters.*	*Includes the arts, religion, scholarship, communications media, sports, entertainment, fashions, fads, and social life.*

	World Affairs	Europe	Africa & The Middle East	The Americas	Asia & The Pacific
Jan. 15					Earthquake tremors are felt in the Philippines and Japan. Communications and transportation are interrupted near Tokyo. The royal family is unharmed.... The American embassy in Beijing learns that Julina Kilen, who was captured by Chinese bandits, has been freed.
Jan. 16	The Dawes Committee of Experts wish to confer with Hjalmar Schacht regarding the financial situation in Germany. Schacht is Controller of the Currency and the head of the Reichsbank in Germany.		The Persian government announces that it will reject a loan backed by the Sinclair Consolidated Oil Corporation that was promised in return for the lease of land in northern Persia.... Oscar S. Straus, former ambassador to Turkey, departs for the Middle East. He intends to visit Palestine in an attempt to reconcile conflicts among the various inhabitants of the region.	Nova Scotian coalminers go on strike.	The death toll in Japan from the earthquake of January 15 stands at 30.... Viscount Takahashi, leader of Japan's Seiyukai Party, proclaims his opposition to the government of Prime Minister Viscount Kiyoura.... England learns that Afghan troops have taken into custody bandits who are suspected of killing British officers and their wives.
Jan. 17		Former Liberal Winston Churchill criticizes the willingness of Britain's Liberal Party leader Herbert Asquith to support the formation of a government led by the Labour Party.... France wants General Charles G. Dawes and the Committee of Experts to impose high taxes on Germany so that, after the German budget is balanced, a surplus will exist for the payment of reparations.	Egyptian premier Yehia Ibrahim Pasha resigns following the triumph of Saad Zaghlul's nationalist Wafd Party at the polls.... The Persian government is reported to be negotiating with American engineering firms to construct roads and railways in Persia.		The U.S. State Department protests Chinese President Tsao Kun's pardoning of a Chinese general held responsible for the death of an American missionary in 1920.
Jan. 18	An official of the Mexican government claims that England and German industrialist Hugo Stinnes are selling weapons to Mexican revolutionaries.... As a result of Italy's questioning of the ability of the League of Nations to resolve its dispute with Greece in 1923, jurists from around the world gather in Geneva to study the covenant of the League of Nations and its relationship to international law.	French Prime Minister Raymond Poincaré and Finance Minister Charles de Lasteyrie press for a 20 percent increase in French taxes as the value of the franc continues to fall.... French Prime Minister Raymond Poincaré states that the Separatists in the Palatinate are not supported by France.... Germany's Krupp Company buys a dockyard and engineering works in order to manufacture steamers and locomotives that, because of the terms of the Treaty of Versailles, cannot be built in Germany.		Two American ships are shelled as they break through the rebel blockade of the port of Tampico, Mexico.... The U.S. Navy cruiser *Richmond* heads for Tampico.	A Filipino newspaper reports that the Colorum, a messianic religious sect that promises the coming of Philippine independence, has established itself in Manila. The Colorum is suspected of killing 24 Filipino policemen on Mindanao.... The legislature of the Philippines adopts a budget that reduces funding for Governor General Leonard Wood's office and provides no money for Wood's yacht.
Jan. 19		The German government hires a former schoolteacher to tell stories to children working in mines and factories.... Germany plans to mortgage the German post office and state-owned railroads to raise money.... The head rabbi of Cracow, Poland, Dr. Osias Thon, predicts that the Polish government will soon grant rights to Polish Jews.		Brazil ratifies agreements reached at the Fourth Pan American Conference in 1923.... Seven U.S. Navy ships are ordered to Mexico.... The rebel blockade of Tampico, Mexico, ends.	
Jan. 20		German police arrest several men thought to be involved with a suspected Separatist plot to take over the Ruhr valley.			

A	B	C	D	E
Includes developments that affect more than one world region, international organizations and important meetings of world leaders.	*Includes all domestic and regional developments in Europe, including the Soviet Union.*	*Includes all domestic and regional developments in Africa and the Middle East.*	*Includes all domestic and regional developments in Latin America, the Caribbean, and Canada.*	*Includes all domestic and regional developments in Asian and Pacific nations (and colonies).*

	U.S. Politics & Social Issues	U.S. Foreign Policy & Affairs, Defense	U.S. Economy & Environment	Science, Technology & Nature	Culture, Leisure & Lifestyle
Jan. 15	Ballots filled out by members of churches belonging to the Federal Churches of Christ in America arrive at the American Peace Award headquarters in New York City. The ballots indicate whether voters approve or disapprove of the adoption of the Bok Peace Plan.		The National Farm Loan Board issues $60 million worth of bonds. Bonds can be purchased at federal land banks.…Senator Robert LaFollette of Wisconsin calls on the Senate to adopt a joint resolution enjoining the Interstate Commerce Commission to lower railroad rates on shipments of crops and agricultural tools and machinery.	James A. Montgomery, president of the American Schools of Oriental Research, reports that British explorer R.E. Stewart Macalister has discovered the oldest artifacts yet found in Jerusalem.	Footwear manufacturers announce that shoe fashions for the coming season will feature suede and lizard and alligator skin.…A discussion of the Baha'i religion takes place at the Community Church on New York City's Park Avenue.…Using volunteers from the audience, Emile Coué demonstrates the use of autosuggestion at New York City's Town Hall.
Jan. 16	The National Negro Democratic Conference Committee warns African Americans that Republican politicians take African-American votes for granted and are no longer concerned with protecting African-American civil rights.…New York City Police Commissioner Richard E. Enright calls for federal legislation banning the sale and possession of handguns.			The northern midwest suffers from subzero temperatures. Snow in Chicago is blamed for a train derailment, one death, and several injuries.…Marquis Raul Pateras Pescara sets a new helicopter record by remaining aloft for more than eight minutes.	
Jan. 17	Former Secretary of the Interior Albert B. Fall denies charges that he profited from leasing naval oil reserves at Teapot Dome, WY, to oilman Harry F. Sinclair.		Crude oil production in the United States increases. A decrease in oil imports is attributed to the revolution in Mexico.		
Jan. 18	The conviction of Dr. William J. Robinson on the charge of selling a book on the subject of birth control is affirmed by the New York Court of Appeals.…Japanese farmers in California are moving to the east and the midwest in search of farmland that they can purchase, rent, or sharecrop, actions prohibited under California law.…President of Yale, Robert Angell, announces that between 1900 and 1920 there has been a 300 percent increase in high school students and calls for an increase in the number of qualified teachers.		The sale of inexpensive Argentine grain to Europe causes the prices of American corn, wheat, and rye to drop. Low wheat prices lead to bank failures in Montana and the Dakotas. President Calvin Coolidge announces that the War Finance Corporation and the Federal Reserve will assist beleaguered banks.		Archbishop Michael Joseph Curley of Baltimore states his opposition to a proposed law that would allow theaters to show films on Sundays. The archbishop bases his opposition to Sunday films on the immoral nature of many movies.…At a meeting of Fundamentalist Protestants, Baptist minister Harry Emerson Fosdick is asked to relinquish his position as preacher in New York City's First Presbyterian Church.
Jan. 19	Hundreds of immigrants held at Ellis Island are allowed to walk outside for the first time since July 1923. Commissioner Henry H. Curran explains that this is the first time that there have been enough guards available to keep detainees from hurting themselves as they explore the grounds.	Secretary Denby admits that the purpose of the navy's planned flight to the North Pole in the dirigible *Shenandoah* is to study the region with the intent of annexing it to the United States for probable use as an airbase.	The Federal Horticultural Board bans the import of Mediterranean fruit fly-infested grapes from Spain.	As a result of a dry summer and warm weather in December, birds and wild animals in New England suffer from a food shortage.	Percival Baxter, governor of Maine, appeals to Will H. Hays, president of the Motion Picture Association of America, to protect animals appearing in motion pictures from abuse.…Presbyterian minister, A. Gordon MacLennan, pastor of Bethany Presbyterian Church in Philadelphia, calls on Reverend Dr. Harry Emerson Fosdick, a Baptist, to cease preaching in New York's First Presbyterian Church.
Jan. 20	Speaking at a dinner given by the National Woman's Party, Florence Kelly, General Secretary of the Consumers' League, argues against the passage of an equal rights amendment.…Under the leadership of Glenn Young, 500 members of the Ku Klux Klan destroy stills and arrest suspected bootleggers in Williamson and Franklin Counties, IL.			The discovery of prehistoric animal statues in an underground cave in southern France is announced.…Medium Nino Pecoraro conducts a séance in order to claim a $2,500 prize offered by *Scientific American* to anyone who can provide objective proof that the spirit world exists. A committee consisting of physicians and their friends and relatives pronounce Pecoraro's performance to be authentic after he converses with his dead brother and makes ectoplasmic hands appear.	Baptist minister Harry Emerson Fosdick addresses a record crowd as a special preacher at New York's First Presbyterian Church.…Edward C. Delafield, President of the Bank of America, announces that the bank will build a 23-story skyscraper on Wall Street.

F	G	H	I	J
Includes campaigns, elections, federal-state relations, civil rights and liberties, crime, the judiciary, education, healthcare, poverty, urban affairs, and population.	*Includes formation and debate of U.S. foreign and defense policies, veterans affairs, and defense spending. (Relations with specific foreign countries are usually found under the region concerned.)*	*Includes business, labor, agriculture, taxation, transportation, consumer affairs, monetary and fiscal policy, natural resources, pollution and industrial accidents.*	*Includes worldwide scientific, medical and technological developments, natural phenomena, U.S. weather and natural disasters.*	*Includes the arts, religion, scholarship, communications media, sports, entertainment, fashions, fads, and social life.*

	World Affairs	Europe	Africa & The Middle East	The Americas	Asia & The Pacific
Jan. 21	The second expert committee charged with finding a workable solution to the payment of reparations by Germany begins its work. The task of the second committee is to identify all sources of German capital located overseas.	Soviet leader Vladimir Ilyich Lenin dies of a stroke....British railroad workers strike. Commuters buy or refurbish bicycles to cope with the interruption in transportation....Robert Clive, British Consul General at Munich, tells the House of Commons that most people living in the Palatinate do not favor the Separatist movement. He maintains that France is behind the move to create a self-governing region in German territory.		A trainload of Mexican troops passes through El Paso, TX, on its way to Juarez, Mexico.	
Jan. 22	The expert committee in charge of stabilizing German finances suggests that the establishment of a gold bank controlled by the international community is the first step toward balancing the German budget and restoring the strength of German money.	Britain's Labor Party leader James Ramsay Macdonald takes office as prime minister. Macdonald's government is the first Socialist Labor government in the history of Britain....Residents of the Baltic region note, with trepidation, sightings of the silk-tailed winter thrush, a bird believed to be a herald of famine, war, and disease.		The Mexican senate studies plans for a civilian peace commission representing all social classes that would attempt to negotiate a settlement between the government of President Alavaro Obregon and the revolutionary government of Adolfo de la Huerta.	The Japanese government announces its intentions to terminate all leases held by foreigners in Yokohama, effectively eliminating the ability of non-Japanese to reside in the city.
Jan. 23		Liverpool suffers from a shortage of coal that might interfere with shipping....Thousands of Russians head to Moscow to view the body of Vladimir Ilyich Lenin.	French general Maxime Weygand travels to Amman to discuss the formation of a Pan-Arabic Confederation with King Hussein of the Hedjaz.	The Coolidge administration hopes to discourage the sale of boats by Americans to the Mexican navy. Under the terms of the international Washington Arms Conference, nations may not sell ships to the navies of other countries, but sales by private citizens are allowed....Puerto Rican delegates meet with President Calvin Coolidge to request self-government for Puerto Rico.	Filipino's celebrate the 25th anniversary of the founding of the Philippine Republic. Marie Bernarda Balitaan, the leader of the Colorum, a religious sect seeking Philippine independence, pledges to work with those who want peace.
Jan. 24		The Soviet city of Petrograd is renamed Leningrad....James O'Grady, MP for Leeds, is named Britain's ambassador to the Soviet Union.			President Calvin Coolidge congratulates Japan's Prince Regent Hirohito on his upcoming marriage.
Jan. 25		France and Czechoslovakia sign a treaty that forms an alliance between the two countries but does not call on them to support one another militarily.			The Bengal legislature calls on the British to free political prisoners currently being held without trial.
Jan. 26	Charles V. Cickrey, General Secretary of Near East Relief, a charitable organization, reports that 95,000 Christian refugees are living in camps in Greece following their departure from Turkey.		Nationalist leader Saad Zaghlul becomes prime minister of Egypt.	An earthquake strikes Ecuador....The former president of Uruguay and the current Minister of War fight a duel over pending legislation that would make military service compulsory for all men.	Auxiliary soldiers are dispatched to the Philippine province of Surigao to restore order after recent violence in the region....Philippine Senator José Clarin severely criticizes Governor General Leonard Wood for ordering the burning of a Filipino town during recent clashes between government police and Filipino rebels.
Jan. 27	Prime Minister Raymond Poincaré of France and Henri Jaspar, foreign minister of Belgium, meet to discuss the findings of the Dawes Committee of Experts.	Vladimir Ilyich Lenin is buried....Yugoslavia and Italy sign the Treaty of Rome. Under the terms of the treaty, Italy takes control of the port of Fiume, whose population is primarily Italian, and Yugoslavia receives the industrial suburb of Sušak, whose population is predominantly Croatian....Prince and Princess Orloff of Russia depart France for the United States. They plan to investigate the case of a young woman claiming to be Grand Duchess Olga, daughter of the late Czar Nicholas.		Five suspected revolutionaries are executed in the town of Juarez, Mexico, by order of the Mexican government....Hundreds of Cuban workers ceremonially plant an olive tree in memory of Vladimir Ilyich Lenin.	

A	B	C	D	E
Includes developments that affect more than one world region, international organizations and important meetings of world leaders.	*Includes all domestic and regional developments in Europe, including the Soviet Union.*	*Includes all domestic and regional developments in Africa and the Middle East.*	*Includes all domestic and regional developments in Latin America, the Caribbean, and Canada.*	*Includes all domestic and regional developments in Asian and Pacific nations (and colonies).*

U.S. Politics & Social Issues	U.S. Foreign Policy & Affairs, Defense	U.S. Economy & Environment	Science, Technology & Nature	Culture, Leisure & Lifestyle	
	State Department officials submit documents to the Senate Foreign Relations subcommittee on the decision to recognize the Soviet Union that purport to show that Communists in the United States and the Soviet Union are working together to plan a revolution in the United States.			The trustees of Albion College meet to discuss whether or not they should expel a female student accused of drinking and smoking. The trustees also discuss whether or not college president, Dr. John W. Laird, who has been accused of flirting with female students and a widow he met on a train, should be removed from his position.	Jan. 21
President Calvin Coolidge asks Congress for $300,000 to remodel the first floor of the Immigration Station at Ellis Island and to purchase more beds and mattresses for the dormitories.…The trial of William H. Anderson, the superintendent of New York's Anti-Saloon League begins. Anderson is charged with forgery.		Nine companies are bidding to win the contract to install safety devices on lines of the New York Central Railroad. The devices will automatically stop a train in the event of open switches or broken rails.…The United Mine Workers of America convention opens in Indianapolis. Miners in soft coal fields seek higher wages. Vice President Philip Murray urges the unionization of all miners.			Jan. 22
Esther Everett Lape, head of the Policy Committee of the Bok Peace Plan prize, testifies before the Senate Policy Committee. She refutes the charge that the jury that chose the winning plan had deliberately selected from among those submitted by League of Nations advocates.…It is announced that the Republican governor of Pennsylvania, Gifford Pinchot, will not run for president.		The Resolutions Committee of the United Mine Workers of American pledges to expel Communists from the union.…The War Finance Corporation will aid failing banks in South Dakota.	A new armored car with bulletproof windows, tear gas, and sneezing gas is tested in Brooklyn.	The North Carolina Board of Education bans the teaching of, and the use of textbooks referring to evolution.	Jan. 23
			General Electric displays both the largest and the smallest light bulbs ever produced at its power plant in Sprague, NJ.	Rudolph Valentino and Marion Davies are named King and Queen of the Movies at a dinner dance given by the Theater Owners' Chamber of Commerce Association in New York City.	Jan. 24
Senator Courtland M. Feuquay of Oklahoma asks the Senate Investigating Committee to examine the lease of mining lands belonging to the Quapaw tribe to the Eagle-Picher Lead Company. The lease was authorized by former Secretary of the Interior Albert B. Fall.	Former ambassador to Germany James W. Gerard attacks the terms of the Treaty of Lausanne and argues that Americans must insist upon independence for Armenia, which it had been granted under Treaty of Sévres.	An explosion in an Illinois mine kills 32 men.		The first Winter Olympics begins at Chamonix, France. The American speed skating team finishes third behind Finland and Norway.	Jan. 25
Representative Albert Johnson claims that both the Senate and the House are in favor of immigration legislation even more restrictive than Johnson's bill, which calls for a quota system under which immigration would be limited to two percent of the number of a nationality living in the United States in 1890.		The United Mine Workers of America vote in favor of collective bargaining as opposed to strikes as the best way to settler labor disputes. Strikes are proclaimed a tactic of Communist labor organizations.…An explosion in a Pennsylvania mine kills 40 men.		Hazel Mackaye reads from her play about the life of suffragist Inez Mulholland. The play, which depicts scenes from the suffrage movement, will be presented in August at a conference of the Student Councils of the National Woman's Party.	Jan. 26
Communists in Wilkes-Barre, PA, are forced by members of the American Legion to end a memorial service for Vladimir Ilyich Lenin. The Communists are also forced to salute the American flag.…A joint committee consisting of the American Federation of Labor, the Moderation League, the Constitutional Liberty League, and the National Association Against the Prohibition Amendment is formed. The goal of the committee is to pressure Congress to amend the Volstead Act.		The Federal Trade Commission charges Westinghouse Electric, General Electric, American Telephone & Telegraph, the Radio Corporation of America, and the United Fruit Company, among others, with acting together to create a monopoly in the making and selling radios and radio communications devices.		Argentine boxer Luis Firpo agrees to a match with African-American boxer Harry Wills.…Siegfried Wagner arrives in New York City. He intends to raise $200,000 to hold the opera festival in Bayreuth.	Jan. 27

F	G	H	I	J
Includes campaigns, elections, federal-state relations, civil rights and liberties, crime, the judiciary, education, healthcare, poverty, urban affairs, and population.	*Includes formation and debate of U.S. foreign and defense policies, veterans affairs, and defense spending. (Relations with specific foreign countries are usually found under the region concerned.)*	*Includes business, labor, agriculture, taxation, transportation, consumer affairs, monetary and fiscal policy, natural resources, pollution and industrial accidents.*	*Includes worldwide scientific, medical and technological developments, natural phenomena, U.S. weather and natural disasters.*	*Includes the arts, religion, scholarship, communications media, sports, entertainment, fashions, fads, and social life.*

	World Affairs	Europe	Africa & The Middle East	The Americas	Asia & The Pacific
Jan. 28		A shipment of food from the United States arrives in Berlin. The food will be used to provide more than 600,000 German children with one 500-calorie meal a day. The meal will consist of bread, milk, and cocoa.…Austria and Turkey sign a treaty regulating relations between the two countries.	Prime Minister Saad Zaghlul forms his new Ministry and announces his political program to the Egyptian Assembly. His chief goal is independence from Britain for both Egypt and the Sudan.	An earthquake strikes Chile. Shocks are felt in Argentina.	
Jan. 29			Crowds cheer as Saad Zaghlul takes office as prime minister of Egypt and presents his cabinet ministers to Egypt's ruler, King Fouad.	Three thousand Doukhobors living in Canada prepare to return to the Soviet Union, where they intend to settle in the Crimea.	
Jan. 30		Ernest Guminger, a supporter of the Separatist movement in the Palatinate, is assassinated.…The Federal Congress of Soviets meets in Moscow. They will select members of the legislature and name a replacement for Vladimir Ilych Lenin.	The Persian newspaper *Mihan* calls for the creation of a Persian republic headed by Prime Minister Reza Khan Sardar Sepah.		
Jan. 31	Britain reconsiders its policy of bombing Iraq.	Belgium plans to reduce the number of troops in the Ruhr valley.		The Mexican government announces that its troops have taken control of Orizaba, the largest city in Vera Cruz.	Eight members of the Colorum, a pro-independence religious cult, are captured in Samar Province.…A Japanese farmer, devastated by his lover's rejection, wrecks a train near Nagoya. Opponents of the Japanese prime minister are on the train. When demands that the prime minister account for the derailing of the train go unanswered, a riot breaks out in the Japanese Diet, leading to its early dissolution.…Swarajists, Indian nationalists led by Mohandas K. Gandhi, take seats as deputies to the All India Legislative Assembly.
Feb. 1		The Belgian War Ministry announces that expenditures for the Belgian army will be reduced.…Great Britain grants recognition to the government of the Soviet Union. Some criticize Prime Minister Ramsay Macdonald for acting too hastily.…France pays the United States $10 million interest on its debt for war supplies.…Italy and the Soviet Union are negotiating a trade agreement.		Governor George W.P. Hunt of Arizona grants permission for Mexican troops to travel through his state.…President Rafael Lopez Gutierrez of Honduras refuses to resign following the end of his term at midnight, January 31. General Tiburcio Carias Andino, who won the plurality of votes in presidential elections held in 1923, leaves Tegucigalpa to raise an army.	
Feb. 2	The Throne of Kandy, used to invest Knights of the Garter, is removed from the throne room at Windsor Castle upon the order of King George. Indian Buddhists have complained that the throne, considered a sacred object by them, should not be used in British ceremonies.	Temperance advocates in Britain report that 300 members of the House of Commons favor their position on alcohol.…Unlike Great Britain, France will not grant unconditional recognition of the Soviet Union. Debts owed to French and to holders of bonds issued by Russia's czarist government must be settled first.…Alexis Ivanovich Rykoff will become the new head of the Soviet Union's Council of Commissars.		Captain Bernier departs Canada to begin preparations for a Canadian exploratory voyage to the arctic before the arrival of the U.S. exploratory mission.…The United States informs the government of Honduras that diplomatic relations between the two countries will cease unless elections are held at once.	

A	B	C	D	E
Includes developments that affect more than one world region, international organizations and important meetings of world leaders.	*Includes all domestic and regional developments in Europe, including the Soviet Union.*	*Includes all domestic and regional developments in Africa and the Middle East.*	*Includes all domestic and regional developments in Latin America, the Caribbean, and Canada.*	*Includes all domestic and regional developments in Asian and Pacific nations (and colonies).*

	U.S. Politics & Social Issues	U.S. Foreign Policy & Affairs, Defense	U.S. Economy & Environment	Science, Technology & Nature	Culture, Leisure & Lifestyle
Jan. 28			The Ford Motor Company's Danish subsidiary will produce automobiles to be sold in the Soviet Union....Standard Oil of New York and Standard Oil of New Jersey announce an increase in the price of gasoline.		Supreme Court Justice William Harmon Black proclaims Fundamentalist minister John Roach Stratton the winner in a debate over evolution with Modernist minister Charles Francis Potter. Stratton opposes the theory of evolution and claims that the theory exerts an immoral influence....The case lodged by baseball player Joe Jackson against his former team, the Chicago White Sox, goes to trial. Jackson is seeking to recover $18,500 in lost salary....A Florida teacher is asked to resign because of complaints that she is teaching her students that the earth is flat.
Jan. 29	William H. Anderson, the head of New York's Anti-Saloon League, is found guilty of forgery.	The United States extends formal recognition to the government of Greece.	The Senate Agriculture Committee approves an amendment that will increase the $50 million intended to provide relief for wheat farmers under the Norbeck-Burtness bill to $75 million. The amendment will also extend the aid to all farmers....Henry Ford refuses to testify before the House regarding his plans for Muscle Shoals.	Doctors in Chicago claim that an 18-year-old girl who has been blind and deaf since infancy has been cured. The girl attributes her cure to her practice of Christian Science.	Former Chicago White Sox baseball player Joe Jackson claims that he is innocent of deliberately trying to lose the 1919 World Series.
Jan. 30			Edward E. Bartlett, Jr., President of the New York Cotton Exchange, calls on the federal government to assist in the eradication of the boll weevil. Bartlett warns that the United States may be overtaken as the world's largest cotton producer by Asian and South American countries.	The fate of a party of Canadian explorers in British Guiana is learned. Several members of the party have died, but they have located a bed of diamonds.	
Jan. 31	The Senate issues a Joint Resolution stating that the leasing of naval oil reserves at Teapot Dome, Wyoming, and Elk Hills, California, was illegal and calls on President Calvin Coolidge to nullify the leases.				At the Winter Olympics, Austria takes first place in pairs figure skating.
Feb. 1	Edward L. Doheny, president of Pan-American Petroleum and Transport Company, testifies before the Senate committee investigating leases of naval oil reserves that he had paid George Creel, chairman of the Bureau of Public Information during the World War, to assist him in the leasing of naval oil reserves from then Secretary of the Navy, Josephus Daniels.	The State Department informs President Rafael Lopez Gutierrez, who has assumed the position of de facto dictator of Honduras, that if he fails to hold new elections, the United States will end all diplomatic connections with Honduras.	The Ku Klux Klan fails in its efforts to change the United Mine Workers of America's constitution, which refuses membership to Klansmen.	A safe whose doors will unlock only when the correct note is sung or produced on a tuning fork is exhibited in Birmingham England....The French firm De Monge is constructing a plane capable of traveling 120 miles per hour that will make possible nonstop flights between Paris and New York.	The U.S. hockey team wins its semi-final match against Sweden at the Winter Olympics in Chamonix. It will compete against Canada in the finals....Johnny Dundee, world featherweight boxing champion, defeats Paul Moran after 15 rounds.
Feb. 2	Former Secretary of the Interior Albert B. Fall refuses to testify before the Senate committee investigating the lease of naval oil reserves....Thirteen members of Pueblo tribes perform ceremonial dances at a luncheon given in their honor by New York's City Club. The Pueblo delegation is traveling the United States to raise support for their opposition to a bill that would deprive them of their lands.	Secretary of State Charles Evans Hughes informs Senators that they will be granted private access to letters written by former Indiana governor James P. Goodrich regarding the Soviet Union but that the letters will not be made public.	The Olds Motor Works is producing four times as many cars as it did one year ago....The Ohio Court of Appeals upholds the expulsion of 881 men from the Brotherhood of Railroad Trainmen in 1920 for staging an unapproved strike....Steel companies are increasing their output....The United Mine Workers of America convention ends in a riot when Alexander Howat, former president of the Kansas district, is not allowed to address the delegates....Philip Morris & Co. reports growth in the tobacco industry.	Canadian professor W.F. Cutler leaves for German East Africa in search of the fossil of the *Gigantosaurus africanus*, the largest dinosaur ever to have lived....Icebergs are sighted in Lake Michigan.	Publisher Cyrus H.K. Curtis endows a music school in Philadelphia....Harvard's indoor polo team loses to West Point by a score of 14–2....The Thomas Jefferson Memorial Foundation announces its plans for the purchase and maintenance of Monticello....Dr. Charles Scanlon, organizer of the Interdenominational Motion Picture Conference, asks Douglas Fairbanks, Mary Pickford, and Will H. Hays, president of the Motion Picture Association of America, to offer their opinions on whether or not the film industry should be placed under the control of the federal government.
	F *Includes campaigns, elections, federal-state relations, civil rights and liberties, crime, the judiciary, education, healthcare, poverty, urban affairs, and population.*	G *Includes formation and debate of U.S. foreign and defense policies, veterans affairs, and defense spending. (Relations with specific foreign countries are usually found under the region concerned.)*	H *Includes business, labor, agriculture, taxation, transportation, consumer affairs, monetary and fiscal policy, natural resources, pollution and industrial accidents.*	I *Includes worldwide scientific, medical and technological developments, natural phenomena, U.S. weather and natural disasters.*	J *Includes the arts, religion, scholarship, communications media, sports, entertainment, fashions, fads, and social life.*

	World Affairs	Europe	Africa & The Middle East	The Americas	Asia & The Pacific
Feb. 3		The Irish consider publishing reports of the Irish Free State's national legislature in Gaelic as well as in English.... German Social Democrat newspapers accuse Communists of attempting of trying to seize control of or to destroy German trade unions in preparation for a coming Communist revolution.		General Tiburcio Carias Andino declares himself head of a new Honduran government. Supporters of Policarpo Bonilla, another candidate in the Honduran elections, form an army.	More than 800 members of the Colorum, a pro-Philippine independence religious sect, are reported to have been killed by Filipino police in Socorro.
Feb. 4	The League of Nations Mixed Commission on Control of Traffic in Arms meets in Geneva to draft a convention to limit the sale of weapons. Although having no power to make official decisions on behalf of the United States, Joseph C. Grew, the United States Ambassador to Switzerland, is in attendance.	Claiming France supports the Separatists in the Palatinate, Germany asks France to disarm members of the movement.... Members of the Chamber of Deputies criticize French Prime Minister Raymond Poincaré's plan to establish economic reforms by decree.		As the Mexican army advances on Vera Cruz, rebel forces prepare to depart.	Tashi Lama, second in importance to the Dalai Lama, is reported to have fled Tibet in an effort to stage a rebellion against the government in Lhasa.... The British government releases Indian nationalist leader Mohandas K. Gandhi from prison because of his poor health. Gandhi was imprisoned for sedition in 1922.
Feb. 5		In Rome, a lioness on the set of the movie *Quo Vadis* mauls an elderly man to death.... In the Soviet Union, small businessmen and their families are being expelled from Moscow. Arrests of Soviet sailors and army officers are taking place.... Romania and the Soviet Union agree to a meeting to discuss trade issues as well as the border between the two countries.		Rebel forces flee Vera Cruz as the Mexican army takes control of the city of Cordoba. General Plutarco Elias Calles announces that, after defeating rebel forces under the command of Hipolito Villa, he will begin his presidential campaign. In Mexico City, a member of the crowd fires into a peace parade.	
Feb. 6	Mexico refuses to discuss the issue of damages to British property incurred during the revolution in Mexico until the British government grants recognition to the government of Mexico as it has to the government of the Soviet Union.... Former U.S. Secretary of State Robert Lansing denies having any knowledge of an alleged agreement that former British Prime Minister David Lloyd George claims was made by former French Prime Minister Georges Clemenceau and President Woodrow Wilson regarding French occupation of the Rhineland.... The new Japanese ambassador to Germany, Kumatore Honda, arrives in Berlin.	Georges Kafandaris becomes Prime Minister of Greece.... France revises its divorce laws. Americans in France will be granted a divorce only on grounds for which they can be divorced in their state of residence.... France's Chamber of Deputies grants Prime Minister Raymond Poincaré the right to institute economic reforms by decree.... Anti-Communist forces in the Ukraine stage an insurrection. Soviet troops in the region support them.		The Mexican army takes control of Vera Cruz. Additional troops are being sent to Tuxpam, where Adolfo de la Huerta, leader of the rebel forces is believed to have fled.... Mexican Congressmen consider extending President Alvaro Obregon's term by two years because of the necessity of preserving political stability in Mexico.	
Feb. 7		Britain's Unemployed Workers' Committee and the Council of the Trade Union Congress submit a list of demands to alleviate the problems of the unemployed, including inexpensive housing, job training, and reduced hours.... French Communists rally to protest the price of bread.	The Persian government clarifies the terms of its granting oil concessions to America's Sinclair Consolidated Oil Corporation. Sinclair Oil has been tentatively granted the right to lease oil concessions in northern Persia in exchange for a $10 million loan, but this agreement must be ratified by the Persian parliament before it can take effect.	American Secretary of State Charles Evans Hughes announces that American troops currently deployed in Nicaragua will be removed following the seating of a new Nicaraguan government in January 1925.	Japan's foreign minister K. Matsui urges the United States not to discriminate against the Japanese or bar Japanese immigration to the United States in the new immigration law being considered before Congress.
Feb. 8	Britain announces that it will grant amnesty to Egyptians imprisoned by military courts.... Vittorio Orlando, Italian representative at the Versailles peace talks concluding the World War, claims that President Woodrow Wilson supported French occupation of the Rhineland in exchange for French support of his opposition to Italian annexation of Fiume.	The government of the Soviet Union is informed of its recognition by Italy.... Archbishop Tikhon, Patriarch of the Russian Orthodox Church, expresses his desire to bring Archbishop Platon, leader of the American Russian Church, to trial in the Soviet Union after Platon declares that the American Russian Church is independent of the Russian Orthodox Church.		A U.S. Navy cruiser is sent to Honduras to protect American lives and property during the ongoing rebellion.	
	A *Includes developments that affect more than one world region, international organizations and important meetings of world leaders.*	B *Includes all domestic and regional developments in Europe, including the Soviet Union.*	C *Includes all domestic and regional developments in Africa and the Middle East.*	D *Includes all domestic and regional developments in Latin America, the Caribbean, and Canada.*	E *Includes all domestic and regional developments in Asian and Pacific nations (and colonies).*

	U.S. Politics & Social Issues	U.S. Foreign Policy & Affairs, Defense	U.S. Economy & Environment	Science, Technology & Nature	Culture, Leisure & Lifestyle
Feb. 3	Former president Woodrow Wilson dies at his home in Washington, DC, at 11:15 A.M. President Calvin Coolidge orders that flags at the White House and on all federal buildings be lowered to half-staff for 30 days.	The army is facing a personnel shortage. Re-enlistment is urged.	The high price of corn forces hog farmers to sell their animals at low prices.…As a result of a decrease in the price of milk, fewer New York farmers keep cows.	Experiments reveal that carbonization under high pressure purifies soft drinks.	Canada takes first place in hockey at the Winter Olympics.…The Reverend Dr. Harry Emerson Fosdick informs the congregation of the First Presbyterian Church in New York City that fossil evidence provides proof of evolution but assures his listeners that evolution is compatible with Christian belief.
Feb. 4	A national campaign to have New York Governor Alfred E. Smith chosen as the Democratic presidential nominee begins in New York City.…The Trade Union Educational League holds a memorial for Vladimir I. Lenin at Madison Square Garden.		The House Commerce Committee approves a $1.5 million appropriation to buy the Cape Cod Canal.…Standard Oil raises the price of gasoline by two cents.…The Standard Oil Company of New Jersey publicly refutes a claim that it has partnered with a British oil syndicate to exploit oil lands in northern Persia while preventing other American oil companies from obtaining similar concessions.	A tornado strikes southern Indiana damaging houses and killing livestock. A blizzard hits eastern Colorado and western Kansas. Sleet and snow fall elsewhere in the midwest.…A Swedish-built car fueled by motor alcohol beats American cars powered by gasoline in a race.	The Millinery Jobber's Association reports that, as bobbed hair is still the fashion for women, small hats will be the style this spring.…The Presbytery of New York acquits the Reverend Dr. Harry Emerson Foster of teaching non-Presbyterian doctrine.
Feb. 5	Bayonne industrialists will build modern apartment houses for their employees.…Federal Judge John C. Knox orders that eight New York City saloons be closed for four months after being presented with evidence that they have been selling liquor.		President Calvin Coolidge supports a higher tariff on wheat.…Prince Orloff of Russia arrives in the United States to discuss the purchase of iron ore from his mines in the Soviet Union with American automobile manufacturers.		Baseball's American League will award a diploma to each season's most valuable player.…The city of Philadelphia outlaws gambling on Mah Jong.…Gertrude Ederle sets a new world and American swimming records at a competition in Miami.…Responding to Palestinian calls for a native Bishop of Jerusalem, the Pope orders the current bishop to return to Rome.…Medals are awarded on the closing day of the Winter Olympics at Chamonix.
Feb. 6	Secretary of the Navy Edwin C. Denby defends his actions in leasing oil in federal naval reserves to oilmen Harry F. Sinclair and Edward L. Doheny. Denby maintains that his lease of naval oil reserves was both legal and necessary because the wells of private oil companies operating on adjoining lands might have drained oil from the government reserves.…Two high schools in Peoria, IL, begin a nationwide campaign to collect money from American high school students to build a memorial to President Woodrow Wilson.		U.S. Treasurer Frank White and Alien Property Custodian Colonel Thomas Miller maintain that all debts owed to the United States by Germany must be paid before individual American citizens and private businesses may sue Germany for damages.		Ontario, Canada, bans boxing matches between African American and white fighters.…The Methodist Council of Boards of Benevolence and the Methodist Board of Sunday Schools plan to launch a radio station that will broadcast nonsectarian Protestant programs.…Radio stations refuse to negotiate with music publishers, who are demanding that stations pay for the right to broadcast music.
Feb. 7	At the annual meeting of the Indian Rights Association, President Herbert Welsh reports that Oklahoma's Indian Probate law is unjustly depriving members of the Cherokee, Choctaw, Chickasaw, Creek, and Seminole tribes of their property.	President Calvin Coolidge orders the Department of Justice to investigate charges that Standard Oil is manipulating gasoline prices.			The Society of American Dramatists announces that radio stations must obtain written consent from authors before performing their plays on the air. The Society plans to sue stations that broadcast plays without consent.
Feb. 8	The Senate passes a joint resolution authorizing special counsel to institute civil and criminal proceedings against those involved in the leasing of federal oil reserves at Teapot Dome, WY, and Elk Hills, CA.…The state of Nevada uses gas for the first time to execute a prisoner.…The state of Texas uses the electric chair for the first time in its execution of five men.		The Federal Trade Commission announces that it will begin an investigation of the rise in gasoline prices in South Dakota.		World flyweight champion Pancho Villa defeats Georgie Marks in a boxing match at Madison Square Garden.…A speech by Bell Telephone's vice president is broadcast coast-to-coast. The radio transmission can be heard as far away as Canada and Cuba.

F	G	H	I	J
Includes campaigns, elections, federal-state relations, civil rights and liberties, crime, the judiciary, education, healthcare, poverty, urban affairs, and population.	*Includes formation and debate of U.S. foreign and defense policies, veterans affairs, and defense spending. (Relations with specific foreign countries are usually found under the region concerned.)*	*Includes business, labor, agriculture, taxation, transportation, consumer affairs, monetary and fiscal policy, natural resources, pollution and industrial accidents.*	*Includes worldwide scientific, medical and technological developments, natural phenomena, U.S. weather and natural disasters.*	*Includes the arts, religion, scholarship, communications media, sports, entertainment, fashions, fads, and social life.*

	World Affairs	Europe	Africa & The Middle East	The Americas	Asia & The Pacific
Feb. 9	Britain sends naval forces to Amoy to prevent conflict between Japan and China....The Soviet Union announces that it will send a delegate to the League of Nations Naval Conference.	The government of Bavaria delays bringing Adolf Hitler to trial because of injuries Hitler sustained during his attempt to overthrow the government of Bavaria in November 1923.		A third U.S. Navy cruiser is sent to Honduras to protect American interests from revolutionary forces....The Chilean Senate and Chamber of Deputies adopt measures that will make President Arturo Alessandri more independent of the legislature.	
Feb. 10		Greek Royalist groups gather in Athens to discuss the best way to maintain the monarchy in the face of an upcoming plebiscite on a new Greek constitution....J.A. Dorten, president of the Rhineland Republic, speaks to a crowd of workers and Separatists in Düsseldorf.		Mexican revolutionary forces flee the city of Guadalajara.	
Feb. 11	Mexico's ambassador to Sweden visits London to discuss British recognition of the government of Mexican President Alvaro Obregon....Charles G. Dawes' Committee of Experts discusses the state of German agriculture and labor with representatives of German farmers and workers.	Bulgaria's parliament ratifies the Treaty of Lausanne, finalizing border disputes among Bulgaria, Greece, and Turkey....The government of the Irish Free State denies that it has held secret trials of Republican leaders, including Eamon de Valera.			
Feb. 12		Austria's Foreign Minister states that Austria should officially recognize the Soviet Union as other European countries have already done.			Japan's Foreign Minister states that Japan wishes to resume relations with the Soviet Union....Moro leaders from the Philippine provinces of Lanao and Zamboanga inform Governor General Leonard Wood that they prefer American rule and, in the event that the Philippines is granted independence, would like to remain under the control and protection of the United States.
Feb. 13	The Dawes committee, having finished its work in Berlin, departs for Paris.	Separatists and German police exchange fire in the Palatinate. Two men are killed; many others are wounded....Employees of Viennese banks and the Viennese stock exchange, in protest against being forced to work overtime for inadequate compensation, have resolved to stop working each day at 4 p.m.		The United States ends diplomatic relations with Honduras.	
Feb. 14	The Latin Press Congress begins in Lisbon with delegates from South America, Spain, Portugal, Italy, and Romania in attendance....The International Conference on Limitation of Naval Armament meets in Rome. The purpose of the conference is to plan for a larger conference on the same topic that will meet in the future.	Friedrich Ebert, president of Germany, proclaims that martial law will end on March 1. Martial law was imposed in November 1923 following a failed attempt to take over the government of Bavaria....In order to save money, prisoners in Prussian jails are given less food and are allowed to bathe only once a month.	Archbishop of Boston, Cardinal O'Connell arrives in Jerusalem for a visit with the Patriarch of Jerusalem....Egyptian government officials rule that Howard Carter has violated his contract with the Egyptian government, leaving the government free to take control of the excavation of the tomb of Tutankhamen.	Mexican president Alvaro Obregon seizes control of Guadalajara.	Japan protests the high interest rate imposed on a multimillion dollar loan by the United States.
Feb. 15	The Dawes Committee of Experts requests Louis Barthou, president of the Reparations Commission, to present French experts who will be able to inform the Committee of French needs and ideas regarding reparations.	Britain's Parliament defeats a proposal to allow Monmouthshire and Wales to passes their own local temperance ordinances.	The Persian government protests statements in the American press to the effect that Persian government officials, including the Prime Minister, were bribed by Sinclair Consolidated Oil into granting it concessions in northern Persia.	The U.S. Navy sends the *Richmond* to rescue Americans trapped in Puerto Mexico before fighting breaks out in the region.	

A	B	C	D	E
Includes developments that affect more than one world region, international organizations and important meetings of world leaders.	*Includes all domestic and regional developments in Europe, including the Soviet Union.*	*Includes all domestic and regional developments in Africa and the Middle East.*	*Includes all domestic and regional developments in Latin America, the Caribbean, and Canada.*	*Includes all domestic and regional developments in Asian and Pacific nations (and colonies).*

U.S. Politics & Social Issues	U.S. Foreign Policy & Affairs, Defense	U.S. Economy & Environment	Science, Technology & Nature	Culture, Leisure & Lifestyle	
William J. Wallace and J.C. Lincoln are nominated as the presidential and vice presidential candidates of the Commonwealth Land Party. The party's goal is to eliminate all private ownership of land.... The charitable organization Near East Relief announces that it will launch a countrywide effort to collect cans of sweetened condensed milk. Milk donation drives will be held in several midwestern and western cities.	The House Appropriations Committee cuts the navy's budget by more than $23 million.	Representative Philip Swing of California encourages the House Irrigation Committee to accept his proposal to build a dam in Boulder Canyon on the Colorado River to protect southern California from floods.... The U.S. Chamber of Commerce recommends that the United States adopt an air safety code.	The U.S. Post Office wins an award from the National Aeronautical Association for its progress in delivering mail by air.	Scarves are a prominent feature of fashion on the Riviera. Skirts are shorter and pleated.... The French practice of wearing evening gowns without stockings is introduced to Palm Beachsociety by Mrs. Charles I. Chapin at the Club de Montmartre.	Feb. 9
Raids on Philadelphia establishments thought to be serving liquor end. Eight-hundred people are under arrest. The raids were ordered by Philadelphia's Public Safety Director Smedley Butler.		A decline in U.S. oil production is predicted.		The American Olympic Committee proposes that individual cities should pay the expenses of the various teams. It is suggested that cities sponsor teams who compete in sports popular in a given locale.... Danish pilot J.P. Hansen dies when, while performing aerial maneuvers for a crowd in Buenos Aires, his plane strikes an antenna and catches fire.	Feb. 10
The Senate passes a resolution calling upon President Calvin Coolidge to ask for the resignation of Edwin C.Denby, Secretary of the Navy.		Prices of lead and zinc rise. The increase in price is attributed to the greater demand for these substances caused by the development of radio.	An expedition led by William Beebe, director of the New York Zoological Society, departs for British Guyana. The team of explorers plan to bring back living specimens of animals and birds, including the hoatzin bird.	In response to Bishop William T. Manning's statement that complete acceptance of the Protestant Episcopal creed is necessary for all members of that church, the Reverend Dr. William Norman Guthrie, of New York City's St. Mark's-in-the-Bouwerie, preaches that belief in the virgin birth and Christ's divinity are secondary in importance to a belief in the kind and human aspect of Christ.	Feb. 11
In a speech delivered at a Lincoln Day dinner, President Calvin Coolidge promises to prosecute those involved in the Teapot Dome scandal, asks for public support of the Mellon tax plan, and restates his warning that the granting of a bonus to veterans will endanger American prosperity.	Crowds in Chicago cheer the return of Lieutenant Corliss Hooven Griffis. Griffis has recently been released from a German prison where he was being held for the attempted kidnapping of Grover Cleveland Bergdoll, the famous World War draft evader.		The sarcophagus of the Pharaoh Tutankhamen is opened. The pharaoh's body is found inside.... The General Electric Company in Schenectady, NY, receives word that a radio broadcast made on January 4 was heard in South Africa, more than 7,000 miles away.	George Gershwin's *Rhapsody in Blue* debuts in New York City.... Reverend William Montgomery Brown, former Protestant Episcopal Bishop of Arkansas and author of the book *Communism and Christianism*, is charged with heresy.	Feb. 12
Secretary of State Charles Evans Hughes makes public his opposition to the exclusion of Japanese immigrants in the proposed immigration bill sponsored by Representative Albert Johnson. Hughes fears such a move would endanger the relationship between the United States and Japan.			Conflict between the Egyptian government and archaeologist Howard Carter regarding control over the objects found in the tomb of Tutankhamen leads Carter to suspend all work on the excavation.	Competition for the Waterloo Cup, also known as the Dog Derby, begins in Britain.	Feb. 13
Equity court Justice Wendell P. Stafford rules that U.S. citizens can seek compensation for losses from the German government before Germany's debt to the government of the United States is paid off.... Dr. Thomas B. Lee, head of New Jersey's State Board of Health urges the use of birth control and the sterilization of criminals and the mentally retarded to lower crime rates in the state.	The War Department gives permission for Lieutenant Russell Lowell Maughan to attempt another nonstop, coast-to-coast flight in June.	The Agricultural Finance Organization is founded to provide financial assistance to northwestern banks and farmers.		Prince and Princess Felix Youssoupoff host a Valentine's Day costume ball in New York City to raise money for Russian refugees.... The General Council of the Presbyterian Church informs missions that they will have to cut their expenses because of a lack of money.	Feb. 14
The House Insular Committee opens hearings on the subject of independence for the Philippines. Representatives King and Cooper state that the Filipinos are capable of governing themselves.	President Calvin Coolidge halts planning for the navy's proposed dirigible flight to the North Pole.			American jewel thief Arthur Hussey (a.k.a "Dapper Don" Collins) is arrested in Paris.... Witnesses testify to the miracles of Pope Pius X as part of an effort to have the late Pope, who died in 1914, canonized.	Feb. 15

F	G	H	I	J
Includes campaigns, elections, federal-state relations, civil rights and liberties, crime, the judiciary, education, healthcare, poverty, urban affairs, and population.	*Includes formation and debate of U.S. foreign and defense policies, veterans affairs, and defense spending. (Relations with specific foreign countries are usually found under the region concerned.)*	*Includes business, labor, agriculture, taxation, transportation, consumer affairs, monetary and fiscal policy, natural resources, pollution and industrial accidents.*	*Includes worldwide scientific, medical and technological developments, natural phenomena, U.S. weather and natural disasters.*	*Includes the arts, religion, scholarship, communications media, sports, entertainment, fashions, fads, and social life.*

	World Affairs	Europe	Africa & The Middle East	The Americas	Asia & The Pacific
Feb. 16	Bok Peace Plan award winner Charles H. Levermore discusses his plan at a meeting of the Foreign Policy Association in New York City.	British dockworkers strike for higher wages. All ports are closed.... Belgians, angered at the high cost of food, riot.		Striking miners in Cape Breton, Nova Scotia, end their month-long work stoppage and return to the mines.	
Feb. 17	Following a meeting in New York City, non-Zionist American Jews agree to work together with the World Zionist Organization, the League of Nations, and the British government to encourage American investment in Palestine.	A meeting of the foreign ministers of the Baltic states ends without any agreements being reached....The Inter-Allied Special Committee takes control of the Rhineland Republic.			
Feb. 18	The Dawes Committee of Experts begins deliberation on a plan to balance the German budget in such a manner that money is left for reparations payments.	Gustav von Kahr resigns as dictator of Bavaira. General Otto von Lossow, commander of the German army in Bavaria, also resigns his post.			India's Legislative Assembly passes a resolution introduced by Indian nationalist Motilal Nehru calling for a conference to reform India's constitution and to discuss greater self-rule for India.
Feb. 19		Yugoslavia's legislature ratifies a treaty with Italy regarding control of the port of Fiume.			
Feb. 20		The trial of General Erich Ludendorff on charges of treason for his role in the attempted takeover of the Bavarian government in November 1923 is denounced as unpatriotic by former German officers.	Archaeologist Howard Carter's permit to excavate the tomb of Tutankhamen is revoked by the Egyptian government. The government intends to assume responsibility for excavating the tomb.	Mexican troops march on Tuxpam.	
Feb. 21	The League of Nations will loan money to Hungary.		Dr. Fuad Shatara, an anti-Zionist, is appointed by King Hussein of the Hedjaz as his envoy to the United States.		
Feb. 22		The British Parliament passes a measure that will put caps on rents until 1928....A mob of 50,000 people in Lisbon calls for a reduction in the cost of living.			Japan's Prince Regent Hirohito and his wife begin their honeymoon.
Feb. 23		The Prime Minister of Albania Ahmed Zog is shot by a student but sustains only minor injuries.... Spanish dictator General Primo Rivera cautions Spanish university professors against making anti-government statements outside of their classes.	The Egyptian government forces its way into the tomb of Tutankhamen by cutting the locks that archaeologist Howard Carter has refused to open.	Railroad workers in Cuba call for a general strike.	
Feb. 24	The majority of votes received by the Policy Committee of the American Peace Award favor implementation of the Bok Peace Plan....Japan is ready to proceed with negotiations for the recognition of the Soviet Union.	Britain's striking dockworkers are ready to accept a settlement.	Nationalist supporters of Prime Minister Saad Zaghloul sweep the elections for the Egyptian senate and win all of the seats except those reserved for senators chosen by King Fouad.		
Feb. 25		President Mustafa Kemal of Turkey announces that the Turkish army is strong enough to defeat any foe.		Cuban dockworkers and railroad workers end their strike.	
	A *Includes developments that affect more than one world region, international organizations and important meetings of world leaders.*	B *Includes all domestic and regional developments in Europe, including the Soviet Union.*	C *Includes all domestic and regional developments in Africa and the Middle East.*	D *Includes all domestic and regional developments in Latin America, the Caribbean, and Canada.*	E *Includes all domestic and regional developments in Asian and Pacific nations (and colonies).*

U.S. Politics & Social Issues	U.S. Foreign Policy & Affairs, Defense	U.S. Economy & Environment	Science, Technology & Nature	Culture, Leisure & Lifestyle	
The appointment of Senator Atlee Pomerene as Special Counsel to prosecute those involved in the leasing of naval oil reserves at Teapot Dome and Elk Hills is approved by the Senate.…Secretary of the Navy Edwin C. Denby resigns.		Prices of wheat and corn fall as the price of coffee rises.	Hugo Gernsback announces his invention of the staccatone, a device that creates music from electricity.		Feb. 16
Spokesmen for the Justice Department and the State Department announce that they have no evidence proving that American arms manufacturers have sold weapons to Mexico despite President Calvin Coolidge's proclamation that such sales would not be allowed.				Johnny Weissmuller sets a record as he swims the 100-yard freestyle in 52.4 seconds.	Feb. 17
The appointment of attorney Owen Roberts as Special Counsel to prosecute those involved in the leasing of naval oil reserves at Teapot Dome and Elk Hills is approved by the Senate.…Louisiana's Senators object to the appointment of an African-American customs collector for New Orleans. In keeping with their wishes, the Senate votes to reject the nomination of Walter L. Cohen.		Speakers at a conference of The American Institute of Mining and Metallurgical Engineers foresee an overall drop in the production of crude oil in the coming months.		Theresa Weld Blanchard wins the U.S. National Women's Figure Skating Championship for the ninth time. Sherwood W. Badger wins the men's title.	Feb. 18
Henry L. Fuqua wins the Democratic nomination for governor of Louisiana over his anti-Ku Klux Klan opponent Hewitt Bouanchaud.…President Calvin Coolidge orders an inquiry into the shooting of Senator Frank L. Greene of Vermont by prohibition agents.	New York's Senator Royal S. Copeland criticizes the Department of the Navy for allowing six of America's 18 battleships to deteriorate.	Prices of hogs in Chicago fall.…Alfred H. Brooks, of the U.S. Geological Survey, predicts that naval oil reserves in Alaska will produce as rich as the reserves at Teapot Dome, WY.	A dinner hosted by the Sphinx Club at New York City's Waldorf-Astoria features a demonstration of the workings of a telephone switchboard.		Feb. 19
Governor of New York Al Smith states that the Volstead Act must be modified.			Bones of prehistoric apes and elephants discovered in China are placed on display at the American Museum of Natural History.		Feb. 20
The Coast Guard anchors off the coast of Massachusetts in an attempt to catch liquor smugglers.…Air mail service begins in Alaska.		The Mixed Claims Commission awards $1 million in damages to American citizens who lost relatives when the *Lusitania* was sunk by a German submarine in 1915.			Feb. 21
	Twenty-four military prisoners at Fort Leavenworth, KS, petition the War Department's Clemency Board for release.			A court in Houston, TX, issues an injunction preventing an African-American fraternal order of Shriners from wearing the same regalia as white Shriners.	Feb. 22
The Sons of Revolution of New Jersey proclaim the Volstead Act to be un-American.…The Senate Judiciary Committee reports that it supports an effort to move presidential inaugurations from March to January.			Norwegian explorer Roald Amundsen announces that, despite the cancellation by the United States of the dirigible *Shenandoah's* arctic flight, he intends to fly to the North Pole.	A meeting of members of the Bahai faith opens in New York City.	Feb. 23
				Argentine heavyweight champion Luis Firpo defeats American boxer Farmer Lodge in five rounds.	Feb. 24
The House of Representatives allots $25,000 for an investigation into Native American affairs.	President Calvin Coolidge announces that he is opposed to any increase pension payments to veterans that would significantly deplete the treasury.				Feb. 25
F *Includes campaigns, elections, federal-state relations, civil rights and liberties, crime, the judiciary, education, healthcare, poverty, urban affairs, and population.*	G *Includes formation and debate of U.S. foreign and defense policies, veterans affairs, and defense spending. (Relations with specific foreign countries are usually found under the region concerned.)*	H *Includes business, labor, agriculture, taxation, transportation, consumer affairs, monetary and fiscal policy, natural resources, pollution and industrial accidents.*	I *Includes worldwide scientific, medical and technological developments, natural phenomena, U.S. weather and natural disasters.*	J *Includes the arts, religion, scholarship, communications media, sports, entertainment, fashions, fads, and social life.*	

	World Affairs	Europe	Africa & The Middle East	The Americas	Asia & The Pacific
Feb. 26	Lord Sydney Olivier, Secretary of State for India, declares in a speech before the House of Lords that, while Britain's Labor government favors eventual home rule for India, the country is not yet ready for self-government.	British cotton spinners threaten to strike as Britain's striking dockworkers return to work.		In Honduras, federal troops and the army of revolutionary general Vicente Tosta reach a temporary cease fire agreement.	
Feb. 27		The Rhineland Republic is abolished.		Honduran revolutionaries under the command of Generals Tiburcio Carias Andino and Gregorio Ferrera attack Tegucigalpa.	
Feb. 28	The Dawes Committee of Experts discusses plans for the control of German railroads.	The Greek legislature rejects a call to overthrow the ruling dynasty.		American marines land in Ceiba, Honduras, to protect American citizens and their property. Representatives of two American businesses, the Rosario Mining Company and the United Fruit Company, claim that rebel forces threatened to seize their property if they failed to pay money to the revolutionaries.	
Feb. 29					A British steamer with 700 passengers on board runs aground near Canton. All the passengers are rescued.
Mar. 1	The committee investigating the payment of German reparations suggests that Germany may not be granted a moratorium on the payment of damages to other countries.	Italy and Czechoslovakia ratify the Treaty of Commerce and Navigation.…Mustafa Kemal speaks before the Turkish National Assembly. In his speech, he stresses the need to separate church and state.			
Mar. 2		Winston Churchill offers to run for a seat in Parliament in order to offset the power of British Socialists.…A minor earthquake hits Lisbon.… Italian Fascists announce names of candidates in the upcoming elections.…Communists attack a group of approximately 1,200 "Young Storm Troops," male students between ages 14 and 18, when they gather in Jena, Germany, to hear a speech. Approximately 200 Communists are arrested.		Honduran government troops are defeated by rebel forces led by General Gregorio Ferrera. Government forces depart the capital of Tegucigalpa, as does the wife of President Rafael Lopez Gutierrez.	
Mar. 3	The U.S. Senate ratifies treaties that protect American rights in the French mandates of Togoland and the Cameroons and in the Belgian mandate of German East Africa.	British shipyard workers at Southampton strike for higher wages.…The Bulgarian government arrests more than 100 Macedonians associated with revolutionary groups that it believes are in league with the government of Yugoslavia.	Egyptian police fail to stop striking workers from invading a soap factory in Alexandria.		

A	B	C	D	E
Includes developments that affect more than one world region, international organizations and important meetings of world leaders.	*Includes all domestic and regional developments in Europe, including the Soviet Union.*	*Includes all domestic and regional developments in Africa and the Middle East.*	*Includes all domestic and regional developments in Latin America, the Caribbean, and Canada.*	*Includes all domestic and regional developments in Asian and Pacific nations (and colonies).*

U.S. Politics & Social Issues	U.S. Foreign Policy & Affairs, Defense	U.S. Economy & Environment	Science, Technology & Nature	Culture, Leisure & Lifestyle	
		Senator Arthur Capper of Kansas urges farmers to organize themselves into cooperatives to better compete in the market.		Ohio's State Director of Education removes the ban on motion pictures starring Mabel Normand.	Feb. 26
Congress commemorates the death of President Warren G. Harding.... Three-thousand men interrupt a meeting of the Ku Klux Klan in Waukesha, WI.		Striking garment workers raid factories in Chicago, where they beat and stab those still at work.			Feb. 27
Senator Edward Edwards of New Jersey calls for an investigation into federal enforcement of the Volstead Act. Edwards claims that public safety is being ignored in the zealous pursuit of alleged violators of the Act.			Surgeons at the University of Pennsylvania Hospital announce that they are able to provide relief from pain to patients suffering from terminal illness by cutting the sensory nerves leading from the spinal column.		Feb. 28
A Senate resolution calls for President Calvin Coolidge to order Secretary of the Treasury Andrew W. Mellon to provide the Public Lands and Surveys Committee with the income tax returns of all people and companies involved in the investigation of the private leasing of federal oil reserves at Teapot Dome and Elk Hills.			The federal government begins an investigation of reports that private mining interests are extracting coal from federal coal reserves in Alabama.	A sleeping sickness antitoxin awakens a New Jersey man after a week of sleep.	Feb. 29
Charles R. Forbes, former head of the Veterans' Bureau, proclaims that he is innocent of fraud and claims that he is the victim of deliberately manufactured charges....Senator Robert LaFollette of Wisconsin withdraws from the North Dakota Republican presidential primaries.	Secretary of State Charles Evans Hughes is named to a commission to negotiate a new treaty with Panama that will give the United States permanent control of territory in the canal zone.	California's Bureau of Animal Industry announces that an outbreak of foot-and-mouth disease in that state has been contained.	Guglielmo Marconi describes his experiments with concentrated radio wave transmissions and warns that government control of radio communications could retard technological advances in the field.	Attorney General of Rhode Island Herbert L. Carpenter announces that he will attempt to stop the scheduled heavyweight championship fight between Jack Dempsey and Harry Wills.	Mar. 1
				Stunt flyer Bertha Morchem is killed while performing in an air show in San Antonio, TX.	Mar. 2
Senators led by Duncan Upshaw Fletcher of Florida voice opposition to the Norbeck-Burtness bill, a farm relief measure that would loan $75 million to northern farmers....Alien Property Custodian Thomas W. Miller and Frank White, U.S. Treasurer, are ordered by an equity court to restore $500,000 owned by the Mechanics Securities Corporation of New York. The funds were seized during the World War under the belief that they belonged to the German government. Previous attempts to recover the money failed when the federal government claimed that money from the fund was to be used to pay debts owed to the U.S. government not to American citizens or companies.	The House Ways and Means Committee discuss bonus payments to veterans. Many Representatives favor granting bonuses in the form of life insurance for all veterans.	Copper prices rise to a new high for 1924.		The play *Juno and the Paycock* by Sean O'Casey debuts at Dublin's Abbey Theatre....Rabbi Nathan Krass of New York City advises Jews to marry other Jews in order to preserve their religion....New York Unitarian minister Reverend Charles Francis Potter holds his first Bible class in which the Scriptures will be studied in a scientific manner....Bishop William T. Manning of the Church of St. John the Divine in New York City urges Christians to read the Bible in order to learn God's intent.	Mar. 3

F	G	H	I	J
Includes campaigns, elections, federal-state relations, civil rights and liberties, crime, the judiciary, education, healthcare, poverty, urban affairs, and population.	*Includes formation and debate of U.S. foreign and defense policies, veterans affairs, and defense spending. (Relations with specific foreign countries are usually found under the region concerned.)*	*Includes business, labor, agriculture, taxation, transportation, consumer affairs, monetary and fiscal policy, natural resources, pollution and industrial accidents.*	*Includes worldwide scientific, medical and technological developments, natural phenomena, U.S. weather and natural disasters.*	*Includes the arts, religion, scholarship, communications media, sports, entertainment, fashions, fads, and social life.*

	World Affairs	Europe	Africa & The Middle East	The Americas	Asia & The Pacific
Mar. 4	The Spanish government announces that Moroccan rebels have attacked Spanish posts at Tizziazza and Azid Demida and shelled a Spanish cruiser, causing the death of its captain and other officers. In response, Spain rushes soldiers to Morocco	Turkey's Grand National Assembly, in accordance with the president of Turkey, Mustafa Kemal, officially abolishes the Muslim caliphate. Members of the House of Osman, rulers of Turkey since the 13th century, are exiled, bringing an end to the Ottoman Empire.... Winston Churchill states that he will run for a seat in Parliament as an anti-Socialist unaffiliated with any party.... Testimony given at the treason trial of Adolf Hitler and General Erich Ludendorff reveals that weapons belonging to the German army were given to Hitler to use in the attempted overthrow of the government.		An earthquake strikes San Jose, Costa Rica, causing great damage.... Mexican elections are scheduled for July 6.	It is announced that Japan now imports substantially more than it exports.
Mar. 5	Following the removal of caliph Abdul Medjid by Turkey's Mustafa Kemal, French newspapers pressure the government of France to support Mulal Jussef, the Sultan of Morocco, as the next Islamic caliph over King Hussein of the Hedjaz.	Bulgaria arrests more suspected Macedonian revolutionaries.... The left wing of the British Labour Party denounces the government's plans to help private enterprise by providing funding for irrigation in the Sudan that would aid in the cultivation of cotton.... Y.M.C.A. officials in Turkey take food to the palace of the former caliph, now in exile, to feed his abandoned harem.		Honduran revolutionaries control all ports on the Atlantic coast.	
Mar. 6		Muslims living in Berlin call for a boycott of Turkey in protest against the abolition of the caliphate by Turkish nationalists led by Mustafa Kemal.... Czechoslovakia's Parliament opens. Following remarks by Prime Minister Antonín Švehla regarding possible graft involving the country's oil industry, a fight breaks out in the chamber, and a Communist deputy hurls a bottle of benzene at Švehla's head.	Pharaoh Tutankhamen's tomb is officially reopened by the Egyptian government.	American forces are recalled from Puerto Cortes, Honduras, as government forces flee.... Mexico's Secretary of Government proposes extending the term for Mexican presidents from four years to 6. Doing so, it is hoped, will deter revolutions by giving the president time to put into effect plans to help the country.... The border between California and Mexico closes at 9 P.M. by order of the United States government.	
Mar. 7	A storm off the coast of Morocco prevents Spain from landing additional troops to combat Moroccan rebels, but Spanish forces do successfully reach the outpost of Tizziazza.... Great Britain ends negotiations with Mexico on the question of British recognition of the Mexican government.	Turkish prime minister General Ismet Inönü forms a new Cabinet.... Britain decides to increase the size of its Home Air Defense while decreasing the size of its air force in the Middle East.... Benito Mussolini officially ratifies a trade agreement between Italy and the Soviet Union.... French Prime Minister Raymond Poincaré reiterates that French troops will not leave the Ruhr valley until all German debts to France have been paid.... Army officers in Greece call for the end of the monarchy.		Mexican revolutionary leader Adolfo de la Huerta goes into exile.... Mexican president Alvaro Obregon predicts an end to the revolution in 20 days.... General Gregorio Ferrera, leader of revolutionary forces, occupies Tegucigalpa, Honduras.... Rebels in the Argentine province of La Rioja attack the home of the provincial governor.	The Japanese Silk Dealer's Association agrees to stop briefly the manufacture of silk in order to raise its price on the world market.
Mar. 8	France disapproves of the nomination of King Hussein of the Hedjaz as the new Caliph. It is feared that Hussein, who receives a subsidy from the British government, will use the position to extend British influence throughout the Middle East.	Bulgaria's Foreign Minister Christo Kalloff denies that Bulgaria is planning to invade Yugoslavia. Kalloff states that Bulgarian troops on the border are intended solely to prevent violence between Bulgarians and Serbs living in Yugoslavia.... Greece formally recognizes the Soviet Union.... The Soviet Union's Council of Commissars will outlaw the practice of bride kidnapping, a common occurrence in the central Asian republics.		Argentine federal troops march on the city of La Rioja to put down a rebellion.... Government troops capture the city of La Ceiba, Honduras.	Police in Bombay shoot at striking cotton mill employees. Four people are killed.
Mar. 9		Italy annexes the port of Fiume on the Yugoslavian coast.			

A	B	C	D	E
Includes developments that affect more than one world region, international organizations and important meetings of world leaders.	*Includes all domestic and regional developments in Europe, including the Soviet Union.*	*Includes all domestic and regional developments in Africa and the Middle East.*	*Includes all domestic and regional developments in Latin America, the Caribbean, and Canada.*	*Includes all domestic and regional developments in Asian and Pacific nations (and colonies).*

U.S. Politics & Social Issues	U.S. Foreign Policy & Affairs, Defense	U.S. Economy & Environment	Science, Technology & Nature	Culture, Leisure & Lifestyle	
President Calvin Coolidge indicates that he supports the McNary-Haugen bill now before Congress. If passed, the bill will allocate $200 million to aid American wheat farmers.…Senator James A. Reed accuses presidential hopeful William G. McAdoo of illegally loaning money to France and Italy during the World War.…Senator Thomas J. Heflin of Alabama charges that oilman Harry F. Sinclair, under investigation in the Teapot Dome affair, placed bets on horse races on behalf of Attorney General Harry M. Daugherty.				A California health official examines the Pittsburgh Pirates baseball team for symptoms of scarlet fever after player Jewell Ens is hospitalized with the disease.	Mar. 4
The House of Representatives postpones other business so that it can debate the proposed lease of the federally owned power plant at Muscle Shoals to Henry Ford.		The prices of wheat, corn, oats, and rye decline.	Chicago's Field Museum receives the world's largest turquoise as a gift from the Grand Vizier of Persia.…Major Edwin H. Armstrong gives a demonstration of the superheterodyne receiver.	Harvard contemplates cutting back on athletic competition. Professors believe athletics requires too much of the students' time.	Mar. 5
The White House states that President Calvin Coolidge, who has previously denied that he will ask Attorney General Harry M. Daugherty to step down while the Senate investigates charges of corruption leveled at Daugherty, may change his mind and request Daugherty's resignation.	Rear Admiral W.C. Cole states that disarmament following the World War has weakened the ability of the United States to protect its territory in the Philippines. To remedy the situation, Cole calls for a naval base to be built at Alameda, CA.…Former Veterans' Bureau head Charles R. Forbes is indicted on charges of conspiracy, fraud, and bribery. He pleads not guilty.	Cleveland residents stand in line at fresh-water springs to collect a gallon of water apiece after the water in Lake Erie is found to be contaminated with chlorine and phenol.…The price of hogs and lambs increases.…The Lago Petroleum Company purchases land owned by the British Equatorial Oil Company in the Lake Maracaibo region of Venezuela.	The tuberculosis vaccine developed by Georges Dreyer is found to be ineffective following use of the vaccine for nearly a year.	The *Giornale d'Italia*, reports that the British government in Palestine is treating Catholics unfairly.	Mar. 6
A federal grand jury charges Thomas B. Felder, Gaston B. Means, and Elmer Jarnecke with conspiracy and obstruction of justice. The indictment alleges that the men attempted to bribe Attorney General Harry M. Daugherty and others in the Justice Department in order to have their clients cleared of charges of mail fraud.		President Calvin Coolidge raises the tariff on wheat.	Radio signals are used to guide aircraft for the first time in history.	Argentine boxer Luis Firpo defeats Italian heavyweight champion Erminio Spalla in a match in Buenos Aires.	Mar. 7
After Attorney General Harry M. Daugherty refuses to supply the names of Congressmen suspected of corruption, the House of Representatives refers the matter to the House Judiciary Committee.…A federal judge orders the destruction of a brewery in Illinois.		Officials of the Baltimore & Ohio Railroad and employees' representatives agree to a plan that will incorporate all of the railroad's workers into a cooperative arrangement in which the workers will share in the company's profits.…The price of crude oil rises to 25 cents per barrel.		The results of a survey taken at the International Perfumery Show are announced. Lilac is the most popular scent among both men and women.	Mar. 8
Oilman Edward L. Doheny declares that the leasing of federal oil reserves at Teapot Dome, WY, and Elk Hills, CA, to private companies was sanctioned by President Woodrow Wilson's Secretary of the Navy, Josephus Daniels.				Baptist minister Henry Roach Stratton attacks New York City's Museum of Natural History for exposing children to the theory of evolution and states that the Bible should also be displayed.	Mar. 9
F *Includes campaigns, elections, federal-state relations, civil rights and liberties, crime, the judiciary, education, healthcare, poverty, urban affairs, and population.*	G *Includes formation and debate of U.S. foreign and defense policies, veterans affairs, and defense spending. (Relations with specific foreign countries are usually found under the region concerned.)*	H *Includes business, labor, agriculture, taxation, transportation, consumer affairs, monetary and fiscal policy, natural resources, pollution and industrial accidents.*	I *Includes worldwide scientific, medical and technological developments, natural phenomena, U.S. weather and natural disasters.*	J *Includes the arts, religion, scholarship, communications media, sports, entertainment, fashions, fads, and social life.*	

	World Affairs	Europe	Africa & The Middle East	The Americas	Asia & The Pacific
Mar. 10	The League of Nations Opium Conference adjourns with Britain and the United States unable to come to terms regarding the best way to reduce opium abuse. The United States argues that all opium production should be limited. Britain maintains that the growing of opium for consumption within a country should not be prohibited.	President of Turkey, Mustafa Kemal, announces that the power of the caliphate will now be held by the Turkish parliament.…The Vatican announces that there is no truth to the rumors that it intends to recognize the Soviet Union.	Muslims attending a conference in Jerusalem recognize the claim of King Hussein of the Hedjaz to the caliphate.	President Rafael Lopez Gutierrez dies of diabetes while trying to flee the revolution in Honduras.	Japanese ambassador Masanao Hanihara urges cooperation between his country and the United States.
Mar. 11	At the opening meeting of the League of Nations Council in Geneva, Charles Cripps, Lord Parmoor of Great Britain, calls upon the United States, Germany, and the Soviet Union to join the League.	Former Bavarian dictator Gustav von Kahr testifies against Adolf Hitler and Erich Ludendorff in their treason trial. Von Kahr states that he found Hitler's ideas ludicrous and denies that he participated in the attempted overthrow of the government in any way.		Mexican troops advance on the Isthmus of Tehuantepec. Rebel forces flee before them.…Followers of General Juan Angel Arias, whose forces control the Honduran capital of Tegucigalpa, bomb the home of revolutionary General Policarpo Bonilla. Fighting erupts in the streets of the capital.…An earthquake strikes Costa Rica. Tremors are recorded as far away as Washington, DC.	
Mar. 12	The League of Nations Council informs Austria that it cannot use the money from a League of Nations loan on public works projects.…Norman H. Davis, chairman of the commission charged with deciding which nation will be awarded control of the Baltic port of Memel, argues that the Council of the League of Nations should give control of the city to Lithuania.	A bomb explodes outside the British embassy in Athens. Police later discover another bomb at the Romanian embassy.	The Muslim Supreme Council offers the caliphate to King Hussein of the Hedjaz.	Mexican Secretary of War Francisco R. Serrano sails to the Isthmus of Tehuantepec to join in the campaign against the remaining rebel forces there.	Pro-independence leaders in the Philippines suggest that General Emilio Aguinaldo be named head of a commission to be sent to the United States for the purpose of securing sovereignty for the Philippines.
Mar. 13	Dr. Adolf Keller asks the League of Nations to allow the Federated Churches of Christ in America to participate, along with the Roman Catholic Church, the Greek Orthodox Church, and the Church of England, in discussions of calendar reform.…Two German insurance companies sue the United States Treasurer and the Alien Property Custodian to recover funds seized during the World War.		The Persian National Assembly opens. The majority of seats are held by members of the Reform Party who support Prime Minster Reza Khan's desire to make Persia into a republic.		
Mar. 14	The Council of the League of Nations allots funds to rescue nearly one-quarter million Albanians from starvation.	The French Senate votes to allow Prime Minister Raymond Poincaré to issue economic measures by decree instead of submitting proposed plans to the Senate and the Chamber of Deputies for approval.…President Friedrich Ebert announces that elections will be held in Germany on May 4.			Japan's foreign minister declares that Japan will not grant recognition to the Soviet Union until it makes amends for closing the Japanese consulate at Vladivostok, arresting Japanese citizens living in the city, and interfering with the Japanese mail.
Mar. 15	The League of Nations Council gives power to the Preparatory Committee of the Opium League to formulate principles to be discussed at upcoming international conferences. The Opium League's goal is to limit (or eradicate) the consumption of opium.	King Victor Emmanuelle III of Italy officially announces that the city of Fiume has been annexed to Italy.	The first parliament in Egyptian history is seated. Only journalists from newspapers favored by the ruling Nationalist Party are allowed to attend.	Mexican troops control the town of Cosamaloapan on the Papaloapan River and clear the tracks of the Vera Cruz & Isthmus Railway.	Indian nationalists in the Legislative Assembly defeat a finance bill proposed by the British government, asserting their right to self-government.

A	B	C	D	E
Includes developments that affect more than one world region, international organizations and important meetings of world leaders.	*Includes all domestic and regional developments in Europe, including the Soviet Union.*	*Includes all domestic and regional developments in Africa and the Middle East.*	*Includes all domestic and regional developments in Latin America, the Caribbean, and Canada.*	*Includes all domestic and regional developments in Asian and Pacific nations (and colonies).*

U.S. Politics & Social Issues	U.S. Foreign Policy & Affairs, Defense	U.S. Economy & Environment	Science, Technology & Nature	Culture, Leisure & Lifestyle	
Secretary of the Navy Edwin Denby resigns.…Oilman Edward L. Doheny refutes charges made by Senator Burton K. Wheeler of Montana that he and other oilmen have provided Mexican revolutionaries with funds to purchase weapons.		Fire damages the Replogle Steel Company's New Jersey plant.		The Associated Glee Clubs of America meet in New York City.	Mar. 10
The California State Grange, the Sons of the Golden West, the California Federation of Labor, and the California Department of the American Legion appeal to the Senate Immigration Committee to prohibit Japanese immigration. Representatives for the organizations argue that the Japanese can never be integrated into American society and argue that they are dangerous to whites.	The American Legion supports the Johnson-McSwain draft bill, which gives the president the power to draft men into the military and to take control of industry in the event of a national emergency.			The Forstmann & Huffmann Company's Fall fabrics consist largely of different weights and weaves of cashmere.…The Pas, a 200-mile dogsled race, begins in Canada.	Mar. 11
	The House of Representatives awards funds to the air force for the purchase of additional planes and recommends that the army be maintained at its present size.	Indiana farmers begin a campaign to pool all of Indiana's wheat harvests.…The Russian-American Mining Corporation affirms that it has acquired the right to mine mica deposits in Siberia.	A strong gale batters Rhode Island and Massachusetts, causing flooding and interrupting rail transport and communications.	Women students at the University of Chicago decide not to form a "man-haters club." They believe the popularity of dating would make it unsuccessful.	Mar. 12
Hearings on the U.S. government's suit to cancel Harry F. Sinclair's lease of federal oil reserves at Teapot Dome, WY, on the grounds that the leases were obtained illegally and to halt drilling on the land begin in Cheyenne.…The Department of Justice and the House of Representatives begin separate investigation of allegations that Congressmen received bribes in exchange for arranging the release of people held in federal prisons.…Chairman of the Democratic National Committee, Charles A. Greathouse, expects Senator Samuel M. Ralston of Indiana to be the Democratic nominee for president.		Wreckage from the schooner *Wyoming* is found off the coast of Nantucket. The crew is believed drowned.…The Baltimore & Ohio Railroad raises the wages of its conductors, yardmen, and switchmen.…The Senate fails to pass a bill that would have granted $50 million in aid to farmers.	Thomas Edison is suggested by Justice Mitchell Erlanger of the New York Supreme Court as an appropriate candidate to investigate the claim of an inventor that he has designed a lamp that can store electricity within it and burn for years.		Mar. 13
John L. Bernstein, representing the Hebrew Immigrants' Aid Society of New York, asks the Senate Immigration Committee to allow the relatives of American citizens to be exempt from quota restrictions.				Dr. John Roach Stratton, minister of the Calvary Baptist Church, proclaims that he will continue to strive to convince Americans that the theory of evolution presented by the Museum of Natural History is untrue and that evidence in support of the theory is either false or self-contradictory.	Mar. 14
				The New York *Herald* and the New York *Tribune* merge to form the New York *Herald Tribune*, edited by Ogden Mills Reid.	Mar. 15

F	G	H	I	J
Includes campaigns, elections, federal-state relations, civil rights and liberties, crime, the judiciary, education, healthcare, poverty, urban affairs, and population.	*Includes formation and debate of U.S. foreign and defense policies, veterans affairs, and defense spending. (Relations with specific foreign countries are usually found under the region concerned.)*	*Includes business, labor, agriculture, taxation, transportation, consumer affairs, monetary and fiscal policy, natural resources, pollution and industrial accidents.*	*Includes worldwide scientific, medical and technological developments, natural phenomena, U.S. weather and natural disasters.*	*Includes the arts, religion, scholarship, communications media, sports, entertainment, fashions, fads, and social life.*

	World Affairs	Europe	Africa & The Middle East	The Americas	Asia & The Pacific
Mar. 16		Veterans in Belgium march to protest against high food prices....The Parisian Senate ratifies the treaty regarding Bessarabia.		Horacio Vasquez is elected president of Santo Domingo.	
Mar. 17	Brazil decides to appoint an ambassador to the League of Nations. It is the first country to do so.	Dublin celebrates St. Patrick's Day without a parade. Most saloons are closed.		Soldiers of the Honduran government's army shoot at the house of the Secretary of the American Legation.	Motilal Nehru declares that the nationalist Swarajist Party refuses to recognize the authority of Britain to regulate Indian affairs.... Manabendra Rath Roy is charged with conspiring to overthrow the British government in India.... Earthquake shocks hit Japan.
Mar. 18	The British government announces that, to demonstrate its commitment to establishing world peace, it has decided not to build a proposed naval base in Singapore....The Soviet newspaper *Izvestia* blames Wellington Koo, China's Minister of Foreign Affairs, for China's delay in granting recognition to the Soviet Union.	On trial for treason in Munich, Adolf Hitler states that his intentions were to march on Berlin and overthrow the government of the German Republic. Co-defendant Erich Ludendorff denies that he intended to take over the government of Germany....Troops of the Irish Free State arrest 10 army officers while searching for the leaders of an attempted mutiny.			India's Legislative Assembly rejects a proposed finance bill for the second time.
Mar. 19	Failure to resolve the status of Mongolia leads China to refuse recognition to the Soviet Union. The Soviet Union's envoy is ordered by the Chinese government to leave Beijing....Turkish Prime Minister Ismet Inönü informs the League of Nations that, as there are no longer any Armenians residing in Turkey, Turkey is not interested in attending a conference to discuss the problem of providing a legal identity to Armenians, no longer possess a national identity.	A Berlin newspaper publishes what it claims is the text of a secret treaty formed between Czechoslovakia and France. Czechoslovakia denies the paper's claims....General Richard Mulcahy, the Minister of Defense of the Irish Free State, resigns.			India's Viceroy and Governor General certify the finance bill rejected by the Legislative Assembly and sends it to the Council of State to be passed into law.
Mar. 20	The League of Nations Non-Partisan Committee begins a campaign in New York City to urge the United States to join the League of Nations and the World Court.	France's Chamber of Deputies passes a bill giving the government the ability to mobilize the army in the event of an external or internal attack without having first to seek permission from the French legislature. Socialists protest the measure.		American troops are fired upon by Honduran forces. The Honduran government tells the American consul, Franklin E. Morales, to call for the withdrawal of American forces.	Japan loses contact with sailors trapped in a sunken submarine.
Mar. 21		The Catholic Young Men's Club in Gubbio, Italy, is attacked. A picture of the pope and a crucifix are burned....Mutinous Irish army officers are released from jail after they agree to surrender weapons and ammunition belonging to the army.	As the formation of a republic is being discussed in the Persian legislature, an anti-Republican mob bursts into the chamber and attacks Republican politicians.	A Mexican gunboat departs New Orleans to attack rebels in Tabasco, Campeche, and the Yucatan.	
Mar. 22		Bus and trolley drivers in London go on strike.		Cuban diplomat General Carlos Garcia-Velez states his intention to overthrow the government of Alfredo Zayas, peacefully if possible.	

A	B	C	D	E
Includes developments that affect more than one world region, international organizations and important meetings of world leaders.	*Includes all domestic and regional developments in Europe, including the Soviet Union.*	*Includes all domestic and regional developments in Africa and the Middle East.*	*Includes all domestic and regional developments in Latin America, the Caribbean, and Canada.*	*Includes all domestic and regional developments in Asian and Pacific nations (and colonies).*

U.S. Politics & Social Issues	U.S. Foreign Policy & Affairs, Defense	U.S. Economy & Environment	Science, Technology & Nature	Culture, Leisure & Lifestyle	
The Universal Negro Improvement Association meets at Madison Square Garden. Speakers urge the establishment of an independent African republic and call upon African Americans to settle there. Those attending are asked to sign a petition to be presented to President Calvin Coolidge and Congress requesting federal aid for the creation of the republic.		A poll taken by *The Literary Digest* indicates that the majority of Americans favor the Mellon Tax Plan.	A blizzard strikes central New York state.	The American Association for Recognition of the Irish Republic calls for a ban on all St. Patrick's Day celebrations. They claim the celebrations are dominated by politicians who have no interest in Irish independence.…The Mah Jong dress, composed of differently colored layers of fabric worn atop one another, debuts in Paris.	Mar. 16
The Senate ratifies the appointment of Walter L. Cohen, an African American, as Controller of Customs of the Port of New Orleans.…The Senate votes down a resolution calling for a single term for the president of the United States.			United States Army fliers leave Los Angeles on a flight around the world.	President Calvin Coolidge makes the first draw for the Davis Cup on the White House lawn with the ambassadors of those nations whose athletes will compete for the Cup in attendance.…Argentine boxer Luis Firpo announces that he will leave the sport following his next match.…New York City holds its annual St. Patrick's Day parade.…Light-heavyweight champion Gene Tunney defeats Jimmy Delaney in St. Paul.	Mar. 17
	The House of Representatives passes the Bonus Bill. The bill will award 20 years of prepaid life insurance to veterans.…The Department of the Navy drafts a new policy for dealing with the lease of naval oil reserves. The policy calls for limiting drilling for oil in reserve lands and for storing emergency reserves above ground in tanks.	Miners at Pennsylvania's Vinton Collieries Company go on strike after learning that the company has cut their pay by one-third.…President Calvin Coolidge requests that the Agricultural Credit Corporation lend money to wheat farmers so that they may diversify their crops.	Three U.S. Army pilots attempting to circumnavigate the globe by air land in Eugene, OR.	The newly created New York *Herald Tribune* begins publication.…Police are called in to control the crowd at the premier of *The Thief of Baghdad,* starring Mary Pickford and Douglas Fairbanks.	Mar. 18
Edwin L. Doheny's attorney denies that his client offered to sell American oil to British companies. He maintains that Doheny did sell oil to the British but that all of the oil had been drilled in Mexico.	Curtis D. Wilbur is sworn in as the new Secretary of the Navy.	Bids are offered for the right to drill for oil on Osage Indian lands in Oklahoma.			Mar. 19
The House Judiciary Committee discusses the Linthicum bill, which will make "The Star-Spangled Banner" the official national anthem of the United States.…Democratic presidential candidate Oscar Underwood claims that William G. McAdoo won the Georgia presidential primary with help from the Ku Klux Klan.		General Electric is charged by the Department of Justice with having violated the Sherman Anti-Trust law by monopolizing the production and sale of light bulbs.…The Railroad Labor Board rules that women cannot hold positions in which they are called upon to move freight.	Four U.S. Army pilots attempting to fly around the world arrive in Seattle, WA.		Mar. 20
The governor of Kentucky signs into law a bill requiring that the Bible be read on a daily basis in Kentucky schools.…The Loyal Legion of Lincoln, an African-American auxiliary of the Ku Klux Klan, is formed at Youngstown, OH.		The Atlantic Coast Line, a southern railroad, announces that, as a result of competition from automobiles, it will cease to run many of its passenger trains.		Gertrude Ederle sets a world record at a swim meet in Buffalo, NY. Ederle swims the 220-yard freestyle in two minutes and 29 seconds.	Mar. 21
	President Calvin Coolidge bans the sale of weapons and ammunition to Honduras.	The Thorndike Company textile mills in Massachusetts will cut working hours to 24 a week.		The National Intercollegiate Football Rules Committee changes the rules of the game. Attempts to score an additional point after making a touchdown must be taken from the three-yard line, not the five-yard line. Kickoffs must take place at midfield, and tees to raise the ball must not be used.	Mar. 22

F	G	H	I	J
Includes campaigns, elections, federal-state relations, civil rights and liberties, crime, the judiciary, education, healthcare, poverty, urban affairs, and population.	*Includes formation and debate of U.S. foreign and defense policies, veterans affairs, and defense spending. (Relations with specific foreign countries are usually found under the region concerned.)*	*Includes business, labor, agriculture, taxation, transportation, consumer affairs, monetary and fiscal policy, natural resources, pollution and industrial accidents.*	*Includes worldwide scientific, medical and technological developments, natural phenomena, U.S. weather and natural disasters.*	*Includes the arts, religion, scholarship, communications media, sports, entertainment, fashions, fads, and social life.*

	World Affairs	Europe	Africa & The Middle East	The Americas	Asia & The Pacific
Mar. 23		Rome celebrates the founding of the Fascist movement in 1919.			
Mar. 24	The United States protests Turkey's closing of the Y.W.C.A. in Istanbul.	Prime Minister Alexandros Papanastasiou proclaims Greece a republic. A plebiscite on the matter will be held in April.... Yugoslavia's Cabinet resigns.		President Alfredo Zayas of Cuba removes General Carlos Garcia-Velez from his position as Ambassador to Great Britain. Garcia-Velez, leader of the Veterans' and Patriots' Association, proclaims that he will soon lead a revolution in Cuba to remove Zayas from office.	
Mar. 25	The Bulgarian National Assembly ratifies the Treaty of Lausanne and a naturalization treaty with the United States.			Mexico names Alberto J. Pani as ambassador to the United States.	
Mar. 26	Members of Britain's House of Lords accuse the Soviet Union of supporting anti-British movements in Ireland, India, Persia, and South Africa.... Spain approves an international treaty against the traffic in women.	French Prime Minister Raymond Poincaré resigns following a narrow defeat for his party in the passage of a pension bill in the Chamber of Deputies.... A landslide near Amalfi, Italy, kills 100 people in surrounding villages, damages houses, and threatens to destroy a famous landmark.	Oscar S. Straus returns to Jerusalem from his meeting in Amman with King Hussein of the Hedjaz. Straus, the former American ambassador to Turkey who is now working with the World Zionist Organization and the British government in Palestine, discussed with Hussein the importance of promoting peace among the various religious groups in Palestine.	Canada's House of Commons castigates the city of Chicago for diverting water from Lake Michigan. Canada maintains that the drainage is lowering the level of the Great Lakes and the St. Lawrence River, interfering with shipping and trade.... Rebel generals including Vincente Tosta, Gregorio Ferrera, and Tiburcio Carias Andino call upon Fausta Davila to become provisional president of Honduras until regular elections can be held.	
Mar. 27		The treason trial of Erich Ludendorff and Adolf Hitler ends. Both men declare themselves patriots concerned only with German freedom. Crowds in Munich applaud their speeches.... Responding to the appeals of French President Alexandre Millerand, Raymond Poincaré resumes his position as prime minister... An earthquake strikes Italy in the area of Naples. No injuries are reported.		General Carlos Garcia-Velez advises his followers in Cuba to be cautious. He warns that the government of President Alfredo Zayas may use the cover provided by their activities to create a "false" revolution that can then be blamed on Garcia-Velez's Veterans' and Patriots' Association.	
Mar. 28				Heavy fighting takes place outside of Tegucigalpa, Honduras.	
Mar. 29	The Policy Committee of the American Peace Award reports that the majority of the 610,558 ballots cast on the Bok Peace Prize Plan favored the plan.	Landslides occur near Amalfi, Italy.			
Mar. 30		The German People's Party adopts a politically conservative platform that calls for the establishment of a democratic monarchy.			
	A *Includes developments that affect more than one world region, international organizations and important meetings of world leaders.*	B *Includes all domestic and regional developments in Europe, including the Soviet Union.*	C *Includes all domestic and regional developments in Africa and the Middle East.*	D *Includes all domestic and regional developments in Latin America, the Caribbean, and Canada.*	E *Includes all domestic and regional developments in Asian and Pacific nations (and colonies).*

U.S. Politics & Social Issues	U.S. Foreign Policy & Affairs, Defense	U.S. Economy & Environment	Science, Technology & Nature	Culture, Leisure & Lifestyle	
			Part of a flock of blackbirds dies in midair while flying over a farm in New Jersey. It is thought that radio waves are the cause.	Acting counter to the orders of Bishop William T. Manning, six barefooted women perform a dance in St. Marks-in-the-Bouwerie as part of a religious service.	Mar. 23
		Waiters go on strike at seven Broadway restaurants and clubs.…The price of wheat drops to its lowest level in nearly a year.	Four human skeletons from the time of the Ice Age are discovered near Los Angeles, CA.	Jean Sibelius's *Symphony No. 7 in C Major* debuts in Stockholm. …Archbishops Patrick J. Hayes and George W. Mundelein are made Cardinals of the Catholic church. …The American public is notified by radio that Tiger, President Calvin Coolidge's cat, is missing and asked for its assistance in his return.	Mar. 24
	President Calvin Coolidge appoints a commission to ascertain the best way of saving oil for the use of the navy and of storing oil for use in wartime.…President Calvin Coolidge designates 7,100 acres of land in Utah as a helium reserve.	The price of hogs and lambs at Chicago is low.	British aviator A. Stuart MacLaren departs Southampton on a flight around the world.	Tiger, President Calvin Coolidge's lost cat, is found and returned to the White House.…The Montreal Canadiens win hockey's Stanley Cup.	Mar. 25
A poll taken by New York City Democrats reveals that there are at least 26 potential Democratic nominees for president.…The Senate Interstate Commerce Committee approves a bill that will restrict radio-broadcasting licenses to two years.…The House Education Committee hears testimony relating to the Sterling-Reed bill, which proposes the creation of a federal Department of Education.…It is revealed that an expert testifying for the defense changed the barrels on the pistol found on Nicola Sacco when he was arrested and charged, along with Bartolomeo Vanzetti, for murder in 1920.		The Senate Interstate Commerce Committee adopts a resolution calling for the lowering of railroad shipping rates for livestock and crops. …The price of wheat reaches a record low.…Census statistics reveal that the birth rate is falling as the death rate is rising.…The House Judiciary Committee favors a constitutional amendment to abolish child labor. Opponents argue that child labor is an issue best left to the states.			Mar. 26
Attorney General Harry M. Daugherty resigns.…Senator William Borah of Idaho proposes that a new international conference be called to discuss armament limits and trade. Borah argues that European markets for American produce are needed to save farmers in the United States.		A bill is introduced into the New York State Assembly to limit women working in stores and industrial facilities to a 48-hour week.	Icebergs are reported in Atlantic shipping lanes.	Dr. William Norman Guthrie, head of the Episcopal church St. Mark's-in-the-Bouwerie, states that, despite the disapproval of Bishop William T. Manning, dances and "pagan" rituals will continue to be part of services at the church.	Mar. 27
The Senate Committee on Territories and Insular Possessions proposes that a plebiscite be held in the Philippines in 1935 to determine whether or not Filipinos desire independence from American rule.	Speaking before the House Committee on Military Affairs, Bernard Baruch argues in support of legislation that would give the president the power to mobilize industry, control production, set prices, allot workers to various industries, and control the railroads.	Twenty-four miners employed by the Yukon-Pocahontas Coal Company are killed, and others are injured when an explosion occurs at the company's mine in Yukon, WV.	Tornadoes hit Kansas and Oklahoma causing eight deaths and significant property damage.	Master Robert II wins Britain's Grand National Steeplechase.	Mar. 28
The House of Representatives allots money to the post office to develop coast-to-coast airmail service.…After learning that the barrels in Nicola Sacco's pistol were switched during preparations for trial, Sacco and Bartolomeo Vanzetti file appeals with the Massachusetts State Supreme Court.			Ohio rivers flood following heavy rainfall. People leave their homes in Pittsburgh. Parents drown trying to rescue their son, who is saved by another.…Explorer Dr. Alexander H. Rice and his wife depart on an exploratory journey to South America.		Mar. 29
	Fifty New York corporations state that they will allow a portion of their younger male employees to attend the Citizens' Military Training Camps in the summer. The purpose of the camps, established by Congress following the World War, is to provide military training for civilians.		A new comet is observed by astronomers at the Royal Observatory at the Cape of Good Hope.	The naval dirigible *Shenandoah* performs in an air show in New Jersey in celebration of Memorial Day.…The Fall River Football Club of Fall River, MA, defeats the Vesper-Buicks of St. Louis to win the American soccer championship.	Mar. 30
F *Includes campaigns, elections, federal-state relations, civil rights and liberties, crime, the judiciary, education, healthcare, poverty, urban affairs, and population.*	G *Includes formation and debate of U.S. foreign and defense policies, veterans affairs, and defense spending. (Relations with specific foreign countries are usually found under the region concerned.)*	H *Includes business, labor, agriculture, taxation, transportation, consumer affairs, monetary and fiscal policy, natural resources, pollution and industrial accidents.*	I *Includes worldwide scientific, medical and technological developments, natural phenomena, U.S. weather and natural disasters.*	J *Includes the arts, religion, scholarship, communications media, sports, entertainment, fashions, fads, and social life.*	

	World Affairs	Europe	Africa & The Middle East	The Americas	Asia & The Pacific
Mar. 31		British airmail pilots go on strike.... London omnibus and tram drivers end a 10-day strike.			
Apr. 1		Government interference and high taxes force an American orphanage and the American Near East Relief Hospital in Turkey to shut down....Erich Ludendorff is found innocent of conspiring to overthrow the German government....Nicola Bonservizi, founder of the Fascist Party in France, is buried in Milan. He was killed by anarchist Ernesto Bonomimi. Benito Mussolini attends the funeral.			
Apr. 2	The League of Nations confirms that it will be responsible for controlling German armaments, as is provided in the Treaty of Versailles. However, the League's Council states, it will depend upon the opinions of military experts from other nations to determine whether or not Germany is abiding by the terms of disarmament.	The Communist Party of the Soviet Union is expelling those members who are deemed insufficiently proletarian in their attitudes. Soviet universities are a special focus of attention....The legislature of the Irish Free State is considering allowing women to choose not to serve on juries....Talks between the Soviet Union and Romania regarding the status of Bessarabia end. Although Bessarabia chose in 1918 to become part of Romania, the Soviet Union demands that a plebiscite be held in the region.	Twelve hundred Muslim pilgrims are rescued after the cargo ship on which they are traveling catches fire in the Red Sea.	The railroad strike in Cuba ends.... Soldiers belonging to various revolutionary factions are doing battle with guns and machetes in the streets of the Honduran capital of Tegucigalpa.	William Morris Hughes, the former prime minister of Australia, maintains that only unity among the English-speaking nations will keep the world at peace, and trumpets Australia's success at maintaining Western civilization in the Pacific. Australia is able to do this, he asserts, only by keeping itself "white."
Apr. 3		The Bulgarian government abolishes the Communist and Labor Parties and seizes property owned by the organizations.			
Apr. 4	A treaty granting Americans rights equal to those of citizens of countries belonging to the League of Nations in the French mandates of Syria and Lebanon is signed.	Anti-Jewish violence breaks out in Romania after students at Bucharest University are put on trial for attempting to kill a Jewish journalist and a Jewish banker....The Belgian government refutes claims in the French press that Belgium has relinquished its right to receive reparations from Germany before other claimants.			
Apr. 5				Rioting between two opposing factions of the governing Conservative Party breaks out in Granada, Nicaragua. Several people are killed....Workers at a Cuban electric plant go on strike.	The United States, Britain, France, Denmark, Italy, and Mexico present damage claims to China on behalf of citizens kidnapped by bandits from a Chinese train in May 1923. The victims remained prisoners of the bandits for more than a month. ...Chinese pirates attack a Portuguese ship. Three men are killed and the ship's captain is injured.
	A *Includes developments that affect more than one world region, international organizations and important meetings of world leaders.*	B *Includes all domestic and regional developments in Europe, including the Soviet Union.*	C *Includes all domestic and regional developments in Africa and the Middle East.*	D *Includes all domestic and regional developments in Latin America, the Caribbean, and Canada.*	E *Includes all domestic and regional developments in Asian and Pacific nations (and colonies).*

U.S. Politics & Social Issues	U.S. Foreign Policy & Affairs, Defense	U.S. Economy & Environment	Science, Technology & Nature	Culture, Leisure & Lifestyle	
		The House Judiciary Committee reports a Constitutional Amendment that will ban child labor.		Parishioners of the Community Methodist Church in Hampden, MA, will, in the absence of their pastor, listen to a sermon broadcast from a Congregational Church in Springfield.…World heavyweight champion Jack Dempsey agrees to appear in 10 films in exchange for $1 million.	Mar. 31
William Jennings Bryan proposes that political campaigns should be funded by the government.…Ku Klux Klan-supported candidates win elections in Tulsa, OK.…L.H. Schwaebe is asked by Assistant Secretary of the Treasury McKinzie Moss to learn the cost of constructing a 180-mile wire fence along the border between the United States and Mexico.…A federal grand jury convenes to hear testimony related to the involvement of former Secretary of the Interior Albert B. Fall in the leasing of naval oil reserves.		In testimony before the House Appropriations Committee William J. Burns, director of the Justice Department's Bureau of Investigation, claims that Communists have infiltrated the American Federation of Labor and are trying to overthrow it.	Despite predictions of good weather, a snowstorm hits the Atlantic coast from Maine to Virginia.	The convention of the Russian Orthodox Church opens in Detroit. Metropolitan Platon denies that the church plans to combine with the Protestant Episcopal Church.	Apr. 1
President Calvin Coolidge appoints Harlan F. Stone as Attorney General.…Proposed immigration legislation is debated in the Senate. Upon learning that the legislation does not impose quotas on immigrants from North and South America, Senator Henry F. Ashurst of Arizona recommends that a quota be placed on Mexican immigrants.…Frederick Wells, an African-American law student at Columbia University, states that he will not be forced by white students into abandoning his room in Furnald Hall, one of Columbia's student residence halls. A cross is seen burning opposite the dormitory at midnight.	Former head of the Veterans' Bureau, Charles R. Forbes, charges that the three grand jury indictments against him were obtained through the use of improper methods, including the hearing of testimony from unsworn witnesses.…American citizens holding property on the Isle of Pines protest the imminent ratification of a treaty that will cede control of the island to Cuba.	Alien Property Custodian Thomas W. Miller suggests that an Alien Property Trade Investment Corporation be created. The corporation would use German funds seized during the World War to promote the sale of American agricultural products in foreign markets.	Ornithologist Frank M. Chapman returns from South America with rare birds and specimens of flora. He intends to build a South American exhibit at the American Museum of Natural History.	Johnny Weissmuller sets a new 100-yard freestyle swimming national record.…Hugo Bezdek, football coach at Penn State, states that the practice of trying to score an additional point after making a touchdown should be done away with. He believes that is unfair to award an entire team with a point won through the ability of only one man.…Friends of the late John Orth, who died recently in New York City, state that proof that he was in fact the missing Archduke Johann Salvatore of Austria, a cousin of Emperor Franz Josef, can be found in a box in Brazil and in a secret letter being held by the Vatican until 1927.	Apr. 2
New York City police guard Furnald Hall at Columbia University following a cross burning across from the residence hall. College officials blame the incident on the Ku Klux Klan. Columbia students circulate a statement declaring that the majority of Columbia's students do not want Frederick Wells, an African-American student, removed from the residence halls.	A federal court decision denies citizenship to men who requested to be released from military obligations during the World War on the grounds that they were not American citizens.		Earthquake tremors strike San Francisco. No damage is caused.	A death mask is made of John Orth in an attempt to establish his identity as Archduke Johann of Austria.…Boxer Tommy Gibbons defeats Jack McFarland in a match in Nashville, TN.…Sybil Bauer sets new world's records in the women's 50- and 150-yard backstroke.	Apr. 3
The Senate Judiciary Committee approves the appointment of Harlan F. Stone as Attorney General of the United States.…A beauty contest in Flushing, Queens, in which a young African-American woman holds third place, is cancelled.					Apr. 4
		A federal court of appeals rules that banks that took customers' money and transferred it to their branches in the Soviet Union during the period when the Soviet government was undertaking the nationalization of banks must reimburse their depositors for their lost funds.…The Kentucky National Guard is dispatched to the Straight Creek camp of the Liberty Coal and Coke Company to quell violence occasioned by a labor dispute.	Following the discovery of human skeletons approximately 25,000 years old, Los Angeles County officials allocate $5,000 to search for additional relics from the Ice Age.…Researchers in psychology at Harvard University attempt to receive thoughts telepathically transmitted from Paris to Cambridge, MA.	The managing editor of the Yale *Daily News* states that college students consider public drunkenness unacceptable behavior.…Argentine boxer Luis Firpo knocks out American fighter Al Reich in a match in Buenos Aires.…"John Orth" is buried under the name Johann Salvatore, the name of a missing archduke of Austria.…Two hundred American Communists gather on West 39th Street, New York City, to witness the christening of Nikolai Lenin Manus.	Apr. 5
F *Includes campaigns, elections, federal-state relations, civil rights and liberties, crime, the judiciary, education, healthcare, poverty, urban affairs, and population.*	G *Includes formation and debate of U.S. foreign and defense policies, veterans affairs, and defense spending. (Relations with specific foreign countries are usually found under the region concerned.)*	H *Includes business, labor, agriculture, taxation, transportation, consumer affairs, monetary and fiscal policy, natural resources, pollution and industrial accidents.*	I *Includes worldwide scientific, medical and technological developments, natural phenomena, U.S. weather and natural disasters.*	J *Includes the arts, religion, scholarship, communications media, sports, entertainment, fashions, fads, and social life.*	

	World Affairs	Europe	Africa & The Middle East	The Americas	Asia & The Pacific
Apr. 6		Two Americans are killed near Tirana, Albania....Four Romanian universities are placed under martial law by the government of Romania. Students participating in and professors advocating anti-Jewish violence will be tried in military courts....Monarchists and Communists both do well in elections in Bavaria. Moderate parties lose votes to parties on the left and right....Prime Minister Benito Mussolini wins the Italian elections.		A new political party forms in the Philippines. The goal of the party, which is led by Manuel Quezon, is immediate independence for the Philippines.	
Apr. 7		The patriarch of the Greek Orthodox Church in Turkey is fined for possessing a Greek flag.	Jan Smuts, prime minister of the Union of South Africa, announces that, because parliament is uncertain whether it still has the support of the people, elections will be held. Smuts's announcement is greeted enthusiastically by members of the Labor and Nationalist Parties.		
Apr. 8		The Turkish government closes French and Italian schools because of their refusal to remove religious symbols from their buildings.			
Apr. 9	The text of the Dawes Plan is made public....Japan and Romania sign a treaty regulating trade between the two countries....Poland plans to establish a permanent delegation to the League of Nations.	The union of Romania and Bessarabia is celebrated in Bucharest, and a national holiday is declared.		Havana's dockworkers go on strike.	
Apr. 10	A League of Nations committee meets in Paris to discuss the problem of ethnic Germans living within Poland.	A Soviet diplomat in Vienna denies that the Soviet Union intends to go to war with Romania over the question of Bessarabia....Earthquake shocks are felt in Orvito, Italy.		Mexico's National Agrarian Party commemorates the death of the party's founder Emiliano Zapata.	
Apr. 11		British ports lock out shipyard workers throughout the country in an effort to end the strike of shipyard workers at Southampton....German industrialists in the Ruhr Valley announce that they will continue to make deliveries to the Allies until the Ruhr situation is finally resolved by the governments of Germany and the occupying forces....Archbishop Zepliak, head of the Roman Catholic Church in the Soviet Union, arrives in Riga after being freed from a Soviet jail.			Japan plans to extend military conscription to the southern part of Sakhalin Island, which is controlled by Japan....Leonard Wood denies that he intends to resign his post as Governor General of the Philippines.
Apr. 12		The government of Spain grants amnesty to Spanish citizens who fled the country in order to avoid military service....Poland receives a loan from France to fund its army.	Arab tribes fight for control of a well near Jerusalem.	Mexican presidential candidate General Calles announces his support for the radical agrarian program of the late Emiliano Zapata.	
Apr. 13		Elections are held in Greece. The majority vote to establish a republic.			The Japanese navy reports that it will need nearly $400 million to replace ships damaged in the earthquake that hit Japan in September 1923.

A	B	C	D	E
Includes developments that affect more than one world region, international organizations and important meetings of world leaders.	*Includes all domestic and regional developments in Europe, including the Soviet Union.*	*Includes all domestic and regional developments in Africa and the Middle East.*	*Includes all domestic and regional developments in Latin America, the Caribbean, and Canada.*	*Includes all domestic and regional developments in Asian and Pacific nations (and colonies).*

U.S. Politics & Social Issues	U.S. Foreign Policy & Affairs, Defense	U.S. Economy & Environment	Science, Technology & Nature	Culture, Leisure & Lifestyle	
	Industrial mobilization for war is practiced in New York City under the direction of banker James L. Walsh, a colonel in the army reserves. Industrialists practice telling plants to convert to munitions production and drawing up contracts at a moment's notice.			An exhibition baseball game at Nashville between the Yankees and the Robins ends in the ninth inning with the score tied when Babe Ruth fans swarm onto the field, making further play impossible.	Apr. 6
The Senate passes a bill limiting radio broadcasting licenses to two years and giving the president the right to control the airwaves in the event of war.		Farmers in Kentucky no longer gather eggs. Prices are too low to justify taking time from other labor to do so.		Two hundred Chicago schoolchildren go on strike calling for the resignation of their principal.	Apr. 7
Washington state's Senator Clarence C. Dill announces that Assistant Secretary of the Navy Theodore Roosevelt, Jr. will be called to testify before the Senate investigating committee regarding his relationship with Harry F. Sinclair and Mammoth Oil.		Southern iron makers plan to lower employees' wages.		The Jacksonville State Normal School in Jacksonville, AL, will bar students who smoke from receiving a teaching certificate from the state.	Apr. 8
Radio broadcasters and their spokesmen appear before the Senate Patents Committee to argue that, because they provide a public service for their listeners, they should not have to pay for the right to broadcast music.	Secretary of the Navy Curtis D. Wilbur and Secretary of Commerce Herbert Hoover testify before the House Committee on Military Affairs in favor of the passage of a law that would give the American president complete control over industry and labor in the event of a war.	Workers digging a tunnel under the Hudson River from New York to New Jersey strike demanding a four-hour day.		An anti-petting bill, which bans parking on the side of the highway, is passed by the New York Assembly.... New Jersey's state boxing commissioner Newton Bugbee says that he will allow a match between white boxer Jack Dempsey and African-American boxer Harry Wills. Bugbee proclaims that race will be no bar to competition so long as Wills behaves properly.	Apr. 9
County Republican conventions in Oklahoma declare their support for Calvin Coolidge as Republican candidate for president.				A fashion show at New York City's McAlpin Hotel reveals that shorter skirts and large picture hats are now the style.	Apr. 10
It is announced that Alabama's Senator Oscar Underwood will appear as a candidate on the ballot in the North Carolina Democratic primaries.		The price of cotton falls.... Colorado bans all crops and livestock from California, which is suffering from an outbreak of foot-and-mouth disease.		A six-week class to prepare young men for marriage begins at Brooklyn, NY's Central Y.M.C.A.	Apr. 11
Ethel Kimball, who posed as "James W. Wilson" when marrying Pearl A. Davis in New Britain, CT, in March, is sentenced to five months in jail for perjury. Pearl Davis is sentenced to one month in prison for subornation of perjury.		Several blast furnaces and sheet mills In Youngstown, OH, will shut down in the coming week. Many of the cities furnaces and mills have already ceased production.		A celebration of Thomas Jefferson's birthday begins in Monticello. The celebration will last for two days.	Apr. 12
The Department of the Interior reports that more than 30,000 Japanese farmers living in California are planning on moving to Mexico, where, unlike California, they will be allowed to own land.		Talks between miners and officials of the Pennsylvania and Hillside Coal and Iron Company result in miners calling off a strike planned for April 14.... The Shoe Workers Protective Union unites with the United Shoe Workers of America to form a new union representing more than 20,000 members.	Italy donates a plane to polar explorer Roald Amundsen to help him in his exploration of the Arctic.	President Calvin Coolidge appoints a committee to formulate an outdoor recreation plan for the nation.... The Palm Sunday parade on the Boardwalk in Atlantic City reveals that silk scarves, sports canes, and brightly colored hats and turbans are the new fashions for women this spring.	Apr. 13

F	G	H	I	J
Includes campaigns, elections, federal-state relations, civil rights and liberties, crime, the judiciary, education, healthcare, poverty, urban affairs, and population.	*Includes formation and debate of U.S. foreign and defense policies, veterans affairs, and defense spending. (Relations with specific foreign countries are usually found under the region concerned.)*	*Includes business, labor, agriculture, taxation, transportation, consumer affairs, monetary and fiscal policy, natural resources, pollution and industrial accidents.*	*Includes worldwide scientific, medical and technological developments, natural phenomena, U.S. weather and natural disasters.*	*Includes the arts, religion, scholarship, communications media, sports, entertainment, fashions, fads, and social life.*

	World Affairs	Europe	Africa & The Middle East	The Americas	Asia & The Pacific
Apr. 14	The government of the United States declares that it will not request that an ambassador from the Irish Free State be sent to Washington. The decision to send such an ambassador must be made by Britain.	Admiral Coundouriotis is appointed the temporary ruler of the Greek republic until a president can be chosen by the Greek Assembly and Senate.... Germany announces that deliveries by German industrialists in the Ruhr Valley to the occupying forces will continue for only two additional months. They will not continue, as the French wish, until a final decision on the matter is reached by the Reparations Committee.		Mexican troops depart Vera Cruz in preparation for an attack on rebel forces in Yucatan.	
Apr. 15	Germany accepts the recommendations of the Dawes Committee's report.	Three men are killed when an airship breaks free from its moorings at Ciampino, Italy.			A severe earthquake strikes the floor of the Pacific Ocean. Tremors are registered in England, Belgium, Italy, Egypt, and Chile.
Apr. 16		Greece commemorates the centennial anniversary of Lord Byron's death.		A blizzard strikes the Canadian provinces of Manitoba, Saskatchewan, and Ontario.	
Apr. 17	Italy announces that it accepts the Dawes Committee's report and its conclusions regarding the payment of reparations.				An editorial in a Japanese newspaper proclaims that the proposed exclusion of Japanese immigrants under new U.S. immigration policies is a deliberate affront and warns the Japanese to prepare for a confrontation with the United States.
Apr. 18		France sentences 12 Germans convicted of committing acts of sabotage in the Ruhr Valley to hard labor in the penal colony of French Guiana for terms ranging from three to 20 years.... The Hungarian Assembly votes in favor of a reconstruction plan suggested, based on suggestions made by the League of Nations.			
Apr. 19		British shipyard workers end their strike.... The Soviet Republic of Georgia announces that Georgian will be its official language. Russian will be used as a secondary language.		Fausto Davila, the provisional president of the Honduras, announces that the country, except for the capital city of Tegucigalpa, is now under government control.	
Apr. 20			Moscow reports that pro-British forces in Afghanistan are fomenting a rebellion against the Emir of Afghanistan.... Two Iraqi politicians who favor a treaty between Iraq and Britain are stabbed.		
Apr. 21		Italian prime minister Benito Mussolini receives the honor of being named a Citizen of Rome.... General Shpak is sentenced to death in the Soviet Union for the role he played in anti-Jewish pogroms. The sentence is later changed to 10 years' imprisonment.		Rebel generals Marcial Cavazos and Lorenzo Alaniz are killed by Mexican government troops near Puebla Nueva.... Mexican presidential hopeful General Plutarco Elias Calles proclaims his support for striking oil workers.... Cuban streetcar conductors and marble and ironworkers go on strike.	The Tokyo Municipal Council authorizes plans to build a network of subways beneath the city.

A	B	C	D	E
Includes developments that affect more than one world region, international organizations and important meetings of world leaders.	*Includes all domestic and regional developments in Europe, including the Soviet Union.*	*Includes all domestic and regional developments in Africa and the Middle East.*	*Includes all domestic and regional developments in Latin America, the Caribbean, and Canada.*	*Includes all domestic and regional developments in Asian and Pacific nations (and colonies).*

Date	U.S. Politics & Social Issues	U.S. Foreign Policy & Affairs, Defense	U.S. Economy & Environment	Science, Technology & Nature	Culture, Leisure & Lifestyle
Apr. 14		The House Naval Committee approves the construction of a navy pier in San Diego, CA. The Committee also authorizes the construction of eight fast cruisers and six gunboats.	Miners employed by the Lehigh Coal and Navigation Company, located in Pennsylvania, go on strike after miners, whose worksite was flooded, were dismissed instead of being given other jobs.	The jawbones of a primate of a species labeled Dryopithecus, or "forest ape," which some scientists believe to have been a common ancestor of humans and apes, are exhibited at the American Museum of Natural History in New York City.	The trial to determine whether or not millionaire Harry K. Thaw is sane and may be released from a mental institution commences.
Apr. 15			Testifying before a House committee investigating the Department of Agriculture, Benjamin C. Marsh of the Farmers' National Council, charges that Secretary of Agriculture Henry Wallace is in league with meat packers and stockyard owners and uses his position to advance their interest over those of the livestock growers.	U.S. Army aviators on a flight around the world leave Seward Bay, AK.	The major league baseball season begins.... Dr. Emanuel Lasker wins world chess championship.
Apr. 16		Former director of the Veterans' Bureau, Charles R. Forbes, and two others are indicted in federal court on charges of attempting to defraud the government of the United States.	Workers at the Vacuum Oil Company in Bayonne, NJ, go on strike. They are demanding a pay increase from the company.	Two U.S. Navy warships are dispatched to the Pacific to search for the best location for an undersea cable connecting Seattle, WA, with Seward, AK.... Dr. L.E. Schmidt of Chicago demonstrates the use of a surgical implement that uses current produced by a radio transmitter to cut through flesh while simultaneously cauterizing blood vessels.	
Apr. 17	The Senate passes a bill that will restrict immigration to the United States. No more than two percent of the number of foreign-born members of a given nationality living in the United Sates in 1890. Japanese will be prevented from permanently settling in the United States.... Representative R. Walton Moore of Virginia asks the House to adopt a resolution in support of the United States joining the World Court.	Major Frederick L. Martin, commander of the army's round-the-world flight team, and Sergeant Alva Harvey are resting after being rescued from the Alaskan wilderness. Mechanical problems forced Martin and Harvey to land, causing them to become separated from the other members of their group.		Arjun Govind Thaker Dass, a Hindu graduate student at Columbia University and Union Theological Seminary who is studying the interaction of music and psychology, plays the sitar for an hour and a half outside the cage of a king cobra at the Bronx Zoo in order to test the effect of music on the snake.	The owner of Metro Pictures, Harry Loew, founds a new motion picture studio, Metro-Goldwyn-Mayer.... The Y.W.C.A. denounces the traditional end-of-summer bathing suit parade at Atlantic City.
Apr. 18	Debate over the Veterans' Bonus Bill begins in the Senate.... California drivers attempt to evade the blockade at Yuma, AZ, rather than submit to inspection and fumigation in an attempt to prevent foot-and-mouth disease, which is currently plaguing California, from spreading beyond its borders.				Clarence H. DeMar wins the Boston Marathon.... Passover begins at sunset.... New York City's West End Presbyterian Church broadcasts an evening communion service for those unable to attend services. Those listening at home substitute white bread for the Eucharist and grape juice for the wine.
Apr. 19		Democrats in the Senate drop plans to allow veterans the option of selecting a cash payment as a bonus in lieu of an insurance policy.	The National Industrial Conference Board announces that unemployment has decreased and wages have increased.	British pilot Stuart MacLaren departs Cairo on the next leg of his round-the-world-flight.	French boxer Georges Carpentier agrees to a ten-round match against American fighter Tommy Gibbons.
Apr. 20			Copper production continues to decline after a brief increase in March.		
Apr. 21	Luke Adams, an African American, is lynched in Norway, SC, after being accused of assaulting a white woman.... It is announced that the Senate Oil Committee will investigate the leasing of federal oil reserves in California to the Honolulu Oil Company.	Major William N. Hensley, Jr. declares that, without Congressional aid, within a few years the United States will not have an air force.	In Chicago, the price of sheep falls to new lows while the price of cattle holds steady.... The production and export of cotton seed oil is in decline.... President of the New York Stock Exchange, Seymour L. Cromwell, warns small investors against speculating on stocks.	Forest fires are burning in the Great Smoky Mountains of Tennessee.	Children role Easter eggs on the White House lawn.... In response to accusations that his writing about sports for money has compromised his status as an amateur athlete, tennis player William Tilden withdraws from both the United States Davis Cup and Olympic teams.

F	G	H	I	J
Includes campaigns, elections, federal-state relations, civil rights and liberties, crime, the judiciary, education, healthcare, poverty, urban affairs, and population.	*Includes formation and debate of U.S. foreign and defense policies, veterans affairs, and defense spending. (Relations with specific foreign countries are usually found under the region concerned.)*	*Includes business, labor, agriculture, taxation, transportation, consumer affairs, monetary and fiscal policy, natural resources, pollution and industrial accidents.*	*Includes worldwide scientific, medical and technological developments, natural phenomena, U.S. weather and natural disasters.*	*Includes the arts, religion, scholarship, communications media, sports, entertainment, fashions, fads, and social life.*

	World Affairs	Europe	Africa & The Middle East	The Americas	Asia & The Pacific
Apr. 22	A meeting of the International Congress for Air Legislation opens in Rome. Representatives of 26 countries are in attendance.			Cuban cigar and cigarette makers, taxicab drivers, and beer wagon drivers go on strike. No Spanish-language newspapers are being printed in Havana.	The Japanese press foresees greater closeness between Japan and the Soviet Union as the result of American immigration legislation that prevents the Japanese from settling in the United States.
Apr. 23		The British Empire Exhibition opens in Wembley, England.…The Soviet Union seizes control of all grain elevators and grain warehouses in the country.…Two express trains collide in Switzerland. All passengers aboard one train burn to death as the train explodes.			At a mass meeting in Osaka, Japan, people call upon American citizens to reject the decision of the U.S. Congress to bar Japanese immigration.…Premier W.F. Massey of New Zealand criticizes the decision of New Zealand's railroad workers to go on strike at a time when the country is anticipating the arrival of a special squadron from the British fleet.
Apr. 24	A Chicago man asks to become a citizen of the League of Nations. He maintains that as a pacifist, he cannot be a citizen of any one country.…German demands that the League of Nations return German colonies seized by the Allies following the World War.	Emma Goldman criticizes the Soviet Union while speaking in front of an audience of workers in Berlin. The crowd shouts her down.…The Bulgaria grants amnesty to Communists who participated in a 1923 revolt against the government.…Talks in London to settle the question of the boundary between Northern Ireland and the Irish Free State dissolve after the two sides find it impossible to come to an agreement.		Mexican federal troops attack rebels in the town of San Cristobal las Casas in Chiapas.	
Apr. 25				The governments of Guatemala, Nicaragua, and El Salvador to agree to participate in talks between warring factions in Honduras.	
Apr. 26		France demands that a member of the Rhineland Separatist movement who is being held by Germany be released.…The Italian government announces that it will allow gambling in resort towns, but visitors will need a permit to visit the casinos.	The Crown Prince of Ethiopia visits Jerusalem.		A steamship sinks off the coast of Korea after hitting a Japanese destroyer. Two hundred Korean students drown.
Apr. 27					Turkey ends its year-long experiment of alcohol prohibition, claiming that the loss of revenue caused by the ban of alcohol led to dangerously high budget deficits.
Apr. 28			Fighting between French troops and Turkish irregulars in northern Syria is reported.		Public protests against proposed changes in U.S. immigration policy that would prohibit Japanese from immigrating to the United States are held throughout Japan.
Apr. 29	The London *Times* urges that Great Britain extend diplomatic recognition to Mexico.				
	A *Includes developments that affect more than one world region, international organizations and important meetings of world leaders.*	B *Includes all domestic and regional developments in Europe, including the Soviet Union.*	C *Includes all domestic and regional developments in Africa and the Middle East.*	D *Includes all domestic and regional developments in Latin America, the Caribbean, and Canada.*	E *Includes all domestic and regional developments in Asian and Pacific nations (and colonies).*

U.S. Politics & Social Issues	U.S. Foreign Policy & Affairs, Defense	U.S. Economy & Environment	Science, Technology & Nature	Culture, Leisure & Lifestyle	
Witnesses testifying before the House Judiciary Committee state that the Volstead Act should be changed to allow the sale and consumption of 2.75 percent beer. The witnesses claim that the Volstead Act is responsible for increasing lawlessness, destroying youth's respect for the law, harming farmers and laborers, and increasing rates of alcoholism and insanity.			Marcel Moreau has found a way to generate heat from sunlight and to regulate its temperature.		Apr. 22
A bill in introduced in the House of Representatives that will grant the Philippines commonwealth status and allow the Filipinos to govern themselves. After 30 years, the Filipinos will vote to determine whether the Philippines should be granted its independence.		The price of cattle, sheep, and hogs declines at the Chicago stockyards.…Prices of wheat, oats, corn, and rye fall.…Mortimer A. Sullivan, mayor of Newport, RI, requests the help of the federal government in alleviating the damage being done to Newport's shore by oil leaking from a tanker that has run aground.		An Ohio schoolteacher commits suicide after his wife bobs her hair.	Apr. 23
	The State Department delays the negotiation of a new treaty between the United States and Panama by one month.	Samuel Gompers, the president of the American Federation of Labor, denounces the Sherman Anti-Trust Act and warns that it may interfere with the production of goods.	Charles E. St. John, a physicist at the Mt. Wilson Observatory in California, declares that his study of the sun confirms part of Albert Einstein's theory of relativity.	Maurice Ravel's, *Tzigane, Concert Rhapsody for Violin and Orchestra* debuts in London.…Director D.W. Griffith sues actor Al Jolson for violating an oral agreement to appear in several of Griffith's motion pictures.	Apr. 24
Candidate for the Republican presidential nomination, Senator Hiram W. Evans announces that he will leave the Republican Party if corruption is not rooted out.	Charles R. Forbes, the former director of the Veterans' Bureau, pleads not guilty to charges that he had conspired to defraud the United States government.		Anthropologists debate the existence of racial superiority at a meeting of the American Philosophical Society in Philadelphia. The majority maintain that there is no superior race.	The Teapot Dome Café opens in Chicago. Patrons are served coffee via pipes, and sugar is kept in derrick-shaped containers.	Apr. 25
A witness testifying before a Senate committee investigating charges brought against Montana Senator Burton K. Wheeler, claims that Wheeler offered to assist oilman Gordon Campbell in obtaining a lease on federal oil lands.…At a meeting of 10,000 Ku Klux Klansmen on Long Island, those present promise to oppose Roman Catholic politician Al Smith's campaign for the presidency.		Workers on five Newark bus lines go on strike to protest longer hours and lower wages.…The National Industrial Conference Board reports that in the past decade the cost of rent has risen by 85 percent.		The Intercollegiate Basketball League announces that it is planning a change in rules.	Apr. 26
Presidential hopeful William McAdoo pledges immediate aid to farmers if he is elected president.…Speaking at a meeting of the National League of Women voters, Carrie Chapman Catt assails the Coolidge administration for showing no interest in joining the League of Nations.		General Motors reports an increase in profits during the first three months of 1924.			Apr. 27
The Board of Directors of the National League of Women Voters adopts a resolution supporting enforcement of the Volstead Act and urging the United States to join the World Court.					Apr. 28
	The proposed bill granting a bonus to veterans is amended to include Puerto Rican auxiliaries who guarded the Panama Canal.	The bodies of 35 dead miners are recovered from a mine in Wheeling, WV.…General Motors reports and increase in the number of automobile exports.		Episcopal priests meet for the first time in conference. Speakers at the conference intend to urge continued belief in the virgin birth of Jesus.	Apr. 29

F	G	H	I	J
Includes campaigns, elections, federal-state relations, civil rights and liberties, crime, the judiciary, education, healthcare, poverty, urban affairs, and population.	*Includes formation and debate of U.S. foreign and defense policies, veterans affairs, and defense spending. (Relations with specific foreign countries are usually found under the region concerned.)*	*Includes business, labor, agriculture, taxation, transportation, consumer affairs, monetary and fiscal policy, natural resources, pollution and industrial accidents.*	*Includes worldwide scientific, medical and technological developments, natural phenomena, U.S. weather and natural disasters.*	*Includes the arts, religion, scholarship, communications media, sports, entertainment, fashions, fads, and social life.*

	World Affairs	Europe	Africa & The Middle East	The Americas	Asia & The Pacific
Apr. 30	Upon returning from a visit to the Middle East, Oscar Straus, the former U.S. ambassador to Turkey, reports that King Hussein of the Hedjaz demands the ouster of the British and French from the region, but promises that if he is allowed to annex Syria and Palestine to his kingdom, he will protect the rights of Christians and Jews living there.			The government of Jamaica proposes that West Indian veterans of the World War be settled by land belonging to the British crown.… Rebel forces in Santa Clara province clash with troops of the Cuban government.…Honduran revolutionaries name General Vicente Tosta provisional president of the nation.	
May 1	Masso Llorens, Deputy for Barcelona, complains to the League of Nations that the Spanish government is prohibiting the use of the Catalan language and is interfering with Catalan councils and juries.	Bakers in the Portuguese army supply bread for the inhabitants of Lisbon whose bakers are on strike.…In the Soviet Union, May Day is celebrated with visits to V. I. Lenin's tomb.…Fighting between police and Communist demonstrators takes place throughout Germany as the police attempt to stop Communists from staging May Day celebrations. Several people are injured or killed.…Britain's Labor Party fails to support the Liberal Party's calls for proportional representation in Parliament.…The Olympic flag is raised in Paris.	France refutes claims that a clash between French troops and Turkish forces has taken place in Syria.	Honduran revolutionaries seize the capital city of Tegucigalpa after a 12-hour battle.	More than 20,000 Japanese workers celebrate May Day in Tokyo, Kyoto, Osaka, and other cities while police watch for signs of violence. To prevent trouble, police arrest several radical leaders before the celebrations begin.
May 2	British Prime Minister Ramsay MacDonald and Belgian Prime Minister Georges Theunis meet to discuss the Dawes Committee's report.	The British airmail pilots strike ends.…The first Jewish Students' World Congress meets in Antwerp.			
May 3		A memorial mass for Irish rebel leaders executed during the 1916 Easter Rising is held in Dublin.		A nationwide general strike is held in Argentina. Workers are protesting a law allowing the government to deduct money from workers' salaries to provide for a national pension fund.	
May 4		The Summer Olympics open in Paris. France defeats Romania in rugby.… Elections are held in Germany.		Canada voices opposition to American plans to build a canal from Chicago to the Gulf of Mexico.…The Cuban government offers amnesty to rebels who cease fighting.	
May 5	German delegates to the Women's International League for Peace and Freedom conference suggest that stability in Europe could best be achieved by joining all the European countries in one, unified state.… Britain asks the United States to give Indians owning real estate in America time to sell their property. Under U.S. law people who cannot become citizens of the United States are not allowed to own U.S. real estate.	The Bavarian Cabinet resigns.		The revolution in Cuba reaches the province of Oriente. The Cuban government dispatches troops.	Chinese pirates kidnap 40 people from a passenger boat after killing the captain and the guard.
May 6					

A	B	C	D	E
Includes developments that affect more than one world region, international organizations and important meetings of world leaders.	*Includes all domestic and regional developments in Europe, including the Soviet Union.*	*Includes all domestic and regional developments in Africa and the Middle East.*	*Includes all domestic and regional developments in Latin America, the Caribbean, and Canada.*	*Includes all domestic and regional developments in Asian and Pacific nations (and colonies).*

U.S. Politics & Social Issues	U.S. Foreign Policy & Affairs, Defense	U.S. Economy & Environment	Science, Technology & Nature	Culture, Leisure & Lifestyle	
Franklin D. Roosevelt is made director of the committee to secure the nomination of Al Smith as the Democratic candidate for president.		Fifteen-thousand workers at the Glen Alden Coal Company go on strike.…The Bethlehem Steel Corporation announces that it will sell $30 million worth of bonds. Proceeds from the sale will be used to improve company properties.	The town of Flicklen, GA, is destroyed by a tornado.		Apr. 30
Assistant Secretary of the Interior Edward C. Finney informs the Senate Oil Committee that Albert B. Fall did not have the permission of President Warren G. Harding to lease naval oil reserves in California to the Honolulu Oil Company.	The Senate passes a bill granting a bonus to veterans in the form of fully endowed insurance policies.	The National Association of Cotton Manufacturers calls for an increase in the cotton goods tariff.…President Calvin Coolidge calls on the Senate Commerce Committee to create reserves in Alaska to protect salmon stocks.		At a conference of the Methodist Episcopal Church, Methodists are urged to renew their devotion to the Methodist creed. The conference also proclaims that the United States should join the World Court.…New York City holds a celebration in Central Park in celebration of National Child Health Day.…Millionaire Harry K. Thaw is released from the mental institution where he has been held for seven years for sexually assaulting and beating a teenager.…Thousands attend the funeral ceremony for Italian actress Eleanora Duse in New York City.	May 1
The trial of oilman Harry F. Sinclair for contempt begins.…The Senate votes to allow radio broadcasts of its meetings.…Assistant Attorney General Albert Ottinger states that Congress has the authority to grant independence to the Philippines. The former vice governor of the Philippines, Newton W. Gilbert, informs the House Committee on Insular Affairs that, while the Filipinos have the ability to govern themselves, the Philippines are not economically ready for independence.	The House of Representatives passes a bill granting a bonus to veterans in the form of fully endowed insurance policies.…President Calvin Coolidge announces that the attempt by naval pilots to circumnavigate the globe will not be aborted as a result of the disappearance of Major Frederick L. Martin, the expedition's commanding officer.				May 2
American Jews meet with the Romanian ambassador to the United States to protest attacks on Jews in several Romanian cities. They ask that the Romanian government end the violence.	The War Department will provide the Cuban government with machine guns and ammunition.	Four companies that manufacture mining machinery are charged in federal court with having formed a monopoly in violation of the Sherman Anti-Trust Act.…Cotton prices fall slightly.	French pilot, Lieutenant Pelletier D'Oisy, lands at Agra, India. D'Oisy is attempting to circumnavigate the globe.		May 3
				A discussion of the works of Sigmund Freud is held at St. Mark's-in-the-Bouwerie in New York City.…The Postmaster General announces that regular, coast-to-coast airmail flights will begin in July.	May 4
The Lehigh Valley Railroad Company files suit in the Supreme Court to prevent the Federal District Court in New York from allowing the Soviet government to sue the company for the loss of munitions purchased by Russia's czarist government and destroyed in an explosion in the railroad's yards in New Jersey.…Calvin Coolidge wins the presidential primaries in Maryland and Texas.	Senator Tasker Lowndes Oddie of Nevada charges that the Veteran's Bureau is run by a ring of corrupt officials for their own profit.		The U.S. Army reports that it has used chlorine gas to cure animal influenza in horses and mules.		May 5
The American Federation of Labor states that in the upcoming presidential election it will favor candidates who support modification of the Volstead Act, a graduated income tax, the abolition of child labor, repeal of the Sherman Anti-Trust Act, America's entry into the League of Nations and the World Court, and an exclusionary immigration policy.	The House Committee on Insular Affairs votes in favor of extending self-rule to the Philippines in the form of a bicameral legislature and a popularly elected governor. The Committee also votes in favor of appointing an American commissioner with the power to suspend acts of the legislature and to call in U.S. troops.	Car sales increase after a decline in April.			May 6

F	G	H	I	J
Includes campaigns, elections, federal-state relations, civil rights and liberties, crime, the judiciary, education, healthcare, poverty, urban affairs, and population.	*Includes formation and debate of U.S. foreign and defense policies, veterans affairs, and defense spending. (Relations with specific foreign countries are usually found under the region concerned.)*	*Includes business, labor, agriculture, taxation, transportation, consumer affairs, monetary and fiscal policy, natural resources, pollution and industrial accidents.*	*Includes worldwide scientific, medical and technological developments, natural phenomena, U.S. weather and natural disasters.*	*Includes the arts, religion, scholarship, communications media, sports, entertainment, fashions, fads, and social life.*

	World Affairs	Europe	Africa & The Middle East	The Americas	Asia & The Pacific
May 7		Winston Churchill proclaims that Socialism is a threat to Britain and calls upon Conservatives and Liberals to work together to defeat Socialism.	The Emir of Afghanistan has regained control of key points, and many members of the rebel forces are reported to be defecting to his side.	The Cuban government reports that they have crushed the rebellion in the province of Santa Clara.	The Australian government reports that it is in favor of increased arms limitation.…A strong earthquake strikes Manila shortly after noon.
May 8	Spain reports that casualties have been suffered in a battle between Spain and Moroccan rebels.	Grand Duke Cyril calls upon loyal Russians to assist him in establishing himself as the new Czar of Russia.		Mexican president Alvaro Obregón orders the sale of state property to raise funds to pay government employees.	
May 9	The London *Times* predicts conflict between Japan and the United States over the issue of Japanese exclusion.	Author H.G. Wells presents a petition to the British Parliament that calls upon the legislative body to allow doctors employed at government maternity clinics to provide patients with birth control information if they ask for it.	Britain's Colonial Office reports that 100 civilians have been killed in a clash with government troops in a town north of Baghdad.	Ricardo Jimenez is inaugurated as the president of Costa Rica.	
May 10	Claiming to be the rightful heir to the throne of Spain, Don Alfonso Louis Jerome de Bourbon asks the League of Nations to present his case to the Spanish people.…The League of Nations rejects the idea proposed by Senator Henry Cabot Lodge that the World Court be abandoned and a new international court created.	Violence erupts in Albania over the question of whether to move the capital from Tirana.			Riots break out across Japan as national elections are held. Gangs fight in the streets and invade candidates' headquarters. Much anti-American sentiment is expressed, and the Kenseikei Party, led by the anti-American Viscount Kato, wins the majority of the vote.
May 11		Elections are held in France. Prime Minister Raymond Poincaré is defeated.…German newspapers urge the imposition of a tariff that would result in forcing American crops out of the German market.… In Rome, thousands view the body of actress Eleanora Duse.			
May 12		Bombs explode in Coimbra, Portugal. The police find more bombs in a rented room in Lisbon.…Earthquake tremors are felt in Munich.		The Cuban government reports that Frederico Laredo Bru, the leader of a group of Cuban rebels, is in hiding.	The London *Daily Telegraph* reports that a cholera epidemic in India that has already killed 10,000 people is spreading to new parts of the country.
May 13		The British government allocates money for the construction of an airship that will be able to fly from Britain to Egypt, India, and Australia.…The government of the Irish Free State offers a reward for information regarding an attack on British soldiers in Queenstown.			
May 14	Japan's Privy Council approves the Treaty of Lausanne. Ratification by the Prince Regent will put the treaty, which has already been ratified by Britain and Italy, into effect.				Proposals for a Japanese-French alliance are abandoned when the governor of French Indochina announces that Japanese immigrants are not needed in Indochina.
May 15	An international conference on immigration opens in Rome.				

A	B	C	D	E
Includes developments that affect more than one world region, international organizations and important meetings of world leaders.	*Includes all domestic and regional developments in Europe, including the Soviet Union.*	*Includes all domestic and regional developments in Africa and the Middle East.*	*Includes all domestic and regional developments in Latin America, the Caribbean, and Canada.*	*Includes all domestic and regional developments in Asian and Pacific nations (and colonies).*

U.S. Politics & Social Issues	U.S. Foreign Policy & Affairs, Defense	U.S. Economy & Environment	Science, Technology & Nature	Culture, Leisure & Lifestyle	
Representative Victor Berger of Wisconsin asks that the World War Espionage Act be repealed.				Episcopal bishop Paul Matthews recommends that those who deny the virgin birth of Jesus be charged with heresy.	May 7
		The price of cotton rises in southern markets....Thirteen ships are trapped in the ice on Lake Superior as a blizzard strikes Duluth, MN.		At a conference of the African Methodist Episcopal Church, women demand the right to participate in the business affairs of the church.	May 8
		Members of the House Agricultural Committee voice their disapproval of the McNary-Haugen bill that would sell surplus crops abroad. They claim that the bill would enlarge the federal payroll and earn money for businessmen and speculators.		The Quadrennial General Conference of the Methodist Episcopal Church rejects pleas that it ordains women as ministers but does vote to ordain women as preachers.	May 9
J. Edgar Hoover becomes head of the Federal Bureau of Investigation....The Ku Klux Klan burns a cross on property belonging to the Roman Catholic Church in Armonk, NY, to protest the building of a new church on the property.		The National Industrial Conference Board reports that the price of clothing has risen over the past two years.		The Association of Museum Directors states its opposition to any efforts to ship the statue Hermes Praxiteles to the United States from Greece. The directors fear that moving the statue may damage it.	May 10
William Jennings Bryan accuses Secretary of the Treasury Andrew Mellon of exerting tyrannical control over the agenda of the Republican Party.	The American Naval Mission to Brazil presents the Brazilian government with plans on how to reorganize Brazil's naval academy and the general staff of the Brazilian navy.	The Labor Bureau predicts that production will decline and unemployment increase in the future if industry continues to expand....Prices for cattle, sheep, and hogs rise at Chicago.	General Electric announces that, together with Harvard University and the University of Maine, it will conduct experiments with fused quartz in an attempt to produce ultraviolet light artificially. The ability to manufacture ultraviolet light indoors will bring an end to rickets.	The Pulitzer Prize in poetry is awarded to Robert Frost. *The Able McLaughlins* by Margaret Wilson wins the prize for best novel. *Hell-Bent fer Heaven* by Hatcher Hughes in named best play....The Church of St. Marks-in-the-Bouwerie holds a service featuring Native American prayers, myths, hymns, and dances from the Omaha, Iroquois, and Zuni cultures.	May 11
Wisconsin Representative Victor Berger calls on President Calvin Coolidge to hold a conference to revise the terms of the Treaty of Versailles.				Nellie Morse wins the Preakness....Walter Hagen wins the Professional Golf Association championship....The American Bible Society reports that in 1923 it distributed more than seven million Bibles, including the first translation of the Bible in Quechua.	May 12
D.C. Stephenson, Grand Dragon of the Ku Klux Klan in Indiana, sues the Klan's Imperial Wizard Hiram W. Evans and two other prominent Klan officials for slander and libel.		The Potomac River floods damaging property in Washington, DC, and Harper's Ferry, VA.	An Italian seismologist announces that he has perfected a device that can predict that an earthquake will strike 15 minutes before the quake begins....A prehistoric whale fossil is discovered in California.	The Actor's Equity Association asks the Methodist Episcopal Church to change its policy excluding actors from church membership and forbidding church members to attend the theater.	May 13
In New York City, 500 men attack Albert Walton, an African American accused of assaulting a young white woman in the hallway of her apartment building. A policeman is able to rescue Walton only after threatening to shoot into the crowd.	The Coast Guard receives a tugboat, a minesweeper, and 13 destroyers from the navy to assist it in ending liquor smuggling by sea.		British flyer Stuart MacLaren arrives at Allahabad, India, on his flight around the world.	Speaking at a convention of the American Booksellers Association, Thomas Dixon, author of *The Clansman*, warns of the perils of government censorship....Babe Ruth is awarded a Master of Swat degree on Babe Ruth Day at Yankee Stadium.	May 14
Kentucky delegates to the Democratic National Convention are instructed to vote for William G. McAdoo. Two delegates are reserved for Oscar Underwood.		The Nashua Manufacturing Company announces that its mills, which produce cotton textiles, will run only three days a week....The Alabama Power Company (APC) informs the Senate Agricultural Committee that the Allied Power Company, of which APC is a part, will pay for the right to buy and sell power produced by federally owned facilities at Muscle Shoals.	Montefiore Hospital announces that a woman suffering from cancer in its advanced stages has been completely cured of the disease through the use of radiation.	Eugene O'Neill's *All God's Chillun Got Wings* debuts at the Provincetown Playhouse in New York City. The play stars actor and former football player Paul Robeson as an African-American man married to a white woman. The Ku Klux Klan protests the play's premiere, and the Salvation Army warns of potential race riots....Evangelist Billy Sunday enters the Mayo Clinic.	May 15

F	G	H	I	J
Includes campaigns, elections, federal-state relations, civil rights and liberties, crime, the judiciary, education, healthcare, poverty, urban affairs, and population.	*Includes formation and debate of U.S. foreign and defense policies, veterans affairs, and defense spending. (Relations with specific foreign countries are usually found under the region concerned.)*	*Includes business, labor, agriculture, taxation, transportation, consumer affairs, monetary and fiscal policy, natural resources, pollution and industrial accidents.*	*Includes worldwide scientific, medical and technological developments, natural phenomena, U.S. weather and natural disasters.*	*Includes the arts, religion, scholarship, communications media, sports, entertainment, fashions, fads, and social life.*

	World Affairs	Europe	Africa & The Middle East	The Americas	Asia & The Pacific
May 16		The House of Commons votes to reject a plan for the nationalization of British mines.…American oilman Harry F. Sinclair receives the right to drill for oil in Italy.…Ras Tafari, Crown Prince of Ethiopia, visits France.	Persian Muslims attack Teheran's Jewish residents. Six people are hurt.	The Argentine consul in New York City advocates closer relations among the nations of the western hemisphere.	Sun Yat-sen's secretary denies rumors that Sun is dead and pronounces him to be alive and in good health.…Chinese bandits in Fukien province attack and capture American, Australian, and Chinese employees of the China Import and Export Company of Shanghai.
May 17		Italy and Czechoslovakia agree to a treaty of friendship between the two nations.…The Polish government states that it intends to make a payment on its debt to the United States.		The Cuban government announces that amnesty will be extended to all Cubans charged with rebellion. The amnesty includes Cuban exiles now living in the United States.	
May 18	Dr. Antonio de Bustamente suggests that the Permanent Court of International Justice meet in the United States.	Residents of Hanover, Germany, vote to keep the city part of the state of Prussia.…Wilhelm II, the former Kaiser of Germany, joins Adolf Hitler's German Fascist Party.			
May 19	Japan agrees to ratify the Lausanne Treaty, thus making it effective.	The Becker Steel Works, one of the largest industries in Germany's Ruhr Valley, declares bankruptcy.…French troops take control of several buildings in Düsseldorf after the city fails to construct barracks that the French army had ordered them to build.			Japan announces that Admiral Saito, its Governor General in Korea, was shot at by Korean rebels. Saito was not harmed.…Japan and French Indochina reach an informal agreement regarding trade.…Three Japanese ocean liners are planning to sail for the United States with Japanese women on board before the new U.S. law excluding immigrants from Japan becomes effective on July 1.
May 20		Students in an anatomy class at Budapest University order that four Jewish classmates be killed so that their bodies may be used for dissection.…The Soviet Union offers to provide money to pay any prewar debts owed to Britain by Russia if the British will in turn help the Soviet Union in securing a loan.…A strike by tobacco workers leads to riots in Athens.	Danish archeologists report finding the remains of a synagogue in which Jesus preached.		
May 21		France sends arms to Romania and Poland to prepare for possible clashes with the Soviet Union over the issue of Bessarabia.…Striking workers riot in the Ruhr Valley. German police and Belgian soldiers are called in to restore order.			
May 22		Igor Stravinsky's *Concerto for Piano, Wind Instruments, and Double-Basses* debuts in Paris.…Anarchist Germaine Breton is jailed in Bordeaux, France.	The Persian government reports that it has been forced to abandon the town of Khoremabab to Lur rebels.	General Angel Flores announces that if he is elected president of Mexico, he will prevent future revolutions by improving economic conditions in Mexico and will also repay all of the country's foreign debts.	
	A *Includes developments that affect more than one world region, international organizations and important meetings of world leaders.*	B *Includes all domestic and regional developments in Europe, including the Soviet Union.*	C *Includes all domestic and regional developments in Africa and the Middle East.*	D *Includes all domestic and regional developments in Latin America, the Caribbean, and Canada.*	E *Includes all domestic and regional developments in Asian and Pacific nations (and colonies).*

U.S. Politics & Social Issues	U.S. Foreign Policy & Affairs, Defense	U.S. Economy & Environment	Science, Technology & Nature	Culture, Leisure & Lifestyle	
The National Legislative Committee of the American Legion implores Congress to override President Calvin Coolidge's veto of the Bonus Bill....Voters in Oregon choose Calvin Coolidge to be the Republican presidential nominee and William G. McAdoo to be the Democratic presidential nominee....Representatives from several national organizations meet in New York City for the All-America Conference. The Conference urges those attending to oppose American recognition of the Soviet Union and all Soviet propaganda and to call for immigration restrictions and the teaching of "unemasculated" American history.		The production of crude oil increases....The International Ladies' Garment Workers Union calls on workers to strike on June 1 if the union's demands for a 40-hour workweek and a guarantee of 40 weeks of employment per year are not met....The Department of Labor announces that unemployment increased in April....Metro Corporation merges with Goldwyn Pictures Corporation.	Blitzen, OR, registers a temperature of 108 F....Dr. Charles Mayo predicts that a cure for cancer will be produced once the germ that causes the disease is found.		May 16
New York Representative Fiorello La Guardia calls on the House to pass a resolution outlawing all future wars.	Congress overrides President Calvin Coolidge's veto of the Veterans' Bonus Bill.	The National Industrial Conference Board reports that the price of coal has decreased over the past five months.		Black Gold wins the Kentucky Derby.	May 17
Members of the Democratic National Committee discuss plans to thwart the nomination of William G. McAdoo.			Professor Yandell Henderson of Yale University suggests that vertical exhaust pipes on automobiles may prevent deaths from carbon monoxide.	Coney Island officially opens for the 1924 season.	May 18
		The price of corn rises at Chicago as wheat sales fall.	Two Australian pilots complete their flight around Australia.	Representatives of the Russian Holy Synod led by Archbishop Nikolai arrive in the United States....Millionaire Harry K. Thaw is declared sane and is released from the mental institution where he was being held. Thaw has been incarcerated in several mental institutions during the past 17 years.	May 19
The House and Senate pass the bill providing for a soldier's bonus over President Calvin Coolidge's veto.	Debate takes place in the House of Representatives regarding the strength of the U.S. Navy in comparison to the navies of Britain and Japan.	Members of the Cloak, Suit and Skirt Manufacturers' Protective Association refuse to meet the demands of members of the International Ladies' Garment Workers Union, who are asking for higher wages, a 40-hour week, and a guaranteed number of weeks of employment.	Officials in Wilmington, DE, call on landowners to cut down wild cherry trees on their property in an effort to stop the spread of caterpillars to threaten to destroy all trees and bushes in the state.	A municipal court in Chicago rules that a wife does not need her husband's permission to bob her hair....Dancer Isadora Duncan is injured in an automobile accident in the Soviet Union.	May 20
The Senate Agriculture Committee rejects Henry Ford's offer to purchase the power plant at Muscle Shoals, AL.	As requests from veterans for bonus payments arrive, the War Department asks newspapers to urge veterans to wait before filing for their bonus allotment....New York Representatives Boylan and La Guardia call upon Congress to pass a resolution asking that Eamon de Valera, in jail in Ireland, be set free.			Baseball player Babe Ruth joins the National Guard....Golfer Bobby Jones wins the Georgia-Alabama Professional Golfers' Association championship title.	May 21
The National Conference on Outdoor Life opens in Washington, DC, with a speech by President Calvin Coolidge. The purpose of the conference is to encourage Americans to take part in sports and outdoor recreation in order to improve the health of citizens.	Charles Wesley Flint, the Chancellor of Syracuse University, joins the U.S. Army Reserve. Flint, in a gesture of support for the Reserve Officers Training Corps (ROTC) program at Syracuse, states that, even though he abhors war, all citizens must be willing to defend the country, if necessary.	The National Electric Light Association reports that less than three percent of farmers are currently receiving electricity generated by a power company.	The Federal Horticultural Board reports that Gypsy moths are spreading from New England to New York and New Jersey.	The General Assembly of the Presbyterian Church meets at Grand Rapids, MI.	May 22
F *Includes campaigns, elections, federal-state relations, civil rights and liberties, crime, the judiciary, education, healthcare, poverty, urban affairs, and population.*	G *Includes formation and debate of U.S. foreign and defense policies, veterans affairs, and defense spending. (Relations with specific foreign countries are usually found under the region concerned.)*	H *Includes business, labor, agriculture, taxation, transportation, consumer affairs, monetary and fiscal policy, natural resources, pollution and industrial accidents.*	I *Includes worldwide scientific, medical and technological developments, natural phenomena, U.S. weather and natural disasters.*	J *Includes the arts, religion, scholarship, communications media, sports, entertainment, fashions, fads, and social life.*	

	World Affairs	Europe	Africa & The Middle East	The Americas	Asia & The Pacific
May 23	Britain agrees to give part of Jubaland, a province of Kenya, to Italy.	The German Nationalist Party led by Adolf Hitler suggests that Prince von Buelow be chosen Chancellor of Germany....Ten thousand Soviet children vow to support the goals of V.I. Lenin in a ceremony at his tomb.			Japanese newspapers call for the boycott of American goods in the event that the bill excluding Japanese immigration to the United States is signed into law.
May 24		Britain celebrates Empire Day.... Roma from throughout Europe celebrate the holiday of their patron saint, Sarah of Egypt, in the French village of Les Saintes Maries de la Mer....King Victor Emmanuel opens the Italian parliament and praises the achievements of Benito Mussolini and the Italian Fascists.			An agent of the China Import and Export Company of Shanghai meets with Chinese bandits to discuss the release of company employees being held captive. An American employee of the company has already died from wounds suffered when the party was attacked on May 16.
May 25	German General Berthold von Deimling urges German entry into the League of Nations.			Nicaragua reports that it fears that former president Emiliano Chamorro will lead an uprising against the present government.	
May 26		Former French Premier Raymond Poincaré vows that he will continue to work to prevent the domination of French government by leftist parties....Attacks on Romanian Jews are taking place throughout the country.			The third Mt. Everest expedition sends its last message before attempting to reach the top of the mountain.
May 27		Benito Mussolini threatens to dissolve Italy's parliament....A bill to nationalize all mineral deposits, lands, and waterways in Great Britain is defeated in the House of Commons.	The London *Times* reports that the Sultans of Nejd and Kuwait have granted concessions to British oil companies.	Mexican troops execute seven men responsible for attacking ranches and burning railroad bridges.	
May 28	Britain asks the Council of the League of Nations to resolve issues regarding control of the region of Mesopotamia.	Former French premier Aristide Briande will assist Socialist deputies in removing President Alexandre Millerand from power.			
May 29		A strike by British coalminers ends....An arsenal in Bucharest explodes. Many Romanians believe the incident is connected to Romania's dispute with the Soviet Union over control of Bessarabia.			The American Vice Consul at Canton travels to Wu-Chow to seek the assistance of Chinese authorities in freeing American missionaries and others abducted by Chinese pirates on the Ho River.
May 30		In a speech before the Italian Chamber of Deputies, Giacomo Matteotti, leader of Italy's Socialists, denounces Fascist violence. Following a brawl between Socialists and Fascists in the Chamber, two members of the opposing parties challenge one another to a duel.		Agents of Mexican revolutionary Adolfo de la Huerta are arrested in the United States. It is believed that they were planning to launch an attack on Mexico at de la Huerta's behest.	
May 31	China grants recognition to the government of the Soviet Union. The Soviet Union agrees to withdraw its troops from Mongolia.	The Soviet Union elects a new Central Executive Committee.... British construction workers in Liverpool go on strike....Edouard Herriot asks for the support of Socialist leader Leon Blum in forming a new French government.			The government of South China protests the sale by an American company of a munitions factory located in Canton to North China. The Chinese maintain that they are the rightful owners of the factory and that the American company has no right to sell it.

A	B	C	D	E
Includes developments that affect more than one world region, international organizations and important meetings of world leaders.	*Includes all domestic and regional developments in Europe, including the Soviet Union.*	*Includes all domestic and regional developments in Africa and the Middle East.*	*Includes all domestic and regional developments in Latin America, the Caribbean, and Canada.*	*Includes all domestic and regional developments in Asian and Pacific nations (and colonies).*

U.S. Politics & Social Issues	U.S. Foreign Policy & Affairs, Defense	U.S. Economy & Environment	Science, Technology & Nature	Culture, Leisure & Lifestyle	
The Senate votes to clear Senator Burton K. Wheeler of Montana of the charges that he accepted bribes in exchange for helping private oil companies secure leases of government lands.		The American Petroleum Institute reports increases in crude oil production in Texas, Oklahoma, and Arkansas.	New York City's health commissioner orders city hospitals to experiment with the use of chlorine gas inhalations for the treatment of colds, pneumonia, and tuberculosis.	The Frick Art Reference Library in New York City opens this afternoon. The library, which contains paintings and photographs of art from throughout the United States and Europe, is intended to help students study works of art that they may not be able to see in person.	May 23
	The Rogers Act, creating the U.S. Foreign Service, becomes law.... Many people refuse to purchase poppies to support American veterans after passage of the Bonus Bill.	The Department of Agriculture reports that 38 million more acres of land will have to be devoted to agricultural production in order to feed the people of the United States in the future.	American aviators attempting to fly around the world arrive in Tokyo.		May 24
President Calvin Coolidge speaks at a ceremony honoring soldiers of the Confederacy and lays a wreath on a monument to the Confederate dead at Arlington National Cemetery.				The Andrew Freedman Home opens in New York City. It will serve as a residence for elderly people who once lived in luxury but lost their fortunes.	May 25
Congress officially passes the Johnson-Reed Immigration Act. The Act restricts the number of immigrants entering the United States from any country to two percent of the members of that nationality living in the United States in 1890. The Act virtually bans immigration from Asia and Africa. No immigration from Japan, China, or India is allowed with the exception of scholars, businessmen, clergymen, and tourists.		The needs of automobile drivers are leading to the depletion of gasoline reserves held by refiners.	The British government asks H. Grindell Matthews to demonstrate conclusively the effectiveness of a device that Matthews claims can stop the engine of an airplane using electric rays.		May 26
	The U.S. Navy successfully tests its new dirigible.	Cigarette production increases in the United States.			May 27
		The American Cotton Manufacturers' Association calls for a higher tariff on cotton imports and rejects proposed federal legislation that would limit child labor.		Chicago police reveal that they have no clues in the kidnapping and murder of Robert Franks.... The Presbyterian General Assembly asks the Rev. Dr. Harry Emerson Fosdick to join the Presbyterian ministry.	May 28
Representative Patrick B. O'Sullivan of Connecticut proposes that the Eighteenth Amendment be repealed....Samuel Gompers, leader of the American Federation of Labor, warns workers not to associate with the National Farmer-Labor Party because of its Communist affiliations.				The Quadrennial General Conference of the Methodist Episcopal Church ends. Delegates vote narrowly to uphold restrictions allowing divorce only in cases of adultery.	May 29
				Veterans march in New York City's Memorial Day parade.	May 30
Former Attorney General Harry M. Daugherty is called to testify before a Senate committee investigating corruption.	A naval air show at Lakehurst, NJ, features "jumping balloons," hydrogen balloons that allow a man, hanging beneath the balloon in a harness, to jump 200 feet into the air and travel a short distance before returning to earth.	Sales of automobile grade sheet metal increase while sales of wire decrease. The lack of demand for wire is blamed on lack of demand on the part of farmers.		The removal of Tikhon, who has encouraged Orthodox churches outside of the Soviet Union to govern themselves, from his position as Patriarch of the Russian Orthodox Church is approved by Gregory VII, Ecumenical Patriarch of Constantinople. It is unclear whether Gregory has the authority to depose Tikhon.	May 31

F	G	H	I	J
Includes campaigns, elections, federal-state relations, civil rights and liberties, crime, the judiciary, education, healthcare, poverty, urban affairs, and population.	*Includes formation and debate of U.S. foreign and defense policies, veterans affairs, and defense spending. (Relations with specific foreign countries are usually found under the region concerned.)*	*Includes business, labor, agriculture, taxation, transportation, consumer affairs, monetary and fiscal policy, natural resources, pollution and industrial accidents.*	*Includes worldwide scientific, medical and technological developments, natural phenomena, U.S. weather and natural disasters.*	*Includes the arts, religion, scholarship, communications media, sports, entertainment, fashions, fads, and social life.*

	World Affairs	Europe	Africa & The Middle East	The Americas	Asia & The Pacific
Jun. 1		Albanian rebels near Tirana after Zog's resignation fails to satisfy their demands. Irregular Yugoslav and Greek forces are on the border, with Italian warships standing by to intervene and the United States seeking League intervention.…Both France and Germany prepare to form new governments.			China recognizes the Soviet Union after Russia agrees to abandon extraterritoriality, allow Chinese purchase of the Chinese Eastern Railway concession, and recognize Mongolian independence. China wants Mongolia.
Jun. 2				Japanese immigration to Canada exceeds the Gentlemen's Agreement quota. Canada contemplates immigration restrictions.	
Jun. 3		Herriot indicates that France will leave the Ruhr once the Dawes Plan is in operation. He also proposes League oversight of a neutral Rhine.…After failed negotiations with nationalists, Marx takes his same government to the Reichstag. There he enjoys Socialist support.		Customs officials seize 12,000 barrels of ale on a barge from Montreal.	
Jun. 4		Britain indicates that its June 15 war debt payments of $69 million will be in gold. This is the first not paid in Liberty Bonds.…A red-led strike begins against British railroads.	Palestine introduces the dinar, last used in the time of Herod, as its currency. Replacing the Egyptian pound, the dinar will be backed by English currency.		Australia completes a four-day stretch in which it has wireless communications with England.…Four Japanese commit suicide over the exclusion law.
Jun. 5		Albanian rebels issue an ultimatum to the government to accept terms. An American warship stands by.		Indications are that U.S. Marines will leave Santo Domingo in July. The new constitutional government should be in place then.	
Jun. 6	Ramsey MacDonald announces an all-empire policy whereby he will seek input on foreign affairs from all dominions.	Berlin's railways declare a 500 billion percent dividend.…The Reichstag accepts the Dawes report, 247–183.…The French left attempts to force President Millerand to resign by blocking his budget.		Cuba's economy is strong enough to allow the government to retire $18 million in war loans. Bond rates are below six percent.	South Australia elects a "radical" government. Extensive social legislation is on tap.
Jun. 7		Mussolini invites five Mediterranean nations to a sea parley to discuss England's needs, the status of Turkey, and rights of other powers.…On the eve of the Republican convention, Republican women consider demanding equality in representation.	The Iraqi constituent assembly rejects the Anglo -Iraq treaty. It wants British agreement in writing the modifications it has agreed to make after ratification.…Well drillers in the Sahara find fish that went underground when the sand swallowed old river systems.		Anti-exclusion rioters in Tokyo block American dances and films.
Jun. 8		A mutiny by Portuguese flyers ends peacefully. The flyers object to the replacement of their favored air service chief.…Latvia prohibits Russian immigrants unless they are just passing through en route to America.…Strikes close Berlin breweries. Other cities cover the city's consumption of four carloads per hour.…Germany begins circulating state money, silver coins worth 38 million gold marks.	Scientists at Ur have cleared the rubble and revealed the Tower of Babel as it looked in 4,000 B.C.E.		

	A	B	C	D	E
	Includes developments that affect more than one world region, international organizations and important meetings of world leaders.	*Includes all domestic and regional developments in Europe, including the Soviet Union.*	*Includes all domestic and regional developments in Africa and the Middle East.*	*Includes all domestic and regional developments in Latin America, the Caribbean, and Canada.*	*Includes all domestic and regional developments in Asian and Pacific nations (and colonies).*

U.S. Politics & Social Issues	U.S. Foreign Policy & Affairs, Defense	U.S. Economy & Environment	Science, Technology & Nature	Culture, Leisure & Lifestyle	
A tri-state gathering of the Ku Klux Klan draws 10,000 Klansmen to Rochester, NY.…California's William G. McAdoo has more than 500 votes for the Democratic nomination, with 110 more collectable. He has 50 percent, but the two-thirds rule requires 732 votes.	Coolidge and Hughes are silent on how they will reply to the Japanese protest that exclusion violates the 1911 commercial treaty.…Immigration authorities block 700 Italian immigrants on the *Dante Alighieri* from landing. They tell a crowd of 1,000 that the would-be immigrants are likely to be deported after the failure in the Supreme Court of the Gottlieb request for family exemption from quotas.	The federal reserve reports a general economic downturn, with prices at May 1922 levels and unemployment increasing. Industry, particularly iron and steel, is down, but agriculture is up.			Jun. 1
By 61–23, the Senate passes a Constitutional amendment allowing the federal government to regulate or ban labor by children under 18. Previously approved by the House, the proposed amendment goes to the states for ratification.…Smith backers say McAdoo has fewer than 450 and some of those are wavering.		The Senate committee majority backs Norris' plan for government ownership of Muscle Shoals fertilizer and munitions plant as the basis for a region-wide power system. The minority prefers to accept Henry Ford's offer to buy the facility. Full Senate debate will begin shortly.		George Wightman, president of the U.S. Lawn Tennis Association, explains to members that he has banned players from writing about tennis because their pay is based on their name, not their skill as writers. By receiving pay for tennis-related work, they cease being amateurs.…Princeton wins the national intercollegiate polo title over Arizona.	Jun. 2
The American Party names its candidates, Gilbert Nations and Charles Randall. It hopes to attract prohibitionists and Klansmen.	Italy signs a treaty allowing the United States to search its ships for liquor.…Japanese begin a boycott of U.S. goods over exclusion.				Jun. 3
Harry Daugherty refuses to appear before congress and explain his personal finances as attorney general. He claims the committee has no jurisdiction and is just trying to blacken his name.	The navy's *Shenandoah* completes a 1,000-mile trip in less than 24 hours, riding out a thunderstorm and having difficulty landing because low fuel makes her light.	The collector of internal revenue notifies the 84,000 income tax payers that June payments will be only half of March installments. The reason is 1924's 25-percent reduction in the income tax.…Utility stocks, led by American Waterworks, set new records.	Representative Kindred reports that 2.75 percent beer has less kick than coffee.…Dr. S.L. Dawes claims that demented aliens, allowed into the United States through neglect at Ellis Island, cost New Yorkers $4.3 million in 1923.	New York City imposes a 20-minute parking limit downtown to ease congestion. Most over-parking violators are from New Jersey and Connecticut.	Jun. 4
Congress finds wrongdoing at Teapot Dome. Edward Doheny's lawyer says even biased Walsh's report shows that the oil leases from the navy are legal.…The House passes a bill establishing a dry bureau to enforce Volstead.…Leopold and Loeb are indicted for the murder of Bobby Franks.		Liberty Bond rates reach record highs. Money rates fall. The economy is awash in money.		New York bars Broadway to cruising cabs to ease congestion.…Bill Tilden says a compromise on the writer rule allows him to compete. Wightman and the USLTA are silent.…In Olympic trials, Johnny Weissmuller breaks the Olympic record for the 100-meter race. Second goes to Duke Kahanamoku.	Jun. 5
Coolidge addresses Howard University's commencement. He says that blacks are as patriotic as anyone is and will develop Africa.…The Prohibition Party names H.P. Faris for president and Miss Marie C. Brehm for vice president.	Secretary Hughes and the Dominion Minister of Justice sign a one-year treaty regulating smuggled liquor and narcotics.	A large Cuban sugar crop drops American prices to their lowest since 1922. Experts say demand for the drop is uncalled for because demand matches even the increased supply.		George Lennox bests Tommy Wright, four gamest to three, in the national marbles championship.…American teenager Helen Wills splits tennis matches against male English stars.…Weissmuller and two other swimmers break Olympic records at U.S. trials.	Jun. 6
Congress adjourns, leaving unfinished business including deficiency appropriations, Muscle Shoals, and more.	The navy announces that next year it will hold maneuvers in the Pacific as it develops a defense of Honolulu.	California is hit by epidemic hoof-and-mouth disease. To save its herds, the industry destroys 50,000 cattle.…Oil men look for a nine billion gallon 1924 to satisfy the 19 million cars expected on the road.		U.S. Olympic hopefuls continue breaking records at the trials. The 100-meter dash, 200-meter swim, and high jump marks are latest to fall.	Jun. 7
Congress authorizes 12 investigations to continue through the summer. The oil lease controversy is not one of them.…McAdoo backers retreat from their claim of an early nomination. They acknowledge a long fight like that of 1912 is likely.…Black organizations want the Republicans to take an anti-Klan stance. They hint at defection to Democrats otherwise.	The army air service tests an amphibian plane that takes off from water and lands on land. The pilot, who flies under the Brooklyn Bridge on the return flight, says performance is satisfactory.…The head of the Reserve Officers Association rebukes those who seek disarmament. Instead, he advocates preparedness.		News photos from the Cleveland Republican convention are transmitted over telephone for the first time.…A Dr. Glover of Toronto claims he has isolated the germ that causes cancer and has 200 cases to support his theory.	An all-Indian conference in Tulsa, OK, draws 10,000.…Two Oregon women, one age 75, complete a 16,000-mile coast-to-coast trip. Next, they will turn around and drive back.	Jun. 8
F *Includes campaigns, elections, federal-state relations, civil rights and liberties, crime, the judiciary, education, healthcare, poverty, urban affairs, and population.*	G *Includes formation and debate of U.S. foreign and defense policies, veterans affairs, and defense spending. (Relations with specific foreign countries are usually found under the region concerned.)*	H *Includes business, labor, agriculture, taxation, transportation, consumer affairs, monetary and fiscal policy, natural resources, pollution and industrial accidents.*	I *Includes worldwide scientific, medical and technological developments, natural phenomena, U.S. weather and natural disasters.*	J *Includes the arts, religion, scholarship, communications media, sports, entertainment, fashions, fads, and social life.*	

	World Affairs	Europe	Africa & The Middle East	The Americas	Asia & The Pacific
Jun. 9	International Telephone and Telegraph invests in recovering European telephone systems. It also seeks a Latin American and another European company not owned by the state. ITT hopes to create international long distance service.	An Italian bishop tires of immodest dress in church. He prohibits bare arms.... The London transport strike begins to crumble. Workers find that the Communists are unable to negotiate for them because government does not recognize any agent for the strikers.	An Arab party formed in Palestine backs the British mandate and government. Mostly agricultural, the party also supports accommodation with the other "races" in Palestine.	Police in Jamaica kill two rioters. Several other people are injured. The violence arises when Kingston tries to use strikebreakers in place of striking municipal workers.... A representative of the Association of American Petroleum Producers in Mexico denies a plot by American oilmen to destabilize Mexico's government as alleged by President Obregon.	
Jun. 10	The Olympic list is closed, with 45 nations participating. Individuals can still sign up to compete on their own.	Millerand's effort to form a cabinet fails. He will resign shortly. Painleve is the favorite to form the new government, with Doumerge second.... Sir Arthur Evans reveals a Minoan aqueduct and palace entrance preserved for 3,000 years.		Flores and Calles backers clash in Queretero. Ten die. Mexican politics is polarizing between conservative and liberal backers of the generals.	
Jun. 11	Previews of the League report on Hungary indicate that the international loan is fully subscribed, with Europeans taking the full offer. Average monthly revenue of 17 million crowns is twice the estimate.	Germany asks the League to have France withdraw from the Saar coal region before the plebiscite. Germany also suggests a police force for the region to thwart unrest.	After British pressure, Iraq ratifies the Anglo-Iraq Treaty. The parliament asks for eventual modification.	George Vernot and Paul Fravel, at the Winnipeg Olympic trials, set Canadian swim records.	The Kato government assumes power in Japan. Although not pro-American, it includes Foreign Minister Baron Shidehara, who is friendly toward the United States.
Jun. 12	The League asks members to help Russian emigrants in Greece. Uruguay says Latin America will welcome them.	Anti-Mussolini Deputy Matteotti disappears in Rome. Socialists implicate the Fascists, but Mussolini assists in the search.	Jews in Algiers protest to Spain after the Moorish ruler of Spanish Morocco flogs a Jew for nonpayment of a debt. Spanish authorities say they are powerless to intervene with the royal family.		
Jun. 13		France's assembly chooses Doumergue over Painleve as new president and Herriott as premier. Doumergue is France's first Protestant president.... London transport workers return to work rather than be fired. The strike fails and ends.			Hawaiian officials propose using Puerto Rican labor to replace the Japanese workers excluded under new immigration law. Free transportation is an inducement.
Jun. 14	The League calls on member governments to hold their armaments expenditures at the current level until a conference on disarmaments can establish lower levels. France, Britain, and Japan are among the powers expressing reluctance to hold the line.	French courts order the press to provide space for rebuttals by artists, actors, authors, and all others whose work receives negative criticism....Italian police patrol Rome to preserve order after the arrests of 15 Fascist leaders implicated in the disappearance of Matteotti.... Reichsbank notes in circulation for the first week of the month reportedly number 27 quintillions.		Mexico reports that General Alvarado is dead. His own forces execute him....American miners in Mexico report losing properties because the United States failed to include them in its land and oil claims convention.	
Jun. 15	International Labor Organization see hope in the Republican world court plank for greater American participation in world affairs.	Austria's imports are still out of balance with exports, but the overseer of Austrian recovery submits a budget to the League for approval....Herriott insists on full reparations in accord with the Dawes Plan and a neutral Rhineland under the League.		Venezuela's president bans radios. He wants to block news of the progress of the country's rebels, says a rebel representative.	Japanese Christians indicate they are ready to sever ties with American organizations.
Jun. 16	The League Council retains control of Austria's finances but defers asking non-League members to consider naval reduction....Britain's MacDonald warns Mexico's Obregon that his government looks with disfavor on Mexico's attempt to expel the British charge d'affairs....Mexico blocks the entry of 60 Japanese at Manzanillo. Japan protests that their papers are in order and their funds are sufficient, $50,000 among the sixty.	The Royal Society for the Prevention of Cruelty to Animals appeals to Prime Minister MacDonald to stop steer roping and wrestling at Tex Austin's international rodeo after a steer roper breaks a cow's leg. The RSPCA also threatens legal action....Herriott allows 7,000 Germans exiled by Poincare to return to the Ruhr. Maginot begins a campaign against disarmament. The allied commission reports Germans are rearming.		The secretary of the Venezuelan legation denies that there is a revolt in his country.	Asian purchases of American silver are heavy. Speculation is that Russia is supplying Asians gold for the purchases. Russia is also buying large amounts of American cotton.
	A *Includes developments that affect more than one world region, international organizations and important meetings of world leaders.*	B *Includes all domestic and regional developments in Europe, including the Soviet Union.*	C *Includes all domestic and regional developments in Africa and the Middle East.*	D *Includes all domestic and regional developments in Latin America, the Caribbean, and Canada.*	E *Includes all domestic and regional developments in Asian and Pacific nations (and colonies).*

U.S. Politics & Social Issues	U.S. Foreign Policy & Affairs, Defense	U.S. Economy & Environment	Science, Technology & Nature	Culture, Leisure & Lifestyle	
The Supreme Court upholds Willis-Campbell, which bars medical prescriptions of malt liquor. The court agrees that the law is appropriate to enforce prohibition.... The court also rejects Oklahoma's attempt to reject the boundary commission report in the Red River dispute with Texas.	Immigration officials, after Congress overturns the Gottlieb Decision, begin admitting the backlog of 9,300 immigrants stuck at Ellis Island and in the harbor.	The Agriculture Department reports crops are the worst in a dozen years. Wheat is down 44 million bushels, but the exchange anticipates 110 million bushels by August.... Four of the seven Liberty Bond issues reach new record levels.			Jun. 9
Senator Borah notifies the convention that he will not be a candidate for vice president. Delegates are split between Capper and Kenyon.	Labor Secretary Davis indicates that he will ask for a law mandating annual registration of aliens. Failure will result in a fine. Current law records aliens only at census time. Davis also says the United States will accept 13,000 aliens over this year's quota.	The Pittston coal strike grows from 5,000 to 10,000 miners protesting a cut in pay.... New York Central tests a new oil-electric engine that provides its own electricity at a third of the cost of steam. It will be used in the switching yard.	Detroit quarantines 15 city blocks. Once it completes 15,000 smallpox vaccinations, the city lifts the quarantine.... Mount Kilauea causes five quakes. An eruption is anticipated.	President Prout of the AAU protests new scoring rules that emphasize first place. Allegedly, the rules hurt the United States and favor Finland.	Jun. 10
The Republicans nominate Borah for vice president. He reiterates that he will not accept. The convention also accepts the Coolidge platform, rejecting that proposed by LaFollette.... Leopold and Loeb plead not guilty to kidnapping and murder. Trial is set for August 4.		A survey of 157 cities shows building permits up more than 10 percent from last year. New York's increase is more than 64 percent.		The flat look creates controversy in the medical community. Some condemn it while others regard it as "hygienic."	Jun. 11
Republicans nominate Coolidge and Dawes. The vice presidential nomination takes three ballots before Dawes beats Hoover after Lowden follows Borah and declines.	An explosion in a 14-inch gun on the USS *Mississippi* kills 48.		The American Medical Association convention hears that automobile fatalities match those from diphtheria and scarlet fever. City killers—industrial accidents, suicide, and exhaust poisoning—are replacing traditional causes of death.		Jun. 12
Presbyterian Reverend Fred Eastman accuses Protestant churches of misconduct in diverting mission funds intended for Indians and Alaskans to rural churches. Home mission aid to 20,000 U.S. churches exceeds $4 million a year.	Coolidge orders veterans and navy and army heads to find $2 million to pay war bonuses. The World War Adjusted Compensation Act, signed over his veto in May, authorizes AEF bonuses, but Congress recessed without authorizing the money.	Richmond and Chicago Federal Reserve banks cut their rediscount rates to four percent. Six others hold to 4.5 percent but several will drop to four percent soon. Money is plentiful.	Experiments on yachters reveal that oxygen both cures and prevents sea sickness.	A group of scientists and artists selected by the Royal Academy begins studying ways to clean art safely and preserve it. Harvard suggests certifying safe paints and canvases.... Olympic hopefuls continue to break records in the run-up to track finals, set for tomorrow. Selection of rowing teams is also finishing.	Jun. 13
Chicago police capture another five of the train robbers, but the leaders are still at large.... Coolidge orders pay raises for federal employees paid despite the absence of budget authority. The cost is $26 million.... Presbyterian home mission officials deny they are misappropriating money.	The U.S. ambassador formally protests to Japan over the continuing boycott of American films. The newspapers are calmer, and Tokyo's police chief warns rioters to stop. Demonstrations move from Tokyo to the west.	Leaders of the U.S. dye industry indicate concern that German companies may take over their business. Bayer officials are in the United States, reportedly trying to buy the Grasselli Chemical Plant.... Ford puts office workers on a five-day week. Factory workers have been on the same schedule for six weeks.	The stethophone sends heartbeats by radio. It has potential to allow diagnosis from long distances.	The U.S. Olympic team has 104 athletes. It is the strongest American team ever.... Bobbed hair is great for barbers, but it plays hob with hair pin sales.... On Flag Day, the president of the U.S. Flag Association accuses noncitizens of shirking their duty.	Jun. 14
Police arrest James Murray, Chicago politician and beer millionaire, as leader of the gas robbers.... The Farmer-Labor Party indicates that its convention will nominate no one, leaving the way clear for LaFollette to run if the Progressives select him first.	Washington indicates that it expects a British protest of its elevating guns because elevating increases their range in violation of the Washington Agreement.	June steel output is 25 million tons, well below capacity of 54 million tons.... Rediscount rates at New York and Boston are 3.5 percent, the worlds lowest and lower even than prewar rates.... The head of the Chandler Company says that trucks are merely an adjunct to railroads and soon will be no competition.	Seventeen balloons take off from Brussels in a race across Europe.... Radio influences the Democratic convention. Plans are to move the keynote speech to an evening hour to bring in more listeners. There will be less interference.	Paris styles for the Olympic Games follow body contours. The corset is passé.	Jun. 15
Kentucky and Texas delegates favor majority rule selection of the Democratic nominee. McAdoo forces are leery of a floor fight although they would like the two-thirds rule revoked.... Farmer-Laborites near a split over participation by American Communists as called for by William Z. Foster.... Raids in San Pedro CA, target I.W.W. headquarters. Police report four "wobblies" tarred and feathered.		The government bans the use of "Havana" and "Tampa" on cigars produced elsewhere.	Three balloons are out of the race. An American radio station, WBZ of Springfield MA, broadcasts messages to the flyers.... Wallace Atwood, president of Clark University, says that Robert Goddard has solved the problem of propellant for his rocket. Goddard will test a liquid-fueled rocket in the summer.		Jun. 16
F *Includes campaigns, elections, federal-state relations, civil rights and liberties, crime, the judiciary, education, healthcare, poverty, urban affairs, and population.*	G *Includes formation and debate of U.S. foreign and defense policies, veterans affairs, and defense spending. (Relations with specific foreign countries are usually found under the region concerned.)*	H *Includes business, labor, agriculture, taxation, transportation, consumer affairs, monetary and fiscal policy, natural resources, pollution and industrial accidents.*	I *Includes worldwide scientific, medical and technological developments, natural phenomena, U.S. weather and natural disasters.*	J *Includes the arts, religion, scholarship, communications media, sports, entertainment, fashions, fads, and social life.*	

	World Affairs	Europe	Africa & The Middle East	The Americas	Asia & The Pacific
Jun. 17	The League accepts a draft treaty outlawing aggressive war. Drafters are 10 Americans, including Generals Bliss and Harbord and Columbia's Prof. Shotwell....The Moscow Opera House hosts Communists from 60 nations as they convene the fifth International.	Two steamers collide off the coast of Norway, killing 17 people, all Norwegians except for one Dane. Fifty members of the Chicago Norwegian male choir, touring Norway, are among the rescuers....Russia executes 12 more for spying....Warrants are out for inhumane cowboys in London.	Jan Smuts, former South African premier and League stalwart, loses his parliamentary seat to a Labour candidate. His South African Party loses heavily in urban districts to a coalition of Nationalists and Labour.		Japan completes an agreement to open a fish cannery in Mexico. Japan and Russia are near agreement over Sakhalin and Manchuria and the Nikolaievsk massacre.
Jun. 18	Britain recalls its ambassador and breaks relations with Mexico.... Interest in the draft treaty barring aggressive war generates requests for 100,000 copies....Zinoviev tells the Communist International that the movement is losing ground in the United States, Britain, Germany, and France. He remains confident of world revolution.	Labour and Liberals combine in the Commons to defeat Stanley Baldwin's proposal for empire preference. The proposals arise from a recent dominion conference on tariffs and disadvantage Britain against the dominion states....Mussolini says all slayers of Matteotti are in custody but he bars private airplane flights lest any flee the country.	An East African trader/ prospector reports finding a Phoenician gold mine in Tanganyika. Near the mine are scores of skulls, presumably those of dead miners.	Canadian postal workers ignore an order to delay 24 hours. Toronto and Montreal walk out, with the rest of Canada expected to follow. The postmaster general vows the mails will move.	
Jun. 19	Japan denies having a secret agreement to sell arms to Russia. Rather, the agreement deals with oil and mineral rights in the Russian sphere. Japan also defers action on Mexican and U.S. immigration slights until after the elections.	The Fascisti arrest Marinelli in the murder of Matteotti. Marinelli is close to Mussolini....France's senate chooses Herriott but rejects his choice for president. It elects De Selves instead.		Canadian strikers seem amenable to settling. The strike that affects two provinces has already provoked the government to call out troops.	Vilhjalmar Stefansson announces plans to retrieve from Wrangel Island a colony consisting of 13 Eskimos and one European. The colony on the island north of Siberia has been in place for three years proves the Arctic island is habitable and wants to establish a British claim to it.
Jun. 20		Fascists hold mass demonstrations and parade in defiance of the disapproval they face due to their complicity in Matteotti's murder....The Hungarian loan is awarded. Only Europeans will participate....After the home secretary intervenes, rodeo officials halt the steer roping competition.	Liberia sues in Germany for the return of a sacred stone allegedly stolen by the German explorer Schomberg.	As election day nears, Mexico's government calls out troops. Speculation is that General Flores is ill and may abandon the field to General Calles.	A bomb attack on Governor General Merlin's dinner party at Canton kills five and injures 28.
Jun. 21	Cummins, the expelled British charge d'affairs, leaves Mexico. Americans and Britons say goodbye. Latin Americans are silent.	Fascist Filipelli admits he ordered Matteotti's kidnapping. He denies he intended any harm to the Socialist....U.S. relief work in Germany ends. Americans provided $5 million in aid.		Puerto Ricans protest the new election law. They contend that it makes the formation of new parties impossible.	
Jun. 22	Herriot and MacDonald call a meeting at Chequers in July to get all allies behind the Dawes Plan.	Britain begins minting 45 million coins for Russia. It receives the metal and payment before minting anything.			The British steamer *Clan MacMillan* out of Glasgow sinks in the Bay of Bengal. The crew is missing.
Jun. 23	Japanese react angrily to the deaths of Japanese citizens in California. They calm when they learn that the killers are Japanese as well and it is not an anti-Japanese crime.... Herriot and MacDonald invite the United States to the Dawes Act parley. They also warn Germany not to resist military control.	Mussolini says he will remain premier because that is how he can best serve his country. He promises to reform the government and make the Fascisti into a legal military organization....Germany's *Schwarzrotgold* opposes right wingers, including Hitler's group, and monarchists. It enrolls 60,000 members in 32 states in two weeks.			
	A *Includes developments that affect more than one world region, international organizations and important meetings of world leaders.*	B *Includes all domestic and regional developments in Europe, including the Soviet Union.*	C *Includes all domestic and regional developments in Africa and the Middle East.*	D *Includes all domestic and regional developments in Latin America, the Caribbean, and Canada.*	E *Includes all domestic and regional developments in Asian and Pacific nations (and colonies).*

U.S. Politics & Social Issues	U.S. Foreign Policy & Affairs, Defense	U.S. Economy & Environment	Science, Technology & Nature	Culture, Leisure & Lifestyle	
McAdoo and Smith forces vow a death struggle over the two-thirds rule. McAdoo says he can win either way.		The Pennsylvania Railroad announces plans to electrify, beginning with a mountainous section between Pittsburgh and Philadelphia. First, it has to find the money.…Gasoline in Omaha drops below 15 cents in a price war.	DeMuyter's *Belgica* is sighted over Ireland. It is the last balloon flying and, thus, the winner. Its flight covers 462 miles.	Governor Smith is recorded for a six-minute talking film, the first to be used in a campaign.	Jun. 17
Farmer-Laborites back LaFollette, nominating a temporary slate that will step aside when the Senator declares. The party shelves the Communist-inspired party platform.…The Lutheran Synod votes for permanent peace and entry of the United States into the World Court.…Democratic leaders stand firm on the two-thirds rule. A long convention is on tap.	Hughes tells Japan that the Gentlemen's Agreement did not limit Congress. The United States retain control of its immigration policy.…China rejects Secretary Hughes' claim to a U.S. interest in the Chinese Eastern Railway. The United States advanced $5 million for maintenance during the war and, Hughes says, has a claim covered by the Washington Agreement. China excludes all westerners and allows only Russia an interest in running the road.	New York's Iron League sues the ironworkers for costing the industry $5 million during a recent strike. The League seeks to have the union declared illegal.…Philadelphia and St. Louis Reserve banks cut their prime rates.	A German inventor successfully broadcasts opera over the telephone without unpleasant interrupting noises.	All-Pueblo Progressive Indians back the Interior Department's efforts to eradicate old Pueblo religion and ritual. The Progressives are Christians who claim that old Pueblos coerce them into unchristian dances.…Boxing promoter Tex Rickard announces plans to revitalize hockey by holding games in Madison Square Garden.	Jun. 18
The Home Missions Council, comprised of 40 Protestant denominations, denies Eastman's charges of diversion of funds. It also votes to shift resources from over-churched areas to underserved regions.…McAdoo forces indicate they will fight an anti-Klan plank in the Democratic platform.…Chlorine gas is used to break up a filibuster in the Rhode Island senate.	The U.S. agreements with France, Togoland, and the Cameroons go into effect. The treaties establish the rights of U.S. citizens and government in the mandates.		RCA's David Sarnoff says that Americans will be able to hear European radio broadcasts in the near future. Sarnoff cites rapid technological change and major improvements in power in the past few months.	Tex Rickard buys the proposed new enlarged Madison Square Garden. He plans several more purchases.	Jun. 19
The Adjutant General prepares to distribute six million blank applications for veterans' bonuses. Another five million are due for distribution later.…Rhode Island Republicans charge Democrats with maintaining thugs in the Senate chamber. The local sheriff says he lacks the money to do anything.…Anti McAdoo forces rally to John W. Davis as the convention opens. Smith claims confidence in victory.	Coolidge announces an investigation into charges that a "naval ring" is getting preferential treatment in navy contracts.…Army Lieutenant Russell Maughan is unable to get off the ground due to fog. This is his third attempt to set the record by flying coast-to-coast in one day.	Five grain companies in the Midwest propose to merge and consolidate with the 5,000 grain elevators in a cooperative owned by farmers themselves. The Farm Bureau looks favorably on the billion-dollar venture.	A German veterinarian claims to have isolated the bacillus that causes hoof and mouth disease.…George C. Mallory and A.C. Irvine conquer Everest. Mallory previously climbed the peak three times.		Jun. 20
The postal service announces a purge of undesirables from its employment. Postal workers are implicated in the $3 million gas-attack train robbery.…New Mexico's Secretary of State Soledad Chacon is acting governor while the governor is at the Democratic convention. She is the first female governor of any state.…Five Southern Methodist bishops oppose merger with Northern Methodists. They contend that merger would help the Northern church but bring no benefit to the Southern one.	An army airplane experiments with broadcasting from the air. Its message from 7,000 feet is heard 25 miles away.…Secretary Hughes reminds China that the $5 million U.S. investment gives the United States a stake in the Chinese railroad.	Florida announces that the 51 mile Connors Highway will open officially in July. The $3 million privately built toll road ties west to east Florida through the Everglades.…Over-expansion in recent years has resulted in 563 U.S. refineries. Now many refineries are idle.	Seven hundred cities agree to a standard fire hose coupling. The standard replaces the 600 sizes that hamper inter-community firefighting efforts.	New York police mount a special effort to keep the convention dry. A raid at the Waldorf nets seven cases of illegal alcohol, and the police chief warns flask carriers that they face arrest.	Jun. 21
The American Civil Liberties Union reports that red activity is on the wane. Right-wing violence is rising, primarily due to the Klan.		Automobile production for the first five months of the year is up 263,000 over the same period in 1923. Estimated total 1924 output is 4.3 million cars.…A survey of 300 issues reveals bond prices are at their highest since 1922.		The U.S. coach names the Olympic team, closely following the results of the trials but replacing a few members. All contenders have been waiting on a ship in France.	Jun. 22
Rhode Island Republicans are in Massachusetts. They refuse to return to Rhode Island until the minority Democrats promise to allow them to enact their legislative program.…Blacks ask Democrats for an anti-Klan plank. They note that it might shift the black vote from Republicans.	Maughan finally makes his single-day coast-to-coast flight. He arrives in San Francisco with 18.5 minutes to spare.…Navy Lieutenants John Price and F.W. Wead narrowly escape death as their engine fails over the Potomac after they set four night-flight records in the seaplane *CS-2*.	Income tax revenue for the first half of the year is $139 million above the same period in 1923.			Jun. 23
F *Includes campaigns, elections, federal-state relations, civil rights and liberties, crime, the judiciary, education, healthcare, poverty, urban affairs, and population.*	G *Includes formation and debate of U.S. foreign and defense policies, veterans affairs, and defense spending. (Relations with specific foreign countries are usually found under the region concerned.)*	H *Includes business, labor, agriculture, taxation, transportation, consumer affairs, monetary and fiscal policy, natural resources, pollution and industrial accidents.*	I *Includes worldwide scientific, medical and technological developments, natural phenomena, U.S. weather and natural disasters.*	J *Includes the arts, religion, scholarship, communications media, sports, entertainment, fashions, fads, and social life.*	

	World Affairs	Europe	Africa & The Middle East	The Americas	Asia & The Pacific
Jun. 24		A tornado strikes Belfast, Ireland.		The United States warn Martinez that he will not have U.S. recognition if he wins the Nicaraguan election. He is running despite a constitutional ban on reelection of presidents.	
Jun. 25	Pershing is feted by Belgium's king and queen. The former AEF commander is in Europe as head of the Battlefield Monuments Commission.	Hungary's loan is open to American bankers, who get a fifth of the $50 million issue. Previously, the entire loan was reserved for Europeans.... Vienna's *Depositen* Bank and its 53 branches fail....After talking with Americans, Doumergue decides that France will establish business relations with Russia.		Marines receive orders to leave Santo Domingo on July 10....Gold, silver, and copper are attracting attention to Canada's mineral belt again after a lull following the initial flurry. The influx of 5,000 miners to northern Manitoba is straining rail transport....Switzerland sends a military commission to assist Colombia's reorganization of its army.	
Jun. 26		The Italian Senate gives Mussolini a vote of confidence on the eve of a pro-Matteotti demonstration. ...Russia prepares for famine but predicts it will not be as severe as that of 1921....Herriott okays the return to the Ruhr of 60,000 Germans Poincare exiled.			
Jun. 27	The International Labor Conference at Geneva hears from Japanese and Cubans on behalf of exploited laborers. A Cuban diplomat denies claims that labor conditions in Cuba are deplorable.	Italy observes a 10-minute work stoppage in memory of Matteotti.			Australia's Premier Bruce says Britain does not understand defense needs of the entire empire. Australia will begin its own defense program....Chinese minister Sze reports that nations have agreed to remit their Boxer indemnity payments. The money will go to Chinese education.
Jun. 28		The British advisor to Hungary on financial affairs says that bootlegging of the old currency has mostly ceased. He anticipates Hungarian control of its finances soon....French deaths for the first quarter exceed births by 24,000....Prussia bans reds from the civil service. It wants no divided loyalties....Sweden opens commercial ties with Russia.		The Inter-American Electrical Communications Conference finishes draft rules on radio and wire telegraph traffic. Other conventions include submarine cables, tariffs, and other communications elements in need of standardization.	
Jun. 29	Haiti prepares to petition the League to end the U.S. Marines occupation. Representatives of 30 nations demonstrate in Lyons in support of Haiti.	The Reichstag agrees to accept allied military control. Agrarians and industrialists press for acceptance and nationalists reluctantly agree.	The Transvaal reports that May gold output is the second most in history. Output is 809,000 fine ounces, valued at £3.5.	The mail strike ends in Toronto. Workers win an investigation into their wage status.	The Philippines delegation to the Democratic convention begins efforts to remove American influence from its representation. Allegedly, those who would represent are those who left the Philippines years before.
Jun. 30		Germany asks a September end to the allied investigation into allegations it is secretly rearming. Rumored militias are mere gymnastic societies, it says.	South Africa suffers a plague of locusts. Swarms miles long are approaching Johannesburg.		
Jul. 1		A cave near Toulouse, France, reveals bones reportedly 6,000 years old....Mussolini is showing signs of strain as an anti-Fascist boycott continues.		Obregon suspends Mexico's debt payment, blaming U.S. oil interests and bankers for exacerbating economic hardships that even prevent Mexico from paying its civil servants.	Japanese crowds take their protests to their ancestors. Demonstrators as the shrines ask for vengeance against the American insult.
	A *Includes developments that affect more than one world region, international organizations and important meetings of world leaders.*	B *Includes all domestic and regional developments in Europe, including the Soviet Union.*	C *Includes all domestic and regional developments in Africa and the Middle East.*	D *Includes all domestic and regional developments in Latin America, the Caribbean, and Canada.*	E *Includes all domestic and regional developments in Asian and Pacific nations (and colonies).*

U.S. Politics & Social Issues	U.S. Foreign Policy & Affairs, Defense	U.S. Economy & Environment	Science, Technology & Nature	Culture, Leisure & Lifestyle	
Odds makers lower the dark horses from four to one to 3.5 to one. Smith holds at 2.5 to one while McAdoo rises to three to one. Dark horses include Davis, Underwood, Glass, and Ralston.		Standard Oil's *Egremont Castle* explodes in Brooklyn after a 200-gallon container of gasoline drops into a hold containing 250,000 gallons. Five men vanish; six are in critical condition.		The fund-raising drive to preserve Monticello has brought in $200,000. The goal is $500,000.	Jun. 24
Presbyterians attribute their inability to attract significant new membership to publicized disputes that hamper evangelization.... Three editors of the *American Standard* are arrested for a religious libel of Al Smith. Police say one is a Klansman....Underwood, Robinson, and McAdoo are formally nominated.	Representative Johnson of Washington predicts that the population will be 200 million in 1974. He says the melting pot has to become history and Japanese exclusion is essential to keep population from becoming excessive.	Forty thousand garment workers strike and begin picketing 2,500 shops. Immediately, three picketers are arrested for assault....The cotton crop is estimated at 11.4 million bales. Prices rise $4 a bale.... Million-dollar storms in Wilmington, DE, unroof 300 houses, kill 5, and injure 20....The government sues 50 gasoline companies for monopoly and extortion.	Professor Calmette reports to the French Academy that he has a vaccine for tuberculosis. He has been researching the vaccine for 20 years.	The U.S. Olympic team arrives in Paris to a tumultuous welcome....Puccini, hot off the success of *Madame Butterfly*, finishes *Turandot*. The new opera will debut in December.	Jun. 25
McAdoo loses the first test vote as the Democrats vote an anti-Klan stance. McAdoo frees his forces to vote as they wish on the Klan plank. Southern delegates fear repudiation will mean the loss of Georgia, Oklahoma, and Texas. F.D. Roosevelt nominates Al Smith, calling him the "Happy Warrior."	Japan's cabinet approves a draft note in response to Hughes on exclusion. The note is conciliatory but expresses dissatisfaction with the U.S. position.	Junkers asks Ford to build all-metal airplanes for passenger service....W.W. Odell of the Bureau of Mines says lignite is an unexploited resource. He attributes the neglect to the fact that the soft coal regions are thinly populated.	Roald Amundsen announces that he will not be flying to the pole this year. He has no money....Detroit officials report that they have inoculated 750,000 against smallpox. They estimate their city is safe for five years.	Presbyterians reject voting rights for women in their synods.	Jun. 26
All nominees are in. McAdoo droops to 5.5 to one against, and the favorite is Smith at one to two....Arkansas becomes the first state to ratify the proposed child labor amendment....A coroner's jury finds that the cause of Bobby Franks' death is Leopold and Loeb.	Immigration commissioner Curran returns from a tour of Europe. He reports that U.S. consuls are ready for a surge when next year's quotas become available. Consulates already show 5,000 would-be immigrants waiting in port cities....Chicago Federal Judge James Wilkinson rules that Syrians and Armenians are eligible for U.S. citizenship. The ruling affects 88,500 Near Easterners.	S.S. Kresge's stock rises 15 points. The chain store's positive sales figures recapture speculators who left last month. Overall, chain store sales are up 15 percent for May while department stores are up one percent and catalog sales decline seven percent.	Radio broadcasts of the convention are pressed onto records.	The U.S. rifle team wins the title and the fencers beat Holland in early Olympic events.	Jun. 27
Alice Paul calls for a women's movement that rejects both parties. Neither has been supportive of women's rights....The convention rejects a pro-League plank. By one vote, the convention avoids condemning the Klan. Georgia switches 1.5 votes. McAdoo forces deny Georgia acted at McAdoo's request.	Budget cutting in the navy results in termination of a third of the Naval Academy's civilian teachers, who vow to sue. Prior to 1914, Annapolis used navy only teachers.	American minters get the contract to produce 24 million of the new Polish zloty....The Industrial Conference Board reports that one-sixth of American wealth is tax exempt. That is $55 billion, an increase of two-thirds in a decade.	A tornado strikes Ohio, killing 72 and injuring 1,500 in Lorain. Five thousand are homeless. Sandusky's death toll, originally reported as more than 100, is actually 6.	The United States win the first Olympic polo game. The United States foils team falls.	Jun. 28
		Railroads across the nation are considering consolidation.			Jun. 29
Seventeen candidates are in the nomination race. McAdoo and Smith remain deadlocked. Davis is moving up....Teapot Dome bribery charges are brought against Fall, two Dohenys, and Sinclair....The NAACP convention rejects both major parties and calls for blacks to support a third party.	Postwar reorganization of the army is finished with the reduction in the size of the general staff....Coolidge announces the new immigrant quotas based on the 1890 census.	Banks report their loans the highest since 1920. Demand deposits in Federal Reserve system banks are up $377 million....Coolidge tells his agency heads to cut next year's expenditures by $83 million. The expected $25 million surplus is too small.	New York's subway link from Manhattan to Brooklyn opens.	A Carpentier-Tunney lightweight fight is announced for July at the Polo Grounds....New York motorists are now required to have a driver's license. The deadline is October 1.	Jun. 30
Davis is now the betting favorite at 2.5 to one. Smith is at three to one and McAdoo has fallen to seven to one....In a New Jersey field guarded by hooded and mounted men, thousands watch as the Klan inducts 400 new members.	Immigrant visas are again available. French police repel crowds storming the Paris consulate. Cuban crowds are also heavy.	The Commerce Department says that industries benefit by adopting simpler standards. In lumber alone the savings is $250 million a year.... Airmail flyers take off from each coast, inaugurating coast-to-coast mail service between San Francisco and New York. The flights completed safely, last a day and a half.			Jul. 1

F	G	H	I	J
Includes campaigns, elections, federal-state relations, civil rights and liberties, crime, the judiciary, education, healthcare, poverty, urban affairs, and population.	*Includes formation and debate of U.S. foreign and defense policies, veterans affairs, and defense spending. (Relations with specific foreign countries are usually found under the region concerned.)*	*Includes business, labor, agriculture, taxation, transportation, consumer affairs, monetary and fiscal policy, natural resources, pollution and industrial accidents.*	*Includes worldwide scientific, medical and technological developments, natural phenomena, U.S. weather and natural disasters.*	*Includes the arts, religion, scholarship, communications media, sports, entertainment, fashions, fads, and social life.*

	World Affairs	Europe	Africa & The Middle East	The Americas	Asia & The Pacific
Jul. 2	The Olympic Games open, with 1,430 athletes representing 45 nations. Olympic officials are already working on the next games, planning to reduce the duration and eliminate unimportant events.		American Zionists meet in Pittsburgh to arrange for raising $500,000 capital to purchase land and create a music conservatory in Palestine as a memorial to Jewish war dead in the World War.	Honduras holds a peaceful election. There is no rioting at the polls, and the new constitution passes.	
Jul. 3	Allied ambassadors reject Germany's call for a time limit to the militarization investigation. They say the duration depends on Germany.…Count von Bernstorff says that Germany would like to join the League but expects France and England to oppose.	German Chancellor Marx explains the Dawes Plan to the state premiers and encourages them to support it.…Ruhr coal operators void the Micum Accord. They say they are unable to supply any more coal to France.	A German firm gets the contract to enlarge the port of Suez.…A display in London contains artifacts discovered by Flinders Petrie at Assiyut, Egypt. It is believed to be the oldest prehistoric settlement, dating to between 8000 and 5000 B.C.E.	A British commission studying the Brazilian government calls for a balanced budget, outside financing, currency and debt reform, and economic development.…U.S. bankers say there is no reason for concern over Mexico's failure to pay. The agreement stands, and Mexico will resume payment when it can.	India's bank rate is down to five percent. It was eight percent in May, 10 percent in February
Jul. 4		Police raid the Reichstag and Prussian Diet and seize papers from the lockers of Communist members.		Canada announces plans to send teams to the far north to investigate weather conditions.	Japanese cabinet members tell the Diet that there is a need for strengthening and modernization of armed forces and an improvement in Japan's naval oil supply. They deny that the September earthquake hurt oil reserves.
Jul. 5	Haiti's target shooting team astounds the experts and ties for second at the Paris Olympics. Their success comes from training by the U.S. Marines.		The Rif in the mountains of Morocco are causing heavy Spanish casualties. The sounds of battle and the smoke of burning villages are visible in Tangiers. Spain acknowledges 400 casualties, including some from friendly fire.	Canadian missionary H.W.G. Stocken of Victoria, BC, is printing the first book in the Blackfoot language, a Bible. He has already developed a phonetic alphabet of 40 letters.…Mexico indicates it will cut the army to 50,000 men and use the savings to pay teachers and low-level civil servants.	
Jul. 6		German bankruptcies are six times those of 1923. Inflation is to blame.…Germany establishes protective tariffs on foodstuffs. Industrialists anticipate comparable protection.…Ludendorff attacks the Dawes Plan. He says it is a Jewish plot to take control of Germany.		Brazilian rebels take Sao Paolo. Rio imposes censorship. The American embassy in Argentina says the unrest is only local.…The preliminary agenda for the General Claims Commission includes the Vera Cruz occupation, the Chamizal dispute over shifting Rio Grande boundaries, and murders of Mexicans in the United States, a total of 350 in seven years prior to 1922.	Authorities arrest 23 Philippine Scouts for joining a secret organization. Earlier authorities allowed Scouts to join and accept Scouts' right to strike over pay issues. Now they fear anti-government demonstrations.
Jul. 7		Charges of animal cruelty against Tex Austin and his cowboys are dropped.…The Reichsbank reports that marks in circulation total 1,126,310, 573,000,000 millions.	Spanish forces relieve Kobadarsa. Seven days of fighting have had a cost of half the garrison dead or wounded.	Brazilian rebels, now numbering 13,000 and including federal forces, march on Rio. Brazilian bonds and coffee futures are down moderately.	
Jul. 8		Little Entente countries meet at Prague. They are prepared to recognize Russia.		Federal forces claim victory in Brazil. Suppressing the rising with artillery and airplanes produces a death toll of 250.	Japan indicates it will abandon dual citizenship. No longer will it expect Japanese-heritage citizens of other countries to serve in its military. The move counters those who say that Japanese are not assimilable.…Strikers against wages at the naval base on Cavite Island are surrendering. U.S. officials rule that they cannot return for 90 days because they were absent without permission for over six days.

A
Includes developments that affect more than one world region, international organizations and important meetings of world leaders.

B
Includes all domestic and regional developments in Europe, including the Soviet Union.

C
Includes all domestic and regional developments in Africa and the Middle East.

D
Includes all domestic and regional developments in Latin America, the Caribbean, and Canada.

E
Includes all domestic and regional developments in Asian and Pacific nations (and colonies).

	U.S. Politics & Social Issues	U.S. Foreign Policy & Affairs, Defense	U.S. Economy & Environment	Science, Technology & Nature	Culture, Leisure & Lifestyle
Jul. 2	Georgia rejects the proposed child labor amendment as a violation of states' rights....LaFollette announces for the presidency on the Progressive ticket....The Klan announces a July 4 rally in New Jersey and promises 40,000 will turn out.	Secretary Hughes shakes up the diplomatic and consular branches of the foreign service under the Rogers Act. Sixty lose their positions as a merit system begins.	Iron production in June was the smallest since 1922.		After a long fight, friends of Newton D. Baker are victorious. The *Encyclopedia Britannica* rewrites its article on the former war secretary to make it less condemnatory.
Jul. 3	Democrats set a record with 61 ballots. Selection of a nominee is still in the air. McAdoo blames favorite sons and demands that they quit the race....The Progressives, meeting in Cleveland, deny credentials to Jacob Coxey, saying that there is no recognized Populist Party in their coalition....Samuel Gompers rejects AFL support of the third party Progressives. He says it weakens labor by dividing it.	The United States announce that flyers from Panama will bomb a derelict schooner off Costa Rica in an exercise.	Cotton prices and oil output continue a slow downward trend....Packard Motors reports $2.3 million in net earnings for the quarter.		Chicago begins horseracing. Police mingle with the crowd to make sure there is no violation of Illinois' ban on gambling.
Jul. 4	Coolidge calls for a Department of Education and federal aid to education....At Little Rock, AR, a Klan rally brings out 10,000, including gubernatorial candidate Lee Cavort. The governor spoke at a veterans' picnic....Tuskegee Institute reports that lynchings have declined, with only five in the first six months of the year....Southern and Northern Methodists agree to merge.	An air show at Mitchell Field features 60 fighting aircraft, parachutists, and the shooting down of a balloon.	Class I railroads show May income down to $60 million from $90 million last May. Gross income is down 12.9 percent. Forty railroads show a loss. Cost cutting continues.		The International Amateur Athletic Federation recognizes four world records by Paavo Nurmi. It chooses not to endorse the Olympic scoring system.
Jul. 5	On the 77th ballot, Smith's total is up to 368. A move begins to have Smith and McAdoo step aside. Dark horses Bryan, Robinson, and Cordell Hull are still in the running....Progressives throw out the Communists and select LaFollette....The New Jersey Klan camp ends. Attendance is at most 10,000. Klansmen beat a non-Klan group. The problem is mosquitoes. In Binghamton, NY, rifle shots disrupt a Klan gathering.	Thirty college presidents send a letter of friendship to Japan. They condemn Congressional inconsideration in enacting anti-Japanese immigration legislation.	Insurance data shows that white-collar crime costs $3 billion a year. A major contributor is the rise in embezzlement by trusted men.		The pocket billiard league announces plans to reduce franchises from 16 to 12. It will concentrate on major cities only....The American Whist league names a new president....Champion Jack Dempsey says his movie obligations will keep him from boxing this year.
Jul. 6	The National Association of Manufacturers asks an end to voter apathy. The NAM says turnout was only 49 percent in 1920....All candidates but McAdoo agree to free their delegates. Even an offer to scrap the two-thirds rule fails to sway him.	The U.S. Army reports that it is having trouble meeting enlistment quotas because of the new requirement that enlistees be 21 years old or, if under 21, have parental consent. The other services are meeting quotas without problems....The United States recalls its minister to Rumania for consultations over Rumania's anti-business oil policy.		Wild fires rage out of control in Tahoe and Sequoia national reserves.	
Jul. 7	McAdoo trails Smith in delegate totals. Cox arrives as titular head of the party to promote harmony.		Crude oil prices are down $1.25 from peak levels. Cotton is at its lowest in three months.		President Coolidge's son, Calvin, Jr., dies of septicemia at age 16. The last time a child died while his father was in office was when Lincoln lost his son.
Jul. 8	In Pennsylvania hooded men fire on black Boy Scouts. A policeman who burns a cross loses his job....McAdoo frees his delegates for Meredith. On the 100th ballot, Davis gets 203.5 votes. Ralston bows out....Fifty thousand needle-trades workers go on strike. Most will return as soon as Morris Hillquit of the ILGWU signs a new contract, but 15,000 nonunion or independent union workers will remain out.		Ford refinances his $5 million loan to Detroit, dropping the interest rate from four to three percent. He first lent the money when Detroit could not find a bank with suitable terms. Ford also plans visits Mexican free cities in search of sites for assembly plants.	French doctors feed cows cod liver oil so the milk they produce will help fight rickets in babies.	The U.S. Olympic team has 98 points. Second place Finland has 54.

F	G	H	I	J
Includes campaigns, elections, federal-state relations, civil rights and liberties, crime, the judiciary, education, healthcare, poverty, urban affairs, and population.	*Includes formation and debate of U.S. foreign and defense policies, veterans affairs, and defense spending. (Relations with specific foreign countries are usually found under the region concerned.)*	*Includes business, labor, agriculture, taxation, transportation, consumer affairs, monetary and fiscal policy, natural resources, pollution and industrial accidents.*	*Includes worldwide scientific, medical and technological developments, natural phenomena, U.S. weather and natural disasters.*	*Includes the arts, religion, scholarship, communications media, sports, entertainment, fashions, fads, and social life.*

	World Affairs	Europe	Africa & The Middle East	The Americas	Asia & The Pacific
Jul. 9	The allies reject Germany's request. They tell Germany that there will be no time limit on the military occupation.	The Little Entente indicates it will have a single foreign policy.... Mussolini imposes press censorship. Opposition papers protest....A malaria epidemic in the Ukraine produces 400,000 cases in five months.		The rebels continue to hold out in Sao Paolo. Federals pound their barracks with artillery and use tanks....Mexico invites American industrialists to examine its facilities....The Mexican army reports that defective Enfield ammunition bought to crush Huerta's rising blinded 50 soldiers. He blames corrupt procurement officials who buy old stock to maximize profits.	Because of their unruly behavior, later defined as mutiny, 190 Filipino Scouts will be discharged and another eight faces court martial.
Jul. 10	Bukharin tells the Communist International that their best means is to infiltrate labor unions and work from there.	Hungarians cheer the news that their loan is oversubscribed in both Europe and the United States.... Trotsky calls for creation of a Russian merchant marine. He sees it as a critical adjunct to the navy and an asset for trade....Turkey breaks with Russia over the spread of Communist propaganda.		Rebels rise in Panama and Rio Grande states of Brazil. In Sao Paolo, the dead litter the streets and food shortages begin.	
Jul. 11					Siberian relics from the Stone Age include a 17,000 skeleton, stags, dinosaurs, and weapons....Hindu-Muslim riots in Delhi kill seven.
Jul. 12	The international advertisers' convention is prepared to open in London....Eight-hundred American lawyers sail for Europe to observe the upcoming conference on the Dawes Plan.	Nationalists criticize the German cabinet harshly for allowing Allied military control in Germany.... German and French Communists meet in Cologne and reject the Dawes Plan for reparations. They also condemn Socialists as tools of world bankers....In Belfast, 30,000 Orangemen parade.		Reportedly, U.S. gold production in 1923 totaled $51 million, half the output of 1915. Canada is gaining on the United States and will soon be the world's number two producer....The death toll in Sao Paolo is up to 400....Fire continues to rage from California to British Columbia.	The current status of the Filipino Scouts is that 206 will face court martial. The mutiny proves larger than expected....Japan abandons its boycott of American films after public demand defeats the effort. Japan seeks to shift trade to Mexico from the United States.
Jul. 13	Communists order demonstrations against war on July 22 in France, Britain, Germany, and the United States.	The Greek assembly orders Sunday closing. It rejects Saloniki Jews' objections.	American Consul Vaughn at Johannesburg reports that implementation of a new air route between the Belgian Congo's Leopoldville and Elizabethville will cut travel time for passengers, mail, and goods over the 1,200 miles separating the two cities from 45 days to two days.	Having won at Sao Paolo, rebels are en route to Santos, port of the government's warships. Federal reinforcements are on their way....The receiver reports that San Domingo is paying its foreign debts too rapidly. It is not providing for ordinary expenses.	
Jul. 14			Primo de Rivera promises peace to the Rif. He warns that they must stop provocations first.	Refugees from Sao Paolo report death totals at 3,000....The wheat crop of the northern hemisphere is down 10 percent.	
Jul. 15	Former British prime minister Baldwin tells the world advertising meeting that if nations would advertise it would promote world peace.	Paris fetes the six American flyers who have completed a flight around the world. They also dine with Pershing....Germany lifts its embargo on grain and flour.		Brazil's government begins arresting officers and policemen in Rio on charges of disloyalty. The American consul asks for warships, but is turned down.	A flood in Kalgan, China, causes $1 million in damage....American Jews commit to supporting the Kai Feng Colony. The colony is home to Chinese Jews.
Jul. 16	With Secretary Kellogg observing, Ramsey MacDonald presides over the opening of the ten-nation allied conference on German reparations and default. Committee work begins.	Ireland's President Cosgrave releases Eamon De Valera and Austin Stack, with additional releases of political prisoners due within a day. The aim is to promote harmony on the eve of the Tailteann (Irish Olympic) games....The around-the-world flyers are in Britain refurbishing their plane for the final leg to New York....Yugoslavia rounds up Communists after the Communist International calls for red action in the Balkans.	Colonel Merian Cooper, after a six-month visit to Persia, reports that the British and Americans have not sewn up Persian oil concessions. Russia, which was strong in north Persia prior to the war, is a significant factor and in a better position than Anglo-Persian, Standard, or Sinclair.	The Pan American Conference on Electrical Communication adopts the convention on inter-American telegraph and other communications methods. The U.S. observer objects that the convention promotes government control rather than private ownership, the U.S. preference....In preliminary results, Saskatchewan votes wet with government control, not saloons.	

A	B	C	D	E
Includes developments that affect more than one world region, international organizations and important meetings of world leaders.	*Includes all domestic and regional developments in Europe, including the Soviet Union.*	*Includes all domestic and regional developments in Africa and the Middle East.*	*Includes all domestic and regional developments in Latin America, the Caribbean, and Canada.*	*Includes all domestic and regional developments in Asian and Pacific nations (and colonies).*

U.S. Politics & Social Issues	U.S. Foreign Policy & Affairs, Defense	U.S. Economy & Environment	Science, Technology & Nature	Culture, Leisure & Lifestyle	
Democrats select Davis after a stampede in his favor begins on the 103rd ballot. Vice presidential nominee is C.W. Bryan, selected on a single ballot. Police report that they arrested no thieves during the convention. Hospitals report they were busy.…Socialists go on record in condemning the Klan by name.		In heavy trading utilities reach new highs. Among the winners are Brooklyn Union Gas, American Waterworks, West Penn, and General Electric.	At a medical association meeting, a claim to have discovered a cancer germ provokes hecklers after the claimant refuses to provide proof.		Jul. 9
Farmer-Laborites reject LaFollette in favor of the Communist William Z. Foster.	Secretary Hughes indicates that the United States agrees with the League treaty to reduce armaments and establish mutual defense. He says the United States cannot participate.…The super dreadnaught Colorado performs well in tests.	An assistant postmaster general reports that airmail flyers have completed two million miles without a fatality. He also says that airmail saves bankers $800,000 annually by allowing lower interest rates.	Marconi says high power radio stations will soon be obsolete. The new radio will rely on short waves. It will provide all day service and be cheap.	Nurmi wins the 1,500- and 5,000-meter races. The United States still leads with a total of 176.5 points to Finland's 103.	Jul. 10
	Authorities corral smugglers after an exchange of gunfire at the Vermont border. Smuggled goods include liquor and Chinese.…The State Department has a draft note ready for the Chinese. It insists that China respect American creditors.…The Department of Labor develops rules to make sure Japanese in Hawaii do not get into the United States.	American investors are putting their money into English ventures. Interest rates are better abroad than at home.	Nathan Straus says that small towns should begin requiring pasteurized milk. Doing so will cut the death rate, which is higher in towns of 1,000–2,500 than in larger ones.	*Queen Mab* wins the Eastern Yacht Club's Vanderbilt Cup for schooners. Smaller class winners are *Mystic* and *Sally Ann*.	Jul. 11
Pueblo Indians tell Indian Commissioner Burke that they will defy his order barring them from teaching their children their traditional ritual and beliefs.	The navy says the airship *Shenandoah* will experiment with a sea mast in August.…Hughes notifies England, France, and Spain that the Tangier agreement is unacceptable. The United States expects protection of its rights.	The post office publishes rates for overseas airmail.…Ford sells its 10 millionth car. Eight million Model T's are on the road.…Mine workers win their 10 year fight with the Coronado Coal Company for damages arising from the company's violence in a coal strike.	A new invention uses radio to set clocks.	The three-cushion league follows the pocket billiards conference in reducing league cities to a dozen.	Jul. 12
A Michigan minister says details are fuzzy but he did preach against the Klan without naming it before he disappeared for 11 days and returned with KKK branded on his back.…Pitman, NJ, Klansmen induct 300 before a crowd of 40,000, burning crosses, and a fireworks American flag.	Rockaway police looking for rum-runners find smuggled immigrants instead, 31 Italians from a ship off shore. The smuggled indicate that they paid up to 3,500 lire for passage.	Sixteen employees buy the Devoe Paint Company. They all are under 40, and the new president is 31.…Gasoline is at 12 cents a gallon in Rochester, NY.		The final U.S. Olympic track and field score is 255. Runner up Finland has 166 points. The United States amasses 12 victories, while setting five world and two Olympic records, its best showing to date.	Jul. 13
		Bankers worry that steady imports of gold will fuel inflation. The six-month intake is more than $243 million.…Connecticut and Massachusetts report improved tobacco crops.			Jul. 14
New Jersey executes four in 40 minutes. It's a state record.	Labor Secretary Davis rules that Hawaiian Japanese are barred by a 1913 order by President Taft. He anticipates appeals on behalf of the 109,000 Japanese in the islands.…Would-be immigrants in Stockholm and elsewhere in Europe storm the consulates to beat the quota limits.	Now that the Red River boundary is defined, the land office issues decisions that allow leases on 36 disputed claims. Nearly 140 disputes remain.…Illinois charters the $26 million grain cooperative formed of the merger of five companies and thousands of cooperatives. Also included are elevators, banks, and railroads.	The University of Chicago reveals a radioscope that measures radium.		Jul. 15
After finding two cases of walking smallpox, the city's 82nd and 83rd cases this year, Cleveland health and police officials cordon off a neighborhood. The 10,000 residents receive involuntary vaccinations.…The Klan takes credit for electing the mayor of Flint, MI, a reformer who promises to clean up the city.…Eugene Debs endorses LaFollette. Burton Wheeler of Montana bolts the "Wall Street" Democrats for LaFollette.		A federal report finds clothing costs too high. Textile and clothing manufacturers blame one another.…Garment workers and manufacturers agree to accept terms proposed by Governor Smith. The 50,000 strikers will return to work tomorrow.	Forest fires in some areas abate due to rain. Forests in eastern Washington, northern Idaho, and California continue to burn.		Jul. 16

F	G	H	I	J
Includes campaigns, elections, federal-state relations, civil rights and liberties, crime, the judiciary, education, healthcare, poverty, urban affairs, and population.	*Includes formation and debate of U.S. foreign and defense policies, veterans affairs, and defense spending. (Relations with specific foreign countries are usually found under the region concerned.)*	*Includes business, labor, agriculture, taxation, transportation, consumer affairs, monetary and fiscal policy, natural resources, pollution and industrial accidents.*	*Includes worldwide scientific, medical and technological developments, natural phenomena, U.S. weather and natural disasters.*	*Includes the arts, religion, scholarship, communications media, sports, entertainment, fashions, fads, and social life.*

	World Affairs	Europe	Africa & The Middle East	The Americas	Asia & The Pacific
Jul. 17	The Olympics continue, with U.S. swimmers, divers, rowers, and boxers enjoying success. Americans are far down the list in the modern pentathlon, won by Sweden.			Brazil bars Associated Press and United Press International from transmitting. It cites bias in the news agencies' dispatches.	To discourage Japanese purchases of foreign goods, the Diet enacts tariffs of 100 percent on 250 luxury imports. Importers and merchants protest that Europeans can no longer expect a European standard of living in Japan.
Jul. 18	France takes a hard line against Germany, suggesting the possibility of unilateral action. Belgium refuses to sign the conference report. The Dawes conference stalls.... MacDonald explains British dislike of the disarmament treaty. He says no nation will disarm unilaterally based on alliances, which are notoriously unreliable.... The 286 million bushel world wheat crop is down 13 percent.	The Soviet Union commits $13 million to refurbish the ruins of the old capital Leningrad. Russia also eases labor rules to combat high unemployment.... The dean of Westminster Abbey blocks a memorial to Lord Byron. He says it is inappropriate in a Christian structure.	In Tehran, a mob beats the American vice consul, Major Imbrie, to death and critically injures his companion, Melin Seymour, living in the consulate after reputedly abusing Iranian laborers. The crowd is outraged that the Americans are taking photos of the site of a miracle.... Spain's Primo de Rivera indicates that Spanish forces in Morocco will abandon the field and move to forts and cities.	Three climbers successfully reach the top of Mount Geilkie. The 10,854 Canadian peak has long defied climbers.	The army formally charges the Filipino Scouts with mutiny.
Jul. 19	Final Olympic point totals are United States 255 and Finland 166.... Australia follows Canada's lead in telling Britain to stop knighting her citizens. The practice creates artificial distinctions that the dominions regard unfavorably.... At the Dawes talks, the committee on sanctions agrees that France can act unilaterally. Another committee decides that bondholders will have first claim to German government assets.	The Catholic Church denies sacraments to women in low cut clothing.... Bavaria's legislature considers a bill to bar Jews from owning land, holding government jobs, teaching school, or changing their names. The law would also banish Jews who arrived in Bavaria after 1914 and confiscate their property.... The Greek cabinet falls. It took office only in March.	"Pussyfoot" Johnson says he will take his prohibitionist campaign to Egypt. The Middle East wants a dry world, he says.		China waits for others to indicate whether they will follow Russia in raising the status of Chinese representatives to ambassador.... Hawaii finds a new crop for land worn out by pineapple and sugar cane. It is the pigeon pea, regarded in India as the staff of life.... The newly created University of Hawaii, allows strong student control and has no racial cliques.
Jul. 20	The allies agree on a plan to evacuate the Ruhr. Control of railroads is contentious because France wants to use some of its own people instead of letting Germans run the roads.	Three American women receive the French Legion of Honor for their efforts in the European relief effort. Americans gave $10 million to the work.... The British Communist Party becomes patron of a unit of the Soviet army.... Anti-monarchist German veterans form the 300,000-member republican *Reichsbanner*.	Martial law in Tehran quiets anti-American demonstrations after the death of the U.S. vice-consul.		
Jul. 21	Bottechia of Italy wins the *Tour de France*, leading every stage of the 3,000-mile race. Sixty of 157 entrants finish.... Bankers say the reparations loan formula is unworkable.	Cholera spreads in Russia and Greece. Bulgaria guards its borders.... Commanders inform Mussolini that reform of the Fascisti is finished. The militia has 373,000 members.	Persia apologizes to the United States and arrests a mullah and 200 others in the death of Imbrie. An army officer is also implicated.		River pirates seize flood relief intended for Canton.
Jul. 22	Kellogg offers a means of defusing the loan crisis. He says Germany is not in default until the reparations commission rules it is. Bankers are not fully satisfied but find it better than allowing unilateral French action.	Russia reports a strong trade for the first half of the year, with nearly 263 million gold rubles changing hands. The largest increase is in trade with the United States.... Berlin police seize Russian and Galician counterfeiters of English and U.S. notes.		Absentee voters shift Vancouver from supporting prohibition to approving government sales.	
Jul. 23	Andrew Mellon works with the Belgians, British, and Americans to find a solution acceptable to France. Meanwhile the plenary session debates when and how to invite Germany.... The head of the U.S. Olympic Committee denies press charges, primarily in France, that the Olympics cause hard feelings.	Mussolini tells the party to purge the Fascisti of undesirables and let the rank and file nominate and elect leaders in fair and open elections.	A British clergyman discussing the Shrine of Venus at Jerusalem's Garden Sepulcher says that the remnant wall there may be part of the one Hadrian erected over Jesus' resurrection tomb.	Federal forces take parts of Sao Paolo and deny an armistice to the rebels.... The Pan American communications conference gives the United States unlimited rights to develop Latin American radio.	The number of Filipino Scouts implicated in the mutiny rises over 500.

A	B	C	D	E
Includes developments that affect more than one world region, international organizations and important meetings of world leaders.	*Includes all domestic and regional developments in Europe, including the Soviet Union.*	*Includes all domestic and regional developments in Africa and the Middle East.*	*Includes all domestic and regional developments in Latin America, the Caribbean, and Canada.*	*Includes all domestic and regional developments in Asian and Pacific nations (and colonies).*

U.S. Politics & Social Issues	U.S. Foreign Policy & Affairs, Defense	U.S. Economy & Environment	Science, Technology & Nature	Culture, Leisure & Lifestyle	
Coolidge's campaign manager says the president will campaign by radio but will not take to the stump. Dawes will do the legwork as Roosevelt did for McKinley.…The Democratic National Committee begins work on rules for 1928. Sentiment is that the two-thirds and unit rules must go.	The navy launches the V-1 submarine, its largest to date. The V-1 has a range equal to that of the fleet.	Crude oil prices continue to fall as stocks increase. Stock prices remain firm.…The ICC rejects a plea by grain producing states for rail rate reductions. The commission cites high grain prices and low railroad profitability. Rail stocks respond positively.		American designers display their wares. The emphasis is on showing the waist. Skirts for daytime wear are 10–12 inches from the floor, but evening attire remains long.…A Philadelphia court rules that theaters must pay royalties to composers. Irving Berlin and nine others are due $500,000.	Jul. 17
West Virginia blocks LaFollette from the ballot. Pennsylvania and Maryland are troublesome as well.…A hundred union miners in Oklahoma raid the nonunion Cambria mine. In a swift raid, they, overpower guards, cut communications, and force the miners out.	The United States warns General Tosta of Honduras that its policy is nonrecognition of all revolutionary leaders as heads of state in Central America. U.S. policy rests on the Treaty of Amity signed by the five Central American nations.…The text of the Sino-Soviet Chinese Eastern Railway agreement arrives in Washington, DC. Officials begin working on a U.S. position.	In yet another setback, the government loses a war profiteering case against U.S. lumber companies.		The U.S. swim team clinches the Olympic title with 116 points, triple the total of second place Sweden.	Jul. 18
Fisk University in Tennessee gets a $1 million bequest. It is the first black university with such a large endowment.	Labor Secretary Davis indicates pleasure that the new immigration law has ended congestion at Ellis Island.…Italy protests the arrest of the commander and seven *Duilio* officers on narcotics smuggling charges.	The head of the garment manufacturers warns the members not to use the recent strike as an excuse to raise prices.	Dr. Abel of Johns Hopkins invents an artificial kidney that circulates blood outside the body and cleanses it.…Judge Olson and Dr. Hickson of Chicago say that criminality arises from brain defects. Eradicating flaws will end crime in two generations.…Brooklyn listeners complain that WNYC interferes with their reception. It operates on a band not authorized by the National Radio Conference.	The owner of the Van Rensselaer house, where Yankee Doodle was written in 1,758, donates the house to New York state.	Jul. 19
Massachusetts frees seven Rhode Island police. Rhode Island Democrats claim the Republicans are behind it.…Because the parties are short of funds, they delay the start of serious campaigning until September.…Mississippi puts shotgun-armed men on its borders to prevent entry of anthrax-bearing animals.	Ambassador Charles Warren clarifies that the claims commission will not act on Vera Cruz claims. It will address individual claims only, leaving government-to-government claims to the diplomats.	Pressed by New York, New Jersey officials begin notifying visitors that many streams are unsafe. Typhoid from drinking tainted water has already become a problem.	A German doctor reports success with his gyrorector. He has worked 20 years on the device to steer airplanes. Another group of Germans report a process to make gold. Unfortunately, it costs $2 million an ounce.	Helen Wills wins Olympic tennis. She is the first American woman to win a title overseas in 17 years.	Jul. 20
Maryland puts LaFollette on the ballot. Rhode Island's governor protests Massachusetts' treatment of Rhode Island police.…Clarence Darrow pleads Leopold and Loeb guilty, hoping psychiatric evidence can save their lives.	The state department declines an offer to select Nicaragua's president. The department merely wants Nicaragua to abide by the Treaty of Amity and hold free elections.	The Brotherhood of Locomotive Engineers purchases a New York bank.	A Chicagoan using a loop aerial receives English radio.	Jack Dempsey dislocates his right elbow and strains his neck in an automobile accident.…Arriving for his bout with Wills, Luis Firpo is detained at Ellis Island over a passport irregularity.	Jul. 21
The governor of Illinois calls out the guard to protect two blacks menaced by a white mob.	Coolidge backs Hughes in saying that the United States is willing to help Europe recover. The United States does expect Europe to be friendly to business.	The ICC prohibits the "Pittsburgh Plus" rate differential charged by U.S. Steel. The practice disadvantages the South especially and nets U.S. Steel $30 million in excess profits.…Ford sets a policy banning alcohol consumption by employees, on or off the job.…Sixty-day loans are at 25 percent, with 90-day rates at 2.75. The rate is lowest since the war.			Jul. 22
	The army orders amphibian planes from Loening. Capable of 120 miles per hour, the three-station planes carry a machine gun and operate from land or water.…The American Monument Commission proposes limited development of overseas cemeteries with government oversight. It opposes the "Gettysburg Plan."	Steel production is up due in part to price reductions. Experts see no fallout from the Pittsburgh Plus ruling.…Federal officials break up an illegal trust controlling imports of sisal from Mexico. Allegedly, the trust has forced prices up from 5.5 to 19 cents. Company officials say their prices are cheaper than other imports.	Marconi works with Britain to construct a beam system to relay radio signals from Britain to the dominions.	Battling Siki, the Senegalese prize fighter, marries a white American. This causes a stir because he is allegedly already married to a Dutch woman.	Jul. 23

F	G	H	I	J
Includes campaigns, elections, federal-state relations, civil rights and liberties, crime, the judiciary, education, healthcare, poverty, urban affairs, and population.	*Includes formation and debate of U.S. foreign and defense policies, veterans affairs, and defense spending. (Relations with specific foreign countries are usually found under the region concerned.)*	*Includes business, labor, agriculture, taxation, transportation, consumer affairs, monetary and fiscal policy, natural resources, pollution and industrial accidents.*	*Includes worldwide scientific, medical and technological developments, natural phenomena, U.S. weather and natural disasters.*	*Includes the arts, religion, scholarship, communications media, sports, entertainment, fashions, fads, and social life.*

	World Affairs	Europe	Africa & The Middle East	The Americas	Asia & The Pacific
Jul. 24	Olympic president De Coubertin says the games are a success. The athletes are polite; the only hooliganism arises in the crowds.	The Sophoulis cabinet takes office in Greece.…Russia offers Black Sea agricultural land for Jewish settlements.	High Commissioner Samuel says the development of British mandate Palestine is progressing smoothly. Palestine is the Jewish national home under the Balfour Declaration.	An explorer in Chile finds an Incan mummy. The 2,000-year-old mummy has false hair and clay on its face.…Canadian Pacific Railway officials are in Copenhagen, Denmark, trying to entice immigrants with cheap farmland.	Tokyo has a draft treaty ready for Russia on China. Tokyo wants oil concessions.
Jul. 25		Greece prepares to evict 50,000 Armenian refugees. It says its own people need the space.…Romania imposes tariff increases averaging 600 percent.…Russia has a famine relief fund of $32 million and seven million sufferers from famine.	Spanish officers express their dislike of the premier's plan to take regular forces out of the front lines in Morocco.	Federals use radio and air-dropped leaflets to warn civilians to leave Sao Paolo. Rumor says German and Italian veterans helped construct the rebel defenses.	
Jul. 26		King George reviews the British war fleet. The fleet consists of 194 ships in 10, four-mile lines.	Britain and Egypt again express competing desires for control of Sudan.…The United States warns Persia that it will break relations unless it gets indemnified for Imbrie's murder. Specifically, the United States wants appropriate honors and an apology for attacks on Imbrie's widow.	Mexico reports that it has a diary of Columbus missing since 1578.…American and Canadian forces capture six con men and $1 million in counterfeit money.…Argentina orders refurbishment of its navy in Quincy, MA.	
Jul. 27	MacDonald pushes for a French commitment to leave the Ruhr. Herriott delays his return to open parliament. He is considering defying Poincare and agreeing to MacDonald's desire.	Authorities shut down a Milan newspaper for editorials about the Matteotti affair.…A Viennese court rules that insults over the phone are not slander. The operator does not qualify as the third party required to change insults to slander.		In Mexico, an ambush kills Federal General Rodriguez Cerillo and his aide.	
Jul. 28		A disastrous storm takes the lives of 52 Ostend fishermen and 22 boats. Fishermen ashore mourn as sabots float ashore.…At the American advertisers' convention in Paris, France, two attendees are decorated with the Legion Cross.		The 130 members of a Canadian alpine club begin simultaneous climbs of six peaks in British Columbia.…Federal tanks and infantry overwhelm Sao Paolo rebels. Brazil resumes shipment of coffee and reopens banks.…Mexican federal forces block American filibusters attempting to unite with Hipolito Villa in Chihuahua.…In Tampico, two girls with bobbed hair come under attack from anti-bob mobs.	Floods in Chihli and Hanon provinces leave millions of Chinese homeless.…Japan agrees that attacks on Japanese in California were not racially motivated. They were due to labor strife instead. Japanese religious leaders organize to promote racial understanding.
Jul. 29	A League commission proposes publishing a catalogue of international scientific films. It touts the educational value of films.	German plans for a canal linking the Black and North Seas receives a cool reception from American bankers. The bankers want to see Europe much more stable before backing such a project.	Tehran is quiet after Persia agrees to all American terms to settle the Imbrie affair.		
Jul. 30	France's final offer on the Ruhr and default is the establishment of a committee, including an American, to decide when default occurs. Herriot reportedly agrees to withdraw from the Ruhr when the loan is floated.	Bavaria prohibits public demonstrations on Constitution Day, August 10, because while Bavaria respects the republican constitution it prefers a monarchy.			
Jul. 31	The sanctions committee agrees to Herriot's default board and coal payment overseer. It also agrees to the French position on payment of reparations in kind.	The Commons receives a bill to settle the boundary between the two Irelands. MacDonald agrees to debate after an 11-week Parliamentary break. His cabinet rides on the contentious issue.…Greece executes 19 Bulgarians who raid across the border. Greece, with Yugoslavian and Rumanian support, is near to invading Bulgaria.	The World Zionist Convention in London agrees in principle to an American plan for the building of Palestine under the mandate. American Jews want non-Zionists on the board while Eastern Europeans want Zionists only. The final decision will come in 1925.	Reports from Brazil indicate Sao Paolo is returning to normal, with refugees streaming back to the battle-scarred city. The rebels have taken the city's money and gone to Paraguay.	

A	B	C	D	E
Includes developments that affect more than one world region, international organizations and important meetings of world leaders.	*Includes all domestic and regional developments in Europe, including the Soviet Union.*	*Includes all domestic and regional developments in Africa and the Middle East.*	*Includes all domestic and regional developments in Latin America, the Caribbean, and Canada.*	*Includes all domestic and regional developments in Asian and Pacific nations (and colonies).*

U.S. Politics & Social Issues	U.S. Foreign Policy & Affairs, Defense	U.S. Economy & Environment	Science, Technology & Nature	Culture, Leisure & Lifestyle	
		Crude oil output is 1.97 million barrels a day, down 15,000 barrels. Prices hold steady.…News of a railroad merger into a Van Swearingen system raises rail stock values. Affected lines are the Erie, Pere Marquette, and Pittsburgh and West Virginia.…The ICC encourages shippers to move bulk items quickly, particularly coal. The railroads need cars for the large fruit crop.	U.S. Steel's Charles Schwab forms the Six-Wheel Company to build trucks and buses. Six wheels will help to save roadbeds and allow larger loads.	Tunney defeats Carpentier. The Frenchman claims he was fouled and demands a rematch.…Airships are a novelty. A test flight of the *Shenandoah* causes a boy to fall off a roof, motorists to collide, and a camper to scald himself.	Jul. 24
LaFollette forces officially label themselves the Progressive Party and establish the Liberty Bell as their emblem. Some Wisconsin Republicans become Progressives.				Chicago barbers threaten to strike. They want higher prices for bobbed hair.…Carpentier says on second thought maybe he was not fouled. He was hit inadvertently by a knee instead.…To speed baseball games, Commissioner Johnson orders 10-day suspensions for trivial delays.	Jul. 25
The front-runner in the Democratic gubernatorial primary in Texas is a Klansman. The Klan in Syracuse, NY, covers the business district with placards reading, "God give us men." New York Socialists denounce the Klan by name and back LaFollette.	The United States and Denmark ratify an agreement on control of liquor traffic.…Rumania responds to a U.S. note but fails to accept a U.S. right to protest its mining law.		The Red Cross reports that it spent $200,000 in the first half of the year. It had more requirements to respond than in any six-month period in its history.	A fashion expert says that short hair is liberating. The bob is here to stay, and long hair will never return.	Jul. 26
An early estimate is that the presidential election will cost $15 million for all campaigns combined. All parties agree they want to attract a record 30 million voters.…New York Socialists select former clergyman Norman Thomas as their candidate for governor.		An engineer's report says that an integrated hydroelectric system using a mix of steam and water power could save 50 million tons of coal annually in the northeast.	An expedition heads out on a naval minesweeper to research little known islands and their inhabitants, flora, and fauna. The Howland, Baker, and other islands under study are south and west of Hawaii.		Jul. 27
A patrol-boat gunner needs 800 shots to bring down a rumrunner. Six hundred of the shots hit the armor-plated converted submarine chaser.		Senator McKellar asks Secretary Wallace to intervene to slow the spread of anthrax in the South.…Drought in Connecticut and western Massachusetts threatens to cost $10 million in losses to the burley tobacco crop.…Urban Pictures, a $10 million business, goes into receivership. The New York company makes educational and scenic films and owns rights to the spirograph, a home projector.	A surgeon restores a man's speech after fixing his broken skull by grafting a bit of shin onto his head.		Jul. 28
Fights in Massachusetts between Klansmen and their opponents injure 50. In one brawl 500 anti-Klansmen square off with 200 Klansmen.		Government reports show chain store sales up five percent. Mail order is up also, but overall wholesale sales are down, with 11 lines of goods at their lowest in five years.		A preview of fall hats shows that the cloche is out. Large and floppy seem to be the fashion.…Babe Ruth hits his 13th homer of the month, tying a record he set in 1921.	Jul. 29
"Get-out-the-Vote" clubs form in Florida cities and in Pittsburgh.…Faced with a split in his ranks, Gompers says the AFL will endorse no candidate. Mine workers back his position, but railroad unions back LaFollette,.	Secretary Wilbur says he is open to discussions with Britain over gun elevations. Britain has formally protested to the United States and Japan that elevating guns increases their range.	According to a representative of the Mechanic and Metals Bank, half of the world's gold is in the United States. Easy credit encourages unwise expansion.			Jul. 30
A million veterans have applied for the bonus. The government processes 1,000 daily but will raise daily processing to 50,000 a day once the 2,000 newly hired clerks are ready to deal with 10 million documents and 80,000 muster rolls.		More than 50 coal mining operations in West Virginia consolidate. The new company has assets between $20 and $25 million.…Studebaker reports that profits for the first half of the year are down $6 million from the same time in 1923.	A Philadelphia diver off Atlantic City's steel pier makes the first broadcast from the bottom of the sea. He describes for Gimbel's radio station listeners of wrecks and other items of interest.…Tests with moths disclose that females avoid whisky but males flock to it.		Jul. 31

F	G	H	I	J
Includes campaigns, elections, federal-state relations, civil rights and liberties, crime, the judiciary, education, healthcare, poverty, urban affairs, and population.	*Includes formation and debate of U.S. foreign and defense policies, veterans affairs, and defense spending. (Relations with specific foreign countries are usually found under the region concerned.)*	*Includes business, labor, agriculture, taxation, transportation, consumer affairs, monetary and fiscal policy, natural resources, pollution and industrial accidents.*	*Includes worldwide scientific, medical and technological developments, natural phenomena, U.S. weather and natural disasters.*	*Includes the arts, religion, scholarship, communications media, sports, entertainment, fashions, fads, and social life.*

	World Affairs	Europe	Africa & The Middle East	The Americas	Asia & The Pacific
Aug. 1	Italy lost 210,000 emigrants in 1923. Rather than go to the United States, now impossible due to quotas, they head to Australia and Central America....The first day of the Williams Institute gathers 225 world scholars and 1,000 interested bystanders. They hear R.H. Tawney anticipate a new Reform Bill era under Britain's Labour Party. Orientalist Sir Valentine Chirol prophesies race war.	A strike by Dublin workers disrupts electricity. Businesses close and litter fills the streets. The Irish Olympics program has to adjust....In the Dail Eireann on the eve of adjournment for the summer, members O'Higgins and Johnson say that England has broken the treaty and the six counties of the Irish Free State should adopt their own republican constitution.		Havana keeps its city lights burning despite an unpaid electric bill of $2.3 million. The American president of the Havana Electric Railway, Light and Power Company backs off threats to cut power after Cuban officials promise payment and mention the risks associated with blackened streets.	
Aug. 2	Allies agree to an implementation strategy for the Dawes Plan. They ask Germany to attend the conference immediately.	Zita, former empress of Austria, refuses to act in the movies. Although in poverty, she stands on her dignity....France declares it has evidence that Germany has 350,000 men training in its illegal army....Belgian Baron Coppee is freed of treason charges after a 61-day trial. Briand testifies on his behalf, and discloses for the first time that the Kaiser wanted a separate peace in 1917....Divers begin raising the German fleet scuttled at Scapa Flow.		Archaeologists in the Yucatan uncover Mayan basketball courts....Facing a typhoid epidemic, the Cuban government prepares to inoculate all Cubans.	China protests Japan's banning of coolie labor. Japan replies that China's note, its seventh, is groundless because Japan bars other nationalities as well as Chinese.
Aug. 3	Lieutenant Wade of the around-the-world flyers sees his effort fall short as his plane crashes into the sea off Iceland.	Lenin's tomb opens and thousands pass by. Soviet scientists say the embalming makes him lifelike....A German shoe expert says shoes should be tight. Loose footwear makes one appear slovenly....European steel producers develop a "convention" to present a united front against low priced U.S. steel....In Berlin, fights break out between nationalists mourning the war dead and Communists.	Spain installs Raisuli as leader of the tribes in its zone. He is to lead 4,000 men in the fight against the Rif in Morocco.	Mexicans murder Rosalie Evans, British citizen fighting to hold her land. The murderers also steal her payroll. Her dispute earlier had caused a diplomatic rift between the two governments.	India reduces its bank rate for the fifth time. Economic conditions are improving....Australia's government indicates it will begin assisting business and industry.
Aug. 4	The German delegation departs for London. Its first priority is evacuation of the Ruhr.	Corfu and Patras have cholera outbreaks, report Italian health officials....The Irish boundary issue is at a crisis. Cosgrave calls British cabinet ministers Henderson and Thomas to Dublin for an emergency meeting.	Liberia bars entry to all associated with Garvey's pan-African organization.	The rebel Fonseca takes San Marcos, a Honduran town near the Nicaraguan border. His small force is moving toward Choluteca. Honduras just recently finished a three-cornered civil war.	
Aug. 5	MacDonald gives Marx the Dawes administration plan. Marx says he has to satisfy his fellow citizens on the military and economic evacuation of the Ruhr but expects an early and positive decision.	Armed men wearing Russian helmets raid a Polish border town. They kill Polish cavalry and take prisoners....Britain and Russia break off negotiations of the commercial and general treaties they have been negotiating for four months. The issue is Russian refusal to compensate for nationalized property. British recognition of Russia remains in place....Cosgrave gets British assurances of action on the boundary. His job is safe as the crisis passes.	Bishop George A. McGuire of the African Orthodox Church and the Bishop of Abyssinia tell Marcus Garvey's convention-goers that the Ethiopian Christ is black. Blacks should burn depictions of a white Christ and Virgin Mary. The script for the King James Bible is of Ethiopian origin.	Newfoundland's premier begins to reverse prohibition.	Japan's air force is upgrading. An Italian subsidiary of a German company is using German plans and building all-metal bombers capable of a round trip to the Philippines with a ton of bombs.
Aug. 6	Germany accepts the Dawes Plan with the reservations Marx indicated earlier. Marx is optimistic and reassures Belgium and France.... Two economies overseen by the League get stronger. Austria is still in crisis but less than before. Hungary has an acceptable budget and a currency benefiting from the rise in Sterling....Trotsky scores American imperialism and calls on the proletariat to fight attempts to Balkanize Europe.	Britain tells Ulster to provide a boundary commissioner or Britain will do it for her. The boundary bill will pass on 30 September.... MacDonald intervenes with negotiators and forces a treaty with the Soviets. The pact acknowledges Russian debts and sends them to a claims commission. Britain agrees to give Russia a loan once the debt amount is set....The supply of Reichsbank notes rises another 201 quintillion in a week. Gold reserves are growing though.	The League receives a report that agrarian Communism works well in the former German colony of Southwest Africa. The Union of South Africa furnishes the communes of its mandate with eight million hectares as well as irrigation, equipment, and schools.... South Africa reports discovery of 50 whites living in near serfdom to the Sebele tribe near the Great Kalahari Desert. They appear to be descendants of Boer pioneers who got lost in the migration of 1878.	The Cuban inoculation program has given shots to 131,381 Havanans.	Floods in India kill 100, leave 50,000 homeless, and cause severe crop damage....Reportedly, the Far East is mired in an economic slump, even Japan. Only Shanghai and Hong Kong show economic life....The Governor of Bengal warns plotters that he knows how to handle them. He says the British will use every weapon at their disposal to quell revolutionary movements.

A	B	C	D	E
Includes developments that affect more than one world region, international organizations and important meetings of world leaders.	*Includes all domestic and regional developments in Europe, including the Soviet Union.*	*Includes all domestic and regional developments in Africa and the Middle East.*	*Includes all domestic and regional developments in Latin America, the Caribbean, and Canada.*	*Includes all domestic and regional developments in Asian and Pacific nations (and colonies).*

	U.S. Politics & Social Issues	U.S. Foreign Policy & Affairs, Defense	U.S. Economy & Environment	Science, Technology & Nature	Culture, Leisure & Lifestyle
Aug. 1	Guarded by Shining Sabres, Marcus Garvey, President General of the African Republic, observes a parade of 3,500 people, including the African Legion, Boy and Girl Scouts, and Black Cross workers. The month-long convention of the Universal Negro Improvement Association is under way.... Massachusetts police are under orders to disarm all who attend Klan meetings. Recent arrestees at Shrewsbury carried clubs, lead pipes, and revolvers.	The August Citizens Military Training Camp at Plattsburgh, NY, has more than 3,000 enrollees from New York, New Jersey, and Delaware. The contingent is the largest for the four-week basic training camp since 1917.		A Johns Hopkins professor calculates that the U.S. population will reach its peak in 2,100 and decline thereafter. Maximum population will be 197 million.	
Aug. 2	Labor endorses La Follette but not his party. Gompers says the AFL has long endorsed individual candidates but not specific parties.... Religious leaders disagree over radio. Some fear it will discourage attendance while others say it will promote religion.	The United States exports $200 million in tobacco a year and imports $100 million worth. It grows a third of the world's crop.	A jeweler comes up with an idea to boost sales. Advertisements and window displays based on birthstones should increase lagging sales.	Sir Ernest Rutherford says the energy stored in atoms may be unreachable because most are stable. Only uranium and thorium have possibilities, and there is no known method of speeding their disintegration sufficiently to release their energy.... The government authorizes 15,500 amateurs to use and experiment with short waves.	Battling Siki, in trouble with immigration authorities, also loses his boxing match. Jack Lynch outpoints him in Rhode Island.
Aug. 3	Bootleggers in Proctorville, OH, dynamite a parked car. The explosion destroys city hall and a nearby house. The mayor and a moonshiner in the municipal building escape with minor injuries.... Garvey calls for a free black Africa with a black God. He cedes Europe and America to whites.		Benjamin Anderson, bank economist, calls tariff reductions to promote imports and reduce the U.S. gold surplus. He says Europe critically needs U.S. credits and the gold standard.		
Aug. 4	The United States indict Garvey for lying to a grand jury about his income tax.... Attendance at citizens' military camps exceeds 33,000 nationally, triple the 1921 record. Omaha is number one, with New York number two.... The AFL commits speakers and funds to campaigning for La Follette.		General Electric offers its 27,000 employees half-year bonuses totaling more than $1.1 million. Profits are at record levels.	Pennsylvania's Eastern State Penitentiary bans radios after it learns that convicts are using them to relay coded messages about drug smuggling into the prison.... Forest fires destroy the mining community of Gold Springs, WY.	Ban Johnson says 1924 is the best year yet for the American League. All clubs are making a profit.... The Navajo adopt Jackie Coogan. The child star's new name is "Talking Eyes."
Aug. 5	After a lengthy hearing, judge rules Leopold and Loeb sane, denies them a jury trial, and prepares to set their penalties. The two have earlier pled guilty.				
Aug. 6	Hempstead, NY, officials allow the Klan to host a carnival. The event is to raise funds for building a church.		A report says last year's petroleum supply was 129.5 million barrels over the previous year. Total supply was 814.4 million barrels including 17.38 million imported barrels. Producing wells totaled 290,000.	The British Association of Medicine meeting at Toronto with hundreds of U.S. attendees hearing Sir David Bruce call for aggressive medicine to eradicate disease. He praises Rockefeller's work against yellow fever and sleeping sickness.	A move to have regattas rowed upstream is rejected. The referee says regattas will continue to be rowed downstream.
	F *Includes campaigns, elections, federal-state relations, civil rights and liberties, crime, the judiciary, education, healthcare, poverty, urban affairs, and population.*	**G** *Includes formation and debate of U.S. foreign and defense policies, veterans affairs, and defense spending. (Relations with specific foreign countries are usually found under the region concerned.)*	**H** *Includes business, labor, agriculture, taxation, transportation, consumer affairs, monetary and fiscal policy, natural resources, pollution and industrial accidents.*	**I** *Includes worldwide scientific, medical and technological developments, natural phenomena, U.S. weather and natural disasters.*	**J** *Includes the arts, religion, scholarship, communications media, sports, entertainment, fashions, fads, and social life.*

	World Affairs	Europe	Africa & The Middle East	The Americas	Asia & The Pacific
Aug. 7				President-elect Calles of Mexico denies plans to talk with Britain about improving relations between the two countries.... Prime Minister Mackenzie-King reminds the Soviet representative, Alexander Zaxikoff, that Canada's recognition accorded last March applies to trade only.	
Aug. 8	The U.S. Navy makes one final effort to find an ice-free base to land supplies in Greenland. The around-the-world flyers are stranded in Iceland because Greenland is their next leg and its waters are ice-bound.	Russia's lack of a head of state forces Labour to break tradition. The Anglo-Russian Treaty does not mention the British king, raising questions of its legality. The treaty is optional for the dominions.		Honduras sends 2,000 troops after the rebel Ferrara.... Mexicans strike in Vera Cruz.	
Aug. 9	The French cabinet holds an all-night session to ratify Herriot's moves in London. MacDonald vows to keep British troops in Cologne until the Germans fulfill their obligations. The commissioners sign the accord and the Dawes Plan goes into effect.	Germany celebrates Constitution Day. At least the Clerical, Democrat, and Socialist parties do. All others boycott the day. Berlin's turnout is only 5,000.... Bulgaria, Rumania, and Yugoslavia agree that they are under threat from Russia, which seeks to subvert the small states and occupy Poland.	An American industrial commission in Persia reports that the country is emerging from a postwar depression and is preparing for significant industrial development.	Before sailing for Europe to drum up business, Calles says he holds no hostility toward U.S. oil companies. He wants to bring prohibition to Mexico and to eliminate gambling on the U.S. border.	
Aug. 10		Germany's June import surplus is 277.8 million gold marks. This is better than previous months.... Russia's Rakovsky says France is next on the list, but France must follow England's lead and recognize Russia before negotiating anything else.		Amapala, Honduras, joins the rebellion. Government troops prepare to take the town back.	
Aug. 11	The flyers' supply ship breaks free of the ice and a supply base in Greenland should be ready in two days.... Britain submits the Mosul question to the League. It also asks Turkey to attend the meeting.	France, Belgium, and Germany hold meetings to work out the details of demilitarizing the Ruhr. They lean toward a commercial treaty as the best tool.... Holland rejects League guarantees as the basis for disarmament.	South Africa looks to expand its cotton production. Experiments have produced a good quality cotton, and exports have risen significantly since the first year, 1921. This year's crop should top last year's 2.3 million pounds by at least 50 percent.	Dr. Alexander Hamilton Rice and his wife are at Para. They are preparing a two-year expedition to find the source of the Orinoco River using a seaplane.	A Japanese mine blast kills 72.
Aug. 12		Cosgrave introduces a bill in the Dail to move on the border dispute as soon as Britain acts. He criticizes anti-treaty British agitators as well as Irish opponents, but he does seek modification of the treaty.	Egyptian forces mass at ports and raid Turkish homes to forestall a Turkish-supported attempt to reinstate the last khedive, Abbas Hilmy Pasha. Sudanese forces fire over the heads of Egyptian forces to kill two mutinying Egyptian Railway Battalion members in service to Sudan. Egypt also has a simmering border dispute over Libya.		
Aug. 13		The Reichsbank increases its gold reserves by 6.3 million gold marks in a week. Its nine-week accrual is 48.8 million.	Britain sends a battleship, cruiser, *Highlanders*, and planes to the Sudan as an inquiry opens into the deaths of the two mutineers. The inquiry reveals that the labor battalion members had engaged in extensive sabotage before the climax of the mutiny.	Mexico declines to accept a British note over the murdered Evans. The Mexican representative says the tone is threatening. He anticipates heavy-handed British action, as is customary by the strong against the weak.	Leaders of the Canton Merchants Volunteer Corps flee after Sun Yat-sen challenges the legality of their purchase of arms. The supplier says he provided arms to Sun Yat-sen only.
Aug. 14				General Ferrera is at Santa Maria in Intibuca with 1,200 men. General Fonseca is 30 miles from Tegucigalpa. Both are in rebellion against the Honduran government and seek to combine their forces.	The American Red Cross sends $100,000 to China to aid in flood and other disaster relief. The flood death toll is 13,115, with 15 million harmed by disasters.

A	B	C	D	E
Includes developments that affect more than one world region, international organizations and important meetings of world leaders.	*Includes all domestic and regional developments in Europe, including the Soviet Union.*	*Includes all domestic and regional developments in Africa and the Middle East.*	*Includes all domestic and regional developments in Latin America, the Caribbean, and Canada.*	*Includes all domestic and regional developments in Asian and Pacific nations (and colonies).*

U.S. Politics & Social Issues	U.S. Foreign Policy & Affairs, Defense	U.S. Economy & Environment	Science, Technology & Nature	Culture, Leisure & Lifestyle	
The Catholic Total Abstinence Union president tells the 52nd annual convention that membership decline threatens the CTAU's existence. He says the hierarchy has lost interest because it misunderstands the union's purpose and thinks the enactment of prohibition makes it moot.		The New York-San Francisco airmail route is taking heavy losses, raising concerns that it may not be affordable and may have to end.…The half-year report on shoe production shows a drop of 30 million pair. Output is 157.8 million pair versus 187.9 million the previous year.	A British scientist predicts that in 100 years there will be a free black state in the United States and a mixed race. Additionally, immigration will alter the politics of the South.		Aug. 7
Connecticut's fire warden says he will arrest anyone who burns a cross without a permit.		The Nickel Plate System, which merges several lines into the fourth-largest in the east, causes no stir among rival lines. The B&O, Pennsylvania, and New York Central have been tracking the deal, and the dealmakers have kept the ICC informed.	The *Shenandoah* successfully moors to the dirigible mast of a naval vessel, dropping 1,000 feet of line in a night test.…From a calm sea, a 15-foot wave appears and knocks hundreds of Coney Island swimmers over. Despite panic, only four suffer harm. The wave is attributed to the screw of a liner off shore.		Aug. 8
Tulsa lawyer Remington Rogers says ex-Governor Walton has no chance of winning the Senate because Democrats will turn from him. Impeached as Governor, Walton also opposes the Klan. The Republicans will carry Oklahoma, says Rogers.	Admiral W.L. Rodgers tells the Institute on Disarmament and Security that the United States should prepare for an aggressive war to take territory it needs when the population reaches 200 million. He cites Henry Pratt Fairchild's estimate that the U.S. population, currently 110 million will surpass China's, currently 400 million, by 2,000.	In June, the federal reserve shipped $600,000 in currency to Europe and brought in over $6.9 million, redeemable in gold. The paper from Europe is mostly that spent by American tourists.		Coney Island roller chairs attract quite a few who prefer to rest their feet, but they have their share of scoffers. Skeptics note that walking is faster and the 75 cents an hour for double occupancy costs will buy seven good hot dogs and a single Bowery one. Alternatively, it pays seven fares from the island plus three lollipops.	Aug. 9
Hiram Evans, Klan imperial wizard, charges La Follette seeks to undermine the people's confidence in government. He also challenges La Follette's war record and says the Klan remains committed to its religious goals.…New York's Fiorello LaGuardia bolts the Republicans, backs La Follette, and declares himself an independent.	Fire in the Great Hickory plant destroys 45 million pounds of gunpowder. The loss totals $28 million.…The first veterans of the Grand Army of the Republic begin arriving at Boston for the annual encampment. Five thousand elderly men are expected.	The AFL announces that its four million members will start a union-label drive in two weeks. The goal is to promote the 50,000 union shops.			Aug. 10
	The United States says it will not send a delegate to the commission on interallied obligations. It will simply have an observer.			Mort than 100 universities will use psychological tests to determine the fitness of applicants for admission. Chicago, Princeton, Dartmouth, Northwestern, and Minnesota are compiling the tests.	Aug. 11
Henry Ford withdraws his name from the Michigan Republican senatorial primary. A reluctant draftee from the first, he waits until the last minute to withdraw.…Klan candidates trail in primaries in Ohio and Arkansas. Both lose.	Coolidge appoints Major General John L. Hines to replace Pershing as chief-of-staff when Pershing retires on September 13. Hines is currently Pershing's deputy and served with Pershing in Mexico and Europe.	The Agricultural Credit Corporation reports that in its first four months it has saved nine banks. By lending $4 million, it safeguards $45 million in deposits as the northwest struggles through a heavy economic downturn.		Rain in Boston fails to dampen the spirits of 4,000 GAR marchers—or the crowds cheering them.…German imperial war bonds should be worthless. After all, the imperial regime is history. However, they are the hot speculative item and at least one speculator turns a $700 purchase into a $170,000 sale.	Aug. 12
After Indiana's governor indicates his opposition, promoters cancel a boxing match between former champion Jack Johnson and Tut Jackson. The governor denies he opposes because the fighters are black. The promoter replaces Johnson with a white football player and two days later cancels the bout due to lack of ticket sales.	Preparations proceed for an all out war against liquor, drugs, and alien smuggling in September. The plan is to take the fight to the 12-mile limit by using four destroyers, 100 patrol boats, and other vessels. The total fleet is 322 ships. The force of 2,000 men will use four-inch guns and machine guns.		Crowds in Central Park hear, above the roar of the engine, the radioed words over of a flyer a mile overhead and reply to him. Radio station WJZ receives the words through a wire tied to the ground receiver and broadcasts them.	The GAR reports that only 65,352 remain on its rolls.	Aug. 13
George S. Rice is head of the new Mine Safety Board in the Department of the Interior at Washington, DC. The board has a broader mandate and greater power than the mine safety committee at the Pittsburgh experimental station that it replaces.…Coolidge accepts his party's nomination. Radio broadcasts the speech.		U.S. banks report they add $18.7 million in new gold during the week. Cash reserves are up $4.4 million.	AT&T and a British company report they are experimenting with a trans-Atlantic radiophone. They think it has commercial possibilities. They see no technological reason restricting the connection of sea and landlines into a global network.	The GAR elects its new commander, selects Grand Rapids, MI, as site of next year's encampment, and votes to ask Congress for a pension increase.…The National Association of Scientific Angling Clubs opens its 16th annual baitcasting tournament.	Aug. 14
F *Includes campaigns, elections, federal-state relations, civil rights and liberties, crime, the judiciary, education, healthcare, poverty, urban affairs, and population.*	**G** *Includes formation and debate of U.S. foreign and defense policies, veterans affairs, and defense spending. (Relations with specific foreign countries are usually found under the region concerned.)*	**H** *Includes business, labor, agriculture, taxation, transportation, consumer affairs, monetary and fiscal policy, natural resources, pollution and industrial accidents.*	**I** *Includes worldwide scientific, medical and technological developments, natural phenomena, U.S. weather and natural disasters.*	**J** *Includes the arts, religion, scholarship, communications media, sports, entertainment, fashions, fads, and social life.*	

	World Affairs	Europe	Africa & The Middle East	The Americas	Asia & The Pacific
Aug. 15	The allies refuse to yield to German entreaties that they accelerate the Ruhr evacuation. Germany prepares to accept the terms, which it does on August 16, with formal signing on August 31.	Bulgaria's foreign minister admits that Bulgarians have crossed into Serbia. He apologizes to Yugoslavia.…Authorities in the Ruhr arrest seven Communists for agitating for a strike.…After a long absence brought on by last year's jailing, De Valera resumes working to establish an Irish republic.…The Tailteann championship goes to the U.S. track and field team. Ireland and Australia follow.	Egypt's cabinet orders its minister in London to protest British action in the Sudan. Egypt challenges Britain's version of events. The high commissioner in Egypt says the cabinet version is incomplete and misleading. Egyptian public opinion is already inflamed.	The warship *Galveston* arrives at La Ceiba, Honduras, to protect American interest.…Armed guards protect the Mexican congress as it opens its session. It has to validate the presidential election results and allocate seats. Agrarians and labor groups intend to contest the seating.	Fighting breaks out between soldiers of two Yunnanese factions near the American Baptist Mission in a Cantonese suburb, Tungshan. The head of the South China naval patrol says all Americans are safe.
Aug. 16			Palestine wants to encourage industrialization. It lifts all duties on heavy machinery.		Governor General Wood and Postmaster General New establish airmail service from the Philippines to points in the United States through San Francisco.
Aug. 17		French steel output is down. Britain's is up but below 1923. Italy is showing signs of economic improvement. German bankers look forward to loans after enactment of Dawes.	Britain warns Egypt that it stands firm on its Sudanese policy that the governor general will take whatever actions he deems necessary.	Barred from coming to the United States, 10,000 Jews stranded in Europe accept General Calles' invitation to immigrate to Mexico. The U.S.-based Refugee Emergency Committee will help with arrangements.	Fighting between police and paraders in Mandalay, Burma, leaves four marchers dead.…A Chinese dike breaks and floods 150 towns.…A new Hyderabad Hindu-Muslim clash injures 300.
Aug. 18	French troops withdraw from the Ruhr towns of Offenbourg and Appenweier. The Dawes-related withdrawal begins.…Around-the-world planes struggle to rise from the water under the heavy load the 825-mile flight to Greenland requires. They remain stuck in Iceland.			Brazil sends a flotilla up the Amazon to quell a mutiny on the antiquated vessels in Amazonas Province. The government discounts the fighting capabilities of the boats, scheduled for scrap.	
Aug. 19		Disturbances at Port Sudan result in the arrest of nine Egyptian officials and some government employees. Martial law is in effect and Highlanders are en route.			Australia opts out of the Anglo-Soviet Accord. The premier points out that Australia was not in on the discussions.
Aug. 20		German Communists and followers of Ludendorff indicate they will oppose ratification of the Dawes agreement.			An earthquake in Turkestan kills 41. Eight thousand are homeless.
Aug. 21	The American planes arrive safely in Greenland, covering 825 miles in about 10 hours. There is no word on the Italian, Locatelli.…Experts tell the League that there are 1,000 poison gases available for use in any future war.	The commissioner for Austria submits a negative report on Austria's recovery. He scolds the government for giving civil servants pay raises even though the budget was in deficit.…Britain debuts a "dreadnaught" plane with a single 1,000 horsepower engine.	Spain reports heavy fighting and growing disaffection in western Morocco. Several rebel columns press the Spanish hard.		
Aug. 22	As the hunt for the missing Italian begins, the American flyers prepare for the next leg, from Greenland to Labrador.	The upcoming Franco-German coal combine promises to be another cause of friction between France and Britain.…French and German Communist deputies shout down Dawes ratification proceedings in France and Germany.		The Canadian dollar reaches par in the United States. Canadian use of American markets for loans and a good wheat crop are reasons for the strong Canadian dollar.	Karakhan, the Communist envoy in Peking, denounces the United States as corrupt at home and violent in Asia.…A bank in Shanghai, owned and operated by women, serves women only. The bank serves as a pawnshop as well as providing a stimulus to savings and women's employment.

A	B	C	D	E
Includes developments that affect more than one world region, international organizations and important meetings of world leaders.	*Includes all domestic and regional developments in Europe, including the Soviet Union.*	*Includes all domestic and regional developments in Africa and the Middle East.*	*Includes all domestic and regional developments in Latin America, the Caribbean, and Canada.*	*Includes all domestic and regional developments in Asian and Pacific nations (and colonies).*

U.S. Politics & Social Issues	U.S. Foreign Policy & Affairs, Defense	U.S. Economy & Environment	Science, Technology & Nature	Culture, Leisure & Lifestyle	
The Presbyterian Mission Board's Reverend John McDowell, one-armed due to a coal mining accident in his youth, says that workers rightly resent uplift programs and welfare work. He calls for fraternal industrialism.	*Shenandoah* heads 500 miles out to sea for battle fleet maneuvers. For the first time, a dirigible will scout enemy vessels for a fleet.	Auto production shows its first increase since spring. It is a sign that the economy is recovering.... Receivers for the $25 million Middle States Oil include former Judge Julius P. Meyer and Joseph P. Tumulty, formerly secretary to Woodrow Wilson. The company entered receivership after a stockholder charged its board, including former Oklahoma Governor Haskell, with fraud and mismanagement.		Abrogast sets another casting record at Buffalo....The president of the Dance Masters Association wants a ban on the "finale hop." It and other suggestive dances should give way to proper dances such as the waltz and tango.	Aug. 15
The National Women's Party determines to back all women running for Congress. The party hopes to elect enough women to establish a bloc in Congress.		Alarmed by a multimillion-dollar robbery in the West, the postal service orders 3,000 armored cars to protect the mails. The cars are bullet and gas proof.		The soda fountain celebrates 50 years since the first opened in Philadelphia. Soda fountains serve five billion drinks and dishes a year....Russian actor/manager Stanislowski says American theater is inartistic and too profit oriented.	Aug. 16
An anti-Klan candidate for sheriff in Childress County, TX, is found alive in his garage with a bullet wound to his head. Officials offer a $100 reward for proof of statements that the Klan rejected his application for membership....Marcus Garvey buys *General Goethals*, the liner that will transport blacks to Africa. He charges 50 cents a head to look at it....The Texas Klan drops its anti-Catholic stance and solicits the Jewish vote. Its candidate is in a tight primary race with "Ma" Ferguson.		The National Association of Manufacturers opposes the child labor amendment. The NAM says child labor is not a federal matter. In fact, the amendment is Socialistic.... The American Federation of Labor has brought in more than $6 million in 14 months and seeks to reach $10 million....General Motors half-year earnings are $23 million. Last year's were $38 million.			Aug. 17
Three hundred women are among the applicants for jobs flying an advertising plane at night. Currently piloted by men, the lighted plane circles Times Square each night at 11:00 when the theaters close.	The United States-Mexico Claims Commission holds its first meeting. Later meetings will establish rules and actually settle claims.	After a year's investigation, *Scientific American* reports that Dr. Abrams' supposed electronic cure for pneumonia and many other illnesses is a sham. The late doctor, who died suddenly of pneumonia in January, was a charlatan.	Washington receives a large volume of requests for buffaloes—singly or in carloads. The letters are in response to Interior Department plans to give away some of the 800 Yellowstone bison, too many for the preserve.		Aug. 18
	Parisians object to new American passport rules. The office is understaffed and new immigration laws increase demand, so business people and travelers have to wait days for their passports.	Stockton, CA, wants government assistance in building a channel to San Francisco Bay. The bill for 14.5 miles of dredging and levee work is $4.6 million, and the city offers to pay half.		Luis Firpo receives a delay of his immigration perjury hearing until after his fight with Wills in September....New York Mayor Hylan prohibits the black and white children appearing together in the opening scene of Eugene O'Neill's *All God's Chillun Got Wings*. The play goes on without the scene.	Aug. 19
Nebraskans form the "La Follette Independent Party." The railway unions' leadership reiterates that the unions will remain neutral in the campaign.		Inquiries by some publishers about Cincinnati lead Postmaster Fisher to speculate that the publishers are planning to move their operations.... The Federal Trade Commission says big tobacco has a monopoly and engages in price fixing.		The Massachusetts post of the American Legion announces opposition to Jack Dempsey's appearing in films. The Legion and other ultra-patriotic groups regard Dempsey as a slacker during the World War.	Aug. 20
Coolidge sends a message to the National Negro Business League. He tells the league that he will uphold the Constitutional rights of blacks.	Immigration Commissioner Curran wants 31 smuggled Italians to get sentences of 20 years each. Held on $10,000 bail, they are shackled and surrounded by armed guards as they move between jail and the courtroom. They are to be an example and deterrent.				Aug. 21
Davis denounces the Klan by name and challenges Coolidge to do the same....Mobs storm the hearing room where Clarence Darrow is pleading for the lives of Loeb and Leopold....Socialists drop out of races and make their slots available for La Follette candidates.	Coolidge says that disarmament must wait until reparations are settled. He supports the World Court though.		As Mars nears Earth, radios around the world are tuned to pick up signals. English and Canadian listeners claim to hear a series of dots. An American stands by in Washington to decode any message.		Aug. 22
F *Includes campaigns, elections, federal-state relations, civil rights and liberties, crime, the judiciary, education, healthcare, poverty, urban affairs, and population.*	G *Includes formation and debate of U.S. foreign and defense policies, veterans affairs, and defense spending. (Relations with specific foreign countries are usually found under the region concerned.)*	H *Includes business, labor, agriculture, taxation, transportation, consumer affairs, monetary and fiscal policy, natural resources, pollution and industrial accidents.*	I *Includes worldwide scientific, medical and technological developments, natural phenomena, U.S. weather and natural disasters.*	J *Includes the arts, religion, scholarship, communications media, sports, entertainment, fashions, fads, and social life.*	

	World Affairs	Europe	Africa & The Middle East	The Americas	Asia & The Pacific
Aug. 23		Stresemann delivers a fiery attack on Reichstag opponents of Dawes. Marx and Luther also point out the perils of nonratification. In France, approval comes 336–204.			Harry Sinclair's agents leave Russia after failing to renew contracts to develop Russian oil in Sakhalin. Russia and Japan are currently negotiating the future of Sakhalin.... Sun Yat-sen attempts to conciliate the volunteers whose arms he seized. He offers to return the weapons if the volunteers will fight "traitors."
Aug. 24	Rather than flying 500 miles to Labrador, the Americans move to another Greenland location to replace engines. They will join the search. The Italian remains missing as warships and planes search 5,000 miles.... The Little Entente announces it will present a united front at the League Treaty Control Committee meetings. It may also seek loans.	Austrian bread prices are up six percent. Austrians worry about a rising cost of living hampering economic recovery.... The Reichstag announces a gold-based bank that will redeem paper marks at a trillion to one. A German banker is in New York seeking a $25 million loan.... Belgians leave Lippewesel and prepare to withdraw from Dortmund.		Deputies challenge the credentials of the delegation from Jalisco. They claim the governor is trying to pack the congress.	
Aug. 25	After three days, searchers rescue Locatelli. The race shifts its end point to Seattle.	Britain's executioner attempts suicide. He has been despondent since resigning after executing a woman.... The Fascists bar membership in the freemasons and all other secret societies.... The first postwar loan to an Austrian company is $3 million to a company holding the state utility monopoly.... London Bridge is falling down. One pier sags four feet.	Britain indicates that an Egyptian note is enough to start negotiations on an accord over the Sudan.		
Aug. 26	The League asks the United States to join the upcoming discussions on arms limitations, not just observe.	Herriot and Poincare debate the Ruhr evacuation policy, with Poincare saying that giving Germany the right to arbitrate will be a disaster. Herriot prevails 181–37 with Poincare's followers abstaining.	A native court martial sentences three Sudanese mutineers to two years apiece.... Liberia protests Marcus Garvey's African plans to the United States. The note says the UNIA is inflammatory.		
Aug. 27		Kameneff says the Dawes Plan endangers Russia. It creates a community of interest among the United States, France, Germany, and Britain.... France and Germany conclude their first postwar agreement. They divide potash sales in the United States.... Spain's king signs an agreement with IT&T for a subsidiary to provide Spanish telephone service.	Heavy fighting on the Wad Lau costs both sides, but the Moroccans check the Spanish advance.	Brazilian forces rout the rebels up the Amazon and force them to flee into the Matto Grosso.... National Lead Company of Delaware spends $30 million for Bolivian tin mines. It appoints Latin American Simon Patino head of the new company. National Lead is the world's leading consumer of tin.	
Aug. 28	The International Law Institute determines that agents of the League enjoy the same immunities as do diplomats.				Rival Chinese armies of 40,000 each face off outside Shanghai. Elsewhere, warlords threaten to disrupt communications and rail service, so American and British ships are en route.
Aug. 29		British miners indicate that they will talk with MacDonald before deciding their posture on reparations coal. Owners yesterday indicated their opposition.... Bulgaria seizes Communist arms. Reports are that Russia has 1,000 agents in Austria preparing to act in Poland and Rumania.... The Reichstag passes the various Dawes bills. London and Paris are relieved. Marx repudiates war guilt.		Canada signs the London agreement and accepts the Dawes Plan.... Honduran rebels take Santa Rosa. Both sides agree to arbitration.	Australia's chief of aviation flies around the continent's perimeter in 22 days. He pays only $5 for repairs.... Indian orders for gold top $1.75 million in the United States. The gold is for jewelry and other decorative items. Indians also purchase $2 million in silver.
	A *Includes developments that affect more than one world region, international organizations and important meetings of world leaders.*	B *Includes all domestic and regional developments in Europe, including the Soviet Union.*	C *Includes all domestic and regional developments in Africa and the Middle East.*	D *Includes all domestic and regional developments in Latin America, the Caribbean, and Canada.*	E *Includes all domestic and regional developments in Asian and Pacific nations (and colonies).*

U.S. Politics & Social Issues	U.S. Foreign Policy & Affairs, Defense	U.S. Economy & Environment	Science, Technology & Nature	Culture, Leisure & Lifestyle	
"Ma" Ferguson wins the Texas Democratic primary by 77,000 votes. She says that she will take advice from "Pa" in some matters but she will be governor.		Expectation is that the trolleys of New York are doomed. There is a scramble for bus franchises in the city. The mayor, having failed to get municipal buses, backs private enterprise.		In a golf exhibition, men golfers beat women 3–1....Veterans and others announce plans for a national conference on the use of parkways as war memorials.	Aug. 23
Socialist Norman Thomas says the Klan has to be really bad if even "Ma" Ferguson can beat it.		Commissioner O'Malley says to buy coal now. Slack time and strikes have cut production by six million tons and a shortage looms....Steel plants are at 50 percent capacity, up from 40 percent a month earlier.	The close-up view of Mars reveals no new information. Previous reports of water and atmosphere are confirmed, as is the absence of life....A tornado in Louisiana rips through a church, killing nine and injuring nine others.		Aug. 24
William Allen White says Kansas Republicans have to denounce the Klan if they are to prevail. In Oklahoma, former-Governor Walton says vice presidential nominee Dawes is unfit and ignorant.		Henry Ford's Detroit, Toledo, and Ironton railroad reports a gain of $1 million. The road records an improvement of 75 percent at a time when most railroads are fading....Kentucky coal mines remain closes as 8,000 miners refuse to work.		The AAU suspends Gertrude Ederle and six other swimmers, all but two indefinitely, after they compete in an unsanctioned meet. ...Walter Johnson of the Washington Senators wins a weather-shortened seven-inning no-hitter. It is the 107th shutout of his career, the sixth of the season.	Aug. 25
Authorities arrest Fahy, a postal inspector and charge him as ringleader of the $2 million postal robbery. Noted for capturing "Big Tim" Murphy, he says professional and criminal enemies are framing him....Texas Democrats work to bar the Klan from their party; Ohio Democrats denounce the Klan. Oklahoma's Governor Trapp says the Klan runs the state Republicans....Henry Ford says the Klan is a patriotic organization.	Coolidge appoints Edgar Sheffield as ambassador to Mexico and James Bancroft to Japan. Both men are Republican lawyers.	Ford tells his railroad employees to save a word each telegram. Workers send more than 15,000 telegrams a month at four cents a word. Shorter telegrams also cut congestion on the system....*Wanderer*, the last New Bedford whaling ship, runs aground on the Middle Ground Shoal in a hurricane. Eight crew members are missing and the whaler is destroyed.	An Italian flyer, Bacola, sets a seaplane altitude record. He reaches 5,500 meters with a load of 250 kg. Centurione, another Italian, sets a record of 4,500 feet with 500 kg. Both planes are Savoia models.	The president of the National Bank of Commerce says that filmmaking has moved from its spoiled child stage to a more mature and stable status....The Prince of Wales parties hard on the *Berengeria*, wilting two collars and dancing the Apache.	Aug. 26
A federal report reveals that 231 cities have adopted zoning ordinances. Thirteen states have model laws....Idaho Democrats condemn the Klan....The Veterans Bureau sets up 51 regional offices to administer veterans' aid....Henry Ford denies praising the Klan.		The post office authorizes insuring of third class mail in the United States and its possessions. C.O.D. is also permitted. Major beneficiaries include film distributors and dealers in photographs and supplies.	A hurricane is blowing up the Atlantic coast. The flyers in Greenland are grounded. Hit by a 100-foot wave, the liner *Arabic* lands with 75 injured passengers. Four other vessels are also damaged....A flyer broadcasts directly from a plane 4,000 feet in the air. His wireless signal reaches 200 miles. Army researchers say they soon can reach 1,000 miles.		Aug. 27
Marcus Garvey tells the UNIA convention that much of blacks' problems are due to members of the race themselves. The UNIA reads W.E.B. Dubois out of the black race.		Car loadings for a week in August total almost a million. The best week of the year is due to grain shipments....Coca-Cola earnings are at $4.13 a share for the quarter. The total is $7.5 million. Net income is $3.15 million.			Aug. 28
Coolidge touts the homely virtues and criticizes secret organizations. He does not cite the Klan by name.	Back at work after a lengthy vacation, a refreshed Coolidge bans the gun elevation plan as provoking an arms race.	The Ford Motor Company reports for tax purposes that it has a surplus of $442 million....The Federal Trade Commission clears an American of charges he monopolizes the Mexican sisal trade.	New York City announces it will open a clinic for treating whooping cough with chlorine gas....A Johns Hopkins researcher says that hard work after 40 shortens life.	The Prince of Wales arrives in New York. Not requiring quarantine, he leaves quickly. He dodges the crowds lining the shores and begins his American holiday in Long Island.	Aug. 29

F	G	H	I	J
Includes campaigns, elections, federal-state relations, civil rights and liberties, crime, the judiciary, education, healthcare, poverty, urban affairs, and population.	*Includes formation and debate of U.S. foreign and defense policies, veterans affairs, and defense spending. (Relations with specific foreign countries are usually found under the region concerned.)*	*Includes business, labor, agriculture, taxation, transportation, consumer affairs, monetary and fiscal policy, natural resources, pollution and industrial accidents.*	*Includes worldwide scientific, medical and technological developments, natural phenomena, U.S. weather and natural disasters.*	*Includes the arts, religion, scholarship, communications media, sports, entertainment, fashions, fads, and social life.*

	World Affairs	Europe	Africa & The Middle East	The Americas	Asia & The Pacific
Aug. 30	The Dawes Plan begins with the appointment of Young as collection agent, the order to withdraw from the Ruhr, and preparations for the first German transfer of reparations.	Three British men and two British women die in a snowstorm on Mount Cervino in the Italian Alps.			As 100,000 armed men gather, a gathering of 52 Chinese merchants' organizations calls for the warlords to try peace. Diplomats warn Peking to order the warlords to cease threatening moves....Hindus and Muslims fight in India—again.... India's wheat crop is off. Only 20 million bushels will be available for export.
Aug. 31	The Filene Prize of 100,000 francs goes to a peace plan that would create a European League within the League of Nations. Theoretically, the smaller league would stabilize currency, production, and debt....After five months and 14 days, the American flyers return to the North American mainland, landing in Labrador.	Hungary, Yugoslavia, and Czechoslovakia report lower than normal harvests....An Italian promoter holds successful races in Germany. The races involve ostrich-drawn sulkies....The Soviets crush a one-day rising in Georgia.	Spanish forces in the Wad Lau are forced back to their bases.	Brazil drives the rebels from Manaos and claims victory.	The warlords outside Shanghai refuse an armistice. The British commander is put in charge of the western ships, including the American ones.
Sep. 1	Germany's first payment under Dawes is 20 million marks, advance payment of loan service charges.		Rivera orders 6,000 reinforcements to Morocco. He admits that the situation is "grave."	Reports from the Virgin Islands indicate that the hurricane has killed at least 80 and injured hundreds of others....In an upbeat annual message, Obregon says the revolt helped to reorganize the army, now reduced to 55,000 people.	Indian provincial legislatures have adjourned without authorizing government salaries or other necessary legislation. Governors act by decree after the sessions fail due obstruction by nationalists.
Sep. 2	On the eve of the Geneva meeting, American Professor Shotwell causes a stir with a plan to outlaw war. Shotwell defines aggressors as those nations that refuse to abide by the rulings of the World court. France and Britain arrive divided over guarantees of military assistance before disarmament. France demands them; Britain refuses.	British conservatives report favorably a proposal to create two autonomous Irish provinces of a single Ireland. De Valera reacts favorably, and Ulster's premier says it deserves study....Naples is astir after Professor Mario di Martino-Fusco disappears. The professor reportedly just discovered new Livy manuscripts.	The World Court denies it has jurisdiction to hear a Greek engineer's claim against Britain over the award of a contract in Palestine despite his prewar Turkish claim. The court says the award is within Britain's mandatory powers.		The Filipino congress votes no confidence in the Secretary of the Interior. The charge against Felipe Agoncillo is that he fails to resist General Wood's appointment of Americans to positions rightfully held by Filipinos.
Sep. 3		Shots fired at Mussolini miss his car and hit the one following. Assailants are unknown....Soviet workers begin agitating against export of Russian grain. They fear that there will be none to prevent them from starving....A court sentences three Ukrainians to death as leaders of the failed rising.	Spain declares a general war against the Moors. For the first time it acknowledges the rising is general.		After skirmishes yesterday, the two large forces arrayed against each other at Shanghai begin a heavy fight, including artillery. Attacks are difficult because the land between the lines consists mostly of rice paddies.
Sep. 4	Maginot says withdrawal of troops from the Ruhr allows Germany to begin industrial mobilization unchecked.	Scholars confirm that Fusco, the recluse, did find the Livy manuscript. Paris scholars split over an antiquarian's claim to have discovered the head of Henry IV....Rome denies the Mussolini assassination report....The Vatican denies rumors that the Pope approves the Turkish effort to remove the crucifix from schools.	In the Rif war, the road from Tetuan to Tangiers falls to Moorish fighters who are headed to Tangiers. Spain vows a fight to the finish.	The Honduran factions accept American mediation and the requirement for a new president.	In China, the defending force blocks the attackers. Calls for an arms embargo begin. In addition, critics note the armies' huge stocks of western arms. So much for the effectiveness of the Washington Treaty.
Sep. 5		Prof. Fusco denies that he found the Livy manuscripts. He says he is retranslating 6th century codices, not the originals.	A modern road opens along the caravan trail between Beirut and Tehran. The road also passes through Damascus and Baghdad.		
Sep. 6		Ludendorff praises himself and Hitler as chosen by God to save the German people. German moderates say the racialist speeches at Weimar are treason and interior minister Jarres should prosecute them or resign.		The merger of Canadian Presbyterians, Congregationalists, and Methodists brings 30 percent of Canadians into a single denomination.	

A	B	C	D	E
Includes developments that affect more than one world region, international organizations and important meetings of world leaders.	*Includes all domestic and regional developments in Europe, including the Soviet Union.*	*Includes all domestic and regional developments in Africa and the Middle East.*	*Includes all domestic and regional developments in Latin America, the Caribbean, and Canada.*	*Includes all domestic and regional developments in Asian and Pacific nations (and colonies).*

U.S. Politics & Social Issues	U.S. Foreign Policy & Affairs, Defense	U.S. Economy & Environment	Science, Technology & Nature	Culture, Leisure & Lifestyle	
Klansmen from Pennsylvania and New York join those in New Jersey to hear Dr. Bernard Bass denounce the Davis candidacy as a conspiracy of the Roman Catholic Church.... The Steuben Society asks German-Americans to back La Follette. The society says parties of Wilson and Harding are unsympathetic to German interests....Socialist Eugene Debs predicts that the La Follette campaign will be the birth of a great Labor Party.	Coolidge lifts the embargo on arms to Cuba. The embargo dates to May when Cuba experienced unrest.			Ocean liners begin setting speed records for the Atlantic crossing after the ban on racing ends.... Officials of a pet cemetery are unable to explain why a woman who wants to disinter her dog finds only an empty box....At .433, Rogers Hornsby of St. Louis is running away in the National League batting race. Ruth leads the American League comfortably too.	Aug. 30
Six thousand blacks watch the UNIA canonize a black Christ....Long Island dedicates its first Jewish synagogue. Two thousand attend the opening of Temple Israel, valued at $100,000 and debt free.		Income taxes bring in $1.8 billion, an increase of $150 million over last year.		Canon Chase claims that Firpo would be deported except that a fight ring is indirectly bribing immigration authorities to keep him in the United States....The Prince of Wales plays polo and races a speedboat. He tells reporters that he has no plans other than to play around and maybe go to a horse race.	Aug. 31
The National Association of Manufacturers sends a get-out-and-vote mailer to 15 million addresses. The mailing is nonpartisan....The 10,000 attendees at the New Jersey Klan rally come from 14 states. Police guard the route but anti-Klan men slash the tires of 100 Klansmen's cars.	Secretary Hughes sends a note to Geneva refusing to appoint an American delegate to the arms reduction conference. He says the American position is already known.		Drivers set new records in the 12.5-mile Pike's Peak Climb. The winner conquers the world's highest road in 18 minutes, 15 seconds despite a badly bent axel.	The long-awaited international horse race featuring the French horse Filene draws a record 60,000 spectators, including the Prince of Wales. Kentucky-bred Wise Counselor edges Filene.	Sep. 1
Texas Democrats nominate "Ma" Ferguson and oust all Klan delegates.	An army fitness board opens hearings on the fitness of an alleged Communist to serve in the reserves. Captain Hibben declines to speak before the board presents the evidence against him....The Army War College says goodbye to retiring Gen. Pershing. It unveils his portrait and gives him a diploma.	The Nickel Plate merger is done but for the formalities. Trading on the yet-to-be railroad begins anyway.		West coast movie studios plan to produce 680 films at a cost of $137 million....In the reformed pocket billiard league, five cities lose franchises. New York has three of the remaining 12 teams....Bill Tilden wins the national tennis championship for the fifth straight year.	Sep. 2
Mayor Curley of Boston prohibits a peace meeting on Boston Common. He wants no pacifist propaganda on Preparedness Day.	Hibben denies that he is a Communist and says somebody misconstrues his relief work in Russia. The inquiry shifts to the issue of what level of free speech an officer has.	The army's former chief signal officer General Squier, loses his suit against AT&T for infringing his patent for a telephony multiplexer. The court rules that he gave the device to the public.	The Weather Service issues long range forecasts for the forest regions. It provides daily updates to state foresters in the East, timber owners in the South, and rangers of the U.S. Forest Service in the west.	John Philip Sousa coaches the band at Philadelphia's Eastern Prison on the proper playing of his compositions. Crowds watch, but rules bar applause.	Sep. 3
Maine Democrats have success in getting women registered to vote. The galvanizing issue is the Klan. The key, though, is a cookbook that brings in the money that women's Democratic clubs use to finance their work....Reportedly, Illinois has eight times as many hold-ups as Pennsylvania and New York combined.	Canada's minister of railways and canals, George Graham, says Chicago is stealing its water. The city is taking 10,0000 feet a second from Lake Michigan despite the absence of any treaty allowing the draining of lake water.	Freight loadings for the third week in August set a new high for the year. The total is near last year's weekly loading....A New York firm indicates it will use London-style gearless gas-electric buses to offer five cent rides in Manhattan with trunk lines to other parts. Transfers cost two cents.	Hetty Green's son says his private station in Massachusetts is sending television pictures 60 feet. He hopes to have a workable system of movies by radio within a year.	Curran says there is no evidence against Firpo except what Chase fraudulently presents. Besides, the matter is out of his jurisdiction....D.W. Griffith fights a ban on his wartime propaganda film *Love and Sacrifice* in London. He denies its portrayal of the American Revolution is anti-British.	Sep. 4
		Gasoline consumption in July is up 107 million gallons from the same month in 1923. Production is up only five million gallons from June 1923. Average daily consumption in July is 25.6 million gallons.	Commerce Secretary Hoover calls for conservation of fish. He says U.S. fishermen are recklessly destroying the littoral food supply.	After consulting with the Labor Department, Curran asks the federal government to issue a warrant for Firpo's arrest on immigration charges. Rickard says he will post bail and the fight will go on.	Sep. 5
		American chemicals are a $62 billion industry. Chemical production accounts for half of U.S. manufacturers. Leading chemicals include chlorine, colloids, and insulin.		Aga Khan's Damask wins the Realization Stakes at Belmont before a crowd of 20,000. The Prince of Wales attends.	Sep. 6

F	G	H	I	J
Includes campaigns, elections, federal-state relations, civil rights and liberties, crime, the judiciary, education, healthcare, poverty, urban affairs, and population.	*Includes formation and debate of U.S. foreign and defense policies, veterans affairs, and defense spending. (Relations with specific foreign countries are usually found under the region concerned.)*	*Includes business, labor, agriculture, taxation, transportation, consumer affairs, monetary and fiscal policy, natural resources, pollution and industrial accidents.*	*Includes worldwide scientific, medical and technological developments, natural phenomena, U.S. weather and natural disasters.*	*Includes the arts, religion, scholarship, communications media, sports, entertainment, fashions, fads, and social life.*

	World Affairs	Europe	Africa & The Middle East	The Americas	Asia & The Pacific
Sep. 7	The Zionist Organization of America's Executive Committee goes on record as opposing Jewish settlement in Mexico or the Crimea. They say that Palestine, which has attracted 2,000 immigrants a month for several months, is the only place where Jews can control their own destiny.	Outraged Turk Rushdi Pasha declares that regardless of the ruling of the mixed commission Turkey will send Constantinople's Greeks to Greece. The commission ruling is that the tens of thousands of Greeks who live in Constantinople before 1918 are entitled to stay.			Manchurian warlord Chang declares war against China. He demotes General Lu, stripping him of rank and honors, and prepares to lead the armies at Shanghai himself.
Sep. 8	The League commission on disarmament begins work. First, it must place disarmament into context with the overall peace project, and the Swedish foreign minister asks codification of international law.		The Spanish forces abandon the Wad Lau line. A contingent cut off between Shessuan and Tetuan manages to break free. A gale in Wad Lau Bay destroys planes and supplies off shore.	A Chilean army junta is in control of the Congress. No opposition arises to the new cabinet.	A multinational force to protect foreign nationals at Shanghai includes Japanese, British, and U.S. forces. A 1,000-man contingent of marines has just arrived. Twenty-two ships are on the scene also.
Sep. 9	The League commissioner reports that Hungary's economy will be able to stand on its own in two years. The currency is already stabilized thanks to League support.	The Georgia revolt failed. Russia executes 24. In Leningrad eight railway workers receive death sentences, while 117 others get various terms for bribery, mismanagement, and corruption. Four are found not guilty.		The chief of Brazil's rebels claims that federals are joining his forces. The government denies the claim.…After the Senate refuses to accept the resignation of Chile's president, he goes to the U.S. embassy.…Honduran rebels begin a march on Tegucigalpa.	Peking expresses concern about the impact of Chang's air force. Japan's cabinet says Japanese forces will not interfere in China.
Sep. 10		Maybe the Georgia revolt has not failed. The Georgian legation in Paris says anti-Communists control most of the state. Other anti-red risings are causing problems in Azerbaijan, Daghestan, and the Caucasus.…Karl Kautsky says rather than blaming the German people, the world should put war guilt on the Kaiser.		At Ceiba, Honduras, 100 troops move from the cruiser to the port to protect U.S. and foreign lives and property.…A new rebellion breaks out in Ecuador. Government troops are en route.	
Sep. 11	Germany pays the second reparations installment of 20 million marks. Reparations overseer Young says the Ruhr will provide the revenue Germany needs to continue payments.…Britain commits to use the fleet to enforce the peace. Work continues in committee on compulsory arbitration.…The League powers move to recognize Georgian independence.	Germany's republican government protests the Hohenzollern claims to lands bringing in annual revenue of $1.425 million. The Hohenzollerns contend that the collection of palaces, castles, and country estates—and the 200,000 acres of land—have revenues of one-sixth of the government's estimate.	A note left by H.G. Evelyn White, who committed suicide in a London cab, says he is victim of an ancient Egyptian curse for taking ancient manuscripts. The story helps to validate those who believe that Lord Carnarvon's death is due to a similar curse for disturbing Tutankhamen's tomb.…Spanish forces concentrate at Tetuan.	Canadian press operators reject terms and go out on strike against the newspapers.	
Sep. 12	The League agrees to accept a conditional British offer of aid to enforce arbitration. It also establishes that agreements do not apply to the United States, which requires direct negotiation of any dispute.	The evacuation of the Ruhr is half done, and France reports it will be completely out well ahead of the deadline.…A report from Paris reveals that financing for the Georgia rebels is coming from international financiers who want to safeguard the Baku oilfields and the three million gallons in storage.…A carpenter assassinates Fascist deputy Casalini. The motive is revenge for Matteotti.…Martino-Fusco, having denied finding the Livy manuscripts, now claims from hiding that he has them and will sell them for $5 million, maybe to an American.	Mecca appeals to the world for aid after a Wahhabi massacre destroys the entire population of Taif, a Hashemite/Hejaz town 70 miles south of Mecca. A recent Wahhabi invasion of Transjordan from Central Arabia fails only due to British use of warplanes against them.		Japan celebrates "Peace Day" as a protest against Defense Day, which the Japanese take as a threat against them and world peace.
Sep. 13	Czechoslovakia's Benes will author the security covenant. The agreement will be open to any nation choosing to adhere to it.	A new problem for France is what to do with African immigrants seeking work. Domestic pressure is for immigration restriction.…Denmark prepares legislation to disband its army and navy. It will totally disarm, retaining only a constabulary and coastal inspectors.…Italy closes its ports and prepares to inspect everyone. It wants to ensure the Livy manuscripts do not leave the country.		The first nation in the world to link all its commercial centers by airmail is Colombia.…Mexican rebels kill 18 soldiers. Then they rob the Jalapa-Teocela train.…Chile banishes reform president Alessandri. Liberal reforms are gone now that the army junta controls the country.	Fighting resumes despite the rain and faulty shells. The Mukden railway is closed in anticipation of fighting between Chang and Wu.…India's legislative assembly defeats civil service reform that would increase British civil servants' pay and open more positions to Indians. The governor has the authority to order changes anyway but is reluctant to put a financial burden on the states.…The Filipino supreme court rules it lacks authority to reinstate a senator suspended for slapping another. A dissenting opinion holds that the Jones Act bars the suspension of an appointed senator.
	A *Includes developments that affect more than one world region, international organizations and important meetings of world leaders.*	B *Includes all domestic and regional developments in Europe, including the Soviet Union.*	C *Includes all domestic and regional developments in Africa and the Middle East.*	D *Includes all domestic and regional developments in Latin America, the Caribbean, and Canada.*	E *Includes all domestic and regional developments in Asian and Pacific nations (and colonies).*

U.S. Politics & Social Issues	U.S. Foreign Policy & Affairs, Defense	U.S. Economy & Environment	Science, Technology & Nature	Culture, Leisure & Lifestyle	
	New York National Guard brigade encampments end with the departure of the 165th Infantry. The camp is available for the 369th Negro Infantry, which camps alone.		A seven-year study of Framingham, MA, by the national tuberculosis association, reveals that two percent of the population has the disease. Intensive disease education has reduced the mortality rate.	The Prince of Wales announces he will sell his string of polo ponies and leave for Canada in mid-September whether the international match is finished or not. After Canada he will go on a year-long world tour.	Sep. 7
	General Hines tells the Veterans of Foreign Wars of plans to humanize the Veterans Bureau. He promises to cut red tape.	Macy's opens a 19-story annex. The department store now employs 7,500 people in 148 departments.		At the New York fur auction, beaver is the top fur for the fall. Ermine is next, mostly as trimming or in short coats.	Sep. 8
The Journeyman Barbers International Union opens its annual convention. Women press for membership, as they have for several years. Prospects are better this year because the bobbed style has brought more women customers into barbershops.			Heavy rains stop the fighting outside Shanghai. Rains also dampen Coolidge's welcome of the around-the-world flyers. He waits four hours in the rain as weather delays their arrival in Washington, DC.	Red and silver fox pelts, prized for neckwear, generate heavy bidding at the fur auction. Sales for the first two days exceed $875,000.	Sep. 9
Because of their ages, rather than death Leopold and Loeb get dual life sentences for murdering and kidnapping Bobby Franks. The judge warns against allowing them parole.	The Army reports that organizations representing 50 million people have indicated that they will participate in Defense Day. The day of military exercises will also test civilian preparedness for a war in the United States. It has generated controversy, with many anti-war objections to the concept.			The Prince of Wales changes his mind. He will stay in the United States until the international polo matches are finished.	Sep. 10
The car taking Loeb and Leopold to Joliet hits a ditch, but the prisoners arrive safely and head to solitary. Loeb's father puts his 12-year-old son to work with the other hands on the family farm. He will not allow his other sons to loaf. The older son is farm manager.			The French military tests an alternative power source for failed airplane engines. Another device of interest converts the fuselage to a parachute.	After a federal judge denies a Mann Act warrant against Firpo, the Argentinean loses a sluggish bout to Wills, who fails to knock him out. Argentina hears a broadcast of the fight, attended by 52,000 quiet patrons. The gate is $462,000.... The Prince of Wales enjoys a fox hunt and a game of polo but does not attend the Wills-Firpo bout, leaving his reserved seat vacant.	Sep. 11
Industry mobilizes nearly 17 million for Defense Day. On his last day of service, Pershing says the day is a success.	The United States receives a plan from the war debt funding commission to spread the French debt out over 67 years at $100 million a year starting in five years. The agent suggests investing half the money in 25-year French business bonds.				Sep. 12
	Pershing officially retires, spending half a day in his office and receiving the thanks of his country through a special order from Coolidge.	To Wall Street, two railroad bond issues sold in New York this week are a harbinger of things to come. Most of Europe, except Germany, seems in need of significant expansion of its rail capabilities.... American railroads resume purchases, buying $60 million worth of stock this week. Included are the Pennsylvania Railroad cars and locomotives for the Missouri Pacific and Illinois Central.	A radio set in the private car of the president of the Seaboard Air Line works well. The railroad sets plans to install radios in all its private cars.	A crowd of 16,500 watches as the United States tops the British 16–5 in the first international polo match.... The fur auction closes a heavy day of muskrat dealing. The day's total is $500,000, and prices for Southern furs are up 30 percent from the spring sale.	Sep. 13

F	G	H	I	J
Includes campaigns, elections, federal-state relations, civil rights and liberties, crime, the judiciary, education, healthcare, poverty, urban affairs, and population.	*Includes formation and debate of U.S. foreign and defense policies, veterans affairs, and defense spending. (Relations with specific foreign countries are usually found under the region concerned.)*	*Includes business, labor, agriculture, taxation, transportation, consumer affairs, monetary and fiscal policy, natural resources, pollution and industrial accidents.*	*Includes worldwide scientific, medical and technological developments, natural phenomena, U.S. weather and natural disasters.*	*Includes the arts, religion, scholarship, communications media, sports, entertainment, fashions, fads, and social life.*

	World Affairs	Europe	Africa & The Middle East	The Americas	Asia & The Pacific
Sep. 14		European grain is down. France's wheat crop is off 18 percent. Germany bans export of wheat.	Spanish forces clear the road between Tetuan and Tangiers of Moors as far as the international zone.		Japan's General Wada cites Defense Day and calls Americans militarists. He argues that Japan needs to strengthen its defenses.
Sep. 15		Fire destroys 35 oil wells at Baku. Damage in millions of rubles is due to short circuits, not sabotage.... The Hohenzollern family claims the Munich art gallery. They relinquish claim to some state jewels, the ones an appraiser rates as worthless.... The Ukraine Government Committee reports that 1,235 pogroms during the civil war killed 70,000 of Russia's six million Jews, producing 200,000 orphans, and displaced half a million more.		Mexico welcomes two commissions. One includes American business people; the other consists of Japanese journalists.	Fighting outside Shanghai becomes increasingly violent, with the first use of hand grenades and machine guns. Japan protests disorder by Chang's forces. Sun prepares to raise an army. Minister Schurman says that aside from the small area of fighting China is quiet.
Sep. 16	A League committee with representatives of 12 nations tentatively accepts the U.S. arbitration proposal. Benes' draft defines an aggressor as one that refuses League or Court arbitration.	Martina-Fusco again claims he has no Livy manuscripts, saying he has only material with references to them.... Peasant revolts in Russia spread to the Crimea. The people are outraged that grain exports leave them with little to eat.... Ulster's leadership again says it will ignore the finding of the commission on the border.		The Brazilian rebels kill a number of federals in taking two Parana River ports.... Explorer Donald MacMillan returns from 15 months in the Arctic. He reports that Eskimo flappers like cigarettes and movies. He also notes that his investigations reveal that Greenland's glaciers are advancing and calving, not retreating as earlier believed.	
Sep. 17	The French win a provision for continuing special alliances. They agree that alliances will remain inactive until the League orders action. The meeting agrees to codify international law and again invites the United States to participate in arms limitation talks.	Germany has a million unemployed, with 540,000 on relief. High ranking Germans reestablish the Colonial League. They call for Germany to have colonies. German nationalists demand that the government send a war guilt demand to the entente or prepare to fall. Police raid Ludendorff's Munich offices.	Professor Bruno Roselli reports progress in uncovering a Roman city buried in the sands near Tripoli. Leptis Magna, abandoned by Romans to the desert in the 5th century, still has baths, statuary, a basilica, and palaces. It once was home to 100,000 to 200,000 people. Excavation is by 200 Arab prisoners of war.		Australia reports a bumper wheat crop.
Sep. 18	The League decides to implement the peace plan only after completion of the arms limitation conference.	Yugoslavia and Lithuania prepare to begin paying their war debts to the United States. Term is 62 years for repayment of Yugoslavia's $61 million and Lithuania's $6 million.... Soviets take Tiflis and massacre 600 leading citizens, including the Metropolitan. Oil men escape. Fighting intensifies in Azerbaijan.... Hungary announces the trial of Karolyi and other exiles for treason.	Archaeologists find two stone tombs, the oldest tombs in Egypt and possibly the oldest stone buildings in the world. They date to 3000 B.C.E. and are of a style unlike most other Egyptian tombs.	In pursuit of rebels, Honduran forces invade Nicaragua and fire on a Nicaraguan town. One villager dies. Nicaragua protests.	Gandhi begins a 21-day fast for peace. He seeks to end Hindu-Muslim fighting.... Tuchun Lu flees, abandoning the defense of Shanghai and precipitating a general withdrawal of forces near to the city. At the same time, Peking formally declares war on Chang. Fighting spreads to the north.
Sep. 19		The Soviet Union organizes new republics by race and ethnicity. The new republics are the Uzbekian and Turkmenian Republics and the autonomous areas of Kaharakirgistan and Tadj.	Belgium establishes a gorilla sanctuary in the Congo. Suggested by Carl Akeley, the preserve will stop the slaughter and allow researchers to live with and study the creatures.		Two Americans are appointed to the board that will disburse Boxer Indemnity relief funds to Chinese institutions. They are John Dewey and Paul Monroe of Columbia University.
Sep. 20		Rumania reports that Russian raids into its territory have caused 600 casualties.... Paris establishes a special department to deal with its 200,000 Moroccans and Africans.	Spanish forces take Gorgues. The Moors can no longer dominate Tetuan from this mountain position.... Nejd Wahabis vow to take the fight to Mecca. They claim that Muslims back their war against Hussein.		
	A *Includes developments that affect more than one world region, international organizations and important meetings of world leaders.*	B *Includes all domestic and regional developments in Europe, including the Soviet Union.*	C *Includes all domestic and regional developments in Africa and the Middle East.*	D *Includes all domestic and regional developments in Latin America, the Caribbean, and Canada.*	E *Includes all domestic and regional developments in Asian and Pacific nations (and colonies).*

U.S. Politics & Social Issues	U.S. Foreign Policy & Affairs, Defense	U.S. Economy & Environment	Science, Technology & Nature	Culture, Leisure & Lifestyle	
Federal officers in Little Rock, AR, serve 69 warrants for liquor violations. Included are state officials, former-Governor Pindall, society matrons, and the state's poet laureate.... James M. Webb, black preacher in Chicago, tells the UNIA that biblical prophecy predicts a black king ruling the world. He calls Garvey a black Moses.		Six western railroads report they are running ahead of last year.... Steel plants are up to 60 percent of capacity, much better than July's 45 percent. Increased rail orders help but account for only seven percent of capacity.	Etienne Oehmichen gets a prize of 40,000 francs for lifting 200 kg one meter for one minute with a helicopter. He adds the record for dead lift to his other helicopter records.	A Syracuse pastor says that by trying to imitate the Prince of Wales Americans are making a mockery of democracy.... A report reveals that "Old Ironsides" is rotting away due to neglect and failure by Congress to appropriate repair funds.	Sep. 14
The National Women's Party protests a ruling by the controller general that a woman civil servant must take her husband's name. The party says there is no legal basis for denying a woman her own name.	Presidents Coolidge and Vasquez exchange greetings over the newly installed cable between the United States and Santo Domingo. Regular service begins tomorrow with reduced rates.	The Lackawanna Railroad reports an improved net income of $6.9 million, despite a lower gross income. The line credits improved efficiencies.	Finsler of Bonn discovers a magnitude seven comet behind the sun. A second sighting, on September 22 at Harvard, validates the discovery.	With Mayor Hylan and Jack Dempsey in attendance, Saks and Company opens its store on Fifth Avenue. The crowds are so great that the management enlists stenographers as sales help. The first item shipped from the store is a silk hat in a leather hatbox for President Coolidge. A rumor that the Prince of Wales is shopping stampedes women men's wear.	Sep. 15
The United States has fewer paupers—78,090 compared to 84,198 in 1910. Per capita, its almshouses are home to fewer poor than at any time in history. The rate is 71.5 per 100,000 compared with 91.5 per 100,000 in 1910 and 132 in 1880. Two thirds are male. Over half are aged between 60 and 80. Almost a third are foreign born.... Blacks tell Coolidge to take a stand on the Klan or prepare for a black bolt from his party to anti-Klan candidates.		Amoskeag Mills asks its 14,000 mill hands to take a pay cut to match the pay level of competing mills. Half of Amoskeag's workers are idle. Some okay a 10 percent cut in exchange for full employment; others say cuts are unnecessary. The hands accept the cut the next day after rejecting a 20 percent possibility.... Fire follows an explosion at Kammerer Company's mine in Sublet, WY. Twelve escape. Rescuers retrieve three bodies near the entrance, but smoke and gas bar penetration into the mine where others are trapped.		The Americans retain the international polo cup. Thirty-thousand spectators include the Prince of Wales, who joins the Americans in the traditional drinking from the cup. Police have trouble spotting the prince because of the thousands dressing in his style, including his gray hat.	Sep. 16
Five ex-soldiers serving life terms in Leavenworth, after seven years of impeccable conduct, receive paroles. The men are part of the group convicted of rioting in Houston, TX, during the war. Forty-nine of the 72 convicted men of the 24th Infantry remain in prison.		Wyoming searchers retrieve 35 bodies from the mine explosion. Eighteen remain unaccounted for and believed buried in the rubble.... Challenging the government ruling, U.S. Steel and other producers nevertheless end "Pittsburgh Plus" pricing. Rather than charge freight to Pittsburgh, they now charge F.O.B. at the producing plant.		In a fight between the light-heavyweight and middleweight champions, Tunney and Greb draw.	Sep. 17
	The American-German Claims Board awards U.S. insurance companies $34.7 million but rules they are not entitled to reimbursement for passenger losses The United States will shift its $24.3 million to the Veterans Bureau.	State, postal, and army air service officials discuss the practicality of airmail to South America from New Orleans or another Gulf port. They find it feasible and expect it to promote inter-American commerce, with U.S. air carriers having the edge. First, six Central American nations have to agree to let the United States penetrate their markets.	The federal government requires parachutes in all planes, including commercial ones. The aim is to protect not only flyers but also the people below.... Major Carl Spaatz sets a record in flying the 540 miles from Selfridge, MI, to the capital in three hours.... Fifteen square miles of Mount Shasta collapse, causing crumbling of the walls of Mud Creek Canyon.	An auction of the 44 ponies used in the international matches brings out Long Island's horsy set. The Prince of Wales' seven polo ponies fetch $18,100. Total proceeds of $114,000 average about $2,800 per horse.	Sep. 18
Gompers confers with La Follette and tells the Progressive that he is sure of the overwhelming majority of the labor vote.	The board allows $97,000 more to survivors in *Lusitania* claims. Insurance companies cannot collect for these cases, but family members can, according to the board's ruling.			English censors agree to the showing of D.W. Griffith's *Love and Hate*, formerly *America*. With all the hate-filled subtitles removed, the film is now acceptable for English schoolchildren.	Sep. 19
Rep. Sol Bloom announces that he will ask Congress to repeal passport requirements. He says 250,000 American travelers are tired of them and they waste $10 million a year in unnecessary passport and visa costs.... In Crisis, James Weldon Johnson tells blacks to cut their ties to the Republicans. They have to keep the bosses guessing if they expect any benefits.... William Allen White files as anti-Klan candidate for Kansas Governor.	Coolidge orders Secretary Wilbur to establish a commission to determine the relative worth of airplanes and battleships.		A new national monument is Carlsbad Caverns in New Mexico. Lowered hundreds of feet by bucket through a hole in the roof, visitors encounter nature's beauty.... Unusual weather conditions, including a hot summer, are causing the Mount Shasta glacier to move slowly down the mountain at five miles per hour The rumbling is audible 100 miles away.	Ty Cobb gets his 200th hit. This is his ninth 200-hit season, breaking the mark he shared with Wee Willie Keeler.... The fur auction concludes with a total sale of more than $3 million, the best since 1919.... Hornsby is still batting .422 and safely ahead in the race. Ruth is leading by only .006.	Sep. 20
F *Includes campaigns, elections, federal-state relations, civil rights and liberties, crime, the judiciary, education, healthcare, poverty, urban affairs, and population.*	G *Includes formation and debate of U.S. foreign and defense policies, veterans affairs, and defense spending. (Relations with specific foreign countries are usually found under the region concerned.)*	H *Includes business, labor, agriculture, taxation, transportation, consumer affairs, monetary and fiscal policy, natural resources, pollution and industrial accidents.*	I *Includes worldwide scientific, medical and technological developments, natural phenomena, U.S. weather and natural disasters.*	J *Includes the arts, religion, scholarship, communications media, sports, entertainment, fashions, fads, and social life.*	

	World Affairs	Europe	Africa & The Middle East	The Americas	Asia & The Pacific
Sep. 21	The League indicates that it will call on outside nations to assist its arms reduction efforts. Missing from the League are Germany, Russia, and the United States.	Britain reports August unemployment and cost of living up. Iron and steel output are down.... Russia has 60,000 troops in the Caucasus. The Georgian rising has failed, but 20,000 guerrillas are in the mountains and disturbances continue in Soviet Armenia, Daghestan, and Azerbaijan.			As the Chekiang navy mutinies and sails away with the fleet, Chang tells foreigners to get out of the battle zone. Fighting for Shanghai is ready to intensify.
Sep. 22		Herriot's 1925 budget has no funding for the French embassy at the Vatican. Poincare and the clerical parties are prepared to fight.	Egypt's cotton crop of 5.9 million cantars (59 million pounds or 1.2 million bales) is below that of the previous two years. Prices rise on reports the government will intervene in the market.		The Dutch government orders a scientific expedition to Sumatra to study the half-ape, half-human Orang Padeks on Poulou Rimau. Authorities disagree over whether they are the lowest humans or apes.
Sep. 23	The drafting commission presents its "ironclad" provision to prevent aggression. The solution, they think, is compulsory arbitration, with both forces treated as aggressors until the League can determine which actually is to blame.	Workmen repairing the baptistery of the Basilica of St. John Lateran in Rome uncover parts of Constantine's church of 324 C.E.... The German cabinet votes to request admission to the League of Nations after settlement of outstanding issues. Germany expects great power treatment. France indicates its opposition.			Two provinces in the Philippines are suffering from locusts, floods, and diseased animals. Starvation confronts 40,000 Filipinos.... Chang is dealing with Russia, offering recognition in return for material. His forces take Chaoyang and attack Shanghai again.... Russian scientist Kozloff uncovers skeletons of unknown species in Mongolia. He also reports tea and wheat that are safe to consume.
Sep. 24	New Zealand wants sanctions lightened. Yugoslavia wants clearer language on cross-border raids. Italy wants to know who controls the aggressor during arbitration.	Trade talks between Germany and Britain flounder as do those between Germany and France. Germany wants most favored nation status as well as tax breaks.... Bulgarians protest G.B. Shaw's *Arms and the Man*. The playhouse manager counters that it ridicules all humanity, not just Bulgarians.... Italian opposition deputies say they will not take their seats under Mussolini. They protest Matteotti and use of the army to repress change.		The Argentine senate asks the government to declare the papal nuncio persona non grata. The senate also wants the Argentine ambassador to the Vatican recalled. The senate is miffed that its preferred candidate for Archbishop of Buenos Aires is instead Apostolic Delegate for all of Latin America.	A Hawaiian territorial grand jury indicts 76 of 173 Filipino strikers for rioting on September 9. The violence killed 20 people.
Sep. 25	Large and small states ask the League of Nations to intervene to stop the fighting in Georgia.	A slide in the Alps kills 15 and buries part of a Swiss village. Then the area floods.... A plane with 10 passengers and their baggage sets a Paris-London speed record. It makes the trip in one hour, 47 minutes.			
Sep. 26	Japan asks that "domestic" issues be subject to arbitration and threatens to reject the agreement when the clause fails. Specifically, Japan wants arbitration of U.S. immigration policy.	Germany protests French imposition of a 26 percent tariff. France says the German government can reimburse exporters and credit the expense to reparations.	Palestine reports the discovery of potash in the Dead Sea. It estimates it can produce potash for half the European price.	Under a reciprocal trade agreement, Canada agrees to admit Australian dried fruit duty free. American producers are upset. In 1922–23, the United States exported 30 million of the 32 million pounds of raisins Canada imported. Canada also imported 1.7 million pounds of currants from the United States and 3.3 million pounds from Greece.	
Sep. 27	Georgia's leaders submit their case to the League of Nations.	An earthquake in Wales alarms miners as mine walls collapse.... Rumania uncovers a cache of arms smuggled into Bessarabia by Russian Communists.... Germany indicates it is ready to join the League of Nations with no reservations and with a neutral foreign policy.	Traditional slave trade continues on the Red Sea between Africa and the Arab world. Britain commits a force of fast ships to stop the traffic.... The French in Morocco prepare for attacks as the Moorish effort continues to drive the Spanish back.... Wahabis reportedly take Mecca.		Demand in a Honolulu high school is high enough that the school will begin classes in Japanese.

A	B	C	D	E
Includes developments that affect more than one world region, international organizations and important meetings of world leaders.	*Includes all domestic and regional developments in Europe, including the Soviet Union.*	*Includes all domestic and regional developments in Africa and the Middle East.*	*Includes all domestic and regional developments in Latin America, the Caribbean, and Canada.*	*Includes all domestic and regional developments in Asian and Pacific nations (and colonies).*

U.S. Politics & Social Issues	U.S. Foreign Policy & Affairs, Defense	U.S. Economy & Environment	Science, Technology & Nature	Culture, Leisure & Lifestyle	
Coolidge cheers 100,000 at the Holy Name Society as he calls for religious tolerance and says the United States will never have a religious test for office. He still avoids naming the Klan.		The New York Federal Reserve Bank relocates five blocks to a new location. It requires 37 armored cars and 300 armed men lining the streets as it moves $3 billion in securities and cash.	MacMillan reports that the Arctic glaciers are bigger and the ice cap is thicker. He also says he has reliable information that Cook planted his flag 500 miles south of the pole.…Darrow says a proposed neuropathic hospital to prevent mental-disease-provoked crime is a good idea.	A three-year American Classical Society study reveals that Latin is still the classical language of choice for secondary school students. It attracts 940,000 compared to 11,000 for Greek.…The Prince of Wales boards his private train and leaves the United States.	Sep. 21
	Among the four promoted to Major General is Douglas MacArthur.	Grain exports top 11 million bushels, 2.8 million bushels above last week. Wheat leads all grains, up more than a million bushels.	MacMillan reports that he found a heavy seam of coal in the Arctic. The report further confirms scientific understanding that the Arctic once had a climate comparable to modern Pennsylvania's.	A regional Salvation Army staff meeting hears a report that flapperhood starts too early. Furthermore, the sowing of wild oats is a fallacy. Most important, there is a noticeable drift from the church.	Sep. 22
Druggists in convention agree that prohibition is ineffective in controlling liquor. It simply hurts druggists' business. As presently enforced, it favors the bootleggers.	Secretary Wilbur appoints Admiral Eberle to head the nine-member board assigned to evaluate the comparative worth of planes and battleships. The board is also to recommend appropriations levels.	American industrialists return from a trade mission to Mexico full of optimism that they have rapport with the Obregon government. They expect trade to revive soon and promise to provide necessary capital.…The U.S. bankers association warns against converting from Liberty bonds to riskier stocks, calls for re-funding of $7.5 billion in long term debt, and commits $250,000 to fighting stock fraud.			Sep. 23
The judge dismisses a suit by the Ponzi trustees against an investor who backs out just in time. He says that the American investment class will inevitably fall for another Ponzi scheme. After all, Ponzi conned both business and government until his scheme finally collapsed of its own weight.		Aircraft production for 1923 is reported at nearly $13 million. That is 94.9 percent above the 1921 figure.…The American Economic Institute prepares to fight government ownership of the railroads, which it fears the Barkley-Howell bill will produce. Railroad unions back the institute.…Issuing $20 million in preferred and one million shares of common stock, Radio Corporation of America becomes the first primarily radio business to appear on the big board. Previously listed firms made radios as a sideline.		Broadway dodges police raids and censorship. *What Price Glory* deletes marines' profanity, and the "Vanities" chorus puts on more clothes.	Sep. 24
Angered by California's ruling that his electors will not appear on the ballot, La Follette declares he will be the Socialist candidate there.…A *Literary Digest* poll shows Coolidge leading La Follette with Davis third. Coolidge's vote is 60 percent above the combined total of the other two.		Canned goods exports are up 27 percent from last year. Dried and evaporated fruit exports are up 177 percent; canned fruits are up 100 percent. Totals should exceed 1922's 545 million pounds. The slump of 1923 is over.	A $4 million cable between New York and the Azores allows transmissions at 1,700 letters a minute. Old technology had a maximum 250 letters a minute.	The Salvation Army commits to educate housewives on thrift. The army believes that poor women's incompetence and ignorance causes many of the horrible conditions they endure.	Sep. 25
	Tchitcherin says the Soviet Union is willing to reopen negotiations on debts. The United States is not interested.		Sir Charles Parsons proposes spending $20 million to sink a shaft 12 miles. He says the venture might reveal new elements and is certainly more valuable than polar exploration.		Sep. 26
		Four states ban Texas cattle infected with hoof-and-mouth disease. This is not related to the California outbreak but is due to South American stock. The USDA quarantines four counties around Houston.	Chicago's WJAZ is built on a truck. The station goes directly to events it wants to broadcast.…A Johns Hopkins researcher says most Nicaraguan jungle creatures are diseased. Urban man is healthier.	An auto show featuring closed models draws crowds. There are more than 200 models. Public taste is shifting toward this style. …Epinard, the French colt, loses another international race. Ladkin noses out Epinard. Wise Counsellor is third.…The New York Giants win the National League for the fourth straight year.	Sep. 27

F	G	H	I	J
Includes campaigns, elections, federal-state relations, civil rights and liberties, crime, the judiciary, education, healthcare, poverty, urban affairs, and population.	*Includes formation and debate of U.S. foreign and defense policies, veterans affairs, and defense spending. (Relations with specific foreign countries are usually found under the region concerned.)*	*Includes business, labor, agriculture, taxation, transportation, consumer affairs, monetary and fiscal policy, natural resources, pollution and industrial accidents.*	*Includes worldwide scientific, medical and technological developments, natural phenomena, U.S. weather and natural disasters.*	*Includes the arts, religion, scholarship, communications media, sports, entertainment, fashions, fads, and social life.*

	World Affairs	Europe	Africa & The Middle East	The Americas	Asia & The Pacific
Sep. 28	The around-the-world flyers arrive in Seattle 175 days after they began their flight. After 27,000 miles, they are finished.	Germany's revenue surplus since April is more than $92 million. Interest rates are expected to drop but stay around 8–10 percent.... France enacts incentives to use checks instead of cash. The move should help contract the currency.			
Sep. 29		Austria's Depositen Bank collapses. One official commits suicide as authorities indict two others. Camillo Castiglioni, the postwar Ponzi of Europe, flees the warrant, seeking refuge in Italy.	Hussein's family flees Mecca for Jeddah. Hussein himself left before the Wahabis arrived....In Morocco, Spanish forces complete a planned withdrawal as Moorish pressure continues.	J.J. Arlitt of Texas offers $50 million in Mexican bonds. Wall Street is surprised. Mexico is still in default on its old bonds. This issue, however, is backed by a tax on oil.	The battles outside Shanghai kill hundreds and cause Japan to reconsider its nonintervention policy. Chang brings in Mongolian troops.
Sep. 30	Great Britain and Turkey agree to accept the League's ruling on who controls Mosul ....League of Nations conferees accept the Japanese demand for arbitration of "domestic" issues. Italy says it broadens the scope but others say it does not weaken sovereignty.				
Oct. 1	All of the major powers express their confidence that the League of Nations protocol is an effective means of stopping war.	Marx announces he will invite Nationalists and Socialists to join a unity government....The Commons defeats an Ulster motion to reject the boundary treaty, and the bill moves forward.			Chang offers $200,000 to anyone who brings Wu or Tsao to him alive. Refugees crowd into Shanghai.
Oct. 2	All speakers at the International Emigration Conference in Prague condemn U.S. immigration policy. A German delegate says 20 million Germans will have to emigrate if Dawes fails....The League Assembly unanimously adopts the peace protocol. China quits the meeting after failing to win a League Council seat.	In a noisy session, Labour MPs accuse MacDonald of receiving stock in a biscuit company. MacDonald earlier this year took heat for accepting an automobile. Despite the hubbub, the Irish bill passes....A French auto show features low-cost, low-power machines wanted by French buyers. Few American models are there.	The fighting around Sheshuan becomes more intense as both sides commit additional forces. Casualties are heavy.		Three hundred representatives of all Indian religions gather to talk of religious tolerance. Hindus ask Muslims to tolerate their music near mosques. Attendees also urge Hindu tolerance of Muslim practices concerning cows.
Oct. 3		A smallpox epidemic hits Amsterdam.	Hussein abdicates the Hashemite throne on demand from Hezaz and Mecca citizens seeking peace with the Wahabi. The Wahabi carry the fight to Transjordan.	Three members of the Rice expedition up the Amazon return to the United States. The rest of the party continues seeking to where none has gone before—at least no white men.	Peking protests Russia's sale of airplanes to Chang. The pressure on Shanghai grows, but defenders hold firm....Japan says its objections to the new peace plan rest not on immigration but on Chinese affairs.
Oct. 4		Castiglioni returns to Austria to face a court in the bank collapse scandal. He offers to repay a third of the $1.4 million he cost the bank.		The annual pilgrimage to the Shrine of Guadalupe draws 100,000 Mexican worshipers.	Australia's premier says nothing in the Geneva protocol binds Australia's handling of its internal affairs. Australians are aroused at Japan's immigration views and determined to keep Australia white.
Oct. 5		British unionists meet and declare their wishes. Among them are nationalization of land, mines, and railways....Moscow says a supposed treaty with Italy for action in the Balkans is a forgery.	Emir Ali refuses to replace his father as caliph but accepts election by the people as King of the Hadj. Emir Zeid is in London, and Hussein's son is there too to learn western ways. The Wahabis are in sacred territory but not yet in Mecca.		A typhoon blows through Luzon, killing seven and doing extensive damage.
Oct. 6	France says German membership in the League of Nations is acceptable if Germany abides by the same rules as everyone else.	Austria's problems getting American loans worsen. The Monarchist Bank fails. Meanwhile, Castiglioni's legal and financial problems cause the press to switch from attacking him to castigating the attorney general for harassing him....Both Liberals and Tories seek to censure MacDonald.		Clashes at Camaguey between police and former president Menocal lead to casualties of seven dead and 60 wounded. The government sends a special train with 400 troops to preserve peace in the area.	
	A *Includes developments that affect more than one world region, international organizations and important meetings of world leaders.*	B *Includes all domestic and regional developments in Europe, including the Soviet Union.*	C *Includes all domestic and regional developments in Africa and the Middle East.*	D *Includes all domestic and regional developments in Latin America, the Caribbean, and Canada.*	E *Includes all domestic and regional developments in Asian and Pacific nations (and colonies).*

U.S. Politics & Social Issues	U.S. Foreign Policy & Affairs, Defense	U.S. Economy & Environment	Science, Technology & Nature	Culture, Leisure & Lifestyle	
The Russell Sage Foundation reports after a five-year study that unemployment is constant at 1–6 million. The study finds that employment bureaus gouge would-be workers.	Embassy officials report there is no way to enforce prohibition in the Philippines. There is no inspection or control, and captains are subject only to small fines, which they pay gladly and offload their cargoes.				Sep. 28
The Rockefeller Foundation donates $1 million to Hampton and Tuskegee Institutes. Robert Russa Moton says the period since 1919 is the best for blacks ever. Public schools now employ 40,000 black teachers and educate two million black students.		Coolidge promotes conservation rather than unlimited development, which vice presidential nominee Dawes wants. Coolidge tells mine owners that the crisis of overproduction will ease when the West develops.... The Agricultural Credit Corporation, formed initially to help stabilize Western banks, moves into agricultural diversification assistance. It provides cattle, sheep, and technical advice.		The Washington Senators win their first American League pennant. Hornsby of St.Louis wins his fifth straight batting title, closing at .423.... A big draw at the closed-car show is the Rolls-Royce manufactured in the United States.... The winner of the Missouri Open Golf Tournament wins $1,275.	Sep. 29
	Storms and floods do extensive damage from South Carolina to New York. High winds and high seas demolish seaside resorts, Pennsylvania is also hard hit.	The Southern Pacific gets permission to purchase the El Paso and Southwestern railroads. It will also build a 175-mile line to link with the Rock Island in Arizona. The cost of having a double track to the Pacific is $57.4 million.			Sep. 30
Judge Thayer denies new trials to Sacco and Vanzetti. Appeal to the Supreme Court is next.		United Light and Power forms from the merger of five Midwestern companies. The new utility provides service to 1.75 million customers in nine states. Its assets are worth $34 million, and it has more than a 340,000-kilowatt capacity plus three billion feet of gas annually.	An X-ray expert says the "artificial sun" has effected 60,000 cures, including rickets, hay fever, and asthma.	Johns Hopkins Hospital rejects the flapper look. Its secretaries cannot wear make up.... Commissioner Landis bans two Giants for offering a Philadelphia pitcher money to throw the pennant-clinching game last week. Three other players are exonerated.	Oct. 1
		Texas bans flights into the area quarantined for hoof-and-mouth disease.... Grain prices rise sharply on reports of low crops abroad and in Canada. Forecasters see a billion dollar wheat crop.	Professor Mailhe of France talks of his efforts to create gasoline from animal and vegetable oils.	Landis says the World Series will go on, even as a blacklisted player says all the Giants were involved and Johnson wants the series cancelled. The investigation continues. Scalpers are asking $50 a ticket as demand for the 37,000 seat Washington stadium reaches 150,000.	Oct. 2
Young Presbyterians say that their problem with the current church is a controversy between modernism and fundamentalism. They also find that the church misstates its creed, is too conservative on social issues, teaches poorly, and tries to force religion on the young.	At the Dayton race meet, an army dirigible launches a plane. The dirigible has capability of mooring the plane.	W.A. Harriman and Company has agreement in principle to handle the Chicatouri, GA, manganese contract. It beats British, German, Dutch, and French firms. Chicatouri generates $100 million a year of sales. It has 100 million tons, a 50-year supply.			Oct. 3
	An army flyer trying for a diving start in the Pulitzer Prize contest dies as his plane crumples and falls 50,000 feet. General Billy Mitchell quickly claims that the planes used at Dayton are old and worn out.		A German researcher reports that bees signal that they have found food by dancing.	A Chicago station broadcasting opera and Shakespeare finds it necessary to rewrite the works to make them interesting over radio.	Oct. 4
New York's Associated Academic Principals agree to take on the issue of teaching religion in school. Previously they have avoided the matter but now seem ready to settle it.	The navy tests the all-metal F4-C and reports it is 50 percent superior to wooden planes.	The Federal Trade Commission reports that a monopoly exists in aluminum. Other industries with unfair practices include vacuum cleaners, washing machines, and brooms.		Massachusetts returns 250,000 magazines to their New York publishers. The magazines are improper for Bostonians.	Oct. 5
Bishop John Hurst says blacks should abandon both parties. La Follette should be their man.... Louisiana Progressives fail to get La Follette on the ballot and appeal to the Supreme Court.... Albert Fall continues to dodge the bullet as a third grand jury adjourns without indicting him.		New York City implements one-way streets, no parking zones, signals every four blocks, and one-hour parking in downtown Manhattan. Merchants applaud the effort to ease congestion.... Railroad and sea shippers seek equity in rate structures.		Ed Wynn is author and composer as well as star of *The Grab Bag*. The production is hilarious, say reviewers.	Oct. 6

F	G	H	I	J
Includes campaigns, elections, federal-state relations, civil rights and liberties, crime, the judiciary, education, healthcare, poverty, urban affairs, and population.	*Includes formation and debate of U.S. foreign and defense policies, veterans affairs, and defense spending. (Relations with specific foreign countries are usually found under the region concerned.)*	*Includes business, labor, agriculture, taxation, transportation, consumer affairs, monetary and fiscal policy, natural resources, pollution and industrial accidents.*	*Includes worldwide scientific, medical and technological developments, natural phenomena, U.S. weather and natural disasters.*	*Includes the arts, religion, scholarship, communications media, sports, entertainment, fashions, fads, and social life.*

	World Affairs	Europe	Africa & The Middle East	The Americas	Asia & The Pacific
Oct. 7		Senator Henri de Jouvenal says that France will create a larger army if the protocol fails....Rumanian Premier Bratianu visits Austria to reestablish cordial relations between the two states and form a Danubian confederation. Rumor says the federation eventually will include Germany.	British Prime Minister MacDonald rejects the proposed Anglo-Egyptian protocol submitted by Egyptian Premier Zaghlul. Control of the Suez Canal is among the issues on which the two countries disagree.		
Oct. 8	Britain defers the empire conference....Japan and Mexico sign a treaty. Japan relinquishes claims for losses during Mexico's revolutions....The Episcopal House of Bishops (Presbyterian) votes to leave the position of Bishop for Mexico vacant because of Mexico's anti-religion stance. The Presbyterians select bishops for North Texas, Nevada, and Hankow.	The International Federation of Motor Clubs invites Germany to join. Recently, Germany rejoined the Olympic movement....The International Peace Conference in Berlin hears a debate over a Pan-European plan....Moscow reports the Ukraine has 50,000 bootleggers who compete with state-run liquor production.	Iraqis are divided over oil concessions. One group sees the benefits of developing Mosul and Baghdad. The nationalists are skeptical, seeing development as exploitation.		War Department officials say that prohibition law for the Philippines is a mistake. The Volstead Act authors did not intend to include the islands. Officials also note that most of the drinking in the Philippines is by foreigners and Americans, not Filipinos.
Oct. 9		The Irish Bill becomes law. Commons dissolves. MacDonald calls elections for October 29....The German cabinet falls, and Marx calls for new elections....In Hungary Magyar deputies riot, bringing the cabinet nearly to collapse.			
Oct. 10	The reparations commission approves the terms of the $200 million German loan. The loan is quickly oversubscribed.	In Britain, nearly 1,500 candidates are up for elections, with the Tories favored and a bitter fight expected....Germany agrees to ship Rumania railroad materiel in partial payment of reparations.	Persia grants Sinclair Oil a concession in the north. In 1923, the deal depended on Sinclair's helping arrange a U.S. loan of $10 million for Persia, but current terms make no mention of that obligation.		Buddhist monks in Burma attack a husband and wife missionary team. The attacks are part of a series that initially targeted police in reprisal for the arrest and conviction of the monks' leader.
Oct. 11		French cardinals ask Herriott to keep the Vatican embassy. They note the patriotism of the church during the war....Herriott indicates he will lay off 20,000 government workers so he can provide pay raises to the remainder....De Valera's Nationalist Party indicates it will participate in British elections by entering candidates in Northern Ireland.	Turkey denies a British allegation that its troops are crossing into the neutral zone in Iraq. The neutral zone is in effect pending League of Nations determination of the border.	Mexico denies it plans to cut the oil tax. American business people sever talks with Mexico.	
Oct. 12	Gold movement is decreasing with little coming to the United States. Demand in India is slacking also.	The Hungarian stock market is unstable due to heavy losses in bank and industrial stocks. The reverberations affect Austria's stock market. Austria's foreign and domestic trade are already lower....German prices continue to rise, primarily due to food shortages caused by poor harvests.	The New York Zoo prepares a 280-foot ship to explore the Sargasso Sea and chart the west coast of Africa. The chart will help to compare the African coast with the east coast of South America....Transvaal sets a new season record for gold output. The reasons are increased efficiency and new mines.		The Shanghai defense forces surrender. Generals flee.
Oct. 13		Castiglioni offers to pay bank depositors 15 billion *kronen* to cover their losses....Liberals and Tories agree that one party or the other will contest seats with Labour opponents. They seek to avoid splitting the anti-Labour vote in three-way contests.	Britain asks Turkey to withdraw its troops on the Iraq border. Turkey denies it has mobilized troops. Unofficial Ankara sources say otherwise....Fighting in Morocco continues as the Moorish army again cuts communications between Tangiers and Tetuan....Wahabis refuse peace and position themselves to lay siege to Mecca. Reports of cholera in their ranks emerge.		Chang begins attacks in the north. In Shanghai, the international contingent lands shore parties to preserve peace in the foreign quarters. Japan maintains troops in Manchuria.
	A *Includes developments that affect more than one world region, international organizations and important meetings of world leaders.*	B *Includes all domestic and regional developments in Europe, including the Soviet Union.*	C *Includes all domestic and regional developments in Africa and the Middle East.*	D *Includes all domestic and regional developments in Latin America, the Caribbean, and Canada.*	E *Includes all domestic and regional developments in Asian and Pacific nations (and colonies).*

U.S. Politics & Social Issues	U.S. Foreign Policy & Affairs, Defense	U.S. Economy & Environment	Science, Technology & Nature	Culture, Leisure & Lifestyle	
	Shenandoah leaves Lakehurst, NJ, on a cross-country test flight. Passengers say it is like sailing the sea but smoother.…Coolidge receives Prof Smiddy, the first Minister Plenipotentiary of the Irish Free State.	Washington radio conference attendees oppose high-powered super radio stations proposed by RCA's David Sarnoff. They fear that stations of up to 50 kilowatts will interfere with small ones.			Oct. 7
General Booth, commander of the Salvation Army, is in the United States en route to Canada. He denies plans to remove his sister as commander of the American branch.…In a south side Chicago immigrant neighborhood, experiencing an influx of blacks, a mob of 100 beat a black man to death with a baseball bat after he allegedly molests a white immigrant girl. Police on the scene in force prevent riots like those of 1919.		A government forecast of a 12.5 million bale cotton crop catches the experts by surprise. The crop is 2.36 million bales above last year's. The price plummets 116–134 points.…In hearings before the Labor Board, 58 railroads oppose the request of their clerks for a six-to 12-cent an hour pay raise.	Former Governor Benjamin O'Dell drives the final rivet in the Hudson River bridge at Peekskill. The privately financed $6 million bridge has a 1,623-foot span, longest in the world until completion of the Philadelphia-Camden bridge two years hence.	The Lutheran Church bans organs with jazzy features—and organists who jiggle the stops to get a jazzy effect. Jazzy music causes churchgoers, particularly children, to lose reverence.	Oct. 8
	Secretary Hughes advises the League of Nations that the United States is willing to consider identity certificates in lieu of passports. The League offered on September 12 to create certificates for Armenian refugees if the United States would accept the alternative paperwork.…Disabled veterans charge the Veterans Bureau with racial and religious discrimination. They blame Klan influence in the bureau.	New York embargoes rail shipments of California juice grapes destined for other cities. Other cities have already embargoed the grapes because they are coming in faster than the yard workers can deal with them. National distribution of juice grapes is a new development of the past few years, and the railroads have not yet established a system of handling them.			Oct. 9
Macon, Georgia's Mercer University, Southern Baptist affiliated, asks a biology professor to resign over his teaching of evolution. Students petition the university to retain the professor, prominent in Georgia scientific circles.…Senator Jones (D-NM) joins a continuing debate over the validity of the *Literary Digest* presidential poll. He notes that 2.8 Republicans to each one Democrat had the opportunity to vote.	A bomb tears the *TC-2* dirigible over Langley Field, VA. Only one dies and four suffer injuries; the blimp uses helium rather than hydrogen.…*Shenandoah* arrives in San Diego safely, having avoided a mountain and struggled with turbulence in a night flight over the Rockies.	The Census Bureau reports that U.S. manufacturers made 3.19 million cars in 1923, an increase of 89 percent over 1921.…The radio conference opposes censorship and monopoly, while agreeing to test the super station and proposes reallocating bandwidths for amateurs, ships, and broadcasters.		Washington wins a seven-game, million-dollar series. Attendance is below that of 1923, the other million-dollar series.…In Boston, Koussevitsky debuts Symphony Hall. An American audience hears the works of Honegger and Vivaldi for the first time.…Connie Mack of the Philadelphia Athletics buys Lefty Groves from the International League's Baltimore Orioles for $106,000. The price is second only to that paid for Ruth.	Oct. 10
Gilbert Nations, American Party presidential candidate, charges the post office with costing him a position on the Maryland ballot by delaying petitions by party members seeking to add his name. Postal officials reply that the petitions had postage due.	During army night maneuvers, a bomber has mechanical problems. Amateur radio buffs help it to find a safe place to land and make repairs.			The Aga Khan's Superlette sets a course mark in winning the Pierrepont at Jamaica.…In other race news, Epinard loses a third time.…The hot fad is radio golf, whose millions of players vie to listen to the greatest number of stations over the widest area.	Oct. 11
			The big German dirigible ZR-3 is under way across the Atlantic. The U.S. Navy is tracking its movement. The ZR-3 is Germany's last gasp at saving its zeppelin factory, ordered closed under the war-ending treaty.		Oct. 12
The Supreme Court says confessions made under duress are inadmissible. They rule in the case of a Chinese national convicted of three murders after police use the third degree on him. The court also declines to hear a trainmen's claim that they have the right to strike, sustaining a lower court conspiracy conviction.		Ford surprises Washington when he withdraws his offer to buy the Muscle Shoals plant. He says there is too much politics involved, but he might yet entertain a government offer.	Professor See of the Naval Observatory says that his observations of eclipses prove Einstein errs. Rather, Newton's theory of gravitation is right and Einstein uses curved space to cover up a mathematical error.		Oct. 13
F *Includes campaigns, elections, federal-state relations, civil rights and liberties, crime, the judiciary, education, healthcare, poverty, urban affairs, and population.*	G *Includes formation and debate of U.S. foreign and defense policies, veterans affairs, and defense spending. (Relations with specific foreign countries are usually found under the region concerned.)*	H *Includes business, labor, agriculture, taxation, transportation, consumer affairs, monetary and fiscal policy, natural resources, pollution and industrial accidents.*	I *Includes worldwide scientific, medical and technological developments, natural phenomena, U.S. weather and natural disasters.*	J *Includes the arts, religion, scholarship, communications media, sports, entertainment, fashions, fads, and social life.*	

	World Affairs	Europe	Africa & The Middle East	The Americas	Asia & The Pacific
Oct. 14		The French Council of War at Nancy sentences several German generals to death for war crimes. As with other trials in France over the past four years, the trials occur in absentia.		A schooner captain raises the U.S. flag on Herald Island, near Wrangel Island where Russians recently raised the Soviet flag. The captain also finds the remains of Stefansson's 1914 expedition.	
Oct. 15	MacDonald calls for an immediate meeting of the League Council to settle the dispute with Turkey.		Wahabis enter Mecca amid reports of looting of homes of the rich and the palace.…An Egyptologist reports that one pharaoh had hardened arteries and another had skin problems. His point is that modern disease plagued the ancients too.	Nicaragua seeks an American advisor to reorganize its national bank and rework its banking laws.…Oil producers and the Mexican government end their dispute. Companies prepare to open new fields.	
Oct. 16		Finland's government sets precedent by providing funds for the statue of Paavo Nurmi at Helsingfors. Finland also plans to build a stadium. The country is enjoying its unprecedented success at the recent Olympics.			In Shanghai, leaderless Chinese troops worry foreigners and Chinese alike. Ten thousand European forces are in the city. In Canton, fighting between workers and merchants has killed more than 1,000 and caused $7 million in damage.
Oct. 17		Russian peasants discover that newspaper reporters are spies for the soviets. They kill 40.…France is interested in buying a zeppelin. Germany says it will build it if it can build one for itself.		Russia withdraws the colony of one American and 13 Eskimos from Wrangel. Rebuffed in his offer of the island to Britain, Stefansson says the American claim is best.	
Oct. 18	French, Spanish, and German diplomats protest Mexican President Obregon's intent to expel eight Puebla merchants who refuse to pay the Mexican income tax. The diplomats argue that the Puebla Chamber of Commerce has ordered all members to boycott the tax as illegal.				
Oct. 19	Mexico orders the expulsion of 100 Chinese. The men are alleged agents of tongs.	German businesses seeking to borrow money abroad find themselves hamstrung by the Dawes Plan. The reparations lien gives reparations first priority, making lower priority loans risky. In addition, Dawes blocks shipment of gold out of Germany, and Germany has little to spare anyway.…Turkey rounds up 2,000 Greeks illegally in Constantinople and places them in camps pending deportation.			Manila's mayor calls out troops and apologizes to the Chinese consul general to head off a race riot. A Filipino kills a Chinese in a business dispute, triggering a near riot with stone throwing and the injury of five Filipinos.…Sun Yat-sen attacks the western powers for hamstringing his revolution. He says Russia is China's best friend, while the United States is lapdog of Great Britain.
Oct. 20		After Marx fails to form a new government, Chancellor Ebert dissolves the *Reichstag* and orders new elections. The campaign will center on foreign policy, particularly the Dawes Plan.	The Soviet envoy says that American experts have failed to balance Persia's budget or correct its financial woes. He blames foreign powers for inciting the southern sheikhs against the Persian government.		Forces of the Peking government stop Chang at Shanhaikwan. Shanghai is quiet. Fifty Indian troops patrol Canton.
Oct. 21		The head of Germany's Nationalist Party says that the ex-Kaiser expects to recover his $5 million estates. The Nationalist further says the Kaiser asked him what chance there is of regaining the throne. The Nationalist favors one of the sons instead of the ex-Kaiser, who has too much political and social baggage.…France evacuates two more zones, Karlsruhe and Mannheim.…Winston Churchill heads a new parliamentary bloc, the Constitutionalists, that includes a dozen liberals.	Osman Digna is free after 22 years in solitary confinement. He is the former head of the "Fuzzy Wuzzy" campaign against Kitchener in the Sudan 40 years ago. He is now on pilgrimage to Mecca.	Cuban storms kill 12 and injure 100.	
	A *Includes developments that affect more than one world region, international organizations and important meetings of world leaders.*	B *Includes all domestic and regional developments in Europe, including the Soviet Union.*	C *Includes all domestic and regional developments in Africa and the Middle East.*	D *Includes all domestic and regional developments in Latin America, the Caribbean, and Canada.*	E *Includes all domestic and regional developments in Asian and Pacific nations (and colonies).*

U.S. Politics & Social Issues	U.S. Foreign Policy & Affairs, Defense	U.S. Economy & Environment	Science, Technology & Nature	Culture, Leisure & Lifestyle	
Connecticut Republican Frank B. Brandagee commits suicide by turning on the gas in his home. His death and another cause worry about what an altered Congressional balance might do if the presidential election produces no clear winner.	Of the 4.5 million eligible war veterans, fewer than a third have asked for the veterans' bonus.…The president of the American-Japan Society resigns over U.S. immigration policy. Viscount Kaneko ends 20 years of promoting friendship between the two nations.		Scientists in Maine demonstrate that chickens develop normally in sunlight but fare poorly in glass-filtered light. The scientists promote windowpanes that do not block violet rays as a cure for rickets in children.		Oct. 14
Indiana Republicans admit that their party is split over the Klan issue. Blacks are moving to the Democrats or Progressives, and Democrats think they can take the state.	Secretary Hughes advises Canada that the United States is not interested in talks over Lake Michigan water only. The talks must include Niagara.	Eight-month freight totals are down 9.7 percent from last year. The west is near last year's total, but eastern freight is off 17 percent.…The Packers and Stockyards Administration charges Swift and Armour discriminate over hogs.	The ZR-3 arrives safely after setting time and distance records. Patents transfer to Goodyear.…Sir Frank Dyson counters See's claims about Einstein, as does Professors Eddington and Eisenhart.	A home expo features electrical homes. Especially exciting is the coalless furnace.…After a lengthy additional stay in the United States, the Prince of Wales is finally in Toronto, where he falls from his horse during a foxhunt.	Oct. 15
The new *Literary Digest* poll shows Coolidge with 36 states, Davis with 10, and La Follette with one. The poll tallies two million ballots in almost all states.…Senator Borah opens hearings on campaign financing. He hears reports that Republicans raised $1.7 million while Progressives amassed $190,500.		A conference of railway executives on consolidation ends with agreement among the New York Central, B&O, and Nickel Plate over consolidation of trunk lines and a plan for eastern railroads. The Pennsylvania Railroad is not totally aboard.			Oct. 16
La Follette charges that the "bread trust" is supporting Republicans clandestinely.…Franklin Roosevelt predicts a Davis victory. He also says Smith will win New York's governorship.	Lillian R. Sire says the flags used to bury American service members are of cheap bunting and have only 40 stars. She says the Veterans Bureau has 300,000 flags with one row missing. The savings is 37 cents a flag.	The Harriman manganese deal with Russia is finished. Unfortunately, Georgia does not recognize Russia's right to deal in Georgian property. Nor has Georgia yielded in the war against Russia.		A paint expert says that red drives men mad. Yellow is good for the shell-shocked, while blue is generally calming.	Oct. 17
La Follette says that the Republicans are amassing a war chest of $10 million. He also alleges a Republican levy on bankers.	Army Lt. Bertrandis sets a new speed record in an army seaplane. His Loening tops 100 miles per hour at Hampton, VA.	Coffee prices are at 55 cents a pound for the finest grades, near to the wartime peak. Supply is 19.5 million pounds, and a shortage looms.	Two amateur radio buffs in London pick up a broadcast from New Zealand. They use homemade equipment.	The smart money moves even more to Coolidge. His odds are now 5–1. Al Smith is 7–5 over Roosevelt in the New York gubernatorial race.	Oct. 18
Rejecting a challenge to the election of "Ma" Ferguson, the Texas Supreme Court rules that women can run for office under the suffrage amendments to the federal and state constitutions.	A former chief of the Veterans of Foreign Wars says the Veterans Administration under Coolidge has betrayed veterans. A third of its funds have been misspent or stolen. The speaker urges rejection of Coolidge for Davis.	Railroad executives cite their contribution to helping the cost of living. Railroad rates have fallen $7 million since 1920 and transit times are half what they were then.	*Shenandoah* begins the return trip from Camp Lewis, WA, to Lakehurst, NJ.	Tex Austin's rodeo is in the news again as two performers suffer injuries. Austin's big problem is his citation for violating Sunday closing laws.…Fifty thousand of the curious flock to the *ZR-3's* hangar. An enterprising hustler collects admission for the free spectacle.	Oct. 19
A new Tong war in Chicago breaks out. One is dead and three injured.…The Supreme Court upholds Nicky Arnstein's right to invoke the Fifth Amendment in a 1920 bankruptcy. Brandeis speaks for the majority in finding self-incrimination protection covers civil as well as criminal cases.	A complaint alleges the War Department sold surplus uniforms at Brooklyn at a loss of $392,000. The department counters that the clothing went to the highest bidder.…A gun flareback on the *Trenton* kills five and injures 17.	Standard of Indiana denies it illegally blocked others from using its cracking process. It says the contracts in question expired and it was voluntarily sharing the information before the government sued it.		Injured in his final race, Epinard retires after his owner refuses a record $300,000 for him. In November he sails for France and a life at stud.	Oct. 20
Democrats tell the Borah committee investigating campaign finance that they expect to spend $750,000 for the campaign. They have collected $548,000. They publish a list of 4,000 donors, none of whom is a beneficiary of the tariff or a banker.…The president of Tammany denies that his organization plans to steal the gubernatorial election from the Republicans, who stand accused of voting irregularities upstate.	Secretary Hughes announces that the United States will participate in the Geneva opium conference.	The government begins its case against Edward Doheny for fraud. The government alleges Doheny's companies bribed Secretary Fall and consequently acquired $100 million in illegal oil leases.…The receiver for New York Railways announces that he is ready to remove 46 miles of light rail tracks and allow the city to replace trains with buses. Not all are ready to change; Park Avenue residents' protest of a proposed bus line on their street is on the city's agenda for two days hence.	Retired stage actress Maude Adams forms a $3.5 million movie company. She plans feature films using a color process she developed herself.…Texas' Dr. House calls for use of "truth serum" in fighting crime. Tests show it works half the time.		Oct. 21

F	G	H	I	J
Includes campaigns, elections, federal-state relations, civil rights and liberties, crime, the judiciary, education, healthcare, poverty, urban affairs, and population.	*Includes formation and debate of U.S. foreign and defense policies, veterans affairs, and defense spending. (Relations with specific foreign countries are usually found under the region concerned.)*	*Includes business, labor, agriculture, taxation, transportation, consumer affairs, monetary and fiscal policy, natural resources, pollution and industrial accidents.*	*Includes worldwide scientific, medical and technological developments, natural phenomena, U.S. weather and natural disasters.*	*Includes the arts, religion, scholarship, communications media, sports, entertainment, fashions, fads, and social life.*

	World Affairs	Europe	Africa & The Middle East	The Americas	Asia & The Pacific
Oct. 22	Church leaders escort the body of Pope Leo XIII from St. Peter's to St. John Lateran. Leo has been at St. Peter's since his 1903 death, but Pope Pius XI wants him permanently in St. John Lateran by the time of St. John Lateran's 16th centennial.	Turkey's camps house 3,000 Greeks awaiting deportation. Greece asks the League to intervene to stop Turkey from expelling Greeks from Constantinople.		Cuban Dominican and Sugar Estates of Oriente merge to create a $90 million sugar organization in Cuba and the West Indies. The firm will control half a million acres and mills generating 2.4 million bags of sugar. Owners are American.	Nuevo Eoija rioters attack Chinese stores and Filipino police as disturbances in the Philippines erupt again.
Oct. 23	The League of Nations begins hearings on mandates established by Versailles. Japan is first to report. It describes its administration of Pacific island mandates. Next, Zionists report on progress in Palestine.	France, Belgium, and Germany indicate a desire to form a steel trust that may include Great Britain. They seek U.S. reaction, which initially is that the combine will not have much impact on the American market. In Germany Socialists denounce the proposal as election-eve pandering.... Italy's anti-Fascist coalition splits over a Communist proposal to establish a second parliament to rival the Fascist one.	*Ha Chalutz*, a story of life as a Jewish pioneer, is finished. Composed by Jerusalem pianist Weinberg, it is the first Palestinian opera.		Christian General Feng rebels and forces President Tsao Kun to flee Peking. Feng calls a conference, seeking an end to the civil war.
Oct. 24	The League of Nations pauses as its secretary general gives Jackie Coogan a letter of thanks for his and Americans' relief contributions. The League cites Near East Relief as well as efforts on behalf of dislocated Greeks.	Britain reveals it has a note from Zinoviev asking British Communists to infiltrate the army and make a revolution. Britain tells Russia to control its international movement or forget about British agreements.		European Jews barred from entering the United States arrive in Mexico. They plan to wait there until they get permission to enter the United States. A New York organization promises to pay their expenses as well as those of a group soon to leave New York, where they are stranded, denied entry.... Canada hangs four convicted of murder in a $160,000 robbery. Two others are spared.	Australia's new trade minister invites U.S. business people to see what the country has to offer. He wants to increase trade in wool and make mutton a popular American table item.... Japanese forces enter North China. Under guard, Tsao Kun shakes up his cabinet and fires General Wu under pressure from Feng. Chang halts fighting.
Oct. 25	The United States agree to sit in on the committee determining the cost of the allied occupation and shares of the income from the Ruhr. The United States claim is $240 million.			Knud Rasmussen, Danish polar explorer, arrives in Seattle after traveling 20,000 miles by dogsled, ship, and foot. He claims to have discovered the origin of the Eskimo, but he will not reveal it. He does reveal a population of fewer than 40,000 that shares a common language from Siberia to Greenland. He also has movies.	Tsao Kun resigns as Wu begins a possibly decisive battle against Chang at Shanhaikwan.
Oct. 26	France determines that a group of Antarctic archipelagos and islands are administratively part of Madagascar. Discovered in the 18th and 19th centuries by French explorers, the islands have never been in any department. They are valuable for whales, seals, and minerals.	Improved Austrian conditions and the German loan lift central European markets. Some stocks rise 20 percent on the expectation that Vienna will play a vital role in financing German rebuilding.... Ulster police arrest De Valera in Londonderry, where he is scheduled to speak. This is De Valera's second arrest this month for being in Northern Ireland.... Russia orders a census of Jews in the Ukraine. It plans farms in the Crimea for those Jews willing to relocate.			Wu is at Tientsin, halfway to Peking, with 38 railway cars full of troops, and talking of raising a 100,000-man army to oust those who ousted him. Shanhaikwan is becoming the pivotal battle, the one to establish which force has credibility.
Oct. 27	Lord Parmoor and Pethi Bey present their respective cases to the League of Nations in the dispute over the border of Iraq. The League will hear the Greek-Turkish dispute next.	Marshal Foch dedicates Lighthouse #3, a Paris home for the war blind donated by Mrs. W.H. Mather and other American women.	Spain withdraws from Sheshuan. The forces in opposition increase as two new groups join the anti-Spain coalition.	In the United States after a post-election vacation in Europe, president-elect Calles predicts a bright future for Mexico. He warns American investors and business people that even as they exploit Mexico's wealth, they must protect the rights of Mexican labor.	A hundred American marines have landed at Taku. They will travel 105 miles to Peking by train. Japan is preparing to add to its forces, but not taking sides. Feng is building his army as Wu moves toward Shanghai.
Oct. 28	Before the League's mandate commission, the commissioner for the Palestinian mandate attributes troubles to Arabs attempting to dominate the region. Sir Herbert Samuel also reports that Palestine holds 40,000 Jewish immigrants, 80 percent of whom reside in towns.	France's Herriott recognizes the Soviet government. Russian émigrés in Paris protest.... Dissident Democrats form a Liberal Union Party. The German electorate now has 14 parties from which to choose.... Berlin police begin rounding up Communist *Reichstag* members.	Facing a growing opposition, Spain tries to bribe the Anjera to remain neutral. The Spanish also send two troops of soldiers. Elsewhere, fighting on the Tangiers-Laraiche road has cut communications and traffic.		Competing armies are entrenching outside Peking. The western powers warn the generals not to cut the route to the sea.
	A *Includes developments that affect more than one world region, international organizations and important meetings of world leaders.*	B *Includes all domestic and regional developments in Europe, including the Soviet Union.*	C *Includes all domestic and regional developments in Africa and the Middle East.*	D *Includes all domestic and regional developments in Latin America, the Caribbean, and Canada.*	E *Includes all domestic and regional developments in Asian and Pacific nations (and colonies).*

U.S. Politics & Social Issues	U.S. Foreign Policy & Affairs, Defense	U.S. Economy & Environment	Science, Technology & Nature	Culture, Leisure & Lifestyle	
	Italy and the United States ratify a treaty protecting American prohibition.	After the Day and Heaton case, over minority protest, Wall Street mandates regular audits of members, signed by all partners. Day and Heaton became insolvent after trusted employee George Christian stole $1 million in securities.	New Jersey courts dismiss a temporary injunction against DeForest and allow the company to begin sales. RCA has lost its control over what other manufacturers can do in the radio market.		Oct. 22
Forty-two former Bull Moosers, including Harold Ickes and Jane Addams, announce for La Follette. They cite the corruption of the Harding-Coolidge administration and the need for a progressive third party to reform politics.…Chief Plentycoos promises Coolidge the Flathead and Crow vote. This year is the first time that Native Americans have the right to vote.…After Tong members stab a court interpreter 12 times, the New York Court of General Sessions solicits volunteers from Columbia University. The court has 50 Tong appeals backlogged.		After internal debate on whether the internal revenue law allows it, some offices release tax information while others refuse. Ford's income tax is $2.4 million. His company's assessment is $18.9 million. John D. Rockefeller, Jr. pays $7.4 million.…Citing eight companies that took a loss, while International Harvester made a profit, Attorney General Stone contends that 1918 action proved futile. Stone seeks to dissolve International Harvester's monopoly of farm equipment.			Oct. 23
The Borah committee hears an uncorroborated secret report that the Republicans have a slush fund. If true, it should shake up the campaign.		The railroad trade association reports that lines have $100 million in pending purchases, including 83 locomotives.…After initially objecting to the disclosure of their incomes, Wall Street leaders develop an interest in seeing how the others are faring.		The Prince of Wales finally heads for home.	Oct. 24
Yonkers police raid Chinese Tongs and take 27 prisoners, including several implicated in murders. Police also find drugs and guns.	A navy seaplane sets a new record of 176 miles per hour more than 100 km. The plane's average for 500 km is 161 miles per hour.	An airplane developed for the Dayton air meet will be safe and economical once it goes into mass production. A kit for home construction of the small craft, the flivver of flight, should be an affordable at $500. The price of a factory-finished plane is $1,500. The engine is inadequate though, not up to European standard.	New York's Health Commissioner asserts that there is no harm from exhaust fumes in the streets. The fresh air dilutes the carbon monoxide. Doctors disagree, citing tiredness as a result of exposure.…*Shenandoah* reaches Lakehurst, NJ, after a 9,000-mile trip.		Oct. 25
A ship from Hong Kong contains crates hiding Chinese, including one dead. Suffering from Beriberi and malnutrition, the Chinese are believed to be recruits for the Tong wars.	A canvass of the Senate by the Non-Partisan League gets only 11 favorable Republican responses. Twenty-five Republicans decline to respond. Of the Democrats, 19 are in favor of U.S. participation on the court.	Ford announces plans to use its own ships to transport its cars and tractors directly from the River Rouge plant to Argentina and other parts of South America.		Seeking to revitalize a largely defunct sport, race walkers ask the AAU to sanction walking. They also want the Olympic Games to reinstate the sport after dropping it in the post-competition reduction of Olympic events.	Oct. 26
The U.S. Supreme Court agrees to hear in January a case seeking to deny New York jurisdiction over the Six Nations. The Federal government seeks to reverse a district court ruling that the state does indeed have jurisdiction.	After being kept aboard ship as an undesirable alien, Countess Karolyi finally receives clearance after a determination that she is not a Communist. Her husband is a Hungarian exile on a lecture tour of the United States.	Twenty-four railways report a profitable September. They net a combined $57 million, compared with $46 million in 1923. The anthracite lines report larger loadings; the other lines are in the black due to cost cutting.	Insanity gas kills another Standard Oil worker. Insanity gas is tetraethyl lead, a component of gasoline. As Standard denies negligence, Dr. Yandell Henderson calls for discontinuing the use of tetra-ethyl lead in gasoline.	Radio fans react favorably to the first day of broadcasts by the Gimbels Department Store's radio station. The station features three bills.	Oct. 27
	Secretary Wilbur lifts the ban on soft drinks on navy ships. The ban by Secretary Daniels predates prohibition and is due to the lack of storage space for soft drink bottles. Intensive lobbying by soft drink manufacturers sways Wilbur.		Professor Tiedjens reports that plants grown under electric light are 50 percent larger. He attributes much of the growth to the increased heat.	The army rules that only one officer can compete for a service football team beginning next year.	Oct. 28

F	G	H	I	J
Includes campaigns, elections, federal-state relations, civil rights and liberties, crime, the judiciary, education, healthcare, poverty, urban affairs, and population.	*Includes formation and debate of U.S. foreign and defense policies, veterans affairs, and defense spending. (Relations with specific foreign countries are usually found under the region concerned.)*	*Includes business, labor, agriculture, taxation, transportation, consumer affairs, monetary and fiscal policy, natural resources, pollution and industrial accidents.*	*Includes worldwide scientific, medical and technological developments, natural phenomena, U.S. weather and natural disasters.*	*Includes the arts, religion, scholarship, communications media, sports, entertainment, fashions, fads, and social life.*

	World Affairs	Europe	Africa & The Middle East	The Americas	Asia & The Pacific
Oct. 29		Early returns give Conservatives 163 seats and a 58-seat majority. Liberals and Labour lose badly, with the latter gaining 73 and the former only 23 seats.	The League of Nations establishes an Iraqi border, orders both sides to withdraw by November 15, and establishes a peacekeeping commission to monitor the border. Peacekeepers include Sweden, Uruguay, and Spain.		Wu continues to advance on Peking despite having his right wing cut by Chang. Russia's financing of Feng tops $3 million. Rumor says Hwang Fu will form the next government.
Oct. 30		Spanish police break up a liberal rally and arrest leading liberals. Protesters want an end to the dictatorship and the implementation of a republic.... The final Conservative majority is 206. Four women win seats.		The Bank of Montreal absorbs Molson Bank. Bank of Montreal, with $735 million in assets, is the third largest in North America. Four banks own 70 percent of Canadian banks' $2.67 billion in resources. Consolidation, a trend begun in 1921, allows Canadian banks to compete with U.S. banks.... Brazilian rebels are gaining in Rio Grande de Sul. The Sao Paolo band controls western Parana. The goal is to combine forces and sever the south from Brazil.	Wu offers peace if Chang will withdraw behind the Great Wall. Chang is reported en route to Peking to make a deal with Feng.
Oct. 31	Czechoslovakia is first to ratify the League protocol on arbitration. Uncertainty prevails over what Britain will do now that it has a Conservative government.		A Belgian company capitalized at 500,000 francs begins testing the feasibility of growing cotton in Ethiopia. The company will commit six million francs once the experiment proves successful.	S.C. Scotte claims to have discovered a subtropical valley in the far north on the British Columbia-Yukon border. He says temperatures rarely dip below freezing and berries and wild fruit are abundant. Scotte says colonization will begin next year	General Huang Fu forms the new cabinet in Peking. Wu tries to seize foreign tax funds. Foreign troops in Tientsin disarm wounded Chinese soldiers.
Nov. 1					Wu abandons his drive on Peking. Peace negotiations begin between Feng and Wu. Tuan Chi-jui heads for the capital to form a new government.
Nov. 2		The Reichsbank is now on gold, with coverage for 44 percent of its outstanding bank notes.... Raouf Bey leads generals seeking to oust Kemal Pasha. Other generals in the anti-Kemal force include the Mosul commander and third army inspector.		Machado is comfortably ahead in the Cuban presidential election, holding a 56,000-vote lead with virtually all returns in. Menocal supporters doubt the legitimacy of the vote.... After completion of the American industrial mission to Mexico, business people led by Texan Harry Lindsley offer 20 scholarships to Mexican students wanting to study in the United States. Mexican authorities are highly pleased at the neighborly gesture.	A volcano erupts beneath the Pacific near the Yaeyama Islands between Formosa and the Loochoo Islands. The captain of the *Miyako Maru* reports the vessel has to dodge boiling muddy water filled with large pumice rocks for 12 miles.
Nov. 3			Tunisia is interested in hiring a California rainmaker. Charles Hatfield shot chemicals into the air. Over the next month, rain totaled two inches. Tunisia has large arid regions.	Menocal charges fraud and intimidation. With a 58,000-vote edge, Machado scoffs and says the election is fair.	
Nov. 4	Henry Morgenthau quits as head of the League's Greek refugee committee after arranging a £6 million loan. The crisis that relocated one million Greeks from Turkey is at an end.	France's Herriott asks his first vote of confidence and survives comfortably, 410–171. MacDonald steps down; Baldwin is the new British prime minister.		Mutinies in Brazil include the crew of a warship and the garrison at Pernambuco.	Wu is at sea, as his protégé, Chi, resumes the central Chinese fighting. Meanwhile, Feng, Chang, and Tuan are negotiating in the north. Tuan negotiates to acquire Wu's forces.
	A *Includes developments that affect more than one world region, international organizations and important meetings of world leaders.*	B *Includes all domestic and regional developments in Europe, including the Soviet Union.*	C *Includes all domestic and regional developments in Africa and the Middle East.*	D *Includes all domestic and regional developments in Latin America, the Caribbean, and Canada.*	E *Includes all domestic and regional developments in Asian and Pacific nations (and colonies).*

U.S. Politics & Social Issues	U.S. Foreign Policy & Affairs, Defense	U.S. Economy & Environment	Science, Technology & Nature	Culture, Leisure & Lifestyle	
A bomb rocks the house of the mayor of Niles, OH. The mayor earlier authorizes the Klan a parade permit.…Arthur Nash, clothing manufacturer, tells the National Association of Religious Liberals that following the Golden Rule is making him rich despite himself.			A blast opens a hole between the two halves of the under-construction Holland Tunnel. Officials cancel the elaborate ceremony, including a triggering signal from Coolidge, because the chief engineer, Clifford Holland, dies two days earlier.…Army flyers blast ionized sand into fog and cause rain.	Two more Big Ten Western Conference schools open new stadiums. The league's commissioner, John L. Griffith, denies that commercialism is a factor in football's growth. He says that large stadiums, led by Ohio State's 72,000-seat facility, merely allow schools to provide athletics for their entire student bodies.	Oct. 29
A *Literary Digest* straw poll gives Coolidge a comfortable victory with 327 votes. Davis polls 165 and La Follette only 39. Republican campaign manager Butler agrees. He says Coolidge can count on the West and should pull in 325 votes.	Turkey's Fethi Bey says that Turkey will not act on the new Turkish-American treaty until the U.S. Senate ratifies it. He further says that the treaty gives the United States the same status as European nations in Turkey. Roberts College is safe. If Turkey wins Mosul, he will allow the United States to compete on equal terms for development rights.	The General Land Office reports that as of the end of 1923 the government has disposed of more than one billion acres, roughly 60 percent of the continental United States. The United States still hold 186 million acres of public lands.…A Cleveland federal judge rules that release of tax information violates no privacy law. The tax collector nevertheless refuses to release the information. A test case is tentatively set for after the election.…With the $57 million purchase of the El Paso Railroad, the Southern Pacific becomes a $2 billion line with 12,370 miles of track.	New York City bans ethyl gasoline, sold in 10,000 stations, as a fifth victim dies.…A dozen fires in the Adirondacks continue to burn. Other fires break out. New York bars hunters and other users from entering the forests. Pennsylvania follows suit the next day.	Commissioner Griffith says the newfangled huddle system for calling plays is just a fad. It will not last.	Oct. 30
In Niles, OH, police guard city officials and business people barricade their shops in anticipation of election-day violence. Some townspeople leave for the duration.…Fundraising totals favor Republicans, who raise $3.7 million to the Democrats' $552,000. Coolidge is now 9–1, with La Follette 15–1 against.		Cities Service separates its utilities from its oil and gas business. The new utility has a value of $100 million.	The state Bureau of Mines denies that tetra-ethyl lead in exhaust fumes is toxic. Standard Oil says it sells the compound only to two experimenters.	Canon Chase's case collapses. After spending $10,000 on the matter, a grand jury declines to indict Firpo on morals charges.	Oct. 31
Niles, OH, erupts as Klan and anti-Klan forces clash. A dozen are injured, nine by gunshot. The governor establishes his command post in Columbus. The militia will withdraw tomorrow as the inquiry begins.		In 1924, electrical utilities have 14.5 million customers, 80 percent of whom are residential. Electricity customers increase 2.18 million in 1923. The gain is 17 percent in the year. California leads with 216,000 new customers.	English scientists wonder if a shifting Gulf Stream accounts for worsening English weather. The water in the English Channel reached its highest average temperature in 1921. It has been cooling a couple of degrees a year.	After attending a Billy Sunday sermon on the wages of sin, an Elmira, NY, woman repents. Her confession leads to the arrest of 14 people and the recovery of many items stolen from parcel post and express packages.	Nov. 1
Loup City, NB, officials arrest a speaker of Polish for violating the state's anti-foreign language law. The Supreme Court has just ruled laws banning teaching foreign languages to be unconstitutional but has not acted on anti-speaking laws enacted during the war.		Class I railroads set a record in September with $116.7 million in net operating income. This is the best since the war. Cost cutting is the reason for the improvement.	The new Pitcairn Flying Field at Bryn Athyn, PA, opens as 20,000 spectators watch stunts by French ace Charles Nungesser. Pitcairn will offer regularly scheduled flights to Chicago, Boston, Detroit, and other cities once the Aero Club builds a clubhouse for commercial flyers.…Los Angeles' pneumonic plague takes another seven lives.		Nov. 2
		American bankers contemplate paying part of Germany's reparations bill. By doing so they hope to acquire the first lien that reparations has on German businesses. Otherwise, their loans are second mortgages.	Fires continue in the Adirondacks and Catskills, endangering large estates. State troopers join firefighters. Two thousand people fight forest fires in Massachusetts. New Jersey and Pennsylvania also have fire problems.	New York's third annual radio show opens when Marconi sends a signal from England that light up a flag at the Grand Central Palace. First-day crowds hit 10,000.	Nov. 3
The presidential election results favor Coolidge over Davis, 379 to 139. La Follette wins Wisconsin as the third party effort fizzles. Jersey City elects Mary T. Norton, the first eastern woman in Congress and first woman Democrat in the House.		The Federal government promotes turkey raising. Annual output is half of the 6.6 million raised in 1900. Good turkeys, says the government, must be free ranging on good soil, protected from predators and weather, and kept in hygienic and sanitary conditions. Other poultry is easier to produce.			Nov. 4

F	G	H	I	J
Includes campaigns, elections, federal-state relations, civil rights and liberties, crime, the judiciary, education, healthcare, poverty, urban affairs, and population.	*Includes formation and debate of U.S. foreign and defense policies, veterans affairs, and defense spending. (Relations with specific foreign countries are usually found under the region concerned.)*	*Includes business, labor, agriculture, taxation, transportation, consumer affairs, monetary and fiscal policy, natural resources, pollution and industrial accidents.*	*Includes worldwide scientific, medical and technological developments, natural phenomena, U.S. weather and natural disasters.*	*Includes the arts, religion, scholarship, communications media, sports, entertainment, fashions, fads, and social life.*

	World Affairs	Europe	Africa & The Middle East	The Americas	Asia & The Pacific
Nov. 5		England's Vickers announces plans to build a zeppelin twice the size of the ZR-3....France and Germany resume negotiating a trade agreement. France offers tariff reductions. The main delay is getting agreement by Lorraine and Ruhr industrialists on a shared iron-coal industry.		The Brazilian revolt spreads as several new garrisons join the rebels. The battleship *Sao Paolo* leaves Rio after suffering damage in fighting with shore forts.	In a surprise move, Feng's troops take the palace and the young Manchu emperor. Motives are unclear. The action has the potential to rouse the nation in protest.
Nov. 6	League of Nations amendments mandating arbitration go into effect. At the League's opium conference western powers counter Dr. Sze's charges about their role in the trade. Also at the League, Germany begins working to reclaim its colonies.	Bavarians attack allied officers in retaliation for France's earlier charging of a visiting German general with war crimes....Former liberal Winston Churchill joins the Tory cabinet as Chancellor of the Exchequer. Austen Chamberlain gets the foreign office. Curzon has a minor role.			
Nov. 7		Seipel refuses to break the League-established Austrian budget. Railway workers strike. The Seipel government falls....Ireland issues amnesties for all civil war offenders....New York business people sign a 15-year agreement to farm 15,000 acres with machinery. They are to teach Russian peasants mechanized agriculture.			Russia claims the Arctic islands north of Siberia and warns that it is prepared to punish invaders. European explorers have routinely ignored such warnings....The government pays 2,000 Manchus severance of $8–10 apiece and orders them to leave the Forbidden City. As they leave, the republican flag rises over the city.
Nov. 8	Mexico is studying an English plan to reestablish amity between the two nations.	Famine plagues the Russian district of Stavrapol.		United States and Mexican delegates meet in Mexico City to develop a means of controlling mail fraud, which has cost $2 million over the past two years. Americans catch gullible Mexicans easily by sending circulars touting nonexistent oil and mining stocks.	
Nov. 9		Germany introduces the gold mark and allows international trade in it, with restrictions. Only banks can trade and there will be no trading in futures....Hans Thyssen and other German steel makers, hard hit by the occupation of the Ruhr, come to the United States seeking business....Some sort of rising is under way in Navarre. Armed men from France cross into Spain and battle constables.			
Nov. 10		On the eve of parliament, the Italian government bans political speeches. The Fascisti are in danger of being ousted....German republicans gain at the expense of monarchists in the Anhalt election.	The United States propose to use the $110,000 Imbrie indemnity to educate Persian students in the United States. Settlement of the indemnity closes the incident.		
Nov. 11	Armistice Day in Ireland sees the Union Jack flying over Irish veterans in Dublin, war cripples parading in Paris, the laying of a wreath at the grave of the unknown soldier and tomb of Wilson in Washington, DC, and silence—at least momentarily—everywhere.				Filipinos do not have to serve three years in the military to become U.S. citizens. A district court judge rules that Filipino civilians can naturalize and hold dual citizenship under the 1905 Autonomy Act.

A	B	C	D	E
Includes developments that affect more than one world region, international organizations and important meetings of world leaders.	*Includes all domestic and regional developments in Europe, including the Soviet Union.*	*Includes all domestic and regional developments in Africa and the Middle East.*	*Includes all domestic and regional developments in Latin America, the Caribbean, and Canada.*	*Includes all domestic and regional developments in Asian and Pacific nations (and colonies).*

U.S. Politics & Social Issues	U.S. Foreign Policy & Affairs, Defense	U.S. Economy & Environment	Science, Technology & Nature	Culture, Leisure & Lifestyle	
By a 2–1 margin, Cincinnati adopts the city manager system. The Republican Hynicka machine is on its way out.…Klan candidates in Colorado win races for both senator and governor. Klan Republicans also win senator or governor in Oklahoma, Indiana, and Kansas. In Texas, Ferguson asks a quick decision after a protest of her victory against Klan opposition.		The Van Sweringens' attempt to consolidate five lines into the Nickel Plate hits a brick wall when minority shareholders block negotiations to lease properties of the smaller lines. Van Sweringen has to start over. This time the strategy will be to purchase the others outright.	In a race between eastbound and westbound radio signals, the eastbound signal wins by a second, traveling the globe in five seconds. The one-second delay is due to slower relay points.		Nov. 5
Albert Bailey George is the first black elected judge in Chicago. Although judges are not elected by district, he will receive an assignment as municipal judge in a black neighborhood.	Secretary of Labor Davis proposes immigration reforms to reduce separation of families. He also proposes enrolling every immigrant in English courses.	Woolworth's reports 10-month gains of 12.4 percent. F.W. Grand reports 23.8 percent gain. Kinneys and Penneys also do well as chain stores continue to grow.	Los Angeles records three more plague deaths and four new cases.	California changes its boxing law to permit boxing matches to last 12 rounds instead of 4. The state is in position to build large boxing venues and attract championship bouts.…Columbia beats Harlem in a crews competition on the Harlem River.	Nov. 6
Republicans report they received nearly $4 million from 80,000 donors. Fundraising expenses are $7,000. Leftover funds will finance an organization to raise funds for the 1928 campaign.	Dutch airplane builder H.G. Fokker arrives in the United States. Fokker builds 500 planes a year, mostly for Latin America. He will build 100 reconnaissance planes for the army at his New Jersey plant.	The annual meeting of American cooperatives represents 333 cooperatives. Annual business tops $15 million.…A post-election 2.3 million-share day is a five-year record for the stock exchange.	A French scientist wins the Osiris Award for his interferometer, which allows study of the stars using light interference.	French poet Jean Richepin wins another Osiris. Jackie Coogan receives another humanitarian award. This time it is the Greek Orthodox Church's Golden Cross of the Order of Jerusalem.	Nov. 7
	Tighter border controls cause would-be immigrants to be creative. The new problem on the Canadian border is those who use airplanes to fly into the United States illegally.	The exchange enjoys its heaviest Saturday since 1906. The market reads the Baldwin and Coolidge victories as good for business.			Nov. 8
New York authorities arrest On Leong for extortion on his arrival from Cleveland. He deserted one Tong for another, causing the war that has taken 15 lives.		Continental Baking Company merges the smaller United Baking into a $500 million concern. Continental offers two shares for one to entice United shareholders.…General Motors' thrift plan pays 8,200 employees $2.4 million. The employees invested $760,000 over five years.	Einstein lauds the Flettner windship. The windship uses wind in a funnel rather than in a sail as its means of propulsion.	Dr. Hereward Carrington, expert on psychics, says only one medium in 100 is not a fraud.	Nov. 9
Gunmen kill Chicago beer king Dion O'Bannion in his flower shop. Six cars block the area, preventing pursuit of the three gunmen.…Bishop Carroll tells the Women's League that Catholics do not want a state church. They prefer, as Americans, separation.…Presbyterians accept Reverend Carlos Fuller. The fundamentalist minority protests admission of the Baptist who denies miracles.	W.B. Shearer gets a court order preventing Secretary Wilbur from proceeding with the destruction of the *Washington* under the Washington Accords. The suit claims Wilbur's action will cost $35 million for an agreement never ratified and already violated by Britain. The suit fails to slow military plans for the event.	A 19 million bushel corn crop is the poorest since 1913. Quality is the lowest in 30 years. The tobacco crop is low too. Potatoes have a record year.…Wall Street records a fifth straight record day.	Eastern forest fires abate. All are out in New York.		Nov. 10
A Baltimore federal judge says that home brew is not illegal if it is not intoxicating.	The chief of army engineers says coastal defenses are obsolete. The war increased gun ranges, and now a railroad-based mobile defense is in order.	Car loadings for October surpass one million a week. It is a record setting month.…Counsel for the Chemical Foundation says fraud does not apply in the wartime sale of dye patents. Both the president and the Congress knew and approved.…On the sixth day of the bull market, stocks are up more than four percent overall as nearly 12 million shares have traded hands. Bond sales are down. Call money is at two percent.	American chemists sponsored by *Scientific American* announce they plan to test the German method of converting mercury to gold. They also seek to lower costs and make the process practical.	New Yorkers gather at Central Park and the Eternal Light churches honor Gold Star Mothers, and the radio broadcasts a bugler playing *Taps*. The city pauses for Armistice Day.	Nov. 11
F	G	H	I	J	
Includes campaigns, elections, federal-state relations, civil rights and liberties, crime, the judiciary, education, healthcare, poverty, urban affairs, and population.	*Includes formation and debate of U.S. foreign and defense policies, veterans affairs, and defense spending. (Relations with specific foreign countries are usually found under the region concerned.)*	*Includes business, labor, agriculture, taxation, transportation, consumer affairs, monetary and fiscal policy, natural resources, pollution and industrial accidents.*	*Includes worldwide scientific, medical and technological developments, natural phenomena, U.S. weather and natural disasters.*	*Includes the arts, religion, scholarship, communications media, sports, entertainment, fashions, fads, and social life.*	

	World Affairs	Europe	Africa & The Middle East	The Americas	Asia & The Pacific
Nov. 12	After five years, the Reparations Board has finished its work. It cuts staff and offices sharply, and lower-level staffers assume the work once done by highly paid administrators.	Austria's rail strike is over....In London, Emma Goldman begins a campaign on behalf of the Russians oppressed by the Bolsheviks. She says her experience in Russia taught her that it is easier to tear down than to build up....German "Peacettes" organize to end all war by 1931....Reds boycott Italy's parliament, which begins work with only 250 members.	Primo de Rivera says he can finish in Morocco by March. Then he can return to Spain and dissolve the dictatorship.		Bubonic plague has killed 4,000 Indians. It has spread to the native quarter of Trimalgiri near Secundrabad.
Nov. 13	The Japanese delegate to the opium conference blocks attempts to blame China by introducing a non-involvement provision. The westerners want opium producing states to institute government monopolies.	Belgium asks France and Britain to join in a new Triple Entente. French opinion is favorable....Glasgow rejects an American low bidder for a British firm asking a higher price for steel. The American price seems an attempt to raid the market....Communists attack a government post at Mesagne, near Brindisi. The government stations nine ships off shore to intervene, if necessary.	At Tanganyika, Africa, scientists uncover bones of a dinosaur twice the size of the Carnegie Diplodocus. The British Museum of Natural History is negotiating with the discoverer. Price should range between £5,000 and £10,000.		In Japan, the Communist Namba, convicted assailant of the prince regent, receives a death sentence. His father has resigned from parliament and his family lives in seclusion due to the disgrace Namba has brought on the family.
Nov. 14				Premier Taschereau asks whether a province has authority to embargo. Canada has an Embargo Commission studying protection of natural resources and a pulpwood industry in Quebec desirous of blocking U.S. companies from Quebec's forests.	
Nov. 15		Mussolini wins his first test vote in parliament. The session is closed to outsiders.		The American Federation of Labor and Mexican Confederation of Labor hold joint meetings on the border—one day in the United States, the next in Mexico. Gompers opens the session with a condemnation of the shooting of a labor deputy in the Mexican congress.	
Nov. 16	The preliminary opium conference staggers to an end as Japan charges Britain with discrimination for refusing to accept the Japanese proposal that national certification is acceptable proof of compliance. Japan also accuses Britain of mercenary motives.	General Barrera suppresses a rising in Barcelona by arresting 300 rebels. Ibanez and other dissidents deny involvement, saying they are waiting for a real revolution....Italy sets penalties for investing abroad....Allies yield control of railroads in the Rhineland to the new German railway company. The roads are the last property held as security for the war debt.		Iceland begins a prohibition enforcement campaign, arresting and imprisoning alcohol smugglers....A Puebla court passes a death sentence on Alejo Garcia and Francisco Ruiz in the death of the American Mrs. Evans. Evans' property dispute with Mexico caused Mexico and Britain to break relations earlier in 1924.	Russo-Japanese negotiations stall as Japan demands an oil monopoly on Sakhalin. Russia accuses Japan of changing terms without giving any assurances of a settlement....Thousands cheer Pancho Villa's return to the Philippines. A native Filipino, Villa is world flyweight boxing champion.
Nov. 17	The League opens a second opium conference. As the Japanese remain obdurate, U.S. delegate Stephen G. Porter claims the right to declare all out war on Asian opium smoking despite the failure of the previous meeting to place it on the agenda....The El Paso/Juarez meeting of labor organizations broadens as labor leaders from Canada, Germany, and Britain join those from the United States and Mexico in a show of solidarity.	Anti-Semitic Berlin vandals destroy the Potsdam monument to 19th-century French Jewish actress Rachel. Her performance before William IV and Nicholas I was prelude to the alliance of the two emperors.		Montreal's Carriage Factories Ltd. reports a second straight annual loss. This year's loss of $59,000 is greater than last year's $43,000, primarily because of a loss in the sale of the company's harness making business.	Feng is tied up in Tientsin, but also tying up traffic through the city. Chang is organizing his army to defend Peking against the Communists should the reds form an army as National University professors propose.

A	B	C	D	E
Includes developments that affect more than one world region, international organizations and important meetings of world leaders.	*Includes all domestic and regional developments in Europe, including the Soviet Union.*	*Includes all domestic and regional developments in Africa and the Middle East.*	*Includes all domestic and regional developments in Latin America, the Caribbean, and Canada.*	*Includes all domestic and regional developments in Asian and Pacific nations (and colonies).*

U.S. Politics & Social Issues	U.S. Foreign Policy & Affairs, Defense	U.S. Economy & Environment	Science, Technology & Nature	Culture, Leisure & Lifestyle	
The county prosecutor says that in Niles, OH, the Klan has armed bands that are in effect county police.…At the AFL convention, the building trades council calls for suspension of the 350,000 carpenters and joiners. The carpenters are in a four-year dispute with sheet metal workers over who installs metal windows.…A counterfeiting ring has cashed more than $1 million in war savings stamps. Authorities take 13 members and seek 80 others in major American cities.	Tchitcherin says he hopes Hughes does retire as the secretary indicated is his desire. It will allow resumption of talks between Russia and the United States.…An infantry regiment tests recall by radio. The unit assembles in two hours.	A would-be player seeking a seat on the exchange offers $100,000.…Stocks trend down early but recover and keep the rally going a seventh day.…L.J. Taber, president of the Grange, says the farmer's problems are economic, not political. He calls for tax relief.	Berkeley astronomer Lauschner confirms that the German Baade has discovered a planet. It has a highly eccentric orbit. Farther out than the other two known minor planets, Albert and Eros, it is 20 million miles away and receding from Earth.	New Jersey heavyweight Charlie Weinert beats Firpo on points in 12 rounds. Weinert is a 13-year veteran who never realized his potential. Firpo once knocked Dempsey out of the ring.	Nov. 12
The Baltimore home brew jury finds the defendant, a representative, not guilty. The feds say they will ignore the ruling and continue prosecuting such cases as violations of Volstead.	The army reports it lost 18 flyers in nine million flight miles in 1923. That averages to a death every 605,000 miles. Injuries occur every 57,480 miles.…The navy signs contracts on a seaplane capable of flying 2,600 miles at 100 miles per hour. It can reach Honolulu or Panama and should revolutionize Pacific defense, particularly in Guam and the Philippines.	So far, the bull market has added $3 billion in value as 59 issues record new highs.…Government lawyers conclude their case against Doheny by noting the secrecy, the bribe, and the fraudulent valuation.		The University of Michigan receives an anonymous donation of 417 rare Arabic, Persian, and Turkish manuscripts, some dating to the 8th century. Some are from the collection of Sultan Abdul Hamid.	Nov. 13
O'Banion's funeral procession includes 1,000 cars and 26 carloads of flowers. His coffin costs $10,000. For the funeral, underworld bosses give up their guns. Police are visible to forestall violence, but the event passes quietly.	The United States and Poland agree on refunding of Poland's $182 million war debt for war supplies, food, and famine relief. This is the fifth refunding completed by the World War Foreign Debt Commission, established in 1922.…The army reserves implement a rule requiring officer candidates to pass an examination before receiving a commission.	Sterling Trust, Ltd., an English company, sells the Alabama and Vicksburg and Vicksburg, Shreveport, and Pacific lines to a New York-New Orleans consortium. Sterling Trust invested in railroads after Reconstruction but no longer owns any U.S. railroads.		The Rockefeller Education Board donates $1 million to the University of Rochester. George Eastman provides an additional $2.5 million. Of 1,600 alumni, 1,200 men have donated a total of $339,000 toward the $10 million fundraising effort.	Nov. 14
Elmira reformatory revokes its no-smoking rule. Some of the 1,200 inmates are able to quit but others lose parole for violating the smoking ban.…Rhode Island politics returns to normal as Republicans agree to return and Democrats agree to drop their filibuster.	A court upholds the navy's right to destroy the *Washington*. Tugs tow the warship from Philadelphia after a sendoff that includes a navy band and a final salute by sailors in formation.				Nov. 15
John J. Chapman, who often objects to Harvard's moves, protests Harvard's decision to appoint a Catholic as Harvard Fellow. Chapman says the Catholic Church seeks to control American education and Harvard has strayed from its traditional "old faith."…A newly formed Jewish council of 250 organizations, representing 250,000 members, condemns the Klan.…Chicago's crackdown on gangsters brings in 1,000.	Coast artillery commander, Major General F.M. Coe, calls for tripling coast defenses and doubling overseas garrisons. Current strength of 12,000 is the lowest since 1907, Coe says, and strength should be 31,500.	Sixty Owens Valley farmers seize the gates to the Los Angeles aqueduct and divert the water to the river. The farmers and the city have a long-standing dispute over Los Angeles' appropriation of valley irrigation water.…The New York Stock Exchange opens a 42-state campaign to wipe out bucketeering and other security swindles. The campaign involves 1,600 NYSE agents and brokers as well as the 240 largest Better Business Bureaus and thousands of bankers.			Nov. 16
Methodists report they support 1,900 missionaries. Helping the overseas efforts are 11,000 native preachers and 10,000 other workers.		California's governor refuses to order troops against the Owens Valley water raiders, who ignore an injunction and keep the water flowing. The Chamber of Commerce endorses their stand, and valley women take food to them.		The AAU awards 28 title events for 1925, confirms 137 event records, and announces plans to affiliate with North and South American national boxing federations. The premier athletic oversight organization also takes control of indoor baseball and racquetball while broadening its efforts on behalf of playgrounds and recreation.	Nov. 17

F	G	H	I	J
Includes campaigns, elections, federal-state relations, civil rights and liberties, crime, the judiciary, education, healthcare, poverty, urban affairs, and population.	*Includes formation and debate of U.S. foreign and defense policies, veterans affairs, and defense spending. (Relations with specific foreign countries are usually found under the region concerned.)*	*Includes business, labor, agriculture, taxation, transportation, consumer affairs, monetary and fiscal policy, natural resources, pollution and industrial accidents.*	*Includes worldwide scientific, medical and technological developments, natural phenomena, U.S. weather and natural disasters.*	*Includes the arts, religion, scholarship, communications media, sports, entertainment, fashions, fads, and social life.*

	World Affairs	Europe	Africa & The Middle East	The Americas	Asia & The Pacific
Nov. 18	Britain asks the League of Nations Council to table discussion of the arbitration protocol. The dominions find it objectionable, and without the United States it is futile. Britain wants to open the way for Coolidge's disarmament conference.... The Reparations Commission allocates shares of prewar German debt to those receiving German territory. Included are Belgium, Poland, Danzig, and Czechoslovakia.... Poland proposes definition of legitimate needs and restriction of production accordingly. Conference delegates, including the Japanese, are amenable.	Defense Minister Rasmussen explains the rationale for dissolving the Danish army and navy. He cites his defense chiefs' admission that a 115,000-person force and a fleet of coast guard boats is unable to stop any invader. Disbanding the military and creating a 7,000 person police force and 600 person police fleet will save $10 million a year.... Austria's Seipel is out. Ramek forms the new government.		Nicaragua selects New York's Abraham Lindberg and Jeremiah Jenks to rewrite its financial and banking laws. Lindberg previously served as Nicaragua's customs deputy and financial agent. Jenks is with New York University.	
Nov. 19	The Unite States introduces the proposal to limit opium production to medicinal uses and to control the traffic.		Sir Lee Stack, head of the Egyptian army, suffers wounds in an assassination attempt in Cairo. After a bomb thrown at his car fails to explode, attackers fire shots at his car, wounding three others. The assailants flee with a $10,000 price on their heads.		After Secretary Weeks rejects Filipino independence, the legislature sits as a commission and declares that the nation is stable. The commission declares that complete and immediate independence is beneficial to both the United States and the Philippines.
Nov. 20	Dawes Plan administrator Owen D. Young says the plan is working. Economic recovery is progressing so well that Germany has already almost met its August 1, 1925, obligation of one billion marks.		Sir Lee Stack, Egypt's army Sirdar, dies of wounds received in the assassination attempt.... Attacks on the Spanish forces at Sheshuan seriously injure General Berenguer. Troop morale is reported low due to refusal to release those who have ended their enlistments.		
Nov. 21		France enacts legislation authorizing the borrowing of $100 million from the Morgan bank. It prepares to issue 25 year bonds at seven percent.... Britain cancels treaties MacDonald established with Russia. The government says the Zinoviev letter is real and Russia is derelict in not apologizing. No break in relations is foreseen.... Russia begins an anti-drug campaign that includes jail or deportation for dealers. Users are penalized also.	Cairo officials apprehend Stack's attackers after a taxi driver confesses and identifies the actual shooter. Britain demands protection for its nationals.		Filipino mobs attack Chinese again. They mob Chinese in Loang and on a sugar estate in San Jose.
Nov. 22		After days of debate led by Orlando, Mussolini wins a vote of confidence 337–17.	Britain demands an apology and $500,000 within 24 hours. It positions warships and infantry and demands that Egypt control demonstrations and evacuate its troops from the Sudan.	Cuban workers are striking at 25 sugar mills. Railroad workers are supporting the strike.	Tuan arrives in Peking to form a new government. Chang and 3,000 men accompany him. Feng is en route. When sworn in tomorrow, Tuan is virtual dictator.
Nov. 23	The League of Nations refuses Egypt the right to appeal to it as Britain sets up a hands-off rule for all others.... South Africa begins an experiment to mint its own coins. It wants to control fluctuations due to a varying exchange rate.	Paris worries that the Egyptian crisis spells out the clear limits of self determination. Still, France recognizes England's rights over the Suez Canal and Sudan.	Egypt agrees to pay the indemnity and apologize. It denies culpability and refuses to evacuate the Sudan.		Gandhi says he has lost power in India. He calls for bending even to the English when it promotes Indian unity.
Nov. 24	The first opium meeting revives when Britain comes around to the Japanese position that each country's internal guarantees should suffice for the other nations.		Britain seizes the Alexandria customs. Zaghlul resigns, and Ziwar takes his place. Egypt indicates it will appeal to the League of Nations.	A Guatemalan oil official sues three Roosevelts, Kermit, Archie, and Richard, for $215,000 for failing to pay the money they promised him for arranging an oil concession.	

A	B	C	D	E
Includes developments that affect more than one world region, international organizations and important meetings of world leaders.	*Includes all domestic and regional developments in Europe, including the Soviet Union.*	*Includes all domestic and regional developments in Africa and the Middle East.*	*Includes all domestic and regional developments in Latin America, the Caribbean, and Canada.*	*Includes all domestic and regional developments in Asian and Pacific nations (and colonies).*

U.S. Politics & Social Issues	U.S. Foreign Policy & Affairs, Defense	U.S. Economy & Environment	Science, Technology & Nature	Culture, Leisure & Lifestyle	
	Shearer sues to save the *Washington*. Again, he loses. He says he will appeal to the Supreme Court.	Coolidge's commission on the agricultural crisis begins work. First on the agenda is the cattle industry. Other concerns include cooperatives, tariffs, and transportation. Commissioners ask Congress to delay legislation until the commission finishes its study.…The bull market continues, with 94 issues setting record highs as more than two million shares trade.	Tuskegee's Dr. George Washington Carver reveals to a women's missionary society the results of his work. He shows 165 peanut products and 100 sweet potato products. He announces that Tuskegee is building a large sweet potato paint factory.	New York Supreme Court Justice John Ford, member of the Clean Books League, says the United States is a dumping ground for foreign "bookleggers" wanting to unload their obscene literature. The Clean Books League wants to return national obscenity laws to 1884.	Nov. 18
The National Founders Association joins with the Grange in an industry-agriculture organization. The new organization's purpose is opposition to radicalism and the closed shop.	Navy data reveals that the government got only half a million dollars for scrapping vessels under construction. The United States spent $153 million on the ships. Under the naval limitation treaty, the United States scrapped 28 vessels for $1.4 million.	The Grange reports that American farm debt tops $14 billion. Farmers must be debt free to compete internationally.			Nov. 19
Congressmen Black defines the Non-Partisan League as hopelessly idealistic in calling for U.S. entry into the League. The Brooklyn Congressman says the United States should wait until Europe becomes decent.	The army's Judge Advocate General rules that the army already has the authority to sell power generated by Muscle Shoals. The decision anticipates completion of the Wilson Dam, which will generate more than 100,000 horsepower, in July 1925.…Major General Mason Patrick, head of the army aviation service, says the United States leads in experimental flight and record setting but fails to develop commercial and military uses. He calls for better military funding and legislation promoting commercial aviation and aircraft manufacture.	The Owens Valley farmers allow water into the aqueduct and all parties share a barbecue after bankers promise an equitable settlement to the 20-year dispute.…Stock market volume tops 2.5 million shares, forcing implementation of emergency rules to handle the unprecedented activity.	At Philadelphia, homeopaths see a demonstration of radium "seeds" as treatment for internal cancers.	The Rochester American Opera, the first composed exclusively of American singers, debuts. Performers trained at the Eastman School of Music sing excerpts from *Pagliacci* and *Boris Godounoff* in English. The hope is to make opera more appealing to American audiences.	Nov. 20
The Grange convention goes on record in opposition to the child labor amendment and the creation of a federal education department.	*Washington* proves tough to sink. On the second day of shelling, two shells finally penetrate her hull.	The Philadelphia Electric Company reports it has a new stoking system that improves plant efficiency 93 percent by capturing gases normally vented to waste and using them to preheat air to the furnaces. When brought on line, the plant will give Philadelphia Electric more generating capacity than Niagara Falls.	Astronomers recalculate the Earth's age at eight billion years. Other astronomers suggest that many planets contain life.		Nov. 21
All leaders of the great train robbery are in captivity. The arrest of George de Sorro, captured in Italy, is the last. He will escape a death sentence for his role in two robbery-related murders.	The army reports development of a method of transmitting maps by radio and creation of a device that teaches code without requiring instructors.			Chicago ties Wisconsin 0–0 and wins its first Big Ten title since 1913. Amos Alonzo Stagg's Maroons finish the year 3–0–3. Red Grange of Illinois leads the league in scoring.	Nov. 22
	The Non-Partisan League counts 60 Senators who support U.S. membership on the World Court. Congress has three court-related bills due this session.	The tobacco industry is moving away from New York to places where women's labor is cheaper. The industry produces 50 billion cigarettes and seven billion cigars a year, and the United States is the world's greatest cigarette user.…The Industrial Board worries at rising government debt on all levels. The federal debt is 1/10 of GNP.			Nov. 23
					Nov. 24

F	G	H	I	J
Includes campaigns, elections, federal-state relations, civil rights and liberties, crime, the judiciary, education, healthcare, poverty, urban affairs, and population.	*Includes formation and debate of U.S. foreign and defense policies, veterans affairs, and defense spending. (Relations with specific foreign countries are usually found under the region concerned.)*	*Includes business, labor, agriculture, taxation, transportation, consumer affairs, monetary and fiscal policy, natural resources, pollution and industrial accidents.*	*Includes worldwide scientific, medical and technological developments, natural phenomena, U.S. weather and natural disasters.*	*Includes the arts, religion, scholarship, communications media, sports, entertainment, fashions, fads, and social life.*

	World Affairs	Europe	Africa & The Middle East	The Americas	Asia & The Pacific
Nov. 25	France opposes a central opium board. This is one of the main planks of the U.S. plan.	With Zaghlul out and the indemnity paid, says public opinion in France, Britain has enough satisfaction and should back off. Italy says the British behavior validates Italian behavior at Corfu.	Italian forces take Arab rebels and gun runners in Syrte. Other successful military actions allow Italy to recapture control of the Mediterranean coast of Tripoli.		
Nov. 26	On British demand, the League of Nations defers hearing the Egyptian protest. The League claims it cannot hear an inquiry from a parliament but must have a Council request.... Japan says it will not ratify the disarmament protocol until it learns what Britain and Italy will do.	France pardons General Nathusius. His conviction for war looting has earlier led to tensions between France and Germany. He now returns to Germany....The Soviet government and Russian émigrés fight over possession of a church on land donated by the czar in Paris. Russia closes the church pending the outcome.	Egypt begins withdrawing troops from Sudan....The Bey of Tunis promises reforms to stabilize his country.		
Nov. 27	Britain and France hold discussions on Africa. France is worried that there are three crises in process on the continent.	Stalin charges Trotsky, who has recently released a book about the revolution, with heresy and of trying to assume Lenin's mantle. Kamineff supports Stalin....Howard Carter defends his rifling through a pharaoh's tomb as necessary for the study of the past....Viennese theaters close, unable to afford the luxury tax.	Spain withdraws from Morocco and implements a blockade. Primo de Rivera is seeking to accomplish through economic pressure what he could not through force of arms.		
Nov. 28	The United States and India exchange harsh words at the opium conference. A U.S. delegate says his country will not compromise with evil.	Ford closes its Belgian plant. It moves to Holland to find lower taxes....France reports a 760,000 ton sugar crop. The yield will make France sugar independent this year....Herriott survives a vote of confidence over election financing. The 299–245 vote is his closest to date....Russia sends a mild-mannered note to Britain expressing regret that trade is off, reiterating that the letter is a forgery, and promising an inquiry.	Two hundred Sudanese troops in Khartoum mutiny. They kill three doctors, barricade themselves in the hospital, cut communications, and engage the British in heavy fighting. In Cairo, arrests continue, with the government taking 35 Zaghlul supporters. The mutiny ends quickly.		A Japanese trade delegation visits Rumania's oil fields, which are currently expanding. The local press reports that Japan is interested in securing oil supplies from Rumania and/or Turkey for an inevitable future fight with the United States. In addition, it helps Japan against Russia in Bessarabia.
Nov. 29	Japan's naval minister says Tokyo is receptive to a concrete proposal with a clear and fair ratio for arms reduction. He says the Pacific should always be a peaceful lake. Optimists read this as a cooling of Japanese upset at U.S. immigration exclusion.	Austria rejects an Italian plan to internationalize the railway station at Innsbruck....Italy contracts for 120,000 tons of Russian oil for 1925....Scots have formed a national movement. They seek independence from Great Britain.		A committee in the United States organizes with the goal of compiling all claims of Americans against Mexico. It intends to amass hundreds of millions in claims since 1864....The United States and Canada suspend hockey matches. The rules of residency are unclear.	Hsuan Tung finds refuge in the Peking Japanese legation. The deposed boy emperor is presumed heading for exile in Japan.
Nov. 30				Calles takes the presidential oath before a crowd that includes labor, agrarians, and a lot of police. Obregon is a rarity, a president who completes a full term....Canada implements a new office, Banking Inspector General. Canada's banking practices are improving and its banks are consolidating, the same as U.S. banks.	
Dec. 1	The chair of the committee working on a "Dawes Plan" for China says the hold up is France, which has not ratified the nine-power customs treaty agreed to in 1921. China also has international debt of $300 million and a sizeable internal debt....France proposes to the debt board a 10-year moratorium on its debt to the United States with payments proportionate to reparations received from Germany. France owes England $623 million and is due $4 billion from several nations.	Estonian Communists seize a post office and railway station. After heavy fighting, the government prevails. Losses include 19 dead and 40 wounded loyalists as well as the minister of communications. Government forces capture 60 reds and blame Moscow.	Quiet returns to the Sudan as British troops withdraw. In Cairo, where British forces remain, sentries fire at prowlers at the ambassador's residence, a student strike fails, and two cabinet ministers resign.	New Mexican president Calles promises to clean up graft and corruption in government....Canada reports population growth of about 500,000 since 1921. Total population is 9.2 million. Increases apply to all provinces but Prince Edward Island....Brazilian rebels rout federal troops at Berra Baracha. They take horses and war supplies.	

A	B	C	D	E
Includes developments that affect more than one world region, international organizations and important meetings of world leaders.	*Includes all domestic and regional developments in Europe, including the Soviet Union.*	*Includes all domestic and regional developments in Africa and the Middle East.*	*Includes all domestic and regional developments in Latin America, the Caribbean, and Canada.*	*Includes all domestic and regional developments in Asian and Pacific nations (and colonies).*

U.S. Politics & Social Issues	U.S. Foreign Policy & Affairs, Defense	U.S. Economy & Environment	Science, Technology & Nature	Culture, Leisure & Lifestyle	
Outside Pittsburgh, a police raid on the suburban West Park mansion of S.W. Morgan uncovers a second story job. The owners live on the first level in appropriate luxury while the upstairs houses cases of liquor and wine and two 100-gallon stills.	Torpedoes, bombs from the air, and underwater shells fail to bring down *Washington*. The guns of *Texas* do the job, and the scrapped battleship sinks. An admiral insists the ship would be floating still had she used her pumps.	H.C. Frick announces plans to spend $2 million electrifying its coke mines to increase output and meet demand from U.S. Steel. Currently running at 55 percent, Frick expects to be at 100 percent soon. The company is re-firing hundreds of ovens and hiring men.		Tex Rickard bans radio from the Garden. He says it has hurt ticket sales.	Nov. 25
	The United States reach agreement with Austria and Hungary on war claims. Belgium and France agree to the United States request for payment of its claim against Germany from Dawes reparations. Other settlements are pending.	The Wall Street rally resumes as steel hits prices not seen in years. Fifty-seven stocks hit new highs.... Attorney General Stone asks the Supreme Court to restrict Chicago's drawing of Lake Michigan water. Stone claims national jurisdiction. Chicago's actions have generated protests from states down to Louisiana and from Canada.	The New Jersey Commissioner of Labor says there is no way to safeguard workers making tetra-ethyl lead. A chemist counters that the workers are just careless.	Leonard Rhinelander sues for an annulment on the basis that his bride lied when she said that she is not partially black. She countersued, saying she cannot give up the man she loves.	Nov. 26
The Tong truce collapses. Murders and attacks occur in the Bronx, Schenectady, Hartford, and various cities in the South.		Production, prices, and employment are all up, says the Federal Reserve....Oil output rises due to new wells in north Texas and Oklahoma and increased output from fields in Wyoming.	The army tests a radio compass. It successfully leads a flyer through fog....After earlier failures, east coast listeners try again to pick up European radio stations. Some claim to hear Liverpool, Madrid, or Newcastle. Most stations say they hear nothing.		Nov. 27
After weeks of talking conciliation, Republicans oust the insurgents from party councils. La Follette, Ladd, Brookhart, and others lose committee assignments.	Labor Secretary Davis reports that the year's illegal immigration topped 850,000, including 35,000 sailors. Both Canada and Mexico provide access but Davis is not sure how. He says there are 10 million Europeans wanting to be Americans, and the United States cannot handle that volume....The President and Secretary Wilbur claim that gun elevation, which they seek on 13 ships as an economy measure, is authorized by the limitation treaty.	Millers and governors of eight states file petitions to break up the Continental Corporation as an illegal trust that eliminates competition in bread making....Postal officials begin developing estimates of costs to run airmail service to Europe. Their first thought is to use the new dirigible, now named *Los Angeles*.		After an eight-year fight, the International League accepts a major league draft....Mrs. Rhinelander denies she is not white and says she never deceived Rhinelander regarding her social status.	Nov. 28
Kansas descendants of Mayflower arrivals protest that the textbooks their children read are pro-British....Sportsmen support the ban of the pump gun.	In his final report, Pershing calls for a larger infantry and air service. He also notes that poison gas and aerial bombing are overrated.	The Chicago carpenters union capitalizes a bank of its own at $5 million. Other unions have previously opened their own banks, particularly railway workers.	The New York City health department abandons tests of chlorine gas as a treatment for colds. Despite what the army claims, it is worthless. In addition, it does no good for whooping cough and asthma. It is also dangerous.	Columbia University acquires 10,000 European law books, bringing its law library to 125,000 volumes. The library has doubled in size in a decade and now has no superior....Crossword puzzles are hot. A Princeton professor proposes using them as textbooks for vocabulary.	Nov. 29
The Society for the Prevention of Cruelty to Animals (S.P.C.A.) says that women are better ambulance drivers than are men. Men, who have driven for the past 30 years, are too dispassionate and businesslike. The New York S.P.C.A. begins with three women drivers.		The postmaster reports that the postal deficit for the year is down 7.5 percent due to efficiencies. Revenues are $573 million, and the deficit is $9.6 million.	London sends photos to New York, using a pen to trace the pictures on a revolving cylinder. In addition, through a process developed by O.F. Jenkins, pictures of text travel from Washington to Boston, where they are printed.	Thirty riders begin the 143-hour, six-day bicycle race at the Garden....In Pittsburgh, a pastor uses a crossword puzzle to hold his listeners. He has them work a puzzle to figure out his sermon.	Nov. 30
Congress reconvenes. One hot agenda item, Howell-Barkley, affects America's two million railroad workers. The bill proposes an arbitration board to replace the Railway Labor Board. Organized labor wants the bill because the current arrangement is weak. Owners say the board is a tool of organized labor, having just granted $5 million in pay raises.	Labor Secretary Davis backtracks on illegal immigration. He says the number is about 175,000. Legal immigration is 870,000, of whom 358,000 are from quota countries and the others from nonquota nations. Total immigration is about one million a year....Army Secretary Weeks says the full-time service can stand no more cuts. He applauds the recent defense exercises and cites the need for more citizen soldiers.	The Dodge Brothers and Ford announce price reductions of $25 to $175 depending on model. Ford's basic four door sedan is down to $660 and, as all models, available through the weekly purchase plan.		Juggler-comedian W.C. Fields headlines at the Hippodrome between rehearsals for a Ziegfield production. Also on the bill is Florence Walton. At the Palace, English dancers Ted Trevor and Dina Harris debut to receptive audiences.	Dec. 1

F	G	H	I	J
Includes campaigns, elections, federal-state relations, civil rights and liberties, crime, the judiciary, education, healthcare, poverty, urban affairs, and population.	*Includes formation and debate of U.S. foreign and defense policies, veterans affairs, and defense spending. (Relations with specific foreign countries are usually found under the region concerned.)*	*Includes business, labor, agriculture, taxation, transportation, consumer affairs, monetary and fiscal policy, natural resources, pollution and industrial accidents.*	*Includes worldwide scientific, medical and technological developments, natural phenomena, U.S. weather and natural disasters.*	*Includes the arts, religion, scholarship, communications media, sports, entertainment, fashions, fads, and social life.*

	World Affairs	Europe	Africa & The Middle East	The Americas	Asia & The Pacific
Dec. 2	Brazil advises Japan that it will issue no more visas for Japanese immigrants. Caught by surprise, Japan regards the issue as serious.	Britain and Germany sign a trade treaty. The treaty is available to dominions but does not obligate them. Still unresolved is the issue of the recovery tax.... Fascists react angrily to Mussolini's order that they clean up and moderate. They continue fighting Communists, killing two while suffering a dozen injured.			
Dec. 3	Chamberlain says he will inform the League of Nations Council of the situation in Egypt. He maintains that the situation is not a League issue and he is informing the council only as a courtesy.	Russia reduces its army to 562,000 and raises military pay. Because army officers now seem trustworthy, dual control of military units ends.	A receiver on the Cape of Good Hope hears a British radio signal. This is the first British radio received in South Africa.		Chang holds his forces near Peking, ready to assist Tuan if Feng attacks. The empress and second consort move to the Japanese embassy with Tuan's approval.
Dec. 4	Britain advises the League of Nations that Egypt's signing of the protocol is insufficient to justify League intervention in what Britain insists is an internal matter.	Britain guards cabinet ministers after reports from Lord Allenby, commissioner for Egypt, that Egyptian Wafd radicals are plotting assassinations in London.	Baldwin says that, despite Egyptian independence, Britain retains treaty obligations to safeguard foreigners. Egypt has failed to do so.	Brazil clarifies its alien restrictions. It bars all immigrants, not just Japanese. The government wants to locate current immigrants before it allows others in.... Bell Telephone of Canada announces plans to issue $20–$25 million in bonds to refinance its debt and expand the Canadian telephone system.	
Dec. 5	The opium conference concludes. Japan is satisfied with inclusion of its provision. China indicates it may file a minority report with the majority report, due December 13.	French ambassador Jules Jusserand says France will pay its entire war debt to the United States. He reminds the United States that 5/6 of the loan was spent there.... France announces a 20-year, $550 million, modernization of its navy.	Andre Citroen, France's Henry Ford, offers nine-day, 2,703 kilometer, automobile tours of the Sahara. The package includes entertainment by jazz bands and nights at oases. Where necessary, Citroen will build hotels.... Courts martial in Sudan result in three executions and one 15-year sentence for mutineers.		
Dec. 6		Sir James Craig, Prime Minister of Northern Ireland, says his government abides by the 1920 government of Ireland agreement and will not participate in boundary discussions. Private citizens and local officials are free to meet the commissioners.... To nip a Communist coup attempt, French police round up 300. Plans are to deport 70 foreign agitators immediately.... Rumania plans to deport 100,000 foreigners and restrict Russians to certain areas.	Tangiers is unable to function because under the Tangiers convention an oversight board has to validate its legislature. The board lacks a quorum because only Spain, France, and England have appointed members. Absent are representatives from the United States, Italy, Belgium, Holland, and Portugal.		
Dec. 7	For Golden Rule Day families in the United States and 24 other nations partake of four-cent meals, with the money saved going to Near East Relief. Orphans in Armenia give up two meals to feed refugees.	Allied recovery taxes for three months total 50 million marks based on the 26 percent recovery tax that German merchants validate for each foreign shipment. Germany wants payments based on exports to the France and Britain.	Ziwar Pasha says in effect "nonsense" to deputies who say his government is illegal because it took a position during the British crisis that the deputies expressly barred.		Chinese bandits kidnap nuns, students, and priests, but Lutheran missionaries elude capture. They also seize an American launch. The bandits release the nuns and priests the next day.

A	B	C	D	E
Includes developments that affect more than one world region, international organizations and important meetings of world leaders.	*Includes all domestic and regional developments in Europe, including the Soviet Union.*	*Includes all domestic and regional developments in Africa and the Middle East.*	*Includes all domestic and regional developments in Latin America, the Caribbean, and Canada.*	*Includes all domestic and regional developments in Asian and Pacific nations (and colonies).*

U.S. Politics & Social Issues	U.S. Foreign Policy & Affairs, Defense	U.S. Economy & Environment	Science, Technology & Nature	Culture, Leisure & Lifestyle	
A Kansas City appeals court upholds the legality of publishing tax information. The case moves quickly to the Supreme Court.				Charlie Chaplin's new bride, actress Lita Grey, is only 16, not 19 as the Mexican marriage license says. She has to attend high school.	Dec. 2
New Jersey issues warrants for eight river police who, according to witnesses, protect and assist bootleggers unloading a lighter. The cargo is valued at $50 million.... The Washington, DC, court follows Kansas City in denying a request to bar publication of tax data.	The U.S. War Debt Commission responds favorably to the suggestion of a moratorium on French debt. Congress has to enact enabling legislation....Labor Secretary Davis calls for restrictions on western hemisphere immigration....Ambassador Kellogg and Secretary Chamberlain sign the agreement granting U.S. citizens the same rights in Palestine as citizens of League nations. This is the first of the mandate protocols.	On the 13th two-million-share day since the election, 74 issues reach new highs. The ticker is now moving fast enough to keep up with the market....William Goldman tells the woolen trade association that their business is suffering because men are buying cheaper clothes. The men use the savings to buy automobiles.	The army's Chief of Health says that chlorine has proven effective in other cities. Maybe New York has not given it a fair test....Researchers announce that they will measure the Woolworth Building during the next high wind. They want to determine if it sways.	The U.S.G.A. announces that it will switch to a new ball in January. The new ball will be larger and lighter....Walter Camp says the off-side and kick-off rules need changing.	Dec. 3
Ford begins razing houses, installing sewers, and repaving streets at Glassmere near Pittsburgh. He is tearing down the old town and building a model city to house the workers at one of the country's largest plate glass plants.		The president of Bethlehem Steel reports his mills running at 70 percent capacity. At mid-summer, they were at 40 percent. Bethlehem is spending $60 million to improve several of its properties....Chain stores report a banner year. Woolworth grosses $180 million for 11 months, while Penneys and Grand are up sharply.	A Nebraska blizzard downs wires and blocks roads. It follows rain, sleet, and ice, and kills a railroad man who slips from an ice-clad ladder.	Milton Academy finds a crossword puzzle for exams. The puzzle is in Latin....New York Justice Benedict, in denying an annulment, decries the Di Lorenzo liberalization of annulment justifications to include fraud. He says the result is an excess of "trial" marriages.	Dec. 4
Governor Bone of Alaska predicts that a statehood request will come in four years. He says the sticking point is voting rights for Native Americans....New Jersey's investigation of the police-bootlegger ring expands to capture the chief of the Weehawken department and a Jersey City broker. Total indictments are at 12....A woman purporting to be Congressman S.A. Kendall's secretary and business partner says he sold war supplies to constituents.	The House Naval Affairs Committee recommends to Coolidge that he recall Marine General Smedley Butler to active service. Butler is currently on loan to Philadelphia as its police chief and has three more years there. The committee notes that extended absences on private business are not good policy. Butler gets one more year....The Pensions Bureau reports that it has paid $6.8 billion in pensions. All but $409 million is for Civil War pensions. The list includes 525,000 people, declining each year although new applications continue.	Secretary Hoover says that additional regulation of radio will be a mistake because the industry is undergoing too much rapid change. He says, however, that federal control of the airwaves is legitimate.			Dec. 5
The Weehawken investigation implicates all six members of the township commission and a major New York bootlegger as well as the police. Reportedly, commissioners receive $700 for the first 200 cases from a boat and $1 per case thereafter....The Six Nations sue for half of New York state. They cite an 18th-century treaty with William Johnson....John D. Rockefeller, Jr. announces plans for a model apartment house, affordable to the working class, in Lenox Hills. His project will include garden plots, a playground, and cross ventilation in all units.	The navy has recruitment woes. It needs 310 submarine officers, but submarine service is unattractive.		Neurologists say that mental instability causes delinquency. They discount poverty as a contributor.		Dec. 6
The Tong war spreads to Springfield, MA. There, two On Leong members fall to a Hip Sing gunman as they leave a gambling den.			A Chicago professor counters that both environment and heredity are important, probably equal, in forming character.	McNamara and Van Kempen win the six-day bicycle race. They set a new record and the crowds are the largest for such an event in the Garden. Of the $200,000 gate, the winning riders get $5,000 each. Promoters get $150,000.	Dec. 7

F	G	H	I	J
Includes campaigns, elections, federal-state relations, civil rights and liberties, crime, the judiciary, education, healthcare, poverty, urban affairs, and population.	*Includes formation and debate of U.S. foreign and defense policies, veterans affairs, and defense spending. (Relations with specific foreign countries are usually found under the region concerned.)*	*Includes business, labor, agriculture, taxation, transportation, consumer affairs, monetary and fiscal policy, natural resources, pollution and industrial accidents.*	*Includes worldwide scientific, medical and technological developments, natural phenomena, U.S. weather and natural disasters.*	*Includes the arts, religion, scholarship, communications media, sports, entertainment, fashions, fads, and social life.*

	World Affairs	Europe	Africa & The Middle East	The Americas	Asia & The Pacific
Dec. 8	The League of Nations Council, meeting in Rome, accepts the British request and postpones discussions of the anti-war protocol. They agree to pursue a codification of international law, as asked by Coolidge, first.	Breton Catholics, having hooted Herriott yesterday, demonstrate more generally against the anti-Catholicism of the Herriott government.…France reads the results of the German elections as favorable to peace. Germans reject extremists on the right and left in favor of Republicans. However, they fail to choose a majority, meaning the government will be a coalition of four parties. Exactly which parties is unclear.			General Wood vetoes Filipino legislation that funds independence activity. The total Filipino budget is $25 million.
Dec. 9	League of Nations members accept the British request to postpone the protocol.	In France, Herriott ridicules Communism in the chamber. Socialists and Communists fight one another, grabbing each other by the throat.			The powers recognize the government as de facto in control of China. Recognition is contingent on the government's adhering to all treaties and agreements previously established.
Dec. 10	Japan quits the opium committee, citing the unacceptability of the American plan's interference with internal affairs.	Russian exiles in European cities back Duke Nicholas as Russia's czar. Czarists in exile number an estimated 300,000.…Britain demands that any nation paying war debts to the United States also pay those it owes Britain.…Albanians rebel. The capital is in panic and the premier in flight.	The mandate report on Palestine is critical of British policy. Pro-Jewish immigration practices understandably cause Arab unrest. The League notes that the two mandatory requirements are contradictory.…Spain enters the final phase of its retreat from Morocco. Troops evacuate Sok-el-Arba and move to Tetuan.		
Dec. 11	New League of Nations discussions deal with the Saar, relief, Morocco, and German arms. The Allied Control Commission reports that Germany has half a million soldiers and is manufacturing arms again.	The Marx cabinet resigns after Stresemann forces the action. He wants to include nationalists in a new government.			
Dec. 12	At the opium conference, England, France, Holland, India, and Portugal align against U.S. attempts to plug "loopholes" in the earlier opium agreement. The major flaw the United States see is lack of import limits.	The Albanian central government denies that tribes are in rebellion. More tribes join the rising.…The OGPU arrests Ukapisti leaders. Ukapisti are Ukrainian leftwing Communist anti-Russian nationalists.	Premier Hertzog tells a Swazi delegation the time has come to incorporate Swaziland and Bechuanaland into South Africa. Incorporation of protectorates requires British approval.	Mexican hero, General Candido Aguilar, says recent treaties with the United States are inequitable and harm Mexican interests. They require revision to reestablish a sense of equity and amity between the two people.	
Dec. 13		Bulgaria rejects its war debt as too large. Successor states' war debts are allied-determined percentages of the total amassed by the Ottoman Empire.…Russia forms colonies for returnees from the United States and Canada. It sets aside 400,000 acres in the Northern Caucasus and Volga and tells representatives in North America what type of settler it wants and how much money they need.	A report leaks that Britain and the United States have evidence of Russian complicity in the death of Egypt's Sirdar. Allegedly, the Communists corrupted Zaghlul, influencing him to attempt revolution.	Puerto Rico's Coll Cuchi asks Calvin Coolidge to intervene against an election judge who commits electoral frauds. The judge engages in massive bribery, to ensure outcomes adverse to labor.	
Dec. 14				President Zayas and Roosevelt's widow dedicate the monument to Teddy Roosevelt at San Juan Hill.	Australia resolves its currency crisis that began with the 1923 contraction of banknotes. It shifts note issuing authority from the tight-money Notes Issue Board to the reorganized Commonwealth Bank, which issues £15 million.

A	B	C	D	E
Includes developments that affect more than one world region, international organizations and important meetings of world leaders.	*Includes all domestic and regional developments in Europe, including the Soviet Union.*	*Includes all domestic and regional developments in Africa and the Middle East.*	*Includes all domestic and regional developments in Latin America, the Caribbean, and Canada.*	*Includes all domestic and regional developments in Asian and Pacific nations (and colonies).*

U.S. Politics & Social Issues	U.S. Foreign Policy & Affairs, Defense	U.S. Economy & Environment	Science, Technology & Nature	Culture, Leisure & Lifestyle	
The House begins work on the Aswell bill that requires ID cards, complete records, and current addresses for all immigrants. Aswell says it will ease deportations.... The Federal Council of Churches denounces war as immoral and calls for discussions in a suitable forum as an alternative.	Commander Drain of the American Legion calls for a universal draft as a guarantor of peace. When he says universal, he means fighting forces, labor, capital, and industries.	The 1924 cotton crop comes in as the fifth best ever. Its value is $1.65 billion. The 13 million bale crop is up three million from last year but three million below the record of 1914.... The offices of a Coffeyville, KS, newspaper blow up. The Klan owners suffer a $75,000 loss.... The Supreme Court upholds a Pennsylvania tax of 1.5 percent on anthracite. Owners had contended that it is inequitable and interferes with interstate commerce.	Seven million hunters help keep wildlife populations at sustainable levels. So says Lee Crandall at the 50th anniversary meeting of the conservationist American Game Protective Association.	Eastman brings his total donations to colleges and universities to more than $58 million when he donates more than $10 million to MIT, the Eastman School of Music, the Rochester Medical School and the Women's College. He sells Kodak stock to them at below face value.... J.B. Duke, the tobacco king, creates a $40 million trust for charity and an institution of higher learning. He offers Durham, NC's Trinity University $6 million and $2 million a year to change its name to Duke University.	Dec. 8
	The United States accept the League of Nations invitation to join the Geneva talks on arms limitation. Talks are set for May 1925.... Britain objects to sharing reparations proceeds with the United States. Hughes indicates the U.S. position will remain that it gets payment from reparations.... Secretary Wilbur announces reconfiguration and additions necessary to realign the fleet to 5–5–3.	The Short Line Association protests the Van Swearingen railroad merger. The 700-member association wants to be part of the consolidation beforehand because it fears unfavorable treatment by the consolidated line.... The Southern Pacific buys the San Antonio and Aransas subject to approval. Southern Pacific formerly held SA&A until the Texas Railroad Commission separated it.		British and American players have a game of chess over the radio.... Professor Alexander McAdie of Boston says Benjamin Franklin's kite experiment is a myth. The electricity would have killed Franklin.	Dec. 9
The Weehawken whiskey ring matter becomes tenser. Already there is background rumbling that the trials will require martial law. Today somebody steals the police blotter and a priest gets threats that he will die if he testifies.... Immigration officials and local police work together to arrest 11 Tong members and prepare them for deportation.		The American Petroleum Institute, meeting at Fort Worth, decides to spend $100,000 a year to publicize its activities.		The American League owners vote unanimously to reelect Landis as baseball commissioner. The move is a sign of conciliation of the long-standing Johnson-Landis feud.... G. De Vilmorin brings the first French historical film, *Miracle of the Wolves*, to New York. France intends a 12-film historical series.... John Bach McMasters leads the Philadelphians who defend Franklin against McAdie's charges.	Dec. 10
The Supreme Court declines to hear a test case on the legality of disclosing tax information.	Congress passes a $111 million navy modernization bill. It provides eight new cruisers and six new gunboats as well as renovation of six battleships.	AT&T announces plans to spend $265 million on expansion in 1925. Cumulative expenditures over five years are $1 billion. The company cites pent up demand after the war.	An insurance expert says that the Gowanus Canal is a fire hazard. Ships routinely release sludge and pollute it.		Dec. 11
Representative Hamilton Fish says the National Disabled Soldiers League is a parasitic organization unrecognized by the Veterans Bureau. Its fundraising letters and sales of pencils prey on disabled veterans.	Coolidge says he will wait to call the arms limitation meeting until he sees sufficient interest in Europe. Secretary Wilbur wants to upgrade the U.S. Navy only as permitted. Competition is too expensive.	With the arrest of 29 more Atlanta brokers, the total number charged with speculation in cotton reaches 100. Georgia law prohibits speculation on futures on margin.			Dec. 12
Edgar Hewett of the Museum of New Mexico blames turbulence among the Pueblo Indians on interference by whites. He particularly condemns women's clubs and white men who use propaganda techniques to confuse Native Americans and lead them from their traditions.... Samuel Gompers dies in San Antonio.	General Patrick acknowledges that planes could not sink a battleship. He says the air corps needs heavier bombs, not heavier planes.	Postmaster General New asks a $66 million postage increase for all classes except letters. Publishers protest that it will kill newspapers. In addition, the method of allocating overhead costs is unfair.		Amateur theatricals are hot. Requests for production rights and royalty information are at an all time high, particularly in small towns around the country, including the South, which 10 years ago had many areas with zero interest in plays.	Dec. 13
The Tong war gets careless. A Tong attacker kills a Chinese-American in his doorway. The victim belongs to neither Tong. His death is a case of mistaken identity.	Demand for immigration papers is up as the new law takes effect. Issuance of first and final papers rises 75 percent. Backlog hits 70,000 applications with one million Europeans awaiting their turn.... The Council of Jewish Women reports it has educated 80,000 foreign women this year.... The battleship *Mississippi* launches an airplane. An explosive catapult fuelled by 14 pounds of smokeless powder gets the plane airborne.		Professor Silvestri restores "The Last Supper." His five-month effort fills in areas Professor Cavenaghi missed during his restoration of 16 years ago.	Isadora Duncan says that if she publishes her love letters, as she is leaning toward doing, she will destroy many families. On the other hand, she is broke and needs money.	Dec. 14
F *Includes campaigns, elections, federal-state relations, civil rights and liberties, crime, the judiciary, education, healthcare, poverty, urban affairs, and population.*	G *Includes formation and debate of U.S. foreign and defense policies, veterans affairs, and defense spending. (Relations with specific foreign countries are usually found under the region concerned.)*	H *Includes business, labor, agriculture, taxation, transportation, consumer affairs, monetary and fiscal policy, natural resources, pollution and industrial accidents.*	I *Includes worldwide scientific, medical and technological developments, natural phenomena, U.S. weather and natural disasters.*	J *Includes the arts, religion, scholarship, communications media, sports, entertainment, fashions, fads, and social life.*	

	World Affairs	Europe	Africa & The Middle East	The Americas	Asia & The Pacific
Dec. 15	The United States claim victory at the opium conference. The first agenda item is the American proposal to suppress the traffic in processed opium.	Austria prepares to introduce a new silver shilling and a smaller bronze coin. The shilling will drop four zeros from the paper currency. Concern rises that it will inflate prices in restaurants and other venues where prices are below the small coin's value.	Spain completes its new defensive line in Morocco. France inquires about helping Spain control the tribes. The rebels' Abd el Krim claims to be a friend of France.	Mexico City reports that more than 55 percent of its 1923 deaths were of children. Officials attribute the rate to ignorance and announce an educational campaign for the federal district's poor.…A U.S. federal court rules in the Oliver railroad case that Mexico cannot be sued. Further, it can operate railroads as it chooses.	Chang prepares to oust Tuan when the dictator abolishes parliament. Tuan has already begun executing officials of the former regime without trials.
Dec. 16	The opium conference preparations are on hold as the delegates take a month's break.	Fighting breaks out on the Albanian border as the ousted premier attempts to recapture his position. Albania accuses Yugoslavia and Greece of aiding the rebels. Britain asks Yugoslavia to block an invasion and warns Albania and Bulgaria against getting too aggressive.	The Spanish commander in Morocco, his troops secure behind the new defensive line, says his new tactic is to starve the tribes to submission. After they submit, he will try to gain their goodwill.		
Dec. 17	Prime Minister Baldwin proposes using the Safeguarding of Industries Act to establish an imperial trading bloc. He would spend up to £1 million a year to bring empire foodstuffs to Britain. Opponents cry that the plan is a general tariff.	Albanian rebels take Scutari and are 15 miles from Tirana. Italy demands Serbian neutrality after reports Serbia is helping Ahmed Zog.…The French Communist Party has only 60,000 members, with only 15,000 paying dues.…After Britain reaffirms its offer to drop France's debt by two thirds, France breaks negotiations with the United States. France is unsure about Britain's condition that the United States not become France's preferred creditor.	Ziwar refuses to call the Egyptian parliament. He says the nation does not really need a forum for debating the situation with Britain.	Nicaragua says baseball is the nation's favorite sport, more popular even than gambling and cock fighting. It plans to send a team to Olympic Games in Costa Rica, marking the first time a Central American team has played outside its borders.	Filipinos ask the League's International Labor Bureau how a country becomes a member. Filipinos hope to use the bureau as the first step toward League of Nations membership and, ultimately, independence.
Dec. 18		Albanian rebels oust the government. Bishop Noli flees.…Britain reports the 1924 birthrate is the lowest in history. At 19 per thousand, it continues the 40-year decline from the 33.5 per thousand recorded in 1883. The cause is "deliberate restrictions."	Meeting in Tel Aviv, Palestinian Jews reject mandate board restrictions on immigration. The meeting establishes an immigrant aid fund and calls for a Zionist fund for building houses for newcomers.		The Japanese arrest a man armed with a knife asking to speak with Ambassador Bancroft about immigration.
Dec. 19	Germany seeks to join the League of Nations and asks what conditions it must meet.	Adolf Hitler, Baron Kreibel, and several Sparticists leave jail after receiving pardons and early release.…Albania protests to the League that Yugoslavia is backing raids into its territory.…Trotsky and his foes in the party near civil war as clashes break out.			Japan expresses its regret at the Bancroft episode. The young man reportedly suffers dementia.
Dec. 20		Yugoslavia extends feelers to traditional enemy Bulgaria for unity against Communism. The other small Balkan states are also desired partners.…American Tobacco Company loses a test case seeking insurance reimbursement for losses suffered in the great 1922 fire at Smyrna. Mussolini calls for March elections and tells parliament to reestablish the old election system in January.		The third Pan American Scientific Conference meets in Lima, Peru. Dr. L.S. Rowe of the United States cites pan-Americanism as ushering in a new age of cooperation.	
Dec. 21		Britain challenges Germany's right to commit to pay the United States. Britain argues that Versailles blocks Germany from choosing what to do with its resources.…The Italian opposition wants the government to step down before the election. Old guard Fascists do not want any election at all. Public opinion supports an election under the pre-Fascist laws.…A Parisian rally of Communists turns out only 5,000. France has been in a red scare for several days, but nothing untoward occurs. In Berlin comparable demonstrations degenerate into riots.	Egypt's student leader, Hilmi Gayar gives up. He denies he is involved in the plot to assassinate the Sirdar and says he went into hiding only to protect himself.	Argentina warns Msgr Borneo to submit his credentials from the Pope or face prison. Argentina claims the right of apostolic appointment as successor state to Spain, which held the right to select its own religious leader.	Chinese students strike. They object to the inclusion of the *Bible* in the course of study at Yale College in Changsha.
	A *Includes developments that affect more than one world region, international organizations and important meetings of world leaders.*	B *Includes all domestic and regional developments in Europe, including the Soviet Union.*	C *Includes all domestic and regional developments in Africa and the Middle East.*	D *Includes all domestic and regional developments in Latin America, the Caribbean, and Canada.*	E *Includes all domestic and regional developments in Asian and Pacific nations (and colonies).*

U.S. Politics & Social Issues	U.S. Foreign Policy & Affairs, Defense	U.S. Economy & Environment	Science, Technology & Nature	Culture, Leisure & Lifestyle	
	The Treasury receives $91.9 million in war debt. Britain pays $91.6 million in U.S. securities. Finland, Lithuania, and Hungary pay their combined $295,000 in cash.... The Mayflower Society backs a strong defense. It says the Pilgrims would agree that pious words on paper mean nothing when nations move toward war.	The Supreme Court rules against the Kansas City Southern Railway, which argues that it receives no benefit from Arkansas' tax on railroads. The court says the state has the power to decide.... Class I railroads report that October set a record of 43 million net ton miles. Recovery in the south and west are responsible. Eastern loadings are down 1.2 percent from 1923.			Dec. 15
Attorney General Stone orders an investigation into New Jersey's enforcement of prohibition.		New York City poultry dealers allege that smugglers are bringing dead and diseased chickens into the city. An absolute embargo on chickens is in effect, as birds die by the thousands of an unidentified cause.	A Paris medical school uses films rather than vivisection to train medical students.	Producers of plays want to bar their actors from radio. Actors Equity takes the issue under consideration.	Dec. 16
New Orleans discovers bubonic plague in rats. Congress receives a request for $275,000 in federal money to keep the disease from spreading to humans.... Roger Baldwin, held for rioting after holding a meeting prohibited by Patterson, NJ, police, says that in criticizing Coolidge he was doing nothing Davis did not do.	The house and senate block inquiries into naval preparedness as Norris attacks Coolidge for supporting Underwood's plan for private operation of the Muscle Shoals plant. Norris claims that giving over Muscle Shoals will make Teapot Dome a "pinhead" in comparison.... Hughes offers to cut war debt repayment to less than 30 percent of the original U.S. claim. He wants to bring Britain around to the U.S. desire for payment from reparations.	New York authorities seize eight truckloads of live diseased chickens and destroy them. Pushcart sales continue. Western poultry prices fall.		To conciliate Commissioner Landis, the American League strips president Ban Johnson of his powers. Johnson has interfered in activities beyond the scope of his job and promises to restrict his actions to league business.	Dec. 17
The warden and deputy at the Atlanta federal penitentiary face charges that they accept bribes to give prisoners easy jobs.... A Charleston, MO, lynch mob of 200 overpowers the sheriff and takes a black prisoner. Before hanging the black, they drag him behind a car.	Hughes denies he offered to cut the total war debt due. He says he merely offered to extend the time of repayment.	An exchange seat sells for $101,000. This is well below the record $115,000 paid in 1920. In 1888, seats sold for around $24,000.... New Jersey and Connecticut join the New York embargo of chickens. They destroy 54,000 pounds.			Dec. 18
Bandits rob banks in Valley View, TX. They then set fire to the town, causing damage estimated at $240,000.... William Green becomes president of the AFL.	American coffee roasters ask the government to seek an agreement with Brazil to lower then stabilize coffee prices and collect market data. The roasters also want the government to begin experimental growing of coffee in Cuba, Puerto Rico, and Hawaii.	The Boston and Maine's president says he is going to drop 1,000 miles of line. Due to stiff competition by buses, trucks, and cars, the 45 percent of the railroad's track generates three percent of revenue. The line will raise $13 million to organize a commercial car service to the affected communities.		Harry Houdini says he can discredit the "psychic," Margery. He promises $5,000 if he fails. He also says *Scientific American* added effects to its results when it tested Margery's powers. He suspects that one of the judges took a bribe.	Dec. 19
The United States Association bans cheap Japanese flags and asks Americans to buy only American-made flags. The colors of the cheap flags run when wet, making the Stars and Stripes closer to the red flag of Communism.... Congress recesses until December 29. The House has passed only three appropriations bills; the Senate has passed none, spending its time on Muscle Shoals.		Despite the lack of chickens, the Christmas feast should cost about what the Thanksgiving meal did. Supplies of turkey, geese, ducks, kids, and pigs are plentiful.	Underwriters report that their tests show no reason to use shingles on roofs. One hundred and 18 cities ban them. Over the past five years, they have cost an average of $1 million a month in losses.		Dec. 20
		The United States spent $117 million on cosmetics in 1923. The total is an increase of $26 million from 1921. Overall drug purchases—cosmetics, preparations, patent medicines—topped $425 million, up from $341 million in 1921.... Night airmail from the Eastern Airlines facility at New Brunswick, NJ, to Chicago will cost eight cents an ounce. Thirty-eight planes will fly the route.	The Committee on Blindness warns of the risks of Christmas. They include air rifles, fireworks, and poison liquor.	Crosswords are a boon to optometrists. Puzzlers learn quickly of any vision problems they might have. Movies had the same impact.	Dec. 21
F *Includes campaigns, elections, federal-state relations, civil rights and liberties, crime, the judiciary, education, healthcare, poverty, urban affairs, and population.*	G *Includes formation and debate of U.S. foreign and defense policies, veterans affairs, and defense spending. (Relations with specific foreign countries are usually found under the region concerned.)*	H *Includes business, labor, agriculture, taxation, transportation, consumer affairs, monetary and fiscal policy, natural resources, pollution and industrial accidents.*	I *Includes worldwide scientific, medical and technological developments, natural phenomena, U.S. weather and natural disasters.*	J *Includes the arts, religion, scholarship, communications media, sports, entertainment, fashions, fads, and social life.*	

	World Affairs	Europe	Africa & The Middle East	The Americas	Asia & The Pacific
Dec. 22	Stresemann asks the League of Nations to grant Germany membership with an exemption from the clause mandating sanctions for aggressors. He says Germany is terribly weak and surrounded by strong neighbors.		Jerusalem opens a free Hebrew school. Capacity is 100 students.... Prince Kemmaldine Hussein leaves Cairo at the head of an automobile expedition into the desert to Quenat and Arkuna. His goal is to find additional oases past the Dakhla Oasis and strengthen Egypt's frontier defenses. He carries movie cameras and a radio capable of reaching Paris.		Gandhi tells Indian National Congress members that each of them has to spin 2,000 yards of yarn a month. If they fall short, the boycott and drive for self-sufficiency will fail. To strengthen the message, he threatens to resign as leader if they spin too little. Gandhi is also moving the INC toward cooperation with the Swarajists and ending the boycott of legislatures, courts, and schools.
Dec. 23	The allies draft a note chiding Germany for failure to disarm as required by treaty. France regards the German note to the League as another instance of German bad faith....Britain polls the dominions and India on the need for an imperial conference on the protocol.	Nintitch returns to Yugoslavia with French and British blessing for his proposal for a union of smaller Balkan states. He prepares to resume negotiations on creation of the anti-Communist bloc.	As requested by Ziwar, King Fuad dissolves parliament. Elections will occur in February.		
Dec. 24	As crowds throng, the Pope strikes three times on the sealed wall of Bernini's Portico at St. Peter's. Thus, he begins history's 23rd jubilee year. Jubilee years occur once a quarter century....Britain decides to remain at Cologne after January 10. France approves this measure of rebuke to recalcitrant Germany. Germany threatens to scrap Dawes in retaliation.	The German cabinet rallies in support of President Ebert, lauding his patriotism after the high court denies Ebert's libel claim. The court upholds a newspaper editor who writes that Ebert's actions during the war were treasonous....Milan police capture an assassin who killed Macedonian Federalist Peter Schankeff. The assassination is retaliation for the assassination of Alexandroff.			Australia reports it sees no need for an imperial conference on the protocol. It can phone in its opinions....In return for recognition, the new Chinese government agrees to abide by old treaties and other commitments. It asks that other governments do the same and promptly implement the Washington Agreement.
Dec. 25				Calles needs $50 million to service Mexico's debt. The legislature complains that he is enacting measures without it. As for federal workers, he tells them to work harder as he reduces the number of holidays....Chile exiles Pedro Ugalde for sedition among the troops.	Japan reports a national debt of $4.27 billion yen. The debt rises $46 million in November.
Dec. 26	France reports the discovery of hundreds of thousands of rifles at the Krupp works. It also reports massive quantities of machine gun parts. Britain says it will let Germany and France work out their differences and it will leave Cologne in August.	The French Senate twice refuses to accept Herriot's bill pardoning 30,000 deserters. It refuses to allow strikers to qualify.			
Dec. 27		Bishop Noli arrives safely in Brindisi, Italy. Victorious, Zog says he has no ill will toward the deposed bishop....Gales with 60–80 miles per hour winds and heavy rains rake England and France, disrupting channel traffic.		Plans are under way for the United States to train Nicaragua's military to replace the U.S. guards at Managua when the marines leave in January. Originally, the United States was to train constabularies for the interior but Congress failed to approve the use of U.S. officers in foreign forces.	An explosion in Otaru Harbor on Hokkaido kills 120 Japanese and injures 300. The victims were transferring cases of dynamite....Indian Muslims, formerly backers of Ibn Saud because of their opposition to the Hashemite family, have switched. The Indian Muslim League now regards Ibn Saud as heretic and the Indian Caliphate Committee is no longer funding him.
Dec. 28		Herriot attempts to jail an editor for revealing state secrets. Opponents claim the move is politically motivated. The paper is a Briand mouthpiece.	Spain announces that it will emulate France in Morocco. It will use a combination of local officials, military rule, and small patrols. Before anything happens, the rebels must give up their weapons.		

U.S. Politics & Social Issues	U.S. Foreign Policy & Affairs, Defense	U.S. Economy & Environment	Science, Technology & Nature	Culture, Leisure & Lifestyle	
	The navy opens an inquiry on how one captain wrote and another published a letter detailing classified information on Navy War College simulated exercises. The games, and the letter, reveal significant weaknesses.	The Bureau of Animal Industry begins surveying the extent of the chicken problem as additional states join the embargo. Inspectors will disinfect coops, railroad cars, and the like. Budget for the effort is $100,000.		Two of the colleges receiving Kodak stock, MIT and Rochester, sell their 187,000 shares for $20.5 million. Eastman thought the total for the four colleges would be $15 million.…Because of heavy demand by crossword enthusiasts, the Los Angeles public library sets time limits on use of its dictionaries.	Dec. 22
Federal agents raid 44 more New Jersey cities and issue additional indictments. Jersey City clergy call for real enforcement and demand that Mayor Hague close saloons.		The NYSE revises its ticker symbols, cutting three-letter ones to a single letter. The purpose is to speed the ticker.…Hudson Motor Company reports December is a record month. Yearly gross of $8 million is approximately the same as the 1923 figure.	New York counts an additional 29 typhoid cases, but medical opinion is that they are of a milder sort. Officials reiterate their warning against uncooked shellfish. Typhoid has killed 159 New Yorkers this year.		Dec. 23
	U.S. officials say there is no need for U.S. representation on the Reparations Commission. Britain set U.S. membership as a condition of the United States sharing reparations under Dawes, but the U.S. position is that it has enough representatives on related boards and commissions and this board's work is virtually finished.	Dollar bills are getting scarce. Secretary Mellon wants to make the silver dollar popular. Bankers cannot convince their customers.			Dec. 24
		W.M. Ritter gives $3 million, a quarter of his fortune, to 124 people, mostly employees of Ritter Lumber. He says he opposes the modern idea of using money to impose individual ideas.	The West records its coldest Christmas in 50 years, with a Colorado temperature reading of -60. Ohio records -14. Five die in Chicago. Upstate New York has a blizzard, but the city has merely a dusting of snow. In Virginia a dam breaks and spills muck, killing 10 with 10 others missing.	Adolph Zukor of Famous Players-Lasky awards Rafael Sabatini's *Scaramouche* the award for best adaptation of a novel to film. The author receives $10,000.	Dec. 25
An explosion destroys the Underwood Colliery powder house in Pennsylvania. The finger quickly points to striking miners. The next day, the miners end the strike.				Michael Long, a "giant of a man," saves his coworker, already buried by sea coal, by holding back another avalanche of sea coal that threatens to bury both of them. Unlike "Big John," Long is saved.	Dec. 26
Los Angeles has a severe traffic problem. It announces that those who drive horses in its central business district will go to jail. Los Angeles also establishes traffic lanes for pedestrians, including no walking and no standing zones, and a ban on jaywalking.…The president of the Stone Mountain Confederate Memorial Association reports that Borglum is on schedule and the monument will be done by Jefferson Davis' birthday, June 3. He also says the Philadelphia Mint is producing five million Stone Mountain half dollars that the association will sell for $1 each to pay for the monument.	C.C. Brigham proposes that West Point use mental tests to identify men suited to be officers in time of war. The Amy is optimistic that this approach will ease its long-standing recruitment problem.			After Rhinelander says he will track his wife's ancestry back 65 years to prove her black blood, the case ends. He gets his annulment, and she gets $300 a month plus attorney's fees.	Dec. 27
Three engineers exploring Mammoth Cave in Kentucky claim to have found traces of a predecessor race to Native Americans. The earlier inhabitants, the engineers say, were vegetarians.		The Farmer-to-Consumer League announces opposition to the Capper-Williams agriculture bill. The League says the bill provides relief only for packers and middlemen and threatens the future of cooperatives.		Hornsby's .4235 is officially the best batting average in baseball this year—and a record.	Dec. 28

F	G	H	I	J
Includes campaigns, elections, federal-state relations, civil rights and liberties, crime, the judiciary, education, healthcare, poverty, urban affairs, and population.	*Includes formation and debate of U.S. foreign and defense policies, veterans affairs, and defense spending. (Relations with specific foreign countries are usually found under the region concerned.)*	*Includes business, labor, agriculture, taxation, transportation, consumer affairs, monetary and fiscal policy, natural resources, pollution and industrial accidents.*	*Includes worldwide scientific, medical and technological developments, natural phenomena, U.S. weather and natural disasters.*	*Includes the arts, religion, scholarship, communications media, sports, entertainment, fashions, fads, and social life.*

	World Affairs	Europe	Africa & The Middle East	The Americas	Asia & The Pacific
Dec. 29		The Irish Free State suspends two majors and dismisses 25 noncommissioned officers and 16 privates. The charge is conspiracy to put unconstitutional pressure on the government, i.e., mutiny.	Abd el Krim reiterates his terms for Spanish surrender. He insists that his Rif forces have humiliated Spain and prospects for a Rif republic could not be brighter.	The Soviet minister to Mexico denies that he is using Mexico as a base to send out Communist propaganda.	In Kalgan, executions for looting and burning continue. The mutinous brigade disbands as authorities execute 489 members.
Dec. 30	American wages are double those in Britain and six times those in Italy. German wages, expected to be lowest, are third after the United States and Britain.	Two liberal cabinet members resign but Mussolini manages to avoid the collapse of his cabinet.... Stresemann says Germany has committed minor infractions to be sure, but the allies are the real threat to Dawes.			
Dec. 31		Police raid the homes of anti-Fascists and seize issues of 11 ant-government newspapers in Rome, Milan, and Turin....Trotsky says he will leave Moscow on his own in a week. Anti-Trotsky forces continue a newspaper blitz.			

A	B	C	D	E
Includes developments that affect more than one world region, international organizations and important meetings of world leaders.	*Includes all domestic and regional developments in Europe, including the Soviet Union.*	*Includes all domestic and regional developments in Africa and the Middle East.*	*Includes all domestic and regional developments in Latin America, the Caribbean, and Canada.*	*Includes all domestic and regional developments in Asian and Pacific nations (and colonies).*

U.S. Politics & Social Issues	U.S. Foreign Policy & Affairs, Defense	U.S. Economy & Environment	Science, Technology & Nature	Culture, Leisure & Lifestyle	
		Shipments of live chickens to New York resume, but only from states not under embargo.		Trinity College trustees vote to accept the gift from tobacco king J.B. Duke, which stipulates that the school change its name to Duke University. Duke University officially begins to operate.	Dec. 29
The American Farm Bureau Federation opposes the postage hike. It says farmers cannot afford increased parcel post. In addition, the increase will do great harm to country newspapers....Green sets out his course for the AFL. He will continue Gompers' conservative approach but abandon third party involvement. His AFL will be anti-Communist but quiet on prohibition.		Hutchinson and West Virginia Coal and Coke merge. The new company has assets of $30 million....General Electric gets out of the utility business. It transfers Electric Bond and Share, which has 100 utilities, to a new company.	A chemist reports that lead in the face powder used by Manchurian women is the fourth leading cause of death among their infants. He also reports that use of lead in consumer products is spreading rapidly and that lead causes dementia in animals.		Dec. 30
In 1924, only 16 lynchings occur, less than half 1923's 33. The number is a record low since Tuskegee Institute has been keeping records. Only one lynching is outside the South. On the bright side, police manage to prevent 45 lynchings.		Dun's reports 20,551 business failures for the year. Total liability is $542.9 million....Five Iowa banks close after runs exacerbated by withdrawal of state and local government funds as well as refusal of surety companies to guarantee their loans.			Dec. 31

F	G	H	I	J
Includes campaigns, elections, federal-state relations, civil rights and liberties, crime, the judiciary, education, healthcare, poverty, urban affairs, and population.	*Includes formation and debate of U.S. foreign and defense policies, veterans affairs, and defense spending. (Relations with specific foreign countries are usually found under the region concerned.)*	*Includes business, labor, agriculture, taxation, transportation, consumer affairs, monetary and fiscal policy, natural resources, pollution and industrial accidents.*	*Includes worldwide scientific, medical and technological developments, natural phenomena, U.S. weather and natural disasters.*	*Includes the arts, religion, scholarship, communications media, sports, entertainment, fashions, fads, and social life.*